Canadian
Edition

Marketing

Canadian
Edition

Marketing

Joel R. Evans
Hofstra University

Barry Berman
Hofstra University

William J. Wellington
University of Windsor

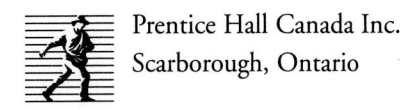

Prentice Hall Canada Inc.
Scarborough, Ontario

Canadian Cataloguing in Publication Data

Evans, Joel R.
    Marketing

Canadian ed.
Includes index.
ISBN 0-13-237678-4

1. Marketing. I. Berman, Barry. II. Wellington, William Joseph Patrick. III. Title.

HF5415.E86 1997   658.8   C96-931703-4

© 1997 Prentice-Hall Canada Inc., Scarborough, Ontario
A Division of Simon & Schuster/A Viacom Company

ALL RIGHTS RESERVED

No part of this book may be reproduced in any form without permission in writing from the publisher.

Prentice-Hall, Inc., Upper Saddle River, New Jersey
Prentice-Hall International (UK) Limited, London
Prentice-Hall of Australia, Pty. Limited, Sydney
Prentice-Hall Hispanoamericana, S.A., Mexico City
Prentice-Hall of India Private Limited, New Delhi
Prentice-Hall of Japan, Inc., Tokyo
Simon & Schuster Southeast Asia Private Limited, Singapore
Editora Prentice-Hall do Brasil, Ltda., Rio de Janeiro

ISBN 0-13-237678-4

Acquisitions Editor: Patrick Ferrier
Developmental Editor: Susan Broadhurst
Copy Editor: Chelsea Donaldson
Production Editor: Mary Ann McCutcheon
Production Coordinator: Deborah Starks
Permissions/Photo Research: Marijke Leupen
Art Direction: Mary Opper
Cover Design: Sputnik Art & Design
Cover Image: Christopher J. Boyle/Photonica
Page Layout: Phyllis Seto

Original English Language edition published by
Prentice-Hall, Inc., Upper Saddle River, New Jersey
Copyright © 1997

1 2 3 4 5   VH   01 00 99 98 97

Printed and bound in USA.

Every reasonable effort has been made to obtain permissions for all articles and data used in this edition. If errors or omissions have occurred, they will be corrected in future editions provided written notification has been received by the publisher.

Visit the Prentice Hall Canada Web site! Send us your comments, browse our catalogues, and more. www.phcanada.com Or reach us through e-mail at phcinfo_pubcanada@prenhall.com

To
Linda, Stacey, and Jennifer
Linda, Glenna, and Lisa
Christine, Roger, and Pamela

Brief Contents

Preface xv

Part 1 An Introduction to Marketing 1
1. Marketing in Contemporary Society 3
2. The Environment in Which Marketing Operates 25
3. Strategic Planning: A Marketing Perspective 51
4. Information for Marketing Decisions 78

Part 2 Broadening an Organization's/Individual's Marketing Scope 107
5. Societal, Ethical, and Consumer Issues 109
6. Global Aspects of Marketing 142

Part 3 Consumer Analysis: Understanding and Responding to Diversity in the Marketplace 173
7. Final Consumer Demographics 175
8. Final Consumer Lifestyles and Decision Making 198
9. Organizational Consumers 226
10. Developing a Target Market Strategy 255

Part 4 Product Planning 287
11. Basic Concepts in Product Planning 289
12. Goods Versus Services Planning 316
13. Conceiving, Developing, and Managing Products 348
14. Branding and Packaging 375

Part 5 Distribution Planning 403
15. Considerations in Distribution Planning and Physical Distribution 405
16. Wholesaling 437
17. Retailing 458

Part 6 Promotion Planning 487
18. The Context of Promotion Planning 489
19. Advertising and Public Relations 517
20. Personal Selling and Sales Promotion 546

Part 7 Price Planning 573
21. Considerations in Price Planning 575
22. Developing and Applying a Pricing Strategy 599

Part 8 Marketing Management 629
23. Pulling It All Together: Integrating and Analyzing the Marketing Plan 631

Appendix
Computer-Based Marketing Exercises A-1

Company and Name Index I-1
Subject Index I-5

Contents

Preface xv

Part 1 An Introduction to Marketing 1

Part 1 Vignette: The Process of Marketing Affects Us All 2

1 Marketing in Contemporary Society 3

Chapter Objectives 3 Overview 4 Marketing Defined 7 The Evolution of Marketing 8
  The Marketing Concept 10 *Selling Versus Marketing Philosophies* 11 *Customer Service* 12 *Customer Satisfaction and Relationship Marketing* 14
The Importance of Marketing 16 Marketing Functions and Performers 17 Format of the Text 20 Marketing in a Changing World: Preparing for the Year 2000 and Beyond 21
  Summary 22 *Key Terms* 22 *Review Questions* 23 *Discussion Questions* 23
Hints for Solving Cases 24

2 The Environment in Which Marketing Operates 25

Chapter Objectives 25 Overview 27 Controllable Factors 28
  Factors Controlled by Top Management 28 *Factors Controlled by Marketing* 31
Uncontrollable Factors 35
  Consumers 35 *Competition* 36 *Suppliers and Distributors* 39 *Government* 40 *The Economy* 42 *Technology* 43 *Independent Media* 44
Attainment of Objectives, Feedback, and Adaptation 45 Marketing in a Changing World: Trends That Will Affect the Future 46
  Summary 47 *Key Terms* 47 *Review Questions* 48 *Discussion Questions* 48
Video Case Soft Image: A Marketing Environment Analysis 49
Case Study Are Good Times Ahead for Planet Reebok? 50

3 Strategic Planning: A Marketing Perspective 51

Chapter Objectives 51 Overview 52 A Total Quality Approach to Strategic Planning 53 Kinds of Strategic Plans 55 Strengthening Relationships Between Marketing and Other Functional Areas 56 The Strategic Planning Process 57
  Defining Organizational Mission 58 *Establishing Strategic Business Units* 58 *Setting Marketing Objectives* 59 *Performing Situation Analysis* 61 *Developing Marketing Strategy* 61 *Implementing Tactical Plans* 68 *Monitoring Results* 68
Devising a Strategic Plan 69
  Sample Outline for a Written Strategic Plan 69 *Labatt: Dealing with a Changing Brewing Market* 71
Marketing in a Changing World: What Business Are We In? 73
  Summary 74 *Key Terms* 75 *Review Questions* 75 *Discussion Questions* 75
Video Case Canadian Boots: Marketing Based on a Distinctive Competency 76
Case Study Schering-Plough: Devising a Marketing Strategy 77

4 Information for Marketing Decisions 78

Chapter Objectives 78 Overview 79 Marketing Information Systems 80
  A Basic Marketing Information System 82 *Commercial Databases* 83 *Database Marketing* 83 *MIS in Action* 87
Marketing Research Defined 88 The Scope of Marketing Research 89 The Marketing Research Process 91
  Issue (Problem) Definition 91 *Secondary Data* 93 *Primary Data* 94 *Data Analysis* 100 *Recommendations* 101 *Implementation* 101
Marketing in a Changing World: Talking to Former Customers 102
  Summary 102 *Key Terms* 103 *Review Questions* 103 *Discussion Questions* 104
Video Case Scanning the Canadian Market: A.C. Neilsen versus IRI 105
Case Study Telogy, Inc.: Coordinating Company Databases 106

x Contents

Part 2 Broadening an Organization's/Individual's Marketing Scope 107

Part 2 Vignette: Ethical Issues and Global Marketing 108

5 Societal, Ethical, and Consumer Issues 109

Chapter Objectives 109   Overview 111
Social Responsibility 112
   *Natural Resources 114   The Landscape 116
   Environmental Pollution 117   Planned Obsolescence
   117   The Benefits and Costs of Social Responsibility
   118*
Ethics 121
   *A Business Perspective 123   A Consumer Perspective
   125   An International Perspective 125   The
   Teachability of Ethics 127*
Consumerism 128
   *Consumer Rights 130   The Responses of Business to
   Consumer Issues 134   The Current Role of
   Consumerism 136*
Marketing in a Changing World: Tough Choices
Ahead 136
   *Summary 137   Key Terms 138   Review Questions
   138   Discussion Questions 139*
**Video Case   Ethicscan: Whose Ethics Matter
Anyway? 140**
**Case Study   Herman Miller: Evaluating the Actions
of an Environmentally Conscious Firm 141**

6 Global Aspects of Marketing 142

Chapter Objectives 142   Overview 143   Why
International Marketing Takes Place 146   The
Scope of International Marketing 148   The
Environment of International Marketing 149
   *The Cultural Environment 150   The Economic
   Environment 151   The Political and Legal
   Environment 153   The Technological Environment 156*
Developing an International Marketing Strategy 157
   *Company Organization 157   Market Entry
   Decisions 160   Standardizing Plans 161   Product
   Planning 162   Distribution Planning 164
   Promotion Planning 165   Price Planning 167*
Marketing in a Changing World: Do You Want
to Work Abroad? 168
   *Summary 169   Key Terms 169   Review Questions
   170   Discussion Questions 170*
**Video Case   When in Japan, Do Like the
Japanese! When in Canada, Do Like the
Japanese? 171**
**Case Study   Can Mercedes Be Less German
and More Global? 172**

Part 3 Consumer Analysis: Understanding and Responding to Diversity in the Marketplace 173

Part 3 Vignette: The Market: The Demands of Satisfying Demand 174

7 Final Consumer Demographics 175

Chapter Objectives 175   Overview 176
Demographics Defined and Enumerated 178
Population Size, Gender, and Age 180
   Marketing Implications 181
Location, Housing, and Mobility 182
   Marketing Implications 183
Income and Expenditures 183
   Marketing Implications 186
Occupations and Education 186
   Marketing Implications 187
Marital Status 188
   Marketing Implications 188
Ethnicity/Race 188
   Marketing Implications 189
Uses of Demographic Data 191   Limitations of
Demographics 191   Marketing in a Changing
World: From Boomers to Xers 193
   *Summary 193   Key Terms 194   Review Questions
   194   Discussion Questions 195*
**Video Case   Marketing to Seniors: Canada's
Fastest-Growing Marketing Is Also Its Most
Lucrative! 196**
**Case Study   Wellcome: The Influence of
Demographic Factors in Taiwan 197**

8 Final Consumer Lifestyles and Decision Making 198

Chapter Objectives 198   Overview 200
Consumer Lifestyles 200
   *Social Characteristics of Consumers 201
   Psychological Characteristics of Consumers 206
   Selected Consumer Lifestyles 208   Marketing
   Implications of Lifestyle Analysis 210   Limitations of
   Lifestyle Analysis 213*
The Final Consumer's Decision Process 213
   *Stimulus 213   Problem Awareness 214   Information
   Search 215   Evaluation of Alternatives 215
   Purchase 215   Post-Purchase Behaviour 216
   Factors Affecting the Final Consumer's Decision Process
   216   Types of Decision Processes 216   Marketing
   Implications of the Final Consumer's Decision Process 220
   Limitations of the Final Consumer's Decision Process 220*
Marketing in a Changing World: REALLY
Understanding Other Cultures 221
   *Summary 221   Key Terms 222   Review Questions
   223   Discussion Questions 223*

Contents xi

Video Case   Do Consumers Have Too Much Choice or Not Enough "Real Choice"? 224
Case Study   Will Twenty-somethings Buy Levi's Dockers? 225

9 Organizational Consumers 226

Chapter Objectives 226   Overview 228   The Characteristics of Organizational Consumers 229
The Nature of Organizational Consumer Purchases 231   The Nature of the Organizational Consumer Market 232   An International Perspective 234
Types of Organizational Consumers 236
Manufacturers as Consumers 237   Wholesalers as Consumers 238   Retailers as Consumers 240   Government as Consumer 240   Nonprofit Institutions as Consumers 242
Key Factors in Organizational Consumer Behaviour 242
Buying Objectives 242   Buying Structure 243   Constraints on Purchases 244
The Organizational Consumer's Decision Process 245
Expectations 245   Buying Process 246   Conflict Resolution 247   Situational Factors 247   Purchase and Feedback 247   Types of Purchases 247   Research on the Organizational Consumer's Decision Process 248
Marketing Implications 248   Marketing in a Changing World: The Quest for Purchasing Partnerships 250
Summary 250   Key Terms 251   Review Questions 251   Discussion Questions 252
Video Case   The Downside of Computer Downsizing 253
Case Study   Steel and Aluminum: The Battle for Auto Makers' Business 254

10 Developing a Target Market Strategy 255

Chapter Objectives 255   Overview 256
Analyzing Consumer Demand 258
Determining Demand Patterns 258   Establishing Possible Bases of Segmentation 259   Identifying Potential Market Segments 270
Targeting the Market 270
Choosing a Target-Market Approach 270   Concentrated Marketing 272   Selecting the Target Market(s) 275
Developing the Marketing Strategy 276
Positioning the Company's Offering 276   Outlining the Appropriate Marketing Mix(es) 276
Sales Forecasting 278
Data Sources 278   Methods of Sales Forecasting 278   Additional Considerations 280
Marketing in a Changing World: Targeting the Interactive Marketplace 282

Summary 282   Key Terms 283   Review Questions 283   Discussion Questions 284
Video Case   Selling Houses in Vancouver with Feng Shui (Wind and Water) 285
Case Study   Teens as Global Comsumers: What Does This Mean for Marketers? 286

Part 4 Product Planning 287

Part 4 Vignette: Products: Satisfying Customer Needs and Wants 288

11 Basic Concepts in Product Planning 289

Chapter Objectives 289   Overview 291
Types of Products 292
Fundamental Distinctions Between Goods and Services 292   Consumer Products 293   Industrial Products 295
Elements of a Product Mix 297   Product Management Organizations 301   Product Positioning 302   The Product Life Cycle 307
Stages of the Traditional Product Life Cycle 307   Evaluating the Product Life-Cycle Concept 309
The International Dimensions of Product Planning 310   Marketing in a Changing World: Even Toyota's Not Infallible 311

Summary 312   Key Terms 313   Review Questions 313   Discussion Questions 313
Video Case   E-ZEEWRAP 314
Case Study   Arm & Hammer Baking Soda: A Positioning Powerhouse 315

12 Goods Versus Services Planning 316

Chapter Objectives 316   Overview 317   The Scope of Goods and Services 318
Categorizing Goods and Services 319
A Goods/Services Continuum 319   Goods and Services Classification Systems 320
Special Considerations in the Marketing of Services 324   The Use of Marketing by Goods and Services Firms 329
A Transition in the Marketing of Services 329   Illustrations of Service Marketing 329
Nonprofit Marketing 332
Nonprofit Versus Profit-Oriented Marketing 332   Classifying Nonprofit Marketing 336   The Extent of Nonprofit Marketing in the Economy 337   Illustrations of Nonprofit Marketing 339
Marketing in a Changing World: Health Care Services—The Thorniest Issue of All 343

Summary 344   Key Terms 345   Review Questions 345   Discussion Questions 345
Video Case   Inside MasterCard 346
Case Study   Olsten Corporation: Creating Differential Advantages for a Service Business 347

13 Conceiving, Developing, and Managing Products 348

Chapter Objectives 348 Overview 349 The Importance of New Products 350 Why New Products Fail 354 New-Product Planning 356
Idea Generation 357 Product Screening 357 Concept Testing 359 Business Analysis 359 Product Development 361 Test Marketing 362 Commercialization 362
Growing Products 363 Mature Products 366 Product Deletion 369 Marketing in a Changing World: Inventors Beware 371
Summary 371 Key Terms 372 Review Questions 372 Discussion Questions 372
Video Case   A Marketer's Nightmare: New Product Flops! 373
Case Study   Can Swatch Make a Comeback? 374

14 Branding and Packaging 375

Chapter Objectives 375 Overview 377 Branding 377
Corporate Symbols 382 Branding Philosophy 383 Choosing a Brand Name 388 The Use of Trademarks 390
Packaging 392
Basic Packaging Functions 394 Factors Considered in Packaging Decisions 394 Criticisms of Packaging 397
Marketing in a Changing World: Marketers Aren't Only Building Brands, They're Building Buildings! 398
Summary 398 Key Terms 399 Review Questions 399 Discussion Questions 400
Video Case Windows 95: Going for the World's Number One Brand 401
Case Study Ralcorp: Is Its Limitation Strategy Really Flattery? 402

Part 5 Distribution Planning 403

Part 5 Vignette: Goods and Services Distribution 404

15 Considerations in Distribution Planning and Physical Distribution 405

Chapter Objectives 405 Overview 407 Distribution Planning 408
The Importance of Distribution Planning 408 Channel Functions and the Role of Distribution Intermediaries 412 Selecting a Channel of Distribution 412 Supplier/Distribution Intermediary Contracts 416 Channel Cooperation and Conflict 417 The Industrial Channel of Distribution 419
International Distribution Planning 420
Physical Distribution 422
The Importance of Physical Distribution 422 Transportation 424 Inventory Management 428
Marketing in a Changing World: Being Aware of the Problem of Export Diversion 432
Summary 433 Key Terms 434 Review Questions 434 Discussion Questions 434
Video Case   Physical Distribution at Vancouver's Port 435
Case Study   CSX: An Intermodal Shipping Strategy 436

16 Wholesaling 437

Chapter Objectives 437 Overview 439 The Importance of Wholesaling 439
Wholesaling's Impact on the Economy 439 The Functions of Wholesalers 440 Wholesalers' Relationships with Suppliers and Customers 441
Types of Wholesaling 443
Manufacturer/Service Provider Wholesaling 443 Wholesale Merchants 446 Agents and Brokers 449
Recent Trends in Wholesaling 451 Marketing in a Changing World: How Manufacturers'/Service Providers' Agents Are Staying the Course 454
Summary 454 Key Terms 455 Review Questions 455 Discussion Questions 455
Video Case   Uniquely Canadian: The Saskatchewan Wheat Pool and Other Co-ops 456
Case Study   The Home-Market Dominance of Japanese Wholesalers 457

17 Retailing 458

Chapter Objectives 458 Overview 460 The Importance of Retailing 461
Retailing's Impact on the Economy 461 Retailing Functions in Distribution 462 The Relationship of Retailers and Suppliers 462
Types of Retailers 464
Ownership 464 Store Strategy Mix 466 Nonstore Operations 470
Considerations in Retail Planning 471
Store Location 472 Atmosphere 473 Scrambled Merchandising 474 The Wheel of Retailing 474 Technological Advances 475
Recent Trends in Retailing 477 Marketing in a Changing World: Invasion of the U.S. Retailers 480
Summary 481 Key Terms 482 Review Questions 482 Discussion Questions 483
Video Case   Wal-Mart: The World's Largest Retailer Comes to Canada 484
Case Study   At Woodworkers Warehouse Stores: No One's Afraid of Home Depot 484

Contents   xiii

Part 6   Promotion Planning 487

Part 6 Vignette: Promotion: Stimulating Marketplace Demand with Information 488

18   The Context of Promotion Planning 489

Chapter Objectives 489   Overview 491   The Importance of Promotion 491   Types of Promotion 493   The Channel of Communication 495   The Source 495
Encoding 497   The Message 497   The Medium 499   Decoding 499   The Audience 500   Feedback 501   Noise 502
Promotion Planning 502
Objectives 502   Budgeting 503   The Promotion Mix 505
International Promotion Considerations 506
The Legal Environment of Promotion 508
Criticisms and Defences of Promotion 511
Marketing in a Changing World: What's Ahead for Integrated Marketing Communications? 512
Summary 512   Key Terms 513   Review Questions 513   Discussion Questions 514
Video Case   Changing the Negative Image of Banks: Is It Possible? 515
Case Study   Can a Firm Succeed by Poking Fun at Itself? 516

19   Advertising and Public Relations 517

Chapter Objectives 517   Overview 519   The Scope and Importance of Advertising 519
The Characteristics of Advertising 522
Developing an Advertising Plan 523
Setting Objectives 523   Assigning Responsibility 524   Establishing a Budget 525   Developing Themes 525   Selecting Media 527   Creating Advertisements 531   Timing Advertisements 531   Considering Cooperative Efforts 532   Evaluating Success or Failure 532
The Scope and Importance of Public Relations 533   The Characteristics of Public Relations 536   Developing a Public Relations Plan 537
Setting Objectives 537   Assigning Responsibility 539   Outlining the Types of Public Relations to Be Used 539   Selecting the Media for Public Relations Efforts 540   Creating Messages 540   Timing Messages 540   Evaluating Success or Failure 540
Marketing in a Changing World: Dos and Don'ts for Using the Web 541
Summary 542   Key Terms 542   Review Questions 543   Discussion Questions 543
Video Case   Creating Advertisements for Radio Shack: "This Place Is Completely Wired" 544
Case Study   Intuit and Intel: Two Different Reactions to Negative Publicity 545

20   Personal Selling and Sales Promotion 546

Chapter Objectives 546   Overview 547   The Scope and Importance of Personal Selling 548   The Characteristics of Personal Selling 549   Developing a Personal Selling Plan 552
Setting Objectives 552   Assigning Responsibility 552   Establishing a Budget 553   Determining the Type(s) of Sales Positions 554   Selecting a Sales Technique 555   Outlining Sales Tasks 556   Applying the Plan 557
The Scope and Importance of Sales Promotion 560   The Characteristics of Sales Promotion 562   Developing a Sales Promotion Plan 563
Setting Objectives 563   Assigning Responsibility 563   Outlining the Overall Plan 563   Selecting the Types of Sales Promotion 565   Coordinating the Plan 565   Evaluating Success or Failure 565
Marketing in a Changing World: Sales Training the 3M Way 568
Summary 568   Key Terms 569   Review Questions 569   Discussion Questions 569
Video Case   Craig Procter: A Super Salesperson 570
Case Study   Sales Promotion in the United States: Does a Free Lunch Work? 571

Part 7   Price Planning 573

Part 7 Vignette: Pricing for Competition 574

21   Considerations in Price Planning 575

Chapter Objectives 575   Overview 576   The Importance of Price and Its Relationship to Other Marketing Variables 577   Price-Based and Nonprice-Based Approaches 579   Factors Affecting Pricing Decisions 580
Consumers 581   Costs 584   Government 586   Criminal Provisions 586   Channel Members 591   Competition 592
Marketing in a Changing World: Will "Pre-Owning" Catch On? 594
Summary 594   Key Terms 595   Review Questions 595   Discussion Questions 596
Video Case   Price Competition in the Energy Business 597
Case Study   Here Come $20 Eyeglasses 598

22   Developing and Applying a Pricing Strategy 599

Chapter Objectives 599   Overview 601   Pricing Objectives 602
Sales-Based Objectives 603   Profit-Based Objectives 603   Status Quo-Based Objectives 604
Broad Price Policy 604   Pricing Strategy 605

xiv   Contents

*Cost-Based Pricing 605   Demand-Based Pricing 611
Competition-Based Pricing 615   Combination Pricing 616*
Implementing a Pricing Strategy 616
Customary Versus Variable Pricing 617   A One-Price Policy Versus Flexible Pricing 617   Odd Pricing 617   The Price-Quality Association 618   Leader Pricing 619   Multiple-Unit Pricing 619   Price Lining 619   Price Bundling 621   Geographic Pricing 621   Purchase Terms 622
Price Adjustments 623   Marketing in a Changing World: Dealing with Non-Paying Customers 624
Summary 625   Key Terms 626   Review Questions 626   Discussion Questions 626

Video Case   Another Discount Priced Airline in Canada? Are You Crazy? 627
Case Study   The Pricing of Beef at Supermarkets 628

Part 8   Marketing Management 629

Part 8 Vignette: Integrated Marketing Plans 630

23   Pulling It All Together: Integrating and Analyzing the Marketing Plan 631

Chapter Objectives 631   Overview 633

Integrating the Marketing Plan 634
Clear Organizational Mission 635   Long-Term Competitive Advantages 636   Precisely Defined Target Market(s) 638   Compatible Long-, Moderate-, and Short-Term Subplans 639   Coordination Among SBUs 639   Coordination of the Marketing Mix 640   Stability Over Time 641
Analyzing the Marketing Plan 642
Benchmarking 643   Customer Satisfaction Research 645   Marketing Cost Analysis 647   Sales Analysis 650   The Marketing Audit 652
Anticipating and Planning for the Future 653
Marketing in a Changing World: Stemming the Tide of Customer Defections 658
Summary 659   Key Terms 659   Review Questions 660   Discussion Questions 660

Video Case   Make-up Art Cosmetics (M.A.C.): A Marketing Strategy of No Strategy 661
Case Study   Full Speed Ahead 662

Appendix

Computer-Based Marketing Exercises   A-1

Company and Name Index   I-1
Subject Index   I-5

Preface

These are very exciting times for all of us. During recent years, we have seen the true arrival of the PC age and the World Wide Web, the steady global movement toward service- rather than production-driven economies, a growing understanding and interest in customer service and customer satisfaction, greater focus on consumer diversity in the marketplace, the emergence of free-market economies in Eastern Europe, business and government grappling with such ethical issues as the consumer's right to privacy, the impact of deregulation on society, and many similar events.

The years ahead promise to be even more intriguing—as the European Union becomes more strongly unified; North American countries make their markets further accessible to one another; opportunities in other foreign countries grow; technological advances continue; and we try to cope with slow-growth economies in various parts of the globe. As we prepare for the rest of this decade and beyond, a thorough understanding and appreciation of marketing becomes critical.

We believe that a good marketing textbook must do several things in order to provide this critical understanding: It should incorporate both traditional and contemporary aspects of marketing, including the careful consideration of environmental factors; address the roles of marketing and marketing managers; and show the relevance of marketing for those who interact with or who are affected by marketing activities (such as consumers). We also believe that presentation is important: A textbook must describe marketing concepts to readers in an interesting, comprehensive, and balanced manner. As we indicate at the beginning of Chapter 1, marketing is truly "an exciting, fast-paced, and contemporary business discipline."

Although the basic, or traditional, components of marketing (such as consumer behavior, marketing research and informations systems, and product, distribution, promotion, and price planning) form the foundation of any introductory-level marketing textbook, contemporary techniques and topics also need to be covered in depth. Among the contemporary topics that are examined in full chapter length in *Marketing*, Canadian Edition, are strategic planning and marketing; societal, ethical, and consumer issues; global marketing; final consumer demographics; final consumer Lifestyles and decision making; organizational consumers (including manufacturers, wholesalers, retailers, government, and nonprofit institutions); goods versus services marketing (including nonprofit marketing); and integrating and analyzing the marketing plan. Environmental effects are noted throughout the book.

Marketing, Canadian Edition, explains all major principles, defines key terms, integrates topics, and demonstrates how marketers make everyday and long-run decisions. Examples based on such diverse organizations as Andersen Consulting, Bata Shoes, Black & Decker, BMW, British Airways, Coca-Cola, Eaton's, Hyatt, Kodak, Lands' End, MCI, Metropolitan Life, Perrier, Pizza Hut, Radio Shack, Swatch, Toyota, United Parcel Service (UPS), Visa, and Wrigley appear in each chapter. The illustrations build on the conceptual material, reveal the exciting and dynamic nature of marketing, cover a wide variety of firms, and involve students in real-life applications of marketing.

A Canadian Tradition Begins

This first Canadian edition of *Marketing* by Evans, Berman and Wellington has been designed to make learning about marketing an enriching and enjoyable experience. Towards this end, *Marketing*, Canadian Edition, contains the following features:

- A lively, easy-to-read writing style.
- A balanced treatment of topics (by size of firm, goods- and service-based firms, profit-oriented and nonprofit firms, final and organizational consumers, etc.).
- Comprehensive coverage of all important marketing concepts, including twelve chapters on the marketing mix (product, distribution, promotion, and price planning).
- A full-colour design throughout the book, including about 145 photos and 140 figures. These visually attractive illustrations are all keyed to the text.
- Part openers that provide integrated overviews of the chapters they contain. These openers each emphasize a different piece of the marketing "puzzle," which ties the various parts of the book together.
- Definitions of marketing terms.
- Early coverage of societal, ethical, and consumer issues, and global marketing (Chapters 5 and 6 respectively).
- Service marketing coverage in the section on product planning (Chapter 12).
- An appendix on computerized exercises that accompany the text. A computer symbol in the relevant chapters keys the exercises to the concepts involved.
- Separate company and name and subject indexes.

These features are contained in each chapter:

- Chapter objectives that outline the major areas to be investigated.
- An opening vignette that introduces the material through a real-world situation.
- An introductory overview to set the tone for the chapter.
- Thought-provoking boxed extracts on key marketing topics.
- Descriptive margin notes that highlight major concepts.
- Boldface key terms that identify important definitions.
- Many flowcharts that demonstrate marketing concepts; and current figures and tables that provide up-to-date information.
- Exciting and useful Internet sites appear in the margin and are easily identifiable by the Web links icon.
- Numerous footnotes to enable the reader to do further research.
- Chapter summaries keyed to chapter objectives. These summaries are followed by a listing of key terms with text page references.
- End-of-chapter questions divided into separate "review" and "discussion" categories.
- Two cases (except Chapter 1, which has an appendix on hints for analyzing cases) that deal with real companies or situations. There are 44 end-of-chapter cases in all, involving all types of companies. One case per chapter has a CBC video component.

Supplements

Marketing, Canadian Edition, is accompanied by a complete set of supplemental learning and teaching aids.

For the Instructor

Instructor's Resource Manual with Transparency Masters. This comprehensive guide contains resource material for each chapter of the text, including suggested sources of additional information, answers to discussion questions and answers to the case and video case questions. It also includes sample syllabi, answers to questions in the student Study Guide, term paper topics, a listing of trade associations and transparency masters.

Instructor's Lecture Manual. This highly detailed lecture guide provides the following for each chapter of the text: eight to ten teaching goals; a complete overview; key terms; approximately fifteen suggested discussion topics not included in the text; a creative, high-involvement class exercise; and a thorough set of lecture notes that cites all tables and figures in the text.

Test Item File. The test item file contains almost 4000 multiple choice, true/false and essay questions and their answers. Questions are coded according to their difficulty and are organized by type (terminology/concept or applied/comprehensive/integrative).

PH Custom Test. This powerful computerized testing package uses a state-of-the-art software program that provides fast, simple and error-free test generation. Tests can be previewed on-screen before printing and can be saved to one of three word processing file formats: WordPerfect, Microsoft Word or ASCII. PH Custom Test can print multiple variations of the same test, scrambling the order of questions and multiple-choice answers.

Electronic Transparencies. All acetates and lecture notes are available on Powerpoint 4.0. The disk is designed to allow you to present the transparencies to you class electronically and may be used as part of a Presentation Manager lecture.

CBC Video Cases. Prentice Hall Canada and the CBC have worked together to bring you 22 segments from such notable CBC programs as *Venture* and *The National Magazine*. Designed specifically to complement the text, this case collection is an excellent tool for bringing students into contact with the world outside the classroom. These programs have extremely high production quality, present substantial content, and have been chosen to relate directly to chapter content.

Computer-Based Marketing Exercises. These eighteen exercises are designed to apply and reinforce specific marketing concepts. The exercises allow students to manipulate marketing factors and see their impact on costs, sales and profits.

For the Student

Study Guide. A comprehensive self-instructional guide, the format of the study guide parallels that of the text. Each chapter contains objectives, an overview, key terms and concepts, true/false questions, completion questions, matching questions, multiple-choice questions, discussion questions and exercises. In addition, chapter 22, "Developing and Applying a Pricing Strategy," contains ten pricing problems. Each part ends with a review quiz, which tests knowledge for all of the chapters in that part.

How Marketing Is Organized

Marketing is divided into eight parts. Part 1 presents marketing in a contemporary society, describes the environment within which it operates, presents strategic planning from a marketing perspective, and discusses marketing information systems and the marketing research process. Part 2 covers the broad scope of marketing: societal, ethical, and consumer issues; and international marketing. Part 3 deals with marketing's central thrust: understanding final and organizational consumers in the diverse marketplace. It examines demographics, life-style factors, consumer decision making, target market strategies, and sales forecasting.

Part 4 encompasses product planning, the product life cycle, goods versus services marketing, new products, mature products, branding, and packaging. Part 5 deals with distribution planning, channel relations, physical distribution, wholesaling, and retailing. Part 6 examines promotion planning, the channel of communication, advertising, public relations, personal selling, and sales promotion. Part 7 covers price planning, price strategies, and applications of pricing. Part 8 integrates marketing planning—including benchmarking and customer satisfaction measurement—and looks to the future.

Particular thanks are due to the following people for reviewing the manuscript and offering many useful suggestions: Gus Cameron, Fanshawe College; Gloria Darroch, Northern Alberta Institute of Technology; Susan Eck, Seneca College; Loreen Gilmour, Algonquin College; Ted Goddard, Conestoga College; and Brian Wrightson, Northern Alberta Institute of Technology.

We hope this first offering of *Marketing*, Canadian Edition, will surpass the needs of new adopters at Canadian colleges and universities. We would really like to know that we have satisfied the needs of the users and would enjoy receiving feedback, especially notes of support and encouragement.

Please feel free to communicate with us. We welcome comments regarding any aspect of *Marketing*, Canadian Edition, or its package: William J. Wellington, Faculty of Business Administration, University of Windsor, 401 Sunset Ave., Windsor, Ontario, Canada, N9B 3P4, E-mail at R87@server.uwindsor.ca, or Joel R. Evans or Barry Berman, Department of Marketing and International Business, Hofstra University, Hempstead, N.Y., 11550-11725, E-mail at MKTJRE@HOFSTRA.EDU or MKTBXB@HOFSTRA.EDU. We promise to reply to any correspondence we receive.

Joel R. Evans
Barry Berman
William J. Wellington
1997

A Brief Walk Through
MARKETING, Canadian Edition

On the following pages, you will find an overview of several distinctive features we have included in Marketing, *Canadian Edition*. These features enable us to present the most complete coverage possible of the field of marketing—and to do so in an interesting, interactive, and contemporary way.

It's all covered—from absolute product failure to yield management pricing.

In Marketing, we introduce and integrate key marketing concepts, many of which have grown in importance in recent years. For this edition, benchmarking, customer satisfaction, ethical theories, the global firm, and integrated marketing communications are just a few of the concepts with expanded coverage.

We look at how "success" may be defined

Benchmarking

*In **benchmarking**, specific points of comparison are set so performance can be measured.*

For a firm to properly assess the effectiveness of its marketing plans, it must set performance standards. That is, it must specify what exactly is meant by "success." One way to do this is to utilize **benchmarking**, whereby a firm sets its own marketing performance standards based on the competence of the best companies in its industry, innovative com-

Customer satisfaction is an underlying theme throughout Marketing.

The largest ongoing research project on customer satisfaction is the annual American Customer Satisfaction Index (ACSI), a joint effort by the University of Michigan and the American Society for Quality Control. To compute ACSI, 30,000 consumers are surveyed about 3,900 goods and services. The surveys cover "perceptions of service, quality, value, how well the good or service lived up to expectations, how it compared to an ideal, and how willing people were to pay more for it." With a maximum score of 100, these were the highest-rated firms in 1995: Dole (90), Mars (89), Clorox (88), CPC International (88), Hershey (88), American Tobacco (87), Heinz (87), Maytag (87), PepsiCo (87), Procter & Gamble (87), Borden (86), Colgate-Palmolive (86), Honda (86), Mercedes-Benz (86), Nestlé (86), Pillsbury (86), Cadbury Schweppes (85), Coca-Cola (85), Dial (85), and Federal Express (85). The average score for all companies was 73.7.[21]

Ethics theories range from egoism to value ethics.

Various ethical theories try to explain why people and organizations act in particular ways. Here are four of them, applied to marketing:

- *Egoism*—a theory asserting that individuals act exclusively in their own self-interest. Example: A product manager postpones investing in improvements for a mature product because he or she expects to be promoted within the next six months and wants to maximize short-term profits.
- *Utilitarianism*—a theory asserting that individual and organizational actions are proper only if these actions yield the greatest good for the most people (the highest net benefit). Example: A pharmaceutical company markets any Health Canada approved drug with some side effects as long as it helps more people combat a particular disease than the number affected by the (minor) side effect.
- *Duty-Based*—a theory asserting that the rightness of an action is not based on its consequences, but rather is based on the premise that certain actions are proper because they stem from basic obligations. Example: A supermarket chain sets below-average prices in a low-income area even though this adversely affects company profits in that community.
- *Virtue Ethics*—a theory asserting that actions should be guided by an individual or organization seeking goodness and virtue ("living a good life"). Example: A virtuous company is totally truthful in its advertising, packaging, and selling efforts—and does not stoop to manipulative appeals to persuade customers.[18]

[18]Gene R. Laczniak and Patrick E. Murphy, *Ethical Marketing Decisions: The Higher Road* (Needham Heights, Mass.: Allyn & Bacon, 1993), pp. 28–42.

The American Marketing Association's ethics code and four theories of ethics are described.

CODE OF ETHICS

Members of the American Marketing Association (AMA) are committed to ethical professional conduct. They have joined together in subscribing to this Code of Ethics embracing the following topics:

Responsibilities of the Marketer
Marketers must accept responsibility for the consequence of their activities and make every effort to ensure that their decisions, recommendations, and actions function to identify, serve, and satisfy all relevant publics: customers, organizations and society.

Marketers' professional conduct must be guided by:
1. The basic rule of professional ethics: not knowingly to do harm;
2. The adherence to all applicable laws and regulations;
3. The accurate representation of their education, training and experience; and
4. The active support, practice and promotion of this Code of Ethics.

Honesty and Fairness
Marketers shall uphold and advance the integrity, honor, and dignity of the marketing profession by:
1. Being honest in serving customers, clients, employees, suppliers, distributors and the public;
2. Not knowingly participating in conflict of interest without prior notice to all parties involved; and
3. Establishing equitable fee schedules including the payment or receipt of usual, customary and/or legal compensation or marketing exchanges.

Rights and Duties of Parties in the Marketing Exchange Process
Participants in the marketing exchange process should be able to expect that:
1. Products and services offered are safe and fit for their intended uses;
2. Communications about offered products and services are not deceptive;
3. All parties intend to discharge their obligations, financial and otherwise, in good faith; and
4. Appropriate internal methods exist for equitable adjustment and/or redress of grievances concerning purchases.

It is understood that the above would include, but is not limited to, the following responsibilities of the marketer:

In the area of product development and management;
- disclosure of all substantial risks associated with product or service usage;
- identification of any product component substitution that might materially change the product or impact on the buyer's purchase decision;
- identification of extra-cost added features.

In the area of promotions,
- avoidance of false and misleading advertising;
- rejection of high pressure manipulation;
- avoidance of sales promotions that use deception or manipulation.

In the area of distribution,
- not manipulating the availability of a product for purpose of exploitation;
- not using coercion in the marketing channel;

- not exerting undue influence over the reseller's choice to handle the product.

In the area of pricing,
- not engaging in price fixing;
- not practicing predatory pricing;
- disclosing the full price associated with any purchase.

In the area of marketing research,
- prohibiting selling or fund raising under the guise of conducting research;
- maintaining research integrity by avoiding misrepresentation and omission of pertinent research data;
- treating outside clients and suppliers fairly.

Organizational Relationships
Marketers should be aware of how their behavior may influence or impact on the behavior of others in organizational relationships. They should not demand, encourage or apply coercion to obtain unethical behavior in their relationships with others, such as employees, suppliers or customers:
1. Apply confidentiality and anonymity in professional relationships with regard to privileged information;
2. Meet their obligations and responsibilities in contracts and mutual agreements in a timely manner;
3. Avoid taking the work of others, in whole, or in part, and represent this work as their own or directly benefit from it without compensation or consent of the originator or owner;
4. Avoid manipulation to take advantage of situations to maximize personal welfare in a way that unfairly deprives or damages the organization of others.

Any AMA members found to be in violation of any provision of this Code of Ethics may have his or her Association membership suspended or revoked.

FIGURE 5-6
The American Marketing Association's Code of Ethics
Reprinted by permission.

- A **multinational firm** is a worldwide player. Although corporate headquarters are in the home nation, the domestic market often accounts for less than 50 per cent of sales and profits—and the firm operates in dozens of nations or more. The business scope and search for opportunities are quite broad (with regard to geography). There are very few Canadian multinationals (examples are The Seagram Company Ltd. and Bombardier Inc.) and most multinational corporations operating in Canada are U.S.-based (such as GM, Ford, Chrysler, and Coca-Cola). Multinationals market items around the world, but usually keep the business culture of their home market. See Figure 6-1.
- A **global firm** is also a worldwide player. Yet, because its domestic sales are low, it places even more reliance on foreign transactions. It has the greatest geographic business scope. Such firms have been more apt to emerge in smaller nations, where the firms have historically needed foreign markets to survive. The quintessential global firm is Switzerland's Nestlé, which derives less than 2 per cent of total sales from its home market, makes products in hundreds of plants all over the world, and has employees from 50 nations at headquarters. As illustrated in Figure 6-2, its brands are among the world's most popular.[3]

[3]Joel R. Evans, "What Does Globalization in Business Really Mean?" *Hofstra Horizons* (Spring 1995), pp. 7–9.

> The range of international marketing options from domestic firm to global firm are discussed and illustrated.

FIGURE 6-1
Coca Cola: A Leading U.S. Multinational
Reprinted by permission

When a well-coordinated promotion mix is involved, a firm is undertaking **integrated marketing communications (IMC)**. An IMC program would be defined as one that "recognizes the value of a comprehensive plan that evaluates the strategic roles of a variety of communication disciplines—advertising, public relations, personal selling, and sales promotion—and combines them to provide clarity, consistency, and maximum communication impact."[12] For example, Frito-Lay has a sales force that visits every store stocking its products, advertises in papers and magazines and on TV, and distributes cents-off coupons. Hitachi has a large technical sales force, advertises in business and trade publications, and sends representatives to trade shows.

Each type of promotion has a distinct function and complements the other types. Ads appeal to big audiences and create awareness; without them, selling is more difficult, time consuming, and costly. The publicity aspect of public relations provides credible information to a wide audience, but content and timing cannot be controlled. Selling has one-to-one contact, flexibility, and the ability to close sales; without it, the interest caused by ads might be wasted. Sales promotion spurs short-run sales and supplements ads and selling.

The selection of a promotion mix depends on company attributes, the product life cycle, media access, and channel members. A small firm is limited in the kinds of ads it can afford or use efficiently; it may have to stress personal selling and a few sales promotions. A large firm covering a sizable geographic area could combine many ads, personal selling, and frequent sales promotions. As products move through the life cycle, promotion emphasis goes from information to persuasion to reinforcement; different media and messages are needed at each stage. Some media may not be accessible (no cigarette ads on TV) or require lengthy lead time (Yellow Pages). In addition, channel members may demand special promotions, sales support, and/or cooperative advertising allowances.

[12]Adapted by the authors from Janet Smith, "Integrated Marketing," *Marketing Tools* (November-December 1995), p. 64.

> The role of integrated marketing communications is amplified.

Because we believe marketing's vital role should be shown in varied situations, we have worked especially hard to present a balance of examples on domestic and international marketing, large and small firms, goods and services, and final consumers and organizational consumers.

Customer service is an important "output" of a marketing system and firms are very conscious of this. McDonald's Restaurants of Canada instituted an incentive program as early as 1993 to encourage improved customer service by its employees. Employee contests for good service are held and the top performers receive prizes in merchandise or McDonald's food discounts. The contests and their results are publicized in-house using posters, newsletters, payroll stuffers, and bulletin board notices.[12]

[12] "Incentives Help to Improve Service," *Strategy*, Vol. 4, No. 11 (February 8, 1993), pp. 22–24.

Nonstop to London. Showers expected upon arrival.

British Airways' new arrival facilities at London's Heathrow and Gatwick airports are making quite a splash. Now, ClubWorld® and First Class passengers can enjoy a hot shower and breakfast or even catch up on business in our private lounge. You'll be off to a flying start. It's the way we make you feel that makes us the world's favourite airline.

BRITISH AIRWAYS
The world's favourite airline®

FIGURE 1-6
Customer Service and British Airways
Reprinted by permission.

This highlights our extensive coverage of domestic and international marketing.

Small firms, as well as large ones, are involved with marketing and strategic planning.

Small firms' goals are often less ambitious, but no less important. For example, Upper Canada Brewing of Toronto is a small regional brewer in an industry dominated by the Labatt and Molson giants. Upper Canada has positioned itself as a Canadian and community brewery. One of their advertising themes is: "Think Globally, Drink Locally." Microbrewery operations by their very nature are small and local and the cost of going to the next level is often not worth the trouble to their owners.[17]

[17] Sean Eckford, "Small Brewers Play Canadian-Ownership Card," *Marketing Magazine* (August 14, 1995), p 4.

Chapter 12, "Goods Versus Services Planning," integrates services marketing into product planning.

Overview

When devising and enacting product plans, a firm must fully comprehend the distinctions between goods and services—beyond the brief coverage in Chapter 11. Although the planning process is the same for goods and services, their differences need to be reflected by the decisions made in the process.

Both final and organizational consumers are important to marketers.

Final consumers *buy for personal, family, or household use;* **organizational consumers** *buy for production, operations, or resale.*

In Chapters 7 to 10, the concepts you need to understand consumers in Canada, the United States, and other nations worldwide; to select target markets; and to relate marketing strategy to consumer behaviour are detailed. Chapters 7 and 8 examine final consumer demographics, lifestyles, and decision making. **Final consumers** buy goods and services for personal, family, or household use.

Chapter 9 centres on the characteristics and behaviour of **organizational consumers**, those buying goods and services for further production, to be used in operating the organization, or for resale to other consumers. Chapter 10 explains how to devise a target-market strategy and use sales forecasts.

xxi

Ethics AND TODAY'S MARKETER

Should Boards of Education Accept Advertising?

In North America, children and young adults annually spend more than U.S.$100 billion and influence their families to spend an additional U.S.$130 billion. Accordingly, marketers are increasingly establishing ties with Canadian and U.S. school boards in order to better attract the school-aged market.

Many school boards see schoolbus advertising as a means of increasing their revenues. Schoolbus advertising began in Colorado Springs, Colorado, and was quickly adopted by school districts throughout the United States, including those in Washington D.C. and New York City. In Canada, The Wellington County Board of Education in Ontario is experimenting with advertising on its fleet of school buses.

Each school board has its own rules governing schoolbus ads. Some restrict ads to the placement of logos on the outside of schoolbuses; these ads resemble travelling billboards. Other boards allow advertisers to place brochures and coupons on racks inside schoolbuses. The Wellington County Board of Education requires that advertising messages be socially responsible. For this reason, their experiment involved an ad for milk. There are also differences in how schoolbus advertising is implemented. Some school boards administer the advertising program themselves. Others, like New York City's Board of Education, plan to develop partnerships with advertising agencies and outdoor media companies. These firms must be willing to absorb all startup costs and to share revenues with the schools.

Supporters of schoolbus advertising say this is a harmless way of offsetting cuts in government funding to schools and rising school costs, and that schoolbus advertising can also involve students in creative projects. Revenue for the Wellington County Board is estimated to be $250 000 for the whole school year. The board sees the situation as a win-win deal for taxpayers, since the messages will be socially responsible and the board will get much-needed revenue. On the other hand, critics feel bus advertising may be perceived as a product endorsement, that it influences students to purchase unnecessary and sometimes unhealthy items, and that it takes advantage of a captive audience.

As a nonpaid marketing advisor to a local school board, develop a position on whether schoolbus advertising should be accepted by the board.

Sources: Based on material in Kemba Johnson, "NY School Buses Learn to Ad," *Advertising Age* (August 14, 1995), p. 10; Betsy Wagner, "Our Class Is Brought To You Today By," *U.S. News & World Report* (April 24, 1995), p. 63; and Laura Medcalf, "The Wellington County Board of Education is the first in Ontario to Experiment with Advertising on its Fleet of School Buses," *Marketing Magazine* (May 1, 1995), p.4.

---

*F*or Marketing, Canadian Edition, we have all-new interactive boxes in each chapter. Each one presents a real-life situation and asks readers to be decision makers and state positions/suggestions.

> The ethics boxes deal with current dilemmas facing marketing managers.

International Marketing in Action

Bata Shoes: Return to the Czech Republic

Bata Ltd., a Toronto-based firm, is the world's largest shoemaker, with factories and retail stores in more than 70 countries all over the world. The chair of Bata is Thomas Bata, a Czechoslovakian expatriate whose family's business was nationalized by the communists in 1945. With the shift in Eastern Europe away from government-run command economies to market economies, Bata was received as a hero when he visited his homeland in 1989. He has since sought to repatriate his family business from the new government.

The deal struck by Bata involves acquiring majority ownership in a manufacturing plant and a number of retail shoe stores. There was no precedent for creating legal entities or laws governing transfers of commercial real estate when Bata began negotiations with the government, and this created some problems. The existing laws were designed to set up retail stores as separate outlets and not to allow retail chains. Further complicating matters was the fact that Bata management had to negotiate with American advisers who had been hired by the Czech government to act on their behalf. Nevertheless, on December 18, 1991, a deal was signed, resulting in Bata acquiring 70 per cent of the stock in a manufacturing plant and a chain of 30 stores with head office in Zlin, the city where the original Bata company had been founded in the late 1800s. Bata has an option to buy the 30 per cent of the stock retained by the government.

With regard to the marketing of shoes, Georgina Wyman, the Canadian manager of the Czechoslovakian operation comments: "You have to constantly remind people of the elements that make a business prosper and reinforce their sensitivity to the marketplace. They're obsessed with having lots of merchandise. You've got to persuade them that the objective is not to have a lot of shoes or huge stores, but to sell shoes that customers want."

Bata has discovered that there are many challenges confronting a marketing-oriented organization in adapting to a culture that is not used to marketing-oriented firms. For example, employees are not used to expressing their thoughts and ideas let alone having anyone being receptive to them. Furthermore, skills and expertise in marketing are lacking among local managers. And, since consumers are not used to much product choice, the price-quality relationship is very strong; promotional price discounting may actually reduce sales volume because the discounted goods are viewed as being inferior in quality.

From 1991 to 1993, the Bata company expanded from thirty retail stores to forty-three and captured 10 per cent of the Czech market with sales of 3.5 million pairs of shoes. Competition has not been a major factor in the marketplace since 1993, but despite this, the operation is just breaking even.

As a consultant to Georgina Wyman, what thoughts do you have on Bata's current and future marketing strategy in Czechoslovakia?

> The international boxes highlight marketing activities around the world.

xxii

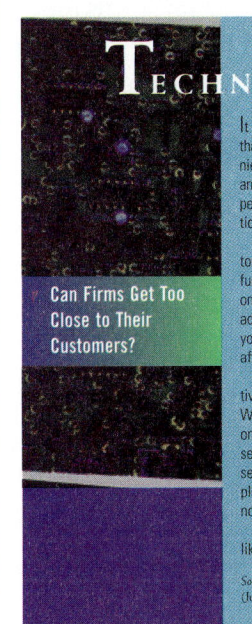

TECHNOLOGY & MARKETING

Can Firms Get Too Close to Their Customers?

It is great that many companies engage in relationship marketing with their customers, and that they stay in regular contact with them. By having good information on customers, companies can tailor marketing efforts to specific customers' needs, provide better follow-up service, and anticipate future customer requests. Yet, with the rapid advances in business technology, some people now feel especially vulnerable to what they perceive as company abuses in their relationships with customers.

Imagine you're sorting through your mail at home when you come across a postcard touting an upcoming sale on shirts at the store where you bought a shirt last week. That's funny, you think. You're sure you didn't give the clerk your address. So how did you end up on the store's mailing list? There's only one explanation: The store must have gotten your address from its credit card database, because you paid with the store's credit card. Since you're tired of being inundated with junk mail, you angrily toss the postcard in the mail—after all, you were just at the store last week!

If firms are truly marketing-oriented, they must recognize that some people are sensitive to information on their behaviour and backgrounds being kept in computerized databases. While one person may prefer that a hotel chain know he or she prefers a nonsmoking room on a high floor, another person may consider that information to be private. Compared to the second person, the first one may value good customer service above privacy or just be less sensitive about who has access to this information. Therefore, companies should train employees who collect customer data to respect a person's request for privacy even if this means not having good information on that person's needs and desires.

As a hotel's marketing manager, present a policy for both acquiring data about customer likes and dislikes and respecting customer privacy.

Source: Based on material in Stephen M. Silverman, "Information Backlash," *Inc. Technology* (June 13, 1995), p. 37.

Please note: Besides these interactive boxes, ethical, international, and technological concepts are integrated into and covered throughout the text.

Because of the growing importance and use of technology by marketers, a full range of technology issues are addressed in these boxes.

VIDEO CASE

Selling Houses in Vancouver with Feng Shui (Wind and Water)

CBC

The Chinese ethnic market in Canada was estimated to be 600 000 people in 1995 and is projected to grow to over 1.3 million by the year 2001. Although the Chinese market represents a little over 4 per cent of the Canadian population, they possess 7.4 per cent of the buying power and the doubling in their size will be accompanied by an increase in their purchasing power. Given the strength and rapid growth of the Chinese community, it is not surprising that marketers are falling all over themselves to offer products and services to this market. For example, *Maclean's* launched a Chinese edition in 1995 as did *Toronto Life*. Toronto Dominion Bank has Chinese Information lines, and in Markham, Ontario, developers are preparing a "Chinese" mall.

However, one of the most interesting approaches to tapping the lucrative Chinese market involves Vancouver real estate, which is among the most expensive in Canada. Building and selling homes in the Vancouver market is big business, especially since the population of British Columbia has been growing due to a major influx of Canadian migrants from Eastern Canada and Chinese immigrants from the Orient. However, success in the Vancouver real estate market means developing a clear understanding of, and dedication to, the Chinese philosophy of Feng Shui.

Builders and architects who have chosen to target the Chinese market have had to adapt their housing designs to Feng Shui in order to sell their products and services to Chinese consumers. Feng Shui is all about keeping energy—and good luck—inside one's house. Keeping "bad" energy out is also important. Feng Shui means that walkways to the house must be skewed so that energy cannot flow right out of the house and into the street. One cannot have a tree in front of the entrance to a house because it may block the flow of energy to and from the house. Doorways must be designed to trap energy and one door must not face another in the house. Stairways cannot face the entrance to the home because this will allow energy to flow out. Bedrooms must be carefully designed so that the head of the bed cannot be seen from the bedroom door, and the location of the head of the bed for the head of the household depends on that person's birthday. If you want to sell your house to a Chinese buyer in Vancouver it will have to pass inspection by a Feng Shui master or be relatively easy to renovate so that it will pass. In fact, many real estate deals are signed with the condition that the house pass inspection by an environmental engineer (read: Feng Shui master). Architects and builders are so responsive to this market situation that virtually all new homes built in Vancouver are now built with Feng Shui in mind.

QUESTIONS

1. What kind of target marketing is involved in appealing to Chinese home buyers (e.g., undifferentiated marketing or differentiated marketing)? Explain your answer.
2. Evaluate the Chinese ethnic market on the basis of the requirements for successful segmentation.
3. What are the pros and cons of designing homes specifically for Chinese buyers?
4. As a marketer giving serious consideration to serving the Chinese ethnic market in Canada, what kinds of problem would you see as being the most difficult to overcome in designing a marketing strategy?

VIDEO QUESTIONS ON FENG SHUI

1. Identify some of the principles of Feng Shui. Discuss some of the problems they present for real estate marketers.
2. Discuss the following comment: Feng Shui is important in the Vancouver real estate market now, but in twenty years it will probably be a mere footnote in history.

Video Source: "Feng Shui," *Venture* (October 8, 1995).
Other Sources: David Leid, "Amazing Grace," *Canadian Business* (May 1996), p. 37; James Pollock, "The Economics of Growing Communities," *Marketing Magazine* (July 3/10, 1995), p. 11; Jennifer Lynn, "Approaching Diversity," *Marketing Magazine* (July 3/10, 1995), p. 11; James Pollock, "Opening Doors of Opportunity," *Marketing Magazine* (September 18, 1995) pp. 17–18; James Pollock, "A Burgeoning Segment," *Marketing Magazine* (September 18, 1995), p. 18; and James Pollock, "Nailing the Niche," *Marketing Magazine* (September 18, 1995), p. 20.

TORONTO DOMINION BANK
www.tdbank.ca/tdbank/

> Each chapter (beginning with Chapter 2) ends with two cases, one of which has an accompanying CBC video and separate video questions—as shown here.

M*arketing, Canadian Edition, has 44 chapter-ending cases. These cases cover a wide range of companies and scenarios. All are new to this edition and extremely current. One case in every chapter has an optional CBC video component.*

*O*ur goal is to reinforce the principles in Marketing, Canadian Edition, in a useful and energetic way. So, we've got all the in-text pedagogy you could want: part vignettes, part openers, chapter objectives, chapter vignettes, highlighted key terms and margin notes, photos and line art, bottom-of-page footnotes, the integrated Changing World of Marketing features, summaries linked to chapter objectives, review and discussion questions—an appendix, and more!

Part 1 Vignette
The Process of Marketing Affects Us All

As we will show throughout *Marketing*, Canadian Edition, organizations come in all sizes and orientations. The diversity of those engaged in marketing is demonstrated by the video cases on different Canadian organizations found at the end of each chapter in this text. The kinds of issues facing these organizations and the forces affecting them are many and varied. This vignette, along with the other part-opening vignettes, previews the cases and relates them to the material to which they pertain. In Part 1, the first video case presents Soft Image, a Montreal software company, and its parent firm Microsoft, the second, Kreb Boots; the third, the market research firms Information Resources Incorporated (IRI) and A. C. Nielsen.

Firms like Soft Image and Microsoft have arisen as a result of the impact of technology on marketing. The human race spawns new technologies that are commercialized, and this leads to new needs and wants, which spawn more new products and take businesses and society in directions never anticipated. Soft Image is a computer technology firm at the cutting edge of computer animation. Using computers to create visual images for movies and television programming is one of the innovative uses that was never fully dreamed of by the originators of computers.

Organizations involved with "marketing" practices come in all sizes and orientations.

Historically, computers have been viewed as tools designed mainly for number crunching and statistical information storage and processing. Today, films like *Toy Story*, *Jurassic Park*, and *The Mask* include computer-animated visual sequences as integral parts of their production. Soft Image is transforming the notion that computers are used only for number crunching and non-creative pursuits. The computer has become an important tool and social force, and its powers are being rapidly enhanced by the software developed by firms like Soft Image and Microsoft. These kinds of forces and their impact on business is something that *Marketing*, Canadian Edition, will examine.

Another critical force that affects marketers is competition. Canadian boot manufacturers like Kreb have survived and flourished in Canada's footwear industry, while Canadian shoe manufacturers have struggled with foreign competition. Developing and marketing products that meet the needs of customers better than any competitor is one of the key factors for survival and success in today's marketplace. Canadian boot manufacturers are innovators and the best producers of quality footwear made to resist the "elements of nature." Understanding that business is almost always conducted in the face of competition is one key aspect of marketing that all would-be marketers must keep in the forefront of their planning.

Dealing with the environment, developing marketing plans and making marketing decisions cannot be undertaken without good information. Acquiring information can be performed by a business itself or may be contracted out to third party market research firms like IRI and A. C. Nielsen. Consumer purchase information is particularly valuable to marketing decisions makers, and these two firms are vying with one another to be the exclusive collectors and providers of this information for the Canadian market. Although IRI and A. C. Neilsen provide marketing information, they also undertake marketing of their own services. In this vein, they compete with one another, and other marketing information providers, and must undertake and understand the process of marketing, even as they play a part in this process.

We hope you enjoy learning about the process of marketing, which will be introduced in the remaining part-opening vignettes and illustrated in video cases on Canadian firms throughout the rest of *Marketing*, Canadian Edition.

Part-opening vignettes engage students in marketing in a very reader-friendly manner and preview the CBC video cases in that part of the text.

In each chapter, the feature entitled "Marketing in a Changing World" demonstrates the kinds of marketing issues that occur in today's tough business environment.

MARKETING IN A CHANGING WORLD
Talking to Former Customers

In today's competitive marketplace, it may not be enough for a firm to focus its efforts on current and prospective customers. It may also be a good idea to research and try to win back various former customers. To do that, a company needs to engage in the sometimes painful task of finding out why these are "former" customers.

Yet because most company owners hate to hear harsh words about their babies, they find the hardest part of tracking lost customers is picking up the phone. Bob Ottley, president of One Step Tree and Lawn Care, hesitated for fear "the negative feedback would be impossible to deal with."

At the same time, Ottley was smart enough to know that he had to talk to former customers if his firm was to survive. Today, One Step has a weekly "cancels" report; and Ottley knows what per cent of cancellations are due to people moving, deciding to mow their own lawns, or no longer being able to afford his service—and switching to a lower-priced competitor. One Step has cut its customer attrition rate in half since it began the "cancels" report. And its leave-behind survey of current customers "puts the idea into their heads that we want to know if there's a problem."

Bruce Grench, chief executive of HDIS (a small mail-order firm that specializes in personal-care products), is another executive who has overcome his qualms. Grench uses six different approaches, from small-group gripe sessions to one-on-one telephone surveys, to gather comments from would-be, current, and former customers. He says, "We kind of look forward to it [contacting former customers], even though it's tough medicine. The hope is that we can find something we're not doing right because it offers us an opportunity." He did; that's why HDIS now offers private-label products for price-conscious customers."[20]

[20]"Where Did We Go Wrong?" *Inc.* (July 1995), p. 91.

XXV

About the Computer Supplement that Accompanies MARKETING, Canadian Edition

As noted in the preface, *Marketing*, Canadian Edition, has a computer supplement available for students: *Computer-Based Marketing Exercises*. It is microcomputer-based and geared to IBM PCs and compatibles. It is also extremely user-friendly, does not require prior computer experience, operates in the Windows environment, and is not dependent on knowledge of such software as Lotus 1-2-3. All directions are contained on computer screens and are self-prompting.

Computer-Based Marketing Exercises is designed to apply and reinforce specific individual concepts in *Marketing*, Canadian Edition, in an interactive manner. The exercises are explained in the appendix at the end of this text; throughout *Marketing*, a computer symbol is used to signify which concepts are related to the exercises. An accompanying master computer diskette (which may be ordered by the instructor) can be used to reproduce student exercise disks. The 18 exercises are as realistic as possible; relate to important marketing concepts; allow students to manipulate marketing factors and see their impact on costs, sales, and profits; are relatively independent of one another; and encourage students to improve computer skills.

The exercises may be handed in as class assignments or used for student self-review/self-learning. Page references to the relevant concepts in *Marketing*, Canadian Edition, are provided for each exercise, both on the computer diskette and in the appendix at the end of this text. Students get to experiment with cross-tabulation tables, bar charts, spreadsheets, graphic scales, data bases, positioning maps, and other learning tools. Graphics quality is high. Here are the exercises:

1. Marketing Orientation.
2. Boston Consulting Group Matrix
3. Questionnaire Analysis
4. Ethics in Action
5. Standardization in International Marketing Strategy
6. Vendor Analysis
7. Segmentation Analysis
8. Product Positioning
9. Services Strategy
10. Product Screening Checklist
11. Economic Order Quantity
12. Wholesaler Cost Analysis
13. Advertising Budget
14. Salesperson Deployment
15. Price Elasticity
16. Key Cost Concepts
17. Performance Ratios
18. Optimal Marketing Mix

We believe this computer supplement greatly enhances text material, further demonstrates the dynamic and exciting nature of marketing, and is an important learning tool in the emerging age of the computer. We welcome your feedback on *Computer-Based Marketing Exercises*.

About the Authors

Joel R. Evans (Ph.D. in Business with majors in Marketing and Public Policy) is the RMI Distinguished Professor of Business and Professor of Marketing and International Business at Hofstra University. Previously, Dr. Evans was department chairperson for seven years. Before joining Hofstra, he worked for United Merchants and Manufacturers, owned a retail mail-order business, and taught at Bernard M. Baruch College and New York University. He has also served as a consultant for such diverse companies as PepsiCo, Nynex, and McCrory.

Dr. Evans is author or editor of numerous books and articles and is active in various professional associations. At Hofstra, he has been honored as a faculty inductee in Beta Gamma Sigma and received two Dean's Awards and the School of Business Faculty Distinguished Service Award. Dr. Evans has also been honored as Teacher of the Year by the Hofstra M.B.A. Association.

Barry Berman (Ph.D. in Business with majors in Marketing and Behavioral Science) is the Walter H. "Bud" Miller Distinguished Professor of Business and Professor of Marketing and International Business at Hofstra University. Previously, Dr. Berman was associate dean of the Hofstra School of Business for seven years. He has served as a consultant to such organizations as the Singer Company, Associated Dry Goods, the State Education Department of New York, and professional and trade groups.

Dr. Berman is author or editor of numerous books and articles and is active in various professional associations. He served as associate editor of the *Marketing Review* for many years. At Hofstra, he has been honored as a faculty inductee in Beta Gamma Sigma and received two Dean's Awards. Dr. Berman has also been honored as Teacher of the Year by the Hofstra M.B.A. Association.

William J. Wellington (Ph.D. in Business Administration) is an Assistant Professor of Marketing at the University of Windsor, where he has taught graduate and undergraduate business students for over ten years. Prior to entering the academic field, Dr. Wellington was employed for three and a half years as a field sales representative for Parke-Davis Canada Ltd., a wholly-owned subsidiary of Warner-Lambert Inc. He received his Ph.D. from Michigan State University in 1989, where he majored in Marketing and Transportation. Dr. Wellington is particularly interested in marketing management, marketing strategy, and marketing education. He has written articles on market segmentation and the use of simulations in marketing education; he won a best paper award at the 1992 conference of the Association for Business Simulation and Experiential Learning.

AN INTRODUCTION TO MARKETING

PART 1

In Part 1, we begin our study of marketing and discuss concepts that form the foundation for the rest of the text.

1 Marketing in Contemporary Society

Here, we show the dynamic nature of marketing, broadly define the term "marketing," and trace its evolution. We pay special attention to the marketing concept, a marketing philosophy, customer service, and customer satisfaction and relationship marketing. And we examine the importance of marketing, as well as marketing functions and performers.

2 The Environment in Which Marketing Operates

In this chapter, we look at the complex environment within which marketing functions, with an emphasis on both the factors that are controllable and those that are uncontrollable to an organization and its marketers. We demonstrate that without adequate environmental analysis, a firm may function haphazardly or be shortsighted.

3 Strategic Planning: A Marketing Perspective

Here, we first distinguish between strategic business plans and strategic marketing plans, and describe the total quality approach to strategic planning. Next, we look at the different kinds of strategic plans and the relationships between marketing and other functional areas. We then present the steps in the strategic planning process in considerable detail. A sample outline for a strategic plan is presented and the actual strategic plan of a small firm is highlighted.

4 Information for Marketing Decisions

In this chapter, we explain why marketing decisions should be based on sound information. We explain the role and importance of the marketing information system—which coordinates marketing research, continuous monitoring, and data storage and provides the basis for decision making. We also describe marketing research and the process for undertaking it. We show that marketing research may involve surveys, observation, experiments, and/or simulation.

Part 1 Vignette
The Process of Marketing Affects Us All

As we will show throughout *Marketing*, Canadian Edition, organizations come in all sizes and orientations. The diversity of those engaged in marketing is demonstrated by the video cases on different Canadian organizations found at the end of each chapter in this text. The kinds of issues facing these organizations and the forces affecting them are many and varied. This vignette, along with the other part-opening vignettes, previews the cases and relates them to the material to which they pertain. In Part 1, the first video case presents Soft Image, a Montreal software company, and its parent firm Microsoft; the second, Kreb Boots; the third, the market research firms Information Resources Incorporated (IRI) and A. C. Nielsen.

Firms like Soft Image and Microsoft have arisen as a result of the impact of technology on marketing. The human race spawns new technologies that are commercialized, and this leads to new needs and wants, which spawn more new products and take businesses and society in directions never anticipated. Soft Image is a computer technology firm at the cutting edge of computer animation. Using computers to create visual images for movies and television programming is one of the innovative uses that was never fully dreamed of by the originators of computers.

Organizations involved with "marketing" practices come in all sizes and orientations.

Historically, computers have been viewed as tools designed mainly for number crunching and statistical information storage and processing. Today, films like *Toy Story*, *Jurassic Park*, and *The Mask* include computer-animated visual sequences as integral parts of their production. Soft Image is transforming the notion that computers are used only for number crunching and non-creative pursuits. The computer has become an important tool and social force, and its powers are being rapidly enhanced by the software developed by firms like Soft Image and Microsoft. These kinds of forces and their impact on business is something that *Marketing*, Canadian Edition, will examine.

Another critical force that affects marketers is competition. Canadian boot manufacturers like Kreb have survived and flourished in Canada's footwear industry, while Canadian shoe manufacturers have struggled with foreign competition. Developing and marketing products that meet the needs of customers better than any competitor is one of the key factors for survival and success in today's marketplace. Canadian boot manufacturers are innovators and the best producers of quality footwear made to resist the "elements of nature." Understanding that business is almost always conducted in the face of competition is one key aspect of marketing that all would-be marketers must keep in the forefront of their planning.

Dealing with the environment, developing marketing plans and making marketing decisions cannot be undertaken without good information. Acquiring information can be performed by a business itself or may be contracted out to third party market research firms like IRI and A. C. Nielsen. Consumer purchase information is particularly valuable to marketing decisions makers, and these two firms are vying with one another to be the exclusive collectors and providers of this information for the Canadian market. Although IRI and A. C. Neilsen provide marketing information, they also undertake marketing of their own services. In this vein, they compete with one another, and other marketing information providers, and must undertake and understand the process of marketing, even as they play a part in this process.

We hope you enjoy learning about the process of marketing, which will be introduced in the remaining part-opening vignettes and illustrated in video cases on Canadian firms throughout the rest of *Marketing*, Canadian Edition.

CHAPTER 1
Marketing in Contemporary Society

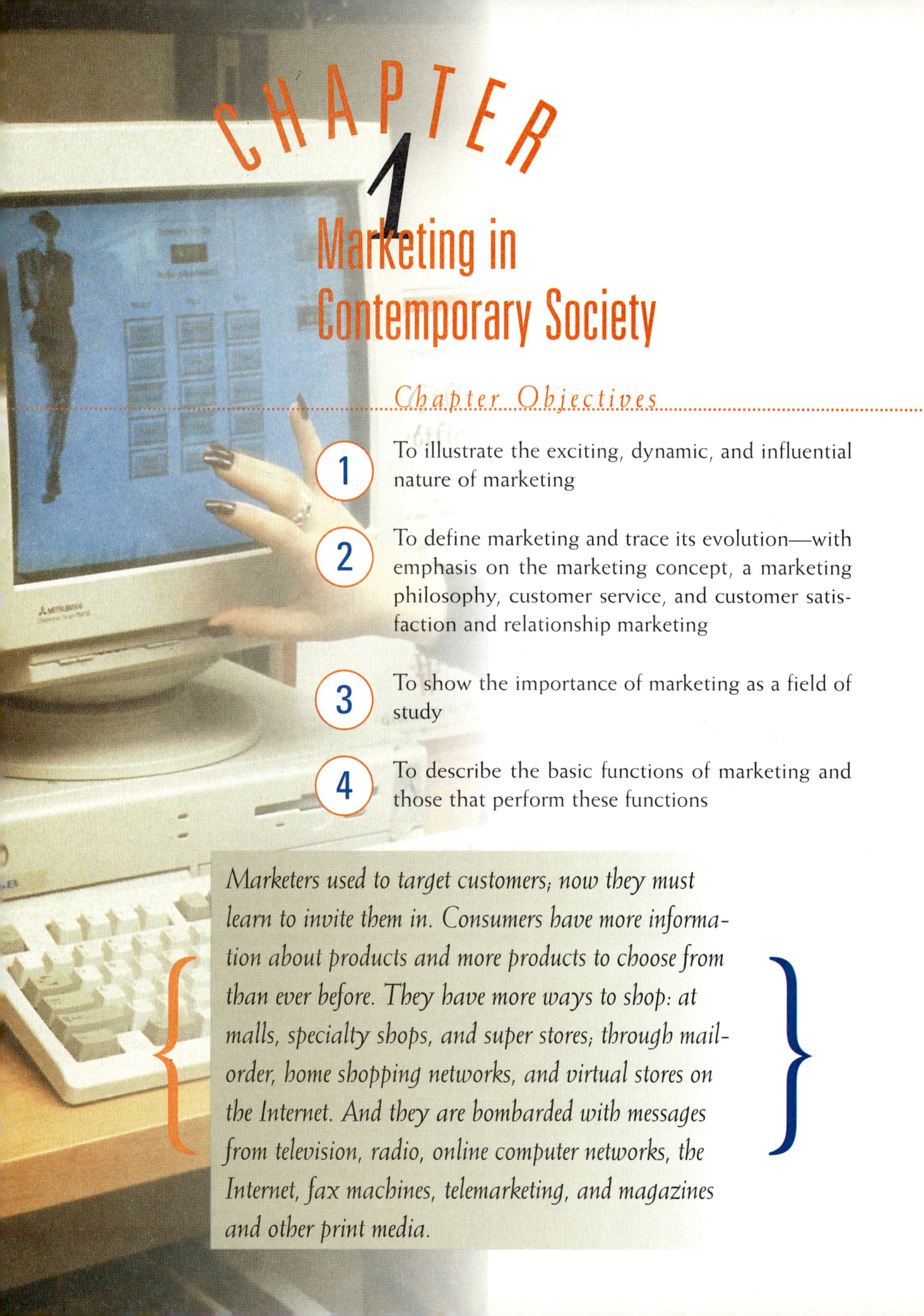

Chapter Objectives

1. To illustrate the exciting, dynamic, and influential nature of marketing

2. To define marketing and trace its evolution—with emphasis on the marketing concept, a marketing philosophy, customer service, and customer satisfaction and relationship marketing

3. To show the importance of marketing as a field of study

4. To describe the basic functions of marketing and those that perform these functions

{ *Marketers used to target customers; now they must learn to invite them in. Consumers have more information about products and more products to choose from than ever before. They have more ways to shop: at malls, specialty shops, and super stores; through mail-order, home shopping networks, and virtual stores on the Internet. And they are bombarded with messages from television, radio, online computer networks, the Internet, fax machines, telemarketing, and magazines and other print media.* }

For marketing-oriented firms, "inviting customers in" is a fundamental part of their business strategies. After all, one of the underpinnings of marketing is a strong interest in consumers—based on a belief that companies cannot succeed unless they understand and satisfy their clientele. How can firms do this in today's high-tech world? They can use information technology such as the Internet and toll-free 800 numbers to keep customers engaged in an ongoing dialogue. In contrast to traditional consumer surveys, "real-time" marketing provides continuous consumer contacts and uses consumer feedback as a critical element in developing and improving products, focuses on customer satisfaction, and refocuses the role of marketing within a firm. Let us look at how Apple Computer, Eaton's, and Federal Express use real-time marketing.

Apple Computer constantly analyzes information from its consumer hotlines for its Macintosh Performa computers. Apple's customer service personnel also use phone conversations with consumers to tell them about new products. On a weekly basis, these personnel identify the top ten consumer issues. The data are used by Apple engineers to design and improve products. For example, because of this feedback system, Apple learned about a particular problem that customers had in setting up Performa systems: Although Apple's instruction manual clearly illustrated how to set up the mouse, some people still thought it served as a foot pedal. After assessing the situation, Apple engineers devised an on-screen "welcome mat" that appears the first time people boot up their Performa computers. This mat introduces them to the basic elements of the Apple system, including the proper set-up and how the mouse functions.

Eaton's uses real-time marketing to issue new credit cards to customers. Instead of filling out long application forms, a customer need only provide a major credit-card number and some personal information to a clerk at an Eaton's sales terminal. The sales terminal then contacts a database operated by Montreal-based Equifax Canada Inc. Ninety per cent of the applicants are approved and issued an Eaton's credit card on the spot. The issued cards can contain a line of credit of up to $3000 and Eaton's promises that if the process of approval takes longer than one minute, the first credit card purchase is free (limited to $1000). As a result of this real-time marketing approach, Eaton's has noted an increase in credit-card usage rates and profitability.

Federal Express provides its larger customers with software and computer terminals to let them track their shipments. National Semiconductor, for instance, can determine if each of its customers worldwide has received the parts ordered by using the software. And a computer company seeking to order parts from National Semiconductor can look at the firm's online catalogue, order parts from Federal Express, and track parts shipping. Federal Express plans to communicate with most customers via real-time systems by the year 2000.[1]

In this chapter, we will learn more about the roles of marketing, see how marketing has evolved over the years, and look at its scope.

APPLE CANADA
www.apple.ca/

EATON'S
www.eatons.com/

EQUIFAX CANADA INC.
www.equifax.com/

NATIONAL SEMICONDUCTOR
www.nsc.com/navigate.html

Marketing is a dynamic field, encompassing many activities.

Overview

Marketing is an exciting, fast-paced business discipline. We engage in marketing activities or are affected by them on a daily basis, both in our business-related roles and as consumers. Okay, but what exactly does "marketing" mean? Well, it is not just advertising or

---

[1] Regis McKenna, "Real-Time Marketing," *Harvard Business Review*, Vol. 73 (July–August 1995), pp. 87–95; Katrina Onstad, "Eaton Credit Corporation Award of Distinction for Technology," *Canadian Business* (Fall 1995 Technology Issue), p. 76.

selling goods and services, although these are aspects of marketing. And it is not just what we do as supermarket shoppers every week, although this too is part of marketing.

As formally defined in the next section, "marketing" encompasses the activities involved in anticipating, managing, and satisfying demand via the exchange process. As such, marketing encompasses all facets of buyer/seller relationships. Specific marketing activities (all discussed later in this chapter) include environmental analysis and marketing research, broadening an organization's scope, consumer analysis, product planning, distribution planning, promotion planning, price planning, and marketing management.

In a less abstract way, here are two examples of real-world marketing—one from a business perspective and one from a consumer perspective.

BUSINESS PERSPECTIVE Marie Jackson, a 1994 B.Comm. with an accounting major and CA certification, has worked for a large accounting firm since graduating from university. She is now ready to open her own practice, but must make a number of decisions: Who should her clients be? What accounting services should she offer? Where should she open her office? How will she attract her clients? What fee schedule should she set? Is it ethical to try to attract clients that she worked with from her old firm? *Each of these questions entails a business-related marketing decision.*

Let's look at some of Marie Jackson's marketing options:

- *Clients*—Marie could target small or medium businesses, nonprofit organizations such as local libraries, and/or individuals (for personal tax and estate planning).
- *Accounting services*—Marie could be a full-service accountant for her clients or specialize in a particular accounting task (such as developing customized accounting software).
- *Office location*—Marie could open an office in a professional building, a small shopping centre, or her home. She could also go on on-site visits to clients, thus making the choice of her office location less important.
- *Attracting clients*—Marie must determine if she is from the "new" school—where it is acceptable to run ads in local newspapers, send out direct-mail pieces to prospective clients, etc.—or from the "old" school—where most forms of promotion are viewed as being unprofessional.
- *Fee schedule*—Marie must rely on her own experience with her previous firm and look at what competitors are doing. Then, she could price similar to others or lower/higher than them (depending on her desired image and a realistic reading of the marketplace).
- *Ethics*—Marie must weigh the personal dilemma of "stealing" clients from her old firm against the difficulty of starting a business from scratch without any client base.

CONSUMER PERSPECTIVE At the same time that Mary Jackson is making decisions about her new accounting practice, Albert Sampson is reappraising his status as an accounting client. He owns a small furniture repair store and has been a client of a mid-sized accounting firm for ten years. Yet he is now unhappy with the firm and feels it takes his business for granted. But before switching accountants, Albert must answer these questions: What kind of firm should he select? What accounting services should he seek? Where should the accounting firm be located? How will he learn more about possible firms? What fees should he be willing to pay? Is it ethical to show prospective firms samples of the work from his present accountant? *Each of these questions addresses a consumer-related marketing decision.*

Let's look at some of Albert Sampson's marketing options:

- *Kind of firm*—Albert could select a small, medium, or large accounting firm. Given his current dissatisfaction, he would probably avoid medium and large firms.
- *Accounting services*—Albert could continue having his accountant perform all accounting tasks for him; or he could take on some of the tasks himself (such as maintaining the ledger books and paying bills).

TECHNOLOGY & MARKETING

Windows 95: Hype or the Real Thing?

Microsoft introduced Windows 95 in August 1995. The launch was accompanied by demonstrations at convention centres, testing by 400 000 trial users, and special promotions by retailers. At its Washington headquarters, Microsoft sponsored a carnival and trade show for 2500. In total, Microsoft spent $150 million on the kickoff.

These are some of Windows 95's heralded benefits: (1) Under DOS and older Windows versions, file names were limited to eight letters, with three more after a period—for example "MKTGTEXT.DOX." In Windows 95, the same file could be "MARKETING, Canadian Edition," a more easily identifiable title. (2) Windows 95 can run up to a dozen or more programs at the same time, versus a maximum of six for the older Windows version. (3) Windows 95-compatible CD-ROMs begin playing as soon as they are inserted in a drive, without entering special commands.

However, some critics say Windows 95's benefits are overstated, and that most benefits will not be noticed unless the user buys new 32-bit versions of existing programs. Even Microsoft acknowledged that much of this software took months to be available and that consumers would have to buy software upgrades. Critics also feel that Microsoft has understated the PC hardware needed to properly run Windows 95, which requires more memory and a larger hard drive than most existing systems have. The cost of such hardware upgrades can easily exceed $900 per computer. And although Windows 95 is the most tested piece of software ever, defects and incompatibilities are still common. Furthermore, Apple has run ads commenting on how hard Windows 95 is to install, compared to easy-to-run Macintosh computers.

As a Microsoft marketing manager, how would you explain Windows 95's benefits and answer the criticisms for a cynical columnist for a newspaper?

Sources: Based on material in Don Clark, "Amid Hype and Fear, Microsoft Windows 95 Gets Ready to Roll," *Wall Street Journal* (July 14, 1995), pp. A1, A9; and Walter S. Mossberg, "Most PC Users Should Take Their Time Moving to Windows 95," *Wall Street Journal* (August 10, 1995), p. B1.

- *Office location*—Albert could look for an accountant that makes on-site visits (as his accountant does now) or seek a firm that has an office near to his store or residence.
- *Information about prospective firms*—Albert could ask prospective firms for references, check out accountants' credentials, interview candidates, and/or require firms to perform a sample task.
- *Fee schedule*—Albert knows he must get "fair" quotes, not "low ball" ones. He recognizes that you get what you pay for; and he wants better service.
- *Ethics*—Albert must determine whether he, as the client, has the right to show any old work to prospective firms—or whether there is a client/accountant relationship that he should not violate.

A MARKETING MATCH For "marketing" to operate properly, buyers and sellers need to find and satisfy each other (conduct exchanges). Do you think that Marie Jackson and Albert Sampson would make a good marketing match? We do—but only if their strategy (Marie) and expectations (Albert) are in sync.

In some way, we are all involved with or affected by marketing.

As these examples show, goods and service providers ("sellers") make marketing-related decisions like choosing who customers are, what goods and services to offer, where to sell these goods and services, the features to stress in ads, and the prices to charge. They also determine how to be ethical and socially responsible, and whether to sell products internationally (in addition to domestically). Marketing-related activities are not limited to industrial firms, large corporations, or people called "marketers." They are taken on by all types of companies and people.

As consumers ("buyers"), the marketing practices of goods and service providers affect many of the choices made by our parents, spouses, other family members, friends and associates, and/or us. For virtually every good and service we purchase, the marketing process affects whom we patronize, the assortment of models and styles offered in the marketplace, where we shop, the availability of knowledgeable sales personnel, the prices we pay, and other factors. Marketing practices are in play when we are born (which doctor our parents select, the style of baby furniture they buy); while we grow (our parents' purchase of a domestic or foreign family car or mini van, our choice of a college or university); while we conduct our everyday lives (the use of a particular brand of toothpaste, the purchase of status-related items); and when we retire (our consideration of travel options, a change in living accommodations).

The formal study of marketing requires an understanding of its definition, evolution (including the marketing concept, a marketing philosophy, and customer service), importance and scope, and functions. These principles are discussed throughout Chapter 1.

Marketing Defined

A broad, integrated definition of marketing forms the basis of this text:

> **Marketing** is the anticipation, management, and satisfaction of demand through the exchange process.

Marketing *includes anticipating demand, managing demand, and satisfying demand.*

It involves goods, services, organizations, people, places, and ideas.

Anticipation of demand requires that a firm do consumer research on a regular basis so it can develop and introduce offerings desired by consumers. Management of demand includes stimulation, facilitation, and regulation tasks. Stimulation motivates consumers to want a firm's offerings due to attractive product designs, distinctive promotion, fair prices, and other strategies. Facilitation is the process whereby the firm makes it easy to buy its offering by having convenient locations, accepting credit cards, using well-informed salespeople, and implementing other strategies. Regulation is needed when there are peak demand periods rather than balanced demand throughout the year or when demand is greater than the supply of the offering. Then, the goal is to spread demand throughout the year or to demarket a good or service (reduce overall demand). Satisfaction of demand involves product availability, actual performance upon purchase, safety perceptions, after-sale service, and other factors. For consumers to be satisfied, goods, services, organizations, people, places, and ideas must fulfil their expectations.

Marketing can be aimed at consumers or at publics. **Consumer demand** refers to the attributes and needs of final consumers, industrial consumers, wholesalers and retailers, government institutions, international markets, and nonprofit organizations. A firm may appeal to one or a combination of these. **Publics' demand** refers to the attributes and needs of employees, unions, shareholders, the general public, government agencies, consumer groups, and other internal and external forces that affect company operations.

Demand *is affected by both* **consumers** *and* **publics**.

The marketing process is not concluded until consumers and publics **exchange** their money, their promise to pay, or their support for the offering of a firm, institution, person, place, or idea. Exchanges must be done in a socially responsible way, with both the buyer and the seller being ethical and honest—and considering the impact on society and the environment.

Exchange *completes the process.*

A proper marketing definition should not be confined to economic goods and services. It should cover organizations (such as the Red Cross), people (for example, politicians), places (Vancouver), and ideas (the value of seat belts). A consumer orientation must be central to any definition. And from a societal perspective, a firm needs to ask whether a good or service should be sold, besides whether it can be sold. Figure 1-1 is an example of organizational marketing, while Figure 1-2 illustrates how a place (Welland, Ontario) can benefit from marketing efforts.

CANADIAN RED CROSS
www.redcross.ca/

FIGURE 1-1
Marketing and the Special Olympics
Marketing not only encompasses goods and services, but also organizations, people, and places.
Reprinted by permission.

Jenny Hubbs, Special Olympics Runner

THAT POUNDING IN YOUR HEART. IT'S PRIDE.

BE PART OF THE LARGEST SPORTS EVENT ON EARTH IN 1995, THE SPECIAL OLYMPICS WORLD GAMES IN CONNECTICUT. YOUR LOCAL PROGRAM NEEDS ATHLETES, COACHES, VOLUNTEERS AND SPONSORS TO PREPARE FOR THE GAMES. JOIN NOW AND GET READY TO BELIEVE.

Special Olympics World Games Connecticut 1995

TO LEARN MORE ABOUT THE WORLD GAMES, CALL 1-800-700-8585

The Evolution of Marketing

Marketing's evolution in an industry, country, or region of the world may be viewed as a sequence of stages: barter era → production era → sales era → marketing department era → marketing company era. In some industries, nations, and regions, marketing practices have moved through each stage and involve a good consumer orientation and high efficiency; in others, marketing practices are still in their infancy.

Marketing's origins can be traced to people's earliest use of the exchange process: the **barter era**. With barter, people trade one resource for another—like food for animal pelts. To accommodate exchanges, trading posts, travelling salespeople, general stores, and cities evolved, along with a standardized monetary system. In the least developed nations of the world, barter is still widely practised.

The modern system of marketing begins with the industrialization of an industry, country, or region. For the world's most developed nations, this occurred with the Industrial Revolution of the late 1800s. For developing nations, efforts to industrialize are now under

Marketing can be traced to the **barter era.**

FIGURE 1-2
Marketing Welland to Business Firms
Marketing can be used for the economic development of communities (places).

Reprinted with permission of Welland Development Commission and Canadian Tire Acceptance Limited.

way. Why is industrialization so important in marketing's evolution? Unless industrialization takes place, exchanges are limited, since people do not have surplus items to trade. With the onset of mass production, better transportation, and more efficient technology, products can be made in greater volume and sold at lower prices. Improved mobility, densely populated cities, and specialization also let more people share in the exchange process: They can turn from being self-sufficient (for example, making their own clothes) to being consumers of what others produce (such as buying clothes in a store or market). In the initial stages of industrialization, output is limited and marketing is devoted to products' physical distribution. Because demand is high and competition is low, firms typically do not have to conduct consumer research, modify products, or otherwise adapt to consumer needs. The goal is to lift production to meet demand. This is the **production era** of marketing.

The next stage takes place as companies expand production capabilities to keep up with consumer demand. At this point, many firms hire a sales force and some use advertising to sell their inventory. Yet, since competition is still rather low, when firms develop new products, consumer tastes or needs receive little consideration. The role of the sales force and advertising is to make consumer desires fit the features of the products offered. For example, a shoe manufacturer might make brown wingtip shoes and use ads and personal selling to convince consumers to buy them. That firm would rarely determine consumer tastes before making shoes or adjust output to those tastes. This is the **sales era** of marketing. It still exists where competition is limited, such as in nations in the process of moving to free-market economies.

As competition grows, supply begins to exceed demand. Firms cannot prosper without marketing input. They create marketing departments to conduct consumer research and advise management on how to better design, distribute, promote, and price products. Unless firms react to consumer needs, competitors might better satisfy demand and leave the firms with surplus inventory and falling sales. Yet, although marketing departments share in decisions, they may be in a subordinate position to production, engineering, and sales departments. This is the **marketing department era**. It still exists where marketing has been embraced, but not as the driving force in an industry or company.

Over the past forty years, firms in a growing number of industries, nations, and regions have recognized marketing's central role; marketing departments at those firms are

In the **production era**, *output increases to meet demand.*

In the **sales era**, *firms sell products without first determining consumer desires.*

The **marketing department era** *occurs when research is used to determine consumer needs.*

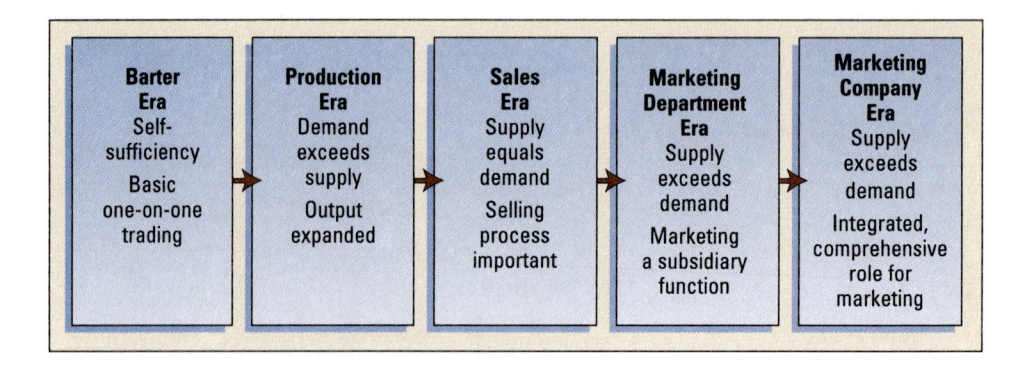

FIGURE 1-3
How Marketing Evolves

Barter Era	Production Era	Sales Era	Marketing Department Era	Marketing Company Era
Self-sufficiency	Demand exceeds supply	Supply equals demand	Supply exceeds demand	Supply exceeds demand
Basic one-on-one trading	Output expanded	Selling process important	Marketing a subsidiary function	Integrated, comprehensive role for marketing

now the equal of others. The firms make virtually all key decisions after thorough consumer analysis: Since competition is intense and sophisticated, consumers must be aggressively drawn and kept loyal to a firm's brands. Company efforts are well integrated and regularly reviewed. This is the **marketing company era**. Figure 1-3 indicates the key aspects of each era in marketing's evolution.

The marketing concept, a marketing philosophy, customer service, and customer satisfaction and relationship marketing are the linchpins of the marketing company era. They are examined here.

The **marketing company era** *integrates consumer research and analysis into all company efforts.*

The Marketing Concept

As Figure 1-4 shows, the **marketing concept** is a consumer-oriented, market-driven, value-based, integrated, goal-oriented philosophy for a firm, institution, or person.[2] Here is an illustration of the marketing concept in action:

The **marketing concept** *is consumer-oriented, market-driven, value-based, integrated, and goal-oriented.*

> How does a $48-million manufacturer compete with global giant Sony? By giving dealers (its customers) what they want. Koss Corporation has been dominant in headphones since it invented "stereo phones" in 1958. Even when Sony came on the scene in the 1980s with its Walkman, which created a market for low-end headphones, Koss was able to triple its sales and stay competitive.
>
> The simple philosophy "anything for the customer" has kept Koss in the game. In 1982, dealers requested that Koss change packaging so the headphones would be visible when hung on display. Koss responded by switching to clear packaging. In 1987, after dealers requested a bigger share of Koss's advertising dollars, the firm, which was spending the bulk of its budget on national print ads, converted most of its ad dollars to cooperative advertising. To meet dealer inventory demand, Koss began electronic data interchange (EDI) in 1989.

FIGURE 1-4
The Marketing Concept

Consumer Orientation, Market-Driven Approach, Value-Based Philosophy, Integrated Marketing Focus, Goal Orientation → Marketing Concept

---

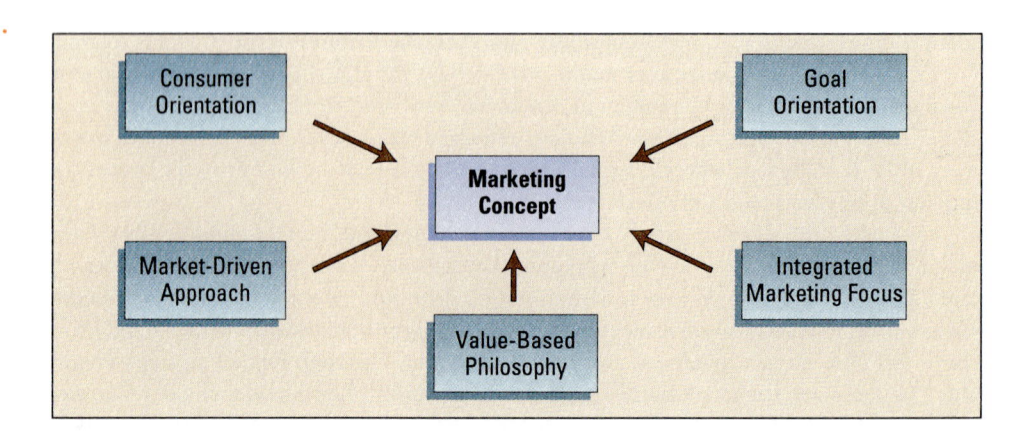

[2]For a comprehensive analysis of the marketing concept, see Frederick E. Webster, Jr., "Defining the New Marketing Concept," *Marketing Management*, Vol. 2 (Number 2, 1994), pp. 23–31.

On a number of occasions, Koss has even gone so far as to alter product features based on one dealer's request. In 1994, Koss built a beefed-up headphone that could take customer abuse to use on store displays for one national record store chain. The store liked the headphones so much it asked Koss to also package them for sale. "We make small changes every day," says CEO Michael Koss. "Even small enhancements like changing the colour or size of packaging help keep us close to our dealers."[3]

The marketing concept's five elements are crucial to the long-term success of a good, service, organization, person, place, or idea: A *customer orientation* means examining consumer needs, not production capability, and devising a plan to satisfy them. Goods and services are seen as means to accomplish ends, not the ends themselves. A *market-driven approach* means being aware of the structure of the marketplace, especially the attributes and strategies of competing firms. A *value-based philosophy* means offering goods and services that consumers perceive to have superior value relative to their costs and the offerings of competitors. With an *integrated marketing focus*, all the activities relating to goods and services are coordinated, including finance, production, engineering, inventory control, research and development, and marketing. A *goal-oriented firm* employs marketing to achieve both short- and long-term goals—which may be profit, funding to find a cure for a disease, increased tourism, election of a political candidate, a better company image, and so on. Marketing helps attain goals by orienting a firm toward pleasing consumers and offering desired goods, services, or ideas.

These are fifteen things that managers can do to ensure that they adhere to the spirit of the marketing concept:

1. Create customer focus throughout the firm.
2. Listen to the customer.
3. Define and cultivate distinctive competencies.
4. Define marketing as market intelligence.
5. Target customers precisely.
6. Manage for profitability, not sales volume.
7. Make customer value the guiding star.
8. Let the customer define quality.
9. Measure and manage customer expectations.
10. Build customer relationships and loyalty.
11. Define the business as a service business.
12. Commit to continuous improvement and innovation.
13. Manage the company culture along with strategy and structure.
14. Grow with partners and alliances.
15. Destroy marketing bureaucracy.[4]

Although the marketing concept lets a firm analyze, maximize, and satisfy consumer demand, it is only a guide to planning. A firm must also consider its strengths and weaknesses in production, engineering, and finance. Marketing plans need to balance goals, customer needs, and resource capabilities. The impact of competition, government regulations, and other external forces must also be evaluated. These factors are discussed in Chapters 2 and 3.

Selling Versus Marketing Philosophies

Figure 1-5 highlights the differences between selling and marketing philosophies. The benefits of a marketing, rather than a sales, orientation are many. Marketing stresses consumer analysis and satisfaction, directs the resources of a firm to making the goods and ser-

With a marketing orientation, selling is used to communicate with and understand consumers.

---
[3]Ginger Trumfio, "Anything for a Customer," *Sales & Marketing Management* (November 1995), p. 25.
[4]Frederick E. Webster, Jr., "Executing the New Marketing Concept," *Marketing Management*, Vol. 3, No. 1 (1994), pp. 9–16.

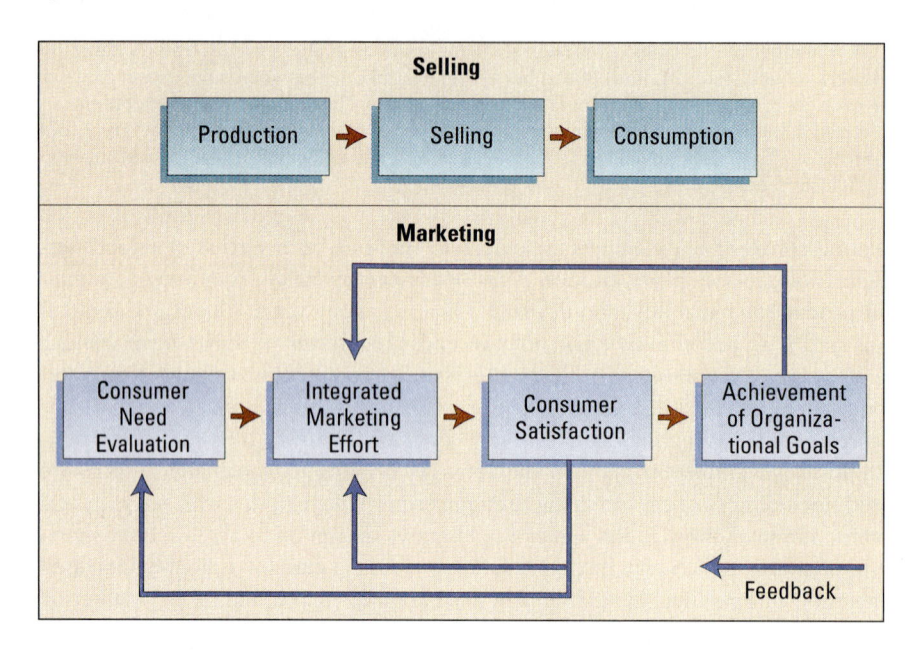

FIGURE 1-5
The Focus of Selling and Marketing Philosophies

vices consumers want, and adapts to changes in consumer traits and needs. Under a marketing philosophy, selling is used to communicate with and understand consumers; consumer dissatisfaction leads to changes in policy, not a stronger or different sales pitch. Marketing looks for real differences in consumer tastes and devises offerings to satisfy them. Marketing is geared to the long run, and marketing goals reflect overall company goals. Finally, marketing views customer needs broadly rather than narrowly (for example, heating as opposed to fuel oil).

As an example, at Wahl Clipper Corporation—which makes electric shavers and hair trimmers—sales have grown at a 16 per cent annual compounded rate for twenty years. Why? According to company president Jack Wahl, "I realized the difference between sales and marketing. That's a big thing for a small company. Sales means simply presenting the product and collecting money. Marketing means stepping back and looking for the needs of the customer, and for the best way to get through to that user."[5]

Customer Service

Customer service *tends to be intangible, but quite meaningful, to many consumers.*

Customer service involves the identifiable, but rather intangible, activities undertaken by a seller in conjunction with the basic goods and/or services it offers.[6] In today's highly competitive marketplace, the level of customer service a firm provides can affect its ability to attract and retain customers more than ever before.

Unless a consumer is happy with *both* the basic good (such as a new auto) or service (such as a car tuneup) offered by a seller *and* the quality of customer service (such as polite, expert sales personnel and punctual appointments), he or she is unlikely to patronize the seller—certainly not in the long run. Imagine your reaction to these situations:

> Stores often tell customers that home deliveries and repairs will be made any time between 8 A.M. and 5 P.M., often effectively killing a workday. Doctors and other health professionals frequently overbook appointments, so patients waste hours waiting to be seen. Federal, provincial, and municipal government agencies are often unreachable on the telephone.[7]
>
> With millions of new buyers, many of them individuals and small businesses, clueless about computers, some manufacturers can't keep up with service complaints and requests for help. The result: hordes of confused and resentful—even outraged—customers.[8]

---

[5]Jerry Flint, "Father Says, 'Jump,'" *Forbes* (August 14, 1995), p. 144.
[6]Peter D. Bennett (Ed.), *Dictionary of Marketing Terms*, Second Edition (Chicago: American Marketing Association, 1995), p. 73.
[7]Theodore D. Kemper, "Good Service Serves the Economy, Too," *New York Times* (January 9, 1994), Section 3, p. 13.
[8]Jim Carlton, "Support Lines' Busy Signals Hurt PC Makers," *Wall Street Journal* (July 6, 1995), p. B1.

International Marketing in Action

Why Is Customer Service at Germany's Deutsche Telekom Lagging Behind?

Customer service at Deutsche Telekom, Germany's phone monopoly, has generally been considered poor. Thus, the German government hoped to privatize the company in 1996 and to let international competitors (such as AT&T and Bell South) offer phone service in Germany as of 1998.

Experts say Deutsche Telekom has a number of customer service problems:

- It is relatively easy to tap into someone's telephone. This encourages fraud and misbilling problems.
- There are only one-quarter the number of pay phones per capita in Germany as compared to the Canadian and U.S. market.
- Although most telephone traffic in industrialized nations is switched by computer, one-half of Telekom's calls use outdated analog systems. Not only is its equipment inefficient and trouble-prone, but also it is incompatible with modern services such as call waiting.
- Deutsche Telekom is often ridiculed with regard to its customer service policies. A popular German television comedy routine, for example, shows Deutsche Telekom employees throwing complaint letters in the garbage.

Even though Deutsche Telekom executives know the firm's problems, they feel that they are due to legal factors beyond their control. For instance, German laws require phone lines to be buried underground rather than strung from poles. This increases the costs and time to service customers. German laws also require German long-distance users to subsidize local rates. Lastly, Deutsche Telekom workers are considered to be government employees; they are, thus, entitled to such benefits as annual five- to six-week paid vacations.

Despite the best intentions, some observers believe that Telekom's new competitors will aim their efforts at large industrial and commercial accounts and their entry into the market will have little impact on small residential customers.

As a Deutsche Telekom executive, what would you do to increase the quality of your customer service?

Source: Based on material in Greg Steinmetz, "Customer-Service Era Is Reaching Germany Late, Hurting Business," *Wall Street Journal* (June 1, 1995), pp. A1, A8.

Yet, firms often have to make customer service tradeoffs. For instance, supermarkets must weigh the potential loss of business if waiting lines are too long versus the cost of opening additional checkout lines.[9]

According to one survey, most people rate the overall level of customer service of businesses as excellent or pretty good, but over 40 per cent rate service as only fair or poor. More than one-third of people say they usually purchase from a business having excellent service but higher prices, rather than a lower-priced competitor with lesser service.[10]

DEUTSCHE TELEKOM
www.dtag.de/dtag/telekom_.html

---

[9]Steve Weinstein, "Rethinking Customer Service," *Progressive Grocer* (May 1995), pp. 63–68.
[10]"Many Consumers Expect Better Service—and Say They Are Willing to Pay for It," *Wall Street Journal* (November 12, 1990), pp. B1, B4.

14 Part 1 *An Introduction to Marketing*

To offer better customer service, some firms are **empowering employees**.

MCDONALD'S CORP.
www.mcdonalds.com/main

This is how several organizations are addressing the issue of customer service: Organizations as diverse as the Winnipeg Blue Bombers and Revenue Canada are **empowering employees**—giving workers broad leeway to satisfy customer requests, and encouraging and rewarding employees for showing initiative and imagination. The Winnipeg Blue Bombers reward their employees with success celebrations to recognize outstanding achievements, whether they are players or other personnel. Revenue Canada has also tried to improve its customer service by empowering employees. More responsibility is being granted to the regions to make decisions. For example, managers are encouraged to consult with the public; make decisions on tax cases by looking at facts rather than the letter of the law; and to consider substance instead of form when administering the Income Tax Act.[11]

Customer service is an important "output" of a marketing system and firms are very conscious of this. McDonald's Restaurants of Canada instituted an incentive program as early as 1993 to encourage improved customer service by its employees. Employee contests for good service are held and the top performers receive prizes in merchandise or McDonald's food discounts. The contests and their results are publicized in-house using posters, newsletters, payroll stuffers, and bulletin board notices.[12]

As Figure 1-6 illustrates, no company is more comprehensive in its approach to customer service than airline giant British Airways:

> The firm tracks some 350 measures of performance, including aircraft cleanliness, punctuality, customer opinions on check-in experiences, the time it takes for a customer to get through when phoning a reservations agent, and customer satisfaction with in-flight and ground services. A monthly report goes to the chief executive officer, the managing director, the chief financial officer, and the top management team responsible for service and performance. The report usually has a section focusing on a particular problem or issue. For example, it might address in-flight food service.[13]

Customer Satisfaction and Relationship Marketing

Firms cannot usually prosper without a high level of **customer satisfaction**.

As previously noted, **customer satisfaction** is a crucial element in successful marketing. It is the degree to which there is a match between a customer's expectations of a good or service and the actual performance of that good or service, including customer service.[14] As one expert says: "Firms that satisfy customers are ones that do their homework. They know a customer satisfaction commitment must be backed up by a complete understanding of the customer, the competition, and the marketplace—and an ability to identify and respond to areas where change is needed."[15] Figure 1-7 shows eleven representative factors that affect overall customer satisfaction.

This is how formidable it can be to keep customers satisfied:

> Do smaller companies give better customer service? The clients of Roberts Express Inc. thought so. In 1983, when sales were $3 million U.S. at this multinational freight company based in Akron, Ohio, Roberts Express was specializing in emergency shipments; customers were spoiled and they enjoyed it. They spoke to service representatives on a first-name basis. Calling in, clients expected to reach a shipping agent who knew their business, even what truck size would best suit their company's products. Roberts Express rarely disappointed its small group of customers.
>
> But as sales doubled annually, that service started to change. Customer service reps and shipping agents who once sat side by side and solved problems by talking over a cubicle wall, now worked in separate buildings. In monthly satisfaction surveys, clients complained that the company had become too large. Customers weren't recognized anymore. "They were saying, 'I'm calling a customer service organization and one of 100 people could pick up the phone,'" recalls Bruce Simpson, president of Roberts Express.

---

[11]"Smart Football," *Manitoba Business*, Vol. 13, No. 2 (March 1991), p. 16; "Revenue Canada Tries to Put on a Happy Face," *Financial Post*, Vol. 5, No. 162 (November 13, 1991), p. 14.
[12] "Incentives Help to Improve Service," *Strategy*, Vol. 4, No. 11 (February 8, 1993), pp. 22–24.
[13]Steven E. Prokesch, "Competing on Service: An Interview with British Airways' Sir Colin Marshall," *Harvard Business Review*, Vol. 73 (November–December 1995), p. 108.
[14]Bennett, *Dictionary of Marketing Terms*, p. 73.
[15]Stanley Brown, "You Can Get Satisfaction," *Sales & Marketing Management* (July 1995), p. 106.

FIGURE 1-6
Customer Service and British Airways
Reprinted by permission.

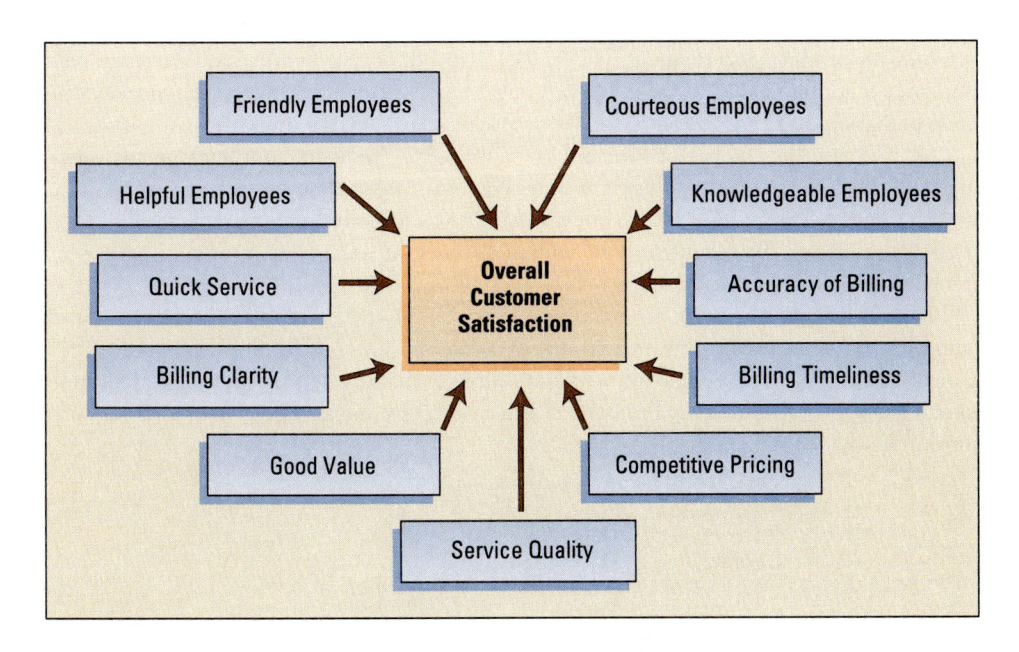

FIGURE 1-7
Factors That Affect Customer Satisfaction
Source: Steven Hokanson, "The Deeper You Analyze, the More You Satisfy Customers," *Marketing News* (January 2, 1995), p. 16. Reprinted by permission of the American Marketing Association.

*Through **relationship marketing**, companies try to increase long-term customer loyalty.*

GREAT PLAINS SOFTWARE
www.gps.com/

To get back to its small-company roots, Roberts started to reorganize into teams. It now has 18 teams that give Roberts a small company feel while allowing it to grow sales. When a customer calls, the team member who picks up the phone owns the service from start to finish. The firm can give personal, immediate service because each team works as a small business for its geographic area. Today, sales are about U.S.$150 million.[16]

Companies with satisfied customers have a good opportunity to convert them into loyal customers who will purchase from them over an extended period. From a consumer perspective, when marketing activities are performed with the conscious intention of developing and managing long-term, trusting customer relations, **relationship marketing** is involved.[17] Why is this so important? According to one observer, "It's far cheaper to hold on to the [customers] you have than to acquire new ones. A happy contingent inside your tent lessens your need to beat the street for business. Loyalists may even drum up fresh prospects for you."[18]

Great Plains Software, a provider of high-end programs for accountants, is one of many firms that has mastered relationship marketing:

How's this for getting close to the customer? Great Plains codes every program in a way that blocks its use after 50 transactions. The customer must call the firm for the code that gets the program running again. At this point, the folks who answer the phones ask questions about the customer's business, computer system, and software requirements. Sound annoying? "Customers don't seem to mind a simple phone call," insists CEO Doug Bergum. Today, Great Plains has some 45 000 buyer profiles in its data bank and personally solicits those likely to upgrade. In 1993, the firm persuaded a phenomenal 42 per cent of the owners of Great Plains Accounting Version 6 to buy new Version 7.

These retention skills got dearly tested when Version 7 turned out to contain bugs. Concerned that his reputation for bug-free products would be ruined, Bergum spent $340 000 to mail new disks to every Version 7 buyer. He also wrote all 2700 Great Plains dealers, admitting that he failed to test Version 7 properly and offering cash compensation to anyone whose business suffered from the glitch. Great Plains' goof may have *enhanced* customer loyalty. More dealers wrote to praise Bergum's response than to claim redress—which amounted to $34 000, less than 0.5 per cent of the sales from Version 7. *Accounting Today* commended Great Plains for being "a model of how problems should be handled." At "Stampede to Fargo," the firm's annual dealer conference, Bergum won the crowd by standing onstage, explaining his mistakes at length, and smashing three fresh eggs on his head.[19]

The Importance of Marketing

Marketing stimulates consumers, costs a large part of sales, employs people, supports industries, affects all consumers, and plays a major role in our lives.

Because marketing stimulates demand, one of its basic tasks is to generate consumer enthusiasm for goods and services. Worldwide, about $35 trillion of goods and services are produced annually, with Canada accounting for approximately $700 billion of that sum.

A large amount of each sales dollar goes to cover the costs related to such marketing activities as product development, packaging, distribution, advertising and personal selling, price marking, and administering consumer credit programs. Some estimates place the costs of marketing as high as 50 per cent or more of sales in certain industries. Yet, it should not be assumed that the performance of some marketing tasks by consumers would automatically lead to lower prices. For example, could a small business really save money by having the owner fly to Windsor to buy a new minivan directly from the maker rather than from a local dealer? Would a family be willing to buy clothing in bulk to reduce a retailer's transportation and storage costs?

Millions of people work in marketing-related jobs in Canada. They include those employed in the retailing, wholesaling, transportation, warehousing, and communications industries and those involved with marketing jobs for manufacturing, service, agricultural, mining, and other industries. Projections indicate future employment in marketing will remain strong.

---

[16] Weld F. Royal, "Keep Them Coming Back," *Inc.* (September 1995), p. 51.
[17] Bennett, *Dictionary of Marketing Terms*, p. 242.
[18] Patricia Sellers, "Keeping the Buyer You Already Have," *Fortune* (Autumn-Winter 1993), p. 56.
[19] Ibid., p. 57.

Marketing activities also involve entire industries, such as advertising and market research. Total annual worldwide advertising expenditures exceed $480 billion. Many agencies, such as WPP Group and Cordiant of Great Britain, Interpublic Group and Omnicom Group of the United States, and Dentsu of Japan have worldwide billings of several billion dollars each. Around $11 billion worldwide is spent yearly on various types of commercial marketing research. Firms such as Nielsen, Information Resources Inc., Research International (Great Britain), and GfK (of Germany) generate yearly revenues of more than $130 million dollars each.

All people and organizations serve as consumers for various goods and services. By understanding the role of marketing, consumers can become better informed, more selective, and more efficient. Effective channels of communication with sellers can also be established and complaints resolved more easily and favourably. Consumer groups have a major impact on sellers.

Because resources are scarce, marketing programs and systems must function at their peak. Thus, by optimizing customer service, inventory movement, advertising expenditures, product assortments, and other areas of marketing, firms will better use resources. Some industries may even require demarketing (lowering the demand for goods and services). For example, a Hydroelectric utility may launch a campaign to encourage consumers to reduce their consumption of electricity.

Marketing strongly affects people's beliefs and lifestyles. In fact, it has been criticized as developing materialistic attitudes, fads, product obsolescence, a reliance on gadgets, status consciousness, and superficial product differences—and for wasting resources. Marketers reply that they merely address the desires of people and make the best goods and services they can at the prices people will pay.

Marketing has a role to play in improving our quality of life. For example, marketing personnel often encourage firms to make safer products, such as child-proof bottle caps. They create public service messages on energy conservation, AIDS prevention, driver safety, alcohol abuse, and other topics. They help new goods, ideas, and services (such as cellular phones, improved nutrition, and ATMs) to be accepted by people and organizations.

A knowledge of marketing is extremely valuable for those not directly involved in a marketing job. For example, marketing decisions must be made by:

- *Doctors*—What hours are most desirable to patients?
- *Lawyers*—How can new clients be attracted?
- *Management consultants*—Should fees be higher, lower, or the same as competitors'?
- *Financial analysts*—What investments should be recommended to clients?
- *Research and development personnel*—Is there consumer demand for a potential "breakthrough" product?
- *Economists*—What impact will the economy have on the way various industries market their offerings?
- *Statisticians*—How should firms react to predicted demographic shifts?
- *Teachers*—How can students become better consumers?
- *City planners*—How can businesses be persuaded to relocate to the city?
- *Nonprofit institutions*—How can donor contributions be raised?

Each of these professions and organizations needs to understand and satisfy patient, client, consumer, student, taxpayer, or contributor needs. And more of them than ever before are now undertaking marketing activities such as research, advertising, and so on.

DENTSU (INFORMATION SERVICES INTERNATIONAL-DENTSU, LTD.)
www.isid.co.jp/index_n.html

Marketing awareness is invaluable for those in non-marketing jobs.

Marketing Functions and Performers

There are eight basic **marketing functions**: environmental analysis and marketing research, broadening an organization's/individual's scope, consumer analysis, product planning, distribution planning, promotion planning, price planning, and marketing management. They are shown in Figure 1-8, which also notes where they are discussed in the text.

*Basic **marketing functions** range from environmental analysis to marketing management.*

18 Part 1 *An Introduction to Marketing*

Here are brief descriptions of the functions:

- *Environmental analysis and marketing research*—Monitoring and adapting to external factors that affect success or failure, such as the economy and competition; and collecting data to resolve specific marketing issues.
- *Broadening an organization's/individual's scope*—Deciding on the emphasis to place, as well as the approach to take, on societal issues and international marketing.
- *Consumer analysis*—Examining and evaluating consumer characteristics, needs, and purchasing processes; and selecting the group(s) of consumers at which to aim marketing efforts.
- *Product planning (including goods, services, organizations, people, places, and ideas)*—Developing and maintaining products, product assortments, product images, brands, packaging, and optional features; and deleting faltering products.
- *Distribution planning*—Forming relations with distribution intermediaries, physical distribution, inventory management, warehousing, transportation, the allocation of goods and services, wholesaling, and retailing.
- *Promotion planning*—Communicating with customers, the general public, and others through some form of advertising, public relations, personal selling, and/or sales promotion.
- *Price planning*—Determining price levels and ranges, pricing techniques, terms of purchase, price adjustments, and the use of price as an active or passive factor.
- *Marketing management*—Planning, implementing, and controlling the marketing program (strategy) and individual marketing functions; appraising the risks and benefits in decision making; and focusing on total quality.

Generally, a firm should first study its environment and gather relevant marketing information. The firm should determine how to act in a socially responsible and ethical manner and consider whether to be domestic and/or international. At the same time, the

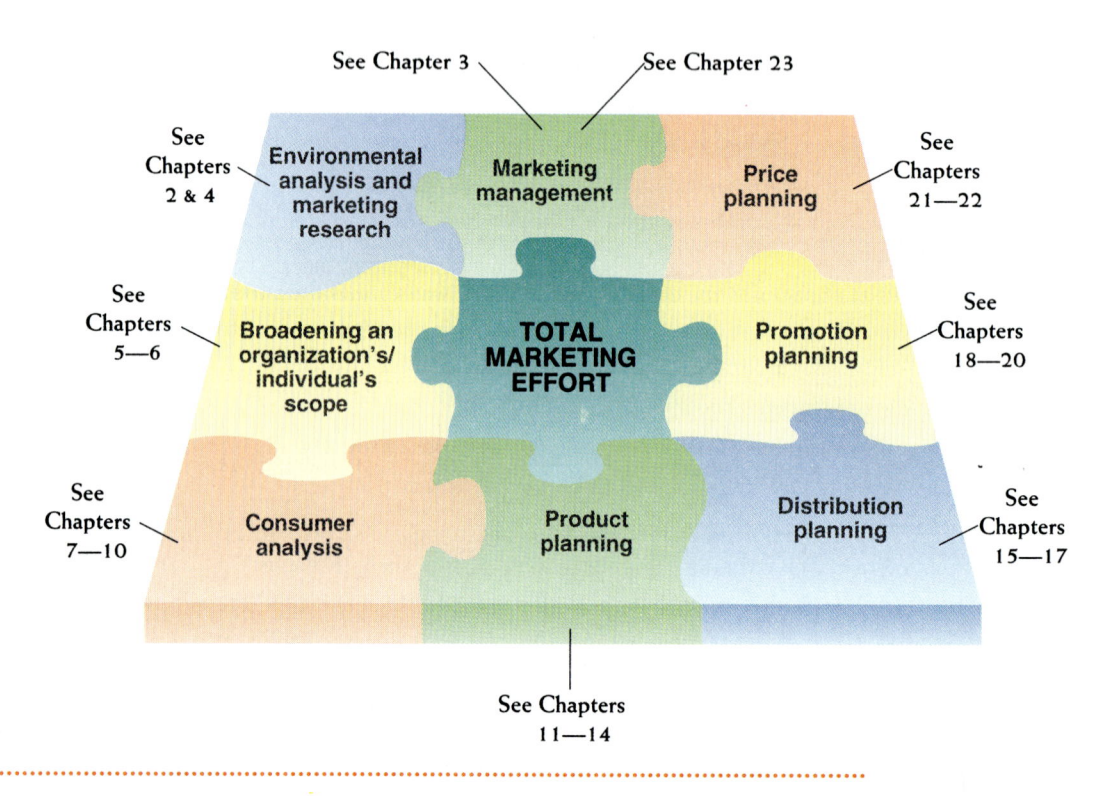

FIGURE 1-8
The Basic Functions of Marketing

firm should analyze potential customers to learn their needs and select the group(s) on which to focus. It should next plan product offerings, make distribution decisions, choose how to communicate with customers and others, and set proper prices. These four functions (in combination, known as the *marketing mix*) should be performed in a coordinated manner, based on environmental, societal, and consumer analysis. Through marketing management, the firm's overall marketing program would be planned and carried out in an integrated manner, with fine-tuning as necessary.

Although many marketing transactions require the performance of similar tasks, such as being ethical, analyzing consumers, and product, distribution, promotion, and price planning, these tasks can be enacted in many ways (for example, a manufacturer could choose to distribute its product via full-service retailers or self-service ones; or a financial-services firm could choose to rely on either telephone sales or in-office visits by salespeople to potential small-business clients).

Ethics AND TODAY'S MARKETER

What Practices Do YOU Believe Are Ethical?

Ethical values in marketing can be determined by using a checklist. Here is an opportunity for YOU to assess your level of marketing ethics.

Respond to these statements on a 1 to 9 scale. For items 1-4, let "1" mean that you completely disagree and "9" mean that you completely agree. For items 5-10, use a "1" for complete agreement and a "9" for complete disagreement:

1. Business ethics and social responsibility are critical to the survival of a business enterprise.
2. Business has a social responsibility beyond making a profit.
3. Good ethics is often good business.
4. Social responsibility and profitability can be compatible.
5. If shareholders are unhappy, nothing else matters.
6. The most important concern for a firm is making a profit, even if it means bending or breaking the rules.
7. To remain competitive in a global environment, business firms will have to disregard ethics and social responsibility.
8. Efficiency is much more important to a firm than whether or not the firm is seen as ethical or socially responsible.
9. Although output quality is essential to corporate success, ethics and social responsibility are not.
10. Communication is more important to the overall effectiveness of a firm than whether it is concerned with ethics and social responsibility.

Items 1 to 4 measure a "good ethics is good business" orientation, items 5 to 8 measure a "profits are not paramount" orientation, and items 9 and 10 measure a "quality and communication" orientation. Summarize and describe your ethical nature by determining your total score, as well as your score on the three individual scales.

Source: Based on material in Anusorn Singhapakdi, Kenneth L. Kraft, Scott J. Vitell, and Kumar C. Rallapalli, "The Perceived Importance of Ethics and Social Responsibility on Organizational Effectiveness: A Survey of Marketers," *Journal of the Academy of Marketing Science,* Vol. 23 (Winter 1995), pp. 49–56.

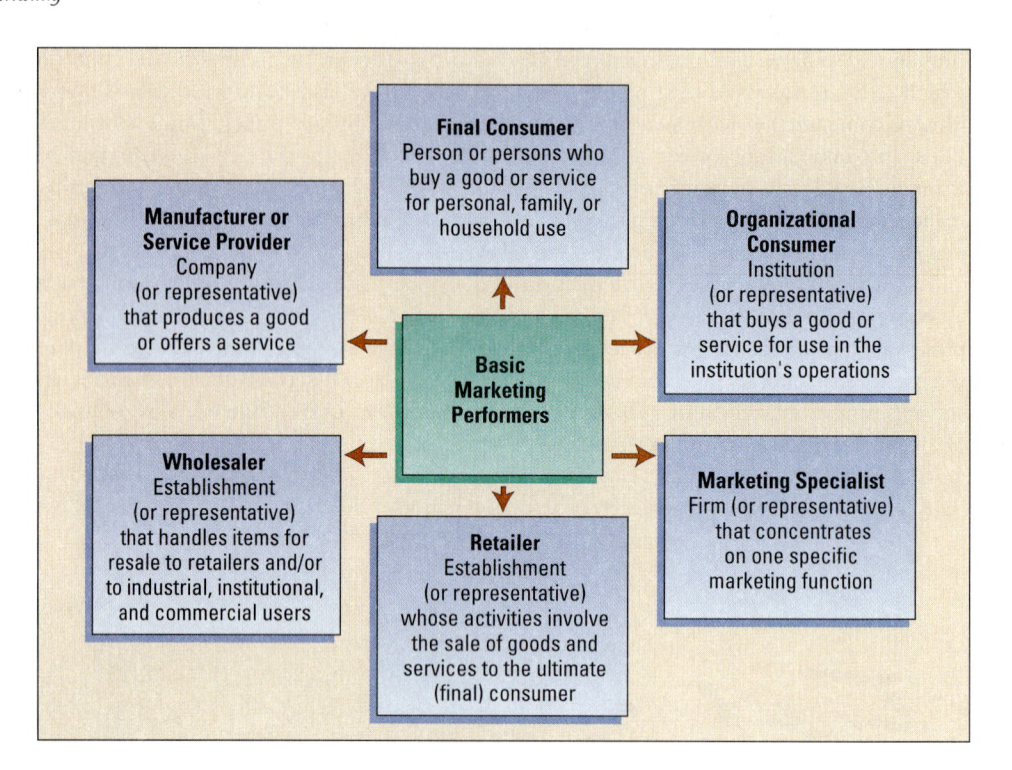

FIGURE 1-9
Who Performs Marketing Functions

Usually at least one **marketing performer** *must undertake each of the basic marketing functions.*

Marketing performers are the organizations or individuals that undertake one or more marketing functions. They include manufacturers and service providers, wholesalers, retailers, marketing specialists, and organizational and final consumers. As Figure 1-9 shows, each performer has a different role. Even though the responsibility for marketing tasks can be shifted and shared in various ways, basic marketing functions usually must be done by one performer or another. They cannot be omitted in many situations.

Sometimes, one marketing performer decides to carry out all—or virtually all—marketing functions (such as Boeing analyzing the marketplace, acting ethically, operating domestically and internationally, seeking various types of customers, developing aerospace and related products, distributing products directly to customers, using its own sales force and placing ads in select media, and setting prices). Yet, for these reasons, one performer often does not undertake all marketing functions:

- Many firms do not have the financial resources to sell products directly to consumers. They need intermediaries to share in the distribution process.
- Marketing directly to customers may require producers of goods and services to offer complementary products or sell the complementary products of other firms so the distribution process is carried out efficiently.
- A performer may be unable or unwilling to complete certain functions and may seek a marketing specialist to fulfil them.
- Many performers are too small to do certain functions efficiently.
- For many goods and services, established distribution methods are in force and it is difficult to set up other methods (such as bypassing independent soda distributors to sell directly to retail stores).
- Some consumers may want to buy in quantity, visit self-service outlets, pay cash, and so on, to save money.

Format of the Text

This book is divided into eight parts. The balance of Part 1 focuses on the marketing environment; developing marketing plans; and the information needed for marketing decisions. Part 2 covers the key topics related to the broadened scope of marketing: societal, ethical, and consumer issues; and international marketing. The discussion in Parts 1 and 2 sets the foundation for studying the specific components of marketing.

Part 3 deals with marketing's central orientation: understanding consumers. It looks at demographics, social and psychological traits, and the decision process of final consumers; organizational consumer attributes and decision making; and developing a target market and sales forecasting. Parts 4 to 7 discuss the elements of the marketing mix (product, distribution, promotion, and price planning) and the actions needed to carry out a marketing program in depth. Part 8 considers the marketing management implications of the topics raised throughout *Marketing* and discusses how to integrate and analyze an overall marketing plan.

Numerous examples and illustrations of actual marketing practices by a variety of organizations and individuals are woven into our discussions. And although such topics as marketing and society, international marketing, organizational consumers, and goods versus service marketing get separate chapter coverage to highlight certain points, applications in these areas are presented throughout the text.

MARKETING IN A CHANGING WORLD
Preparing for the Year 2000 and Beyond

A daunting challenge for any organization is to examine the changing world so as to plan for the future. Thus, in each text chapter, we will look at some of the key events that are affecting or will affect marketing decision making.

Experts at Batelle, a leading research institute, feel these technologies are most apt to "bring rich rewards" to firms that are capable of developing and marketing them in the next decade:

- *Genetic mapping*—New treatments for ailments ranging from AIDS to Alzheimer's disease may be on the way.
- *Super materials*—Scientists will increasingly produce new materials with almost any desired characteristic.
- *High-density energy sources*—Batteries the size of sugar packets will bring many new, revolutionary products to life.
- *Digital HDTV*—Digital high-definition television could be the next "hot" item in the entertainment industry.
- *Miniaturization*—It will be possible to carry around a laptop computer the size of a pocket calculator. This computer will be interactive and wireless.
- *Smart manufacturing*—Factory assembly lines will more often be controlled by smart devices and systems rather than people.
- *Anti-aging goods and services*—New developments will range from aging creams that may actually work to an effective cure for baldness.
- *Medical treatments*—There will be new diagnostic tools that use extremely accurate sensors to detect diseases at very early stages.
- *Hybrid-fuel vehicles*—Research on alternative fuels will be stepped up.
- *Edutainment*—Computer software and other products will increasingly meld education and entertainment features.[20]

[20]Douglas E. Olesen, "The Top 10 Technologies for the Next 10 Years," *Futurist* (September–October 1995), pp. 9–13.

SUMMARY

In this and every chapter in the text, the summary is linked to the objectives stated at the beginning of the chapter.

1. *To illustrate marketing's exciting, dynamic, and influential nature* Marketing may be viewed from both business and consumer perspectives; and it influences us daily. As goods and service providers, we make such marketing-related decisions as choosing who customers are, what goods and services to offer, where to sell them, what to stress in promotion, what prices to charge, how to be ethical and responsible, and whether to operate internationally. As consumers, the marketing process affects whom we patronize, choices in the marketplace, where we shop, the availability of sales personnel, the prices we pay, and other factors.

2. *To define marketing and trace its evolution—with emphasis on the marketing concept, a marketing philosophy, customer service, and customer satisfaction and relationship marketing* Marketing involves anticipating, managing, and satisfying demand via the exchange process. It includes goods, services, organizations, people, places, and ideas.

The evolution of marketing can be traced to people's earliest use of barter in the exchange process (the barter era); but it has truly developed since the Industrial Revolution, as mass production and improved transportation have enabled more transactions to occur. For many firms, the evolution of modern marketing can be traced through four stages or "eras": production, sales, marketing department, and marketing company. Yet, in less-developed and developing countries, marketing practices are still in the early stages of development.

The marketing concept requires organizations or individuals to be consumer-oriented, market-driven, value-based, integrated in their efforts, and goal-oriented. A marketing philosophy means assessing and responding to consumer wants, to real differences in consumer tastes, and to long-run opportunities and threats; such a philosophy also requires coordinated decision making.

To prosper today, firms must emphasize customer service: the identifiable, rather intangible, acts performed by a seller in conjunction with the basic goods and/or services being offered. A number of firms now empower employees so as to improve the level of customer service. Customer satisfaction occurs when consumer expectations are met or exceeded; then firms have an opportunity to attract loyal customers by paying attention to relationship marketing.

3. *To show the importance of marketing as a field of study* Marketing is a crucial field for several reasons: it stimulates demand; it involves a lot of money and employs a large number of people; it involves entire industries, such as advertising and marketing research; all organizations and people are consumers in some situations; and finally, it has an impact on our beliefs and lifestyles and influences the quality of our lives. Some marketing knowledge is therefore valuable to all of us, regardless of occupation.

4. *To describe the basic functions of marketing and those that perform these functions* The major marketing functions are environmental analysis and marketing research; broadening an organization's or individual's scope; consumer analysis; product, distribution, promotion, and price planning; and marketing management. Responsibility for performing these tasks can be shifted and shared in several ways among manufacturers and service providers, wholesalers, retailers, marketing specialists, and consumers. Due to costs, assortment requirements, specialized abilities, company size, established distribution methods, and consumer interests, one party usually does not perform all functions.

KEY TERMS

marketing (p. 7)
consumer demand (p. 7)
publics' demand (p. 7)
exchange (p. 7)
barter era (p. 8)
production era (p. 9)

sales era (p. 9)
marketing department era (p. 9)
marketing company era (p. 10)
marketing concept (p. 10)
customer service (p. 12)
empowering employees (p. 14)

customer satisfaction (p. 14)
relationship marketing (p. 16)
marketing functions (p. 17)
marketing performers (p. 20)

Review Questions

1. How does marketing influence us daily both in our business roles and as consumers?
2. Explain the following:
    a. Anticipation of demand.
    b. Management of demand.
    c. Satisfaction of demand.
    d. Exchange process.
3. Distinguish between consumer and publics' demand.
4. Give an example of a good, service, organization, person, place, and idea that may be marketed.
5. Describe the five eras of marketing.
6. What are the five components of the marketing concept? Give an example of each component.
7. What is customer service? Why is it so important to any firm?
8. What is customer satisfaction? Why is it so important to any firm?
9. What are the basic functions performed by marketing?
10. Why do most consumers *not* buy products directly from manufacturers?

Discussion Questions

1. a. As Marie Jackson, CA, what business-related marketing decisions would you make? Why?
    b. As Albert Sampson, accounting client, what consumer-related marketing decisions would you make? Why?
    c. Develop a plan for Marie Jackson to attract Albert Sampson as a client.
2. Does the presence of a marketing department mean a firm is following the marketing concept? Explain your answer.
3. As the manager of a full-service hotel chain, how would your customer services differ from those offered by a limited-service hotel chain? Why?
4. Develop a seven-item questionnaire to assess the quality of a firm's customer satisfaction efforts.
5. Examine the technologies that the Batelle Institute experts predicted would bring rich rewards. Provide your assessment as to why these experts felt they would be so lucrative.

Hints for Solving Cases

Each chapter, from 2 through 23, ends with two short cases—a total of 44. All cases are intended to build on text discussions, improve your reasoning skills, and stimulate class discussions.

The cases in *Marketing*, Canadian Edition, describe actual marketing scenarios faced by a variety of organizations and individuals. The facts, situations, and people are all real. The questions following each case are designed to help you pinpoint major issues, foster your analysis, cite alternative courses of future action, and develop appropriate marketing strategies. The information necessary to answer the questions may be drawn from the case and the text chapter to which the case relates.

One case per chapter also has a video component, which your professor may or may not assign. The material in the text is sufficient to answer the first four questions regarding a case; there are two other questions for the case that pertain to its video.

These hints should be kept in mind when solving a case:

- Read (observe) all material carefully. Underline or take notes on important data and statements.
- List the key issues and company actions detailed in the case.
- Do not make unrealistic or unsupported assumptions.
- Read each question following the case. Be sure you understand the thrust of every question. Do not give similar answers for two distinct questions.
- Write up tentative answers in outline form. Cover as many aspects of each question as possible.
- Review relevant material in the appropriate chapter of the text. In particular, look for information pertaining to the case questions.
- Expand your tentative answers, substantiating them with data from the case and the chapter.
- Reread the case and your notes to be sure you have not omitted any important concepts in your answers.
- Make sure your answers are clear and well-written, and that you have considered their ramifications for the organization.
- Reread your solutions at least one day after developing your answers. This ensures a more objective review of your work.
- Make any necessary revisions.
- Be sure your answers are not a summary ("rehash") of the case, but that you have presented a real analysis and recommendations.

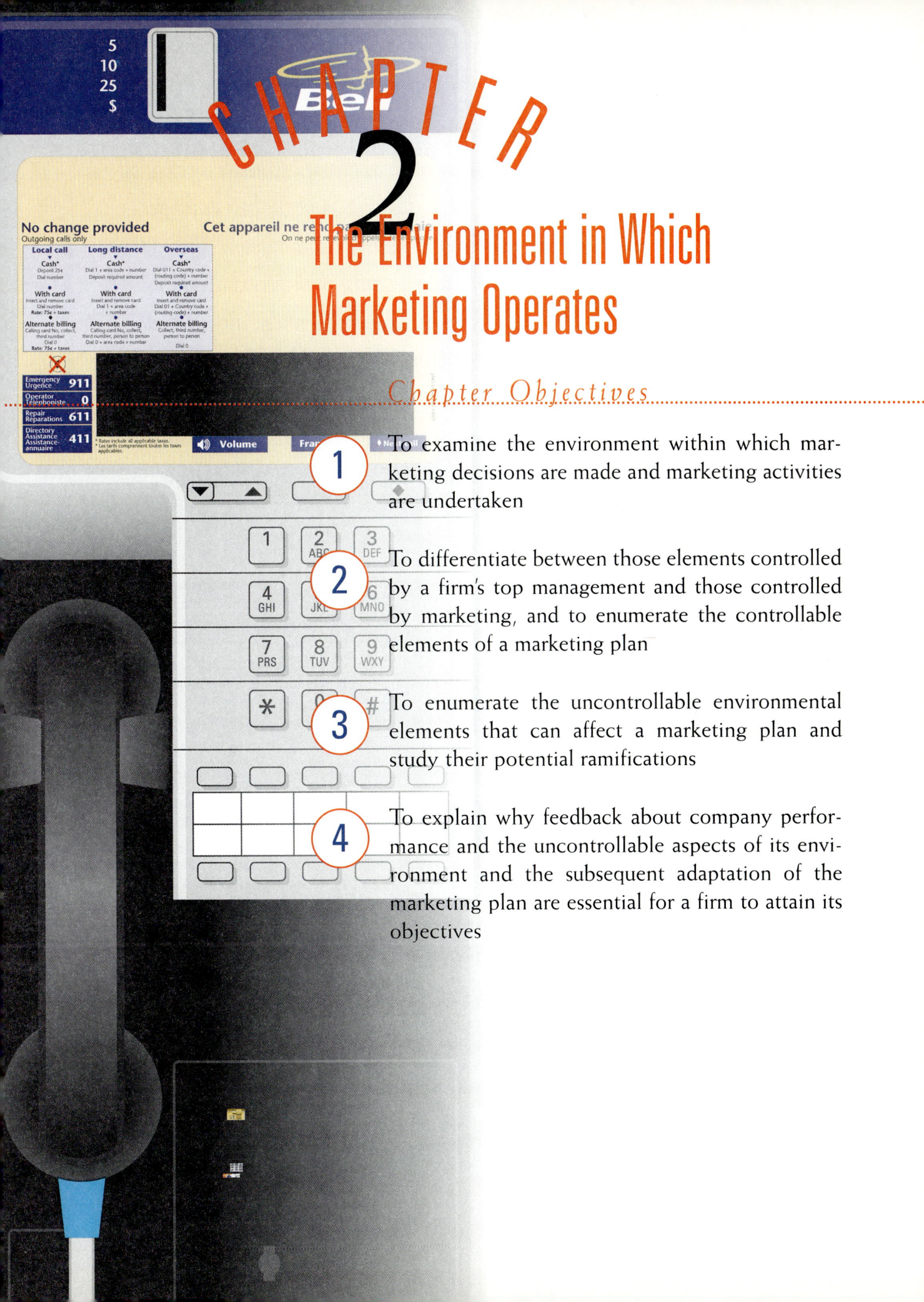

CHAPTER 2
The Environment in Which Marketing Operates

Chapter Objectives

1. To examine the environment within which marketing decisions are made and marketing activities are undertaken

2. To differentiate between those elements controlled by a firm's top management and those controlled by marketing, and to enumerate the controllable elements of a marketing plan

3. To enumerate the uncontrollable environmental elements that can affect a marketing plan and study their potential ramifications

4. To explain why feedback about company performance and the uncontrollable aspects of its environment and the subsequent adaptation of the marketing plan are essential for a firm to attain its objectives

> *Pitches by Bell Canada, Unitel, and Sprint Canada, as merciless as they are amusing, pose a challenge worthy of biblical scholars: Each claims to have the best deal offering incentives such as frequently called number discounts, U.S. rates, custom calling cards, peak-period discounts, off-peak discounts, itemized billing services, air-miles, etc. Sorting through the many offers could easily cost more time than most people actually spend on the phone. But one thing rings clear to almost every viewer: That staid bastion of bureaucracy, Ma Bell, has turned into one determined competitor.*

At one time, competitors were more genteel. They would not mention a direct competitor in an ad—or even think about saying something disparaging in public. Now, the rules of conduct have changed. Let's look at the new competitive tactics.

Bell Canada ads talk about sticking with a company that has always brought reliable service and quality. One ad notes how a Bell calling card's electromagnetic strip allows you to use 60 000 pay phones while the competitors cards allow access to 0. Bell has also taken aim at its competition by showing ads where people have who have tried the "other guys" returned to Bell because they did not achieve the savings promised and have had service problems. Sprint Canada has used Candace Bergen as a spokesperson, promising that with Sprint you will "go the distance," and Unitel promises that "doing business with a phone company will never be the same." Bell, Sprint, and Unitel have all engaged in telemarketing campaigns and direct mail campaigns that compare long distance savings. Bell has been particularly adept at retaining customers by using billing information to tailor custom calling plans to the actual behaviour of the individual. Sprint and Unitel do the same thing to retain their existing customers, but the key to their success is in aggressively switching customers from Bell Canada.[1]

Some competition involves blatant ripoffs. The Cowichan First Nations people have been selling hand-knit sweaters since the 1880s. They use designs trademarked in Canada: the thunderbird, the whale, the eagle, and the deer. The sweaters were popular with the many Japanese tourists who visited British Columbia every year, and the Cowichans hoped to capitalize on this popularity by selling them in the Japanese market. They were stunned to find Cowichan-brand sweaters already being sold in Japan. These sweaters were imported into the Japanese market from New Zealand. The Kiwi copies are machine-made and much

BELL CANADA
www.bell.ca/
UNITEL
www.unitel.com/

---

[1] "Psst, Wanna Buy Some Long-Distance?" *Canadian Business* (October 1994), p. 98.

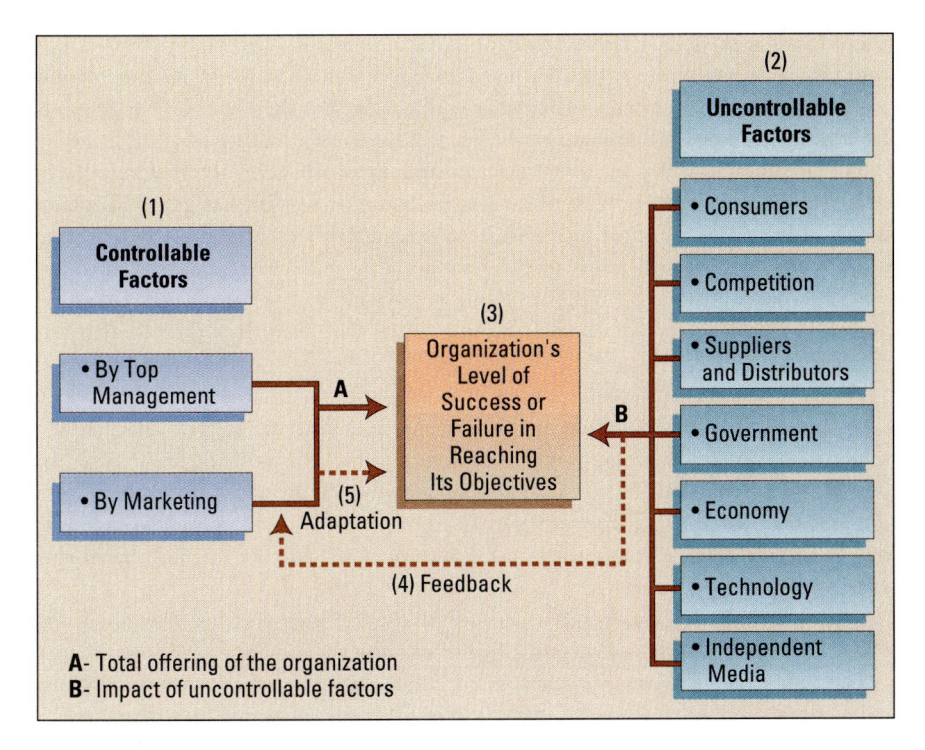

FIGURE 2-1
The Environment Within Which Marketing Operates

less expensive than the hand-made Cowichan originals. The Cowichans had not ensured international protection for their trademark. The copies have made strong in-roads into the Japanese market. Now the Cowichans are fighting back by identifying their sweaters as the genuine article using tags signed by the knitters. The problem is: How do you fight a brand with the same name as yours?

In the United States firms often resort to filing law suits as a competitive tactic. Take Cyrix's feud with Intel. Although Cyrix's sales are a small fraction of Intel's (Cyrix's 1994 sales were U.S.$250 million versus Intel's sales of U.S.$11.5 billion), this has not prevented Cyrix from voluntarily running up more than U.S.$20 million in legal bills. According to Cyrix's top marketing executive, "I can't say we encourage our people to think ill of Andy Grove [Intel's chief executive], but we did put Intel's tombstone in our lobby atrium, and we make sure the flowers stay fresh."[2]

In this chapter, we will study the complex environment in which marketing decisions are made. We will see that an organization's level of success (or failure) is related not only to its marketing efforts, but also to the external environment in which it operates and its ability to adapt to environmental changes.

Overview

The environment within which marketing decisions are made and enacted is depicted in Figure 2-1. **The marketing environment** consists of five parts:

1. Controllable factors.
2. Uncontrollable factors.
3. The organization's level of success or failure in reaching its objectives.
4. Feedback.
5. Adaptation.

The **marketing environment** *consists of* **controllable factors, uncontrollable factors,** *organizational performance, feedback, and* **adaptation.**

Controllable factors are those directed by an organization and its marketers. First, several broad, fundamental decisions are made by top management. Then, marketing man-

---
[2]Jaclyn Fierman, "When Genteel Rivals Become Mortal Enemies," *Fortune* (May 15, 1995), pp. 90-100; "Woolly Bully," *Canadian Business* (February 1996), p. 22.

agers make specific decisions based on these guidelines. In combination, these factors result in an overall strategy or offering (A in Figure 2-1). The major **uncontrollable factors** are beyond the control of an individual organization, but they have an impact on how well an organization does (B in Figure 2-1).

The interaction of controllable factors and uncontrollable factors determines an organization's **performance**, or level of success or failure, in reaching its goals. **Feedback** occurs when a firm makes an effort to monitor uncontrollable factors and assess its strengths and weaknesses. **Adaptation** refers to the changes in a marketing plan that an organization makes to comply with the uncontrollable environment. If a firm is unwilling to consider the entire environment in a systematic manner, it will likely lack direction and may have disappointing results.

When analyzing the environment, an organization should consider it from two perspectives: the macroenvironment and the microenvironment. The **macroenvironment** refers to the broad demographic, societal, economic, political, technological, and other forces that an organization faces. The **microenvironment** refers to the forces close to an organization that have a direct impact on its ability to serve customers, including distribution intermediaries, competitors, consumer markets, and the capabilities of the organization itself.[3]

Both the **macroenvironment** *and the* **microenvironment** *must be understood.*

Throughout this chapter, the various parts of Figure 2-1 are described and drawn together so the complex environment of marketing can be understood. In Chapter 3, the concept of strategic planning is presented. Such planning establishes a formal process for developing, implementing, and evaluating marketing programs in conjunction with the goals of top management.

Controllable Factors

The organization and its marketers can manage **controllable factors**.

Controllable factors are internally directed by an organization and its marketers. Some of these factors are directed by top management; these are not controllable by marketers, who must develop plans to satisfy overall organizational goals. In situations involving small or medium-sized institutions, both broad policy and marketing decisions are often made by one person, usually the owner. Even in those cases, broad policies are typically set first and marketing plans must adjust to them. For example, a person could decide to open an office-supply store selling products to small businesses (broad policy) and stress convenient hours, a good selection of items, quantity discounts, and superior customer service (marketing plan).

Factors Controlled by Top Management

Although top management is responsible for numerous decisions, five are of extreme importance to marketers: line of business, overall objectives, the role of marketing, the role of other business functions, and corporate culture. They have an impact on all aspects of marketing. Figure 2-2 shows the types of decisions in these areas.

A firm's **line of business** *refers to its business category.*

The **line of business** refers to the general goods/service category, functions, geographic coverage, type of ownership, and specific business of a firm. The general goods/service category is a broad definition of the industry in which a firm seeks to be involved. It may be energy, transportation, computing, or any number of others. The functions of the business outline a firm's position in the marketing system—from supplier to manufacturer to wholesaler to retailer—and the tasks it seeks to do. A firm may want to be in more than one of these positions. Geographic coverage can be a neighbourhood, city, county, or province, or it could be defined as regional, national, or international. The type of ownership can range from a sole proprietorship, partnership, or franchise to a multi-unit corporation. The specific business is a narrow definition of the firm, its functions, and its

---

[3]Peter D. Bennett (Ed.), *Dictionary of Marketing Terms*, Second Edition (Chicago: American Marketing Association, 1995), pp. 159, 177.

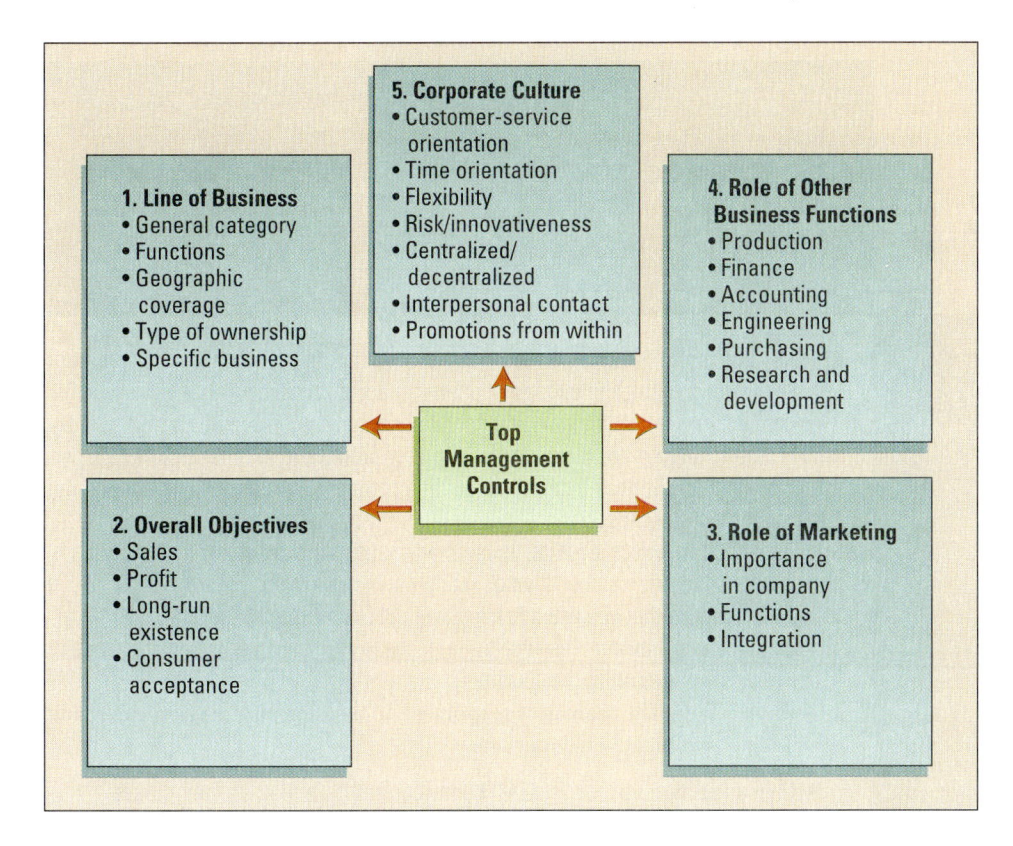

FIGURE 2-2
Factors Controlled by Top Management

1. Line of Business
- General category
- Functions
- Geographic coverage
- Type of ownership
- Specific business

2. Overall Objectives
- Sales
- Profit
- Long-run existence
- Consumer acceptance

5. Corporate Culture
- Customer-service orientation
- Time orientation
- Flexibility
- Risk/innovativeness
- Centralized/ decentralized
- Interpersonal contact
- Promotions from within

Top Management Controls

4. Role of Other Business Functions
- Production
- Finance
- Accounting
- Engineering
- Purchasing
- Research and development

3. Role of Marketing
- Importance in company
- Functions
- Integration

operations; for example, a particular dry cleaners might define itself as a local full-service dry cleaner specializing in outerwear).

Overall objectives are the broad, measurable goals set by top management. A firm's success or failure is often determined by comparing these objectives with actual performance. Usually, a combination of sales, profit, and other goals is stated by management for short-run (one year or less) and long-run (several years) periods. Most firms cite customer acceptance as a key goal with a strong effect on sales, profit, and long-run existence.

Top management determines the role of marketing by noting its importance, outlining its activities, and integrating it into a firm's overall operation. Marketing's importance is evident when marketing people have decision-making authority, the rank of the chief marketing officer is equal to that of other areas (usually vice-president), and proper resources are given. It is not considered important by a firm that gives marketing people advisory status, places marketing personnel in a subordinate position (like reporting to the production vice-president), equates marketing with sales, and withholds the funds needed for research, promotion, and other marketing tasks. The larger marketing's role, the greater the likelihood that a firm has an integrated marketing organization. The smaller its role, the greater the possibility that a firm undertakes marketing tasks on a project, crisis, or fragmented basis.

The roles of other business functions and their interrelationships with marketing need to be defined clearly to avoid overlaps, jealousy, and conflict. Production, finance, accounting, engineering, purchasing, and research and development departments each have different perspectives, orientations, and goals. This is discussed further in Chapter 3.

Top management strongly influences a firm's corporate culture: the shared values, norms, and practices communicated to and followed by those working for the firm. **Corporate culture** may be described in terms of:

- *A customer-service orientation*—Is the commitment to customer service clearly transmitted to employees?
- *A time orientation*—Is a firm short- or long-run oriented?
- *The flexibility of the job environment*—Can employees deviate from rules? How formal are relations with subordinates? Is there a dress code?

Corporate culture involves shared values, norms, and practices.

Ethics AND TODAY'S MARKETER

How Does Corporate Culture Influence Ethical Behaviour?

Surveys of recent M.B.A. graduates found that, in many cases, they feel pressure from their companies to engage in unethical and sometimes illegal behaviour. For example, a management trainee at a consumer products company was told to make up the data to support the introduction of a new product. In another situation, a person was asked to overlook a safety defect in a product and to ship items that did not meet published specifications.

According to ethics experts, these new managers are subjected to four commandments: (1) Performance is what really counts, so make your numbers. (2) Be loyal, and show us that you are a team player. (3) Don't break the law. (4) Don't overinvest in ethical behaviour. The first three of these commandments become troublesome when combined with the fourth.

Here is how the managers responded to a series of questions involving ethical and unethical behaviour:

- Only a few believe that "sleazy" behaviour will be a drag on their career.
- Less than a third believe their firms respect or encourage "whistle blowing."
- When asked what offences would result in punishment, they rarely mention unethical behaviour. Instead, such infractions as poor performance, failure at being a team player, stealing, or drinking on the job were noted.
- Many executives fear repercussions from doing what they see as the right thing.

Although many of the managers worked in firms with formal ethics programs, in general, these programs had little effect on their behaviour or attitudes.

As an ethical compliance manager for a bank, how would you help institute a corporate culture that values high moral principles?

Source: Based on material in Joseph L. Badaracco, Jr., and Allen P. Webb, "Business Ethics: A View From the Trenches," *California Management Review*, Vol. 37 (Winter 1995), pp. 8–28.

- *The level of risk/innovation pursued*—Is risk-taking fostered?
- *The use of a centralized/decentralized management structure*—How much input into decisions do middle managers have?
- *The level of interpersonal contact*—Do employees freely communicate with one another?
- *The use of promotions from within*—Are internal personnel given preference as positions open?

For example, IBM Canada is trying to change its corporate culture in order to get better in touch with its customers. For starters, the blue suits are out and dressing for the firm's customers is in. The elimination of IBM's dress code was an important symbol of change for both employees and customers alike. Employees are encouraged to speak their minds and management communicates news to employees directly and provides a forum for comments and suggestions.[4]

The "ten commandments" listed below are what many experts recommend to firms that wish to foster a nurturing corporate culture:

IBM CANADA
www.can.ibm.com/

[4]Tamsen Tillson, "Be it Ever So Humble," *Canadian Business* (June 25, 1995), Special Technology Issue, pp. 26–32.

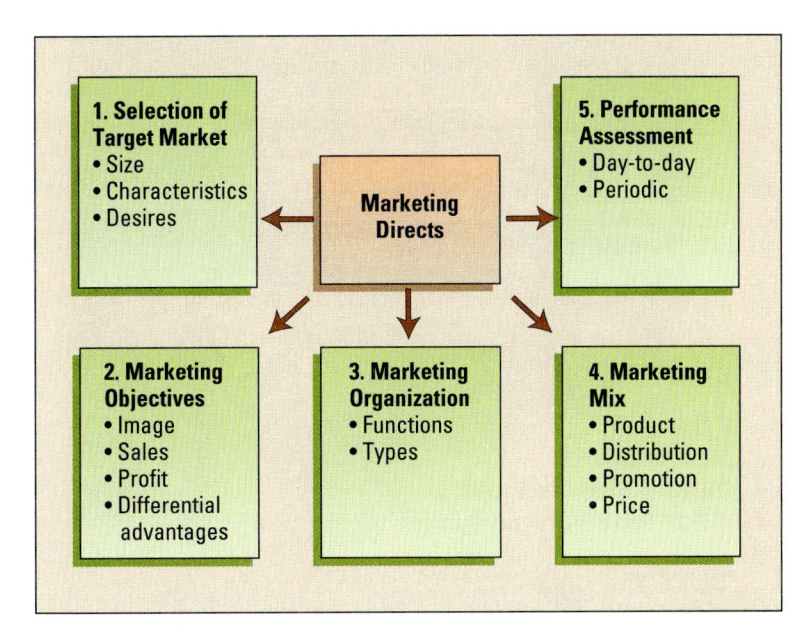

FIGURE 2-3
Factors Controlled by Marketing

1. Seek consensus—don't bark orders.
2. Set broad visions, then give people the freedom needed to carry them out.
3. Make sure people have the resources and support they need to succeed.
4. Spend more time in the field with employees than in your office.
5. Spend some time with employees off the job, too.
6. Monitor progress on projects—don't micro manage.
7. Be quick to give ambitious employees increased responsibilities.
8. Make sure all employees are continuously learning and growing.
9. Reward people for reaching personal, not just financial, goals.
10. Before criticizing someone for "failing," find out why he or she fell short of expectations.[5]

After top management sets company guidelines, the marketing area begins to develop the factors under its control.

Factors Controlled by Marketing

The major factors controlled by marketing personnel are the selection of a target market, marketing objectives, the marketing organization, the marketing mix, and assessment of the marketing plan. These factors are shown in Figure 2-3.

One crucial marketing-related decision involves selecting a target market. The **target market** is the particular group(s) of customers a firm proposes to serve, or whose needs it proposes to satisfy, with a particular marketing program. When selecting a target market, a company usually engages in some form of **market segmentation**, which involves subdividing a market into clear subsets of customers that act in the same way or that have comparable needs.[6] A company can choose a large target market or concentrate on a small one, or try to appeal to both with separate marketing programs for each. Generally, these questions must be addressed before devising a marketing approach: Who are our customers? What kinds of goods and services do they want? How can we attract them to our company?

At marketing-oriented firms, the choice of a target market has an impact on all other marketing decisions. For example, a book publisher appealing to the high school science market would have a different marketing approach from one appealing to the adult fiction market. The first firm would seek an image as a prestigious, well-established publisher; specialize product offerings; make presentations to high school book-selection committees;

*A **target market** is the customer group to which an organization appeals. **Market segmentation** is often used in choosing a target market.*

---
[5]Geoffrey Brewer, "The New Managers," *Performance* (March 1995), p. 32.
[6]Bennett, *Dictionary of Marketing Terms*, pp. 165–166.

FIGURE 2-4
The Marketing of Differential Advantages
Reprinted with permission of 3M Canada.

Differential advantages *consist of the firm's unique features that attract consumers.*

sell in large quantities; offer durable books with many photos and line drawings that could be used for several years; and so on. The second firm would capitalize on well-known authors or publish books on hot topics to establish an image; have books on a variety of subjects; use newspaper ads and seek favourable reviews; distribute via bookstores; sell in small quantities (except if large bookstore chains are involved); de-emphasize durability, photos, and line drawings and produce books as efficiently as possible.

Marketing objectives are more customer-oriented than those set by top management. Marketers are quite interested in the image consumers hold of a firm and its products. From a marketing perspective, sales goals will reflect a desire to foster brand loyalty (repeat purchases), encourage growth (through new-product introductions), and appeal to unsatisfied market segments. Profit goals may be related to long-term customer loyalty. Most importantly, marketers seek to create **differential advantages**, the unique features in a firm's marketing program that cause consumers to patronize that firm and not its competitors. Without differential advantages, a firm would have a "me-too" philosophy and offer the consumer no reasons to select its offerings over competitors'. Differential advantages can be based on a distinctive image, new products or features, product quality, customer service, low prices, availability, and other factors. For example, Snapple is known for its offbeat beverages, Harvey's restaurants make hamburgers a beautiful thing, Zellers is known for its low prices, and the Toronto Dominion Bank's VISA credit cards are "everywhere you want to be." Figure 2-4 shows how 3M markets its differential advantages.

A **marketing organization** *may be functional, product-oriented, or market-oriented.*

A **marketing organization** is the structural arrangement that directs marketing functions. It outlines authority, responsibilities, and tasks to be accomplished. As illustrated in Figure 2-5, an organization may be functional, with jobs assigned in terms of buying, selling, promotion, distribution, and other tasks; product-oriented, with product managers for each product category and brand managers for each brand, in addition to functional categories; or market-oriented, with jobs assigned by geographic market and customer type, in addition to functional categories. A single firm may use a combination of these forms.

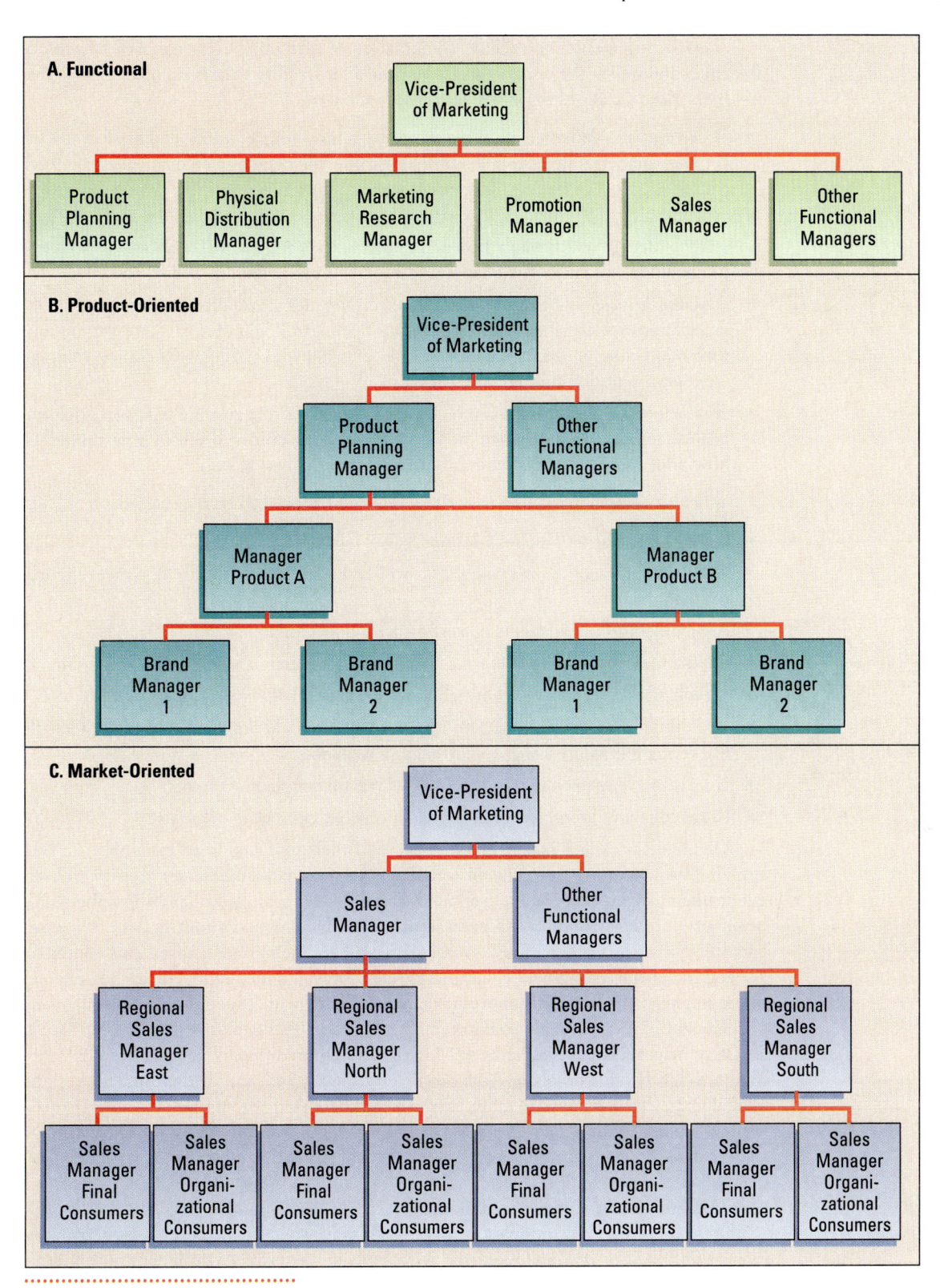

FIGURE 2-5
Illustrations of Marketing Organizations

*The **marketing mix** consists of four elements: product, distribution, promotion, and price.*

A **marketing mix** is the specific combination of marketing elements used to achieve objectives and satisfy the target market. Finding a satisfactory marketing mix requires that managers make decisions regarding four major variables:

- *Product decisions*—What goods, services, organizations, people, places, and/or ideas to market, the number of items to sell and their quality, the degree of innovativeness pursued, packaging, product features, warranties, when to drop existing offerings, and so on.
- *Distribution decisions*—Whether to sell via intermediaries or directly to consumers, how many outlets to sell through, how to interact with other channel members, what terms to negotiate, the functions to assign to others, supplier choice, and so on.
- *Promotion decisions*—The most appropriate combination of promotional tools (ads, public relations, personal selling, sales promotions, etc.), whether to share promotions with others, the image to pursue, the level of personal service, media choice, message content, promotion timing, and so on.
- *Price decisions*—Overall price levels, the range of prices, the relation between price and quality, the emphasis on price, how to react to competitors, when to offer discounts, how prices are computed, what billing terms to use, and so on.

When devising a marketing mix, these questions should all be considered:

- Is the target market precisely defined?
- Does the total marketing program, as well as each element of the mix, meet the target market's needs?
- Are marketing-mix elements consistent with one another?
- Do the elements add up to form a harmonious, integrated whole?
- Is each marketing-mix element being put to its best use?
- Does the marketing mix build on the firm's cultural and tangible strengths? Does the marketing mix imply a way to correct any weaknesses?
- Is a distinctive personality in the competitive marketplace created?
- Is the company protected from the most obvious competitive threats?[7]

OLYMPUS
www.olympusamerica.com/alt/index.html

Olympus, a leading maker of cameras and other products, is an example of a firm applying the marketing-mix concept well. It has distinct marketing mixes for different target markets, such as beginners, serious amateurs, and professional photographers. For beginners, it offers very simple cameras with automatic focus and a built-in flash. The cameras are sold in all types of stores, such as discount and department stores. Ads appear on TV and in general magazines. The cameras retail for well under $100. For serious amateur photographers, Olympus has more advanced cameras with superior features and many attachments. The cameras are sold in camera stores and finer department stores. Ads are in specialty magazines. The cameras sell for several hundred dollars. For professional photographers, Olympus has even more advanced cameras with top-of-the-line features and attachments. The cameras are quite expensive and are sold through select camera stores, with ads appearing in trade magazines. In sum, Olympus markets the right products in the right stores, promotes them in the right media, and has the right prices for its various target markets. See Figure 2-6.

Performance assessment involves monitoring and evaluating marketing activities.

The last factor directed by marketers is extremely important: Performance assessment is the monitoring and evaluation of overall and specific marketing effectiveness. Evaluations need to be done regularly, with both the external environment and internal company data being reviewed. In-depth analysis of performance should be completed at least once or twice each year. Strategy revisions need to be enacted when the external environment changes or the company encounters difficulties.

---

[7]Benson P. Shapiro, "Rejuvenating the Marketing Mix," *Harvard Business Review*, Vol. 63 (September–October 1985), p. 34. See also Walter van Waterschoot and Christophe Van den Bulte, "The 4P Classification of the Marketing Mix Revisited," *Journal of Marketing*, Vol. 56 (October 1992), pp. 83–93.

FIGURE 2-6
Focused Marketing Mixes
The Olympus Stylus camera is a simple device for beginners, while the Olympus IS-3 is a sophisticated device for advanced camera buffs. A distinct marketing mix is used with each camera.
Reprinted by permission.

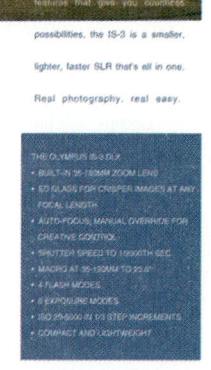

Uncontrollable Factors

Uncontrollable factors are the external elements affecting an organization's performance that cannot be fully directed by that organization and its marketers. A marketing plan, no matter how well conceived, may fail if uncontrollable factors have too adverse an impact. Thus, the external environment must be regularly observed and its effects considered in any marketing plan. Contingency plans relating to uncontrollable variables should also be a key part of a marketing plan. Uncontrollable factors that especially bear studying are consumers, competition, suppliers and distributors, government, the economy, technology, and independent media. These are shown in Figure 2-7.

Uncontrollable factors *influence an organization and its marketers but are not fully directed by them.*

Consumers

Although a firm has control over its selection of a target market, it cannot control the changing characteristics of its final or organizational consumers. A firm can react to, but not control, consumer trends related to age, income, marital status, occupation, race, education, place and type of residence, and the size of organizational customers. For example, health insurers who provide drug plans, out-of-province medical benefits, eyeglasses, and other special services must deal with the fact that many of their largest business customers are downsizing; thus, there are fewer employees to be insured there.

Organizations need to understand consumer trends, interpersonal influences, the decision process, and consumer groups.

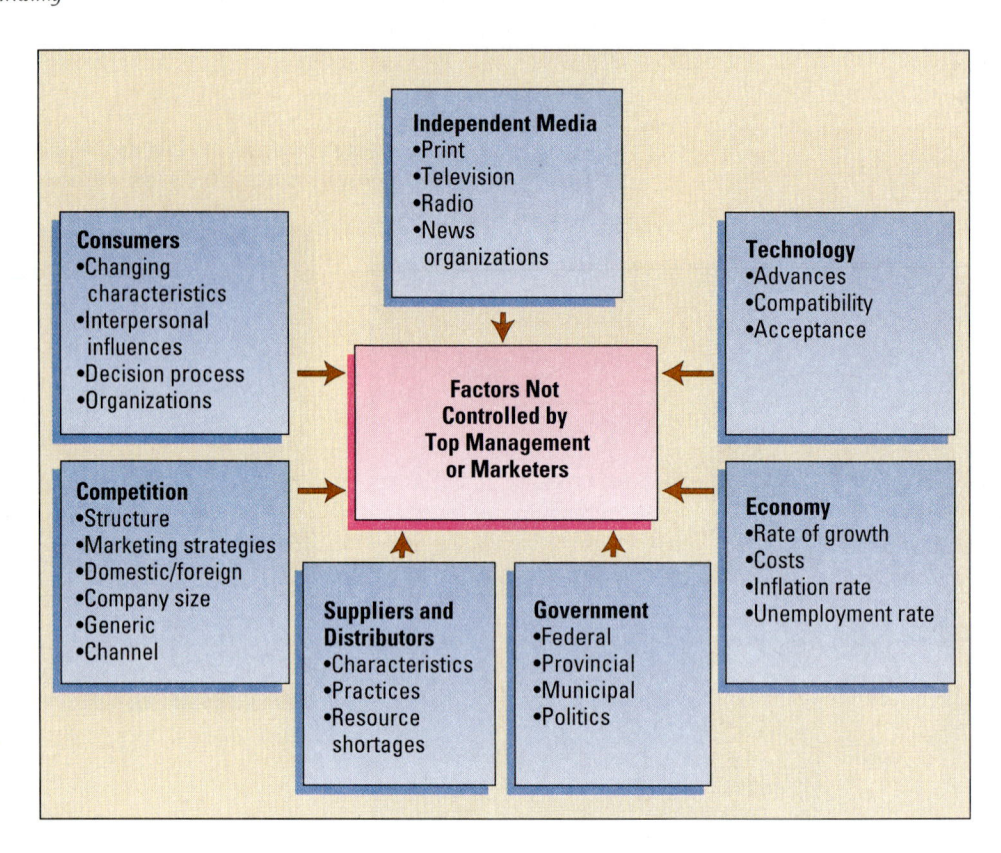

FIGURE 2-7
Uncontrollable Factors

[Diagram: Factors Not Controlled by Top Management or Marketers, surrounded by: Independent Media (Print, Television, Radio, News organizations); Technology (Advances, Compatibility, Acceptance); Economy (Rate of growth, Costs, Inflation rate, Unemployment rate); Government (Federal, Provincial, Municipal, Politics); Suppliers and Distributors (Characteristics, Practices, Resource shortages); Competition (Structure, Marketing strategies, Domestic/foreign, Company size, Generic, Channel); Consumers (Changing characteristics, Interpersonal influences, Decision process, Organizations).]

Interpersonal influences on consumer behaviour need to be understood. People's purchases are affected by the corporate culture at their jobs as purchasing agents; their family, friends, and other social contacts; and the customs and taboos shaping culture and society. For instance, in some parts of Canada, liquor sales are more regulated (as to outlets, prices, other goods that can be sold, and days open) than in other parts.

People act differently in buying various types of goods and services. In the case of company cars, a purchasing agent carefully searches for information on a number of models, ranks several alternatives, selects a favourite, negotiates terms, and finally completes the purchase. On the other hand, with an inexpensive meal, a person looks at his or her watch, sees it is lunch time, and goes to a nearby fast-food outlet. Because of these differences, the consumer decision process—the steps people go through when buying products—affects the way that products are marketed.

Today, consumer-rights groups speak out on behalf of consumers at public hearings, at shareholder meetings, and before the media. To avoid negative consequences brought on by active consumer groups, a firm must communicate with customers on relevant issues (such as a product recall), anticipate problems (such as delays in filling orders), respond to complaints (such as unsatisfactory customer service), and maintain good community relations (such as sponsoring neighbourhood projects).

Competition

The competitive environment often affects a company's marketing efforts and its success in reaching a target market. Thus, firms need to assess the following characteristics of their competitive environment:

- The industry structure.
- Their competitors' marketing strategies.
- The nationality of their competitors (domestic or foreign).
- The size of their competitors.
- Generic competition.
- Channel competition.

International Marketing in Action

Bata Shoes: Return to the Czech Republic

Bata Ltd., a Toronto-based firm, is the world's largest shoemaker, with factories and retail stores in more than 70 countries all over the world. The chair of Bata is Thomas Bata, a Czechoslovakian expatriate whose family's business was nationalized by the communists in 1945. With the shift in Eastern Europe away from government-run command economies to market economies, Bata was received as a hero when he visited his homeland in 1989. He has since sought to repatriate his family business from the new government.

The deal struck by Bata involves acquiring majority ownership in a manufacturing plant and a number of retail shoe stores. There was no precedent for creating legal entities or laws governing transfers of commercial real estate when Bata began negotiations with the government, and this created some problems. The existing laws were designed to set up retail stores as separate outlets and not to allow retail chains. Further complicating matters was the fact that Bata management had to negotiate with American advisers who had been hired by the Czech government to act on their behalf. Nevertheless, on December 18, 1991, a deal was signed, resulting in Bata acquiring 70 per cent of the stock in a manufacturing plant and a chain of 30 stores with head office in Zlin, the city where the original Bata company had been founded in the late 1800s. Bata has an option to buy the 30 per cent of the stock retained by the government.

With regard to the marketing of shoes, Georgina Wyman, the Canadian manager of the Czechoslovakian operation comments: "You have to constantly remind people of the elements that make a business prosper and reinforce their sensitivity to the marketplace. They're obsessed with having lots of merchandise. You've got to persuade them that the objective is not to have a lot of shoes or huge stores, but to sell shoes that customers want."

Bata has discovered that there are many challenges confronting a marketing-oriented organization in adapting to a culture that is not used to marketing-oriented firms. For example, employees are not used to expressing their thoughts and ideas let alone having anyone being receptive to them. Furthermore, skills and expertise in marketing are lacking among local managers. And, since consumers are not used to much product choice, the price-quality relationship is very strong; promotional price discounting may actually reduce sales volume because the discounted goods are viewed as being inferior in quality.

From 1991 to 1993, the Bata company expanded from thirty retail stores to forty-three and captured 10 per cent of the Czech market with sales of 3.5 million pairs of shoes. Competition has not been a major factor in the marketplace since 1993, but despite this, the operation is just breaking even.

As a consultant to Georgina Wyman, what thoughts do you have on Bata's current and future marketing strategy in Czechoslovakia?

Source: Adapted from Sonja Sinclair, "The Best Revenge," *Canadian Business* (March 1994), pp. 20–31.

BATA LTD.
www.bata.com/

Monopoly, oligopoly, monopolistic competition, and *pure competition are the main types of competitive structure.*

A company may operate under one of four possible competitive structures: monopoly, oligopoly, monopolistic competition, or pure competition. With a **monopoly**, just one firm sells a given good or service and has a lot of control over its marketing plan. This occurs in Canada when a firm has a patent (exclusive rights to a sell a product it invented for a fixed number of years, such as for new pharmaceutical products), is a public utility (such as local phone or natural gas companies), or is a Crown corporation (such as Canada Post). In an **oligopoly**, a few firms—usually large ones—account for most industry sales and tend to engage in nonprice competition. For example, General Motors, Ford, Chrysler, Honda and Toyota account for about 95 per cent of Canadian auto sales. In **monopolistic competition**, there are several firms in an industry, each trying to offer a unique marketing mix—based on price or nonprice factors. This is the most common Canadian industry structure, followed by oligopoly. Service stations, beauty salons, stores, garment makers, computer-clone makers, and furniture makers are some firms facing monopolistic competition. In **pure competition**, many firms sell virtually identical goods or services and they are unable to create differential advantages. This occurs rarely in Canada. It is most common for selected food items and commodities (and happens if numerous small firms compete with each other).

After analyzing its industry's competitive structure, a firm needs to study the strategies of competitors. Specifically, it should look at their target markets and marketing mixes, their images, their differential advantages, which markets are saturated and which are unfulfilled, and the extent to which consumers are content with the service and quality provided by competitors.

Foreign competition is intensifying.

BANK OF MONTREAL
www.bmo.com/

MOLSON
www.molson.com/

LABATT
www.labatt.com/

MILLER BREWING COMPANY
www.careermosaic.com/cm/miller

INTERBREW S.A.
www.environics.ca/pr/clients/interbr.html

Both domestic and foreign competition need to be examined. For instance, in Canada, Investors Group competes with the Bank of Montreal, Canada Trust, Canada Life Insurance, and others—besides traditional brokerage firms—for financial-services business. Many Canadian, American and West European industries are mature; the amount of domestic competition is stable. In some industries, competition is rising due to the popularity of innovations like notebook PCs. In others, domestic competition is intensifying as a result of government deregulation. For instance, witness all the companies offering long-distance telephone services in Canada.[8]

Foreign competitors play a major role in many industries in North America. In the early 1980s the Canadian brewing industry was owned and dominated by three major breweries: Molson, Labatt and Carling-O'Keefe, who controlled over 90 per cent of the market. Now, Molson owns Carling-O'Keefe and in turn is controlled by the Miller Brewing Company of the United States. In 1995 Labatt was purchased by a Belgian firm, Interbrew S.A., leaving micro brewers as the only Canadian-owned brewing companies—and they have less than 15 per cent market share. Foreign-based firms are doing well at capturing large market shares across North America—50 per cent for steel, 65 per cent for clothing, 75 per cent for shoes, and up to 98 per cent for some consumer electronics.

At the same time, competition in foreign markets is intensifying for Canadian-based firms as rivals stress innovations, cost cutting, good distribution and promotion, and other factors. Many of the industries in which Canadian firms have international dominance are related to the harsh winter climate. For example, Canadian firms excel in the areas of snowmobiles, hockey equipment, and winter boot manufacturing. Of course, the energy and mining industries of Canada are very strong competitors too.

For many industries, there has been a trend toward larger firms because of mergers and acquisitions, as well as company sales growth. Over the last decade, mergers and acquisitions have involved telecommunications firms (AT&T acquiring Unitel, a long distance phone company), food firms (Nestlé acquiring Perrier), pharmaceuticals firms (Bristol-Myers merging with Squibb), transportation firms (Canadian Airlines joining with American Airlines), consumer-products firms (Sony buying CBS Records), retailers (Wal-mart acquiring Woolco), and numerous others. Canadian sales have been growing for such firms as Onex Corp., BC Sugar Refinery, Cott Corp., and Rider Group Inc.—each of which

---

[8]"Psst, Wanna Buy Some Long-Distance?" p. 98.

were among the top 10 fastest growing firms in Canada in 1994, with sales of over 500 million dollars.[9]

For small firms, major differential advantages include personal service, a focus on under-served market segments, an entrepreneurial drive, and flexibility; cooperative ventures and franchising allow such firms to buy in quantity and operate more efficiently. Among large firms, widespread distribution, economies of scale, well-known brands, mass-media ads, and low to moderate prices are commonly used competitive tactics.

Every organization should define its competition generically, meaning as broadly as possible. Direct competitors are similar to the firm with regard to their line of business and marketing approach. Indirect competitors are different from the firm, but still compete with it for customers. Both types of competitors should be studied and accounted for in a firm's marketing plan. For instance, a movie theatre not only competes with other theatres (direct competitors), but with video stores, TV and radio shows, video games, sporting events, live music concerts, plays, amusement parks, bookstores, restaurants, and schools (indirect competitors all). A theatre owner might ask, "What can I do to compete with this variety of entertainment and recreation forms, in terms of movie selection, prices, hours, customer service, refreshments, and parking?"

Competition should be defined generically—as widely as possible.

A company also needs to study the competition from its channel members (resellers). Each party in the distribution process has different goals and would like to maximize its control over the marketing mix. Some wholesalers and retailers carry their own brands besides those of manufacturers.

Suppliers and Distributors

Many firms rely on their suppliers and distributors (wholesalers and retailers) to properly run their own businesses. Without their ongoing support, it would be difficult, if not impossible, for a company to succeed.

Suppliers and distributors can have a dramatic impact on an organization.

Suppliers provide the goods and services that firms need to operate, as well as those that they resell to their own customers. In general, a firm is most vulnerable when there are relatively few suppliers; specific goods and services are needed to run a business or satisfy customer demand; competitors would gain if the firm had a falling out with a supplier; suppliers are better attuned to the desires of the marketplace; suppliers informally take care of maintenance and repair services; the turnaround time to switch suppliers is lengthy; or suppliers have exclusive access to scarce resources.

Firms that cannot market their products directly to consumers need distributors (be they wholesalers or retailers). In general, a firm is most vulnerable when there are relatively few distributors in an area; the distributors carry many brands; shelf space is tight; the firm is unknown in the marketplace; particular distributors account for a large portion of the firm's revenues; distributors help finance the firm; distributors are better attuned to the marketplace; or other competitors are waiting in the wings to stock the distributors.

Among the supplier/distributor practices that a firm should regularly study are: delivery time or requests, product availability, prices, flexibility in handling special requests, marketing support, consistency of treatment, returns policies, and other services. Unsatisfactory performance by a supplier or distributor in one or more of these areas could have a lasting impact on the firm's ability to enact its marketing plans.

Regardless of suppliers' good intentions, a firm's ability to carry out its plans can be affected by the scarcity of particular resources. Over the past twenty-five years, sporadic shortages and volatile price changes have occurred for a variety of basic commodities, such as home heating oil, other petroleum-based products, plastics, synthetic fibres, aluminum, chrome, silver, tungsten, nickel, steel, glass, grain, fertilizer, cotton, and wool. And despite efforts at conservation, some raw materials, processed materials, and component parts may remain or become scarce over the next decade.[10]

Resource shortages and/or rapid cost increases require one of three actions. First, substitute materials could be used in constructing products, requiring intensified research and

---

[9]"Performance 500: The Top 10," *Canadian Business* (June 1996), pp. 143–148.
[10]William B. Wagner, "Establishing Supply Service Strategy for Shortage Situations," *Industrial Marketing Management*, Vol. 23 (1994), pp. 393–401.

Table 2-1
Key Canadian Federal Government Legislation Affecting Marketers

Access to Information Act	Gasoline Handling Act
Bankruptcy Act	Government Corporations Operations Act
Boards of Trade Act	Hazardous Products Act
Broadcasting Act	Income Tax Act
Bulk Sales Act	Industrial Design Act
Canada Agricultural Products Standards Act	Lobbyists Registration Act
Canada Business Corporations Act	Maple Products Industry Act
Canada Cooperative Association Act	Official Languages Act
Canada Corporations Act	Patent Act
Canada Dairy Products Act	Pension Fund Societies Act
Canadian Human Rights Act	Precious Metals Marking Act
Competition Act (Bill C–2)	Public Servants Invention Act
Consumer Packaging and Labelling Act	Shipping Conferences Exemption Act
Copyright Act	Tax Rebate Discounting Act
Department of Consumer and Corporate Affairs Act	Textile Labelling Act
	Timber Marking Act
Electricity Inspection Act	Trade Marks Act
Fish Inspection Act	Weights and Measures Act
Food and Drugs Act	Winding-Up Act
Gas Inspection Act	

Canadian federal legislation involves international and interprovincial commerce. Each province and municipality has its own regulations, as well.

product testing. Second, prices could be raised for products that cannot incorporate substitute materials. Third, firms could abandon products where resources are unavailable and demarket others where demand is greater than it is able to satisfy.

Government

Governmental bodies have a great impact on marketing practices by placing (or removing) restrictions on specified activities. In any country, government rulings can be on a national, provincial/state, and/or local level.

In Canada there are myriad federal legislative acts affecting the practice of business and marketing, as shown in Table 2-1.

A key piece of legislation is the Competition Act, Bill C–2, which was passed in 1986. It is administered by the Director of Investigation and Research and the director's staff at the Competition Bureau, which is part of Industry Canada. Industry Canada is responsible for administering the federal legislation passed specifically for the purpose of regulating business. Currently, deceptive marketing practices covered in the Competition Act include: misleading advertising, promotional contests, bait-and-switch selling, multi-level marketing, and pyramid selling plans.

The purpose of the act is to insure healthy competition in the Canadian marketplace by promoting the provision of information about goods and services to both consumers and businesses. Most complaints are made by consumers and handled by the marketing practices branch of the Competition Bureau, but complaints from competitors are made as well and lead to actions more frequently than consumer complaints. Competitor complaints often involve detailed information and if not evaluated, could lead to widespread adoption of the marketing practice in question. Each complaint is considered by an assessment officer and then one of three options is undertaken: the file is closed if the complaint is deemed to not fall under the act or does not fall within the priorities of the marketing practices branch, the subject may be asked to provide more information about the complaint in hopes that this will result in the marketing practice being stopped; or an inquiry into the case may be undertaken.

When an inquiry is undertaken the company whose marketing practice is called into question is contacted for an explanation. The company is able to make its case voluntarily and most companies respond by providing details. The process is designed to create a climate of cooperation, and to avoid involving the courts. If it appears that an offence has been committed then a formal inquiry may be undertaken. The cases which are pursued usually display three characteristics: there is considerable harm done in the marketplace; the case has value in terms of jurisprudence; or the resolution of the case may result in significant deterrence.[11]

In June 1995 the Competition Bureau put forward a discussion paper on issues dealing with competition policy which might call for amendments to the Competition Act. These issues include notifiable merger transactions; the protection of confidential information; mutual assistance with foreign competition law agencies; misleading advertising and deceptive marketing practices; "regular price" claims and price discrimination and promotional allowances; prohibition orders; deceptive telemarketing solicitations; and finally access to the Competition Tribunal.

This discussion paper generated some immediate action because Canada and the United States signed a Competition Policy agreement in August 1995 so that the two countries could cooperate to enforce laws on deceptive marketing practices and competition. The Competition Bureau in Canada will cooperate with the U.S. Federal Trade Commission and the Antitrust division of the U.S. Department of Justice. The two countries will notify one another about investigations that involve both jurisdictions and about enforcement proceedings that might affect the interests of the other nation. The agreement also calls for sharing of investigative information and evidence and cooperation in locating witnesses.[12]

In addition to federal regulation and agencies, each province and municipal government in Canada has its own legal environment. Provincial and municipal laws may regulate where a firm is allowed to locate, the hours open, the types of items sold, if prices must be marked on every item sold, how goods must be labelled or dated, and so on. Provincial and municipal governments may also provide incentives, such as small business assistance, for firms to operate there. Examples of key provincial legislation include: the Franchises Act in Alberta, the Environmental Protection Act in Ontario, the Licensing Act in Prince Edward Island, and the Consumer Protection Act in Quebec. The latter is of particular concern for marketers because it contains a ban on all child-directed advertising. As such, marketers of products designed for children are faced with a very difficult task as they are not allowed to advertise directly to the users of their products.

Because the United States is Canada's largest trading partner, it is important for Canadian marketing managers to understand the U.S. federal legislative environment as well as their own. The U.S. legislation can be divided into three groups: antitrust, discriminatory pricing, and unfair trade practices; consumer protection; and deregulation. Laws in the first group protect smaller firms from anti-competitive acts by larger ones. These laws seek a "level playing field" for all by barring firms from using marketing practices that unfairly harm competitors. Laws in the second group help consumers deal with deceptive and unsafe business practices. They protect consumer rights and restrict certain marketing activities (like banning cigarette ads from TV and radio). Laws in the third group have deregulated various industries to create a more competitive marketplace. They allow firms greater flexibility in enacting marketing plans. The Federal Trade Commission (FTC) is the major U.S. regulatory agency monitoring restraint of trade and enforcing rules against unfair methods of competition and deceptive business practices.

The political environment often affects legislation. Should certain goods and services be prohibited from advertising on TV? Should mail-order sales to out-of-province cus-

---

[11]Rachel Larabie-Lesieur, "Ottawa's Competition Act, How It Works," *Marketing Magazine* (May 1, 1995), p. 15; and Industry Canada Internet Site (http://info.ic.gc.ca) (June 1996).
[12]Tom Messer and James Pollock, "Canada, U.S. Agree to Share Deceptive Marketing Info," *Marketing Magazine* (August 21–28, 1995), p. 3; and Industry Canada Internet Site (June 1996).

tomers be taxed? Should provincial governments become more active in handling consumer complaints? Marketing issues such as these are typically discussed via the political process before laws are enacted (or not enacted). Both firms and consumer groups may market their positions on such issues to government officials. A strength of Canada's political system is its continuity, which lets organizations and individuals develop strategies for long periods of time.

One of the biggest legal and political challenges facing Canada and other countries is how to privatize organizations that were formerly run by the government:

Privatization is changing the number of businesses in Canada and elsewhere.

> The obstacles to privatization are numerous. They include lack of a free-market culture; confusion over who owns the enterprises and what they're worth; poor physical infrastructure, which discourages foreign investment; the absence of a legal framework governing the conduct of business; and shortage of investment capital. After privatization, consequences can include higher prices for basic goods and services, large-scale layoffs, loss of national assets to foreign buyers, and the possible closure of vital industries.[13]

The Economy

The rate of growth in a nation's or region's economy can have a big impact on a firm's marketing efforts. A high growth rate means the economy is strong and the marketing potential large. Quite important to marketers are consumer perceptions—both in the business and final consumer sectors—regarding the economy. For instance, if people believe the economy will be good, they may spend more; if they believe the economy will be poor, they may cut back. In uncertain times, many organizational consumers are interested in preserving their flexibility. Figure 2-8 shows how one firm tried to capitalize on this tendency.

Economic growth is measured by the **Gross Domestic Product**.

A country's economic growth is reflected by changes in its **Gross Domestic Product (GDP)**, which is the total annual value of goods and services produced in a country less net foreign investment. These are the estimated 1996 GDPs (in U.S. dollars) for ten selected nations in order of size: United States, $7.4 trillion; Japan, $5.3 trillion; Germany, $2.3 trillion; France, $1.5 trillion; Italy, $1.2 trillion; Brazil, $950 billion; Canada, $630 billion; Mexico, $375 billion; India, $370 billion; and Thailand, $175 billion.[14] In recent years, the yearly growth in most of these nations has been 3 per cent or less; and when certain industries, such as autos and housing, slow down, repercussions are felt in other areas, such as insurance and home furnishings. Canada is expected to have real GDP growth averaging about 2 to 4 per cent annually during the rest of the 1990s—but the rate could be lower if federal and provincial budget deficits are not reduced.

Several business costs—like raw materials, unionized labour wages, taxes, interest rates, and office (factory) rental—are generally beyond any firm's control. If costs rise by a large amount, marketing flexibility may be limited because a firm often cannot pass along all of the increase; it might have to cut back on marketing activities or accept lower profit margins. If costs are stable, marketers are better able to differentiate products and expand sales because their companies are more apt to invest in marketing activities.

Real income *describes earnings adjusted for inflation. Both inflation and unemployment affect purchases.*

From a marketing perspective, what happens to a consumer's real income is critical. While actual income is the amount earned by a consumer (or his/her family or household) in a given year, **real income** is the amount earned in a year adjusted by the rate of inflation. For example, if a person's actual income goes up by 4 per cent in a year (from $40 000 to $41 600) and the rate of inflation (which measures price changes for the same goods and services over time) is 4 per cent for the year, real income remains constant [($41 600) − ($41 600/1.04) = $40 000]. If actual income increases exceed the inflation rate, real income rises and people can buy more goods and services. If actual income increases are less than the inflation rate, real income falls and people must buy fewer goods and services.

A high rate of unemployment can adversely affect many firms because people who are unemployed are likely to cut back on nonessentials wherever possible. Low unemployment often means substantial sales of large-ticket items, as consumers are better off, more optimistic, and more apt to spend earnings.

---

[13]Christopher McIntosh, "To Market, to Market," *Futurist* (January–February 1994), p. 24.
[14]Louis Richmond, "Global Growth Is on a Tear," *Fortune* (March 20, 1995), p. 108.

FIGURE 2-8
Marketing Flexibility to Organizational Consumers
Reprinted by permission.

Technology

Technology refers to the development and use of machinery, products, and processes. Individual firms, especially smaller ones with limited capital, must usually adapt to technological advances (rather than control them).

Many firms depend on others to develop and perfect new technology, such as computer microchips; only then can they use the new technology in their products, such as automated gas pumps at service stations, talking toys, or electronic sensors in smoke detectors for office buildings. The inventor of new technology often secures patent protection, which excludes competitors from using that technology (unless the inventor licenses rights for a fee).

In a number of areas, companies have been unable to achieve practical technological breakthroughs. For example, no firm has been able to develop and market a cure for the common cold, a good-tasting non-tobacco cigarette, a commercially acceptable electric car, or a truly effective and safe diet pill.

When new technology first emerges, it may be expensive and in short supply, both for firms using the technology in their products and for final consumers. The challenge is to mass produce and mass market the technology efficiently. In addition, some technological advances require employee training and consumer education before they can succeed. Thus, an emphasis on user-friendliness can speed up the acceptance of new technology.

Technology *includes machinery, products, and processes.*

TECHNOLOGY & MARKETING

Should Canadian Marketers Tap the Internet?

In 1995 the Internet became a mainstream medium for marketers. Estimates indicate that there are 27 million North American Internet users, and that number is growing daily. Globally, the rate of adoption of Internet usage is growing 10 to 15 per cent a month!

The attraction of the Internet for both buyers and sellers is its interactive nature. Unlike the traditional media of newsprint, radio, television, magazines and outdoor advertising, which are essentially one-way communications, the Internet allows two-way communication between marketer and customer. Furthermore, the "market" access of the Internet is equal (at least so far) for all marketers. A small firm can compete with a large firm by having a good Web site, a 1-800 number (for transaction security) and a vendor's account with VISA or Mastercard. The Web site is like a store front, so its design and presentation are critical. In this regard large firms may assert an advantage by paying multimedia designers as much as $100 000 for a top-notch site. Still, do-it-yourselfers can save money and satisfy their creative fantasies by designing their own pages using packaged software. It is also pleasing to know that such software will be getting better and cheaper in the future so that updating and changing Web pages will be even easier.

It seems the wheel-of-retailing has come full circle. The new technology promises on-line catalogue shopping. These catalogues may possess sound and motion and be able to listen to their customers, but in other ways this is just catalogue shopping the way it was over 100 years ago. For the marketer, reaching customers and creating demand interactively on the Internet will present a number of new challenges, but the goods and services will still have to be physically distributed. It seems unlikely that the technology to move goods and services will be able to keep pace with the technology to move information.

How would you design an "electronic store front" for an auto dealer?

Source: Based on Angela Kryhul, "The Internet Makes the Mainstream," *Marketing Magazine* (December 18–25, 1995), p. 11; Jim McElgunn, "Smoke and Mirrors," *Marketing Magazine* (December 18–25, 1995), pp. 11–12; Tony Spencer, "Setting Up a Virtual Store," *Marketing Magazine* (December 18–25, 1995), p. 12; Christopher E. Erickson, "Copyright and New Media Marketing," *Marketing Magazine* (December 18–25, 1995), p. 14; and Tony Long, "Telecommunications and New Media Renovate the Old-Style Bazaar," *Marketing Magazine* (December 18–25, 1995), p. 15.

Certain advances may not be compatible with goods and services already on the market or may require retooling by firms wanting to use them in products or operations. Every time an auto maker introduces a significantly new car model, it must invest hundreds of millions of dollars to retool facilities. Each time a firm buys new computer equipment to supplement existing hardware, it must see if the new equipment is compatible (Can it run all the computer programs used by the firm and "talk" to the firm's existing machines?).

To flourish, technological advances must be accepted by each firm in the distribution process (manufacturer/service provider, wholesaler, retailer). Should any of the firms not use a new technology, its benefits may be lost. If small retailers do not use electronic scanning equipment, cashiers will still have to ring up prices by hand even though packages are computer-coded by manufacturers.

Independent Media

Independent media *affect perceptions of products and company image.*

Independent media are not controlled by a firm, yet they influence government, consumer, and publics' perceptions of that firm's products and overall image. Media can provide positive or negative coverage when a firm produces a new product, pollutes the air, mislabels products, contributes to charity, or otherwise performs a newsworthy activity. Coverage may be by print media, TV, radio, or news organizations. To receive good coverage, a firm should willingly offer information to independent media and always try to get its position written or spoken about.

Although the media's coverage of information about a firm is beyond that firm's control, paid advertising is not. Ads may be rejected by the media, but if they are accepted, they must be presented in the time interval and form stipulated by the firm.

Attainment of Objectives, Feedback, and Adaptation

An organization's success or failure in reaching objectives depends on how well it directs its controllable factors and deals with the impact of uncontrollable factors. As shown in Figure 2-1, the interaction of an organization's total offering and its uncontrollable environment determines how well it does.

To optimize its marketing efforts and secure its long-run existence, a firm must get **feedback**—information about the uncontrollable environment, the organization's performance, and how well the marketing plan is received. Feedback is gained by measuring consumer satisfaction, looking at competitive trends, evaluating relationships with government agencies, studying the economy and potential resource shortages, monitoring the independent media, analyzing sales and profit trends, talking with suppliers and distributors, and utilizing other methods of acquiring and assessing information.

Feedback *provides information that lets a firm* **adapt** *to its environment.*

After evaluating feedback, a company—when necessary—needs to engage in **adaptation**, thereby fine-tuning its marketing plan to be responsive to the surrounding environment, while continuing to capitalize on differential advantages. A firm should look continually for new and attainable opportunities that fit its overall marketing plan and respond to potential threats by revising its marketing policies. For instance:

> In Atlantic Canada there are approximately 116 co-op food and general merchandise stores. The Price Club and Real Atlantic Superstores are opening in the Maritimes as part of the "bigger is better" trend in retailing that is sweeping across the rest of Canada. The typical victims of the bigger stores have been medium-sized food and general merchandise stores like the Atlantic co-ops.
>
> Co-ops and the Price Club operate in a similar fashion, in that fees for shopping in the outlet are often charged and some exclusivity is associated with them because a membership is required. However, the co-ops operate differently from the Price-Club in a number of ways. Some co-ops use direct charges where shoppers pay weekly fees ($3 to $5) and then buy their merchandise for essentially no mark-up. Another approach to operation allows members and non-members to shop in the store and keeps pricing similar to that of the competition. However, members receive dividends based on store profits at the end of the year.
>
> The secret to success for the co-ops is their customer loyalty. The Price Club plans to charge a $40.00 annual fee to secure loyalty from its customers as well. The co-ops plan to fight back by letting their shoppers know that they are stockholders and consumers in these stores. Their advertising slogan is "It's your store for shopping," and they mean that quite literally. They will also tell their customers that while the operating profits of the Atlantic co-ops will stay in Atlantic Canada, this will not be the case for the competition.[15]

In preparing for the future, a firm must avoid **marketing myopia**—a shortsighted, narrow-minded view of marketing and its environment. It is a "self-inflicted and avoidable harm caused to an organization due to a lack of attention to and poor implementation of marketing concepts and principles." These are some major warning signs:

Marketing myopia *is an ineffective marketing approach.*

- *We-know syndrome*—An ongoing assumption that the correct answers to crucial questions are always known.
- *Me-tooism*—Occurs when goods and services are too similar to those of competitors and there is no competitive advantage.
- *Monopricis*—Occurs when a firm's primary (or only) marketing/competitive tool is changing prices.
- *Customerphobia*—The fear of having a close relationship with and really caring about consumers and their wants.

---

[15]Mark Higgins, "Owners and Consumers," *Marketing Magazine* (November 6, 1995), pp. 14–15.

- *Fax-me complex*—Occurs when the firm is completely dominated by tasks that require immediate attention (crises).
- *Hypermentis*—Occurs when executives devote too much of their time to thinking, studying, and planning while they take little action.
- *Global idiosis*—The lack of ability or willingness to compete in the international marketplace.
- *If it works, don't fix it*—Occurs when business is very good, but no one knows why and everyone is hesitant to make changes.
- *Interfunctionalphobia*—A lack of mutual understanding, integration, and cooperation among a firm's various functional areas.
- *Short-run fetish*—Occurs when decisions are too biased toward the short-run, thus sacrificing long-run performance.[16]

MARKETING IN A CHANGING WORLD
Trends That Will Affect the Future

Futurists have tried to identify environmental trends that will greatly influence how marketers do business in the world during the next several years. Here are several of them. Are we ready? Do you agree with all of these predictions?

- *Cocooning*—More people at home because they are working there, or they "cashed out," and retired early because of corporate downsizing. They are not going out as much; they are taking delivery of products rather than shopping, spending leisure time at home, focusing on home entertainment (watching videos, playing video games, surfing the Internet), and working out on home exercise equipment. This trend will produce more home renovation business and result in furniture upgrades. The home office will be fully equipped with faxes, cellular phones, computers, modems, and interactive television.
- *Consumer spending*—Recession-weary people will break-out and treat themselves. The upper-income earners will buy pricey, upscale products while lower-income earners will look to warehouse stores and non-branded merchandise.
- *Staying alive*—The fitness rage of the eighties is over, but the long term, health, nutrition, fitness, stress management, meditation, holistic approach to life is here. Wellness programs, new age remedies, organic foods and longevity centres will be in demand.
- *Wildering*—People will go for more outdoor activities. Hiking boots, backpacks, and off-road vehicles should be in demand.
- *One-on-one marketing*—Customized marketing as marketers use advanced technology to get to know their customers intimately and try to establish a long-term relationship by serving as many needs as possible using this knowledge.
- *Globalnomics*—The Canadian economy will become more integrated with the international economy as international trade barriers fall. Tourism, vacationing, and travel will grow.
- *Moving targets*—Marketers will try some new target-market approaches by aiming at women with products not traditionally marketed to them, e.g. cars. Men will also be targeted with non-traditional products such as food and household products. Marketers will rediscover mass marketing by lumping the baby boomers and Generation X segments together.
- *Save our society*—Demand for ethical business practices, lifelong education, and training and environmental conservation will heat up throughout society.[17]

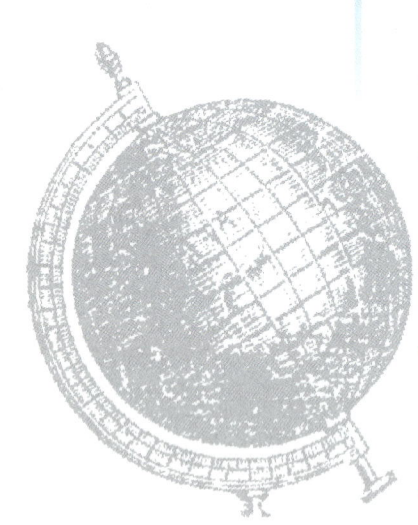

---

[16]John H. Antil, "Are You Committing Marketcide?" *Journal of Services Marketing*, Vol. 6 (Spring 1992), pp. 45–53.
[17]Marvin J. Cetron, *An American Renaissance in the Year 2000* (New York: St. Martin's Press, 1994); and Jo Marney, "Towards the Next Millennium," *Marketing Magazine* (July 24, 1995), p. 17.

SUMMARY

1. *To examine the environment within which marketing decisions are made and marketing activities are undertaken* The marketing environment consists of controllable factors, uncontrollable factors, the organization's level of success or failure in reaching its objectives, feedback, and adaptation. The macroenvironment includes the broad societal and economic forces that a firm faces, while the microenvironment refers to the forces that more directly affect a firm's ability to serve its customers.

2. *To differentiate between those elements controlled by a firm's top management and those controlled by marketing, and to enumerate the controllable elements of a marketing plan* Controllable factors are the internal strategy elements directed by a firm and its marketers. Top management decides on the line of business, overall objectives, the role of marketing and other business functions, and the corporate culture. These decisions have an impact on all aspects of marketing.

The major factors directed by marketing personnel are the selection of a target market (the group(s) of customers a firm proposes to serve); marketing objectives, which are more customer-oriented than those set by top management; the marketing organization; the marketing mix, which is a specific combination of product, distribution, promotion, and price decisions; and performance assessment, which involves monitoring and evaluating marketing outcomes. It is important for marketing personnel to strive to create differential advantages—the unique features that cause consumers to patronize a firm and not its competitors.

3. *To enumerate the uncontrollable environmental elements that can affect a marketing plan and study their potential ramifications* Uncontrollable factors are the external elements affecting a company's performance that cannot be fully directed by the top management and marketers of a firm. Any marketing plan, no matter how well conceived, may fail if uncontrollable factors influence it too much.

Among the key uncontrollable variables are changing consumer traits, interpersonal influences on consumer behaviour, the consumer decision process, and consumer groups; the competitive structure of the industry in which a firm operates (monopoly, oligopoly, monopolistic competition, or pure competition) and such competitor attributes as marketing strategies, country of origin, size, generic competition, and channel competition; suppliers and distributors, their traits and practices, and resource shortages; government legislation and the political environment; the rate of economic growth (as measured by the GDP and real income), the costs of doing business, and other economic factors; technology, which refers to the development and use of machinery, products, and processes; and independent media, the communication vehicles not controlled by the firm.

4. *To explain why feedback about company performance and the uncontrollable aspects of its environment and the subsequent adaptation of the marketing plan are essential for a firm to attain its objectives* A firm's level of success or failure in reaching its goals depends on how well it directs and implements its controllable factors and the impact of uncontrollable factors on the marketing plan. When enacting a marketing strategy, a firm should obtain feedback (information about both its overall and marketing performance and the uncontrollable environment) and adapt the strategy to be responsive to the surrounding environment while continuing to exploit its differential advantages. Marketing myopia, a shortsighted view of marketing and its environment, must be avoided.

KEY TERMS

marketing environment (p. 27)
controllable factors (p. 27)
uncontrollable factors (p. 27)
organizational performance (p. 27)
feedback (p. 27)
adaptation (p. 27)
macroenvironment (p. 28)
microenvironment (p. 28)
line of business (p. 28)

corporate culture (p. 29)
target market (p. 31)
market segmentation (p. 31)
differential advantages (p. 32)
marketing organization (p. 32)
marketing mix (p. 34)
monopoly (p. 38)
oligopoly (p. 38)
monopolistic competition (p. 38)

pure competition (p. 38)
Gross Domestic Product (GDP) (p. 42)
real income (p. 42)
technology (p. 43)
independent media (p. 44)
feedback (p. 45)
adaptation (p. 45)
marketing myopia (p. 45)

Review Questions

1. Explain the environment within which marketing operates.
2. Differentiate between the "macroenvironment" and the "microenvironment."
3. Why are the factors controlled by top management usually considered uncontrollable by marketing personnel?
4. What criteria would you use to assess the role of marketing in a company?
5. Why should a firm select a target market before developing a specific marketing mix?
6. What is the most important marketing objective for an organization? Why?
7. Describe the four components of the marketing mix.
8. Why are suppliers an important uncontrollable factor for many companies?
9. What is the intent of the Competition Act, Bill C–2?
10. How do the independent media affect a firm's marketing practices?

Discussion Questions

1. How does a firm's corporate culture influence the performance of its personnel? Relate your answer to a small taxi service that caters to corporate accounts.
2. What are the differential advantages for each of these? Explain your answers.
   a. Your college or university.
   b. People magazine.
   c. A local printing service.
3. Distinguish between the marketing mixes used by Cadillac and Saturn, two car lines of General Motors.
4. Deregulation represents both opportunities and potential problems for companies. Offer several examples of both for the cable TV industry.
5. Comment on this statement: "By defining competition in generic terms, acquiring information about the uncontrollable environment, and modifying strategy when necessary, an organization will avoid marketing myopia and guarantee its long-term success."

VIDEO CASE

Soft Image: A Marketing Environment Analysis

Soft Image (Soff Imajh in French), a Montreal software company, is a world leader in technology. It was purchased by Microsoft in 1994 for $130 million because Bill Gates, CEO of Microsoft, saw Soft Image's products as the wave of the future. Soft Image had advanced its software technology years ahead of Microsoft's and Gates realized that Microsoft would never be able to catch up. His solution was simple: he bought Soft Image and Microsoft caught up immediately. The problem with computer technology and its related software, is that it is changing so rapidly that no one knows where it is going.

Soft Image is a computer animation software company. They are on the leading edge of this technology and have animated advertising spots for soft drink cans as well as the dinosaurs for the blockbuster film *Jurassic Park*. The customers for Soft Image have largely been film makers and video game firms who have big budgets and special needs. Bill Gates acquired the company because he felt that animation technology would be something that home computer users would be dabbling in in the future. Gates is banking on the notion that there is a powerful desire on the part of consumers to go beyond playing games and movies on their computers. He believes computer users will want to use computers to create their own games and films and to customize existing games and films to their own needs. The technology of Soft Image is what the consumers will need to reach this new level of computer sophistication.

The business computer market is almost totally saturated with equipment. There are plenty of replacements and upgrades, but very little new growth. On the other hand, the home computer market is expected to expand at a rate of 15 per cent per year. The entertainment factor is one of the driving forces. Video games represent a $4 billion industry for Sega of Japan and Sonic the Hedgehog is Sega's superstar character in this market. Soft Image provides the software tools which enable Sonic the Hedgehog to spin out of trouble. The future in games involves three dimensional graphics and interactive television.

Now, Microsoft is betting that a young generation of computer savants will get as much fun out of designing games as playing them. Today's game players are continually demanding more and more sophistication and realism from video games. The demand for virtual reality games promises to be very strong and Soft Image has the technology to deliver them. Furthermore, Soft Image will be able to offer a package so that computer users can design games for themselves.

Imagine consumers designing their own virtual reality, limited solely by their dreams and the amount of RAM they have in their computers. Soft Image is placed to seize this future—and therefore, so is Microsoft.

QUESTIONS
1. Evaluate the "future" for Soft Image in reference to the futurists' predictions provided in this chapter.
2. Explain the impact of technology on Soft Image's marketing strategy.
3. Assess Soft Image's differential advantages.
4. Assess the "risk" taken by Bill Gates in acquiring Soft Image.

VIDEO QUESTIONS ON SOFT IMAGE
1. Comment on Soft Image's position in the software industry.
2. Analyze Soft Image's current target-market strategy.

Video Source: "Soft Image," *Venture* (February 20, 1994).

CASE STUDY
Are Good Times Ahead for Planet Reebok?

American Paul Fireman became aware of Reebok (then a small British shoe maker) at a 1979 Chicago trade show and quickly purchased the exclusive rights to sell Reebok running shoes in North America. Fireman acquired Reebok in 1984 and later renamed it Reebok International.

After Fireman's acquisition, Reebok's first major new-product success was its Freestyle line of aerobic shoes. To avoid directly competing against Nike, Reebok targeted Freestyle shoes at the female market; and Freestyle became one of the best-selling shoes in history. It was instrumental in pushing Reebok's sales from U.S.$3.5 million in 1982 to U.S.$919 million in 1986—and in giving Reebok a sales edge over Nike. Reebok kept this sales advantage over Nike until 1990.

Since Nike has surged ahead, Reebok is now the world's second-largest athletic shoe maker (with a global market share of 24 per cent versus Nike's 33 per cent). In 1994, Reebok sales were U.S.$3.28 billion and net profit was 7.7 per cent of sales; Nike had U.S.$3.79 billion in sales and a net profit of 7.9 per cent of sales. The only other true global competitor is Adidas, with a 10 per cent market share. Let's now look at Reebok's and Nike's marketing strategies.

There are several similarities in the marketing strategies of the two firms: Each has a similar philosophy in terms of product design, marketing, and production. Both Reebok and Nike design and market their products, but use subcontractors (located in low-cost countries) to produce their footwear and apparel items. This approach lowers plant investment costs and reduces the risks associated with wide variations in demand. Both Reebok and Nike also make extensive use of athletes to endorse their products. Reebok features Grant Connell (tennis), Frank Thomas (baseball), Emmitt Smith (football), and Shaquille O'Neal (basketball), while Nike features André Agassi and Pete Sampras (tennis); Ken Griffey, Jr. (baseball); Troy Aikman (football); and Michael Jordan, Charles Barkley, and Shawn Kemp (basketball). Reebok's signing of Shaquille O'Neal was important due to his appeal to males aged 18 and under, a group accounting for one-quarter of total U.S. athletic footwear sales.

There are also some key differences between Reebok's and Nike's marketing strategies: Although the firms are in the same general industry, they often appeal to different market segments. Reebok's major market is still women's fitness shoes and apparel; and its product line includes lower-priced casual shoes. In contrast, Nike places greater attention on higher-priced shoes for males. And until recently, Nike had a much stronger group of endorsers in the basketball market than Reebok.

Even though Reebok's overall performance is generally strong, it has had some problems: Nike's market share is much higher than Reebok's. Nike has entered Reebok's core market—women's fitness footwear. And despite the signing of Shaquille O'Neal, Reebok has not yet been as successful in the basketball shoe and apparel segment. Lastly, Reebok has been unable to move quickly into such fast-growing markets as hiking and outdoor gear.

Reebok made extensive use of the 1996 Summer Olympics to boost its image. More than 3000 Olympic athletes wore Reebok footwear and apparel; and it had advertising exclusivity in the athletic footwear category on NBC's Olympics telecasts. Reebok also used the Olympics to introduce a new advertising slogan, "This is my planet, Planet Reebok."

During March 1996, Reebok introduced Mobius, a new line of footwear and apparel products that cuts across all performance categories. The Mobius line was devised to give Reebok a more integrated presence across all sports areas.

QUESTIONS
1. Develop appropriate marketing objectives for Reebok.
2. Describe the competitive environment for the athletic shoe and apparel business. What are the implications of this for Reebok?
3. What would you do to take market share away from Nike?
4. Reebok plans to enter the soccer shoe market that is currently dominated by Adidas. Present a marketing mix for Reebok to do so.

Source: The data from this case is drawn from Gary Hoover, Alta Campbell, and Patrick J. Spain (Eds.), *Hoover's Handbook of American Business 1995* (Austin, Texas: Reference Press, 1995), pp. 912–913; Jeff Jensen, "Better Days Ahead for Planet Reebok," *Advertising Age* (June 26, 1995), p. 4; and Kenneth Labich, "Nike vs. Reebok: A Battle for Hearts, Minds, and Feet," *Fortune* (September 18, 1995), pp. 90–106; Nike Internet Site. Geoffrey Smith, "Reebok Is Tripping Over Its Own Laces," *Business Week* (February 26, 1996), pp. 62–66.

CHAPTER 3
Strategic Planning: A Marketing Perspective

Chapter Objectives

1. To define strategic planning and consider its importance for marketing

2. To describe the total quality approach to strategic planning and show its relevance to marketing

3. To look at the different kinds of strategic plans and the relationships between marketing and the other functional areas in an organization

4. To describe thoroughly each of the steps in the strategic planning process: defining organizational mission, establishing strategic business units, setting marketing objectives, performing situation analysis, developing marketing strategy, implementing tactics, and monitoring results

5. To show how a strategic plan may be devised and applied

{ According to Roberto Goizueta, Coca-Cola's chair and chief executive officer, "You can't stumble if you're not moving. And if you stumble and make a decision that doesn't pan out, then you move quickly to change it. But it's better than standing still." }

Although Coca-Cola has always had a reputation as a successful marketer, until recently its strategic planners were slow to respond to changes in the marketplace. Thus, the firm did not enter India until the late 1980s; at the same time, it was sluggish in dealing with the popularity of private-label soda in Great Britain; and in the early 1990s, it virtually ignored iced teas, new-age juices, and flavoured waters. By the time Coca-Cola responded in each of these instances, its competitors were able to garner a sizable market share.

Today, Coca-Cola uses a much quicker, more aggressive approach in its market-planning activities. For example, the firm now markets such new drinks as Mountain Blast Powerade sports drink and Strawberry Passion Awareness Fruitopia fruit drink; and it has developed and introduced new packaging and promotions. Says Roberto Goizueta, "Nothing energizes an organization like speed."

In the not-too-distant past, some marketing analysts saw PepsiCo as the "hot" soft-drink company most likely to come out with new products and the best advertising campaigns. Now, they credit Coca-Cola with these qualities. Even arch-rival PepsiCo acknowledges Coca-Cola's new-found strength. PepsiCo's head of marketing states that "Coke has definitely raised the bar."

One good example of Coca-Cola's peppy approach to planning involves Japan, the firm's most profitable market. Japanese consumers are noted for demanding new products at breakneck speed; and while soda companies typically launch a total of 700 to 800 new drinks per year, few last for more than a month. Until 1993, Coca-Cola did not keep pace with its competitors. Then, it set up a product development centre that reduced the launch time for new drinks from 90 days to 30 days. Because of this, Coca-Cola now releases 50 new products per year in Japan—and its Japanese development centre serves all of Asia. A similar strategy is also being used for North America and Europe.

Coca-Cola's increased responsiveness applies equally to the withdrawal of slow-selling products. Formerly, the firm would take its time in discontinuing poor-sellers. Thus, ViProMin, a fortified tomato juice launched in the 1960s, was distributed by Coca-Cola for several years despite poor sales. Some analysts feel the slow-withdrawal strategy was caused by Coca-Cola's unwillingness to publicly acknowledge defeat. Now, Coca-Cola is better able to shrug off failure. That is why the firm's Japanese "lactic-based" drink was quickly pulled after the product's initial sales growth slowed.

Coca-Cola's superior planning is quite evident in Eastern Europe. When the Soviet Union collapsed, Coca-Cola rapidly built manufacturing, distribution, and marketing facilities from scratch. In contrast, PepsiCo kept using its old network of inefficient state-run bottlers. Furthermore, Coca-Cola's aggressive strategy has given its products the image as the "milk of capitalism," especially among the young. Not surprisingly, Coca-Cola's current sales in Eastern Europe greatly exceed those of Pepsi.[1]

In this chapter, we will consider strategic planning from a marketing perspective and review in depth each of the steps in the strategic planning process. We will also examine the use of strategic planning by both small and large firms.

Overview

As described in Chapter 2, the environment within which marketing operates includes a number of factors directed by top management and others directed by marketing. To coordinate these factors and provide guidance for decision making, it is helpful to employ a formal strategic planning process. To marketers, such a process consists of two main components: a strategic business plan and a strategic marketing plan.

---

[1] Robert Frank, "Coca-Cola is Shedding Its Once-Stodgy Image with Swift Expansion," *Wall Street Journal* (August 22, 1995), pp. A1, A5.

A **strategic business plan** "describes the overall direction an organization will pursue within its chosen environment and guides the allocation of resources and effort. It also provides the logic that integrates the perspectives of functional departments and operating units, and points them all in the same direction." It has (1) an external orientation; (2) a process for formulating strategies; (3) methods for analyzing strategic situations and alternatives; and (4) a commitment to action.[2]

A **strategic marketing plan** outlines the marketing actions to undertake, why those actions are needed, who is responsible for carrying them out, when and where they will be completed, and how they will be coordinated. Thus, a marketing plan is carried out within the context of a firm's broader strategic plan.

Strategic planning involves both **strategic business plans** *and* **strategic marketing plans**.

There are a number of reasons why marketers need an appreciation of the relationship between strategic planning and marketing. One, strategic planning gives direction to a firm's efforts and better enables it to understand marketing research, consumer analysis, and product, distribution, promotion, and price planning. It is a hierarchal process, moving from company-wide guidelines down to specific marketing decisions. Two, a strategic plan ensures each company division has clear goals that are integrated with the firm's overall goals. Three, different functional areas are encouraged to coordinate efforts. Four, strategic planning forces a firm to assess its strengths and weaknesses and to consider environmental opportunities and threats. Five, the alternative actions or combinations of actions a firm can take are outlined. Six, a basis for allotting resources is set. Seven, the value of having a procedure for assessing performance can be shown.

Marketing's role in strategic planning is indeed a crucial one:

Marketing should have a key role in strategic planning.

> In industry after industry, the opportunity today is clear. It is now possible for companies to focus directly on achieving the full potential of customer relationships. Doing so will require executives to abandon outdated management models. But, as with prior shifts in management thinking, those who act early will reap disproportionate rewards.[3]
>
> Strategic planning should stress market information, market-segment definition, and market targeting. All company activities should be built around the goal of creating the desired position with a well-defined set of customers. Separate market segments should be the subject of separate plans that focus on developing customer relationships that emphasize the firm's distinctive competence. [Marketing's] contribution to strategic planning and implementation begins with the analysis of market segments and an assessment of a firm's ability to satisfy customer needs. This includes analyzing demand trends, competition, and in industrial markets, competitive conditions. Marketing also plays a key role by working with top management to define business purpose in terms of customer-need satisfaction. In a market-oriented view of the strategic planning process, financial goals are seen as results and rewards, not the fundamental purpose of business.[4]

In Chapter 3, we discuss a total quality approach to strategic planning, various kinds of strategic plans, relationships between marketing and other functional areas, and the strategic planning process—and show how strategic planning may be applied. Chapter 23, which concludes the text, deals with how marketing plans are integrated and analyzed using a total quality framework.

A Total Quality Approach to Strategic Planning

When devising strategic plans, any firm—small or large, domestic or international, manufacturing or services driven—should adopt a total quality perspective. **Total quality** is a process- and output-related philosophy, whereby a firm strives to fully satisfy customers in an effective and efficient manner. To flourish, a total quality program needs all of the following:

All firms should adopt a **total quality** *approach, thereby becoming more process- and output-oriented in satisfying consumers.*

---

[2]Peter D. Bennett (Ed.), *Dictionary of Marketing Terms*, Second Edition (Chicago: American Marketing Association, 1995), p. 276.

[3]Alan W. H. Grant and Leonard A. Schlesinger, "Realize Your Customers' Full Profit Potential," *Harvard Business Review*, Vol. 59 (September–October 1995), p. 72.

[4]Frederick E. Webster, Jr., "The Rediscovery of the Marketing Concept," *Business Horizons*, Vol. 31 (May-June 1988), pp. 37–38.

- *A process-related philosophy*—Total quality is based on all the activities undertaken to create, develop, market, and deliver a good or service to the customer. A firm gains a competitive advantage if it can offer the same quality good or service at a lower cost or if it can offer a better-quality good or service than other companies.
- *An output-related philosophy*—Although process-related activities give a good or service its value, usually the consumer can only judge the total quality of the finished product. Many consumers care about what they buy, rather than how it was made.
- *Customer satisfaction*—To the consumer, total quality refers to how well a good or service performs. Thus, customer service is a key element in a person's ultimate satisfaction, which is affected by the gap between that person's expectations of product performance and actual performance.
- *Effectiveness*—To a marketer, this means how well various marketing activities (such as adding new product features) are received by consumers.
- *Efficiency*—To a marketer, this involves the costs of various marketing activities. A firm is efficient when it holds down costs, while offering consumers the appropriate level of quality.
- *Customer focus*—From a total quality perspective, a firm views the consumer as a partner and seeks input from that partner as it creates, develops, markets, and delivers a good or service.
- *Top management commitment*—Because a total quality program must be believed in by everyone who works for and comes into contact with a firm, senior executives must be dedicated to making it work and make sure corners are not cut in an attempt to be more efficient. In the best firms, "total quality" becomes ingrained as part of the corporate culture.
- *Continuous improvement*—In most cases, today's total quality will become tomorrow's suboptimal quality; so, a firm must continuously improve. A complacent firm will be hurt by the dynamics of the marketplace and fast-paced technological and global trends.
- *Employee support and involvement*—For a total quality program to work, employees must buy into it. Empowering employees not only gets them involved in the total quality process, but it also assures that customer problems are promptly addressed and resolved in the customer's favour.
- *Supplier and distributor support and involvement*—Due to their involvement in creating total quality, both suppliers and resellers can have a dramatic effect on it. They too must buy into a firm's efforts at total quality.

For a total quality program to work, every party in the process must participate.

Figure 3-1 shows how a successful total quality program works. At the left are the participants in a total quality program, who together engage in the process of creating total quality. There is an interchange among the parties and between the parties and the process. A good's or service's effectiveness and efficiency both influence and are influenced by the total quality process, and the output of the process is total quality. Both process and outcome are regularly improved.

If consumers feel a good or service has superior quality, they will buy it; when the experience with a good or service is positive, the result is customer satisfaction, which is one measure of effectiveness. Finally, the level of customer satisfaction affects the consumer's future input into the total quality process, as represented by the feedback loop in the figure. The fact that the consumer appears three times in the diagram (consumer input, consumer purchase, and customer satisfaction) is evidence of the importance of the consumer in total quality.

As one expert notes, "To see things truly from the customer's perspective is to stand at the end of a long sequence of events, all of which have to mesh smoothly. Hotel clerks may be charming and attentive, but if the computer system is down, their courtesy isn't going to help much. Within any company, TQM theory holds, is a whole chain of 'internal customers' like the hotel clerk, ending with the person at the cash register, credit card in hand. The trick is to get everyone working together while keeping the ultimate cus-

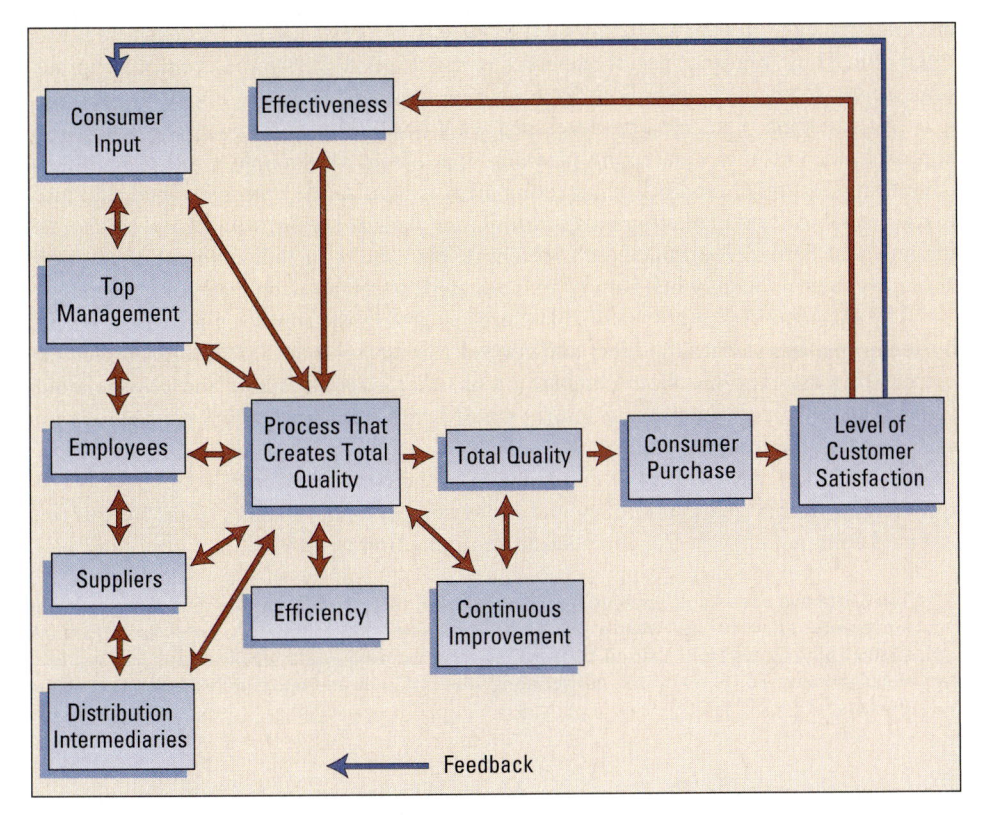

FIGURE 3-1
The Keys to a Successful Total Quality Program

tomer in focus." To Siemens (the German-based industrial firm), "Quality is when your customers come back and your products don't."[5]

Kinds of Strategic Plans

Strategic plans can be categorized by their duration, scope, and method of development. They range from short-run, specific, and department generated to long-run, broad, and management generated.

Plans may be short-run (typically one year), moderate in length (two to five years), or long run (five to ten or even fifteen years). Many firms rely on a combination: Short-run and moderate-length plans are more detailed and operational in nature than long-run plans.

At Japan's Canon Corporation (which makes cameras, business machines, and optical products), short-run plans show a "numerical expression of management activities during defined operating periods;" moderate-length plans "develop strategies to achieve the direction and goals defined by long-range plans, to provide guidelines for short-range plans, and to ensure optimum resource procurement and allocation;" and long-run plans are "more a vision or concept rather than plans, in the sense that they provide the direction and goals for a firm to pursue in a rapidly changing environment, and they lead to the achievement of qualitative innovations in every aspect of operations."[6]

The scope of strategic marketing plans also varies. There may be separate marketing plans for each of a firm's major products; a single, integrated marketing plan encompassing all products; or a broad business plan with a section devoted to marketing. Separate marketing plans by product line are often used by consumer-goods manufacturers; a single,

Short-run plans are precise; long-run plans outline needs.

CANON CORPORATION
www.cancom.com/

Consumer-products firms often have plans for each line.

---

[5]Frank Rose, "Now Quality Means Service Too," *Fortune* (April 22, 1991), pp. 97–108; and Earl Naumann and Patrick Shannon, "What Is Customer-Driven Marketing?" *Business Horizons*, Vol. 35 (November–December 1992), p. 44. See also John Shea and David Gobeli, "TQM: The Experience of Ten Small Businesses," *Business Horizons*, Vol. 38 (January–February 1995), pp. 71–77.
[6]Toshio Nakahara and Yutaka Isono, "Strategic Planning for Canon; The Crisis and the New Vision," *Long Range Planning*, Vol. 25 (February 1992), p. 67.

integrated marketing plan is often employed by service firms; and a broad business plan is often utilized by industrial-goods manufacturers. A firm's diversity and the number of distinct market segments it seeks both have a strong influence here.

Last, strategic plans may be developed via a bottom-up, top-down, or combination approach. In bottom-up marketing planning, input from salespeople, product managers, advertising personnel, and other marketing areas is used to set objectives, budgets, forecasts, timetables, and marketing mixes. Bottom-up plans are realistic and good for morale. Yet it may be hard to coordinate each bottom-up plan and to include different assumptions about the same concept when setting an integrated, company-wide marketing plan.

Bottom-up plans foster employee input; top-down plans are set by top management.

The shortcomings of bottom-up plans are resolved in the top-down approach, whereby senior managers centrally direct and control planning activities. A top-down plan can use complex assumptions about competition or other external factors and provide a uniform direction for the marketing effort. Yet, if input from lower-level managers is not actively sought, morale may suffer.

The solution may be to use a combination of the two approaches, with senior executives setting overall goals and policy and marketing personnel forming plans for carrying out marketing policies. As the chief executive of one firm remarked:

> You can't have a workable strategy forced down from the top. Empowering middle managers is a necessity. They manage what we as a corporation want to accomplish. To make them think strategically comes from sharing the direction and from having a set of supportive organizational systems. So it's real work, not sermons, that makes us and our middle managers strategic thinkers.[7]

Strengthening Relationships Between Marketing and Other Functional Areas

The perspectives of marketing and other functional areas need to be reconciled.

An organization's strategic planning must accommodate the distinct needs of marketing and other functional areas. This is not always simple, due to the different orientations of each area, as shown in Table 3-1. Marketing people may seek tailor-made products, flexible bud-

Table 3-1
The Orientations of Different Functional Areas

FUNCTIONAL AREA	MAJOR STRATEGIC ORIENTATION
Marketing	To attract and retain a loyal group of consumers through a unique combination of product, distribution, promotion, and price factors
Production	To utilize full plant capacity, hold down per-unit production costs, and maximize quality control
Finance	To operate within established budgets, focus on profitable items, control customer credit, and minimize loan costs for the company
Accounting	To standardize reports, detail costs fully, and routinize transactions
Engineering	To develop and adhere to exact product specifications, limit models and options, and concentrate on quality improvements
Purchasing	To acquire items via large, uniform orders at low prices and maintain low inventories
Research and development	To seek technological breakthroughs, improvements in product quality, and recognition for innovations
Personnel	To hire, motivate, supervise, and compensate employees in an efficient manner
Legal	To ensure that a strategy is defensible against challenges from the government, competitors, channel members, and consumers

---

[7] Manab Thakur and Luis Ma. R. Calingo, "Strategic Thinking Is Hip, But Does It Make a Difference?" *Business Horizons*, Vol. 35 (September–October 1992), p. 47.

gets, non-routine transactions, many product versions, frequent purchases, customer-driven new products, employee compensation incentives, and aggressive actions against competitors. These may conflict with the goals of other functional areas to seek mass production (production), well-established budgets (finance), routinized transactions (accounting), limited models (engineering), infrequent orders (purchasing), technology-driven new products (research and development), fixed employee compensation (personnel), and passive actions against competitors (legal).

Top management makes sure every functional area sees the need for a balanced view in company decision making and has a say in the decisions that are made. Although some degree of tension among departments is inevitable, conflict can be lessened by encouraging interdepartmental contact; seeking employees with both technical and marketing expertise; forming multifunctional task forces, committees, and management-development programs; and setting goals for each department that take the other departments into account.[8]

The Strategic Planning Process

As Figure 3-2 illustrates, the **strategic planning process** has seven interrelated steps: defining organizational mission, establishing strategic business units, setting marketing objectives, performing situation analysis, developing marketing strategy, implementing tactics, and monitoring results. Because the process encompasses both strategic business planning and strategic marketing planning, it is usually conducted by a combination of senior company executives and marketers.

This process is applicable to small and large firms, consumer-products and industrial-products firms, goods- and services-based firms, domestic and international firms, and profit-oriented and nonprofit-oriented institutions. While planning at each step in the process may differ by type of organization, using a thorough strategic plan is beneficial for any organization.

The steps in strategic planning are discussed in the following sections.

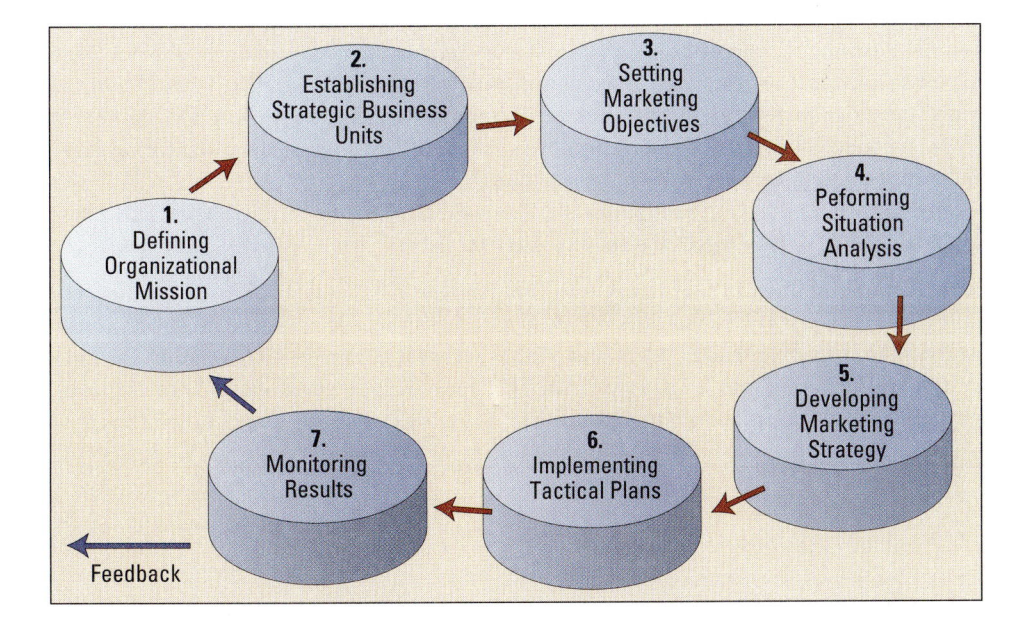

*The **strategic planning process** includes steps from defining a mission to monitoring results.*

FIGURE 3-2
The Strategic Planning Process

---

[8]See Jeen-Su Lim, "Vital Cross-Functional Linkages with Marketing," *Industrial Marketing Management*, Vol. 21 (May 1992), pp. 159–165; Victoria L. Crittenden, "Close the Marketing/Manufacturing Gap," *Sloan Management Review*, Vol. 33 (Spring 1992), pp. 41–51; and Michael D. Hutt, Beth A. Walker, and Gary L. Frankwick, "Hurdle the Cross-Functional Barriers to Strategic Change," *Sloan Management Review*, Vol. 36 (Spring 1995), pp. 22–30.

Defining Organizational Mission

A firm sets its direction in an **organizational mission.**

An **organizational mission** is a long-term commitment to a type of business and a place in the market. It "describes the scope of the firm and its dominant emphasis and values," based on that firm's history, current management preferences, resources, and distinctive competences, and on environmental factors.[9]

An organizational mission can be expressed in terms of the customer group(s) served, the goods and services offered, the functions performed, and/or the technologies utilized. It is more comprehensive than the line-of-business concept noted in Chapter 2. And it is considered implicitly whenever a firm seeks a new customer group or abandons an existing one, introduces a new product (good or service) category or deletes an old one, acquires another company or sells one of its own businesses, engages in more marketing functions (a wholesaler opening retail stores) or in fewer marketing functions (a small innovative toy maker licensing its inventions to an outside company that produces, distributes, and promotes them), or shifts its technological focus (a phone manufacturer placing more emphasis on cellular phones).

Here are two diverse illustrations of clear organizational missions:

> Lands' End is a leading international direct merchant of traditionally styled, casual clothing for men, women, and children, accessories, shoes, and soft luggage. Its products are offered through regular mailings of a monthly catalogue and four specialty catalogues. Lands' End is known for providing products of exceptional quality at prices representing honest value, enhanced by a commitment to excellence in customer service.[10]

B.C. SUGAR REFINERY LTD.
www.bcsugar.com/

LANTIC SUGAR
www.lanticsugar.com

> B.C. Sugar Refinery Limited has decided that a "sugar diet" is just what it needs for success. It is Canada's largest sugar company and the third largest in North America. In 1990 B.C. Sugar had holdings in specialty chemicals and oil and natural gas. The firm decided to exit these ventures and proceeded to buy up 50 per cent of a larger competitor, Lantic Sugar of Montreal, followed by purchasing the remaining 50 per cent a year-and-a-half later. The firm believes that by sticking to its core business coupled with the reduction of trade barriers to the U.S. market they can enjoy something even sweeter than their product, success.[11]

Organizations that diversify too much may lack a clear sense of direction. For example, Jostens—the maker of class rings, yearbooks, and other items targeted to high school and university students—was extremely profitable for four decades. Then, it launched Jostens Learning Corporation in 1989, even though its senior executives did not have expertise in educational software. Jostens' software business flopped, largely because of the high startup costs for clients and intense competition; and the firm lost $16 million in 1994. As one analyst observed, "Nobody was taking a hard look at what was going on—nobody seemed to be asking the right questions."[12]

JOSTENS LEARNING CORPORATION
www.jlc.com/

Establishing Strategic Business Units

Strategic business units *are separate operating units in an organization.*

After defining its mission, a firm may form strategic business units. Each **strategic business unit (SBU)** is a self-contained division, product line, or product department in an organization with a specific market focus and a manager with complete responsibility for integrating all functions into a strategy.[13] An SBU may include all products with the same physical features or products bought for the same use by customers, depending on the mission of the organization. Each SBU has these general attributes:

- A specific target market.
- Its own senior marketing executive.
- Control over its resources.

---

[9]Bennett, *Dictionary of Marketing Terms*, p. 67. See also James Krobe Jr., "Do You Really Need a Mission Statement?" *Across the Board* (July–August 1995), pp. 17–21.
[10]*Lands' End 1995 Annual Report.*
[11]"The Top Ten Performers," *Canadian Business* (June 1994), p. 110.
[12]Kenneth Labich, "Why Companies Fail," *Fortune* (November 14, 1994), pp. 52–54.
[13]Subhash C. Jain, *Marketing Planning & Strategy*, Fourth Edition (Cincinnati: South-Western, 1993), pp. 15–19.

- Its own marketing strategy.
- Clear-cut competitors.
- Distinct differential advantages.

The SBU concept lets companies identify those business units with the greatest earnings potential and allocate to them the resources needed for their growth. For instance, at General Electric, every SBU must have a unique purpose, identifiable competitors, and all its major business functions (manufacturing, finance, and marketing) within the control of that SBUs manager. Units not performing up to expectations are constantly reviewed and, if necessary, consolidated with other units, sold, or closed down.[14]

The proper number of SBUs depends on a firm's organizational mission, its resources, and the willingness of top management to delegate authority. A small or specialized firm can have as few as one SBU, a diversified one up to 100 or more. Thus, Johnson Controls has the four SBUs depicted in Figure 3-3; General Electric has twelve SBUs—ranging from aircraft engines to lighting to information services; Dover has 70 SBUs— ranging from elevators to garbage trucks to welding torches; and Johnson & Johnson has 165+ SBUs— related to consumer, pharmaceutical, and professional products.[15]

Setting Marketing Objectives

A firm needs overall marketing objectives, as well as goals for each SBU. Objectives are often described in both quantitative terms (dollar sales, percentage profit growth, market share, etc.) and qualitative terms (image, level of innovativeness, industry leadership role, etc.).

Marketing objectives may include quantitative and qualitative measures.

FIGURE 3-3
The SBUs of Johnson Controls
Reprinted by permission.

[14]Noel M. Tichy and Stratford Sherman, *Control Your Destiny or Someone Else Will* (New York: Doubleday, 1993).
[15]*General Electric 1995 Annual Report*; Phillip L. Zweig, "Who Says the Conglomerate Is Dead?" *Business Week* (January 23, 1995), pp. 92–93; and Brian O'Reilly, "J&J Is on a Roll," *Fortune* (December 26, 1994), pp. 178–192.

International Marketing in Action

Understanding the Marketing Strategies of U.S. and South African Firms

To successfully compete in foreign markets, Canadian marketing managers must understand how businesses compete. Very often, the marketing approach of a nation will require adjustments in the way a firm does business. The United States and South Africa represent excellent market opportunities for Canadian firms since both countries do business in English, one of Canada's official languages. These are some of the ways in which the marketing strategies used in the United States and South Africa differed.

- U.S. firms focus more on competitive advantage and identifying target markets as key components in their strategies. In contrast, South African firms place more emphasis on company positioning and taking advantage of trends and opportunities as market strategy components.
- With regard to target marketing approaches, South African firms have a greater tendency to focus on the entire market (rather than individual customers or multiple segments).
- In terms of demand-based strategies, U.S. firms are more apt to try to take customers from competitors and attract new users to the market.
- In terms of pricing, U.S. firms engage in more penetration pricing (aimed at charging a lower price to capture the mass market) than South African firms.
- U.S. firms use market research and online data bases more than their South African counterparts, while South African firms make greater use of product portfolio analysis and formal planning procedures.
- South African firms use more financial managers and external consultants.

As a marketing manager for a small Canadian manufacturer who wants to market internationally, what could you learn from the above findings?

Source: Based on material in Michael H. Morris and Leyland F. Pitt, "Implementing Marketing Strategies in the U.S. and South Africa," *Long Range Planning*, Vol. 27 (February 1994), pp. 56–71.

For example, Quaker Oats Company's eight key goals are: (1) "Provide total shareholder returns that exceed the cost of equity and the S&P 500 stock index over time." (2) "Maintain a robust financial position from strong operating cash flows, while generating economic value via the use of leverage." (3) "Aggressively market brands for leadership positions. We assess our strength by our ability to grow, acquire, or maintain brands that are number one or two in their categories." (4) "Profitably grow the volume of key brands at better-than-industry-average rates by offering greater value to the customer." (5) "Enhance productivity and efficiency in every element of our business." (6) "Develop mutually beneficial, interdependent relationships with our trade customers to improve the economic return of both parties." (7) "Build high-performance teams of resourceful, motivated, and productive employees." (8) "Raise the productivity of low-return businesses or divest them."[16]

Small firms' goals are often less ambitious, but no less important. For example, Upper Canada Brewing of Toronto is a small regional brewer in an industry dominated by the Labatt and Molson giants. Upper Canada has positioned itself as a Canadian and commu-

---

[16] *Quaker Oats Company 1995 Annual Report*.

nity brewery. One of their advertising themes is: "Think Globally, Drink Locally." Microbrewery operations by their very nature are small and local and the cost of going to the next level is often not worth the trouble to their owners.[17]

Performing Situation Analysis

In **situation analysis**, also known as SWOT analysis, an organization identifies its internal strengths (S) and weaknesses (W), as well as external opportunities (O) and threats (T). Situation analysis seeks to answer: Where is a firm now? In what direction is it headed? Answers are derived by recognizing the company's strengths and weaknesses relative to its competitors, studying the environment for opportunities and threats, assessing the firm's ability to capitalize on opportunities and to minimize or avoid threats, and anticipating competitors' responses to company strategies.

Situation analysis can, and should be, conducted at any point in a firm's life. For instance, when Ann Bayley, President of Iceculture Inc., started her business it was to provide ice bowls as a free add-on to her husband's catering business. Ann has been quick to recognize opportunities and Iceculture is now a $100 000 business going beyond weddings and hospitality events to include winter carnival displays. Iceculture got into the winter carnival business when Ann offered to supply ice carving as a backup to worried Winter Carnival organizers in Grand Bend, Ontario who had planned a carnival but did not plan on a lack of snow. Winter carnivals have now become a major growth market for Iceculture. Of course, the product does have one important problem, customers complain that it melts. Ann plans to seize this opportunity by launching fake ice.[18]

Sometimes, situation analysis reveals weaknesses or threats that cannot be overcome, and a company opts to drop or sell a product line or division. Thus, in 1995, General Mills sold its restaurant division—comprised of the Red Lobster, Olive Garden, and China Coast chains. Why? Fifty-five per cent of General Mills' food profits were being used to fund the restaurant business; and the firm decided to focus instead on its leading food brands: Wheaties, Cheerios, Betty Crocker baking products, Yoplait yogurt, and others.[19]

Situation analysis investigates a firm's strengths, weaknesses, opportunities, and threats.

Developing Marketing Strategy

A **marketing strategy** outlines the way in which the marketing mix is used to attract and satisfy the target market(s) and achieve an organization's goals. Marketing-mix decisions centre on product, distribution, promotion, and price plans. A separate strategy is necessary for each SBU in an organization; these strategies must be coordinated.

A marketing strategy should be explicit to provide proper guidance. It should take into account a firm's mission, resources, abilities, and standing in the marketplace; the status of the firm's industry and the product groups in it (such as light versus ice beer); domestic and international competitive forces; such environmental factors as the economy and population growth; and the best opportunities for growth—and the threats that could dampen it.

Four strategic planning approaches are presented next: the product/market opportunity matrix, the Boston Consulting Group matrix, the General Electric business screen, and the Porter generic strategy model.

A good marketing strategy provides a framework for marketing activities.

THE PRODUCT/MARKET OPPORTUNITY MATRIX The **product/market opportunity matrix** identifies four alternative marketing strategies to maintain and/or increase sales of business units and products: market penetration, market development, product development, and diversification (see Figure 3-4).[20] The choice of an alternative depends on the market saturation of an SBU or product and the firm's ability to introduce new products. Two or more alternatives may be combined.

*The **product/market opportunity matrix** involves **market penetration, market development, product development,** and **diversification** options.*

---

[17]Sean Eckford, "Small Brewers Play Canadian-Ownership Card," *Marketing Magazine* (August 14, 1995), p 4.
[18]Tim Falconer, "Freeze Play," *Canadian Business* (September 1995), p. 100.
[19]Leah Rickard, "General Mills Gathers Rewards of Change," *Advertising Age* (July 10, 1995), p. 4; and Richard Gibson, "General Mills Gets in Shape for Turnaround," *Wall Street Journal* (September 26, 1995), pp. B1, B4.
[20]H. Igor Ansoff, "Strategies for Diversification," *Harvard Business Review*, Vol. 35 (September–October 1957), pp. 113–124.

62   Part 1   *An Introduction to Marketing*

FIGURE 3-4
The Product/Market Opportunity Matrix
Source: Adapted from H. Igor Ansoff, "Strateges for Diversification," *Harvard Business Review, Vol. 35* (September–October 1957), pp. 113–124.

Market penetration is effective when the market is growing or not yet saturated. A firm seeks to expand the sales of its present products in its present markets through more intensive distribution, aggressive promotion, and competitive pricing. Sales are increased by attracting non–users and competitors' customers and raising the usage rate among current customers. United Parcel Service is a good example of a firm that has pursued a market penetration strategy. UPS (see Figure 3-5) is the world's largest package-delivery firm. It advertises extensively on TV and in magazines. Low prices and extensive distribution are centrepieces of its strategy.

FIGURE 3-5
UPS: The Leader in Package Delivery
Reprinted by permission

Market development is effective when a local or regional business looks to widen its market, new market segments are emerging due to changes in consumer lifestyles and demographics, and innovative uses are discovered for a mature product. A firm seeks greater sales of present products from new markets or new product uses. It can enter new geographic markets, appeal to market segments it is not yet satisfying, and reposition existing products. New distribution methods may be tried; promotion efforts are more descriptive. For example, UPS is stepping up efforts around the world, where client use of delivery services tends to be much less frequent than in North America.

Product development is effective when an SBU has a core of strong brands and a sizable consumer following. A firm develops new or modified products to appeal to present markets. It stresses new models, better quality, and other minor innovations closely related to entrenched products—and markets them to loyal customers. Traditional distribution methods are used; promotion stresses that the new product is made by a well-established firm. For example, UPS now offers more shipping choices than ever before, including GroundSaver, GroundTrac, 3 Day Select, Next Day Air, 2nd Day Air, and Worldwide Expedited Package services.

Diversification is used so a firm does not become too dependent on one SBU or product line. The firm becomes involved with new products aimed at new markets. These products may be new to the industry or new only to the company. Distribution and promotion orientations are both different from those usually followed by the firm. UPS has diversified by gaining a 15 per cent stake in Mail Boxes Etc., the leading North American neighbourhood mailing and business service-centre franchiser.[21]

THE BOSTON CONSULTING GROUP MATRIX The **Boston Consulting Group matrix** lets a firm classify each SBU in terms of its market share relative to major competitors and annual industry growth (see Figure 3-6). A firm can see which SBUs are dominant—compared to competitors—and whether the industries in which it operates are growing, stable, or declining. The matrix identifies four types of SBUs: star, cash cow, question mark, and dog, and offers strategies for each of them.[22]

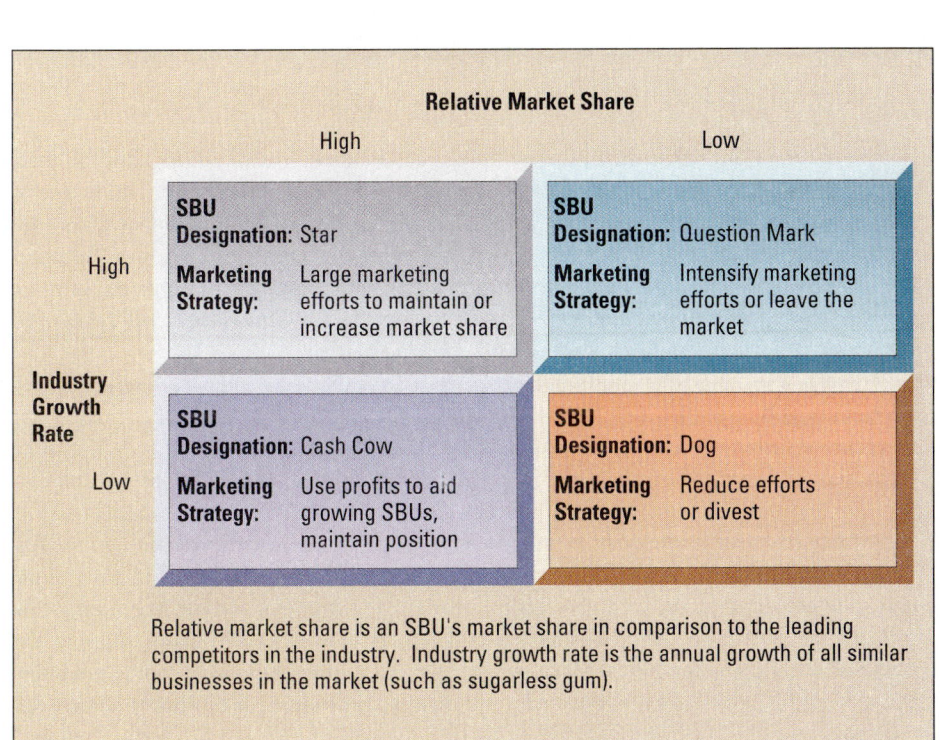

The **Boston Consulting Group matrix** *uses market share and industry growth to describe* **stars**, **cash cows**, **question marks**, *and* **dogs**.

FIGURE 3-6
The Boston Consulting Group Matrix
Source: Adapted from Bruce D. Henderson, "The Experience Curve Reviewed: IV. The Growth Share Matrix of the Product Portfolio" (Boston: Boston Consulting Group, 1973). *Perspectives* No. 135.

Relative Market Share

Industry Growth Rate	High (Relative Market Share)	Low (Relative Market Share)
High	**SBU Designation:** Star — **Marketing Strategy:** Large marketing efforts to maintain or increase market share	**SBU Designation:** Question Mark — **Marketing Strategy:** Intensify marketing efforts or leave the market
Low	**SBU Designation:** Cash Cow — **Marketing Strategy:** Use profits to aid growing SBUs, maintain position	**SBU Designation:** Dog — **Marketing Strategy:** Reduce efforts or divest

Relative market share is an SBU's market share in comparison to the leading competitors in the industry. Industry growth rate is the annual growth of all similar businesses in the market (such as sugarless gum).

---

[21] Gary Hoover, Alta Campbell, and Patrick J. Spain (Eds.), *Hoover's Handbook of American Business 1995* (Austin, Texas: Reference Press, 1994), pp. 1062–1063.

[22] See *Perspectives on Experience* (Boston: Boston Consulting Group, 1972); and D. Sudharshan, *Marketing Strategy: Relationships, Offerings, Timing & Resource Allocation* (Englewood Cliffs, N.J.: Prentice Hall, 1995), pp. 244–253.

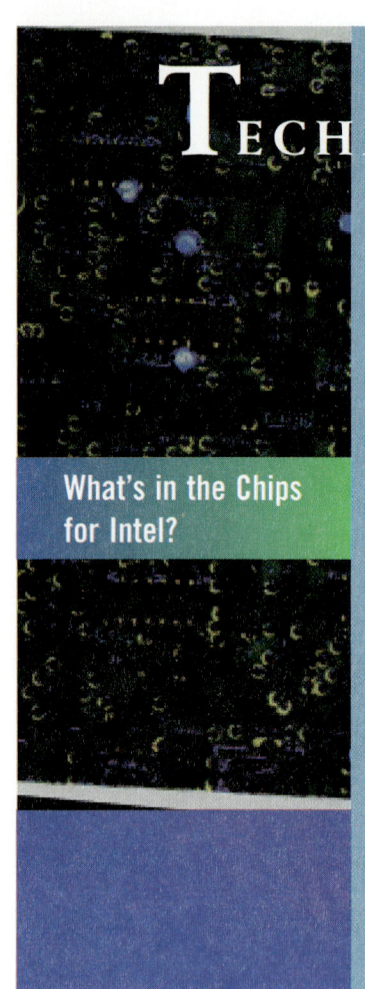

TECHNOLOGY & MARKETING

What's in the Chips for Intel?

Due to its estimated 75 per cent of the microprocessor chip market, Intel Corporation has the advantage of economies of scale (lower per-unit costs than competitors) and high profits. As a result, the firm regularly generates all the cash it needs for new-product development. And because the investment required to develop new microprocessor chips is growing quite rapidly, this places a tough burden on Intel's competitors. According to industry experts, the capital spending needed to devise the Pentium chip was U.S.$5 billion. This was five times the amount needed for the 486 chip and 50 times that for the 386 chip. In general, plant and equipment costs double every four years.

Some analysts say that Intel will become the world's most profitable company by the year 2000. They estimate that Intel's annual earnings may reach U.S.$8 billion to U.S.$11 billion in that year. Few large firms have been able to match Intel's recent five-year average earnings growth rate of 37 per cent. In addition, company executives suggest that microprocessor chips are less vulnerable than other products to the business cycle.

Much of Intel's strategy revolves around an observation made in 1965 by Intel's then chairman, Gordon E. Moore. This observation, now known as Moore's Law, states that the number of transistors that can be placed on a chip doubles every 18 months or so. Making smaller circuits also means that chips get faster, consume less energy, become more reliable, and cost less. For example, Intel's new P6 chip has 254 times more computing power per U.S.$100 in cost than the Intel 8086 chip used by IBM in its initial PC sold in 1981.

As a marketing analyst, what do you think Intel must do to meet the year 2000 profit goals noted above?

Source: Based on material in Don Clark, "A Big Bet Made Intel What It Is Today; Now, It Wagers Again," *Wall Street Journal* (July 7, 1995), pp. A1, A6; and Brent Schlender, "Why Andy Grove Can't Stop," *Fortune* (July 10, 1995), pp. 88–98.

The assumption is that the higher an SBU's market share, the better its long-run marketplace position because of rather low per-unit costs and high profitability. This is due to economies of scale (larger firms can automate or standardize production, service tasks, distribution, promotion, and so on), experience (as operations are repeated, a firm becomes more effective), and better bargaining power. At the same time, the industry growth rate indicates a firm's need to invest. A high growth rate means a big investment will be needed to maintain or expand the firm's position in a growing market.

A **star** is a leading SBU (high market share) in an expanding industry (high growth). The main goal is to sustain differential advantages in the face of rising competition. A star can generate substantial profits but requires financing for continued growth. Market share can be kept or increased through intensive advertising, product introductions, greater distribution, and/or price reductions. As industry growth slows, a star becomes a cash cow.

A **cash cow** is a leading SBU (high market share) in a mature or declining industry (low growth). It often has loyal customers, making it hard for competitors to woo them. Since sales are steady, without high costs for product development and the like, a cash cow produces more cash (profit) than needed to keep its market share. Profits support the growth of other company SBUs. Marketing is oriented to reminder ads, periodic price discounts, keeping up distribution channels, and offering new styles or options to encourage repurchases.

A **question mark** is an SBU that has had little impact (low market share) in an expanding industry (high growth). There is low consumer support, differential advantages are weak, and competitors are leaders. To improve, a big marketing investment is needed in the face of strong competition. A firm must decide whether to beef up promotion, add distributors, improve product attributes, and cut prices—or to abandon the market. The

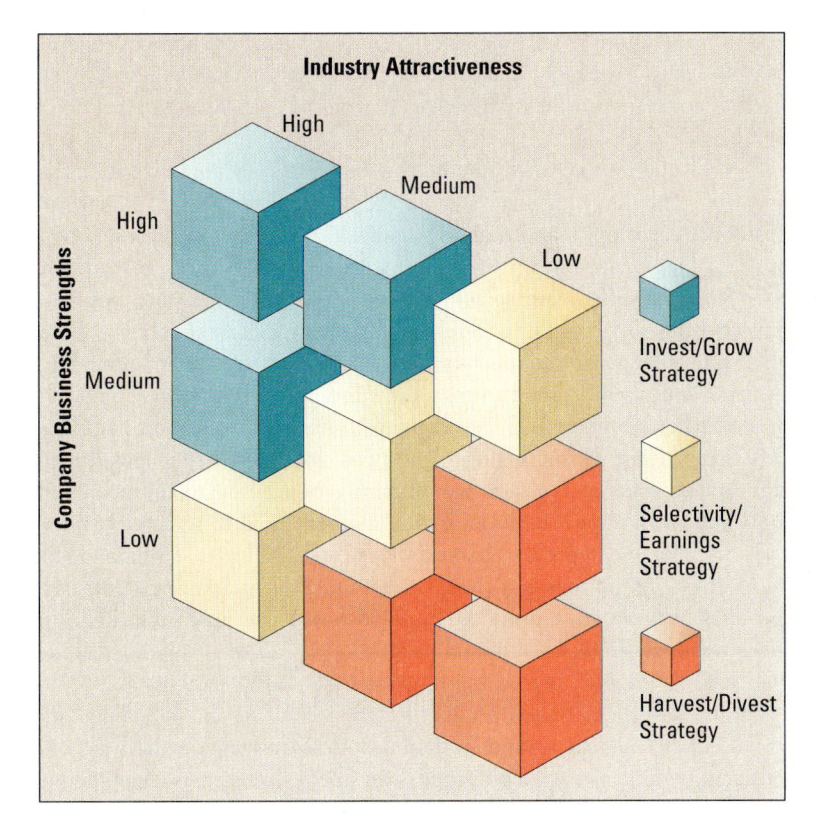

FIGURE 3-7
The General Electric Business Screen
Source: *Maintaining Strategies for the Future Through Current Crises* (Fairfield, Ct.: General Electric, 1975).

choice depends on whether a firm believes the SBU can compete successfully with more support and what that support will cost.

A **dog** is an SBU with limited sales (low market share) in a mature or declining industry (low growth). Despite time in the marketplace, a dog has a small customer following—and lags behind competitors in sales, image, and so on. A dog usually has cost disadvantages and few growth opportunities. A firm with such an SBU can appeal to a specialized market, harvest profits by cutting support services, or exit the market.

Dylex Ltd. is the parent firm of the women's fashion clothiers Fairweather and Braemar, men's clothiers Tip Top and Harry Rosen, as well as Biway and Thrifty's. It also has a holding in Club Monaco. Elliott Wahle, the CEO, takes pride in being a builder and he is determined to market Dylex's products so they build share. Wahle believes that Dylex has a responsibility to provide an environment where its divisions will be allowed to grow. Maintaining customer loyalty and store branding are the approaches Wahle believes will build market share. For example, Tip Top and Fairweather's might be treated as "Cash Cow SBUs." As for growth, developing products for an aging population and capitalizing on the casual-business attire market are two fertile areas for Dylex. In this regard, Club Monaco might be considered a "Question Mark SBU." Wahle decided that Dylex should divest the "Dog SBUs" of Braemar and Harry Rosen divisions to concentrate on the remaining retail divisions. The focus on growth and market share for Dylex falls right in line with the principles suggested by the Boston Consulting Group matrix. Dylex will be seeking growth opportunities to "build on the diversity of the Dylex portfolio."[23]

DYLEX LTD.
www.dylex.com/

THE GENERAL ELECTRIC BUSINESS SCREEN The **General Electric business screen** categorizes SBUs and products in terms of industry attractiveness and company business strengths. It involves more variables than the product/market opportunity matrix or the Boston Consulting Group matrix. Industry attractiveness factors include market size and growth, competition, technological advances, and the social/legal environment. Company business strength is measured according to differential advantages, market share,

The **General Electric business screen** *measures industry attractiveness and company business strengths.*

---

[23] James Pollock, "At Bat for Dylex," *Marketing Magazine* (November 13, 1995), pp. 1, 12; and "Dylex to Unload Rosen and Braemar Stakes," *Marketing Magazine* (February 19, 1996), p. 1.

patent protection, marketing effectiveness, control over prices, and economies of scale. An SBU may have high, medium, or low industry attractiveness, as well as high, medium, or low company business strengths; it would be positioned accordingly on the business screen in Figure 3-7.[24]

SBUs in green are investment/growth areas. They are in strong industries and performing well. They are similar to stars in the Boston Consulting Group matrix. Full marketing resources are proper, and high profits are expected. Innovations, product-line extensions, product and image ads, distribution intensity, and solid price margins are pursued.

SBUs in yellow are selectivity/earnings areas. They are not positioned as well as investment/growth ones. An SBU may be strong in a weak industry (like a cash cow), okay in a somewhat attractive industry, or weak in an attractive industry (like a question mark). A firm wants to hold the earnings and strength of cash cows, and use marketing to maintain customer loyalty and distribution support. For question marks, a firm must decide whether to raise its marketing investment, focus on a specialized market niche, acquire another business in the industry, or trim product lines. The medium/medium SBU is an opportunity to appeal to under-served segments and to selectively invest in marketing.

SBUs in red represent harvest/divest areas. They are similar to dogs in the Boston Consulting Group matrix. A firm can minimize its marketing effort, concentrate on a few products rather than a product line, divest, or close down the SBU. Profits are harvested because investments are minimal.

Bausch & Lomb applies the fundamentals of the business screen: It has "a heritage of technical achievement and product excellence dating to 1853. The company markets personal health, medical, biomedical, and optics products on the basis of quality and differentiated benefits. Its strategic focus is on selected segments of global health care and optical markets where it is advantaged with superior technology, low production costs, and established brand names. Products have earned worldwide consumer recognition and are frequently recommended by health-care professionals."[25]

The **Porter generic strategy model** *distinguishes among cost leadership, differentiation, and focus strategies.*

THE PORTER GENERIC STRATEGY MODEL The **Porter generic strategy model** identifies two key marketing planning concepts and the options available for each: competitive scope (broad or narrow target) and competitive advantage (lower cost or differentiation). The model, shown in Figure 3-8, pinpoints these basic strategies: cost leadership, differentiation, and focus.[26]

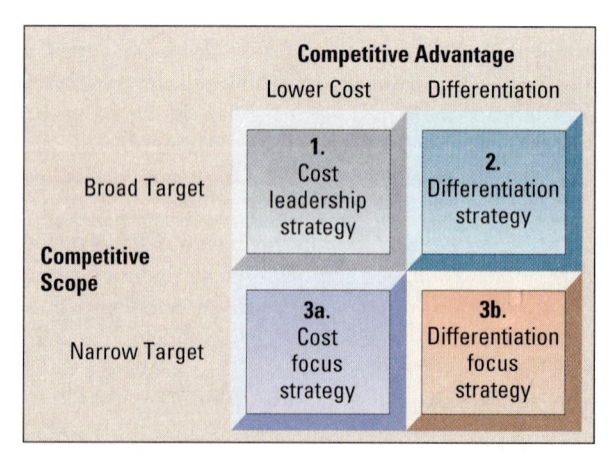

FIGURE 3-8

The Porter Generic Strategy Model

Source: Michael E. Porter, *Competitive Advantage: Creating and Sustaining Superior Performance* (New York: Free Press, 1985), p. 12. Reprinted with the permission of The Free Press, a division of Macmillan Inc. Copyright © 1985 by Michael E. Porter.

---

[24]See Derek F. Abell and John S. Hammond, *Strategic Market Planning* (Englewood Cliffs, N.J.: Prentice-Hall, 1979), pp. 211–227; and David A. Aaker, *Strategic Market Management* (New York: Wiley, 1995), pp. 164–167.
[25]*Bausch & Lomb 1992 Annual Report*; and *Bausch & Lomb 1994 Annual Report*..
[26]Michael E. Porter, *Competitive Advantage: Creating and Sustaining Superior Performance* (New York: Free Press, 1985), pp. 11–26; and Michael E. Porter, *Competitive Strategy: Techniques for Analyzing Industries and Competitors* (New York: Free Press, 1980), pp. 34–46. See also Steven P. Schnaars, *Marketing Strategy: A Customer-Driven Approach* (New York: Free Press, 1991), pp. 112–131.

With a cost-leadership strategy, an SBU aims at a broad market and offers goods or services in large quantities. Due to economies of scale, a firm can reduce per-unit costs and have low prices. This gives it higher profit margins than competitors, better response to cost rises, and/or the ability to attract price-conscious consumers. Among those using cost leadership is Royal Airlines. The latter has been called Canada's most efficient carrier. Royal began operations in 1992 and is fanatically dedicated to keeping overhead low and revenue and profits high. In fact, its managers speak with pride as they mention how they have borrowed heavily from management approaches developed by famous cost controlling firms like Wal-Mart. To keep revenues high, Royal focuses on international flights to the Caribbean and other warm-weather destinations in the winter, and serves European and cross-Canada destinations in the summer. This focus on the tourist segment at peak flying times allows them to have fully booked flights and flexible scheduling, which keep costs down and revenues high.[27]

In a differentiation strategy, an SBU aims at a large market by offering goods or services that are viewed as distinctive. The goods or services have a broad appeal, yet are perceived by consumers as unique by virtue of features, availability, reliability, etc.; price is less important. Among those using differentiation are Astoria Airlines of Montreal, Federal Express, Seiko, Caterpillar Tractor, and Harry Rosen's menswear stores. Harry Rosen offers men's fashion clothing with an upscale image and good quality.[28]

With a focus strategy, an SBU (which could be a small firm) seeks a narrow market segment by offering low prices or a unique product. It can control costs by concentrating on a few key products aimed at specific consumers or by having a specialist reputation and serving a market unsatisfied by competitors. Samsung is a South Korean producer of inexpensive consumer electronics; James Izatt of Vancouver develops turf-growing systems for golf courses and sports fields, which he then licenses.[29]

The Porter model shows that a small firm can profit by concentrating on one competitive niche, even though its total market share may be low. A firm does not have to be large to do well.

EVALUATION OF STRATEGIC PLANNING APPROACHES The strategic planning approaches just discussed are widely used—at least informally. Many firms assess alternative market opportunities; know which products are stars, cash cows, question marks, and dogs; recognize what factors affect performance; understand their industries; and realize they can target broad or narrow customer bases. Formally, strategic planning models are most apt to be used by larger firms; and the models are adapted to the needs of the specific firm employing them.

Strategic models have pros and cons, and should be only part of planning.

The major strengths of these approaches are that they let a firm analyze all SBUs and products, study the effects of various strategies, learn the opportunities to pursue and the threats to avoid, compute marketing and other resource needs, focus on meaningful differential advantages, compare performance against designated goals, and discover principles for improving. Competitors' actions and long-term trends can also be followed.

The major weaknesses of these approaches are that they may be hard to use (particularly by a small firm), may be too simplistic and omit key factors, are somewhat arbitrary in defining SBUs and evaluative criteria (like relative market share), may not be applicable to all companies and situations (a dog SBU may actually be profitable and generate cash), do not adequately account for environmental conditions (like the economy), may overvalue market share, and are often used by staff planners rather than line managers.

These techniques only aid planning. They do not replace the need for managers to study each situation and base marketing strategies on the unique aspects of their industry, firm, and SBUs.

---

[27]Tamsen Tillson, "On a Wing and a Prayer," *Canadian Business* (October 1995), pp. 90–100.
[28]James Pollock, "At Bat for Dylex."
[29]Kerry Banks, "Blade Runner," Canadian Business (February 1996), p. 104.

Implementing Tactical Plans

*A marketing strategy is enacted using **tactical plans**.*

A **tactical plan** specifies the short-run actions (tactics) that a firm undertakes in implementing a given marketing strategy. A tactical plan has three basic elements: specific tasks, a time frame, and resource allocation.

The specific tasks relate to the marketing mix and may be aimed at creating a variety of combinations, from high quality, high service, low distribution intensity, personal-selling emphasis, and above-average prices to low quality, low service, high distribution intensity, advertising emphasis, and low prices. Each SBU has a distinct marketing mix, based on its target market and strategic emphasis. The individual mix elements must be coordinated for each SBU and conflicts among SBUs minimized.

The time frame may mean being the first to introduce a product, bringing out a product when the market is most receptive, or quickly reacting to a competitor's strategy to catch it off guard. A firm must balance its desire to be an industry leader with clear-cut competitive advantages against its concern for the risks of innovation. Marketing opportunities exist for limited periods of time, and the firm needs to act quickly.

Resource allocation (or marketing investments) can be classed as order processing or order generating. Order-processing costs are associated with recording and handling orders, such as order entry, computer-data handling, and merchandise handling. The goal is to minimize those costs, subject to a given level of service. Order-generating costs, such as advertising and personal selling, produce revenues. Reducing them may have a harmful effect on sales and profits. Thus, a firm should estimate sales at various levels of costs and for various combinations of marketing functions. Maximum profit rarely occurs at the lowest level of expenditure on order-generating costs.

Tactical decisions differ from strategic decisions in several key ways:

- They are less complex and more structured.
- They have a much shorter time horizon.
- They require a considerably lower resource commitment.
- They are enacted and adjusted more often.

At Frito-Lay, tactical planning means preparing its delivery people and its retailers for new product introductions, aggressively promoting its products, maintaining its profit margins—while not giving competitors any opportunities to win market share through lower prices, and servicing its retail accounts very well. How do Frito-Lay personnel avoid complacency in light of such a strong position? As its chief executive says, "I wake up every morning thinking, I haven't sold one bag of Fritos yet. We're always raising the bar on ourselves and our future."[30]

Monitoring Results

*Performance is evaluated by **monitoring results**.*

Monitoring results involves comparing the actual performance of a firm, business unit, or product against planned performance for a specified period. Actual performance data are then fed back into the strategic planning process. Budgets, timetables, sales and profit statistics, cost analyses, and image studies are just some measures that can be used to assess results.

When actual performance lags behind plans, corrective action is taken. For instance, "if implementation problems persist, it is not (in most instances) because employees mean to do the wrong thing. It is because they do not know the right thing to do. The first task in making strategy work, then, is to identify the right behaviour—that is, behaviour that reduces costs, improves quality, pleases customers, and adds to profitability."[31]

Some plans must be revised due to the impact of uncontrollable factors on sales and costs. Many far-sighted firms develop contingency plans to outline their responses in advance, should unfavourable conditions arise. (Techniques for evaluating marketing effectiveness are covered in Chapter 23.)

---

[30]Robert Frank, "Frito-Lay Devours Snack-Food Business," *New York Times* (October 27, 1995), pp. B1, B4.
[31]Steven J. Heyer and Reginald Van Lee, "Rewiring the Corporation," *Business Horizons*, Vol. 35 (May–June 1992), p. 21.

Ethics AND TODAY'S MARKETER

Is Genentech Too Aggressive with Its Marketing?

Genentech, a biotechnology company, has always been an aggressive marketer. Some observers feel that it may be *too* aggressive. One industry expert familiar with G. Kirk Raab, Genentech's chief executive officer, says "Within the law, Kirk will take it as close to the edge as he can." As a result, the U.S. Food and Drug Administration has been investigating Genentech's marketing practices, particularly its sale of approved drugs for non-approved uses or at higher-than-approved dosage levels.

An example of a questionable Genentech strategy is its use of a database of patients who have particular illnesses. Genentech pays nurses and doctors' assistants as much as $50 per patient for information on the person's illness, current treatment, and outcome. Its heart attack registry, for instance, includes detailed questions about Genentech's clot-buster for heart attack patients (TPA), but not about those patients who are receiving other medicines or treatments. According to sources critical of Genentech, the firm has used this database to exaggerate the effectiveness of TPA and understate its drawbacks (which include the increased likelihood of a stroke and high drug costs). Genentech even promoted a seminar with a malpractice attorney to warn doctors of the liability associated with using an inferior substitute product.

Perhaps the greatest source of controversy concerns Genentech's marketing of Protropin, its growth hormone product. In an indictment, a Genentech executive was accused of providing a $224 000 research grant and consulting fee to a doctor who prescribed high doses of Protroprin. And while Genentech has also funded charities that screen school-aged children who are very short, Genentech does not disclose its funding to either the schools or parents. Critics say Genentech is selling its growth hormone to about twice the number of children that would benefit from the product.

As a marketing manager for Protropin, where do you draw the line between ethical and unethical behaviour?

Source: Based on material in Ralph T. King, "In Marketing of Drugs, Genentech Tests Limits of What Is Acceptable," *Wall Street Journal* (January 10, 1995), pp. A1, A6.

Devising a Strategic Plan

Having a written strategic plan encourages executives to carefully think out and coordinate each step in the planning process, pinpoint problem areas, be consistent, tie the plan to goals and resources, measure performance, and send a clear message to employees and others. A sample outline for a written strategic plan and an application of strategic planning by a small firm are presented next.

Written documents aid strategic planning and are useful for all sorts of firms.

Sample Outline for a Written Strategic Plan

What are the ingredients of a good strategic plan? Here is a brief list:

- It should affect the consideration of strategic choices.
- It should force a long-range view.
- It should make the resource allocation system visible.
- It should provide methods to help strategic analysis and decision making.

Table 3-2
A Sample Outline for a Written Strategic Plan—From a Marketing Perspective

Using as much detail as possible, please address each of these points for your firm:

1. **Organizational Mission**
   (a) In 50 words or less, describe the current mission of your organization.
   (b) In 50 words or less, describe how you would like your organizational mission to evolve over the next five years. The next ten years.
   (c) Is your firm on track regarding the mission statements in (a) and (b)? Explain your answer.
   (d) Discuss the organizational mission in terms of your target market(s), your functions performed, and your overall style of marketing.
   (e) Discuss the organizational mission in terms of company diversification.
   (f) How is the organizational mission communicated to employees?

2. **Strategic Business Units**
   (a) State the present organizational structure of your firm.
   (b) Assess the present organizational structure.
   (c) How would you expect the organizational structure to evolve over the next five years? The next ten years?
   (d) Does your firm have strategic business units? If yes, describe them. If no, why not?
   (e) Does your firm have a separate marketing plan for each target market, major product, and so on? Explain your answer and relate it to (d).
   (f) Does each product or business unit in your firm have a marketing manager, proper resources, and clear competitors? Explain your answer.

3. **Marketing Objectives**
   a) Cite your organization's overall marketing goals for the next one, three, five, and ten years.
   (b) Cite your organization's specific marketing goals by target market and product for the next one, five, and ten years:
   - Sales.
   - Market share.
   - Profit.
   - Image.
   - Customer loyalty.
   (c) What criteria will be used to determine whether goals have been fully, partially, or unsatisfactorily reached?

4. **Situation Analysis**
   (a) Describe the present overall strengths, weaknesses, opportunities, and threats (SWOT) facing your organization.
   (b) How do you expect the factors noted in your answer (a) to change over the next five to ten years?

- It should be a basis for managing a firm or SBU strategically.
- It should provide a communication and coordination system both horizontally (between SBUs and departments) and vertically (from senior executives to front-line employees).
- It should help a firm and its SBUs cope with change.[32]

Table 3-2 presents a sample outline for a written strategic plan from a marketing perspective. This outline may be used by firms of any size or type.

---
[32] Aaker, *Strategic Market Management*, pp. 17–18.

Table 3-2 (continued)

(c) For each of the key products or businesses of your firm, describe the present strengths, weaknesses, opportunities, and threats.
(d) How do you expect the factors noted in your answer to (c) to change over the next five to ten years?
(e) How will your firm respond to the factors mentioned in the answers for (a) to (d)?

5. Developing Strategy
   (a) Describe the target market, marketing mix, and differential advantages for each of your products or businesses.
   (b) Does your firm have sufficient resources and capabilities to carry out its marketing strategy? Explain your answer.
   (c) Compare your firm's strategy with those of leading competitors.
   (d) Describe your use of these strategic approaches: market penetration, market development, product development, and diversification.
   (e) For each product or business, detail the characteristics of your firm's present customers, as well as those who should be sought in the future.
   (f) Categorize each of your products or businesses as a star, cash cow, question mark, or dog. Explain your reasoning.
   (g) What is the impact of the categorization cited in (f) on your strategy?
   (h) For each product or business, which of these approaches is most apt: invest/grow, selectivity/earnings, or harvest/divest? Explain your reasoning.
   (i) For each of your products or businesses, which of these approaches is most appropriate: cost leadership, differentiation, cost focus, or differentiation focus? Explain your reasoning.
   (j) Describe how the plans for all of your firm's products or businesses are coordinated.

6. Implementation
   (a) Describe the procedures to activate your firm's strategy.
   (b) For each product or business, how does your firm ensure that the strategy is implemented as intended with regard to the target market and marketing mix?
   (c) Do marketing personnel have appropriate authority (i.e., are they empowered) and resources to implement plans? Explain your answer.
   (d) Are ongoing marketing budgets sufficient? Does your organization differentiate between order-generating and order-processing costs? Explain your answers.
   (e) How do you expect competitors to react as you implement your strategy?
   (f) Are there contingency plans in case of unexpected results?

7. Monitoring Results
   (a) Describe the procedures used by your firm to monitor steps 1 to 6.
   (b) For each company product or business, is planned performance compared with actual performance on a regular basis? Explain your answer.
   (c) Is a SWOT analysis conducted regularly? Explain your answer.
   (d) How are performance results communicated through the organization?
   (e) What procedures do you use to respond to the findings of performance reviews?

Labatt: Dealing With a Changing Brewing Market

Labatt Brewing Company has the reputation in Canada as "the savviest marketer in sudsland." Earning and keeping this reputation has not been easy and will not get any easier. Labatt has been brewing beer in Canada since 1847. It brews and markets a number of well-known national brands of beer including: Cold-Filtered Genuine Draft, Labatt Ice, Labatt 50, Labatt Blue, Blue Light, Labatt Extra Dry, Labatt Lite, John Labatt Classic, Wildcat, and Labatt 0.5. In addition, Labatt also brews and markets Budweiser, Bud Light, Carlsberg, and Carlsberg Light brands of beer under license. Labatt's main competitor and the market leader is Molson Brewery, which is owned by the U.S.-based Miller Brewing Company. Labatt and Molson comprise 94 per cent of the Canadian brewing industry.

Aside from battling each other, both these companies must prepare to handle major upheavals in their competitive environment caused by expected changes in interprovincial

Labatt's reputation as a "savvy" brewer comes from having a detailed strategic plan.

trade barriers for beer, a ruling by GATT (General Agreement on Tariffs and Trade) that trade barriers to beer from the United States be removed, and the emergence of microbrewing and home brewing. In the face of competition from Molson and the expected changes, Labatt's strategic planning will be very important to its future.

ORGANIZATIONAL MISSION In June of 1995 Labatt was acquired in a friendly takeover by Interbrew S.A., a Belgian brewing conglomerate. This acquisition has resulted in the company returning to its 1847 roots: Interbrew S.A. was quite specific in stating that they wanted no part of any of the other businesses Labatt was involved in, and let it be known that companies in the entertainment division were for sale.

ESTABLISHING STRATEGIC BUSINESS UNITS In 1993, Labatt was a multinational conglomerate with annual sales of $2.135 billion and 5700 employees in its two main businesses of brewing and entertainment. Labatt had a strong sales base in Canada, which accounted for 84 per cent of company revenues, while the brewing operations accounted for 84 per cent of Labatt's total sales as well. One of two large brewers in Canada, Labatt operated 10 breweries and marketed 36 brands of ale and lager while holding a 44.5 per cent share of the Canadian market as of March 1994. Molson held a market share of just under 50 per cent at that time. Labatt also exports beer to 20 other countries including the United States. However, with the takeover by Interbrew S.A. in June 1995, the plan is for Labatt to have one main SBU: brewing.

SETTING MARKETING OBJECTIVES Labatt has a number of marketing goals but their main objective is to overtake Molson to become the number one brewer in Canada. As of November 1995, Molson's market share of the Canadian beer market was 47 per cent while Labatt's share was in the mid-40 per cent range. To achieve this main objective Labatt has set two secondary objectives for themselves. The first is to hold on to the market share of their flagship brand, Labatt Blue. The second objective is to introduce new products to quickly gain market share and then hold onto the gains.

PERFORMING SITUATION ANALYSIS Beer distribution in Canada is unique in that each of the ten provinces has independent control over beer distribution. The two major markets for beer, Quebec and Ontario, have very diverse distribution channels. In Quebec, beer is sold through company-owned and independent beer distributors, while in Ontario, all beer is sold through Brewers Warehousing Corporation, which is owned by the brewers themselves. The distribution of beer in the remaining provinces of Canada is through outlets owned and operated by the provincial governments—except in Alberta where distribution is similar to that in Quebec. In Ontario, the largest beer market, there is virtually no price competition between brands of beer so that nonprice factors have become critical to marketing beer in this province.

Across Canada several microbreweries have been asserting themselves in the large metropolitan markets, and brew-your-own-beer operations are also growing into a significant competitive threat through their low price positioning. The microbreweries are growing at a tremendous rate; Sleeman Brewery of Guelph, Ontario recently merged with Okanagan Spring Brewery of Vernon, British Columbia. Moosehead Breweries from Dartmouth, Nova Scotia is competing aggressively while identifying itself as the only "Canadian" brewery left since Interbrew S.A.'s takeover of Labatt.

One microbrewery, Pacific Western Brewery in Prince George, British Columbia, has even had the audacity to market its products in Japan. Japanese consumers are well disposed towards Canadian beers and in 1993 Canadian beers held an impressive 21 per cent market share among imported beers against brands from the United States, Australia, Belgium, The Netherlands, Germany, and Mexico.

The Canadian beer market itself has been experiencing no volume growth in consumption. Labatt and Molson have been looking at foreign markets for their growth potential and have made strong inroads in the United States and Japan. However, the competition in Canada is expected to be fierce when Canada complies with a GATT ruling to eliminate trade barriers to American beer. In order for the Canadian brewing industry to compete against foreign beers there needs to be a level playing field for brewers within Canada, which means that interprovincial trade barriers for beer will have to be eliminated too.

OKANAGAN SPRING BREWERY
www.okspring.com/

MOOSEHEAD
www.cybernetone.com/Moosehead/

DEVELOPING MARKETING STRATEGY In order to accomplish the objective of becoming number one in market share in Canada, Labatt's CEO Hugo Powell is employing a number of approaches. In the past five years, Labatt and Molson have combined to introduce 40 new products or line extensions. Labatt has been very successful with this strategy: 25 per cent of its current sales are from products introduced since 1992.

The marketing strategy Labatt has been pursuing is to offer unique products to gain market share, which must then be held. Labatt has presented innovative new products while holding the number one beer brand position with Labatt Blue. However, Blue's market share recently fell to 16.5 per cent from its peak of 19 per cent in the late 1980s. Brand loyalty to beer can be very strong, particularly in the 19- to 29-year-old age group, which is influenced heavily by advertising. A new advertising campaign aimed at this group was successful in reversing Blue's falling market share.

Labatt is preparing to meet the expected environmental changes through product innovations based on research on consumer wants and needs and cost cutting measures.

IMPLEMENTING TACTICAL PLANS To strengthen Labatt's flagship brand, Blue, and introduce new products, the critical marketing tools are advertising, sales promotion, public relations, and personal selling. Labatt's is marketing internationally with a great deal of success by concentrating on innovative products like Labatt Ice Beer. The latter made the strongest market-share gains in the Japanese market recently and the Labatt method of brewing ice beer has been licensed to several foreign breweries in the South American market. Labatt has already brought out Wildcat Beer as a low-price product to position the firm for potential price competition and has plans for cost-cutting measures such as standardizing bottles and reducing administrative staff.

MONITORING RESULTS Every quarter, Hugo Powell goes before the board of directors of Labatt to give a report. He describes the company's position at the time and provides targets to meet in the next two quarters. One board member has described Powell as a very focused individual who provides specific targets, specific reasons for the targets, and the specific means of accomplishing these targets. Given Labatt's commitment to planning, involvement with sound marketing principles, and its reputation as "the savviest marketer in sudsland," it is a good bet that the company will handle changes to its industry quite well.[33]

MARKETING IN A CHANGING WORLD
What Business Are We In?[34]

According to Peter Drucker, the long-time management guru, "What to do" (organizational mission) is the main challenge now facing top management. The story is a familiar one: A firm that was a superstar only yesterday finds it is stagnant, frustrated, and in trouble. This phenomenon is not confined to Canadian and American firms. It is common in Japan and Germany, the Netherlands and France, Italy and Sweden. The root cause of nearly every one of these crises is not that things are being done poorly. It is not even that the wrong things are being done. Usually, the right things are being done—but fruitlessly.

---

[33] Mark Stevenson, "My Dear, Beer Friend," *Canadian Business* (March 1994), pp. 52–58; "Historical Report, John Labatt Ltd.," *Financial Post Datagroup* (Nov. 5, 1993); Conference Board of Canada, *The Canadian Brewing Industry: An Assessment of the Impacts of Liberalized Interprovincial Trade in Canada* (June 1990), pp. 1–32; "Powell Brings New Angle to the Beer Biz," *Strategy*, Vol. 3 (July 13, 1992), pp. 1, 19; "Labatt Battles to Stay on Track," *Financial Post*, Vol. 86 (June 20–22, 1992), p. 5; "How U.S. Beer Will Uncap the Canadian Market," *Financial Times of Canada*, Vol. 80 (November 11–17, 1991), pp. 1, 4; "Labatt's Blues: Can the Savviest Marketer in Sudsland Revive the Flagging Fortunes of Canada's Top Brew?," *Report on Business Magazine*, Vol. 7 (June 1991), pp. 40–48; "Labatt Could Cut 100 Managers, Sources Say," *Financial Post*, Vol. 3 (January 16, 1991), p. 3; Douglas Faulkner, "Powell's Big Picture," *Marketing Magazine* (November 20, 1995), p. 12–13; Stan Sutter, "Labatt Deal Gives Interbrew a North American Beachhead," *Marketing Magazine* (June 19, 1995), p. 6; James Pollock, "Labatt Stronger After Buyout by Interbrew," *Marketing, Magazine* (June 19, 1995), p. 3; "Belgian Beer Giant Poised to Take Over Labatt," *Marketing Magazine* (June 12, 1995), p. 10; Taka Aoki, "Canadian Brewers on Leading Edge of Japan's Import Surge," *Marketing Magazine* (August 21–28, 1995), p. 5.

[34] The material in this section is based on Peter F. Drucker, "The Theory of the Business," *Harvard Business Review*, Vol. 72 (September–October 1994), pp. 95–104.

This occurs when the assumptions that a firm makes about its mission no longer fit reality. These are assumptions that shape its behaviour, dictate its decisions about what to do and what not to do, and define what a firm deems meaningful results. The assumptions relate to markets; customer and competitor values and behaviour; technology and its dynamics; and company strengths and weaknesses. They are what Drucker calls a company's "theory of the business."

To remedy the situation, Drucker suggests that a company needs to assess its current business [organizational mission] regularly—and decide what it really should be. Here is how a firm can do this:

- "Every three years, an organization should challenge every product, every service, every policy, every distribution channel with the question, 'If we were not in it already, would we be going into it now?'"
- The firm should "study what goes on outside the business, especially with regard to non customers. The first signs of fundamental change rarely appear within one's own organization or among one's own customers. Almost always they show up first among one's non-customers."
- "To diagnose problems early, managers must pay attention to warning signs. A theory of the business always becomes obsolete when a firm attains its original goals. Attaining one's objectives is not cause for celebration; it is cause for new thinking."
- To establish, maintain, or reorient an organizational mission does not require genius, but hard work. "It is not being clever; it is being conscientious. It is what CEOs are paid for."

SUMMARY

1. *To define strategic planning and consider its importance for marketing* Strategic planning encompasses both strategic business plans and strategic marketing plans. Strategic business plans describe the overall direction firms will pursue within their chosen environment and guide the allocation of resources and effort. Strategic marketing plans outline what marketing actions to undertake, why those actions are needed, who is responsible for carrying them out, when and where they will be completed, and how they will be coordinated.

Strategic planning provides guidance via a hierarchal process, clarifies goals, encourages cooperation among departments, focuses on strengths and weaknesses (as well as opportunities and threats), examines alternatives, helps allocate resources, and points up the value of monitoring results.

2. *To describe the total quality approach to strategic planning and its relevance to marketing* A total quality approach should be used while devising and enacting business and marketing plans. With this approach, a firm adopts a process- and output-related philosophy, by which it strives to fully satisfy consumers in an effective and efficient manner. There is a customer focus; a top management commitment; emphasis on continuous improvement; and support and involvement from employees, suppliers, and channel members.

3. *To look at the different kinds of strategic plans and the relationships between marketing and other functional areas in an organization* A firm's strategic plans may be short run, moderate in length, or long run. Strategic marketing plans may be for each major product, presented as one company-wide marketing plan, or considered part of an overall business plan. A bottom-up, top-down, or combined management approach may be used.

The interests of marketing and the other key functional areas in a firm need to be accommodated in a strategic plan. Departmental conflict can be reduced by improving communications, employing personnel with broad backgrounds, establishing interdepartmental development programs, and blending departmental goals.

4. *To describe thoroughly each of the steps in the strategic planning process* First, a firm defines its organizational mission—the long-term commitment to a type of business and a place in the market. Second, it establishes strategic business units (SBUs), which are self-contained divisions, product lines, or product departments with specific market focuses and separate managers. Third, quantitative and qualitative marketing objectives are set. Fourth, through situation analysis, a firm identifies its internal strengths and weaknesses, as well as external opportunities and threats.

Fifth, a firm develops a marketing strategy—to outline the way in which the marketing mix is used to attract and satisfy the target market(s) and accomplish organizational goals. Every SBU has its own marketing mix. The approaches to strategy planning include the product/market opportunity matrix, the Boston Consulting Group matrix, the General Electric business screen, and the Porter generic strategy model. They should be viewed as planning tools that aid decision making; they do not replace the need for executives to engage in hands-on planning for each situation.

Sixth, a firm uses tactical plans to specify the short-run actions necessary to implement a given marketing strategy. At this stage, specific tasks, a time horizon, and resource allocation are operationalized. Seventh, a firm monitors results by comparing actual performance against planned performance; and this information is fed back into the strategic planning process. Adjustments in strategy are made as needed.

5. *To show how a strategic plan may be devised and applied* Strategic planning works best when it is done systematically and comprehensively. This is exemplified by Labatt Brewing Company, one of Canada's finest brewers.

KEY TERMS

strategic business plan (p. 53)
strategic marketing plan (p. 53)
total quality (p. 53)
strategic planning process (p. 57)
organizational mission (p. 58)
strategic business unit (SBU) (p. 58)
situation analysis (p. 61)
marketing strategy (p. 61)

product/market opportunity matrix (p. 61)
market penetration (p. 61)
market development (p. 61)
product development (p. 61)
diversification (p. 61)
Boston Consulting Group matrix (p. 63)
star (p. 63)

cash cow (p. 63)
question mark (p. 63)
dog (p. 63)
General Electric business screen (p. 65)
Porter generic strategy model (p.66)
tactical plan (p. 68)
monitoring results (p. 68)

Review Questions

1. What are the benefits of strategic planning?
2. Explain Figure 3-2, which deals with the total quality approach.
3. Distinguish between bottom-up and top-down strategic plans. What are the pros and cons of each?
4. Why are conflicts between marketing and other functional areas inevitable? How can these conflicts be reduced or avoided?
5. Under what circumstances should a company consider reappraising its organizational mission?
6. What is a strategic business unit? Why is this concept so important for strategic planning?
7. In situation analysis, what is the distinction between strengths and opportunities and between weaknesses and threats? How should a firm react to each of these factors?
8. Compare the BCG Matrix, the General Electric business screen, and the Porter generic strategy models.
9. Explain how tactical decisions differ from strategic decisions.
10. What are the ingredients of a good strategic plan?

Discussion Questions

1. Do you think your college or university is following a total quality approach? Why or why not? What total quality recommendations would you make for your school?
2. Comment on this statement: "In the market-oriented view of the strategic planning process, financial goals are seen as results and rewards, not the fundamental purpose of business."
3. What issues should a small airline study during situation analysis? How could it react to them?
4. Give a current example of each of these strategic approaches: market development, product development, market penetration, and diversification. Evaluate the strategies.
5. Develop a rating scale to use in analyzing the industry attractiveness and company business strengths of a small stock brokerage firm, a medium-sized management consulting firm, or a large auto supplies manufacturer.

VIDEO CASE

Canadian Boots: Marketing Based on a Distinctive Competency

Seeking a competitive advantage in a business or an industry is often the key to success. In economic terms, if a nation can establish an absolute advantage in the manufacture of any good, its industry will thrive. If a nation can establish a comparative advantage, its industries will survive. Canada appears to have an absolute competitive advantage in making boots—in particular, winter boots!

Canada has the coldest climate in the world. To live and work in this climate people need warm footwear. When Canada signed on to GATT (General Agreement on Trade and Tariffs) in the mid 1970s it was expected that the footwear industry would completely disappear. However, this has not been the case at all. The shoe industry has virtually disappeared, but the boot industry is thriving. Canada has a niche as the world's best maker of all-weather and winter boots.

At the Acton rubber plant in Actonville, Quebec they are turning out toe rubbers, a Canadian invention. About 90 per cent of the toe rubbers sold in Canada are produced in this plant and they are designed to fit over those foreign shoes that Canadians are buying. But toe rubbers are just the start. Canadian boot makers specialize in making military boots, fire fighter's boots, construction boots, safety boots, letter carrier's boots and of course, everyday winter boots. The demand for boots has been very strong in recent years because although scientists have said the planet is undergoing a global warming, the weather seems more volatile than ever. Places like Dallas and Atlanta have been getting snowstorms more often. The United States isn't the only market for Canadian boots; people in Australia and Chile are frequent customers too, despite their usually mild climates.

Although 80 per cent of the footwear sold in Canada is imported, the domestic shoe industry is still an $850 million business employing 12 000 workers. This is down from 16 000 20 years ago, but given the impact of competition and the trends to automation and corporate downsizing a 25 per cent workforce reduction is not unusual. Canada's competition in the shoe industry comes from two main sources: Brazil, which makes low-cost shoes and Italy, which makes higher-priced stylish shoes. Canadian shoes have trouble finding a market because they are not particularly cheap or stylish. However, when it comes to boots worn to protect against the weather, Canadians buy Canadian.

Kreb, who also manufactures in Actonville, Quebec, invented vulcanized waterproof workboots. Kreb specializes in making construction boots, safety boots, and military boots. The Actonville plant uses modern manufacturing techniques and is a model of efficiency. They will process and ship an order in three to four weeks which ten years ago would have taken three to four months! This dramatic improvement in productivity contributes to the excellence the Canadian boot industry has established for itself.

What is it that really gives Canadians the upper hand in the boot industry? The explanation, according to one plant manager, is: Canadians know the winter! Days with temperatures of –31° C are not uncommon in Canada. Manufacturers have to make products that can routinely stand up to this kind of weather. Canadian firms' experience with extreme weather conditions give them the edge in producing the highest quality products. For this reason, Canadian boots are sought after all over the world—in any country where people contend with snow.

QUESTIONS

1. Evaluate the competitive advantage Canadian boot makers appear to have. Do you think it will be sustainable over time?
2. Canadians buy imported shoes but domestically manufactured boots. How might you account for this difference in buyer behaviour?
3. Threats from imported boots were not discussed much in the case. However, it seems likely they exist or will exist in the future. Discuss where such threats might originate in the future and what form they are likely to take.
4. Comment upon the apparent marketing strategies employed by Canadian boot manufacturers.

VIDEO QUESTIONS ON CANADIAN BOOTS

1. What other market opportunities might be available to Canadian boot manufacturers as a result of their apparent excellence in manufacturing winter boots?
2. Canadian boot manufacturers are successful because they serve specific niches. Evaluate this statement and give some examples of these niches, as presented in the video.

Video Source: "Boots," Venture (December 25, 1994).

CASE STUDY

Schering-Plough: Devising a Marketing Strategy

Schering-Plough (SP) is a diversified pharmaceutical manufacturer. It markets prescription and over-the-counter drugs (OTC) for a variety of illnesses including asthma and allergies, cancer and infectious diseases, and skin disorders. SP also markets disposable contact lenses and foot-care and sun-care products. Among its best-known OTC brands are Coricidin, Afrin, Dr. Scholl's, Coppertone, and Solarcaine.

To get a picture of Schering-Plough, let's look at each of these facets of its marketing strategy: the new-product development process, cost containment, and the importance of the OTC drug segment.

SP is committed to research to discover innovative drugs that offer important cost-effective therapeutic advantages. Therefore, in 1994, it spent U.S.$620 million on research, about 13.3 per cent of its total revenues. SP is working hard to streamline the new-product discovery process. For example, SP now makes better decisions as to whether to go ahead with or drop a product at an early stage in the development process. SP recognizes that since it costs hundreds of million of dollars to develop a new pharmaceutical product, it can only back the most promising projects. As an alternative to developing and testing new products itself, SP also actively seeks to acquire and license drug products developed by other firms. SP's most successful new product ever is Claritin, an antihistamine. Worldwide sales of Claritin increased 71 per cent between 1993 and 1994 alone. This drug captured the number one position in its market after less than 18 months on the market (with close to a 40 per cent market share).

SP recognizes that any marketing strategy in the health care field must reflect government concerns about cost containment, the increasing use of pharmacy benefit management (involving firms that buy drugs for hospitals and pharmacies at large discounts), and the expanding market share of low-cost generic brands. SP is working hard to profitably offer drugs at prices acceptable to pharmacy benefit management organizations. These organizations typically negotiate for discounts that are as much as 40 per cent off prevailing drug prices. SP has been able to sustain its profitability by becoming more efficient as a manufacturer and as a marketer. Over the last several years, SP's cost of sales as a per cent of sales revenue has gone from 24 per cent to 20 per cent; and its selling, general, and administrative expenses have gone from 43 per cent to 39 per cent of sales revenues.

SP has leading market positions in several big OTC markets. These include drugs to alleviate allergy symptoms (Afrin), coughs and colds (Drixoral and Coricidin), and female health products (Gyne-Lotrimin). Unlike prescription drugs, these products are advertised directly to final consumers. Advertising for OTC drugs is regulated by Health Canada's Health Protection Branch.

Recently, Health Canada has expressed concern over a new practice in the pharmaceutical industry of using direct-to-consumer advertising of information on diseases to get the public to seek advice from their physicians. As practised it does not violate any laws or regulations but Health Canada believes this is a back-door approach to advertising prescription drugs. A significant decision for SP is knowing when to use direct-to-consumer advertising of disease information and when to switch a drug from prescription to OTC status. For example, two years after SP switched Gyne-Lotrimin to OTC status, its sales more than doubled.

QUESTIONS

1. Evaluate Schering-Plough's overall marketing strategy.
2. How could the Boston Consulting Group matrix be used in identifying possible strategies for Schering-Plough?
3. Apply the Porter generic strategy model to Schering-Plough.
4. Present several suggestions as to how Schering-Plough could evaluate its performance.

Source: The data from this case is drawn from D. P. Hamacher, "Step Up to Better Foot Care Sales," *Drug Topics* (March 20, 1994), pp. 68–69; Cyndee Miller, "Drug Firms Boost Pitch Directly to Consumers," *Marketing News* (November 21, 1994), pp. 1, 16; Jennifer Reingold, "Schering-Plough: Great Expectations," *Financial World* (December 6, 1994), p. 20; Edward A. Wyatt, "Counter Moves," *Barron's* (July 18, 1994), pp. 20–22, and Laura Medcalf, "Pushing the Limits," *Marketing Magazine* (March 4, 1996), pp. 10, 12.

CHAPTER 4
Information for Marketing Decisions

Chapter Objectives

1. To show why marketing information is needed

2. To explain the role and importance of marketing information systems

3. To examine a basic marketing information system, commercial databases, database marketing, and examples of MIS in action

4. To define marketing research and its components and to look at its scope

5. To describe the marketing research process

{ *At a time when growing numbers of publishing firms are racing to develop databases to market their products better, Reader's Digest Association is years ahead. Its files, started 40 years ago in much simpler form, now hold data on an astounding 100 million households worldwide (half of which are in the United States). The database is the organization's lifeblood. Virtually all company operations are connected to it. And the Association neither rents nor sells its list of names.* }

Reader's Digest Association has one of the largest private consumer databases in the world. These files are updated continuously to reflect information about subscribers to the firm's magazines, books (both general interest and reference), interactive CDs (reference and cook books), recorded music cassettes, and videocassettes.

The main source of names for the Association's database is *Reader's Digest*, with a monthly worldwide circulation of 28 million—including 1.2 million in Canada. Two-thirds of *Reader's Digest* readers renew their subscriptions annually; and five million new subscriptions are sold throughout the world each year. *Reader's Digest* has the largest circulation among Canadian magazines (*Reader's Digest* in English and *Selection du Reader's Digest* in French) and the second largest circulation among U.S. magazines, behind only *Modern Maturity*, a magazine mailed to all members of the American Association of Retired Persons.

Reader's Digest has been expanding its global circulation. In total, the magazine publishes 45 editions in 17 different languages; and it has the largest circulation of any magazine in Britain, Finland, Germany, Mexico, and Southeast Asia. The Association publishes its general interest books and CDs in 11 languages and its condensed books in 12 languages.

In 1989, the Association began to acquire special-interest magazines. It now publishes *American Health*, *Family Handyman*, *Moneywise* (in Great Britain), *New Choices for Retirement Living*, and *Travel Holiday*. According to the company, its main goal in these acquisitions was to strengthen its database. As of 1994, three million additional names had been added to the firm's database because of the acquisitions.

Although the Association's management of its database is well respected, even this company has, on occasion, had difficulties in using it efficiently. Several years ago, for example, the firm had trouble coordinating offers from its various divisions. Thus, a *Reader's Digest* subscriber with an interest in travel might receive offers for travel books, a video on a foreign country, and a subscription to *Travel Holiday*. At that time, many people in the database felt so inundated with the direct mail offers that the firm's "hit rate" in getting new business fell off. After realizing the consumer discontent, the Association reduced its promotional mailings in the book and home entertainment business. It also became more selective in the use of its promotional mailings.[1]

In this chapter, we will look at the value of marketing information, explain the role of a marketing information system (which gathers, analyzes, disseminates, and stores relevant marketing data), and describe the marketing research process. We will also take another peek at database marketing.

READER'S DIGEST ASSOCIATION
www.ima.org/members/rrr01.html

Overview

It is essential for a firm to have appropriate information before, while, and after making (and enacting) marketing decisions if it wants to accurately assess strengths, weaknesses, opportunities, and threats; tailor its actions to the marketing environment; and maximize its performance. Good information enables marketers to:

Firms make better marketing decisions when they have good information.

---

[1] Deirdre Carmody, "Lifeblood of Reader's Digest Is 40-Year-Old Database," *New York Times* (May 16, 1995), pp. D1, D7; Gary Hoover, Alta Campbell, and Patrick J. Spain (Eds.) *Hoover's Handbook of American Business 1995* (Austin, TX: Reference Press, 1994), pp. 910–911; and *Canadian Advertising Rates and Data* (August 1995).

- Gain a competitive edge.
- Reduce financial and image risks.
- Determine consumer attitudes.
- Monitor the environment.
- Gather competitive intelligence.
- Coordinate strategy.
- Measure performance.
- Improve advertising credibility.
- Gain management support for decisions.
- Verify intuition.
- Improve effectiveness.

Relying on intuition, executive judgment, and past experience is not enough:

> In markets that are growing more slowly and are saturated with competition, businesses prosper by following two strategies. First, they learn more and more about the characteristics and location of their customers. Second, they use that knowledge to develop better goods or services and reduce unsuccessful marketing efforts.[2]

The **scientific method** *requires objectivity, accuracy, and thoroughness.*

Marketing information is collected using the **scientific method**—incorporating objectivity, accuracy, and thoroughness. Objectivity means information is gathered in an open-minded way. Judgments are not reached until all data are collected and analyzed. Accuracy refers to the use of carefully constructed research tools. Each aspect of information gathering, such as the study format, the sample, interviewer training, and tabulation of responses, must be well planned and executed. Thoroughness describes the comprehensive nature of information gathering. Mistaken conclusions may be reached if probing is not intense enough.

In this chapter, two vital aspects of marketing information are covered: marketing information systems and marketing research. A marketing information system guides all of a firm's marketing-related information efforts and stores and disseminates data on a continuous basis. Marketing research involves gathering and analyzing information on specific marketing issues.

Marketing Information Systems

The collection of marketing information should not be a rare event that occurs only when data are needed about a specific marketing topic. Research done this way exposes the firm to numerous risks:

- Opportunities may be missed.
- There may be a lack of awareness of environmental changes and competitors' actions.
- It may not be possible to analyze data over several periods.
- Marketing plans and decisions may not be properly reviewed.
- Data collection may be disjointed.
- Previous studies may not be stored in an easy-to-use format.
- Time lags may result whenever a new research study is required.
- Actions may be reactionary rather than anticipatory.

A **marketing information system** *regularly gathers, analyzes, disseminates, and stores data.*

Thus, it is essential for any firm, regardless of its size or type, to devise and employ some form of marketing information system to aid decision making. A **marketing information system (MIS)** is "a set of procedures and methods designed to generate, analyze, disseminate, and store anticipated marketing decision information on a regular, continuous basis."[3]

---

[2]Peter Francese, "Managing Market Information," *American Demographics* (September 1995), p. 59.
[3]Adapted by the authors from Robert A. Peterson, *Marketing Research*, Second Edition (Dallas: Business Publications, 1988), p. 31; and Peter D. Bennett (Ed.), *Dictionary of Marketing Terms*, Second Edition (Chicago: American Marketing Association, 1995), p. 167.

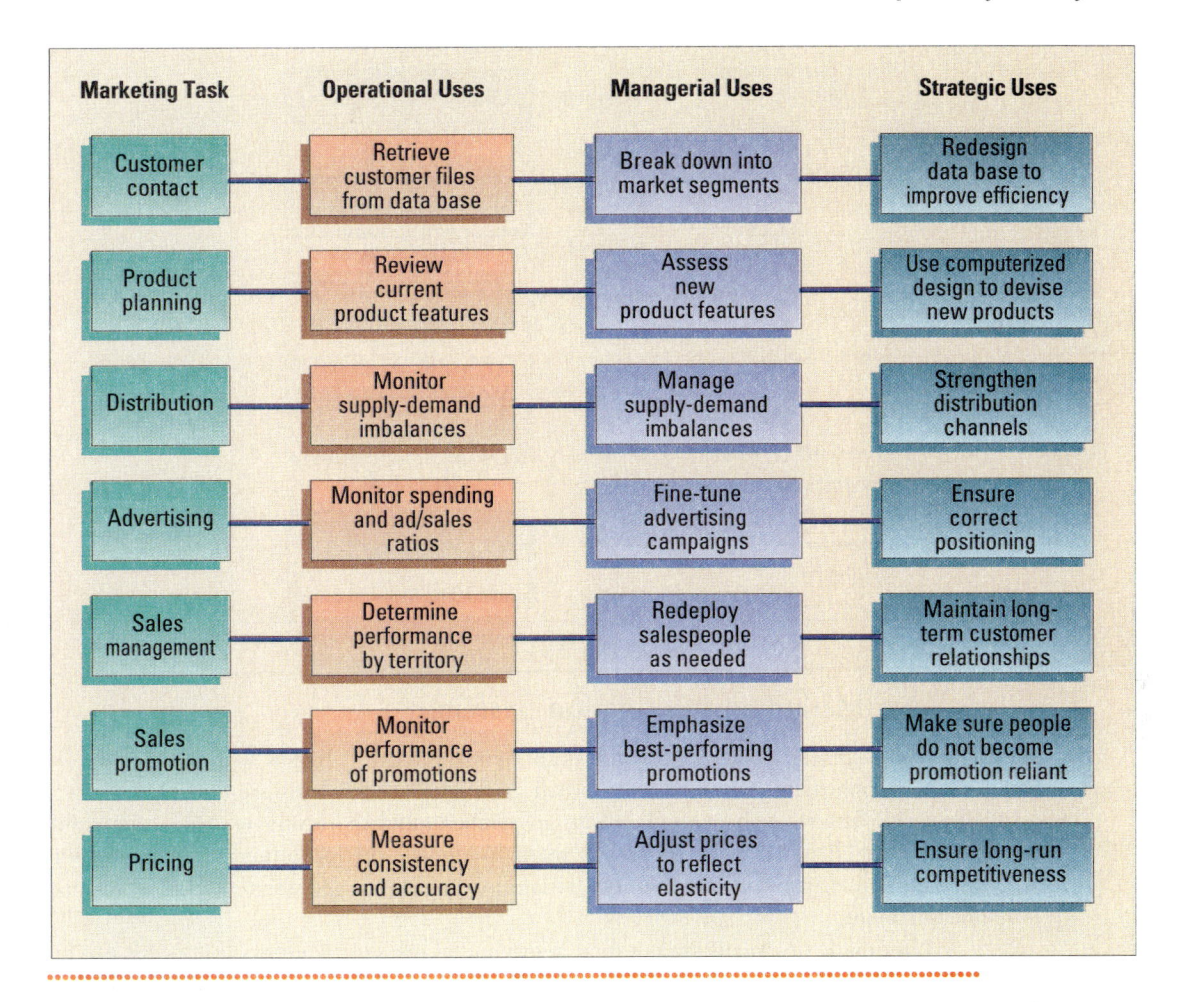

Marketing Task	Operational Uses	Managerial Uses	Strategic Uses
Customer contact	Retrieve customer files from data base	Break down into market segments	Redesign data base to improve efficiency
Product planning	Review current product features	Assess new product features	Use computerized design to devise new products
Distribution	Monitor supply-demand imbalances	Manage supply-demand imbalances	Strengthen distribution channels
Advertising	Monitor spending and ad/sales ratios	Fine-tune advertising campaigns	Ensure correct positioning
Sales management	Determine performance by territory	Redeploy salespeople as needed	Maintain long-term customer relationships
Sales promotion	Monitor performance of promotions	Emphasize best-performing promotions	Make sure people do not become promotion reliant
Pricing	Measure consistency and accuracy	Adjust prices to reflect elasticity	Ensure long-run competitiveness

FIGURE 4-1
Uses of a Marketing Information System

Source: Adapted by the authors from Rajendra S. Sisodia, "Marketing Information and Decision Support Systems for Services," *Journal of Services Marketing*, Vol. 6 (Winter 1992), pp. 51–64.

To establish an MIS, a firm should:

- Aggressively amass data from internal company documents, existing external documents, and primary studies (when necessary).
- Analyze the data and prepare appropriate reports—in terms of the company mission, strategy, and proposed tactics.
- Disseminate the analyzed data to the right marketing decision makers in the company. They will vary on the basis of the particular topics covered.
- Store data for future use and comparisons.
- Seek out all relevant data that have either current or future marketing ramifications—not just data with specific short-term implications.
- Undertake ongoing data collection, analysis, dissemination, and storage.

Figure 4-1 shows how an information system can be used operationally, managerially, and strategically for several aspects of marketing.

In the following sections, the components of a basic marketing information system, commercial databases, database marketing, and examples of MIS in action are presented.

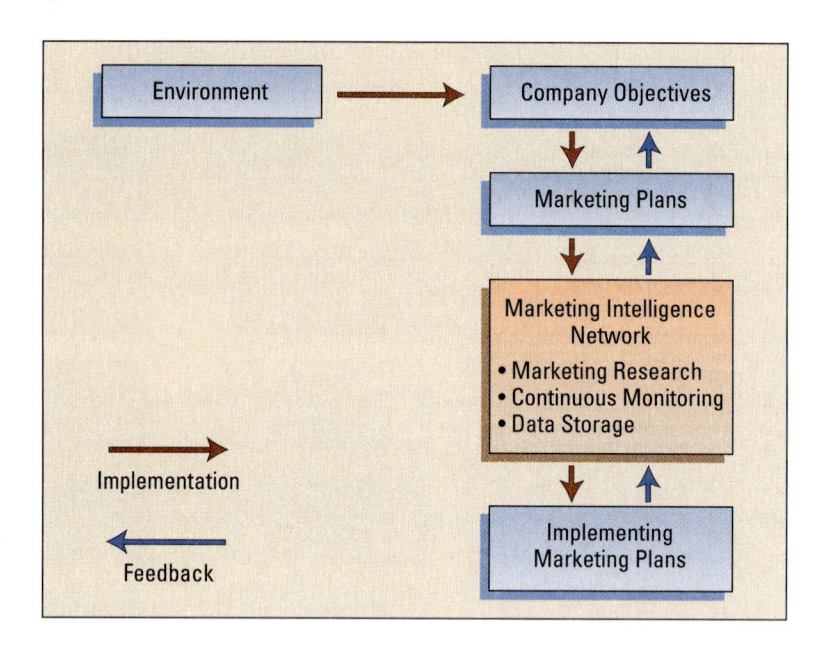

FIGURE 4-2
A Basic Marketing System

A Basic Marketing Information System

Figure 4-2 presents a basic marketing information system. It begins with a statement of company objectives, which provide broad guidelines. These goals are affected by environmental factors, such as competition, government, and the economy. Marketing plans involve the choice of a target market, marketing goals, the marketing organization, the marketing mix (product, distribution, promotion, and price decisions), and performance measurement.

After marketing plans are outlined, a firm's total marketing information needs can be specified and satisfied with a **marketing intelligence network**, which consists of marketing research, continuous monitoring, and data storage. **Marketing research** is used to obtain information on particular marketing issues (problems). Information may be retrieved from storage (existing company data) or acquired by collecting external secondary data and/or primary data. **Continuous monitoring** is used to regularly study a firm's external and internal environment. It can entail subscribing to trade publications, observing news reports, getting constant feedback from employees and customers, attending industry meetings, watching competitors' actions (competitive intelligence), and compiling periodic company reports. **Data storage** involves retaining all types of relevant company records (such as sales, costs, personnel performance, etc.), as well as information collected through marketing research and continuous monitoring. These data aid decision-making and are kept for future reference. Marketing research should be considered as just one part of an ongoing, integrated information system.

Depending on a firm's resources and the complexity of its information needs, a marketing intelligence network may or may not be computerized. Small firms can do well without computerizing; they merely need to read industry publications, attend trade shows, observe competitors, talk with suppliers and customers, track performance, and store the results of these efforts. In any event, information needs must be stated and regularly reviewed, data sources must be identified, personnel must be given information tasks, storage and retrieval facilities must be set up, and data must be routed to decision makers. The keys to a successful MIS are consistency, completeness, and orderliness.

Marketing plans should be enacted based on information obtained from the intelligence network. For example, by continuous monitoring, a firm could ascertain that a leading competitor intends to cut prices by 7 per cent during the next month. This would give the firm time to explore its own marketing options (e.g., switch to cheaper materials, place larger orders with suppliers to get discounts, or ignore the cuts) and select one. If monitoring is not done, the firm might be caught by surprise and forced to just cut prices, without any other choice.

A marketing intelligence network includes marketing research, continuous monitoring, and data storage.

A basic MIS generally has many advantages: it allows the firm to organize and store data over long time periods; gain a broad perspective on their business; avoid crises; coordinate their marketing plans; make decisions more quickly; and perform cost-benefit analysis. However, forming an information system is not easy. Initial time and labour costs may be high, and setting up a sophisticated system can be complex.

Commercial Databases

Because companies need current, comprehensive, and relatively inexpensive information about the environment in which they operate, many specialized research firms offer ongoing **commercial databases** with information on population traits, the business environment, economic forecasts, industry and company performance, and other items. Databases may include newspaper and magazine articles, business and household addresses culled from Yellow Pages and other sources, industry and company news releases, government reports, conference proceedings, indexes, patent records, and so on. The research firms sell access to their databases to clients, usually for a relatively low fee.

Commercial databases *can provide useful ongoing information.*

Databases are typically available in printed form; on computer disks, CD-ROMs, or tapes; and "online" using a computer and a modem. There are commercial database firms that concentrate on tracking and clipping newspaper and magazine articles on an orderly basis; unlike computerized databases, these firms actually look for information on subjects specified by clients. They offer their services for a fee. The annual *Burwell Directory of Information Brokers* cites over 1200 information brokers in the United States, Canada and about 44 other nations.

Firms such as Pro CD Inc. and American Business Information (ABI) provide business and household addresses in CD-ROM format. ABI and Pro CD Inc. gather data from phone directories, annual reports, and government agencies; ABI makes 14 million calls per year and sends out more than 700 000 mail surveys to keep its databases current. *Canada Phone*, a $119 CD sold by Pro CD Inc., contains over 12 million Canadian phone listings including households and businesses. The *Canada Phone* CD allows users to conduct a number of database searches. ABI sells a U.S.$39.95 CD which contains data on 70 million U.S. households, while a U.S.$2500 CD has data on 10 million businesses. ABI has over 400 000 customers—from small, single-person firms to giant corporations.[4]

Many companies and libraries subscribe to one or more online computerized databases, whereby users are charged a fee based on the time spent using the database. A few of the well-known computerized database services available to Canadians are America Online, CompuServe, Prodigy, World Linx Telecommunications, WEB, UUNET Canada, and Delphi. A full list of Internet resources and Internet access providers can be found in "The 1996 Canadian Internet Directory." This directory is available from Prentice-Hall Canada Inc. and lists over 300 Canadian Internet service providers along with hundreds of Canadian sources of information on the Internet. With these services, the user can do a search on a particular topic or company, generate the names and abstracts of relevant articles or reports, and then print out the information. Full articles or reports may also be accessed and printed, but doing so could be expensive.

UUNET CANADA
www.uunet.ca/

Figure 4-3 highlights the power of information and how cheap and readily available commerical databases are for consumers and business people alike.

Database Marketing

In conjunction with their marketing information systems, growing numbers of firms are using database marketing to better identify target markets and more efficiently reach them. **Database marketing** is "an automated system to identify people—both customers and prospects—by name, and to use quantifiable information about them to define the best possible purchasers and prospects for a given offer at a given point in time."[5]

Through **database marketing**, *companies can better reach and interact with customers.*

---

[4]Jacqueline M. Graves, "Building a Fortune on Free Data," *Fortune* (February 6, 1995); American Business Information brochures; and *Canada Phone User Guide* (Danvers, Mass: ProCD Incorporated, 1995) pp.1–5.
[5]Susan K. Jones, *Creative Strategy in Direct Marketing* (Lincolnwood, Ill.: NTC Publishing, 1991), p. 5.

84 Part 1 *An Introduction to Marketing*

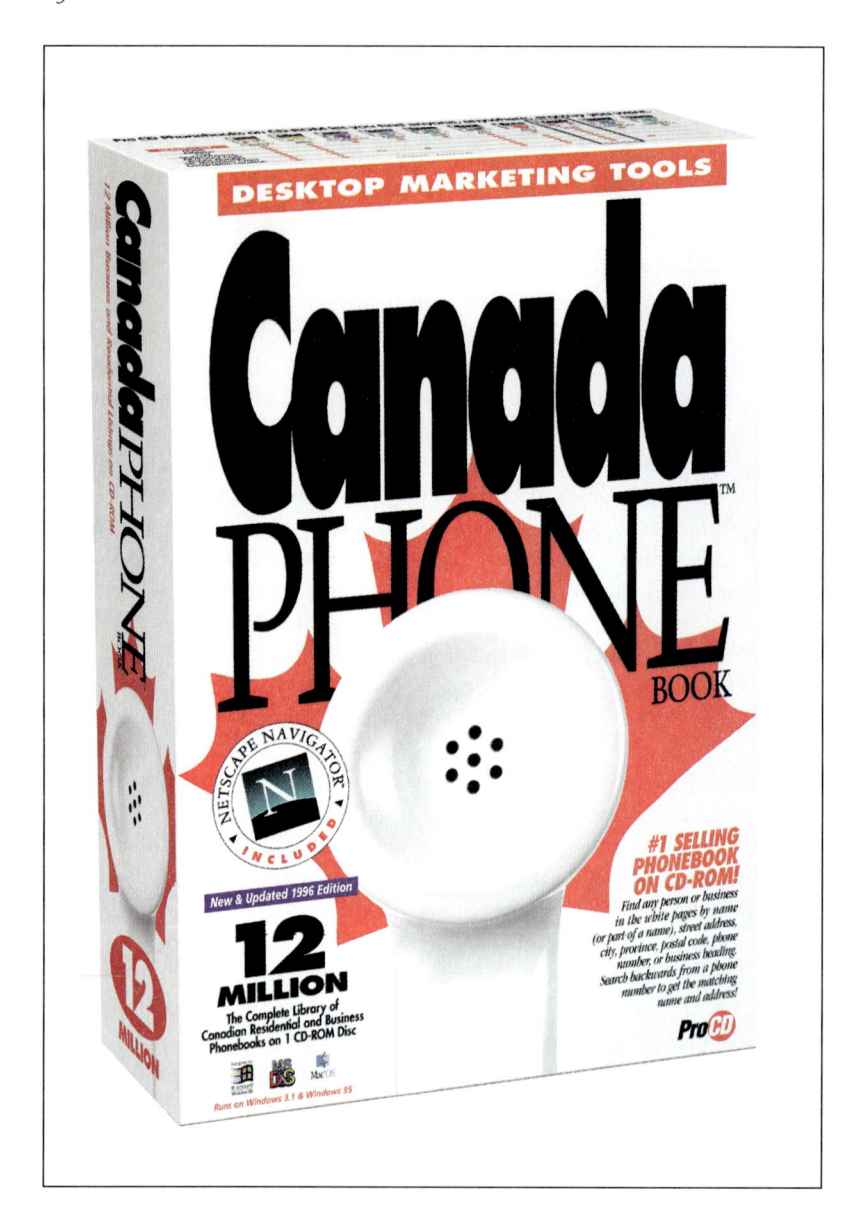

FIGURE 4-3
The Power of Information
Reprinted with permission of ProCD Inc.

FIGURE 4-4
Fully Integrated Database Marketing
Source: Robert Shaw and Merlin Stone, *Data-Base Marketing: Strategy & Implementation* (New York, Wiley, 1990). Reprinted by permission of Gower Publishing Company Limited.

CANADIAN DIRECT MARKETING ASSOCIATION
www.westminster.ca/cdma/

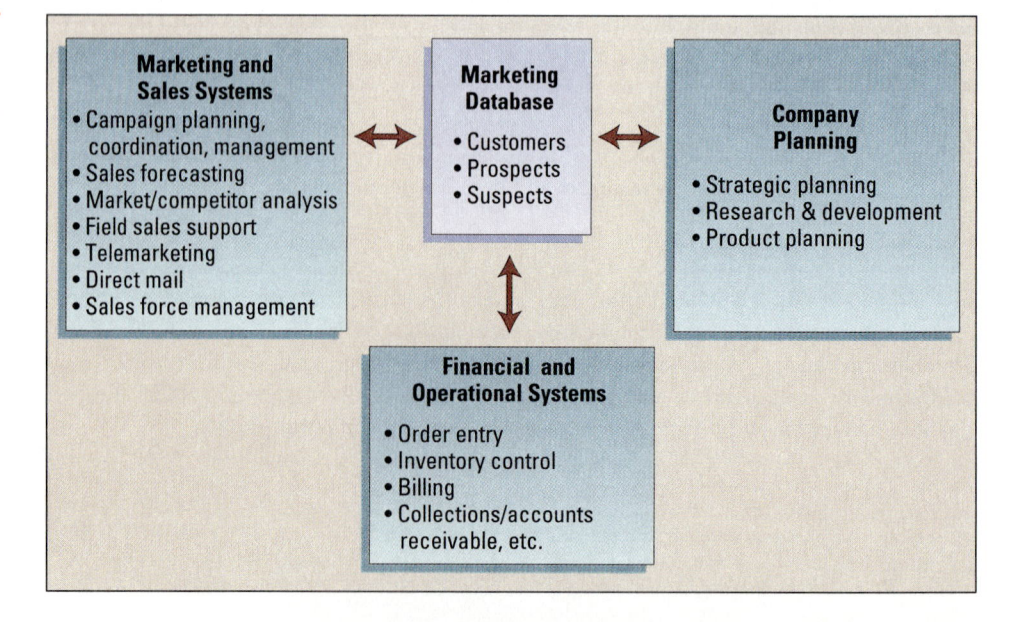

Marketing and Sales Systems
- Campaign planning, coordination, management
- Sales forecasting
- Market/competitor analysis
- Field sales support
- Telemarketing
- Direct mail
- Sales force management

Marketing Database
- Customers
- Prospects
- Suspects

Company Planning
- Strategic planning
- Research & development
- Product planning

Financial and Operational Systems
- Order entry
- Inventory control
- Billing
- Collections/accounts receivable, etc.

Ethics AND TODAY'S MARKETER

How Can Direct Marketers Resolve the Privacy Paradox?

The growth in database-driven information has the Canadian Direct Marketing Association (CDMA) worried. So much so that it has backed away from its long-time stance in favour of industry self-regulation, and taken the unusual step of asking the federal government to legislate its discipline.

The CDMA wants the industry minister to establish minimum standards of conduct to ensure that anyone collecting or using consumer information does so in a manner that protects the privacy of individuals. In a letter to the minister, the CDMA stated: "In an age of information technology, inter-relation of databases and the amassing of transactional data, national legislation appears to be the only practical way of providing comprehensive protection to every Canadian." The CDMA has a privacy code for its member companies but only 80 per cent of the direct marketers in Canada are members of the CDMA. Canadian direct response sales were approximately $9.2 billion in 1995 but not all sectors of the industry have compulsory privacy codes.

Codes such as those developed by the Canadian Standards Association (CSA), are mainly based on guidelines from the international Organization for Economic Co-operation and Development (OECD). These guidelines indicate that firms should identify how they plan to use personal information they collect and get permission from individuals to collect, use, and disclose this information. More importantly, the consumers themselves should be able to gain access to the information which has been collected from them.

The CDMA has only one recourse in dealing with member companies that violate the voluntary code of privacy, which is to oust them. Chastisement of member organizations is not a particularly powerful deterrent and throwing paying members out is harmful to the CDMA as well as the offending firm. The CDMA sees legislation as the only way in which the conduct of marketers can be controlled effectively. What's more, non-member direct marketers who often hurt the industry would also be subject to legislative discipline.

Not all firms feel that legislation is necessary to protect privacy. American Express is an example of a firm that carefully guards its customers' right to privacy. In 1974, it was the first company that offered customers the right not to be on a mailing list. And in 1978, American Express adopted a series of privacy principles requiring employees to collect only the data absolutely needed. The firm still reviews its data-collection activities each year; and everyone with access to customer information receives customer privacy training. American Express even distributes brochures to consumers explaining how they can refuse to provide the information requested on warranty cards.

Is legislation the only way for marketers to solve the privacy paradox?

Source: Based on material in James Pollock, "Direct Marketers Want to Regulate How Consumer Data Is Used," *Marketing Magazine* (October 16, 1995), p. 12; Jeffrey Casey, "The Privacy Paradox," *Link* (May 1995), pp. 19–22; and Judith Waldrop, "The Business of Privacy," *American Demographics* (October 1994), pp. 46–54.

Database marketing creates a bank of information about individual customers (taken from orders, inquiries, external lists), uses it to analyze buying and inquiry patterns, and creates the ability to target goods and services more accurately to specific customers (see Figure 4-4). It may be used to promote the benefits of brand loyalty to customers at risk from competition. It can fuel sales growth by identifying customers most apt to buy new goods and services. It can increase sales effectiveness. It can support low-cost alternatives to traditional sales methods, including telemarketing and direct mail, which can be important in markets where margins are eroding.[6]

Database marketing is especially useful in the relationship marketing process. A company can identify those customers with which it would most like to have long-term relationships, learn as much as possible about them (such as demographics and purchase behaviour), tailor its marketing efforts toward them, and follow up to learn the level of customer satisfaction. A firm might even compute a "lifetime value" for specific customers, based on their purchase history with the company—and plan its marketing efforts accordingly.[7]

When setting up a database, each actual or potential customer is given an identifying code. Then, contact information (name, address, phone number, fax number, e-mail address, industry code, and demographic data) and marketing information (source and date of contacts with firm, purchase history, product interests, and responses to offers) are entered and updated for each customer. The information should be distributed to marketing decision makers in the firm and kept in the MIS, and company efforts should be coordinated so customers are not bombarded with mailings and there is a consistent image.

In practice, database marketing actually works like this:

1. You may think you're just sending in a coupon, filling out a warranty card, or entering a sweepstakes. But to a marketer, you're also volunteering information about yourself—data that gets fed into a computer, where it's combined with more information from public records.

2. Using sophisticated statistical techniques, the computer merges different sets of data into a coherent, consolidated database. Then, with powerful software, brand managers can "drill down" into the data to any level of detail they require.

3. The computer identifies a model consumer for a chosen product based on the common characteristics of high-volume users. Next, clusters of consumers who share those characteristics—interests, incomes, brand loyalties, for instance—can be identified as targets for marketing efforts.

4. The data can be used in many ways: to determine the values of coupons and who should get them; to develop new products and ensure that the appropriate consumers know about them; to tailor ad messages and aim them at the right audience.

5. Cash-register scanners provide reams of information about exactly what shoppers are buying at specific stores. Merged with the manufacturer's data, this intelligence helps to plan local promotional mailings, fine-tune shelf displays, and design store layouts.

6. The database is continually updated with information collected from product-oriented clubs, responses to coupons, calls to 800 numbers, and sweepstakes entries, as well as with new lists from outside sources.[8]

Although often associated with a computerized MIS, database marketing may also be used by small, non-computerized firms: A company might ask potential and existing customers for their names, addresses, phone and fax numbers, e-mail addresses, and product interests as they contact them, and these data could be entered on large index cards. Consumers could be enticed to provide data by means of a monthly raffle that awards a small prize to the winner. The firm would alphabetize the cards, keep them in a file cabinet, and update the records from sales receipts. Separate mailings could be sent to regular customers and to non-customers from the database.

---

[6] Robert Shaw and Merlin Stone, *Data-Base Marketing: Strategy & Implementation* (New York: Wiley, 1990), p. 4. See also Mary Lou Roberts, "Expanding the Role of the Direct Marketing Database," *Journal of Direct Marketing*, Vol. 6 (Spring 1992), pp. 51–60; and Terry G. Vavra, "The Data-Base Marketing Imperative," *Marketing Management*, Vol. 2 (Number 1, 1993), pp. 47–57.

[7] See Timothy J. Keane and Paul Wang, "Applications for the Lifetime Value Model in Modern Newspaper Publishing," *Journal of Direct Marketing*, Vol. 9 (Spring 1995), pp. 59–66.

[8] Coopers & Lybrand Consulting, "Data-Base Marketing: How It Works," *Business Week* (September 5, 1994), pp. 56–57.

MIS in Action

Worldwide, millions of organizations now use some form of MIS in their decision making, and the trend is expected to continue. In fact, as a result of computer networking, progressive firms (and divisions within the same firm) around the globe are transmitting and sharing their marketing information with each other—quickly and inexpensively.

One recent study on the use of MIS by large business firms discovered that:

- More than three-quarters have a marketing information system. Of those that do, over 95 per cent are computer-based.
- Nearly 80 per cent use computers to produce reports; and two-thirds store marketing data in their computers.
- All gather customer data, three-quarters are involved with competitive intelligence, and 37 per cent track government actions.
- More than 70 per cent use annual reports, sales call reports, and purchased reports to amass competitive intelligence. Just over one half hire clipping services.[9]

Information systems are being applied today in various settings.

In Sweden, financial institutions have taken the lead in developing MIS:

During the late 1970s, the banking community took an innovative step by organizing a business intelligence (BI) research company called Upplysnigs Centralen (UC Research). It provides fee-based BI services for banks and their major customers, such as database services consisting of public and published information on firms and individuals; proactive intelligence gathering, using participating banks' overseas offices to answer specific and time-urgent requests; and the use of some 3000 business agents around the world who can be tapped for specific expertise or information."[10]

In Japan today, almost all major firms engaged in international business have an internal intelligence unit:

Typically, it is located in the planning or research departments. Some 10 to 20 employees are assigned responsibilities at company headquarters; but intelligence gathering is company-wide, with virtually every employee participating (from the president to salespeople). Intelligence collection and dissemination are well developed at most Japanese firms. However, it is the ability—almost culturally inherent—for sharing intelligence that makes MIS use in Japanese firms so effective.[11]

Among the specific firms with superior marketing information systems are NutraSweet, Northern Telecom, Johnson & Johnson, and United Cigar Stores. Each devotes considerable time and resources to its system. Here are examples of how they apply MIS.[12]

Because NutraSweet's patent protection on its aspartame-based artificial sweeteners has expired in both Europe and the United States, the company is now vulnerable to the actions of competitors. Yet, it remains, by far, the industry leader. Why? It regularly gathers competitive intelligence regarding competitors' prices, expansion plans, and advertising campaigns—and then stores this information in a computer databank. In response to its MIS findings, NutraSweet has cut costs and improved customer service.

Northern Telecom installed its first Enterprise Support System software in 1990 as part of the firm's restructuring towards a more centralized system. Now Northern Telecom

---

[9] Eldon Y. Li, "Marketing Information Systems in the Top U.S. Companies: A Longitudinal Analysis," *Information & Management*, Vol. 28 (January 1995), pp. 13-31.

[10] Jan P. Herring, "Business Intelligence in Japan and Sweden: Lessons for the U.S.," *Journal of Business Strategy*, Vol. 13 (March–April 1992), p. 45.

[11] Ibid., p. 47.

[12] Michael Haddigan, "Competitor Intelligence Considered More Vital Now," *Marketing News* (October 9, 1995), p. 3; Jay Finegan, "Taking Names," *Inc.* (September 1992), pp. 121–130; Robert C. Blattberg and John Deighton, "Interactive Marketing: Exploiting the Age of Addressability," *Sloan Management Review*, Vol. 33 (Fall 1991), pp. 10–11; Mark Stevenson, "He Sees All He Knows All," *Canadian Business* (Spring 1994), Special Technology Issue; and *General Host Corporation 1994 Annual Report.*.

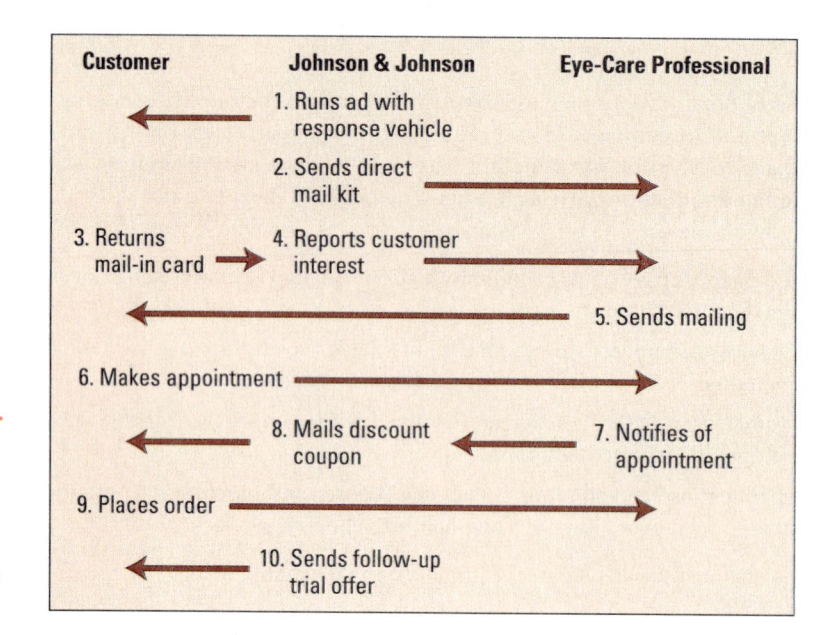

FIGURE 4-5
A Database Marketing Program for Acuvue Contact Lenses

Source: Robert C. Blattberg and John Deighton, "Interactive Marketing: Exploring the Age of Addressability," *Sloan Management Review*, Vol. 33 (Fall 1991), p. 10. *Reprinted by permission.*

Customer	Johnson & Johnson	Eye-Care Professional
←	1. Runs ad with response vehicle	
	2. Sends direct mail kit	→
3. Returns mail-in card →	4. Reports customer interest	→
←	5. Sends mailing	
6. Makes appointment		→
←	8. Mails discount coupon	7. Notifies of appointment ←
9. Places order		→
←	10. Sends follow-up trial offer	

has adopted a new support system to enable it to gather and utilize information along product lines and market lines. Importantly, the new system allows managers to cross-reference data along products and markets. The system currently holds information on the company's finances, personnel records, and customer satisfaction surveys. The system is set up so that information is available to hundreds of users instead of just the firm's executives, although only the executives can access all of the information.

Johnson & Johnson, the maker and marketer of consumer, professional, and health-related products that are sold around the globe, employs a variety of marketing information systems to enhance its performance. For instance, when the Acuvue line of disposable contact lenses was launched, the firm developed and implemented the database marketing program shown in Figure 4-5. The success of that program was due to the company's recognizing that two databases were necessary: one for potential customers and another for eye-care professionals (who had to be properly encouraged and supported).

United Cigar Stores has installed an enterprise support system which enables senior and middle managers to "log onto the system and check sales at any of its 476 stores." For example, a marketing manager can compare weekly or monthly sales against set targets, and if there is a discrepancy, he or she

> can drill down through the data to find the division, region or district where sales are slackening.... [A manager can] cross-reference by store type or product line to see if, perhaps, it's cigarette sales at hotel locations in Ontario that are causing the problem.... [The manager] can even search by promotion, to find out, for example, if a two-pack cigarette discounting program is dragging down revenue instead of boosting it."

One manager has commented "Upper management has had difficulty staying in touch, obtaining accurate, timely data. Now the information is much closer at hand."

Marketing Research Defined

Marketing research involves collecting, tabulating, and analyzing data about specific marketing issues.

Marketing research involves systematically gathering, recording, and analyzing information about specific issues related to the marketing of goods, services, organizations, people, places, and ideas. It may be done by an outside party or by the firm itself. As indicated earlier, marketing research should be one component of a firm's marketing information efforts.

Marketing research data may be obtained form different sources: the firm itself, an impartial agency (such as the government), or a research specialist working for the firm. The information thus obtained may be applied to any aspect of marketing that requires information to aid decision making. To be effective, however, marketing research must be conducted methodically, following a sequence of tasks: gathering the data, recording it, and analyzing it. Furthermore, the research findings must be communicated to the proper decision maker(s) in the firm.

A firm's decision to use marketing research does not mean it must engage in expensive projects like test marketing and national consumer attitude surveys. It may get enough data by analyzing internal sales reports or from informal meetings with customer-service personnel. Marketing research *does* require an orderly approach and adherence to the scientific method.

For each marketing issue studied, the amount and cost of research depend upon the kinds of data needed to make informed decisions, the risk involved in making those decisions, the potential consequences of the decisions, the importance of the issue to the firm, the availability of existing data, the complexity of the data-gathering process for the issue, and other factors.

The Scope of Marketing Research

Companies annually spend about U.S.$8 billion worldwide for data gathered by marketing research firms. The top 25 research firms account for more than U.S.$4 billion of that amount, with over 1000 firms responsible for the rest.[13] These amounts are in addition to research sponsored by government and other institutions and to internal research efforts of firms themselves—which also run into the billions of dollars each year.

According to the American Marketing Association's most recent Survey of Marketing Research, these are the topical areas in which companies are most apt to engage in or sponsor research efforts: industry/market characteristics and trends, product satisfaction, market-share analyses, segmentation studies, brand awareness and preference, purchase intentions, and concept development and testing. And, on average, the surveyed companies spend 1 per cent of their revenues on marketing research.[14]

Five aspects of marketing research merit special discussion. These involve the rapid rise in customer satisfaction studies, the use of state-of-the-art technology, the application of single-source data collection, ethical considerations, and the complexities of international marketing research.

Companies now participate in more customer satisfaction research than ever before, in keeping with the customer focus noted in Chapter 1. This form of research has more than doubled in recent years, with some firms doing their own studies and others hiring outside specialists. For instance, Whirlpool sends surveys on appliance satisfaction to 180 000 households each year. It also pays hundreds of consumers per year to "fiddle" with computer-simulated products at its Usability Lab. Whirlpool's research also extends to its European marketplace. On the other hand, the Walker Group and Maritz Marketing Research, two U.S.-based research firms, each generate worldwide revenues of several million dollars by doing customer satisfaction studies for clients. As a Maritz executive remarked, the company's success is "due to the quality movement in the country, global competitiveness, and a desire to get back to basics and make the marketing orientation more customer-driven."[15]

Over the last decade, significant technological innovations have been applied to marketing research, as these examples indicate:

- Toronto-based Internationational Surveys Ltd. (ISL) has developed PC Meter, a system which is loaded onto home computers (by permission of the users) and is designed to monitor the activities of computer users while they "surf" on the Internet.

Global marketing research expenditures total several billion dollars each year.

AMERICAN MARKETING ASSOCIATION
www.ama.org/

INTERNATIONAL SURVEYS LTD.
www.npd.com/ww.htm

---

[13]Jack Honomichl, "The Honomichl 50," *Marketing News* (June 5, 1995), Special Section.
[14]Thomas C. Kinnear and Ann R. Root (Eds.), *1994 Survey of Marketing Research* (Chicago: American Marketing Association, 1995), pp. 38, 49.
[15]Sally Solo, "How to Listen to Consumers," *Fortune* (January 11, 1993), pp. 77, 79; Laura Loro, "Customer Is Always Right," *Advertising Age* (February 10, 1992), p. 26; and "1995 Directory of Customer Satisfaction Measurement Firms," *Marketing News* (October 23, 1995), Special Section.

- Advanced Neurotechnologies has designed MindTrack, to detect emotional responses to ads and other forms of communication. MindTrack detects brainwaves using sensors attached to a headband; people are exposed to an ad campaign or a TV show and quantitative digital results appear.
- More companies are using facsimile machines to get responses to marketing surveys. In general, faxed responses are obtained quicker; response rates are higher due to the ease of return; and answer quality approximates that for other methods of transmission.[16]

Single-source data collection *is a result of high-tech advances.*

INFORMATION RESOURCES INC.
www.iric.com

Technological advances have facilitated **single-source data collection**—whereby research firms track the activities of individual consumer households from the programs they watch on TV to the products they purchase at stores. For instance, via its BehaviorScan service, Information Resources Inc. (IRI) monitors the viewing habits and shopping behaviour of thousands of households in various markets. Microcomputers are hooked to household TVs and note all programs and ads watched. Consumers shop in supermarkets and drugstores with scanning registers and present cashiers with shoppers

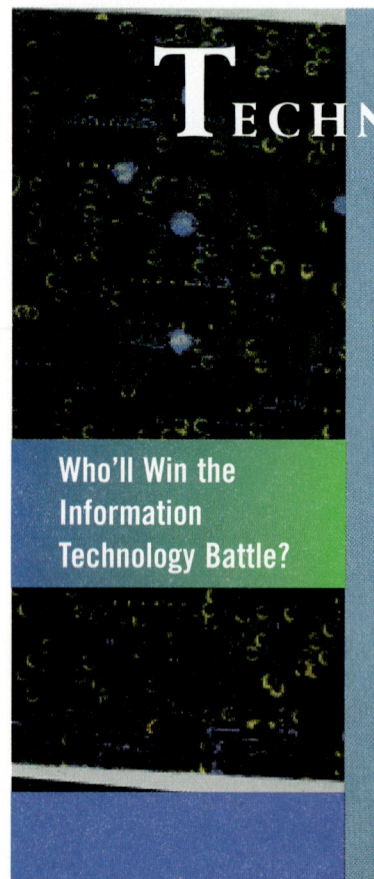

TECHNOLOGY & MARKETING

Who'll Win the Information Technology Battle?

Electronic data linkages between firms let them reduce their inventory levels and order-processing times. Companies joined by such data linkages can also eliminate duplicate functions that occur in billing and purchasing. According to the author of a book on customer-supplier alliances, 30 to 40 per cent of savings from these alliances come from improving joint processes.

With electronic linkages, firms can gather and study information as products go from raw materials to finished goods to retailer shelves. In many cases, the most influential companies in a value chain are those that have the best knowledge of the marketplace. In particular, managers need to ask three questions: What information drives our business? Who has that information? What is it worth?

MicroAge and W.W. Grainger are two examples of firms that understand the value of information. MicroAge shifted from being a wholesaler that stocked Apple, Compaq, Hewlett-Packard, and IBM computers to a producer of computers tailored to individual consumer needs. Instead of selling systems produced by single companies, MicroAge now assembles computers using parts from over 500 companies. MicroAge relies on its knowledge of customer needs, as well as the costs, features, and compatibilities of different manufacturers' products.

W.W. Grainger, which describes itself as a distributor of maintenance, repair, and operating supplies, has an average order size of U.S.$129. Unlike competitors, the firm is able to tailor its services to customer needs. Based upon the desires of individual customers, Grainger might offer electronic ordering and payment capabilities or even perform a customer's inventory management functions. According to a Grainger vice-president, "On sales calls these days, we're seldom talking about why the motor we sell is better than someone else's motor; we talk about value-added services."

As a W.W. Grainger product manager, describe how a marketing information system can be used to maximize its value-added services.

Source: Based on material in Thomas A. Stewart, "The Information Wars: What You Don't Know Will Hurt You," *Fortune* (June 12, 1995), pp. 119–120.

---

[16]James Pollock, "Measured Growth," *Marketing Magazine* (Jan. 15, 1996), p. 16; Kelly Shermach, "Respondents Get Hooked Up and Show Their Emotions," *Marketing News* (August 28, 1995), p. 35; and John P. Dickson and Douglas L. MacLachlan, "Fax Surveys?" *Marketing Research*, Vol. 4 (September 1992), pp. 26–30.

cards (resembling credit cards). Cashiers enter each consumer's identification code, which is electronically keyed to every item bought. Via computer analysis, viewing and shopping behaviour are then matched with such information as age and income.

Due to the unethical practices of some firms, many potential respondents are averse to participating in marketing research projects. To turn the situation around, researchers need to avoid such practices as these:

- Unrealized promises of anonymity.
- False sponsor identification.
- Selling or fundraising under the guise of research.
- Misrepresenting research procedures.
- Observational studies without informed consent.
- Asking overly personal questions.
- Selling consumer demographic information for database use without consent.
- Misportraying research findings in ads and other communications.[17]

With more and more firms striving to expand their foreign endeavours, international marketing research is becoming increasingly important. And this can be quite challenging. The language of the survey, respondent selection, and interviewer training are among the many areas that require special consideration. Consider this example:

> Firms deciding how to market to the 350 million consumers in Eastern Europe and Central Asia increasingly do marketing research there. Yet designing and conducting this research is difficult. Often, people have never been surveyed before. Communications systems, especially phone service, may be primitive by Western standards. Secondary data from government agencies and trade associations may be lacking or unavailable. Thus, companies must be adaptable.
>
> When it did research, Kodak could not find relevant consumer data, a photography trade association, or pictures of local cameras for use in a questionnaire. So, to gather data on camera usage and preferences, Kodak took part in a multi-client survey devised by SRG International Ltd., a research firm. The survey was conducted in nine former Soviet republics; since each had its own language, nine questionnaire versions were prepared.[18]

The Marketing Research Process

The **marketing research process** consists of a series of activities: defining the issue or problem to be studied; examining secondary (previously collected) data; generating primary (new) data if necessary; analyzing information; making recommendations; and implementing findings.

Figure 4-6 presents the complete process. Each step is completed in order. For example, secondary data are not examined until a firm states the issue or problem to be studied, and primary data are not generated until secondary data are thoroughly reviewed. The dashed line around primary data means these data do not always have to be collected. Many times, a firm can obtain enough information internally or from published sources to make a marketing decision without gathering new data. Only when secondary data are insufficient should a firm generate primary data. The research process is described next.

The **marketing research process** *consists of steps from issue definition to implementation of findings.*

Issue (Problem) Definition

Issue (problem) definition is a statement of the topic to be investigated. Without a focused definition of the issue or problem, irrelevant and expensive data may be gathered. A good

Research efforts are directed by **issue definition**.

---

[17] Gene R. Laczniak and Patrick E. Murphy, *Ethical Marketing Decisions: The Higher Road* (Needham Heights, Mass.: Allyn and Bacon, 1993), pp. 53–68.

[18] Lourdes Lee Valeriano, "Western Firms Poll Eastern Europeans to Discern Tastes of Nascent Consumers," *Wall Street Journal* (April 27, 1992), pp. B1–B2; Richard W. Stevenson, "Teaching the Hard Sell of Soap to Eastern Europe," *New York Times* (February 18, 1993), pp. D1, D7; and R. Craig Endicott, "European Dream Captivates Researchers," *Advertising Age* (October 18, 1993), p. S–6.

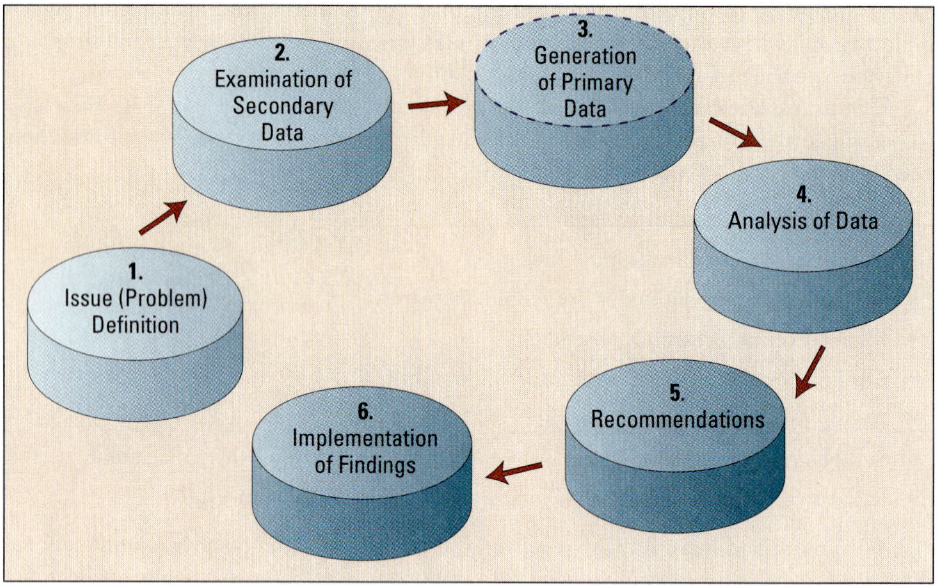

FIGURE 4-6
The Marketing Research Process

Exploratory research *looks at uncertain topics;* conclusive research *is better defined.*

problem definition directs the research process to collect and analyze appropriate data for the purpose of decision making.

When a firm is uncertain about the precise topic to be investigated or wants to informally study an issue, exploratory research is used. The aim of **exploratory research** is to gain ideas and insights, and to break broad, vague problem statements into smaller, more precise statements.[19] Exploratory research, also called "qualitative research," may involve in-depth probing, small group discussions, and understanding underlying trends.

Once an issue is clarified, conclusive research, also called "quantitative research," is used. **Conclusive research** is the structured collection and analysis of data pertaining to a specific issue or problem. It is more focused than exploratory research, and requires larger samples, and more limited questions in order to provide the quantitative data to make decisions. Table 4-1 contrasts exploratory and conclusive research.

Table 4–1
Examples of Exploratory and Conclusive Research

VAGUE RESEARCH TOPIC	EXPLORATORY RESEARCH	PRECISE RESEARCH TOPIC	CONCLUSIVE RESEARCH
1. Why are sales declining?	1. Discussions among key personnel to identify major cause	1. Why is the turnover of sales personnel so high?	1. Survey sales personnel and interview sales managers
2. Is advertising effective?	2. Discussions among key advertising personnel to define effectiveness	2. Do adults recall an advertisement the day after it appears?	2. Survey customers and non-customers to gauge advertising recall
3. Will a price reduction increase revenues?	3. Discussions among key personnel to determine the level of a price reduction	3. Will a 10 per cent price reduction have a significant impact on sales?	3. Run an in-store experiment to determine effects

[19]Bennett, *Dictionary of Marketing Terms,* p. 103.

Secondary Data

Secondary data consist of information not collected for the issue or problem at hand but for some other purpose; this information is available within a firm or externally. Whether secondary data fully resolve an issue or problem or not, their low cost and availability mean that primary data should not be collected until a thorough secondary data search is done.

Secondary data have been previously gathered for purposes other than the current research.

ADVANTAGES AND DISADVANTAGES Secondary data have these general advantages:

- Many types are inexpensive because primary data collection is not involved.
- Data assembly can be fast, especially for published or company materials.
- There may be several sources and perspectives available.
- A source (such as the government) may obtain data a firm could not get itself.
- There is high credibility for data assembled by independent sources.
- They are helpful when exploratory research is involved.

Secondary data also have these general disadvantages:

- Available data may not suit the current research purpose because it is too general or incomplete.
- Information may be dated or obsolete.
- The methodology used in collecting the data (such as the sample size, date of the research, etc.) may be unknown.
- All the findings of a research study may not be made public.
- Conflicting results may exist.
- Because many research projects are not repeated, the reliability of data may not be proven.

SOURCES OF SECONDARY DATA There are two major sources of secondary data. Internal secondary data are available within a firm. External secondary data are available outside a firm. Most companies use both of these sources.

Internal Secondary Data Before spending time and money searching for external secondary data or collecting primary data, the information contained inside a firm should be reviewed. Internal sources include budgets, sales figures, profit-and-loss statements, customer billings, inventory records, prior research reports, and written reports.

A firm's records or past studies comprise internal secondary data.

At the beginning of the business year, most firms set detailed budgets for the next twelve months. The budgets, based on sales forecasts, outline planned expenditures for every good and service during the year. By examining the sales of each division, product line, item, geographic area, salesperson, time of day, day of week, and so on and comparing these sales with prior periods, overall performance can be measured. Through profit-and-loss statements, actual achievements can be measured against profit goals by department, salesperson, and product. Customer billings provide information on credit transactions, sales by region, peak selling seasons, sales volume, and sales by customer category. Inventory records show the levels of goods bought, manufactured, stored, shipped, and/or sold throughout the year.

Prior research reports, containing findings of past marketing research efforts, are often stored and retained for future use. When a report is used initially, it is primary data. Later reference to that report is secondary in nature because it is no longer employed for its original purpose. Written reports (ongoing data stored by a firm) may be compiled by top management, marketing executives, sales personnel, and others. Among the information attainable from such reports are typical customer complaints.

External Secondary Data If a research issue or problem is not resolved through internal secondary data, a firm may use external secondary data sources. There are government and nongovernment sources.

Government and nongovernment sources make available external secondary data.

All levels of government in Canada distribute various types of economic and business statistics. Statistics Canada is the most important source of external secondary information in Canada. The Statistics Canada catalogue provides a listing of all the facts and figures on Canada's business, economic, and social environment. The catalogue lists sources on trade, income, employment, education, and detailed industry information, all of which have been collected by or for Statistics Canada. Aside from its regular written publications, Statistics Canada disseminates data on CD, diskettes, computer printouts, microfiche, microfilm, and magnetic tape. Direct online access is available through Statistics Canada's Internet website, which gives access to copies of "The Daily," StatsCan's newsletter, and to CAN-SIM, Statistics Canada's machine-readable database and retrieval system.

Industry Canada has an online Internet website called Strategis, which is billed as Canada's largest business website. This site provides access to an Industry Canada database that contains:

- 60 000 reports
- 500 000 pages of searchable text
- 2 gigabytes of statistical data
- hot links to Canadian and international business information databases.

Users of the website are told that the database can assist them with decisions such as: identifying opportunities for growth, exploring new markets, finding partners, forming alliances, finding and developing new technologies or processes, and assessing the risks of new ventures.

When using government data, particularly Census statistics, the research date must be noted. There may be a lag before government data are released.

There are three kinds of nongovernment secondary data: regular publications; books, monographs, and other nonregular publications; and commercial research houses. Regular publications contain articles on diverse aspects of marketing and are available in libraries or by subscription. Some are quite broad in scope (such as *Canadian Business*); others are more specialized (*Canadian Advertising Rates and Data*). Periodicals are published by publishing companies, as well as by professional and trade associations.

Books, monographs, and other literature are also published by conventional publishing companies, as well as by professional and trade associations. These materials deal with special topics in depth and are compiled on the basis of interest by the target audience.

Various commercial research houses conduct periodic and ongoing studies and make results available to many clients for a fee. The fee can run as high as the tens of thousands of dollars, depending on the extent of the data. That kind of research is secondary when a firm purchasing the data acts as a subscriber and does not request specific studies pertaining only to itself; in this way, commercial houses provide a number of research services more inexpensively than if data are collected for a firm's sole use. Some examples of research houses are A.C. Nielsen Canada, Canadian Facts, Dun & Bradstreet Canada, and Burke International Research. Figure 4-7 shows one subscription service provided by commercial research houses. A great many others are also available.

DUN & BRADSTREET CANADA
www.dbisna.com/

Lists of commercial research firms and research services available in Canada can be found quickly from two sources: 1) *Marketing Magazine* annually publishes a "Guide to Market Research Services." This guide lists private research organizations in Canada, explains how to contact them, and in many cases gives a brief description of the type of information they trade in. 2) *The International Member & Marketing Services Guide* is an annual publication of the American Marketing Association in Chicago, Illinois. It contains a list of market research firms and services indexed alphabetically and geographically by country. This guide lists private research organizations throughout the world. It also provides details on how to contact these firms, and gives a brief description of the type of services they specialize in.

Primary Data

Primary data *relate to a specific marketing issue.*

Primary data consist of information gathered to address a specific issue or problem at hand. Such data are needed when a thorough analysis of secondary data is insufficient for a proper marketing decision to be made.

FIGURE 4-7
Retail Store Auditing by Burke Marketing Services
Burke auditors regularly visit a national sample of stores to provide clients with data about sales, inventories, brand distribution, prices, displays, and so on.
Reprinted by permission.

Advantages and Disadvantages

Primary data have these general advantages:

- They are collected to fit the precise purpose of the current research topic.
- Information is current.
- The methodology of data collection is controlled and known by the firm.
- All findings are available to the firm, which can maintain their secrecy.
- There are no conflicting data from different sources.
- A study can be replicated (if desired).
- When secondary data do not resolve all questions, collecting and analyzing primary data are the only ways to acquire information.

Primary data also have these general disadvantages:

- Collection may be time consuming.
- Costs may be high.
- Some types of information cannot be collected (e.g., *Census* data).
- The company's perspective may be limited.
- The firm may be incapable of collecting primary data.

RESEARCH DESIGN If a firm decides primary data are needed, it must devise a **research design**—which outlines the procedures for collecting and analyzing data. A research design includes the following decisions.

*The **research design** outlines data collection.*

Who Collects the Data? A company can collect data itself or hire an outside research firm for a specific project. The advantages of an internal research department are its knowledge of company operations, total access to company personnel, ongoing assembly and storage of data, and high commitment. The disadvantages of an internal department are the continuous costs, narrow perspective, possible lack of expertise on the latest research techniques, and potentially excessive support for the views of top management. The strengths and weaknesses of an outside research firm are the opposite of those for an inside department.

Internal or outside personnel can be used.

What Information Should Be Collected? The kinds and amounts of data to be collected should be keyed to the issue (problem) formulated by the firm. Exploratory research requires different data collection from conclusive research.

Who or What Should Be Studied? First, the people or objects to be studied must be stated; they comprise the population. People studies generally involve customers, company personnel, and/or distribution intermediaries. Object studies usually centre on company and/or product performance.

Sampling the population saves time and money.

Second, the way in which people or objects are selected must be decided. Large and/or dispersed populations usually are examined by **sampling**, which requires the analysis of selected people or objects in the designated population, rather than all of them. It saves time and money; and when used properly, the accuracy and level of representation of the sample can be measured.

The two approaches to sampling are probability and nonprobability. With a probability (random) sample, every member of the designated population has an equal or known probability of being chosen for analysis. For example, a researcher may select every fiftieth person in a phone directory. With a nonprobability sample, members of the population are chosen on the basis of convenience or judgment. For instance, an interviewer may select the first 100 residence students entering a university cafeteria. A probability sample is more accurate; but, it is more costly and difficult than a nonprobability sample.

Third, the sample size studied must be set. Generally, a large sample will yield greater accuracy and cost more than a small sample. There are methods for assessing sample size in terms of accuracy and costs, but a description of them is beyond the scope of this text.

What Technique of Data Collection Should Be Used? There are four basic primary-data collection methods: survey, observation, experiment, and simulation.

A survey communicates in person, over the phone, or by mail.

A **survey** gathers information from respondents by communicating with them. It can uncover data about attitudes, purchases, intentions, and consumer traits. However, it is subject to incorrect or biased answers. A questionnaire is used to record survey responses. A survey can be conducted in person, by phone, or by mail.

A personal survey is face-to-face and flexible, can elicit lengthy replies, and reduces ambiguity. It is relatively expensive, however, and bias is possible because the interviewer may affect results by suggesting ideas to respondents or by creating a certain mood during the interview. A phone survey is fast and relatively inexpensive, especially with the growth of discount telephone services. Responses are usually brief, and nonresponse may be a problem. It must be verified that the desired respondent is the one contacted. Some people do not have a phone, or they have unlisted numbers. The latter problem is now overcome through computerized, random digit-dialing devices.

A mail survey reaches dispersed respondents, has no interviewer bias, and is relatively inexpensive. Nonresponse, slowness of returns, and participation by incorrect respondents are the major problems. The technique chosen depends on the goals and needs of the specific research project. See Figure 4-8.

A nondisguised survey reveals its purpose, whereas a disguised one does not.

A survey may be nondisguised or disguised. With a nondisguised survey, the respondent is told a study's real purpose; in a disguised survey, the person is not. The latter may be used to indirectly probe attitudes and avoid a person's answering what he or she thinks the interviewer or researcher wants to hear or read. The left side of Figure 4-9 is a nondisguised survey showing the true intent of a study on sports car attitudes and behaviour. The right side of the figure shows how the survey can be disguised: By asking about sports car owners in general, a firm may get more honest answers than with questions geared right at the respondent. The intent of the disguised study is to uncover the respondent's actual reasons for buying a sports car.

A semantic differential uses bipolar adjectives.

A **semantic differential** is a list of bipolar (opposite) adjective scales. It is a survey technique with rating scales instead of, or in addition to, traditional questions. It may be disguised or nondisguised, depending on whether the respondent is told a study's true purpose. Each adjective in a semantic differential is rated on a bipolar scale, and average scores for all respondents are computed. An overall company or product profile is then devised. The profile may be compared with competitors' profiles and consumers' ideal ratings. Figure 4-10 shows a completed semantic differential.

Chapter 4 Information for Marketing Decisions   **97**

FIGURE 4-8
Consumer Surveys at Stanley Works
Roundtable discussions with consumers are used to spark reactions to company products, such as the Stanley Closet Organizer.
Reprinted by permission.

Nondisguised	Disguised
1. Why are you buying a sports car?	1. Why do you think people buy sports cars?
2. What factors are you considering in the purchase of a sports car?	2. What factors do people consider in the purchase of a sports car?
3. Is status important to you in a sports car? ____ Yes ____ No	3. Are people who purchase sports cars status-conscious? ____ Yes ____ No
4. On the highway, I will drive my sports car ____ within the speed limit. ____ slightly over the speed limit. ____ well over the speed limit.	4. On the highway, sports car owners drive ____ within the speed limit. ____ slightly over the speed limit. ____ well over the speed limit.

FIGURE 4-9
Nondisguised and Disguised Surveys

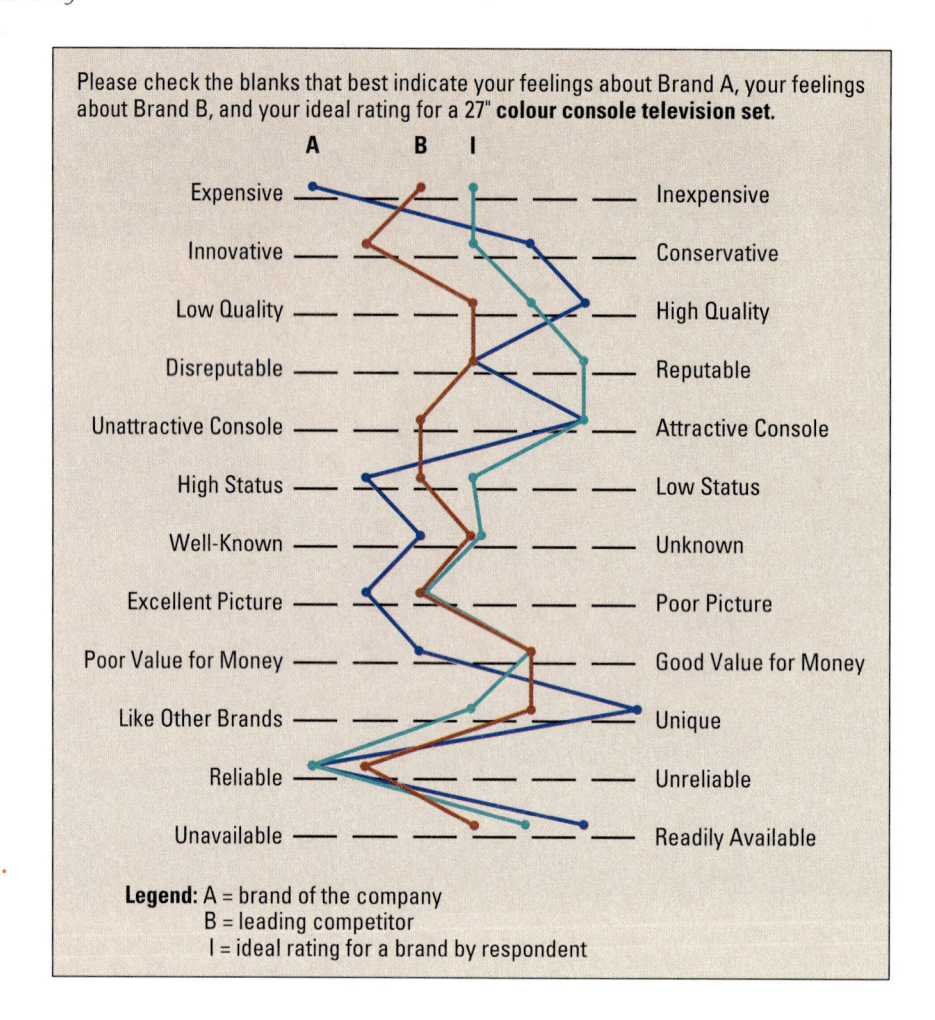

FIGURE 4-10
A Semantic Differential for a Colour Television

> Please check the blanks that best indicate your feelings about Brand A, your feelings about Brand B, and your ideal rating for a 27" **colour console television set.**
>
> | Expensive | — | Inexpensive |
> | Innovative | — | Conservative |
> | Low Quality | — | High Quality |
> | Disreputable | — | Reputable |
> | Unattractive Console | — | Attractive Console |
> | High Status | — | Low Status |
> | Well-Known | — | Unknown |
> | Excellent Picture | — | Poor Picture |
> | Poor Value for Money | — | Good Value for Money |
> | Like Other Brands | — | Unique |
> | Reliable | — | Unreliable |
> | Unavailable | — | Readily Available |
>
> **Legend:** A = brand of the company
> B = leading competitor
> I = ideal rating for a brand by respondent

*In **observation**, behaviour is viewed.*

Observation is a research method whereby present behaviour or the results of past behaviour are observed and noted. People are not questioned and cooperation is unnecessary. Interviewer and question bias are minimized. Observation is often used in actual situations. The major disadvantages are that attitudes cannot be determined and observers may misinterpret behaviour.

In disguised observation, a consumer is unaware he or she is being watched. A two-way mirror, hidden camera, or other device may be used. With nondisguised observation, a participant knows he or she is being observed. Human observation is carried out by people; mechanical observation records behaviour through electronic or other means, such as a movie camera filming customer reactions to a sales presentation in a store.

*An **experiment** varies marketing factors under controlled conditions.*

An **experiment** is a type of research in which one or more factors are manipulated under controlled conditions. A factor may be any element of marketing from package design to advertising media. In an experiment, just the factor under study is varied; all other factors remain constant. For example, to evaluate a new package design for a product, a manufacturer could send new packages to five retail outlets and old packages to five similar outlets; all marketing factors other than packaging remain the same. After one month, sales of the new package at the test outlets are compared with sales of the old package at the similar outlets. A survey or observation is used to determine the reactions to an experiment.

An experiment's key advantage is that it can show cause and effect—such as whether a new package is the cause of increased sales. It is also methodically structured and en-

International Marketing in Action

Is Rummaging Through Trash in Argentina "Marketing Research?"

After evaluating its garbage-digging research technique, the Dynamics Group consulting firm decided to expand its market-surveillance activities from 400 to 1650 residences in greater metropolitan Buenos Aires, Argentina. The bulk (no pun intended) of the firm's research results come from studying disposable packaging.

As Dynamics Group's research director says, "By analyzing disposable containers, we can certify that this is real consumption and not what somebody felt like saying or what they 'thought' was right for a survey. The people in this study don't know that we are studying their garbage so the information is totally objective." Among the firm's clients are food and beverage marketers such as Coca-Cola, Argentina's largest dairy products marketer, a major pasta maker, and two big wine and meat marketers. Dynamics Group is now seeking to attract marketers of health and beauty aids, household cleaning products, and paper goods.

Dynamics Group provides clients with data on brand share gains and losses, key competitors, and customer loyalty. It can also furnish data on associated consumption (such as what food item was consumed with a specific type of beverage), the impact of advertising campaigns (measured by the amount of the advertised product in the trash), and product usage by day of week. Discarded newspapers, magazines, and cable television guides can also give marketers data on media availability by household.

As a Coca-Cola de Argentina spokesperson states, "We can get information about sales from Nielsen, but this shows us more about end consumption." For example, an analysis of garbage data suggested that people in poorer areas of Argentina consumed more expensive wines and champagnes on weekends, while the opposite pattern occurred in wealthier areas.

What types of data would you, as a brand manager for an Argentine pasta maker, want to obtain through the garbage-digging method? Why?

Source: Based on material in Mike Galetto, "Turning Trash to Research Treasure," *Advertising Age* (April 17, 1995), p. J–16.

---

acted. Key disadvantages are the rather high costs, frequent use of contrived settings, and inability to control all factors in or affecting a marketing plan.

Simulation is a computer-based method to test the potential effects of various marketing factors using a software program rather than real-world applications. A model of the controllable and uncontrollable factors facing the firm is first constructed. Different combinations of the factors are then fed into a computer to determine their possible impact on an overall marketing strategy. Simulation requires no consumer cooperation and can handle many interrelated factors. However, it may be complex and hard to use; does not measure actual attitudes, behaviour, and intentions; and is subject to the accuracy of the assumptions made.

Simulation *enables marketing factors to be analyzed using a computer model.*

Table 4-2
The Best Uses of Primary Data-Collection Techniques

TECHNIQUE	MOST APPROPRIATE USES
1. Survey	When determining consumer or distribution intermediary attitudes and motivations toward marketing-mix factors; measuring purchase intentions; relating consumer traits to attitudes
2. Observation	When examining actual responses to marketing factors under realistic conditions; interest in behaviour and not in attitudes
3. Experiment	When controlling the research environment is essential and establishing a cause-and-effect relationship is important
4. Simulation	When deriving and analyzing many interrelationships among variables

Research expenses range from personnel time to marketing costs.

How Much Will the Study Cost? Table 4–2 shows the best uses for each kind of primary data collection.

The overall and specific costs of a study must be clearly outlined. These costs may include executive time, researcher time, support-staff time, pre-testing, computer usage, respondent incentives (if any), interviewers, supplies, printing, postage or phone expenses, special equipment, and marketing expenses (such as advertising).

A study's expected costs should be compared with the expected benefits to be derived. Suppose a consumer survey costing $10 000 would let a firm improve the package design of a new product. With the changes suggested by research, the firm would lift its first-year profit by $30 000. Thus, the net increase due to research is $20 000 ($30 000 profit less $10 000 in costs).

How Will the Data Be Collected? The people needed to collect the data outlined in the research design must be determined and the attributes, skills, and training of the data-collection force specified. Too often, this important phase is improperly planned, and data are collected by unqualified people.

Interviewers administer surveys or respondents fill them out.

Data collection can be administered by research personnel or can be self-administered. With administered collection, interviewers ask questions or observers note behaviour; they record answers or behaviour and explain questions (if asked) to respondents. With self-administered collection, respondents read questions and write their answers. There is a trade-off between control and interviewer probing (administered) versus privacy and limited interviewer bias (self-administered).

How Long Will the Data-Collection Period Be? The time frame within which data are collected must be stipulated, or else a study can drag on. Too long a time frame may lead to inconsistent responses and secrecy violations. Short time frames are easy to set for personal and phone surveys. Mail surveys, observation, and experiments often require much more time to implement; nonetheless, time limits must be defined.

When and Where Should Information Be Collected? The day and time of data collection must be set. It must also be decided if a study will be done on or off a firm's premises. The desire for immediacy and convenience have to be weighed against the need to contact hard-to-reach respondents at the proper time.

DATA COLLECTION After the research design is thoroughly detailed, data are actually collected. Those engaged in data collection must be properly supervised and follow directions exactly. Responses or observations must be entered correctly.

Data Analysis

Data analysis *consists of coding, tabulation, and analysis.*

In **data analysis**, the information on questionnaires or answer forms is first coded and tabulated and then analyzed. Coding is the process by which each completed data form is numbered and response categories are labelled. Tabulation is the calculation of summary data

1. Do you drink coffee?	☐ Yes	01	300
	☐ No	02	200
2. In general, how frequently do you drink coffee? (Check only one answer.)	☐ Two or more times per day	03	142
	☐ Once per day	04	84
	☐ Several times per week	05	42
	☐ Once or twice per week	06	20
	☐ One to three times per month	07	12
	☐ Never	08	200
3. During what time of day do you drink coffee? (Check all answers that apply.)	☐ Morning	09	270
	☐ Lunch time	10	165
	☐ Afternoon	11	100
	☐ Dinner time	12	150
	☐ Evening	13	205
	☐ None	14	200

Coding: Questionnaires numbered A001 to A500. Each response is labeled 01 to 14 (e.g., Morning is 09, Evening is 13). Question 3 is a multiple-response question.

Tabulation: Total responses are shown above right.

Analysis: 60% drink coffee. About 28% drink coffee two or more times daily (representing 47% of all coffee drinkers); almost 25% of coffee drinkers (74 people) consume coffee less than once per day. 90% of coffee drinkers consume coffee in the morning; only one-third consume it in the afternoon.

Recommendations: The coffee industry and individual firms need to increase the advertising geared toward noncoffee drinkers, as well as infrequent coffee drinkers. Emphasis should also be placed on lifting coffee consumption during afternoon hours.

Implementation of findings: New, more aggressive advertising campaigns will be developed and the annual media budgets devoted to increasing overall coffee consumption will be expanded. One theme will stress coffee's value as an afternoon "pick-me-upper."

FIGURE 4-11
Data Analysis, Recommendations, and Implementation of Findings for a Study on Coffee

for each response category. Analysis is the evaluation of responses, usually by statistical techniques, as they pertain to the specific issue or problem under investigation. The relationship of coding, tabulation, and analysis is shown in Figure 4-11.

Recommendations

Recommendations are suggestions for future actions that are based on marketing research findings. They are typically presented in written (sometimes, oral) form to marketing decision makers. The report must be written for the audience that reads it. Thus, technical terminology must be defined.

After recommendations are passed on to the proper decision makers, the research report should be kept in the data storage part of a firm's marketing intelligence network. It may then be retrieved in the future, as needed.

Implementation

A research report represents feedback for marketing managers, who are responsible for implementing any changes that may be necessary. If the findings are ignored, the research has little value. If decisions are based on the results, then marketing research has great value and the organization benefits in the short and long run.

Marketing managers are most apt to implement research findings if they have input into the research design, broad control over marketing decisions, and confidence that results are accurate.

MARKETING IN A CHANGING WORLD
Talking to Former Customers

In today's competitive marketplace, it may not be enough for a firm to focus its efforts on current and prospective customers. It may also be a good idea to research and try to win back various former customers. To do that, a company needs to engage in the sometimes painful task of finding out why these are "former" customers.

Yet because most company owners hate to hear harsh words about their babies, they find the hardest part of tracking lost customers is picking up the phone. Bob Ottley, president of One Step Tree and Lawn Care, hesitated for fear "the negative feedback would be impossible to deal with."

At the same time, Ottley was smart enough to know that he had to talk to former customers if his firm was to survive. Today, One Step has a weekly "cancels" report; and Ottley knows what per cent of cancellations are due to people moving, deciding to mow their own lawns, or no longer being able to afford his service—and switching to a lower-priced competitor. One Step has cut its customer attrition rate in half since it began the "cancels" report. And its leave-behind survey of current customers "puts the idea into their heads that we want to know if there's a problem."

Bruce Grench, chief executive of HDIS (a small mail-order firm that specializes in personal-care products), is another executive who has overcome his qualms. Grench uses six different approaches, from small-group gripe sessions to one-on-one telephone surveys, to gather comments from would-be, current, and former customers. He says, "We kind of look forward to it [contacting former customers], even though it's tough medicine. The hope is that we can find something we're not doing right because it offers us an opportunity." He did; that's why HDIS now offers private-label products for price-conscious customers."[20]

SUMMARY

1. *To show why marketing information is needed* Marketing information lets a firm accurately assess its strengths, weaknesses, opportunities, and threats; operate properly in the marketing environment; and maximize performance. Reliance on intuition, judgment, and experience are not sufficient. The scientific method requires objectivity, accuracy, and thoroughness in research projects.

2. *To explain the role and importance of marketing information systems* Collecting marketing information should not be viewed as an infrequent occurrence. Acting in that way can have negative ramifications, especially with regard to misreading the competition and other external factors that can affect a firm's performance.

A marketing information system (MIS) is a set of procedures to generate, analyze, disseminate, and store anticipated marketing decision information on a regular, continuous basis. It can aid a company operationally, managerially, and strategically.

3. *To examine a basic marketing information system, commercial databases, database marketing, and examples of MIS in action* The key aspect of a basic MIS is the marketing intelligence network, which consists of continuous monitoring, marketing research, and data storage. The intelligence network is influenced by the environment, company goals, and marketing plans; and it affects the implementation of marketing plans. Marketing research should be considered as just one part of an ongoing, integrated information system. An MIS can be used by both small and large firms, and does not have to be computerized.

Specialized research firms offer valuable information through commercial databases that contain information on the population, the business environment, the economy, industry and company performance, and other factors. Databases are available in printed form; on computer diskettes, CD-ROMs, or tapes; and via online hookups.

[20]"Where Did We Go Wrong?" *Inc.* (July 1995), p. 91.

An increasing number of firms are looking to database marketing to improve their interactions with customers. Database marketing involves setting up an automated system to identify and characterize customers and prospects and then using quantifiable information to better reach them.

Marketing information systems are being used by firms of every size and type.

4. To define marketing research and its components and to look at its scope Marketing research entails systematically gathering, recording, and analyzing data about specific issues related to the marketing of goods, services, organizations, people, places, and ideas. It may be conducted internally or externally.

Expenditures on marketing research run into the billions of dollars annually. Five key aspects of marketing research are particularly noteworthy: customer satisfaction studies, the use of advanced technology, single-source data collection, ethical considerations, and the intricacies of international research.

5. To describe the marketing research process It has a series of activities: defining the issue or problem to be studied, examining secondary data, generating primary data (when needed), analyzing data, making recommendations, and implementing findings. Many considerations and decisions are needed at each stage of the process.

Exploratory (qualitative) research is used to develop a clear definition of the study topic. Conclusive (quantitative) research looks at a specific issue in a structured manner. Secondary data—not gathered for the study at hand but for some other purpose—are available from internal and external (government, nongovernment, commercial) sources. Primary data—collected specifically for the purpose of the investigation at hand—are available through surveys, observation, experiments, and simulation. Primary data collection requires a research design: the framework for guiding data collection and analysis. Primary data are gathered only if secondary data are inadequate. Costs must be weighed against the benefits of research. The final stages of marketing research are data analysis—consisting of coding, tabulating, and analyzing; recommendations—suggestions for future actions based on research findings; and the implementation of findings by management.

KEY TERMS

scientific method (p. 80)
marketing information system (MIS) (p. 80)
marketing intelligence network (p. 82)
continuous monitoring (p. 82)
data storage (p. 82)
commercial databases (p. 83)
database marketing (p. 83)
marketing research (p. 88)

single-source data collection (p. 90)
marketing research process (p. 91)
issue (problem) definition (p. 91)
exploratory research (p. 92)
conclusive research (p. 92)
secondary data (p. 93)
primary data (p. 94)
research design (p. 95)

sampling (p. 96)
survey (p. 96)
semantic differential (p. 96)
observation (p. 98)
experiment (p. 98)
simulation (p. 99)
data analysis (p. 109)

Review Questions

1. Why is marketing information necessary? What may result if managers rely exclusively on intuition?
2. What is the scientific method? Must it be used each time a firm does research? Explain your answer.
3. Describe the elements of a basic marketing information system.
4. Distinguish between commercial databases and database marketing.
5. What is single-source data collection?
6. Differentiate between conclusive and exploratory research. Give an example of each.
7. What are the pros and cons of secondary data?
8. When is primary data collection necessary?
9. Outline the steps in a research design.
10. Under what circumstances should a firm use surveys to collect data? Observation? Explain your answers.

Discussion Questions

1. A small jeweller wants to get information on the average amounts that consumers spend on gold jewelry, the incomes and occupations of gold jewelry consumers, the times of year when gold jewelry purchases are heaviest and lightest, sales of the leading competitors, the criteria people use in choosing gold jewelry, and consumer satisfaction. Explain how the firm should set up and implement a marketing intelligence network. Include internal and external data sources in your answer.

2. How could a firm use a modified version of Johnson & Johnson's database marketing program as shown in Figure 4-5? Apply your answer to a firm marketing expensive attaché cases to business customers via office-supply stores.

3. Pizza Hut is an internationally oriented fast-food chain. Pierre's Pizza is an independent local European fast-food restaurant. If both wanted to gather data about their respective competitors' marketing practices, how would your research design differ for each?

4. Develop a five-question disguised survey to determine attitudes toward the reputations of colleges and universities in your area. Why use a disguised survey for this topic?

5. Comment on the ethics of disguised surveys. When would you recommend that they not be used?

VIDEO CASE

Scanning the Canadian Market: A.C. Neilsen versus IRI

Information on markets and competitors is an absolute must for marketing decision makers. Suppliers of this information control a valuable resource and should be able to profit handsomely. However, marketing decision makers in Canada have reduced spending on Canadian market research in recent years. Despite this, market research billings in Canada range between $110 and $120 million annually. Now A.C. Neilsen of Canada and Information Resources Incorporated (IRI), two major rivals in the marketing research business in the United States, are squaring off in Canada over access to grocery-store scanner information. More competition in what has been a declining market in Canada is bound to be intense and IRI has brought the Canadian government into the fray, a sure sign of the level of intensity of the competition and the potential for profit.

Grocery-store scanner information is one of the most important sources of consumer and product information available to packaged-goods marketers. Every store that uses UPC codes to scan product prices is a source of valuable marketing information. The scanner information collected is not restricted to price alone; the date of purchase, the brand purchased, the package size, plus any associated coupon-usage behaviour is recorded with each transaction. The scanner information can then be cross-referenced with demographic information on consumers, such as income, age, dwelling type, house value, occupation, race/ethnicity, sex, as well as product marketers' information on selling space devoted to the brand and related advertising and promotional campaigns, couponing and in-store promotional campaigns. This information is critical to the formulation and evaluation of marketing strategies by packaged-goods marketers.

In the United States and Canada A.C. Neilsen has been a long-term supplier of retail-sales and market-share information, and was the dominant firm in the industry until IRI came on the scene in 1979. Information Resources Incorporated began using UPC scanner data at this time and quickly stole 50 per cent of A.C. Neilsen's U.S. customers. Aside from basic information on what is being purchased and by whom, IRI has developed a unique marketing strategy model for its clients. Their strength is in having developed unique and specialized software to complement their gigantic database of scanner data. As such, IRI provides their U.S. clients with a great deal of customized advice on marketing strategy. However, IRI was unable to provide these same services in Canada because A.C. Neilsen had signed exclusive long-term contracts with many retailers, giving them an effective monopoly. IRI complained to Canada's Competition Bureau that Neilsen's contracts were restraining trade and should be considered illegal under Bill C-2. An investigation was launched and the case went before Canada's Competition Tribunal.

The result: as of August 30, 1995 all contracts for scanner data are limited to a maximum of 18 months duration. A.C. Neilsen's monopoly is broken. Price and service incentives for manufacturers to insist on A.C. Neilsen (or any firm for that matter) as the preferred supplier of scanner data are also prohibited. The most controversial aspect of the tribunal's ruling is that A.C. Neilsen must provide IRI with historical data dating back 18 months on request. This will allow IRI to provide a historical background for any new clients that they sign up.

Will competition make the marketplace work better? IRI presents a service that has been shown to be extremely valuable to its U.S. clients. However, one disturbing spectre looms. The American operations of A.C. Neilsen and IRI have been losing money over the last few years. Only "foreign" operations like Canada have been making money for A.C. Neilsen, and this situation has just taken a turn for the worst. The competitive situation mandated by Canada's Competition Tribunal promises to give purchasers of market research more choice; however, the price of that choice is yet to be determined, and there is no guarantee it will be less than the current costs.

QUESTIONS

1. Comment on the fact that A.C. Neilsen and IRI are having a difficult time operating profitably. What are some of the implications?
2. Identify and discuss some of the marketing decisions which could be made on the basis of the market research information supplied in the scanner data.
3. What types of information would you, as a marketing manager, like to have, which are not available in the scanner data described?
4. Put yourself in the position of A.C. Neilsen's Canadian manager. Accepting the ruling of Canada's Competition Tribunal, what type of approach would you use to maintain your clients and blunt the impact of IRI's market entry on your firm?

VIDEO QUESTIONS ON NEILSEN SAGA

1. As a potential purchaser of A.C. Neilsen's scanner data on your products and your competitor's products, evaluate the data as a source of competitive advantage for your firm.
2. Discuss the strengths and weaknesses of the marketing information offered by scanner technology.

Video Source: "Nielsen Saga," *Venture* (November 27, 1994).
Other Sources: James Pollock, "Tribunal Orders Scanner Data Market Be Opened," *Marketing Magazine*, (Sept. 11, 1995), p. 3; James Pollock, "IRI Challenges Nielsen's Niche," *Marketing Magazine* (October 16, 1995), p. 13; and James Pollock, "Research Billings Remain Steady," *Marketing Magazine* (January 15, 1996) p. 18.

CASE STUDY
Telogy, Inc.: Coordinating Company Databases

Telogy is a manufacturer of electronic testing and measurement products. On an average day, it receives customer service calls from as many as 60 current or prospective customers. The typical caller requests data on price, product availability, or product specifications for one or more of Telogy's 3000 products.

Prior to 1993, none of Telogy's databases were integrated. Accordingly, customer service personnel had to query multiple databases to get the necessary information. For example, information on pricing was contained in one database, while customer information was in another. In some cases, it took customers at least 15 to 20 minutes to obtain essential data. If a sales representative had to be contacted, the process could take as long as a day. And in most cases, Telogy had no idea if the caller was an existing or a prospective customer unless it asked.

Telogy's old system also did not provide the firm with information deemed vital to running its business. The company had a hard time learning what types of products a client bought, whether these items were purchased or leased, and what types of problems, if any, were encountered. Telogy also missed many sales opportunities due to the poor level of integration of its old marketing information system. A particularly embarrassing problem was that in some cases an item was sold out between the time an order was placed with a salesperson and the time the order was transferred to the shipping department.

So, Telogy decided that it needed to centralize its database. This would enable customer desires to be better matched with specific products, the firm's order-processing system could be simplified, and each of Telogy's salespeople could have access to data on customer leads, product availability, and pricing.

Telogy's new software now lets its order-processing and marketing departments have access to the same data at the same time. This eliminates the problem with orders being sold out during the time between a customer's ordering with a sales representative and the order-processing department receiving that order. And by centralizing information on product availability and pricing, sales reps can better service customers and process orders. Although the software conversion process took ten months (the delay was caused by having to change computer systems), sales training averaged only four hours per person.

Telogy's $500 000 system enables its customer-support personnel to look up any customer's file, and quickly determine whether a caller is a prospective or past customer. And if the customer calls customer support and then decides to place an order, the customer-support representative can instantaneously send that information to the sales department without re-keying the order. This system also allows Telogy's telemarketing sales group to better profile their accounts based on past order histories, and to more easily pass along data to the firm's outside sales force.

Besides setting up a new database, Telogy has automated its outside sales force. Each of the firm's sales reps now has a notebook PC equipped with word processing and spreadsheet software, an e-mail system, and a sales-tracking system with key customer profile data. As a result, sales reps can record orders more quickly and spend more time selling.

There are many ways to evaluate the success of Telogy's new database. One way is to analyze how inventory is used. Thus, in comparing sales and inventory levels under the old and new information systems, Telogy computed that its sales revenues increased by 15 per cent and inventory levels were reduced by 10 per cent.

QUESTIONS

1. List and discuss the benefits of an integrated database beyond those discussed in this case.
2. Describe how Telogy's database can be used in strategic planning. Refer to Figure 4-5 in your answer.
3. How can Telogy use its new database as part of a database marketing system?
4. Discuss three other measures (beyond inventory utilization) that can be used to assess Telogy's new database system.

Source: The data from this case was drawn from Melissa Campanelli, "On the Right Track," *Sales & Marketing Management* (August 1995), pp. 47–51.

BROADENING AN ORGANIZATION'S / INDIVIDUAL'S MARKETING SCOPE

PART 2

In Part 2, we present an expanded perspective on marketing—one that is necessary today.

5 Societal, Ethical, and Consumer Issues

In this chapter, we examine the interaction of marketing and society. We begin by exploring the concept of social responsibility and discussing the impact of company and consumer activities on natural resources, the landscape, environmental pollution, and planned obsolescence. Next, there is an in-depth discussion of ethics from several vantage points: business, consumer, international, and teachability. We then turn to consumerism and consider the basic rights of consumers: to information, to safety, to choice in product selection, and to be heard. We also note the current trends related to the role of consumerism.

6 Global Aspects of Marketing

Here, we place marketing into a global context—important for both domestic and international firms, regardless of their size. First, we distinguish among domestic, international, and global marketing. Then, we see why international marketing takes place and how widespread it is. We assess cultural, economic, political, legal, and technological factors. We conclude by looking at the stages in the development of an international marketing strategy: company organization, market entry decisions, degree of standardization, and product, distribution, promotion, and price planning.

Part 2 Vignette
Ethical Issues and Global Marketing

Marketers need to be aware that the importance of social responsibility, ethical behaviour and consumer responsibility vary in different countries and cultures. In Part 2 we will encounter two Canadian perspectives on ethics and competing cultures. The first illustrates business ethics and social responsibility through David Nitkin and his firm Ethicscan; the second examines how culture affects the way in which business is conducted in North America and is based on the views of author James Fallows. Ethical behaviour in business and society is a hot topic in the media and other influential Canadian institutions. In as much as cultural institutions help shape ethical norms of society, global marketers must be aware of the impact of culture on how they do business in foreign markets. The guidelines for proper conduct when interacting with other people and organizations derive from the codes of ethics that people and organizations have adopted. It is often commented that "when self-interest comes in, ethics go out."

The importance of ethics and the need for a social conscience is the subject of the video case on Ethicscan and David Nitkin, who is working to make Canadian firms conduct their businesses more ethically. The adoption of the marketing concept implies ethical conduct because it forces firms to take a long-term view of society and their role in that society. However, a "code of conduct" that defines ethics would be very helpful to businesses, especially to new businesses. David Nitkin is trying to help firms develop such ethical codes of conduct, which seem to be of more recent concern to the public.

> *Marketers need to be aware that the importance of social responsibility, ethical behaviour and consumer responsibility may vary in different countries and cultures.*

Marketing firms are aware that perceptions about their ethical conduct can affect their corporate image, and thus the sale of their goods and services. Therefore, firms want to be perceived as being ethical. Of course, being perceived as ethical and actually being ethical are not necessarily the same. Given that ethics have a cultural component, what is acceptable in Canada may be more or less acceptable in another nation.

Social changes affecting ethical standards produce both problems and opportunities for businesses. Some firms find themselves criticized for operating with formerly acceptable practices. For example, cosmetics manufacturers have tested their products on animals for years. They reason that the testing is designed to protect their consumers. However, animal rights activists consider this testing unethical because it harms the animals. Companies like the Body Shop have capitalized on this concern by developing and promoting products that have not been tested on animals.

The impact of culture on how business is conducted is illustrated by an interview with business author James Fallows, who lived in Japan and discussed his experience there in the book *Looking at the Sun*. Because Japan is the second largest trading partner of both Canada and the United States, it is important for us to understand how the Japanese do business. After all, Japan is an important market for our products and an important competitor for us as we deal with our largest trading partner, the United States! The way in which Japanese firms do business is very much conditioned by their culture, and Canadians firms are no different. A difficulty occurs when firms seeking opportunities try to do business in markets with different cultures. Fallows discusses how the cultural differences between Japan and Western nations have affected their trading relationships and means of doing business. He also examines how international competitiveness can be affected by the way firms do business. Taking a fundamental approach to marketing by analyzing each nation or culture with the idea of offering goods and services customized to them is one notion on how marketing should be practised.

These video cases illustrate that the process by which marketers seek to understand how to conduct business ethically in their own culture is useful for helping them understand how to conduct business in foreign markets.

CHAPTER 5
Societal, Ethical, and Consumer Issues

Chapter Objectives

1. To consider the impact of marketing on society

2. To examine social responsibility and weigh its benefits and costs

3. To look into the role of ethics in marketing

4. To explore consumerism and describe the consumer bill of rights

5. To discuss the responses of manufacturers, retailers, and trade associations to consumerism and study the current role of consumerism

{ *Cigarettes represent the quintessential example of an ethical dilemma involving marketing and society in Canada. It seems remarkable that a product that has no redeeming characteristics and little consumer value is accepted in the marketplace. Yet despite extensive negative advertising and severe restrictions on their use, cigarettes have not disappeared from the market.* }

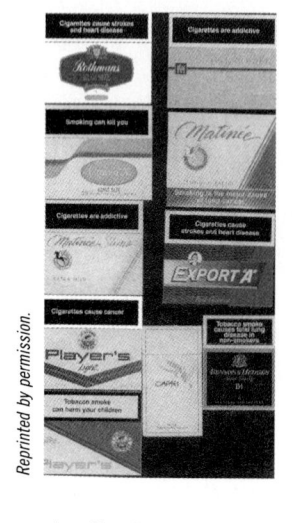

The distribution and sale of tobacco is regulated at all government levels —federal, provincial, and municipal. Like all regulated products, tobacco is heavily taxed. This presents governments with a serious dilemma, because the taxes represent a source of significant revenue while being designed to discourage consumption. The taxes seem as habit-forming for governments as cigarettes are for consumers. However, high taxes can only work to discourage consumption if consumers have no recourse in the marketplace. In 1994, the federal government actually lowered tax rates to discourage the business of cigarette smuggling in Canada. Cigarettes produced in Canada and exported into the United States were returning to Canada illegally, giving smugglers a fine profit, smokers a good deal, and the government reduced revenues coupled with the increased costs of trying to enforce customs regulations. Non-smoker groups and parents were upset because the cheaper cigarettes made them more readily affordable by teenagers, who are extremely vulnerable to picking up the habit.

Tobacco producers and distributors seem to be faced with an ethical situation with a clear resolution. They knowingly produce and sell a product which appears to be harmful to its users. The clear course of action for most firms who find they produce and sell a product which has harmful effects is to withdraw this product from the marketplace. However, the tobacco firms continue to distribute and sell their product. Why? Simply stated, the product is legal and in demand by consumers. Tobacco's harmful effects are still denied by the tobacco industry and have yet to be established in a court of law. Still, why haven't tobacco producers withdrawn the product based on the current evidence of harm (sufficient enough to justify product warnings in Ontario such as "Smoking can kill you," and "Smoking is dangerous to unborn children")? The problem is, the tobacco industry is essentially a single-product business and market withdrawal means the end of the industry, with all of its economic repercussions.

The tobacco industry has not been totally irresponsible. In 1972, Canadian tobacco firms voluntarily withdrew their advertising from broadcast media (radio and television), which have the greatest impact on younger people. The tobacco firms continued to advertise in the print and outdoor media and by sponsoring special events. However, in 1988 the federal government passed the Tobacco Products Control Act, which had a blanket prohibition on the advertising of any tobacco product whatsoever. The purpose of the law was to protect Canadians from the health risks associated with tobacco use. The prohibition of advertising was intended to prevent the tobacco industry from persuading people to use tobacco products. The tobacco industry felt the law was stifling the ability of manufacturers to compete on a brand basis and as such was a threat to their freedom of expression. As such they chose to challenge the Tobacco Products Control Act in court.

On Sept 21, 1995 the Supreme Court of Canada struck down the Tobacco Products Control Act as being in contravention of Canada's Charter of Rights and Freedoms. Bans on freedom of expression are only acceptable under the charter if they are reasonable and are so justified. The general opinion was that the degree to which tobacco advertising was informational was being unduly restricted and that preventing the dissemination of information was an unacceptable outcome of the legislation.

Now what do the tobacco firms do with their court victory? During the 1960s tobacco advertising and promotion amounted to almost $100 million, and prior to the Tobacco Products Control Act in 1988 the spending of the three largest Canadian tobacco companies was about $80 million. After the passing of the Tobacco Products Control Act the tobacco companies maintained some awareness of their products through sponsorship programs. The future promises to be interesting. The tobacco companies have been given free reign to advertise but the sentiments of the non-smoking majority of the population has prompted the government to prepare new regulations to curtail the tobacco companies. The Non-Smokers' Rights Association feels that tobacco should be subject to the Hazardous Products Act, and its marketing fall completely under government control.

For their part, the tobacco companies have not rushed to start advertising again. They claim they merely want the right to compete among themselves for existing tobacco customers. This does not seem unethical but it hardly seems possible to target smokers with promotional appeals that do not reach non-smokers.

The ethical standards of the media will also be put to the test: will they accept tobacco advertising again given public sentiment and the potential that the revenue might be short-lived? All in all, the tobacco industry presents marketers with a great many issues associated with business ethics and social responsibility. Should ethical conduct be mandated by the government through regulation? Or should self-regulation by businesses be the norm? Or is it consumer sovereignty that should dictate standards? Smokers and non-smokers have rights alike. If a consumer wants a product and will use it responsibly so that no one else will come to harm, shouldn't it be available?[1]

In this chapter, we will study several issues relating to the interaction of marketing with society as a whole, as well as with consumers. We will also show how ethics and marketing are interwoven.

Overview

Individually (at the company level) and collectively (at the industry level), the activities involved with marketing goods, services, organizations, people, places, and ideas can strongly affect society. They have the potential for both positive and negative consequences for such things as:

Marketing can have both a positive and a negative impact on society.

- The quality of life (standard of living).
- Natural resources, the landscape, and environmental pollution.
- Consumer expectations and satisfaction with goods and services.
- Consumer choice.
- Innovation.
- Product design and safety.
- Product durability.
- Product and distribution costs.
- Product availability.
- Communications with consumers.
- Final prices.
- Competition.
- Employment.
- Deceptive actions.

In Canada and many other highly industrialized nations, marketing practices have made a wide variety of goods and services available at relatively low prices and in convenient locations. At the same time, the relative lack of modern marketing practices in Eastern Europe, Africa, and other parts of the world have often led to fewer product choices, higher prices, and less convenient shopping locations. For example:

> Developments in Russia, its former republics, and other Eastern European nations clearly indicate that the lack of basic possessions (appliances, electrical goods, autos, and so on) has contributed greatly to the high level of dissatisfaction among citizens. In many developing nations, citizens have been viewed as simply producers of infrastructure, heavy industry, and public housing, while citizens as consumers have been ignored.[2]

---

[1] Laura Medcalf and Andrea Haman "After The Ad Ban," *Marketing Magazine* (October 2, 1995), pp. 1,4; Bob Reaume, "Reviewing the Big Picture," *Marketing Magazine* (October 9, 1995), p. 20; Andrea Haman, "Groups Want Tougher Tobacco Measures," *Marketing Magazine* (October 16, 1995), p. 4; and Eric Swetsky, "Through the Smoke," *Marketing Magazine* (November 27, 1995), p. 14.

[2] Orose Leelakulthanit, Ralph Day, and Rockney Walters, "Investigating the Relationship Between Marketing and Overall Satisfaction with Life in a Developing Country," *Journal of Macromarketing*, Vol. 11 (Spring 1991), p. 19.

Yet, even in Canada and other nations where marketing is quite advanced, marketing acts can create unrealistic consumer expectations, result in costly minor product-design changes, and adversely affect the environment. Thus, people's perceptions of marketing are mixed, at best. Over the years, studies have shown that many people feel cheated in their purchases due to deception, the lack of proper information, high-pressure sales pitches, and other tactics. Consumers may also believe they are being cheated when prices are increased. Waiting in store lines and poor customer service are two more key areas of consumer unhappiness.

Firms need to realize that consumer displeasure is not always made known to them. Only a small percentage of disgruntled consumers take time to voice their complaints. However, few dissatisfied customers who do not complain will buy a product again. In contrast, many who complain and have their complaints resolved do buy again:

> A gripe from a customer gives a firm the chance to retain that business. Solving a complaint can mean holding on not only to that customer, but also to the 11 or 12 others the customer will likely tell about a negative experience. "If we have a customer who's not happy, other prospective customers hear about it. Bad news is like gossip. It travels quickly because it's a little juicier and people seem to remember it more," says David Heppe, sales and marketing manager of a medical-equipment maker.[3]

In this chapter, the discussion is broken into three broad areas: *social responsibility*—which deals with issues concerning the general public and the environment, employees, channel members, shareholders, and competitors; *ethics*—which entails firms deciding upon and doing what is morally correct with regard to society and individual consumers; and *consumerism*—which focuses on the rights of consumers.

Social Responsibility

Social responsibility *aids society. The* **socioecological view of marketing** *considers voluntary and involuntary consumers.*

Social responsibility involves a concern for "the consequences of a person's or firm's acts as they might affect the interests of others."[4] Corporate social responsibility means weighing the impact of company actions and behaving in a way that balances short-term profit needs with long-term societal needs. This calls both for firms to be accountable to society and for consumers to act responsibly— for example, disposing of trash properly, wearing seat belts, not driving after drinking, and not being abusive to salespeople. See Figure 5-1.

From a marketing perspective, social responsibility also encompasses the **socioecological view of marketing**. According to this view, firms, their customers, and others should consider all the stages in a product's life span in developing, selling, purchasing, using, and disposing of that product. And the interests of everyone affected by a good's or service's use, including the involuntary consumers who must share the consequences of someone else's behaviour, should be weighed. For example, how much of a scarce resource should a firm use in making a product? What should be the rights and responsibilities of smokers and nonsmokers (as involuntary consumers) to one another?

As one observer noted:

> In marketing, much debate has centred on the role and scope of marketing in society, and particularly marketing's role in the quality of life. A basic premise of societal marketing, as a philosophy guiding marketing efforts, is the creation of consumer satisfaction of particular consumer segments in society with the minimal social cost to society. In other words, marketers guide the development of goods and services that meet certain needs of consumer groups in a manner that may not tax other publics through pollution, product hazards, environmental clutter, energy depletion, etc.[5]

---

[3]Weld F. Royal, "Cashing in on Complaints," *Sales & Marketing Management* (May 1995), p. 88.
[4]Peter D. Bennett (Ed.), *Dictionary of Marketing Terms*, Second Edition (Chicago: American Marketing Association, 1995), p. 267.
[5]Joseph Sirgy, "Can Business and Government Help Balance the Quality of Life of Workers and Consumers?", *Journal of Business Research*, Vol. 22 (June 1991), p. 332.

FIGURE 5-1
A Socially Responsible Ad
Reprinted by permission of Joseph E. Seagram & Sons, Inc.

To respond to the socioecological view of marketing, many firms are now applying a concept known as "design for disassembly" (DFD)—whereby their products are designed to be disassembled in a more environmentally friendly manner once they have outlived their usefulness. With DFD, firms use fewer parts, less materials, snap-fits instead of screws, and more recycled materials. The pioneer DFD product was BMW's Z1 limited-production two-seat roadster (see Figure 5-2). It had an all-plastic exterior that could be removed from the metal chassis in 20 minutes. All major "skin" components—doors, bumpers, and panels (front, rear, and side)—were made of recyclable plastic. Among the current worldwide crop of DFD products are Siemens coffee pots, Caterpillar tractors, Xerox copiers, Kodak cameras, Hewlett-Packard workstations, BMW 3 Series autos, IBM PCs, and Northern Telecom phones.[6]

There are times when social responsibility poses dilemmas for firms and/or their customers because popular goods and services have potentially adverse effects on consumer or societal well-being. Examples of items that offer such dilemmas are tobacco products, no-return beverage containers, food with high taste appeal but low nutritional content, crash diet plans, and liquor.

Until the 1960s, it was generally felt that marketing's role was limited to satisfying customers and generating profits. Such resources as air, water, and energy were seen as limitless. Responsibility to the general public was rarely considered. Many firms now realize

NORTHERN TELECOM
www.nortel.com/

---
[6]Gene Bylinsky, "Manufacturing for Reuse," *Fortune* (February 6, 1995), pp. 102–112.

FIGURE 5-2
BMW's "Design for Disassembly"
Reprinted by permission.

WEYERHAUSER CANADA
www.saic.com/fed/uscompanies/labor/n_z/Weyerhaeuser_Company.html

they should be responsive to the general public and the environment, employees, channel members, shareholders, and competitors—as well as customers. Table 5–1 shows how marketing can be socially responsible in these areas.

This is how Weyerhauser, the forest products firm, views its societal role:

Our [business] customers expect: Products that consistently satisfy their performance needs. Dependability. Quality assurance, responsive service, and timely delivery—every time. Innovative, value-adding solutions. Suppliers that meet their own customers' standards of environmental responsibility and continuous improvement. *Our employees expect*: A safe work environment. To be respected, valued, rewarded, and listened to. To have the authority to set goals and use their skills to satisfy the customer. To be part of a winning team. To receive and give feedback. To work for a company that is ethical, well-managed, and competitive. *Our communities expect*: Forests to last forever. Clean air and water. Industry support for local jobs. Conservation of precious resources. Protection of fish, wildlife, and unique and special places. Economically viable communities. Affordable housing. Elimination of waste. Good corporate citizenship. *Our shareholders expect*: Continued management focus on creating shareholder value. Consistent improvement in operating performance. Prudent capital expenditures. A clear understanding of the company's plans and direction for the future. Clear, concise, meaningful information about the company.[7]

Company and consumer activities have a significant impact on natural resources, the landscape, pollution, and planned obsolescence. These areas are discussed next.

Natural Resources

Today, we are aware that our global supply of natural resources is not unlimited. Both consumer behaviour and marketing practices have contributed to some resource shortages: "The 25 per cent of the world population in industrialized nations consumes 70 per cent of the world's resources that are used annually. As developing nations boost economic growth, demand will skyrocket."[8]

Nonetheless, resource waste goes on. Canadians annually throw out 1400 pounds of trash per person. This includes large amounts of paper, food, yard waste, aluminium, glass, plastic, tires, appliances, copper, furniture, and clothing. How do other nations compare? Americans discard 1600 pounds of trash per person, the Japanese 900 pounds, the Germans

---

[7] *Weyerhaeuser 1994 Annual Report.*
[8] Emily T. Smith, "Growth Vs. Environment," *Business Week* (May 11, 1992), p. 66.

Table 5-1
Illustrations of Socially Responsible Marketing Practices

Regarding the General Public and the Environment
Community involvement
Contributions to nonprofit organizations
Hiring hard-core unemployed
Product recycling
Eliminating offensive signs and billboards
Properly disposing of waste materials
Using goods and services requiring low levels of environmental resources

Regarding Employees
Ample internal communications
Employee input into decisions
Employee training about social issues and appropriate responses to them
No reprisals against employees who uncover questionable company policies
Recognizing socially responsible employees

Regarding Channel Members
Honouring both verbal and written commitments
Fairly distributing scarce goods and services
Accepting reasonable requests by channel members
Encouraging channel members to act responsibly
No coercion of channel members
Cooperative programs addressed to the general public and the environment

Regarding Shareholders
Honest reporting and financial disclosure
Publicity about company activities
Shareholder participation in setting socially responsible policy
Explaining social issues affecting the company
Earning a responsible profit

Regarding Competitors
Adhering to high standards of performance
Avoiding illegal or unethical acts to hinder competitors
Cooperative programs for the general public and environment
Avoiding actions that would lead competitors to waste resources

---

825 pounds, the British 800 pounds, and the French 675 pounds. In the less-developed Ivory Coast, about 400 pounds per person are discarded.[9] Sadly, Canada and the United States, having only 5 per cent of the world's population, generate one-half of the world's trash.

Combined, Canadians and Americans create 416 million tonnes of garbage (a little more than 50 per cent of which comes from business and industry) and 186 million tonnes of hazardous wastes and spend about $145 billion each year on garbage collection and disposal to manage this waste. Despite the ambitious use of recycling programs by almost every Canadian municipality there is a long way to go to rival the formal recycling

---

[9]Ferdinand Protzman, "Garbage," *New York Times* (July 12, 1992), Section 3, p. 1; and *Statistical Abstract of the United States 1995* (Washington, D.C.: U.S. Bureau of the Census, 1995).

Resource depletion can be slowed by reducing consumption, improving efficiency, limiting disposables, and lengthening products' lives.

program in Germany, where 80 per cent of all packaging materials—from aluminium to paper—must be recycled.[10]

The depletion of natural resources can be reduced if the consumption of scarce materials is lessened and more efficient alternatives are chosen; fewer disposable items—such as soda cans, pens, and cigarette lighters—are bought; products are given longer life spans; and styles are changed less frequently. Convenient recycling and repair facilities, better trade-in arrangements, and simpler packaging can also contribute to more efficient resource use.

Progressive actions require cooperation among business, shareholders, government, employees, the general public, consumers, and others. They also involve changes in lifestyles and corporate ingenuity:

> This is perhaps the ultimate recycling system: a popcorn bag becomes a seat belt, a seat belt becomes a shirt, a shirt becomes a sheet of packaging film, the packaging film becomes a videotape, the videotape becomes an X-ray, and (after many more metamorphoses) may become a popcorn bag again.[11]

The Landscape

Garbage dumps, discarded beverage containers, and unsightly billboards are examples of items marring the landscape. In Canada, about two-thirds of discarded materials are disposed of in dumps and landfills. But currently, many communities are not allowing new dumps and landfills, existing ones are closing for environmental reasons, and recycling efforts are being stepped up at existing facilities. In several areas of Europe and Japan, landfills are already at capacity—hence, these regions have a greater interest in recycling and incineration.[12]

Dumps and littering have become major factors in marring the landscape. Various communities have enacted rules to lessen them.

At one time, virtually all beverage containers were recycled. Then, no-return bottles and cans were developed; and littering at roadsides and other areas became a major problem. To reduce litter, most beverage containers are designed for recycling or reuse and municipal recycling programs are widespread through provincial support and encouragement. Still, aside from enforcement of littering laws, consumers are ultimately responsible for container disposal. The labour and bottle-sorting costs associated with refillable container returns leads to higher beverage prices and consumers have not been enthusiastic about purchasing beverages in these containers when given the choice of one-way packaging.

At one time the Ontario Government asked soft drink manufacturers to maintain a minimum of 30 per cent of their volume in refillable packaging. Despite offering discounts on these types of containers, the producers were unable to meet these targets or even come close to being profitable. As such, the Ontario government backed off on legislating any packaging requirements and turned their attention to consumer education and the aggressive use of recycling programs. Other ways to reduce the marring of the landscape include limits or bans on billboards and roadside signs, fines for littering, and better trade-ins for autos and appliances. Neighbourhood associations, merchant self-regulation, area planning and zoning, and consumer education can also help. Keeping the landscape attractive is a cooperative effort. A merchant cleanup patrol cannot overcome pedestrians who throw litter on the street rather than in waste baskets.

---

[10]Mark Stevenson, "Waste Not," *Canadian Business* (January 1994) pp. 20–26; David Fischer, "Turning Trash into Cash," *U.S. New & World Report* (July 17, 1995), p. 43; Jeff Bailey, "Curbside Recycling Comforts the Soul, But Benefits Are Scarce," *Wall Street Journal* (January 19, 1995), pp. A1, A8; "A Guilt-Free Guide to Garbage," *Consumer Reports* (February 1994), pp. 91–113; and Marilyn Stern, "Is This the Ultimate in Recycling?" *Across the Board* (May 1993), pp. 28–31.

[11]*DuPont 1994 Annual Report.*

[12]*Statistical Abstract of the United States 1995*; George C. Lodge and Jeffrey F. Rayport, "Knee-Deep and Rising: America's Recycling Costs," *Harvard Business Review*, Vol. 69 (September–October 1991), pp. 128–139; and Subrata N. Chakravarty, "Dean Buntrock's Green Machine," *Forbes* (August 2, 1993), pp. 96–100.

Environmental Pollution

Environment Canada is the major federal government agency involved with pollution; a number of provincial environment ministries and departments are also active in this area. Numerous other nations have their own government agencies to deal with this issue.

Environmental pollution can be generated by spray-can propellants, ocean dumping of industrial waste, lead from gasoline and paint, pesticides, factory emissions, improper disposal of garbage, and other pollutants. As one observer noted:

> To those doubting the wisdom of pollution control—those who believe there is a conflict between economic growth and environmental protection—let them see the Vistula River in Poland; over 80 per cent is so corrosive that it is useless for even cooling machinery. Let them see sulphur dioxide levels in Krakow, so high that 500-year-old monuments have crumbled in just 40 years. Pollution is not an economic shortcut. In the long run, it will only drain economies and make living conditions unproductive.[14]

While greater attention is being paid to it, environmental pollution will be a big challenge for the foreseeable future. Government and industry in Canada, the United States, Western Europe, and Japan spend a combined total of more than $300 billion annually on environmental protection. In addition, anti-pollution expenditures have gone up dramatically in several less-developed nations in Latin America, Asia, and Africa.

Both government and business actions are needed to reduce dangerous environmental pollution.

Among the voluntary activities of companies and associations are:

- New PCs, printers, monitors, and other devices automatically power down when not in use to reduce air pollution and conserve energy (see Figure 5-3).
- Western Canada's Unique Tire Recycling Inc. has developed a method to recycle tires, a waste product which many landfills refuse to accept.
- 3M devotes 15 per cent of its overall research-and-development budget to projects involving environmental protection.
- Japan's Ebara Corporation uses its own technology to remove harmful sulphur dioxides and nitrogen oxides from power plants more efficiently.
- A number of firms have joined together to form the Global Environmental Management Initiative (GEMI), with the goal of fostering an exchange of information about environmental protection programs.
- Sun Co., the parent of Sunoco, was the first big firm to sign the Coalition for Environmentally Responsible Economies (CERES) principles—which were drawn up by the National Wildlife Federation, among others.[15]

3M
www.mmm.com/

Planned Obsolescence

Planned obsolescence is a marketing practice that capitalizes on short-run material wearout, style changes, and functional product changes.

In material planned obsolescence, firms choose materials and components that are subject to comparatively early breakage, wear, rot, or corrosion. For example, the makers of disposable lighters and razors use this form of planned obsolescence in a constructive manner by offering inexpensive, short-life, convenient products. However, there is growing resistance to material planned obsolescence because of its effects on natural resources and the landscape.

Planned obsolescence *can involve materials, styles, and functions.*

---

[14] William K. Reilly, "Environment, Inc.," *Business Horizons*, Vol. 35 (March–April 1992), p. 9.

[15] Jerry Jasinowski, "Business Is America's Leading Environmentalist," *Christian Science Monitor* (April 21, 1995), p. 19; Bruce Headlam, "Rubber Baron," *Canadian Business* (December 1994), p. 146; Richard A. Westin, "Global Climate Change," *Columbia Journal of World Business*, Vol. 27 (Spring 1992), p. 82; Lee M. Thomas, "The Business Community and the Environment: An Important Partnership," *Business Horizons*, Vol. 35 (March–April 1992), p. 24; and Faye Rice, "Who Scores Best on the Environment," *Fortune* (July 26, 1993), pp. 114–118.

FIGURE 5-3
"Powering Down"
Reprinted by permission.

In style planned obsolescence, a firm makes minor changes to differentiate this year's offering from last year's. Since some people are style-conscious, they are willing to discard old items while they are still functional so as to acquire new ones with more status. This is common with fashion items and cars.

With functional planned obsolescence, a firm introduces new product features or improvements to generate consumer dissatisfaction with currently owned products. Sometimes, features or improvements may have been withheld from an earlier model to gain faster repurchases. A style change may accompany a functional change to raise consumer awareness of a "new" product. This form of planned obsolescence occurs most often with high-tech items such as computers.

Marketers reply to criticisms in this fashion: Planned obsolescence is a response to people's desires and is not coercive; without product turnover, people would be disenchanted by the lack of choices; consumers like disposable items and often discard them before they lose their effectiveness; firms use materials that hold down prices; and competition requires firms to offer the best products possible and not hold back improvements. A number of firms have enacted innovative strategies with regard to planned obsolescence. For example, Kodak and Fuji have programs for recycling their single-use disposable cameras, after people take them to photo processing labs. Canon has a factory in China that reconditions and refills used copier cartridges. SKF of Sweden is a worldwide bearings maker; to increase the life of its products, it has added more preventative maintenance services.

The Benefits and Costs of Social Responsibility

Social responsibility has benefits as well as costs; these need to be balanced.

Socially responsible actions have both benefits and costs. Among the benefits are improved worker and public health, as reflected in fewer and less severe accidents, longer life spans, and less disease; cleaner air; better resource use; economic growth; a better business image; an educated public; government cooperation; an attractive, safe environment; an enhanced standard of living; and self-satisfaction for the firm. Many of these benefits cannot be quantified. Nonetheless, expectations are that Canadian anti-pollution legislation and other nations' laws (e.g. the U.S. Clean Air Act) will ultimately save thousands of lives each year, protect food crops, reduce medical costs, and lead to clearer skies.

Although some social-responsibility expenditures are borne by a broad cross-section of firms and the general public (through taxes and higher product prices), the benefits of many environmental and other programs are enjoyed primarily by those living or working in affected areas. The costs of socially responsible actions can be high. For instance, the Canadian environmental industry accounted for $11 billion of business in 1994, employed 92 000 people and is growing at about 6 per cent per year. The industry is heavily driven by government regulation and the costs represent about 2.1 per cent of Canada's Gross Domestic Product.[16]

Various environmentally questionable products that are efficient have been greatly modified or removed from the marketplace, such as leaded gasoline. Because of various legal restrictions and fears of lawsuits, new-product planning tends to be more conservative; and resources are often allotted to prevention rather than invention. Furthermore, trade-offs have to be made in determining which programs are more deserving of funding. Figure 5-4 summarizes the benefits and costs of social responsibility.

For socially responsible efforts to be effective, all parties must partake in the process—sharing benefits and costs. This means business, consumers, government, channel members, and others. The rest of the 1990s promises to see the further emergence of **green marketing**, whereby the goods and services sold, and the marketing practices involved in their sale, take into account environmental ramifications for society as a whole. To succeed in green marketing, firms will have to take care not to mislead consumers or create unrealistic expectations about their products' "green" features.

Green marketing *efforts will expand during this decade.*

Benefits
Worker and public health
Cleaner air
Efficient use of resources
Economic growth
Improved business image
Government cooperation
Public education
Attractive environment
Better standard of living
Self-satisfaction of firm

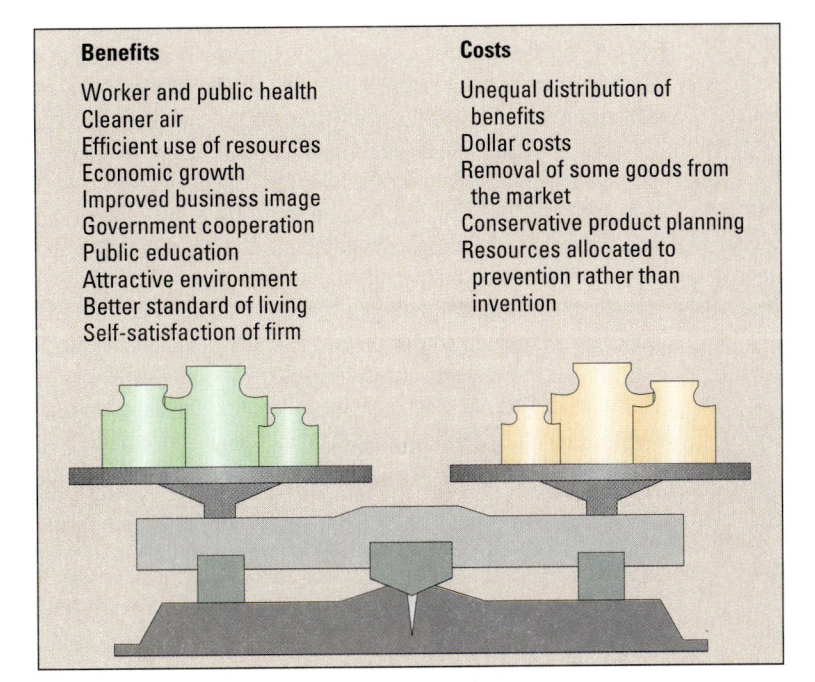

Costs
Unequal distribution of benefits
Dollar costs
Removal of some goods from the market
Conservative product planning
Resources allocated to prevention rather than invention

FIGURE 5-4
The Benefits and Costs of Social Responsibility

---

[16]"The Big Clean-Up: Once Dismissed as More of a Movement Than a Business, the Fast-Growing Environmental Industry Is Cashing In On a Multibillion-dollar Market" *Report on Business Magazine*, Vol.11 (November 1994), pp. 45–56.

Ethics AND TODAY'S MARKETER

How Much Should Regulations Be Regulated?

In recent years, this question has been asked repeatedly: "How much government regulation is enough?"

In 1993 the Ontario Department of the Environment issued regulations requiring a 40 per cent reduction of the maximum allowable discharge of organochlorine compounds by 1996. Ontario pulp and paper makers will have to reduce the compounds by 70 per cent by the year 2000. The changes were expected to cost industry from $600 million to $1.2 billion and covered 27 pulp and paper mills, eight of which used chlorine. The Ontario Provincial Government does not plan a total ban on chlorine but incentives will be offered to eliminate its use. The regulations will also require cuts in suspended solids in pulp-mill effluent, reduction in oxygen-depleting biological waste, and several other discharge limits. Ontario's rules are not as strict as British Columbia's, where the forest industry must eliminate chlorine use by 2002.

WC Wood (Guelph, Ontario) may be forced to move production south of the border or out of Ontario because it has exceeded provincial regulations for chlorofluorocarbons (CFCs), which erode the ozone layer. WC Wood took over the production of appliances from several companies that closed recently. Ontario's Environment Minister is sympathetic to the company's situation and is looking at alternatives to deal with the situation and keep the company from moving.

In Quebec, six business groups united to oppose Quebec legislation setting up an environmental protection office to keep watch on pollution. Legislators wanted to give more autonomy and authority to the new body which was being created to investigate companies breaking pollution laws. The Quebec Manufacturers Association stated that businesses could not understand how the new protection office would work. Opposition to the bill comes from both the Quebec Mining Association and the Quebec Association of Forest Industries, who believe it would create two competing bureaucracies which would further complicate environmental regulation.

Critics of government regulation feel that many rules are too costly, have little positive effect on society, inhibit firms from being innovative, and lead to more goods and services being produced in foreign markets. Some even suggest that a strict cost-benefit analysis be conducted before any new rules are enacted. This would ensure that "regulations do more good than harm."

On the other side, there are numerous strong advocates of government regulations. They are quite concerned that important regulations affecting deceptive business practices, marketplace competition, drinking-water purity, food safety, and worker health may be dropped as a result of anti-regulation forces. Such actions could have long-term detrimental affects on consumer and worker quality of life.

What do you think about limiting Canadian government regulations? Why?

Sources: Based on material in Linda Grant, "Shutting Down the Regulatory Machine," *U.S. News & World Report* (February 13, 1995), pp. 70–72. "Ontario Toughening Organochlorine Rules" *Globe & Mail*, Metro edition (February 2, 1993), p. B7; "Ozone rules may cause plant to move (WC Wood Co Ltd)," *Globe & Mail*, Metro edition (August 1, 1991), p. B3; "Pollution Office Opposed: Quebec Firms Say It's Confusing," *Globe & Mail*, Metro edition (May 28, 1992), p. B3.

Ethics

In any marketing situation, **ethical behaviour** based on honest and proper conduct ("what is right" and "what is wrong") should be followed. This applies both to situations involving company actions that affect the general public, employees, channel members, shareholders, and/or competitors and to situations involving company dealings with consumers.

Figure 5-5 outlines an ethical decision/action process—with a moral decision structure, decision-maker traits, situational factors, and outcomes. The preeminent organization for marketing in Canada and the United States is the American Marketing Association, which provides information and guidelines for managers who practice marketing. Figure 5-6 shows the code of ethics of the American Marketing Association.

Of particular importance in the study of ethics are answers to these two questions: How do people determine whether an act is ethical or unethical? Why do they act ethically or unethically?[17] People determine whether given actions are ethical or not through their upbringing, education, job environment, lifelong experiences, and others' responses to their behaviour. In addition, people may apply their own cognitive reasoning skills to decide what is morally acceptable. People act ethically or unethically based on their expectations of the rewards or punishments—financial, social, and so forth—flowing from their actions. They consider both the magnitude of the rewards or punishments (such as the size of a raise or the maximum fine that could be imposed on a company) and the likelihood of their occurrence (such as the probability of getting a large raise or having a large fine imposed on the firm).

Ethical behaviour *involves honest and proper conduct.*

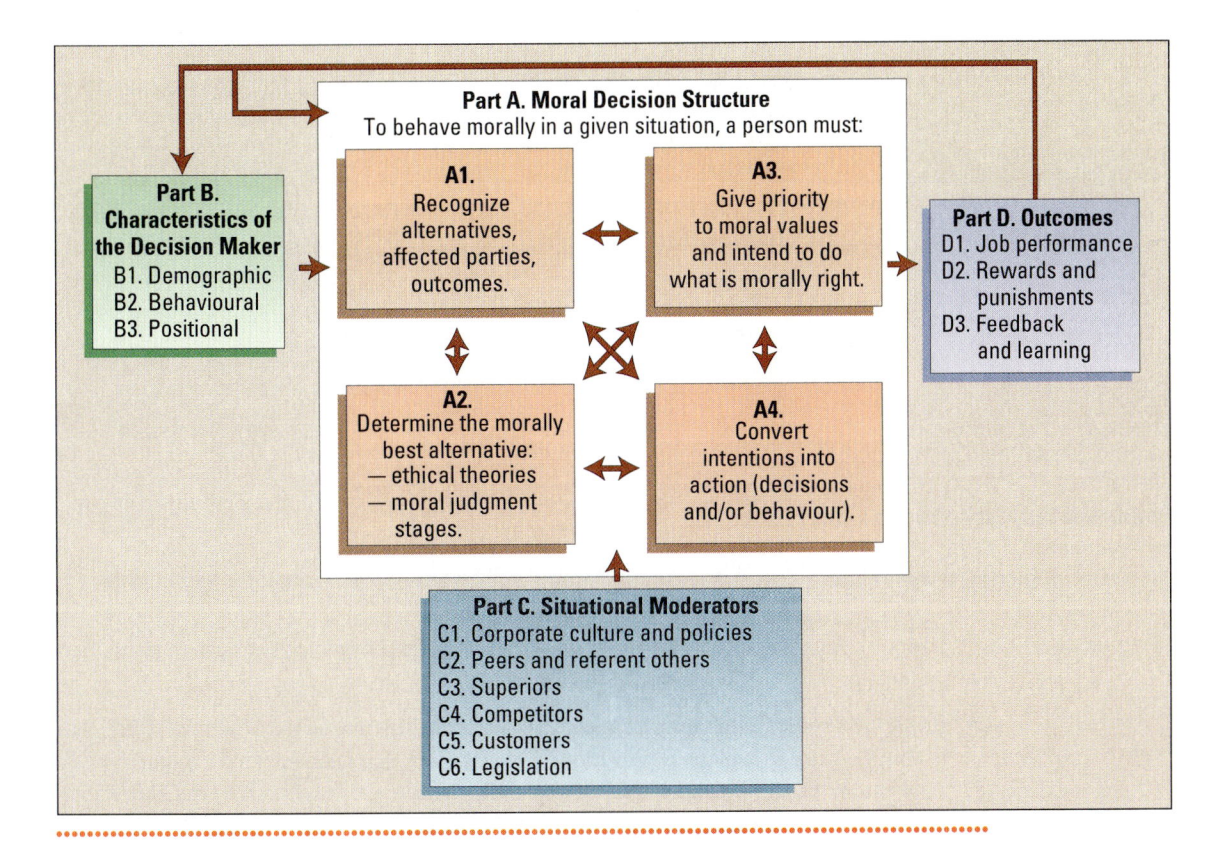

Part A. Moral Decision Structure
To behave morally in a given situation, a person must:

- **A1.** Recognize alternatives, affected parties, outcomes.
- **A2.** Determine the morally best alternative:
  — ethical theories
  — moral judgment stages.
- **A3.** Give priority to moral values and intend to do what is morally right.
- **A4.** Convert intentions into action (decisions and/or behaviour).

Part B. Characteristics of the Decision Maker
B1. Demographic
B2. Behavioural
B3. Positional

Part C. Situational Moderators
C1. Corporate culture and policies
C2. Peers and referent others
C3. Superiors
C4. Competitors
C5. Customers
C6. Legislation

Part D. Outcomes
D1. Job performance
D2. Rewards and punishments
D3. Feedback and learning

FIGURE 5-5
An Ethical Decision/Action Process

Source: Thomas R. Wotruba, "A Comprehensive Framework for the Analysis of Ethical Behavior, with a Focus on Sales Organizations," *Journal of Personal Selling & Sales Management*, Vol. 10 (Spring 1990), p. 31. *Reprinted by permission.*

---

[17] Shelby D. Hunt, "Foundations of the Hunt-Vitell Theory of Ethics," presented at the 1995 AMA Faculty Consortium on Ethics and Social Responsibility in Marketing" (Hempstead, N.Y.: Hofstra University).

CODE OF ETHICS
Members of the American Marketing Association (AMA) are committed to ethical professional conduct. They have joined together in subscribing to this Code of Ethics embracing the following topics:

Responsibilities of the Marketer
Marketers must accept responsibility for the consequence of their activities and make every effort to ensure that their decisions, recommendations, and actions function to identify, serve, and satisfy all relevant publics: customers, organizations and society.

Marketers' professional conduct must be guided by:

1. The basic rule of professional ethics: not knowingly to do harm;
2. The adherence to all applicable laws and regulations;
3. The accurate representation of their education, training and experience; and
4. The active support, practice and promotion of this Code of Ethics.

Honesty and Fairness
Marketers shall uphold and advance the integrity, honor, and dignity of the marketing profession by:

1. Being honest in serving customers, clients, employees, suppliers, distributors and the public;
2. Not knowingly participating in conflict of interest without prior notice to all parties involved; and
3. Establishing equitable fee schedules including the payment or receipt of usual, customary and/or legal compensation or marketing exchanges.

Rights and Duties of Parties in the Marketing Exchange Process
Participants in the marketing exchange process should be able to expect that:

1. Products and services offered are safe and fit for their intended uses;
2. Communications about offered products and services are not deceptive;
3. All parties intend to discharge their obligations, financial and otherwise, in good faith; and
4. Appropriate internal methods exist for equitable adjustment and/or redress of grievances concerning purchases.

It is understood that the above would include, but is not limited to, the following responsibilities of the marketer:

In the area of product development and management,
- disclosure of all substantial risks associated with product or service usage;
- identification of any product component substitution that might materially change the product or impact on the buyer's purchase decision;
- identification of extra-cost added features.

In the area of promotions,
- avoidance of false and misleading advertising;
- rejection of high pressure manipulation.
- avoidance of sales promotions that use deception or manipulation.

In the area of distribution,
- not manipulating the availability of a product for purpose of exploitation;
- not using coercion in the marketing channel;
- not exerting undue influence over the reseller's choice to handle the product.

In the area of pricing,
- not engaging in price fixing;
- not practicing predatory pricing;
- disclosing the full price associated with any purchase.

In the area of marketing research,
- prohibiting selling or fund raising under the guise of conducting research;
- maintaining research integrity by avoiding misrepresentation and omission of pertinent research data;
- treating outside clients and suppliers fairly.

Organizational Relationships
Marketers should be aware of how their behavior may influence or impact on the behvior of others in organizational relationships. They should not demand, encourage or apply coercion to obtain unethical behavior in their relationships with others, such as employees, suppliers or customers:

1. Apply confidentiality and anonymity in professional relationships with regard to privileged information;
2. Meet their obligations and responsibilities in contracts and mutual agreements in a timely manner;
3. Avoid taking the work of others, in whole, or in part, and represent this work as their own or directly benefit from it without compensation or consent of the originator or owner;
4. Avoid manipulation to take advantage of situations to maximize personal welfare in a way that unfairly deprives or damages the organization of others.

Any AMA members found to be in violation of any provision of this Code of Ethics may have his or her Association membership suspended or revoked.

FIGURE 5-6
The American Marketing Association's Code of Ethics
Reprinted by permission.

Ethics theories range from egoism to value ethics.

Various ethical theories try to explain why people and organizations act in particular ways. Here are four of them, applied to marketing:

- *Egoism*—a theory asserting that individuals act exclusively in their own self-interest. Example: A product manager postpones investing in improvements for a mature product because he or she expects to be promoted within the next six months and wants to maximize short-term profits.

- *Utilitarianism*—a theory asserting that individual and organizational actions are proper only if these actions yield the greatest good for the most people (the highest net benefit). Example: A pharmaceutical company markets any Health Canada approved drug with some side effects as long as it helps more people combat a particular disease than the number affected by the (minor) side effect.

- *Duty-Based*—a theory asserting that the rightness of an action is not based on its consequences, but rather is based on the premise that certain actions are proper because they stem from basic obligations. Example: A supermarket chain sets below-average prices in a low-income area even thought this adversely affects company profits in that community.

- *Virtue Ethics*—a theory asserting that actions should be guided by an individual or organization seeking goodness and virtue ("living a good life"). Example: A virtuous company is totally truthful in its advertising, packaging, and selling efforts—and does not stoop to manipulative appeals to persuade customers.[18]

Ethical issues in marketing can generally be divided into two categories: process-related and product-related.[19] **Process-related ethical issues** involve "the unethical use of marketing strategies or tactics." Examples include bait-and-switch advertising, price fixing, selling products overseas that have been found unsafe in Canada, and bribing purchasing agents of large customers. **Product-related ethical issues** involve "the ethical appropriateness of marketing certain products." For example, as was discussed in the opening of the chapter, should tobacco products be marketed? More specifically, should cigarettes be sold? Should there be restrictions on their sales? Should cigarette ads be allowed? Should cigarette taxes be raised to discourage use? Should smoking be banned in offices, restaurants, and any other public places?

Marketers need to consider **process-related** *and* **product-related ethical issues**.

These comments sum up the complexity of many ethical issues:

> Some employees may believe unethical activity is in the company's best interest and is thus expected of them—or will at least be tolerated. Top management wants employees to be ethical and tells them so, but some people may not believe it, thinking instead that requests to be ethical are simply window dressing. Because of their loyalty to their company, they engage in unethical conduct. Some employees act unethically because they may believe this conduct is in their self-interest. Those who want to get ahead sometimes seek ways to distinguish themselves by outperforming others. Such employees may believe that unethical conduct is a way to improve their performance and is, thus, in their self-interest. Other employees may not always know they're doing something unethical. There certainly is a sense in which ethics is a matter of opinion—an art rather than a science. Where is the line between the sharp deal and the shady deal? Between profit maximization and social irresponsibility? Between clever advertising and fraud? These can sometimes be difficult questions for an employee to answer.[20]

Thus, to maintain the highest possible ethical conduct by employees, the senior executives in a firm must make a major commitment to ethics, communicate standards of conduct to every employee (perhaps via a written ethics code), reward ethical behaviour, and discourage unethical behaviour.

Next, ethics is examined from four vantage points: a business perspective, a consumer perspective, an international perspective, and a pedagogical perspective.

A Business Perspective

Most of the firms listed in the *Canadian Business 500* and in the U.S. *Fortune 500* have formal ethics codes. Some codes are general and, thus, similar to organizational mission statements; others are specific and operational. In contrast, French, British, and German firms are less apt to have formal codes; acceptable standards of behaviour are more implied. Why? According to one North American ethics expert: "Society guarantees people the right to determine their moral values and obligations, but it really doesn't offer guidelines on how to fulfil them. Thus, it depends less on roles and traditions and more on laws and formal statements of ethics."[21]

Many companies have ethics codes; some have implicit standards.

---

[18]Gene R. Laczniak and Patrick E. Murphy, *Ethical Marketing Decisions: The Higher Road* (Needham Heights, Mass.: Allyn & Bacon, 1993), pp. 28–42.

[19]Gene R. Laczniak, Robert F. Lusch, and William A. Strang, "Ethical Marketing: Perceptions of Economic Goods and Social Problems," *Journal of Macromarketing*, Vol. 1 (Spring 1981), p. 49.

[20]John Collins, "Why Bad Things Happen to Good Companies—And What Can Be Done," *Business Horizons*, Vol. 33 (November–December 1990), p. 18.

[21]Joanne B. Ciulla, "Why Is Business Talking About Ethics?: Reflections on Foreign Conversations," *California Management Review*, Vol. 34 (Fall 1991), pp. 73–76.

One of the most complex aspects of business ethics is how to decide what is ethical. To address this, the following scale was devised and tested with a variety of marketing personnel. The scale suggests that business people would make better decisions if they consider whether a specific marketing action (is):[22]

Fair ___ ___ ___ ___ ___ ___ ___	Unfair
Just ___ ___ ___ ___ ___ ___ ___	Unjust
Culturally Acceptable ___ ___ ___ ___ ___ ___ ___	Culturally Unacceptable
Violates an Unwritten Contract ___ ___ ___ ___ ___ ___ ___	Does Not Violate an Unwritten Contract
Traditionally Acceptable ___ ___ ___ ___ ___ ___ ___	Traditionally Unacceptable
Morally Right ___ ___ ___ ___ ___ ___ ___	Not Morally Right
Violates an Unspoken Promise ___ ___ ___ ___ ___ ___ ___	Does Not Violate an Unspoken Promise
Acceptable to My Family ___ ___ ___ ___ ___ ___ ___	Unacceptable to My Family

Cause-related marketing has good and bad points.

MARY KAY COSMETICS
www.marykay.com/

Cause-related marketing is a somewhat controversial practice. With it, profit-oriented firms contribute specific amounts to given nonprofit organizations for each consumer purchase of certain goods and services during a special promotion (such as sponsorship of a sport for the 1998 Winter Olympics). It has been used by such firms as Imperial Oil (Safe Kids Canada Campaign), Bell Canada (Kids Help Phone) and Kellogg Canada Inc. (Muscular Dystrophy Association of Canada). Advocates feel cause-related marketing stimulates direct and indirect contributions and benefits the images of both the profit-oriented firms and the nonprofit institutions involved they support. Critics feel there is too much commercialism on the part of nonprofit groups and implicit endorsements for sponsor products.

- According to a recent survey, CEOs of large business firms overwhelmingly feel it is always wrong to use misleading advertising or labelling, sell goods and services that have poor safety, dump banned or flawed products in foreign markets, and cause environmental harm.

- Mary Kay Cosmetics was one of the first companies to halt product testing on animals. As its vice-chairperson noted, "Our goal was to take the high ground. The decision meant putting a hold on new products for a while, which meant lost sales. Ethical decision making, by its very nature, is relative—what will be the effect of our decision on others? Is the decision right, not only for us, but also for society? Ethical corporate conduct is not easy and can be costly, but I believe ethics is good business."

- Leasing of automobiles in Canada involves many intermediaries and hefty commission payments. This has led to excessive leasing costs which are hidden from consumers; sometimes these hidden costs are over 20 percentage points higher than personal bank loan rates. In fact, for vehicles with lower sticker prices, the Canadian Bankers Association found that leasing actually cost more, and interest rates of over 30 per cent were being charged on some contracts. Consumers were unable to detect or understand this fact because of the complexity of the leasing contracts. To respond to

---

[22]Eric Reidenbach, Donald P. Robin, and Lyndon Dawson, "An Application and Extension of a Multidimensional Ethics Scale to Selected Marketing Practices and Marketing Groups," *Journal of the Academy of Marketing Science*, Vol. 19 (Spring 1991), p. 84.

this issue, many Canadian car dealerships will provide customers with computer printouts comparing the costs of "leasing" versus "buying." This allows customers to determine the "real" costs of leasing.[23]

A Consumer Perspective

Just as businesses have a responsibility to act in an ethical and a societally oriented way, so do consumers. Their actions affect businesses, other consumers, the general public, and the environment. In marketing transactions, ethical standards can truly be maintained only if both sellers and buyers act in a mutually respectful, honest, fair, and responsible manner.

Consumers should act as ethically towards businesses as they expect to be treated by businesses.

Yet, especially with regard to broad societal issues, consumers may find it hard to decide what is acceptable. Daniel Yankelovich, an expert in the area, says a society goes through seven stages to form a consensus on major issues:

1. People begin to become aware of an issue.
2. They develop a sense of urgency about it.
3. They start exploring choices for dealing with the issue.
4. There is resistance to costs and trade-offs—leading to wishful thinking.
5. The pros and cons of alternatives are weighed.
6. People take a stand intellectually.
7. A responsible judgment is made morally and emotionally.[24]

In terms of consumer perceptions about whether specific activities on their part are proper, a large-scale study on ethical beliefs offers some interesting insights: First, people have a rather high level of ethical concern about some acts that could be done by consumers (with ethical concern measured as strongly agreeing—answer 1—or agreeing—answer 2—that given actions are wrong). See Table 5-2. Second, ethical perceptions are affected by how often consumers themselves engage in these actions, whether deceitful or fraudulent behaviour is involved, and the degree to which sellers are harmed. Third, the strongest ethical concerns belong to older people with lower levels of education and income; younger, better educated, and more affluent people have less concern.[25]

An International Perspective

Assessing ethical standards in an international setting is complex, due to several factors. First, different societies have their own views of acceptable behaviour regarding interpersonal conduct, communications, and business practices. Second, there may be misunderstandings due to linguistic differences. Third, in less-developed nations, there may be less concern for social and consumer issues than for improving the level of industrialization. Fourth, in their self-interest, governments in some nations may devise questionable rules to protect domestic firms. Fifth, executives are usually more aware of ethical standards in their home nations than in foreign ones. Sixth, international ethical disputes may be hard to mediate; under whose jurisdiction are disputes involving firms from separate nations?

Ethical decisions can be complicated on an international level.

Here are some views of the ethical challenges on the international level:

---

[23]Mark Stevenson, "What's In It For Me?", *Canadian Business* (December 1993) pp. 54–60; Jan Larson, "If You're Not Committed, Don't Bother," *American Demographics* (December 1994), pp. 16–17; Gene R. Laczniak, Marvin W. Berkowitz, Russell G. Booker, and James P. Hale, "The Ethics of Business: Improving or Deteriorating?" *Business Horizons*, Vol. 38 (January–February 1995), p. 43; Richard C. Bartlett, "Mary Kay's Foundation," *Journal of Business Strategy*, Vol. 16 (July–August 1995), p. 16; Jonathan Dahl, "Before You Use the Hotel Phone, Read This," *Wall Street Journal* (August 2, 1994), pp. B1, B4; and Phil Edmonston, *Lemon-Aid New Car Guide 1992*, (Toronto: Stoddart), pp. vi–vii.

[24]Daniel Yankelovich, "How Public Opinion Really Works," *Fortune* (October 5, 1992), p. 103.

[25]James A. Muncy and Scott J. Vitell, "Consumer Ethics: An Investigation of the Ethical Beliefs of the Final Consumer," *Journal of Business Research*, Vol. 24 (June 1992), pp. 297–311.

Table 5-2
Selected Consumer Beliefs About Their Own Ethical Behaviour

	STRONGLY BELIEVE IT IS WRONG 1	2	3	4	STRONGLY BELIEVE IT IS NOT WRONG 5
Changing price-tags on merchandise in a retail store	81%	16%	1%	0%	2%
Drinking a can of soda in a supermarket without paying for it	71%	28%	1%	0%	1%
Using a long-distance telephone access code that does not belong to you	65%	30%	3%	1%	1%
Reporting a lost item as "stolen" to an insurance company in order to collect the money	58%	34%	5%	2%	1%
Giving misleading price information to a clerk for an unpriced item	53%	42%	3%	1%	1%
Getting too much change and not saying anything	42%	45%	6%	5%	1%
Observing someone shoplifting and ignoring it	38%	43%	15%	4%	1%
Stretching the truth on an income-tax return	34%	41%	12%	10%	3%
Joining a record club just to get some free records without any intention of buying	29%	41%	13%	13%	4%
Using computer software or games you did not buy	12%	25%	39%	18%	6%
Returning merchandise after trying it and not liking it	8%	14%	15%	46%	16%
Taping a movie off the TV	4%	9%	20%	37%	30%

Note: There are some rounding errors in the above percentages.
Source: James A. Muncy and Scott J. Vitell, "Consumer Ethics: An Investigation of the Ethical Beliefs of the Final Consumer," *Journal of Business Research*, Vol. 24 (June 1992), p. 303. Reprinted by permission of Elsevier Science Publishing Company, Inc. Copyright (c) 1992.

- Business executives generally feel there are just minor differences in ethics as practised in Canada, the United States, and Northern Europe. However, there are "some departures" in ethical practices when doing business in Southern Europe—such as Italy and Spain—and a "tremendous" difference in the underdeveloped nations. With the latter, "it's difficult. You'll be tested constantly, and, at times, you'll think you've lost business."
- "The Japanese are a special case. Take gift giving. It is an important part of how they conduct themselves. There is little thought given to the idea: 'Give me the business and I'll give you a gift.'"
- "A kind of noblesse oblige (honour) still exists among the business classes in Canada, Great Britain, Australia, and perhaps Germany. Conversely, in the United States, where there is a less entrenched business group, the prevailing attitude is that you make it whatever way you can."
- Canadians (or any other non-Americans) who work for U.S.-owned multinationals or do business with U.S. firms should be aware that the United States has legislation governing moral business conduct outside the United States, in the form of the Foreign Corrupt Practices Act. This act prohibits improper sales tactics by U.S. firms in international markets and is applicable to any employee of the firm regardless of whether or not they are a U.S. citizen or a U.S. resident.[26]

[26]Andrew W. Singer, "Ethics: Are Standards Lower Overseas?" *Across the Board* (September 1991), pp. 31–34.

International Marketing in Action

Marketing in Russia and the U.S.: Understanding Russian and American Ethics

A four-quadrant matrix may be used to compare the ethical values of Russian and American business people:

- *Quadrant I*—Consists of practices viewed as ethical by both Russians and Americans. These include keeping one's word, maintaining trust, competing fairly, and receiving rewards that are commensurate with performance.
- *Quadrant II*—Consists of practices viewed as unethical by business people in both countries. These include gangsterism, racketeering and extortion; black market activity; price gouging; and refusing to pay bills.
- *Quadrant III*—Consists of practices viewed as ethical by Russians, but unethical by Americans. These include showing personal favouritism, making "grease" payments (to facilitate transactions), manipulating data, fixing prices, and ignoring "senseless" laws and regulations.
- *Quadrant IV*—Consists of practices viewed as ethical by Americans, but not by Russians. These include maximizing profits, high salary differentials between management and workers, employee layoffs, and whistle blowing (reporting poor company practices to others).

By understanding this matrix, Russian and American business people can acquire a better appreciation for each other's behaviour. Nonetheless, American firms doing business in Russia (and vice versa) must still decide whether Russian managers are accountable to Russian or American ethical standards.

As marketing manager for a Canadian firm selling cosmetics in Russia and the U.S., use the above information to devise an ethical code for both your U.S. and Russian operations.

Source: Based on material in Sheila M. Puffer and Daniel J. McCarthy, "Finding the Common Ground in Russian and American Business Ethics," *California Management Review,* Vol. 37 (Winter 1995), pp. 29–46.

Firms that market internationally need to keep three points in mind: One, *core business values* provide the foundation for worldwide ethics codes. Core values are company principles "that are so fundamental they will not be compromised" in any foreign markets. These include non-maleficence (to not knowingly do harm), promise-keeping, non-deception, and protection of societal and consumer rights. Two, *peripheral business values* are less important to the firm and may be adjusted to foreign markets. These relate to local customs in such areas as buyer-seller exchanges, selling practices, and so forth. Three, when possible, *ethnocentrism*—perceiving other countries' moral standards in terms of one's own country—must be avoided.[27]

The Teachability of Ethics

Given the impact of societal values, peer pressure, self-interest, personal ambitions, and fear of failure on people's sense of ethically acceptable behaviour, there has been consid-

Ethical concepts can be communicated.

---

[27]Gene R. Laczniak, "Observations Concerning International Marketing Ethics," presented at the 1995 AMA Faculty Consortium on Ethics and Social Responsibility in Marketing (Hempstead, N.Y.: Hofstra University); and Laczniak and Murphy, *Ethical Marketing Decisions: The Higher Road,* p. 218.

erable debate as to whether ethics can be taught—in either a classroom or a business setting. For example, none of the statements reported in Table 5-2 on questionable consumer activities had the study's respondents in full agreement.

Nonetheless, what can be transmitted to people are:

- Clear ethics codes.
- Role models of ethical people.
- Wide-ranging examples of ethical and unethical behaviour.
- Specified punishments if ethical behaviour is not followed.
- How vigilant professors and top management are regarding such issues as cheating on tests, misleading customers, and other unethical practices.
- The notion that ethical behaviour will never put a person in jeopardy (for instance, a salesperson should not be penalized for losing a customer if that salesperson is unwilling to exaggerate the effectiveness of a product).

Consumerism

Consumerism protects consumers from practices that infringe upon their rights.

Whereas social responsibility involves firms' interactions with all of their publics, consumerism focuses on the relations of firms and their customers. **Consumerism** encompasses "the wide range of activities of government, business, and independent organizations that are designed to protect people from practices that infringe upon their rights as consumers."[28]

Consumer interests are most apt to be served in industrialized nations, where people's rights are considered important, and governments and firms have the resources to address consumer issues. In less-developed nations and those just turning to free-market economies, consumer rights have not been as well respected, due to fewer resources and to other commitments; the early stages of consumerism are just now emerging in many of these nations.

Consumerism as practised in Canada is rooted to the consumerism movement in the United States, where it has evolved through four distinct eras, and is now in a fifth. The first era was in the 1900s and focused on the need for a banking system, product purity, postal rates, antitrust, and protection against product shortages. Emphasis was on business protection against unfair practices. The second era lasted from the 1930s to the 1950s. Issues were product safety, bank failures, labelling, misrepresentation, stock manipulation, deceptive ads, credit, and consumer refunds. Consumer groups, such as Consumers Union and Consumers' Research, grew, as did the amount of legislation related to consumer issues. Issues were initiated but seldom resolved.

U.S. President Kennedy declared a **consumer bill of rights**: *to information, to safety, to choice, and to be heard.*

The third era began in the early 1960s and lasted to 1980. Ushering in this era was President Kennedy's **consumer bill of rights**: granting consumers the right to information, to safety, to choice in product selection, and to be heard (see Figure 5-7). These rights apply to people in any nation or economic system. Other events also contributed to the rise of interest in consumer issues: Thousands of children were born with birth defects after their mothers were prescribed the drug thalidomide. Several books on such topics as marketing's ability to influence people, dangers from unsafe autos, and funeral industry tactics were published. Consumers became more discontented with product performance, the way firms handled complaints, and deceptive and unsafe practices; and they set higher—perhaps unrealistic—standards. Self-service shopping and more complex products caused uncertainty for some. The media publicized poor practices more often. Government intervention expanded; in particular, the U.S. Federal Trade Commission extended its activities on consumer issues.

---

[28]Bennett, *Dictionary of Marketing Terms*, p. 62.

- To be informed and protected against fraudulent, deceitful, and misleading statements, advertisements, labels, etc.; and to be educated as to how to use financial resources wisely.

- To be protected against dangerous and unsafe products.

- To be able to choose from among several available goods and services.

- To be heard by government and business regarding unsatisfactory or disappointing practices.

FIGURE 5-7
Consumers' Basic Rights

Following on the American example, Canadian consumerism really took wing in this era. In fact, Canada made history when the federal government established Consumer and Corporate Affairs Canada in 1968, thereby becoming the first nation to establish a federal government agency to oversee consumer rights. Canadian consumerism has a strong expression through the electronic media through public affairs shows such as the *Fifth Estate* and *Market Place*. The Consumers' Association of Canada gained a strong following in the 70s, but this following waned as consumerism moved into its fourth era.

During the 1980s, consumerism entered a mature fourth era, which emphasized business deregulation and self-regulation. Nationally, no major consumer laws were enacted and budgets of federal and provincial agencies concerned with consumer issues were cut. Provincial and local governments remained active, but in general, the federal government believed that most firms took consumer issues into account when devising and applying their marketing plans. Indeed, fewer firms did ignore consumer input or publicly confront consumer groups. Cooperation between business and consumers was better; and confrontations were less likely. It was in this mature phase that what in the 1970s would have been unthinkable, happened in Canada. The Consumers' Association of Canada went broke from a lack of public support and had to be bailed out with federal government money in 1988.

In the 1990s, the federal government is still involved with consumer issues. Its goal is to balance consumer and business rights. Consumer protection derives most strongly from the Competition Act but the enforcement practices in Canada have changed in the 1990s. Instead of criminal prosecution the Competition Bureau has adopted a policy of "alternative case resolution," whereby misinformation given to consumers can be offset in one of two ways: A firm can be asked to comply with an "undertaking" or be subject to a "consent prohibition order."

An undertaking is essentially a voluntary action on the part of a business. It involves stopping the business practice in question and making sure the practice does not happen again. The process is usually completed with corrective advertising and sometimes restitution to consumers. A consent prohibition order is a much stronger response to firms that have misrepresented their products or themselves. In this circumstance a written order may be given.

In all cases where firms are involved with alternative case resolution methods, admissions of guilt to offences under the Competition Act are not assumed. Any contraventions of the Competition Act can be prosecuted by Canada's attorney general and cases which are referred for prosecution cannot be resolved under an alternative case resolution approach. Unfair business tactics, product safety, and health issues are the areas of greatest concern.

Today, more firms are willing to address consumer issues and resolve complaints than ever before. In this climate of cooperation, the Consumers' Association of Canada again found itself in financial difficulty, despite ceasing the publication of *Canadian Consumer Magazine* in 1993. Without their own media voice, the Consumers' Association is forced to rely on "getting into the news" of other public media.

In the following sections, we will discuss consumer rights, business response to consumer issues, and the current role of consumerism.

Consumer Rights

As noted, consumer rights fall into four categories: information and education, safety, choice, and the right to be heard.

CONSUMER INFORMATION AND EDUCATION The right to be informed includes protection against fraudulent, deceitful, or grossly misleading information, advertising, labelling, pricing, packaging, and so on; and being given enough information to make good decisions. The key federal law protecting consumers is the Competition Act (Bill C-2), which was discussed in Chapter 2.

An important consideration for consumers, and a key source of product information, is the product warranty. The Competition Act, along with a number of pieces of provincial legislation, governs the use and liability associated with product warranties. A **warranty** is an assurance to consumers that a product meets certain standards. An express warranty is explicitly stated, such as a printed form showing the minimum mileage for truck tires. An implied warranty does not have to be stated to be in effect; a product is assumed to be fit for use and packaged properly, and to conform to promises on the label. The Marketing Practices Branch of the Competition Bureau can monitor product-accompanying information as to the warrantor's identity and location, exceptions in warranty coverage, and how people may complain. A full warranty must cover all parts and labour for a given period. A limited warranty may have conditions and exceptions, as well as a provision for labour charges. The courts have ruled that implied warranties may not be disclaimed. Figure 5-8 shows the full warranty provided by Lands' End, a direct marketer.

*A **warranty** assures consumers that a product will meet certain standards.*

Many provinces have laws relating to consumer information. For instance, cooling-off laws (allowing people to reconsider and, if they desire, cancel purchase commitments made in their homes with salespeople) are now in force. Unit-pricing laws, that let people compare the prices of products coming in many sizes (such as small, medium, large, and economy), are likewise on a province-by-province basis.

Government actions involving consumer information are also increasing internationally. For instance, in Hungary, an Eastern European nation with rapid growth in advertising, Home Shopping Budapest—a mail-order firm—was fined $1.25 million (U.S.) for misleading ads. Said one observer, "Until now, there was a feeling the government's attitude was laissez faire. But they've shown they're ready to intervene and rather powerfully."[29]

Unfortunately, the existence of good information does not mean consumers will use it in their decision making. At times, the information is ignored or misunderstood, especially by those needing it most (such as the poor); thus, consumer education is essential. In Canada there is no national policy focusing on consumer education. This is in contrast to the United States where many states, including Illinois, Oregon, Wisconsin, Florida, Kentucky, and Hawaii, require public high school students to take a consumer education course. In both Canada and the United States hundreds of public information programs are conducted by all levels of government, as well as by private profit and nonprofit groups. The programs typically cover how to purchase goods and services; key features of credit agreements, contracts, and warranties; and consumer protection laws.

---

[29]Ken Kasriel, "Hungary Cracks Down on Ad Claims," *Advertising Age* (June 22, 1992), pp. I-1, I-31; and Christopher Condon, "Hungary Regulations Could Polish Industry Image," *Advertising Age* (October 11, 1993), pp. I–6.

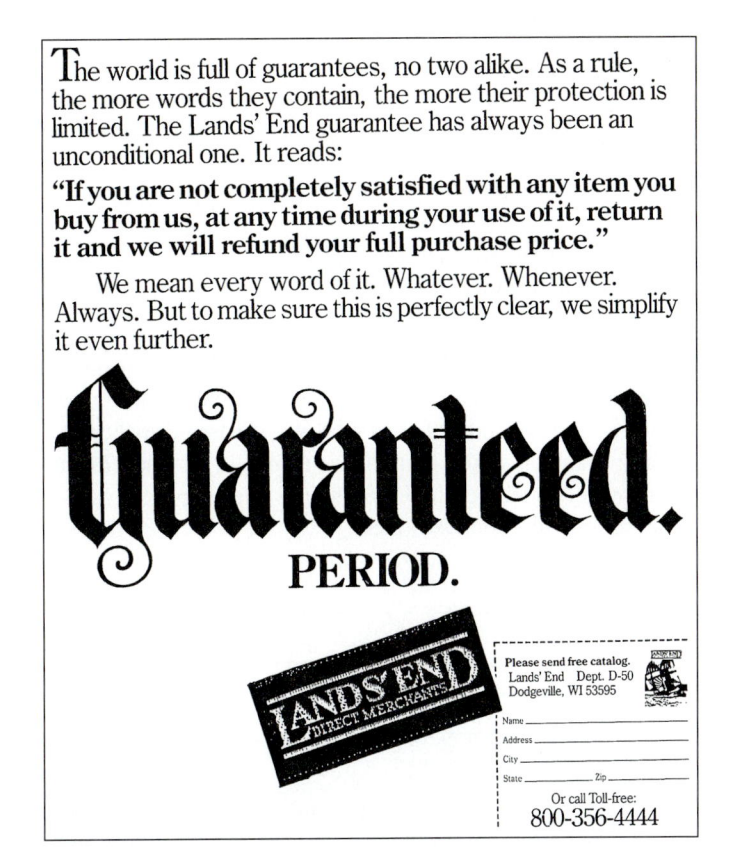

> The world is full of guarantees, no two alike. As a rule, the more words they contain, the more their protection is limited. The Lands' End guarantee has always been an unconditional one. It reads:
>
> **"If you are not completely satisfied with any item you buy from us, at any time during your use of it, return it and we will refund your full purchase price."**
>
> We mean every word of it. Whatever. Whenever. Always. But to make sure this is perfectly clear, we simplify it even further.
>
> # Guaranteed.
> ## PERIOD.
>
> LANDS' END DIRECT MERCHANTS
>
> Please send free catalog.
> Lands' End Dept. D-50
> Dodgeville, WI 53595
>
> Name
> Address
> City
> State   Zip
>
> Or call Toll-free:
> 800-356-4444

FIGURE 5-8
The Lands' End Full Warranty
Reprinted by permission.

CONSUMER SAFETY Every year, millions of people worldwide are hurt and thousands killed in incidents involving products other than motor vehicles. The yearly cost of product-related injuries is several billion dollars. Critics believe up to one-quarter of these injuries could be averted if companies made safer, better-designed products.

The Hazardous Products Act is the key piece of Canadian legislation dealing with product safety. The Act provides jurisdiction over tens of thousands of products—including TVs, bicycles, lamps, appliances, toys, sporting goods, ladders, furniture, housewares, and lawn mowers. It also regulates structural items in homes such as stairs, retaining walls, and electrical wiring. A number of other major products are regulated by laws, such as the Food and Drug Act, which regulates the marketing of food, drugs, and cosmetics.

Under the Hazardous Products Act, if the attorney general finds a product to be a hazard, he or she can order a firm to bring the product into conformity with the applicable safety rule, repair the defect, exchange the product for one meeting safety standards, or refund the purchase price. Firms found breaking safety rules can be fined, and executives can be held accountable as well. **Product recall**, whereby firms are asked to recall and modify (or discontinue) unsafe products, is an important enforcement tool. A single recall may entail millions of units of a product.

Consumers also have the right to sue the maker or seller of an injurious product. A legal action on behalf of many affected consumers is known as a **class-action suit**. However, consumer lawsuits are more common in the United States than in Canada. Each year in the United States, 20 000 consumer lawsuits are filed in federal courts and 90 000 are filed in state courts; these include both individual and class-action suits.[30]

Yet this American trend to legal action by consumers is spreading internationally:

> Japanese consumers have been docile. But now, consumer consciousness is rising. That's causing government to take a hard look at consumer protection. The Social Democratic Party is even drafting Japan's first product-liability law. Such efforts could alter the cushy atmosphere

The Hazardous Products Act allows for several enforcement tools, including **product recall**.

A **class-action suit** *can be filed on behalf of many consumers.*

---

[30] Paula Mergenhagen, "Product Liability: Who Sues," *American Demographics* (June 1995), pp. 48–54.

132 Part 2 *Broadening an Organization's / Individual's Marketing Scope*

Japanese firms enjoy at home. For years, they've been shielded from product-liability suits. Japanese legal procedures put the burden of proof on plaintiffs, while limiting access to evidence. In 50 years, consumers have won only 150 product-liability cases. In the United States, American and other firms have lost tens of thousands of such suits."[31]

A firm can reduce the negative effects of product recalls, as well as the possibility of costly class-action suits, by communicating properly when it learns a product is unsafe. This means voluntarily telling affected consumers, citing specific models that are unsafe, making fair adjustment offers (repair, replacement, or refund), and quickly and conveniently honouring those offers.

When consumers have several alternatives available to them, they are given the right to choose.

CONSUMER CHOICE The right to choose means people have several products and brands from which to select. (Figure 5-9 shows how one company—British Air—uses choice as a selling point for its services.) As noted earlier, the lack of goods and services (of any brand) is a key consumer concern in less-developed and newly free-market nations—where demand often far outstrips the supply for such items as coffee, bread, jeans, shoes, cosmetics, and fresh meat.

FIGURE 5-9
The Right to Choose
Reprinted by permission.

[31]Ted Holden and Hiromi Uchida, "Consumers Start Telling It to the Judge," *Business Week* (March 9, 1992), p. 50. See also Paul A. Herbig and Frederick A. Palumbo, "Japanese Consumer Protection," *Journal of Consumer Marketing*, Vol. 11, No. 1 (1994), pp. 5–14.

Governments in many industrialized countries have taken various actions to enhance the already extensive consumer choices available:

- Patent rights have time bounds; when they run out, all firms can use the patents.
- Noncompetitive business practices, like price fixing, are banned.
- Government agencies review proposed company mergers; in some cases, they have stopped mergers if they felt industry competition would be lessened.
- Restrictions requiring franchisees to purchase all goods and services from their franchisers have been reduced.
- The media are monitored to ensure that advertising space or time is made available to both small and large firms.
- Imports are allowed to compete with domestic-made items.
- Various service industries have been deregulated to foster price competition and encourage new firms to enter the marketplace.

A high profile example of Canadian consumers insisting on the right to choose became evident in 1995. The Cable TV industry (Rogers Cable, Videotron, Trillium Cable, and others), with the blessing of the Canadian Radio-Television and Telecommunications Commission (CRTC), attempted to introduce a group of new specialty pay channels in the marketplace. The channels were bundled with existing pay channels and cable subscribers were told they had to pay extra or lose some of their existing services. The backlash from subscribers was swift and sure. They did not mind having new pay services available but they wanted the right to choose these channels without giving up their current services. The outcry was reported in the public media and brought to the attention of both provincial and federal members of Parliament. Eventually, the cable industry relented and "unbundled" these services. However, the industry is in a quandary because they need a large subscriber base to make these channels economically viable and they had not planned on having to work so hard to market them.[32]

In Canada, consumer choice for some product categories is so extensive that some wonder if there are too many options. For example, specialty athletic footwear stores such as Footlocker often carry over 200 different brands and styles of running shoes. Electronic superstores like the Future Shop may offer between forty and fifty makes and models of VCRs. According to one prominent social scientist: "We are racing toward 'overchoice'—the point at which the advantages of diversity and individualization are cancelled by the complexity of the buyer's decision-making process."[33]

CONSUMERS' RIGHT TO BE HEARD The right to be heard means people should be able to voice their opinions (sometimes as complaints) to business, government, and other parties. This gives consumers input into the decisions affecting them. The Department of Consumer and Corporate Affairs was amalgamated into Industry Canada in 1993. This move, coupled with the demise of the Consumers' Association of Canada, could be seen as a threat to consumers' ability to be heard. However, provincial agencies and large municipalities have their own Consumer Affairs offices, as do many corporations. Each encourages consumer input.

There are various federal, provincial, and local agencies involved with consumers.

There are also several consumer groups representing the general public or specific consumer segments. They are motivated in their efforts to publicize consumer opinions and complaints, speak at government and industry hearings, and otherwise generate consumer input into the decision processes of government and industry. Because a single consumer rarely has a significant impact, consumer groups frequently become the individual's voice.

---

[32]Jim McElgunn, "A Shot in The Dark on Specialty TV," *Marketing Magazine* (February 13, 1995), p. 11.
[33]Lena Williams, "Free Choice: When Too Much Is Too Much," *New York Times* (February 14, 1990), p. C10.

The Responses of Business to Consumer Issues

Firms have become much more responsive to consumers, yet questions remain about the effects of consumerism on firms.

Over the last thrity-five years, the business community has greatly increased its acceptance of the legitimacy and importance of consumer rights; many firms now have real commitments to address consumer issues in a positive manner. Nonetheless, a number of companies have raised reasonable questions about consumerism's impact on them. They particularly wonder why there isn't a *business' bill of rights* to parallel the consumer's. Here are some of the questions that business people raise:

- Why do different provinces, municipalities, and nations have different laws regarding business practices? How can a national or international company be expected to comply with all of these laws?
- Don't some government rules cause unnecessary costs and time delays in new-product introductions that outweigh the benefits of these rules?
- Is it the job of business to ensure that consumers obey laws (such as not littering) and use products properly (such as wearing seat belts)?
- Isn't business self-regulation preferable to government regulation?
- Are multimillion dollar jury awards to consumers getting out of hand?

TECHNOLOGY & MARKETING

Can Firms Get Too Close to Their Customers?

It is great that many companies engage in relationship marketing with their customers, and that they stay in regular contact with them. By having good information on customers, companies can tailor marketing efforts to specific customers' needs, provide better follow-up service, and anticipate future customer requests. Yet, with the rapid advances in business technology, some people now feel especially vulnerable to what they perceive as company abuses in their relationships with customers:

Imagine you're sorting through your mail at home when you come across a postcard touting an upcoming sale on shirts at the store where you bought a shirt last week. That's funny, you think. You're sure you didn't give the clerk your address. So how did you end up on the store's mailing list? There's only one explanation: The store must have gotten your address from its credit card database, because you paid with the store's credit card. Since you're tired of being inundated with junk mail, you angrily toss the postcard in the mail—after all, you were just at the store last week!

If firms are truly marketing-oriented, they must recognize that some people are sensitive to information on their behaviour and backgrounds being kept in computerized databases. While one person may prefer that a hotel chain know he or she prefers a nonsmoking room on a high floor, another person may consider that information to be private. Compared to the second person, the first one may value good customer service above privacy or just be less sensitive about who has access to this information. Therefore, companies should train employees who collect customer data to respect a person's request for privacy even if this means not having good information on that person's needs and desires.

As a hotel's marketing manager, present a policy for both acquiring data about customer likes and dislikes and respecting customer privacy.

Source: Based on material in Stephen M. Silverman, "Information Backlash," *Inc. Technology* (June 13, 1995), p. 37.

Selected responses to consumer issues by manufacturers, retailers, and trade associations are discussed next.

MANUFACTURERS Numerous manufacturers have long-standing programs to handle consumer issues. Almost every product package you buy in Canada today has a toll-free number or an address where you can write for consumer information. This has been the response to consumerism and represents tremendous progress for businesses.

In the area of product recalls, many firms are now doing a better job. For instance, in April 1996 the Ford Motor Company of Canada issued recalls for 859 000 cars sold in Canada to fix faulty ignition switches responsible for spontaneous car fires in hundreds of cars. The estimated cost of the recall is $40 million. The recall also involved 7.9 million vehicles sold in the U.S. and cost estimates for the recall there ranged in the area of $U.S.200 million.

Recalls can even be good for business. LifeScan, a Johnson & Johnson company, makes meters that diabetics use to monitor their sugar levels. When one meter was found to be defective, LifeScan voluntarily recalled its entire product line and notified 600 000 customers within 24 hours. Because of how it handled the recall, LifeScan's market share has increased by 7 per cent since that incident.[34]

Despite manufacturers' interest in consumer issues, there are still times when their performance could be better. As a case in point, "Many times, product design is severely deficient in the area of human interface, with insufficient attention paid to how people use— and learn to use—the things in their lives. PCs. Phone systems. Toys requiring assembly. Upscale autos. Even light switches. They all can cause havoc for a person who doesn't read what's in an accompanying 500-page manual, written in 'engineerese.'"[35]

RETAILERS Various retailers have expressed a positive concern about consumer issues, some for several decades. Loblaws has pioneered a number of important consumer trends in Canada including low-cost generic products (so-called no-name products), high-quality store brands (President's Choice Brands) and Green Products to name a few.

Although relatively new to Canada, Wal-Mart has in-store signs to inform consumers about environmentally safe products. It has also run newspaper ads encouraging suppliers to make more environmentally sound products. At 7-Eleven Japan, three times a week, top executives sample foods sold at the chain. The firm's president says, "I won't sell what I wouldn't eat."[36]

Retailers and consumer groups have opposing views regarding **item price removal**— whereby prices are marked only on store shelves or aisle signs and not on individual items. Numerous retailers, particularly supermarkets, want to use item price removal because computerized checkouts allow them to computer scan prices through premarked codes on packages. They say this reduces labour costs and that these reductions can be passed on to consumers. Consumer groups believe the practice is deceptive and will make it harder for them to guard against misrings (i.e., when the scanner charges the wrong price for an item—usually a sale item that is charged at the regular price).

With **item price removal**, *prices are displayed only on shelves or signs.*

TRADE ASSOCIATIONS Trade associations represent groups of individual firms. Many have been quite responsive to consumer issues through such actions as coordinating and distributing safety-related research findings, setting up consumer education programs, planning product standards, and handling complaints. For example, in 1996 Quebec pharmacies launched Pharm-Action, a consumer product-information program which provides information sheets on health-related issues to consumers. The Canadian Direct Marketing Association sets industry guidelines and emphasizes that direct marketers concern themselves with building relationships with clients as opposed to just "making sales". The Canadian Chamber of Commerce and its provincial and municipal counterparts are also very important business associations who are concerned with consumer issues. All members of the Chambers of Commerce subscribe to a code of business conduct.

---

[34]Transport Canada Internet Website (http://www.tc.gc.ca/vehiclerecalls/.\VRNOV95e.htm); and Tim Triplett, "Product Recall Spurs Company to Improve Customer Satisfaction," *Marketing News* (April 11, 1994), p. 6.
[35]Howard Schlossberg, "Design Disability," *Marketing Management*, Vol. 1 (Spring 1992), p. 6.
[36]Karen Lowry Miller, "Listening to Shoppers' Voices," *Business Week: Reinventing America* (1992), p. 69.

BETTER BUSINESS BUREAU
www.bbb.org/index.html

The Better Business Bureau (BBB) is the largest and broadest business-run Canadian trade association involved with consumer issues. It publishes educational materials, handles complaints, supervises arbitration panels, makes available a Consumer Affairs Audit, outlines ethical behaviour, publicizes unsatisfactory practices and the firms involved, and has nationwide offices. It supports self-regulation as a substitute to government regulation. Nationwide, the BBB handles thousands of arbitration cases each year. These cases— many involving cars—are decided by impartial arbitrators. Rulings are usually binding on participating firms but not on consumers.

Trade associations may vigorously oppose potential government rules. In the opening of the chapter we saw how the Canadian Tobacco Manufacturers' Council (funded by tobacco firms) successfully challenged the Tobacco Products Control Act. Now the council must work with two other trade groups, the Association of Canadian Advertisers and the Institute of Canadian Advertisers, to develop advertising which will be acceptable to the various media. In this instance, these organizations will be acting somewhat for consumers by insuring that the targeting of the promotion is restricted to adults as much as possible.[37]

The Current Role of Consumerism

In the 1980s, with the Conservative government in Parliament reflecting a more conservative Canadian public, the role of government in regulating business was reduced. The feeling was that government had become too big, impeded business practices, and caused unnecessary costs; as a result, some government agency functions were limited and budgets cut. Consumerism issues were not as important as other factors, such as unemployment, the rate of inflation, industrial productivity, and separatist movements in Quebec and Western Canada.

Consumerism efforts have picked up, after a relative lull in the 1980s.

After a decade of a "hands-off" approach, a growing number of government leaders, consumer activists, and business leaders in Canada felt that the balance between business and consumer rights had tipped a little too much in favour of business. The federal government's posture toward consumer-related issues is now slightly more aggressive than in the 1980s; provinces and municipalities are still heavily involved.

In many countries outside of Canada, government, industry, and consumer groups are stepping up their efforts relating to consumer rights. Some nations are making real progress, while others still have a very long way to go. The worldwide challenge of the late 1990s will be for government, business, and consumer groups to work together so the socioecological view of marketing, ethical behaviour, consumer rights, and company rights are in balance.

MARKETING IN A CHANGING WORLD
Tough Choices Ahead

It is now harder than ever to make good societal, ethical, and consumer-oriented decisions. Here are two views as to why this is so:

Marketing was easier when the economy was expanding and consumer income was growing. For decades after World War II, marketing strategies generally were built around the development of growth markets. Satisfying customers was important, but never as important as it has become in the 1990s, with the competitive pressures of largely static markets. Previously, ethical problems

---

[37]Andrea Haman, "Tobacco Ad Code Gives Firms the PR High Ground," *Marketing Magazine*, (January 1–8, 1996), p. 2.

were less apparent, not because people did not care, but because society's expectations were different and there was a simple rule for rating marketing practices: *caveat emptor* [let the buyer beware], within the rule of law. If it was legal to sell a product that might be harmful or not live up to seller promises, then marketing the product was acceptable because the decision to buy was the consumer's.

Today, there is widespread concern about ethics in public and private life extending to many areas—politics, education, health, as well as business. The current period may be called the "ethics era." For marketers, this has meant that standards of acceptable marketing practice have shifted along a continuum, from a position wherein producer interests were paramount to a position wherein consumer interests are more favoured. Society's expectations have changed so that if *caveat emptor* ever was truly an adequate way to evaluate marketing ethics, this is no longer the case.[38]

Ethical issues are no longer just about what's right and what's wrong. Increasingly, we must choose between two things that are right, such as doing everything we can to save lives or allowing people to die with dignity. Good moral leadership in the next century will be grounded in centuries-old ethics concepts that may never change. Yet, it must also be flexible, adaptable, and inventive. Already, new dilemmas face us at every turn: How should software be protected from unlicensed copying? Only people living in a computer age would want to know.... Should public school children get free condoms? Before AIDS, the question would have seemed scandalous. Should you and I clone ourselves? The question has yet to come up—but it will.[39]

SUMMARY

1. *To consider the impact of marketing on society* Marketing actions can positively or negatively affect many aspects of society, such as the quality of life and consumer expectations. Various studies have shown that people's perceptions of marketing are mixed. Firms need to recognize that many dissatisfied consumers do not complain; they simply do not repurchase offending products.

2. *To examine social responsibility and weigh its benefits and costs* Social responsibility involves a concern for the consequences of a person's or firm's actions as they might affect the interests of others. It encompasses the socioecological view of marketing, which looks at all the stages of a product's life and includes both consumers and nonconsumers. Social responsibility can pose dilemmas when popular goods and services have potentially adverse effects on consumer or societal well-being.

Consumers and marketing practices have led to some resource shortages. To stem their depletion, cooperative efforts among business, shareholders, government, employees, the general public, consumers, and others are needed. Garbage dumps and landfills are marring the landscape. As a result, many areas have laws to rectify the situation. Dangerous pollutants need to be removed and safe ones found to replace them; environmental pollution will be an issue for the foreseeable future. Planned obsolescence is a heavily criticized practice that encourages material wearout, style changes, and functional product changes. Marketers say it responds to consumer demand; critics say it increases resource shortages, is wasteful, and adds to pollution.

Socially responsible actions have such benefits as worker and public health, cleaner air, and a more efficient use of resources. They also have many costs, such as the unequal distribution of benefits, dollar expenditures, and conservative new-product planning. Benefits and costs need to be weighed. Green marketing will continue gaining popularity.

3. *To look into the role of ethics in marketing* Ethical behaviour, based on honest and proper conduct, comes into play when people decide whether given actions are ethical or unethical and when they choose how to act. Egoism, utilitarianism, duty-based, and virtue ethics theories help explain behaviour. Marketing ethics can be divided into two categories: process-related and product-related.

---

[38]Craig Smith, "Marketing Strategies for the Ethics Era," *Sloan Management Review*, Vol. 36 (Summer 1995), p. 85.
[39]Rushworth M. Kidder, "Tough Choices: Why It's Getting Harder to Be Ethical," *Futurist* (September–October 1995), pp. 29–30.

Ethics may be examined from four vantage points: a business perspective, a consumer perspective, an international perspective, and in terms of their teachability. A major difficulty of ethics in business is setting boundaries for deciding what is ethical. For high ethical standards to be kept, both consumers and firms must engage in proper behaviour. For various reasons, ethical standards in an international setting are especially complex. There has been a lot of debate as to whether ethics can be taught.

4. *To explore consumerism and describe the consumer bill of rights* Consumerism deals with the relations of firms and their consumers. It comprises the acts of government, business, and independent organizations that are designed to protect people from practices that infringe upon their rights as consumers.

Consumerism has seen five eras: early 1900s, 1930s to 1950s, 1960s to 1980, 1980s, and 1990 to the present. The third was the most important and began with U.S. President Kennedy's announcement of a consumer bill of rights—to information, to safety, to choice, and to be heard. The interest now is in balancing consumer and business rights—in Canada as well as in other countries.

The right to be informed includes consumer protection against fraudulent, deceitful, grossly misleading, or incomplete information, advertising, labelling, pricing, packaging, or other practices. Consumer education involves teaching people to spend their money wisely.

The concern over the right to safety arises from the large numbers of people who are injured or killed in product-related accidents. The Hazardous Products Acts is the protective legislation which gives the federal government the power to order recalls or modifications on a wide range of products; other agencies oversee such products as food, pharmaceuticals, and cosmetics.

The right to choose means consumers should have several products and brands from which to select. In Canada, some observers wonder if there is too much choice.

The right to be heard means consumers should be able to voice their opinions (and complaints) to business, government, and other parties. A number of government agencies and consumer groups provide this voice.

5. *To discuss the responses of manufacturers, retailers, and trade associations to consumerism and study the current role of consumerism* Many firms and associations are reacting well to consumer issues. A small number intentionally or unintentionally employ unfair, misleading, or dangerous practices.

The 1990s is witnessing more consumer activism than did the 1980s but less than in the 1960s and 1970s. Government, business, and consumers will continue working together to resolve consumer issues.

KEY TERMS

social responsibility (p. 112)
socioecological view of marketing (p. 112)
planned obsolescence (p. 117)
green marketing (p. 119)
ethical behaviour (p. 121)

process-related ethical issues (p. 123)
product-related ethical issues (p. 123)
cause-related marketing (p. 124)
consumerism (p. 128)
consumer bill of rights (p. 128)

warranty (p. 130)
product recall (p. 131)
class-action suit (p. 131)
item price removal (p. 135)

Review Questions

1. What are some of the areas in which marketing practices have the potential for both positive and negative consequences for society?
2. Define the term social responsibility. What are its implications for marketers?
3. Explain the responsibilities of both business and consumers according to the socioecological view of marketing.
4. Describe the pros and cons of planned obsolescence as a marketing practice.
5. What is ethical behaviour? Distinguish among the egoism, utilitarianism, duty-based, and virtue ethics theories.
6. Why is cause-related marketing a controversial practice?
7. Why are ethical standards of conduct particularly complex for international marketers?
8. How does consumerism differ from social responsibility?
9. Explain the consumer bill of rights.
10. Describe the current role of consumerism.

Discussion Questions

1. From a company's perspective, why is hidden consumer dissatisfaction a particular problem? How would you go about uncovering hidden dissatisfaction?
2. Present a seven-point ethics guide for operating internationally.
3. How would you teach marketing ethics to a class of second-year university business majors? What topics would you discuss? Why?
4. As an executive for a leading toy manufacturer, how would you implement a product recall if you discover that one of your toys could easily be swallowed by children under age 3?
5. Do consumers in Canada have too many goods and services from which to choose? Why or why not?

VIDEO CASE

Ethicscan: Whose Ethics Matter Anyway?

David Nitkin is a self-appointed corporate ethics watchdog. He considers himself on the leading edge of corporate responsibility. He publishes the *"Corporate Ethics Monitor"* six times a year. Working from the basement of his house he researches the ethical behaviour (or lack thereof) of Canadian businesses. He then publishes his findings in the *Corporate Ethics Monitor* in which he names the worst polluter, the best employer and identifies firms which invest in nations governed by oppressive regimes. He gathers his information from responses to mailings, received faxes, and direct from the private sector.

Nitkin is not the only investigator concerned with ethics. He himself has been investigated by oil companies and airlines and he claims to have been threatened by some companies as well. The *Corporate Ethics Monitor* has 300 subscribers, businesses who pay $300 per year to see if Nitkin is writing about them or about their competitors. In addition to writing and publishing his newsletter, Nitkin also operates his own consulting business to perform ethical checks and audits for clients. One of his clients was the Body Shop, which has a specific policy of not carrying cosmetic products that have been brought to market as a result of animal testing. The Body Shop hired Nitkin to check the backgrounds of a number of their suppliers to make sure that the suppliers were in compliance with the no animal testing policy. They really did not want to risk having the policy blow up in their faces because of the actions of an unscrupulous supplier.

Not everyone feels that David Nitkin is an ethical paramour. Terence Corcoran, a business press writer, views Nitkin's activities as almost akin to blackmail. Nitkin criticizes companies, who then hire him as a consultant to help them get their house in order. If they don't hire him, he writes a scathing exposé. If they do hire him, he can write about how they have become socially responsible. Is this type of business practice ethical? Corcoran feels Nitkin and others like him are imposing political correctness and leftist ideologies on businesses. It is Corcoran's view that corporation's exist to make profits, not to make society a better place. Corcoran feels that ethical conduct should be legislated. If a firm is operating legally, that's all the ethics they need.

Nitkin, on the other hand, does not see any conflict of interest on his part. He is carrying out his mission to make the world a better place by exposing corrupt or questionable business practices where he finds them, and by consulting with businesses who wish to operate in a more socially responsible manner.

QUESTIONS
1. If Nitkin himself was subjected to the same type of Ethicscan he puts other businesses through, what do you think the findings would be?
2. Evaluate this statement: "Business ethics is just a societal fad that will fade into obscurity in the face of economic hardship and technological progress, thereby resigning David Nitkin and the *Corporate Ethics Monitor* to the sociological scrap heap where they belong."

VIDEO QUESTIONS ON ETHICSCAN
1. How would you assess The Body Shop's use of Nitkin's services? Do you think there is an important need for the services Nitkin provides?
2. What is your opinion of Corcoran's view of ethics? What are the marketplace implications for those businesses who agree with him?

BODY SHOP INTERNATIONAL
www.the-body-shop.ca/

Video Source: "Ethicscan," *Venture* (January 16, 1994).

CASE STUDY

Herman Miller: Evaluating the Actions of an Environmentally Conscious Firm

Michigan-based Herman Miller is a leading maker of contemporary-styled furniture and furniture systems for offices and, to a lesser extent, for health-care facilities. Its annual sales exceed U.S.$1.1 billion, making it the second-largest U.S. manufacturer of office furniture (after Steelcase). One of its best-known products is an office system, consisting of an integrated desk and wall unit, that is used when office space is both limited and costly.

In 1982, long before most firms were concerned with environmental issues, Herman Miller built an U.S.$11 million waste-to-energy plant that continues to provide a large portion of its power needs. Instead of burning waste products in landfills, the firm uses its trash to supply all the electricity it needs to heat and air-condition its central factory. Its waste-to-energy plant has reduced the amount of trash the firm discards in landfills by 90 per cent.

Years in advance, the firm set a goal of sending no trash to landfills as of 1995. To reach the goal, it used reduced quantities of packaging and worked with materials that were recyclable. Today, even Herman Miller's scrap fabric is shredded and made into insulation for car-roof linings and dashboards. Not only does this recycling process help the environment, it also saves the firm U.S. $50 000 in annual dumping fees. Overall, according to the vice-president of the Michigan Audubon Society, "Herman Miller has been doing a superb job."

According to the United Nations' Food and Agricultural Organization, 17 million hectares of rain forest are destroyed each year. In March 1990, when Herman Miller's research manager realized that the firm's use of rosewood and Honduran mahogany had resulted in the destruction of tropical rain forests, the company decided not to purchase additional rosewood—a vital ingredient in the company's U.S.$2300 signature-piece chair. As a result, the chair is now made from walnut and cherry woods. According to the firm's chief executive, "We are sharing the growing concern about the tropical rain forests."

The firm's new environmental policy requires that it use only wood from sustained-yield forest sources. This policy was developed in conjunction with the International Hardwood Products Association (IHPA) and the International Timber Trade Organization, a multigovernment agency.

Herman Miller's mission statement highlights its environmental concern: "We are a company that services the built environment with facilities, goods, and services that improve the quality of life and with policies and practices that sustain our environment." Based upon its recycling program, Herman Miller was honoured with the 1993 Waste Reduction Award from California's Integrated Management Board. It also received the Wildlife Federation Corporate Conservation Council's 1993 Environmental Achievement Award.

Herman Miller's concern with social responsibility extends to employees and customers. As such, it spent U.S.$800 000 for two incinerators to burn 98 per cent of the toxic solvents that are emitted from its painting and varnishing operations. These furnaces are effective beyond the standards of the U.S. Clean Air Act.

Herman Miller is not content with its environmental actions. The company presently only recycles about 15 per cent of its corrugated cardboard; the balance is burned in its energy plant. It also feels that it needs to burn more of the sawdust that is accumulated as a by-product of producing wooden furniture.

Unlike other companies, Herman Miller does not promote its environmental efforts to its customers. According to its senior vice-president for sales, "green marketing is a ploy that may eventually wear thin with customers."

QUESTIONS

1. Comment on Herman Miller's actions in terms of the socioecological view of marketing.
2. Develop other strategies that Herman Miller can use to increase its social responsibility efforts.
3. Evaluate Herman Miller's refusal to purchase additional rosewood from a product-related ethical issue perspective.
4. Should Herman Miller promote its environmental policies to its customers? Explain your answer.

Source: The data in this case are drawn from Joseph A. Azzarello, "Long-Time Environmental Leadership Pays Off in Many Ways at Herman Miller," *Total Quality Environmental Management* (Winter 1992/1993), pp. 187–191; *Herman Miller, Inc. and Subsidiaries 1994 Annual Report;* and Faye Rice, "Who Scores Best on the Environment," *Fortune* (July 26, 1993), pp. 114–122.

CHAPTER 6
Global Aspects of Marketing

Chapter Objectives

1. To define domestic, international, and global marketing

2. To explain why international marketing takes place and study its scope

3. To explore the cultural, economic, political, legal, and technological environments facing international marketers

4. To analyze the stages in the development of an international marketing strategy

Paddling down cow paths in flip-flop sandals or paddling a canoe through piranha-infested creeks, Iraci Macedo da Costa Queiroz lugs from door to door what rain forest dreams are made of: Mesmerize cologne, Forever Fragrance perfume, and Cool Confidence deodorant. With no doorbells to ring at the riverside shanties on stilts, this Avon lady of the Amazon claps her hands and calls out cheerily: "Hi, Honey! I'm here!"

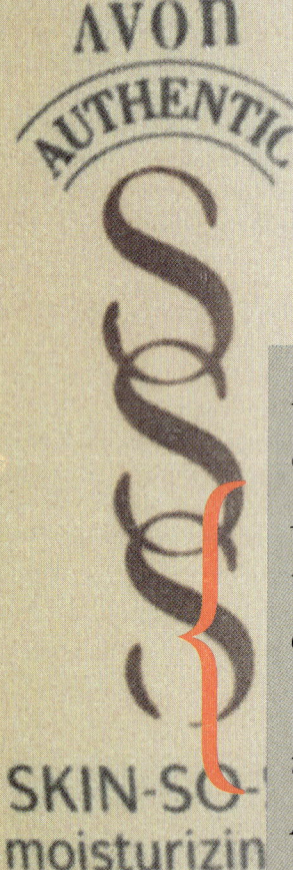

U.S.-based Avon Products is the world's largest cosmetics firm. In recent years, its annual North American sales have fallen slightly, but foreign sales have risen rapidly (except in Western Europe). As such, foreign sales account for more than 60 per cent of Avon's total revenues. Today, Avon is especially focused on growth opportunities in such emerging markets as Brazil, Argentina, Mexico, China, and Poland. As Avon's chief executive officer says, "we see great promise in these markets, and we feel the growth is sustainable."

North American opportunities for Avon have stagnated as a result of more women being in the workforce than at home. This trend makes it more difficult for Avon not only to reach customers, but also to hire qualified salespersons. In North America the firm has tried to attract new customers with its Avon Select program, which lets customers order cosmetics through a direct-mail catalogue or a toll-free phone number. Unfortunately, sales through this innovative program have been quite low. And Avon's plan to motivate the North American sales force to work harder by cutting their commissions and sales incentives also have not worked out well. Instead of motivating the sales force, the plan led to poor morale and sales. Under Avon's new president, Christina A. Gold, the old commission structure and bonus system was reinstituted.

Although Avon has had problems in North America with its direct selling strategy, this approach has proven ideal for its emerging markets. For example, many countries, such as China and Argentina, lack well-developed infrastructures and distribution systems. And the high potential income is a large attraction for sales representatives. In all, Avon is doing business in about thirty developing countries; and the revenues Avon generates in those nations alone exceed its North American revenues. Its newest markets are India, South Africa, and Vietnam, all targeted to start operations by 1997.

Avon's largest market in the world, after North America, is Brazil. Avon's Brazilian sales reached $1 billion in 1995, double the 1993 level. Avon has 480 000 "beauty consultants" in Brazil; this is more than double the size of Brazil's army—and double the number of Amway distributors in the North American market. A typical Brazilian sales representative earns between $250 and $700 a month selling Avon products, based on a 30 per cent commission rate. This compares favourably with a national average income of $250 a month in Brazil. "For housewives, there is emancipation," says Eliana Maria Machado de Silva, who supervises 1000 Avon salespeople in the Amazon region. "They start to have their own financial life. They discover themselves. They gain self confidence."

Avon knows the Brazilian market is diverse. So, to reach affluent Sao Paulo residents who live in high-security buildings, Avon advertises on cable TV; it sells to consumers in the Amazon by allowing its salespeople to trade anti-wrinkle cream for three grams of gold dust.[1]

In this chapter, we will explore the environment facing international marketers and see how to develop an international marketing strategy.

Overview

International business transactions generate trillions of dollars in yearly global sales. And virtually every nation engages in significant international business, whether it be Canada with over $345 billion in yearly exports and imports of goods and services, the United States with over U.S.$1.5 trillion in imports and exports, Namibia (in southern Africa) with U.S.$3 billion in exports and imports, or Tonga (in the South Pacific) with U.S.$100

Due to its impact, international marketing concepts should be understood by all types of firms.

---

[1] James Brooke, "Who Braves Piranha Waters? Your Avon Lady!" *New York Times* (July 7, 1995), p. A4; and Veronica Byrd and Wendy Zellner, "The Avon Lady of the Amazon," *Business Week* (October 24, 1994), pp. 93–96.

million in exports and imports. In many areas, the marketplace has a wide variety of foreign firms competing with domestic ones.

Whether a firm is small or large, operates solely in its home nation or in both the home market and abroad, markets goods or services, and is profit- or nonprofit-oriented, it needs to grasp key international marketing concepts and to devise and enact a proper strategy. This means having a broadened marketing perspective.

> Most small...businesses never had to look to exports for increased market share. For forty-five years, the domestic market...provided large profits.... Firms grew accustomed to being contacted directly by companies overseas for new technology, quality products, and 'know-how.' Times are changing, however. Small-business owners are starting to review their marketing strategies. They see quality competition from the East, price competition from less-developed countries with cheaper labour, and looming competition from 'Fortress Europe... Firms of all sizes are now thinking globally.[2]

Domestic marketing encompasses a firm's efforts in its home country. **International marketing** involves marketing goods and services outside a firm's home country, whether in one or several markets. **Global marketing** is an advanced form of international marketing in which a firm addresses global customers, markets, and competition. It is practised by both multinational and global firms.

A company may act domestically, internationally, or both; efforts vary widely. Here is the range of options that may be pursued:

- A **domestic firm** restricts its efforts to the home market. The firm believes its base market is both large enough and responsive enough to meet its sales and profit goals.

Domestic marketing *involves the home nation,* **international marketing** *embraces foreign activities, and* **global marketing** *has a worldwide focus.*

FIGURE 6-1
Coca Cola: A Leading U.S. Multinational
Reprinted by permission

[2]Bonnie Heineman Wolfe, "Finding the International Niche: A 'How To' for American Small Business," *Business Horizons*, Vol. 34, No. 2 (March-April 1991), p. 13. Reprinted with permission of the Foundation for the School of Business at Indiana University.

- An **exporting firm** is just embarking on sales expansion beyond its home borders. This company recognizes that the home market is no longer adequate for it fully to meet revenue and profit goals. A firm typically uses exporting when it seeks to sell its traditional products in foreign markets, often through distribution and sales intermediaries. A relatively low percentage of its business is outside the domestic market.
- An **international firm** goes beyond just exporting existing products. It makes modifications in those items for foreign markets or introduces new products there; the firm knows it must more aggressively cultivate foreign markets. There remains enough strength in the firm's domestic market for that market to remain the dominant one for the company.
- A **multinational firm** is a worldwide player. Although corporate headquarters are in the home nation, the domestic market often accounts for less than 50 per cent of sales and profits—and the firm operates in dozens of nations or more. The business scope and search for opportunities are quite broad (with regard to geography). There are very few Canadian multinationals (examples are The Seagram Company Ltd. and Bombardier Inc.) and most multinational corporations operating in Canada are U.S.-based (such as GM, Ford, Chrysler, and Coca-Cola). Multinationals market items around the world, but usually keep the business culture of their home market. See Figure 6-1.
- A **global firm** is also a worldwide player. Yet, because its domestic sales are low, it places even more reliance on foreign transactions. It has the greatest geographic business scope. Such firms have been more apt to emerge in smaller nations, where the firms have historically needed foreign markets to survive. The quintessential global firm is Switzerland's Nestlé, which derives less than 2 per cent of total sales from its home market, makes products in hundreds of plants all over the world, and has employees from 50 nations at headquarters. As illustrated in Figure 6-2, its brands are among the world's most popular.[3]

A firm may be **domestic, exporting, international, multinational,** *or* **global**.

BOMBARDIER INC.
www.sea-doo.com/sd/bombardier/index.html

CHRYSLER CANADA
www.chrysler.com/

FIGURE 6-2
Nescafé by Nestlé: A Leading Global Firm
Reprinted by permission

[3] Joel R. Evans, "What Does Globalization in Business Really Mean?" *Hofstra Horizons* (Spring 1995), pp. 7–9.

146 Part 2 *Broadening an Organization's Individual's Marketing Scope*

As we move into the 21st century, it is clear that more domestic firms will need to become exporters and then international in orientation. And multinational firms will need to become more global, thereby acting without boundaries and without being dominated by a home-country-based corporate culture.

This chapter looks at why international marketing occurs, its scope, its environment, and the components of an international marketing strategy.

Why International Marketing Takes Place

There are several reasons why countries and individual firms are engaging in greater international marketing efforts than ever before. These are shown in Figure 6-3 and discussed next.

Countries trade items in which they have a **comparative advantage**.

According to the concept of **comparative advantage**, each country has distinct strengths and weaknesses based on its natural resources, climate, technology, labour costs, and other factors. Therefore, nations can benefit by exporting the goods and services for which they have relative advantages and importing the ones for which they have relative disadvantages. Comparative advantages may generally be grouped into two categories: those related to the physical environment of a country (such as natural resources and climate) and those related to the socioeconomic development of a country (such as technological advances or low labour costs). Canada's comparative advantages lie in its natural resources. Industries that take advantage of these resources include: agriculture, forestry, oil and gas, and mining.

The domestic economy and demographics affect international efforts.

Economic and demographic trends vary by country. A firm in a nation with adverse domestic conditions (like high inflation) and/or a small or stagnant population base can stabilize or increase sales by marketing products in more favourable foreign markets. Thus, the Canadian market is attractive due to rather low inflation, moderate unemployment rates, and relative political stability, as well as the relative affluence of the population. Developing and less-developed countries are potentially lucrative markets due to their population growth; over 90 per cent of world population growth is there. For example, Heinz now targets developing and less-developed nations because of their population growth and nutrition needs. Its brands are established in Africa, China, and the Pacific Rim.

Home competition may lead to international efforts.

Competition in a firm's domestic market may become intense and lead it to expand internationally. For example, Gennum Corporation of Burlington, Ontario manufactures integrated circuits for hearing aids. Competing against Siemens AG and Philips Electronics NV, Gennum realized it would have to employ a niche strategy to survive. Gennum's approach was so successful that Siemens AG and Philips Electronics ceased being competitors and became customers. Gennum's non-Canadian revenues represent 90 per cent of the company total; and the company is planning more niche products. Remaining successful will require Gennum to continue to find customers worldwide.[4]

SIEMENS USA
www.siemens.com/

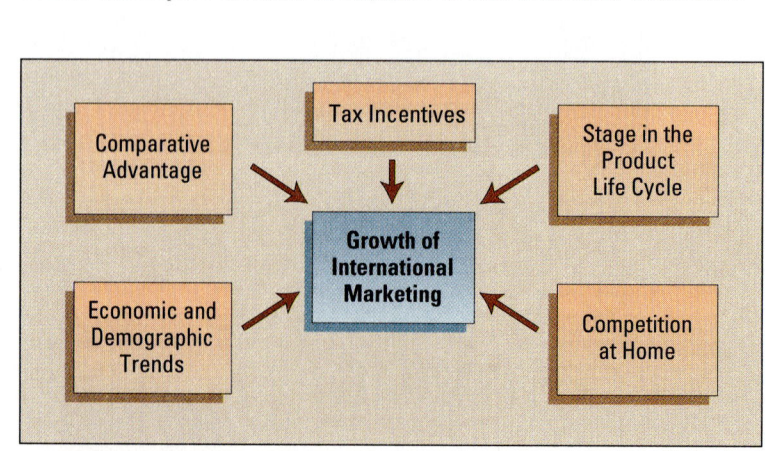

FIGURE 6-3
Why International Marketing Occurs

Comparative Advantage → Growth of International Marketing ← Tax Incentives
Economic and Demographic Trends → Growth of International Marketing ← Stage in the Product Life Cycle
→ Growth of International Marketing ← Competition at Home

---

[4] Alexander Ross and Randall Litchfield, "Circuit Stars," *Canadian Business* (December 1993), p. 34.

Because products are often in different stages of their life cycles in different nations, exporting may be a way to prolong the cycles. For instance, the Canadian market for beer products has been essentially flat, for health and social reasons. To stimulate beer sales, Canada's two largest brewers, Labatt and Molson, have heightened their efforts in Japan. Imported beers are popular because Japanese consumers are well disposed to them and they are cheap, since Japan's currency, the yen, is strong.

International marketing can also be used to dispose of discontinued goods, seconds, and manufacturer remakes (products that have been repaired). These items can be sold abroad without spoiling the domestic market for full-price, first-quality items. However, firms must be careful about selling unsafe products in foreign markets. This can lead to ill will on the part of the governments there.

International marketing may extend the product life cycle or dispose of discontinued items.

International Marketing in Action

Is India the Next Big Marketing Opportunity?

India—with its 900 million people—is the second most-inhabited nation in the world. Yet, for a long time, foreign companies did not view the Indian market as a very attractive one, due largely to the low annual per capita income and the restrictions placed on foreign businesses by the government.

Since the early 1990s, the situation has changed; foreign firms have invested billions of dollars in India, and 95 per cent of the respondents to a recent survey said they intend to expand their investments. Here is why:

- India's middle-class market is huge (more than 200 million people).
- Household appliance sales are growing at a double-digit rate. Refrigerator sales are growing at a 15 per cent annual rate and sales of colour TVs are growing at an 18 per cent rate.
- India has opened its doors to foreign products by reducing the highest duty rate from 120 to 65 per cent. It also plans to lower duties on imported capital goods.
- Taxes on companies that are incorporated abroad but that earn income in India have been reduced from 65 per cent to 55 per cent.
- To foreign investors, India offers low labour costs and the availability of skilled management and technical personnel. A third resource, research and development opportunities, is tied to the availability of skilled personnel.

Foreign firms do need to be aware of the fragmented nature of the Indian market and of the differences in labour costs, distribution alternatives, and tax rates among Indian regions. Three popular areas for foreign investments are Bombay, Bangalore, and New Delhi. Each one has unique advantages: Bombay is valued for its commercial infrastructure, Bangalore for its software expertise, and New Delhi for the presence of the central government.

As an international marketing consultant, draw up a checklist of factors for Westinghouse's appliance business to consider when investing in India.

Source: Based on material in Philip Banks and Ganesh Natarajan, "India: The Next Asian Tiger?" *Business Horizons*, Vol. 38 (May–June 1995), pp. 47–50; and Sally D. Goll, "India's Growing Middle Class Buys Stuff Firms' Dreams Are Made Of," *Wall Street Journal* (July 28, 1995), p. B4C.

Some countries entice foreign firms to invest by offering tax incentives in the form of low property, import, and income taxes for an initial period. In addition, multinational firms may adjust revenue reports so their largest profits are recorded in nations with the lowest tax rates.

The Scope of International Marketing[5]

Canada is the world's eighth-largest goods and services exporter and seventh-largest importer.

The world's leading export countries are the United States, Japan, United Kingdom, Germany, and France. Together, they account for more than U.S.$2 trillion annually in goods and services exports. Canada ranks about eighth in the world in exports and 1994 Canadian merchandise exports exceeded $213 billion, an amount equalling 28.4 per cent of the Canadian Gross Domestic Product and 3.5 to 4.0 per cent of world merchandise exports. The leading Canadian exports are newsprint, wood pulp, timber, grain, crude petroleum, natural gas, ferrous and nonferrous ores, and motor vehicles.

The United States is also the world's largest importer, followed by Japan, Germany, France, and Great Britain, with Canada ranking seventh. In 1994, Canadian imports were $202 billion—3.6 per cent of total world imports. Leading Canadian imports are processed foods, beverages, petroleum, chemicals, industrial machinery, motor vehicles, durable consumer goods and computers.

Canada has a merchandise **trade surplus,** *while the U.S. has a* **trade deficit.**

As a result of the high level of exports in 1994, Canada had a merchandise **trade surplus** of Cdn$11 billion. This surplus is due mainly to seven factors:

- The low value of the Canadian dollar (averaging U.S.$.73).
- The Goods and Services Tax (GST) 7 per cent, which replaced the former manufacturer's sales tax of 13 per cent. Unlike the latter, the GST is not applied to export goods and thus functions as a value-added tax in the production and distribution of both goods and services within Canada.
- Major productivity gains in Canadian manufacturing.
- Canada's abundance of natural resources and a comparative advantage in their production, which results in large exports of these materials.
- The Canada-U.S. Autopact, which allows essentially free movement of Canadian or U.S. manufactured automobiles and auto parts between the two countries.
- The U.S.-Canada Free Trade Agreement has allowed free movement of all goods and services between Canada and the United States, effectively expanding our market to include an additional 260 million people.
- NAFTA—the North American Free Trade Agreement—has allowed for freer movement of all goods and services between Canada, the United States, and Mexico. This gives Canadian firms access to a North American market of 380 million people.

In contrast, Canada's largest trading partner, the U.S., had a 1995 merchandise **trade deficit**—the amount by which the value of imports exceeds the value of exports—of U.S.$200 billion. This was by far the greatest merchandise deficit of any country, and set a U.S. record. Because the U.S. is Canada's largest trading partner and U.S. merchandise trade deficits have been so high, Canadians must be aware of, and able to react to, any trade retaliation activities undertaken by American companies and U.S. federal and state governments.

---

[5]The data cited in this section are from *Market Research Handbook 1995*, Statistics Canada, Minister of Industry, Science and Technology; *The 1996 Canadian Global Almanac* (Toronto: MacMillan Canada); *The Canada - U.S. Free Trade Agreement*, Copy 1—12-87, (External Affairs Canada); "U.S. Trade Facts," *Business America* (May 1995), pp. 17–18; Terence Roth, "Gordian Knot," *Wall Street Journal* (September 30, 1994), p. R4; James Aley, "New Lift for the U.S. Export Boom," *Fortune* (November 13, 1995), pp. 73–78; and Brian Bremner and Edith Hill Updike, "'Made in America' Isn't the Kiss of Death Anymore," *Business Week* (November 13, 1995), p. 62.

The Environment of International Marketing

Even though the marketing principles described in this book are applicable to international marketing strategies, there are often major environmental differences between domestic and foreign markets—and marketing practices may have to be adapted accordingly. Each market should be studied separately. Only then can a firm decide how much of its domestic marketing strategy can be used in foreign markets and what elements should be modified.

Here's how 3M is expanding globally:

> We like to get in ahead of competitors. We call this our FIDO approach (First In Defeats Others). We start small, with a modest investment, and gradually build a local presence. We make a little, sell a little, and plough profits back into the business. We pick out a few product lines that address the country's most pressing needs—often in the infrastructure. Then, we build up our local capability. Of course, these days when a company goes into a new market, it doesn't have as much time to make a little, sell a little, test it, and see how it all works. Opportunities are shorter than they used to be and competition is more intense. We have to make a bigger commitment than we did in the past.[6]

To gain insight into the global marketplace, useful resources such as these may be consulted:

- Statistics Canada sources such as: *The Canadian International Merchandise Trade Database* (for information on Canadian imports and exports of commodities); *The World Trade Database* (uses UN supplied data for approximately 160 countries and has information beginning in 1970); *TIERS —Trade Information and Enquiry Retrieval System* (a microcomputer-usable trade database with import and export commodity data for Canada.)

- The Internet has the *World Factbook* (published by the Central Intelligence Agency of the U.S. no less) plus sources such as: the UN, World Bank, General Agreement on Trade and Tariffs (GATT), and North American Free Trade Agreement (NAFTA).

- The United Nations (UN) *Statistical Year Book* has information on member countries and is available in many libraries. Aside from the UN, the Organization for Economic Cooperation and Development (OECD) located in Paris, France, and the European Union (EU) located in Brussels, Belgium are also able to provide international trade statistics and market information.

- Independent publishing sources include: Gower, which publishes the *World Index of Economic Forecasts* and the *Yearbook of International Trade Statistics* ; and Euromonitor, which publishes *International Marketing Data and Statistics* and *European Marketing Data and Statistics*.

- The Canadian Chamber of Commerce has a relationship with Chambers of Commerce in foreign nations and can put researchers seeking information in touch with these foreign Chambers.

Canadian businesses can also access U.S. sources of information which are very useful as well. Such sources include:

- National Trade Data Bank (NTDB)—a "one-stop" source for international business data collected by 17 U.S. government agencies. It is updated and released monthly on two CD-ROM disks, with a total of 100,000 documents. The NTDB is also available via the Internet.

- Trade Information Center Fax Retrieval Hotline (1-800-USA-TRADE)—provides general information, listings of U.S. state and private organizations, and business contacts. It is accessed through touch-tone phones.

- Export Yellow Pages—a free directory of U.S. manufacturers, banks, service firms, and trading companies looking to do business internationally. It is distributed through local U.S. Department of Commerce offices.[7]

---

[6]Harry Hammerly, "Matching Global Strategies with National Responses," *Journal of Business Strategy*, Vol. 13 (March-April 1992), p. 10.
[7]"Growing a Global Business," *Wall Street Journal*, 1995 advertising supplement sponsored by Sprint Business.

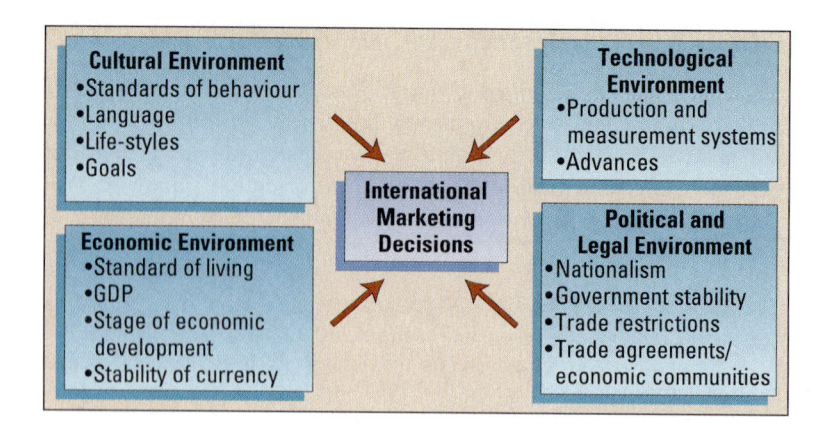

FIGURE 6-4
The Environment Facing International Marketers

[Figure 6-4: Diagram showing four environments converging on International Marketing Decisions:
- **Cultural Environment**: Standards of behaviour, Language, Life-styles, Goals
- **Technological Environment**: Production and measurement systems, Advances
- **Economic Environment**: Standard of living, GDP, Stage of economic development, Stability of currency
- **Political and Legal Environment**: Nationalism, Government stability, Trade restrictions, Trade agreements/economic communities]

The major cultural, economic, political, legal, and technological environments facing international marketers are discussed next. See Figure 6-4.

The Cultural Environment

*Inadequate information about foreign **cultures** is a common cause of errors.*

International marketers need to be aware of each foreign market's cultural environment. A **culture** consists of a group of people sharing a distinctive heritage. It teaches behaviour standards, language, lifestyles, and goals; is passed down from one generation to another; and is not easily changed. Almost every country has a different culture; continental differences exist as well. A firm unfamiliar with or insensitive to a foreign culture may try to market goods or services that are unacceptable to that culture. For example, beef and unisex products are rejected by some cultures.

Table 6-1 shows the errors a firm engaged in international marketing could commit due to a lack of awareness about foreign cultures. Sometimes, the firm is at fault because it operates out of a domestic home office and gets little local input. Other times, especially in less-developed countries, information may be limited because a low level of population data exist and mail and phone services are poor. In either case, marketing research—to determine hidden meanings and the ease of pronunciation of brand names and slogans, the

Table 6-1

Illustrations of Errors in International Marketing Because of a Lack of Cultural Awareness

In the Czech Republic, Eurotel portable phones did poorly when introduced because they were perceived as walkie-talkies.

Japanese cars had engine trouble in China, where drivers turn off their motors when stopped at red lights. Inasmuch as the air-conditioning in these cars kept going with the motors off, the engines malfunctioned.

At the Moscow Pizza Hut, consumers did not purchase the Moscva Seafood Pizza, with sardines and salmon. "Russians have this thing. If it's their own, it must be bad."

Pepsodent failed in Southeast Asia when it promised white teeth to a culture where black or yellow teeth are symbols of prestige.

Maxwell House advertised itself as the "great American coffee" in Germany, although Germans have little respect for American coffee.

In Mexico, a U.S. airline meant to advertise that passengers could sit in comfortable leather seats; but the phrase used in its Spanish translation ("sentando en cuero") meant "sit naked."

African men were upset by a commercial for men's deodorant that showed a happy male being chased by women. They thought the deodorant would make them weak and overrun by women.

Source: Compiled by the authors from various publications.

Table 6-2

Illustrations of Cultural Opportunities for International Marketers

Globally, the greatest growth in ready-to-eat cereal sales is in Latin America, where there is new interest in convenience foods.

After one year of employment, in most European countries people receive 20 to 25 days of vacation (compared to 10 days for Canadians and Americans). This means an emphasis on travel, summer homes, and leisure wear.

Japanese consumers are attracted by high-tech vending machines—such as those that play music, talk, dispense free products at random, and use splashy rotating signs.

Worldwide, consumers want the "American look" provided by Levi's jeans.

At Domino's outlets in Australia, the favourite pizzas are those with prawns and pineapple.

In China, the most popular colour is red—indicating happiness. Black elicits a positive response because it denotes power and trustworthiness.

French Canadians drink more soda, beer, and wine than their English-speaking counterparts.

Nigerians believe "good beer only comes in green bottles."

British consumers insist on cake mixes that require their adding fresh eggs, as Betty Crocker mixes sold there do.

Source: Compiled by the authors from various publications.

LEVI STRAUSS
www.levi.com/

rate of product consumption, and reasons for purchases and nonpurchases—would not be fully effective.

Cultural awareness can be improved by employing foreign personnel in key positions, hiring experienced marketing research specialists, locating offices in each country of operations, studying cultural differences, and responding to cultural changes. Table 6-2 shows several cultural opportunities.

This is how Samsung, Korea's largest firm, is improving cultural awareness among its executives:

> Overseas-bound managers attend a month-long boot camp to get lessons on table manners, dancing, and avoiding sexual harassment. In addition, 400 bright junior employees are sent abroad for a year. Their decidedly un-Korean mission: Goof off. "International exposure is important, but you have to develop international tastes. You have to goof off at the mall and watch people." The program costs U.S.$80 000 a year per person and takes key people out of their jobs. But Samsung is convinced cultural immersion will pay off in more astute judgments about what customers want.[8]

SAMSUNG
www.samsung.com/

The Economic Environment

A nation's economic environment indicates its present and potential capacity for consuming goods and services. Measures of economic performance include the standard of living, the Gross Domestic Product (GDP), the stage of economic development, and the stability of currency.

The **standard of living** refers to the average quantity and quality of goods and services that are owned and consumed in a given nation. According to United Nations Organization for Economic Cooperation and Development (OECD) data, the United States has the highest standard of living of any industrialized country in the world, and Canada ranks second. By examining a nation's per-capita ownership and consumption across a range of goods and services, a firm can estimate the standard of living there (regarding the average *quantity* of goods and services). Table 6-3 compares data for eleven diverse countries.

The quality of life in a nation is measured by its **standard of living**.

[8] "Korea's Biggest Firm Teaches Junior Execs Strange Foreign Ways," *Wall Street Journal* (December 30, 1992), p. 1.

Table 6-3
Ownership and Consumption in Eleven Countries

	PASSENGER CARS (per 100 People)	TV SETS (per 100 People)	RADIOS (per 100 People)	DAILY NEWSPAPER CIRCULATION (per 100 People)	TELEPHONE LINES (per 100 People)	ENERGY CONSUMPTION (Kilograms per Year per Person)
Brazil	8	21	44	6	7	800
Canada	46	64	100	23	59	10 900
China	.2	3	19	4	1	800
France	41	50	89	21	52	5 500
Great Britain	35	43	115	40	45	5 400
India	.3	4	8	3	1	340
Italy	48	42	79	11	41	4 000
Japan	31	61	91	59	47	4 750
Nigeria	.9	8	11	2	1	210
Russia	7	37	60	NA	15	6 400
United States	55	81	212	25	56	10 800

NA = Not available.
Source: United Nations data; Statistics Canada *Market Research Handbook 1995*; and authors' estimates.

The total value of goods and services produced in a nation is its **Gross Domestic Product**.

As noted in Chapter 2, the **Gross Domestic Product (GDP)** is the total value of goods and services produced in a country each year. Total and per-capita GDP are the most frequently used measures of a nation's wealth because they are regularly published and easy to calculate and compare with other nations. But per-capita GDP may be misleading. The figures are means and not income distributions; a few wealthy citizens may boost per-capita GDP, even though the bulk of the population has low income. And due to price and product-availability differences, the same income purchases a different standard of living in each nation. An income of U.S.$33 000 in Canada yields the same standard of living as an income of U.S.$30 000 in the United States, U.S.$13 200 in Brazil, U.S.$11 100 in Poland, U.S.$6900 in China, U.S.$6600 in India, and U.S.$5100 in Uganda.[9]

Marketing opportunities often can be highlighted by looking at a country's stage of economic growth. One way to classify growth is to divide nations into industrialized, developing, and less-developed groups.[10] See Figure 6-5.

Countries can be classified as **industrialized, developing**, *and* **less developed**.

Industrialized countries have high literacy, modern technology, and a per-capita income of several thousand dollars. They can be placed into two main subgroups: established free-market economies and newly emerging free-market economies. The former include Canada, the United States, Japan, Australia, and countries in Western Europe; they have a large middle class, annual per-capita GDP of U.S.$12 000 and up, and plentiful goods and services to satisfy their needs. The latter include Russia and its former republics, as well as other nations in Eastern Europe; although industrialized, they have a smaller middle class, annual per-capita GDP of U.S.$5000 to U.S.$8000, and insufficient goods and services to satisfy all of their needs.

In **developing countries**, education and technology are rising, and per-capita GDP is about U.S.$2000 to U.S.$4000. Included in this grouping are many Latin American

---
[9] Peter Fuhrman and Michael Schuman, "Where Are the Indians? The Russians?" *Forbes* (July 17, 1995), pp. 126, 128.
[10] Peter D. Bennett (Ed.), *Dictionary of Marketing Terms*, Second Edition (Chicago: American Marketing Association, 1995), various pages.

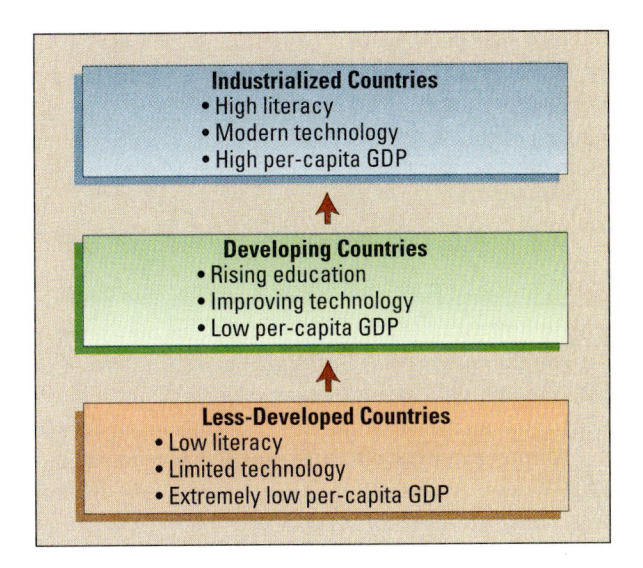

FIGURE 6-5
The Stages of Economic Development

nations. Although developing countries are striving to build their industries, consumers there are limited in what they can purchase (due to the scarcity and relatively high prices of goods and services). These countries account for 20 per cent of world population and almost one-third of its income.

Less-developed countries include a number of nations in Africa and South Asia. Compared to other nations, literacy is lower and technology is more limited. Per-capita GDP is below U.S.$1500 (sometimes less than U.S.$500). These nations have two-thirds of the world's population but under 15 per cent of world income. According to UN data, people in the most affluent one-fifth of the world have 65 times greater per-capita GDP than those in the bottom one-fifth.

The greatest marketing opportunities often occur in industrialized nations due to their higher incomes and standards of living. However, industrialized countries have slower rates of population growth, and sales of some product categories may have peaked. In contrast, developing and less-developed nations tend to have more rapidly expanding populations but now purchase few imports. There is long-run potential for international marketers in these nations. For example, Brazilians have only 80 cars per 1000 population and Indians 3 per 1000. The 1.2 billion people of China have 2.3 million cars—compared to 1.7 million cars in Denmark, a country with just over 5 million people.

Currency stability should also be considered in international transactions because sales and profits could be affected if a foreign currency fluctuates widely relative to a firm's home currency. For example, during 1995, the value of the Mexican peso against the Canadian dollar fell from 2.38 to 4.85 pesos per dollar—in January 1996, a Mexican consumer had to spend 485 of his or her pesos to buy a $100 Canadian good that cost 238 pesos in January 1995. This decline in the peso's value meant Mexican goods became cheaper for consumers in other nations, while foreign products became more expensive for Mexicans. As a result, foreign firms had some difficulty exporting products to Mexico during this period because their prices became too high.

In recent years, the currencies of both industrialized countries and developing and less-developed nations have fluctuated—some dramatically. As a rule, the currencies of established free-market industrialized countries have been more stable than those of other nations.

Currency stability affects foreign sales and profit.

The Political and Legal Environment

Every nation has a unique political and legal environment. Among the factors for international marketers to study are nationalism, government stability, trade restrictions, and trade agreements and economic communities.

Nationalism involves a host country's attempts to promote its interests.

Nationalism refers to a country's efforts to become self-reliant and raise its stature in the eyes of the world community. At times, a high degree of nationalism may lead to tight restrictions on foreign firms as governments seek to foster the development of domestic industry at their expense. In the past, some nations have even seized the assets of multinational firms, revoked their licenses to operate, prevented funds transfers from one currency to another, increased taxes, and/or unilaterally changed contract terms.

Government stability must be studied in terms of two elements: consistency of business policies and orderliness in installing leaders. Do government policies regarding taxes, company expansion, profits, and so on, remain relatively unchanged over time? Is there an orderly process for selecting and installing new government leaders? Firms will probably not function well unless both factors are positive. Thus, although Nestlé, PepsiCo, and CPC International have made large investments in developing nations, other food companies have stayed away from some less-developed and developing countries.

A firm can protect itself against the adverse effects of nationalism and political instability. Prior to entering a foreign market, it can measure the potential for domestic instability (riots, government purges), the political climate (stability of political parties, manner of choosing officials), and the economic climate (financial strength, government intervention)—and avoid nations deemed unsuitable.

For example, the October 30, 1995 Quebec referendum on sovereignty had powerful effects on the value of the Canadian dollar (it rose to 75.25 cents on the day after the referendum, from a close of U.S.73.58 cents the previous day) and the assessment of business risk in Canada. The closeness of the outcome of the referendum (50.6 per cent to 49.4 per cent) means that foreign investors in Canada are likely to be relatively cautious about how and where they invest, expecially with respect to direct investment in Quebec. Even within Canada, a number of domestic firms are uncertain about how their business interests might be affected by a sovereign Quebec. Southam Inc. has put plans to build a new printing plant in Montreal on hold until the political and economic situation in Quebec stabilizes. However, since the sovereignty question remains open, most Canadian business firms shy away from making any official policy statements on sovereignty for fear of causing the very market instability they want to avoid.[11]

To assist firms with international marketing the Department of Foreign Affairs and International Trade operates "The Trade Commissioner Service," which provides information on marketing research and market development for Canadian firms interested in doing business internationally. Industry Canada's Strategis website is also a useful source of information on doing business internationally. In addition, the federal government provides direct assistance for firms who wish to market internationally through the Export Development Corporation. This corporation enables firms to operate with less risk by providing loans, guarantees, insurance, and other types of financial aid. Risks can also be reduced by using foreign partners, borrowing money from foreign governments or banks, and/or utilizing licensing, contract manufacturing, or management contracting (which are covered later in the chapter).

Tariffs, trade quotas, embargoes, and local content laws are forms of trade restrictions.

Another aspect of the international political and legal environment involves trade restrictions. The most common one is a **tariff**, which is a tax placed on imported products by a foreign government. The second major restriction is a **trade quota**, which sets limits on the amounts of products that can be imported into a country. The strictest form of trade quota is an **embargo**, which disallows entry of specified products into a country. The third major restriction involves **local content laws**, which require foreign-based firms to set up local plants and use locally made components. The goal of tariffs, trade quotas, and local content laws is to protect both the economies and the domestic employment of the nations involved. Embargoes may also have political ramifications, as with the UN embargoes on Iraqi oil and on weapons sales to Bosnia, Croatia, and Serbia. Here are some further examples:

---

[11]Gail Chiasson, "Walking on Eggshells," *Marketing Magazine* (March 18, 1996), p. 9; Cathy Taylor, "Not Taking Sides: U.S. Marketers Steer Clear of Quebec Politics," *Marketing Magazine* (March 18, 1996), p. 10; and Eric Siblin, "It's No, By a Hair: Federalists Win—Only by One Point," *The Daily News Worldwide* (Tuesday, October 31, 1995), Internet address, http://www/cfn.cs.dal.ca/Media/TodaysNews/quevec1.html.

- There are Canadian tariffs on imported clothing, poultry, dairy products, beer and malt products, liquor, wine, sugar, tobacco, tires, pleasure craft, appliances, steel, and other items. The tariffs raise import prices relative to domestic items.
- Many European nations have pacts with Japan that set voluntary quotas on certain goods exported by Japan to those nations. The agreements limit the sales of VCRs, autos, TVs, quartz watches, and machine tools.
- To stimulate domestic production, in 1984 Brazil placed an embargo on most foreign computer products. The embargo was not lifted until 1990, with some microcomputers still barred until 1992.
- In Italy, food products cannot be called pasta unless they are made from durum wheat, which is the country's major wheat crop.

Some barriers among nations have been reduced through trade agreements and economic communities. In 1948, twenty-three nations, including Canada and the United States, signed the General Agreement on Tariffs and Trade (GATT) to foster multilateral trade. By 1994, 115 nations participated in GATT. From its inception, GATT talks helped lower tariffs on manufactured goods. But member nations got bogged down because trade in services, agriculture, textiles, and investment and capital flows was not covered; and GATT let members belong to regional trade associations (economic communities) with fewer trade barriers among the nations involved in those associations than among those not involved.

On January 1, 1995, after eight years of difficult negotiations, GATT was replaced by the **World Trade Organization (WTO)**. About 125 nations have joined the WTO, whose mission is to open up international markets even further and promote a cooperative atmosphere around the globe. These are some of the provisions of the WTO:

The **World Trade Organization** *seeks to eliminate trade barriers. GATT set up the most-favoured nation principle.*

- Thousands of tariffs are to be reduced globally by about 40 per cent.
- Intellectual-property protection (such as copyright and patent rights) is to be enacted worldwide. The agreement specifies twenty years protection for patents and up to fifty years for copyrights. This will help book, software, movie, and pharmaceutical companies combat piracy.
- There are tougher rules regarding price dumping in foreign markets to discourage firms from selling at below-market prices in foreign countries.
- New rules apply to global agricultural and textile-products transactions.
- Some nations have agreed to open up their markets for legal and accounting services, as well as computer software. However, Canada did not secure much access to the foreign markets that are closed to Canadian banks and securities firms, such as those in Japan and other Asian countries.
- Three-person arbitration panels are to rule on disputes between countries.
- Economic communities are still permitted.[12]

In contrast to the WTO, which promotes free trade around the world, each **economic community** promotes free trade among its member nations—but not necessarily with nonmembers. As a result, the best interests of the WTO and of economic communities may clash.

The two leading **economic communities** *are the* **European Union** *and the* **North American Free Trade Agreement.**

The two leading economic communities are the European Union and the North American Free Trade community. The **European Union (EU)**, also called the Common Market, consists of Austria, Belgium, Denmark, Finland, France, Germany, Great Britain, Greece, Ireland, Italy, Luxembourg, the Netherlands, Portugal, Spain, and Sweden. And other European nations are expected to join the EU within the next five years. EU rules call for no trade restrictions among members; uniform tariffs with nonmembers; common product standards; and a free flow of people and capital. The aim is for members to have

---

[12]"The Trade Pact's Key Provisions," *Wall Street Journal* (December 2, 1994), p. A8; Paul Lewis, "Trade in Financial Services Is Dealt a Setback by U.S.," *New York Times* (June 30, 1995), pp. D1, D4; and Eduardo Lachica, "U.S. May Be Losing Its Trade-Bully Status," *Wall Street Journal* (October 13, 1995), p. A11.

an open marketplace, as exists among provinces in Canada. One of the EU's biggest challenges is installing a common currency, which will not occur until the turn of the century.

In 1988, Canada and the United States reached agreement on a free-trade pact. They then turned to negotiating a free-trade accord with Mexico. On January 1, 1994, the **North American Free Trade Agreement (NAFTA)** was enacted, creating an economic community that links Canada, the United States, and Mexico; over the next several years, tariffs and other trade restrictions among the three countries are to be removed. The NAFTA community and the EU are about the same size in both total GDP and total population (until the EU adds more members). There have been some very preliminary discussions about expanding NAFTA to include such emerging Latin American nations as Brazil and Chile. But it is quite unlikely that NAFTA will expand in the near future.

Other economic communities include the Andean Pact (with five Latin American members), the Association of South East Asian Nations (with six members), the Caribbean Common Market (with more than a dozen members), the Central American Common Market (with five members), the Gulf Cooperation Council (with six Arabic members), the Economic Community of West African States (with 16 members), and Mercosur (with four Latin American members).

As many nations in Eastern Europe and elsewhere have moved to more open economies, they have become more interested in increasing their world trade. They are deregulating industries, encouraging foreign investment, and seeking trade agreements with free-market nations. In 1990, Eastern Europe's Council for Mutual Economic Assistance announced its own demise— members did not want to be hampered by a "ramshackle trading system." Since then, a number of Eastern European countries have expressed interest in eventually gaining entry into the European Union.[13]

The Technological Environment

International marketing may require adjustments in technology.

Technological factors such as these affect international marketing:

- Technology advances vary around the world. For example, outside Canada and the United States, cable TV is more limited. Even in Western Europe, only one-third of households have cable TV (compared to 74 per cent in Canada and two-thirds in the United States).

- Foreign workers must often be trained to run equipment unfamiliar to them.

- Problems occur if equipment maintenance practices vary by nation or adverse physical conditions exist, such as high humidity, extreme hot or cold weather, or air pollution.

- Electricity and electrical power needs may vary by nation and require product modifications. For example, Canadian appliances work on 110 volts; European appliances work on 220 volts.

- Although the metric system is used by 95 per cent of the world's population, our largest trading partner, the United States, still relies on ounces, pounds, inches, and feet. Thus, Canadian auto makers, food processors, beverage bottlers, and many other firms make items using metric standards—and then list U.S. and metric measures side-by-side on labels and packages.

On the plus side, various technological advances are easing the growth of international marketing. Such advances involve transactions (automatic teller machines), order processing (computerization), communications (TV satellites, facsimile machines, the Internet), and production (multiplant innovations).

---

[13]Tim Carrington, "Anxiety Grows as Comecon's End Nears," *Wall Street Journal* (July 20, 1990), p. B6; Richard W. Stevenson, "East Europe Says Barriers to Trade Hurt Its Economies," *New York Times* (January 25, 1993), pp. A1, D5; and Nathaniel C. Nash, "European Union Offers Timetable for Talks with Applicants," *New York Times* (December 17, 1995), Section 1, page 17.

TECHNOLOGY & MARKETING

How Should PCs Be Marketed in Developing Countries?

Until recently, both companies and consumers in less-developed nations were unable to purchase PCs and related items due to their high prices. But now very affordable PCs and computer networks are flooding the market. Throughout Latin America, the sales of PCs are hot—with annual growth rates of 25 per cent and more.

Some experts attribute the strong sales to the technological advances of the new PCs (which let businesses use PCs for functions that formerly could only be undertaken by expensive mainframe computers): "Technology is quite reasonably priced for most people, except in the very, very poor nations." Other experts see the high inflation rates in many less-developed countries as an impetus to computer sales. According to that theory, many firms and individuals would rather buy PCs now on the assumption that they will be much more expensive in the future.

Let's look at PC and workstation sales in Chile: From 1991 to 1995, the annual sales of PCs and workstations in Chile grew from U.S.$55 million to U.S.$200 million. Still, there were fewer than four PCs for every 100 people as of the end of 1995 (compared to Canada where 25 per cent of Canadian households have a PC). Much of Chile's PC sales growth is from small businesses that use computers to track inventories or prepare invoices, from larger firms that use computers to dispatch their salespeople or to track sales of important products, and from electronic banking. In addition, "Chile's export-promotion agency recently connected 160 PCs around the world to a group of Compaq Computer Corp. servers back at its Santiago headquarters, allowing prospective buyers to see exactly what's available, when, and what price."

As the marketing vice-president for a PC manufacturer, what would you do differently in Chile than in Canada?

Source: Based on material in Scott McCartney and Jonathan Friedland, "Computer Sales Sizzle as Developing Nations Try to Shrink PC Gap," *Wall Street Journal* (June 29, 1995), pp. A1, A8 and Statistics Canada, *Market Research Handbook 1995*, p. 232.

Developing an International Marketing Strategy

The vital parts of an international marketing strategy are explored next: company organization; market entry decisions; the degree of standardization; and product, distribution, promotion, and price planning.

Company Organization

A firm has three organizational formats from which to choose: exporting, joint venture, and direct ownership. They are compared in Figure 6-6.

With **exporting**, a firm reaches international markets by selling products made in its home country directly through its own sales force or indirectly via foreign merchants or agents. In direct selling, a firm situates its sales force in a home office or foreign branch offices. This method is favoured when customers are easy to locate, concentrated, or come to the seller. With indirect selling, a firm hires outside specialists to contact customers. The specialists may be based in the home or foreign country. Indirect selling is best if customers are hard to locate or dispersed, a potential exporter has limited funds, and/or local customs are unique.

An exporting structure requires minimal investment in foreign facilities. There is no foreign production by the firm. The exporter may modify packages, labels, or catalogues at its domestic facilities in response to foreign market needs. Exporting embodies the lowest level of commitment to international marketing. Most smaller firms that engage in

Exporting *lets a firm reach international markets without foreign production.*

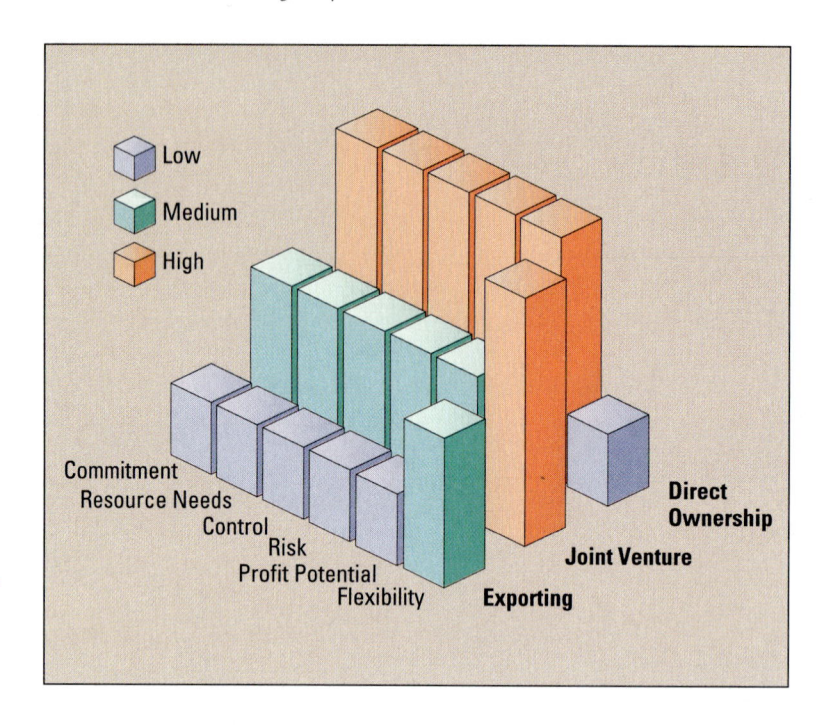

158 Part 2 *Broadening an Organization's Individual's Marketing Scope*

FIGURE 6-6
Alternate Company Organizations for International Marketing

*A **joint venture** can be based on licensing, contract manufacturing, management contracting, or joint ownership.*

international marketing rely on exporting. For example, IP Constructors Ltd. specializes in making oil and gas processing equipment that removes water and other contaminants from wellheads at its two Calgary plants. Although Calgary and the province of Alberta are at the heart of the Canadian oil industry, IP Constructors Ltd. makes over 97 per cent of its sales overseas.[14]

With a **joint venture** (also known as a strategic alliance), a firm agrees to combine some aspect of its manufacturing or marketing efforts with those of a foreign company so as to share expertise, costs, and/or connections with important persons. As experts observe: "In this period of advanced technology and global markets, implementing strategies quickly is essential. Forming alliances is often the fastest, most effective method of reaching objectives. However, without the proper partner, a company should not undertake an alliance, even for the right reasons. Partners must be compatible and willing to trust one another."[15]

Here are examples of firms engaged in international joint ventures:

- Credit Suisse (Switzerland) and CS First Boston (United States) are partners in ventures that offer financial services around the world. See Figure 6-7.

- Airbus Industrie, a jet maker, is owned and operated by Aerospatiale (France), Deutsche Airbus (Germany), British Aerospace, and Construcciones Aeronauticas (Spain). It gets financial support from members' governments.

- Charoen Pokphand (Thailand) has a telecommunications venture with Nynex (United States) and a retailing venture with Wal-Mart (United States).

- CanWest Global Communications (Canada) has a 50 per cent stake in television network La Red Television (Chile)[16]

---

[14]William J. Holstein and Kevin Kelly, "Little Companies, Big Exports," *Business Week* (April 13, 1992), p. 71. See also Stephanie N. Mehta, "Small Companies Look to Cultivate Foreign Business," *Wall Street Journal* (July 7, 1994) p. B1; Alexander Ross and Randall Litchfield, "Clean Machines," *Canadian Business* (December 1993), p. 34.

[15]Bruce A. Walters, Steve Peters, and Gregory G. Dess, "Strategic Alliances and Joint Ventures: Making Them Work," *Business Horizons*, Vol. 37 (July-August 1994), p. 5.

[16]Patrick J. Spain and James R. Talbot, *Hoover's Handbook of World Business 1995-1996* (Austin, Texas: Reference Press, 1995), various pages; Joyce Barnathan, Pete Engardio, and John Winzenburg, "Asia's New Giants," *Business Week* (November 27, 1995), p. 78; Geri Smith and John Pearson, "The New World's Newest Trade Bloc," *Business Week* (May 4, 1992), p. 51; and Ian McGugan, "A Boom Heard Around the World," *Canadian Business* (January 1995), pp. 58–70.

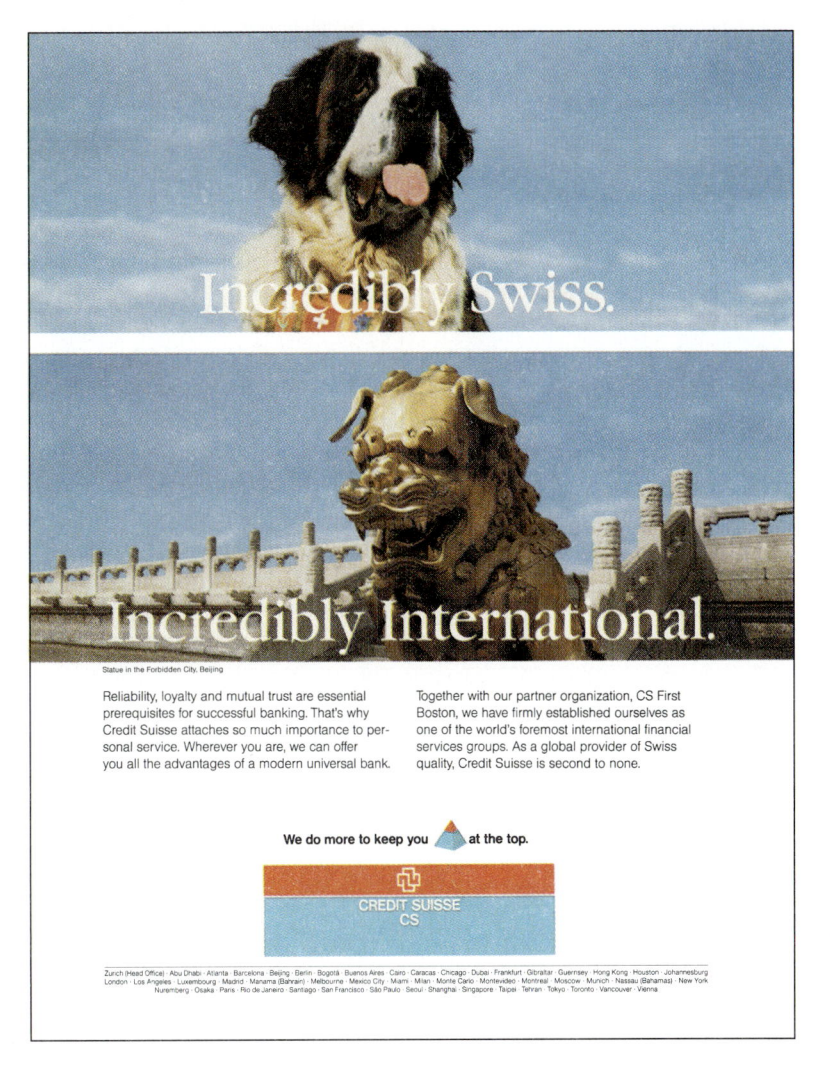

FIGURE 6-7

A Joint Venture that Is "Incredibly International"

A joint venture may lead to reduced costs and favourable trade terms from a foreign government if products are made locally and some degree of foreign ownership is set. Thus, joint ventures between Japanese and Canadian firms are growing because Japanese firms see them as lowering the possibility of trade restrictions. Canadian firms view the ventures as a means of opening the Japanese market and as a way of observing and learning from potential competitors.

A joint venture can involve licensing, contract manufacturing, management contracting, or joint ownership. Licensing gives a foreign firm the rights to a manufacturing process, trademark, patent, and/or trade secret in exchange for a commission, fee, or royalty. Coca-Cola and PepsiCo license products in some nations. Under contract manufacturing, a firm agrees to have a foreign company make its products locally. The firm markets the products itself and provides management expertise. This arrangement is common in book publishing. In management contracting, a firm acts as a consultant to foreign companies. Delta Hotels of Toronto has a management contract with the Cuban resort hotel, Delta Los Brisas. Delta supplies the management and marketing knowledge, and its state-owned Cuban partner, Cubanacan SA, provides the property, operating materials and labour.[17] With joint ownership, a firm produces and markets products in partnership with a foreign company so as to reduce costs and spread risk. General Electric has a majority

---

[17] Tamsen Tillson, "Rooms at the Revolution," *Canadian Business* (February 1996), pp. 75–76.

Direct ownership *involves total control of foreign operations and facilities by a firm.*

MAGNA INTERNATIONAL
www.magnaint.com/Magna/

A firm needs to determine which and how many foreign markets to do business in.

interest in Tungsram, a Hungarian light-bulb maker. Sometimes, a government may require joint ownership with local businesses as a condition for entry. In Japan, outsiders must use joint ownership with Japanese firms. Domestically, the Canadian government regulates foreign investment and requires outsiders to use joint ownership with Canadian firms for new ventures.

With **direct ownership**, a firm owns production, marketing, and other facilities in one or more foreign nations without any partners. The firm has full control over its international operations in those nations. Thus, Toronto's Magna International Corporation opened a U.S.$20 million auto-parts plant in Puebla, Mexico in 1993. A wholly owned subsidiary may also be established. In Canada, John Labatt (Labatt breweries) is a subsidiary of Interbrew S.A. of Belgium and Imperial Oil Ltd. (Esso gasoline and service stations) is a subsidiary of Exxon Corporation of Texas. Similarly, foreign facilities of Canadian-based firms annually yield revenues of billions of dollars.

Under direct ownership, a firm has all the benefits and risks of owning a foreign business. There are potential labour savings and marketing plans are more sensitive to local needs. Profit potential may be high, although costs may also be high. There is a possibility of nationalistic acts, and government restrictions are apt to be stricter. This is the riskiest organization form.

Companies often combine formats. For instance, a firm could use exporting in a country with a history of taking over the assets of foreign businesses and direct ownership in one with tax advantages for construction. McDonald's (Canadian sales of $1.6 billion in 1994) combines company-operated stores (19 per cent of outlets), franchisee-operated stores (70 per cent of outlets), and affiliate-operated stores—whereby McDonald's owns 50 per cent or less of the assets, with the rest owned by resident nationals (11 per cent of outlets). Company stores are largely in Canada, the United States, France, Great Britain, and Germany; franchisee outlets are mostly in Canada, the United States, France, Germany, and Australia; and affiliate restaurants are common in Latin America, Japan, and other Pacific nations. McDonald's has outlets in more than 70 countries outside North America; they generate nearly 50 per cent of system-wide sales.[18]

Market Entry Decisions

There are a number of factors to consider in deciding which and how many foreign markets a firm should enter.

Which Market(s) to Enter

- Are there cultural similarities between the foreign country and the company's home market? How important is this?
- Are there language similarities between the foreign country and the firm's home market? How important is this?
- Is the standard of living in the foreign country consistent with the goods and services the company would offer there?
- How large is the foreign market for the goods and services the firm would offer there? Is it growing? What is the regional potential (e.g., Eastern Europe)?
- Is the technology in the foreign market appropriate for the firm to do business? Is the country's infrastructure appropriate?
- Are there enough skilled workers in the foreign country?
- Are the media in the foreign country adequate for the firm's marketing efforts?
- What is the level of competition in the foreign market?
- What are the government restrictions the firm would face in the foreign market? The economic communities?

---

[18]Hoover, Campbell, and Spain, *Hoover's Handbook of American Business 1995*, pp. 744–745; and "Performance 500," *Canadian Business* (June 1995), p. 106.

- How stable are the currency and government in the foreign market?
- Is the overall business climate in the foreign country favourable to a firm?

HOW MANY MARKETS TO ENTER

- What are the firm's available resources?
- How many foreign markets could the firm's management and marketing personnel properly oversee and service?
- How diverse are multiple foreign markets? What is the geographic proximity?
- What are the marketing economies of scale from being regional or global?
- Are exporting arrangements possible? Are joint ventures?
- What are the firm's goals regarding its mix of domestic and foreign revenues?
- How extensive is competition in the firm's home market?

Standardizing Plans

A firm engaged in international marketing must determine the degree to which plans should be standardized. Both standardized and nonstandardized plans have benefits and limitations.

With a **standardized (global) marketing approach**, a firm uses a common marketing plan for all nations in which it operates—because the firm assumes that worldwide markets are becoming more homogeneous due to better communications, more open country borders, the move to free-market economies, and other factors. This approach downplays differences among foreign markets. There are marketing and production economies—product design, packaging, advertising, and other costs are spread over a large product base. A uniform image is presented, training foreign personnel is easier, and centralized control is applied. Yet, standardization is insensitive to individual market needs, and input from foreign personnel is limited:

> The increase in global markets and global competition is attributed to many factors. The pressures for growth in slow-growth home markets are driving companies around the world to seek new geographic markets. Converging customer tastes and requirements, the need to gain scale from world market development, shortening product life cycles, and expanding financial markets all have made globalization more necessary and feasible. Government changes, too, are freeing up or encouraging increased global competition.
>
> Yet, the world economy remains mostly local both in market characteristics and in marketing and competitive requirements. Regional conditions and tastes vary to the point where local customization is necessary—often in products and usually in marketing [especially in Canada with its multicultural make-up.] Many industries can support a business on a local country or regional basis; they need not garner scale from cross-country or cross-region participation. Product development and production technologies, too, are helping provide the flexibility to adjust products for local needs. Finally, as much as government actions are stimulating cross-border competition, they are restricting it as well.[19]

With a **nonstandardized marketing approach**, a firm sees each nation or region as distinct, and requiring its own marketing plan. This strategy is sensitive to local needs and means grooming foreign managers, as decentralized control is undertaken. It works best when distinctive major foreign markets are involved and/or a firm has many product lines. For instance, although Bausch & Lomb has such "global" brands as Ray-Ban sunglasses, its strategy is tailored to individual markets: "In Europe, Ray-Bans tend to be flashier, more avant garde, and costlier. In Asia, the company redesigned them to better suit the Asian face—with its flatter bridge and higher cheekbones—and sales took off. Ray-Ban commands an awesome 40 per cent of the world market for premium-priced ($40 to $250) sunglasses."[20]

In recent years, more firms (including Bausch & Lomb) have turned to a **glocal marketing approach**—which stands for *think global and act local*. Under this approach, combin-

*Under a **standardized approach**, a common marketing plan is used for each nation. Under a **nonstandardized approach**, each country is given a separate marketing plan. A **glocal approach** is a combination strategy.*

BAUSCH & LOMB
www.bausch.com/

[19] Marc C. Particelli, "A Global Arena," *Journal of Consumer Marketing*, Vol. 7 (Fall 1990), pp. 43–52.
[20] Rahul Jacob, "Trust the Locals, Win Worldwide," *Fortune* (May 4, 1992), p. 76.

ing standardized and nonstandardized efforts lets a firm attain production efficiencies, have a consistent image, have some home-office control, and still be sensitive and responsive to local needs. To U.S.-based CPC International (the maker of such brands as Hellmann's Mayonnaise, Knorr soups, Mueller's pasta, Skippy peanut butter, and Mazola corn oil), a glocal approach is "the best of both worlds":

> *We are emphatically global* in our strategy of building a few core businesses worldwide; in the way we share technology, coordinate purchasing, and maximize other CPC worldwide resources; in our application of financial strength to seize opportunities wherever they may be; in our ability to spot worldwide trends before they become locally obvious; in the geographic spread of our businesses that helps us offset economic difficulties in one market with rapid growth in another. At the same time, *we are decisively local* in our detailed understanding of cultures, consumer trends, and competitive environments in fifty-nine countries; in our ability to adapt our products to local eating habits and our marketing programs to local cultural nuances and developing trends; in the entrepreneurial energy that thrives in local CPC teams empowered to act quickly and take risk where we, as the local "home team," have a competitive advantage.[21]

When determining a marketing approach, a firm should evaluate whether differences among countries are sufficient to warrant changes in marketing plans, which elements of marketing can be standardized, whether the size of each foreign market would lead to profitable adaptation, and if modifications can be made on a regional rather than a country basis.

Product Planning

International product planning (including both goods and services) can be based on straight-extension, product-adaptation, backward-invention, and/or forward-invention strategies.

Straight extension, product adaptation, backward invention, *and* **forward invention** *are basic methods of international product planning.*

In a **straight-extension** strategy, a firm makes and markets the same products for domestic and foreign sales. The firm is confident successful products can be sold abroad without modifications in the product, its brand name, packaging, or ingredients. This simple approach capitalizes on economies of scale in production. Apple markets the same PCs in Canada, the United States, and Mexico. Coca-Cola and PepsiCo use straight extension to "cross multitudes of national, regional, and ethnic taste buds trained to a variety of deeply ingrained local preferences of taste, flavour, consistency, effervescence, and aftertaste."[22] Beer makers also use straight extension; and imported beer often has a higher status than domestic beer. Yet, a straight-extension strategy does not take into account differences in customers, laws, customs, technology, and other factors.

With a **product-adaptation** strategy, domestic products are modified to meet foreign-language needs, taste preferences, climates, electrical requirements, laws, and/or other factors. It is assumed that new products are not needed and minor changes are sufficient. This is the most often-used strategy in international marketing: For example, Knorr Products' food packages are printed in the languages of the nations in which they are sold, as shown in Figure 6-8. This is how Boeing used product adaptation in marketing its 737 jet in the Mideast, Africa, and South America:

> The runways in developing [and less-developed] countries were too short to accommodate the jet, and too soft, made of asphalt instead of concrete. Boeing's engineers redesigned the wings to allow shorter landings and added thrust to the engines for quicker takeoffs. Boeing also redesigned the landing gear and installed low-pressure tires so the plane would stick to the ground when it touched down.[23]

With **backward invention**, a firm appeals to developing and less-developed nations by making products less complex than the ones it sells in its domestic market. This includes

---

[21] *CPC International 1994 Annual Report.*
[22] Kate Bertrand, "The Pan-American Marketing Motherlode," *Business Marketing* (December 1992), p. 31; and Theodore Levitt, "The Globalization of Markets," *Harvard Business Review*, Vol. 61 (May-June 1983), pp. 92–102.
[23] Andrew Kupfer, "How to Be a Global Manager," *Fortune* (March 14, 1988), p. 52.

Ethics AND TODAY'S MARKETER

Why Aren't International Codes of Conduct More Effective?

As a condition for doing business with U.S. retailer J.C. Penney, Canadian and other suppliers around the world are required to sign a code of conduct. This code forbids suppliers from violating any local labour law, including the hiring of underage children. The penalty for violating a contract condition is the immediate loss of J.C. Penney's current and future business. According to many industry observers, enforcing such contract clauses is at best very hard and at worst impossible.

As an example, Guatemala is a country with a long history of firms using illegal child labour and paying workers below the minimum wage. Despite codes of conduct, labour-law violations are rampant there. Nonetheless, in 1994, 400 Guatemalan firms exported U.S.$591 million worth of clothing to the United States.

Guatemalan government labour officials estimate that half of the country's apparel workers are paid below the minimum wage. And one government official says there are 300 000 illegally employed minors in Guatemala. Visits to Guatemalan factories that supply J.C. Penney have turned up children under the age of 14 (the minimum legal age to work), workers who are paid below the country's minimum wage of $2.80 per day, and workers who are forced to toil overtime on an unpaid basis.

According to one market analyst, "Setting standards is 5 per cent of the work; ensuring compliance is 95 per cent." J.C. Penney's difficulty in enforcing standards is compounded by having suppliers in over 50 countries. Many of these suppliers also hire subcontractors to complete their projects. In many cases, J.C. Penney does not even know which factory has produced its products. And some retailers, including Wal-Mart, rely on suppliers to self-police the retailer's code of conduct.

As a clothing buyer for J.C. Penney who does business with Guatemala-based factories, how would you make Penney's international code of conduct more effective?

Source: Based on material in Bob Ortega, "Conduct Codes Garner Goodwill for Retailers, But Violations Go On," *Wall Street Journal* (July 3, 1995), pp. A1, A14.

---

manual cash registers and nonelectric sewing machines for consumers in countries without widespread electricity and inexpensive washing machines for consumers in low-income countries. Whirlpool affiliates now build and sell an inexpensive "world washer" in Brazil, Mexico, and India. It is compact, is specially designed (so it does not tangle a sari), handles about one-half the capacity of a regular Canadian washer, and accommodates variations in component availability and local preferences.

In **forward invention**, a company develops new products for its international markets. This plan is riskier and more time-consuming and requires higher capital investments than other strategies. It may also provide the firm with great profit potential and, sometimes, worldwide recognition for innovativeness. Ford's mid-sized Mondeo car was introduced in Western Europe in 1993. The firm spent U.S.$6 billion and used five design studios to develop this front-wheel-drive car, priced at U.S.$18 000 in Europe. Ford introduced modified versions (named the Ford Contour and Mercury Mystique)—slightly longer and with more chrome—in Canada and the United States in 1994. Today, annual North American sales of the two cars total nearly 100 000 units.[24]

---

[24] Alex Taylor III, "Ford's $6 Billion Baby," *Fortune* (June 28, 1993), pp. 76–81; Richard W. Stevenson, "Ford Sets Its Sights on a 'World Car,'" *New York Times* (September 27, 1993), pp. D1, D4; and Hoover, Campbell, and Spain, *Hoover's Handbook of American Business 1995*, pp. 520–521.

FIGURE 6-8
A Modification Strategy for Knorr Products
CPC International markets its Knorr food products around the world. In many cases, it offers specially adapted versions of Knorr sauces, soups, and bouillons—tailored to the tastes of foreign consumers.
Reprinted by permission.

Distribution Planning

Channel members and physical distribution methods depend on customs, availability, costs, and other factors.

International distribution planning encompasses the selection and use of resellers and the physical movement of products. A company may sell directly to customers or hire outside distribution specialists—depending on the traditional distribution relationships in a country, the availability of appropriate resellers, differences in distribution practices from those in the home country, government restrictions, costs, and other factors. For example:

- In Brazil, PepsiCo markets soft drinks through the domestic Brahma Beer and Soda Company because of Brahma's extensive distribution network.
- Amway sells its household products in Japan via hundreds of thousands of local distributors (who are also customers); as in Canada, the distributors earn a commission on their sales.
- Loewen Group Inc. is a Burnaby, B.C.-based funeral service company. Loewen group identifies and takes over funeral homes across Canada and the United States. Most funeral homes are independent businesses and operate within the confines of provincial/state and municipal regulations. Loewen usually leaves the existing management in control to conserve funds for further takeovers.[25]

Physical distribution in international markets often requires special planning: Processing marine insurance, government documents, and other papers may take time. Transportation modes may be unavailable or inefficient. A nation may have inadequate docking facilities, poor highways, or too few motor vehicles. Distribution by ship is slow and subject to delays. Inventory management should take into account the availability of warehousing and the costs of shipping in small quantities.

[25]"Performance 500," *Canadian Business* (June 1995), p. 100.

Even product availability can be a significant problem. Thus, in Cuba, Toronto's Delta Hotels and Resorts in Havana faced difficulties simply finding basic foodstuffs like fruits, vegetables, eggs, and seafood. Cuban suppliers had shortages or just simply did not get around to making deliveries. Many of the suppliers were afraid they would not be paid. The distribution system for perishables is government-regulated with its associated bureaucracy. Instead of being able to buy lettuce from a farmer next door, Delta had to purchase from a distant produce market, thus extending the time from when the lettuce was picked to when it was available to Delta to as much as four days—hardly fresh lettuce. In response Delta now sponsors its own nearby farms and markets to get fruit and vegetables both fresh and fast. The Cuban government is letting landowners sell up to 20 per cent of their products on the open market as well. Still, Delta must bring in 10 to 12 per cent of its operating supplies from outside of Cuba.[26]

Promotion Planning

Promotion campaigns can be global, nonstandardized, or glocal.[27] Figures 6-9 and 6-10 show examples of nonstandardized and glocal ads.

Firms sometimes use globalized promotion for image purposes: Coca-Cola's "polar bear" TV and print ads have been used around the world, as have various IBM television

International promotion planning depends on the overlap of audiences and languages and the availability of media.

FIGURE 6-9

Klorin by Colgate-Palmolive: A Nonstandardized Approach to Advertising

This ad appeared in Sweden; and the Klorin brand is not marketed in Colgate-Palmolive's U.S. marketplace.
Reprinted by permission.

[26]Tamsen Tillson, "Rooms at the Revolution."
[27]See Madu Agrawal, "Review of a 40-Year Debate in International Advertising," *International Marketing Review*, Vol. 12 (Number 1, 1995), pp. 26–48.

FIGURE 6-10
A Global Visa Ad
The Visa card is a global symbol that appears in this ad. The copy is adapted to the markets in which various ads appear. The ad depicted here appeared in French-speaking Europe.
Reprinted by permission.

ads that highlight its vast computing strengths. At Revlon, "the intent is to make Revlon more of a global name. All Revlon North America advertising, for all products, whether they are cosmetics, skin care, hair care, or Almay, will be used worldwide."[28]

Companies marketing in various European nations often find that some standardization is desirable due to overlapping readership, listeners, and viewers. For instance, German TV shows are received by a large percentage of Dutch households and *Paris Match* magazine has substantial readership in Belgium, Switzerland, Luxembourg, Germany, Italy, and Holland.

There are also reasons for using nonstandardized promotion. Many countries have distinctions that are not addressed through a single promotion campaign. These differences include customs, language, the meaning of colours and symbols, and literacy rates. For instance, alcoholic products are banned in some Middle East nations. As a result, Stroh, Heineken, and others market nonalcoholic beers there. Yet, even with nonalcoholic beer, advertising is forbidden. The promotional emphasis is on store displays, special promotions, and contests. As Stroh's international general manager said: "The challenge is how do you position a beer-like product not as a beer? One has to be quite sensitive."[29]

---

[28]Pat Sloan, "Revlon Eyes Global Image; Picks Y&R," *Advertising Age* (January 11, 1993), pp. 1, 41.
[29]Tara Parker-Pope, "Nonalcoholic Beer Hits the Spot in Mideast," *Wall Street Journal* (December 6, 1995), pp. B1, B3.

Media may be unavailable or inappropriate. In a number of nations, there are few TV sets, ads are restricted, and/or mailing lists are not current. National pride sometimes requires that individual promotions be used. Even within regions that have perceived similarities, such as Western Europe and Latin America, there are differences.

Standardized strategies seem most appropriate and effective if a product is utilitarian and the message is informational. Reasons for buying or using the good or service are rational—and less apt to vary in different cultures. Glue, batteries, and gasoline are such products. A standardized approach would also appear appropriate and effective if a brand's identity and desirability are integrally linked to a specific national character. Coca-Cola and McDonald's are marketed worldwide as quintessential American products; Chanel is a quintessential French product.

For most products, it is generally more appropriate and effective to adapt or modify strategies and campaigns to local customs and cultures.

- Often, product usage varies according to the culture. This applies to most foods, and beverages such as coffee and tea.
- For many products, benefits are more psychological than tangible, requiring an understanding of the psychologies of different cultures. Sweets, snacks, and clothing are products with intangible benefits.
- When there is an emotional appeal, advertisers must recognize the vast differences in emotional expression that exist in the world. Some societies are demonstrative and open; others are aloof or private.
- Perhaps the riskiest method of selling is humour. There are differences in humour even within a culture—not to mention those that exist among cultures. In addition, advertisers must consider a multicultural, adaptable, and flexible strategy or campaign if a brand is in different stages of development or of varying stature across different markets.
- A commercial for a mature market may not work well in a developing one.
- A commercial to support a brand's leadership in a market where it is number one may not have the characteristics to succeed in a market where it is number five.
- A commercial in a market where the product/brand is unique has quite a different task than a commercial where competition is intense.[30]

Price Planning

The basic considerations in international price planning are whether prices should be standardized, the level at which prices are set, the currency in which prices are quoted, and terms of sale.

Price standardization is hard unless a firm operates within an economic community, such as the EU. Taxes, tariffs, and currency exchange charges are among the costs a firm incurs in international marketing. For example, a 1995 Chrysler Jeep Cherokee made in Toledo, Ohio, had a factory price of U.S.$19 100. After an adjustment to reflect the U.S. dollar-Japanese yen exchange rate, the price became U.S.$20 433. Shipping to Chiba, Japan, raised the price to U.S.$20 633. Customs fees lifted the price to U.S.$21 315. The Japanese distributor's profit drove the price to U.S.$22 884. "Homologation" (the inspections and modifications needed to meet Japan's standards) and added options sent the price to U.S.$25 909. The final sticker price at a Nagoya, Japan, dealer was U.S.$31 372.[31]

When setting a price level, a firm would consider such local economic conditions as per-capita GDP. For this reason, many firms try to hold down prices in developing and less-developed countries by marketing simplified product versions or employing less-expensive local labour. On the other hand, prices in such industrialized countries as France and Germany can reflect higher product quality and the added charges of international marketing.

Major decisions in international price planning involve standardization, price levels, currency choice, and sales terms. **Dumping** *is disliked by host countries.*

---
[30] McCollum Spielman Worldwide, "Global Advertising: Standardized or Multicultural?" *Topline* (Number 37, 1992), pp. 3–4.
[31] Sheryl WuDunn, "An Uphill Journey to Japan," *New York Times* (May 16, 1995), p. D1.

Some firms set lower prices abroad to enhance their international presence and sales or to remove excess supply from their home markets and preserve the prices there. **Dumping** occurs if a firm sells a product in a foreign country at a price much lower than that prevailing in its home market, below the cost of production, or both. In Canada and many other nations, duties may be levied on products "dumped" by foreign firms.

If a firm sets prices on the basis of its own nation's currency, the risk of a foreign currency devaluation is passed along to the buyer, allowing better control. But this strategy also has limitations. Consumers may be confused or unable to convert a price into their currency, or a foreign government may insist that prices be quoted in its currency. While Dow Chemical only uses German marks in European transactions to "insulate itself from sharp currency swings," Canondale (a U.S. bicycle maker) does business in thirteen European currencies.[32]

Finally, terms of sale need to be set. This involves such judgments as what fees or discounts channel intermediaries get for the tasks they perform, when ownership is transferred, what payment form is required, how much time customers have to pay bills, and what constitutes a proper refund policy.

MARKETING IN A CHANGING WORLD
Do You Want to Work Abroad?

In today's global marketplace, one of the key career decisions that you may have to make involves whether you want to work abroad at some point. In some firms, international assignments are becoming part of a manager's normal work rotation; in others, they are used to groom junior executives for fast-track job advancement. The goal for these firms, in either case, is to develop managers who are "world wise" and have a better and closer understanding of foreign markets.

To prepare for a foreign job assignment, these are some things you should accomplish:

- Learn a foreign language well.
- Study the cultures of foreign countries.
- Travel abroad.
- Study abroad.
- Join and become active in your college's or university's international business organization.

If you are working for a company and asked about undertaking a specific foreign assignment, these are some questions you should ask:

- What specific job is being offered?
- How long will the assignment be?
- What will the compensation be?
- What standard of living will the company support?
- What will your next job be after you return home?[33]

---

[32]Scott McMurray and Robert L. Simison, "Dow Chemical to Use Only the Mark for All of Its Business Dealings in Europe," *Wall Street Journal* (September 28, 1992), p. A5C; and Robina A. Gangemi, "Invoicing in 13 Currencies," *Sales & Marketing Management* (November 1995), p. 101.

[33]Grace W. Weinstein, "Before Saying Yes to Going Abroad," *Business Week* (December 4, 1995), pp. 130–132.

SUMMARY

1. *To define domestic, international, and global marketing* Domestic marketing encompasses a firm's efforts in its home country. International marketing involves goods and services traded outside a firm's home country. Global marketing engages a firm in operations in many nations. Companies may be placed into one of five categories: domestic firm, exporting firm, international firm, multinational firm, or global firm. For any type of company (whether domestically or internationally oriented) to succeed in today's competitive marketplace, it must understand key international marketing concepts and act appropriately.

2. *To explain why international marketing takes place and study its scope* International marketing occurs because nations want to exchange goods and services in which they have comparative advantages for those in which they do not. Firms seek to minimize adverse economic conditions and attract growing markets, avoid domestic competition, extend the product life cycle, and get tax breaks. In 1994 Canada ranked about eighth in the world with exports exceeding $213 billion. At the same time Canadian imports were about $202 billion giving Canada an $11 billion trade surplus. The NAFTA agreement combined with the low value of the Canadian dollar are the main reasons behind Canada's trade surplus. The United States is Canada's largest economic trading partner.

3. *To explore the cultural, economic, political, legal, and technological environments facing international marketers* The cultural environment includes the behaviour standards, language, lifestyles, and goals of a country's citizens. The economic environment incorporates a nation's standard of living, GDP, stage of economic development, and currency stability. The political and legal environment includes nationalism, government stability, trade rules, and trade agreements and economic communities such as the World Trade Organization, European Union, and the North American Free Trade community. The technological environment creates opportunities and problems, and varies by country.

4. *To analyze the stages in the development of an international marketing strategy* In developing a strategy, a firm may stress exporting, joint ventures, or direct ownership of operations. Each approach has a different level of commitment, resources, control, risk, flexibility, and profit.

When deciding on which and how many foreign markets to enter, a company should consider several factors. These include cultural and language similarities with the home market, the suitability of the standard of living, consumer demand, its own available resources, and so on.

A firm may adopt a standardized (global), nonstandardized, or glocal marketing approach. Its decision would depend on the differences among the countries served, which marketing elements can be standardized, the size of each market, and the possibility of regional adaptation.

Product planning may extend existing products into foreign markets, modify them, produce simpler items for developing nations, or invent new products for foreign markets. Distribution planning looks at channel relations and sets a network for direct sales or channel intermediaries. Physical distribution features would also be analyzed and adjustments made. Promotion planning would stress global, mixed, or glocal campaigns. Price planning involves whether prices should be standardized, what the price level should be, what currency prices should be quoted in, and terms of sale.

KEY TERMS

domestic marketing (p. 144)
international marketing (p. 144)
global marketing (p. 144)
domestic firm (p. 145)
exporting firm (p. 145)
international firm (p. 145)
multinational firm (p. 145)
global firm (p. 145)
comparative advantage (p. 146)
trade deficit (p. 148)
trade surplus (p. 148)
culture (p. 150)
standard of living (p. 151)

Gross Domestic Product (GDP) (p. 152)
industrialized countries (p. 152)
developing countries (p. 152)
less-developed countries (p. 152)
nationalism (p. 154)
tariff (p. 154)
trade quota (p. 154)
embargo (p. 154)
local content laws (p. 154)
World Trade Organization (WTO) (p. 155)
economic community (p. 155)
European Union (EC) (p. 155)
North American Free Trade Agreement (NAFTA) (p. 155)

exporting (p. 157)
joint venture (strategic alliance) (p. 158)
direct ownership (p. 160)
standardized (global) marketing approach (p. 161)
nonstandardized marketing approach (p. 161)
glocal marketing approach (p. 161)
straight extension (p. 162)
product adaptation (p. 162)
backward invention (p. 162)
forward invention (p. 162)
dumping (p. 167)

Review Questions

1. Distinguish among domestic, international, and global marketing.
2. Explain the concept of comparative advantage.
3. How can a firm improve its cultural awareness?
4. How can a country's GDP be a misleading indicator of marketing opportunities?
5. Differentiate among industrialized, developing, and less-developed countries.
6. If the value of the Kenyan shilling goes from 42 shillings per Canadian dollar to 50 shillings per Canadian dollar, will Canadian products be more or less expensive in Kenya? Why?
7. Define each of the following:
   a. Local content law.
   b. Tariff.
   c. Embargo.
8. What are the pros and cons of exporting versus joint ventures?
9. Why would a firm use a nonstandardized international marketing strategy? What are the potential disadvantages of this strategy?
10. Distinguish among these product-planning strategies: straight extension, product adaptation, backward invention, and forward invention. When should each be used?

Discussion Questions

1. Cite three basic differences between marketing in Canada and marketing in Mexico.
2. In China, there are two cars per 1000 people, compared with 455 per 1000 people in Canada. What are the ramifications of this from a marketing perspective?
3. What are the advantages and disadvantages of a country belonging to an economic community such as the European Union?
4. Develop a ten-question checklist by which a cable television network could determine which and how many foreign markets to enter.
5. Provide a current example of an international ad that you consider to be "global." Evaluate the ad.

VIDEO CASE

When in Japan, Do Like the Japanese!
When in Canada, Do Like the Japanese?

James Fallows has lived in Japan and has written a book entitled *Looking at the Sun*. In his book he compares the economies and ways of doing business in Japan and the West. The foundation of western economies, according to Fallows, is consumer sovereignty, with a focus on individual welfare and the understanding of market forces. Most of the marketing principles used in Canada and the United States are based on this philosophy. In contrast, Japan uses state-sponsored capitalism. According to this view, production and material economics are the source of strength and growth for an economy. The Japanese approach to business is a form of peacetime military structure. Business is "war" for them. Home markets must be protected, not opened. Foreign markets are invaded, captured, and held. The producer is seen as the creator of wealth and the one who offers employment security. As part of this "peacetime" military structure is the notion of "employees for life." Soldiers (employees) are never laid off from their jobs, although they might be fired. The requirement of an employee for life is loyalty to one's company (like a soldier's loyalty to their country). A person who quits a company in Japan will have a difficult time getting hired somewhere else because they have a stigma of disloyalty attached to them (much like a soldier who has committed treason). Getting fired is an even worse situation for an employee (soldiers who have lost battles get relieved).

Japan takes an imperialistic approach to trade. They import raw materials and export finished goods. The Japanese mind set views business as part of the nation's productive might. The independence of Japan depends on Asia's industrial structure being dependent on Japan. Therefore the Japanese have sought to dominate the Asian continent economically and have been successful at doing so. Japan is Canada's second-largest trading partner: Canada imports $11.3 billion of Japanese goods and exports $9.5 billion in Canadian goods to Japan. In 1994 Japanese firms had $5.8 billion in direct investments in Canada, compared to $3 billion of direct investment in Japan by Canadian firms. The United States is also an important trading partner of Japan's, with whom they have a U.S.$50 billion trade deficit. In 1996, U.S. President Clinton, like almost every other U.S. president in the previous twenty years, called for open Japanese markets in order to eliminate this trade deficit. Of course, open by the western definition means acceptance of consumer sovereignty and western-style economic policies.

Fallows suggests that dealing with Japan successfully means operating more on their terms. This means using protectionist policies, subsidies, and a producer orientation. That is, do like the Japanese do!

There is an important myth that the Japanese do everything well and North American firms do not. On a micro level Japanese consumers as individuals are very much like North Americans, except they seem to demand higher levels of quality and expect to receive them. As such, the production orientation of Japanese companies serves them well in producing quality products rapidly. However, Japanese consumers are also used to paying high retail prices for merchandise, whereas North Americans expect to have low prices with their quality. The authoritarian approach to business and production orientation used in East Asia is not acceptable to westerners. In fact, the successful Japanese firms and products have developed the ability to tap into western consumer sovereignty.

Will the Japanese dominate Canadian markets the way they have Asian markets? James Fallows thinks that Canada's multicultural make-up will enable us to be more resilient in our trade relations with Japan. As well, Canada has plenty of what the Japanese need: natural resources. Our strong productive capacity in this area coupled with our small (in global terms) consumer market for finished goods, means that the imbalance in value of exporting raw materials and importing finished trade goods will be offset by the volume of raw materials exported. After all, we do not serve as Japan's only market for the finished goods produced from the raw materials we supply them.

QUESTIONS

1. Discuss the differences between Japanese business philosophy and western business philosophy.
2. From your own experience, think of some examples of real market products of both the western and Japanese business philosophies and how the products are different or the marketing approaches are different as a result of these philosophies.
3. Discuss Fallows' views that protectionism is the way to deal with Japan, or any other nation for that matter.
4. Advise a Canadian company what aspects they must consider if they are to market in Japan?

VIDEO QUESTIONS ON JAMES FALLOWS

1. Discuss James Fallows' comment that Canada is resilient to trade with Japan due to our multicultural make-up.
2. Discuss whether Canadian firms can do business the Japanese way in Canada.

Video Source: "James Fallows," *Venture* (March 27, 1994).
Other Sources: Peter Foster, "What Makes Samurai Run?" *Canadian Business* (March 1994), pp. 72–73; *Market Research Handbook 1995*, Statistics Canada, Minister of Industry, Science and Technology; *The 1996 Canadian Global Almanac* (Toronto: MacMillan Canada).

CASE STUDY

Can Mercedes Be Less German and More Global?

During 1994, Germany's Mercedes staged a major turnaround, earning a net profit of 1.85 billion marks (U.S.$1.35 billion) on sales of 70.7 billion marks (U.S.$51.61 billion), a 2.6 per cent profit margin. In contrast, during 1993, it lost 1.2 billion marks (U.S.$876 million) on sales of 64.7 billion marks (U.S.$47.23 billion). On average, Mercedes' 1994 profit per vehicle was about 2000 marks (U.S.$1460). By comparison, Germany's Volkswagen earned a profit margin of only 0.2 per cent and had an average profit per car of 48 marks (U.S.$35) in 1994.

Despite its return to profitability, Mercedes is concerned about the high value of the German mark relative to other European currencies and the U.S. dollar. According to Helmut Werner, chair of Mercedes-Benz AG, the high appreciation in the value of the German mark against other European currencies is just as much of a threat to the firm as a falling dollar: "The fundamental problem of German exporters is that we are producing in a country with a hard currency and selling in countries with soft currencies." He concluded that the value of the U.S. dollar needs to move up by about 25 per cent for the firm to make satisfactory profits on cars sold to the U.S. market.

The combination of the mark's strength and recent wage agreements makes German labour 15 to 17 per cent more costly than labour in other European markets. These high costs put Mercedes at a significant disadvantage in such important European markets as Italy and Great Britain. As a result, to guard against the rising costs of German labour and parts, Mercedes plans to make the firm less German and more global. Thus, the firm intends to build more than 10 per cent of all Mercedes outside Germany (in North America, Latin America, and Asia). And between 1995 and 1998, it aims to double the amount of supplies it buys outside Germany. A look at Mercedes' financial statements shows the rising importance of its non-German operations: Foreign subsidiaries now account for 38 per cent of total net profit and non-German sales comprise 62 per cent of overall company sales.

Mercedes also hopes to continue streamlining its manufacturing operations to make itself more efficient. In 1994, it saved about 3.0 billion marks (U.S.$2.2 billion) due to lower factory and lower materials costs. And the firm wants to obtain additional reductions by having its suppliers perform more work.

German labour unions have not taken kindly to Mercedes' globalization plans. For example, unions strongly protested the Mercedes' decision to situate a new Swatchmobile minicar plant in France. Although Mercedes originally assumed that placing the plant in France instead of Germany would save the company about 500 marks (U.S.$365) per car, these savings have been revised upward by 50 marks (an additional U.S.$37). German labour is also sensitive to Mercedes' decision to build its first U.S. plant (in Tuscaloosa, Alabama). In an effort to keep additional Mercedes plants (for the firm's A-1 line) in Germany, German workers recently agreed to a 1 per cent reduction in wages.

Amidst all of these changes in its German-based strategy, Mercedes has been a major advocate of a single currency for Europe. The firm views a single currency as a way to reduce some of the pressure for it to turn to operations outside Germany—and Europe. As Helmut Werner says, "There is a danger that Europe will fall back from an internal market to a large number of individual markets if the currency situation does not become more predictable."

QUESTIONS

1. Evaluate the statement by Helmut Werner that: "The fundamental problem of German exporters is that we are producing in a country with a hard currency and selling in countries with soft currencies."
2. What opportunities and threats does Mercedes face by virtue of the European Union (EU)?
3. What are the pros and cons of Mercedes' globalization strategy?
4. Evaluate the pros and cons of Mercedes' using a straight-extension versus a product-adaptation strategy.

Source: The data in this case is drawn from Audrey Choi, "For Mercedes, Going Global Means Being Less German," *Wall Street Journal* (April 27, 1995), p. B4.

CONSUMER ANALYSIS

PART 3

UNDERSTANDING AND RESPONDING TO DIVERSITY IN THE MARKETPLACE

In Part 3, we see why consumer analysis is so essential and discuss consumer characteristics, needs, profiles, and decision making—and how firms can devise marketing plans responsive to today's diverse global marketplace.

7 Final-Consumer Demographics
This chapter is devoted to final consumer demographics, the objective and quantifiable characteristics that describe the population. We examine population size, gender, age, location, housing, mobility, income, expenditures, occupations, education, marital status, and ethnicity/race—for Canada, the United States, and a number of other countries around the globe.

8 Final-Consumer Lifestyles and Decision Making
Here, we investigate final consumer lifestyles and decision making, useful concepts in explaining why and how consumers act as they do. Lifestyles encompass various social and psychological factors, many of which we note here. By studying the decision process, we see how consumers move from stimulus to purchase or nonpurchase.

9 Organizational Consumers
In this chapter, we focus on the organizational consumers that purchase goods and services for further production, use in operations, or resale to other consumers. We look at how they differ from final consumers and at their individual characteristics, buying objectives, buying structures, constraints on purchases, and decision processes.

10 Developing a Target Market Strategy
We are now ready to discuss how to plan a target-market strategy. Consumer-demand patterns and segmentation bases are examined; and undifferentiated marketing (mass marketing), concentrated marketing, and differentiated marketing (multiple segmentation) are explained and contrasted. The requirements for successful segmentation and the importance of positioning are also considered. We conclude with a discussion of sales forecasting.

Part 3 Vignette
The Market: The Demands of Satisfying Demand

Marketing is the anticipation, management and satisfaction of demand through the exchange process. You must understand the reasons for, and sources of, demand before undertaking any marketing program. The Part 3 video cases present Canadian situations of managing demand.

The aging face of demand is the subject of the first video case. Although the seniors market is very large and possesses the highest amount of disposable income, marketers worldwide have responded to it slowly. One reason for the lack of response is that marketing practitioners, being much younger than the seniors market, have difficulty relating to it. Aging has important implications for marketers because it produces changes in the needs and wants of people and consequently in the choice of products and services used. Understanding how aging affects consumption behaviour is one factor marketers need to consider when they undertake the development of a marketing mix. Given that seniors represent a market of significant disposable income and absolute size, serving their needs and wants represents a tremendous business opportunity.

The reasons for, and the sources of, demand must be understood before any marketing program is undertaken.

Another important demand consideration for marketers involves understanding how consumers make choices. Very few firms have a monopoly in the market; the philosophy of a market economy is based on having choices. The second video case considers the market philosophy in Canada, which has been criticized for its lack of choices. However, in other areas, the market economy is too responsive. For some products, such as running shoes, consumers are confused by the number of brands to choose from. Baskin Robbins stocks 31 flavours at each store, and 600 to 700 more are kept in rotation. However, some flavours are much more popular than others and are kept on hand. With 50 flavours on hand that are completely changed once a month, it would take one year to present 600 flavours to one store's customers. Do consumers really take ice cream that seriously? What does that say about them? Understanding how consumers make their choices when faced with brand proliferation is useful to marketers. It might help them avoid engaging in costly activities that actually impede market efficiency rather than improve it.

The third video case presents an expanded view of the notion of "customer." Marketers must recognize that governments, businesses, manufacturers, retailers, professionals and non-profit charities also represent a source of demand greater than the individual consumer market. Understanding the needs, wants and buying behaviour of organizational consumers is just as important. However, organizational buying behaviour often involves many individuals and a slower, much more complex buying process.

Acquisition of computer systems by businesses is one area in which understanding organizational buying behaviour is critical to success. Given that computer technology is undergoing rapid change accompanied by cost and price reductions, computer system purchasing is a very unsettling and risky process, as is computer system development and maketing. Buyers and sellers making decisions involving large expenditures exxperience a great deal of stress when the marketing environment undergoes rapid and volatile changes.

Finally, applying what we can learn about the characteristics of consumers to the development of a marketing strategy is the process of target marketing. The last video case discusses the application of target marketing to Vancouver's ethnic Chinese market; it explains how the target market drives the development of a marketing strategy. Design, development, pricing, distribution-location and promotion of homes are all being driven by the principle of Feng Shui. In the marketplace, Feng Shui is extremely important to the buying behaviour of Chinese purchasers and a non-issue for other home buyers. Consequently, offering this attribute does not diminish the demand for homes for the whole market, but it appeals to Chinese buyers.

CHAPTER 7
Final Consumer Demographics

Chapter Objectives

1. To show the importance and scope of consumer analysis

2. To define and enumerate important consumer demographics for the Canadian population and other countries: size, gender, and age; location, housing, and mobility; income and expenditures; occupations and education; marital status; and ethnicity/race

3. To examine trends and projections for these important demographics and study their marketing implications

4. To present examples of consumer demographic profiles

5. To consider the limitations of demographics

{ *Perhaps never before have marketers trying to reach women worldwide felt so unsure about what women want and need. Thirty years ago, even fifteen years ago, it was fairly easy. Most women did not work outside the home, and advertising featured them worrying about spotless dishes and clean floors.* }

Today, such trends as increased participation by women in the workforce, couples having fewer children, and many women's greater focus on career opportunities are having an impact around the globe. For example, research in Australia shows that only 7 per cent of families fit the "traditional" family structure of a working father, a mother at home, and two school-age children.

Here's how marketers throughout the world are responding to the changing demographics of women:

- In Spain, firms are beginning to capitalize on the shortage of time for women. Home food delivery is now a growth industry; it was practically nonexistent less than a decade ago. One firm alone, TelePizza, has annual sales of $55 million. Campofrío, a leading food marketer, uses the theme "Let Roteta cook" for its Cocina Placer line of microwaveable entrées. Roteta is a well-known Basque chef who has created many of the recipes for this food line. The concept of the ad campaign is that women can leave food preparation to a highly-regarded chef.

- When General Motors Spain introduced the Opel Corsa, the firm relied on special presentations to female journalists. It also advertised the product in such women's magazines as the Spanish *Vogue* and *Cosmopolitan*. The ads told the story of a woman going through the day, undertaking different activities, and driving her Corsa. The Corsa model became the fifth best-selling car in Spain—with 46 per cent female buyers, the highest proportion of any Opel model.

- According to the Bureau for Market Research at the University of South Africa, as of the year 2011, women will make up 42.3 per cent of the South African workforce, a significant increase from 38.6 per cent in 1991 and 21.1 per cent in 1989. As a result, the sales of convenience foods have increased and will continue to do so. And ads that once depicted women in the home now focus on other roles. More and more firms are also promoting job opportunities for women. One ad, for example, showed a young woman in coveralls and safety glasses welding machinery together. The ad, sponsored by Caltex, a gasoline retailer, described job openings for young people.

- In another South African illustration, Lever Brothers used a unique twist in its TV campaign for Sunlight Micro dishwashing liquid. In the ad, a woman in an evening dress passes the dirty dishes on to a gold-coloured male robot, instead of a nearby female domestic. "Sorry, these are a bit greasy, Arthur," she stated, advising him that Sunlight would make his job easier. The ad was developed since images of the housewife "in a tradition role" did not test well, according to Lever Brothers' marketing director.[1]

We have just looked at a few of the demographic changes occurring in Spain and South Africa—and how marketers are responding to them. In this chapter, we will focus on a number of important consumer demographic trends in Canada and elsewhere, and consider the marketing implications of these trends.

LEVER BROTHERS
www.leverbrothers.com/

Consumer analysis is crucial in the diverse global marketplace.

Overview

As discussed in Chapters 1 and 2, the consumer is the central focus of marketing. To devise good marketing plans, it is important to study consumer attributes and needs, lifestyles, and purchase processes and then make proper marketing-mix decisions.

---

[1] Laurie Freeman, Susan Hack, Deborah Klosky, Geoffrey Lee Martin, Ann Marsh, and Jack Russell, "Changing Demographics: Women," *Advertising Age International* (October 17, 1994), pp. I–14, I–16.

Chapter 7 *Final Consumer Demographics* **177**

The scope of consumer analysis includes the study of who buys, what they buy, why they buy, how they make decisions to buy, when they buy, where they buy, and how often they buy.[2] For example, a university student (who) purchases textbooks (what) because they are required for various classes (why). The student first looks up the book list at the school store and decides whether to purchase new or used books for each course (how). Then, just before the first week of classes (when), the student goes to the school store to buy the books (where). The student does this three times per year— fall, spring, and summer (how often).

An open-minded, consumer-oriented approach is imperative in today's diverse global marketplace so a firm can identify and serve its target market, minimize consumer dissatisfaction, and stay ahead of competitors. Why is this so important? As Seagate, a leader in computer data-storage products, puts it: "People buy expectations, not just things. Customer satisfaction is dependent not only on our products, but on continuously improving our way of doing business."[3] Figures 7-1 and 7-2 illustrate two creative ad campaigns aimed at different types of consumers.

In Chapters 7 to 10, the concepts you need to understand consumers in Canada, the United States, and other nations worldwide; to select target markets; and to relate marketing strategy to consumer behaviour are detailed. Chapters 7 and 8 examine final con-

FIGURE 7-1
Creatively Appealing to the Final Consumer of Today
Reprinted by permission.

---

[2]Adapted from Leon G. Schiffman and Leslie Lazar Kanuk, *Consumer Behaviour*, Fifth Edition (Englewood Cliffs, N.J.: Prentice-Hall, 1994), p. 7.
[3]*Seagate 1992 Annual Report*, p. 9.

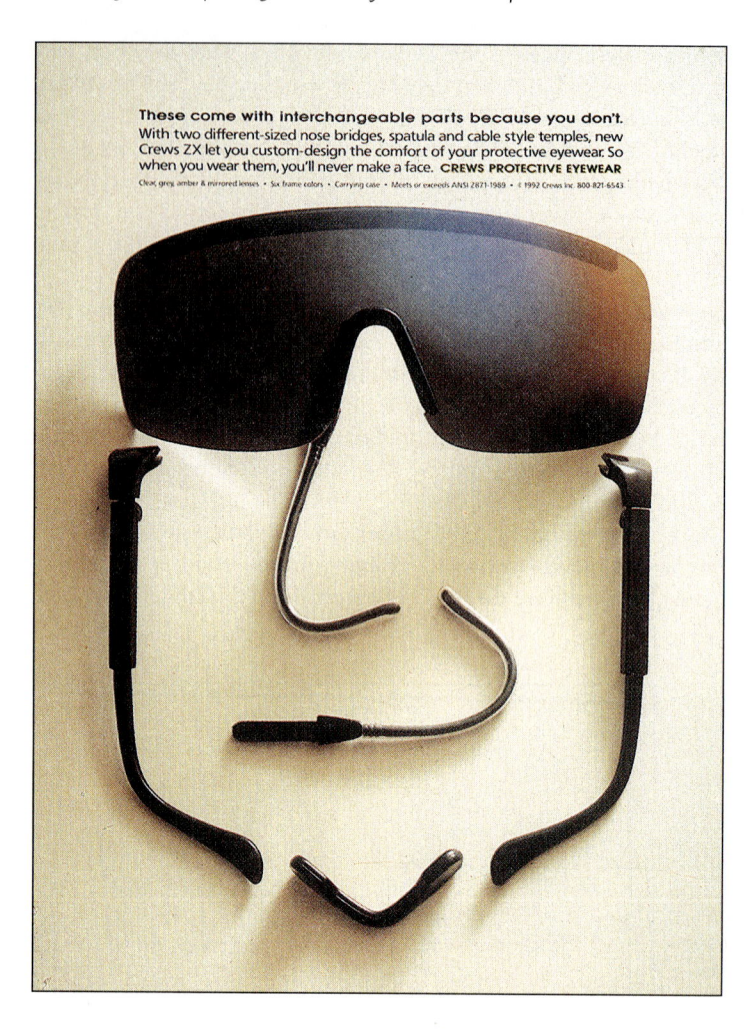

FIGURE 7-2
Creatively Appealing to the
Organizational Consumer of Today
Reprinted by permission.

Final consumers *buy for personal, family, or household use;* **organizational consumers** *buy for production, operations, or resale.*

Consumer demographics *are population characteristics that are easy to identify and measure.* **Demographic profiles** *may be formed.*

sumer demographics, lifestyles, and decision making. **Final consumers** buy goods and services for personal, family, or household use.

Chapter 9 centres on the characteristics and behaviour of **organizational consumers**, those buying goods and services for further production, to be used in operating the organization, or for resale to other consumers. Chapter 10 explains how to devise a target-market strategy and use sales forecasts.

Demographics Defined and Enumerated[4]

Consumer demographics are objective and quantifiable population characteristics. They are relatively easy to identify, collect, measure, and analyze—and show diversity around the globe. The demographics covered in Chapter 7 are population size, gender, and age; location, housing, and mobility; income and expenditures; occupations and education; marital status; and ethnicity/race.

As shown in Figure 7-3, after separately examining various demographic factors a firm can form a **consumer demographic profile**—a demographic composite of a consumer group. By establishing consumer profiles, a firm can pinpoint both attractive and declining market opportunities. For example, in highly industrialized nations, the population is growing more slowly, people are older, incomes are higher, more people work in white-

---

[4]Unless otherwise indicated, the data presented in this chapter are all from *Market Research Handbook 1995*, Statistics Canada, Minister of Industry, Science and Technology; *The 1996 Canadian Global Almanac* (Toronto: MacMillan Canada); the U.S. Bureau of the Census (various publications); the United Nations (various publications); *International Marketing Data and Statistics 1995* (Great Britain: Euromonitor, 1995); *American Demographics* (various issues); and *World Almanac and Book of Facts 1996* (Mahwah, N.J.: World Almanac Books, 1995).

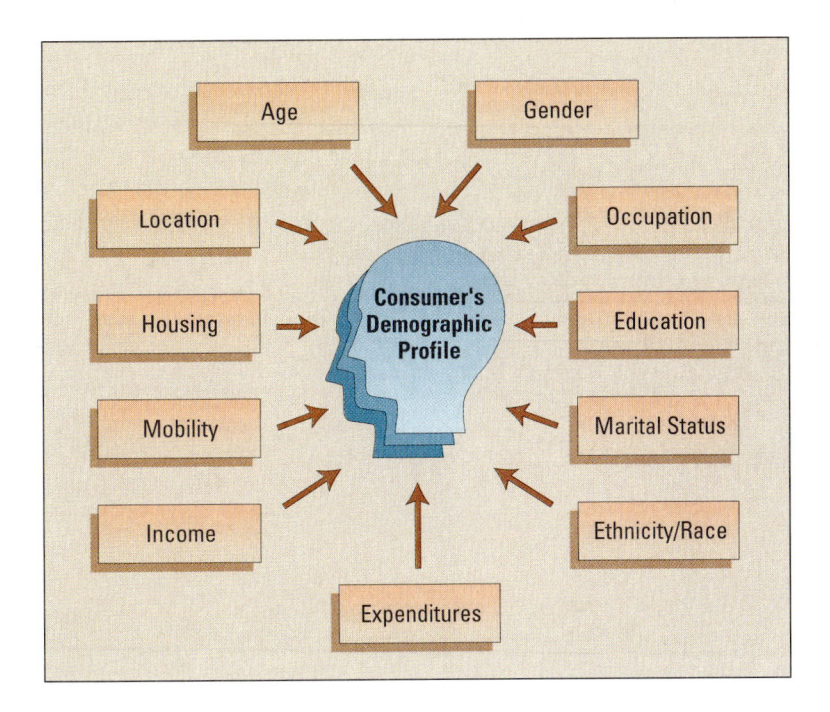

FIGURE 7-3
Factors Determining a Consumer's Demographic Profile

collar jobs, and there are smaller households than in less-developed and developing countries. Together, these factors have a great impact on the goods and services that are offered and on marketing strategies for these items.

Several secondary sources offer data on consumer demographics. For both Canadian and U.S. demographics, a key source is the *Census of Population*, (undertaken by Statistics Canada in Canada) a federal government research project in both countries. Census information provides a wide range of national, provincial/state, and local data via printed reports, computer tapes, microfiche, CD-ROM diskettes, and online databases. Many marketing research firms and provincial/state data centres arrange census data by postal (zip) code, provide forecasts, and update information.

Since complete census data are gathered only once every five years in Canada, and once every decade in the U.S., they must be supplemented by Statistics Canada (U.S. Bureau of the Census) estimates and statistics from chambers of commerce, public utilities, and others. The *Canada Yearbook*, and *The Market Research Handbook*. published by Statistics Canada, along with *Canadian Markets*, published by the *Financial Post* contain a great deal of useful information. *The Canadian Global Almanac* (Published by Macmillan Canada) is also a quick reference source for demographic information.

American Demographics is a monthly magazine dealing mostly with U.S. demographic trends. The *Survey of Buying Power* (published annually by *Sales & Marketing Management*) has current Canadian and U.S. data by metropolitan area and state/province, including retail sales by merchandise category, personal disposable income, and five-year estimates. Other U.S. secondary sources are *Editor & Publisher Market Guide*, *Rand McNally Commercial Atlas & Market Guide*, *Standard Rate & Data Service*, local newspapers, and regional planning boards.

The United Nations (UN), Euromonitor, and the Organization for Economic Cooperation and Development (OECD) are sources of international demographic data. The UN publishes a *Statistical Yearbook* and a *Demographic Yearbook*. Euromonitor publishes *International Marketing Data and Statistics*. OECD issues ongoing demographic and economic reports. In highly industrialized nations, demographic data are fairly accurate because actual data are collected on a regular basis. In less-developed and developing nations, demographic data are often based on estimates rather than actual data. Throughout this chapter, information is provided on Canadian, American and worldwide demographics. A broad cross-section of country examples is provided to give the reader a good sense of the demographic diversity that exists around the globe.

ORGANIZATION FOR ECONOMIC CO-OPERATION AND DEVELOPMENT (OECD)
www.oecd.org/

TECHNOLOGY & MARKETING

What's the Deal with Online Census Data?

Need Canadian or U.S. demographic data in a hurry? In Canada you can subscribe to *Statistics Canada Daily* by e-mail by contacting listproc@statcan.ca with the message: subscribe daily Yourfirstname Yourlastname. *The Daily* is a publication containing announcements about products, services as well as information on new data and releases by Statistics Canada. You can also visit Statistics Canada's Home Page on the World Wide Web, which contains media releases, provides frequently requested statistics, product and service catalogues and issues of *The Daily*.

Of course, the real service comes from the Canadian Socio-Economic Information Management System (CANSIM), Statistics Canada's computerized database and information retrieval service. CANSIM is composed of three basic databases: Census Summary Data Service, Cross-Classified Database and Time Series Database. It is available online (for a fee) through modem-equipped PCs that can access Statistics Canada regional offices or one of the national data transmission networks operating in Canada.

In the United States, census statistics are now available to anyone free of charge with a computer, a modem, and a public-domain graphic interface software package called Mosaic. During its first six months of operation, over one million inquiries—an average of 5500 per day—were made to the U.S. Bureau of the Census' Internet site. And this number is expected to rise dramatically as more people learn about the service. In the near future, some Census Bureau reports will *only* be available online as the Bureau attempts to promote electronic access as a way of better serving consumers and to reduce its printing and paper costs.

Marketers interested in analyzing detailed demographic data about a specific state need only "Enter the Main Data Bank" at the initial menu and select "Statistical Abstract Summaries by States." They are then able to review data on income levels, births and deaths, business failures, and even social insurance programs. Large sets of data can be downloaded by users to their own computers for further analysis.

Another popular program offered at the Census Bureau's Internet site is County Business Patterns. This site features state- and county-based data on employment, payrolls, and establishments. Census Bureau news releases can also be accessed by both subject and date.

As a marketing researcher, how would you use online versus published Statistics Canada or U.S. Census Bureau reports?

Source: Based on material in Jackson Morton, "Census of the Internet," *American Demographics* (March 1995), pp. 52-53; and Jim Carroll and Rick Broadhead, 1996 *Canadian Internet Directory* (Toronto: Prentice-Hall Canada).

Population Size, Gender, and Age

Relatively speaking, the Canadian population is expanding slowly. There are also many firstborns, more women than men, and a rising average age.

CANSIM
www.mun.ca/library/databases/cansimguide.html

The world population is expected to grow from 5.7 billion in 1995 to 6.2 billion in 2000, an increase of 1.5 per cent annually. Over the same period, Canada's population is expected to grow from 29 million to 31 million, an annual increase of 1.4 per cent. The U.S. population is expected to grow from 263 million to 275 million, an annual increase of 1 per cent. Thus, the Canadian population will drop from .508 per cent of the world population in 1995 to .5 per cent of the world population in the year 2000, while the U.S. population will drop from 4.6 per cent of the world population to 4.4 per cent over the same time period. Figure 7-4 shows world population distribution by region for 1990 and 2000.

Newborns account for less than 2 per cent of the population in industrialized nations (1.33 per cent in Canada and 1.5 per cent in the United States)—compared to up to 4 per cent or more in nations such as Afghanistan, Syria, and Zaire. For industrialized countries, a large proportion of births are firstborns.

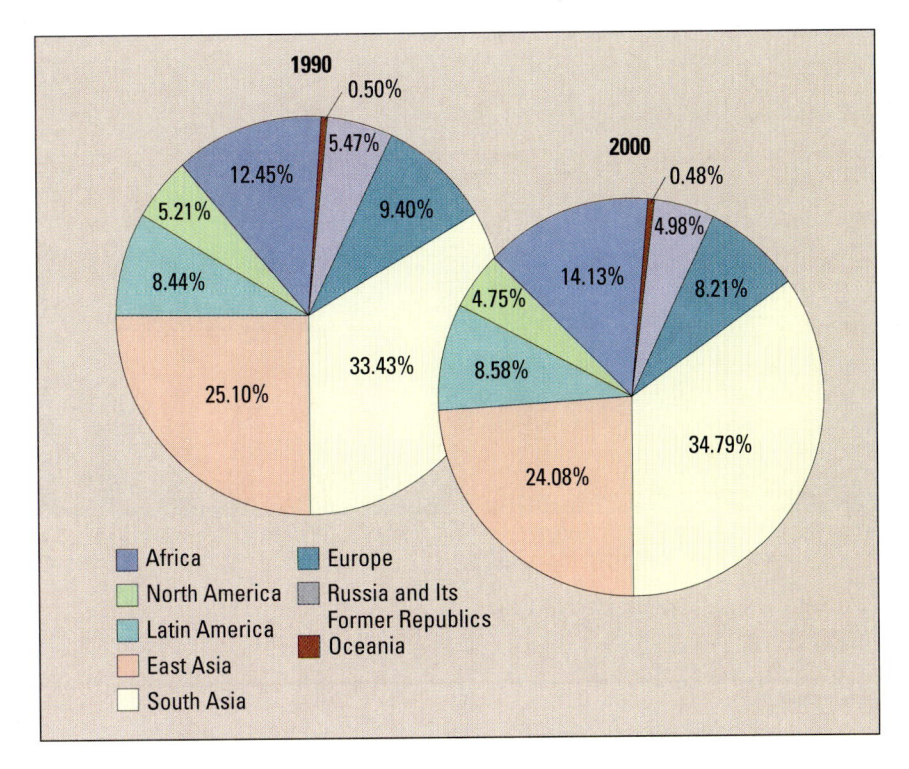

FIGURE 7-4
The World's Population Distribution, 1990 and 2000
Source: U.S. Bureau of the Census.

Worldwide, males and females comprise roughly equal percentages of the population. Yet in many industrialized countries, females comprise well over one-half of the population—mostly due to differences in life expectancy. For example, the life expectancy for newborn females is 82 in Canada, 80 years in Italy, 80 in the United States, and 74 in Russia; it is 75 years for newborn males in Canada, 76 in Italy, 73 in the United States, and 64 in Russia.

The populations in industrialized nations are older than those in less-developed and developing nations. Today, the median age of the population is about 35 years in Canada, 37 years in Japan, 36 in Italy and Great Britain, 34 in the United States, 25 in China, 23 in Brazil, 20 in Mexico, and 16 in Nigeria.

Marketing Implications

Around the world, there are opportunities for marketing all types of goods and services. However, in industrialized countries, the low rate of population growth means that firms there need to focus on specific opportunities, such as firstborns, females, and expanding age groups. There will be heightened battles among firms for market share in industrialized nations.

The number of firstborns is significant because parents have many initial purchases to make, for such items as furniture, clothing, and transportation (stroller, car seat, and so on). On average, parents in industrialized nations spend thousands of dollars (including food, clothing, furniture and bedding, toys, health care, child care, and other items) to raise a first child to just his or her first birthday, far more than on each later child. And today's parents are much more likely to bring their babies with them when they travel.

In Canada, there are about 300 000 more females than males in the total population while in the United States, there are over 6 million more females than males in the total population. This has important implications for marketers of clothing, household services, appliances, cars, and other items. Accordingly, more and more companies are gearing their appeals to women. Special interest should be paid to older females, who greatly outnumber their male counterparts.

The shifting age distribution in industrialized countries brings many possibilities. For example, colleges and universities are increasing their recruitment of older, nontraditional students. Sports and recreation companies are becoming more oriented toward the

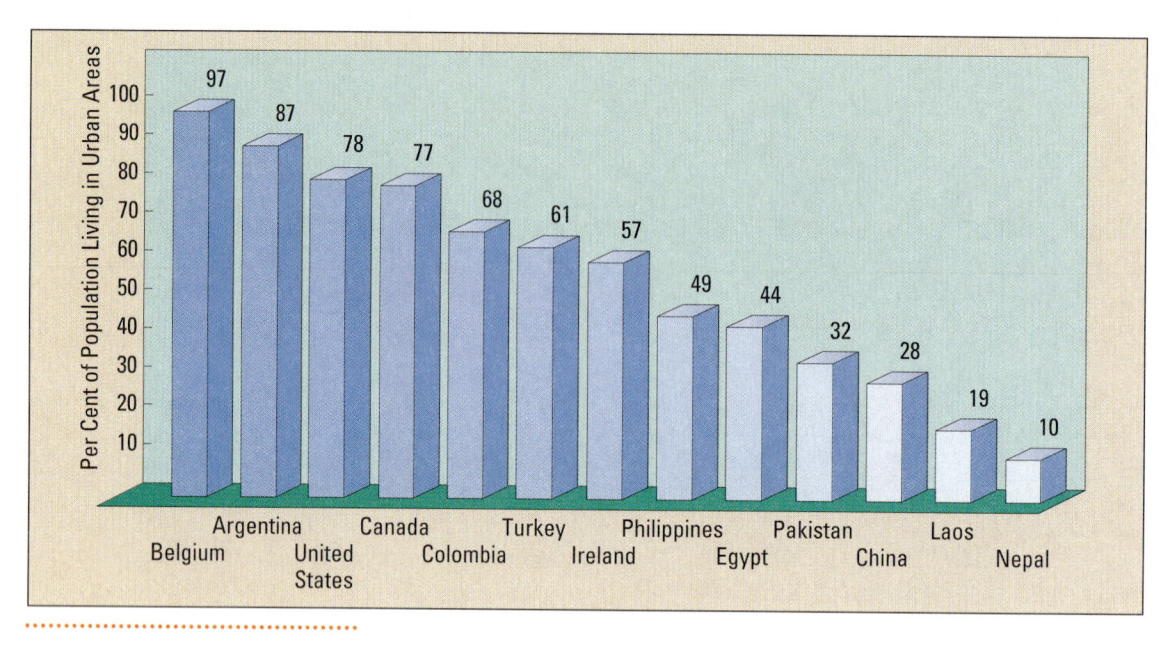

FIGURE 7-5
The Urbanization of Selected Countries
Source: United Nations

over-45 age group. The over-65 age group represents a growing market for food, medical care, vacation homes, telephone services, travel, entertainment, and restaurants.

On the other hand, the much higher rate of population growth—usually across both genders and all age groups—in less-developed and developing countries means that company opportunities there will be broad-based. There will be openings for companies to substantially increase the overall sales of food, clothing, autos, communications equipment, financial services, and a host of other goods and services—rather than fight over market share or carve up very small market segments. For example, from 1990 to 2000, the total populations in China, Nigeria, and Brazil are expected to rise by 160 million, 42 million, and 28 million people, respectively.

Location, Housing, and Mobility

During this century, there has been a major move of the world population to large urban areas and their surrounding suburbs. As of 1996, over 15 cities had at least 10 million residents each—led by Tokyo/Yokohama and Mexico City. But, as Figure 7-5 shows, the level of urbanization varies greatly by country.

Today, 77 per cent of the Canadian population resides in urban areas and approximately 80 per cent of the population lives within 160 kilometres of the U.S. border. The population is concentrated in twenty-five **Census Metropolitan Areas** or CMAs (Statistics Canada defines a CMA as a main labour-market area of an urban area with at least 100 000 people) and 115 **Census Agglomeration Areas** (Statistics Canada defines a CA as a main labour-market area of an urban area with at least 10 000 people and less than 100 000 people).

In the United States 80 per cent of the U.S. population resides in 19 per cent of the land area, often in Metropolitan Statistical Areas (MSAs) or Consolidated Metropolitan Statistical Areas (CMSAs). The U.S. Census Bureau defines a Metropolitan Statistical Area (MSA) as being relatively freestanding and not closely associated with other metropolitan areas. It contains either a city of at least 50 000 population or an urbanized area of 50 000 population (with a total population of 100 000+). Its population can exceed one million. There are 250 MSAs in the United States. As defined by the U.S. Census Bureau, a Consolidated Metropolitan Statistical Area (CMSA) has two or more overlapping and/or interlocking urban communities, known as Primary Metropolitan Statistical Areas

The world is becoming more urban. Canadian urban areas are classed as **Census Metropolitan Areas** *and* **Census Agglomeration Areas**.

(PMSAs), with a total population of at least one million. CMSAs comprise the 18 largest U.S. metropolitan areas and hold over a third of the national population. The biggest CMSA is New York-Northern New Jersey-Long Island, New York-New Jersey-Connecticut with 20 million people and 15 interlocking communities.

In many parts of the world, the majority of people own the homes in which they reside. Here are some examples: Canada, 63 per cent; Bangladesh, 91 per cent; Paraguay, 81 per cent; New Zealand, 74 per cent; Greece, 73 per cent; Finland, 68 per cent; United States, 65 per cent; and Sri Lanka, 61 per cent.

Globally, many people own homes and population mobility is high on a worldwide basis.

The worldwide mobility of the population is quite high; annually, millions of people emigrate from one nation to another and hundreds of millions move within their nations. During the last decade, more than 2 million people have legally emigrated to Canada, while 8 million people emigrated to the United States. Among Canadian and U.S. residents, 15 to 20 per cent of all people move annually. In Canada the population is moving to the far west with virtually every province having had a net loss of population in 1994 with the exception of British Columbia, which has had a substantial gain. While B.C. has been a net gainer of 31 000 people, Quebec (-13 000) Alberta (-6000) and Newfoundland (-5500) have had the greatest decreases. U.S. population mobility varies by region: From 1990 to 2000, the highest growth will be in the Mountain, Pacific, South Atlantic, and Southwest regions.

Marketing Implications

When a nation's population is urbanized, marketing programs are more cost efficient, it is easier to offer goods and services to large groups of consumers, and mass distribution and advertising are possible. In some regions of the world, suburban shopping has been growing, leading to branch outlets in suburbs and improved transportation and delivery services.

The continuing interest in home ownership offers sales potential for such home-based items as furniture, appliances, carpeting, and insurance. Specially modified products for those occupying small homes and for apartment owners, such as space-efficient washers and dryers, are growing in importance. Because some large-ticket home purchases are greatly affected by the economy, firms need to monitor economic conditions carefully.

Population mobility offers openings for well-advertised global, national, or regional brands; retail chains and franchises; and major credit cards— among others. Their names are well known when consumers relocate and represent an assurance of quality. For example, Crest toothpaste, Heineken beer, British Airways, Honda, McDonald's, and Visa are recognized and successful worldwide, as well as throughout Canada and the United States. Shopper's Drug Mart stores do good business in Florida because a number of Canadian "Snowbirds" who winter there or have relocated there patronize them.

Companies often refocus their marketing programs as they anticipate the growth of certain geographic areas and the decline of others. For instance, in Canada, marketing efforts directed at consumers in British Columbia have risen dramatically. Similarly, in the United States, marketing efforts directed at consumers in such states as Arizona, Texas, Florida, and Georgia have risen dramatically. Still, firms should be aware of the possibility of oversaturation in these areas. Regions being abandoned by some firms, like Quebec and the Maritimes in Canada and the Northeast in the U.S., should be reviewed by comparing population trends with competition levels.

HONDA
www.honda.com/toc/

SHOPPER'S DRUG MART
www.lifebrand.com/

VISA
www.visa.com/cgi-bin/vee/vw/main.html?2+0

Income and Expenditures

Consumer income and expenditure patterns are valuable demographic factors when properly studied. In examining them, these points should be kept in mind:

- Personal income is often stated as GDP per capita—the total value of goods and services produced in a nation divided by its population size. This does not report what people really earn and it inflates per-capita income if a small portion of the population is affluent. A better measure is median income—the income for those at the fiftieth

Country-by-country income data are hard to compare.

percentile in a nation; it is a true midpoint. Yet median incomes are rarely reported outside Canada and the United States.

- Personal income can be expressed as family, household, and per capita. Because families are larger than households and per-capita income is on an individual basis, these units are not directly comparable. Income can also be stated in pretax or after-tax terms, which are not directly comparable.

- Since prices differ by country, a comparison of average incomes that does not take purchasing power into effect will be inaccurate.

- Economic growth is cyclical; at any given time, some countries will be performing well while others are struggling.

- Although the definition of poverty varies greatly by nation, one billion people in the world suffer from malnutrition, illiteracy, and disease.

During the 1960s and early 1970s, real income in Canada and the U.S. rose considerably. Growth then slowed; and from 1981 to 1983, real income fell in Canada. Between 1983 and 1990, real income rose moderately in both Canada and the U.S.—before falling again in 1991. Since then, it has fluctuated slightly each year. Thus, in sum, real Canadian and U.S. income has gone up rather little over the last twenty-five years.

The most recent data for Canada indicates a median family income of $47 719 for 1992 and average family income of $53 676. The top 20 per cent of families had over $92 000 in average family income, the next 20 per cent had an average family income of $54 505, and the bottom 20 per cent had an average family income of $11 171.

In contrast, in 1995 the U.S. median after-tax family income was between U.S.$33 000 and U.S.$34 000. Although the top one-fifth of families averaged U.S.$80 000 (with the top 1 per cent averaging U.S.$400 000+ per family)—and 14 per cent of all families had incomes of U.S.$75 000 and over, the bottom fifth averaged U.S.$13 000— and 8 million families were at the poverty level. According to recent studies, the top one-fifth of U.S. families have total annual incomes that are nearly fifteen times those of the lowest one-fifth. And the OECD reports that the United States has the greatest spread between high-income and low-income families of any industrialized nation in the world.[5]

Worldwide, these are the annual household income distributions:[6]

	% EARNING U.S. $20 000+	% EARNING UNDER U.S.$5000
Industrialized countries	65	3
Latin America	27	24
Middle East	18	22
Former Socialist economies	17	21
East Asia/Pacific	4	73
Sub-Saharan Africa	2	75
South Asia	1	75

Changes in the **cost of living** *are measured by a* **consumer price index.**

The slowdown in real Canadian and U.S. income growth has occurred because income rises have been virtually offset by higher prices. This has led to a higher **cost of living**, the total amount consumers annually pay for goods and services.

Over the last twenty-five years in Canada, the greatest price increases have been for recreation, education, alcohol, and tobacco products; the smallest have been for clothing and food. In the U.S. the greatest price increases have been for medical care, auto insurance, and tobacco products; the smallest have been for phone services, apparel and upkeep, and household furnishings.

Many nations monitor their cost of living by means of a **consumer price index** (CPI), which measures monthly and yearly price changes (the rate of inflation) for a broad range

---

[5]See Joseph Spiers, "Why the Income Gap Won't Go Away," *Fortune* (December 11, 1995), pp. 65–70; and Keith Bradsher, "Widest Gap in Incomes? Research Points to U.S.," *New York Times* (October 27, 1995), p. D2.
[6]Chip Walker, "The Global Middle Class," *American Demographics* (September 1995), p. 44.

of consumer goods and services. Since 1983, the overall annual rise in the Canadian CPI has been under 5 per cent (except for 1989-1992, when it rose on average by 6 per cent). In 1995, the CPI rose less than 5 per cent in Canada, the United States, France, Great Britain, and Germany. It went up by 10 per cent or more in many developing and less-developed countries.

Global consumption patterns have been shifting. In industrialized nations, the proportion of income that people spend on food, beverages, and tobacco has been declining. The percentage spent on medical care, personal business, and recreation has been rising. In less-developed and developing nations, the percentage of spending devoted to food remains high. Canadians spend 15.6 per cent of income on food, beverages and tobacco and 1.9 per cent on health care. Americans spend 18 per cent of income on food, beverages, and tobacco and 16 per cent on medical care. In contrast, Argentines spend 40 per cent of income on food, beverages, and tobacco and 4 per cent on medical care, while Pakistanis spend 47 per cent of income on food, beverages, and tobacco and 5 per cent on medical care.

International Marketing in Action

How Would YOU Do Business in Zambia?

Zambia's economic fortunes have changed dramatically over the past thirty years. At the time of its independence from Great Britain in 1964, the country had the highest standard of living in Black Africa. Unfortunately, Zambia then fell victim to a decline in the price of copper (the country's major export) and years of political control by a dictator.

Now, after holding a multi-party election and enacting economic controls proposed by the International Monetary Fund, Zambia's economic future looks promising. With its Central Africa location, Zambia has common borders with eight other countries; it is an ideal location as a distribution hub, with easy access to 250 million consumers.

Zambia has worked hard to become more attractive to foreign investors. There are no longer restrictions on foreign exchange and investment; new business ventures are exempt from customs duties and sales taxes; firms can take after-tax profits out of the country; and a low income-tax rate (a 15 per cent flat tax) is in effect. The nation's annual budget emphasizes such major infrastructure projects as road rehabilitation and rural electrification. The areas luring the most foreign investment are agriculture, mining, and tourism.

Here are some of the key demographic characteristics of Zambia:

- It has a population of 8.1 million people.
- The population density is very low, as Zambia's area is approximately the size of Ontario.
- The annual population growth rate is 3.7 per cent.
- The total GDP is U.S.$3.5 billion, and per capita income is about U.S.$425.
- Its annual inflation rate was reduced from over 200 per cent in 1992 to 35 per cent in 1995.

As an international marketing consultant, what opportunities would you recommend pursuing in Zambia? Why?

Source: Based on material in Christina Lamb, "Zambia: A Model for Africa," *Fortune* (July 24, 1995), Special Advertising Section.

*Consumption reflects **disposable income** and **discretionary income**.*

Disposable income is a person's, household's, or family's total after-tax income to be used for spending and/or savings. **Discretionary income** is what a person, household, or family has available to spend on luxuries, after necessities are bought. Classifying some product categories as necessities or luxuries depends on a nation's standard of living. In Canada and the United States, autos and phones are generally considered necessities; in many less-developed countries, they are typically considered luxuries.

Marketing Implications

Several marketing implications regarding consumer income can be drawn:

- Companies need to be quite careful in drawing conclusions about the income levels in different countries. Terms must be properly defined and purchasing power, as well as income levels, assessed.
- There is great income diversity between countries. Thus, firms' goods, services, and marketing strategies should be consistent with the income levels in the targeted nations.
- There is tremendous income diversity within countries. This means that, even in the same country, some firms can prosper by focusing on lower-income consumers while others succeed by targeting upper-income consumers.
- The cost of living affects the discretionary income that people have available to spend. For goods and services perceived as luxuries, consumers need to have discretionary income available.

U.S.-based Whirlpool is a good example of a firm that understands how to react to consumer income levels. It knows that outside Canada, the United States, and Western Europe, the middle-class consumer is quite different. A consumer has to work 40 to 45 days to afford a washing machine in Poland, 35 days in the Czech Republic, and 30 days in Hungary—versus five days in Western Europe. As a result, Whirlpool arranges for more financing in Eastern Europe.[7]

WHIRLPOOL
www.whirlpool.com/

Occupations and Education

The trend to white-collar and service occupations is continuing in industrialized countries.

The labour force in industrialized nations continues to move to white-collar and service occupations. In less-developed and developing nations, many jobs still involve manual work and are more often agriculture-based.

The total Canadian labour force (people over 15 who are eligible to work) is 14.5 million people. The employed labour force in Canada amounts to 12.5 million people, compared with 125 million in the U.S., 64 million in Japan, 28 million in Germany, 26 million in Great Britain, 22 million in France, and 20 million in Italy. For the last 30 years, the per cent of Canadian workers in service-related, technical, and clerical white-collar jobs has risen; the per cent as managers, administrators, and sales workers has been relatively constant; and the per cent as unskilled workers has dropped. Four hundred and thirty-five thousand Canadian workers have an agriculture-related job.

Women are a large and growing percentage of the worldwide labour force; they make up 45 per cent of the Canadian labour force.

Another change in the labour force throughout the world has been the increase in the number and percentage of working women. For example, in 1971, 3 million women comprised 34 per cent of the total Canadian labour force. Today, 6.5 million women account for 45 per cent of the labour force, and 53 per cent of adult women in both Canada and the U.S. are working. In Japan and Great Britain as well, one-half of adult women are in the labour force, while 60+ per cent of adult women are in the Swedish labour force.

Unemployment rates, which reflect the percentage of adults in the total labour force not working, vary widely by nation. For instance, during 1995, the Canadian unemployment rate was about 10 per cent but falling. In comparison, the 1995 unemployment rate in the U.S. was 6 per cent, while those in Belgium, Finland, France, Great Britain, and Italy exceeded 10 per cent; Spain's rate was 22 per cent. Some worldwide unemployment has

---

[7] Rahul Jacob, "The Big Rise," *Fortune* (May 30, 1994), pp. 74–90.

been temporary, due to weak domestic and international economies. Other times, depending on the nation and industry, many job losses have been permanent. Unemployment is often accompanied by cutbacks in discretionary purchases.

Great strides are being made globally to upgrade educational attainment; but, the level of education tends to be much higher in industrialized nations than in less-developed and developing ones. One measure of educational attainment is the literacy rate—the percentage of people in a country who can read and write. Canada's literacy rate is 99 per cent and in industrialized nations the literacy rate exceeds 95 per cent. Here are the rates for some less-developed and developing nations: Bolivia, 78 per cent; Cambodia, 74 per cent; Chad, 30 per cent; China, 78 per cent; Morocco, 50 per cent; and Saudi Arabia, 62 per cent.

Another measure of educational attainment is the level of schooling completed. In Canada 16.7 per cent of people ages 25 to 64 years have graduated from university. In comparison to other large industrialized nations, the United States is the most educated. A higher percentage of U.S. adults has finished high school and university than in Canada, France, Germany, Great Britain, Italy, or Japan (see Figure 7-6).

The sharp increase in working women and higher educational attainment have generally contributed to the growing number of people in upper-income brackets; the rather high unemployment rates in some nations and industries and slow-growth economies have caused other families to have low incomes.

Global education levels are going up.

Marketing Implications

The occupations and education of the population have marketing implications. A greater number and percentage of the total population are in the labour force than before, and this workforce needs transportation, clothing, restaurants, and personal services; stores have opportunities in commercial centres; and the market for job-oriented goods and services is growing and the shift in jobs means different needs and aspirations in consumer purchases.

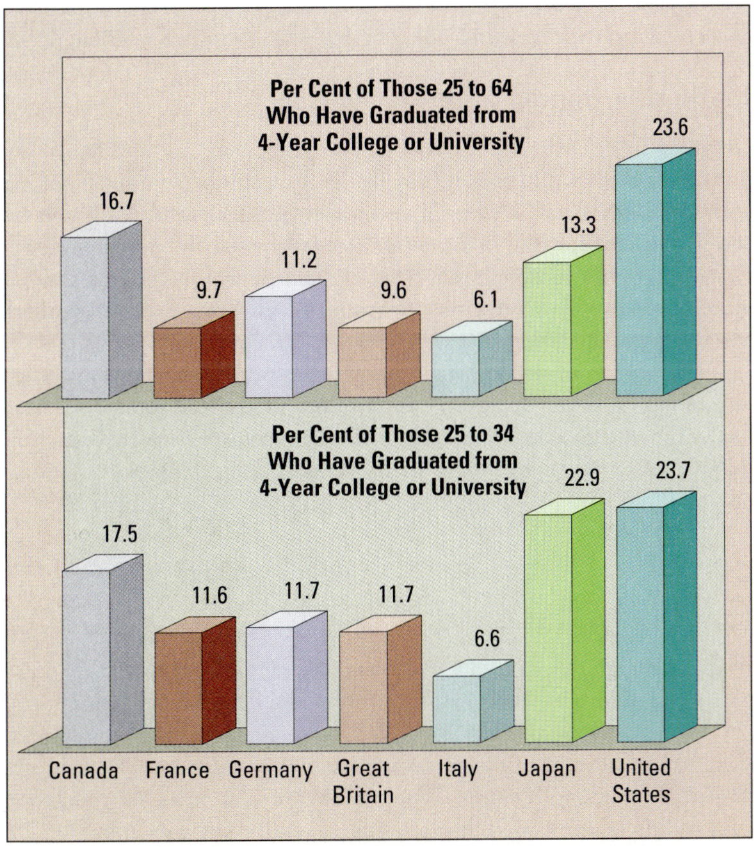

FIGURE 7-6
Educational Attainment by Country

NOTE: These statistics are from 1991, the latest common date available.

Source: Organization for Economic Cooperation and Development data, as reported in *The Condition of Education 1994* (Washington, D.C.: U.S. Department of Education, 1994), p. 70.

Per Cent of Those 25 to 64 Who Have Graduated from 4-Year College or University

Canada	France	Germany	Great Britain	Italy	Japan	United States
16.7	9.7	11.2	9.6	6.1	13.3	23.6

Per Cent of Those 25 to 34 Who Have Graduated from 4-Year College or University

Canada	France	Germany	Great Britain	Italy	Japan	United States
17.5	11.6	11.7	11.7	6.6	22.9	23.7

Because working women have less time for shopping and operating the home, they tend to be interested in convenience and customer service. They often cannot shop during weekdays and many require evening and weekend store hours, efficient store layouts, and mail-order and phone purchases. Such time-saving devices as microwave ovens and food processors, prepared foods, pre-wrapped goods, and special services (such as automatic teller machines), appeal to working women. Also, child-related services, such as daytime child care, are particularly important for them. Yet, too few firms help employees in this area, leaving a prime opening for specialized firms to market these services.

As the population's education level rises, firms need to respond in terms of better information, better product quality, better customer service, enhanced safety and environmental controls, greater accuracy in learning and meeting consumer expectations, and improved consumer-complaint departments. At the same time, companies marketing in less-developed and developing countries need to keep the literacy rates of those areas in mind and adapt products, packaging, promotion messages, and operating instructions accordingly.

Marital Status

Marriage and family remain important.

Marriage and family are powerful institutions worldwide; but in some nations they are now less dominant than they once were. Although 165 000 couples get married each year, only 60 per cent of Canadian adults are married; the percentage of married adults in many other nations is much higher. The average Canadian age at first marriage is 28 years for males and 26 years for females—up from 27.7 and 24.7 in 1960. Thus, the average Canadian family size has gone from 3.9 in 1961 to 3.0 in 1994. The male and female ages at first marriage are much lower in less-developed and developing nations; and the average family is bigger there.

*A **family** has related persons residing together. A **household** has one or more persons who may not be related.*

A **family** is a group of two or more persons residing together who are related by blood, marriage, or adoption. A **household** is a person or group of persons occupying a housing unit, whether related or unrelated. In many nations, average household size has been dropping. Of the 10 million Canadian households, 23 per cent are one-person units, with family households accounting for 73 per cent. Figure 7-7 shows household data for several nations.

Marketing Implications

Despite changes over the last thirty or so years, marriage and family are still vital institutions around the world and in Canada. This creates opportunities for industries associated with weddings (such as caterers and travel agents), family life (such as financial services and full-sized cars), and divorce (such as attorneys). When marriages occur later in individuals' lives, those people have better financial resources and two-income families are more prevalent. This presents opportunities for firms involved with clothing, furniture, entertainment, and recreation.

The growth of single-person households provides opportunities for home and home furnishings industries and those that produce specialized products. These implications also apply to divorced and widowed persons. For example, smaller households have a demand for smaller homes, appropriate-sized furnishings and appliances, and single-serving food packages.

Ethnicity/Race

*Demographically, **ethnicity/race** is one measure of a population's diversity with regard to language, country of origin, or race.*

From a demographics perspective, **ethnicity/race** is studied to determine the existence of diversity among and within nations in terms of language and country of origin or race.

Worldwide, there are over 200 different languages spoken by at least 1 million people each—and twelve of those are spoken by 100+ million people each (including Mandarin, English, Hindi, and Spanish). Thus, there are vast linguistic differences among nations. Even within nations, there is often linguistic diversity. For example, Canada (English and

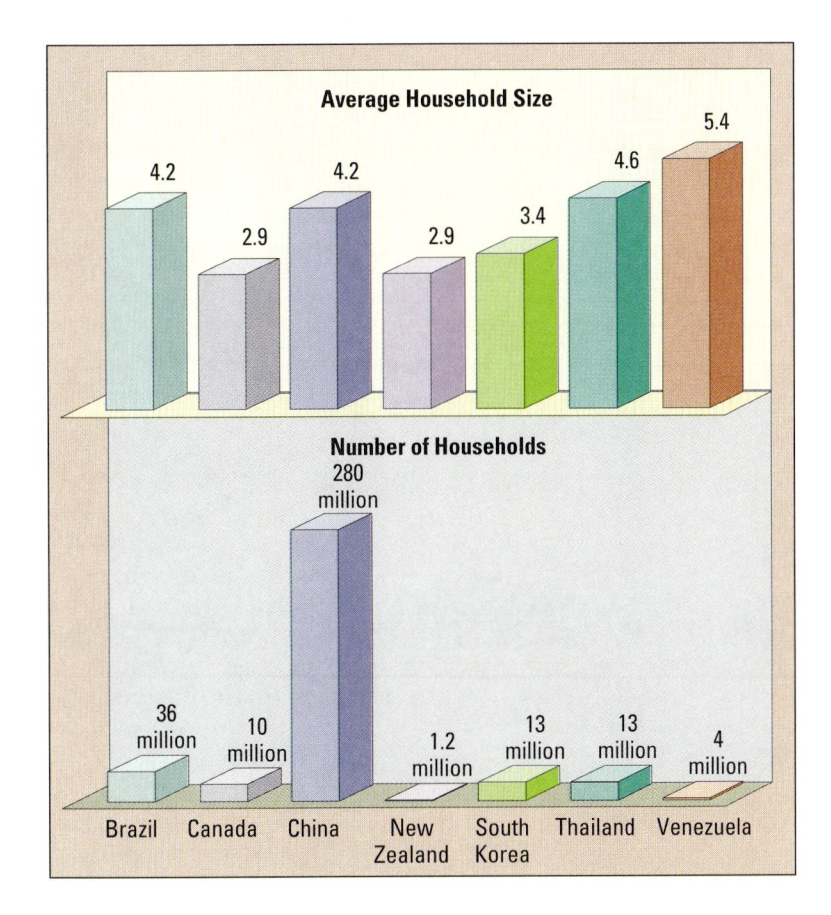

FIGURE 7-7
Household Data by Country

NOTE: These statistics are from 1993, the latest common date available.

Source: *International Marketing Data and Statistics, 1995* (Great Britain: Euromonitor, 1995), p. 429; and authors' estimates.

French), Chad (French and Arabic), India (Hindi and English), and Peru (Spanish and Quechua) all have two official languages. One of the issues facing the European Community in its unification drive is the multiplicity of languages spoken in the fifteen member nations.

Most nations consist of people representing different ethnic and racial backgrounds. For instance, among those living in the Philippines are Malays, Chinese, Americans, and Spaniards. Sometimes, the people in various groups continue to speak in the languages of their countries of origin, even though they may have resided in their current nations for one or two generations.

Canada is comprised of people from virtually every ethnic group in the world. Statistics Canada measures ethnic origin, which is defined as the ethnic or cultural group to which the respondent or the respondent's ancestors belonged on first coming to North America. The 1996 Census in Canada was the first time that "race" was measured as a census category. The 1993 Canadian population was 20.8 per cent British, 22.8 per cent French, 3.4 per cent German, 2.8 per cent Italian and 1.7 per cent aboriginal people.

Marketing Implications

The ethnic/racial diversity of the world's population means firms must be careful not to generalize or stereotype—either in dealing with multiple nations or in marketing to different ethnic/racial groups within the same nation. Companies marketing goods and services in Canada might miss some prime opportunities if they do not research and adapt to the racial/ethnic characteristics of the marketplace:

- Marketers can reach specific ethnic groups in Canada with specialized media. Figure 7-8 shows an ad for one such medium. *Marketing Magazine's* "1995 Guide to Ethnic Marketing Services" lists the following marketing-service providers that specialize in ethnic marketing services in Canada: eight advertising agencies, three consultant services, three creative services, one direct mail service, three magazines, two media bro-

FIGURE 7-8
Marketing to a Diverse Marketplace
Reprinted with permission of Eyetalian Magazine.

> SUCCESSFUL, YOUNG, AND PROFESSIONAL.
>
> THEIR PARENTS HELPED BUILD OUR CITIES AND NOW THEY HELP RUN THEM.
>
> THE EYETALIAN IS YOUR ONLY DIRECT ACCESS TO THIS EXCLUSIVE MARKET.
>
> **The eyetalian magazine**
>
> WATCH OUT FOR A NEW DESIGN IN THE FALL. WITH ITS SIGHTS SET ON A NEW GENERATION OF ITALIAN CANADIANS.
>
> "Elegant and fun to read" **Bronwyn Drainie,** The Globe and Mail
> "Re-imagining and redefining the immigrant experience altogether"
> **Naomi Klein,** The Toronto Star
> "Inspired" **Elizabeth Renzetti,** The Globe and Mail
>
> Contact Nicholas Bianchi @ 416-787-9598 or 1-800-689-5145

kers, two market research firms, seven newspapers, five radio stations, seven television services and one translation service.[8]

- Vancouver, Toronto, and Montreal are home to over 80 per cent of Canada's ethnic population (about 2.1 million people). Italian and Chinese people represent over half of this market.

- The purchasing power and population growth rate of ethnic markets are expected to be greater than those for the Canadian market as a whole by the year 2000. For example, population growth among Italian, Chinese, East Indian, Portuguese, Greek, and Polish ethnic groups is expected to be 33 per cent, growing from 2.1 million in 1995 to 2.8 million people by the year 2000.[9]

- "For those approaching target marketing correctly, the benefits are there. One of Canada's major banks showed a 400 per cent increase over five years in its Chinese business when it took an aggressive marketing approach. Besides showing Chinese in their mass marketing material, they also developed Chinese-language ads, direct-mail and in-branch materials, and took a highly visible role supporting community events. Another advertiser, an automaker, saw a 25 per cent boost in sales to the Chinese market due to an integrated ethnic-marketing approach."[10]

---

[8] "Guide to Ethnic Marketing Services," *Marketing Magazine* (July 3/10 1995), pp. 12–14.
[9] Charles Laughlin, "Speaking in Tongues," *Link* (October 1993), p. 15; "The Economics of Growing Communities," *Marketing Magazine,* (July 3/10, 1995), p. 11.
[10] Jennifer Lynn, "Approaching Diversity," *Marketing Magazine* (July 3/10, 1995), p. 11.

Uses of Demographic Data

As we noted at the beginning of the chapter, after studying individual demographics a firm can form consumer demographic profiles to better focus marketing efforts. Here, three examples of demographic profiles are presented.

Profiles of the Canadian, American, and Mexican populations can be contrasted:

	CANADA	**UNITED STATES**	**MEXICO**
Annual population growth (%)	1.4	1.0	1.9
Life expectancy (years)	78	77	74
Median age (years)	35	34	20
Urban population (%)	77	80	71
Income ratio of top fifth of population to bottom fifth	8.3	15	14
Working women as part of total labour force (%)	45	46	37
Literacy rate (%)	99	96	90
Average household size	2.9	2.7	5.6

The typical working woman in Japan is married, in her middle- to late-forties, and has children in school. A two-income family can pay for the children's education and meet housing costs. The husband's earnings go to cover housing, household, and other ongoing expenses; the wife's earnings go for children's education, personal needs, social life, and savings. "Japanese women control the household purse strings. Most husbands handed over the pay packet and got an allowance. Today, even with direct deposit, most women know exactly how much their husbands make, but only a few men know what their wives earn." A full-time working woman spends seven hours per day on the job, 3.5 hours on household chores and child care, and less than three hours on herself.[11]

One of the best indicators of consumer buying trends and the underlying interplay of needs, tastes, and desires is the rate at which people buy certain household goods and appliances. It comes as no surprise that 98 per cent of households in Canada have a colour television. That figure drops to 81.5 per cent for microwave ovens and to 79 per cent for VCRs. In the have-not category are automatic dishwashers (46 per cent), compact disk players (41 per cent) and home computers (25 per cent). Households with children are twice as likely to have a video camera (26 per cent versus 13 per cent), a home computer (38 per cent versus 20 per cent) and, of course, a mortgage (55 per cent versus 27 per cent).[12]

Limitations of Demographics

In applying demographic data, these limitations should be noted:

- Information may be old. In Canada, a full census is done only once every five years and there are time lags before data are released.
- Data on various demographics may be unavailable in some nations, especially less-developed and developing ones.
- Summary data may be too broad and hide opportunities and risks in small markets or specialized product categories.
- Single demographics may not be useful. A demographic profile may be needed.
- The psychological or social factors influencing people are not considered.

Demographic data may be dated, unavailable, or too general, may require profile analysis, and may not consider reasons for behaviour.

---

[11] Sandra T. W. Davis, "Japan's Working Women Are a 'New Breed' of Consumer," *Marketing News* (August 17, 1992), p. 12.
[12] George Vasic, "Why Today's Luxuries Are Tomorrow's Necessities," *Canadian Business* (June 1995), p. 159.

Ethics AND TODAY'S MARKETER

Should Boards of Education Accept Advertising?

In North America, children and young adults annually spend more than U.S.$100 billion and influence their families to spend an additional U.S.$130 billion. Accordingly, marketers are increasingly establishing ties with Canadian and U.S. school boards in order to better attract the school-aged market.

Many school boards see schoolbus advertising as a means of increasing their revenues. Schoolbus advertising began in Colorado Springs, Colorado, and was quickly adopted by school districts throughout the United States, including those in Washington D.C. and New York City. In Canada, The Wellington County Board of Education in Ontario is experimenting with advertising on its fleet of school buses.

Each school board has its own rules governing schoolbus ads. Some restrict ads to the placement of logos on the outside of schoolbuses; these ads resemble travelling billboards. Other boards allow advertisers to place brochures and coupons on racks inside schoolbuses. The Wellington County Board of Education requires that advertising messages be socially responsible. For this reason, their experiment involved an ad for milk. There are also differences in how schoolbus advertising is implemented. Some school boards administer the advertising program themselves. Others, like New York City's Board of Education, plan to develop partnerships with advertising agencies and outdoor media companies. These firms must be willing to absorb all startup costs and to share revenues with the schools.

Supporters of schoolbus advertising say this is a harmless way of offsetting cuts in government funding to schools and rising school costs, and that schoolbus advertising can also involve students in creative projects. Revenue for the Wellington County Board is estimated to be $250 000 for the whole school year. The board sees the situation as a win-win deal for taxpayers, since the messages will be socially responsible and the board will get much-needed revenue. On the other hand, critics feel bus advertising may be perceived as a product endorsement, that it influences students to purchase unnecessary and sometimes unhealthy items, and that it takes advantage of a captive audience.

As a nonpaid marketing advisor to a local school board, develop a position on whether schoolbus advertising should be accepted by the board.

Sources: Based on material in Kemba Johnson, "NY School Buses Learn to Ad," *Advertising Age* (August 14, 1995), p. 10; Betsy Wagner, "Our Class Is Brought To You Today By," *U.S. News & World Report* (April 24, 1995), p. 63; and Laura Medcalf, "The Wellington County Board of Education is the first in Ontario to Experiment with Advertising on its Fleet of School Buses," *Marketing Magazine* (May 1, 1995), p. 4.

- The purchase-making process is not explained.
- Demographics do not provide insights into what motivates people to make purchase decisions. Why do people with similar demographic profiles buy different products or brands?

For these reasons, Chapter 8 examines the psychological and social factors affecting consumer behaviour and the decision process consumers use.

MARKETING IN A CHANGING WORLD
From Boomers to Xers

Two of the key age groups that today's marketers must continually strive to understand and satisfy are *Baby Boomers* and *Generation Xers*. In some cases, the first group includes the parents of the second group.

Baby boomers are people born between 1947 and 1965 (with the peak birth rate occurring in 1959), in the aftermath of World War II. They are generally divided into two groups: older and younger boomers. By the year 2000, the 7 million Canadian and 77 million U.S. baby boomers will range in age from 35 to 54, be in their peak earnings years, and dominate consumer spending.

The older baby boomers grew up with the "Vietnam War, the Civil Rights Movement, and economic expansion." The younger group of boomers grew up with stagflation, wage-and-price controls, and government spending freezes. Overall, baby boomers are "well-educated, high-tech parents who suffer from a lack of leisure time. Despite their financial worries, most can expect a healthy, active, and fun-filled retirement."[13]

Generation Xers—a term coined by marketers and disliked by most in this group (don't YOU dislike this name?)—are people born between 1965 and 1976, a period also known as the "baby bust." By the year 2000, Generation Xers will range in age from 24 to 35 and be embarking on major life changes: getting married, having children, and moving along career ladders. In contrast to baby boomers, Generation Xers "are more apt to have participated in household chores at an earlier age, so they are more knowledgeable about products at a comparable age. They are more apt to seek a balance of work and leisure activities. They are more diverse and more accepting of diversity, whether it be defined by ethnicity or by sexual preference. And while they are not anti-advertising, they are repulsed by insincerity—and they are experts at spotting it."[14]

SUMMARY

1. *To show the importance and scope of consumer analysis* By analyzing consumers, a firm is better able to determine the most appropriate audience to which to appeal and the combination of marketing factors that will satisfy this audience. This is a critical task given the diversity in today's global marketplace. The scope of consumer analysis includes who, what, why, how, when, where, and how often.

2. *To define and enumerate important consumer demographics for the Canadian population and other countries* Consumer demographics are objective and quantifiable population statistics. They include size, gender, and age; location, housing, and mobility; income and expenditures; occupations and education; marital status; and ethnicity/race.

3. *To examine trends and projections for these important demographics and study their marketing implications* The world population is 5.7 billion people and rising by 1.5 per cent annually. Canada's population is 29 million people and increasing by 1.4 per cent each year. In many nations, a large proportion of births are firstborns. Worldwide, the number of men and women is roughly equal. However, women generally live longer than men; and the average age of populations in industrialized nations is higher than in less-developed and developing countries.

There has been a significant movement of the world population to large urban areas. The level of urbanization does vary by country, with 77 per cent of Canadians living in urban areas. In many countries, the majority of people own the home in which they live, with almost two-thirds of the Canadian population residing in homes they own. Each year, millions of people emigrate from one country to another and hundreds of millions move within their countries. About 240 000 people move to Canada from abroad every year; and about 15 to 20 per cent of the Canadian population moves annually. Essentially, the only area of population growth in Canada is in the province of British Columbia, while the populations of Quebec and Newfoundland have been shrinking.

For several reasons, comparing countries' personal income data can be rather difficult. The 1992 Canadian after-tax median family income was $47 719—with the top one-fifth of families having after-tax incomes averaging $92 000 and the bottom one-fifth having after-tax incomes averaging $11 171. Many nations measure their cost of living and rate of inflation using a consumer price index. There are differences in consumption patterns between people in industrialized nations and in less-developed and developing

---

[13] Patricia Braus, "The Baby Boom at Mid-Decade, *American Demographics* (April 1995), pp. 40–45; Harvey Schachter, "Power Shift," *Canadian Business* (August 1995), p. 21.
[14] Karen Ritchie, "Marketing to Generation X," *American Demographics* (April 1995), pp. 34–39.

countries. When assessing consumption patterns, the distinction between disposable-income spending and discretionary-income expenditures should be kept in mind.

In industrialized nations, the labour force is continuing its movement to white-collar and service occupations; many more jobs in less-developed and developing nations still entail manual work and are agriculture-based. The total employed Canadian civilian labour force is 12.5 million people. Throughout the world, women comprise a significant portion of the labour force (45 per cent in Canada). Unemployment rates vary widely among nations, based on economic conditions and industry shifts. Globally, educational attainment has gone up—though there are great variations among countries. In Canada, a much larger percentage of the population is now graduating high school and attending college or university than did thirty years ago.

Marriage and family are powerful institutions, although less dominant than in the past for some nations. Three-fifths of Canadian adults are married, with couples waiting until they are older for marriage and having fewer children than in prior decades. A family consists of relatives living together. A household consists of a person or persons occupying a housing unit, related or not. In many nations, both family and household size have declined, due to the growth in single-person households and other factors.

Demographically, ethnicity/race is important as it pertains to the diversity of people among and within nations. Globally, over 200 languages are spoken by at least 1 million people; and some nations have two or more official languages. Most countries have populations representing different ethnic and racial groups. Statistics Canada measures ethnic origin which is defined as the ethnic or cultural group to which the respondent or the respondent's ancestors belonged on first coming to North America. The 1993 Canadian population was 20.8 per cent British, 22.8 per cent French, 3.4 per cent German, 2.8 per cent Italian and 1.7 per cent aboriginal people.

Each of these demographics has marketing implications, which are discussed in the chapter.

4. *To present examples of consumer demographic profiles* After looking at demographic factors separately, a firm may develop a consumer demographic profile—a composite description of a consumer group based upon key demographics. Three examples of such profiles are provided.

5. *To consider the limitations of consumer demographics* Data may be obsolete or unavailable for some nations; hidden trends or implications may not be evident in the statistics; single demographic statistics are often not useful; and demographics do not explain the factors affecting behaviour, consumer decision making, and motivation.

KEY TERMS

final consumers (p. 178)
organizational consumers (p. 178)
consumer demographics (p. 178)
consumer demographic profile (p. 178)
Census Metropolitan Area (CMA) (p. 182)

Census Agglomeration Area (CA) (p. 182)
cost of living (p. 184)
consumer price index (CPI) (p. 184)
disposable income (p. 186)
discretionary income (p. 186)

family (p. 188)
household (p. 188)
ethnicity/race (p. 188)

Review Questions

1. How does the use of consumer demographics aid marketing decision making?
2. What is the value of a consumer demographic profile?
3. Distinguish between final and organizational consumers.
4. Compare the worldwide and Canadian trends with regard to population growth. Why is this meaningful to marketers?
5. In Canada, how does a Census Metropolitan Area (CMA) differ from a Census Agglomeration Area (CA)?
6. Cite several reasons why it is difficult to contrast personal income data by country.
7. Distinguish between the terms "cost of living" and "consumer price index."
8. In addition to the examples cited in the text, what goods and services should grow as the number of working women and working mothers increases?
9. What is a family? Why are Canadian families getting smaller?
10. Describe the major limitations of demographics.

Discussion Questions

1. Comment on this statement and its marketing ramifications: "Even though the world is getting smaller, there remains tremendous demographic diversity in the marketplace."
2. The biggest CMA in Canada is Toronto, with 4.4 million people. What are the pros and cons of marketing products there? Recommend a marketing approach for a local bank.
3. Discuss the country household data in Figure 7-7 and its implications for marketers.
4. Using the *Census of Population*, develop a demographic profile of the people residing in the CA or CMA nearest to where you live. What are the marketing overtones of this profile?
5. As the owner-operator of a prospective camera store in Canada, what demographic factors would you study? Describe the demographic profile of your ideal consumer.

VIDEO CASE

Marketing to Seniors: Canada's Fastest-Growing Market Is Also Its Most Lucrative!

With almost flat population growth in Canada, where can marketers go to find a fast-growing and attractive market opportunity? They do not have to go far, just simply appeal to the oldest market in Canada, seniors! The seniors market is defined as people 50 years of age and over. In 1985 the 50 and over market in Canada was 25 per cent of the total population; in 1996 this number was estimated at about 26 per cent, or 7.8 million people; by 2006, 32-34 per cent of the population, or 10.3 million Canadians, will be over 50 years of age. This substantial increase in the senior population provides major marketing opportunities in retirement housing and medical care. It also means special opportunities for retailers that specialize in the seniors' market, such as travel agencies, cosmetic firms, clothing firms, and automobile companies.

Aside from using products normally associated with aging, the over 50s have 75-80 per cent of the discretionary income in the country and they spend 28 per cent of their discretionary income. Today's seniors have paid their mortgages, have no school-aged children, and have saved like crazy because of the scarcity psychology that they developed as a result of living through a depression and a world war. The net wealth of the country is concentrated in the hands of people over 50.

Furthermore, today's seniors are not just a bunch of wealthy old crocks sitting on porches waiting to expire! They are in better health than ever before and they are active in their communities as volunteers, political activists, and educators. As such, they are not particularly comfortable with being referred to as "seniors." They are very individualistic and insist on making their own decisions. Canada's seniors have tremendous amounts of free time on their hands and they spend more of it on sports, hobbies, reading, watching TV, and shopping than any other age group.

These people are a marketer's dream, yet a great number of Canadian marketers have not paid enough attention to them. Advertising is aimed at younger audiences and seniors are rarely portrayed favourably in ads. Seniors really do see themselves as being much younger and do not identify with "old" people. American marketers, on the other hand, have not been overlooking this market. State tourism representatives from the Southern U.S. see the Canadian seniors market as a very desirable market and pursue them with great vigor. Busch Gardens, Florida sent its band to the Great Canadian Maturity Show in Toronto. There, they entertained among display booths presenting other products: recreational vehicles, automobiles, cosmetics, canes, travel agents, and even a psychic.

Marketing to seniors presents its own challenges. Marketers need to realize that seniors see themselves as still young, so advertising and promotional portrayals must present this. Marketing aimed at people between 75 and 80 years old is better accepted using a person who is 60. Appealing to the psychology and social maturity of this market is more important than appeals related to their demographic make-up. Senior buyers tend to be more brand loyal than younger buyers and they value integrity, so promotion should contain a lot of factual information. Emotional appeals are quite effective but they should not be patronizing or shallow. Seniors seem to use coupons more, watch TV newscasts, read heavily, and enjoy television. They also tend to respond more favourably to direct-response promotions. Seniors are a group that marketers can build a relationship with and this means doing lots of research on this market. Canadian marketers need to get in touch with today's older citizens so they can be prepared for tomorrow's bumper crop of seniors.

Who knows, in ten or fifteen years when you turn on TSN, you may find it stands for "The Seniors Network" instead of "The Sports Network"!

QUESTIONS

1. Describe how a supermarket chain could better attract and service the growing senior-citizen market.
2. Discuss the marketing implications of the increased aging of the Canadian population.
3. Find an advertisement that you believe is targeted to seniors. Discuss how and why it works.
4. What are the advantages and disadvantages of applying the demographic data presented in this case?

VIDEO QUESTIONS ON SENIORS MARKETING

1. Describe a product not mentioned in the case that you think would be particularly appropriate and appealing to the seniors market, and discuss how you would market it.
2. Discuss some of the reasons why marketers have been slow to react to the seniors market and what marketers need to do to successfully serve this market.

Video Source: "Seniors Marketing," *Venture* (April 10, 1994).
Other Sources: Today's Seniors (October 1995); and Eric Miller, "A 24-Point Guide to Mature Minds," *Marketing Magazine* (May 15, 1995), p. 29.

CASE STUDY

Wellcome: The Influence of Demographic Factors in Taiwan

Many parts of Asia are seen as markets with substantial long-run potential. Some analysts even predict that over the next decade more people will become affluent in Asia than anywhere else in the world.

Some forecasters see particularly high growth in Asian grocery marketing, especially for supermarkets. Currently, only 20 per cent of people shop in a supermarket at least once a week in Malaysia, as compared with 35 per cent in Taiwan, and 80 per cent in Hong Kong. In contrast, the average Canadian shopper makes 2.2 trips to a supermarket per week and spends a weekly total of $110.00. As the Gross Domestic Product per capita rises, market analysts forecast that supermarket usage by Asians will significantly increase.

One way to predict the potential number of supermarkets in Asian countries is by extrapolating data from the mature supermarket industry in Canada, using the following formula. Let us apply the formula to Taiwan:

$$\text{Potential number of supermarkets in Taiwan} = \frac{\text{Population of Taiwan}}{\text{Number of people per supermarket in Canada}} \times \frac{\text{Per capita income in Taiwan}}{\text{Per capita income in Canada}}$$

$$= \frac{21\ 500\ 000}{7750} \times \frac{\$10\ 600}{\$22\ 200}$$

$$= 2774 \times .48$$

$$= 1332$$

Thus, based on this formula, there currently is room for 1332 supermarkets in Taiwan.

One supermarket chain, Dairy Farm (owned by Wellcome, a Hong Kong-based firm with $8 billion in sales), opened its first store in Taiwan in 1987. Dairy Farm's Taiwanese market strategy was to open stores earlier than competitors and to establish economies of scale in advertising, warehousing, and distribution. Dairy Farm now has eighty supermarkets in Taiwan and sees the potential for an additional 250 to 300 markets over the next decade. Although Dairy Farm's Taiwanese stores are small by Canadian standards, they have a large selection of merchandise when compared to the mom-and-pop store competitors in Taiwan.

Among Asian countries, several supermarket executives feel Taiwan will soon represent a more important market than Hong Kong:

- In 1997, Hong Kong is to return to the jurisdiction of China, after being a British Crown Colony.
- There are now 21.5 million people in Taiwan, 25 per cent under the age of 15. The adult population has a literacy rate of 93 per cent.
- Some economic forecasters predict that, in the future, Taiwan's GDP per capita will be higher than Australia's. In 1994, Taiwan had a GDP per capita of $10 600, a strong increase over the 1993 level. In comparison, the per-capita GDP for Australia was $19 100 in 1994.
- An additional advantage of the Taiwanese market is its high population density. Taiwan has 1540 people per square mile versus 620 in Great Britain and 72 in the United States.

One obstacle to achieving supermarket success in Taiwan is the long supply chain and the poor infrastructure (roads, warehouses, and communications systems). These drawbacks limit expansion opportunities to the larger cities. Another problem relates to the difficulty in getting suppliers to become more efficient. For example, Dairy Farm found that after operating in Taiwan for over seven years, only 10 per cent of its products are delivered to its central warehouse on pallets.

QUESTIONS

1. Comment on the Taiwanese demographic data presented in this case. Besides supermarkets, what other kinds of firms should pursue this market? Why?
2. What kinds of demographic data would be useful in evaluating a particular site in Taiwan as a potential supermarket location?
3. What do you think about the formula used to determine the potential number of supermarkets in Taiwan?
4. Apply the formula to any other country in Asia and compare the results to those shown here for Taiwan.

Source: Data in this case drawn from Kevin Coupe, "You Can't Cook a Turkey in a Wok," *Progressive Grocer* (October 1994), pp. 59–60; "62nd Annual Report of the Grocery Industry," *Progressive Grocer* (April 1995), p. 43; and Statistics Canada, *Market Research Handbook 1995*, p. 203.

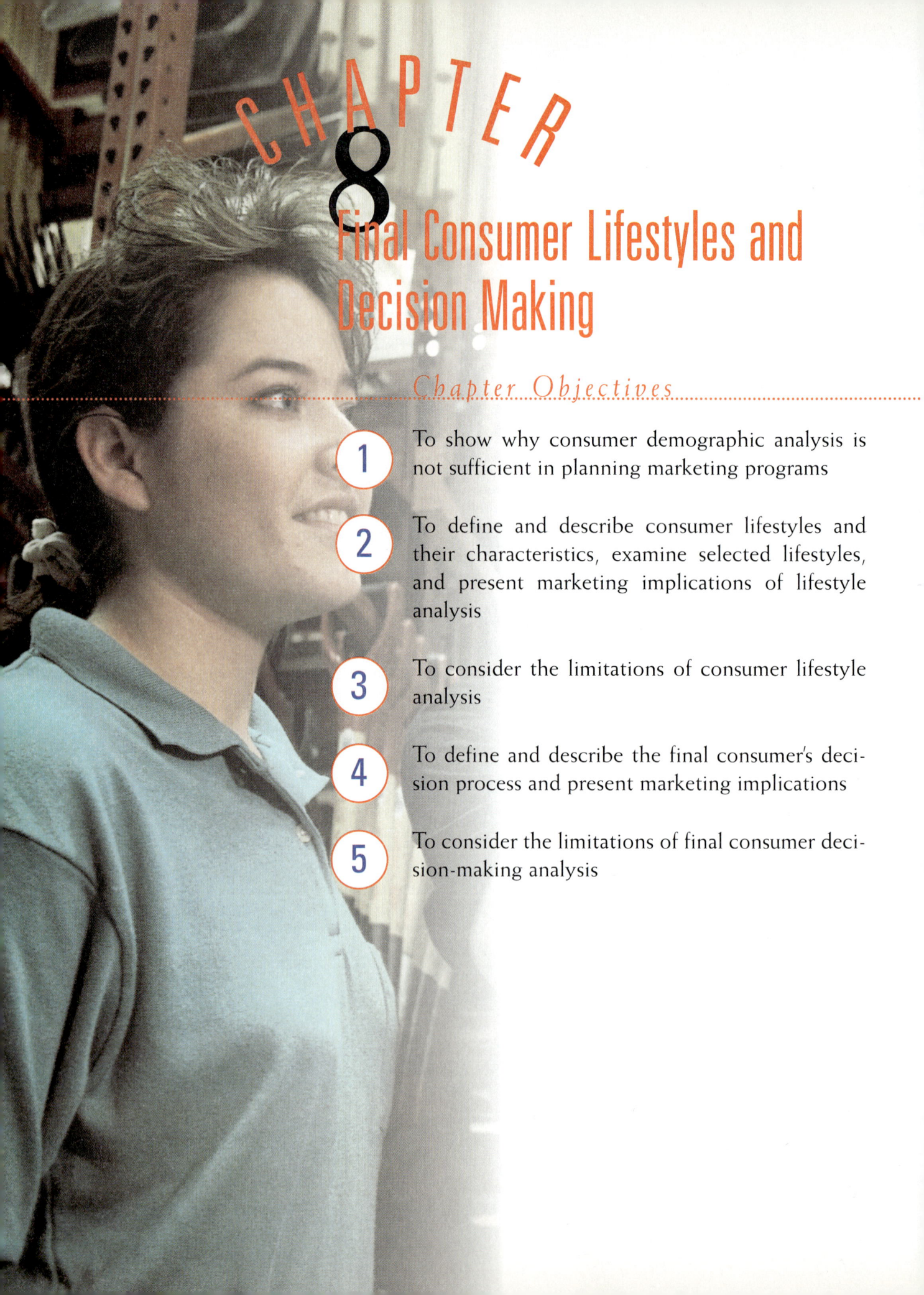

CHAPTER 8
Final Consumer Lifestyles and Decision Making

Chapter Objectives

1. To show why consumer demographic analysis is not sufficient in planning marketing programs

2. To define and describe consumer lifestyles and their characteristics, examine selected lifestyles, and present marketing implications of lifestyle analysis

3. To consider the limitations of consumer lifestyle analysis

4. To define and describe the final consumer's decision process and present marketing implications

5. To consider the limitations of final consumer decision-making analysis

> With an automatic teller machine, you can bank without a banker. With computer software, you can pick a mutual fund without a broker or design a patio deck without an architect. With an online service, you can plan a trip to Paris without a travel agent. You can do these activities when you want— days, nights, or weekends. "In many industries," observes Chris Meyer, a vice-president at Mercer Management Consulting, "you get more choice, more control, and more convenience by doing things yourself."

In greater numbers, North American consumers are transporting goods in their own trucks, renovating their homes with their own tools, and managing their own finances with financial software. Although the size of the do-it-yourself market is open to some debate, one U.S. study found that if the value of the time spent on such projects was included (based on the cost of a professional), the do-it-yourself market would amount to 40 per cent of the United States' Gross Domestic Product. In Canada the GST has fuelled the trend toward do-it-yourself projects, since Canadians want to avoid paying tax on top of already-high labour charges for renovation work.

A glimpse at the do-it-yourself market in the home-repair industry suggests that the size of the overall market is huge. Each year, Canadians spend upwards of $13.1 billion on renovations, and about 60 per cent of North American homeowners undertake at least one repair or home renovation project. Let's look at how Home Depot and its Canadian subsidiary, Aikenhead's, are catering to this large consumer lifestyle segment.

According to one marketing expert, Home Depot has done more than any company in North America to spread the gospel of do-it-yourself to the masses. The chain now operates over 410 warehouse-size stores in North America. Its sales, which hit U.S.$15 billion in 1995, have grown at a compound rate of 40 per cent. To help people buy tools for tasks with which they have little experience, Home Depot employs experienced carpenters, plumbers, and electricians as sales associates. Besides helping customers select the appropriate items, these associates teach clinics on such topics as how to plant a tree, install a lighting fixture, or even replace a toilet bowl. They are paid solely on the basis of salary and are encouraged to sell a low-cost replacement part (such as a 15-cent washer) instead of an entire faucet, if the replacement part will suffice.

Aikenhead's of Toronto, owned by Home Depot, is trying to cash in on the do-it-yourself boom in Canada by emulating some of Home Depot's approaches to retailing. Aikenhead's plans to open warehouse stores in the metropolitan Toronto area and then

HOME DEPOT
www.homedepot.com/

expand throughout Canada. Part of the approach involves merchandising at low prices and with low operating costs. Aikenhead's has tried to accomplish this by securing low prices from suppliers and fast delivery which will allow them to minimize inventory carrying costs. As part of the low-cost strategy, Aikenhead's prefers dealing direct with manufacturers over dealing through wholesale intermediaries, which often inflate costs. Like Home Depot, Aikenhead's will employ a customer service orientation and staff tradespeople to advise their customers.[1]

By learning more about customers than just their demographics (such as their activities and interests), companies can better pinpoint market needs, reasons for purchases, and changing lifestyles and purchase behaviour patterns. In this chapter, we will study the way consumers live and spend time and money—as well as how they make purchase decisions.

Overview

Demographics leave many questions unanswered.

Demographic data are often insufficient aids in planning marketing programs for final consumers because these data do not address issues such as:

- Why do consumers act as they do?
- Why do consumers with similar demographic characteristics act differently?
- To whom do consumers look for advice prior to purchasing?
- Under what situations do families (households) use joint decision making?
- Why does status play a large role in the purchase of some products and a small role in the purchase of others?
- How do different motives affect consumer decisions?
- How does risk affect consumer decisions?
- Why do some consumers act as innovators and buy products before others?
- How important are purchase decisions to consumers?
- What process do consumers use when shopping for various products?
- How long will it take for consumers to reach purchase decisions?
- Why do consumers become brand loyal or regularly switch brands?

To answer these and other questions, marketers, in increasing numbers, are going beyond just demographics in studying final consumers. They are using demographic data in conjunction with and as part of consumer lifestyle and decision-making analysis. The latter two topics are the focus of this chapter.

*Consumer **lifestyles** describe how people live. In making purchases, people use a decision process with several stages.*

A **lifestyle** represents the way in which a person lives and spends time and money. It is based on the social and psychological factors that have been internalized by that person—as well as his or her demographic background.[2] These factors overlap and complement each other; they are not independent or exclusive of one another. The consumer's decision process involves the steps a person uses in buying goods and services: stimulus, problem awareness, information search, evaluation of alternatives, purchase, and post-purchase behaviour. Demographics, social factors, and psychological factors all affect the process.

Consumer Lifestyles

The social and psychological characteristics that help form final-consumer lifestyles are described next.

---

[1]Ronald Henkoff, "Why Every Red-Blooded Consumer Owns a Truck," *Fortune* (May 29, 1995), pp. 86–100; "Do-it-yourselfers Spawn Home-Specialty Shopping Centres," *Profit: The Magazine for Canadian Entrepreneurs*, Vol.10 (January/February 1991), p.7; "GST Creating a Rising Nation of Do-it-yourselfers: Small Business Hurt as Canadians Turn Handymen," *Calgary Herald* (July 25, 1992), p. J12; "Retailer Hammers Home Message to Suppliers: Aikenhead's is Levelling Fines to Ensure Product Deliveries," *Globe & Mail* (March 31, 1992), pp. B1, B17.

[2]Peter D. Bennett (Ed.), *Dictionary of Marketing Terms*, Second Edition (Chicago: American Marketing Association, 1994), p. 154.

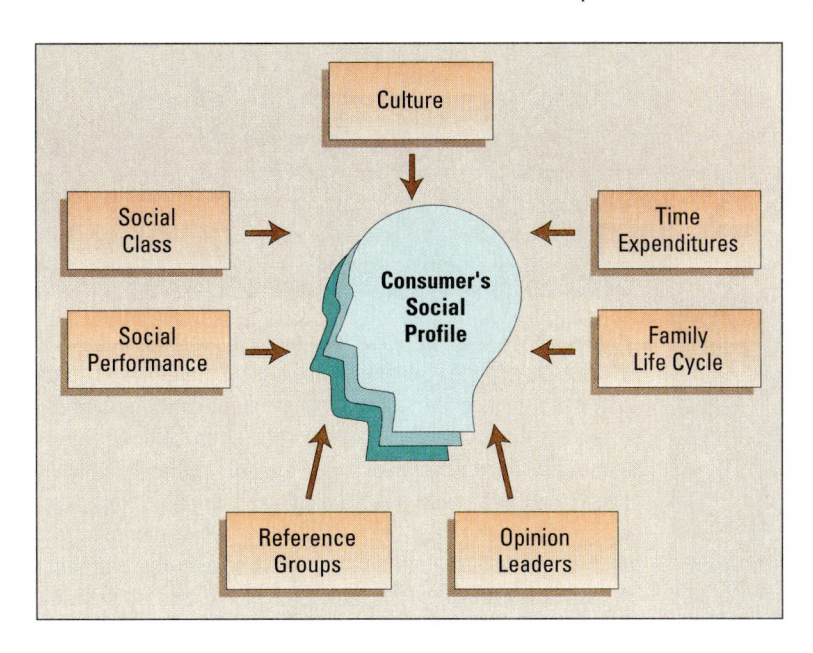

FIGURE 8-1
Factors Determining a Consumer's Social Profile

Social Characteristics of Consumers

The social profile of a final consumer is based on a combination of culture, social class, social performance, reference groups, opinion leaders, family life cycle, and time expenditures (activities). See Figure 8-1.

As discussed in Chapter 6, a **culture** comprises a group of people who share a distinctive heritage, such as Canadians or Americans. People learn about socially proper behaviour and beliefs through their culture. As a nation, Canada was founded upon the principles of "Law, Order, and Good Government," in contrast to the United States which enshrined "life, liberty and the pursuit of happiness" in their constitution. Canadians' culture can be characterized as follows: support collective responsibility, have confidence in social institutions such as education, health care, and the police, place importance on consensus, willing to accept difference and diversity, health conscious, pessimistic and skeptical, value driven, frugal, seeking personalization, brand disloyal, informed buyers.[3] However, slower economic growth, the strong influence of American culture, the rising tide of foreign immigration, and a maturing Canadian population may be signalling changes in some of these values.

*Each **culture** transmits socially acceptable behaviour and attitudes.*

From a cultural perspective, consumers often have a difficult time when there are dramatic changes in their way of living. This is exemplified by the current situation in eastern Germany.

> People have been propelled into a new consumer society and have had to learn its ways quickly. They remain confused by the huge product choice that has been available to them since the 1990 reunification. Many express the need to relearn consumption and feel inadequate for the task. Not that they get much help; stores may still be poorly laid out, and distribution problems still cause some basics to be out of stock. Sales assistants generally are not equipped to advise consumers, and product literature is absent at the point of sale. Yet, the desire to own Western products and luxury items is strong. People are optimistic they will learn to cope with modern consumer society. Yet, they also feel the old way of life, with basic necessities subsidized by the state, had positive points, too.[4]

---

[3] Elliott Ettenberg, "Les blokes Canadiens," *Marketing Magazine* (March 13, 1995), p. 8; Graham Watt, "History and the Canadian Way," *Marketing Magazine* (May 1, 1995), p. 8; Shirley Roberts, "New Consumer Attitudes," *Strategy* (April 14, 1994), p. 4; " A Common Border Does Not Mean Shared Values," *Marketing Magazine*, (January 25, 1993), p 3.

[4] Carla Millar and Christine Restall, "The Embryonic Consumer of Eastern Europe," *Marketing Management*, Vol. 1 (Spring 1992), pp. 48–49.

Ethics AND TODAY'S MARKETER

What Should Be Done with Unethical Consumers?

Although we often dwell on the unethical practices of business people, consumers can also engage in unethical activities. For example, in a retail setting, there are many opportunities for unethical behaviour by consumers. These include deliberately misrepresenting where an item was bought in order to get an exchange at a local store, returning merchandise beyond a store's posted return period, misrepresenting a price at another store as a bargaining tactic, buying an item (such as a notebook PC to be used during an out-of-town vacation) with the intention of returning it, offering to pay a retailer in cash to avoid payment of sales taxes, and shoplifting. In Canada it is estimated that retailers lose about $3 billion in goods to shoplifting and bookkeeping errors (about 1.5 per cent of sales) with about one-half of this amount accounted for by customers, about one-quarter by employees and the other quarter due to bookkeeping errors and other causes.

Many consumers try to rationalize their unethical practices as a way of reducing self-blame or to make the activities appear more socially acceptable. Let's look at how people typically seek to rationalize the act of shoplifting:

- *Denial of responsibility*—"It's not my fault, I had no other choice."
- *Denial of injury*—"What's the big deal? Nobody will miss it."
- *Denial of victim*—"It's their fault; if they had been fair with me, I would not have done it."
- *Condemning the condemners*—"It's a joke they should find fault with me, after the ripoffs they have engineered."
- *Appealing to higher loyalties*—"To some, what I did may appear wrong, but I did it for my family."

These excuses can also be used to rationalize other unethical practices. For instance, denial of injury can be used to suggest that stores plan for consumer shoplifting in setting their original prices.

As vice-president of operations for a retail chain, how would you try to get shoppers to understand that they too have a responsibility to be ethical?

Source: Based on material in David Strutton, Scott J. Vitell, and Lou E. Pelton, "How Consumers May Justify Inappropriate Behaviour in Market Settings: An Application on the Techniques of Neutralization," *Journal of Business Research*, Vol. 30 (July 1994), pp. 253–260; "Retail Council of Canada's Annual Survey," *Globe & Mail*, Metro Edition (April 11, 1995), p. B13 ; "Retailers Get Upper Hand on Five-Finger Discounts," *Globe & Mail*, Metro Edition (April 19, 1994), p. B7.

Social class *separates society into divisions.*

Social class systems reflect a "status hierarchy by which groups and individuals are classified on the basis of esteem and prestige."[5] They exist virtually everywhere and separate society into divisions, informally or formally grouping those with similar values and lifestyles. Such systems in industrialized nations have a larger middle class, greater interchange among classes, and less rigidly defined classes than those in less-developed and developing nations. Social classes are based on income, occupation, education, and type of dwelling. Each social class may represent a distinct target market for a firm. Table 8-1 shows an informal social class structure.

[5]Bennett, *Dictionary of Marketing Terms*, p. 265. See also Chip Walker, "The Global Middle Class," *American Demographics* (September 1995), pp. 40–46.

Table 8-1
The Informal Social Class Structure

CLASS	SIZE	CHARACTERISTICS
Upper Class		
Upper-upper	0.3%	Social elite; inherited wealth; exclusive neighbourhoods; summer homes; children attend best schools; money unimportant in purchases; secure in status; spending with good taste
Lower-upper	1.2%	Highest incomes; earned wealth; often business leaders and professionals; college or university educated; seek best for children; active socially; insecure; conspicuous consumption; money unimportant in purchases
Upper-middle	12.5%	Career-oriented; executives and professionals earning well over $50 000 yearly; status tied to occupations and earnings; most educated, but not from prestige schools; demanding of children; quality products purchased; attractive homes; socially involved; gracious living
Middle Class		
Middle class	32%	Typical Canadians; average-earning white-collar workers and the top group of blue-collar workers; many university educated; respectable; conscientious; try to do the right thing; home ownership sought; do-it-yourselfers; family focus
Working class	38%	Remaining white-collar workers and most blue-collar workers; working class lifestyles; some job monotony; job security sought more than advancement; usually high school education; close-knit families; brand loyal and interested in name brands; not status-oriented
Lower Class		
Upper-lower	9%	Employed, mostly in unskilled or semiskilled jobs; poorly educated; low incomes; rather difficult to move up the social class ladder; protective against lower-lower class; standard of living at or just above poverty; live in affordable housing
Lower-lower	7%	Unemployed or most menial jobs; poorest income, education, and housing; the bottom layer; present-oriented; impulsive as shoppers; overpay; use credit

Sources: This information is derived from Richard P. Coleman, "The Continuing Significance of Social Class in Marketing," *Journal of Consumer Research*, Vol. 10 (December 1983), pp. 265-280; James F. Engel, Roger D. Blackwell, and Paul W. Miniard, *Consumer Behaviour*, Seventh Edition (Hinsdale, Ill.: Dryden, 1993), pp. 117-119; and William L. Wilkie, *Consumer Behaviour*, Third Edition (New York: Wiley, 1994), pp. 344-351.

Social performance refers to how a person carries out his or her roles as a worker, family member, citizen, and friend. One person may be an executive, have a happy family life, be active in the community, and have many friends. Another may never go higher than assistant manager, be divorced, not partake in community affairs, and have few friends. Many combinations of social performance are possible—such as vice-president and divorced. The ad in Figure 8-2 is oriented to a person's interest in social performance.

A **reference group** is one that influences a person's thoughts or actions. For many goods and services, these groups have a large impact on purchases. Face-to-face reference groups, such as family and friends, have the most effect. Yet, other—more general—groups also affect behaviour and may be cited in marketing products. Ads showing goods and services being used by college students, successful professionals, and pet owners often ask viewers to join the "group" and make similar purchases. By pinpointing reference groups that most sway consumers, firms can better aim their strategies.[6]

Firms want to know which persons in reference groups are **opinion leaders**. These are people to whom other consumers turn for advice and information via face-to-face communication. They tend to be expert about a product category, socially accepted, longstanding members of the community, gregarious, active, and trusted; and they tend to seek approval from others. They normally have an impact over a narrow product range and are perceived as more believable than company-sponsored information.

Social performance *describes how people fulfil roles.*

Reference groups *influence thoughts and behaviour.*

Opinion leaders *affect others through face-to-face contact.*

[6] See Basil G. Englis and Michael R. Solomon, "To Be *and* Not to Be: Lifestyle Imagery, Reference Groups," *Journal of Advertising*, Vol. 24 (Spring 1995), pp. 13–28.

FIGURE 8-2
Appealing to a Consumer's Social Performance
Reprinted by permission.

The **family life cycle** *describes life stages, which often use* **joint decision making**. *The* **household life cycle** *includes family and nonfamily units.*

The **family life cycle** describes how a family evolves through various stages from bachelorhood to solitary retirement. At each stage, needs, experience, income, family composition, and the use of **joint decision making**—the process whereby two or more people have input into purchases—change. The number of people in different life-cycle stages can be obtained from demographic data. Table 8-2 shows the traditional family life-cycle and its marketing relevance. The cycle's stages apply to families in all types of nations—both industrialized and less-developed/developing; but, the marketing opportunities in Table 8-2 are most applicable for industrialized countries.

When using life-cycle analysis, the people who do not follow a traditional pattern because they do not marry, do not have children, become divorced, have families with two working spouses (even if there are very small children), and so on, should be noted. They are not adequately reflected in Table 8-2, but may represent good marketing opportunities. For that reason, the concept of the **household life cycle**—which incorporates the life stages of both family and nonfamily households—is taking on greater significance.[7] Table 8-3 shows the current status of Canadian households.

---

[7]Robert E. Wilkes, "Household Life-Cycle Stages, Transitions, and Product Expenditures," *Journal of Consumer Research*, Vol. 22 (June 1995), pp. 27–42.

Table 8-2
The Traditional Family Life Cycle

STAGE IN CYCLE	CHARACTERISTICS	MARKETING OPPORTUNITIES
Bachelor, male or female	Independent; young; early in career; low earnings, low discretionary income	Clothing; auto; stereo; travel; restaurants; entertainment; status appeals
Newly married	Two incomes; relative independence; present- and future-oriented	Apartment furnishings; travel; clothing; durables; appeal to enjoyment and togetherness
Full nest I	Youngest child under 6; one to one-and-a-half incomes; limited independence; future-oriented	Goods and services for the child, home, and family; durability and safety; pharmaceuticals; day care; appeal to economy
Full nest II	Youngest child over 6, but dependent; one-and-a-half to two incomes; at least one spouse set in career; future-oriented	Savings; home; education; family vacations; child-oriented products; some luxuries; appeal comfort and long-term enjoyment
Full nest III	Youngest child living at home, but independent; highest income level; thoughts of future retirement	Education; expensive durables for children; replacement and improvement of parents' durables; appeal to comfort and luxury
Empty nest I	No children at home; independent; good income; thoughts of self and retirement	Vacation home; travel; clothing; entertainment; luxuries; appeal to self-gratification
Empty nest II	Retirement; less income and expenses; present-oriented	Travel; recreation; new home; health-related items; less interest in luxuries; appeal to comfort at a low price
Sole survivor I	Only one spouse alive; actively employed; present-oriented; good income	Immersion in job and friends; interest in travel, clothing, health, and recreation areas; appeal to productive citizen
Sole survivor II	Only one spouse alive; retired; some feeling of futility; less income	Travel; recreation; pharmaceuticals; security; appeal to economy and social activity

Table 8-3
The Current Status of Canadian Family and Nonfamily Households

HOUSEHOLD STATUS	PERCENTAGE OF ALL CANADIAN HOUSEHOLDS	
Total Husband and Wife Families	77.1	
Married couples, no children		29.3
Married couples, with children		47.8
Total Families of Common-law Couples	9.9	
Unmarried couples, no children		5.8
Unmarried couples, with children		4.1
Total Lone-Parent Families	13	
Female Parent		10.7
Male parent		2.3

Source: Computed by the authors from Statistics Canada, *Marketing Research Handbook*, 1995 p. 156.

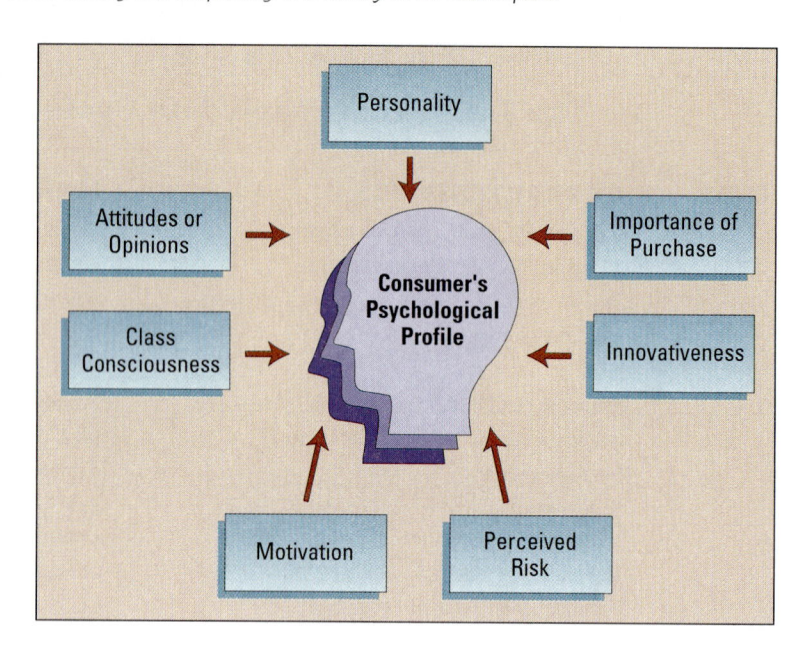

FIGURE 8-3
Factors Determining a Consumer's Psychological Profile

Time expenditures *reflect time allocated to the work week, to family care, and to leisure.*

Time expenditures refer to the activities in which a person participates and the time allocated to them. Such activities include work, commuting, personal care, home maintenance, food preparation and consumption, childrearing, social interactions, reading, shopping, self-improvement, recreation, entertainment, vacations, and so on. Although the average work week for an individual's primary job has stabilized at 35 to 40 hours weekly, more people are working at two jobs. Canadians enjoy TV, phone conversations, pleasure driving, swimming, sightseeing, walking, bicycling, attending spectator events, reading, and playing outdoor games and sports.

Psychological Characteristics of Consumers

The psychological profile of a final consumer involves his or her personality, attitudes (opinions), class consciousness, motivation, perceived risk, and innovativeness, as well as the importance of the purchase. See Figure 8-3.

A **personality** *describes a person's composite internal, enduring, psychological traits.*

A **personality** is the sum total of the enduring internal psychological traits that make a person unique. Self-confidence, dominance, autonomy, sociability, defensiveness, adaptability, and emotional stability are selected personality traits. Personality has a strong impact on an individual's behaviour. For example, a self-confident and sociable person often will not purchase the same goods and services as an inhibited and aloof person. It is necessary to remember that a personality is made up of many traits operating in association with one another. See Figure 8-4.

Attitudes *can be positive, negative, or neutral.*

Attitudes (opinions) are an individual's positive, neutral, or negative feelings about goods, services, firms, people, issues, and/or institutions. They are shaped by demographics, social factors, and other psychological characteristics. One role of marketing is to generate favourable attitudes; given the intensive competition in many industries, a firm cannot normally succeed without positive consumer attitudes. When studying attitudes, two concepts should often be measured—the attitude itself and the purchase intention toward a firm's brand. For example: (1) Do you like brand A? Would you buy brand A in the future? (2) How does brand A compare with other brands? Would you buy brand A if it were priced higher than other brands?

Class consciousness *is low for inner-directed persons and high for outer-directed ones.*

Class consciousness is the extent to which a person seeks social status. It helps determine his or her interest in social-class mobility, use of reference groups, and the importance of prestige purchases. Inner-directed people want to please themselves and are generally attracted by products that perform well functionally. They are not concerned with social mobility, rely on their own judgment, and do not value prestige items. Outer-directed people want to please the people around them. Upward social mobility, reference group

FIGURE 8-4
Marketing to the Uninhibited
Reprinted by permission.

approval, and ownership of prestige items are sought. These people are generally attracted by products providing social visibility, well-known brands, and uniqueness. Functional performance may be less important.

Motivation involves the positive or negative needs, goals, and desires that impel a person to or away from certain actions, objects, or situations.[8] By identifying and appealing to people's **motives**—the reasons for behaviour—a firm can produce positive motivation. For example:

Motivation is a drive-impelling action; it is caused by motives.

MOTIVES	MARKETING ACTIONS THAT MOTIVATE
Hunger reduction	Television and radio ads just before mealtimes
Safety	Smoke detector demonstrations in stores
Sociability	Perfume ads showing social success due to products
Achievement	Use of consumer endorsements in ads specifying how much knowledge can be gained from an encyclopedia
Economy	Newspaper coupons advertising sales
Social responsibility	Package labels that emphasize how easy it is to recycle products

Each person has distinct motives for purchases, and these change by situation and over time. Consumers often combine economic (price, durability) and emotional (social acceptance, self-esteem) motives when making purchases.

[8]Bennett, *Dictionary of Marketing Terms*, pp. 179–180.

Perceived risk *is the uncertainty felt by the consumer.*

Perceived risk is the level of uncertainty a consumer believes exists as to the outcome of a purchase decision; this belief may or may not be correct. Perceived risk can be divided into six major types:

1. *Functional*—risk that a product will not perform adequately.
2. *Physical*—risk that a product will be harmful.
3. *Financial*—risk that a product will not be worth its cost.
4. *Social*—risk that a product will cause embarrassment before others.
5. *Psychological*—risk that one's ego will be bruised.
6. *Time*—risk that the time spent making a purchase will be wasted if the product does not perform as expected.[9]

Because high perceived risk can dampen customer motivation, companies must deal with it even if people have incorrect beliefs. Firms can lower perceived risk by giving more information, having a reputation for superior quality, offering money-back guarantees, avoiding controversial ingredients, and so on.

A person willing to try a new good or service that others perceive as risky exhibits **innovativeness**. An innovator is apt to be young and well educated, and to have above-average income for his or her social class. He or she is also likely to be interested in change, achievement-oriented, open-minded, status-conscious, mobile, and venturesome. Firms need to identify and appeal to innovators when introducing a new good or service.

Innovativeness *is trying a new product others see as risky.*

The **importance of a purchase** affects the time and effort a person spends shopping for a product—and the money allotted. An important purchase means careful decision making, high perceived risk, and often a large amount of money. An unimportant purchase means less decision time (an item may be avoided altogether) and low perceived risk, and it is probably inexpensive.

The **importance of a purchase** *determines the time, effort, and money spent.*

Selected Consumer Lifestyles

Many distinct consumer lifestyles are expected to continue, including: family values, voluntary simplicity, getting by, "me" generation, blurring of gender roles, poverty of time, and component lifestyles.

A **family values** lifestyle emphasizes marriage, children, and home life. It encourages people to focus on children and their education; family autos, vacations, and entertainment; and home-oriented products. Yet, as previously noted, the traditional family is becoming less representative of Canadian households. Thus, firms need to be careful in targeting those who say they follow this lifestyle. They should also keep in mind that a family values lifestyle remains the leading one in many nations outside of Canada. For instance, in Italy, less than one-third of women are in the labour force and the divorce rate is about one-sixth that of Canada.

In some households, **family values** *have a great impact.*

Voluntary simplicity is a lifestyle in which people have an ecological awareness, seek product durability, strive for self-reliance, and buy simple products. People with this lifestyle are cautious, conservative, and thrifty shoppers. They do not buy expensive cars and clothing, hold on to products for long periods, and rarely eat out or go on pre-packaged vacations. They like going to a park or taking a vacation by car, are more concerned with product toughness than appearance, and believe in conservation. They tend to be attracted to rational appeals and no-frills retailing.

Voluntary simplicity *is based on ecological awareness and self-reliance.*

Getting by is a frugal lifestyle pursued by people because of economic circumstances. Those who are getting by seek product durability, self-reliance, and simple products. But, unlike with voluntary simplicity, they do so because they must. In less-developed and developing nations, most people have this lifestyle; a much smaller proportion do in industrialized countries. Getting by consumers are attracted to well-known brands (to reduce perceived risk), do not try new goods and services, rarely go out, and take few vacations. They look for bargains and tend to patronize local stores. They rarely believe they have any significant discretionary income.

When economic circumstances are tough, people place more emphasis on **getting by.**

---

[9]Leon G. Schiffman and Leslie Lazar Kanuk, *Consumer Behaviour*, Fifth Edition (Englewood Cliffs, N.J.: Prentice-Hall, 1994), pp. 562–564.

FIGURE 8-5
Blurring Gender Roles
Today, more men and women are engaging in nontraditional activities.
Reprinted by permission of SPX Corporation

A **"me" generation** lifestyle stresses being good to oneself, self-fulfillment, and self-expression. It involves less pressure to conform, as well as greater diversity; there is also less interest in responsibilities and loyalties. Consumers with this lifestyle want to take care of themselves. They stress nutrition, exercise, and grooming. And they buy expensive cars and apparel, and visit full-service stores. These people are more concerned with product appearance than durability, and some place below-average value on conservation if it will have a negative effect on their lifestyle.

Because many women are working, more men are assuming the once-traditional roles of their wives, and vice versa, thus **blurring gender** roles: "Men are doing more shopping and housework, but only because women are making them change. Knowing how men are changing—and how they aren't—is the key to targeting them. Meanwhile, more women are learning how to buy cars, program VCRs, and use power tools."[10] See Figure 8-5.

The prevalence of working women, the long distances between home and work, and the large number of people working at second jobs contribute to a **poverty-of-time** lifestyle in many households. For them, the quest for financial security means less free time. This lifestyle leads people to greater use of time-saving goods and services. Included are convenience foods, quick-oil-change services, microwave ovens, fast-food restaurants, mail-order retailers, one-hour film processing, and professional lawn and household care.

Today, more people are turning to a **component lifestyle**, whereby their attitudes and behaviour depend on particular situations rather than an overall lifestyle philosophy. For example, consumers may take their children with them on vacations (family values), engage in trash recycling programs (voluntary simplicity), look for sales to save money (getting by), take exercise classes ("me" generation), share food-shopping chores (blurring gender roles), and eat out on busy nights (poverty of time). As the Roper Organization, a research firm, has noted:

The "me" generation stresses self-fulfillment.

Blurring gender roles involves men and women undertaking nontraditional duties.

A poverty of time exists when a quest for financial security means less free time.

With a component lifestyle, consumer attitudes and behaviour vary by situation.

---
[10]Diane Crispell, "The Brave New World of Men," *American Demographics* (January 1992), pp. 38, 43.

Consumer behaviour is becoming more individualistic and less defined by reference to easily identified social groups. People are piecing together "component lifestyles" for themselves, choosing goods and services that best express their growing sense of uniqueness. A consumer may own a BMW but fill it with self-service gas. Buy take-out fast food for lunch but good wine for dinner. Own expensive photo equipment and low-priced home stereo equipment.[11]

Marketing Implications of Lifestyle Analysis

Over the years, analysis of the social and psychological characteristics of final consumers has increased dramatically. In this section, we present both general and specific applications of lifestyle analysis in marketing.

Several organizations are involved with defining and measuring consumer lifestyles. They sell this information to client firms, who use it to improve their marketing efforts. Here are some well-known North American services:

- *VALS (Values and Lifestyles)* is a research program sponsored by SRI International. SRI's VALS 2 classification categorizes consumers into eight basic lifestyle groups: actualizers, fulfilleds, believers, achievers, strivers, experiencers, makers, and strugglers.
- *PRIZM (Potential Rating Index by Zip Market)* is a program that relies on census data and examines consumer lifestyles by postal code. It uses about sixty different neighbourhood designations, such as blue blood ("old money"), to describe lifestyles.

These services have been used by companies marketing financial instruments, cars, health-care products, appliances, women's girdles, liquor, food, and other items.

Studies of consumer lifestyles around the world have been conducted.

- *Yankelovich Monitor* tracks over 50 social trends annually, including accommodation to technology, the need for control, and responsiveness to fantasy. Impermanent consumer profiles are developed, such as "the new establishment," the "discontented," and "traditionalists"— and describe people in terms of their response to the changing environment.
- *The Bureau of Broadcast Measurement* (BBM) conducts a Radio Product Measurement study of several thousand respondents on a regular basis in Vancouver, Toronto, and Montreal, with occasional measurements in Winnipeg, Edmonton, and Calgary. The surveys measure lifestyles and shopping behaviour. Lifestyles are categorized as: active, traditional, insecure, and career-driven while shopping behaviour is categorized as: impulse, pro-advertising, early adopter, and uninvolved.[12]
- *Target Mail* of Toronto has a database of more than 200 000 consumers from across Canada, entitled Target Lifestyle Changes. The consumers are surveyed and asked to report whether they or a family member have undergone a major lifestyle change in the past six months or will be undergoing one in the upcoming year.[13]

Here are some findings for firms to consider when planning their marketing mixes:

- Although North American men go to shopping centres somewhat more often than women, the latter spend nearly 25 per cent more time in a shopping centre per visit (and stop at more stores). Two-thirds of North American women make apparel decisions on their own, compared with 48 per cent of men.
- Russian households prefer and trust ads from western firms over those from local companies. On average, Russians view television nearly three hours per day and enjoy the commercials. Billboards have not been very popular there.
- European women are less likely than North American women to diet and exercise, are more apt to smoke, and have higher self-esteem and optimism for the future.
- In India, the husband in lower-class families usually initiates decisions for appliances and furniture and the wife is more responsible for initiating clothing decisions. For

---

[11]"Thirty-One Major Trends Shaping the Future of American Business," *Public Pulse*, Vol. 2, No. 1 (1988), p. 1.
[12]"RPM Adds to Radio's Sales Arsenal,"*Marketing Magazine* (May 4, 1992) p. 2.
[13]"Harvesting the Power of Synchrographics." *Marketing Magazine* (November 30, 1992), p 10.

International Marketing in Action

A Moving Target: Understanding Consumer Behaviour in Eastern Europe

A North American Pet Food producer presented a new cat food to former communist Eastern Europeans in an ad showing a Persian cat with a jewelled collar eating cat food off of fine china. The reaction was strong and negative: Western pets eat better than Eastern Europeans. Understanding consumer behaviour in international markets is difficult enough due to cultural and social differences, but when cultural and social change is occurring rapidly it becomes nearly impossible. When formerly communist Eastern European markets first opened up in the early 1990s marketers merely had to translate their product packaging and get the products on the retail shelf to enjoy record sales.

A market which had lots of demand and few products to satisfy it was a new experience to western marketers—as new as having products to fill demand was to Eastern European consumers. Now formerly communist Eastern Europeans are faced with a wide variety of products to fill their demand and are faced with something they have not experienced before: choice.

The nature of consumer behaviour and the approach to influencing consumers used in the West is much different from what is required in Eastern Europe. Western consumers have been inundated with product choice and variety and have come to accept these as a natural condition. Promotional efforts in western markets feature puffery and persuasive advertising efforts to convince people to try new products. Formerly communist Eastern European consumers are not used to choice but are used to receiving persuasive messages about making choices, the choices the government wanted them to make! Consequently, the approach to promotion employed by Western marketers needs to be adjusted.

Interestingly, the old approach is what appears to work for these new consumers. Eastern Europeans are responding to a consumer education approach to product marketing, not the usual propaganda approach which is reminiscent of the former communist government. Post-communist European society bears some similarity to post-World War II North American society: couples marry at young ages, divorce rates are low, women work at home and raise families, and children live with their parents until they marry. And a simple, honest approach to promoting products (reminiscent of North American advertising in the 1950s) seems to work.

As for research on consumer behaviour, it has its own unique problems. Because of past conditioning, consumers tell researchers in Poland what they (the consumers) believe the researchers want to hear, as opposed to what they really feel. Therefore, researchers have to adjust their approach to questioning so they get honest responses and not socially-expected responses.

One thing marketers discovered early on was that Eastern Europeans were very responsive to sales promotions that involved giveaways. However, response rates have been falling as Eastern Europeans, like their North American brethren, have discovered that you generally get what you pay for.

As a marketing manager for a Canadian firm considering marketing a packaged-good product in Slovenia, what approach would you take to keep up with the changes in consumer behaviour?

Source: Based on material in Normandy Madden, "Former Eastern Bloc Consumers Now Savvy To Marketing Wiles," *Marketing Magazine*, (May 29, 1995), p. 6.

middle-class families, the wife has more influence over all three types of products. For upper-class families, the wife is the initiator for clothing, but there is greater sharing of influence between the husband and wife for appliances and furniture.

- The Japanese are less satisfied with the overall quality of their lives than North Americans. They are much less pleased with regard to housing, leisure time, and income.[14]

Marketing opportunities related to family values, voluntary simplicity, getting by, "me" generation, blurring of gender roles, poverty of time, and component lifestyle concepts are shown in Table 8-4.

Table 8-4
Selected Marketing Opportunities of Consumer Lifestyles

LIFESTYLE CATEGORY	MARKETING OPPORTUNITIES IN APPEALING TO THE LIFESTYLE
Family values	Family-oriented goods and services Educational devices and toys Traditional family events "Wholesome" entertainment
Voluntary simplicity	Goods and services with quality, durability, and simplicity Environmentally safe products Energy-efficient products Discount-oriented retailing
Getting by	Well-known brands and good buys ("value") Video rentals and other inexpensive entertainment Do-it-yourself projects such as "knock-down" furniture Inexpensive child care
"Me" generation	Individuality in purchases Luxury goods and services Nutritional themes Exercise- and education-related goods and services.
Blurring of gender roles	Unisex goods, services, and stores Couples-oriented advertising Child-care services Less male and female stereotyping
Poverty of time	Mail-order and phone sales Service firms with accurate customer appointments Labour-saving devices One-stop shopping
Component lifestyle	Situational purchases Less social-class stereotyping Multiple advertising themes Market niching

[14]Dottie Enrico, "Sex Matters," *Newsday* (December 13, 1992), p. 88; Adi Ignatius, "Lifestyle Pitch Works in Russia Despite Poverty," *Wall Street Journal* (August 21, 1992), pp. B1, B4; Cyndee Miller, "No Exercise, and They Like to Smoke," *Marketing News* (August 17, 1992), p. 13; Cynthia Webster, "Observation of Marital Roles in Decision Making: A Third-World Perspective" in Robert P. Leone and V. Kumar (Eds.) *1992 AMA Educators' Proceedings* (Chicago: American Marketing Association, 1992), p. 517; Robert Levine, "Why Isn't Japan Happy?" *American Demographics* (June 1992), pp. 58–60.

A. The Decision Process

Stimulus → Problem Awareness → Information Search → Evaluation of Alternatives → Purchase → Post-Purchase Behavior

B. Factors Affecting the Process

Demographics ↔ Social and Psychological Factors

Arrows connect all the elements in the decision process and show the impact of demographics, social factors, and psychological factors upon the process.

Arrows show feedback.
(a) Shows the impact of social and psychological factors on certain demographics such as family size, occupation, and marital status.
(b) Shows the impact of a purchase on social and psychological factors such as social class, social performance, and attitudes.

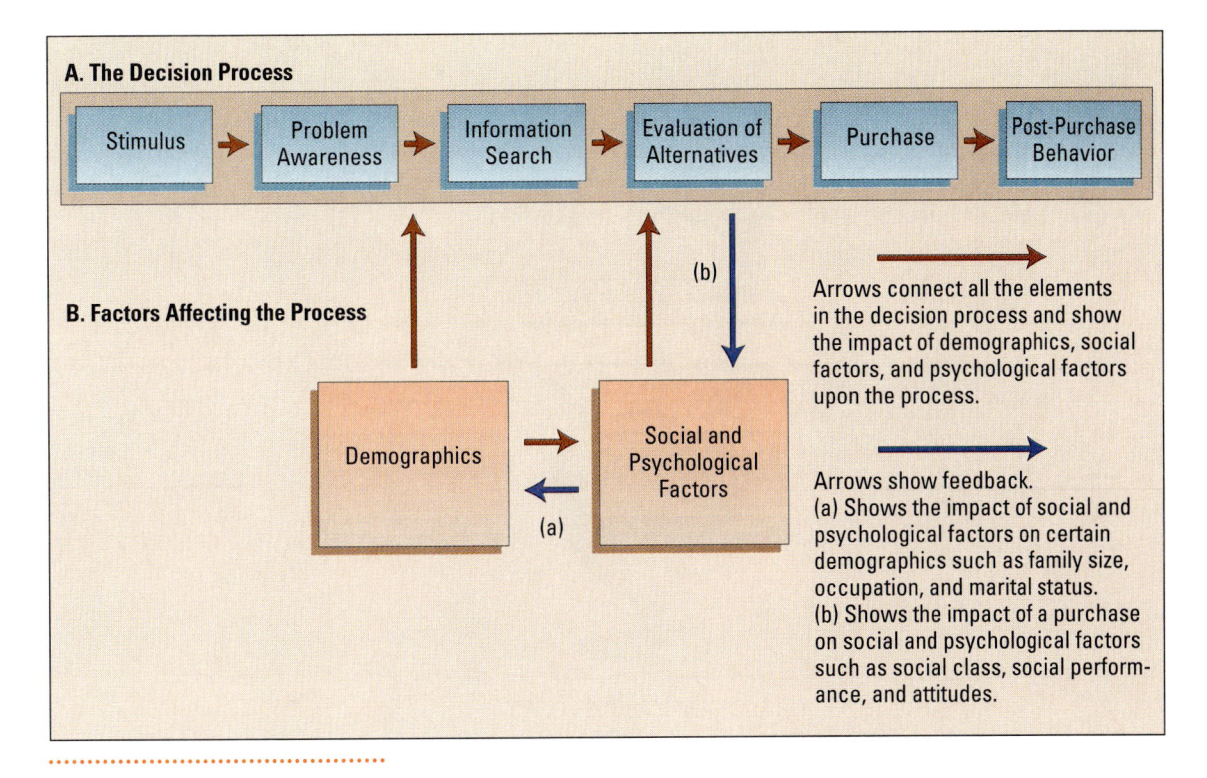

FIGURE 8-6
The Final Consumer's Decision Process

Limitations of Lifestyle Analysis

Unlike demographics, many of the social and psychological aspects of final-consumer lifestyles are difficult to measure, somewhat subjective, usually based on the self-reports of consumers, and sometimes hidden from view (to avoid embarrassment, protect privacy, convey an image, and other reasons). In addition, there are still some ongoing disputes over terminology, misuse of data, and reliability.

Social and psychological factors can be difficult to measure.

The Final Consumer's Decision Process

The **final consumer's decision process** is the way in which people gather and assess information and choose among alternative goods, services, organizations, people, places, and ideas. It consists of the process itself and factors affecting it. The process has six stages: stimulus, problem awareness, information search, evaluation of alternatives, purchase, and post-purchase behaviour. Demographic, social, and psychological factors affect the process. Figure 8-6 shows the total consumer decision-making process.

When a consumer buys a good or service, decides to vote for a political candidate or donate to a charity, and so on, he or she goes through a decision process. Sometimes, all six stages in the process are used; other times, only a few steps are necessary. For example, the purchase of an expensive stereo requires more decision making than the purchase of a new music video.

At any point in the decision process, a person may decide not to buy, vote, or donate—and, thereby, end the process. A good or service may turn out to be unneeded, unsatisfactory, or too expensive.

*The **final consumer's decision process** has many stages and various factors affect it.*

Stimulus

A **stimulus** is a cue (social, commercial, or noncommercial) or a drive (physical) meant to motivate a person to act.

*A **stimulus** is a cue or drive intended to motivate a consumer.*

FIGURE 8-7
A Manufacturer-Sponsored Commercial Stimulus
Reprinted by permission of Wm. Wrigley Jr. Company.

A *social cue* occurs when someone talks with friends, family members, co-workers, or another interpersonal source not affiliated with a seller. A *commercial cue* is a message sponsored by a seller—such as that shown in Figure 8-7—to interest a person in a particular good, service, organization, person, place, or idea. Ads, personal selling, and sales promotions are commercial cues. They are less regarded than social cues because people know they are seller-controlled. A *noncommercial cue* is a message from an impartial source, such as Consumer Reports or the government. It has high believability because it is not affiliated with the seller. A *physical drive* occurs when a person's physical senses are affected. Thirst, hunger, and fear cause physical drives.

A person may be exposed to any or all of these stimuli. If sufficiently stimulated, he or she will go to the next step in the decision process. If not, the person will ignore the cue and delay or terminate the decision process for the given good, service, organization, person, place, or idea.

Problem Awareness

Problem awareness *entails recognition of a shortage or an unfulfilled desire.*

At the **problem awareness** stage, a consumer recognizes that the good, service, organization, person, place, or idea under consideration may solve a problem of shortage or unfulfilled desire.

Recognition of shortage occurs when a consumer realizes a repurchase is needed. A suit may wear out. A man or woman may run out of razor blades. An eye examination may be needed. A popular political candidate may be up for re-election. It may be time for a charity's annual fund-raising campaign. In each case, the consumer recognizes a need to repurchase.

Recognition of unfulfilled desire occurs when a consumer becomes aware of a good, service, organization, person, place, or idea that has not been patronized before. Such an item may improve status, appearance, living conditions, or knowledge in a manner not tried before (luxury auto, cosmetic surgery, proposed zoning law, encyclopedia), or it may offer new performance features not previously available (laser surgery, tobacco-free cigarettes). Either way, a consumer is aroused by a desire to try something new.

Many consumers hesitate to act on unfulfilled desires due to the greater risk entailed. It is easier to replace a known product. Whether a consumer becomes aware of a problem of shortage or of unfulfilled desire, he or she will act only if the problem is perceived as worth solving.

Information Search

Next, an **information search** requires listing the alternatives that will solve the problem at hand and determining their characteristics.

*An **information search** determines alternatives and their characteristics.*

A list of alternatives does not have to be written. It can be a group of items a consumer thinks about. With an internal search, a person has experience in the area being considered and uses a memory search to list choices. A person with minimal experience will do an external search to list alternatives; this can involve commercial sources, noncommercial sources, and/or social sources. Often, once there is a list of choices, items (brands, companies, and so on) not on it do not receive further consideration.

The second phase of information search deals with the attributes of each alternative. This information can also be generated internally or externally, depending on the expertise of the consumer and the level of perceived risk. As risk increases, the information sought increases.

Once an information search is completed, the consumer must determine whether the shortage or unfulfilled desire can be satisfied by any alternative. If one or more choices are satisfactory, the consumer moves to the next decision. The process is delayed or discontinued when no alternative provides satisfaction.

Evaluation of Alternatives

There is now enough information for a consumer to select one alternative from the list of choices. This is easy when one option is clearly the best across all attributes: A product with excellent quality and a low price will be a sure choice over an average-quality, expensive one. The choice is usually not that simple, and a consumer must carefully engage in an **evaluation of alternatives** before making a decision. If two or more alternatives seem attractive, the individual needs to determine which criteria to evaluate and their relative importance. Alternatives are then ranked and a choice made.

Evaluating alternatives consists of weighing features and selecting the most desired product.

Decision criteria are the features a person deems relevant—such as price, style, quality, safety, durability, status, and warranty. A consumer sets standards for various features and forms an attitude toward each alternative according to its ability to meet the standards. In addition, each criterion's importance is set because the multiple attributes of a given product are usually of varying weight. For example, a consumer may consider shoe prices to be more important than style and select inexpensive, nondistinctive shoes.

A consumer now ranks alternatives from most to least desirable and selects one. Ranking is sometimes hard because alternatives may have technical differences or be poorly labelled, new, or intangible (as is the case when evaluating two political candidates). On these occasions, options may be ranked on the basis of brand name or price, which is used to indicate overall quality.

In situations where no alternative is satisfactory, a decision to delay or not make a purchase is made.

Purchase

After choosing the best alternative, a person is ready for the **purchase act**: an exchange of money, a promise to pay or support in return for ownership of a specific good, the performance of a specific service, and so on. Three considerations remain: place of purchase, terms, and availability.

*The **purchase act** includes deciding where to buy, agreeing to terms, and seeing if the item is available.*

Although most items are bought at stores, some are bought at school, work, and home. The place of purchase is picked in the same way as a product. Choices are noted, attributes detailed, and a ranking done. The best locale is chosen.

Purchase terms involve the price and method of payment. Generally, a price is the amount (including interest, tax, and other fees) a person pays to gain the ownership or use of a good or service. It may also be a person's vote, time investment, and so on. The payment method is the way a price is paid (cash, short-term credit, or long-term credit).

Availability refers to the timeliness with which a consumer receives a product that he or she buys. It depends on stock on hand (or service capacity) and delivery. Stock on hand relates to a seller's ability to provide a good or service when requested. For items requiring delivery, the period from when an order is placed by a consumer until it is received and the ease with which an item is transported to its place of use are crucial.

A consumer will make a purchase if these elements are acceptable. However, dissatisfaction with any one may cause a consumer to delay or not buy, even though there is no problem with the good or service itself.

Post-Purchase Behaviour

Post-purchase behaviour often embodies further buying and/or re-evaluation. **Cognitive dissonance** *can be reduced by proper consumer after-care.*

Once a purchase is made, a person may engage in **post-purchase behaviour**, in the form of further purchases and/or re-evaluation of the original purchase. Many times, one purchase leads to others: A house purchase leads to the acquisition of fire insurance, a PC purchase leads to the acquisition of computer software.

A person may also re-evaluate a purchase after making it: Does performance match expectations? Satisfaction usually leads to a repurchase when a good or service wears out, another contribution when a charity holds a fundraising campaign, and so on, and leads to positive communication with other people interested in the same item. Dissatisfaction can lead to brand switching and negative communication.

Dissatisfaction is often due to **cognitive dissonance**—doubt that a correct decision has been made. A person may regret a purchase or wish another choice was made. To overcome dissonance, a firm must realize the process does not end with the purchase. Follow-up calls, extended warranties, and ads aimed at purchasers can reassure people.

Factors Affecting the Final Consumer's Decision Process

The decision process is affected by demographic, social, and psychological factors.

Demographic, social, and psychological factors affect the way final consumers make choices and can help a firm understand how people use the decision process. For example, an affluent consumer would move through the process more quickly than a middle-income one because he or she faces less financial risk. An insecure consumer would spend more time making a decision than a secure one.

By knowing how these factors influence decisions, a firm can fine-tune its marketing strategies to cater to the target market and its purchase behaviour, and answer these questions: Why do two or more people use the decision process in the same way? Why do two or more people use it differently?

Types of Decision Processes

Final-consumer decision making can be categorized as **extended**, **limited**, *or* **routine**.

Each time a person buys a good or service, donates to a charity, and so on, he or she uses the decision process. This may be done subconsciously, without the person being aware of it. Some situations allow a person to move through the process quickly and de-emphasize or skip certain steps; others may require a thorough use of each step. A consumer may use extended, limited, or routine decision making—based on the degree of search, level of experience, frequency of purchase, amount of perceived risk, and time pressure. See Figure 8-8.

Extended consumer decision making occurs when a person fully uses the decision process. Much effort is spent on information search and evaluation of alternatives for expensive, complex items with which a person has little or no experience. Purchases are made infrequently. Perceived risk is high, and the purchase is important. A person has time available to make a choice. Purchase delays often occur. Demographic, social, and psy-

	Degree of Search	Level of Prior Experience	Frequency of Purchase	Amount of Perceived Risk	Time Pressure

Extended Consumer Decision Making

Limited Consumer Decision Making

Routine Consumer Decision Making

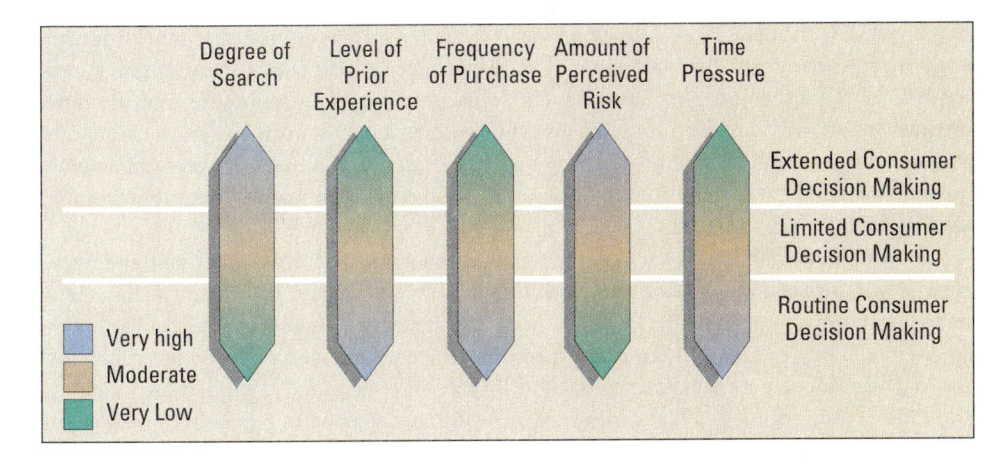

- Very high
- Moderate
- Very Low

FIGURE 8-8
The Three Types of Final-Consumer Decision Processes

chological factors have their greatest impact. Extended decision making is often involved in picking a college, a house, a first car, or a location for a wedding.

Limited consumer decision making occurs when a person uses every step in the purchase process but does not spend a great deal of time on some of them. The person has previously bought a given good or service, but makes a fresh decision when it comes under current purchase consideration—due to the relative infrequency of purchase, the intro-

MICROSOFT CANADA
www.microsoft.com/canada/

TECHNOLOGY & MARKETING

Will Computers Ever Be Truly "User Friendly?"

Why is the increased market penetration of PCs accompanied by such high levels of consumer frustration with their computers? Aren't PCs supposed to be "user friendly?"

Problems often occur because of the complications arising from the wide range of peripherals (such as a modem, CD-ROM player, and mouse) that may be bought to accompany a PC. Many peripherals claim to be fully compatible with a given PC; but they are produced by different firms and often need adjustments in dip switches, memory organization, and interrupt settings that are beyond the capability of most novices. Thus, many consumers have reported spending as much as two days with an "easy-to-install" peripheral such as a CD-ROM player. According to the marketing vice-president for one peripherals manufacturer, "Getting these things to work together is a lot like putting a Chevy engine and a Ford transmission into a Rolls Royce body."

Advanced computer capabilities such as simultaneously displaying graphics and music, jumping from one program to another, and playing audio-based CDs have also made computers more complicated. IBM says it gets 200 000 calls per month on its customer support line.

Microsoft has observed PC users through one-way mirrors in its "usability" labs, and even invested $90 000 in staff time to study how five families used PCs in their homes—to better understand the frustrations of computer novices. To the firm's surprise, its staff found that some people did their budgets with word processing software instead of spreadsheets because the spreadsheets were too intimidating. Microsoft is using the taped sessions to show its programmers the types of problems faced by consumers. It hopes the information will result in more user-friendly products.

As a product manager for Conner Peripherals, a producer of tape drives that back up PC hard drives, describe how you would make your products as user friendly as possible for the first-time customer.

Source: Based on material in Julie Pitta, "New Hope for Computer Illiterates?" *Forbes* (January 16, 1995), pp. 88-89.

duction of new models, or an interest in variety. Perceived risk is moderate, and a person is willing to spend some time shopping. The thoroughness with which the process is used depends on the amount of prior experience, the importance of the purchase, and the time pressure facing the consumer. Emphasis is on evaluating a list of known choices, although an information search may be done. Factors affecting the decision process have some impact. A second car, clothing, gifts, home furnishings, and an annual vacation typically need limited decision making.

Routine consumer decision making occurs when a person buys out of habit and skips steps in the process. He or she spends little time shopping and often rebuys the same brands (or brands bought before). In this category are items with which a person has much experience. They are bought regularly, have little or no perceived risk, and are relatively low in price. Once a person realizes a good or service is depleted, a repurchase is made. The time pressure to buy is high. Information search, evaluation of alternatives, and post-purchase behaviour are normally omitted, as long as a person is satisfied. Factors affecting the process have little impact because problem awareness typically leads to a purchase. Examples of items routinely purchased are the daily newspaper, a haircut by a regular stylist, and weekly grocery items.

The way the decision process is used varies by country.

There are several differences between consumers in industrialized nations and those in less-developed and developing ones. In general, consumers in less-developed and developing countries:

- Are exposed to fewer commercial and noncommercial cues.
- Have access to less information.
- Have fewer goods and services from which to choose.
- Are more apt to buy a second choice if the first one is not available.
- Have fewer places of purchase and may have to wait in long lines.
- Are more apt to find that stores are out of stock.
- Have less purchase experience for many kinds of goods and services.
- Are less educated and have lower incomes.
- Are more apt to rebuy items with which they are only moderately satisfied (due to the lack of choices).

Because many consumers—in both industrialized nations and less-developed nations—want to reduce shopping time, the use of complex decision making, and risk, most purchases are made using routine or limited decision making. Thus, consumers often rely on low-involvement purchasing and/or brand loyalty.

Low-involvement purchasing *is often used when buying unimportant products.*

With **low-involvement purchasing**, a consumer minimizes the time and effort expended in both making decisions about and shopping for those goods and services he or she views as unimportant. Included are "those situations where the consumer simply does not care and is not concerned about brands or choices and makes the decision in the most cognitively miserly manner possible. Most likely, low involvement is situation-based and the degree of importance and involvement may vary with the individual and with the situation."[15] In these situations, consumers feel little perceived risk, are passive about getting information, act fast, and may assess products after (rather than before) buying.

Firms can adapt to low-involvement purchasing by using repetitive ads to create awareness and familiarity, stressing the practical nature of goods and services, having informed salespeople, setting low prices, using attractive in-store displays, selling in all types of outlets, and offering coupons and free samples. Table 8-5 compares the traditional high-involvement view of consumer behaviour with the newer low-involvement view.[16]

Brand loyalty *involves consistent repurchases of and preference for specific brands.*

Once a consumer tries one or more brands of a good or service, **brand loyalty**—the consistent repurchase of and preference for a particular brand—may develop. Brand loyal-

---

[15] Bennett, *Dictionary of Marketing Terms*, p. 157.
[16] See also Stephen L. Vargo, "Consumer Involvement: An Historical Perspective and Partial Synthesis" in Barbara B. Stern and George M. Zinkham (Eds.), *1995 AMA Educators' Proceedings* (Chicago: American Marketing Association, 1995), pp. 139–145.

Table 8-5

High-Involvement View of Active Consumers Versus Low-Involvement View of Passive Consumers

TRADITIONAL HIGH-INVOLVEMENT VIEW OF ACTIVE CONSUMERS	NEWER LOW-INVOLVEMENT VIEW OF PASSIVE CONSUMERS
1. Consumers are information processors.	1. Consumers learn information at random.
2. Consumers are information seekers.	2. Consumers are information gatherers.
3. Consumers are an active audience for ads and the effect of ads on them is *weak*.	3. Consumers are a passive audience for ads and the effect of ads on them is *strong*.
4. Consumers evaluate brands before buying.	4. Consumers buy first. If they do evaluate brands, it is done after the purchase.
5. Consumers seek to maximize satisfaction. They compare brands to see which provide the most *benefits* and buy based on detailed comparisons.	5. Consumers seek an acceptable level of satisfaction. They choose the brand least apt to have *problems* and buy based on few factors. Familiarity is key.
6. Lifestyle characteristics are related to consumer behaviour because the product is closely tied to a consumer's identity and belief system.	6. Lifestyle characteristics are not related to consumer behaviour because the product is not closely tied to a consumer's identity and belief system.
7. Reference groups influence behaviour because of the product's importance to group norms.	7. Reference groups have little effect on behaviour because the product is unlikely to be related to group norms.

Source: Henry Assael, *Consumer Behaviour and Marketing Action*, Fourth Edition (Boston: PWS-Kent, 1992), p. 104. Reprinted by permission of Wadsworth, Inc.

ty allows the consumer to reduce the amount of time, thought, and risk required when buying a given good or service. Brand loyalty can develop for simple items such as gasoline (due to low-involvement purchasing) and for complex items like autos (to minimize the risk of switching brands).

Canadians are less brand loyal than they used to be. A recent survey indicated that 57 per cent of shoppers would buy a product on sale rather than their favourite brand. In comparison, only 45 per cent of shoppers felt this way in 1989. Approximately 56 per cent of Canadian shoppers think generics are as good as national brands, compared to 52 per cent in 1989. Sixty per cent of U.S. adults say they "try to stick with well-known brands." And a lot of people are loyal to one brand of cigarettes, mayonnaise, toothpaste, coffee, hot cereal, ketchup, film, soap, salad dressing, beer, auto, perfume, and gasoline. In Great Britain, France, and Germany, 74 per cent, 54 per cent, and 52 per cent of adults (respectively) say "Once I find a brand, it is very difficult to get me to change brands." In India and China, 35 per cent and 28 per cent of adults (respectively) consider themselves to be "brand loyalists"—who buy name brands and remain true to them.[17]

How can companies generate and sustain customer loyalty? Here is the way Zeller's and the Royal Bank of Canada have tackled this issue:

> Zeller's offers all its customers a Club Z card, which entitles them to build up points on all merchandise purchases at Zeller's. These points can be redeemed in merchandise selected from the retailers Club Z catalogue. Part of the secret of the success of Club Z is that merchandise purchases are credited no matter how they are paid for (cash, Zeller's Card, VISA, Master Card, etc.). The Club Z approach rewards store loyalty without constraining purchase behaviour. Most other frequent-purchase programs require the use of a credit card.

---

[17]"Brand Loyalty Declining, Study Shows," *Marketing Magazine* (April 27, 1992), p 2; Adrienne Ward Fawcett, "Lifestyle Study: The Latest Results of DDB Needham's 18-Year Survey," *Advertising Age* (April 18, 1994), p. 13; Leo Burnett, U.S.A. Research Department, "Consumer Buying Patterns: Beyond Demographics," *Progressive Grocer* (May 1995), pp. 135–138; Nancy Giges, "Europeans Buy Outside Goods, But Like Local Ads," *Advertising Age* (April 27, 1992), pp. I-1, I-26; and Leah Rickard, "Ex-Soviet States Lead World in Ad Cynicism," *Advertising Age* (June 5, 1995), p. 3.

RADIO SHACK
www.tandy.com/

ROYAL BANK
www.royalbank.com/

Another example is the Royal Bank's VISA Classic II card. Launched in the spring of 1996, the card targets value-conscious consumers, such as young families and students. The idea is for participating retailers to give customers savings discounts of up to 25 per cent and other bonuses when they use the card to make purchases. Participating retailers include: Radio Shack, Music World, Cotton Ginny, and Domino's Pizza, among others. Of course, the VISA card is good at nonparticipating retailers as well, and any card usage allows customers to build up points which can be exchanged for gift certificates on merchandise from Radio Shack or Eaton's.[18]

Marketing Implications of the Final Consumer's Decision Process

Over the years, the marketing implications of the final consumer's decision process have been studied in many settings, as these present-day illustrations indicate:

- When acquiring information for a car purchase, people read articles in newspapers and magazines, talk to friends and relatives, and consider their previous experience. On average, men spend fourteen weeks thinking about a new-car purchase; and 32 per cent visit a closed showroom so they can look at models and learn about sticker prices. Once the actual "hunt" starts, men average fourteen shopping days to buy a car and visit five dealers. Two-thirds of men say they have a good time when buying a new car.

- Nearly a third of Chinese consumers are "enthusiastic shoppers," who enjoy shopping and like to price-bargain. They prepare complete shopping lists before shopping, consult with friends and neighbours prior to making major purchases, and are often innovators and opinion leaders. About 15 per cent of Chinese consumers are "passive shoppers," who consider shopping to be a necessary burden. They are casual shoppers, do not prepared detailed lists before shopping, and do not like price bargaining. They are conservative in their purchase of new products.

- Supermarket shoppers in eastern Germany are impulsive. They are more likely to make brand choices after they enter a store than are consumers in the Netherlands, western Germany, Spain, France, Italy, or Great Britain.

- For several reasons, "substantial time often elapses between the time people recognize the need for a product and the time they actually purchase it." People may believe they do not have enough time to devote to the decision. They may feel shopping is an unpleasant experience. They may experience perceived risk. They may need advice from others that is not readily available. They may not know how to gather adequate information about products and their attributes. They may expect prices to fall or improved products to be introduced later.

- Satisfied consumers discuss their experiences with far fewer people than dissatisfied ones. Yet, according to one auto-industry consultant, "It costs you five times as much to get a new customer as to keep an old one."[19]

Limitations of the Final Consumer's Decision Process

Much of purchase behaviour is hidden or subconscious.

The limitations of the final consumer's decision process for marketers lie in the hidden (unexpressed) nature of many elements of the process; the consumer's subconscious performance of the process or a number of its components; the impact of demographic, social, and psychological factors on the process; and the differences in decision making among consumers in different countries.

---

[18]Lara Mills, "Royal Bank Rolls Out New Customer Loyalty Card," *Marketing Mazazine* (May 13, 1996), p. 4.
[19]"How Men Buy Cars," *Ad Week* (September 18, 1995), p. 21; and "How Guys Buy Cars," *Advertising Age* (September 18, 1995), p. 3; Zhengyuan Wang, C. P. Rao, and Angela D'Auria, "Measuring Chinese Personal Values and Shopping Behaviour: An Empirical Comparison of the Rokeach Value Survey and Perceived Attribute Importance," in Brian T. Engelland and Alan J. Bush (Eds.), *Marketing: Advances in Theory and Thought* (Evansville, Ind.: Southern Marketing Association, 1994), pp. 378–381; "In-Store Promotion Sways Consumers," *Advertising Age* (May 25, 1992), p. I–24; Raymond Serafin and Cleveland Horton, "Auto Makers Focus on Service," *Advertising Age* (July 6, 1992), pp. 3, 33; Eric A. Greenleaf and Donald R. Lehmann, "Reasons for Substantial Delay in Consumer Decision Making," *Journal of Consumer Research*, Vol. 22 (September 1995), pp. 186–199.

MARKETING IN A CHANGING WORLD
REALLY Understanding Other Cultures[20]

As we discussed before, and again in this chapter, marketers need to do a first-rate job of grasping and appealing to the global marketplace. As such, they must understand other cultures—because of their broad impact on the demographics and lifestyles of potential customers, and the way they make consumption decisions. With this in mind, let us explore the distinctions between North American and Japanese cultures in greater detail.

According to Koichiro Naganuma, the Japanese chairman of Asatsu/BBDO (an advertising agency):

> In most western countries, the individual is seen as separate from, and often more important than, the larger community. We Japanese view ourselves as one homogeneous family. Our shared history, traditions, and national cultural identity give us a very strong sense of community. Consequently, the nature of communication within the Japanese culture reflects a commonality of thought, attitude, and circumstance, in what is often an unspoken language understood by us. In contrast to the Japanese, westerners are direct in face-to-face interaction, conversation, and expression. Western advertising, therefore, tends to fix on a target audience and address it with direct messages which seek to affect the attitude of that audience. Conversely, in the same manner that Japanese find it awkward and even disrespectful to maintain eye contact during conversation, our advertising shuns the directness of the western method, seeking instead to create a positive, welcoming atmosphere around the product. The Japanese prefer to come to an understanding with little actual conversation. For example, North Americans spend six-and-a-half hours in conversation a day, almost double the amount of time we [Japanese] spend conversing with each other.

Here are some further comparisons of the North American and Japanese cultures:

- North Americans fight for their beliefs. Japanese value harmony.
- North Americans get the facts straight. Japanese prefer unspoken agreements.
- North Americans display their emotions. Japanese hold back their emotions.
- North Americans are humour-oriented. Japanese are pun-oriented.
- North Americans make a long story long. Japanese make a short story short.
- North Americans are interested in *what* is spoken. Japanese are interested in *who* is speaking.

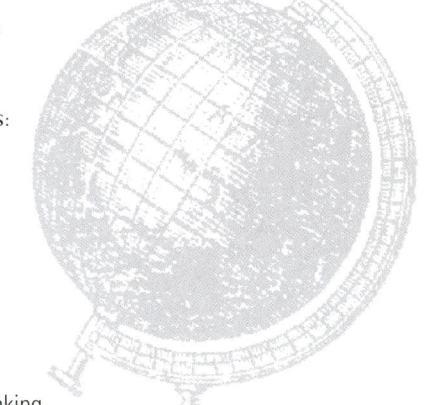

SUMMARY

1. *To show why consumer demographic analysis is not sufficient in planning marketing programs* Demographic data do not explain why consumers act as they do, why demographically similar consumers act differently, how motives and risks affect decisions, and how long it takes people to reach purchase decisions. Many firms now analyze the social and psychological aspects of final-consumer lifestyles, as well as the way in which consumers make decisions—in conjunction with demographics—and then develop descriptive consumer profiles.

2. *To define and describe consumer lifestyles and their characteristics, examine selected lifestyles, and present marketing implications of lifestyle analysis* A final consumer's lifestyle is the way in which a person lives and spends time and money. It is a function of the social and psychological factors internalized by that person, along with his or her demographic background. Consumer

---

[20]The material in this section is based on Hideo Ishikawa and Koichiro Naganuma, "Exploring Differences in Japan, U.S. Cultures," *Advertising Age* (September 18, 1995), pp. I–8.

social profiles are made up of several elements, including culture, social class, social performance, reference groups, opinion leaders, the family life cycle, and time expenditures. Psychological profiles are based on a combination of personality, attitudes (opinions), the level of class consciousness, motivation, perceived risk, innovativeness, and purchase importance.

These seven lifestyle types are expected to continue, with their popularity often differing by country. A family values lifestyle emphasizes marriage, children, and home life. With voluntary simplicity, people have an ecological awareness, seek material simplicity, strive for self-reliance, and buy inexpensive product versions. Getting by is a frugal lifestyle brought on because of economic circumstances. The "me" generation stresses being good to oneself, self-expression, and the acceptance of diversity. With blurring gender roles, more husbands are assuming the once traditional roles of their wives, and vice versa. A poverty of time occurs for some consumers because the quest for financial security means less free time as the alternatives competing for time expand. In a component lifestyle, consumer attitudes and behaviour depend on particular situations, rather than on an overall lifestyle philosophy. The various marketing implications of these consumer lifestyles are discussed further in the text.

3. *To consider the limitations of consumer lifestyle analysis* Many lifestyle concepts are difficult to measure, somewhat subjective, based on self-reports by consumers, and sometimes hidden from view. There are disputes over terms, misuse of data, and reliability.

4. *To define and describe the final consumer's decision process and present marketing implications* The final consumer's decision process is the procedure by which those consumers collect and analyze information and make choices among alternatives. It consists of the process itself and the factors affecting it (demographic, social, and psychological). It can be delayed or terminated by the consumer at any point.

The process has six steps: stimulus, problem awareness, information search, evaluation of alternatives, purchase, and post-purchase behaviour. There are three types of process: extended, limited, and routine. The way people make decisions varies widely between industrialized nations and less-developed and developing nations. Consumers often reduce shopping time, thought, and risk through low-involvement purchasing (for goods and services viewed as unimportant) and brand loyalty (the consistent repurchase of and preference toward a brand).

The marketing implications of the final consumer's decision process have been detailed for years. Several current applications are discussed in the text..

5. *To consider the limitations of final-consumer decision-making analysis* The limitations of the decision process for marketers lie in the unexpressed nature of many parts of the process; the subconscious nature of many consumer actions; the impact of demographic, social, and psychological factors; and the international differences in consumer decision making.

KEY TERMS

lifestyle (p. 200)
culture (p. 201)
social class (p. 202)
social performance (p. 203)
reference group (p. 203)
opinion leaders (p. 203)
family life cycle (p. 204)
joint decision making (p. 204)
household life cycle (p. 204)
time expenditures (p. 206)
personality (p. 206)
attitudes (opinions) (p. 206)
class consciousness (p. 206)

motivation (p. 207)
motives (p. 207)
perceived risk (p. 208)
innovativeness (p. 208)
importance of a purchase (p. 208)
family values (p. 208)
voluntary simplicity (p. 208)
getting by (p. 208)
"me" generation (p. 209)
blurring gender roles (p. 209)
poverty of time (p. 209)
component lifestyle (p. 209)
final consumer's decision process (p. 213)

stimulus (p. 213)
problem awareness (p. 214)
information search (p. 215)
evaluation of alternatives (p. 215)
purchase act (p. 215)
post-purchase behaviour (p. 216)
cognitive dissonance (p. 216)
extended consumer decision making (p. 216)
limited consumer decision making (p. 216)
routine consumer decision making (p. 216)
low-involvement purchasing (p. 218)
brand loyalty (p. 218)

Review Questions

1. Why are demographic data alone frequently insufficient for marketing decisions?
2. How does social class affect an individual's lifestyle and purchases?
3. Distinguish between the traditional family life cycle and the household life cycle.
4. How does class consciousness differ for inner-directed and outer-directed people? What does this signify for marketers?
5. Distinguish between actual risk and perceived risk. How may a firm reduce each type of perceived risk for a new arthritis pain reliever?
6. Compare the voluntary simplicity lifestyle with the getting by lifestyle.
7. Differentiate among social, commercial, and noncommercial stimuli. Provide specific examples of each.
8. What causes cognitive dissonance? How can it be reduced?
9. Draw a flowchart showing the steps in routine purchase behaviour.
10. Define low-involvement purchasing and explain its use by consumers. Give an example.

Discussion Questions

1. Canadian culture emphasizes collective responsibility, confidence in social institutions such as education, health care, and the police, consensus, willingness to accept difference and diversity, health consciousness, pessimism, and skepticism; Canadian consumers are value-driven, frugal, seeking personalization, brand disloyal, and informed buyers. What are the implications of this for firms marketing the following goods and services?
   a. Motorcycles.
   b. Tanning salons.
   c. Adult education.
   d. Vacation travel.
2. Give examples of current advertisements targeting the:
   a. Upper-middle class.
   b. Working class.
   c. Upper-lower class.
3. Distinguish between Tables 8-2 and 8-3. What are the marketing implications of your answer?
4. A large cereal manufacturer has hired you as a marketing consultant. It is particularly interested in learning more about the concept of a component lifestyle and developing an appropriate strategy.
   a. Explain the relevance of the component lifestyle concept for the cereal industry.
   b. Suggest various ways in which the cereal manufacturer can appeal to component lifestyles.
5. In this chapter, several distinctions are made between consumers in industrialized countries and those in less-developed nations with regard to the final consumer's decision process. How would you deal with these distinctions when marketing to consumers in less-developed and developing countries?

VIDEO CASE

Do Consumers Have Too Much Choice or Not Enough "Real Choice"?

In marketing, one of the inalienable rights of consumers is "the freedom to choose." In the past the cry for more freedom to choose was often echoed by consumers and consumer groups in the marketplace. In many areas marketers have responded to these cries quite vigorously. In fact, so vigorously that consumers are raising a new complaint: they have too much to choose from and their decision-making abilities are being overwhelmed. At Athlete's World, a Toronto specialty store, consumers are presented with over 250 pairs of running shoes. One of the salespeople wryly comments that the ugliest-looking shoes are often the best sellers, indicating appearance dominates over substance in this market situation.

Retailers who offer this bewildering variety say that even with hundreds of choices, some people are still not satisfied and go looking elsewhere. Retailers cannot compete successfully unless they offer all the brand names. One criticism is that the reason for all the choice is that marketers do not really understand their marketplace. Marketers counter by noting that there is truth to this criticism but the lack of understanding is not for lack of trying, but because consumers are very fickle. In the case of having 300 shoe choices, only about 150 will really sell, but the retailer does not know which 150 it will be.

A helpful salesperson is often the key for the consumer. Even a knowledgeable consumer like Orville Lee, a running back for the Toronto Argonauts with a fair bit of experience, was a bit bewildered when confronted with the variety of products in Athlete's World. On the advice of a salesperson, he found himself purchasing a pair of shoes promoted by Bo Jackson, another professional football player.

Canadian consumers live in a marketplace that appears to be a "mecca" of choice. They can choose from over 250 different types of running shoes, hundreds of satellite TV channels, and forty different kinds of coffee offered by the Second Cup Coffee franchise. Baskin Robbins Ice Cream built a retail chain by offering thirty-one flavours and more, meaning a total inventory of 600 to 700 flavours, which are rotated in and out of their stores throughout the year. The consumer's head spins faster than a CD ROM drive when he or she tries to buy a computer, given all the different hardware and software options presented to them. Even the apparently simple issue of processor types and speeds is very confusing, never mind the risk of obsolescence in the future.

This phenomenon is not unique to Canada. Reports of consumers being "irritated and bewildered" by choice have been made in the United States, United Kingdom, France, Germany, and Italy. Interestingly, the issue is not purely one of choice alone, but of the existence of so many "me-too" products in the marketplace. Consumers are faced with multiple brands and products on store shelves and end up making product comparisons that often turn out to be meaningless because they find different brands of packaged goods have essentially the same ingredients. Marketers find the failure rate of new products to be about 90 per cent, so to avoid risk there is a tendency is to bring out new products which are minor variations of existing products with established track records. This contributes to brand and product proliferation without adding meaningfully to consumer choice. The basic benefit provided by a laundry detergent has not been meaningfully enhanced despite being offered in over 100 different brands in Britain. Many consumers long for the days when soap was soap, shampoo was shampoo, and toilet paper was toilet paper.

To the extent that new products present new benefits consumer choice is enhanced, but the extent to which me-too products proliferate in the market place, consumer choice is not enhanced and is, in reality, being stymied.

QUESTIONS

1. Given your reading so far, what advice would you give marketers so they do not offer "too much choice"?
2. Suggest some ways marketers could respond to and perhaps even capitalize on this issue.
3. There are clearly consumers who seem to like all the choices and consumers who are confused by them. In light of theory on the consumer's decision process, how might these two groups differ? Refer to each element in Figure 8-7 for your answer.
4. When it comes to consumer goods, are you "pro-choice" or not? Discuss your views and support them with marketing theory.

VIDEO QUESTIONS ON TOO MUCH CHOICE

1. Based on consumer behaviour principles, what advice could you have given Toronto Argonaut running back Orville Lee to help him with his purchase decision?
2. Think about your experiences as a consumer. Present and discuss two examples you encountered for each of the following situations: too much choice, not enough choice, about the right amount of choice.

Video Source: "Too Much Choice," *Venture* (May 5, 1994).
Other Source: Based on material in Virginia Matthews, "Too Much Choice On Store Shelves Leaves Euro Consumers Crabby," *Marketing Magazine*, April 22, 1996, p. 6.

CASE STUDY

Will Twenty-somethings Buy Levi's Dockers?

Levi Strauss is in the midst of a major advertising campaign for its Dockers pants. Dockers is currently the best-selling brand of men's pants in the world, with over $1 billion in annual wholesale sales. Of Levi Strauss' total advertising budget, about one-quarter is spent on Dockers.

As an addition to its traditional Dockers line of khaki slacks, Levi's recently introduced a new high-fashion khaki line called Dockers Authentics. A cross between khakis and jeans, Dockers Authentics sell for U.S.$45 to $48 (versus U.S.$35 for Levi's regular khakis). Levi Strauss is targeting Dockers Authentics at Generation-Xers. Levi Strauss realizes that its traditional Dockers brand appeals to an older population group and wants to broaden the brand's appeal beyond baby boomers. Without a successful product aimed at Generation X, the Docker name will become associated with an aging audience.

Levi Strauss is hoping to send the message to men in their twenties that its new khakis are cool. The firm's goal for its advertising campaign is to encourage men to wear khakis in place of jeans and to view Dockers Authentics as a more formal alternative to jeans. And in an attempt not to appear too trendy, Levi's new ads promote Dockers Authentics on the basis of tradition and comfort, not as current fashion.

Levi has used an innovative series of promotions for Dockers Authentics. Early promotions, for example, were based around sponsored rock concerts in six cities. Prior to each concert, Dockers projected a four-minute Much Music-style video featuring Dockers Authentics on the side of a nearby building. Each advertisement had the tag line: "Khakis with a blue-jean soul."

Dockers Authentics are being featured in special "Authentics" departments in department stores located in large metropolitan markets. The special departments are placed with other mid-priced collections of clothing aimed at young men. Retail analysts expect the Authentics line to compete against Calvin Klein and other brands.

Levi Strauss expects the sales of its Dockers, Dockers Authentics, and Levi's jeans to benefit from the shift to more casual clothing styles on weekends and at work. According to a major marketing research study, almost 90 per cent of all workers say they are "dressing down." Even IBM, once noted for a rigid dress code, has adapted its standards to include more relaxed clothing styles. The study also found that interest in men's suits was down, but interest in casual apparel (like no-iron cotton slacks and sweaters) was up.

Levi Strauss is determined to capitalize on this trend with its casual clothing line. Early research by the company found that although human resources managers favoured casual clothing policies, those managers needed Levi's help to convince top management to change their dress codes. So the company developed a four-page newsletter filled with reasons why more casual dress codes should be enacted. For example, it noted that letting employees dress casually was a cost-free employee benefit. The newsletter also contained case histories of firms that successfully adopted casual dress codes. In total, Levi Strauss mailed the newsletter to 42 000 human resources managers. Levi Strauss also produced a video on the "Fine Art of Dressing." And in fall 1995, it started hosting casual-dress fashion shows at the Dockers shops that the firm owns.

Levi did have one advertising slip up. In late 1995, it pulled a Dockers' ad from city bus shelters in San Francisco and New York after it was accused of encouraging vandalism. Each ad had a pair of Dockers placed behind a glass plate. Under the pants (seemingly in anticipation of their theft) was the message: "Apparently, they were very nice pants."

QUESTIONS

1. Which family life-cycle stage is most likely to purchase Dockers? Dockers Authentics? Explain your answers.
2. What forms of perceived risk accompany the purchase of Dockers Authentics by a first-time purchaser? A loyal customer?
3. sWhat consumer lifestyles are associated with "dressing down?" Explain your answer.
4. What type of decision process would be used in the purchase of Dockers Authentics? Explain your answer.

Sources: The data in this case are drawn from Alice Z. Cuneo, "Levi's Dons New Men's Wear Appeal," *Advertising Age* (April 24, 1995), p. 12; Cyndee Miller, "A Casual Affair," *Marketing News* (March 13, 1995), pp. 1-2; and Kevin Whitelaw, "Gobbling Up the Gen-X Market," *U.S. News & World Report* (October 9, 1995), p. 68.

CHAPTER 9
Organizational Consumers

Chapter Objectives

1. To introduce the concept of industrial marketing

2. To differentiate between organizational consumers and final consumers and look at organizational consumers from an international perspective

3. To describe the different types of organizational consumers and their buying objectives, buying structure, and purchase constraints

4. To explain the organizational consumer's decision process

5. To consider the marketing implications of appealing to organizational consumers

{ *In 1989, Fred Brunk, vice-president of sales at Fluid Management, a supplier of display shelving for paint, wanted to grow the company's domestic sales. What was missing from his portfolio were the big retailers such as Wal-Mart, which would bring him larger volumes. Six years later, Brunk got his wish—domestic sales doubled, from $20 million to $40 million, thanks to an increase in volume to the mass merchants. But what Brunk did not count on were the tremendous expectations of these companies.* }

For many small firms, large retailers represent a great opportunity, but selling to them is often more complicated than expected. As Fluid Management's Fred Bunk says, "Even when the details are in place, such as the specific needs of the company and negotiated prices, you have to constantly watch when new stores are opening. There must always be a salesperson ready at a moment's notice to make a trip to the retailer's headquarters." And while Fluid Management's eight-member sales force may not be able to visit each of Wal-Mart's thousands of stores, the firm's chief executive officer is willing to go to Wal-Mart's Bentonville, Arkansas, headquarters as often as needed.

Here are some other complexities in selling to big accounts like Wal-Mart:

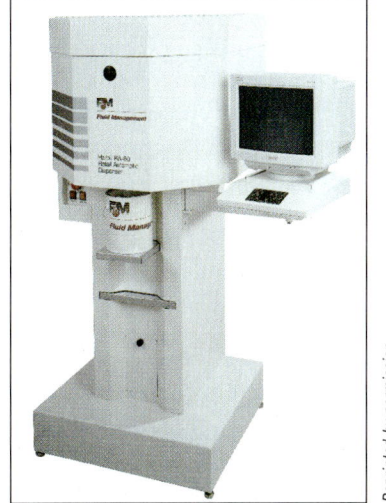

- Wal-Mart does not purchase from wholesalers. Thus, small firms must service the firm directly. This could be especially tough for a small supplier selling a narrow product line.
- Most small manufacturers do not have the resources to set up offices near to Wal-Mart stores.
- Some large retailers require that suppliers take back excess inventories, seek extended payment policies, and even ask that suppliers handle data collection responsibilities. Other demands may include requiring rebates on purchases, adhering to an automatic return policy, and dictating that a supplier give donations to the retailers' favourite charities. A number of small manufacturers say the demands that large retailers place on them are so great that they would lose money selling to those retailers.
- A small supplier's current customers may resent it selling to firms such as Wal-Mart that are viewed as direct competitors.
- The loss of a key account could drive a small supplier into bankruptcy.

So, why bother? There are major benefits for a small firm selling to a large retailer.

Reprinted by permission.

WAL-MART
www.wal-mart.com/

First, there is the huge sales potential. For example, after Wal-Mart began to upgrade the paint departments in its stores, Fluid Management received more business from Wal-Mart in two months than the firm otherwise received in an entire year. Second, small suppliers can use their contracts with large buyers as a means of getting increased financing or better terms from banks. Third, it may be less costly to sell to large retailers based on their high average sales and the delivery of big orders to a single distribution centre instead of to a number of small stores.[1]

In this chapter, we will study much more about the characteristics and behaviour of organizational consumers such as Wal-Mart. We will also discuss the different types of organizational customers, their buying objectives, buying structure, and purchase constraints.

Overview

Firms involved with organizational consumers use **industrial marketing**.

As defined in Chapter 7, organizational consumers purchase goods and services for further production, use in operations, or resale to others. In contrast, final consumers buy for personal, family, or household use. Organizational consumers are manufacturers, wholesalers, retailers, and government and other nonprofit institutions. When firms deal with organizational consumers, they engage in **industrial marketing**, as shown in these examples.

Purchasing executives around the world spend trillions of dollars annually for the goods and services their companies require. According to one estimate, "On average, manufacturers shell out 55 cents of each dollar of revenues on goods and services, from raw materials to overnight mail. By contrast, labour seldom exceeds 6 per cent of sales, overhead 3 per cent."[2]

Although purchasing executives at large corporations often deal with major suppliers, in North America over 100 000 small businesses sell goods and services to these big companies. As one purchasing director noted, "We've discovered that smallness just equates with quality. A tiny company just tends to pay more attention. After all, it's risking everything on a small output. Sloppiness can be ruinous." One-third of the largest North American companies use formal programs for seeking out small suppliers. Why then do only a little over 100 000 of the millions of small North American firms sell to big corporations? Many feel there is a "nightmare of paperwork, pre-qualifying inspections, mazes to find the right contact, and the time involved before the contract is signed."[3]

POLAROID
www.polaroid.com/

For a long time, Polaroid Corporation earned its reputation (and considerable profits) by making and marketing self-developing cameras for final consumers. But in recent years, due to the popularity of inexpensive 35-mm cameras and the growth of one-hour photo developing labs, Polaroid has reduced its focus on final consumers. Today, Polaroid places greater emphasis on products for organizational consumers, including digital scanners, medical imaging systems, photo ID systems, and security systems.[4] And as Figure 9-1 shows, Polaroid now advertises some of its cameras to such organizational consumers as real-estate brokers.

Bombardier Inc. of Montreal "is an international powerhouse in transportation equipment" and had sales of about $7.1 billion in 1995. Most Canadians think of Bombardier as making snowmobiles and Sea-Doo water craft. However, Bombardier also designs and manufactures mass-transit vehicles, rail cars, and just happens to be the leading executive jet manufacturer in the world. Bombardier owns Canadair, Learjet Inc., Short Brothers PLC and de Havilland Inc. The market for the products of these jet and turboprop manufacturers is small passenger commuter airlines, business jet operators, national heads of state, and a handful of entrepreneurs. In the age of the Internet, which allows executives to communicate online, why is Bombardier expecting to make any sales at all? Because in the increas-

---

[1]Allison Lucas, "Can You Sell to Wal-Mart?" *Sales & Marketing Management* (August 1995), p. 14.
[2]Shawn Tully, "Purchasing's New Muscle," *Fortune* (February 20, 1995), pp. 75–76.
[3]Arthur Bragg, "How to Sell in the Big Time," *Sales & Marketing Management* (February 1990), pp. 42–44; and Michael Selz, "Some Suppliers Rethink Their Reliance on Big Business," *Wall Street Journal* (March 29, 1993), p. B2.
[4]Gary Hoover, Alta Campbell, and Patrick J. Spain, *Hoover's Handbook of American Business 1995* (Austin, Texas: Reference Press, 1994), pp. 880–881.

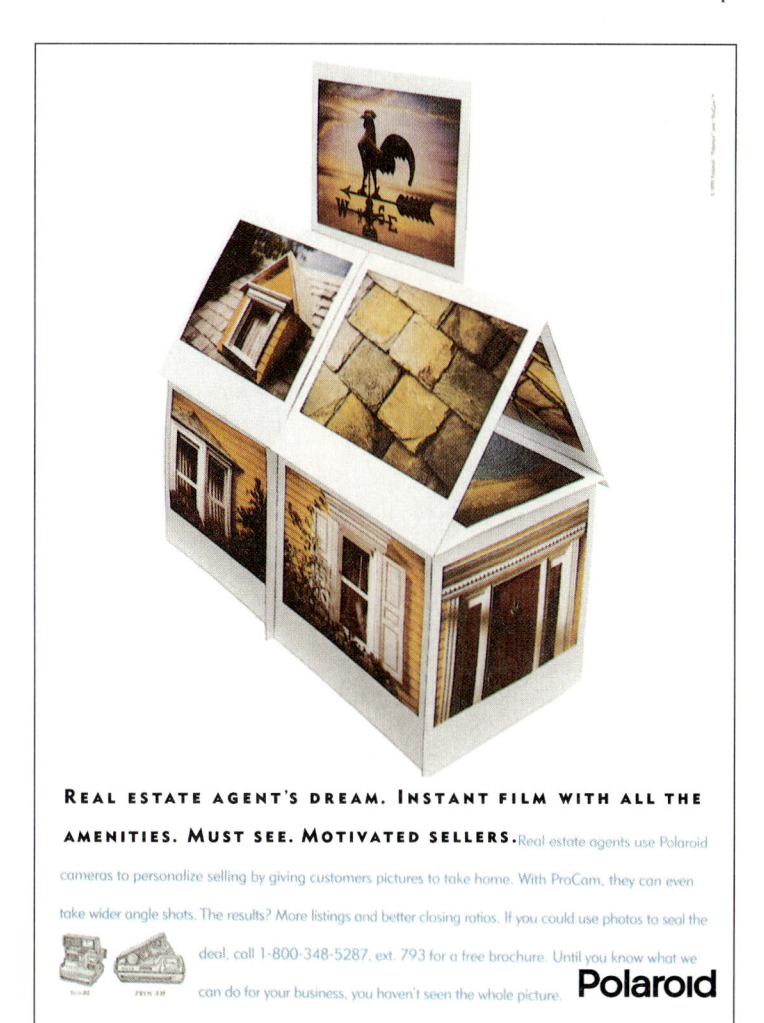

FIGURE 9-1
At Polaroid: A Heightened Emphasis on Industrial Marketing
As Polaroid's core consumer photography business has stagnated, it has turned to imaginative approaches to industrial marketing.
Reprinted by permission.

ingly global economy, people will still have to travel on business, especially if it is big business. And big businesses are more likely to need the travelling flexibility and the office in the sky facilities of computers, fax machines and satellite communication links afforded by corporate jets.[5] See Figure 9-2.

Andersen Consulting, a division of Arthur Andersen & Co., has annual revenues of $3.5 billion and nearly 30 000 consultants in about 50 countries. Its specialties are technical consulting—with which it first became involved in 1954 when helping General Electric install its initial computer—and strategic planning. Its Method/1 approach is a widely-used process for teaching clients how to handle any type of computer project in a systematic and cost-efficient manner.[6]

In this chapter, organizational consumers are distinguished from final consumers and an international perspective is provided. The various types of organizational consumers are described. Key factors in organizational consumer behaviour are presented. The organizational consumer's decision process is outlined, and marketing implications are offered.

GENERAL ELECTRIC
www.ge.com/

The Characteristics of Organizational Consumers

Organizational consumers differ from final consumers in several key ways. As shown in Table 9-1, these differences are due to the nature of their purchases and the nature of the market. Organizational consumer characteristics also vary by nation.

---

[5]Daniel Stoffman, "Bombardier's Billion-Dollar Space Race," *Canadian Business* (June 1994) p. 90–101.
[6]Lee Berton, "Big Six's Shift to Consulting Services," *Wall Street Journal* (September 21, 1995), pp. B1, B4.

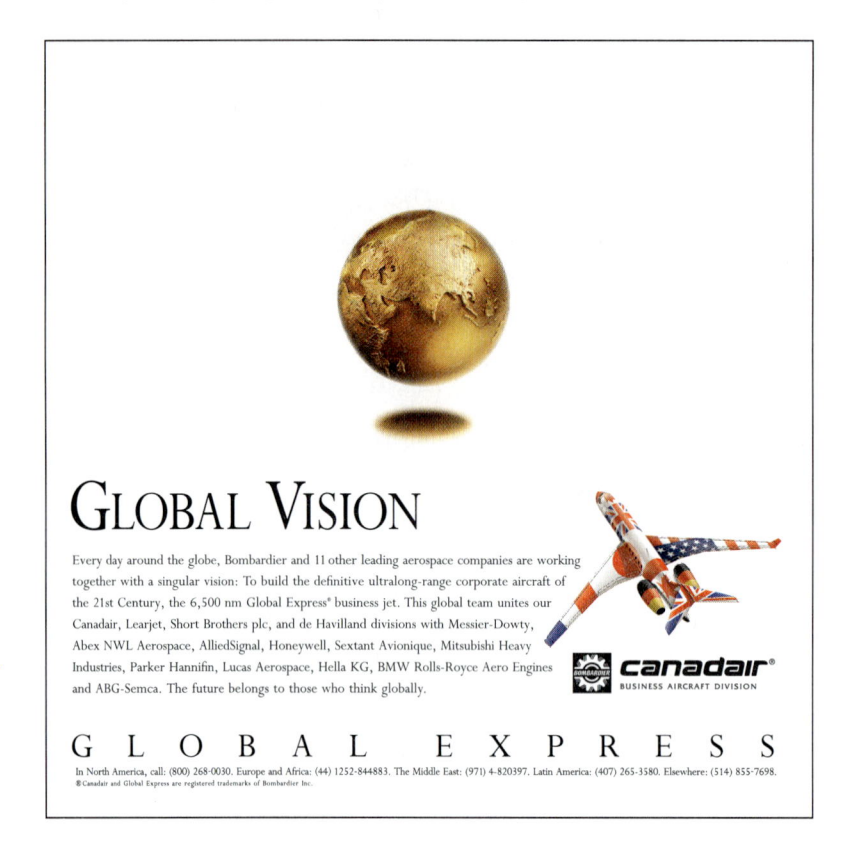

FIGURE 9-2
Industrial Marketing for Corporate Jets
Reprinted with permission of Bombardier Aerospace.

GLOBAL VISION

Every day around the globe, Bombardier and 11 other leading aerospace companies are working together with a singular vision: To build the definitive ultralong-range corporate aircraft of the 21st Century, the 6,500 nm Global Express® business jet. This global team unites our Canadair, Learjet, Short Brothers plc, and de Havilland divisions with Messier-Dowty, Abex NWL Aerospace, AlliedSignal, Honeywell, Sextant Avionique, Mitsubishi Heavy Industries, Parker Hannifin, Lucas Aerospace, Hella KG, BMW Rolls-Royce Aero Engines and ABG-Semca. The future belongs to those who think globally.

canadair®
BUSINESS AIRCRAFT DIVISION

GLOBAL EXPRESS

In North America, call: (800) 268-0030. Europe and Africa: (44) 1252-844883. The Middle East: (971) 4-820397. Latin America: (407) 265-3580. Elsewhere: (514) 855-7698.
®Canadair and Global Express are registered trademarks of Bombardier Inc.

Table 9-1

Major Differences Between Organizational and Final Consumers

DIFFERENCES IN PURCHASES

Organizational consumers

1. Buy for further production, use in operations, or resale to others. Final consumers buy only for personal, family, or household use.
2. Commonly purchase installations, raw materials, and semifinished materials. Final consumers rarely purchase these goods.
3. Often buy on the basis of specifications and technical data. Final consumers frequently buy based on description, fashion, and style.
4. Utilize multiple-buying and team-based decisions more often than final consumers.
5. Are more apt to apply formal value and vendor analysis.
6. More commonly lease equipment.
7. More frequently employ competitive bidding and negotiation.

DIFFERENCES IN THE MARKET

Organizational consumers

1. Derive their demand from that of final consumers.
2. Have demand states that are more subject to cyclical fluctuations than final consumer demand.
3. Are fewer in number and more geographically concentrated than final consumers.
4. Often employ buying specialists.
5. Require a shorter distribution channel than do final consumers.
6. May require special relationships with sellers.
7. Are more likely than final consumers to be able to make goods and undertake services as alternatives to purchasing them.

The Nature of Organizational Consumer Purchases

Organizational and final consumers vary in the way they use goods and services and in the items they buy. Organizational consumers purchase capital equipment, raw materials, semifinished goods, and other products for use in further production or operations or for resale to others. Final consumers, by contrast, usually acquire finished items (and are not involved with million-dollar purchases of plant and equipment) for personal, family, or household use. As a result, organizational consumers are more apt to use specifications, multiple-buying decisions, value and vendor analysis, leased equipment, and competitive bidding and negotiation than are final consumers.

Many organizational consumers rely on product specifications in purchase decisions and do not consider alternatives unless they meet minimum standards, such as engineering and architectural guidelines, purity, horsepower, voltage, type of construction, and construction materials. Final consumers more often purchase on the basis of description, style, and colour.

Organizational consumers often use **multiple-buying responsibility**, whereby two or more employees formally participate in complex or expensive purchase decisions. For example, a decision to buy computerized cash registers may involve input from computer personnel, marketing personnel, the operations manager, a systems consultant, and the controller. The firm's president might make the final choice about the system's characteristics and the supplier. Though final consumers use multiple-buying responsibility (joint decision-making), they employ it less frequently and less formally.

Multiple-buying responsibility *may be shared by two or more employees.*

A lot of organizational consumers use value analysis and vendor analysis. In **value analysis**, organizational consumers thoroughly compare the costs and benefits of alternative materials, components, designs, or processes so as to reduce the cost/benefit ratio of purchases.[7] They seek to answer such questions as: What is the purpose of each good or service under purchase consideration? What are the short-run and long-run costs of each alternative? Is this purchase necessary? Are there substitute goods or services that could perform more efficiently? How long will a good or service last before it must be replaced? Can uniform standards be set to ease reordering?

Value analysis *reduces costs;* **vendor analysis** *rates suppliers.*

In **vendor analysis**, organizational consumers thoroughly assess the strengths and weaknesses of current or new suppliers in terms of quality, customer service, reliability, and price.[8] Satisfaction with current vendors often means customer loyalty. Figures 9-3 and 9-4 illustrate value analysis and vendor analysis.

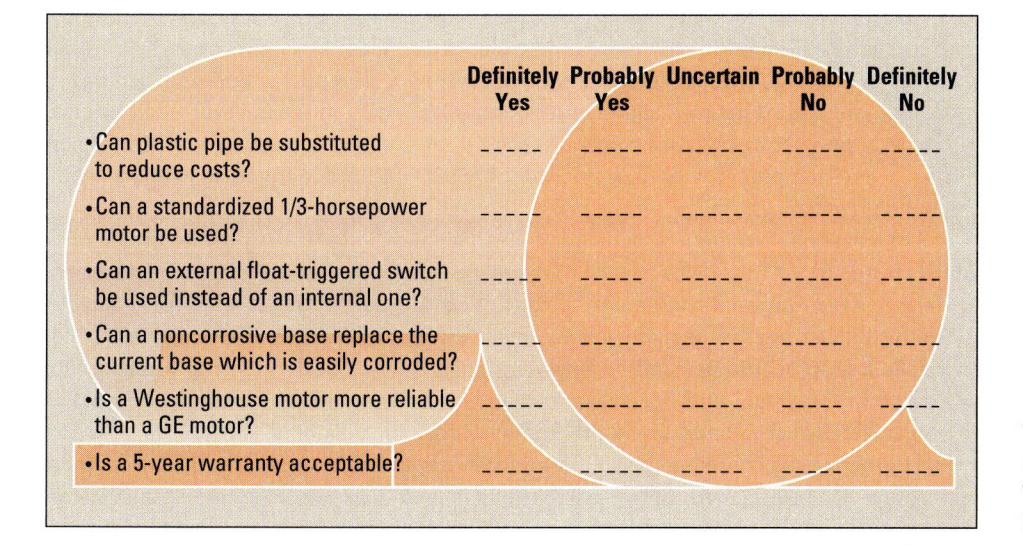

	Definitely Yes	Probably Yes	Uncertain	Probably No	Definitely No
• Can plastic pipe be substituted to reduce costs?	-----	-----	-----	-----	-----
• Can a standardized 1/3-horsepower motor be used?	-----	-----	-----	-----	-----
• Can an external float-triggered switch be used instead of an internal one?	-----	-----	-----	-----	-----
• Can a noncorrosive base replace the current base which is easily corroded?	-----	-----	-----	-----	-----
• Is a Westinghouse motor more reliable than a GE motor?	-----	-----	-----	-----	-----
• Is a 5-year warranty acceptable?	-----	-----	-----	-----	-----

FIGURE 9-3
Value Analysis by a Purchaser of an Electrical Pump

---

[7]Peter D. Bennett (Ed.), *Dictionary of Marketing Terms*, Second Edition (Chicago: American Marketing Association, 1995), pp. 297–298.

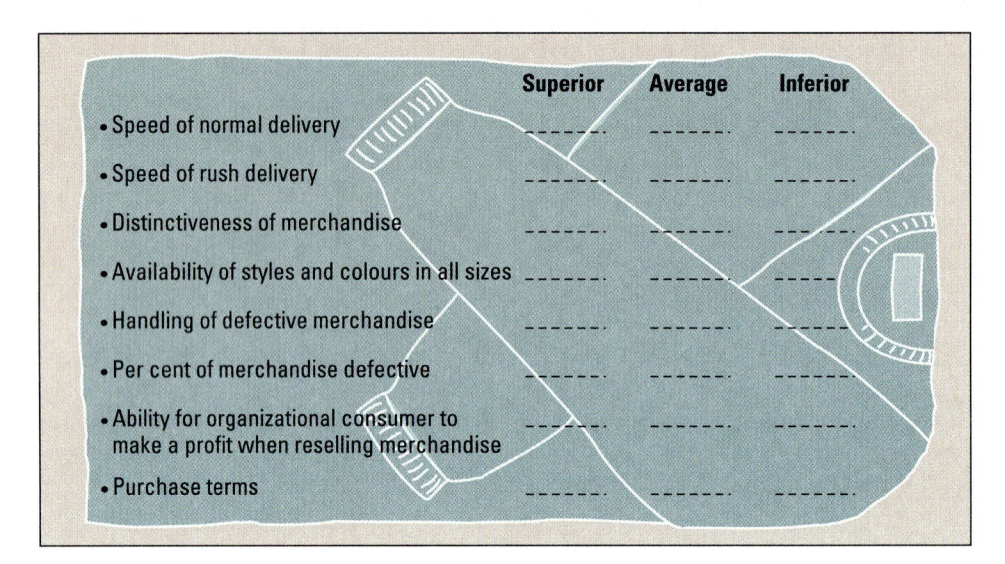

FIGURE 9-4
Vendor Analysis of a Sweater Supplier by a Purchaser

	Superior	Average	Inferior
• Speed of normal delivery	------	------	------
• Speed of rush delivery	------	------	------
• Distinctiveness of merchandise	------	------	------
• Availability of styles and colours in all sizes	------	------	------
• Handling of defective merchandise	------	------	------
• Per cent of merchandise defective	------	------	------
• Ability for organizational consumer to make a profit when reselling merchandise	------	------	------
• Purchase terms	------	------	------

*In **competitive bidding**, sellers submit price bids; in **negotiation**, the buyer bargains to set prices.*

*Organizational consumers **derive demand** from their own customers. With the **accelerator principle**, final-consumer demand impacts on many organizational consumers.*

Organizational consumers of all sizes frequently lease major equipment. Each year, Canadian firms spend over $15 billion in leasing equipment (measured by the original cost of the equipment). Commonly leased equipment include aircraft, computers, office machinery, and trucks and trailers. The worldwide use of commercial leasing is rising rapidly. Final consumers are less involved with leasing; it is most common in apartment and auto leasing.

Organizational consumers often use competitive bidding and negotiation. In **competitive bidding**, two or more sellers submit independent price quotes for specific goods and/or services to a buyer, who chooses the best offer. In **negotiation**, a buyer uses bargaining ability and order size to get sellers' best possible prices. Bidding and negotiation are mostly used for complex, custom-made goods and services.

The Nature of the Organizational Consumer Market

Derived demand occurs for organizational consumers because the quantity of the items they purchase is often based on the anticipated level of demand by their subsequent customers for specific goods and services. For example, the demand for the precision rivets used in cruise ships is derived from the demand for new cruise ships, which ultimately is derived from the demand for cruises. Firms know that unless demand is generated at the end-user level, distribution pipelines become clogged and resellers will not buy fresh goods and services. Organizational consumers' price sensitivity depends on end-user demand. If end users are willing to pay higher prices, organizational consumers will not object to increases. However, if end-user demand is low, organizational consumers will reduce purchases, even if suppliers lower their prices. Figure 9-5 illustrates derived demand for major household appliances.

Organizational consumers' demand tends to be more volatile than final consumers'. A small change in the final demand for highly processed goods and services can yield a large change in organizational consumers' demand. This is a due to the **accelerator principle**, whereby final-consumer demand affects many layers of organizational consumers. For example, a drop in auto demand by final consumers reduces dealer demand for cars, auto maker demand for steel, and steel maker demand for iron ore. In addition, capital purchases by organizational consumers are highly influenced by the economy.

Organizational consumers are fewer in number than final consumers. In Canada, there are about 35 000 manufacturing establishments, 65 000 wholesaling establishments (including manufacturer-owned facilities), and 206 000 retailing establishments, as compared with 10 million final-consumer households. In some industries, large organizational consumers dominate, and their size and importance give them bargaining power in dealing with sellers.

---

[8] Ibid., p. 299. See also Stephanie Gruner, "The Smart Vendor-Audit Checklist," *Inc.* (April 1995), pp. 93–95.

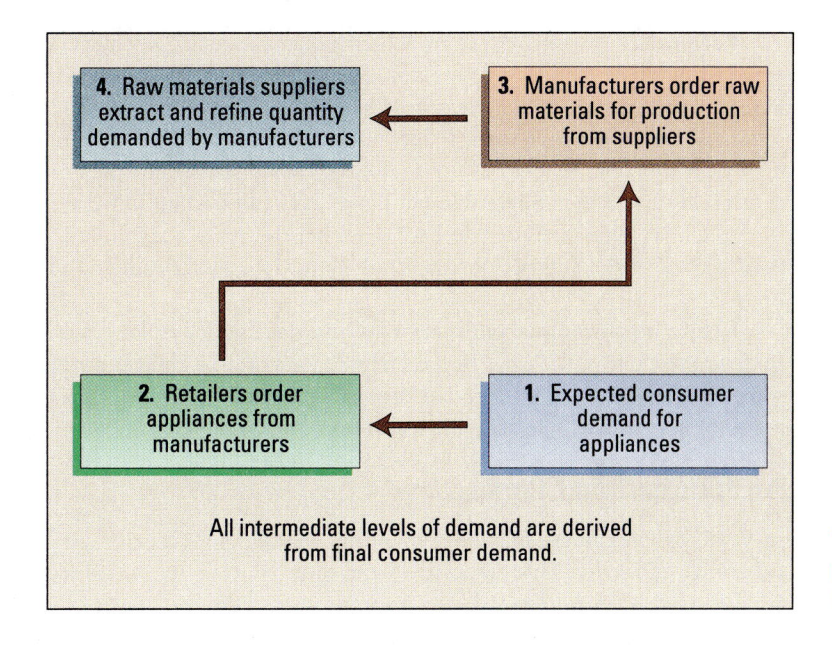

FIGURE 9-5
Derived Demand for Major Appliances

[Figure: Flow diagram showing derived demand]
- 1. Expected consumer demand for appliances
- 2. Retailers order appliances from manufacturers
- 3. Manufacturers order raw materials for production from suppliers
- 4. Raw materials suppliers extract and refine quantity demanded by manufacturers

All intermediate levels of demand are derived from final consumer demand.

Over the last several years a number of global firms have exercised this bargaining power. For example, Xerox has gone from dealing with 5000 suppliers to 500, Motorola from 10 000 to 3000, Ford from 10 000 to 2300, and Texas Instruments from 22 000 to 14 000. And Allied Signal has gone from buying valves, pipes, and fittings from more than 400 suppliers to just one. This practice has severely affected those dropped, causing some to go out of business and others to invest considerable amounts to upgrade their facilities and products. Furthermore, the suppliers that are kept are expected to meet the highest levels of quality and customer service—while holding prices down.[9]

Organizational consumers tend to be geographically concentrated. For instance, two provinces (Ontario and Quebec) contain 70 per cent of the nation's manufacturing plants. Some industries (such as steel, wood, petroleum, rubber, auto, and tobacco) are even more geographically concentrated.

Because of their size and the types of purchases they make, many organizational consumers use buying specialists. These people often have technical backgrounds and are trained in supplier analysis and negotiating. Their full-time jobs are to purchase goods and services and analyze purchases. Expertise is high.

Inasmuch as many organizational consumers are large and geographically concentrated, purchase complex and custom-made goods and services, and use buying specialists, distribution channels tend to be shorter than those for final consumers. For example, a laser-printer maker would deal directly with a firm buying 100 printers; a salesperson from the manufacturer would call on the firm's purchasing agent. A company marketing printers to final consumers would distribute them through retail stores and expect final consumers to visit those stores.

Organizational consumers may require special relationships. They may expect to be consulted while new products are developed; want extra customer services, such as extended warranties, liberal returns, and free credit; and want close communications with vendors. Systems selling and reciprocity are two specific tactics used in industrial marketing. In **systems selling**, a combination of goods and services is provided to a buyer by one vendor. This gives a buyer one firm with which to negotiate and an assurance of consistency among various parts and components. For example, Hewlett-Packard uses systems selling for its laser printers, personal computers, and servicing.

WEB LINKS

XEROX
www.xerox.com/

Organizational consumers tend to be large and geographically concentrated.

Systems selling offers single-source accountability.

---

[9] John R. Emshwiller, "Suppliers Struggle to Improve Quality as Big Firms Slash Their Vendor Rolls," *Wall Street Journal* (August 16, 1991), pp. B1–B2; Kathleen Kerwin and Bill Vlasic, "A Shrinking Supply of Suppliers," *Business Week* (January 8, 1996), p. 83; Tully, "Purchasing's New Muscle," p. 79; and *Market Research Handbook 1995*, Statistics Canada (Ottawa: Minister of Industry, Science, and Technology).

In **reciprocity**, *suppliers purchase as well as sell.*

PEPSI
www.pepsi.com/

Foreign organizational consumers must be carefully studied.

Reciprocity is a procedure by which organizational consumers select suppliers that agree to purchase goods and services, as well as sell them. In Canada, the Competition Bureau monitors reciprocity because of its potential lessening of competition. However, in international marketing efforts, sellers may sometimes have to enter into reciprocal agreements (in this case, known as countertrade). For instance, in 1973, because of currency restrictions in the then Soviet Union, PepsiCo began trading soft-drink syrup concentrate for Stolichnaya vodka. Since then, it has exchanged syrup concentrate for more than a million cases of vodka and two Russian-built ships. Its countertrade in today's Russia remains high.[10]

Finally, organizational consumers may produce goods and services themselves, if they find purchase terms, the way they are treated, or available choices unacceptable. They may sometimes suggest to suppliers that they will make their own goods or perform services as a way of improving their bargaining positions.

An International Perspective

As with final consumers, many dissimilarities exist among organizational consumers around the world, and sellers must understand and respond to them. In this section, several topics are discussed: attitudes toward foreign firms as suppliers, the effects of culture on negotiating styles and decision making, the impact of a nation's stage of economic development, the need for an adaptation strategy, and the opportunities available due to new technology.

Firms doing business in foreign markets need to know how organizational consumers in those markets perceive the goods and services of firms from different countries. The attitudes of purchasing agents in foreign nations to Canadian products are often quite positive, especially with regard to high-technology items, professional services, raw materials, and industrial machinery. Likewise, many Canadian firms believe the product quality and/or prices for some foreign goods and services are better than those of Canadian suppliers. That is why Bombardier's Canadair subsidiary is having Sextant Avionique of France supply the flight-control systems for its new Global Express Airplane.

National culture has a large impact on the way organizational consumers negotiate and reach decisions. Here is an illustration:

> The Chinese believe that one should build the relationship and, if successful, transactions will follow. Westerners build transactions and, if they are successful, a relationship will follow. This difference underlies many negotiating failures.
>
> In China, negotiating responses may be riddled with contradictions. Westerners will see illogical behaviour, evasion, deviousness perhaps, where none may be intended. Disentangling these communications supplies much of the challenge that is China. The deadline-driven, transcontinental executive may find it hard to slow down to the pace required to share "a loaf of bread, a jug of wine, and Tao," but marketing in China requires the patient building of relationships. Not that China is slow. The pace can simultaneously be fast and slow. Those involved in negotiations know how long they can drag when the Chinese side is consulting internally or has other reasons for delay, and yet how swiftly they move on other occasions.[11]

The stage of economic development in foreign countries affects the types of goods and services purchased by organizational consumers there. Many less-developed and developing nations do not yet have the infrastructure (electricity, roads, transportation systems, skilled workers) to properly use state-of-the-art machinery and equipment. In addition, such machinery and equipment may be too expensive for customers in those markets to afford. On the other hand, there is substantial long-term growth potential in those nations due to the scarcity of industrial goods and services. Firms marketing to less-developed and developing nations need to be patient and flexible in dealing with organizational consumers.

When marketing goods and services to organizational consumers in foreign markets, firms have to consider how much to adapt their strategies to address the unique charac-

---

[10] Nathaniel Gilbert, "The Case for Countertrade," *Across the Board* (May 1992), p. 44. See also Peter W. Liesch, "Government-Mandated Countertrade in Australia," *Industrial Marketing Management*, Vol. 23 (October 1994), pp. 299–305.

[11] Tim Ambler, "Reflections in China: Re-Orienting Images of Marketing," *Marketing Management* (Summer 1995), pp. 24, 25–26.

International Marketing in Action

Does Country of Origin Affect Industrial Buyers?

In the past, most country-of-origin studies looked at the impact of where a product was made on industrial buyers' quality perceptions. But a more recent study assessed country-of-origin effects by distinguishing between where a good was designed and where it was assembled. That study investigated the perceptions of members of the Canadian Association of Purchasing Managers.

The study suggests that, in general, products designed and assembled in industrialized countries have higher evaluations than those designed and assembled in developing and less-developed nations. Among seven industrialized nations, Japan, Germany, the United States, and Canada rank highest as countries of origin for design and assembly. France, Italy, and Belgium have lower ratings on these two criteria. South Korea, a rapidly industrializing nation, rates almost as highly as France and Italy as a country of assembly and was slightly higher than Belgium.

Country of design is a more important cue to purchasing managers than country of assembly for all three product categories evaluated: computer systems, fax machines, and ballpoint pens. It appears that purchasing managers perceive a large difference in design and assembly capabilities based on a country's stage of economic development. And this perceived difference is greater in design than assembly capabilities.

Although brand name has a significant impact in terms of perceived quality and perceived value for both computer systems and fax machines, it has much less impact than both country-of-origin cues. Brand name has no impact on the evaluation of ballpoint pens. In summary, according to this study, brand name plays a limited role as a predictor of quality or purchase value.

As a consultant to a South Korean-based maker of electronic components, how would you incorporate the results of this study into your recommended marketing plan?

Source: Based on material in Sadrudin A. Ahmed, Alain d'Astous, and Mostafa El Adraoui, "Country-of-Origin Effects on Purchasing Managers' Product Perceptions," *Industrial Marketing Management*, Vol. 23 (October 1994), pp. 323–332.

---

teristics and needs of those customers. Because large organizational consumers can account for a significant part of any firm's overall revenues, selling firms are often quite willing to be responsive to customers' desires—by employing personnel who fluently speak the language of the foreign markets, utilizing the most appropriate negotiating styles, and adapting product features and customer service as requested. In general, it is more likely that selling firms will engage in meaningful adaptation of their marketing efforts if a potential customer order is big, the good or service being marketed is complex, and the business cultures and stage of economic development in their domestic and foreign markets are dissimilar.

With the new technology now available, there are more opportunities to market to international organizational consumers than ever before. For example, the Internet, e-mail, fax machines, satellite TV, and video conferencing all facilitate buyer-seller communications—and tear down the barriers caused by weak transportation infrastructures, differences in time zones, and the inability for both parties to see each other in regular phone calls. See Figure 9-6.

FIGURE 9-6
All the World's a Stage—for Business
From *Canadian Business* 1996 Performance 500, p. 176. Reprinted by permission of ADCOM Inc.

The **Standard Industrial Classification (SIC)** *provides information on Canadian and foreign organizational consumers.*

Types of Organizational Consumers

In devising a marketing plan aimed at organizational consumers, it is necessary to research their attributes: areas of specialization, size and resources, location, and goods and services purchased. As shown in Figure 9-7, organizational consumers can be placed into five broad major categories: manufacturers, wholesalers, retailers, government, and nonprofit.

The Canadian **Standard Industrial Classification (SIC)** for Companies and Enterprises contains information about most organizational consumers. The 1980 Canadian SIC, compiled by Statistics Canada, assigns organizations to eighteen sector classifications: (A) food, beverage, and tobacco; (B) wood and paper; (C) energy; (D) chemicals, chemical products, and textiles; (E) metallic minerals and metal products; (F) machinery and equipment (except electrical machinery); (G) transportation equipment; (H) electrical and electronic products; (I) construction and related activities; (J) transportation services; (K) communications; (L) finance and insurance; (M) general services to business; (N) government services; (O) education, health, and social services; (P) accommodation, restaurants, and recreation services; (Q) food retailing; and (R) consumer goods and services. Within these groups, there are over 1000 more specific industry classifications, such as computer programming and system services, tea and coffee processing, and automobile recyclers. Canadian data by SIC code are available from Statistics Canada, and various provincial government and commercial publications.

The U.S. uses an SIC code system with eleven classifications: (1) agricultural, forestry, and fishing; (2) mining; (3) construction; (4) manufacturing; (5) transportation, communi-

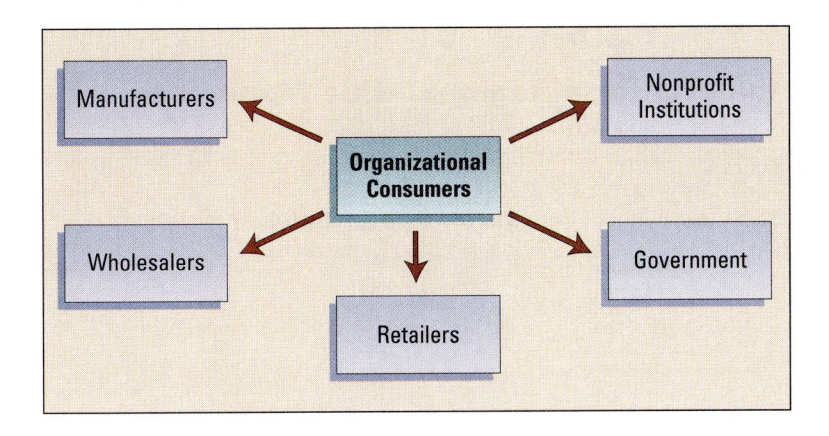

FIGURE 9-7
Types of Organizational Consumers

cation, electric, gas, and sanitary services; (6) wholesale trade; (7) retail trade; (8) finance, insurance, and real estate; (9) services; (10) public administration; and (11) nonclassifiable establishments. The *U.S. Industrial Outlook* (last published in 1994), the *Annual Survey of Manufacturers*, and the monthly and annual *Current Business Reports* are U.S. Department of Commerce documents with data on hundreds of industries. *Moody's Industry Review* (weekly), *Standard & Poor's Industry Surveys* (weekly), *Predicast's Forecasts* (quarterly), and *Dun's Census of American Business* (annual) also provide data by SIC code and/or geographic area. Data on government institutions are available on a local, state, and federal level from the *Census of Governments*.

With the advent of NAFTA, Canada, Mexico and the United States are cooperating to harmonize the SIC code systems of the three nations into a North American Industrial Classification System (NAICS). Considerable data on industrial activity and companies in other nations are also available in the context of the SIC code. Dun & Bradstreet's yearly *Principal International Businesses* directory lists 50 000 firms in 140 different nations. *Predicasts F&S Index Europe* annually cites articles with industry and company data by nation for Western and Eastern Europe, and Russia and the former Soviet republics. *Dun's Latin America's Top 25 000* annually provides data on companies in thirty-five countries. The U.S. Department of Commerce's *Global Trade and Economic Outlook* has information on a number of international industries.

End-use analysis, by which a seller determines the proportion of sales made to organizational consumers in different industries, is one way in which SIC data can be employed. Table 9-2 shows end-use analysis for a glue manufacturer (in this example, the seller). First, the firm ascertains the current relative importance of various categories of its customers—9-2(A). It then applies end-use analysis to make an overall sales forecast by estimating the expected growth of each customer category in its geographic area—9-2(B).

Next, several characteristics of manufacturers, wholesalers, retailers, government, and nonprofit organizations as consumers are described.

With **end-use analysis**, *a seller studies sales made in different industries.*

Manufacturers as Consumers

Manufacturers produce products for resale to other consumers. The *Canadian Standard Industrial Classification Manual* lists twenty-nine major two-digit industry segments that manufacture goods. Each may be divided into three-digit groups and then into four-digit subgroupings. Thus, SIC 16 includes textile products; 162, textile products manufacturing; and 1621, carpets, mats, and rugs manufacturing. Table 9-3 shows the twenty-nine two-digit groups.

In Canada, 60 per cent of manufacturers have twenty or more workers. The annual costs of their materials are $209 billion. Their expenditures for plant and equipment (from trucks to generator sets) are billions of dollars each year. They annually use billions of BTUs of energy and their annual net sales (including shipments between firms in the same industry category) exceed $330 billion.

By knowing where different industries are located, a firm can concentrate its efforts and not worry about covering geographically dispersed markets. Because manufacturers'

Manufacturers *make items for resale to others.*

Table 9-2

End-Use Analysis for a Regional Glue Manufacturer

(A) SIMPLE END-USE ANALYSIS

SIC Code	Industry Classification of Customers	Current Total Sales (in Per Cent)[a]
07	Wood and wood products	25
08	Wood and paper products	13
15	Plastic and rubber	15
55	Printing and publishing	17
85	Apparel	10
86	Household furniture and other consumer goods	20
	Total	100

(B) APPLYING END-USE ANALYSIS TO SALES FORECASTING

SIC Code	Industry Classification of Customers	Per Cent of Current Total Sales	Estimated Annual Percentage Growth Rate of Industry[b]	Overall Sales Growth Percentage for Glue Manufacturer[c]
07	Wood and wood products	25	+1.8	+0.45
08	Wood and paper products	13	+2.0	+0.26
15	Plastic and rubber	15	+3.0	+0.45
55	Printing and publishing	17	+1.9	+0.32
85	Apparel	10	-2.0	-0.20
86	Household furniture and other consumer goods	20	+3.2	+0.64
	Total estimated sales increase			+1.92

[a] Firm examines its sales receipts and categorizes them by SIC group.
[b] Firm estimates growth rate of each category of customer (in its geographic area) on the basis of trade-association and government data.
[c] Firm multiplies per cent of current sales in each SIC group by expected growth rate in each industry to derive its own expected sales for the coming year. It expects sales to increase by 1.92 per cent during the next year.

purchasing decisions tend to be made centrally at headquarters or at divisional offices, the seller must identify the location of the proper decision makers.

As consumers, manufacturers buy a variety of goods and services, including land, capital equipment, machinery, raw materials, component parts, trade publications, accounting services, supplies, insurance, advertising, and delivery services. For example, Boeing has long- and short-term contracts with suppliers that total $56 billion; and it buys equipment, raw materials, component parts, finished materials, and services from thousands of different subcontractors and other businesses.[12]

Wholesalers as Consumers

Wholesalers *buy or handle merchandise and its resale to nonfinal consumers.*

Wholesalers buy or handle merchandise and its subsequent resale to organizational users, retailers, and other wholesalers. They do not sell significant volume to final users but are involved when services are marketed to organizational consumers. Table 9-4 lists the major

[12] Jeff Cole, "Boeing's Bid to Avoid Swings in Business Falls Short of Hopes," *Wall Street Journal* (February 16, 1993), pp. A1, A12.

Table 9-3
Canadian Manufacturing Industries

SIC CODE	INDUSTRY NAME	SIC CODE	INDUSTRY NAME
01	Food	21	Non-Ferrous Metals & Primary Metal Products
02	Beverages	22	Fabricated Metal Products
03	Tobacco	25	Agricultural, Construction and Industrial Machinery
04	Other Agricultural Products	26	Commercial, Professional & Institutional Furniture, Machinery & Equipment
06	Forestry	30	Motor Vehicles and Motor Vehicle Parts and Accessories
07	Wood and Wood Products	31	Other Transportation Equipment
08	Wood and Paper Products	32	Tires
09	Wood, Wood Products & Paper, Integrated Operations	35	Household Appliances and Electrical Products
10	Petroleum and Natural Gas	36	Electronic Equipment and Computer Services
11	Other Fuels	40	Real Estate Developers, Builders, and Operators
12	Electricity	44	Building Materials
15	Plastic and Rubber	55	Printing and Publishing
16	Textiles	85	Apparel
17	Chemicals and Other Chemical Products	86	Household Furniture and Other Consumer Goods
20	Iron, Steel, and Related Products		

Source: Statistics Canada, *Canadian Standard Industrial Classification For Companies And Enterprises 1980* (Ottawa: Minister of Supply and Services Canada, 1986).

Table 9-4
Canadian Wholesaling and Related Industries

SIC CODE	INDUSTRY NAME	SIC CODE	INDUSTRY NAME
01	Food	31	Other Transportation Equipment
02	Beverage	32	Tires
03	Tobacco	35	Household Appliances and Electrical Products
04	Other Agricultural Products	36	Electronic Equipment and Computer Services
07	Wood and Wood Products	44	Building Materials
08	Wood and Paper Products	45	Air Transport
10	Petroleum and Natural Gas	46	Railway Transport
11	Other Fuels	47	Water Transport
12	Electricity	48	Truck Transport
16	Textiles	49	Urban Transit and Other Passenger Transport
17	Chemicals and Other Chemical Products	50	Storage and Other Services Incidental to Transport
21	Non-Ferrous Metals and Primary Metal Products	55	Printing and Publishing
22	Fabricated Metal Products	56	Postal and Courier Services
25	Agricultural, Construction, and Industrial Machinery	58	Telecommunication Carriers
26	Commercial, Professional, and Institutional Furniture, Machinery, and Equipment	85	Apparel
30	Motor Vehicles and Motor Vehicle Parts and Accessories	86	Household Furniture and Other Consumer Goods

Source: Statistics Canada, *Canadian Standard Industrial Classification For Companies And Enterprises 1980* (Ottawa: Minister of Supply and Services Canada, 1986).

industry groups in wholesaling, as well as related transportation industries and business services. Chapter 16 has a broad discussion of wholesaling.

Canadian wholesalers are most prominent in Ontario and Quebec. Annual wholesaling and related sales (excluding manufacturer wholesaling) exceed $248 billion. Sales are largest for food products ($44 billion); coal and petroleum products ($32 billion); motor vehicles and accessories ($22.8 billion); machinery and equipment ($21 billion); electrical machinery ($19.4 billion); lumber and building materials ($17.4 billion); and farm products ($14.8 billion).

As consumers, wholesalers buy or handle many goods and services, including warehouse facilities, trucks, finished products, insurance, refrigeration and other equipment, trade publications, accounting services, supplies, and spare parts. A major task in dealing with wholesalers is getting them to carry the selling firm's product line for further resale, thereby placing items into the distribution system. For new sellers or those with new products, gaining cooperation may be difficult. Even well-established manufacturers may have problems with their wholesalers because of the competitive nature of the marketplace, wholesalers' perceptions that they are not being serviced properly, or wholesalers' lack of faith in the manufacturers' products.

Retailers as Consumers

Retailers sell to the final consumer.

Retailers buy or handle goods and services for sale (resale) to the final (ultimate) consumer. They usually obtain goods and services from both manufacturers and wholesalers. Table 9-5 lists the major industry groups in retailing, as well as several related service businesses that cater to final consumers. Chapter 17 has a broad discussion of retailing.

Annual Canadian retail sales exceed $200 billion. Chains operate about 20 per cent of all retail stores, accounting for about 40 per cent of total retail sales. A large amount of retailing involves auto dealers, food stores, general merchandise stores, eating and drinking places, gas stations, furniture and home furnishings stores, and apparel stores.

As consumers, retailers buy or handle a variety of goods and services, including store locations, facilities, interior design, advertising, resale items, insurance, and trucks. Unlike wholesalers, they are usually concerned about both product resale and the composition of their physical facilities (stores). This is because final consumers usually shop at stores, whereas wholesalers frequently call on customers. Thus, retailers often buy fixtures, displays, and services to decorate and redecorate stores.

Getting retailers to stock new items or continue handling current ones can be difficult because store and catalogue space is limited and retailers have their own goals. Many retail chains have evolved into large and powerful customers, not just "shelf stockers." Some are so powerful that they may even charge *slotting fees* just to carry manufacturers' products in their stores. For instance:

> Nowadays, most supermarket-savvy manufacturers chalk them up as a cost of doing business. But if fees for shelf-space had been around in the 1980s, products like granola, herbal tea, and yogurt might never have made it into stores and kitchens. These so-called slotting fees [charged by retailers for providing shelf-space] can often exceed $40 000 per retail chain per item, which adds up to millions of dollars for national distribution.[13]

Retailers (and wholesalers) sometimes insist that suppliers make items under the retailers' (or wholesalers') names. For private-label manufacturers, the continued orders of these customers are essential. If a large retailer or wholesaler stops doing business with a private-label manufacturer, then that firm has to establish its own identity with consumers—and it may even go out of business due to its lack of marketplace recognition.

Government as Consumer

Government purchases and uses a variety of routine and complex products.

Government consumes goods and services in performing its duties and responsibilities. Federal (1), provincial (10), territorial (2), and municipal (6006) units together account for the greatest volume of purchases of any consumer group in Canada with total expenditures

---

[13]Bernice Kanner, "Shelf Control," *New York* (January 22, 1990), p. 22.

Table 9-5

Canadian Retailing and Retailed Industries

SIC CODE	INDUSTRY NAME	SIC CODE	INDUSTRY NAME
02	Beverages	61	Consumer and Business Financing Intermediaries
10	Petroleum and Natural Gas	62	Investment Intermediaries
30	Motor Vehicles and Motor Vehicle Parts and Accessories	63	Insurers
31	Other Transportation Equipment	64	Other Financial Intermediaries
32	Tires	65	General Services to Business Management
36	Electronic Equipment and Computer Services	80	Accommodation Services
40	Real Estate Developers, Builders, and Operators	81	Food and Beverage Services
42	Special Trade Contracting	82	Entertainment, Recreation and Amusement Services
43	Services Incidental to Construction and Building Operations	84	Food Retailing
44	Building Materials	87	Specialty Merchandise Retailing
49	Urban Transit and Other Passenger Transport	88	General Merchandise Retailing
57	Telecommunication Broadcasting	89	Other Consumer Services
60	Deposit Accepting Intermediaries		

Source: Statistics Canada, *Canadian Standard Industrial Classification For Companies And Enterprises 1980* (Ottawa: Minister of Supply and Services Canada, 1986).

of $153 billion on goods and services each year. The federal government accounts for 22 per cent of this, the provincial governments for 33 per cent and the territorial and local governments for the remaining 45 per cent. The biggest budget shares (including employee wages) go for operations, capital outlays, military services, postal services, education, highways, public welfare, health care, police, fire protection, sanitation, and natural resources. The major SIC codes for government are government services (70); education (75); and health and social services (76).[14]

Governmental consumers buy a wide range of goods and services, including food, military equipment, office buildings, subway cars, office supplies, clothing, and vehicles. Some purchases involve standard products offered to traditional consumers; others, such as highways, are specially made for a government customer. Bombardier is one of the large Canadian firms which has its own marketing specialists dedicated to making government sales.

Some firms are unaccustomed to the bureaucracy, barriers, political sensitivities, and financial constraints of selling to government consumers. To aid them, the federal government publishes the *Weekly Bulletin of Business Opportunities*, which contains opportunities for businesses to sell to government. As noted earlier, the major government organization in Canada which undertakes buying is the federal agency, Supply and Services Canada. Each government unit (federal, provincial, and municipal) and division typically has a

---

[14]Statistics Canada, *Market Research Handbook 1995* (Ottawa: Minister of Industry Science and Technology); and Statistics Canada, *1991 Census Dictionary* (Ottawa: Minister of Industry Science and Technology), Catalogue 92-301E; and Statistics Canada, *Canadian Standard Industrial Classification For Companies And Enterprises 1980* (Ottawa: Minister of Supply and Services Canada, 1986).

purchasing department. Every one of these purchasing departments will gladly divulge their procurement policies to anyone who wishes to supply goods and services.

The size of the government market in Canada is further enlarged by the fact that the federal, provincial, and local governments own some of the nation's largest corporations. In fact, thirty-nine of the top 500 Canadian Corporations are government owned. These thirty-nine corporations had combined sales of $55 billion in 1995, combined net income of $686 million ($4.3 billion if Ontario Hydro's mammoth $3.6 billion loss is discounted) and utilized $165 billion in assets. The heavy asset base is due to the fact that eighteen of these companies are public utilities (power companies or telephone companies). Referred to as "Crown" corporations, some of these companies include: Petro Canada, Canadian National Railways, Canada Post, Canadian Wheat Board, Canadian Broadcasting Corporation, Canadian Commercial Corporation, Atomic Energy of Canada Ltd. Cape Breton Development Corporation, Via Rail Canada Inc. (all owned by the federal government), Ontario Hydro, Ontario Lottery Corporation, Liquor Control Board of Ontario (all owned by the province of Ontario), and Hydro-Quebec.[15]

The buying behaviour of these corporations is very much like that of privately owned corporations; however, large contracts are awarded in a fashion very similar to government bid purchasing. Further, political considerations affect the decision-making behaviour of these organizations more often than for privately owned corporations.

Nonprofit Institutions as Consumers

Nonprofit institutions function in the public interest.

Nonprofit institutions act in the public interest or to foster a cause, and do not seek financial profits. Hospitals, charitable organizations, museums, universities, political parties, civic organizations, and parks are nonprofit institutions. They buy goods and services in order to run their organizations and also buy items for resale to generate additional revenues to offset costs.

There are many national and international nonprofit institutions, such as the Canadian Cancer Society, the Liberal, Progressive Conservative, New Democratic, Bloq Québécois and Reform parties, the Boy Scouts and Girl Guides, chambers of commerce, and the Red Cross. Hospitals, museums, and universities, due to fixed sites, tend to be local nonprofit institutions.

There are no separate SIC codes for nonprofit- versus profit-oriented firms. However, firms in the 75 (Education) and 76 (Health and Social Services) SIC categories are often nonprofit in nature.

Key Factors in Organizational Consumer Behaviour

Organizational consumer behaviour depends on buying objectives, buying structure, and purchase constraints.

Buying Objectives

Organizational buying objectives relate to availability, reliability, consistency, delivery, price, and service.

Organizational consumers have several distinct goals in purchasing goods and services. Generally, these organizational buying objectives are important: availability of items, reliability of sellers, consistency of quality, delivery, price, and customer service. See Figure 9-8.

Availability means a buyer can obtain items when needed. An organizational consumer's production or resales may be inhibited if products are unavailable at the proper times. Seller reliability is based on its fairness in allotting items in high demand, nonadversarial relationships, honesty in reporting bills and shipping orders, and reputation. Consistency of quality refers to buyers' interest in purchasing items of appropriate quality on a regular basis. For example, drill bits should have the same degree of hardness each time they are bought. Delivery goals include minimizing the length of time from order

---

[15]"Performance 500," *Canadian Business* (June 1995), p. 104-127.

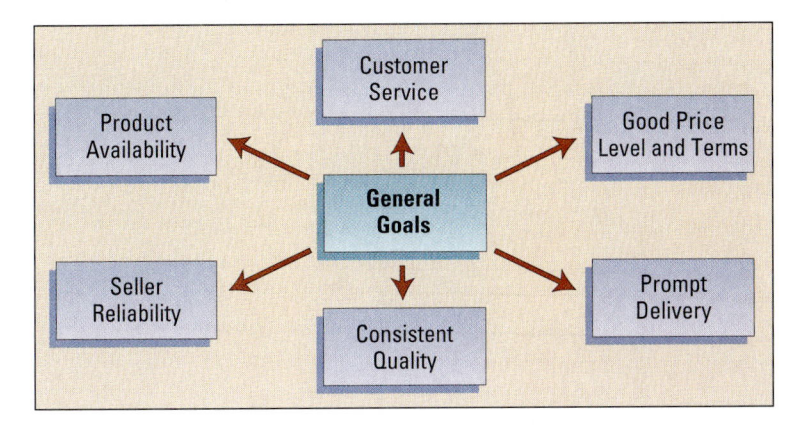

FIGURE 9-8
Goals of Organizational Consumers

placement to the receipt of items, minimizing the order size required by the supplier, having the seller responsible for shipments, minimizing costs, and adhering to an agreed-on schedule. Price considerations involve purchase prices and the flexibility of payment terms. Customer service entails the seller's ability or willingness to satisfy special requests, to have staff ready to field questions when needed, to promptly address problems, and to have an ongoing dialogue with customers.

Industrial marketers must recognize that price is only one of several considerations for organizational consumers; and it may be lower in importance than availability, quality, service, and other factors:

> Cutting purchasing costs has surprisingly little to do with browbeating suppliers. Purchasers at companies like Moore Business forms and Chrysler aim to reduce the total cost—not just the price—of each part or service they buy. They form enduring partnerships with suppliers that let them chip away at key costs year after year. Purchasing companies are also packing once-fragmented purchases of goods and services into companywide contracts for each.[16]

With regard to more specific goals, manufacturers are concerned about quality standards for raw materials, component parts, and equipment. Some like dealing with many suppliers to protect against shortages, foster price and service competition, and be exposed to new products. Others have been reducing the number of suppliers from which they buy, to foster better relationships, cut ordering inefficiencies, and have more clout with each supplier.[17]

Wholesalers and retailers consider further salability (their customers' demand) to be the highest priority. If possible, they seek buying arrangements whereby the number of distribution intermediaries that can carry goods and services in a geographic area is limited. They also seek manufacturers' advertising, transportation, and warehousing support.

Salability and exclusivity are keys for wholesalers and retailers.

Government consumers frequently set exact specifications for some products they buy; as large-volume buyers, they can secure them. Government consumers may sometimes consider the economic conditions in the geographic areas of potential sellers. Contracts may be awarded to the firms with the higher unemployment in their surrounding communities.

Nonprofit consumers stress price, availability, and reliability. They may seek special terms in recognition of their nonprofit status.

Buying Structure

The buying structure of an organization refers to the formality and specialization used in the purchase process. It depends on the organization's size, resources, diversity, and for-

The organization's buying structure depends on its attributes.

---
[16]Tully, "Purchasing's New Muscle," p. 76; Shona McKay, "A Paper Tiger in the Paperless World," *Canadian Business* (April 1996), pp. 25–29.
[17]See Cathy Owens Swift, "Preferences for Single Sourcing and Supplier Selection Criteria," *Journal of Business Research*, Vol. 32 (February 1995), pp. 105–111.

TECHNOLOGY & MARKETING

GE Plastics: Business-to-Business Marketing Through the Internet

One of the key uses of the Internet is for customer support. Because a firm can use the Internet to communicate with thousands (millions) of current and potential users of a product with a small customer support staff, it is a very cost-effective way of disseminating product information to customers.

GE Plastics is ideally suited to the Internet since almost all of its customers have PCs with modems. Although the firm will not divulge the costs in setting up its Internet site, one analyst estimated them at up to $150 000.

GE Plastics was the first *Fortune 500* firm to use the Internet in a major marketing effort. Its Internet site provides its engineer, designer, and scientist customers with instant access to crucial product and technical information, design guidelines, and graphics. Customers can also communicate and exchange ideas within five newsgroup forums (automotive, building and construction, computers, design, and plastics) that collect information from a variety of sources. This information is updated on a weekly basis.

GE Plastics went online in October 1994. It first had to digitize roughly 1500 pages of technical literature. An additional challenge it faced was that Internet standards at the time did not allow for a variety of page layouts. So, it had to find other ways of making documents look good. GE Plastics also hired a software developer to simplify the commands relating to accessing, searching, retrieving, and saving data on the Internet. According to the software developer, "The steps GE took to ease user access to the Internet are highly unusual. Most of the businesses establishing a presence on the Internet leave it up to users to find their own way."

As the customer support manager for GE Plastics, develop specific criteria to evaluate the success of the firm's Internet site.

Source: Based on material in Thayer C. Taylor, "Marketing: The New Generation," *Sales & Marketing Management* (February 1995), pp. 43–44.

---

mat. The structure is apt to be formal (i.e., separate department) for a large, corporate, resourceful, diversified, and departmentalized organization. It will be less formal for a small, independently owned, financially limited, focused, and non-departmentalized organization.

Large manufacturers normally have specialized purchasing agents who work with the firms' engineers or production department. Large wholesalers tend to have a single purchasing department or a general manager in charge of operations. Large retailers tend to be quite specialized and have buyers for each narrow product category. Small manufacturers, wholesalers, and retailers often have their buying functions completed by the owner-operator.

As mentioned previously, each government unit (federal, provincial, and municipal) and division typically has a purchasing department. Supply and Services Canada is the federal office responsible for centralized procurement and coordination of purchases. In a nonprofit organization, there is usually one purchasing department, or a member of the operations staff performs buying functions.

Constraints on Purchases

Derived demand is the key constraint on organizational purchases.

For manufacturers, wholesalers, and retailers, derived demand is the major constraint on purchase behaviour. Without the demand of consumers, production halts and sales drop as the backward chain of demand comes into play (final consumers —>retailers—>wholesalers —>manufacturers).

Manufacturers also are constrained by the availability of raw materials and their ability to pay for large-ticket items. Wholesalers and retailers are limited by the finances available to make purchases, as well as by the level of risk they are willing to take. In this case, risk refers to the probability that wholesalers or retailers will be able to sell the products they buy in a reasonable time and at a satisfactory profit. Products like fashion clothing have higher risks than such staple items as vitamins and disposable diapers.

Government consumers are constrained by the budgeting process. Approval for categories of purchases must normally be secured well in advance, and deviations must be explained. Budgets must be certified by legislative bodies. For many nonprofit consumers, cash flow (the timing of the money they have coming in versus the money they spend) is the major concern.

The Organizational Consumer's Decision Process

Organizational consumers use a decision-making procedure in much the same way as final consumers. Figure 9-9 shows the **organizational consumer's decision process**, with its four components: expectations, buying process, conflict resolution, and situational factors.[18]

An **organizational consumer's decision process** *is like a final consumer's.*

Expectations

Purchasing agents, engineers, and users bring a set of organizational consumer expectations to any buying situation: "These expectations refer to the perceived potential of alternative suppliers and brands to satisfy a number of explicit and implicit objectives."[19]

For purchases to be made, buyers must have positive expectations of such supplier attributes as product availability and quality, vendor reliability, delivery time, price, and cus-

Expectations are based on buyers' backgrounds, information, perceptions, and experience.

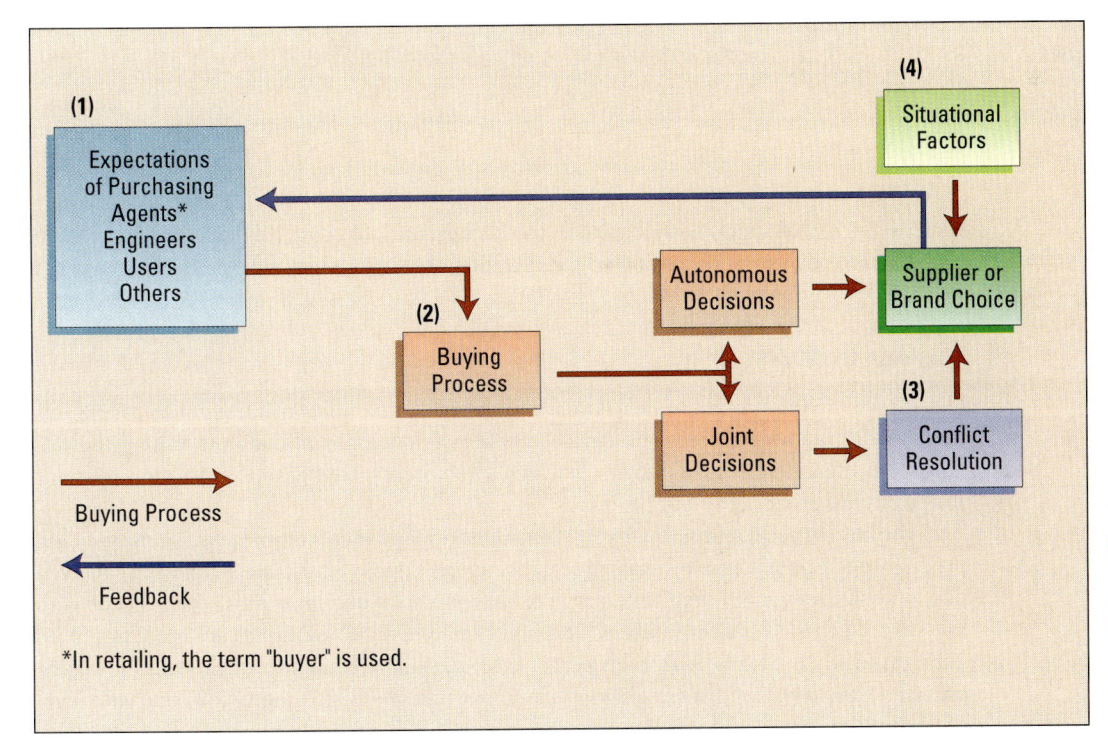

FIGURE 9-9
The Organizational Consumer's Decision Process

Source: Adapted from Jagdish N. Sheth, "A Model of Industrial Buyer Behaviour," *Journal of Marketing,* Vol. 37 (October 1973), pp. 50–56.

[18]The material in this section is drawn from Jagdish N. Sheth, "A Model of Industrial Buyer Behaviour," *Journal of Marketing,* Vol. 37 (October 1973), pp. 50–56.
[19]Ibid., p. 52.

FIGURE 9-10
Meeting Organizational Consumers' Expectations
Reprinted with permission of IBM Canada Ltd.

tomer service. Expectations are based on the backgrounds of those participating in the buying process, the information received, perceptions, and satisfaction with past purchases. See Figure 9-10.

Buying Process

Autonomous or joint decision-making is based on product and company buying factors.

During the buying process, a decision as to whether to consider making a purchase is initiated, information gathered, alternative suppliers evaluated, and conflicts among the different representatives of the buyer resolved. The process itself is similar to the final consumer buying process in Figure 8-6.

The buying process may involve autonomous (independent) or joint decisions based on product-specific and company-specific factors. *Product-specific buying factors* include perceived risk, purchase frequency, and time pressure. Autonomous decisions most often occur with low perceived risk, routine products, and high time pressure. Joint ones are more apt to be undertaken when dealing with high perceived risk, seldom-bought products, and low time pressure. *Company-specific buying factors* are an organization's basic orientation, size, and level of decision-making centralization. Autonomous decisions most often occur when the buyer has a high technology or production orientation, is small, or is highly centralized. Joint ones are more likely with a low technology or production orientation, large organization, and little centralization in decision making.

As noted earlier in the chapter, competitive bidding is often used with organizational consumers: Potential sellers specify in writing all terms and conditions of a purchase in addition to the product attributes they offer; the buyer then selects the best bid. With *open bidding*, proposals can be seen by competing sellers. With *closed bidding*, contract terms are kept secret and sellers are asked to make their best presentation in their first bids. Bidding is used in government purchases to avoid charges of bias or unfair negotiations, and bids for government purchases tend to be closed.

Conflict Resolution

Joint decision-making may lead to conflicts due to the diverse backgrounds and perspectives of purchasing agents, engineers, and users. **Conflict resolution** is then needed to make a decision. Four methods of resolution are possible: problem solving, persuasion, bargaining, and politicking.

Problem solving, persuasion, bargaining, and politicking lead to **conflict resolution**.

Problem solving occurs when members of a purchasing team decide to acquire further information before making a decision. This is the best procedure. Persuasion takes place when each member of a team presents his or her reasons why a particular supplier or brand should be selected. In theory, the most logical presentation should be chosen. However, the most dynamic (or powerful) person may persuade others to follow his or her lead.

Under bargaining, team members agree to support each other in different situations, with less attention paid to the merits of a purchase. One member may select the supplier of the current item; in return, another member would choose a vendor the next time. The last, and least desired, method of conflict resolution is politicking. With it, team members try to persuade outside parties and superiors to back their positions, and seek to win at power plays.

Situational Factors

A number of **situational factors** can interrupt the decision process and the actual selection of a supplier or brand. These include "temporary economic conditions such as price controls, recession, or foreign trade; internal strikes, walkouts, machine breakdowns, and other production-related events; organizational changes such as merger or acquisition; and *ad hoc* changes in the marketplace, such as promotional efforts, new-product introduction, price changes, and so on, in the supplier industries."[20]

Situational factors *affect organizational consumer decisions.*

Purchase and Feedback

After the decision process is completed and situational factors are taken into account, a purchase is made (or the process terminated) and a product is used or experienced. The level of satisfaction with a purchase is then fed back to a purchasing agent or team, and the data are stored for future use.

To maintain customer satisfaction and ensure continued purchases, regular service and follow-up calls by sellers are essential. As one study concluded: "Industrial salespeople today are generally younger, better educated, and more professional in their handling of business activities than in the past. That higher level of education is something that both purchasers and sales professionals benefit from. Both sides appear to be more sensitive to the other's responsibilities. Among purchasers and suppliers interested in developing partnerships, it's not unusual to see sales professionals attending purchasing courses, purchasing agents attending sales courses, and even purchasers and suppliers attending seminars together."[21]

Types of Purchases

A **new-task purchase process** is needed for expensive products an organizational consumer has not bought before. A lot of decision making is undertaken, and perceived risk is high. This is similar to extended decision-making for a final consumer. A **modified-rebuy purchase process** is employed for medium-priced products an organizational consumer has bought

Organizational buyers use a **new-task process** *for unique items,* **modified rebuys** *for infrequent purchases, and* **straight rebuys** *for regular purchases.*

---

[20] Ibid., p. 56.
[21] Derrick C. Schnebelt, "Turning the Tables," *Sales & Marketing Management* (January 1993), p. 23.

infrequently before. Moderate decision-making is needed. This type of purchase is similar to limited decision making for a final consumer. A **straight-rebuy purchase process** is used for inexpensive items bought regularly. Reordering, not decision making, is applied because perceived risk is very low. This process is like a routine purchase for a final consumer.

Research on the Organizational Consumer's Decision Process

Throughout the world, the organizational consumer's decision process has been heavily researched. Here are a sampling of the findings:

- There are significant differences in the way that decisions are made by Russian purchasing managers who are 40 years of age or less and those who are over 40. The younger managers see entrepreneurs, flexibility, and autonomy rising; their older counterparts do not.[22]

- Nigerian purchasers of capital equipment rely mostly on salesperson visits and manufacturers' catalogues for information; joint decision-making is used during all stages of the decision process; and dissatisfaction with existing suppliers is a key reason a detailed decision process is triggered.[23]

- Some Eastern European purchasing agents, due to their lack of experience in a free-market economy, are having a tough time adjusting to situations in which they have more autonomy and a greater voice in decisions.[24]

- High-tech purchasing agents are apt to stick with existing suppliers if they feel there would be switching costs and compatibility issues with any changes to new vendors. "Out" vendors have the best opportunity to woo these purchasing agents when technological advances are rapid and decisions are important (causing the agents to be more open in vendor analysis).[25]

Marketing Implications

There are many similarities, as well as differences, between organizational and final consumers.

Although organizational and final consumers have substantial differences (as mentioned earlier), they also have similarities. Both can be described demographically; statistical and descriptive data can be gathered and analyzed. Both have different categories of buyers, each with separate needs and requirements. Both can be defined by using social and psychological factors, such as operating style, buying structure, purchase use, expectations, perceived risk, and conflict resolution. Both use a decision process, employ joint decision-making, and face various kinds of purchase situations.

Industrial marketers must develop plans that reflect the similarities, as well as the differences, between organizational and final consumers. In their roles as sellers, manufacturers and wholesalers may also need two marketing plans—one for intermediate buyers and another for final consumers.

Finally, it must be recognized that purchasing agents or buyers have personal goals, as well as organizational goals. They seek status, approval, promotions, bonuses, and other rewards. And as noted in Figure 9-9, they bring distinct expectations to each buying situation, just as final consumers do.

---

[22] John F. Veiga and John N. Yanouzas, "Emerging Cultural Values Among Russian Managers: What Will Tomorrow Bring?" *Business Horizons*, Vol. 38 (July-August 1995), pp. 20–27.

[23] E. D. Bamgboye, "Equipment Buying in Nigeria," *Industrial Marketing Management*, Vol. 21 (August 1992), pp. 181–185.

[24] Johan Roos, Ellen Veie, and Lawrence S. Welch, "A Case Study of Equipment Purchasing in Czechoslovakia," *Industrial Marketing Management*, Vol. 21 (August 1922), pp. 257–263; and Dale A. Lunsford and Bradley C. Fussell, "Marketing Business Services in Central Europe," *Journal of Services Marketing*, Vol. 7 (Number 1, 1993), pp. 13–21.

[25] Jan B. Heide and Allen M. Weiss, "Vendor Consideration and Switching Behaviour for Buyers in High-Technology Markets," *Journal of Marketing*, Vol. 59 (July 1995), pp. 30–43.

Ethics AND TODAY'S MARKETER

Is Environmental Impact an Issue for Purchasing Agents?

How important is social responsibility—a concern for the environmental impact associated with an industrial good or service—to purchasing managers? According to one study, organizations can be placed into four categories:

- *Type I (Founder's Ideals)*—Social responsibility is an extension of the founder's ideals and values. A social mission for such firms is clearly articulated. This mission often acts as a second "bottom line" by which the firm would be evaluated. For example, "What we're trying to do is to suspend the standard rules in purchasing, which are to get the job done as quickly as possible and as cheaply as possible."
- *Type II (Symbolism)*—Socially-responsible buying is indirectly tied to company success. Firms in this group want to discourage further government regulation. For example, "Now that we buy socially responsible products, people perceive us as green. This is important in getting the company name to where we want it to be."
- *Type III (Opportune)*—Socially responsible purchasing is seen as a way to lower costs or to increase sales. In one such firm, the purchase of a socially responsible product reduced costs by 70 per cent. Thus, "We do not buy socially irresponsible products, but it isn't as you say for a moral reason. It's for hassle avoidance more than anything else."
- *Type IV (Restraint)*—There is no deliberate plan as to socially responsible purchasing. And there are negligible "bottom-line" benefits to buying socially-responsible products. For example, "If a supplier that we've worked with for twenty years before all the environmental concerns came up didn't share our views, it was hard. I feel much more like an extension of the supplier."

As a product manager for recycled paper, how would you use the preceding typology in marketing to book publishers?

Source: Based on material in Minette E. Drumwight, "Socially Responsible Organizational Buying: Environmental Concern as a Noneconomic Buying Criterion," *Journal of Marketing*, Vol. 58 (July 1994), pp. 1–9.

One leading consultant offers these suggestions for industrial marketers:

- Understand how your customers run their business.
- Show how your good or service fits into your customer's business.
- Make sure the benefits you sell stay current.
- Know how customers buy and fit your selling to their buying process.
- When selling, reach everyone on the customer's side involved in the buying decision.
- Communicate to each decider the message that will address his or her chief concerns.
- Be the person or firm with whom your customers prefer to have a relationship.
- Be sure everything you do is consistent with your chosen level of quality, service, price, and performance.
- Understand your competitors' strengths and weaknesses.
- Strive to dominate your niche.

Industrial marketing strategies should be insightful.

- Train your people in each aspect of your business and your customers'.
- Have a distribution system that meets your needs and your customers'.
- Seek new markets and new applications for your existing products.
- Enhance your products with customer service.
- Have your goals clearly in mind.[26]

MARKETING IN A CHANGING WORLD

The Quest for Purchasing Partnerships[27]

In an era when so many purchasing companies are cutting down on the number of suppliers from which they will buy, industrial marketers must be sure they have a strong appreciation of what makes good "purchasing partnerships"—and they must do so from the buyer's point of view.

Purchasing partnerships are "informal or formal agreements between sellers and buyers, in which buyers receive quality products per customer requirements and sellers become primary suppliers. Through such arrangements, partners are able to plan requirements on a mutually beneficial time schedule with mutually satisfactory pricing."

According to a recent study, organizational consumers want to achieve these specific benefits (in the order listed) from purchasing partnerships: better communication, better prices, better quality products, better delivery schedules, development of trust with suppliers, and better forecasting and planning. With regard to communication, organizational consumers expect that purchasing partnerships will result in "more attention" and vendors who "know our business."

Here's what two study participants remarked:

In business, a relationship is worth a great deal. It is invaluable because the companies can grow together, share information for good planning, and stabilize the pricing environment. We then enter a trust relationship.

Suppliers with ongoing partnerships feel more secure about future business. Consequently, they don't build in contingency costs, and this reduces the cost of our materials. A good working relationship allows for better parts design, standardization, and packaging.

To measure their suppliers' performance, organizational consumers review the quality of the products; on-time delivery; competitive pricing; personnel responsiveness; how well needs, technology, and design are understood; and the ability to resolve problems.

SUMMARY

1. *To introduce the concept of industrial marketing* When firms market goods and services to manufacturers, wholesalers, retailers, and government and other nonprofit institutions, industrial marketing is used.

2. *To differentiate between organizational consumers and final consumers and look at organizational consumers from an international perspective* Organizational consumers buy goods and services for further production, use in operations, or resale to others; they buy installations, raw materials, and semifinished materials. They often buy on the basis of specifications, use joint decision making, apply formal value and vendor analysis, lease equipment, and use bidding and negotiation. Their demand is generally derived from that of their consumers and can be cyclical. They are fewer in number and more geographically

---

[26] F. Michael Hruby, "Seventeen Tips (Not Just) for Industrial Marketers," *Sales & Marketing Management* (May 1990), pp. 68–76.

[27] The material in this section is based on Eugene H. Fram, "Purchasing Partnerships: The Buyer's View," *Marketing Management* (Summer 1995), pp. 49–55.

concentrated. They may employ buying specialists, expect sellers to visit them, require special relationships, and make goods and undertake services rather than buy them.

There are distinctions among organizational consumers around the globe.

3. *To describe the different types of organizational consumers and their buying objectives, buying structure, and purchase constraints* Organizational consumers may be classified by area of specialization, size and resources, location, and goods and services purchased. The major types of organizational consumers are manufacturers, wholesalers, retailers, government, and nonprofit organizations. The SIC system provides information on organizational consumers in Canada and the rest of the world.

These consumers have general buying goals, such as product availability, seller reliability, consistent quality, prompt delivery, good prices, and superior customer service. They may also have more specific goals, depending on the type of firm involved. An organization's buying structure refers to its level of formality and specialization in the purchase process. Derived demand, availability, further salability, and resources are the leading purchase constraints.

4. *To explain the organizational consumer's decision process* The process involves buyer expectations, the buying process, conflict resolution, and situational factors. Of prime importance is whether an organization uses joint decision making and, if so, how. Some form of bidding may be used with organizational consumers (most often with government).

If conflicts arise in joint decisions, firms may use problem solving, persuasion, bargaining, or politicking to arrive at a resolution. Situational factors can intervene between a decision to buy and an actual purchase. Such factors include strikes, economic conditions, and organizational changes.

New task, modified rebuy, and straight rebuy are the different purchase situations facing organizational consumers.

5. *To consider the marketing implications of appealing to organizational consumers* Organizational consumers and final consumers have many similarities and differences. Industrial marketers must understand them and adapt marketing plans accordingly. Dual marketing campaigns may be necessary for manufacturers and wholesalers that sell to intermediate buyers and have their products resold to final consumers.

Purchasing agents and buyers have personal goals, such as status, promotions, and bonuses; these may have a large impact on decision making.

KEY TERMS

industrial marketing (p. 228)
multiple-buying responsibility (p. 231)
value analysis (p. 231)
vendor analysis (p. 231)
competitive bidding (p. 232)
negotiation (p. 232)
derived demand (p. 232)
accelerator principle (p. 232)

systems selling (p. 233)
reciprocity (p. 234)
Standard Industrial Classification (SIC) (p. 236)
end-use analysis (p. 237)
manufacturers (p. 237)
wholesalers (p. 238)
retailers (p. 240)
government (p. 240)

nonprofit institutions (p. 242)
organizational consumer's decision process (p. 245)
conflict resolution (p. 247)
situational factors (p. 247)
new-task purchase process (p. 247)
modified-rebuy purchase process (p. 247)
straight-rebuy purchase process (p. 247)

Review Questions

1. Describe five of the most important differences between organizational and final consumers.
2. Distinguish between vendor analysis and value analysis.
3. What is the relationship between derived demand and the accelerator principle?
4. How is the Standard Industrial Classification a useful marketing tool?
5. What are the most important general organizational consumer buying objectives?
6. For manufacturers, wholesalers, and retailers, what is the major constraint on their purchase behaviour? Why?
7. On what basis are organizational consumer expectations formed?
8. How do product-specific and company-specific buying factors affect the use of autonomous or joint decision making?
9. Which is the worst form of conflict resolution? The best? Explain your answers.
10. Cite several suggestions that industrial marketers should keep in mind when developing and enacting their strategies.

Discussion Questions

1. As a university's purchasing agent, what would you have to do to get useful competitive bids from suppliers of new dormitory furniture?
2. As a chemical manufacturer's liaison to China, how would you handle the cultural relationships that would be necessary to win over prospective Chinese business clients?
3. A packaging firm knows its current sales are allocated as follows: 15 per cent to wine manufacturers (SIC code 0223), 20 per cent to sugar and chocolate confectionery manufacturing (SIC code 0173), 30 per cent to soft drink manufacturers (SIC code 0211), 25 per cent to tea and coffee processors (SIC code 0174), and 10 per cent to fish and other seafood processing (SIC code 0112). The firm expects next year's industry sales growth in these categories to rise as follows: wine manufacturing, 5 per cent; sugar and chocolate confectionery manufacturing, 2 per cent; soft drinks, 3 per cent; tea and coffee, 0 per cent; and seafood processing, -5 per cent. According to end-use analysis, by how much should the packaging firm's sales increase next year? Explain your answer.
4. Describe a floral arranger's decision process in choosing a transportation firm to use to ship its products to retailers. Does this process entail a new task, modified rebuy, or straight rebuy? Explain your answer.
5. "It must be understood that organizational purchasing agents or buyers have personal as well as company goals." Comment on this statement.

VIDEO CASE

The Downside of Computer Downsizing

Manufacturers of computer systems are performing incredible feats of magic year-in and year-out. Computers are becoming smaller and smaller, cheaper and cheaper, and more and more powerful. It seems new technological marvels are announced on a daily basis and are less costly than ever before. Meanwhile, business people considering the purchase of computer systems are faced with a difficult and complex decision. Which "computer" systems should they recommend to their CEOs to ensure their firm remains productive and competitive? The speed of technological change is so fast and bewildering that computer systems ordered today are seemingly rendered obsolete and inadequate tomorrow. Competition is moving at such a rate that systems are being made obsolete in only eighteen months.

The confusion is not limited to purchasers of computers either. Manufacturers, consultants, and distributors are confused too. In business, time is of the essence and speedy decision making an absolute requirement. Making good decisions depends on having good, up-to-the-minute information. The ability to assess and access such information is directly related to the computer hardware and software at the manager's command. The better the computerized information support system, the better—and quicker—are the firm's decisions, thus conferring a competitive advantage upon the business. Therefore, the capabilities of a firm's computer hardware and software systems, and the ease with which managers can use them, are directly related to firm competitiveness.

However, what is a firm to do when any computer system they purchase will be obsolete in a mere eighteen months? Perhaps the solution is for purchasers to take a hard look at their business and determine what kinds of decisions they must routinely make and what they need to know to make these decisions. Then they will be better able to determine whether their firm needs to have a state-of-the-art system or can manage with a simpler "state-of-need" system.

A lot of purchasing agents worry because once an investment is sunk into a computer system which is becoming obsolete, the costs cannot be recovered. Add the costs of employee training to the hardware and software costs and the importance of the decision becomes even greater. Leasing may seem like a good way out to the purchasing manager, but what about manufacturers and distributors who grant these leases? How can they determine a residual value for equipment that will not only be obsolete but potentially have a higher price tag as used equipment than new equipment? It seems purchasing managers can salve their consciences with a lease, but not their firm's pocketbook. It looks as if computer downsizing has only one side: the down side.

QUESTIONS

1. Relationship marketing is commonly viewed as the way to conduct business-to-business dealings. Discuss how relationship marketing principles could be applied to the marketing of computer systems to businesses.
2. Present a vendor analysis checklist to help a purchasing agent to evaluate competing computer systems.
3. Take a computer supplier's point of view. How would you sell your systems knowing they are likely to become obsolete very rapidly?
4. Consider your own point of view. Discuss how you are dealing with the reality that the computer system you use as a marketing student is either obsolete right now, or will be in about eighteen months!

VIDEO QUESTIONS ON COMPUTER DOWNSIZING

1. Which kind of business person stands to benefit most from the dilemma of computer downsizing and how will they benefit?
2. What kinds of actions might you recommend to computer systems buyers to partially overcome the down side of computer downsizing?

Video Source: "Computer Downsizing," *Venture* (December 5, 1993).

CASE STUDY

Steel and Aluminum: The Battle for Auto Makers' Business

There is a huge battle for market share in auto-manufacturing materials between aluminum and steel makers. The car industry is especially important for steel makers since this industry accounts for as much as one-third of total steel sales for some steel makers.

Steel proponents say that the use of steel results in a safer vehicle since steel (as opposed to aluminum) actually becomes stronger in a crash. Steel is also much less costly than aluminum. For example, a steel hood weighing fifty pounds costs U.S.$17.50 in material costs, while a comparable hood made of aluminum has a material cost of U.S.$35 (even though it weighs only twenty-five pounds). The steel manufacturers are also quick to cite the long-term experience that car makers have had with steel. Lastly, the labour costs in recycling steel are much lower than for aluminum, since scrap steel can be collected with a heavy magnet. The primary benefit to the use of aluminum over steel is in terms of aluminum's weight and ease of forming shapes; aluminum can be extruded while steel must be stamped.

Aluminum has been making significant headway in the auto industry. Since 1980, the proportion of aluminum in an average car has gone from 3.5 per cent to 7 per cent. And in 1995, 15 000 Audi A-8 luxury cars with aluminum frames were sold in Germany. This model was made in partnership with the Aluminum Corporation of America (Alcoa). Honda also sells some aluminum-based cars.

In the near future, the use of aluminum could skyrocket. Ford and Chrysler have created prototype cars made from aluminum. And Ford executives predict that, as of the year 2000, a leading auto maker will begin mass producing an aluminum-based luxury car. In an effort to further increase the inroads made by aluminum, Alcoa recently offered to invest U.S.$1 billion in a partnership with any auto maker willing to produce a high-volume aluminum car.

General Motors, Ford, and Chrysler have joined forces to form the Partnership for a New Generation of Vehicles. This group wants to build a fuel-efficient car (that gets up to eighty miles a gallon) that is priced at a comparable level to existing autos. Failing this, the development of non-fossil fuel burning electrical cars for the California market is a further impetus for weight savings, because the less energy required to move these cars means less recharging time. In addition, the group wants to reduce vehicle weight as a means of increasing fuel efficiency. Currently, 55 per cent of the overall weight of the average car is comprised of steel.

The steel industry is not taking aluminum's initiatives lying down. Steel makers are well aware of their loss in market share in the beverage can market over the past twenty years—as aluminum rapidly replaced steel in containers—and this market is currently worth U.S.$5 billion per year.

According to a Chrysler purchasing executive, "Steel has changed more in the last five years than in the last twenty-five years. You can get more strength with lighter kinds of steel." Unlike the aluminum industry, where each company has developed its own production technologies, thirty-one steel makers from around the world are combining to finance new research. One goal is to make a lighter variation of steel that is still strong enough to be dent-resistant.

Both the steel and aluminum industries are concerned about the increasing use of plastics and composites (such as mixtures of carbon fibre) that are being used by car makers. Plastics are currently not strong enough for car bodies and composites are very costly. But, due to engineering advances, it is expected that their use in cars will rise dramatically in the near future.

QUESTIONS

1. Use value analysis to compare aluminum and steel for use in car frames.
2. Describe the importance of derived demand in the sale of steel and aluminum to the auto industry.
3. What other organizational consumers—besides auto makers—should steel firms address? How?
4. What organizational buying objectives should steel makers concentrate on fulfilling? Why?

FORD
www.ford.com/

Source: The data in this case are drawn from Erle Norton and Gabriella Stern, "Steel and Aluminum Vie Over Every Ounce in a Car's Construction," *Wall Street Journal* (May 9, 1995), pp. A1, A14.

Chapter 10
Developing a Target Market Strategy

Chapter Objectives

1. To describe the process of planning a target-market strategy

2. To examine alternative demand patterns and segmentation bases for both final and organizational consumers

3. To explain and contrast undifferentiated marketing (mass marketing), concentrated marketing, and differentiated marketing (multiple segmentation)

4. To show the importance of positioning in developing a marketing strategy

5. To discuss sales forecasting and its role in target marketing

{ *"As the world becomes closer due to technological advances in transportation and telecommunications, and with multinational companies expanding worldwide, increasingly there is a great interest in whether individuals in different parts of the world are more alike than different,"* says Thomas A. W. Miller, senior vice-president of Roper Starch Worldwide. }

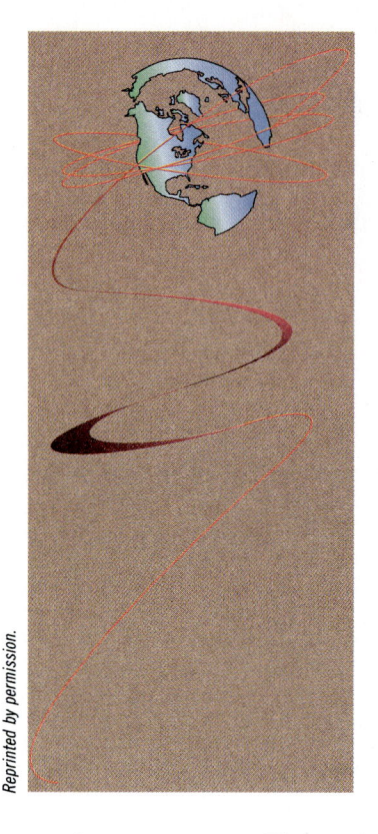

Roper Starch Worldwide (a marketing research firm) recently conducted a series of studies on global trends. In all, it surveyed nearly 40 000 adults. According to this research, four major shopping styles of consumers are found throughout the world: deal makers, price seekers, brand loyalists, and luxury innovators. And the shopping styles of consumers are heavily influenced by where they live.

Let's look at these four consumer segments and their characteristics.

- *Deal makers*—They enjoy the buying process. This is an educated group, with a median age of 32 years and average affluence and employment. Deal makers make up 29 per cent of all consumers.

- *Price seekers*—They place major emphasis on the product. This group has the highest per cent of retirees, the lowest education level, and an average level of affluence. Price seekers constitute 27 per cent of all consumers.

- *Brand loyalists*—They agree that a brand gives good value for the money. This is the least affluent group and is mostly male. Brand loyalists have a median age of 36 and hold average education and employment. They make up 23 per cent of all consumers.

- *Luxury innovators*—They seek brands that are prestigious and new. This is the most affluent and educated group, with the highest proportion of executives and other professionals. Luxury innovators are mostly male and have a median age of 32. They constitute 21 per cent of all consumers.

The above segment percentages are global figures that vary greatly by country. For example, in Mexico, 35 per cent of consumers are deal makers, 23 per cent are price seekers, 20 per cent are luxury innovators, and 19 per cent are brand loyalists. In the United States, 37 per cent of consumers are deal makers, 36 per cent are price seekers, 17 per cent are luxury innovators, and 11 per cent are brand loyalists. In Saudi Arabia, 40 per cent of consumers are deal makers, 34 per cent are luxury innovators, 15 per cent are brand loyalists, and 9 per cent are price seekers. In the Czech Republic, 27 per cent of consumers are price seekers, 26 per cent are luxury innovators, 24 per cent are brand loyalists, and 23 per cent are deal makers. As Thomas Miller notes:

> Price seekers exist more in competitive, developed markets, where shoppers generally cannot haggle or negotiate. Deal makers are more often in developing markets that have less brand competition and a tradition of open-air markets, where the process is half the fun. America straddles the two styles because of our more heterogeneous culture and also because shoppers can bargain at many retail outlets and even large category-killer stores.[1]

In this chapter, we will examine each step involved in planning a target-market strategy and the related topic of sales forecasting. Lifestyle segmentation is only one of the ways in which a company may appeal to a target market.

Overview

After gathering data on consumer traits, desires, and decision making; company and industry attributes; and environmental factors; a firm is ready to select the target market(s) to

---

[1] Kelly Shermach, "Portrait of the World," *Marketing News* (August 28, 1995), pp. 20–21; and Leah Rickard, "Ex-Soviet States Lead World in Ad Cynicism," *Advertising Age* (June 5, 1995), p. 3.

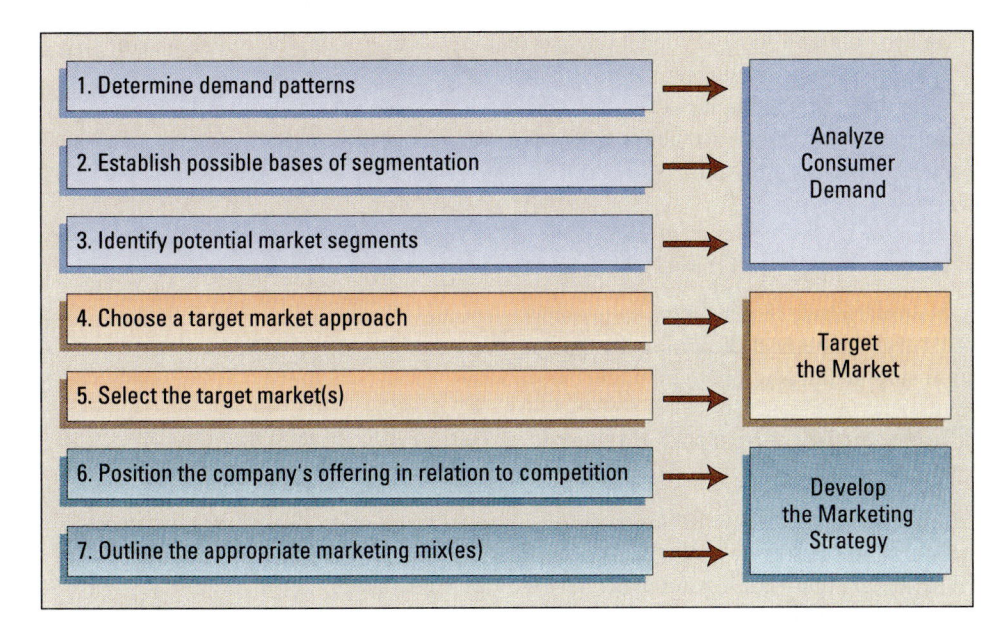

FIGURE 10-1
The Steps in Planning a Target-Market Strategy

1. Determine demand patterns
2. Establish possible bases of segmentation
3. Identify potential market segments
→ Analyze Consumer Demand

4. Choose a target market approach
5. Select the target market(s)
→ Target the Market

6. Position the company's offering in relation to competition
7. Outline the appropriate marketing mix(es)
→ Develop the Marketing Strategy

---

which it will appeal and for which it will develop a suitable strategy. The total **market** for a particular good or service consists of all the people and/or organizations who desire (or potentially desire) that good or service, have sufficient resources to make purchases, and are willing and able to buy. Firms often use **market segmentation**—dividing the market into distinct subsets of customers that behave in the same way or have similar needs. Each subset could possibly be a target market.

Developing a **target-market strategy** consists of three general phases: analyzing consumer demand, targeting the market, and developing the marketing strategy. These phases break down into the seven specific steps shown in Figure 10-1 and described throughout this chapter. First, a firm determines the demand patterns for a given good or service, establishes bases of segmentation, and identifies potential market segments. For example, do prospective consumers have similar or dissimilar needs and desires? What consumer characteristics, desires, and behaviour types can be best used to describe market segments?

Second, a firm chooses its approach and selects its target market(s). It can use undifferentiated marketing (mass marketing)—targeting the whole market with a single basic marketing strategy intended to have mass appeal; concentrated marketing—targeting one well-defined market segment with one tailored marketing strategy; or differentiated marketing (multiple segmentation)—targeting two or more well-defined market segments with a marketing strategy tailored to each segment.[2]

Third, a firm positions its offering relative to competitors and outlines the proper marketing mix(es). Of particular importance here is attaining **product differentiation**, whereby "a product offering is perceived by the consumer to differ from its competition on any physical or nonphysical product characteristic, including price." When differentiation is favourable, it yields a differential advantage. A firm may be able to achieve a key differential advantage by simply emphasizing how its offering satisfies existing consumer desires and needs better than competitors do. However, sometimes, demand patterns may have to be modified for consumers to perceive a firm's product differentiation as worthwhile. Thus, Tylenol is promoted as an alternative to aspirin for persons who cannot take aspirin (appealing to existing consumer needs), whereas Dove is marketed as a nonsoap bar cleanser with moisturizing qualities (modifying consumer perceptions of soap's role). If targeted consumers do not believe that moisturizing is a meaningful product attribute, then they will probably not buy Dove—no matter how much better a job of moisturizing it does com-

*A **market** is all possible consumers for a good or service. Through **market segmentation**, it can be subdivided.*

*In a **target-market strategy**, a firm first studies demand.*

*Targeting approaches are **undifferentiated**, **concentrated**, and **differentiated marketing**.*

*The marketing strategy is then actually developed, with emphasis on **product differentiation**.*

---

[2] Peter D. Bennett (Ed.), *Dictionary of Marketing Terms*, Second Edition (Chicago: American Marketing Association, 1995), p. 166.

pared to competing soaps. Given the fact that Dove is the industry leader, moisturizing is clearly a desirable attribute.[3]

In this chapter, the steps in a target-market strategy are detailed—as they pertain to both final and organizational consumers. Sales forecasting and its role in developing a target-market strategy are also examined.

Analyzing Consumer Demand

The initial phase in planning a target market strategy (analyzing consumer demand) consists of three steps: determining demand patterns, establishing possible bases of segmentation, and identifying potential market segments.

Determining Demand Patterns

Demand patterns show if consumer desires are similar for a good or service. People may demonstrate **homogeneous, clustered,** or **diffused demand**.

A firm must first determine the **demand patterns**—the uniformity or diversity of consumer needs and desires for particular categories of goods and services—it faces in the marketplace. A firm faces one of the three alternative demand patterns shown in Figure 10–2 and described here for each good or service category it markets.

With **homogeneous demand**, consumers have rather uniform needs and desires for a good or service category. A firm's marketing tasks are straightforward—to identify and satisfy the basic needs of consumers in a superior way. For instance, business customers in the express mail-delivery market are most interested in rapid, reliable delivery and reasonable prices. A firm such as United Parcel Service (UPS) appeals to customers by convincing them it is better than competitors in these areas. As competition picks up, firms may try to modify consumer demand patterns so new-product features become desirable and homogeneous demand turns to clustered demand, with only one or a few firms marketing the new features.

UPS
www.ups.com/about/story.html

With **clustered demand**, consumer needs and desires for a good or service category can be divided into two or more clusters (segments), each having distinct purchase criteria. A firm's marketing efforts must be geared toward identifying and satisfying the needs and desires of a particular cluster (or clusters) in a superior way. For example, in the auto market, people can be grouped by their interest in price, car size, performance, styling, handling, sportiness, and other factors. Thus, auto makers offer luxury cars, economy cars, full-sized family cars, high-performance vehicles, and sports cars—each appealing to a particular cluster of consumer needs and desires. Clustered demand is the most prevalent demand pattern.

With **diffused demand**, consumer needs and desires for a good or service category are so diverse that clear clusters (segments) cannot be identified. A firm's marketing efforts are

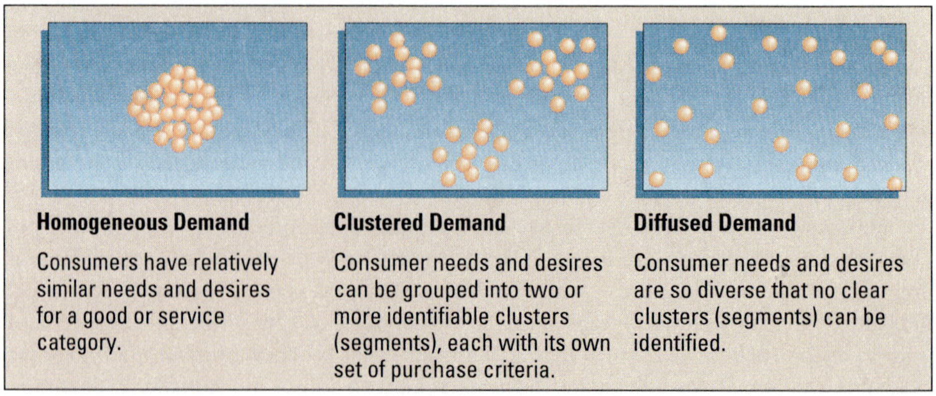

FIGURE 10–2
Alternative Consumer Demand Patterns for a Good or Service Category

Homogeneous Demand	Clustered Demand	Diffused Demand
Consumers have relatively similar needs and desires for a good or service category.	Consumer needs and desires can be grouped into two or more identifiable clusters (segments), each with its own set of purchase criteria.	Consumer needs and desires are so diverse that no clear clusters (segments) can be identified.

---

[3]Peter R. Dickson and James L. Ginter, "Market Segmentation, Product Differentiation, and Marketing Strategy," *Journal of Marketing*, Vol. 51 (April 1987), pp. 1–10; and "Superbrands '96: Category Charts," *Superbrands 1996: Brandweek's Marketers of the Year* (October 6, 1995), p. 129.

complex because product features are harder to communicate and more product versions may be offered. For example, consumers have diverse preferences for lipstick colours; even the same person may desire several colours, to use on different occasions or just for variety. Thus, cosmetics firms offer an array of lipstick colours. It would be nearly impossible for a firm to succeed with one colour or a handful of colours. To make marketing strategies more efficient, firms generally try to modify diffused consumer demand so clusters of at least moderate size appear.

Firms today often try to perform a balancing act with regard to consumer demand patterns. Just as the world marketplace is now getting closer due to more open borders and enhanced communications, there is also more information available on the diversity of the marketplace through customer databases, point-of-sale scanning in supermarkets, and other emerging data-collection techniques. On the one hand, some firms are looking for demand patterns that let them standardize (perhaps even globalize) their marketing mixes as much as possible—to maximize efficiency, generate a well-known image, and use mass media. On the other hand, some companies are searching for demand patterns that let them pinpoint more specific market segments—to better address the consumer needs in those segments.

Establishing Possible Bases of Segmentation

Next, a company studies possible bases for segmenting the market for each of its products or product lines. Some of these are shown in Table 10-1. The firm must decide which of these segmentation bases are most relevant for its particular situation.

Table 10-1
Possible Bases of Segmentation

BASES	EXAMPLES OF POSSIBLE SEGMENTS
Geographic Demographics	
Population (people or organizations)	
Location	Maritimes, Quebec, Ontario, Western Canada; domestic, international
Size	Small, medium, large
Density	Urban, suburban, rural
Transportation network	Mass transit, vehicular, pedestrian
Climate	Warm, cold
Type of commerce	Tourist, local worker, resident; SIC codes
Retail establishments	Downtown shopping district, shopping mall
Media	Local, regional, national
Competition	Underdeveloped, saturated
Growth pattern	Stable, negative, positive
Legislation	Stringent, lax
Cost of living/operations	Low, moderate, high
PERSONAL DEMOGRAPHICS	
A. Final Consumers	
Age	Child, young adult, adult, older adult
Gender	Male, female
Education	Less than high school, high school, college, university
Mobility	Same residence for 2 years, moved in last 2 years
Income	Low, middle, high
Occupation	Blue-collar, white-collar, professional

Table 10-1 (Cont.)

Marital status	Single, married, divorced, widowed
Household size	1, 2, 3, 4, 5, 6, or more
Ethnicity	Anglophone, Francophone, European, Asian

B. Organizational Consumers

Industry designation	SIC codes; end-use analysis
Product use	Further production, use in operations, resale to others
Institutional designation	Manufacturer, wholesaler, retailer, government, nonprofit
Company size	Small, medium, large
Industry growth pattern	Slow, moderate, high
Company growth pattern	Slow, moderate, high
Age of company	New, 5 years old, 10 years old or more
Language used	English, French, Chinese

CONSUMER LIFESTYLES

Social class (final consumers)	Lower-lower to upper-upper
Family life cycle (final consumers)	Bachelor to solitary survivor
Buying structure	Informal to formal, autonomous to joint
Usage rate	Light, medium, heavy
Usage experience	None, some, extensive
Brand loyalty	None, some, total
Personality	Introverted-extroverted, persuasible-nonpersuasible
Attitudes	Neutral, positive, negative
Class consciousness	Inner-directed, outer-directed
Motives	Benefit segmentation
Perceived risk	Low, moderate, high
Innovativeness	Innovator, laggard
Opinion leadership	None, some, a lot
Importance of purchase	Little, a great deal

Geographic demographics describe towns, cities, provinces, regions, and countries.

GEOGRAPHIC DEMOGRAPHICS Geographic demographics are basic identifiable characteristics of towns, cities, provinces or states, regions, and countries. A company may use one or a combination of the geographic demographics cited in Table 10-1 to describe its final or organizational consumers.

A segmentation strategy could be geared to geographic differences. For example, Japanese mail-order shoppers spend twice as much per order as their North American counterparts. Per-capita chocolate consumption in Western Europe is two to four times that in Canada and the United States; and per-capita consumption of bottled water in Italy is seven times that in Canada and the United States. Germans want laundry detergents that are gentle on rivers, and will pay a premium for them; Greeks want small packages to keep down the cost per store visit. Less than 5 per cent of all the life insurance sold in the world is bought by people in Africa and Latin America. Canada and Mexico account for over one-half of steel-mill products exported by U.S. firms. Among Canada's twenty-five Census Metropolitan Areas (CMAs), annual per-household expenditures on food are highest in Toronto, Ontario ($6457) and lowest in Saskatoon, Saskatchewan ($4348); annual household expenditures on furnishings are highest in Edmonton, Alberta at $1562 compared to only $1032 in Winnipeg, Manitoba; the best-dressed Canadians appear to be in Thunder Bay, Ontario where annual household expenditures on clothing were $2637, while the people in Saskatoon, Saskatchewan were most likely to make the worst-dressed list with expenditures of only $1780; those well-dressed people in Thunder Bay, Ontario are also voracious readers, spending $338 on reading material, while another hotbed of

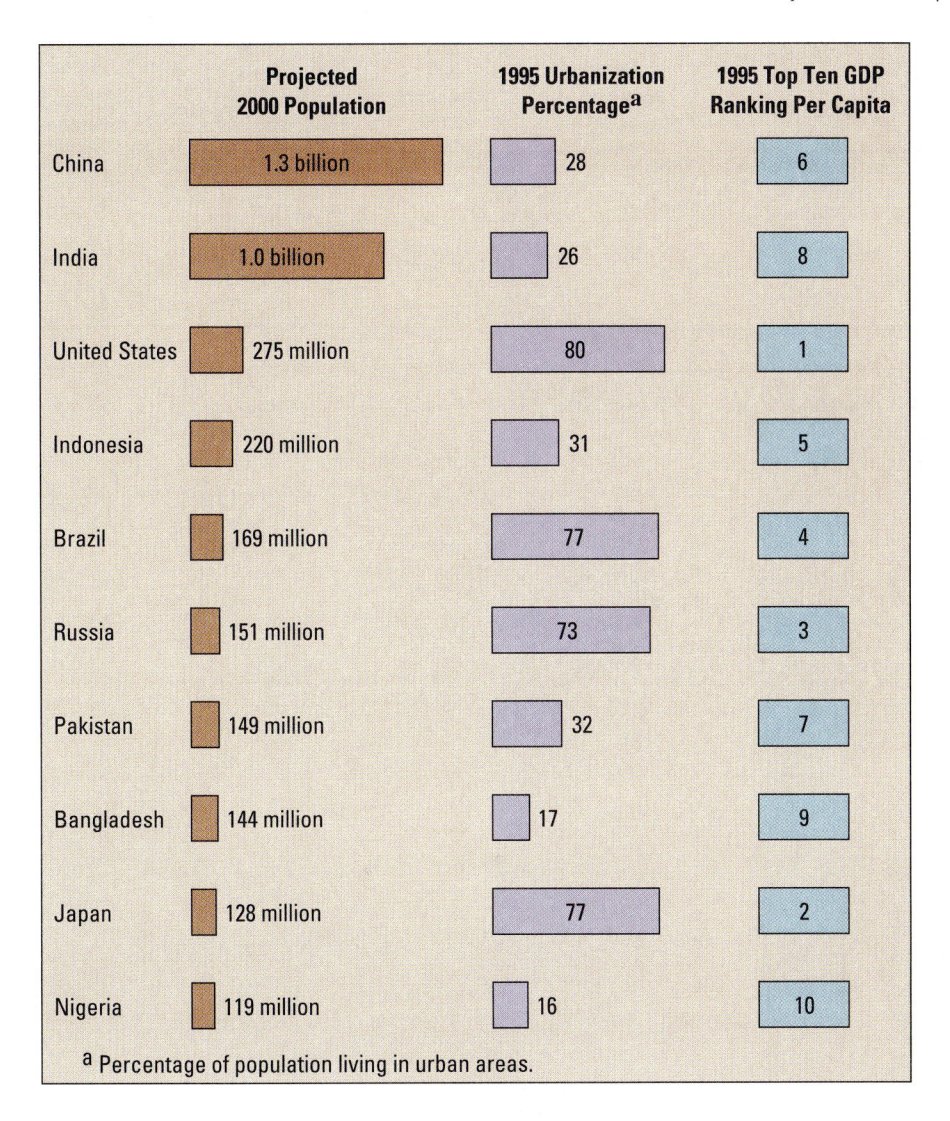

Country	Projected 2000 Population	1995 Urbanization Percentage[a]	1995 Top Ten GDP Ranking Per Capita
China	1.3 billion	28	6
India	1.0 billion	26	8
United States	275 million	80	1
Indonesia	220 million	31	5
Brazil	169 million	77	4
Russia	151 million	73	3
Pakistan	149 million	32	7
Bangladesh	144 million	17	9
Japan	128 million	77	2
Nigeria	119 million	16	10

[a] Percentage of population living in urban areas.

FIGURE 10-3
Comparing the Ten Most Populated Countries in the World
Sources: Compiled by the authors from the U.S. Bureau of the Census, International Database.

readers can be found in Ottawa-Hull where household expenditures are $309 annually; as for consuming hedonistic products, annual expenditures on tobacco and alcohol are highest in Halifax, Nova Scotia ($1751) while the people of Saskatoon spend the least with only $1131 annual household expenditures on these products.[4]

Figure 10-3 indicates the population size, urbanization, and per-capita GDP ranking of the ten most populated nations of the world. Figure 10-4 shows a demographic map of Canada.

PERSONAL DEMOGRAPHICS Personal demographics are basic identifiable characteristics of individual final consumers and organizational consumers and of groups of final consumers and organizational consumers. They are often used as a segmentation base because groups of people or organizations with similar demographics may have similar needs and desires that are distinct from those with different backgrounds. Personal demographics may be viewed singly or in combinations.

Personal demographics *describe people and organizations. They should be used in studying final and organizational consumers.*

---

[4] Sheryl WuDunn, "Japanese Do Buy American: By Mail and a Lot Cheaper," *New York Times* (July 3, 1995), pp. 1, 43; "Who Has the Sweetest Tooth?" *Advertising Age* (July 17, 1995), p. I-3; "Data Watch," *Advertising Age* (February 15, 1993), p. I-22; E. S. Browning, "In Pursuit of the Elusive Euroconsumer," *Wall Street Journal* (April 23, 1992), p. B1; "U.S. Share of Worldwide Insurance Market in Decline," *National Underwriter* (October 5, 1992), pp. 41–43; Marcia Mogelonsky, "America's Hottest Markets," *American Demographics* (January 1996), pp. 20–31; "1995 Survey of Buying Power," *Sales & Marketing Management* (1995), various pages; and Statistics Canada, *Market Research Handbook 1995*, (Ottawa: Minister of Industry Science and Technology), pp. 243–473.

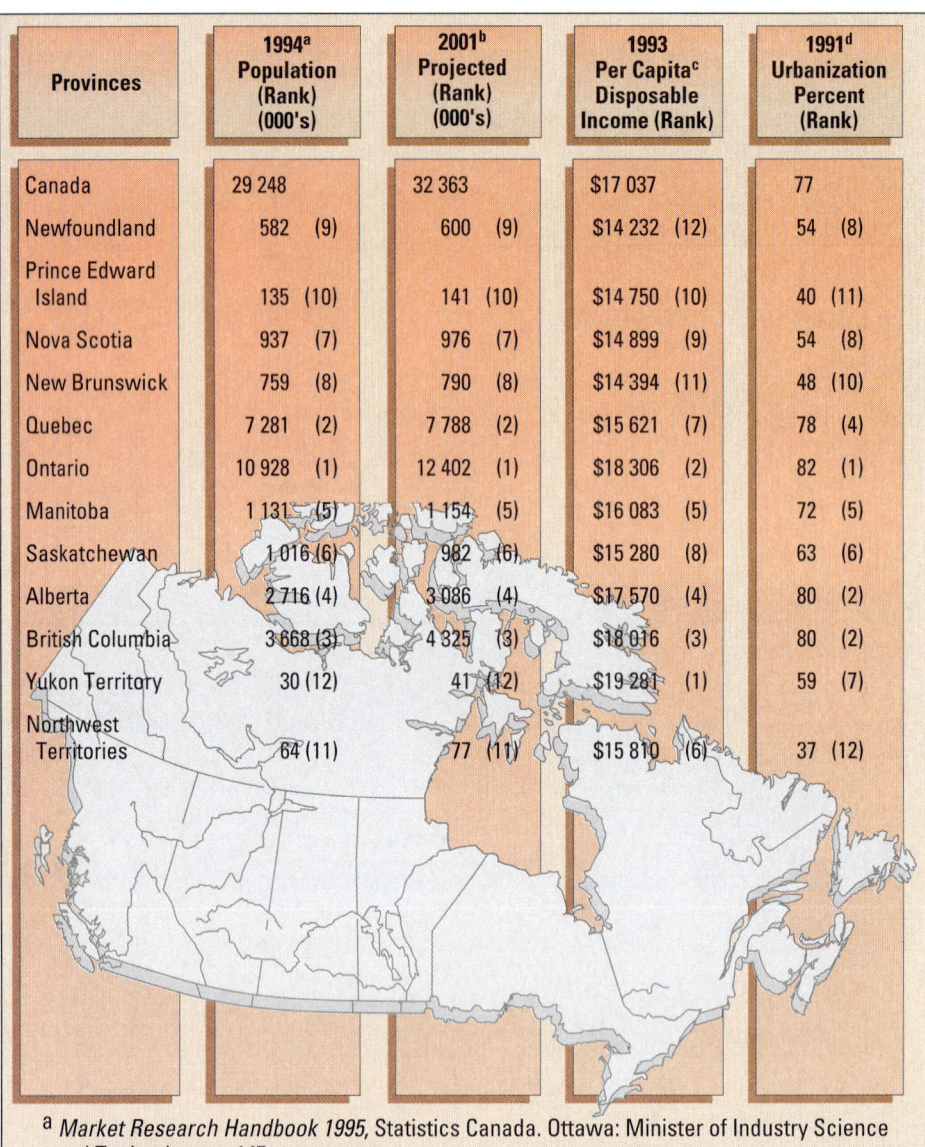

Provinces	1994[a] Population (Rank) (000's)	2001[b] Projected (Rank) (000's)	1993 Per Capita[c] Disposable Income (Rank)	1991[d] Urbanization Percent (Rank)
Canada	29 248	32 363	$17 037	77
Newfoundland	582 (9)	600 (9)	$14 232 (12)	54 (8)
Prince Edward Island	135 (10)	141 (10)	$14 750 (10)	40 (11)
Nova Scotia	937 (7)	976 (7)	$14 899 (9)	54 (8)
New Brunswick	759 (8)	790 (8)	$14 394 (11)	48 (10)
Quebec	7 281 (2)	7 788 (2)	$15 621 (7)	78 (4)
Ontario	10 928 (1)	12 402 (1)	$18 306 (2)	82 (1)
Manitoba	1 131 (5)	1 154 (5)	$16 083 (5)	72 (5)
Saskatchewan	1 016 (6)	982 (6)	$15 280 (8)	63 (6)
Alberta	2 716 (4)	3 086 (4)	$17 570 (4)	80 (2)
British Columbia	3 668 (3)	4 325 (3)	$18 016 (3)	80 (2)
Yukon Territory	30 (12)	41 (12)	$19 281 (1)	59 (7)
Northwest Territories	64 (11)	77 (11)	$15 810 (6)	37 (12)

[a] *Market Research Handbook 1995*, Statistics Canada. Ottawa: Minister of Industry Science and Technology, p. 147.

[b] *Market Research Handbook 1995*, Statistics Canada. Ottawa: Minister of Industry Science and Technology, p. 577 (Projection 3).

[c] *Market Research Handbook 1995*, Statistics Canada. Ottawa: Minister of Industry Science and Technology, p. 187.

[d] *Market Research Handbook 1995*, Statistics Canada. Ottawa: Minister of Industry Science and Technology, p. 152.

FIGURE 10–4
Demographic Map of Canada

Final Consumers As noted in Table 10-1, several personal demographics for final consumers may be used in planning a segmentation strategy.

Applications of personal demographic segmentation are plentiful. In Latin America, 14 per cent of all urban households are headed by an "emerging professional elite," people with professional and executive professions. More than one-half of this group is university educated. The "emerging professional elite" represents a strong market for major appliances, credit card services, consumer electronics, and cars.[5]

---

[5] Jeffrey D. Zbar, "Gallup Offers New Take on Latin America," *Advertising Age* (November 13, 1995), p. 21.

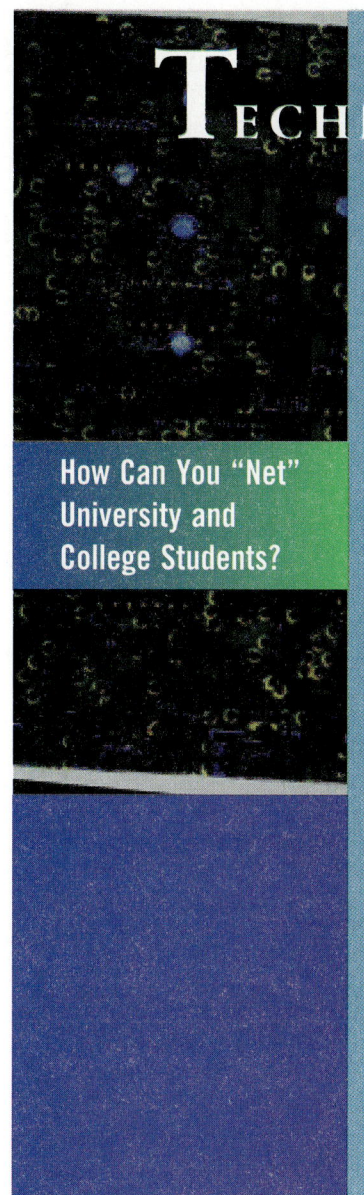

TECHNOLOGY & MARKETING

How Can You "Net" University and College Students?

The Internet is a particularly effective medium for providing information and promotions targeting university and college students. Unlike other populations, a very large proportion of students are computer literate. And currently more than 35 per cent of full-time university and college students own PCs. At many American universities, such as the University of Wisconsin-Madison, students can access the Internet directly from their dormitory rooms simply by hooking up their PC to a special phone jack. Students at York University's Calumet College residence in Toronto are part of a trial project called Intercom Ontario, which involves direct network communications including Internet access for an entire community. The students will have access to Apple computers in the common areas of the residence as well as have hand-held remote-control Newton Message Pads to tap into the World Wide Web. Intercom is specifically interested in measuring actual levels of usage (particularly among students). Before expanding and pricing their services, Intercom might well refer to a survey by Roper College Track, which shows that Internet use among college students doubled between 1994 and 1995 alone.

One important Internet site aimed at the university market is *Link* magazine's *Digital Campus*. Introduced in fall 1995, *Digital Campus* already has a circulation of one million plus. *Digital Campus* shows a rendering of a university campus—complete with a library, a bookstore, a student union, and an athletic stadium. Each building in the *Digital Campus* represents an information and service site. For example, students who browse through the bookstore can view flight schedules for Northwest Airlines, apply for an AT&T Universal credit card, order Paco Rabanne men's fragrance, and request free samples of many products.

By clicking on the "Specialized Bicycles" icon in the bookstore, students can enter a sweepstakes to win an $800 RockHopper bike, download a screen saver for their computer, and correspond with the manufacturer (via e-mail) about mountain biking. Students can even use a ZIP code-based locator service that lists the nearest authorized Specialized Bicycles' dealer. Specialized Bicycles' marketing director say this about *Digital Campus*, "If you want to play the game, you've got to speak the language."

As the promotion manager for a magazine subscription service, assess the pros and cons of using *Digital Campus* as a vehicle for reaching the university market.

Source: Based on material in "Hot Wiring the College Crowd," *Promo* (July 1995), pp. 62–63; and Saul Chernos, "Intercom tries to figure what consumers really want," *Marketing Magazine*, (April 24, 1995), p. 18.

In Canada, the United States and other western nations, Clairol and many other companies are now placing greater emphasis on wooing consumers in the early stages of middle age. This group is quite large and particularly interested in slowing the aging process. See Figure 10-5.

Procter & Gamble marketed specially designed Luvs Deluxe Diapers for Boys and Luvs Deluxe Diapers for Girls. Radio Station EZ Rock FM 97.3 in Toronto, Ontario is targeting the 329 000 women 35-44 (8.5 per cent of the population) who live in the area.[6]

At "A Buck or Two," a discount store chain, value-conscious consumers are attracted by low prices: many items are $5 or less. The firm locates in mall locations, sells many irregulars and factory overruns, and has few employees in each store. In contrast, American Express attracts upper-income consumers with its platinum card. These consumers pay an

---

[6]Maria Mallory, Dan McGraw, Jill Jordan Siedler, and David Fischer, "Women on a Fast Track," *U.S. News & World Report* (November 6, 1995), pp. 60–72; and Jim McElgunn, "Where the Girls Are," *Marketing Magazine* (February 26, 1996), pp. 11–12.

264 Part 3 *Consumer Analysis: Understanding and Responding to Diversity in the Marketplace*

FIGURE 10–5
Wooing Consumers in Early Middle Age
Reprinted by permission.

annual fee of a few hundred dollars and charge tens of thousands of dollars per year; in return, they get special services (such as a worldwide valet service to help them shop, plan trips, and so on) and a high credit line.

There are approximately 600 000 Chinese in Canada and the market is expected to grow to 1.3 million by 2001. This segment represents a lot of buying power with personal income of $27 675 compared to $24 329 for an average Canadian. Marketers have responded with specialized goods and services—including the Toronto Dominion Bank's Chinese information phone lines and *Maclean's* Magazine Chinese edition.[7]

Organizational Consumers Table 10-1 also shows several personal demographics for organizational consumers that may be used in planning a segmentation strategy.

The easiest way to segment organizational consumers is by their industry designation. As an illustration, if a firm studies the information-services industry, it would learn it has over 26 000 North American businesses, with a total of one million employees, and that global information-services revenues are divided as follows: North America, 48 per cent; Europe, 33 per cent; Asia/Pacific, 17 per cent; Latin America, 1.5 per cent; and Middle East/Africa, 0.5 per cent. The businesses offer electronic information, systems integration, data processing, network services, programming, and consulting and training.[8]

---

[7]James Pollock, "Opening Doors of Opportunity," *Marketing Magazine* (September 18, 1995), p. 17–18; James Pollock, "A Burgeoning Segment," *Marketing Magazine*, (September 18, 1995) p. 18; and James Pollock, "Nailing the Niche," *Marketing Magazine* (September 18, 1995), p. 20.

To access potential organizational consumers by institutional type, some sellers rely on trade directories—such as the *Canadian Trade Index* with 15 000 Canadian manufacturers, *Hoover's Masterlist of Major Latin American Companies* with 1250 businesses, *ABC Europ Production* with 100 000 European manufacturers, and *Scott's Directories* with 53 800 Canadian manufacturers. Mailing lists of organizational consumers are also available. *Canadian Business Information* lists 1.08 million Canadian businesses, including 21 883 big businesses (more than fifty employees), 1 028 079 small businesses (less than fifty employees), 144 657 professionals, and 75 847 business services. And American Business Lists' U.S. lists cite hundreds of thousands of manufacturers and wholesalers, over one million retailers, one million professional service businesses, and 450 000 membership organizations.

Organizational consumers may be divided into small, medium, and large categories. Some companies prosper by marketing goods and services to smaller customers, while others focus on medium and/or large accounts. For example, Panasonic has a line of inexpensive fax machines for small customers that cost a few hundred dollars, while Pitney Bowes markets fax machines that cost up to $5000 and can handle 1200 pages of text and store 1000 phone numbers. In Canada 97.9 per cent of business locations have under 50 employees, 2 per cent have 50 to 499 employees, and 0.1 per cent have 500 or more employees. Fifty per cent of Canadian business locations have annual revenues of less than $500 000, 18 per cent have annual revenues between $500 000 and $999 999, 22 per cent have annual revenues of $1 million or more and the revenues for the remaining ten per cent are unknown.[9]

Growth patterns in various industries may give an indication of a firm's future success in marketing to businesses in those industries and provide a good segmentation base. According to the International Trade Administration of the U.S. Department of Commerce, which makes forecasts for North American industries, electronic information services, health services, pre-recorded music, semiconductors, and surgical and medical instruments are fast-growing industries. Aircraft, paper industries machinery, personal leather goods, farm machinery, and newspapers are slow-growing industries.

CONSUMER LIFESTYLES Lifestyles are the ways in which people live and spend time and money; and many lifestyle factors can be applied to both final and organizational consumers. Table 10–1 listed a number of lifestyle segmentation bases; except where indicated, these factors are relevant when segmenting either final or organizational consumer markets.

Final consumers may be segmented by social class and stage in the family life cycle. In North America, the posh Four Seasons hotel chain appeals to upper-middle-class and upper-class guests with luxurious accommodations, whereas the Choice Hotels (formerly Journey's End) chain appeals to middle-class and lower-middle-class consumers with reasonable rates and limited services (such as no restaurant). To attract families with children, various Club Med resorts have day-camp programs.

Final- and organizational-consumer market segments may be based on their usage rate—the amount of a product they consume. People or organizations can use very little, some, or a great deal. A **heavy-usage segment** (at times known as the **heavy half**) is a consumer group that accounts for a large proportion of a good's or service's sales relative to the size of the market. For instance, women buy 85 per cent of all greeting cards. Heavy yogurt consumers eat nearly double the amount consumed by average yogurt consumers. Manufacturers, wholesalers, and retailers account for over 90 per cent of all equipment leasing, while government and nonprofit organizations make less than 10 per cent of equipment leases.[10] Sometimes, a heavy-usage segment may be attractive because of the volume it consumes; other times, the competition for consumers in that segment may make other opportunities more attractive.

Final-consumer and organizational-consumer segments each can be described on the basis of lifestyle factors.

CLUB MED
www.world.net/clubmed/welcome.html

A **heavy-usage segment** *has a rather large share of sales.*

---

[8] *U.S. Industrial Outlook 1994* (Washington, D.C.: U.S. Department of Commerce, 1994), pp. 25-1–25-8.
[9] *Statistical Abstract of the United States 1995* (Washington, D.C.: U.S. Department of Commerce, 1995), various pages; Karen Maru File, "Is There a Trillion-Dollar Family Business Market?" *Industrial Marketing Management*, Vol. 24 (August 1995), pp. 247–255; and "A Catalogue of Sales Leads," *Canadian Business Information* (March 1996), pp. 24–29.

FIGURE 10-6
Applying Benefit Segmentation to Office Furniture
The ad on the left targets people who are interested in comfort, while the one on the right targets people who are attracted to environmentally-friendly products.
Reprinted by permission.

Benefit segmentation *groups consumers based on their reasons for using products.*

Consumer motives may be used to establish benefit segments. **Benefit segmentation** groups people into segments on the basis of the different benefits they seek from a product. It was first popularized in the late 1960s when Russell Haley divided the toothpaste market into four segments: sensory—people wanting flavour and product appearance; sociable—people wanting bright teeth; worrier—people wanting decay prevention; and independent—people wanting low prices. Since then, benefit segmentation has been applied in many final and organizational consumer settings[11] Figure 10-6 shows how benefit segmentation is used to market office furniture.

BLENDING DEMOGRAPHIC AND LIFESTYLE FACTORS It is generally advisable to use a mix of demographic and lifestyle factors to set up possible bases of segmentation. A better analysis then takes place. Two broad classification systems are the **VALS (Values and Lifestyles) program**, which divides final consumers into lifestyle categories; and the **Social Styles model**, which divides the personnel representing organizational consumers into lifestyle categories.

VALS *and the* **Social Styles model** *describe market segments in terms of a broad range of factors.*

In North America, the current VALS 2 typology, shown in Figure 10-7, seeks to explain why and how people make purchase decisions, and places them into segments based on self-orientation and resources. Principle-oriented people are guided by their beliefs; status-oriented people are influenced by others; and action-oriented people are guided by a desire for activity, variety, and risk-taking. People's resources include their education, income, self-confidence, health, eagerness to buy, intelligence, and energy level; and resources rise from youth to middle age and fall with old age. Here are descriptions of

---

[10]Gerri Hirshey, "Happy [ ] Day to You," *New York Times Magazine* (July 2, 1995), p. 27; Henry Assael and David F. Poltrack, "Can Demographic Profiles of Heavy Users Serve as a Surrogate for Purchase Behavior in Selecting TV Programs?" *Journal of Advertising Research*, Vol. 34 (January-February 1994), pp. 11–17; "Brewing Up a Storm," *Advertising Age* (May 15, 1995), pp. 1–3; *Statistical Abstract of the United States 1995*, various pages; and *U.S. Industrial Outlook 1994*, various pages.

[11]Russell I. Haley, "Benefit Segmentation: A Decision-Oriented Research Tool," *Journal of Marketing*, Vol. 32 (July 1968), pp. 30–35; Russell I. Haley, "Benefit Segments: Backwards and Forwards," *Journal of Advertising Research*, Vol. 24 (February–March 1984), pp. 19–25; James W. Harvey, "Benefit Segmentation for Fund Raisers," *Journal of the Academy of Marketing Science*, Vol. 18 (Winter 1990), pp. 77–86; P. J. O'Connor and Gary L. Sullivan, "Market Segmentation: A Comparison of Benefits/Attributes Desired and Brand Preference," *Psychology & Marketing*, Vol. 12 (October 1995), pp. 613–635; and Chatrathi P. Rao and Zhengyuan Wang, "Evaluating Alternative Segmentation Strategies in Standard Industrial Markets," *European Journal of Marketing*, Vol. 29 (Number 2, 1995), pp. 58–75.

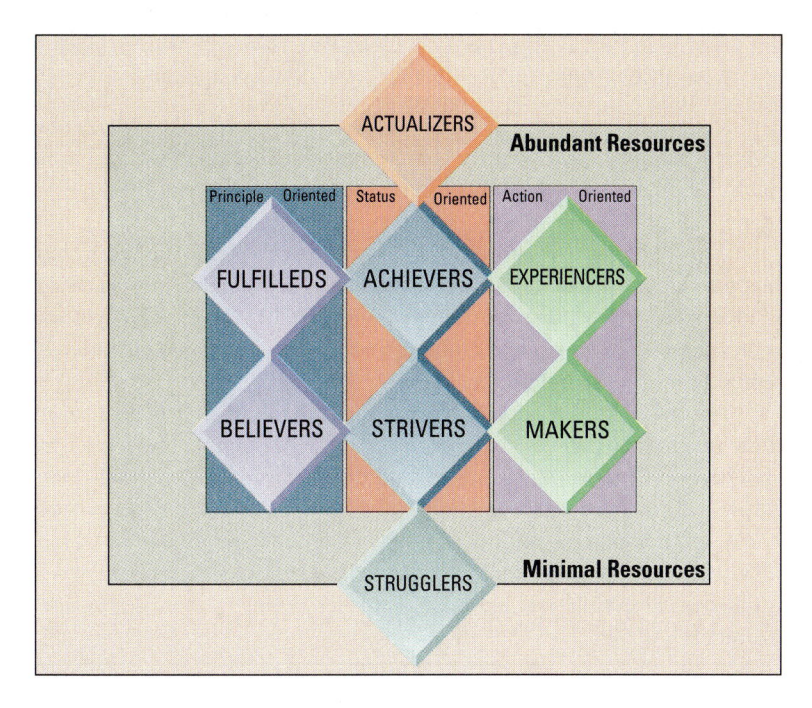

FIGURE 10-7
The VALS 2 Network
Reprinted by permission of SRI International, Menlo Park, California.

the basic VALS 2 segments (in terms of adult characteristics):

- *Actualizers*—Highest resources. Successful, sophisticated. Can indulge in any self-orientations. Have a taste for the finer things in life. Comprise 8 per cent of population. Ninety-five per cent have at least some university education. Median age of 43.
- *Fulfilleds*—Principle-oriented, abundant resources. Mature, satisfied, comfortable, and reflective. Mostly professional and well educated. As consumers, concerned with functionality, value, and durability. Comprise 11 per cent of population. Eighty-one per cent have at least some university education. Median age of 48.
- *Believers*—Principle-oriented, lower resources. Follow routines organized around homes, families, and social or religious organizations. Want domestic products and known brands. Resources sufficient for needs. Comprise 16 per cent of population. Six per cent have at least some university education. Median age of 58.
- *Achievers*—Status-oriented, second-highest resources. Committed to jobs and families, and satisfied with them. Like to be in control. Favour established products that demonstrate their success to peers. Comprise 13 per cent of population. Seventy-seven per cent have at least some university education. Median age of 36.
- *Strivers*—Status-oriented, lower resources. Values similar to achievers but fewer resources. Unsure of themselves. Concerned about approval from others. Most-desired goods and services generally beyond reach. Comprise 13 per cent of population. Twenty-three per cent have at least some university education. Median age of 34.
- *Experiencers*—Action-oriented, acquiring resources. Young, enthusiastic, and rebellious. Seek variety and excitement. Spend much of income on clothing, fast food, music, movies, and videos. Comprise 12 per cent of population. Forty-one per cent have at least some university education. Median age of 26.
- *Makers*—Action-oriented, lower resources. Live in a traditional context of family, work, and physical recreation. Unimpressed by possessions. Like do-it-yourself projects. Comprise 13 per cent of population. Twenty-four per cent have at least some university education. Median age of 30.
- *Strugglers*—Lowest resources (too few to include in any self-orientation). Chronically poor, ill-educated, older, and low in skills. Concerned about health, safety, and secu-

268 Part 3 *Consumer Analysis: Understanding and Responding to Diversity in the Marketplace*

rity. Brand loyal and cautious. Comprise 14 per cent of population. Three per cent have at least some university education. Median age of 61.[12]

In conjunction with SRI International (VALS' developer), Market Statistics has devised a high-tech way to use the VALS 2 model—called GeoVALS. Through GeoVALS, the eight VALS 2 market segments can be broken down by metropolitan area, city, and postal code.[13]

The VALS system is so popular that it is also being applied in Japan, and tailored to people there. For example, ryoshiki ("socially intelligent") innovators are career-oriented, middle-aged innovators; ryoshiki adapters are shy and look to ryoshiki innovators; tradition adapters are young and affluent; and low pragmatic are attitudinally negative and oriented to inexpensive products.[14]

According to the Social Styles model, highlighted in Figure 10-8, social styles affect how people react to various stimuli on and off the job. This model looks at two traits—assertiveness and responsiveness—and divides organizational personnel into "analyticals," "drivers," "amiables," and "expressives." Assertiveness is the degree to which a person states views with assurance, confidence, and force, and the extent to which he or she tries to direct others' actions. Responsiveness is the extent to which a person is affected by appeals, influence, or stimulation and how his or her feelings, emotions, or impressions are shown to others:

- *Analyticals*—Low in both assertiveness and responsiveness. Like facts and details. Money- and numbers-oriented. Work well alone. Stay under control. Interested in processes. Risk avoiders.
- *Expressives*—High in both assertiveness and responsiveness. Personality opposites of analyticals. Use hunches to make decisions. Need to be with people. Focus on gener-

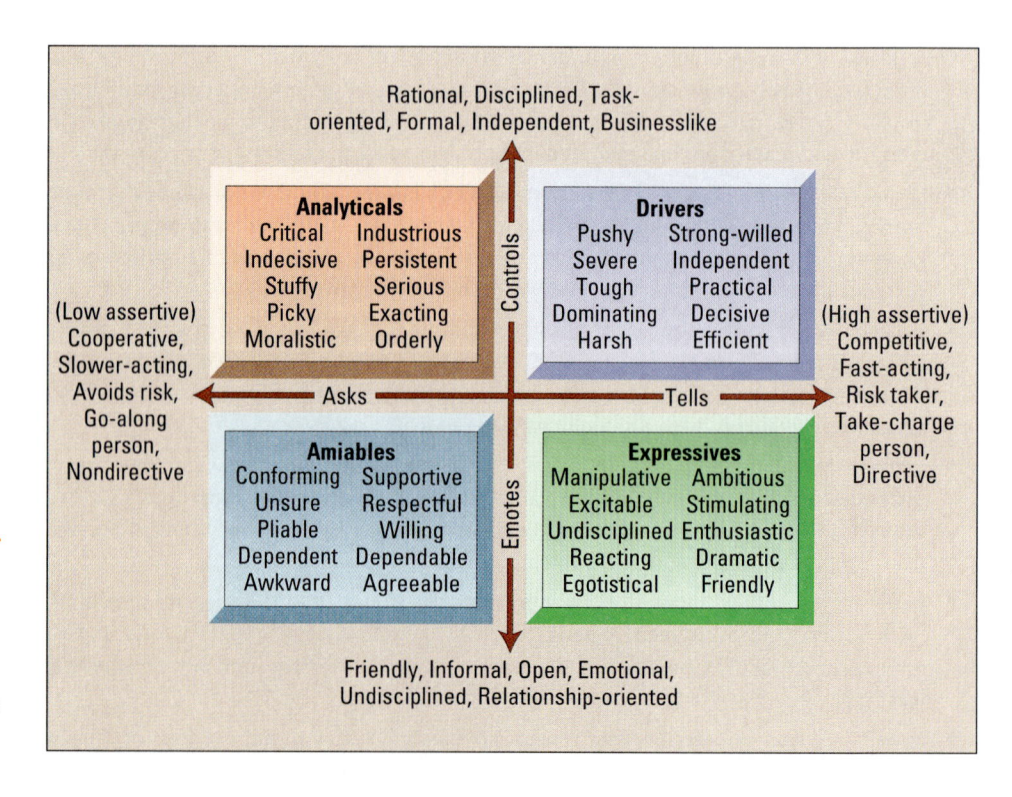

FIGURE 10–8
The Social Styles Model for Organizational Consumers

Sources: Wilson Learning Corporation and Tracom Corporation. Reprinted by permission of Crain Communications Inc., from Tom Eisenhart, "How to Really Excite Your Prospects," *Business Marketing* (July 1988).

Rational, Disciplined, Task-oriented, Formal, Independent, Businesslike

Analyticals
Critical   Industrious
Indecisive   Persistent
Stuffy   Serious
Picky   Exacting
Moralistic   Orderly

Drivers
Pushy   Strong-willed
Severe   Independent
Tough   Practical
Dominating   Decisive
Harsh   Efficient

(Low assertive) Cooperative, Slower-acting, Avoids risk, Go-along person, Nondirective ← Asks — Controls — Tells → (High assertive) Competitive, Fast-acting, Risk taker, Take-charge person, Directive

Amiables
Conforming   Supportive
Unsure   Respectful
Pliable   Willing
Dependent   Dependable
Awkward   Agreeable

Expressives
Manipulative   Ambitious
Excitable   Stimulating
Undisciplined   Enthusiastic
Reacting   Dramatic
Egotistical   Friendly

Emotes

Friendly, Informal, Open, Emotional, Undisciplined, Relationship-oriented

---

[12] SRI International, Menlo Park, California.
[13] "The Best 100 Sources for Marketing Information," *American Demographics* (January 1995), p. 29.
[14] Lewis C. Winters, "International Psychographics," *Marketing Research*, Vol. 4 (September 1992), pp. 48–49.

alities. Thrive on freedom from outside control. Risk-takers, but seek approval for themselves and their firms.
- *Drivers*—Low in responsiveness and high in assertiveness. Get right to the point. Limited time. "Hard chargers." Self-motivated and impatient. Work well alone. Risk-takers. Success-oriented.
- *Amiables*—Low in assertiveness and high in responsiveness. Team players. Like to build relationships. Friendly and loyal. Need support from others. Careful. Less time-oriented. Can be indecisive. Risk avoiders.[15]

The Social Styles model has been used to classify personnel within industries—including banking, computers and precision instruments, chemicals, pharmaceuticals, telecommunications, aerospace, utilities, and industrial and farm equipment. In all cases, the analyticals segment is the largest.

International Marketing in Action

How Do Americans, Argentines, and Venezuelans Spend Their Money?

Roper Reports Americas tracks people's activities in the United States and leading Latin American markets, including Argentina and Venezuela. The data it compiles help to highlight target-market opportunities in these markets. The data reported below refer to urban adults aged 18 and older.

In a typical month, people in Argentina and Venezuela are more likely than those in the United States to perform job-related duties at home (32 per cent Argentina, 28 per cent Venezuela, and 25 per cent U.S.), make an international phone call (11 per cent Argentina, 14 per cent Venezuela, and 8 per cent U.S.), and take a vacation for four or more days (14 per cent Argentina, 10 per cent Venezuela, and 6 per cent U.S.).

On the other hand, in a given month, people in Argentina and Venezuela are less likely than those in the United States to buy clothing for themselves (38 per cent Argentina, 41 per cent Venezuela, and 48 per cent U.S.), use a credit card (21 per cent Argentina, 17 per cent Venezuela, and 44 per cent U.S.), and send or receive a fax at work (7 per cent Argentina, 7 per cent Venezuela, and 15 per cent U.S.).

There are also significant differences between Argentine and Venezuelan consumers. Consumers in Argentina are more apt to buy recorded music (23 per cent in Argentina versus 10 per cent in Venezuela). In contrast, consumers in Argentina are less apt than their Venezuelan counterparts to go away for a weekend (15 per cent in Argentina versus 21 per cent in Venezuela).

As a marketing consultant who works with small Canadian companies that want to market products in the United States, Argentina, and Venezuela, how would you use these findings?

Source: Based on material in Ignacio Galceran and Jon Berry, "A New World of Consumers," *American Demographics* (March 1995), pp. 26–33.

---

[15]Tom Eisenhart, "How to Really Excite Your Prospects," *Business Marketing* (July 1988), pp. 44–45 ff.; and Raymond E. Taylor, Lorraine A. Krajewksi, and John R. Darling, "Social Style Application to Enhance Direct Mail Response," *Journal of Direct Marketing*, Vol. 7 (Autumn 1993), pp. 42–53.

270 Part 3 *Consumer Analysis: Understanding and Responding to Diversity in the Marketplace*

Consumer profiles are used in identifying market segments.

Identifying Potential Market Segments

After establishing possible bases of segmentation, a firm is ready to construct specific consumer profiles—which identify potential market segments for that firm by aggregating consumers with similar characteristics and needs and separating them from those with different characteristics and needs. For example, a supermarket could segment female and male shoppers in terms of their in-store behaviour. In general, on each visit, women spend more time shopping, buy more items, are more apt to bring children, and more often use a shopping list than men; and they are equally apt to shop in the evening.

A photocopier manufacturer could group the office-copier market into benefit segments, such as: basic copying (satisfied with simple, inexpensive machines that make up to 99 black-and-white copies of a single page at a time); extensive copying (satisfied with mid-priced machines that make up to 100 or more one- or two-sided copies of multiple pages and then collate them); and desktop publishing (satisfied with expensive, sophisticated machines that make high-quality colour copies in large quantities). Both domestic and international prospects for each segment are bright.

Targeting the Market

The second phase in planning a target-market strategy consists of choosing the proper approach and selecting the target market(s).

Choosing a Target-Market Approach

A firm now decides upon undifferentiated marketing (mass marketing), concentrated marketing, or differentiated marketing (multiple segmentation). These options are shown in Figure 10-9 and Table 10-2, and are discussed next.

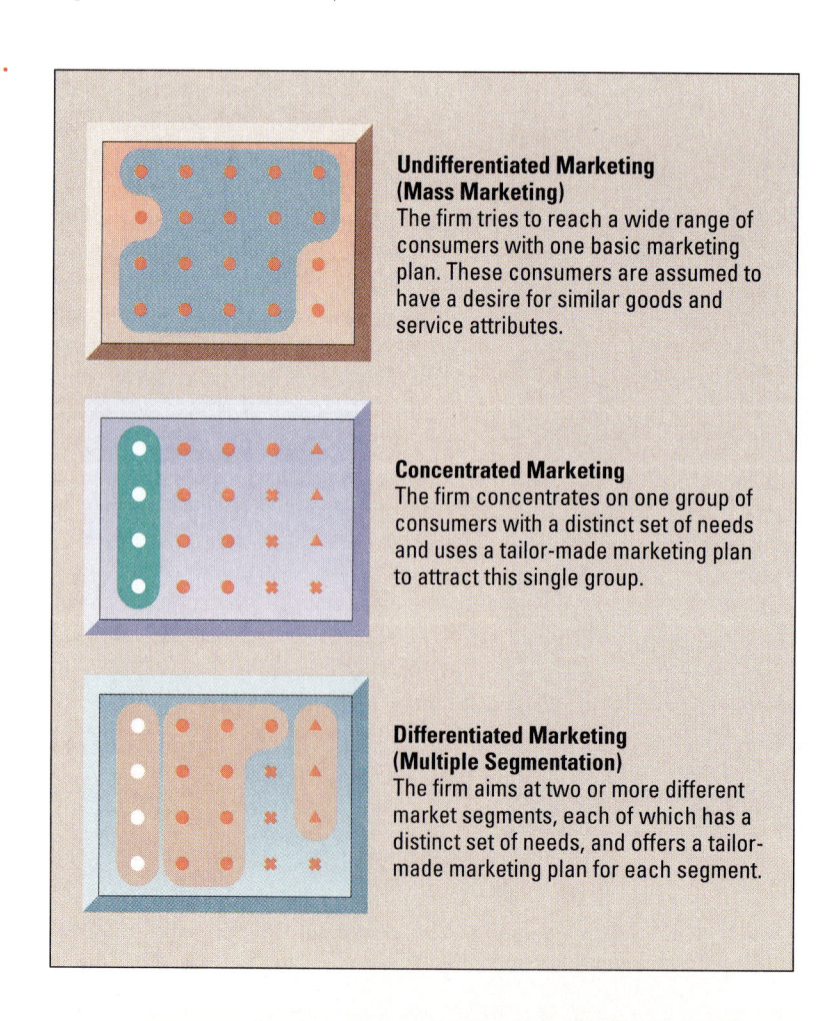

FIGURE 10-9
Contrasting Target-Market Approaches

Undifferentiated Marketing (Mass Marketing)
The firm tries to reach a wide range of consumers with one basic marketing plan. These consumers are assumed to have a desire for similar goods and service attributes.

Concentrated Marketing
The firm concentrates on one group of consumers with a distinct set of needs and uses a tailor-made marketing plan to attract this single group.

Differentiated Marketing (Multiple Segmentation)
The firm aims at two or more different market segments, each of which has a distinct set of needs, and offers a tailor-made marketing plan for each segment.

Table 10-2
Contrasting Target-Market Approaches

STRATEGIC FACTORS	APPROACHES		
	Undifferentiated Marketing	*Concentrated Marketing*	*Differentiated Marketing*
Target market	Broad range of consumers	One well-defined consumer group	Two or more well-defined consumer groups
Product	Limited number of products under one brand for many types of consumers	One brand tailored to one consumer group	Distinct brand or version for each consumer group
Distribution	All possible outlets	All suitable outlets	All suitable outlets—differs by segment
Promotion	Mass media	All suitable media	All suitable media—differs by segment
Price	One "popular" price range	One price range tailored to the consumer group	Distinct price range for each consumer group
Strategy emphasis	Appeal to a large number of consumers with a uniform, broad-based marketing program	Appeal to one specific consumer group with a highly specialized but uniform marketing program	Appeal to two or more distinct market segments with different marketing plans catering to each segment

UNDIFFERENTIATED MARKETING (MASS MARKETING) An undifferentiated marketing (mass marketing) approach aims at a large, broad consumer market using one basic marketing plan. With this approach, a firm believes consumers have very similar desires regarding product attributes or opts to ignore differences among segments. An early practitioner of mass marketing was Henry Ford, who sold one standard car at a reasonable price to many people. The original Model T had no options and came only in black.

Mass marketing was popular when large-scale production started, but the number of firms using a pure undifferentiated marketing approach has declined in recent years. Competition has grown, and firms need to stimulate consumer demand by appealing to specific segments. In addition, improved marketing research can better pinpoint different segments' desires, and total production and marketing costs can be reduced by segmentation.

Before engaging in undifferentiated marketing, a firm must weigh several factors. Large total resources are needed to mass produce, mass distribute, and mass advertise. At the same time, per-unit production and marketing costs may be lower, because a limited product line is offered and different brand names are not employed. These savings may allow low competitive prices.

A major goal of undifferentiated marketing is to maximize sales—that is, a firm tries to sell as many units of an item as possible. Regional, national, and/or international goals are set. Diversification is not undertaken.

For pure mass marketing to succeed, a large group of consumers must have a desire for the same product attributes (homogeneous demand), so a firm can use one basic marketing program. Or, demand must be so diffused that it is not worthwhile for a firm to aim marketing plans at specific segments; the firm would try to make demand more homogeneous. Under undifferentiated marketing, different consumer groups are not identified and sought. For example, if all consumers buy Windsor salt for its freshness, quality, storability, availability, and fair price, a pure mass-marketing strategy is then proper. However, if various consumers want attractive decanters, low-sodium content, larger crystals, and smaller-sized packages (as they now do), Windsor would be unable to appeal to all consumers using one basic marketing mix.

With undifferentiated marketing, a firm appeals to a broad range of consumers with one basic marketing plan.

With undifferentiated marketing, a firm sells through all possible outlets. Some resellers may be displeased if a brand is sold at nearby locations and insist on carrying additional brands to fill out their product lines. It may be hard to persuade them not to carry competing brands. The shelf space a firm gets is based on its brand's popularity and the promotion support it provides.

An undifferentiated marketing strategy should take both total and long-run profits into account. Firms sometimes become too involved with revenues and lose sight of profits. For example, for several years, A&P's sales rose as it competed with Safeway for leadership in North American supermarket sales. A&P incurred large losses during that period. Only when it began to close some unprofitable stores and stop pursuing sales at any cost did it regain profitability.

A firm and/or its products can ensure a consistent, well-known image with a mass marketing approach. Consumers have only one image when thinking of a firm (or a brand), and it is retained for a number of years.

TV Guide is an example of undifferentiated marketing in action. It is a magazine with television program listings, descriptions, and evaluations, as well as current events and articles on personalities, shows, and the industry. Each week, 14 million copies are sold in North America (down from 18 million a decade ago). It is advertised on TV and in newspapers and stores. It is inexpensive and available through subscription or at a number of stores and newsstands. The concept of the product, a TV listing magazine, is the same throughout North America. In the U.S., the only regional differences are in program listings (program descriptions, articles, and features remain the same). Canada has its own edition of *TV Guide* which has uniquely Canadian articles and features, but as in the U.S. these remain the same in all regions of the country.

To be more competitive, *TV Guide* now includes cable-TV listings and VCR-Plus codes (for easy taping), and it has moved all feature stories to the front of the magazine. *TV Guide* is recognized as the standard in the field. Consumers of varying backgrounds and lifestyles buy it for the completeness of its listings and the interesting stories.

Concentrated Marketing

With concentrated marketing, a firm appeals to one segment using a tailored marketing plan.

By means of a concentrated-marketing approach, a firm aims at a narrow, specific consumer segment with one specialized marketing plan catering to the needs of that segment. Concentrated marketing is often appropriate if demand is clustered or if diffused demand can be clustered by offering a unique marketing mix.

Concentrated marketing has become more popular, especially for smaller firms, because the firm does not have to mass produce, mass distribute, or mass advertise. It can succeed with limited resources and abilities by focusing efforts. This method does not usually maximize sales; the goal is efficiency—attracting a large portion of one segment at controlled costs. The firm wants recognition as a specialist and does not diversify.

A firm using concentrated marketing must do better than its competitors in tailoring a strategy for its segment. Areas of competitor strength should be avoided and weaknesses exploited. For instance, a new vendor selling standard office stationery would have a harder time distinguishing itself from competitors than a new vendor that provides customers with free recycling services for the office stationery it sells.

When there are two or more attractive market segments from which a firm may choose, it should select the one with the greatest opportunity—while being alert to these two factors:

*To avoid the **majority fallacy**, a company can enter a smaller, but untapped, market segment.*

1. The largest segment may not be the best option, due to heavy competition or high consumer satisfaction with competitor offerings. A firm entering this segment may regret it due to the **majority fallacy**, which causes some firms to fail if they go after the largest market segment because competition is intense (see Figure 10–10).

2. A potentially profitable segment may be one ignored by other firms. As an example, in the United States Frank Perdue is very successful in the poultry business. This is due to its being the first chicken processor to see a market segment desiring superior quality, an identifiable brand name, and a guarantee—and with a willingness to pay premium prices. Previously, chicken was sold as an unbranded commodity.

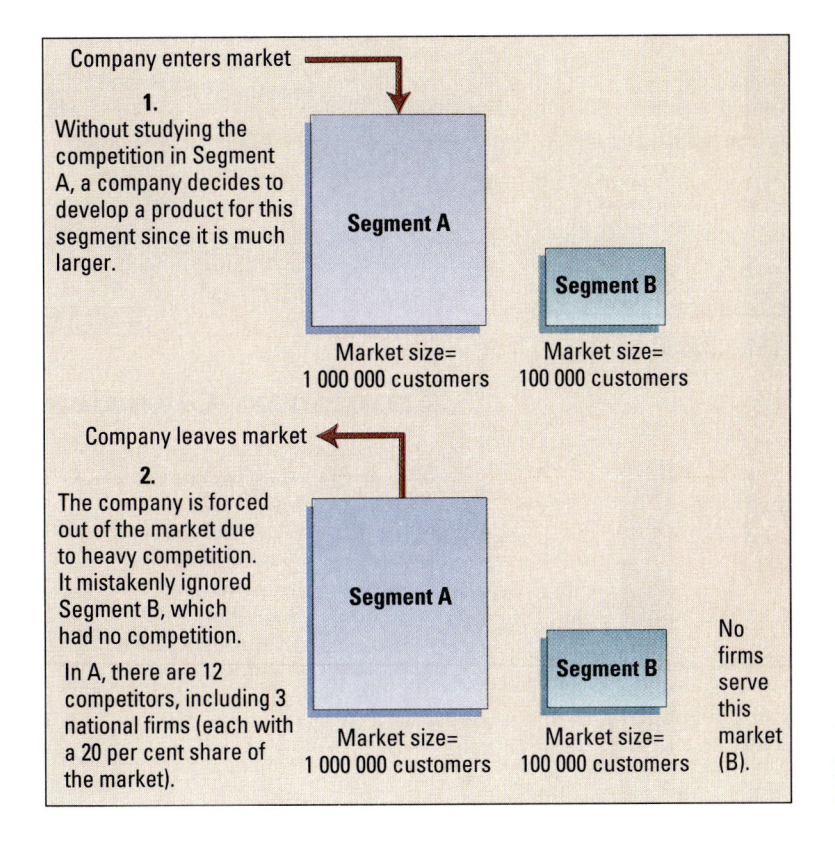

FIGURE 10–10
How the Majority Fallout Occurs

1. Without studying the competition in Segment A, a company decides to develop a product for this segment since it is much larger.

Company enters market → Segment A
Market size = 1 000 000 customers

Segment B
Market size = 100 000 customers

2. The company is forced out of the market due to heavy competition. It mistakenly ignored Segment B, which had no competition.

In A, there are 12 competitors, including 3 national firms (each with a 20 per cent share of the market).

Company leaves market ← Segment A
Market size = 1 000 000 customers

Segment B
Market size = 100 000 customers

No firms serve this market (B).

Concentrated marketing can enable a firm to maximize per-unit profits, but not total profits, because only one segment is sought. It also allows a firm with low resources to vie effectively for specialized markets. There are many local and regional firms that do not have the finances to compete nationally or internationally but that profitably compete in their own markets with national and international companies. However, minor shifts in population or consumer tastes can sharply affect a firm engaging in concentrated marketing.

By carving out a distinct niche through concentrated marketing, a firm may foster a high degree of brand loyalty for a current offering and also be able to develop a product line under a popular name. As long as the firm stays within its perceived area of expertise, the image of one product will rub off on another: Even though it makes several car models, Porsche aims only at the upscale segment of the market—people interested in styling, handling, acceleration, and, of course, status.

DIFFERENTIATED MARKETING (MULTIPLE SEGMENTATION) In differentiated marketing (multiple segmentation), a firm appeals to two or more distinct market segments, with a different marketing plan for each. This approach combines the best aspects of undifferentiated marketing and concentrated marketing: A broad range of consumers can be sought and efforts focused on satisfying identifiable consumer segments. Differentiated marketing is appropriate to consider if there are two or more significant demand clusters, or if diffused demand can be clustered into two or more segments and satisfied by offering unique marketing mixes to each one.

Some firms appeal to each segment in the market and achieve the same market coverage as with mass marketing. Mita markets photocopiers ranging from the simple and inexpensive to the sophisticated and expensive, thus separately appealing to small and large businesses. Other firms appeal to two or more, but not all, market segments. Dylex Limited operates several different apparel outlets: Fairweather and Braemar for women, Tip Top for men, and Biway and Thrifty's for families, thus aiming at several—but not all—apparel segments. And Switzerland's SMH markets Swatch watches for teenagers and young adults, Hamilton watches for adults attracted by classic styles, and upscale Blancpain, Omega, and Tissot brands. See Figure 10-11.

In differentiated marketing, two or more marketing plans are tailored to two or more consumer segments.

274 Part 3 *Consumer Analysis: Understanding and Responding to Diversity in the Marketplace*

FIGURE 10-11
Differentiated Marketing in Action: Targeting Final Consumers
These two watch brands are both marketed by SMH, but they are targeted at different market segments.
Reprinted by permission.

Firms may use both mass marketing and concentrated marketing in their multiple segmentation strategies. They could have one or more major brands aimed at a wide range of consumers (the mass market) and secondary brands for specific segments. Maclean Hunter publishes *Maclean's* magazine for general audiences, *Chatelaine* for women, and *Pharmacist News* and *Marketing Magazine* for more specialized segments.

Multiple segmentation requires thorough analysis. The company must have the resources and abilities to produce and market two or more different sizes, brands, or product lines. This can be costly, especially with high-technology products. However, if a firm sells similar products under its own and retailer brands, added costs are small.

Differentiated marketing lets a firm reach many goals. For one thing, it can maximize sales: Procter & Gamble is the world leader in laundry products—with such brands as Tide, Bold, Dash, Cheer, Gain, Oxydol, Era, Ivory Snow, and Ariel; and Boeing leads in the global commercial aircraft business, offering planes with different sizes and configurations (including the 737, 747, 757, 767, and 777). Recognition as a specialist can continue if the firm has separate brands for items aimed at separate segments or has a narrow product line: Whirlpool has a clear image under its own label; few people know it also makes products for Sears under the latter's Kenmore brand. Multiple segmentation lets a firm diversify and minimize risks because all emphasis is not placed on one segment: Honda's motorcycles and small engines (for lawn mowers and outboard motors) provide an excellent hedge against a drop in the sales of its cars.

Differentiated marketing does not mean a firm has to enter segments where competitors are strongest and be subjected to the majority fallacy. Its goals, strengths, and weaknesses must be measured against its competitors. A firm should target only those segments it can handle. And the majority fallacy can work in reverse. If a firm enters a segment before a competitor, it may prevent the latter from successfully entering that segment in the future.

Differentiated marketing requires the existence of at least two consumer segments (with distinct desires by each), and the more potential segments that exist, the better the opportunity for multiple segmentation. Firms that start with concentrated marketing often turn to multiple segmentation and pursue other segments after they become established in one segment.

Wholesalers and retailers usually find differentiated marketing by their suppliers to be attractive. It lets them reach multiple segments, offers some brand exclusivity, allows orders to be placed with fewer suppliers, and may enable them to carry their own private brands. For the selling firm, several distribution benefits exist. Items can be placed with competing resellers under different brands; shelf space is given to display various sizes, packages, and/or brands; price differentials among brands can be maintained; and competitors may be discouraged from entering a distribution channel. Overall, differentiated marketing places the seller in a good bargaining position.

Multiple segmentation can be profitable because total profits should rise as a firm increases the number of segments it services. Per-unit profits should also be high if a firm does a good job of creating a unique marketing plan for each segment. Consumers in each segment would then be willing to pay a premium price for the tailor-made offering.

Even though serving diverse segments lessens the risks from a decline in any one segment, extra costs may be incurred by making product variations, selling in more channels, and promoting more brands. The firm must weigh the revenues gained from selling to multiple segments against the costs.

A company must be careful to maintain product distinctiveness for each market segment and guard its overall image. Many consumers still perceive various General Motors' divisions as having "look-alike" cars, and IBM's image has been affected by its past weak performance in the home-PC segment.

Selecting the Target Market(s)

At this point, a firm must decide which segment(s) offer the best opportunities and how many segments it should pursue. In evaluating market segments, a firm must review its goals and strengths, competition, segment size and growth potential, distribution requirements, necessary expenditures, profit potential, company image, and ability to create and sustain differential advantages, as well as any other factors that are relevant.

A company now chooses which and how many segments to target.

Based on the target-market approach chosen, the firm then decides whether to pursue one or more segments (or the mass market). For example, due to the high costs of entering the office PC market and the existence of several well-defined demand clusters, it is most likely that a firm new to that industry would start with a concentrated marketing effort. On the other hand, a new sweater-maker could easily use differentiated marketing to target boys, girls, men, and women with its products.

REQUIREMENTS FOR SUCCESSFUL SEGMENTATION For concentrated marketing or differentiated marketing plans to succeed, the selected market segment(s) have to meet five criteria:

Effectiveness requires segments that are distinct, homogeneous, measurable, large enough, and reachable.

1. There must be *differences* among consumers, or mass marketing would be the appropriate strategy.
2. Within each segment, there must be enough consumer *similarities* to develop an appropriate marketing plan for that segment.
3. A firm must be able to *measure* consumer attributes and needs in order to form groups. This may be hard for some lifestyle attributes.
4. A segment must be *large enough* to produce sales and cover costs.

The shortcomings of segmentation need to be considered.

5. The members of a segment must be *reachable* in an efficient way. For example, young women can be reached via *Teen* magazine. It is efficient because males and older women do not read the magazine.

LIMITATIONS OF SEGMENTATION Although segmentation is often a consumer-oriented, efficient, and profitable marketing technique, it should not be abused. Firms could fall into one or more traps. For example, companies may:

- Appeal to segments that are too small.
- Misread consumer similarities and differences.
- Become cost inefficient.
- Spin off too many imitations of their original products or brands.
- Become short-run instead of long-run oriented.
- Be unable to use certain media (due to the small size of individual segments).
- Compete in too many segments.
- Confuse people.
- Get locked into a declining segment.
- Be too slow to seek innovative possibilities for new products.

Developing the Marketing Strategy

The third phase in planning a target-market strategy includes two steps: positioning the company's offering relative to competitors and outlining the appropriate marketing mix(es).

Positioning the Company's Offering

A good or service must be carefully positioned against competitors.

Once a firm selects its target market(s), it must identify the attributes and images of each competitor and select a position for its own offering.

For example, a firm considering entry into the office PC market could describe the key strengths of some of the major competitors as follows:

- *IBM*—Reliability, service, range of software applications, product variety.
- *Apple*—Ease of use, graphics, desktop publishing, innovativeness.
- *Compaq*—Innovativeness, construction, monitor quality, competitive pricing.
- *Dell*—Low prices, range of accessories carried, direct marketing experience.

In positioning itself against these competitors, the firm would need to present a combination of customer benefits that are not being offered elsewhere and that are desired by a target market. Customers must be persuaded that there are clear reasons for buying the new firm's computers. It is not a good idea for the firm to go head-on against big, well-known competitors.

As one alternative, the firm could focus on small businesses that have not yet bought a computer and that need a personal touch during both the purchase process and the initial use of the product. It could thus market fully configured PC systems, featuring IBM clones that are installed by the seller (complete with software libraries and customized programs), in-office training of employees, and a single price for a total system. The positioning emphasis would be "to provide the best ongoing, personalized customer service possible to an underdeveloped market segment, small-business owners."

A fuller discussion of product positioning appears in Chapter 11.

Outlining the Appropriate Marketing Mix(es)

The marketing mix must be attractive to the target market.

The last step in the target-marketing process is for a firm to outline a marketing-mix plan for each customer group it is targeting. Marketing decisions relate to product, distribution, promotion, and price factors.

Ethics AND TODAY'S MARKETER

Wheelchair Advertising: Targeting Your Market With Billboard Bob's

Bob Gerrie offers marketers a unique specific targeting vehicle—vehicle as in wheelchair with a billboard on it. Disabled in a car crash, Bob has turned his handicap into a business opportunity. Based in Toronto, Bob has a 50 cm by 75 cm weatherproof sign board on the back of his wheelchair. He rents this space at a rate of $295 for seven days of exposure. He goes further than simply displaying an ad, however. Bob will hand out coupons and flyers and talk up his client's business too. This unique personal selling touch is certainly a rare commodity in advertising. As for targeting, although Bob may not be ambulatory, he is certainly very mobile. He takes his wheelchair to where the crowds are to provide maximum exposure for his client's message. Local businesses have been the ones who have utilized his services so far. However, Bob is looking for other people in wheelchairs to join his company and expand his business. He has also given some thought to having wheelchairs with corporate logos to supplement the advertising business.

One concern which Bob has had to deal with is the notion that people are responding to his promotional efforts out of sympathy. His position is very professional: he is selling advertising, period. In addition, Bob gets a lot of exposure for his clients but not in a typical fashion. Although it is not considered polite, it is human nature to stare at people in wheelchairs, and Bob is capitalizing on this.

Despite these issues, the advertisers who have hired Bob report that feedback has been very positive and effective. Representatives of organizations for people with disabilities also feel Bob's business is an excellent idea. It shows the public that a wheelchair is a useful tool and shows the person in the wheelchair engaged in meaningful and useful work. Certainly advertisers feel good about supporting Bob while targeting their message to the people living in the areas where they do business. It seems like a winning approach for everyone concerned.

As the marketing manager for a local food store, discuss how you might use Bob Gerrie's services and discuss the possible concerns associated with their use.

Source: Based on material in Peter Kenter, "How Bob Gerrie Used His Wheelchair to Create a Vehicle for Advertising," *Marketing Magazine* (March 11, 1996), p. 6.

Here is a logical marketing-mix plan for a firm entering the office PC market and concentrating on small-business owners:

- *Product*—Good-quality, Pentium-based IBM clone with expansion capability; very user-friendly, with a simple keyboard layout; high-resolution colour monitor; four-speed CD-ROM player and suitable speakers; one gigabyte hard drive; basic software library; customized software; and more.
- *Distribution*—Direct calls and installations at customers' places of business; follow-up service calls.
- *Promotion*—Emphasis on personal selling and direct mail; hands-on, on-site training programs; customer referrals.
- *Price*—Average to above-average; customers presented with nonprice reasons for purchase; positioning linked to high value for the price relationship; price of computer, software, and service bundled together.

Sales Forecasting

*A **sales forecast** predicts company sales over a specified period.*

As a firm plans a target-market strategy, it should forecast its short-run and long-run sales to that market. A **sales forecast** outlines expected company sales for a specific good or service to a specific consumer group over a specific period of time under a specific marketing program. By accurately projecting sales, a firm can better set a marketing budget, allot resources, measure success, analyze sales productivity, monitor the environment and competition, and modify marketing efforts.[16]

A firm should first study industry forecasts; they can strongly affect any company's sales. Next, analysis of the sales potential for the product outlines the upper limit for the firm, based on its marketing and production capacity. A sales forecast then enumerates a firm's realistic sales. The forecast is also based on the expected environment and company performance. Figure 10-12 shows this sales-forecasting process.

A sales forecast should take into account demographics (such as per-capita income), the economy (such as the inflation rate), the competitive environment (such as promotion levels), current and prior sales, and other factors. When devising a forecast, precision is required. A forecast should break sales down by good or service (model 1, 2, 3, etc.), consumer group (for example, adult female), time period (July through September), and type of marketing plan (intensive advertising).

Data Sources

Several external secondary sources may be consulted to obtain some of the data needed for a sales forecast. Government agencies provide data on global, national, regional, and local demographic trends; past sales by industry and product; and the economy. Trade associations publish various statistics and often have libraries for member firms. General and specialized media, such as *The Financial Post* and *Ward's Automotive Reports*, do regular forecasts.

A firm can also obtain data from present and future customers, executives, salespeople, research studies and market tests, and internal records. These data will usually centre on company rather than industry predictions.

Methods of Sales Forecasting

Sales forecasting methods range from simple to sophisticated. Among the simple ones are trend analysis, market-share analysis, jury of executive or expert opinion, sales-force sur-

FIGURE 10-12
Developing a Sales Forecast

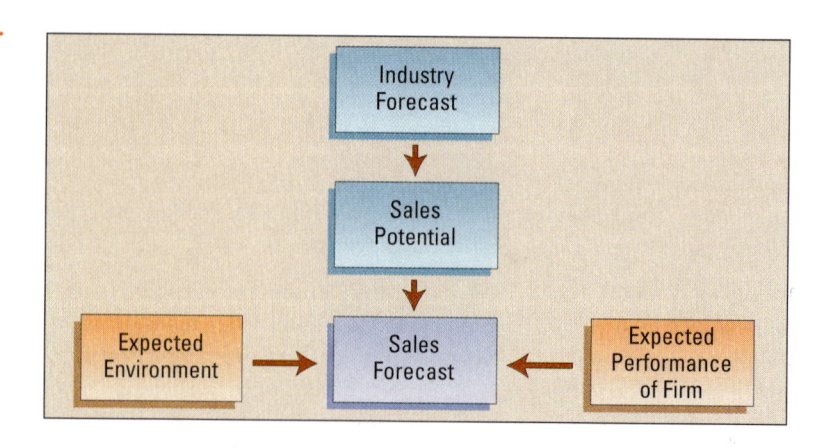

[16]See Paul A. Herbig, John Milewicz, and James E. Golden, "The Do's and Don'ts of Sales Forecasting," *Industrial Marketing Management*, Vol. 22 (February 1993), pp. 49–57; Theodore Modis, "Life Cycles: Forecasting the Rise and Fall of Almost Anything," *Futurist* (September–October 1995), pp. 20–25; and John B. Mahaffie, "Why Forecasts Fail," *American Demographics* (March 1995), pp. 34–40.

Table 10-3
Applying Sales Forecasting Techniques

TECHNIQUE	ILLUSTRATION	SELECTED POTENTIAL SHORTCOMINGS
Simple trend analysis	This year's sales = $2 million; company trend is 5% growth per year; sales forecast = $2 100 000.	Industry decline not considered.
Market-share analysis	Current market share = 18%; company seeks stable market share; industry forecast = $10 000 000; company sales forecast = $1 800 000.	New competitors and greater marketing by current ones not considered.
Jury of executive opinion	Three executives see strong growth and three see limited growth; they agree on a 6% rise in this year's sales of $11 million; sales forecast = $11 680 000	Change in consumer attitudes not uncovered.
Jury of expert opinion	Groups of wholesalers, retailers, and suppliers meet. Each group makes a forecast; top management utilizes each forecast in forming one projection.	Different beliefs by groups about industry growth.
Sales force survey	Sales personnel report a competitor's price drop of 10% will cause company sales to decline 3% from this year's $7 million; sales forecast = $6 790 000.	Sales force unaware a competitor's price cut will be temporary.
Consumer survey	85% of current customers indicate they will repurchase next year and spend an average of $1000 with the firm; 3% of competitors' customers indicate they will buy from the firm next year and spend an average of $800; sales forecast = $460 000.	Consumer intentions possibly not reflecting real behaviour
Chain-ratio method	Unit sales forecast for introductory marketing text = (number of students) x (% annually enrolled in marketing) x (% buying a new book) x (expected market share) = (500 000) x (0.07) x (0.87) x (0.11) = 3350.	
Market buildup method	Total sales forecast = region 1 forecast + region 2 forecast + region 3 forecast = $2 000 000 + $7 000 000 + $13 000 000 = $22 000 000.	Incorrect assumption that areas will behave similarly in future.
Test marketing	Total sales forecast = (sales in test market A + sales in test market B) x (25) = ($1 000 000 + $1 200 000) X (25) = $55 000 000.	Test areas not representative of all locations.
Detailed statistical analyses	Simulation, complex trend analysis, regression, and correlation.	Lack of understanding by management; all factors not quantifiable.

veys, and consumer surveys. Among the more complex ones are the chain-ratio technique, market buildup method, and statistical analyses. Table 10-3 illustrates each. By combining two or more techniques, a firm can have a better forecast and minimize the weaknesses in any one method.

With **simple trend analysis**, a firm forecasts sales on the basis of recent or current performance. For example, if sales have risen an average of 10 per cent annually over the last five years, it will forecast next year's sales to be 10 per cent higher than the present year's. Although the technique is easy to use, the problems are that sales fluctuations, changing consumer tastes, changing competition, the economy, and market saturation are not considered. A firm's growth may be affected by these factors.

Market-share analysis is similar to simple trend analysis, except that a company bases its forecast on the assumption that its share of industry sales will remain constant. However, all firms in an industry do not progress at the same rate. Market-share analysis has the same weaknesses as simple trend analysis, but relies more on industry data—and it would let an aggressive or declining firm adjust its forecast and marketing efforts.

A **jury of executive or expert opinion** is used if the management of a firm or other well-informed persons meet, discuss the future, and set sales estimates based on the group's

A jury of executive opinion has informed people estimate sales.

experience and interaction. By itself, this method relies too much on informal analysis. In conjunction with other methods, it is effective because it enables experts to directly interpret and respond to concrete data. Because management lays out goals, sets priorities, and guides a firm's destiny, its input is crucial.

The employees most in touch with consumers and the environment are sales personnel. A sales-force survey allows a firm to obtain input in a structured way. Salespeople are often able to pinpoint trends, strengths and weaknesses in a firm's offering, competitive strategies, customer resistance, and the traits of heavy users. They can break sales forecasts down by product, customer type, and area. However, they can have a limited perspective, offer biased replies, and misinterpret consumer desires.

Many marketers feel the best indicators of future sales are consumer attitudes. By conducting a consumer survey, a firm can obtain information on purchase intentions, future expectations, consumption rates, brand switching, time between purchases, and reasons for purchases. However, consumers may not reply to surveys and may act differently from what they say.

*With the **chain-ratio method**, general data are broken down. The **market buildup method** adds segment data.*

In the **chain-ratio method**, a firm starts with general market information and then computes a series of more specific information. These combined data yield a sales forecast. For instance, a maker of women's casual shoes could first look at a trade association report to learn the industry sales estimate for shoes, the percentage of sales from women's shoes, and the percentage of women's shoe sales from casual shoes. It would then project its own sales of casual women's shoes to its target market. This method is only as accurate as the data plugged in for each market factor. It is useful, since it gets management to think through a forecast and obtain different information.

Opposite to the chain-ratio method is the **market buildup method,** by which a firm gathers data from small, separate market segments and aggregates them. For example, the market buildup method lets a company operating in four urban areas develop a forecast by first estimating sales in each area and then adding the areas. With this method, a firm must note that consumer tastes, competition, population growth, and media differ by geographic area. Segments of equal size may present dissimilar sales opportunities; they should not be lumped together without careful study.

Test marketing is a form of market buildup analysis in which a firm projects a new product's sales based on short-run, geographically limited tests. The company usually introduces a new product into one or a few markets for a short time and carries out a full marketing campaign there. Overall sales are then forecast from test-market sales. However, test areas may not be representative of all locales; and test-market enthusiasm may not carry into national distribution. Test marketing is discussed further in Chapter 13.

There are a number of detailed statistical methods for sales forecasting. Simulation allows a firm to enter market data into a computer-based model and forecast under varying conditions and marketing plans. With complex trend analysis, the firm includes past sales fluctuations, cyclical factors (such as economic conditions), and other factors when looking at sales trends. Regression and correlation techniques explore mathematical links between future sales and market factors, such as annual family income or derived demand. These methods depend on reliable data and the ability to use them correctly. A deeper discussion is beyond the scope of this text.

Additional Considerations

A forecast for a product that has been in the market for a while is usually quite accurate.

The method and accuracy of sales forecasting depend on the newness of a firm's offering. A forecast for a continuing good or service could be based on trend analysis, market-share analysis, executive and expert opinion, and sales-force surveys. Barring major alterations in the economy, industry, competition, or consumer tastes, the forecast should be relatively accurate.

A forecast for an item new to the firm but that already has a track record in the industry could be based on trade data, executive or expert opinion, sales-force and consumer surveys, and test marketing. The first year's forecast should be somewhat accurate, the ensuing years more so. It is hard to project first-year sales precisely, since consumer interest and competition may be tough to gauge.

A forecast for a good or service new to both the firm and the industry should rely on sales-force and consumer surveys, test marketing, executive and expert opinion, and simulation. The forecast for the early years may be highly inaccurate, since the speed of consumer acceptance cannot be closely determined in advance. Later forecasts will be more accurate. While an initial forecast may be imprecise, it is still needed for setting marketing plans, budgeting, monitoring the environment and competition, and measuring success.

A company must consider **sales penetration**—the degree to which a firm is meeting its sales potential—in forecasting sales. It is expressed as:

Sales penetration shows whether a firm has reached its potential. Diminishing returns may result if it seeks nonconsumers.

Sales penetration = Actual sales/Sales potential

A firm with high sales penetration needs to realize that **diminishing returns** may occur if it seeks to convert remaining nonconsumers because the costs of attracting them may outweigh revenues. Other products or segments may offer better potential. An illustration is shown in Table 10–4.

A company must always keep in mind that factors such as economic conditions, industry conditions, company performance, competition, and consumer tastes may change and lead to an inaccurate forecast unless the forecast is revised.

Table 10-4
Illustrating Sales Penetration and Diminishing Returns

YEAR 1
- Sales potential = $1 000 000
- Actual sales = $600 000 (60 000 units)
- Selling price = $10/unit
- Total marketing costs = $100 000
- Total production costs (at $8/unit) = $480 000
- Sales penetration = $\frac{\$600\ 000}{\$1\ 000\ 000}$ = 60%
- Total profit = $600 000 − ($100 000 + $480 000) = $20 000

YEAR 2
- Sales potential = $1 000 000
- Actual sales = $700 000 (70 000 units)
- Selling price = $10/unit
- Total marketing costs = $150 000
- Total production costs (at $8/unit) = $560 000
- Sales penetration = $\frac{\$700\ 000}{\$1\ 000\ 000}$ = 70%
- Total profit = $700 000 − ($150 000 + $560 000) = −$10 000

In year 1, sales penetration is 60% and the firm earns a $20 000 profit. In year 2, the firm raises marketing expenditures to increase sales penetration to 70%; as a result, it suffers diminishing returns—the additional $100 000 in actual sales is more than offset by a $130 000 rise in total costs (from $580 000 in year 1 to $710 000 in year 2).

MARKETING IN A CHANGING WORLD
Targeting the Interactive Marketplace[17]

As companies look ahead to further advances in interactive technology—and the fascinating new marketing opportunities that will accompany such advances, they also need to think about the alternative target-market approaches they could pursue. After all, just like other consumer markets, the interactive marketplace will encompass all sorts of potential segments.

With this in mind, Arbitron's NewMedia Pathfinder Study recently examined the U.S. interactive marketplace. Arbitron surveyed thousands of American adults and included 612 variables related to demographics, lifestyles, current media experiences, and expectations. What did it find? Well, the research firm did come up with some catchy segment names, as well as a lot of implications for marketers. There are fast laners (14 per cent of all respondents), diverse strivers (5 per cent), savvy sophisticates (11 per cent), family-focused (15 per cent), bystanders (16 per cent), sports fanatics (11 per cent), moral Americans (11 percent), and the settled set (17 per cent).

Let's highlight a few of these segments:

- *Fast laners* are mostly Generation Xers and teens. They are more open to new technology.
- *Savvy sophisticates* are high-income, well-educated baby boomers. They are confident and innovative. More own and use PCs than any other group.
- *Family-focused* consumers are mostly price-oriented women with average income and below-average involvement with PCs and technology.
- *Bystanders* are lowest in confidence and innovativeness. They tend to be baby boomers with an above-average number of children living at home.

As summarized in the *Marketing News*, "Home shopping channels appeal most to fast laners, diverse strivers, family-focused, and bystanders. Infomercials have only average appeal among family-focused and well below-average appeal among bystanders. Savvy sophisticates show the heaviest involvement with online and print catalogues. They do not see TV as a purchasing medium." Furthermore, "Internet shoppers are pioneers more in the way they shop than in what they buy."

SUMMARY

1. *To describe the process of planning a target-market strategy* After collecting information on consumers and environmental factors, a firm is ready to select the target market(s) to which it will appeal. A potential market contains people with similar needs, adequate resources, and a willingness and ability to buy.

Developing a target-market strategy consists of three general phases, comprising seven specific steps: analyzing consumer demand—determining demand patterns (1), establishing bases of segmentation (2), and identifying potential market segments (3); targeting the market—choosing a target market approach (4) and selecting the target market(s) (5); and developing the marketing strategy—positioning the company's offering relative to competitors (6) and outlining the appropriate marketing mix(es) (7). Of particular importance is product differentiation, whereby a product offering is perceived by the consumer to differ from its competition on any physical or nonphysical product characteristic, including price.

2. *To examine alternative demand patterns and segmentation bases for both final and organizational consumers* Demand patterns indicate the uniformity or diversity of consumer needs and desires for particular categories of goods and services. With homogeneous demand, consumers have relatively uniform needs and desires. With clustered demand, consumer needs and desires can be classified into two or more identifiable clusters (segments), with each having distinct purchase requirements. With diffused demand, consumer needs and desires are so diverse that clear clusters (segments) cannot be identified.

The possible bases for segmenting the market fall into three categories: geographic demographics—basic identifiable characteristics of towns, cities, provinces, regions, and countries; personal demographics— basic identifiable characteristics of individual final consumers and organizational consumers and groups of final consumers and organizational consumers; and lifestyles—patterns by which people (final consumers and those representing organizational consumers) live and spend time and money. It is generally advis-

---

[17]The material in this section is based on Kelly Shermach, "Study Identifies Types of Interactive Shoppers," *Marketing News* (September 25, 1995), p. 22.

able to use a combination of demographic and lifestyle factors to form possible segmentation bases. Although the distinctions between final and organizational consumers should be kept in mind, the three broad segmentation bases could be used in both cases.

After establishing possible segmentation bases, a firm is ready to develop consumer profiles. Such profiles identify potential market segments by aggregating consumers with similar characteristics and needs.

3. *To explain and contrast undifferentiated marketing (mass marketing), concentrated marketing, and differentiated marketing (multiple segmentation)* Undifferentiated marketing aims at a large, broad consumer market using one basic marketing plan. In concentrated marketing, a firm aims at a narrow, specific consumer group with one specialized marketing plan catering to the needs of that segment. With differentiated marketing, a firm appeals to two or more distinct market segments, with a different marketing plan for each. When segmenting, a firm must understand the majority fallacy: The largest consumer segment may not offer the best opportunity since it often has the greatest number of competitors.

In selecting its target market(s), a firm should consider its goals and strengths, competition, segment size and growth potential, distribution needs, required expenditures, profit potential, company image, and ability to develop and sustain a differential advantage.

Successful segmentation requires differences among and similarities within segments, measurable consumer traits and needs, large enough segments, and efficiency in reaching segments. It should not be abused by appealing to overly small groups, using marketing inefficiently, placing too much emphasis on imitations of original company products or brands, confusing consumers, and so on.

4. *To show the importance of positioning in developing a marketing strategy* In positioning its offering against competitors, a firm needs to present a combination of customer benefits that are not being provided by others and that are desirable by a target market. Customers must be persuaded that there are clear reasons for buying the firm's products rather than those of its competitors.

The last step in the target-marketing process is for a firm to develop a marketing mix for each customer group to which it wants to appeal.

5. *To discuss sales forecasting and its role in target marketing* Short- and long-run sales should be forecast in developing a target-market strategy. This helps a firm compute budgets, allocate resources, measure success, analyze productivity, monitor the environment and competition, and adjust marketing plans. A sales forecast describes the expected company sales of a specific good or service to a specific consumer group over a specific time period under a specific marketing program.

A firm can obtain sales-forecasting data from a variety of internal and external sources. Forecasting methods range from simple trend analysis to detailed statistical analyses. The best results are obtained when methods and forecasts are combined. A sales forecast should consider the newness of a firm's offering, sales penetration, diminishing returns, and the changing nature of many factors.

KEY TERMS

market (p. 257)
market segmentation (p. 257)
target-market strategy (p.257)
undifferentiated marketing (mass marketing) (p. 257)
concentrated marketing (p. 257)
differentiated marketing (multiple segmentation) (p. 257)
product differentiation (p. 257)
demand patterns (p. 258)
homogeneous demand (p. 258)

clustered demand (p. 258)
diffused demand (p. 258)
geographic demographics (p. 260)
personal demographics (p. 261)
heavy-usage segment (heavy half) (p. 265)
benefit segmentation (p. 266)
VALS (Values and Lifestyles) program (p. 266)
Social Styles model (p. 266)
majority fallacy (p. 272)

sales forecast (p. 278)
jury of executive or expert opinion (p. 279)
chain-ratio method (p. 280)
market buildup method (p. 280)
sales penetration (p. 281)
diminishing returns (p. 281)

Review Questions

1. Distinguish between the terms "market" and "market segmentation."
2. What are the three general phases in planning a target market strategy?
3. Explain this comment: "Sometimes a firm can achieve a key differential advantage by simply emphasizing how its offering satisfies existing consumer desires and needs better than its competitors do. Sometimes demand patterns must be modified for consumers to perceive a firm's product differentiation as worthwhile."
4. Differentiate among homogeneous, clustered, and diffused consumer demand. What are the marketing implications?
5. Describe five personal demographics pertaining to organizational consumers.
6. What is the majority fallacy? How can a firm avoid it?
7. Cite the five key requirements for successful segmentation.
8. Why is sales forecasting important when developing a target-market strategy?
19. Contrast the jury of executive opinion and the chain-ratio methods of sales forecasting.
10. Why are long-run sales forecasts for new products more accurate than short-run forecasts?

Discussion Questions

1. How could an international manufacturer of personal beepers apply geographic-demographic segmentation?
2. Develop a personal-demographic profile of the students in your marketing class. For what goods and services would the class be a good market segment? A poor segment?
3. Describe several potential benefit segments for a firm marketing maintenance services to business clients.
4. Develop a marketing strategy for a utility-vehicle manufacturer that wants to appeal to experiencers (as described in VALS 2). How should the strategy differ if the target market is strivers?
5. If a firm has a sales potential of $4 000 000 and attains actual sales of $2 400 000, what does this signify? What should the firm do next?

VIDEO CASE

Selling Houses in Vancouver with Feng Shui (Wind and Water)

The Chinese ethnic market in Canada was estimated to be 600 000 people in 1995 and is projected to grow to over 1.3 million by the year 2001. Although the Chinese market represents a little over 4 per cent of the Canadian population, they possess 7.4 per cent of the buying power and the doubling in their size will be accompanied by an increase in their purchasing power. Given the strength and rapid growth of the Chinese community, it is not surprising that marketers are falling all over themselves to offer products and services to this market. For example, *Maclean's* launched a Chinese edition in 1995 as did *Toronto Life*. Toronto Dominion Bank has Chinese Information lines, and in Markham, Ontario, developers are preparing a "Chinese" mall.

However, one of the most interesting approaches to tapping the lucrative Chinese market involves Vancouver real estate, which is among the most expensive in Canada. Building and selling homes in the Vancouver market is big business, especially since the population of British Columbia has been growing due to a major influx of Canadian migrants from Eastern Canada and Chinese immigrants from the Orient. However, success in the Vancouver real estate market means developing a clear understanding of, and dedication to, the Chinese philosophy of Feng Shui.

Builders and architects who have chosen to target the Chinese market have had to adapt their housing designs to Feng Shui in order to sell their products and services to Chinese consumers. Feng Shui is all about keeping energy—and good luck—inside one's house. Keeping "bad" energy out is also important. Feng Shui means that walkways to the house must be skewed so that energy cannot flow right out of the house and into the street. One cannot have a tree in front of the entrance to a house because it may block the flow of energy to and from the house. Doorways must be designed to trap energy and one door must not face another in the house. Stairways cannot face the entrance to the home because this will allow energy to flow out. Bedrooms must be carefully designed so that the head of the bed cannot be seen from the bedroom door; and the location of the head of the bed for the head of the household depends on that person's birthday. If you want to sell your house to a Chinese buyer in Vancouver it will have to pass inspection by a Feng Shui master or be relatively easy to renovate so that it will pass. In fact, many real estate deals are signed with the condition that the house pass inspection by an environmental engineer (read: Feng Shui master). Architects and builders are so responsive to this market situation that virtually all new homes built in Vancouver are now built with Feng Shui in mind.

QUESTIONS

1. What kind of target marketing is involved in appealing to Chinese home buyers (e.g., undifferentiated marketing or differentiated marketing)? Explain your answer.
2. Evaluate the Chinese ethnic market on the basis of the requirements for successful segmentation.
3. What are the pros and cons of designing homes specifically for Chinese buyers?
4. As a marketer giving serious consideration to serving the Chinese ethnic market in Canada, what kinds of problem would you see as being the most difficult to overcome in designing a marketing strategy?

VIDEO QUESTIONS ON FENG SHUI

1. Identify some of the principles of Feng Shui. Discuss some of the problems they present for real estate marketers.
2. Discuss the following comment: Feng Shui is important in the Vancouver real estate market now, but in twenty years it will probably be a mere footnote in history.

TORONTO DOMINION BANK
www.tdbank.ca/tdbank/

Video Source: "Feng Shui," *Venture* (October 8, 1995).
Other Sources: David Leid, "Amazing Grace," *Canadian Business* (May 1996), p. 37; James Pollock, "The Economics of Growing Communities," *Marketing Magazine* (July 3/10, 1995), p. 11; Jennifer Lynn, "Approaching Diversity," *Marketing Magazine* (July 3/10, 1995), p. 11; James Pollock, "Opening Doors of Opportunity," *Marketing Magazine* (September 18, 1995) pp. 17–18; James Pollock, "A Burgeoning Segment," *Marketing Magazine* (September 18, 1995), p. 18; and James Pollock, "Nailing the Niche," *Marketing Magazine* (September 18, 1995), p. 20.

CASE STUDY

Teens as Global Consumers: What Does This Mean for Marketers?

The worldwide teen (and pre-teen) market is huge. In Europe, Latin America, and the Pacific Rim, there are over 200 million teens—with Mexico, Brazil, and Argentina together having 57 million 10- to-19-year-olds. Canada has 3.9 million citizens aged 10 to 19 years old while the United States has 35 million people in this age group.

A recent study by Darsey Masius Benton & Bowles (DMB&B) of more than 6500 teens in twenty-six countries concluded that "teens around the world are living very parallel lives." Similarities can be seen in dress (baggy Levi's or Diesel jeans, Doc Martens or Nike shoes, T-shirt, and leather jacket), dining habits (Coca-Cola and Big Macs), and even in the popularity of the same rock groups (such as the Red Hot Chili Peppers). See Table 1. A common explanation of the similarity in teen behaviour is that the worldwide media (including MTV, the Internet, and satellite television) closely bind teens, the same stores exist in multiple geographic markets, and global events such as the Olympics are appealing to people all around the world.

The DMB&B study also revealed that teens throughout the world cited the United States as having the greatest influence in fashion and culture. When asked to state which nation had the most impact on their fashion and culture, 54 per cent of American teens, 80 per cent of European teens, 80 per cent of teens from the Far East, and 87 per cent of Latin American teens said the United States. This "Americanization" has had direct benefits for U.S. firms. Still, "Americanization" is not complete. For example, Canadian teens only watch an average of 16.9 hours of television per week compared to an average of 21.6 hours of viewing by American teens. It would appear that American teens "tune-in" a bit more often than their Canadian counterparts.

Still, some experts implore marketers to be aware of the importance of regional or country-based differences. As DMB&B's senior vice-president and director of strategic planning says, "I'm in no way advocating one-size-fits-all communications or advertising. That's just foolish. There will always be local forces that you can't ignore." For example, American advertisers need to realize that although ads aimed at the U.S. market tend to use a lot of superlatives, many Europeans and Asians like more subtle forms of persuasion. Europeans and Asians also dislike comparative ads, whereby advertisers compare their offerings to other products or brands.

In Canada there are important differences in consumption habits between Anglophone and Francophone teenagers in Quebec, and Anglophone teenagers in the other provinces of Canada. For example, 32 per cent of Francophone teenagers 12 to 17 years of age report consuming beer, compared to 21 per cent for Quebec Anglophones and 15 per cent of Anglophones outside Quebec. Among all Quebec teenagers in this age group, 16 per cent report consuming fast food once a week while 27 per cent of teenagers in the rest of Canada report having fast food at least once a week. The fast-food visits must not be good for the stomach because 27 per cent of teens outside of Quebec also report consumption of upset stomach tablets while for Quebec residents, 13 per cent of Francophone teens and 12 per cent of Anglophone teens report consumption of upset stomach tablets.

Other experts say that even though a global teen consumer exists, with the exception of Levi's, America no longer dominates teen culture. They feel the emergence of the European Union has brought European teens closer together. They also see greater influence coming from Europe, Asia, and Latin America.

Table 1
Teenage Wearing Habits In Selected Countries (Per Cent of Teens Who Wear Selected Clothing)

	UNITED STATES	EUROPE	LATIN AMERICA	ASIA	CHINA
Jeans	93	94	86	93	48
T-shirt	93	89	59	96	22
Running shoes	80	79	65	69	36
Blazer	42	43	30	27	43
Denim jacket	39	57	41	23	7

Source: "Teen Interests Appear to be Universal," *Advertising Age* (July 17, 1995), p. A3. Reprinted by permission, Darsey Masius Benton & Bowles.

Sources: The data in this case are drawn from "Teen Interests Appear to be Universal," *Advertising Age* (July 17, 1995), p. A3; Shawn Tully, "Teens: The Most Global Market of All," *Fortune* (May 16, 1994), pp. 90–97; Cyndee Miller, "Teens Seen as the First Truly Global Consumers," *Marketing News* (March 27, 1995), p. 9; Francois Vary, "Getting Down to Details with PMB'94," *Marketing Magazine*, (February 20, 1995) p. 14; "Freeze Frame: A Marketing-Nielsen Update on Television," *Marketing Magazine*, (April 3, 1995), p. 18; and Pierre Audet, "The Realistic Generation," *Marketing Magazine* (February 20, 1995), p. 13.

QUESTIONS
1. How can the product differentiation concept be applied to the teen market?
2. Comment on the "Americanization" versus the "need to reflect cultural differences" theories from the perspective of determining demand patterns.
3. Discuss the "need to reflect cultural differences" theories from the perspective of the establishment of bases for segmentation in light of the differential findings on Canadian teen consumption behaviour.
4. Does the teen market represent a heavy-usage segment? Explain your answer.

PRODUCT PLANNING

PART 4

To adhere to the marketing concept, a firm needs to devise, enact, and monitor a systematic marketing plan. This plan centres on the four elements of the marketing mix: product, distribution, promotion, and price. We present these elements in Parts 4 to 7, with Part 4 concentrating on product planning.

11 ### Basic Concepts in Product Planning
Here, we define tangible, augmented, and generic products and distinguish among different types of consumer and industrial products (both goods and services). We look at product mix strategies and product management organizations in detail. We also study product positioning and the product life cycle in depth. The chapter concludes with a look at the international dimensions of product planning.

12 ### Goods Versus Services Planning
Now, we look at the scope of goods and services, and introduce a goods/services continuum. We review goods and services classification systems. Then, we study the special considerations in the marketing of services. We also see that service marketing has lagged behind goods marketing and why this is changing. At this point, our discussion turns to nonprofit marketing and how it is distinct from profit-oriented marketing. We examine how nonprofit organizations can be classified, as well as the role of nonprofit marketing in the economy.

13 ### Conceiving, Developing, and Managing Products
In this chapter, we look at products from their inception to their deletion. We discuss the types of new products, reasons for new-product failures, and the new-product planning process. We explain the growth of products in terms of the adoption and diffusion processes, and note several methods for extending the lives of mature products. We also offer product deletion strategies.

14 ### Branding and Packaging
Here, we look at the branding decisions that centre on corporate symbols, the branding philosophy, the choice of brand names, and the use of trademarks. We also consider the six basic functions of packaging: containment, usage, communication, market segmentation, channel cooperation, and new-product planning.

Part 4 Vignette
Products: Satisfying Customer Needs and Wants

Marketers offer products to satisfy customer needs and wants in exchange for the customer's money or products.

Part 4 focuses on designing products to satisfy customers' demands. The first video case discusses a marketer who understands his product and his customers. Jim Scharf is an entrepreneur with a keen eye for product innovation. His approach to marketing is one of product orientation. Finding unmet needs and wants—and developing goods and services to satisfy them—is central to product orientation. However, he also realizes the importance of the other aspects of the marketing mix. Therefore, when he developed his E-ZEEWRAP plastic wrap dispenser, it was designed as a way to sell plastic wrap. Designed to overcome the problems of tangling, snarling and uneven tearing associated with most plastic wraps and their dispensers, it was simply satisfying an incompletely met need.

The second case examines how Canada Trust manages its Mastercard service in relation to its customers. Financial services are among the most important services in Canada's economy, accounting for two-thirds of Canada's GDP. Credit services available to the mass market via credit cards have been one of the most significant marketing innovations of this century—each Canadian holds an average of two major credit cards. The video case illustrates the marketing of credit cards and shows that the product concept associated with credit cards is very sophisticated. The basic concept of delayed payment combined with "instant" buying power has been enhanced by a variety of other features, including consumer protection services for card purchases, insurance services, frequent usage rewards and enhanced ability to make non-personal transactions.

New product development is the subject of the third case, which points out that when it comes to product development, marketing managers must be prepared to cope with failure more often than success. The video takes you to the Museum of Flops in Ithaca, New York, where the curator, Robert McMath, is an excellent source of information and a consultant for new product development. The museum contains samples of over 80 000 commercialized ventures, each with its own "lesson" of failure. The products failed for a variety of reasons: poor product concepts, good product concepts that were not technically feasible, poor packaging, inappropriate branding and bad timing.

The last video case discusses branding, one of the most powerful concepts of modern product marketing. In the most basic sense, brand names identify products just as branding cattle identified ownership in the Old West and prevented cattle rustling. Its modern equivalent, counterfeit branding, is much more lucrative because branding has more power than mere identification. The video cases presents the case of Microsoft, which wants to become the world's number one brand, replacing Coca Cola.

Why is this recognition so important? The brand is the bridge between target market, product positioning and product concept. Brands are personalized images and are often entities unto themselves. In fact, for many products the brand name defines the product category. For example, one uses an IBM or a Mac computer with a DOS, Windows 95 or Mac operating system. Each of these terms refer to trademarked product identifiers. A good brand name can provide an extra launch for new products associated with the name. Hence, Microsoft launched Windows 95 as an upgrade replacement for its earlier Windows version. In cases such as this, the new product must be able to live up to, or surpass, the previous image of the brand. In its most basic sense, branding allows consumers to purchase goods holistically and efficiently. In the absence of branding, every purchase transaction would require intensive product inspection. If every transaction in our society involved this, it could take an entire day just to buy weekly groceries for a family!

CHAPTER 11
Basic Concepts in Product Planning

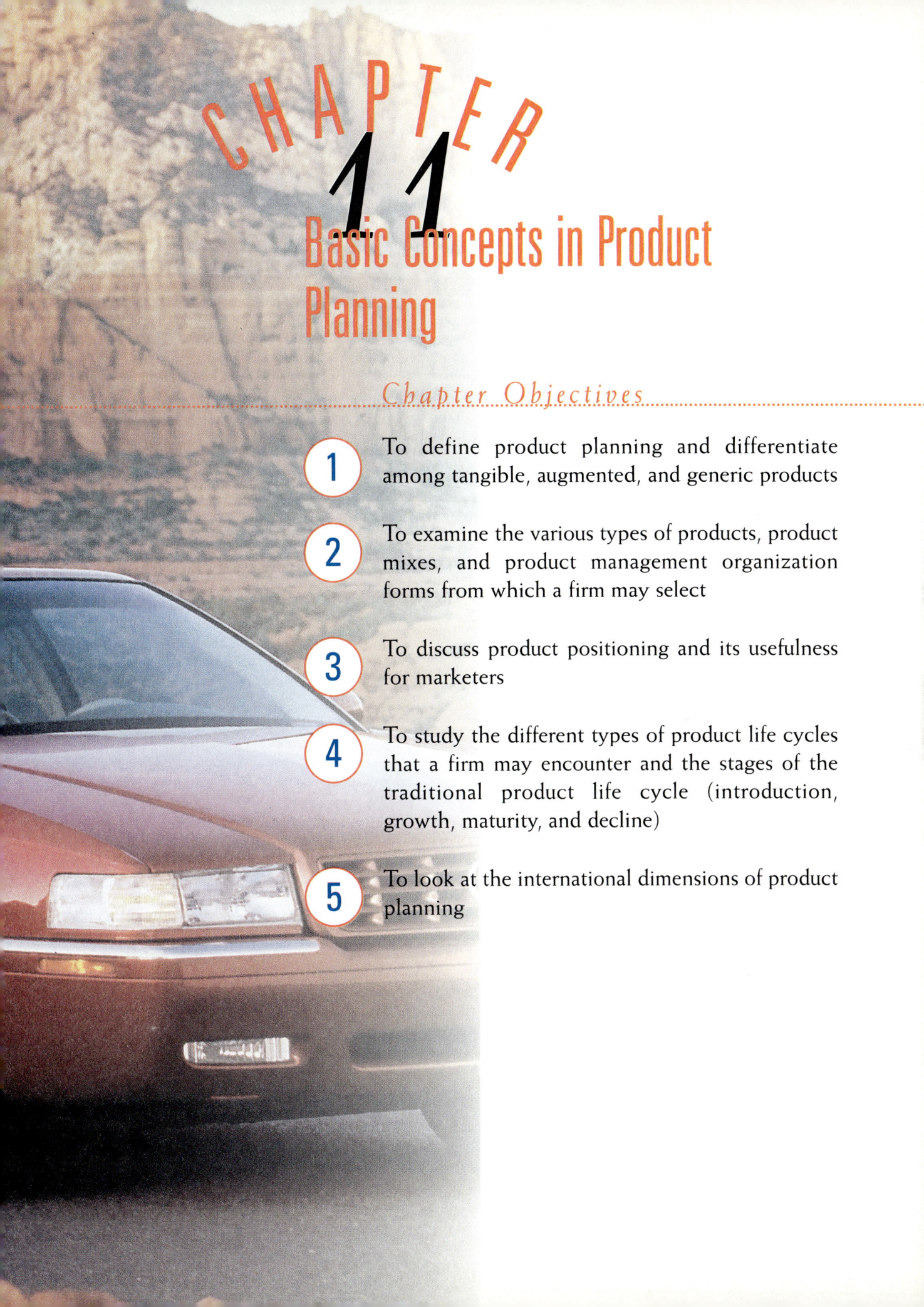

Chapter Objectives

1. To define product planning and differentiate among tangible, augmented, and generic products

2. To examine the various types of products, product mixes, and product management organization forms from which a firm may select

3. To discuss product positioning and its usefulness for marketers

4. To study the different types of product life cycles that a firm may encounter and the stages of the traditional product life cycle (introduction, growth, maturity, and decline)

5. To look at the international dimensions of product planning

> *Upon his appointment as General Motors' (GM's) head of marketing, Ronald L. Zarrella stated that although GM had some of the most recognized car names in the world—from the Buick Roadmaster to the Cadillac Fleetwood—it had failed to keep many of the models up-to-date enough to be competitive with rivals. "We have too many models and vehicle lines," he said, adding that he counted as many as seventy-seven different car and light-truck varieties in GM's lineup. Zarrella also said a GM survey found that 35 per cent of people shopping for cars didn't even consider a GM model.*

GENERAL MOTORS OF CANADA
www.gm.com/index.htm

Reprinted by permission.

Because of GM's weak product positioning strategy, Ronald Zarrella was hired away from Bausch & Lomb and given the job of revamping General Motors' marketing approach. No longer would the company's various divisions be so muddled in consumers' minds.

Zarrella announced that the company's seven vehicle divisions would each become more focused and consistent: "We can't escape the fact that the way our vehicle products have been targeted in the past, many are right on top of one another." To accomplish this, he planned to recruit more marketers to sharpen GM's strategy and to serve as brand managers for the divisions. And to provide inducement for change, each divisional marketing manager will have greater profit-and-loss responsibility.

Here is Zarrella's product-positioning vision for GM's vehicle divisions:

- *Chevrolet*—This is GM's high-volume and light-truck division. Chevrolet should offer dependability, reliability, and the widest range of models.
- *Pontiac*—This is GM's sportiest brand. Pontiac should represent youthfulness and spirit and feature "in-your-face styling."
- *Saturn*—It should target import buyers and younger buyers. Saturn needs to stand for "dependability, intelligence, and friendliness." Saturn needs also to retain its "overall shopping, buying, and ownership experience."
- *Oldsmobile*—It should represent the logical trade-up alternative for Saturn owners as they become more affluent and want larger cars. Oldsmobile should compete for market share with Audi, Acura, and entry-level Infiniti and Lexus purchasers.
- *Buick*—It should represent GM's "premium American car." Buick should offer products that are "substantial, distinctive, powerful, mature." Buick needs to target baby boomers in their 50s.

- *Cadillac*—GM's luxury car division. Cadillac should represent "sophisticated, highly perfected cars." Cadillac needs to compete against Mercedes, BMW, Jaguar, and Lexus "in all of the markets of the world." Cadillac is especially seen as attracting foreign buyers willing to pay for a large, luxury automobile.
- *GMC*—This is GM's "premium truck brand with differentiated products from Chevrolet." High-end sports-utility vehicles are in the domain of GMC. These vehicles need to be differentiated from Chevrolet's mainstream truck business.

Ronald Zarrella also sees Saturn, Chevrolet, and Cadillac as global divisions that should sell more cars and light trucks outside of North America. And he intends to convey brand identities through easy-to-remember ads, like those used by consumer products manufacturers such as Procter & Gamble.[1]

In this chapter, we will look at several basic product-planning decisions a firm must make, including those involving product management organizations and product positioning.

Overview

Product planning is systematic decision making relating to all aspects of the development and management of a firm's products, including branding and packaging. Each product consists of a bundle of attributes (features, functions, benefits, and uses) capable of exchange or use, usually in a mix of tangible and intangible forms. Thus, a product may be an idea, a physical entity (a good), a service, or any combination of the three. It exists for the purpose of exchange in the satisfaction of individual and organizational objectives.[2]

Product planning *means devising and managing* **products** *that satisfy consumers.*

A well-structured product plan lets a company pinpoint opportunities, develop appropriate marketing programs, coordinate a mix of products, maintain successful products as long as possible, reappraise faltering products, and delete undesirable products.

A firm should define its products in three distinct ways: tangible, augmented, and generic. By considering all three definitions, the company is better able to identify consumer needs, competitive offerings, and distinctive product attributes. This is illustrated in Figure 11-1.

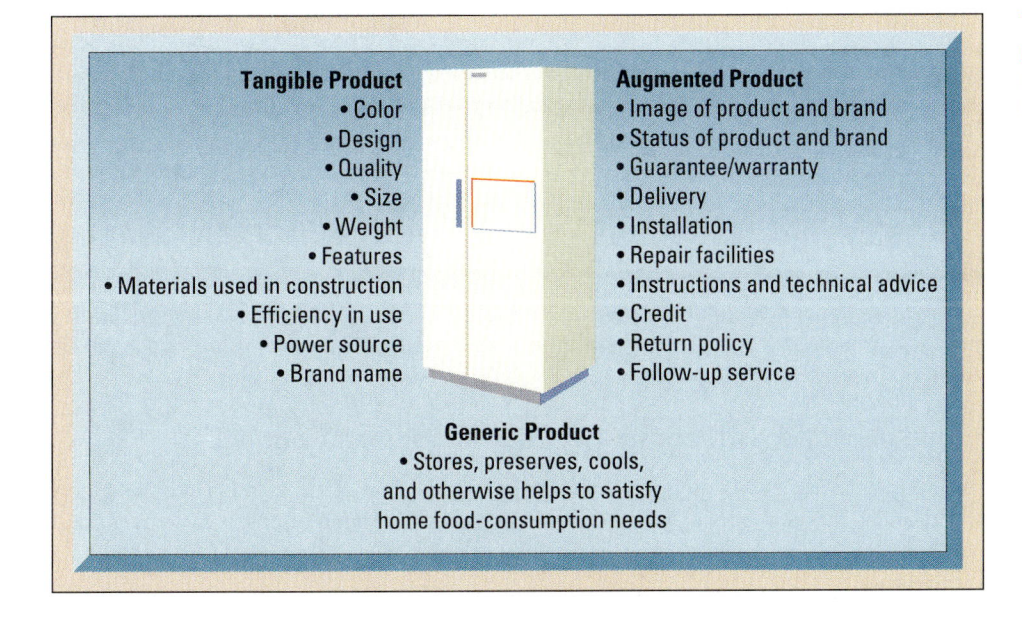

Tangible Product
- Color
- Design
- Quality
- Size
- Weight
- Features
- Materials used in construction
- Efficiency in use
- Power source
- Brand name

Augmented Product
- Image of product and brand
- Status of product and brand
- Guarantee/warranty
- Delivery
- Installation
- Repair facilities
- Instructions and technical advice
- Credit
- Return policy
- Follow-up service

Generic Product
- Stores, preserves, cools, and otherwise helps to satisfy home food-consumption needs

FIGURE 11-1
Illustrating the Three Product Definitions

---

[1]Gabriella Stern, "GM's New Marketing Chief Seeks Clarity Amid Muddle of Overlapping Car Lines," *Wall Street Journal* (May 1, 1995), pp. A3, A5.
[2]Peter D. Bennett (Ed.), *Dictionary of Marketing Terms*, Second Edition (Chicago: American Marketing Association, 1995), p. 219.

A **tangible product** *has precise specifications, while an* **augmented product** *includes image and service features.*

A **tangible product** is a basic physical entity, service, or idea; it has precise specifications and is offered under a given description or model number. Windows 95 software, a Caterpillar diesel engine, *Canadian Business* magazine, a seven-day Caribbean cruise on the QE2 (Queen Elizabeth 2), and a proposal to cut provincial income taxes by 15 per cent are examples of tangible products. Colour, style, size, weight, durability, quality of construction, price, and efficiency in use are some tangible product features.

An **augmented product** includes not only the tangible elements of a product, but also the accompanying cluster of image and service features. For example, one political candidate may receive more votes than another because of charisma (augmented product), despite identical party platform issues (tangible product). Rolex watches are popular chiefly due to the image of luxury and status they convey. At Cummins Engine, offering augmented products means "helping our customers be successful, not simply supplying them with quality engines. Increasingly, the value we bring to customers can be described as *smart power*, which is a value-added package of products, information systems, and support services that provides improved performance and business solutions to our customers."[3]

A **generic product** *centres on consumer benefits.*

A **generic product** focuses on what a product means to the customer, not the seller. It is the broadest definition and is consistent with the marketing concept:

- "In the factory we make cosmetics, and in the drugstore we sell hope." (Charles Revson, founder of Revlon)
- "We know our customers come to us to buy more than bearings and steel. They come to us looking for solutions." (Timken Company)

When applying the generic product concept, several points should be kept in mind. First, because a generic product is a consumer view of what a product represents, a firm should learn what the product means to the consumer before further product planning—as shown in Figure 11-2. Second, inasmuch as people in various nations may perceive the same product (such as a car) in different generic terms (such as basic transportation versus comfortable driving), a firm should consider the impact of this on a possible global strategy.

This chapter provides an overview of product planning. It examines the basic areas in which a firm must make decisions: product type(s), product mix, product management organization, and product positioning. It also covers the product life cycle and its marketing relevance, and presents considerations for international marketers. Chapter 12 covers the planning involved in marketing goods versus services. Chapter 13 presents an in-depth discussion of how to manage products over their lives, from finding new product ideas to deleting faltering products. Chapter 14 concentrates on two specialized aspects of product planning: branding and packaging.

Types of Products

The initial product-planning decision is choosing the type(s) of products to offer. Products can be categorized as goods or services and as consumer or industrial. Categorization is important because it highlights the differences in the characteristics of products and the resulting marketing implications.

Fundamental Distinctions Between Goods and Services

Goods marketing *relates to selling physical products.* **Service marketing** *includes rented-goods services, owned-goods services, and nongoods services.*

Goods marketing entails the sale of physical products such as furniture, heavy machinery, food, and stationery. Service marketing encompasses the rental of goods, servicing goods owned by consumers, and personal services such as vehicle rentals, house painting, and accounting.

Four attributes generally distinguish services from goods: intangibility, perishability, inseparability from the service provider, and variability in quality. Their impact is greatest for personal services, which are usually more intangible, more perishable, more dependent

[3]*Cummins Engine Company 1994 Annual Report.*

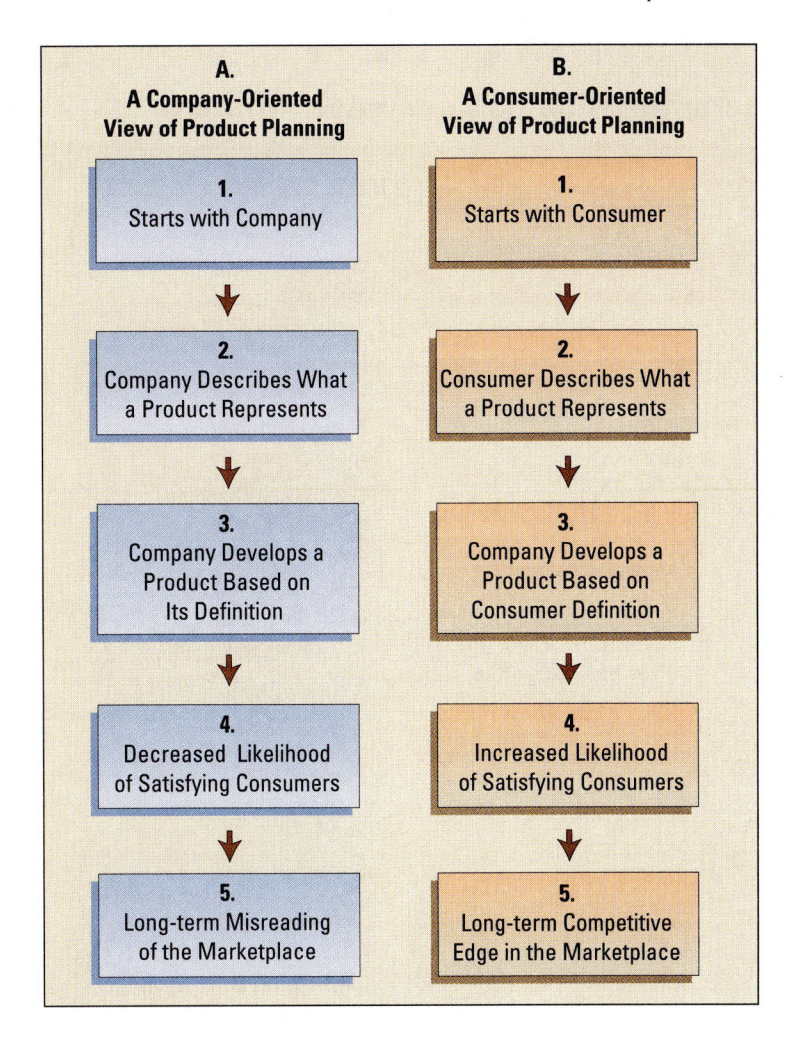

FIGURE 11-2

Applying the Generic Product Concept
In A, the firm is not properly employing the generic product concept and does not understand its customers' needs. In B, the firm is properly using the generic product concept and is successful with its customers.

Source: Adapted by the authors from Leon G. Schiffman and Elaine Sherman, "Value Orientations of New-Age Elderly: The Coming of an Ageless Market," *Journal of Business Research,* Vol. 22 (March 1991), p. 193.

on the skills of the service provider (inseparability), and have more quality variations than rented- or owned-goods services.

The sales of goods and services are frequently connected. For instance, a tractor manufacturer may provide—for an extra fee—extended warranties, customer training, insurance, and financing. In goods marketing, goods dominate the overall offering and services augment them. In service marketing, services dominate the overall offering and goods augment them.

The distinctions between goods and services planning are more fully discussed in Chapter 12.

Consumer Products

Consumer products are goods and services destined for the final consumer for personal, family, or household use. The use of a good or service designates it as a consumer product. For example, a calculator, dinner at a restaurant, phone service, and an electric pencil sharpener are consumer products only if purchased for personal, family, or household use.

Consumer products may be classed as convenience, shopping, or specialty products, based on shoppers' awareness of alternative products and their characteristics prior to a shopping trip and how extensively people will search for the product. Thus, which class a product belongs in depends on shopper behaviour. See Table 11-1.

Convenience products are those bought with a minimum of effort because a consumer has knowledge of product attributes prior to shopping and/or is pressed for time. The person does not want to search for much information and will accept a substitute (Libby's instead of Green Giant corn) rather than visit more than one store. Marketing

Consumer products are final-consumer goods and services.

Convenience products are purchased with minimum effort and are categorized as staples, impulse products, and emergency products.

Table 11-1
Characteristics of Consumer Products

CONSUMER CHARACTERISTICS	TYPE OF PRODUCT		
	Convenience	*Shopping*	*Specialty*
Knowledge prior to purchase	High	Low	High
Effort expended to acquire product	Minimal	Moderate to high	As much as needed
Willingness to accept substitutes	High	Moderate	None
Frequency of purchase	High	Moderate or low	Varies
Information search	Low	High	Low
Major desire	Availability without effort	Comparison shopping to determine best choice	Brand loyalty regardless of price and availability
Examples	(a) Staple: cereal	(a) Attribute-based: name-brand clothes	Hellmann's mayonnaise
	(b) Impulse: candy	(b) Price-based: budget hotel	
	(c) Emergency: tire repair		

tasks centre on distribution at all available outlets, convenient store locations and hours, the use of mass advertising and in-store displays, well-designed store layouts, and self-service to minimize purchase time. Resellers often carry many brands.

Convenience products can be subdivided into staples, impulse products, and emergency products. Staples are low-priced and routinely purchased on a regular basis, such as detergent, mass transit, and cereal. Impulse products are items or brands a person does not plan to buy on a specific store trip, such as candy, magazines, or lottery tickets. According to a recent study, 70 per cent of brand decisions at supermarkets are made in the stores.[4] Emergency products are bought out of urgent need—such as an umbrella in a rainstorm and aspirin for a headache.

Shopping products are those for which consumers feel they lack sufficient information about product alternatives and their attributes (or prices), and therefore must acquire further knowledge in order to make a purchase decision. People will exert effort searching for information because shopping products are bought infrequently, have large purchase prices, or require comparisons. The marketing emphasis is on full assortments (such as many colours, sizes, and options), the availability of sales personnel, the communication of competitive advantages, informative ads, well-known brands (or stores), distributor enthusiasm, and customer warranties and follow-up service to reduce perceived risk. Shopping centres and downtown business districts ease shopping behaviour by having many adjacent stores.

Shopping products may be attribute- or price-based. With attribute-based shopping products, consumers get information on product features, performance, and other factors. Items with the best combination of attributes are bought. Sony electronics and Calvin Klein clothes are marketed as attribute-based shopping products. With price-based shopping products, people feel the choices are relatively similar and shop for the best prices. Budget hotels and low-end electronics are marketed as price-based shopping products.

Shopping products require an information search.

SONY CANADA
www.bccc.com/partners/Sony.html

[4]"POPAI's 1995 Study: 'More Purchase Decisions Made In-Store,'" *Promo* (October 1995), p. 15.

TECHNOLOGY & MARKETING

Will Cars of the Future Be Smarter Than Their Drivers?

Passenger car makers have come up with many new optional features that add convenience, safety, and comfort for drivers and their passengers. Let's look at some of these innovations.

Several car makers have begun to market devices based on satellite-linked navigational systems. GM's system, Guidestar, uses a voice synthesizer that provides directions to lost motorists. Guidestar is currently available on some Oldsmobile models as a $2000 option. Volvo's Dynaguide Info System is similar to Guidestar, but also includes specific traffic report information. Not to be outdone, Lincoln's Remote Emergency Satellite Cellular Unit (RESCU) will notify the nearest police department, fire department, medical unit, and tow truck in the event of an emergency. The unit dials 911 and then uses satellite information to tell the rescuing unit your car's exact location. RESCU is available as an option on the Lincoln Continental.

Another safety-related option would properly adjust driver and passenger headrests every time the car is started. The option, in final development by Lear Seating, uses ultrasonic sensors that determine the proper positions and adjust each headrest automatically. Improperly positioned headrests provide little protection from whiplash.

Other options are designed to ease the tasks of driving. The Mitsubishi Galant LS and Infinity I30, for example, include a single transmitter that controls a garage door, car doors, and windows. Robert Bosch Corporation, a major parts supplier, has devised an electronic rain sensor that automatically turns the windshield wipers on and closes the sunroof at the first sign of rain or snow. The sensor then continually adjusts the windshield wiper speed based on weather conditions.

As a marketing consultant to Oldsmobile, develop a brief report on how Guidestar and other options can be used as part of a product life-cycle strategy.

Source: Based on material in Kathleen Kerwin, "The Smart Cars Ahead," *Business Week* (May 1, 1995), p. 158 E-6.

Specialty products are particular brands, stores, and persons to which consumers are loyal. People are fully aware of these products and their attributes prior to making a purchase decision. They will make a significant effort to acquire the brand desired and will pay an above-average price. They will not buy if their choice is unavailable: Substitutes are unacceptable. The marketing emphasis is on maintaining the attributes that make the products so unique to loyal consumers, reminder ads, proper distribution (Hellmann's mayonnaise and *Canadian Business* require different distribution to loyal customers: supermarkets versus home subscriptions), brand extension to related products (such as Hellmann's tartar sauce), product improvements, ongoing customer contact (such as *Nintendo Power* magazine for owners of Nintendo game consoles), and monitoring reseller performance.

Because many people may view the same products differently, the preceding classification is excellent for segmentation. For example, Tylenol pain reliever may be a convenience product for some people (who will buy another brand if Tylenol is unavailable), a shopping product for others (who read ingredient labels), and a specialty product for still others (who insist on Tylenol). Johnson & Johnson, maker of Tylenol, must understand how Tylenol fits into the various categories and plan its marketing strategy accordingly.

Consumers are loyal to **specialty products**.

JOHNSON & JOHNSON
www.jnj.com/homepage.htm

Industrial Products

Industrial products are goods and services purchased for use in the production of other goods or services, in the operation of a business, or for resale to other consumers. A customer may be a manufacturer, wholesaler, retailer, or government or other nonprofit organization.

Industrial products *are organizational consumer goods and services.*

Table 11-2
Characteristics of Industrial Products

TYPE OF PRODUCT

CHARACTER-ISTICS	Installations	Accessory Equipment	Raw Materials	Component Materials	Fabricated Parts	Supplies	Services
Degree of consumer decision making	High	Moderate	Low	Low	Low	Very low	Low to high
Per-unit costs	High	Moderate	Low	Low	Low	Very low	Low to moderate
Rapidity of consumption	Very low	Low	High	High	High	High	Low to high
Item becomes part of final product	No	No	Sometimes	Yes	Yes	No	Sometimes
Item undergoes changes in form	No	No	Yes	Yes	No	No	Sometimes
Major consumer desire	Long-term facilities	Modern equipment	Continuous, low-cost, graded materials	Continuous, low-cost, specified materials	Continuous, low-cost, fabricated materials	Continuous, low-cost, efficient supplies	Efficient, expert services
Examples	Production plant	Forklift truck	Coal	Steel	Thermostat	Machinery repair, accounting	

Industrial products may be categorized by the degree of decision making involved in a purchase, costs, consumption rapidity, the role in production, and the change in form. Since industrial-product sellers tend to visit customers, store shopping behaviour is often not a factor. Installations, accessory equipment, raw materials, component materials, fabricated parts, business supplies, and business services are types of industrial products—as shown in Table 11-2.

Installations and accessory equipment are expensive and do not become part of the final product.

Installations and **accessory equipment** are capital goods. They are used in the production process and do not become part of the final product. Installations are nonportable, involve considerable consumer decision making (usually by upper-level executives), are very expensive, last many years, and do not change form. The key marketing tasks are direct selling from producer to purchaser, lengthy negotiations on features and terms, having complementary services such as maintenance and repair, tailoring products to buyers' desires, and offering technical expertise and team selling (in which various salespeople have different areas of expertise). Examples are buildings, assembly lines, major equipment, large machine tools, and printing presses.

Accessory equipment consists of movable goods that require moderate consumer decision making, are less costly than installations, last many years, and do not become part of the final product or change form. The key marketing tasks are tying sales to those of installations; providing various choices in price, size, and capacity; having a strong distribution channel or sales force; stressing durability and efficiency; and having maintenance and technical support. Examples are drill presses, trucks, vans, and lathes.

Raw materials, component materials, and fabricated parts are consumed in production.

Raw materials, component materials, and **fabricated parts** are used up in production or become part of final products. They are expense rather than capital items. They require limited consumer decision making, are low cost on a per-unit basis, and are rapidly consumed. Raw materials are unprocessed primary materials from extractive and agricultural industries—minerals, coal, and crops, for example. Component materials are semimanufactured goods that undergo further changes in form—steel, textiles, and basic chemicals, for example. Fabricated parts are placed in products without changes in form—electric motors, thermostats, and microprocessors, for example. The major marketing tasks for materials and parts are to ensure consistent quality, continuity in shipments, and prompt delivery; pursue reorders; have competitive prices; seek long-term contracts; use assertive distributors or sales personnel; and meet buyer specifications.

Industrial supplies are convenience goods used in a firm's daily operations. They can be maintenance supplies, such as light bulbs, cleaning materials, and paint; repair supplies, such as rivets, nuts, and bolts; or operating supplies, such as stationery, pens, and business cards. They require little consumer decision making, are very low cost on a per-unit basis, are rapidly consumed, and do not become part of the finished product. Marketing emphasis is on availability, promptness, and ease of ordering.

Industrial supplies are used daily, and industrial services are classified as maintenance and repair, and business advisory.

Industrial services involve maintenance and repair services, and business advisory services. Maintenance and repair services (such as janitorial services and machinery repair) usually involve little consumer decision making, are rather inexpensive, and are consumed quickly. They may become part of a final product (for example, keeping for-sale equipment in good working condition) or involve a change in form (for example, janitorial services converting a dirty office into a clean one). The key marketing thrust is on consistent, efficient service at a reasonable price. Business advisory services (such as accounting and legal services) may involve a moderate to high level of consumer decision making when these services are first purchased. Ongoing costs tend to be low to moderate, while benefits may be long-lasting. These services do not become part of the final product. The major marketing task is to present an image of expertise and convey the reasons for a client to use the service.

Elements of a Product Mix

After determining the type(s) of products to offer, a firm needs to outline the variety and assortment of those products. A **product item** is a specific model, brand, or size of a product that a company sells, such as a college course on the principles of marketing, a General Motors truck, or Sony 3.5-inch diskettes for PCs. Usually a firm sells a group of closely related product items as part of a **product line**. In each product line, the items have some common characteristics, customers, and/or uses; they may also share technologies, distribution channels, prices, related services, and so on.[5] As an example, Revlon markets lipstick, eye makeup, and other cosmetics. Caterpillar makes several different tractor models. Prentice Hall Canada publishes a number of college and university textbooks on marketing. Many local lawn-service firms offer lawn mowing, landscaping, and tree-trimming services.

A product item is a specific model; a product line has related items; a product mix is all a firm's lines.

PRENTICE HALL CANADA
www.phcanada.com

The **product mix** consists of all the different product lines a firm offers. For instance, Heinz markets ketchup, tuna fish, low-calorie foods, frozen french fries, soup, pet food, and various other food products in over 200 countries around the globe. Metropolitan Life operates North America's largest life insurer (MetLife), as well as its biggest franchised real-estate broker (Century 21). The Seagram Company Ltd. is a global multinational with two major product lines: wines and spirits with brand names such as Crown Royal whisky and Chivas Regal scotch, and beverages such as Tropicana juices and Seagram's coolers and mixers.[6]

A product mix can be described in terms of its width, depth, and consistency. The width of a product mix is based on the number of different product lines a company offers. A wide mix lets a firm diversify products, appeal to different consumer needs, and encourage one-stop shopping. A narrow mix requires lower resource investments and does not call for expertise in different product categories.

A product mix has levels of width, depth, and consistency.

---

[5]Bennett, *Dictionary of Marketing Terms*, p. 222.
[6]Mark Stevenson, "Can This Marriage Survive?" *Canadian Business* (October 1994), p. 26.

298 Part 4 *Product Planning*

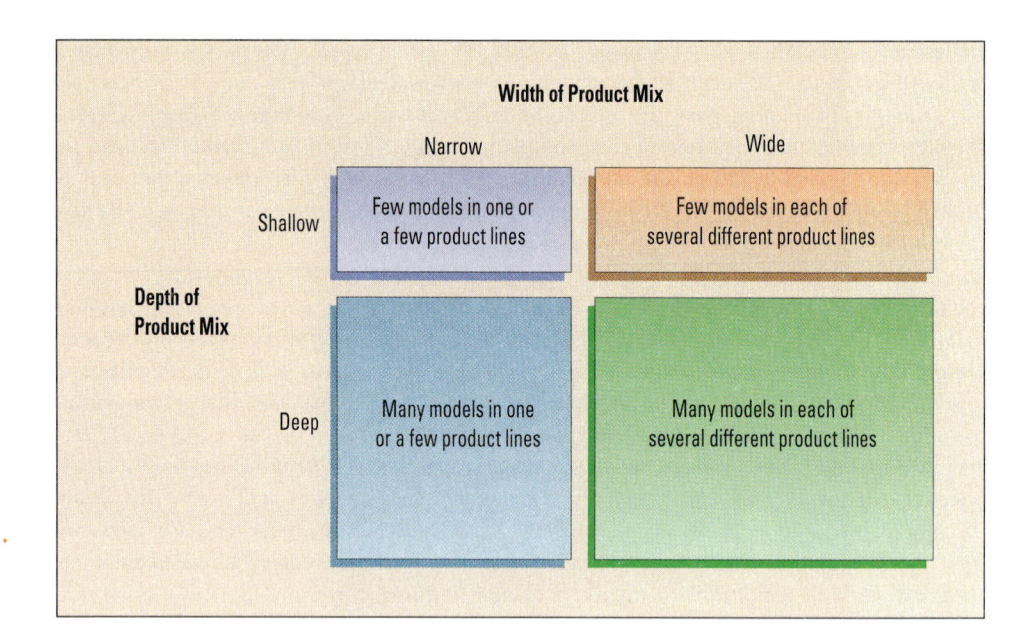

	Width of Product Mix	
	Narrow	**Wide**
Shallow	Few models in one or a few product lines	Few models in each of several different product lines
Deep	Many models in one or a few product lines	Many models in each of several different product lines

(Depth of Product Mix)

FIGURE 11-3
Product Mix Alternatives

FIGURE 11-4
ConAgra's Product Mix
ConAgra's diversification across the food chain expands opportunities and balances results. About half of ConAgra's earnings are from branded food products, and about half are from food service, processing, and distribution businesses.
Reprinted by permission.

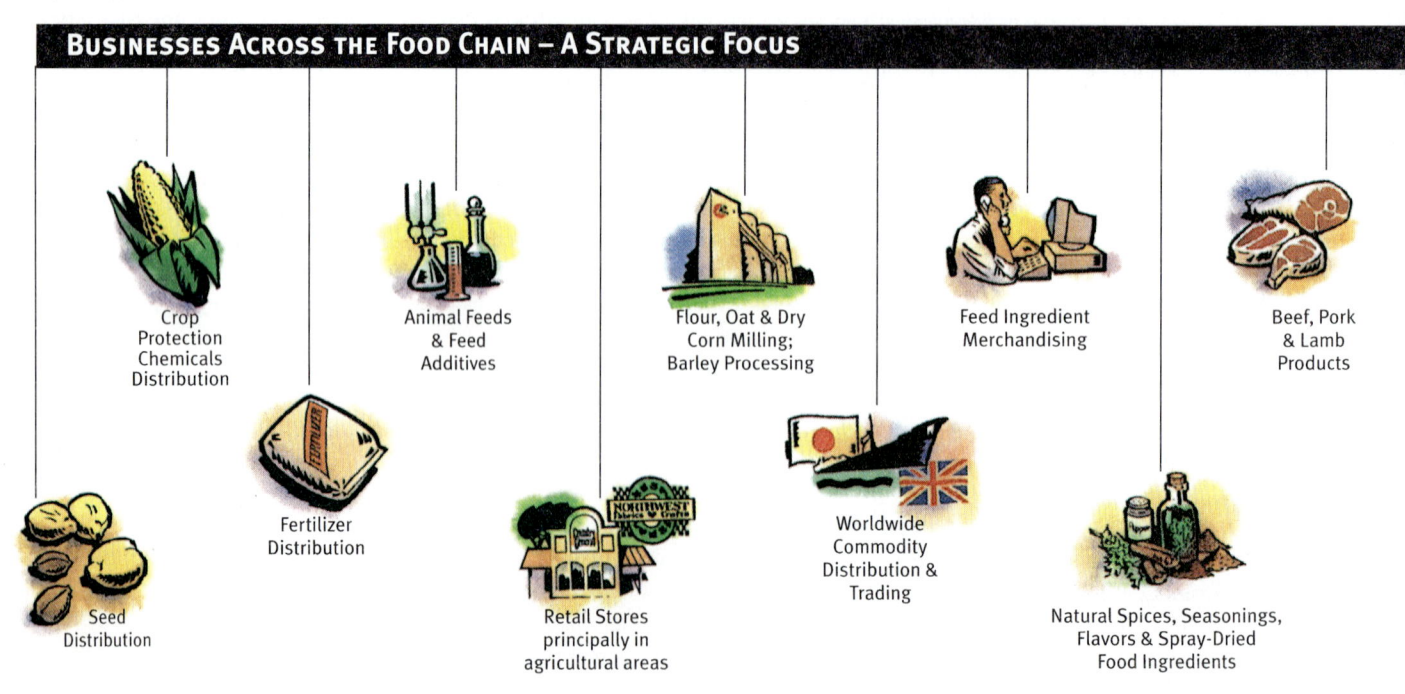

BUSINESSES ACROSS THE FOOD CHAIN – A STRATEGIC FOCUS

- Crop Protection Chemicals Distribution
- Seed Distribution
- Fertilizer Distribution
- Animal Feeds & Feed Additives
- Retail Stores principally in agricultural areas
- Flour, Oat & Dry Corn Milling; Barley Processing
- Worldwide Commodity Distribution & Trading
- Feed Ingredient Merchandising
- Natural Spices, Seasonings, Flavors & Spray-Dried Food Ingredients
- Beef, Pork & Lamb Products

The depth of a product mix is based on the number of product items within each product line. A deep mix can satisfy the needs of several consumer segments for the same product, maximize shelf-space, discourage competitors, cover a range of prices, and sustain dealer support. A shallow mix imposes lower costs for inventory, product alterations, and order processing; and there are no overlapping product items.

The consistency of a product mix is based on the relationship among product lines in terms of their sharing a common end-use, distribution outlets, consumer group(s), and price range. A consistent mix is generally easier to manage than an inconsistent one. It allows a firm to concentrate on marketing and production expertise, create a strong image, and generate solid distribution relations. However, excessive consistency may leave the firm vulnerable to environmental threats, sales fluctuations, or decreased growth potential, since emphasis is on a limited product assortment. Figure 11-3 shows product mix alternatives in terms of width and depth. Figure 11-4 highlights ConAgra's broad product mix. Figure 11-5 displays Jergen's deep product line of hand soaps.

Product-mix decisions can have both positive and negative effects on companies,[7] as these examples demonstrate:

- Wrigley's strategy is to concentrate on chewing-gum products and not to market even closely related items such as hard candies: "If you are thinking of chewing gum, you are thinking Wrigley's." The firm is so successful that it dominates the sugared gum and sugar-free gum markets with nearly a 50 per cent market share of the North American gum market; and Extra, Doublemint, Spearmint, and Juicy Fruit are among the world's best-known brands. Wrigley's annual total sales are U.S.$1.7 billion, 40 per cent of which comes from sales outside the United States.[8]
- Bombardier Corporation is booming because of its product-mix diversification strategy. The firm began in the 1960s as the maker of Ski-Doo snowmobiles. Now,

FIGURE 11-4 (cont.)

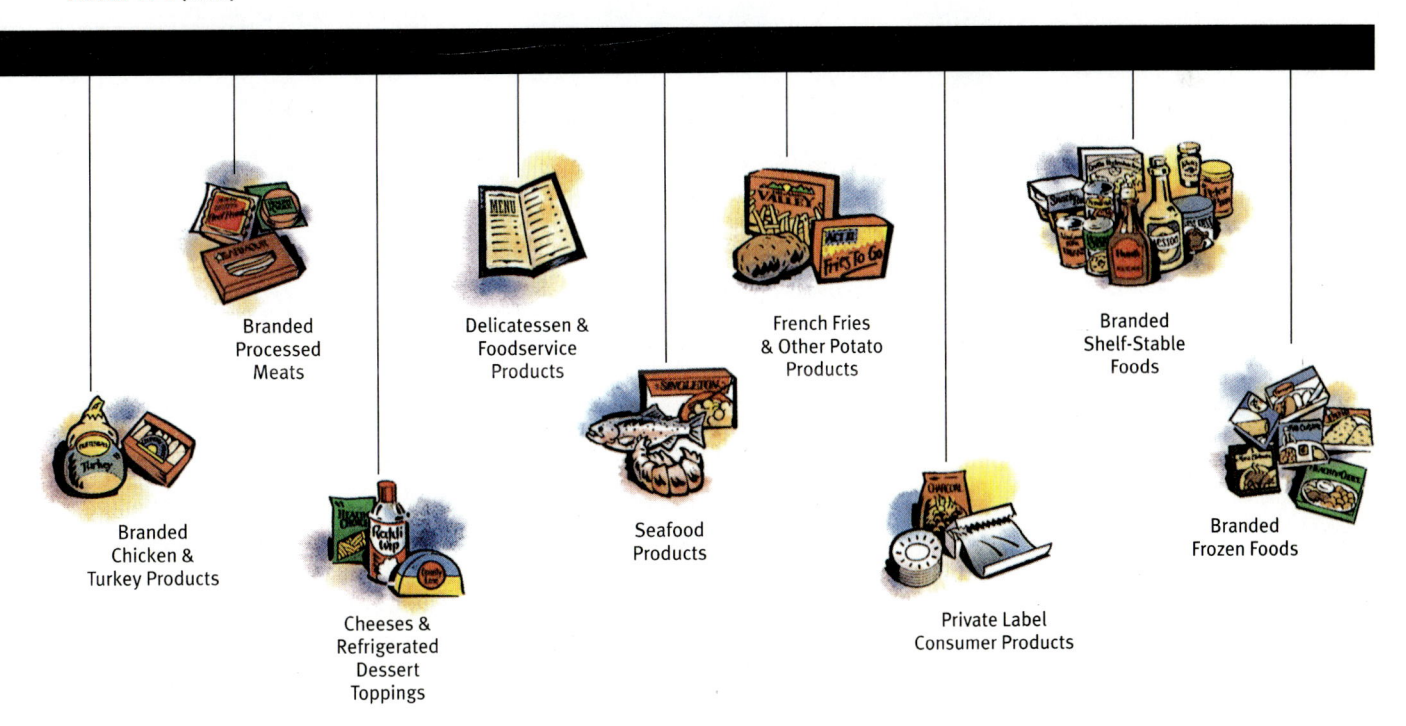

Branded Chicken & Turkey Products

Branded Processed Meats

Cheeses & Refrigerated Dessert Toppings

Delicatessen & Foodservice Products

Seafood Products

French Fries & Other Potato Products

Private Label Consumer Products

Branded Shelf-Stable Foods

Branded Frozen Foods

---

[7]See John A. Quelch and David Kenny, "Extend Profits, Not Product Lines," *Harvard Business Review*, Vol. 72 (September–October 1994), pp. 153–160.
[8]"Wm. Wrigley Jr. Co.," *Advertising Age* (September 27, 1995), p. 62.

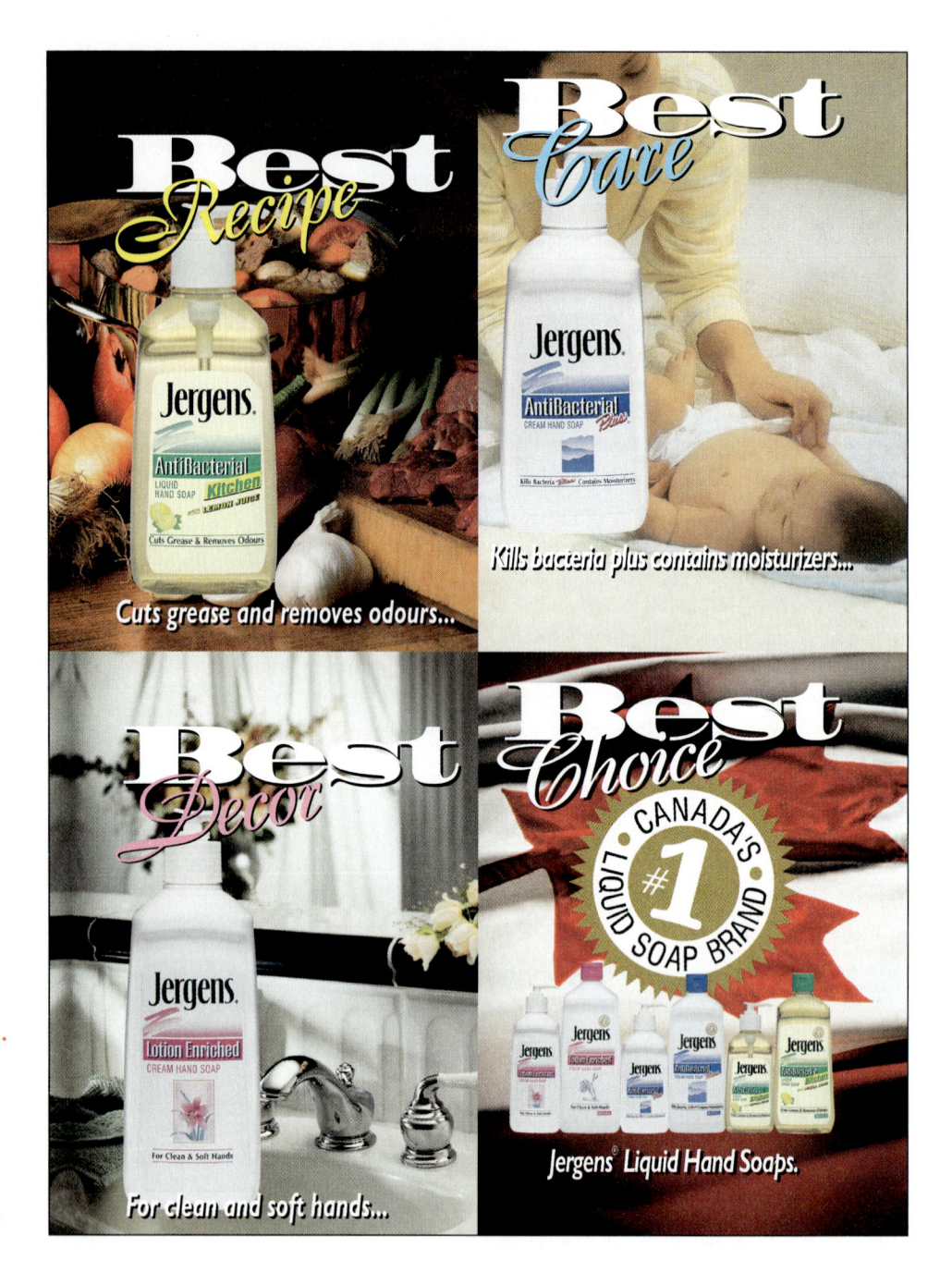

FIGURE 11-5
Jergens' Deep Product Line
By offering a wide variety of hand soaps Jergens has become Canada's leader in the liquid hand soap market.

Reprinted with permission of Jergens Canada Inc., designed by CREATIVE ART + DESIGN

Bombardier manufactures aircraft for commuter airlines and corporate air fleets, railroad and subway cars, and Sea-Doo personal watercraft—as well as Ski-Doo snowmobiles. Its annual revenues have gone from $11 million in 1964 to $7.1 billion today.[9]

- H.J. Heinz Co. of Canada dominates the Canadian jarred baby-food market, worth about $110 million, with an 80 per cent market share. The company recently launched a new niche product branded Heinz Toddler, which was designed for children one to two years old. The new product line has ten meals, a cereal, and three desserts, and it is hoped it will dominate this niche market, estimated to have $1.5 million in sales potential. The new product line replaces the less successful Good 'n Chunky line of canned baby foods, which never really caught on. The action is being taken in

[9]Patrick J. Spain and James R. Talbot (Eds.), *Hoover's Handbook of World Business 1995-1996* (Austin, Texas: Reference Press, 1995), pp. 138–139.

Table 11-3
Comparing Product Management Organizations

CHARACTERISTICS

ORGANIZATION	Staffing	Ideal Use	Permanency
Marketing manager system	Key functional areas of marketing report directly to a senior marketer with a lot of authority.	A company makes one product line, has a dominant line, or uses broad category marketing managers.	The system is ongoing.
Product (brand) manager system	There is a layer of middle managers, with each focusing on a single product or a group of related products	A company makes many distinct products, each requiring expertise.	The system is ongoing.
Product planning committee	Senior executives from various functional areas participate.	The committee should supplement another product organization.	The committee meets irregularly.
New-product manager system	Separate middle managers focus on new products and existing products.	A company makes several existing new products, and substantial time, resources, and expertise are needed for new products.	The system is ongoing, but new products are shifted to product managers after introduction.
Venture team	An independent group of company specialists guides all phases of a new product's development.	A company wants to create vastly different products from those currently offered and needs an autonomous structure to aid development.	The team disbands after a new product is introduced, with responsibility going to a product manager.

response to Gerber Canada (which controls the other 20 per cent of the market), who was first into this market niche with a microwaveable product line called Gerber Graduates.[10]

- Because TRW's product mix had grown to more than 100 categories of high-technology industrial goods and services, some of these products were not performing up to company goals. As a result, TRW decided to sell off businesses generating $500 million in annual sales, including its popular computer repair and servicing division.[11]

Product Management Organizations

A firm may select from among several organizational forms of product management, including: marketing manager, product manager, product planning committee, new-product manager, and venture team.[12] See Table 11-3.

Under a **marketing manager system**, an executive is responsible for overseeing a wide range of marketing functions (such as research, target marketing, planning for existing and new products, distribution, promotion, pricing, and customer service) and for coordinating with other departments that perform marketing-related activities (such as warehousing, order filling, shipping, credit, and purchasing). It works well for firms with a line of similar products or one dominant product line, and for smaller firms that want centralized con-

*One person is directly in charge of a host of marketing tasks, including product planning, with a **marketing manager system**.*

---

[10]"Heinz Food for Toddlers," *Strategy* (June 28, 1993), p. 4.
[11]Gary Hoover, Alta Campbell, and Patrick J. Spain (Eds.), *Hoover's Handbook of American Business* (Austin, Texas: Reference Press, 1994), pp. 1044–1045.
[12]The definitions in this section are drawn from Bennett, *Dictionary of Marketing Terms*, various pages.

Middle managers handle new and existing products in a category in the **product manager system**.

trol of marketing tasks. It may be less successful if there are several product lines and they require different marketing mixes—unless there are category marketing managers, with each responsible for a broad product line.

Ontario Lottery Corporation, Pepsi Cola, and Christie Brown (maker of Oreo cookies and Ritz crackers, among others) have used some form of marketing manager system.[13]

With a **product (brand) manager system**, there is a level of middle managers, each of whom is responsible for planning, coordinating, and monitoring the performance of a single product (brand) or a small group of products (brands). The managers handle both new and existing products and are involved with all the marketing activities related to their product or group of products. The system lets all products or brands get adequate attention. It works well when there are many distinct products or brands, each needing special marketing attention. But, it has two potential shortcomings: lack of authority for the product manager and inadequate attention to new products. Labatt's Breweries, Procter & Gamble, and Black & Decker have used product managers.[14]

A **product planning committee** *has top executives involved part time.*

A **product planning committee** is staffed by high-level executives from various functional areas in a firm, such as marketing, production, engineering, finance, and research and development. It handles product approval, evaluation, and development on a part-time basis. Once a product is introduced, the committee usually turns to other opportunities and completely gives that product over to a product manager. This system lets management have strong input into product decisions; but, because the committee meets irregularly and must pass projects on to line managers, this method functions best as a supplement to other methods. It is utilized by many large and small firms.

A **new-product manager system** *has separate middle managers for new and existing products.*

A **new-product manager system** has product managers to supervise existing products and new-product managers to develop new ones. It ensures enough time, resources, enthusiasm, and expertise for new-product planning. Once a product is introduced, it is given to a product manager who oversees the existing products in that line (or brand). The system can be costly, incur conflicts, and cause discontinuity when an item is introduced. Kraft General Foods, General Electric, and Johnson & Johnson have used new-product managers.

A **venture team** *is an autonomous new-product department.*

A **venture team** is a small, independent department comprised of a broad range of specialists, drawn from the marketing, finance, engineering, and other functional departments, who are involved with a specific new product's entire development process. Team members work on the team full time and act in a relatively autonomous manner. The team disbands when its new product is introduced, and the product is then managed within the firm's regular management structure. A venture team ensures there are proper resources, a flexible environment, expertise, and continuity in new-product planning. It is valuable if a firm wants to be more far-sighted, reach out for truly new ideas, and foster creativity. It is also expensive to establish and operate. Xerox, Ault Foods, Campbell Soup, and 3M have used venture teams.

The correct organization for a particular firm depends on the diversity of its offerings, the number of new products it introduces, its level of innovativeness, company resources, management expertise, and other factors. A combination organization may be highly desirable; among larger firms, this is particularly common.

Product Positioning

Distinctive and desirable product features must be communicated to the marketplace.

Critical to a firm's product-planning efforts is how the items in its product mix are perceived in the marketplace. The firm must work hard to make sure that each of its products is perceived as providing some combination of unique features (product differentiation) and that these features are desired by the target market (thereby converting product differentiation to a differential advantage).

When a product is new, a company must clearly communicate its attributes: What is it? What does it do? How is it better than the competition? Who should buy it? The goal

---

[13]See "The Dynamics of Category Management," *Promo/Progressive Grocer Special Report* (December 1994); "Interview with Tom Dawley, Marketing Director of Online Products Ontario Lottery Corp," *Strategy* (June 27, 1994), p.9; and "Mr Christie gives Teddy a Canadian Ad Flavour," *Marketing Magazine* (January 21, 1991), p.3.
[14]"Career Labatt Man Set to Fill New VP Slot," *Marketing Magazine* (December 21–28, 1992), p 2.

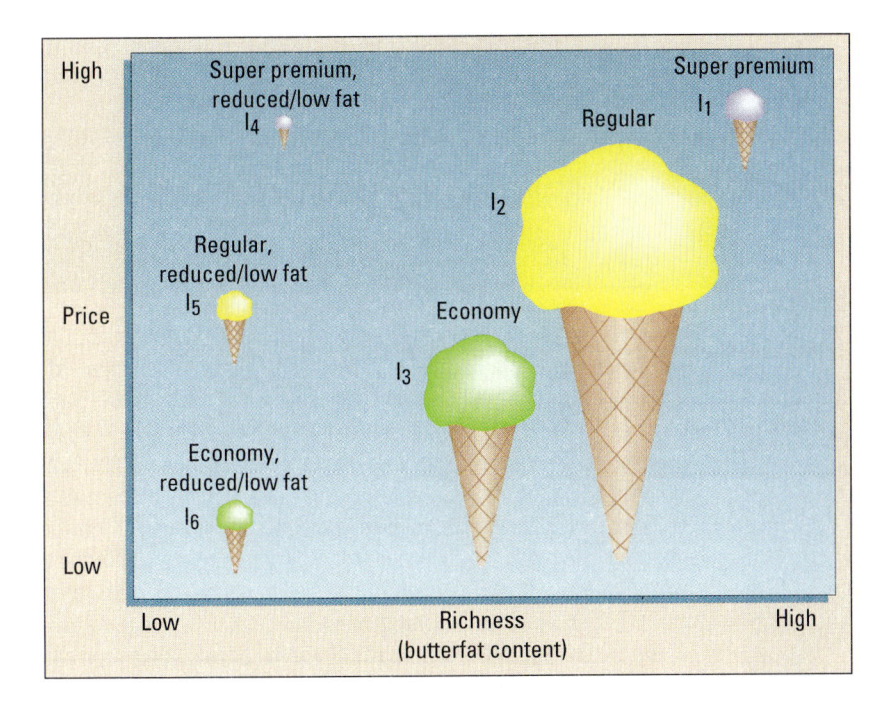

FIGURE 11-6
The Product Positioning of Ice Cream

is to have consumers perceive product attributes as the firm intends. When a product has an established niche in the market, a company must regularly reinforce its image and communicate the reasons for its success. Once consumer perceptions are formed, they may be hard to alter. And it may also be tough later to change a product's niche in the market (for instance, from low price, low quality, to high price, high quality).

Through **product positioning**, a firm can map each of its products in terms of consumer perceptions and desires, competition, other company products, and environmental changes. Consumer perceptions are the images of products, both a firm's and competitors', in people's minds. Consumer desires refer to the attributes that people would most like products to have—their **ideal points**. If a group of people has a distinctive "ideal" for a product category, that group is a potential market segment. A firm will do well if its products' attributes are perceived by consumers as being close to their ideal.

Competitive product positioning refers to people's perceptions of a firm relative to competitors. The goal is for the firm's products to be perceived as "more ideal" than competitors'. *Company product positioning* shows a firm how consumers perceive that firm's different brands (items) within the same product line and the relationship of those brands (items) to each other. The goal is for each of the firm's brands to be positioned near an ideal point, yet not too close to one another in the consumer's mind—the brands should appeal to different ideal points (market segments).

A firm must monitor the environmental changes that may alter the way its products are perceived. Such changes could include new technology, shifts in consumer lifestyles, new offerings by competitors, and negative publicity.

Product positioning is illustrated in Figure 11-6, which depicts the ice cream marketplace in terms of the consumer desires regarding two key ice-cream attributes: price and richness (level of butterfat content). In this figure, there are six ideal points (target markets)—I1-I6, each associated with a specific type of ice cream. Here is a brief description of the six categories:

- *I1—super premium*. The creamiest, richest ice cream (butterfat content of 15 to 18 per cent) with the highest price. Häagen-Dazs, Movenpick's, Richard D's, Laura Secord, and Ben & Jerry's are in this grouping. This segment is the fastest growing and represents about 3 per cent of Canadian ice cream sales.
- *I2—regular*. A creamy, rich ice cream (butterfat content of 10 to 12 per cent) with an average to slightly above-average price. Sealtest, Breyers, Natrel, and Baskin Robbins are positioned here.

Product positioning maps out *consumer perceptions of product attributes.* **Ideal points** show the *most preferred attributes.*

Both competitive and company product-positioning are important.

Ethics AND TODAY'S MARKETER

Old Dutch Potato Chips Expands Their Product Market to Ontario and Finds a "Chippy" Response from Hostess Frito-Lay

Faced with a maturing market for potato chips in Western Canada, Winnipeg-based Old Dutch Foods Ltd. decided to head east to the Ontario market. At the time, Old Dutch was the market leader in Western Canada with sales of $115 million and market shares of nearly 60 per cent in Manitoba, Saskatchewan, and Alberta respectively and 40 per cent in British Columbia. However, the Canadian chip market is worth over $1 billion in annual sales, with a great majority of these sales to be found in the large and lucrative, but fairly mature, Ontario chip market. Hostess Frito-Lay of Toronto and Humpty-Dumpty Foods Ltd. of Montreal were comfortably in control of Eastern Canada with 45 per cent of the market each, and were not too pleased to discover Old Dutch was planning to move in.

Old Dutch expected a bit of a battle, maybe price cutting, promotional contests, in-store promotional displays, trade incentives, trade inventory loading, the usual. However, the tactic Hostess Frito-Lay chose came as a complete surprise to Old Dutch: the sales representatives from Hostess Frito-Lay went to all of the retailers who had purchased Old Dutch potato chips and bought up their inventory! Since Old Dutch was trying to supply Ontario from its Winnipeg base and did not have an extensive truck fleet, they could not replenish chip supplies quickly enough. The power of the tactic was that Old Dutch had been promoting its product to Ontario consumers and creating demand, but because there was no shelf-stock, consumers could not try the product and became dismayed and disenchanted. Dismay was also the reaction of Old Dutch, because the purchase of their stocks from some eighty-two retailers was rumoured to have occurred as a result of coercion on the part of Hostess Frito-Lay.

The activity was clearly anti-competitive and Old Dutch complained to the Federal Competition Bureau. At this point, Hostess Frito-Lay ceased buying up the product. When the Competition Bureau investigated they concluded that since the tactic was no longer being employed, they did not need to take action and the issue was closed. Curiously, Old Dutch was accused of employing this same tactic when Miss Vickie's, a small Ontario potato chip manufacturer, attempted to penetrate the Western market.

As the marketing manager of Old Dutch potato chips, how would you proceed now?

Source: Based on "Crunch Time," *Report on Business Magazine*, Vol. 8 (December 1991), pp. 48–52; "Chipping Away for More Share," *Playback Strategy*, Vol. 2 (July 15, 1991), pp. 1–2; "Hostess on Buying Binge of Rival's Potato Chips: Consumers Blocked from Product, Old Dutch Manager Says," *Globe & Mail*, Metro edition (July 3, 1991), p. B3; "Bureau Checking Chips," *Globe & Mail*, Metro edition (July 13, 1991), p. B4.

FRITO-LAY
www.fritolay.com/

- I_3—*economy*. An average ice cream (butterfat content of 10 per cent) at a below-average price. Private-label brands fit here.
- I_4—*super premium, reduced or low fat*. A flavourful ice cream with a high price for moderately health-conscious consumers (butterfat content of 5 to 10 per cent). The reduced-fat versions of the leading super premiums go here.
- I_5—*regular, reduced or low fat*. A good-quality ice cream for more health-conscious consumers (butterfat content of less than 8 per cent) at an average price. Weight Watcher's, Light n' Lively, and Sealtest Parlour 1% are positioned here.

FIGURE 11-7
Wrigley's Spearmint Chewing Gum: Pure Chewing Satisfaction
Reprinted by permission of the Wm. Wrigley Jr. Company.

- *I6—economy, reduced or low fat.* An average ice cream for more health-conscious consumers (butterfat content of 4 to 8 per cent) at a below-average price. Private-label brands fit here.

An examination of competitive product positioning reveals that there are competing products in each market niche. In some instances, the marketplace is saturated. Nonetheless, the companies in the industry have done a good job in addressing the needs of the various consumer segments and in differentiating the products offered to each segment.

Breyers, Sealtest, and Light n' Lively are all marketed by Unilever. From an analysis of company product positioning, it is clear that Unilever serves the customers in its markets well. However, it must continue to differentiate carefully between Breyers (the "all natural" ice cream) and Sealtest (the "ice-cream parlor" ice cream).

By undertaking product-positioning analysis, a company can learn a great deal and plan its marketing efforts accordingly, as these examples show:

- Wrigley is always on the lookout for positioning opportunities for its chewing gums. Because of the negative attention placed on cigarette smoking, Wrigley recently embarked on a very creative marketing strategy for Wrigley's Spearmint gum—positioning it with the phrase, "When you can't smoke, enjoy pure chewing satisfaction." See Figure 11-7.

- Air Canada believes numerous travellers perceive airlines as indifferent and impersonal. To remedy this, it is emphasizing the quality of its service—depicted in ads by the worldwide symbol for outstanding service, the red carpet. See Figure 11-8.

- When marketing its photocopiers and fax machines, Japan's Konica is faced with the knowledge that many potential customers are unfamiliar with the company and its product lines. As a result, the firm has run ads such as the one shown in Figure 11-9—whereby Konica positions its products by aligning itself with another well-known name, in this case, Dutch Boy paint (from Sherwin-Williams). Konica must be careful that its positioning message does not get lost in these ads.

FIGURE 11-8
Air Canada: A Customer-Service Positioning Approach

Reprinted by permission.

FIGURE 11-9
Konica Business Machines: Gaining Positioning Credibility by Affiliating Itself with the Dutch Boy Name

Reprinted by permission.

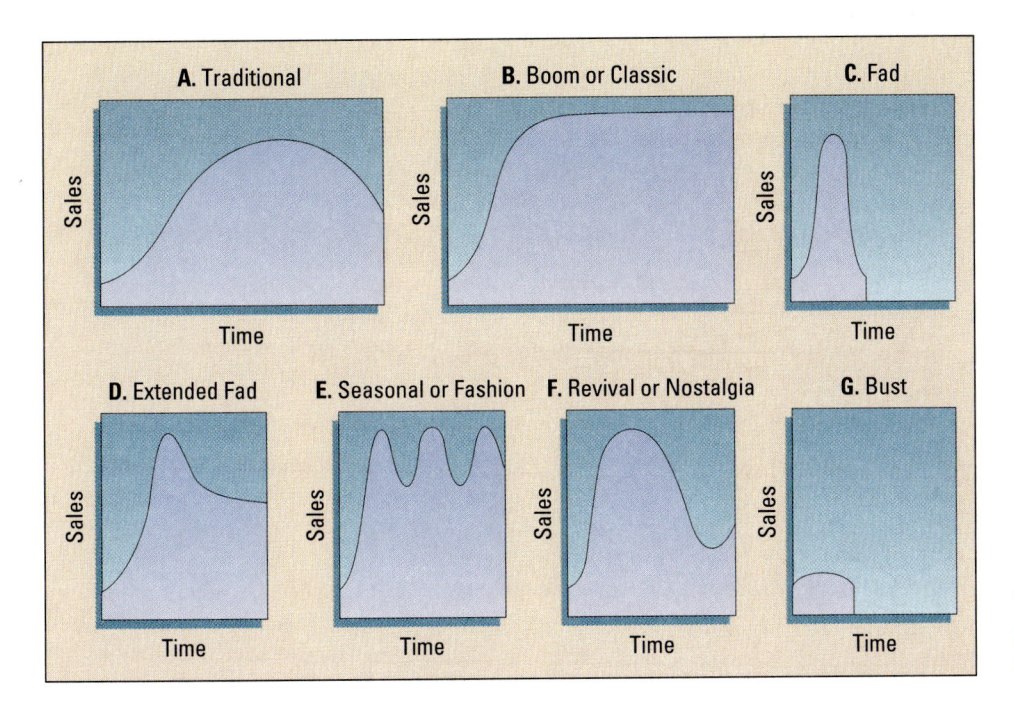

FIGURE 11-10
Selected Product Life-Cycle Patterns

The Product Life Cycle

The **product life cycle** is a concept that attempts to describe a product's sales, competitors, profits, customers, and marketing emphasis from its inception until it is removed from the market.

From a product-planning perspective, there is interest in the product life cycle for several reasons.

1. Some product lives are shorter than before.
2. New products often require high marketing and other investments.
3. An understanding of the concept lets a firm anticipate changes in consumer tastes, competition, and support from resellers and adjust its marketing plan accordingly.
4. The concept enables a firm to consider the product mix it should offer; many firms seek a **balanced product portfolio**, whereby a combination of new, growing, and mature products is maintained.

The life-cycle concept can be applied to a product class (watches), a product form (quartz watches), or a brand (Seiko quartz watches). Product forms generally follow the traditional life cycle more faithfully than product classes or brands.

As Figure 11-10 shows, product life cycles vary greatly, in both duration and shape. A *traditional cycle* has distinct periods of introduction, growth, maturity, and decline. A *boom*, or *classic, cycle* describes a very popular product that sells well for a long time. A *fad cycle* represents a product with quick popularity and a sudden decline. An *extended fad* is like a fad, but residual sales continue at a lower level than earlier sales. A *seasonal* or *fashion cycle* results if a product sells well in nonconsecutive periods. With a *revival* or *nostalgia cycle*, a seemingly obsolete product achieves new popularity. A *bust cycle* occurs for a product that fails.

Stages of the Traditional Product Life Cycle

The stages and characteristics of the traditional product-life cycle are shown in Figure 11-11 and Table 11-4, which both refer to total industry performance during the cycle. The performance of an individual firm may vary from that of the industry, depending on its specific goals, resources, marketing plans, location, competitive environment, level of success, and stage of entry.

*The **product life cycle** describes each stage in a product's life.*

*Companies often desire a **balanced product portfolio**.*

Product life cycles may be traditional, boom, fad, extended fad, seasonal, revival, or bust.

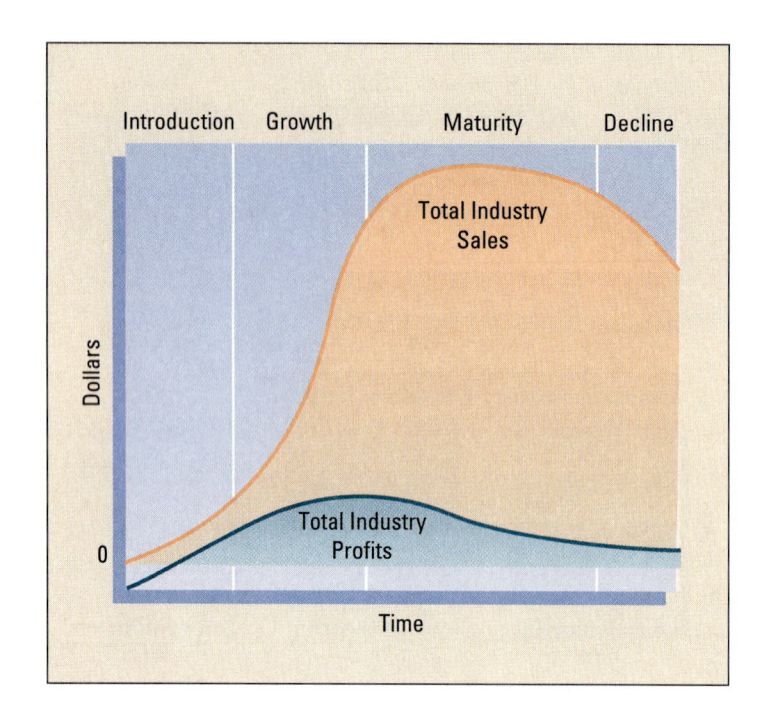

FIGURE 11-11
The Traditional Product Life Cycle

In the **introduction stage**, *the goal is to establish a consumer market.*

During the **introduction stage** of the product life cycle, a new product is introduced to the marketplace and the goal is to generate customer interest. The rate of sales growth depends on a product's newness, as well as its desirability. Generally, a product modification gains sales faster than a major innovation. Only one or two firms have entered the market, and competition is minimal. There are losses due to high production and marketing costs; and cash flow is poor. Initial customers are innovators who are willing to take risks, can afford to take them, and like the status of buying first. Because one or two firms dominate and costs are high, only one or a few basic product models are sold. For a rou-

Table 11-4
The Characteristics of the Traditional Product Life Cycle

	STAGE IN LIFE CYCLE			
CHARACTERISTICS	*Introduction*	*Growth*	*Maturity*	*Decline*
Marketing goal	Attract innovators and opinion leaders to new product	Expand distribution and product line	Maintain differential advantage as long as possible	(a) Cut back, (b) revive, or (c) terminate
Industry sales	Increasing	Rapidly increasing	Stable	Decreasing
Competition	None or small	Some	Substantial	Limited
Industry profits	Negative	Increasing	Decreasing	Decreasing
Customers	Innovators	Resourceful mass market	Mass market	Laggards
Product mix	One or a few basic models	Expanding line	Full product line	Best-sellers
Distribution	Depends on product	Rising number of outlets/distributors	Greatest number of outlets/distributors	Decreasing number of outlets/distributors
Promotion	Informative	Persuasive	Competitive	Informative
Pricing	Depends on product	Greater range of prices	Full line of prices	Selected prices

tine item like a new cereal, distribution is extensive. For a luxury item like a new boat, distribution is limited. Promotion must be informative, and free samples may be desirable. Depending on the product and choice of consumer market, a firm may start with a high status price or low mass-market price.

Over the **growth stage** of the product life cycle, a new product gains wider consumer acceptance, and the marketing goal is to expand distribution and the range of available product alternatives. Industry sales increase rapidly as a few more firms enter a highly profitable market that has substantial potential. Total and unit profits are high because an affluent (resourceful) mass market buys distinctive products from a limited group of firms and is willing to pay for them. To accommodate the growing market, modified versions of basic models are offered, distribution is expanded, persuasive mass advertising is utilized, and a range of prices is available.

*During the **growth stage**, firms enlarge the market and offer alternatives.*

During the **maturity stage** of the product life cycle, a product's sales growth levels off and firms try to maintain a differential advantage (such as a lower price, improved features, or extended warranty) for as long as possible. Industry sales stabilize as the market becomes saturated and many firms enter to capitalize on the still sizable demand. Competition is at its highest. Thus, total industry and unit profits drop because discounting is popular. The average-income mass market makes purchases. A full product line is made available at many outlets (or through many distributors) and many prices. Promotion becomes very competitive.

*In the **maturity stage**, companies work hard to sustain a differential advantage.*

In the **decline stage** of the product life cycle, a product's sales fall as substitutes enter the market or consumers lose interest. Firms have three options. They can cut back on marketing, thus reducing the number of product items they make, the outlets they sell through, and the promotion used; they can revive a product by repositioning, repackaging, or otherwise remarketing it; or they can drop the product. As industry sales decline, many firms exit the market since customers are fewer and they have less money to spend. The product mix focuses on best-sellers, selected outlets (distributors) and prices, and promotion that stresses—informatively—availability and price.

*In the **decline stage**, firms reduce marketing, revive a product, or end it.*

The bulky, electric-powered portable calculator is a good example of a product form that moved through the life cycle. It went from an exclusive, expensive item to a widespread, moderately priced item to a mass-marketed, inexpensive item to obsolescence. Today, earlier versions of the portable calculator have been replaced by technologically advanced product forms—such as credit-card sized, solar-powered calculators.

Evaluating the Product Life-Cycle Concept

The product life cycle provides a good framework for product planning; but, it has not proven very useful in forecasting. In using the product life-cycle concept, these key points should be kept in mind:

1. The stages, the time span, and the shape of the cycle (such as flat, erratic, or sharply inclined) vary by product.

2. Such external factors as the economy, inflation, and consumer lifestyles may shorten or lengthen a product's life cycle.

3. A firm may do better or worse than the industry "average" at any stage in the cycle. Just because an industry is in the growth stage for a product does not mean every firm that enters the market will succeed, nor does the decline stage mean lower sales for every firm.

4. A firm may not only be able to manage a product life cycle, it may also be able to extend it or reverse a decline. Effective marketing may lure a new market segment, find a new product use, or foster better reseller support.

5. As Figure 11-12 illustrates, firms may engage in a **self-fulfilling prophecy**, whereby they predict falling sales and then ensure this by reducing or removing marketing support. With proper marketing, some products might not fail.

*A **self-fulfilling prophecy** may occur when a firm anticipates declining sales and reduces marketing efforts.*

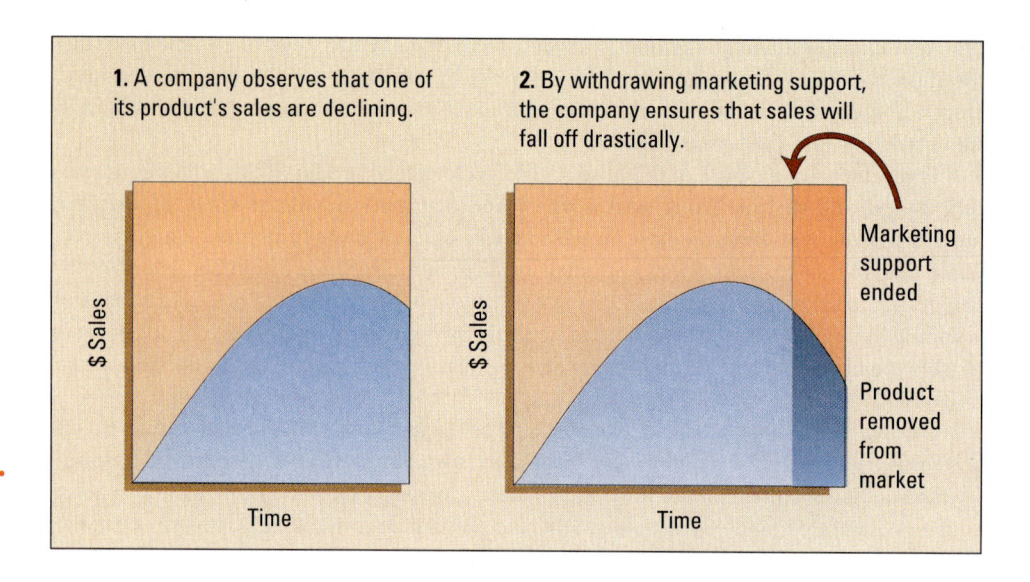

FIGURE 11-12
A Self-Fulfilling Prophecy

1. A company observes that one of its product's sales are declining.
2. By withdrawing marketing support, the company ensures that sales will fall off drastically.

Marketing support ended
Product removed from market

The International Dimensions of Product Planning

When an international product plan is being devised, the following points should be kept in mind:

- Although a firm may offer the same products in countries around the globe, these products can have distinct generic meanings in different countries.
- In developing and less-developed countries, product "frills" are often less important than in industrialized countries.
- Due to their intangibility, perishability, inseparability, and variability, international marketing efforts for services are often more complex than those for goods.
- The concept of convenience, shopping, and specialty products is less valid in markets where distribution is limited or consumers have few choices.
- Installations and accessory equipment may be hard to ship overseas.
- Marketing all of the items in a wide and/or deep product mix may not be appropriate, or economically feasible, on an international basis.
- The diversity of international markets may necessitate a decentralized product management organization, with some executives permanently assigned to foreign countries.
- For many products, there are differences in product positioning and consumer ideal points by country or region. Simple positioning messages travel better than more complicated ones.
- Some products are in different stages of their life cycles in developing and less-developed countries than in industrialized countries.
- Expectations regarding goods/services combinations (discussed in the next chapter) may differ by country.
- A product modification or minor innovation in a home market may be a major innovation internationally, necessitating different marketing approaches.
- The characteristics of the market segments—innovators, early adopters, early majority, late majority, and laggards—in the diffusion process (covered in Chapter 13) often differ by country.
- Even though global branding and packaging may be desirable, various nations may have special needs or requirements.

International Marketing in Action

Are the Positioning Factors Used by MBA Students Universal?

As consumers, how do MBA students decide upon a product's positioning? To answer this question, a marketing research study was conducted to evaluate the importance of brand name, price, physical appearance, and retailer reputation as indicators of product quality for consumer electronics. A questionnaire was completed by 640 beginning MBA students from thirty-eight mostly western industrialized countries and Japan. The respondents were matched on such factors as age, education, professional goals, and income; and they were separated into four cultural groups: North American countries (Canada and the U.S.), EU member countries, European countries not belonging to the EU, and others.

The researchers found that brand-name cues are more important than price or physical appearance—regardless of cultural group. And price and physical appearance are more important than a retailer's reputation in positioning a product's overall quality. The findings support the notion that the value of certain product positioning cues does not vary by culture.

The study's authors suggest that culture or country boundaries are less important in product positioning than these five factors:

- The more consumers rely on a particular quality cue, the more they also want information from other sources.
- Consumers who are willing to accept certain forms of risk also tend to use positioning cues the most.
- Brand-prone consumers are less price sensitive.
- The use of brand and price as signals increases when people have a greater intention to buy a product or when they perceive product benefits as high.
- The use of specific positioning cues decreases as a consumer's education increases and when the consumer is more technologically oriented.

As a Sony Discman marketing manager responsible for the Canadian and the U.S. markets, how would you use these results in catering to educated young adults?

Source: Based on material in Niraj Dawar and Philip Parker, "Marketing Universals: Consumers' Use of Brand Name, Price, Physical Appearance, and Retailer Reputation as Signals of Product Quality," *Journal of Marketing*, Vol. 58 (April 1994), pp. 81–95.

MARKETING IN A CHANGING WORLD

Even Toyota's Not Infallible[15]

With its stable of Toyota and Lexus vehicles, Toyota has been one of the most respected manufacturers in the world for decades. Toyota is admired for its ability to read the market, its deep product mix, the quality of its vehicles, its ability to position its models in the marketplace (especially the upscale Lexus brand), and its strong customer following. And lest we forget, Toyota's annual sales exceed U.S.$100 billion and it is very profitable.

Yet, despite its prowess, this manufacturing dynamo recently had a major stumble in its home Japanese market with the redesigned Corolla. What does this signify? Careful product planning turns into successful product planning only if the consumer says so.

TOYOTA
www.toyota.com/

[15] The material in this section is based on Andrew Pollack, "The Risks of Cutting Too Far," *New York Times* (December 21, 1995), pp. D1, D8.

For years, Japanese car makers built base models that were luxurious by other makers' standards. The Toyota Corolla was Japan's best-selling car for twenty-six years. Thus, when Toyota—worried that sticker prices had grown too steep—did a full remodelling and stripped features from the Corollas it sells in Japan, consumers rebelled. Toyota responded by restoring some of the removed features in a mid-year replacement model.

Before the remodelling, a basic Toyota Corolla sold for U.S.$10 700 in Japan. Standard features included an AM-FM stereo, self-adjusting air-conditioning, and bumpers painted so they matched the car's colour. The remodelled Corolla sold for U.S.$9750 due to a simplified engine, an AM mono radio, partially vinyl seats, black bumpers, and manual-control air-conditioning. Said one dealer, the car "looked cheaper" and "the interior was much poorer."

Once Toyota saw the consumer reaction to the redesign, it had a revamped Corolla at dealer showrooms within five months. The remodelled U.S.$10 400 basic Corolla included full-fabric seats, power windows, automatic door locks, and a driver's airbag (which is not legally mandated in Japan). As Toyota learned, "cutting costs too much—or too obviously—can backfire, turning consumer off," even if prices are cut, too.

SUMMARY

1. To define product planning and differentiate among tangible, augmented, and generic products Product planning systematically allows a firm to pinpoint opportunities, develop marketing programs, coordinate a product mix, maintain successful products, reappraise faltering ones, and delete undesirable products.

Products should be defined in a combination of ways. A tangible product is a basic physical entity, service, or idea with precise specifications; it is offered under a given description or model number. An augmented product includes not only tangible elements, but also the accompanying cluster of image and service features. A generic product focuses on the benefits a buyer desires; this concept looks at what a product means to the consumer rather than the seller.

2. To examine the various types of products, product mixes, and product management organization forms from which a firm may select Goods marketing entails the sale of physical products. Service marketing includes goods rental, servicing goods owned by consumers, and personal services. Goods and services often differ in terms of intangibility, perishability, inseparability from the service provider, and variability in quality.

Consumer products are goods and services for the final consumer. They can be classified as convenience, shopping, and specialty items. These products are differentiated on the basis of consumer awareness of alternatives prior to the shopping trip and the degree of search and time spent shopping. Industrial products are goods and services used in the production of other goods or services, in the operation of a business, or for resale. They include installations, accessory equipment, raw materials, component materials, fabricated parts, business supplies, and business services. They are distinguished on the basis of decision making, costs, consumption, the role in production, and the change in form.

A product item is a specific model, brand, or size of a product sold by a firm. A product line is a group of closely related items sold by a firm. A product mix consists of all the different product lines a firm offers. The width, depth, and consistency of the product mix are important.

A firm may choose from or combine several product management structures, including: marketing manager system, product (brand) manager, product planning committee, new-product manager system, and venture team. Each has particular strengths and best uses.

3. To discuss product positioning and its usefulness for marketers A firm must ensure that each of its products is perceived as providing some combination of unique features and that they are desired by the target market. Through product positioning, a firm can map its offerings with regard to consumer perceptions, consumer desires, competition, its own products in the same line, and the changing environment. Competitive positioning, company positioning, and consumers' ideal points are key concepts.

4. To study the different types of product life cycles that a firm may encounter and the stages of the traditional product life cycle The product life cycle seeks to describe a product's sales, competitors, profits, customers, and marketing emphasis from its inception until its removal from the market. Many firms desire a balanced product portfolio, with products in various stages of the life cycle. The product life cycle has several derivations, ranging from traditional to fad to bust. The traditional cycle consists of four stages: introduction, growth, maturity, and decline. During each stage, the marketing objective, industry sales, competition, industry profits, customers, and the marketing mix change. While the life cycle is useful in planning, it should not be used as a forecasting tool.

5. To look at the international dimensions of product planning If a firm intends to market products internationally, several points should be kept in mind, including the distinctive generic meanings of products in different nations and the complexity of marketing services in foreign markets.

KEY TERMS

product planning (p. 291)
product (p. 291)
tangible product (p. 292)
augmented product (p. 292)
generic product (p. 292)
goods marketing (p. 292)
service marketing (p. 292)
consumer products (p. 293)
convenience products (p. 293)
shopping products (p. 294)
specialty products (p. 295)
industrial products (p. 295)

installations (p. 296)
accessory equipment (p. 296)
raw materials (p. 296)
component materials (p. 296)
fabricated parts (p. 296)
industrial supplies (p. 296)
industrial services (p. 297)
product item (p. 297)
product line (p. 297)
product mix (p. 297)
marketing manager system (p. 301)
product (brand) manager system (p. 302)

product planning committee (p. 302)
new-product manager system (p. 302)
venture team (p. 302)
product positioning (p. 303)
ideal points (p. 303)
product life cycle (p. 307)
balanced product portfolio (p. 307)
introduction stage of the product life cycle (p. 308)
growth stage of the product life cycle (p. 309)
maturity stage of the product life cycle (p. 309)
decline stage of the product life cycle (p. 309)
self-fulfilling prophecy (p. 309)

Review Questions

1. Why is it so important to understand the concept of a generic product?
2. Distinguish between a consumer product and an industrial product.
3. How can the same product be a convenience, shopping, and a specialty product? What does this mean to marketers?
4. What are the similarities and differences between raw materials and component parts?
5. What is a wide/shallow product mix? State the advantages and disadvantages of such a mix.
6. Under what circumstances is a product manager system appropriate? A new-product manager system?
7. What is the role of product positioning for a new product? A continuing product?
8. How do competitive positioning and company positioning differ? Give an example of each.
9. Explain the basic premise of the product life cycle. What is the value of this concept?
10. What is the key marketing objective during the growth stage of the product life cycle? Why?

Discussion Questions

1. For each of the following, describe the tangible, augmented, and generic product:
   a. A review course for the Graduate Management Aptitude Test (GMAT).
   b. A computer mouse.
   c. A *Tragically Hip* CD.
   d. Highway paving materials.
2. Identify, describe, and differentiate between two product lines offered by the Pepsi Cola company. Refer to the definition of "product line" offered in the chapter to support your answer.
3. Evaluate the product mix for ConAgra, shown in Figure 11-4.
4. What product management organization would you recommend for a large firm that makes, installs, and services home security systems? The firm is thinking about getting involved with auto alarms, fire detectors, and/or television satellite dishes. Explain your answer.
15. How has the positioning of the cellular telephone changed since the product has been on the market? Why?

VIDEO CASE
E-ZEEWRAP

Jim Scharf is an entrepreneur with a capital E: E as in E-ZEEWRAP. His company, Jim Scharf Holdings Ltd., markets a unique plastic food wrap dispenser branded as E-ZEEWRAP and the plastic wrap refills that go into it. Jim has no misconceptions about his product whatsoever. He says he is marketing plastic food wrap. The E-ZEEWRAP dispenser is the means by which he gets the wrap into his customers hands and obtains some customer loyalty on repurchases, where the real money is made. In this regard, one has to recognize that Jim Scharf has a very clear understanding of the concept his product represents to people. His customers seem to perceive the product concept in the same fashion too, and this is driving his success. E-ZEEWRAP is a product with $2.5 million in sales in Canada and Scharf wants to market it in the United States.

At first glance, one might not recognize Scharf as the astute businessperson that he is. He is often found working his 4000-acre farm near Perdue, Saskatchewan, 60 kilometres west of Saskatoon. Aside from growing lentils and wheat on the farm, Jim and his wife, Bruna, grow businesses. Some of the inventions that they have developed and marketed include a hoe to clear grain from the corners of trucks and the Looney Nest dollar-coin holder, which had sales of $500 000 when it was introduced.

However, Jim and Bruna have had to put aside their inventive and farming activities for a while to concentrate on the job of marketing E-ZEEWRAP. This plastic wrap dispenser holds a 1000-foot (30-metre) roll of plastic wrap, but is only twice the size of other boxed rolls that hold about one tenth of that amount. The dispenser is made by an injection moulder in Swift Current, Saskatchewan and then trucked to Perdue, where it is assembled and packaged in an 8000-square-foot facility that acts as plant, office, and warehouse for Jim Scharf Holdings Ltd.

Jim Scharf began marketing E-ZEEWRAP via direct-response marketing using television advertising to demonstrate the advantages of the product. Because Jim could not afford the out-of-pocket expenses for the TV air time in Canada, he made a unique arrangement. He cut the TV stations in on the profits and sales of the product created by the advertising. Many of the television stations took him up on his offer and were rewarded with more revenue than if they had charged directly for the air time. The product first retailed for $50 in 1986 but more recent versions have been priced in the $20–$30 range. Physical distribution was through mail delivery. The success in Canada made it possible for Scharf to move from direct-response marketing to retail distribution through outlets such as Canadian Tire and K-mart.

Jim has chosen to pursue the same strategy to penetrate the United States, developing demand with direct-response promotion and then distributing the product through conventional retailers. He has set up a barter deal with Turner Broadcasting System (TBS Superstation and CNN), trading product for some advertising air time. However, because of the size of the market, Jim's busy schedule, and the competition for air time, he cannot work the same kind of revenue-sharing deal for all the TV air time he needs. Therefore, he needs a $4-million loan from his bank to buy the U.S. television air time to launch his product.

Success for E-ZEEWRAP is not solely dependent on obtaining this loan; Jim has secured a distribution agreement from True Value Hardware, a 7000-store national chain in the U.S., and Wal-Mart and others are considering handling the product as well. Scharf is currently the major employer in Perdue, Saskatchewan and it looks like employment prospects are about to get better. In fact, Scharf is looking at taking his experience with plastic wrap to the next level, packaging and distributing noodles!

QUESTIONS

1. Describe E-ZEEWRAP's product-planning strategy from the perspective of the generic product concept.
2. How would you characterize Jim Scharf Holdings' product mix? Explain your answer.
3. What stage of the product life cycle is E-ZEEWRAP currently at in Canada? Explain your answer.
4. The case does not touch upon competitive products very much. Identify and evaluate some potentially serious competitive threats that E-ZEEWRAP might face and articulate some responses to these threats. Justify your answer.

VIDEO QUESTIONS ON E-ZEEWRAP

1. In the video, one of the questions of concern posed to Jim Scharf by his bankers focused on competition. Discuss the kind of competition E-ZEEWRAP faces in terms of the concepts of direct and indirect product competition. Provide detailed examples of competing brands and products as much as possible.
2. Develop a positioning map for E-ZEEWRAP. Do you think the current positioning is effective? Justify your opinion.

Video Source: "E-ZEEWRAP," *Venture* (November 12, 1995).
Other Source: "The Enterprising Entrepreneur (E-ZEEWRAP Plastic Wrap Dispenser)," *Saskatchewan Business* (April 1992), p. 12.

CASE STUDY

Arm & Hammer Baking Soda: A Positioning Powerhouse

Baking soda (sodium bicarbonate) was originally formulated for use in kitchens in the 1830s by Dr. Austin Church, a physician. In the 1840s, Dr. Church's brother-in-law, John Dwight, marketed baking soda as a time-saver for homemakers who made yeast-based breads and biscuits. When the product was combined with vinegar, buttermilk, or molasses, it released carbon dioxide, which created an instant leavening agent. Early in its history, baking soda was also used to neutralize stomach acids. Over time, other household uses were discovered. These include baking soda's use as a refrigerator freshener, garage floor cleaner, toothpaste ingredient to deter the formation of plaque, and fire extinguisher for grease-based fires. Many of these applications were discovered by consumers who communicated them to Dwight & Church, the parent company of Arm & Hammer.

Marketing research studies show that 90 percent of North American households have at least one box of baking soda in their home. Each year, 450 million kilograms of baking soda are sold in North America alone. And Arm & Hammer has the lion's share of sales for this product category in the U.S. and in Canada where they use both the Arm & Hammer Baking Soda and Cow Brand Baking Soda brand names.

In Canada Arm & Hammer has been faced with two positioning issues in the consumer market. First, the company wants to phase out the Cow Brand name and present a single image, Arm & Hammer's. They plan to do this by more prominently displaying the Arm & Hammer logo, while downplaying the Cow Brand name and image on the packaging. The second positioning issue involves a response to an aggressive competitor. Sifto has been making strong competitive moves by distributing their product in packaging with claims that it is more "pure" than competing brands. Arm & Hammer has taken them to court in Ontario over the issue and Sifto has been told to dampen down their claims.

Arm & Hammer Baking Soda is not solely focused on home-based uses; the product has over 300 significant industrial applications. For example, more baking soda is used as an ingredient in cattle feed than for any other application. Beef cattle are given baking soda to speed up digestion of their high-energy, low-fibre diet. And dairy cows are fed baking soda to increase their milk production. Baking soda has also been applied as a cleaning agent for the interior of the Statue of Liberty, as an ingredient in kidney dialysis solutions, and to reduce environmental pollution.

At Arm & Hammer, sales of baking soda for environmental applications have grown more than 25 per cent a year for the past five years. According to a spokesperson for Church & Dwight, "The possibilities for sodium bicarbonate to react favourably on the environment are almost infinite." Baking soda is even used to keep such toxic materials as lead and copper out of drinking water, help prevent acid rain, reduce smokestack emissions, and clean building façades. Let's look at these environmental applications.

Until ten years ago, lead pipes were commonly used in water systems. Unfortunately, when these pipes begin to corrode, lead leaches into the public's drinking water. Baking soda, when added to the water supply, bonds with the dissolving lead to produce a coating on the inside of lead pipes. This coating prevents further leaching of lead into the drinking water. In the past, phosphates were used by many municipalities to prevent lead contamination. However, unlike baking soda, phosphates had a detrimental effect on the ecosystem.

In recent years, factories and municipal waste plants in more than sixty cities have begun to use baking soda to help prevent acid rain. Using technology developed by Church & Dwight, these factories and plants now shoot baking soda into smokestacks and flues. The baking soda effectively absorbs acid gases before they enter the air. As a result, acid rain emissions have been controlled.

Baking soda is also being utilized to remove grime, paint, and graffiti from buildings. Unlike sandblasting and chemical solvents, baking soda does not damage the surface or release dangerous chemical fumes.

According to the president of the nationwide Earth Day Network, "It [Baking soda] is a perfect example of using an environmentally sound product to make money. We'd be in much better shape if we realized what's good for the environment is also good for business."

QUESTIONS

1. Describe Arm & Hammer's product mix based on its width, depth, and consistency.
2. What product management organization is most appropriate for Church & Dwight? Explain your answer.
3. Present a product positioning strategy for Arm & Hammer's baking soda to deal with Sifto's baking soda.
4. Evaluate the success of Arm & Hammer's baking soda from the perspective of the product life-cycle concept.

Source: The data in this case are drawn from Suzanne Hamlin, "Baking Soda to the Rescue!" *New York Times* (July 19, 1995), pp. C1, C6; "Judge Rules Sifto Must Alter Packaging," *Globe & Mail*, Metro edition (September 28, 1994), p. B7; and "Arm & Hammer Muscles in on Maud: Namesake Is Downplayed in New Marketing of Baking Soda," *Marketing Magazine* (October 12, 1992), p.3.

CHURCH & DWIGHT CO. INC
www.envirolink.org/orgs/edn/ChurchRs.html

CHAPTER 12
Goods Versus Services Planning

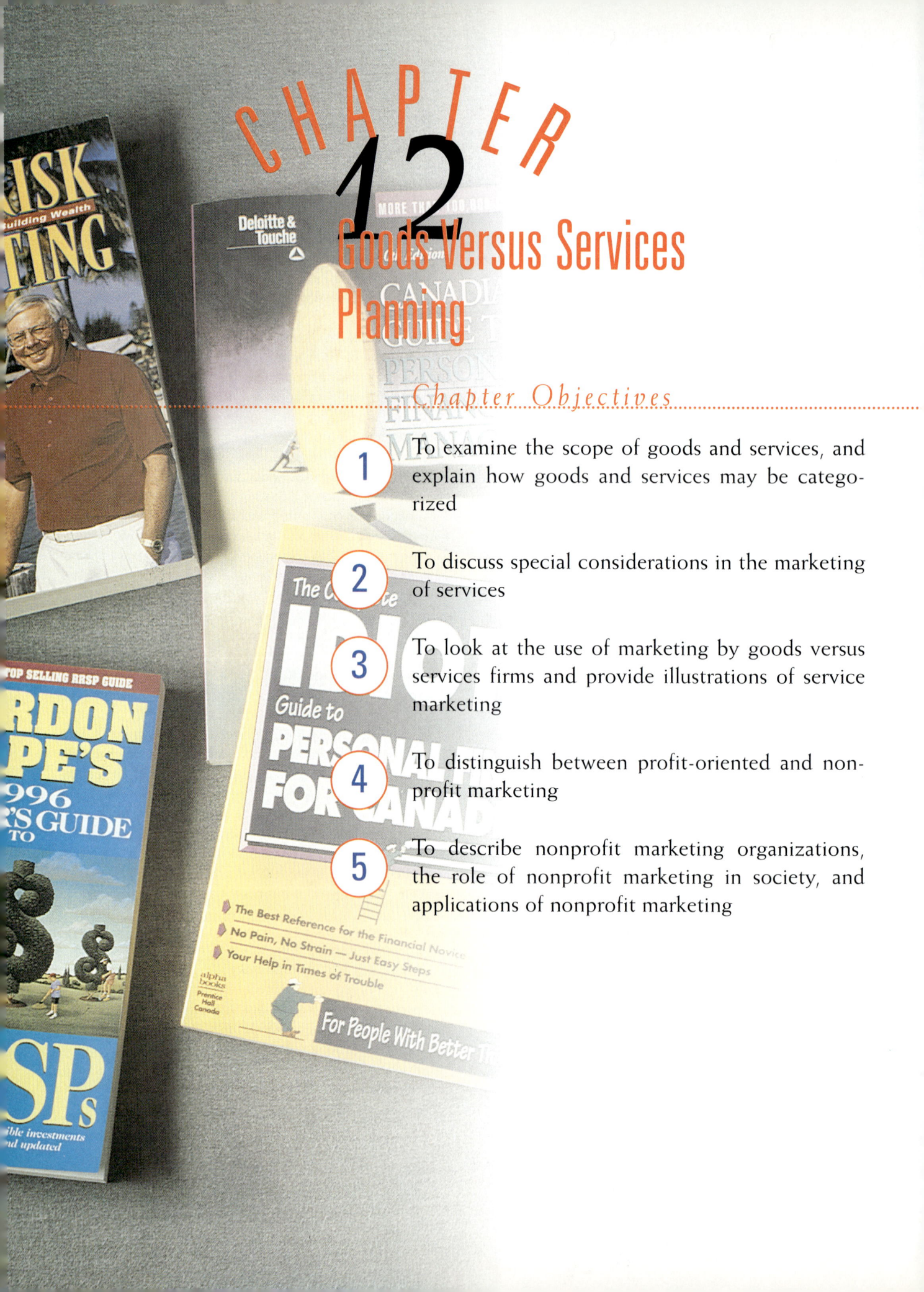

Chapter Objectives

1. To examine the scope of goods and services, and explain how goods and services may be categorized

2. To discuss special considerations in the marketing of services

3. To look at the use of marketing by goods versus services firms and provide illustrations of service marketing

4. To distinguish between profit-oriented and nonprofit marketing

5. To describe nonprofit marketing organizations, the role of nonprofit marketing in society, and applications of nonprofit marketing

> *In Canada, the industries that are winning the fast-growing, job adding, tax-paying race are those that involve services, technology, and the environment.*

The services sector has had tremendous growth in the last thirty years in North America and promises to grow well in the rest of the world. Globalization is seen as an important trend that will affect service-industry growth and will be fueled by technology. One report indicates that there are as many as 20 000 unfilled positions available in Canada for people who design, develop, and write computer programs. A Statistics Canada survey on trends in employment compared the growth of service jobs between 1960 and 1990 in Canada and the U.S. The study indicated that 72 per cent of all employment was in the service sector in 1990 as compared to 1960 when 55 per cent of employed Canadians and 58 per cent of employed Americans worked in services.

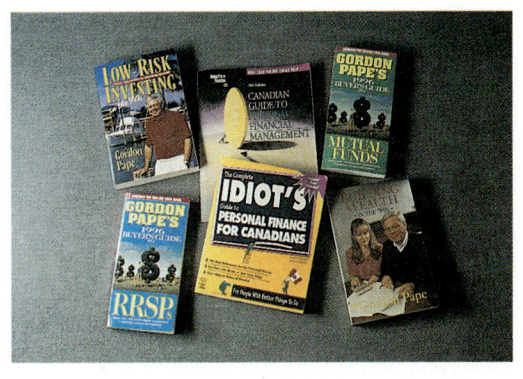

Canada's population is aging and they have less need of physical goods and more need of services as a result. The hottest growth services are in personal finance—services such as estate planning and financial planning for retirement. Other growth areas are business services, community services, health care services, personal services, and even funeral services.

Despite the growth in service jobs, productivity in service industries has not kept pace, even with the advances in modern technology. A study of ten large U.S. firms that had 10 000 or more personal computers was carried out by Nolan, Norton & Co. The results of the study indicated that employee cost in learning involved lost productivity worth between U.S.$6000 and $15 000, while the annual amortization expenses of the hardware and software was U.S.$2000 to $6500 per workstation. Productivity has begun to increase over the past three or four years due to increased electronic data interchanges coupled with the concept of mobile offices. The trend to downsizing in companies has also contributed to productivity gains because firms have fewer staff, and this has been offset by an increasing use of local and wide-area networks, which provide quick access to information.

Thus, service industries driven by technology, globalization, and an aging population present a tremendous opportunity, as they promise to exceed their pace of growth since 1960.[1]

In this chapter, we will study key concepts pertaining to the marketing of services. We will also focus on the differences and similarities between goods and services marketing.

Overview

When devising and enacting product plans, a firm must fully comprehend the distinctions between goods and services—beyond the brief coverage in Chapter 11. Although the

---

[1] Katrina Onstad and Tamsen Tillson, "Get 'Em While They're Hot," *Canadian Business* (April 1996), pp. 37–55; "Service Sector Jobs Double in 30 Years," *Globe & Mail*, Metro edition (June 9, 1993), p. B3; and "Modern Technology Fails to Bring About Productivity Boom," *Financial Post*; (April 24–26, 1993), p.18.

planning process is the same for goods and services, their differences need to be reflected in the decisions made during planning.

Chapter 12 covers the scope of goods and services, a goods/services continuum, goods and services classifications, special considerations in service marketing, and the use of marketing by goods and services firms. Also included is information on nonprofit marketing because most nonprofits (such as universities, health facilities, and libraries) are involved with services.

The Scope of Goods and Services

Goods marketing involves the sale of **durable** *and* **nondurable goods**.

Goods marketing entails the sale of physical products. **Durable goods** are physical products that are used over an extended period of time, such as furniture and heavy machinery. **Nondurable goods** are physical products made from materials other than metals, hard plastics, and wood; they are more quickly consumed or worn out; or they become dated, unfashionable, or otherwise unpopular. Examples are food and office supplies.

Service marketing covers **rented-goods**, **owned-goods**, *and* **nongoods services**.

Service marketing includes the rental of goods, the alteration, maintenance, or repair of goods owned by consumers, and personal services. **Rented-goods services** involve the leasing of goods for a specified period of time—such as auto, hotel-room, office-building, and tuxedo rentals. **Owned-goods services** involve alterations to, or maintenance or repair of, goods owned by consumers, such as house painting, clothing alterations, lawn care, equipment maintenance, and machinery repair. **Nongoods services** involve personal service on the part of the seller, such as accounting, legal, consulting, and tutoring services; they do not involve goods.

Overall, the value of manufacturers' shipments of Canadian-made nondurable goods slightly exceeds that of durable goods. The leading durable products are transportation equipment, electronic and electrical equipment, machinery, and fabricated metal products. Among Canadian final consumers, 52 per cent of expenditures are on services, 26 per cent are on nondurables led by food products, and 22 per cent are on durable and semi-durable goods. Because nondurables are bought more often and consumed more quickly, sales are more influenced by ads and sales promotions.

Service marketing is huge in industrialized nations, and accounts for two-thirds of the total output of the Canadian economy.

In industrialized nations, services generally account for well over one-half of the GDP. In developing and less-developed nations, services account for a lower share of GDP; goods production (including agricultural items and extracted resources) is more dominant. Yet, even in these countries, the role of services is growing rapidly. In Canada services-producing industries account for 66 per cent of the total output of the economy, at $360 billion. The United States is the world's leading service economy: services account for U.S.$ 4.5 trillion in annual output, or 60 per cent of the GDP. On an international level, the United States is by far the leading service exporter.

Three-quarters of the spending on services in Canada is by the business sector in such areas as transportation and storage; communications; wholesale trade; retail trade; finance; insurance and real estate; and community, business, and personal services. In contrast, the non-business sector accounts for the remaining quarter of service expenditures in categories such as government services and community and personal services. Among the leading Canadian service industries are finance; insurance and real estate; community, business, and personal services; and transportation and storage services. More than 78 per cent of the private-sector Canadian labour force is in service jobs. Among the other nations with at least 50 per cent of their labour forces in service jobs are Australia, Great Britain, France, Japan, Germany and the United States.[2]

These reasons have been cited for the worldwide growth of final-consumer services: the rising living standard of the population; the complex goods that require specialized installation and repair; consumers' lack of technical skills; the high purchase prices of items

---

[2]Bureau of Economic Analysis, U.S. Commerce Department; and *Statistical Abstract of the United States 1995* (Washington, D.C.: U.S. Department of Commerce, 1995), various pages. See also Fanglan Du, Paula Mergenhagen, and Marlene Lee, "The Future of Services," *American Demographics* (November 1995), pp. 30–47; Statistics Canada, *The Daily* (April 30, 1996); and Statistics Canada, *The Daily* (January 29, 1996).

that can be rented rather than bought; and the greater need for health care, child care, and educational services. In the industrial sector, here are some of the services experiencing the greatest growth: computer repair and training, management consulting, engineering, and equipment leasing. There are 612 000 people in Canada working in business services and these services are worth $68 billion to the nation's economy.[3]

The scope of services is sometimes underestimated because services may be lumped together with goods in assigning revenues. The **hidden service sector** encompasses the delivery, installation, maintenance, training, repair, and other services provided by firms that emphasize goods sales. For instance, although IBM is a manufacturer, its Integrated Systems Solutions division now generates billions of dollars in revenues. Through outsourcing, IBM "takes back a company's data-processing operations and then sells back computing services, or simply runs the operation for a fixed annual fee." In 1994 Air Canada signed an agreement for $800 million in contracts over a seven-year period with Advantis Canada. Advantis is a subsidiary of IBM Canada and will be composed of employees who formerly worked for IBM Canada, Air Canada, and the Gemini airline reservation system. Advantis will operate in conjunction with ISM Information Systems Management, IBM's outsourcing company.[4]

*The **hidden service sector** refers to services offered by goods-oriented firms.*

AIR CANADA
www.aircanada.ca/

Categorizing Goods and Services

Goods and services can be categorized in two ways. They can be located on a goods/services continuum; and they can be placed into separate classification systems.

A Goods/Services Continuum

A **goods/services continuum** categorizes products along a scale from pure goods to pure services. With pure goods, the seller offers the consumer only physical goods without any accompanying services. With pure services, the seller offers the consumer only nongoods services without any accompanying physical goods. Between the two extremes, the seller would offer a combination of goods and services to the consumer.

Figure 12-1 shows a goods/services continuum with four different examples. In each one, a pure good is depicted on the far left and a pure service is depicted on the far right. Moving from left to right within each example, the combined good/service offerings become more service-oriented. For example, a computer diskette is usually marketed as a pure good—a product free from defects. With most computer software, there is a telephone hotline to answer questions. A PC is typically set up (configured) by the seller, preloaded with software, and accompanied by on-site servicing. Computer programming involves labour-intensive service on a physical good. Systems design entails professional consultation regarding a client's information system needs; the seller provides a pure service and does not sell or service goods.

*With a **goods/services continuum**, products are positioned from pure goods to pure services.*

Several things can be learned from a goods/services continuum. First, it applies to both final-consumer and organizational-consumer products. Second, most products embody goods/services combinations; the selling firm must keep this in mind. Third, each position along the continuum represents a marketing opportunity. Fourth, the bond between a goods provider and its customers becomes closer as the firm moves away from marketing pure goods. Fifth, a firm must decide if it is to be perceived as goods- or services-oriented.[5]

Whether it is goods- or services-oriented, a company needs to specify which are its core services and which are peripheral—and then decide what level of peripheral services

---

[3] Statistics Canada, *The Daily* (January 29, 1996).
[4] "Advantis Takes Over Air Canada IS," *Computing Canada* (September 1, 1994), pp. 1,4; and Ira Sager, "The View from IBM," *Business Week* (October 30, 1995), p. 145.
[5] See Ralph W. Jackson, Lester A. Neidell, and Dale Lunsford, "An Empirical Investigation of the Differences in Goods and Services as Perceived by Organizational Buyers," *Industrial Marketing Management*, Vol. 24 (March 1995), pp. 99–108.

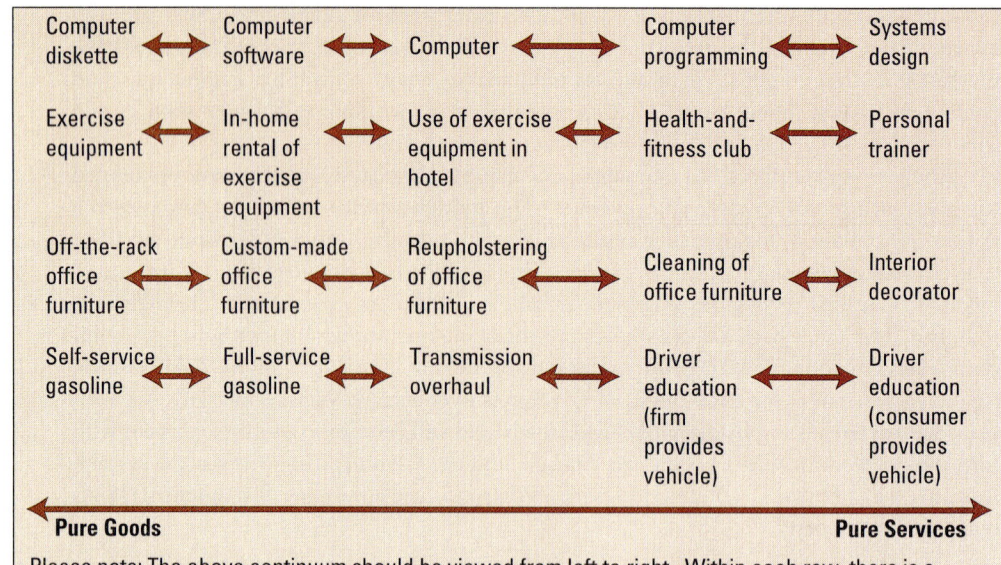

FIGURE 12-1
Illustrating the Goods/Services Continuum

Pure Goods ←——————————————————————————————————————→ Pure Services
Computer diskette ↔ Computer software ↔ Computer ↔ Computer programming ↔ Systems design
Exercise equipment ↔ In-home rental of exercise equipment ↔ Use of exercise equipment in hotel ↔ Health-and-fitness club ↔ Personal trainer
Off-the-rack office furniture ↔ Custom-made office furniture ↔ Reupholstering of office furniture ↔ Cleaning of office furniture ↔ Interior decorator
Self-service gasoline ↔ Full-service gasoline ↔ Transmission overhaul ↔ Driver education (firm provides vehicle) ↔ Driver education (consumer provides vehicle)

Please note: The above continuum should be viewed from left to right. Within each row, there is a consistent pattern from pure good to pure service. When comparing different rows, there is somewhat less consistency due to the diversity of the examples shown.

---

*By adding **peripheral services** to their **core services**, firms can create a competitive advantage.*

to offer. **Core services** are the basic services that firms must provide to their customers to be competitive. At Casio, core services include prompt delivery, credit, advertising support, and returns handling for the retailers that carry its watches in 150 nations around the globe. At Federal Express, core services involve taking phone orders, picking up packages, tracking them, shipping them overnight, and delivering them the next morning or afternoon.

Peripheral services are supplementary (extra) services that firms provide to customers. Casio's peripheral services are extended credit terms and advice on how to set up displays for its retailers, and a toll-free phone number for consumer inquiries. Federal Express' peripheral services include giving shipping advice to customers, making address labels and special packaging materials available, and tracing packages in transit. Although these services may increase a firm's costs, require added employee and management skills, and be time-consuming, they may also help a company create and sustain a competitive advantage.[6]

FEDERAL EXPRESS
www.fedex.com/

Goods and Services Classification Systems

Goods may be classified as to market, durability, value added, goals, regulation, distribution channel, and customer contact.

Figure 12-2 shows a detailed, seven-way classification system for goods. It is useful in demonstrating the diversity of goods marketing.

In selecting a market segment, a goods seller should remember that final and organizational consumers have similarities and differences. The same good may be offered to each segment. The major distinctions between the segments are the reasons for purchases, the amount bought, and the features desired.

Durable-goods marketers have a particular challenge. On the one hand, they want to emphasize the defect-free, long-running nature of their products. On the other hand, inasmuch as they need to generate repeat business from current customers, they must continually strive to add unique features and enhance the performance of new models—and then convince people to buy again while the durable goods they own are still functional. For

---

[6]See James C. Anderson and James A. Narus, "Capturing the Value of Supplementary Services," *Harvard Business Review*, Vol. 73 (January–February 1995), pp. 75–83.

Chapter 12 *Goods Versus Services Planning* 321

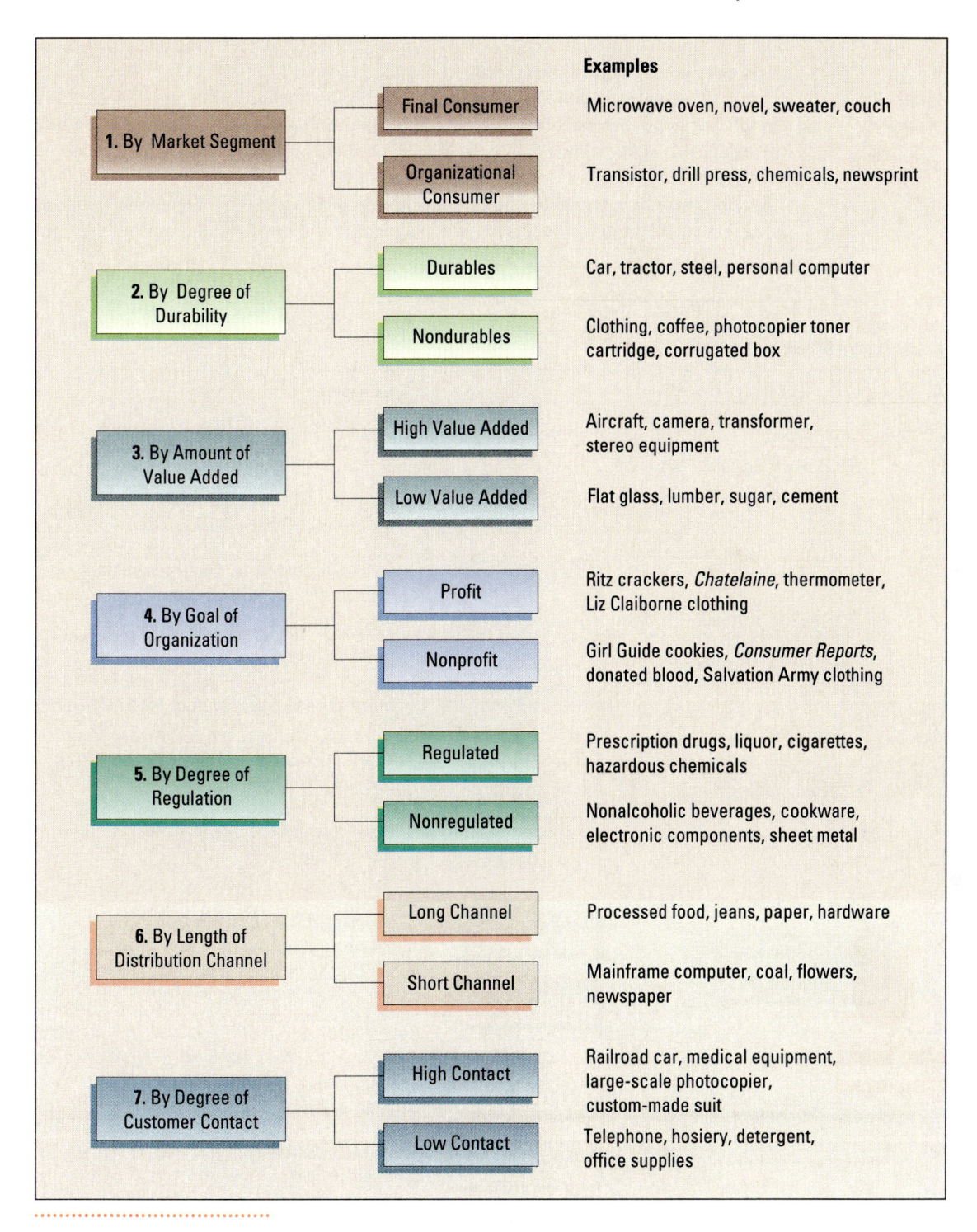

Category	Subcategory	Examples
1. By Market Segment	Final Consumer	Microwave oven, novel, sweater, couch
	Organizational Consumer	Transistor, drill press, chemicals, newsprint
2. By Degree of Durability	Durables	Car, tractor, steel, personal computer
	Nondurables	Clothing, coffee, photocopier toner cartridge, corrugated box
3. By Amount of Value Added	High Value Added	Aircraft, camera, transformer, stereo equipment
	Low Value Added	Flat glass, lumber, sugar, cement
4. By Goal of Organization	Profit	Ritz crackers, *Chatelaine*, thermometer, Liz Claiborne clothing
	Nonprofit	Girl Guide cookies, *Consumer Reports*, donated blood, Salvation Army clothing
5. By Degree of Regulation	Regulated	Prescription drugs, liquor, cigarettes, hazardous chemicals
	Nonregulated	Nonalcoholic beverages, cookware, electronic components, sheet metal
6. By Length of Distribution Channel	Long Channel	Processed food, jeans, paper, hardware
	Short Channel	Mainframe computer, coal, flowers, newspaper
7. By Degree of Customer Contact	High Contact	Railroad car, medical equipment, large-scale photocopier, custom-made suit
	Low Contact	Telephone, hosiery, detergent, office supplies

FIGURE 12-2
A Classification System for Goods

nondurable goods marketers, the key task is to engender brand loyalty, so consumers rebuy the same brands.

High value-added goods are those where manufacturers convert raw materials or components into distinctive products. The more value firms add to the goods they sell, the better the chance for a goods-based differential advantage. Low value-added goods are those where manufacturers do little to enhance the raw materials or components they extract or buy. These firms often must compete on price, since their goods may be seen as com-

322 Part 4 *Product Planning*

modities. Superior customer service can be a major differential advantage and enable marketers of low value-added goods to avoid commodity status.

For the most part, goods-oriented firms are profit-oriented. Sometimes, as noted in Figure 12-2, goods are marketed by nonprofit organizations—usually as a way of generating revenues to support their activities. Nonprofit marketing is discussed in depth later in this chapter.

Goods may be grouped by the extent of government regulation. Some items, such as those related to the health and safety of people and the environment, are highly regu-

FIGURE 12-3
A Classification System for Services

Classification	Category	Examples
1. By Market Segment	Final Consumer	Tutoring, taxi, car wash, life insurance
	Organizational Consumer	Management consulting, machinery repair, accounting services, legal services
2. By Degree of Tangibility	Rental Goods	Car rental, boat rental, hotel room rental, tool rental
	Owned Goods	Television repair, watch repair, plumbing repair
	Nongoods	University education, tutoring, legal services
3. By Skill of Service Provider	Professional	Legal services, medical services, accounting services, management consulting
	Nonprofessional	Taxi, uniformed security, janitorial, shoe shining
4. By Goal of Service Provider	Profit	Hospitals, insurance firms, executive recruiting, airlines
	Nonprofit	Crown Corporations, universities, libraries, museums
5. By Degree of Regulation	Regulated	Mass transit, hospitals, insurance firms, utilities
	Nonregulated	Computer time sharing, catering, lawn care, house painting
6. By Degree of Labour Intensiveness	Equipment-Based	Automated car wash, computer time sharing, dry cleaning, air travel
	People-Based	Executive recruiting, tennis instruction, accounting, uniformed security
7. By Degree of Customer Contact	High Contact	Universities, large appliance repair, air travel, hotels
	Low Contact	Lawn care, motion picture entertainment, janitorial service, automated car wash

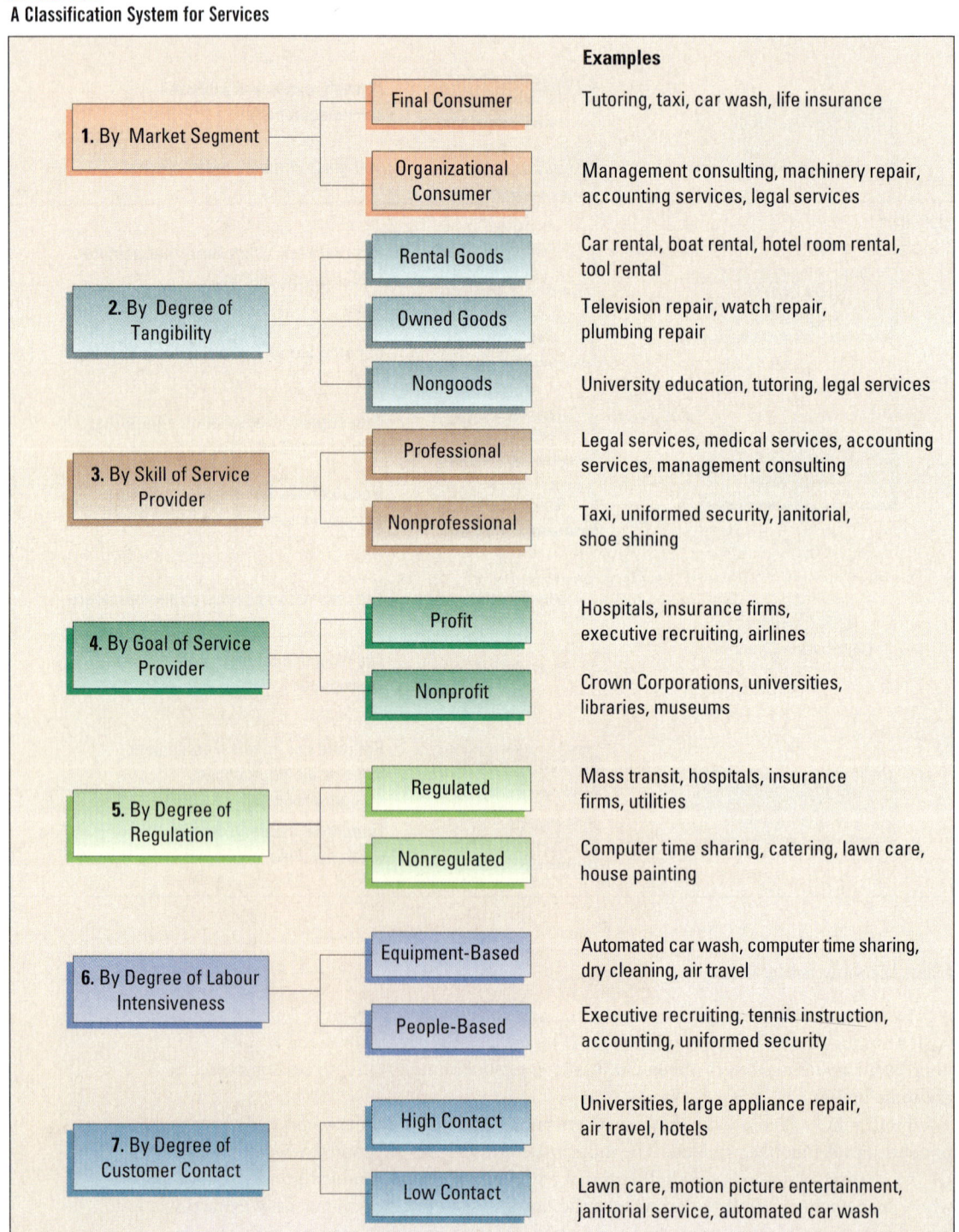

lated. Others, generally those not requiring special health and safety rules, are subject to less regulation.

Distribution channel length refers to the number of intermediaries between goods producers and consumers. Final-consumer goods tend to have more intermediaries than organizational-consumer goods due to the size and importance of the latter. Furthermore, goods that are complex, expensive, bulky, and perishable are more apt to have shorter channels.

Goods may be classified by the degree of customer contact between sellers and buyers. Contact is greater for sophisticated equipment, items requiring some training, and custom-made goods. In these instances, proper employee training is needed. Low customer contact is required for goods that consumers are able to buy and use with little assistance from sellers.

A good would normally be classified on a combination of the factors in Figure 12-2. *Chatelaine* magazine appeals to final consumers, is nondurable, has a high added value, is profit-oriented, is subject to few regulations, is sold through newsstands (long channel) and home delivery (short channel), and has low customer contact.

Figure 12-3 displays a detailed, seven-way classification system for services. It is helpful in showing the diversity of service marketing.

As with goods, final and organizational consumers have similarities and differences in their use of services. Both groups can counter high prices or poor service by doing some tasks themselves. The major differences between the segments are the reasons for the service, the quantity of service required, and the complexity of the service performed.

In general, the less tangible a service, the less services marketing resembles goods marketing. For nongoods services, 2nd performance can only be judged after the service is completed. Rentals and owned-goods services involve physical goods and may be marketed in a manner somewhat similar to goods.

Services may be provided by persons of greatly varying skills. For services requiring high skill levels, customers are quite selective in picking a provider. That is why professionals often achieve customer loyalty. For services requiring low levels of skill, the range of acceptable substitutes is usually much greater.

Service firms may be profit- or nonprofit-oriented. Nonprofit service marketing may be undertaken by government or private organizations. The major distinctions between profit- and nonprofit-oriented marketing are noted later in this chapter.

Services may be classed by the extent of government regulation. Some firms, such as insurance companies, are highly regulated. Others, such as caterers and house painters, are subject to limited regulation.

The traditional view of services has been that they are performed by one person for another. However, this view is too narrow. Services do differ in labour intensity—for example, automated versus teller-oriented bank services. Labour intensity rises if highly skilled personnel are involved or services must be provided at the customer's home or business. Some labour-intensive services may be done by do-it-yourself consumers—for example, home repair.

Services may be grouped by their degree of customer contact. If contact is high, training personnel in interpersonal skills is essential, in addition to the technical schooling needed to perform a service properly. An appliance repair person or a car mechanic may be the only contact a person has with a firm. If contact is low, technical skills are most essential.

A service would typically be classified using a combination of the factors in Figure 12-3. A firm tutoring students for graduate school entrance examinations appeals to final consumers, has an intangible service, requires skill by the service provider, is profit-oriented, is not regulated, has many trainers, and has high customer contact. A company may also operate in more than one part of a category (this also applies to goods marketers): A CA (Chartered Accountant) may have both final and organizational consumer clients.

Services may be classified as to market, tangibility, skill, goals, regulation, labour intensity, and customer contact.

Special Considerations in the Marketing of Services

Services differ from goods in terms of **intangibility**, **perishability**, **inseparability**, *and* **variability**.

CANADA TRUST
www.canadatrust.com/ct/disclaim.html

Services have four attributes that typically distinguish them from goods (as noted in Chapter 11): higher intangibility, greater perishability, inseparability of the service from the service provider, and greater variability in quality. Their effect is greatest for personal services.

The **intangibility** of services means they often cannot be displayed, transported, stored, packaged, or inspected before buying. This occurs for repair services and personal services; only the benefits to be derived from the service can be described. The **perishability** of services means many of them cannot be stored for future sale. If a painter who

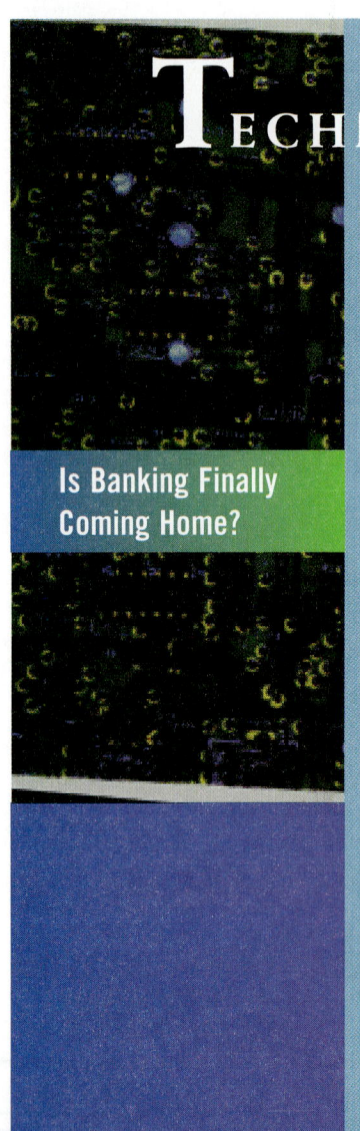

TECHNOLOGY & MARKETING

Is Banking Finally Coming Home?

Home banking services can now be conducted around-the-clock by phone or a modem-equipped personal computer. Consumers can use either their phones or PCs to transfer money between accounts, to verify their balances, and even to apply for credit cards. Although many consumers do engage in phone-based banking, banking by computer has not taken off. According to a recent study, only one per cent of consumers bank using their personal computers. Thus, there is much debate over the potential of home banking on PCs.

Some experts say consumers will soon embrace computers for home banking functions. As a manager at one large accounting firm says, "The Nintendo generation will be coming into substantial amounts of money by the time they're ready to do their personal banking, and then you'll see this market explode."

In Canada, Toronto Dominion Bank, Bank of Montreal, the Royal Bank, VanCity Credit Union, and Canada Trust are prominent financial institutions that have Internet Web sites; Toronto Dominion's Web site was rated as one of the top 100 sites in the world by *Interactive Age Magazine*. This has prompted a number of international customers to open accounts after visiting the site. The Web site has information such as RRSP data, economic reports, and TD Green Machine locations. TD Bank considered the Web site as a new channel of distribution for their services with the particular advantage that a Web site is not an intrusive form of marketing. Furthermore, the Web site allows TD to display a large quantity of information to clients who access the site while the costs of providing the information are significantly less than if hard copies were made available to all of the interested individuals. Still, TD has, for the moment, stopped short of online commerce.

In anticipation of the growth of home banking by PC in the United States, Bank America and Nations Bank recently purchased Meca Software, a developer of personal finance software. And twelve other banks have begun to offer updated home banking service via PC through Intuit's *Quicken* personal finance software.

Other experts wonder about the growth of computer-based home banking services. Even though Citibank reduced the fees for customers who use its home banking products, the bank's management still has doubts as to the long-term growth of PC-based home banking. As Citibank's marketing director says, "People will still want branches to get advice and seek help with financial planning." And the fees that many banks charge to use home banking services (ranging from $8 to $20 per month) are an additional deterrent to customer interest. Furthermore, the electronic payment of bills is now most suitable only for bills that are due periodically (such as utility and mortgage bills).

As the marketing manager for Toronto Dominion Bank, what marketing strategies (aside from a price reduction) would you enact to introduce computer-based home banking services?

Source: Based on material in David Menzie "TD Bank Opens a Branch in Cyberspace," *Marketing Magazine,* (June 19, 1995, p. 11; and Timothy L. O'Brien, "Home Banking: Will it Take Off This Time?" *Wall Street Journal* (June 8, 1995), pp. B1, B4.

needs eight hours to paint a single house is idle on Monday, he or she will not be able to paint two houses on Tuesday; Monday's idle time is lost. A service supplier must try to manage consumer usage so there is consistent demand over various parts of the week, month, and/or year.

The **inseparability** of services means a service provider and his or her services may be inseparable. When this occurs, the service provider is virtually indispensable, and customer contact is often considered an integral part of the service experience. The quality of machinery repair depends on a mechanic's skill and the quality of legal services depends on a lawyer's ability. **Variability** in service quality—differing service performance from one purchase occasion to another—often occurs even if services are completed by the same person. This may be due to a service firm's difficulty in problem diagnosis (for repairs), customer inability to verbalize service needs, and the lack of standardization and mass production for many services.

In planning its marketing strategy, a service firm needs to consider how intangible its offering is, how perishable its services are, how inseparable performance is from specific service providers, and the potential variability of service quality. Its goal would be to prepare and enact a marketing strategy that lets consumers perceive its offering in a more tangible manner, makes its services less perishable, encourages consumers to seek it out but enables multiple employees to be viewed as competent, and makes service performance as efficient and consistent as possible.

Service intangibility can make positioning harder. Unlike goods positioning, which stresses tangible factors and consumer analysis (such as touching and tasting) prior to a purchase, much service positioning must rely on performance promises (such as how well a truck handles after a tune-up), which can only be measured once a purchase is made. But, there are ways to use positioning to help consumers perceive a service more tangibly. A firm can:

- Associate an intangible service with tangible objects better understood by the customer.
- Focus on the relationship between the company and its customers. It can sell the competence, skill, and concern of its employees.
- Popularize the company name.
- Offer tangible benefits, such as Scudder Funds of Canada promoting specific reasons for people to buy mutual funds from it. See Figure 12-4.
- Establish a unique product position, such as 24-hour, on-site service for the repair of office equipment.[7]

Service intangibility makes positioning decisions more complex.

Service intangibility may be magnified if only a small portion of the provided service is visible to the consumer. For example, in-shop repairs are normally not seen by consumers. Although a repair person may spend two hours on a facsimile machine and insert two parts priced at $35, when the consumer sees a bill for $145, he or she may not appreciate the service time involved. Thus, a firm must explain how much time is needed to render each aspect of service—and the tasks performed—to make that service more tangible to customers.

Because of service perishability, a service firm needs to match demand and supply patterns as well as it can. Thus, it might have to alter the timing of consumer demand and/or exert better control over the supply of its service offering. It should try to avoid situations in which excess demand goes unsatisfied and cases in which excess capacity causes an unproductive use of resources. To better match demand with supply, a firm can:

Services often cannot be stored for later sale, so demand must be carefully matched with supply.

- Market similar services to segments having different demand patterns.
- Market new services with different demand patterns from existing services.
- Market new services that complement existing ones.

---

[7]Gordon H. G. McDougall and Douglas W. Snetsinger, "The Intangibility of Services: Measurement and Competitive Perspectives," *Journal of Services Marketing*, Vol. 4 (Fall 1990), pp. 27–40.

FIGURE 12-4
Scudder Funds of Canada: Offering Tangible Benefits
Reprinted with permission of Scudder Canada Investor Services.

- Market service "extras" during nonpeak periods.
- Market new services not affected by existing capacity constraints.
- Train personnel to perform multiple tasks.
- Hire part-time employees during peak periods.
- Educate consumers to use services during nonpeak periods.
- Offer incentives and price reductions in nonpeak periods.[8]

---

[8]Leonard L. Berry, A. Parasuraman, and Valarie A. Zeithaml, "Synchronizing Demand and Supply in Service Businesses," *Business*, Vol. 34 (October–December 1984), pp. 36–37; James L. Heskett, W. Earl Sasser, Jr., and Christopher W. L. Hart, *Service Breakthroughs* (New York: Free Press, 1990), pp. 135–158; and Donald J. Shemwell, Jr. and J. Joseph Cronin, Jr., "Services Marketing Strategies for Coping with Demand/Supply Imbalances," *Journal of Services Marketing*, Vol. 8 (Number 4, 1994), pp. 14–24.

The existence of a close relationship between service provider and consumer makes employee interpersonal skills important. The workforce must be trained to interact well with people in such diverse situations as selling and performing services, handling payments, and delivering repaired goods. Generally, more personal involvement, personal contact, and customer input are needed to market services than to market goods. Thus, employee empowerment can be quite beneficial. Those who participate in the marketing of complex services often act as *relationship managers*. As such, the quality of the relationship between a firm's employees and its customers "determines the probability of continued interchange between those parties in the future." Greyhound Courier Express, the courier division of Greyhound Lines of Canada is trying to build customer loyalty through a one-to-one relationship with shippers and decision makers. Greyhound had the names of the companies they have dealt with in their database, but not the names of the shippers or decision makers of these firms. Using a $3.6 million Sweepstakes promotion Greyhound encouraged shippers to register their names to build a database so these individuals could be contacted personally along with their companies.[9]

Many customers of personal service firms become loyal to a particular employee rather than the company. If that person leaves the firm, he or she may take some customers too. That is why it is important for a firm to show its customers that multiple employees are equally capable of providing excellent service.

By their nature, many services have the potential for great variability in their quality. It is hard for lawn care firms to mow lawns in exactly the same way each week, for marketing consultants to make sales forecasts for clients that are always accurate, and for each airline flight to arrive on time. But what service firms can do is strive to make their performance as efficient and consistent as possible. One solution to the issue of high costs (inefficiency) and low reliability (performance variability) is the **industrialization of services** by using hard, soft, and hybrid technologies.[10] Service reliability can also be improved by setting high-level standards and by tying employee pay and promotions to performance levels.

Hard technologies substitute machinery for people. An example is the implementation of an electronic credit authorization system to replace manual credit checks. Hard technologies cannot be as readily applied to services requiring extensive personal skill and contact, such as medical, legal, and hairstyling services. *Soft technologies* substitute pre-planned systems for individual services. For example, travel agents sell pre-packaged vacation tours to standardize transportation, accommodations, food, and sightseeing. *Hybrid technologies* combine both hard and soft technologies. Examples include muffler repair and quick oil-change shops.

This is how the Bank of Nova Scotia industrialized its services to improve the Customer Service Centre that supports its VISA card and banking services for customers and branches. In 1990 the Centre began receiving so many customer inquiries by mail and telephone that the paper-based system of responding was overwhelmed. The bank decided to use technology to help solve the problem, so a computer system using IBM's ImagePlus imaging technology, running on an AS/400 minicomputer linked to fifty networked PCs was put in place. The bank set up a pilot team of eight people doing day-to-day work in the VISA centre to enable a hands-on system development approach. The system evolved and was customized as a result of this development approach, resulting in improvements in: customer service, operating efficiency, employee morale, and productivity. Other imaging applications for Scotiabank include: VISA sales draft processing, mortgage discharging, automated draft retrievals, and processing of chargebacks.[11]

Interpersonal skills are crucial for service businesses.

GREYHOUND COURIER EXPRESS
www.greyhound.ca/courier.html

The **industrialization of services** *can lower inefficiency and excessive variability using hard technologies, soft technologies, or hybrid technologies.*

BANK OF NOVA SCOTIA
www.scotiabank.ca/

---

[9] Lawrence A. Crosby, Kenneth R. Evans, and Deborah Cowles, "Relationship Quality in Services Selling: An Interpersonal Influence Perspective," *Journal of Marketing*, Vol. 54 (July 1990), p. 68; and "Greyhound: A Plan To Hold Its Ground," *Strategy* (September 6, 1993) p. 15. See also David E. Bowen and Edward E. Lawler III, "Empowering Service Employees," *Sloan Management Review*, Vol. 36 (Summer 1995), pp. 73–84.

[10] Theodore Levitt, *The Marketing Imagination* (New York: Free Press, 1983), pp. 50–71; and James S. Hensel, "Service Quality Improvement and Control: A Customer-Based Approach," *Journal of Business Research*, Vol. 20 (January 1990), pp. 43–54. See also Myron Magnet, "Good News for the Service Economy," *Fortune* (May 3, 1993), pp. 46–52.

[11] "Using People to Drive Success (How One of Canada's Leading Banks Built a Successful Imaging Application)," *I.T. Magazine* (September 1993), pp. 18–22.

FIGURE 12-5

A Service Blueprint for an X-Ray

This service blueprint depicts the thirteen steps involved in a typical hospital's X-ray process. The steps can be completed in under one hour and they require multiple employees. Without such a blueprint, the X-ray process would probably be less systematic, more time-consuming, and less efficient.

Source: Stephen H. Baum, "Making Your Service Blueprint Pay Off!" *Journal of Services Marketing,* Vol. 4 (Summer 1990), p. 49. Reprinted by permission.

◇ Physician task
○ Patient-care professional task
△ Unit-supportperson task
▢ Technical specialist task

Steps: Order X-Ray → Enter and Print Order → Pull or Set Up Folder → Ready Patient → Transport Patient → Adjust Machine and Take X-Ray → Develop and Queue Film → Read X-Ray → Transcribe Diagnosis → Review Report → Return File and Report → File Folder; with Return Patient branch.

A **service blueprint** *enhances productivity.* **Service gaps** *must be reduced.*

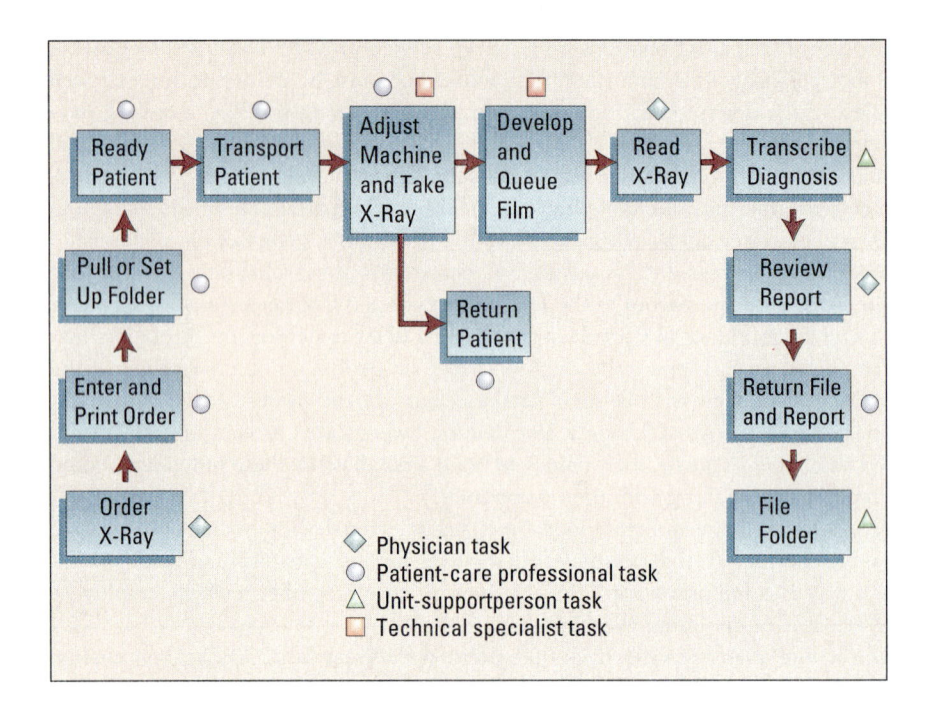

To industrialize their services better, many firms use a **service blueprint**, which is a visual portrayal of the service process: "It displays each subprocess (or step) in the service system, linking the various steps in the sequence in which they appear. A service blueprint is essentially a detailed map or flowchart of the service process."[12] Figure 12-5 shows how a service blueprint can be used in administering an X-ray to a patient.

While planning their marketing strategies, it is also important for firms to understand service quality from the perspective of their customers. They must try to minimize any possible **service gaps**—the difference between customer expectations and actual service performance. Consumer expectations regarding service companies cover these ten areas:

1. *Tangibles*—facilities, equipment, personnel, communication materials.
2. *Reliability*—ability to perform a desired service dependably and accurately.
3. *Responsiveness*—willingness to provide prompt service and assist customers.
4. *Competence*—possession of the necessary skills and knowledge.
5. *Courtesy*—respect, politeness, and friendliness of personnel.
6. *Credibility*—honesty, trustworthiness, and believability of service performers.
7. *Security*—freedom from risk, doubt, or danger.
8. *Access*—ease of contact.
9. *Communication*—keeping customers informed and listening to comments.
10. *Understanding the customer*—knowing the customer's needs.[13]

---

[12] Valarie A. Zeithaml, A. Parasuraman, and Leonard L. Berry, *Delivering Quality Service* (New York: Free Press, 1990), p. 158. See also Susan J. Devlin and H. K. Dong, "Service Quality from the Customers' Perspective," *Marketing Research* (Winter 1994), pp. 5–13.

[13] Zeithaml, Parasuraman, and Berry, *Delivering Quality Service,* pp. 18–22.

The Use of Marketing by Goods and Services Firms

Goods and services firms have differed in their use of marketing, but service firms are now better adapting to their special circumstances than in the past.

A Transition in the Marketing of Services

Service firms have tended to lag behind manufacturers in the use of marketing for several reasons.

1. Many service firms are so small that marketing specialists cannot be afforded.
2. Because manufacturers often have a larger geographic market, they can more efficiently advertise.
3. A lot of service firms are staffed by people with technical expertise in their fields but limited marketing experience.
4. Strict licensing provisions sometimes limit competition among service firms and therefore the need for marketing; in most industries, manufacturers have faced intense competition for years.
5. Consumers have held some service professionals, such as doctors and lawyers, in such high esteem that marketing has not been needed.
6. In the past, some professional associations banned advertising by members; this was changed by various court rulings that now permit it.
7. There are still service professionals who dislike marketing, do not understand it, or question the use of marketing practices, such as advertising, in their fields.
8. Many manufacturers have only recently set up services as profit centres.

The low use of marketing for services has been due to small firm size, an emphasis on technical expertise, limited competition, negative attitudes, and other factors.

Over the next few years, the use of marketing for services will continue to rise, due to a better understanding of the role of customer service in gaining and retaining consumers; worldwide service opportunities; deregulation in the banking, transportation, and communication industries; competition among service providers; consumer interest in renting/leasing rather than buying, the aggressive marketing of services by firms that once focused on manufacturing (such as IBM), the advent of high-technology services (such as video conferencing), the growing number of do-it-yourselfers because of high service costs, and the number of service professionals with formal business training.

Service providers' use of marketing practices is expected to continue increasing in the future.

Illustrations of Service Marketing

This section examines the use of marketing by hotels, auto repair and servicing firms, and lawyers. The examples represent rented-goods services, owned-goods services, and non-goods services. They differ in their degrees of tangibility, service provider skill, labour intensiveness, and customer contact. But in all three instances the use of marketing practices is expanding.

Hotels may target one or more market segments: business travellers, through tourists (who stay one night), regular tourists (who stay two or more nights), extended-stay residents (who stay up to several months or longer), and conventioneers. Each requires different services. The business traveller wants efficient service, a desk in the room, and convenient meeting rooms. A through tourist wants a convenient location, low prices, and quick food service. A regular tourist wants a nice room, recreational facilities, and sightseeing assistance. An extended-stay resident wants an in-room kitchen and other apartment-like amenities. Conventioneers want large meeting rooms, pre-planned sightseeing, fax machines, computer access, and hospitality suites.

To attract and keep customers, hotels are upgrading, adding new services, opening units in emerging markets around the world, and improving marketing efforts. As shown in Figure 12-6, elaborate, distinctive lobby areas and immaculate grounds are popular among U.S. resort hotels. First-run movies that can be viewed in the room, frequent-stay

FIGURE 12-6
The Hyatt Touch
Reprinted by permission.

bonus plans, and special promotions are some of the amenities offered. For example, Commonwealth Hospitality Ltd. (Holiday Inns of Canada) has a database of business travellers and their companies, and promotes directly to corporate travel managers. Sheraton has the largest international frequent-stay program, with a database of over one million members.[14]

Hotels' marketing efforts now rely more on research, publicity, TV ads, well-conceived slogans, personal attention for consumers, and product positioning. The Heritage Inns Marketing Association in Atlantic Canada has come up with an innovative marketing idea. This organization of forty-seven innkeepers who manage heritage properties joined together to promote their inns to affluent travellers. In the spring of 1994, some representatives of the organization took part in a cruise ship promotion, distributing information to travel agents along the coastline of New England. The Heritage Inns Marketing Association followed up with other initiatives such as advertisements in New England, Ontario, and Quebec newspapers and publications, a bilingual brochure, and training sessions for operators of Nova Scotia's CheckIns. These efforts have resulted in more frequent visitor referrals among the organization's inns. The goal is to promote their accommodations as a single and reliable brand and this means eligibility standards and regulations for the organization's

---

[14]Laura Koss-Feder, "Pricier Hotels Are Piling on the Extras," *Business Week* (October 23, 1995), p. 138; Alan Salomon, "Hotels Rise in Emerging Markets as Business Occupies Vacancies," *Advertising Age* (October 16, 1995), pp. I-20, I-22; Chad Rubel, "Hotels Help Lodgers Who Help Themselves," *Marketing News* (May 8, 1995), p. 615; and "Cutting the Fat in Tough Times: Competition Hot for Hotel Sector," *Globe & Mail*, Metro edition (February 22, 1994), pp. C1, C4.

members are fairly strict. The Heritage Inns Marketing Association wants to position its Atlantic Canada Inns as world-class quality products.[15]

Hotels are even trying to resolve consumer complaints more effectively. For instance, business travellers are quite concerned about overbooking, long waiting lines, late check-in times, and unresponsive or discourteous staff. In response, many of today's hotels arrange for alternative accommodations if they are overbooked, have computerized check-ins or offer one-minute check-ins or the room is free, offer express check-out (with bills placed under room doors or mailed to guests' businesses or homes), serve free drinks and provide baggage handling if check-in times are late.[16]

Repair and servicing firms operate in a variety of product categories, including motor vehicles, computers, TVs and appliances, industrial equipment, watches and jewellery, and a host of others. These firms fix malfunctioning products, replace broken parts, and provide maintenance. We will highlight the auto repair and servicing industry.

Auto repairs and servicing are carried out via manufacturer-owned or sponsored dealers and independent service centres.[17] New-car dealers actually generate over 85 per cent of their profits from parts and servicing. In total, $11.6 billion is spent annually on Canadian auto repairs and servicing (including parts and labour) at new-car dealers and independent service outlets. For example, General Motors cars can be repaired and serviced on the firm's Mr. Goodwrench program, available at approved GM dealerships; independent repair and maintenance shops; tire, muffler, and battery outlets; mass merchants (such as Sears); and service stations. Independents handle many makes and models. Among the largest independent specialists are Jiffy Lube (oil and lubricating fluids), Midas (mufflers), and Aamco (transmissions).

How has the auto repair and servicing business changed? According to the executive director of the Gasoline and Automotive Services Association, "The old type of gas station with the dirty rags and cigar-smoking mechanic no longer exists. We have evolved due to the technology needed to service, repair, and diagnose modern-day vehicles. It has forced shops to upgrade their tools and equipment. Where it may have cost several thousand dollars in the past, now it can cost several hundred thousand dollars." In addition, there has been an influx of companies such as quick-oil-change firms:

> You can do it on your lunch hour. Usually at the dealerships, you have to check your car in for the day. The average length of time that a car stays on the road is far longer than it used to be. When you start holding cars longer, you try to maintain them better, so you're more likely to change the oil regularly.[18]

In 1977, the U.S. Supreme Court ruled that lawyers could not be prohibited from advertising their services. This ruling resulted in a boom in advertising of U.S. legal services and this trend has spread to Canada where provincial law societies now allow law firms to engage in advertising. Prior to this, the extent of lawyer advertising was limited to a simple yellow pages ad with the name, address, phone number, and legal specialty of a lawyer or their firm. It is estimated that 20 to 30 per cent of new clients now choose their attorneys on the basis of the latter's marketing efforts; the rest rely on personal referrals.[19] Thus, many attorneys advertise in the Yellow Pages and have printed brochures. Some advertise in newspapers and magazines; and some even use TV and radio ads. Various law firms send out newsletters, employ public relations firms, and have sessions where partners and associates practice selling services to clients.

Lawyers have been very innovative in their marketing efforts but not all of these efforts have been well received. For example, in 1993 Ontario's Law Society of Upper

---

[15]"Inns for All Reasons: Hoteliers Rely on Branding to Compete in the Travel Market," *Marketing Magazine* (October 31, 1994), p. 15.

[16]"Cutting the Fat in Tough Times: Competition Hot for Hotel Sector," pp. C1,C4; and James S. Hirsch, "Now Hotel Clerks Provide More Than Keys," *Wall Street Journal* (March 5, 1993), pp. B1, B6.

[17]Bureau of Economic Analysis, U.S. Commerce Department; Julie Edelson Halpert, "Who Will Fix Tomorrow's Cars?" *New York Times* (November 7, 1993), Section 3, p. 4; and authors' estimates.

[18]Du, Mergenhagen, and Lee, "The Future of Services, " p. 35.

[19]Jennifer Fulkerson, "When Lawyers Advertise," *American Demographics* (June 1995), pp. 54–55.

Canada was concerned about the use of fictitious names used by legal firms to be first in the telephone directory and about the level of professionalism in lawyers' ads. One fictitious name was Action Law (10 A's) of Etobicoke, Ontario. In addition, several ads showed drawings of people with bandaged heads and handcuffed hands. The use of fictitious names was seen as creating harmful competition between practising lawyers. The ads were criticised because they contributed to the negative image that lawyers are greedy and self-serving and only interested in profiting from the troubles of their clients.[20]

A growing number of firms even hire jury consultants: "Target marketing tools aren't just for business. They are also being used in courtrooms to help attorneys understand what motivates jury decisions. Target marketers use focus groups to understand consumers; jury consultants use mock juries to understand jurors."[21] Overall, lawyers spend 4 per cent of gross revenues on marketing activities—up from 1 per cent a few years ago.

Law clinics and franchised law firms have grown. These firms concentrate on relatively routine legal services. They have large legal staffs, convenient locations (such as in shopping centres), standardized fees and services (about $100 or so for a simple will), and plain fixtures and furniture. The largest franchised firms have hundreds of attorneys, cover a wide geographic area, advertise heavily, and set fees in advance and in writing.

Legal-services marketing has met with resistance from a number of attorneys. They criticize price advertising for stressing price at the expense of quality and mass-marketing techniques as eliminating personal counselling. They feel the public's confidence in the profession is falling, information in ads may be inaccurate, and excessive consumer expectations are created. Most lawyers still do not advertise in mass media; they rely totally on referrals.

Nonprofit Marketing

Nonprofit marketing serves the public interest and does not seek financial profits.

Nonprofit marketing is conducted by organizations and individuals that operate in the public interest or that foster a cause and do not seek financial profits. It may involve organizations (Crown corporations, charities, unions, trade associations), people (political candidates), places (resorts, convention centres, industrial sites), and ideas ("stop smoking"), as well as goods and services. See Figure 12-7.

Although nonprofit organizations conduct exchanges, they do not have to be in the form of dollars for goods and services. Politicians request votes in exchange for promises of better government services. Canada Post wants greater use of postal codes in exchange for improved service and lower rate hikes. The Canadian Red Cross seeks funds to help victims of all kinds of disasters.

Prices charged by nonprofit organizations often have no relation to the cost or value of their services. The Brownies and Girl Guides of Canada sell cookies to raise funds; only part of the price goes to pay for the cookies. In contrast, the price of a chest X-ray at an overseas health clinic may be below cost or free.

Due to its unique attributes, marketing by nonprofit organizations rates a thorough discussion from a product-planning perspective. In the following sections, nonprofit marketing is compared with profit-oriented marketing, a classification system is given for nonprofit marketing, and the extent of nonprofit marketing in the economy is examined. Three detailed examples of nonprofit marketing are also presented.

Nonprofit Versus Profit-Oriented Marketing

Nonprofit marketing has both similarities with and distinctions from profit-oriented marketing.

There are a number of marketing similarities between nonprofit and profit-oriented firms. In today's uncertain and competitive arena, nonprofit organizations must apply appropriate marketing concepts and strategies if they are to generate adequate support, financial or otherwise.

With both nonprofit and profit-oriented organizations, people usually can choose among competing entities; the benefits provided by competitors differ; consumer seg-

---

[20]"Yellow Pages Ploy Irks Law Body," *Globe & Mail*, Metro edition (January 25, 1993), p. B5.
[21]Joe Schwartz, "Marketing the Verdict," *American Demographics* (February 1993), p. 52.

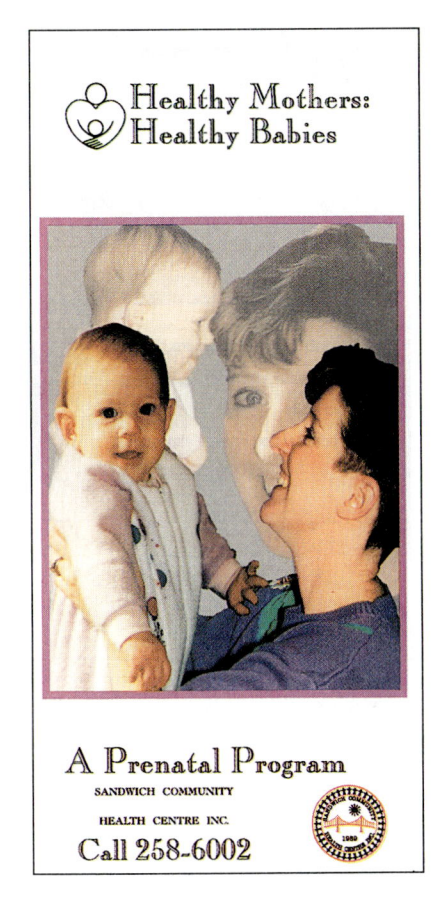

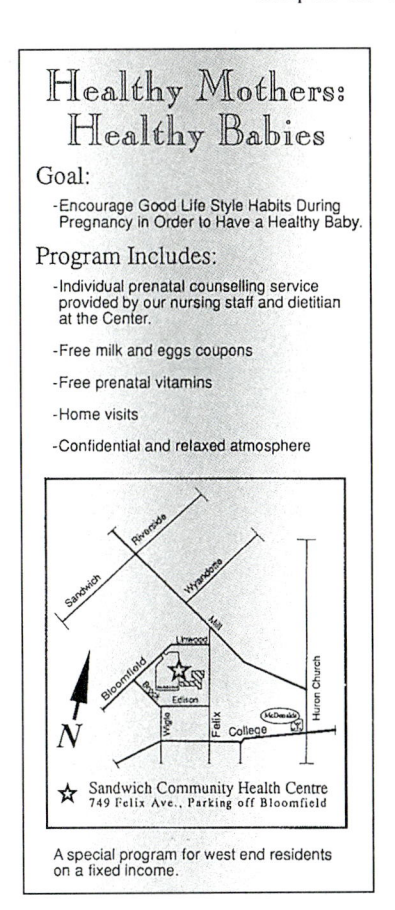

FIGURE 12-7

Nonprofit Marketing in Action

Nonprofit marketing is very broad in scope and growing in stature. In this leaflet, the Sandwich Community Health Centre in Windsor, Ontario, promotes its "Healthy Mothers: Healthy Babies" prenatal program.

Reprinted with permission of Sandwich Community Health Centre Inc.

ments may have distinct reasons for their choices; people are lured by the most desirable product positioning; and they are either satisfied or dissatisfied with performance. Figure 12-8 shows how a political candidate could target various voter segments using a well-conceived marketing mix and careful product positioning (party platform, past record, and personal traits). This approach is like the one a profit-oriented firm would use.

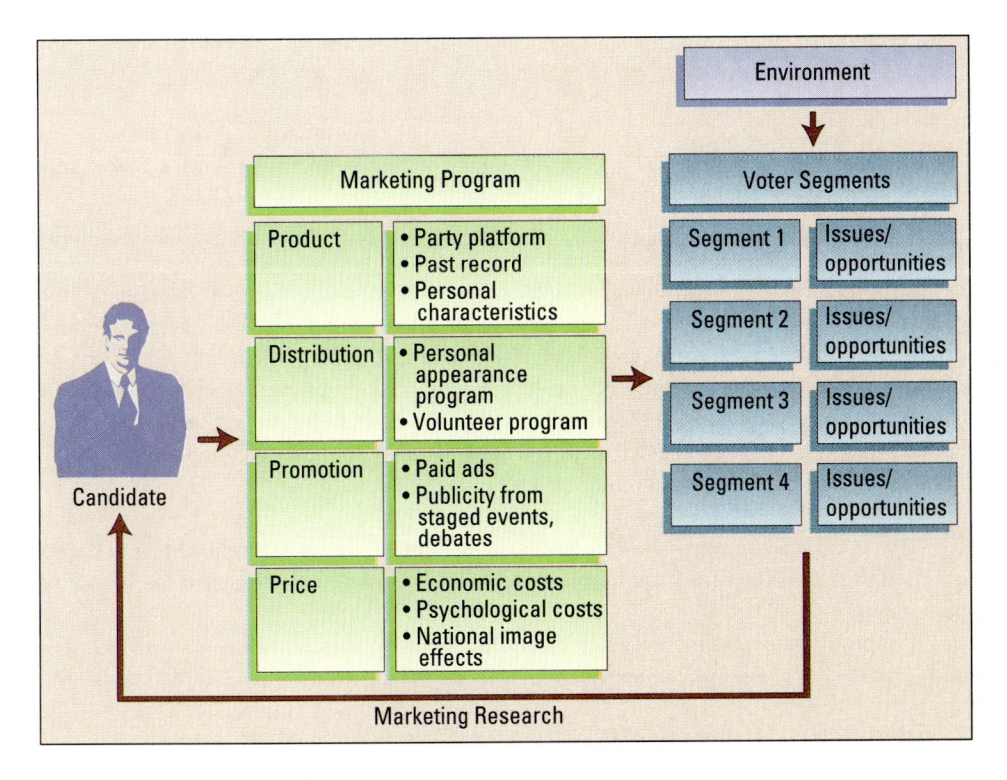

FIGURE 12-8

The Political Marketing Process

Source: Adapted by the authors from Phillip B. Niffenegger, "Strategies for Success from the Political Marketers," Journal of Consumer Marketing, Vol. 6 (Winter 1989), p. 46. Reprinted by permission.

International Marketing in Action

How Can Middle East Tourism Be Increased?

Market analysts agree that the most promising areas for the development of Middle East tourism are Egypt, Israel, Jordan, and Lebanon. In one recent year, Egypt's tourist revenues were U.S.$1.03 billion, versus U.S.$1.67 billion for Israel and U.S.$532 million for Jordan. No data were available for Lebanon.

One key to developing and promoting tourism in the region is joint tourist efforts by Egypt, Israel, and Jordan. Tourist officials in each of these countries feel the overall region will be more attractive to tourists who can visit two or three of these countries on a single trip. The Israeli Ministry of Tourism forecasts that Israel's 1993 record of two million tourists could easily double or even triple by 1998.

Some tour officials see Jordan as particularly gaining from this alliance. Jordan has the spectacular ancient city of Petra, world-class beaches, and a modern capital. Until recently, these attractions were not accessible by Israelis. Today, demand is so great that Jordan has been forced to limit the number of visitors to Petra. At the same time, there is also a shortage of hotels and taxis. And while Jordanian land is cheap, hotel development is impeded by the lack of an infrastructure.

Lebanon is another potential bright spot. Before its civil war in 1975, Lebanon had close to 570 hotels, impressive ski resorts, and great beaches. Many of these facilities were destroyed, but foreign investors are now renovating and rebuilding the hotels that were wrecked. Lebanon is working with the World Tourism Organization and the United Nations Development Program to develop pamphlets depicting its important archeological treasures.

As a marketing consultant retained by a hotel chain that operates hotels in Israel, Jordan, Egypt, and Lebanon, develop a plan for increasing tourism in the area.

Source: Based on material in Mary A. Kelly, "Tourists Return to Calmer Middle East," *Advertising Age* (April 17, 1995), p. I-12.

A couple of years ago, a well-known Calgary company was faced with a 30 per cent decline in demand in spite of offering a high quality product. The firm hired a marketing director who carefully studied Calgary's demographics. He recommended targeting higher income, fewer-children families, and improving customer service with the installation of a dedicated telephone line for regular customers. In addition, a direct-mail and telemarketing campaign of current and past customers was undertaken including a follow-up telephone call to 50 000 individuals who were targeted with a specially designed brochure. What kind of organization was this, a luxury car dealership? No, the nonprofit Calgary Philharmonic Orchestra. The result of the marketing efforts was sales of 11 000 tickets, a sell-out of three-quarters of the orchestra's regular fifty-five concerts, as well as all of the Saturday Night Pop's concerts; and there was a retention rate of 90 per cent of the 1994/95 season's ticket subscribers for the 1995/96 season.[22]

There are also some basic differences in marketing between nonprofit and profit-oriented organizations. They are highlighted in Table 12-1 and described in the following paragraphs.

Nonprofit marketing includes organizations, people, places, and ideas, as well as goods and services. It is much more apt to be involved with social programs and ideas than is prof-

[22]"Calgary Orchestra Hits Right Marketing Notes," *Marketing Magazine* (August 15, 1994), p. 4.

it-oriented marketing. Examples include AIDS prevention, recycling, highway safety, family planning, gun control, and energy conservation. The use of marketing to increase the acceptability of social ideas is referred to as **social marketing**.[23]

The nonprofit exchange process can include nonmonetary and monetary transactions. Nonmonetary transactions can be votes, volunteers' time, blood donations, and so forth. Monetary transactions can be donations, magazine subscriptions, tuition, and so on. Sometimes, nonprofit marketing does not generate revenues in day-to-day exchanges; instead, it may rely on infrequent fundraising efforts. In addition, a successful marketing campaign may actually lose money if services or goods are provided at less than cost. Thus, operating budgets must be large enough to serve the number of anticipated clients, so none are poorly treated or turned away.

Goals may be complex because success or failure cannot be measured in purely financial terms. A nonprofit organization might have this combination of goals: raise $250 000 from government grants, increase client usage, find a cure for a disease, change public attitudes, and raise $750 000 from private donors. Goals must include the number of clients to be served, the amount of service to be rendered, and the quality of service to be provided.

The benefits of nonprofit organizations may not be allotted on the basis of consumer payments. Only a small portion of the population contracts a disease, requires humanitarian services, visits a museum, uses a public library, or goes to a health clinic in a given year; yet the general public pays to find cures, support fellow citizens, or otherwise assist nonprofit organizations. Many times, the people who would benefit most from a nonprofit organization's activities may be the ones least apt to seek or use them. This occurs for libraries, health clinics, remedial programs, and others. With profit-oriented organizations, benefits are usually distributed equitably, based on consumers' direct payments in exchange for goods or services.

Crown corporations fall generally within the terms of reference of nonprofit organizations. They are owned and operated by the government in the public interest and they are

Nonprofit marketing is broad in scope and frequently involved with **social marketing**.

Consumer benefits may not be related to their payments.

Table 12-1
The Basic Differences Between Nonprofit and Profit-Oriented Marketing

NONPROFIT MARKETING	PROFIT-ORIENTED MARKETING
1. Nonprofit marketing is concerned with organizations, people, places, and ideas, as well as goods and services.	1. Profit-oriented marketing is largely concerned with goods and services.
2. Exchanges may be nonmonetary or monetary.	2. Exchanges are generally monetary.
3. Objectives are more complex because success or failure cannot be measured strictly in financial terms.	3. Objectives are typically stated in terms of sales, profits, and recovery of cash.
4. The benefits of nonprofit services are often not related to consumer payments.	4. The benefits of profit-oriented marketing are usually related to consumer payments.
5. Nonprofit organizations may be expected or required to serve economically unfeasible market segments.	5. Profit-oriented organizations seek to serve only those market segments that are profitable.
6. Nonprofit organizations typically have two key target markets: clients and donors.	6. Profit-oriented organizations typically have one key target market: clients.

---

[23] See Alan R. Andreasen, "Social Marketing: Its Definition and Domain," *Journal of Public Policy & Marketing*, Vol. 13 (Spring 1994), pp. 108–114; and Patricia Braus, "Selling Good Behavior," *American Demographics* (November 1995), pp. 60–64.

CANADIAN NATIONAL
www.cn.ca/

Nonprofit organizations must satisfy **clients** *and* **donors**.

often expected, or required, to serve markets that profit-oriented firms find uneconomical. For example, Canada Post must have rural post offices and Canadian National must offer freight rail service to some sparsely populated areas. Crown corporations are given the same tax treatment as profit organizations but because they serve in the public interest they are usually only marginally profitable at best. This usually gives profit-oriented, privately-owned firms an edge; they can concentrate on the most lucrative market segments.

Profit-oriented firms have one major target market—clients (customers)—to whom they offer goods and services and from whom they receive payment; a typical nonprofit organization has two: **clients**, to whom it offers membership, elected officials, locations, ideas, goods, and services, and **donors**, from whom it receives resources (which may be time from volunteers or money from foundations and individuals). There may be little overlap between clients and donors.

Private nonprofit organizations have been granted many legal advantages. These include tax-deductible contributions, exemptions from most sales and real-estate taxes, and reduced postal rates. Profit-oriented firms often feel they are harmed competitively by these legal provisions.[24]

Classifying Nonprofit Marketing

The classification of nonprofit marketing may be based on tangibility, structure, goal, and constituency.

As shown in Figure 12-9, nonprofit organizations may be classified in terms of tangibility, structure, goals, and constituency. An organization would be classed by a combination of factors. For example, postage stamps for collectors are tangible, distributed by Canada Post (a Crown corporation), intended to reduce Canada Post's usual operating losses, and aimed at the general public.

As already noted, nonprofit marketing may involve organizations, people, places, ideas, goods, and services. Organizations include foundations, universities, religious institutions, and government; people include politicians and volunteers; places include resorts and industrial centres; ideas include family planning and multiculturalism; goods include postage stamps and professional journals; and services include medical care and education.

Nonprofit organizations may have a government-affiliated, private, or cooperative structure. The federal government markets military service to recruits, and owns and operates Crown corporations (such as Canadian National Railways, Canada Post, and Atomic Energy of Canada), and other goods and services; provincial governments market tourism and hospitals; local governments market libraries and sports arenas. Government marketing is also used to secure support for tax increases, programs, and legislative initiatives. Private organizations market religions, charities, social services, and other goods and services. They also use marketing to increase membership and donations. Cooperative organizations (such as the Better Business Bureau) aid consumers and businesses; their success depends on securing a large membership base and performing their function efficiently.

Overall nonprofit marketing goals may be divided into health (increase the number of nonsmokers), education (increase usage of the local library), welfare (list more job openings at the Canada Employment Centre office), and other (finding leaders for Scouts Canada) components.

Nonprofit organizations usually require the support of both clients/users and donors. Clients/users are interested in the direct benefits they get by participating in an organization, such as their improved health, education, or welfare. Donors are concerned about the efficiency of operations, success rates, the availability of goods and services, and the recognition of their contributions. For each constituency, an organization must pinpoint its target market. For example, the Easter Seal Society would focus on households with direct mail during the Easter campaign season and seek funds from corporate donors during the rest of the year. Figure 12-10 shows some of the differing interests of clients and donors.

---

[24]Edward T. Pound, Gary Cohen, and Penny Loeb, "Tax Exempt!" *U.S. News & World Report* (October 2, 1995), pp. 36–51; and John R. Emshwiller, "More Small Firms Complain About Tax-Exempt Rivals," *Wall Street Journal* (August 8, 1995), pp. B1–B2.

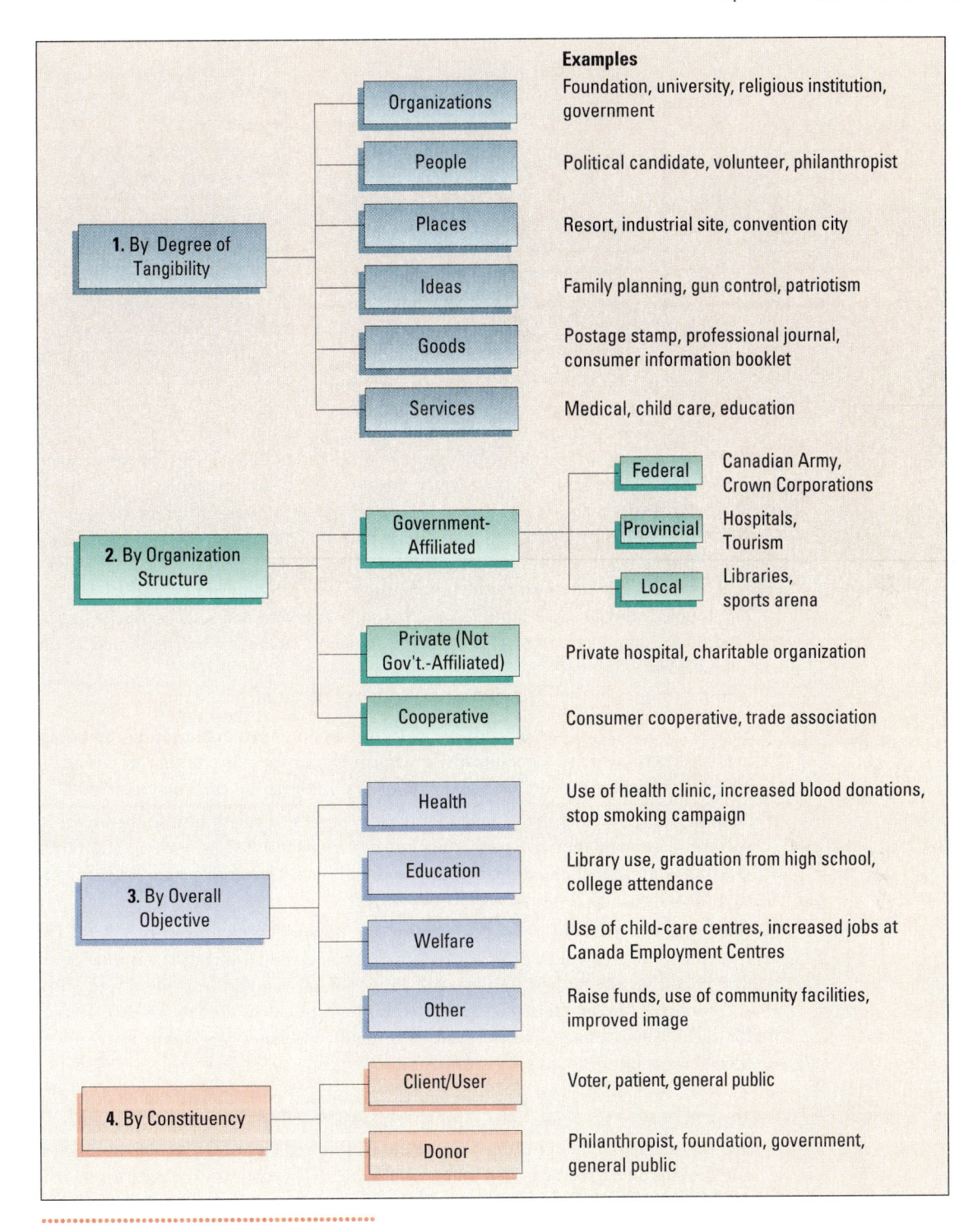

FIGURE 12-9
A Classification System for Nonprofit Marketing

1. By Degree of Tangibility

Category	Examples
Organizations	Foundation, university, religious institution, government
People	Political candidate, volunteer, philanthropist
Places	Resort, industrial site, convention city
Ideas	Family planning, gun control, patriotism
Goods	Postage stamp, professional journal, consumer information booklet
Services	Medical, child care, education

2. By Organization Structure

Category		Examples
Government-Affiliated	Federal	Canadian Army, Crown Corporations
	Provincial	Hospitals, Tourism
	Local	Libraries, sports arena
Private (Not Gov't.-Affiliated)		Private hospital, charitable organization
Cooperative		Consumer cooperative, trade association

3. By Overall Objective

Category	Examples
Health	Use of health clinic, increased blood donations, stop smoking campaign
Education	Library use, graduation from high school, college attendance
Welfare	Use of child-care centres, increased jobs at Canada Employment Centres
Other	Raise funds, use of community facilities, improved image

4. By Constituency

Category	Examples
Client/User	Voter, patient, general public
Donor	Philanthropist, foundation, government, general public

The Extent of Nonprofit Marketing in the Economy

Worldwide, millions of organizations and people engage in nonprofit marketing. In 1994, individual Canadian tax filers claimed $3.39 billion in charitable donations on their taxes. This represented a 1 per cent increase in donations over 1993. A total of 5 344 480 tax filers reported charitable donations, but this number was down 3 per cent from 1993 donations. The most generous Canadians are over 65 years of age, giving an average of $890 to

There are millions of nonprofit organizations in the world and their use of marketing is increasing.

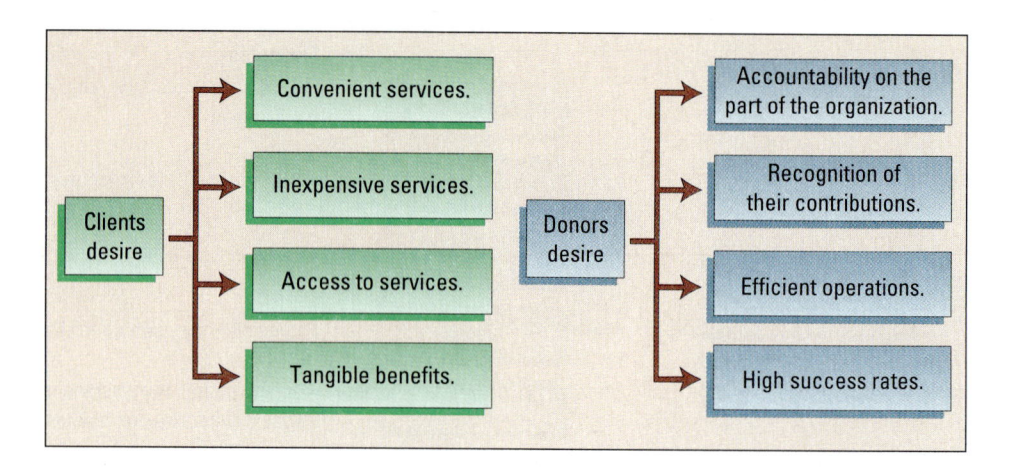

FIGURE 12-10
Clients Versus Donors

```
Clients desire → Convenient services.
              → Inexpensive services.
              → Access to services.
              → Tangible benefits.

Donors desire → Accountability on the part of the organization.
             → Recognition of their contributions.
             → Efficient operations.
             → High success rates.
```

charity in comparison to the national average of $634 for all of Canada. The most generous donors live in Alberta where the average donation was $812 per taxfiler. By definition, charitable donations can only be claimed if they are made to nonprofit organizations.

Nonprofit organizations often use direct-mail solicitation for donations and the Canadian Direct Marketing Association reports that nearly one-third of all revenues reported by direct marketers go to the fundraising efforts of nonprofit organizations.

Employment in Canadian nonprofit sectors such as health and social services, education, and public administration was 2.8 million people in 1995, which represented 25 per cent of industrial employees.[25]

These examples further demonstrate the scope of nonprofit marketing:

- Scouts Canada is just one of a number of Canadian nonprofit organizations that operates an Internet site. It contains a summary of the history of scouting in Canada, a directory of regional council offices, and general information on scouting activities.
- After a survey showed that 92 per cent of the world's population was unaware of its social and humanitarian activities, the United Nations enacted its first major advertising campaign. Ninety advertising agencies in thirty nations donated their time, and they sought U.S.$53 million in free media space.
- Many countries use tourism boards to market themselves to foreign travellers. The French Ministry of Tourism spends tens of millions of dollars annually on promotion. The British Tourist Authority works with airlines, hotels, and credit-card firms to create and publicize special offers. The Spanish Tourism Institute has used the slogan, "Passion for Life." The German Tourist Board distributes brochures describing lower-priced accommodations.
- The City of Thunder Bay set up a company comprised of ninety charitable nonprofit organizations. The company was called Thunder Bay Lottery and the City gave it a $50 000 start-up loan. The idea was for the City to reduce its charity expenses without causing any reduction in funding of charities. The company started up in June 1993 and within six months had repaid the start-up loan. The lottery sells $2 tickets for weekly draws with a $10 000 grand prize and ten second prizes worth $100. The profits from the lottery are allocated to the ninety member charities and $220 000 was made available in 1993.
- The Canadian Council on Smoking and Health annually sponsors National Non-Smoking Week, a key part of a national public education campaign that has these five objectives: to educate Canadians about the dangers of tobacco use; to prevent people from becoming addicted to tobacco; to help smokers quit; to ensure a smoke-free environment for non-smokers; and to help Canada become a smoke-free society.

---

[25]Statistics Canada, *The Daily* (December 13, 1995); John Gustavson, "CDMA Well-Positioned to Take on Tough Issues," *Marketing Magazine* (September 16, 1991), p. 22; Statistics Canada, *The Daily* (April 30, 1996).

The week was founded in 1977 and is held annually during the third week of January. The Wednesday of this week is designated as Weedless Wednesday, when people are encouraged to stop smoking for one day (in the hope that they will quit for life).[26]

Illustrations of Nonprofit Marketing

This section examines marketing by Canada Post, Canadian universities, and the United Way of Canada. The activities of these organizations differ in their degree of tangibility, structure, objectives, and constituencies.

Canada Post is a Crown corporation, owned 100 per cent by the federal government, and has $2.5 billion in assets. It was created by the federal government in 1981 when the Canada Post Corporation Act was passed. Currently, Canada Post employs 62 578 people and had revenues of $4.7 billion in 1995 but incurred a loss of $68 million on these sales. Canada Post handles 11.8 billion letters and parcels each year and provides 18 500 retail outlets to access postal services. The postal system in Canada has 900 000 locations from which mail can enter the postal system and these points are serviced by a fleet of over 6000 vehicles. Canada Post faces intense competition in the most lucrative parts of the market from alternative document and information transfer services, such as private couriers, facsimile machines, direct-funds transfer, and telecommunications firms (many of which provide e-mail services). As a Crown corporation, Canada Post is constrained because it must deliver all mail, no matter how uneconomical. Consequently, Canada Post often loses money on its operations.[27]

To protect itself against competition and stimulate demand, Canada Post has tried marketing its services using a mix of continuing and new offerings, extensive advertising, and different ways of pricing. For example, one of its new marketing initiatives was to open "Connexions" marketing resource centres in Winnipeg and Toronto to provide more information and assistance to Canadian direct-mail marketers. The Connexions centres have on-site assistance for individuals who want to market through the mail. Some of the features include English and French direct marketing videotapes, interactive video stations, a direct-marketing reference library, seminars and lectures by experts in direct marketing, and names of suppliers that direct marketers can use.

Canada Post invests $300 to $400 million each year in information technology to analyze and track every segment of the postal system. Canada Post is hoping to be able to use this system to become the main supplier of delivery services for catalogue retailers such as Sears.

Canada Post has a subsidiary, Purolator Courier, which competes head-to-head with FedEx and UPS and operates as an autonomous unit that can select its service areas so that it can operate profitably. Of course, Canada Post also operates Xpresspost, its own courier service that allows overnight delivery of packages and letters. Through the Priority Post service customers have a less expensive two- to three-day delivery option available throughout Canada.

In order to operate more effectively on the international scene Canada Post is a partner (along with the postal administrations of Germany, France, The Netherlands, Sweden, and TNT of Australia) in GD Express Worldwide, a courier that serves nearly 200 countries. In addition, Canada Post has access to Electronic Data Interchange services through an agreement with the Brussels-based International Post Corporation (a firm in which Canada Post holds shares along with twenty-one other postal administrations).

Canada Post has a Mail Management Services division, which is designed to assist business customers in managing internal mail systems. Canada Post will consult on, or even assume responsibility for, these operations. Recently, Canada Post signed an agreement with IBM to explore opportunities in electronic commerce.

[26]Jim Carroll and Rick Broadhead, *1996 Canadian Internet Directory*, (Scarborough: Prentice Hall Canada), p. 252; Nan O'Neal, "UN Taps Ad Group," *Advertising Age* (October 29, 1990), p. 12; "Thunder Bay Wins! With Local Lottery," *Strategy* (March 7, 1994), pp. 1, 28. "National Non-Smoking Week 1996," *Canadian Council on Smoking and Health Home Page* (www.ccsh.ca).

[27]"Performance 500," *Canadian Business* (June 1996) pp. 152–153; "Cost of Canada Post Merge Service No Hit," *Marketing Magazine* (May 31, 1993), p. 4; and "DM Centre Connects," *Strategy* (March 22, 1993), p. B7.

Ethics AND TODAY'S MARKETER

Are North American Arthritis Organizations Risking a Backlash?

Nonprofit organizations are increasingly licensing their names and symbols for use with certain products, entering into cooperative arrangements and collecting fees or donations based on product sales. According to the president of the U.S.-based Arthritis Foundation, "It is the prototype for future relationships between nonprofit organizations and corporate America."

In Canada, the Arthritis Society has established a fundraising effort in conjunction with Meditrust Pharmacy Inc., a mail-order pharmacy in Toronto, Ontario. The Canadian Arthritis Society sent a letter to all of its members informing them of the alliance between the society and Meditrust. For their part, Meditrust puts Arthritis Society information in with every arthritis medication delivery and at the end of each year, Meditrust makes a donation to the Arthritis Society to support research. However, retail pharmacists are upset with the arrangement because they see it as an endorsement of Meditrust by the Canadian Arthritis Society. The retail pharmacists claim that mail-order delivery of medication prevents personal interaction between the pharmacist and the patients and puts patients at risk.

Proponents of this type of relationship say both groups win. The company increases its visibility and sales, and gains increased credibility. At the same time, the nonprofit organization expands its membership roster and upgrades its research efforts.

However, licensing arrangements by nonprofit organizations are not without critics. Some question whether any nonprofit organization should endorse products. There is also the question of which products should be endorsed. For example, should a nonprofit organization endorse a product that is of better value or a product that has a higher royalty rate? Still others feel that donations may suffer if the nonprofit organization derives too much of its funds from licensing arrangements.

As a marketing consultant to the Canadian Arthritis Society, present a policy for selecting and controlling cooperative arrangements between profit and nonprofit organizations.

Sources: Based on material in Jeff Smyth, "Nonprofits Get Market Savvy," *Advertising Age* (May 29, 1995), pp. 1, 7; "McNeil Finds Cause to Celebrate," *Promo* (August 1994), p. 23; and Andrea Haman, "Pharmacists Angered by Charity's Link to Meditrust," *Marketing Magazine*, (October 16, 1995), p. 2.

Canada Post has become very customer-service conscious and can be reached by customers through a 1-800 number, on the Internet, and of course, by mail. The comments, complaints, and suggestions that arise from these contacts are analyzed via enquiry management systems and the goal of the corporation is to respond as quickly as possible. The feedback is seen as important to corporation's drive to improve its services and better serve its customers. In this regard, Canada Post strives to achieve its objective of being a customer-driven organization.[28]

Colleges and universities realize that the population trends in many industrialized nations (such as smaller households and a relatively low birth rate) have been affecting their enrolment pools, especially with the number of 18- to 24-year-olds falling in some areas. In 1995, Canadian universities had a drop in full-time student enrolment from a peak

---

[28] "The Post Office and the Power of Information: Microchips Move the Mail," *Globe & Mail*, Metro edition (June 23, 1992), p. B22; and *Canada Post Corporation Home Page*, June 1996 update.

of 576 500 in 1994 to 574 300, the first such drop since 1978. Coupled with almost flat growth rates of 1 per cent in 1993 and 1994, this is a sign that enrolments have reached a plateau and may trend downwards. In light of federal and provincial cutbacks in post-secondary funding, in conjunction with tuition-fee increases to offset these cuts, the outlook is for further enrolment drops at the very time when universities need more students and the fees they pay to maintain their funding levels. Thus, Canadian universities are targeting new markets and using marketing strategies more than ever before.[29]

For example, early in the summer of 1995 the University of Calgary was offered a $2.2-million additional share of provincial funding under the provision that enrolment was boosted by 450 students. In order to take advantage of the situation the University had to act quickly. The fastest course of action was to relax admission standards and then inform students about this. The University undertook a $100 000 promotional campaign entitled "65 per cent and You're In." The result was an increase of 1000 students.

Many universities are actively seeking nontraditional students: Today, 32 per cent of Canadian university students attend part time; many of them are over 25 years old. This market demands convenient sites and classes that do not infringe on work hours. At the University of Windsor, the Division of Continuing Education is specifically designed to provide academic advice and support to part-time and nontraditional students. This division funds and coordinates the course offerings at campuses in Chatham and Sarnia, Ontario as well as locations in Windsor that are off the main campus. In addition, the University of Windsor has a distance education program through which students may obtain a Bachelor of Commerce degree as well as take credit courses towards other degrees.[30]

Traditional students are also being sought vigorously. Schools are no longer relying on the usual recruitment tools—high school visits, open houses, calendars, posters, and brochures—but are pursuing mass media campaigns such as the one by the University of Calgary. The University of Western Ontario placed an eight-page glossy colour tabloid in the *Globe and Mail* to attract students. The tabloid discussed Western's 118-year-old history as a leading Canadian university and presented Western's educational disciplines as continuing the tradition of being on the leading edge. Virtually every university maintains an Internet Web site that potential students can visit , and a number of universities distribute recruiting films or videocassettes, costing tens of thousands of dollars (and up) to produce, to high schools.

UNIVERSITY OF WESTERN ONTARIO
www.uwo.ca/

The heightened use of marketing is not limited to recruiting undergraduate students. Universities are seeking to retain their student populations longer by encouraging growth of their graduate programs. *Canadian Business Magazine* routinely carries advertising for executive MBA programs offered by Queen's University and the University of Western Ontario. The University of Windsor has a Co-op MBA program targeted specifically at students with non-business degrees and no work experience and has produced posters, ads, and brochures based on the theme "Earn As You Learn." (See Figure 12-11.) Simon Fraser University goes after mature students with its Harbour Centre Campus in downtown Vancouver. The target is well-educated, mid-career adults who want courses specifically tailored to their workplace requirements. At the Harbour Centre, the executive MBA is marketed by direct mail and newspaper ads, and large companies like BC Hydro and CP Rail have been approached with degree programs designed for their employees.[31]

This is a crucial time for the United Way of Canada. Located in Ottawa, the national organization is affiliated with 120 local United Way-Centraides whose annual fundraising efforts yielded $235 million in 1994. Most donations come from deductions made from workers' paycheques. In contrast, such organizations as the Salvation Army generate most of their donations from non-workplace sources. The 120 local organizations used the money they raised to fund 3976 different agencies, which provide the following services:

---

[29]Statistics Canada, *The Daily* (January 8, 1996); Terry Bullick, "Recruitment 101," *Marketing Magazine* (March 11, 1996), p. 8.
[30]University of Windsor Internet Home Page, June 1996.
[31]Terry Bullick, "Recruitment 101," p. 8.

FIGURE 12-11

The Marketing of Higher Education

Reprinted with permission of University of Windsor, graphic design by Steve Daigle.

- Services to families;
- Services to youth and children;
- Services to senior citizens;
- Services for the disabled;
- Help for the disadvantaged;
- Social and community planning.[32]

The burden on the services funded by United Way-Centraides promises to grow larger as the federal and provincial governments in Canada make drastic cuts to existing social programs such as welfare, unemployment insurance, old age security, the Canada Pension Plan and medical care. The reduction in funding has not been in response to a reduction in need. Fortunately, the United Way-Centraides are finding some unique sources of support.

For example, in Calgary a "loaned representative" program was used to enable the local Centraide to acquire the talent of some of Calgary's best organizations. Various firms loaned some of their employees to the United Way for thirteen weeks in the fall. During this period, the firms paid the salaries of these employees, who worked for the United Way on projects, in public relations, and making presentations. The loaned employees underwent intensive training programs with the United Way and then coordinated fundraising

---

[32] United Way of Canada Internet Site.

campaigns which produced almost 60 per cent of the $11.9 million in funds that were raised in Calgary in 1993. The payoff for the firms was the experience, training, and personal network links their employees gained from the activity.[33]

For years, the United Way has had an outstanding marketing orientation. In Canada, the United Way has undertaken some excellent promotional initiatives which are clearly visible to the public. For example, it conducted a "Bay Day X" promotion with The Bay Stores, in which the United Way received a percentage of the Bay's sales for a one-day period. In the United States it is well known for its long-run association with the National Football League (NFL) and the touching ads that appear during NFL games. In addition, an Internet Web site was constructed to inform the public as well as the various United Way-Centraides about what the United Way of Canada was doing.[34]

As well, employees in affiliated chapters are trained in marketing. Periodic conferences are held, such as a yearly marketing and advertising conference. Affiliated chapters present United Way home videos, films, and slide-show programs to potential contributors and volunteers. The United Way of America published a book, *Competitive Marketing*, so all United Way chapters and other charitable groups could learn from it.

The United Way's present situation can be summed up thus: "Keen competition and urgent need cry out for creativity. For an organization that has thrived on automatic generosity, that is a challenge."[35]

MARKETING IN A CHANGING WORLD
Health Care Services—The Thorniest Issue of All[36]

As the 21st century approaches, by far the toughest issue we must address is how health care services will be marketed. Health care costs in Canada topped $20 billion in 1995. The rate of increase in these costs has been about 5 per cent per year.

And the future promises to be more expensive, not less, thanks to the development of expensive medical technologies combined with population demographics. By the year 2006, it has been estimated that 32 to 34 per cent of the population, or 10.3 million Canadians, will be over 50 years of age—and one of their major demands as consumers will be for health care products.

Not surprisingly, the issue of health care costs is front and centre right now. Some ideas put forward to control costs are:

- Putting physicians on salary rather than paying fee-for-service;
- Limiting extra-billing;
- Initiating user fees for higher income people;
- Capping malpractice-suit payouts to lower insurance costs;
- Creating a two-tiered medical system where people can opt out and pay privately.

---

[33]"Volunteer Work Is Training Ground for Managers," *This Week In Business* (June 27, 1994), p. F16; and Keith H. Hammonds and Morton D. Sosland, "Even the United Way Is Struggling to Make Ends Meet," *Business Week* (November 5, 1990), p. 102.

[34]United Way of Canada Internet Site.

[35]Hammonds and Sosland, "Even the United Way Is Struggling to Make Ends Meet," p. 102.

[36]Material in this section is based on Statistics Canada, *1995 Market Research Handbook* (Ottawa: Minister of Supply Services); *Today's Seniors* (October 1995); Eric Miller "A 24-Point Guide To Mature Minds," *Marketing Magazine* (May 15, 1995), p. 29; Garth Turner, "A Private Cure for Public Health Care," *Canadian Business* (January 1996), p. 13; Andrea Haman, "It's New Blue Cross vs. Old Blue Cross in Ontario," *Marketing Magazine* (September 4, 1995), p. 2; and "Private Health Insurance Re-Emerges: The Canada America Healthcare Plan Gives Canadians The Opportunity To Escape Surgical Waiting Lists By Accessing American Hospitals And Clinics," *Canadian Insurance* (July, 1993) pp. 26–27.

This last approach would mean higher income Canadians could divert their tax contributions to a private plan and not pay into provincial health care plans, thereby imposing a market discipline on public health care and giving rise to a private health care system. This notion is unpopular among proponents of universal health care.

Still, a two-tiered system of medical care is emerging on its own. Because of cutbacks in the Canadian health care system people have long waits for elective surgical procedures (like hernias), diagnostic tests (like CT scans, angiograms) and treatment, even in potentially serious instances where cardiac problems may be suspected. The marketplace has responded to this situation with private health insurance plans such as the Canada America Healthcare Plan and Blue Cross, offering Canadians coverage for medical procedures in the United States. Consequently, wealthier Canadians have access to both Canada's health care system and the free-enterprise American system.

There are two certainties for the Canadian health care market: the demand for services will continue to grow, making it appear attractive; and funding to support this market will be spread ever thinner and will have to be managed much more carefully.

SUMMARY

1. *To examine the scope of goods and services, and explain how goods and services may be categorized* Goods marketing encompasses the sales of durable and nondurable physical products; service marketing involves goods rental, goods alteration, maintenance, or repair, and personal services. In Canada, consumer expenditures on nondurable goods are slightly higher than those for durable goods. Services account for a very large share of the GDP in industrialized nations, 66 per cent of Canada's GDP, and a smaller share in developing and less-developed nations. Both final-consumer and business services have seen significant growth in recent years. The scope of services is sometimes underestimated due to the hidden service sector.

With a goods/services continuum, products can be positioned on a scale from pure goods to goods/services combinations to pure services. Much can be learned by studying this continuum, including its use for final and organizational consumer products, the presence of unique marketing opportunities, and the changing relationship between sellers and buyers as pure goods become goods/services combinations. Both goods- and services-oriented firms need to identify core and peripheral services.

Goods can be classed by market, product durability, value added, company goal, degree of regulation, distribution channel length, and extent of customer contact. Services can be classed by market, level of tangibility, service provider skill, service provider goals, degree of regulation, labour intensiveness, and amount of customer contact. A firm would be categorized on the basis of a combination of these factors.

2. *To discuss the special considerations in the marketing of services* Services are generally less tangible, more perishable, less separable from their provider, and more variable in quality than goods that are sold. The effect of these factors is greatest for personal services. Service firms need to enact strategies that enable consumers to perceive their offerings more tangibly, make their offerings less perishable, encourage consumers to seek them out but enable multiple employees to be viewed as competent, and make performance as efficient and consistent as possible. Such approaches as the industrialization of services, the service blueprint, and gap analysis enable service firms to better devise and implement marketing plans by improving their performance.

3. *To look at the use of marketing by goods versus services firms and provide illustrations of service marketing* Many service firms have lagged behind manufacturers in the use of marketing because of their small size, the larger geographic coverage of goods-oriented companies, their technical emphasis, less competition and the lack of need for marketing, the high esteem of consumers for certain service providers, past bans on advertising, a dislike of marketing by some service professionals, and the reluctance of some manufacturers to view services as profit centres. Yet, for a number of reasons, this has been changing and the marketing of services is now expanding greatly. The marketing practices of hotels, repair and servicing firms, and lawyers are highlighted.

4. *To distinguish between nonprofit and profit-oriented marketing* Nonprofit marketing is conducted by organizations and people that operate for the public good or to foster a cause and not for financial profits. It is both similar to and different from profit-oriented marketing. These are some of the differences: Nonprofit marketing is more apt to involve organizations, people, places, and ideas. Nonprofit firms' exchanges do not have to involve money, and goals can be hard to formulate. The benefits of nonprofit firms may be distributed unequally, and economically unfeasible market segments may have to be served. Two target markets must be satisfied by nonprofit organizations: clients and donors.

5. *To describe a classification system for nonprofit marketing, the role of nonprofit marketing in the economy, and applications of nonprofit marketing*

Nonprofit organizations can be classed on the basis of tangibility, organization structure, objectives, and constituency. A nonprofit organization would be categorized by a combination of these factors. Worldwide, there are millions of organizations and people engaged in nonprofit marketing. Nonprofit organizations play a key roll in the Canadian economy, employing 25 per cent of industrial employees. Funding for nonprofits comes from corporations, government, and individuals. In 1994 5.3 million individual Canadian tax filers claimed $3.39 billion in charitable donations on their taxes. The marketing practices of Canada Post, Canadian universities, and the United Way of Canada are highlighted.

KEY TERMS

goods marketing (p. 318)
durable goods (p. 318)
nondurable goods (p. 318)
service marketing (p. 318)
rented-goods services (p. 318)
owned-goods services (p. 318)
nongoods services (p. 318)
hidden service sector (p. 319)

goods/services continuum (p. 319)
core services (p. 320)
peripheral services (p. 320)
intangibility of services (p. 324)
perishability of services (p. 324)
inseparability of services (p. 324)
variability in service quality (p. 325)

industrialization of services (p. 327)
service blueprint (p. 328)
service gap (p. 328)
nonprofit marketing (p. 332)
social marketing (p. 335)
clients (p. 336)
donors (p. 336)

Review Questions

1. Differentiate among rented-goods services, owned-goods services, and nongoods services.
2. What is a goods/services continuum? Why should firms be aware of this concept?
3. Distinguish between core and peripheral services. What is the marketing role of each?
4. How can a service be positioned more tangibly?
5. Describe how hard, soft, and hybrid technologies may be used to industrialize services.
6. Why have service firms lagged behind manufacturers in the development and use of marketing strategies?
7. What are some of the similarities and differences in the marketing efforts of nonprofit and profit-oriented organizations?
8. When is an organization engaged in social marketing?
9. Discuss the factors that may be used to classify nonprofit marketing.
10. How do the goals of clients and donors differ?

Discussion Questions

1. Present a goods/services continuum related to entertainment. Discuss the implications of this continuum for a firm interested in developing a marketing plan in the entertainment field.
2. Give several ways that a car rental agency can match demand and supply on days following holidays.
3. Draw and discuss a service blueprint for an insurance broker dealing with small-business clients.
4. Present five objectives that could be used to evaluate the effectiveness of public television broadcasting.
5. Discuss several innovative fundraising programs for the Canadian Heart and Stroke Foundation.

VIDEO CASE
Inside MasterCard

Banks and trust companies in Canada represent one of the most important service institutions in the economy. They are key facilitators for businesses and private citizens alike. One of the most useful financial and retailing innovations, and an important source of revenue and profits for banks, trust companies, and large retail institutions, is the credit card.

The ability to delay payment for goods and services, the security of not having to carry cash to make purchases, the freedom to buy on impulse and seize a bargain are all important benefits conferred by credit cards. The word "convenience" sums up the appeals of some of the more universally accepted credit cards like MasterCard, Visa, and American Express. In Canada (population 29 million +) there are 25 million VISA and MasterCards and credit card usage is very big business. (To encourage the acquisition and use of the cards financial and retailing institutions have joined together to arrange a host of features and benefits to induce the use of the cards for the purchase of specific retail products.) For example, Toronto Dominion Bank and General Motors have combined to produce a joint credit card that gives buyers rebates on GM cars based on the amount of purchases made on their Visa cards. Canadian Tire and MasterCard have a joint card which allows purchasers to build up "bonus points" that are redeemable for Canadian Tire merchandise. Previously, purchasers could only build up these points on Canadian Tire credit cards and Canadian Tire cards were not accepted elsewhere.

Credit card usage creates revenue for financial institutions in three fundamental ways. First, companies charge various annual fees depending on the credit limits of the cards and other features. Secondly, financial institutions charge high interest rates on unpaid credit card balances. In the case of Canada Trust, which typically has $1 billion in outstanding balances, this quickly amounts to a large revenue stream. Finally, retailers pay a percentage fee to the credit card issuers based on the dollar volume of the transaction associated with the credit card. The advantage to the retailer is that they make a credit sale without assuming any risk themselves. The financial institutions assume the risk.

The inducement to have credit cards in the market is very strong and Canada Trust makes a special effort every year to approve and ship as many cards as possible prior to the Christmas season. However, before approving and shipping these cards they are fairly careful to check the credit histories of the applicants with the credit bureau, an independent organization that routinely keeps six-year credit histories on people.

Canada Trust believes in relationship marketing as they deal with card holders who present problems. They provide customer service with a toll-free phone line. This receives almost 10,000 calls per day at its MasterCard centre and deals with the loss or theft of an average of 300 cards per day! Canada Trust views their customers as major assets and makes every attempt to quickly replace lost or stolen cards. For people who have gotten themselves into financial distress and are late in payment the approach is to request payment but the situation is handled very delicately. A number of gentle reminders and requests are made and litigation does not usually occur until the account is more than 6 months past due. Canada Trust wants to maintain as positive a relationship as possible with their cardholders.

Credit cards are now a critical element for all marketers in the current Canadian economy and will likely be more critical to the economy of the future. It seems clear that the age-old promotional theme of "Don't Leave Home Without It" as presented by American Express, has had a strong carryover in creating demand for all credit cards. And now, with mail order services, home shopping networks and internet shopping convenience all fuelled by the use of credit cards, the new slogan might become: "Without it, you'll have to leave home."

QUESTIONS
1. Describe credit cards in terms of the goods/services continuum shown in Figure 12-1.
2. Discuss some of the ways that credit card issuers differentiate themselves from their competitors. Define the kind of offering a credit card represents.
3. Discuss the kinds of ethical issues surrounding credit cards from financial institutions, their acceptance by retailers, and their use by consumers. In cases of fraud and abuse, who should bear the costs and responsibilities and in what proportions?
4. Explain how market forces might account for the disparity between credit card interest rates and loan interest rates. Do you think the differences are really justified and why?

VIDEO QUESTIONS ON INSIDE MASTERCARD
1. Is Canada Trust's approach to handling customer problems a good example of relationship marketing? Why or why not? Use the discussion from the chapter to support your answer.
2. Discuss some of the ways in which Canada Trust segments the market for its MasterCard products. Can you think of an unserved segment which could be appealed to and what features a "new MasterCard" might contain that could appeal to this segment?

Video Source: "Inside MasterCard," *Venture* (December 10, 1995).

Other Sources: "Canadian Tire Introduces MasterCard," *Marketing Magazine*, (July 24, 1995) p. 1; "TD, GM Launch Credit Card: Joint Visa Lets Users Build Rebates to Buy or Lease New Cars," *Globe & Mail* (March 10, 1993), p. B2; "Amex Leaves Attitude at Home: Company Tries to Alter Ivory Tower," *Globe & Mail* (March 14, 1994), pp. B1, B5; Gwyn Gill, "Banks Turn to Bold Marketing," *Marketing Magazine* (July 5/12, 1993), p. 17; and "Credit Card Rates Too High, Federal Minister Charges: Committee Revisits the Idea of Promoting Cap," *Globe & Mail* (November 19, 1991), pp. B1, B10.

CASE STUDY

Olsten Corporation: Creating Differential Advantages for a Service Business

Olsten Corporation is North America's largest provider of home health-care services and one of the world's leading providers of staffing services. The firm operates 1200 offices in the U.S., Canada, Mexico, and Great Britain and has annual revenues of U.S. $2.3 billion. The firm is divided into two major divisions: health care services and staffing services.

Olsten's health-care service unit provides home health care, management services for hospital-based home-health agencies, and institutional staffing in the United States and Canada. This unit is comprised of Olsten Kimberly Quality Care (U.S. and Canada) and ASB Meditest (U.S.). It serves over 400 000 patient accounts through a variety of compensation systems (such as Medicare and Medicaid). Forty-seven per cent of Olsten's total revenues are health-care based.

The company's staffing services unit is comprised of Olsten Staffing Services (U.S. and Canada), Office Angels (Great Britain), and Olsten STAFF (Mexico). This unit provides temporary office employees (including clerical, accounting, legal, technical, and production specialties) in the United States, Canada, Great Britain, and Mexico. It serves over 100 000 client accounts in business, industry, and government. Fifty-three per cent of Olsten's total revenues are in staffing services.

Several industrywide developments have affected the market for temporary workers: the ability of clients to "test drive" a temporary employee, clients' desire to reduce the number of temporary suppliers with which they deal, the increased popularity of "vendor-on-premises" contracts, and the growing concern over cost containment by clients. Each of these developments has a positive impact on Olsten.

Many firms like initially hiring an employee on a temporary basis. This allows the firm to see how well a worker performs without having to make a formal job offer, explain why a worker is fired, and so forth. Employees also like to "test drive" an employer or see the differences in job dynamics in different industries. According to a survey by the National Association of Temporary Staffing Services (NATSS), three-quarters of respondents said they became temporary workers as a way of looking for a full-time position. And 40 per cent of those respondents stated that they received permanent job offers.

A lot of firms are reducing the number of temporary agencies with which they deal. These firms favour this approach because it increases their bargaining power. A national partnership with a major manufacturer or bank could be worth $100 million per year to Olsten. As partners, agencies also are expected to develop special electronic billing and training for their leading clients. In one such partnership with Columbia/HCA Healthcare, Olsten now manages the home health agencies at twenty-two Columbia/HCA hospitals.

With "vendor-on-premises" contracts, temporary agencies set up offices at each major client's factory or office. This enhances the customer service provided. For instance, Olsten operates offices at AT&T, Bristol-Myers Squibb, and the computer services unit of General Electric. Olsten hires, trains, and schedules the temporary workers for these clients.

Temporary workers are a means of cost containment for firms. Client firms need only pay for temporary workers in busy seasons or provide coverage for time periods corresponding to regular employees' absences. Health care employees can even be hired on a temporary basis during a person's illness.

QUESTIONS

1. Classify Olsten's two divisions based on the dimensions of Figure 12-3.
2. Discuss the difficulties in the marketing of temporary services based on their intangibility, perishability, inseparability, and variability.
3. How can Olsten industrialize its services? Discuss specific concepts that relate to hard, soft, and hybrid technologies.
4. What are the pros and cons of a "vendor-on-premises" contract to Olsten? What are the pros and cons of a "vendor-on-premises" contract to a manufacturer?

Source: The data in this case are drawn from James Aley, "The Temp Biz Boom: Why It's Good," *Fortune* (October 16, 1995), p. 53; Barnaby J. Feder, "Bigger Roles for Suppliers of Temporary Workers," *New York Times* (April 1, 1995), p. 39; *Olsten Corporation 1994 Annual Report*; and "Temp Work on the Rise—for Now," *Newsday* (October 18, 1995), p. A39.

CHAPTER 13
Conceiving, Developing, and Managing Products

Chapter Objectives

1. To examine the types of new product opportunities available to a firm

2. To detail the importance of new products and describe why new products fail

3. To present the stages in the new-product planning process

4. To analyze the growth and maturity of products, including the adoption process, the diffusion process, and extension strategies

5. To examine product deletion decisions and strategies

Ask just about any company these days to give up its facsimile machine and you're in for a fight. For most businesspeople today, it's difficult to remember what life was like before fax machines made it possible to send documents easily and cheaply across the country or around the world. Final consumers are also finding uses for the fax machine. They order take-out food, request a song on the radio, and make mail-order purchases via fax.

According to a recent survey, two-thirds of North American adults have either received or sent a fax message at some point (usually at work). Yet, even though PC sales have successfully made the transition from office to home, just 7 per cent of North American households now own a freestanding fax machine. In contrast, 28.8 per cent of Canadian households own PCs and 42 per cent of these computers have a modem.

The survey just cited also indicates that fax machine manufacturers will have to work awfully hard to increase their market penetration in the home market. Seventy-one per cent of North American adults feel there is no benefit to being able to send and receive faxes at home. Of the 28 per cent who believe there are benefits to having a fax machine at home, only 11 per cent (equal to 3 per cent of all North American adults) think there is a great benefit. Among the key benefits to home faxes are ease of use, flexibility (they allow individuals to work at home), convenience (not having to leave home to send a fax), and speed (compared to mail or express carriers).

According to the survey, among people who would purchase fax equipment for home use, one-half of them would prefer a fax machine built into their home computer. (Note: While a built-in computer fax modem can generally be bought for less than $100, it cannot be used to send documents that are not part of a computer file—but a fax modem can receive noncomputerized documents). One quarter would buy a freestanding machine and 25 per cent do not know what type of machine they would purchase.

Many consumers are also uncertain about the cost of a freestanding fax machine, where they would buy it, and the name of a good brand. On average, consumers expect to pay $640 for a freestanding machine—double today's real "street prices." Price expectations vary with the person's previous experience with fax machines. More experienced shoppers plan to pay less (an average price of $540) than nonusers (an average price of $860). The place to shop for a freestanding fax machine that people mention most is electronics stores (35 per cent of respondents), followed by office supply stores (15 per cent), and then mail-order catalogues (12 per cent). Most people do not know the name of a good brand of fax machine; some even mention names of firms that do not produce freestanding fax machines.[1]

In this chapter, we will study how new products are developed, the factors causing rapid or slow growth for new products, how to manage mature products, and what to do when existing products falter. As our home fax discussion illustrates, it takes a lot of work—and persistence—to stay ahead.

Overview

While any product combines tangible and intangible features to satisfy consumer needs, a **new product** involves a modification of an existing product or an innovation the consumer perceives as meaningful. To succeed, a new product must have desirable attributes, be unique, and have its features communicated to consumers. Marketing support is therefore necessary.[2]

Product planning involves **new products** *and existing products.*

---

[1] Susan Reda, "Home Faxes Fail to Strike," *Stores* (April 1995), pp. 28–29; and Statistics Canada, *The Daily* (Friday, January 12, 1996).

[2] See Roger J. Calantone, C. Anthony Di Benedetto, and Ted Haggbloom, "Principles of New Product Management: Exploring the Beliefs of Product Practitioners," *Journal of Product Innovation Management*, Vol. 12 (June 1995), pp. 235–247.

New products may be **modifications**, **minor innovations**, *or* **major innovations**.

Modifications are alterations in or extensions of a firm's existing products and include new models, styles, colours, features, and brands. **Minor innovations** are items not previously marketed by a firm that have been marketed by others. For example, the Toronto Dominion Bank introduced a Visa TD Gold Travel Card that is not affiliated with any major airline or other travel service. Instead, cardholders create their own travel package with points built up on the basis of their dollar purchases.[3]

Major innovations are items not previously sold by any firm (like the first cellular telephone). If a firm works with major innovations, the costs, risks, and time required for profitability all rise. Overall, most new products are modifications; few are major innovations.

New products may be conceived of and developed by a company itself or purchased from another firm. A company may buy a firm, buy a specific product, or sign a licensing agreement (whereby it pays an inventor a royalty fee based on sales). Acquisitions may reduce risks and time demands, but they rely on outsiders for innovations and may require large investments.

Early in a product's life, there is usually strong sales growth, as more people purchase and repurchase. This is an exciting time; and if a product is popular, it can last for quite a while. Later, the market becomes more saturated and competition intensifies. At that point, a firm can maintain high sales by adding features that provide convenience and durability, using new materials in construction, offering a range of models, stressing new packaging, and/or adding customer services. It can also reposition a product, enter untapped geographic markets, demonstrate new uses, offer new brands, set lower prices, use new media, and/or appeal to new segments. At some point, however, firms must decide whether these items have outlived their usefulness and should be dropped.

The Importance of New Products

A firm's product policy should be future-oriented and recognize that products, no matter how successful, tend to be mortal—they usually cannot sustain a peak level of sales and profits indefinitely. "Innovation can give a company a competitive advantage and profits, but nothing lasts forever. Success brings on imitators, who respond with superior features, lower prices, or some other new way to draw customers. Time ultimately renders nearly all advantages obsolete."[4] So, replacements should be constantly planned and a balanced product portfolio pursued—by both small and large firms.

New products offer differential advantages.

Introducing new products is important for several reasons. Desirable differential advantages can be attained. For example, the Seiko Kinetic Quartz watch is the first quartz watch that does not require a battery or have to be wound. It is advertised as "No more batteries. No more winding. No more hassles." (See Figure 13-1.) Goodyear's "smart tire" for trucks is embedded with a computer chip allowing drivers to easily see the wear and air pressure of tires; this improves tire life and fuel efficiency.

New products lead to sales growth or stability.

New products may be needed for continued growth. That is why Quaker Oats has a new line of rice cakes; due to their poor taste, earlier Quaker Rice Cakes did not attain company goals—as Quaker admits in Figure 13-2. At Timken, a nearly 100-year-old U.S.-based maker of industrial roller bearings, "Today's bearing is a dramatically different product than it was ten years ago, and we would be very surprised if the 2005 version is anything like we're making today." By thinking like this, Timken still holds a one-third share of the world market for tapered roller bearings.[5]

QUAKER OATS COMPANY
www.quaker-oats.com/

BLACK & DECKER
www.blackanddecker.com/

For firms with cyclical or seasonal sales, new products can stabilize revenues and costs. Union Carbide manufactures medical-testing equipment, to reduce its dependence on cyclical chemicals. Black & Decker has cut back on lawn mowers and looks for new opportunities in less seasonal products (such as power tools for the home).

---

[3]Andrea Haman, "TD Piles on Features in New Travel Card," *Marketing Magazine* (June 5, 1995), p. 4.
[4]Jeffrey R. Williams, "How Sustainable Is Your Competitive Advantage?" *California Management Review*, Vol. 34 (Spring 1992), p. 29.
[5]Eric S. Hardy, "The Soul of an Old Company," *Forbes* (March 13, 1995), pp. 70–71.

Chapter 13 *Conceiving, Developing, and Managing Products* **351**

FIGURE 13-1
Creating a Differential Advantage
Reprinted by permission. Courtesy of Seiko Corporation of America.

Planning for growth must take into consideration the time it takes for a new product to move from idea stage to commercialization. For instance, in 1983, Canadian Brian Maxwell came up with the idea for a food bar for exercise enthusiasts that would let them fuel up for long workouts while circumventing the stomach problems that often accompany eating while exercising. He immediately began experimenting with various recipes; it took three years and 800 experimental recipes to find one that worked: "For three years, people would say the texture wasn't right, the bar was upsetting their stomachs, or there was something wrong with the taste." At that point, Maxwell and his partner, Jennifer Biddulph, invested their life savings to contract for a 50 000-bar production run and start a mail-order business. In 1989, they opened their first plant. And in 1993, Powerfood Inc. became a PriceCostco vendor. Today, the maker of PowerBar has annual revenues of more than $30 million and does business in thirty countries.[6]

New products can take time.

New products can lead to larger profits and give a company better control over a marketing strategy. For example, the new Lincoln line of cars is quite popular, so the cars have been selling at close to the sticker price, with dealers earning gross profits of up to $10 000 on each car sold. Because there are fewer Lincoln dealers relative to lower-priced cars, they do not use much price discounting and have firm command over their marketing efforts.

New products can increase profits and control.

To limit risk, many firms seek to reduce dependence on one product or product line. That is why many movie theatres converted to multiplexes; their revenues are not tied to any one film's performance. Hewlett-Packard makes electronic components and test equip-

Risk may be lessened through diversity.

[6]Tod Jones, "The Power of Persistence," *Price Costco Connection* (June 1995), p. 15.

FIGURE 13-2
Better-Tasting Rice Cakes from Quaker Oats
Reprinted by permission.

New products may improve distribution.

Technology can be exploited.

KODAK
www.kodak.com/homePage.shtml

Waste materials can be used.

ment, medical electronic equipment, and analytical instrumentation—in addition to its core computing and printing products; and it regularly adds new products. Turtle Wax, the world's leader in car care products, now makes shoe polish, household cleaners, and fabric protectors.

Firms may try to improve the efficiency of their established distribution systems by placing new products in them. They can then spread advertising, sales, and distribution costs among several products, gain dealer support, and discourage other companies from entering the market. Manufacturers like Neilsen-Cadbury's, Unilever, and Revlon can place new products in many outlets quickly. Service firms, such as banks, also can efficiently add new products (financial services) into their distribution networks.

Firms often seek technological breakthroughs. For instance, Kodak has developed a line of digital cameras that create electronic images, and which promise to revolutionize the photodeveloping business. This may well mean the demise of traditional film-based cameras—and the core of Kodak's business. To remain viable, Kodak has chosen to embrace digital technology, as it did with VCRs and camcorders, which replaced "film based" movie cameras in the 1980s. Kodak is now a leading producer of videotapes.[7]

Sometimes, firms want to find uses for waste materials from existing products—to aid productivity or be responsive to environmental concerns. Just over a decade ago, the chicken industry found that "we have four billion broilers, and the consumer generally doesn't want the necks and backs. What do we do? We grind them into baloney and hot dogs."[8] The sales of these products have skyrocketed since then. For environmental and

[7]Deborah McKay-Stokes, "Old Products and New Processes," *Marketing Magazine* (April 24, 1995), p. 15.
[8]R. Kleinfield, "America Goes Chicken Crazy," *New York Times* (December 9, 1984), Section 3, p. 9.

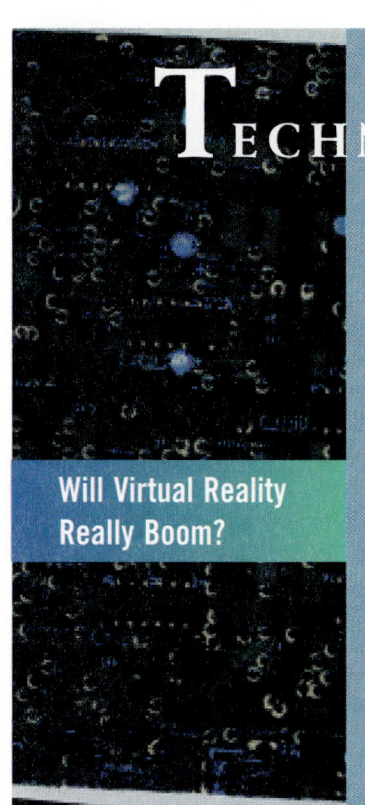

TECHNOLOGY & MARKETING

Will Virtual Reality Really Boom?

There used to be a common saying among computer programmers: "Virtual reality can be fast, pretty, or cheap—but you can choose only two of the three." Thus, an interactive simulation that was fast and had excellent graphics was also costly. For example, a realistic computer simulation for pilot training used to cost U.S.$2 million or more.

In 1990, Silicon Graphics introduced an U.S.$80,000 workstation that was able to reproduce realistic backgrounds that simulated motion. This hardware changed forever the "two-of-three" rule.

Using Silicon Graphics equipment, three young programmers (aged 29 to 35) started Paradigm Simulation. Since then, Paradigm software has been used by the U.S. government to test missile designs, the Federal Aviation Administration to evaluate new flight-control console designs, and an Italian firm to develop a model of a Renaissance city for an educational project.

Until recently, the landing lights at an airport could be simulated only by writing 3000 lines of computer code. With Paradigm software, these lights can now be added by simply moving a cursor to an icon labelled "Light Lobes" and clicking a mouse button. Customers can even adjust the size and intensity of the landing lights through another window. Similarly, users can adjust the time of day, weather conditions, add special effects like explosions, and even include computer-controlled objects such as highway traffic.

Paradigm's software prices range from U.S.$3500 to U.S.$40 000. Although the software for ship design is especially costly, architectural renderings can be simulated with a U.S.$10 000 program. The hardware needed to run Paradigm's most popular software costs approximately U.S.$300 000. Paradigm's total sales exceed U.S.$5 million, and are 40 per cent defence-related.

As a marketing manager for Paradigm, develop a concept test to evaluate a new application of its virtual-reality business software.

Source: Based on material in R. Lee Sullivan, "Virtual Reality Made Easy," *Forbes* (January 2, 1995), pp. 66–67.

---

cost reasons, Johnson Controls makes auto batteries from recycled lead and plastic; Reynolds Metals uses recycled paperboard in foil and wax paper packaging; and Scotch-Brite steel wool pads are made from recycled bottles and packaged in recycled paper.

Companies may bring out new products to respond to changing consumer demographics and lifestyles. For example, Royal Plastics markets a basic 500-square-foot plastic house targeted at underdeveloped nations. At a cost of U.S.$30 a square foot for construction, it is priced right for these markets. Added to the fact that many of the homes are built in tropical climates where termites and dampness are very hard on wood-frame construction, it is a product well positioned to meet people's needs. And CP8 Oberthur is planning to market "smart" cards in Canada. These cards are embedded with computer chips and memory chips and will allow electronic storage and transfer of money and personal information (like health history on health cards). This will allow consumers more convenience and more security when using credit cards.[9]

New products are sometimes developed in response to government mandates. In 1990, the Ontario provincial government mandated that all new cars sold in the province be equipped with daytime running lights. Prior to this, North American manufacturers had no experience with this type of feature on automobiles. They had to scramble to come up

JOHNSON CONTROLS
www.johnsoncontrols.com/

New products respond to consumer needs.

Government mandates are addressed.

---

[9] Gail Chiasson, "Tardit To Head Up New Smart Card Venture In Canada," *Marketing Magazine* (August 21–28, 1995), p. 4; and Katrina Onstad, "The Midas Touch," *Canadian Business* (December 1995), p. 40.

with technologies to deal with this requirement. As a result of the Ontario legislation, foreign manufacturers have essentially equipped all automobiles for the Canadian market with daytime running lights. And General Motors has been selling automobiles in the United States with daytime running lights, promoting this as a safety feature, even though it is not required there by law.

In a more recent example, the CRTC mandated that all broadcasters establish a V-Chip rating system for use in televisions. The V-Chip is a computer chip embedded in a television tuner, which is designed to allow parents to choose the acceptable ratings of programs coming into their homes. This means broadcasters must develop a rating system for programs and send these signals along with the program so that the V-Chip can decode them and block the signals if programmed to do so. Rating signal systems can rate a whole program or parts of a program. For example, the V-Chip can be set to block out an entire broadcast or just parts of a broadcast that contain too much violence or sex.[10]

Good long-run new-product planning requires systematic research and development, matching the requirements of new-product opportunities against company abilities, emphasizing consumer desires, properly spending time and money, and defensive—as well as offensive—planning. A firm must accept that some new products may fail; a progressive firm will take risks:

> Innovation is a risky business, and failure is commonplace. Rewarding success is easy, but rewarding intelligent failure is more important. Don't judge people strictly by results; try to judge them by the quality of their efforts. People should take intelligent business risks without also risking their compensation or their careers.[11]

And there has been some criticism of the negative effects of many Canadian firms' short-run, bottom-line orientation on their level of innovativeness (and willingness to take risks).

Why New Products Fail

Despite better product-planning practices today than ever before, the failure rate for new products is quite high. According to the consulting firm of Booz, Allen, & Hamilton, an average of 35 per cent of new industrial and consumer products fail. Others say the rate may be even greater.[12]

*With **absolute product failure**, costs are not regained. With **relative product failure**, goals are not met.*

Product failure can be defined in both absolute and relative terms. **Absolute product failure** occurs if a firm is unable to regain its production and marketing costs. It incurs a financial loss. **Relative product failure** occurs if a firm makes a profit on an item but that product does not reach profit goals and/or adversely affects a firm's image. In computing profits and losses, the impact of the new product on the sales of other company items must be measured.

Even firms with good new-product records have had failures along the way. These include "light" pizza (Pizza Hut), Crystal Pepsi (PepsiCo), Bic perfume, McLean Deluxe (McDonald's), "new" Coke (Coca-Cola), Premier smokeless cigarettes (R.J. Reynolds) and *Junior* (the Universal movie starring Arnold Schwarzenegger, Danny DeVito, and Emma Thompson).

---

[10]Susan Ellsworth, "V-Chips and Audience Numbers," *Marketing Magazine* (January 22, 1996), p. 19; and "TV Forced to Code Shows for Violence: CRTC Has Ordered Broadcasters to Establish a V-Chip System by September 1 To Help Parents Control What Their Children Watch," *Vancouver Sun* (March 15, 1996), pp. A1, A10.

[11]"How Can Big Companies Keep the Entrepreneurial Spirit Alive?" *Harvard Business Review*, Vol. 73 (November–December 1995), p. 190.

[12]See Cyndee Miller, "Survey: New Product Failure Is Top Management's Fault," *Marketing News* (February 1, 1993), p. 2; Erik Jan Hultink and Henry S. J. Robben, "Measuring New Product Success: The Difference That Time Perspective Makes," *Journal of Product Innovation Management*, Vol. 12 (November 1995), pp. 392–405; James Dao, "From a Collector of Turkeys, A Tour of a Supermarket Zoo," *New York Times* (September 24, 1995), Section C, p. 12; and Ulrike de Brentani, "New Industrial Service Development: Scenarios for Success and Failure," *Journal of Business Research*, Vol. 32 (February 1995), pp. 93–103.

Numerous factors may cause new-product failure. The key ones are lack of a differential advantage, poor planning, poor timing, and excessive enthusiasm by the sponsor. Illustrations of poor performance due to those factors follow.

Leading to failure are lack of an advantage, poor planning and timing, and excess enthusiasm.

Vancouver's Harvard Capital Corporation thought they had a sure winner with the "Spud Stop," a french fry vending machine, till they filed for bankruptcy in October 1994. The concept of bringing french fries to the masses in every location where there are vending machines is very alluring. The differential advantage of delivering a desired product with the convenience of a vending machine was very appealing to investors. The problem is that fast food outlets are easy to access too and very good at making french fries.

The "Spud Stop" machines were designed to deliver fries in 50 seconds by mixing dehydrated potato powder with water, producing thirty-two potato strands, dipping the strands in oil and then putting them in a box. But the machines could not deliver on their potential. For example, a "Spud Stop" machine was tested in Sedgewick Hall at the University of British Columbia. The students found that the machine would often begin smoking, the quality of the fries dispensed was often less than acceptable, and there were sanitation problems as well. In one instance the fire department was called and this resulted in the removal of the machine. Despite investments of over $10 million, Harvard Capital was unable to make a product which was able to deliver on its promise.[13]

Thermalux was the only North American maker of aerogels, "special substances that look like glass, feel like styrofoam, and are as light as a feather. They are great insulators." Despite the apparent potential of the product, after two years of poor planning, Thermalux had no customers; its aerogels remained "a solution looking for a problem." At first, it thought refrigerator makers would be the best market since they were under pressure to avoid using insulation materials made from certain fluorocarbons and to cut energy use. But the company underestimated competition from other insulation-materials firms. It also had a tough time setting the prices of its aerogels; and when aerogel insulation was tested in refrigerators, it did not show the benefits expected. Finally, Thermalux could not produce aerogels in sufficient quantity.[14]

Poor timing led to the failure of Zap Mail by Federal Express. When it was introduced, Federal Express expected its Zap Mail (which was essentially a facsimile machine service) to change the way business customers sent documents. With it, a customer could send a copy of a document almost anywhere in Canada or the United States in under two hours. The sender called a Federal Express operator, who had a courier pick up a document and take it to a Zap Mail office, which forwarded a copy to a receiving site. The copy was delivered by courier. Yet, within three years, Zap Mail was off the market. Although Federal Express felt Zap Mail would be successful, it failed for three reasons: computer modems let customers communicate instantly and without a delivery firm; many clients did not believe two-hour service (at a high price) was better than overnight service; and as Zap Mail started, inexpensive fax machines began to flood the market.[15]

Excessive enthusiasm caused RCA to overinvest in its videodisc player, causing a loss of nearly $600 million before the product was dropped. RCA felt the player's superior picture quality and low price would lead to success with the mass market. It underestimated consumer interest in recording programs (which the videodisc player could not do, but a VCR could). Firms with more focused goals, such as Hitachi, have done well marketing videodisc players to business customers as aids in sales training and point-of-purchase displays. Pioneer has laser videodisc players that "marry the superb sound of audio compact discs with crisp pictures." Philips has interactive players.[16]

---

[13]David Baines, "The Frying Game," *Canadian Business* (September 1994), pp. 32–36; and "Harvard Flunks Out," (editorial) *Canadian Business* (December 1994), p. 22.
[14]John R. Emschwiller, "Thermalux Seeks Customers for a New Technology," *Wall Street Journal* (February 15, 1991), p. B2.
[15]Federal Express Corporation reports.
[16]Sandra Salmans, "RCA Defends Timing of Videodisc Canceling," *New York Times* (April 6, 1984), pp. D1, D15; Marcia Watson, Jeff Kemph, and Judith Steele, "Marketing Muscle and the Videodisc," *Business Marketing* (June 1985), pp. 130–140; Brian O'Reilly, "Pioneer's Bright Picture," *Fortune* (August 13, 1990), p. 89; and "How to Sell Yourself on a CD-Interactive Player from Philips," *Wall Street Journal* (May 1, 1992), p. A13.

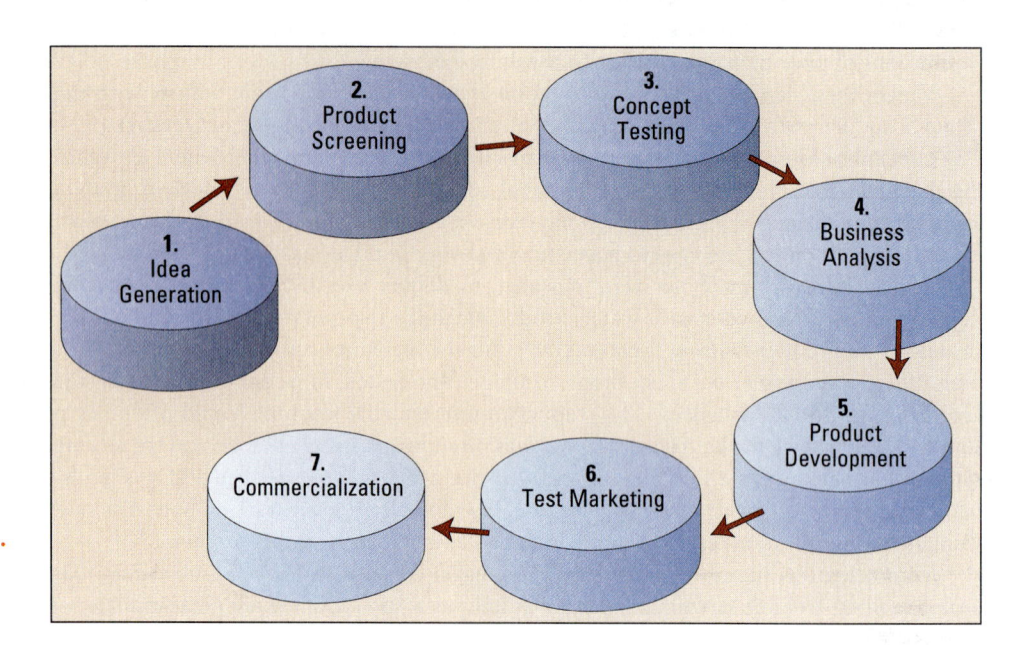

FIGURE 13-3
The New-Product Planning Process

The **new-product planning process** *moves goods and services from ideas to commercialization.*

New-Product Planning

The **new-product planning process** involves a series of steps from idea-generation to commercialization. See Figure 13-3. During the process, a firm generates ideas, evaluates them, weeds out poor ones, obtains consumer feedback, develops the product, tests it, and brings it to market. An idea can be terminated at any time, and costs rise as the process goes on. The process could be used by firms of any size or type, and applies to goods and services.

Booz, Allen, & Hamilton says it generally takes a firm an average of seven well-defined ideas to yield one commercially successful new product. But this number can be much higher. A study of new-product managers found that it took nearly seventy-five ideas to yield one successful new product. In the pharmaceuticals industry, it may take up to 10 000 compounds to come up with one drug that is approved by government regulators.[17]

During the new-product planning process, a firm tries to balance such competing goals as these:

- A systematic process should be followed; however, there must be flexibility to adapt to each unique new-product opportunity.
- The process should be thorough, yet not unduly slow down introductions.
- True innovations should be pursued, yet fiscal constraints must be considered.
- An early reading of consumer acceptance should be sought, but the firm must not give away too much information to potential competitors.
- There should be an interest in short-run profitability, but not at the expense of long-run growth.[18]

Figure 13-4 highlights 3M's perspective on new-product planning: The "unique 3M culture, passed on from generation to generation, has resulted in more than 60 000 small miracles that make our lives safer, easier, better."

---

[17]Miller, "Survey: New Product Failure Is Top Management's Fault," p. 2; T. Erickson and L. Brenkus, *Healthcare R & D: Tools and Tactics* (Cambridge, Mass.: Arthur D. Little, October 1986), meeting notes; Laura Jereski, "Block That Innovation!" *Forbes* (January 18, 1993), p. 48; and Lara Mills, "The New Rx for Drug Marketing," *Marketing Magazine* (September 11, 1995), p. 15.

[18]See Robert G. Cooper and Elmo J. Kleinschmidt, "Benchmarking the Firm's Success Factors in New Product Development," *Journal of Product Innovation Management*, Vol. 12 (November 1995), pp. 374–391; and James M. Higgins, "Innovate or Evaporate," *Futurist* (September–October 1995), pp. 42–48.

FIGURE 13-4
The 3M Approach to New-Product Planning
Reprinted by permission.

Idea Generation

Idea generation is a continuous, systematic search for new product opportunities. It involves new-idea sources and ways to generate ideas.

Sources of ideas may be employees, channel members, competitors, outside inventors, customers, government, and others. *Market-oriented sources* identify opportunities based on consumer needs and wants; laboratory research is used to satisfy them. Light beer, many ice cream flavours, and easy-to-open soda cans have evolved from market-oriented sources. *Laboratory-oriented sources* identify opportunities based on pure research (which seeks to gain knowledge and indirectly leads to specific new-product ideas) or applied research (which uses existing scientific techniques to develop new-product ideas). Penicillin, antifreeze, and synthetic fibres have evolved from laboratory sources.

Methods for generating ideas include brainstorming (small-group sessions to come up with a variety of ideas), analyzing current products, reading trade publications, visiting suppliers and dealers, and doing surveys. An open perspective is key: different people should be consulted; many ideas should be offered; and ideas should not be criticized, no matter how offbeat:

> Think of the *worst* possible idea you can for a new soup. How about a soup with rocks in it? Or a soup made of green slime? Terrible ideas, right? Maybe not. Thinking about a soup with rocks in it could inspire you to invent a new, extra-chunky brand of soup. Thinking about green slime soup could lead you to create a new $100-million line of "Slime Soups" for young boys, who we know like anything and everything that's "gross."[19]

Idea generation *is the search for opportunities.*

Product Screening

Once a firm spots potential products, it must screen them. In **product screening**, poor, unsuitable, or otherwise unattractive ideas are weeded out. Today, many firms use a new-

Product screening *weeds out undesirable ideas.*

[19]Bryan W. Mattimore, "Eureka! How to Invent a New Product," *Futurist* (March–April 1995), p. 34.

FIGURE 13-5
A New-Product Screening Checklist

General Characteristics of New Products	Rating
Profit potential	_____
Existing competition	_____
Potential competition	_____
Size of market	_____
Level of investment	_____
Patentability	_____
Level of risk	_____
Marketing Characteristics of New Products	
Fit with marketing capabilities	_____
Effect on existing products (brands)	_____
Appeal to current consumer markets	_____
Potential length of product life cycle	_____
Existence of differential advantage	_____
Impact on image	_____
Resistance to seasonal factors	_____
Production Characteristics of New Products	
Fit with production capabilities	_____
Length of time to commercialization	_____
Ease of production	_____
Availability of labor and material resources	_____
Ability to produce at competitive prices	_____

product screening checklist for preliminary analysis. In it, they list the attributes deemed most important and rate each idea on those attributes. The checklist is standardized and allows ideas to be compared.

Figure 13-5 shows a new-product screening checklist with three major categories: general characteristics, marketing characteristics, and production characteristics (which can be applied to both goods and services). In each category, there are several product attributes to assess. They are scored from 1 (outstanding) to 10 (very poor) for each product idea. In addition, the attributes would be weighted because they vary in their impact on new-product success. The checklist yields an overall score for every idea. Here is an example of how a firm could develop overall ratings for two product ideas. Remember, in this example, the best rating is 1 (so, 3 is worse than 2):

1. Product idea A gets an average rating of 2.5 on general characteristics, 2.9 on marketing characteristics, and 1.4 on production characteristics. Product idea B gets ratings of 2.8, 1.4, and 1.8, respectively.

2. The firm assigns an importance weight of 4 to general characteristics, 5 to marketing characteristics, and 3 to production characteristics. The best overall rating is 12 [$(1 \times 4) + (1 \times 5) + (1 \times 3)$]. The poorest possible overall average rating is 120 [$(10 \times 4) + (10 \times 5) + (10 \times 3)$].

3. Idea A gets an overall rating of 28.7 [$(2.5 \times 4) + (2.9 \times 5) + (1.4 \times 3)$]. B gets an overall rating of 23.6 [$(2.8 \times 4) + (1.4 \times 5) + (1.8 \times 3)$].

4. Idea B's overall rating is better than A's because of its better marketing evaluation (the characteristics judged most important by the firm).

In screening, patentability must often be determined. A **patent** grants an inventor of a useful product or process exclusive selling rights for a fixed period. An invention may be patented if it is a "useful, novel, and nonobvious process, machine, manufacture, or composition of matter" and not patented by anyone else. Separate applications are needed for

*A **patent** gives exclusive selling rights to an inventor.*

protection in foreign markets. Many nations have simplified matters by signing patent cooperation treaties; however, some do not honour such treaties. Today, Canada and the other members of the World Trade Organization grant patents that last for twenty years from the date that applications are filed. In 1992–93, 26 865 patent applications were filed in Canada and 17 247 were granted. Only 12 per cent of the patent applications were filed by Canadians and only 7 per cent of the applications that were granted went to Canadians. The remaining 88 per cent of applications and 93 per cent of patents granted involved foreign nationals (mainly U.S., European, and Japanese) of which 50 per cent were from the U.S.[20]

A company should answer several questions regarding patents during the screening stage. For example:

- Can the proposed new product be patented by the firm?
- Are competitive items patented?
- When do competitors' patents expire?
- Are patents on competing items available under a licensing agreement?
- Would the firm be free of patent liability (infringement) if it introduced the proposed new product?

Concept Testing

Next, a firm needs consumer feedback about the new-product ideas that pass through screening. **Concept testing** presents the consumer with a proposed product and measures attitudes and intentions at an early stage of the new-product planning process.

Concept testing is a quick, inexpensive way to assess consumer enthusiasm. It asks potential consumers to react to a picture, written statement, or oral product description. This lets a firm learn initial attitudes prior to undertaking costly, time-consuming product development. Heinz, Kodak, Sony, and Sunbeam are among those using concept testing. Figure 13-6 shows a concept test for prepaid telephone cards to be used with pay phones. This card is popular in Europe and becoming so in Canada, where 1995 sales are estimated to be in the $8 million range.[21]

Concept testing generally asks consumers these types of questions:

Concept testing *determines customer attitudes before product development.*

- Is the idea easy to understand?
- Would this product meet a real need?
- Do you see distinct benefits for this product over those on the market?
- Do you find the claims about this product believable?
- Would you buy the product?
- How much would you pay for it?
- Would you replace your current brand with this new product?
- What improvements can you suggest in various attributes of the concept?
- How frequently would you buy the product?
- Who would use the product?[22]

---

[20]Teresa Riordan, "Patents," *New York Times* (June 12, 1995), p. D2; Neil Gross, "New Patent Office Pending," *Business Week* (October 23, 1995), p. 130; Masaaki Kotabe, "A Study of Japanese Patent Systems," *Journal of International Business Studies*, Vol. 23 (First Quarter 1992), pp. 147–168; and "Patents," in *Resource Book For Science and Technology Consultations, Volume I*, Secretariat for Science and Technology Review, Industry Canada (June 1994), Internet Download.
[21]Gail Chiasson, "The Line On Calling Cards," *Marketing Magazine* (September 4, 1995), p. 18.
[22]Adapted from Philip Kotler, *Marketing Management: Analysis, Planning, Implementation, and Control*, Eighth Edition (Englewood Cliffs, N.J.: Prentice-Hall, 1994), p. 331.

FIGURE 13-6
A Brief Concept Test for a Proposed New Telephone Service

> A U.S. long-distance telephone-service company is considering the introduction of a pre-paid card for use with pay phones. Here's how it would work: The caller inserts the card (resembling a credit card) in a special slot at a pay phone and leaves it there during a call; the cost of the call is automatically deducted from the value of the card. The caller does not have to stock up on change and pays a slightly discounted rate. The card is like cash; can be bought in denominations of $10, $25, $50, and $100; and is discarded when used up. This telephone card is already popular in Europe.
>
> **Would you please answer some questions to give us a better idea of the pre-paid telephone card's marketability?**
>
> 1. React to the overall concept of a pre-paid telephone card.
>
> 2. In what situations would the pre-paid telephone card be most beneficial to consumers?
>
> 3. What else would you like to know about this concept?
>
> 4. Do you have any suggestions about the features of the pre-paid telephone card?
>
> 5. How likely would you be to purchase a pre-paid telephone card within the next year? Check one answer.
> Very likely ____ ____ ____ ____ ____ Very unlikely
> Why? _____

Business Analysis

At this point, a firm does business analysis for the new-product concepts that have thus far been deemed attractive. **Business analysis** involves the detailed review, projection, and evaluation of such factors as consumer demand, production costs, marketing costs, break-even points, competition, capital investments, and profitability for each proposed new product. It is much more detailed than product screening.

Business analysis looks at demand, costs, competition, etc.

Here are some of the considerations at this planning stage:

CRITERIA	SELECTED CONSIDERATIONS
Demand projections	Short- and long-run sales potential; speed of sales growth; price/sales relationship; seasonality; rate of repurchases
Production cost projections	Total and per-unit costs; startup vs. continuing costs; estimates of raw materials and other costs; economies of scale; break-even points
Marketing cost projections	Product planning (patent search, product development, testing); promotion; distribution; marketing research; break-even points
Competitive projections	Short-run and long-run market shares of company and competitors; competitors' strengths and weaknesses; potential competitors; likely strategies by competitors in response to firm
Capital investment projections	Need for new equipment and facilities vs. use of existing facilities and resources
Profitability projections	Time to recoup initial costs; short- and long-run total and per-unit profits; reseller needs; control over price; return on investment; risk

Because the next step is expensive and time-consuming, critical use of business analysis is essential to eliminate marginal items.

Product Development

During **product development**, an idea for a new product is converted into a tangible form and a basic marketing strategy is identified. Depending on the product involved, this stage in the planning process encompasses product construction, packaging, branding, positioning, and consumer attitude and usage testing.

Product construction decisions include the type and quality of materials comprising the product, the method of production, production time, production capacity, the assortment to be offered, and the time needed to move from development to commercialization. Packaging decisions include the materials used, the functions performed, and alternative sizes and colours. Branding decisions include the choice of a name, trademark protection, and the image sought. Product positioning involves selecting a target market and positioning the new good or service against competitors and other company offerings. Consumer testing studies perceptions of and satisfaction with the new product.

If a modification is involved, product-development costs may be relatively low. However, an innovation may be costly (up to several million dollars or more) and time consuming (up to four years for a new car). And this is true of services, as well as goods:

> AlphaNet Telecom of Toronto supplies in-room hotel fax services and has a near monopoly on this market. In 1994 it supplied 8400 fax machines to 120 major North American hotels including chains such as Hyatt, Westin, Hilton, Loews, and Fairmont. AlphaNet Telecom also has arrangements to serve Hong Kong, Singapore, Japan, Indonesia, Australia, and New Zealand, with more countries under negotiation. Fax machines are installed in the hotels at cost but AlphaNet Telecom receives much of the usage revenue. AlphaNet is building its installed customer base and has added such services as FollowFax, which gives subscribers a permanent fax number.[23]

Besides being costly and time consuming, product development can be complicated. For example:

> Boeing's traditional method for designing new aircraft has three phases. First, engineers design a plane's shape and components. Then, they hand blueprints to manufacturing experts, who plan the production of components and final assembly. Finally, the manufacturing plan goes to tooling specialists who design specialized production machinery. Since the phases are completed in sequence, they take a long time and the system forces each group to turn out reams of corrections, consuming millions of hours a year in engineering time.
>
> Once final drawings are ready, carpenters and artisans go to work. They build a full-scale mock-up of the plane incorporating replicas of every part. Converted for the first time from drawings to three-dimensional reality, parts don't necessarily fit. Electricians stringing mock

Product development *focuses on devising an actual product and a broad marketing strategy.*

ALPHANET TELECOM
www.alphanet.net/about/about.htm

---

[23]"AlphaNet Delivers Room Service (In-Room Hotel Fax Service)," *Financial Times of Canada*, (June 11–17, 1994), pp. 4–5.

instrument wires through the model, for instance, may discover that a structural beam gets in the way. Result: more expensive changes, as engineers redesign the beam so it has a hole in the centre and tool makers reconfigure machines to accommodate the fix. Similar mistakes inevitably plague construction of the first few planes. And since subsequent planes must be tailored to the customer, Boeing goes through a minor version of the same tortuous process with each order.[24]

Test Marketing

Test marketing occurs in selected areas and observes real performance.

Test marketing involves placing a fully developed new product (a good or service) in one or more selected areas and observing its actual performance under a proposed marketing plan. The purpose is to evaluate the product and pre-test marketing efforts in a real setting prior to a full-scale introduction. Rather than just study intentions, test marketing lets a firm monitor actual consumer behaviour, competitor reactions, and reseller interest. After testing, the firm could decide to go ahead, modify the product and then go ahead, modify the marketing plan and then go ahead, or drop the product.

Many companies routinely use test marketing to help introduce new products and refine their marketing strategies. McDonald's, in particular, tests new products regularly by bringing out "special" offerings and gauging consumer response. Consumer products firms are much more apt to engage in test marketing than industrial products firms:

> In consumer products, test marketing is a science dominated by marketing consultants, database collection firms, and electronic test marketing services. The business is so sophisticated that Information Resources Inc. of Chicago, which runs several electronic test markets, not only measures what every member of its participating households buys but also identifies exactly which television ads propelled them into stores.
>
> By contrast, the test marketing of business-to-business products has only recently become a widespread practice. In the past, a manufacturer created a product, ran it by a few executives, and hoped customers would buy it. Thus, manufacturers often spent huge sums on parts and labour to fix any problems that cropped up after installation. Now, a growing number of manufacturers in such diverse industries as computers, electronics, industrial chemicals, cleaning equipment, maintenance products, and insurance have begun intensive on-site tests of new products. In most cases, these tests are conducted with anywhere from five to fifty clients and last from two to six months.[25]

The test-marketing process requires several decisions: when to test, where to test, how long to test, what test information to acquire, and how to apply test results. Figure 13-7 shows the criteria to weigh in making the choices.

Although test marketing has been beneficial in many cases, some firms now question its effectiveness and downplay or skip this stage in new-product planning. Their dissatisfaction arises from test marketing's cost, the time delay required before full introduction, the fact that it may provide information to competitors, the inability to predict national (global) results based on limited test-market areas, and the impact of such external factors as the economy and competition on test results. Test marketing can even allow nontesting competitors to catch up with an innovative firm by the time a product is ready for a full rollout.

Commercialization

Commercialization involves a major marketing commitment.

When testing goes well, a firm is ready to introduce a new product to its full target market. This involves **commercialization** and corresponds to the introductory stage of the product life cycle. During commercialization, the firm enacts a total marketing plan and works towards production capacity. Among the factors to be considered are the speed of acceptance by consumers and distribution intermediaries, the intensity of distribution (how many outlets), production capabilities, the promotion mix, prices, competition, the time until profitability, and commercialization costs.

---

[24]Shawn Tully, "Can Boeing Reinvent Itself?" *Fortune* (March 8, 1993), p. 72. See also Alex Taylor III, "Boeing Sleepy in Seattle," *Fortune* (August 7, 1995), pp. 92–98.

[25]Aimee L. Stern, "Testing Goes Industrial," *Sales & Marketing Management* (March 1991), p. 30. See also Steve Blount, "It's Just a Matter of Time," *Sales & Marketing Management* (March 1992), pp. 32–43.

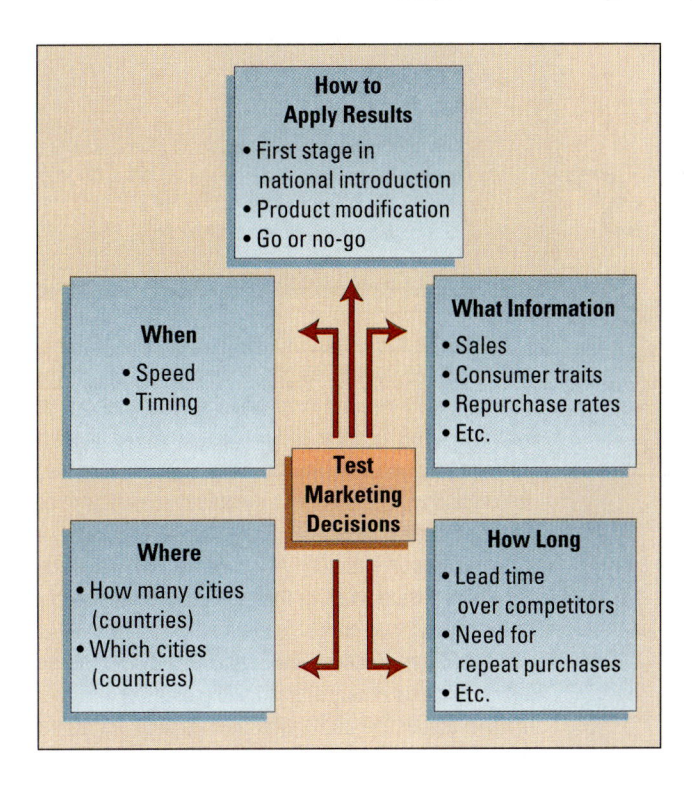

FIGURE 13-7
Test Marketing Decisions

Commercialization may require large outlays and a long-term commitment. For example, manufacturers may spend an average of $5 million for a national rollout in both Canadian and U.S. supermarkets—nearly half on consumer promotion and the rest on product costs, market research costs, and promotions for supermarkets. Yet, commercialization costs can go much higher. When Coca Cola Canada launched PowerAde, a new sports drink, in Canada, it paid $1 million for its promotional campaign alone (which included TV and print ads, coupons, and in-store promotions).[26]

The commercialization of a new product sometimes must overcome consumer and reseller reluctance because of ineffective prior company offerings. Diet Coke's test marketing of new sweeteners in Canada encountered consumer resistance because of the failure of New Coke.[27] The same thing happened to Texas Instruments, which encountered resistance in the business computer market after it bowed out of the home computer market.

COCA COLA CANADA
www.cocacola.com/

Growing Products

Once a new product is commercialized, the goal is for consumer acceptance and company sales to rise rapidly. This occurs in some cases; in others, it may take a long while. The growth rate and total sales level of new products rely heavily on two related consumer behaviour concepts: the adoption process and the diffusion process. In managing growing products, a firm must understand these concepts and plan its marketing efforts accordingly.

The **adoption process** is the mental and behavioural procedure an individual consumer goes through when learning about and purchasing a new product. It consists of these stages:

1. *Knowledge*—A person (organization) learns of a product's existence and gains some understanding of how it functions.
2. *Persuasion*—A person (organization) forms a favourable or unfavourable attitude about a product.

*The **adoption process** explains the new-product purchase behaviour of individual consumers.*

---

[26]Douglas Faulkner, "The Coca-Cola Kid," *Marketing Magazine* (August 14, 1995), p. 24.
[27]"Coke Quietly Tests New Diet Sweetener," *Marketing Magazine* (June 12, 1995), p. 7.

Ethics AND TODAY'S MARKETER

Oil Companies, Auto Companies and the Impact of GM's Electric Car, the "Impact"

GM's new electric car, the Impact, is a "zero emission vehicle" that eliminates the pollutants emitted by gas-powered cars. This would seem like a marketer's dream. Invent a truly needed product to solve a serious societal problem and profit by it. However, until recently, GM worked on the Impact only because large U.S. states such as California had set a mandate that 2 per cent of the cars offered for sale in 1998 have zero emissions. Research on electric cars has been going on for over 75 years but until California set a mandate, the automobile companies never came through. Can the automakers come through and produce a successful electric car and do they even want to? GM is unsure whether they can produce such a car. That is why the late 1996 launch of the Impact was conducted in just two states— California and Arizona—and in limited quantities. Because the auto companies have not been able to produce a commercially viable car, many states have pulled back from insisting on electric vehicles. Why is there a question about whether the auto companies want to produce such a vehicle as opposed to whether it is technically feasible?

The top five U.S. oil companies in 1995 were Exxon (U.S.$110 billion in sales), Mobil (U.S.$67 billion in sales), Texaco (U.S.$36 billion in sales), Chevron (U.S.$32 billion in sales) and Amoco (U.S.$27 billion in sales). In 1995 the largest U.S. auto companies were General Motors (U.S.$169 billion in sales), Ford (U.S.$137 billion in sales) and Chrysler (U.S.$53 billion in sales). Considering, GM, Ford and Exxon are 1, 2, 3 as the largest U.S. corporations it becomes very clear that there is a lot at stake for oil companies and automobile firms if electric cars are produced. Given the inertia behind gasoline powered vehicles, well understood and well produced by the world's automobile companies, and fuelled very profitably by the products of oil companies, it seems clear that without a mandate, electric vehicles will not be produced no matter how needed they are.

The potential for economic havoc is high if one considers what would happen to the oil industry were electric vehicles to become widely used. Oil would still be in demand but nowhere near the current levels. The interests of the oil companies would not be served if the automotive companies produced electric cars. However, this may happen despite the threat to the oil firms. After all, the automobile companies will continue even if the "power" plant of their vehicles were to change. In fact, in an atmosphere of mandated innovation, the opportunity for gaining competitive advantage is extremely attractive. The first company to produce a viable car will become the market leader or in the case of GM, remain the leader!

Unlike electric cars based on traditional gas-powered car designs, the Impact has been designed from scratch. Thus, it has some innovative features: It is so aerodynamic that it has half the resistance of traditional cars. A dashboard meter constantly recalculates the remaining distance before the car must be recharged (based on the amount of electricity remaining and the rate of electric usage). The fuel cost is low compared to gas-powered cars. The cost of charging the Impact's batteries averages U.S.$1.70; this works out to half the fuel cost per kilometre of a comparably sized gas-based vehicle.

Despite these innovations, the Impact has some major handicaps that greatly limit the market potential for the car. As with most electric-powered vehicles, the Impact has a limited driving range between charges (110 to 140 kilometres). Although the car can be fully charged in two to three hours with a special 220-volt outlet, with regular household voltage, the recharging time is about ten hours. The Impact is also

Ethics AND TODAY'S MARKETER (cont.)

only being offered as a two-seater. Many analysts feel these characteristics would limit buyers to consumers needing a car to drive short distances and households that already own one or two cars. And it is priced at over U.S.$30 000.

From the perspective of a GM marketing manager, discuss the kinds of impact an innovation like the Impact may have on the marketplace and society.

Sources: Based on material in Matthew L. Wald, "Future Shock: Driving an Electric Prototype," *New York Times* (April 2, 1995), Section F, p. 1; and Rebecca Blumenstein and Gabriella Stern, "GM to Announce Plans for Selling Electric Car, Truck," *Wall Street Journal* (January 4, 1996), p. 3.

3. *Decision*—A person (organization) engages in actions that lead to a choice to adopt or reject a product.
4. *Implementation*—A person (organization) uses a product.
5. *Confirmation*—A person (organization) seeks reinforcement and may reverse a decision if exposed to conflicting messages.[28]

The rate (speed) of adoption depends on consumer traits, the product, and the firm's marketing effort. Adoption is faster if consumers have high discretionary income and are willing to try new offerings; the product has low perceived risk; the product has an advantage over other items on the market; the product is a modification and not an innovation; the product is compatible with current consumer lifestyles or ways of operating a business; product attributes can be easily communicated; product importance is low; the product can be tested before a purchase; the product is consumed quickly; the product is easy to use; mass advertising and distribution are used; and the marketing mix adjusts as the person (organization) moves through the adoption process.

The **diffusion process** describes the manner in which different members of the target market often accept and purchase a product. It spans the time from product introduction through market saturation and affects the total sales level of a product as it moves through the life cycle:

*The **diffusion process** describes when different segments are likely to purchase.*

1. Innovators are the first to try a new product. They are venturesome, willing to accept risk, socially aggressive, communicative, and worldly. It must be determined which innovators are opinion leaders—those who influence others. This group is about 2.5 per cent of the market.
2. Early adopters are the next to buy a new product. They enjoy the prestige, leadership, and respect that early purchases bring—and tend to be opinion leaders. They adopt new ideas but use discretion. This group is about 13.5 per cent of the market.
3. The early majority is the initial part of the mass market to buy a product. They have status among peers and are outgoing, communicative, and attentive to information. This group is about 34 per cent of the market.
4. The late majority is the second part of the mass market to buy. They are less cosmopolitan and responsive to change, and include people (firms) with lower economic and social status, those past middle age (or set in their jobs), and skeptics. This group is about 34 per cent of the market.

[28] Everett M. Rogers, *Diffusion of Innovations*, Third Edition (New York: Free Press, 1982), pp. 164–175.

5. Laggards purchase last, if at all. They are price-conscious, suspicious of change, low in income and status, tradition bound, and conservative. They do not adopt a product until it reaches maturity. Some sellers ignore them because it can be hard to market a product to laggards. Thus, concentrated marketing may do well by focusing on products for laggards. This group is about 16 per cent of the market.[29]

Growth for a major innovation often starts slowly because there is an extended adoption process and the early majority may be hesitant to buy. Sales may then rise quickly. As an illustration, the PC was first marketed in 1977; yet, by the end of 1981, less than 10 per cent of North American businesses and under 2 per cent of North American households owned one. Consumers were hesitant to make a purchase due to high initial prices, the perceived difficulty of mastering the PC, its early image as a game console, and the limited software. Sales then grew dramatically, going from 1.1 million units in 1981 to over 7.5 million in 1984; inexpensive models entered the market, PCs became more user-friendly, the product lost its game image, and software became widely available.

By 1995, North American businesses owned about 40 million PCs and North American households nearly 40 million. In contrast, at that time, a total of 40 million PCs were owned by organizational and final consumers in the European Union and fewer than 20 million PCs were owned by organizational and final consumers in Japan. Why has ownership been so low in Japan? It is due to skepticism about the benefits of PCs among Japanese businesspeople; limited office and household space; and rather high prices (compared to North America).[30]

For minor innovations or product modifications, growth is usually much faster. Therefore, marketers often prefer to launch these kinds of products as opposed to developing "innovations." As an example, in the spring of 1996, Gillette introduced SensorExcel™ for women with a $2.5 million multi-media rollout. The SensorExcel is a premium adaptation from the Sensor line of razors for men.[31] See Figure 13-8.

These products are among those now in the growth stage of the product life cycle. They represent good opportunities for firms: CD-ROM software, cellular phones and related phone services, anti-lock car brakes, men's hair-colouring products, solar-powered products, generic drugs, plain-paper fax machines, stereo TVs, international financial services, adult education, rechargeable batteries, subnotebook PCs, and business-to-business video conferencing.

Mature Products

Proper marketing can let mature products maintain high sales.

Products are in the maturity stage of the life cycle when they reach the late majority and laggard markets. Goals turn from growth to maintenance. Because new products are so costly and risky, more firms are placing marketing emphasis on mature products with steady sales and profits, and minimal risk.

In managing mature products, a firm should examine the size, attributes, and needs of the current market; untapped market segments; competition; the potential for product modifications; the likelihood of new company products replacing mature ones; profit margins; the marketing effort required for each sale; reseller attitudes; the promotion mix; the impact of specific products on the overall product line; each product's effect on company image; the number of years remaining for the products; and the management effort needed.

Popular mature brands offer several benefits for companies.

Having a popular brand in a mature product category has many benefits. First, the life cycle may be extended almost indefinitely. Budweiser beer, Coke Classic soft drink, Goodyear tires, Ivory soap, Lipton tea, Maxwell House coffee, Life Savers mints, Sherwin-Williams paints, and Quaker Oats oatmeal are among the leaders in their product categories; each is well over seventy-five years old. Second, the brand attracts a loyal customer

---

[29]Ibid, pp. 246–261.
[30]*Industrial Outlook 1994* (Washington, D.C.: U.S. Department of Commerce, 1993), pp. 26-16–26-21; Jim Carlton, "Foreign Markets Give PC Makers a Hearty Hello," *Wall Street Journal* (September 15, 1995), pp. B1, B4; and authors' estimates.
[31]"Gillette Readies Launch Of Women's Razor," *Marketing Magazine*, (December 11, 1995), p. 5.

FIGURE 13-8
Introducing the New Sensor Excel™ for Women
Reprinted with permission of Gillette Canada.

group and has a stable, profitable position in the market. Third, the likelihood of future low demand is greatly reduced; this is a real risk for new products. Fourth, a firm's overall image is enhanced, allowing the firm to extend a popular name to other products. Fifth, it allows for more control over marketing efforts and more precision in sales forecasting. Sixth, mature products can be used as cash cows to support spending on new products. However, some marketing support must be continued if a mature product is to remain popular.

Successful industries and companies market products that stay in maturity for long periods, as the following illustrate:

- The paper clip was invented in 1899 by Norwegian Johan Vaaler. Since then, "several hundred inventors have patented paper clips in every conceivable shape—square, round, oval, triangular, teardrop, and arrowhead." Today, it is more popular than ever due to its ease of use, flexible applications, and large customer following. It seems that after nearly 100 years, there is still nothing to match a paper clip. Twenty billion are sold yearly.[32]

---

[32]Amal Kumar Naj, "Hey, Get a Grip! Your Basic Paper Clip Is Like a Mousetrap," *Wall Street Journal* (July 24, 1995), pp. A1, A5.

FIGURE 13-9
Promoting Customer Loyalty to a Mature Brand
Reprinted by permission.

- Chlorine is a chemical produced by the electrolysis of brine. It is used to process organic chemicals and in the production of pulp, paper, and other industrial goods. In industrialized nations, chlorine is a mature or declining product—it has stable sales in the United States and negative sales growth in Canada, Japan, and Europe. But, sales are growing in Asia, Latin America, Africa, and the Middle East. Thus, chlorine producers' marketing efforts are now quite aggressive in developing and less-developed nations.[33]

- "Whether clothes are lean or loose, short or long, there's a common thread running through much of today's fashion: Lycra—DuPont's trademark for spandex fibre that started out in the 1950s as a substitute for rubber in girdles." After sales stagnated for a while, the fibre gained attention in the 1980s with the advent of cycling pants and leggings, and technological advances that let Lycra fibres be used in sheer hosiery. Lycra is now "in everything from long, willowy cotton and linen sheaths by Liz Claiborne's Lizsport to crewneck bodysuits from Anne Klein II and tank dresses from designer Donna Karan's DKNY division." In certain parts of Europe, the Lycra name has a consumer recognition rate of 98 per cent; and expansion in Latin America and the Far East are under way.[34]

- For decades, Ralston Purina has dominated the pet food market with its Purina Dog Chow and Purina Cat Chow. Although it regularly adds updated product versions, the company also encourages its customers to seek a consistent diet for their pets by regularly buying its mature brands. Figure 13-9 shows how Ralston Purina promotes customer loyalty to Purina Dog Chow.

There are many options available for extending the mature stage of the product life cycle. Table 13-1 shows seven strategies and gives examples of each.

---

[33]"Chloralkali Industry Sees Changes," *Chemical Marketing Reporter* (September 21, 1992), pp. 3, 16.
[34]Pat Sloan, "Lycra Stretches Fashion Appeal," *Advertising Age* (November 2, 1992), pp. 3, 36.

Table 13-1
Selected Strategies for Extending the Mature Stage of the Product Life Cycle

STRATEGY	EXAMPLES
1. Develop new uses for products	Jell-O used in garden salads WD-40 used in the maintenance of kitchen appliances
2. Develop new product features and refinements	Zoom lenses for 35mm cameras Battery-powered televisions
3. Increase the market	Bell Canada's 1-800 & 1-888 phone services for small businesses International editions of major magazines
4. Find new classes of consumers for present products	Nylon carpeting for institutional markets Johnson & Johnson's baby shampoo used by adults
5. Find new classes of consumers for modified products	Industrial power tools altered for do-it-yourself market Inexpensive copy machines for home offices
6. Increase product usage among current users	Multiple packages for soda and beer Discounts given for making more long-distance phone calls
7. Change marketing strategy	Greeting cards sold in supermarkets Office furniture promoted in mail-order catalogues

Not all mature products can be revived or extended. Consumer needs may disappear, as when frozen juice replaced juice squeezers. Lifestyle changes may lead to less interest in products, such as teller services in banks. Better and more convenient products may be devised, such as when CD players replaced record players. The market may be saturated and further marketing efforts may be unable to garner enough sales to justify time and costs, which is why Japan's NEC has a diminished role in consumer electronics.

Product Deletion

Products should be deleted from a firm's offerings if they offer limited sales and profit potential, reflect poorly on the firm, tie up resources that could be used for other opportunities, involve large amounts of management time, create reseller dissatisfaction due to low inventory turnover, and divert attention from long-term goals.

Products need to be deleted if they have consistently poor sales, tie up resources, and cannot be revived.

However, there are many points to weigh before deleting a product: As a product matures, it blends in with existing items and becomes part of the total product line (mix). Customers and distribution intermediaries may be hurt if an item is dropped. A firm may not want competitors to have the only product for customers. Poor sales and profits may be only temporary. Or the marketing strategy, not the product, may be the cause of poor results. Thus, a systematic procedure should be used to handle faltering products.

As these examples show, low-profit or rapidly declining products are often dropped or de-emphasized:

- After seven years on the market, the Cadillac Allante, a U.S.$62 000 General Motors' two-seat luxury roadster, was discontinued due to weak sales. Although the car was profitable, only 2000 units were sold during its last year. And the Allante was very complicated to build, with undercarriages made in Detroit and bodies and interiors made in Italy.
- The Scott Paper Company decided to drop the White Swan brand of facial tissues and paper towels in Atlantic Canada and Quebec because they could not see significant product differentiation in the facial tissue and paper towel markets. The reduction in the number of products would allow Scott Paper to focus its efforts on building national and international brands, like Scotties facial tissues and Scott towels.[35]

[35]"Scott Trims White Swan Product Line," *Marketing Magazine* (September 25, 1995), p. 1.

International Marketing in Action

Why Did Unilever Lose the Power?

Dutch-British Unilever is one of the world's global giants, with annual sales of nearly U.S.$50 billion—including U.S.$11 billion from laundry detergents alone. Yet the firm recently suffered a major embarrassment with its new Power detergent, which featured a "patented, stain-annihilating, manganese-based catalyst known as Accelerator. Just months after it was introduced, Power had to be pulled from the market because it damaged clothes. "It's the greatest marketing setback we've seen," said Sir Michael Perry, Unilever's chairperson.

Why did this happen? According to one expert, "The [U.S.]$300 million Power introduction is a cautionary tale highlighting the pressure multinational firms face to come up with winning products that work internationally—and roll them out faster. With only half of [Procter & Gamble's] detergent sales, Unilever was desperate to parlay its technology breakthrough into a greater market share."

Specifically, here's what Unilever did:

- It ignored a pre-introduction warning from arch-rival Procter & Gamble that Power could damage clothes.
- It was so enthusiastic that it skipped test marketing and placed Power into full commercialization right after product development.
- It was a victim of its own efficiency. Until recently, it took Unilever up to three years to roll out a new product in sixteen European countries. Today, such a rollout is done in a few months, leaving no real chance to catch product errors early in commercialization.
- It decided not to create a strong new brand and "piggybacked" Power onto two of its existing brands, hence Omo Power and Persil Power.
- It underestimated the marketing blitz that P&G would use to call public attention to Power's potentially damaging effect on clothing.

As Unilever's laundry detergent manager, how would you avoid such errors, while still being an aggressive competitor?

Source: Laurel Wentz, "Unilever's Power Failure a Wasteful Use of Haste," *Advertising Age* (March 6, 1995), p. 42.

- "If business is a jungle, then the rise and fall of the typewriter is one of its more cherishable demonstrations of evolution, of the little creature that could. As Smith Corona filed for bankruptcy protection last week [July 1995], one of the final signals in the triumph of PCs and software over the typewriter [originally patented in 1868] was at hand."[36]

During deletion, customer and distributor needs must be considered.

In discontinuing a product, a firm must take replacement parts, the notification time for customers and resellers, and the honouring of warranties/guarantees into account. For example, a company planning to delete its line of office telephones must resolve these questions: Who will make replacement parts? How long will they be made? How soon before the actual deletion will an announcement be made? Will distributors be alerted early enough so they can line up other suppliers? How will warranties be honoured? After they expire, how will repairs be handled?

[36]Francis X. Clines, "An Ode to the Typewriter," *New York Times* (July 10, 1995), p. D5.

MARKETING IN A CHANGING WORLD

Inventors Beware

Gemstar Corporation was started with a U.S.$50 000 loan, as founders Henry Yuen and Daniel Kwoh (then co-workers at TRW) developed VCR Plus—a hand-held device that lets TV viewers easily program their VCRs by entering a code number obtained from a television program listing guide. More than three million VCR Plus units (at about U.S.$60 each, retail) were sold in the first two years alone. The product is now being marketed in the United States, Canada, Europe, Japan, and Latin America. In addition, some VCR makers bundle VCR Plus with their products (and pay Gemstar to do so).

Sounds simple, right? You invent a product, prepare a marketing plan, and—presto—you're a millionaire. Unfortunately, it's not so simple. In fact, according to experts, for every patented invention that succeeds, about 98 fail. And sometimes, inventors may be disheartened about what others say about their ideas and mistakenly give up—although the ideas may later prove to be blockbusters: "As recently as 1977, Kenneth Olsen, the founder of the Digital Equipment Corporation (DEC), told the World Future Society, 'There is no reason for any individual to have a computer in his or her home.'"[37]

These are some of the hard challenges facing today's inventors:

- *Acquiring marketing and business prowess*—Technical proficiency does not guarantee "business smarts."
- *Financing a startup*—Banks, venture capitalists, and others may be reluctant to underwrite a new product unless the inventor has a track record or collateral to back up a loan.
- *Marketplace clutter*—This can be a double whammy. How do you get resellers to carry new products when existing shelf space is tight? How do you get consumers to pay attention, since thousands of new products come out yearly?
- *Marketplace skepticism*—So many products have been "hyped" that consumers are often unwilling to believe that new items can really do what they say.
- *Inaccurate forecasting*—This means budget projections about sales, profits, and so forth will tend to be off target (as will inventor earnings).

SUMMARY

1. *To examine the types of new-product opportunities available to a firm* Product management entails creating and overseeing products over their lives. New products are modifications or innovations that consumers see as substantive. Modifications are improvements to existing products. Minor innovations have not been previously sold by the firm but have been sold by others. Major innovations have not been previously sold by anyone.

2. *To detail the importance of new products and describe why new products fail* New products are important because they may foster differential advantages, sustain sales growth, require a lot of time for development, generate large profits, enable a firm to diversify, make distribution more efficient, lead to technological breakthroughs, allow waste products to be used, respond to changing consumers, and address government mandates.

When a firm suffers a financial loss, a product is an absolute failure. When it makes a profit but does not attain its goals, a product is a relative failure. Failures occur because of such factors as a lack of a significant differential advantage, poor planning, poor timing, and excessive enthusiasm by the product sponsor.

3. *To study the stages in the new-product planning process* New-product planning involves a comprehensive, seven-step process. During idea generation, new opportunities are sought. In product screening, unattractive ideas are weeded out using a new-product screening checklist. At concept testing, the consumer reacts to a proposed idea. Business analysis requires a detailed evaluation of demand, costs, competition, investments, and profits. Product development converts an idea into a tangible form and outlines a marketing strategy. Test marketing, a much-debated technique, involves placing a product for sale in selected areas and observing performance under actual conditions. Commercialization is the sale of a product to the full target market. A new product can be terminated or modified at any point in the process.

---

[37]Laura Pedersen, "Invented a Gadget? Don't Quit Your Job," *New York Times* (September 10, 1995), Section 3.

372 Part 4 *Product Planning*

4. To analyze the growth and maturity of products, including the adoption process, the diffusion process, and extension strategies Once a new product is commercialized, the firm's goal is consumer acceptance and for company sales to rise as rapidly as possible. However, the growth rate and sales level for a new product are dependent on the adoption process—which describes how a single consumer learns about and purchases a product—and the diffusion process—which describes how different members of the target market learn about and purchase a product. These processes are faster for certain consumers, products, and marketing strategies.

When products mature, company goals turn from growth to maintenance. Mature products can provide stable sales and profits and loyal consumers. They do not require the risks and costs of new products. There are several factors to consider and alternative strategies from which to choose when planning to sustain mature products. It may not be possible to retain aging products if consumer needs disappear, lifestyles change, new products make them obsolete, or the market becomes too saturated.

5. To examine product deletion decisions and strategies At some point, a firm may have to determine whether to continue a faltering product. Product deletion may be difficult because of the interrelation of products, the impact on customers and resellers, and other factors. It should be done in a structured manner; and replacement parts, notification time, and warranties should all be considered in a deletion plan.

KEY TERMS

new product (p. 349)
modifications (p. 350)
minor innovations (p. 350)
major innovations (p. 350)
absolute product failure (p. 354)
relative product failure (p. 354)

new-product planning process (p. 356)
idea generation (p. 357)
product screening (p. 357)
patent (p. 358)
concept testing (p. 359)
business analysis (p. 360)

product development (p. 361)
test marketing (p. 362)
commercialization (p. 362)
adoption process (p. 363)
diffusion process (p. 365)

Review Questions

1. Distinguish among a product modification, a minor innovation, and a major innovation. Present an example of each for a hospital.
2. Give four reasons why new products are important to a company.
3. Explain the new-product planning process.
4. How does product screening differ from business analysis?
5. What are the major tasks during product development?
6. What are the pros and cons of test marketing?
7. How can a firm speed a product's growth?
8. Is the maturity stage a good or bad position for a product to occupy? Why?
9. Cite five ways in which a firm could extend the mature stage of the product life cycle. Provide an example of each.
10. Why is a product deletion decision so difficult?

Discussion Questions

1. Comment on the following statement: "We never worry about relative product failures because we make a profit on them. We only worry about absolute product failures."
2. Develop a ten-item new-product screening checklist for a CD-ROM software developer. How would you weight each item?
3. Construct a fifty- to seventy-five-word concept statement and six pertinent questions relating to potential consumer interest in new contact lenses that could be left in the eyes for one year without ever having to be removed. Whom would you question in your concept test? Why? What would you expect to learn from this test?
4. Differentiate between the commercialization strategies for a product modification and a major innovation. Relate your answers to the adoption process and the diffusion process.
5. Select a product that has been in existence for twenty or more years and explain why it has been successful for so long.

VIDEO CASE

A Marketer's Nightmare: New Product Flops!

There is an old saying, "success has many parents, but failure is an orphan." Unfortunately, orphans are the rule in marketing new products, not the exception. With failure should come learning, and there is plenty of learning in the marketplace, according to most statistics. Between 80 and 90 per cent of all new products fail. This means marketing must be approached by tough-minded people with poker player's instincts for knowing when to call and when to fold.

In Ithaca, New York, the New Product Showcase and Learning Centre (better known as the Museum of Flops) represents a monument to folly and a set of object lessons for marketers. The saying, "those who forget the past are doomed to repeat it," is the raison d'être of this institution. Robert McMath, the museum's curator, spent a great deal of time as a market researcher before assuming his role as the custodian of this ominous supermarket. The museum contains 80 000 "odd" items, and there will be more to come! A guided tour of the learning centre presents a number of fascinating products and product concepts, some of which do not seem all that bad (like Campbell's no-salt tomato soup and Short and Sassy shampoo). The need seems apparent: low-salt food and shampoo for short hair, but these products fouled up on the timing. People just did not buy them when they were put on the market. Timing is also a factor in brand names like Republican Choice Coffee with former U.S. President George Bush's face on the label. Its popularity fell as fast as his did, maybe even faster.

On the other hand, one finds products that made it into the marketplace for reasons it is hard for an experienced marketer to fathom, let alone a casual observer. There just does not seem to be a need for products offered in certain forms. For example, aerosol ketchup? toaster chicken patties? toaster eggs? Canada's Cold Buster Bar? Richard Simmons' Salad Spray? and Spray-U-Thin, a weight loss product? The aerosol ketchup cans exploded after a while as the corrosive ketchup placed under pressure ate through the metal can. The toaster chicken would drip fat into the toaster and set it on fire. As for Cold Buster Bars, toaster eggs, salad spray and Spray-U-Thin, one's imagination is sufficient to understand why they failed.

The museum contains a host of products for which the need is apparent but the brand-name decisions seem hard to relate to. For example, Warheads candy and Harley Davidson Heavy Beer certainly tap into commonly satisfied needs. The candy and beer markets are huge, so the concepts of these products are quite viable. However, the brand name Warhead certainly does not evoke an image of candy and a beer named after a motorcycle seems to be stretching an excellent brand image a bit too far.

Robert McMath is available to tell you what went wrong with all the products in the museum and to provide a history lesson on what not to do. As for what makes success, the answers are a lot more elusive.

QUESTIONS

1. In many ways, had common sense prevailed, perhaps a lot of the products in the "Museum of Flops" would never had made it to marketplace to fail. Discuss some of the reasons why marketers cannot simply rely on common sense.
2. Look at the examples in the case and identify all the products that failed due to bad timing. Identify at least one other product (not in this case) that you know of, or can find in the business press, that probably failed for this reason. Describe the details of this product failure and relate how timing was the problem.
3. As a future marketing manager who will undoubtedly be in charge of new product development, and supervising other people involved in new product development, discuss the kinds of lessons you have learned from this case that will better enable you to perform and manage in this capacity.
4. Reread the case on the examples of toaster eggs, Harley Davidson Beer and Short and Sassy shampoo. Consider each of these products in light of the various stages of new product development presented in Chapter 13. If this process were applied to these products, at which stages might some warning signs have been evident to a marketing manager and what might those warning signs have been?

VIDEO QUESTIONS ON FLOPS

1. Discuss some of the "marketing" lessons that your video visit to the New Product Showcase and Learning Centre imparted to you and relate them to the "causes" of new product failure discussed in Chapter 13.
2. Imagine, (perhaps wildly) that you had conceived of aerosol ketchup. What needs could it fill, what advantages might it have had over existing products? Make a case why this product should be developed and launched.

Video Source: "Flops," Venture (February 20, 1994).

CASE STUDY

Can Swatch Make a Comeback?

Swatch is owned by SMH, the firm that produces such well-known and highly respected Swiss watches as Blancpain, Omega, and Tissot. In 1983, SMH revolutionized the watch industry by introducing Swatch in North America. The original Swatch marketing strategy combined the use of advanced technology (drawn from the U.S. $16 000 Concord Delirium model), low-cost production (the average Swatch included fifty-one parts instead of an industry average of ninety-one, and had a plastic case and band), and the marketing of a constant stream of new models (and dropping older models). Unlike other watches, Swatch was not sold in jewellery stores (which the company felt were not progressive enough) or discount stores (which SMH thought would tarnish the product's Swiss image).

Because Swatch was seen as a fashion accessory and not just a timekeeping mechanism, its young customers were encouraged to buy more than one at a time. In addition, limited-edition Swatch watches were sold as collectors' items; and some of them highly escalated in value. For example, a limited-edition Swatch designed by a pop artist (one of 140), sold at Sotheby's for U.S.$45 000—the record for a Swatch sold at auction. Since 1983, over 150 million inexpensive Swatch watches have been sold, at an average retail price of U.S.$50.

Swatch's runaway success did not go unnoticed at Timex, a leading North American competitor with a traditionally high market share in this price range. Timex, with annual sales of U.S.$600 million, introduced its own Guess? line of watches with metal cases and leather bands. Timex correctly reasoned that Swatch's plastic watch cases and bands and bright colours were not as attractive as its new Guess? product line to many people. According to Timex, its Guess? line sold U.S.$75 million in watches in 1994—versus Swatch's sales of U.S.$20 to $30 million. In addition, market leader Fossil sold U.S.$100 million in watches in 1994. According to Timex's chief executive, "The world passed Swatch by as fashion watches moved away from plastic." In addition to poor sales, Swatch lost 1800 of its 3000 North American distribution outlets between 1994 and 1995.

Swatch is now fighting back with a revitalized marketing strategy. As Swatch's founder and head says, "We were stupid enough to continue letting department stores sell the product as a fashion item alone. We forgot to market Swatch not only as an emotional product but also as a technically advanced product." The overriding question facing Swatch is whether the firm's typical watch product is a fad whose time has passed or whether it can be regenerated.

Swatch recently hired the former head of Swatch in Italy to turn the company around. It has introduced a line of heavier metal watches (priced at U.S.$55 to U.S.$75)—designed to appeal to older customers. Although its earlier ads were cute and provocative, Swatch's current ads simply portray its watches against a metal backdrop. Swatch's new head of North American marketing, in commenting about its older ads, noted, "We were trying to be crazy, a little provocative, and it didn't work [in North America for very long]." To drive home its new products and revised target market strategy, Swatch doubled its 1994 advertising budget in 1995 (to around U.S.$12 million). And Swatch invested U.S.$40 million to become the official timekeeper for the 1996 Summer Olympic Games in Atlanta. SMH hoped the Olympic Games expenditure would result in the general public perceiving the Swatch name more as a precision timekeeping mechanism than as a fashion item.

QUESTIONS

1. Characterize Swatch's current watch model as a modification, a minor innovation, or a major innovation over the original design. Explain your answer.
2. Describe the differential advantages of Swatch's current watch models. What results must these watches achieve to be deemed a "success?" Why?
3. What other strategies can Swatch use to prolong the maturity stage of the product life cycle for its watches?
4. Discuss the diffusion process as it pertains to Swatch watches.

SWATCH
www.swatch-art.com/

Source: The data in this case are drawn from Joshua Levine, "Swatch Out!" *Forbes* (June 5, 1995), pp. 150–152.

CHAPTER 14
Branding and Packaging

Chapter Objectives

1. To define and distinguish among branding terms and to examine the importance of branding

2. To study the key branding decisions that must be made regarding corporate symbols, the branding philosophy, the choice of brand names, and the use of trademarks

3. To define and distinguish among packaging terms and to examine the importance of packaging

4. To study the basic functions of packaging, key factors in packaging decisions, and criticisms of packaging

{ *Louis Vuitton, the French maker of luxury products, has had to fight against fake goods since the very beginnings of the company. In 1896, Georges Vuitton created the famous "LV" monogram (in honour of his father, Louis Vuitton) precisely to stop counterfeiting of the canvas used to cover his baggage trunks.* }

Genuine bag at left, fake at right. Reprinted by permission of Louis Vuitton Malletier.

Each year, according to the International Anti-Counterfeiting Coalition, companies around the world lose hundreds of billions of dollars on products that are either outright counterfeits or pirated versions of trademarked or copyrighted materials. Counterfeit products involve everything from Louis Vuitton leather bags to Head & Shoulders Shampoo.

Because counterfeiting is a serious problem, the Louis Vuitton Malletier company invests considerable resources to fight against this fraud throughout the five continents. For instance, by taking steps to dismantle illegal manufacturing and distribution networks, the firm tries to remove the sources of operations, which are sometimes very professionally organized. Thus, it initiates seizures of fake goods around the world with the assistance of local police and customs officials, and systematically takes legal action.

One of the most lucrative markets for the Louis Vuitton Malletier company is the United States and the firm is very focused on acting against counterfeit products in this market. The firm's anti-counterfeiting fight stretches from New York to Texas and from California to Florida, where the various forms of counterfeiting take place: importers and wholesalers in Los Angeles, New York City, and Atlanta; specialized retail stores in tourist areas; street vendors in New York City; and flea markets in Florida and middle America. Most counterfeit goods are imported from Southeast Asia, mainly South Korea, via Los Angeles.

There is close cooperation between Louis Vuitton Malletier and U.S. officials (customs and FBI officials, as well as state and local authorities) to conduct raids, seize counterfeit goods, and arrest offending parties. Intellectual property rights are strongly regarded in the United States and this has resulted in the recent passage of tougher federal and state anti-counterfeiting laws (especially in New York, California, and Florida), which reflects a growing recognition of the problem and aids companies in the battle against counterfeiting.

At the same time, Louis Vuitton Malletier tries to increase consumers' awareness of counterfeiting. As the firm says, "It goes without saying that the poor quality of the counterfeits has nothing in common with the superb craftsmanship that sets apart the genuine Louis Vuitton products. Thus, the actual and potential clients must be aware that Louis Vuitton products are exclusively sold at the company's stores and leased departments in upscale department stores. A Louis Vuitton product bought in a flea market, in the street, or even at 'home parties' is definitely a fake."

The company even issues consumer tips: "Know a fake when you see one. Some details easily help you to distinguish an authentic Louis Vuitton bag from a counterfeit. A genuine Louis Vuitton always has a leather trim, never plastic; and never bears any patch logo on the outside." See the photos above.

Trademark owners and consumers both lose in counterfeiting. The rightful trademark owners must incur costs to investigate the source of the counterfeit products, make consumers aware of the counterfeit products, and offer restitution. Consumers also lose in terms of poorer quality products, possible safety risks, and the inconvenience in returning products.[1]

---

[1] 1996 correspondence from Louis Vuitton Malletier and Laurel Wentz, "Cachet and Carry," *Advertising Age* (February 12, 1996), pp. I-15–I-16, I-18.

Next, we will study various aspects of both branding and packaging. We will see how firms decide such issues as what corporate symbols to use, what emphasis to place on manufacturer versus private brands, and the basic functions of packaging.

Overview

When conceiving, developing, and managing its products, a firm needs to make and enact a variety of decisions regarding the brand and package used with each item. A **brand** is a name, term, design, symbol, or any other feature that distinguishes the goods and services of one seller from those of other sellers. A **package** is a container used to protect, promote, transport, and/or identify a product.[2] It may consist of a product's physical container, an outer label, and/or inserts.

In this chapter, the various types of brand designations, key branding decisions, the basic functions of packaging, key packaging decisions, and selected criticisms of packaging are discussed.

Brands identify a firm's products; packages are product containers that serve many functions.

Branding

An important part of product planning is *branding*, the procedure a firm follows in researching, developing, and implementing its brand(s). As just noted, a brand is a name, term, design, or symbol (or combination of these) that identifies the products of a seller or group of sellers. By establishing well-known brands, firms gain acceptance, distributor cooperation, and above-average prices.

There are four types of brand designation:

1. A **brand name** is a word, letter (number), group of words, or letters (numbers) that can be spoken. Examples are Labatt's Blue, Windows 95, and Lipton Cup-a-Soup.
2. A **brand mark** is a symbol, design, or distinctive colouring or lettering that cannot be spoken. Examples are Lexus' stylized L crest, Ralston Purina's checkerboard, and Prudential's rock.
3. A **trade character** is a brand mark that is personified. Examples are Qantas Airlines' koala bear, McDonald's Ronald McDonald, and the Pillsbury Doughboy.
4. A **trademark** is a brand name, brand mark, or trade character or combination thereof that is given legal protection. When it is used, a registered trademark is followed by ®. Examples are Scotch Brand® tape and MasterCard®.

*Branding involves **brand names**, **brand marks**, **trade characters**, and **trademarks**.*

Brand names, brand marks, and trade characters do not offer legal protection against use by competitors, unless registered as trademarks. Trademarks ensure exclusivity for trademark owners or those securing their permission and provide legal remedies against firms using "confusingly similar" names, designs, or symbols. With the exception of Labatt's Blue, all of the previous examples are registered trademarks. Trademarks are discussed more fully later in the chapter.

Branding started during the Middle Ages, when craft and merchant guilds required producers to mark goods so output could be restricted and inferior goods traced to their producer. The marks also served as standards for quality when items were sold outside the local markets in which the guilds operated. The earliest and most aggressive promoters of brands in North America were patent medicine manufacturers. Examples of current well-known brands that started more than 100 years ago are Vaseline Petroleum Jelly and Pillsbury's Best Flour. The best known Canadian brand names in the world in 1995 were Molson's and Seagram's.[3]

MASTERCARD
www.canadatrust.com/ct/credit/index.html

Worldwide, there are now millions of brand names in circulation. Each year, Canadian advertisers spend over $9 billion advertising their brands.[4] Permanent media expenditures

---

[2]Peter D. Bennett (Ed.), *Dictionary of Marketing Terms*, Second Edition (Chicago: American Marketing Association, 1995), pp. 27, 201.
[3]World Line, "Coke, Marlboro Still the World's Top Brands," *Marketing Magazine* (July 24, 1995), p. 5.
[4]Jim McElgunn, "CARD Releases New Figures on Ad Spending," *Marketing Magazine*, (September 25, 1995), p. 6.

FIGURE 14-1
The Most Popular and Powerful Brand in the World
Reprinted by permission.

ADIDAS
www.adidas.com/

(such as company logos, stationery, brochures, business forms and cards, and vehicular and building signs) for brands are another large marketing cost. For instance, when Allied-Signal decided to remove its hyphen and become AlliedSignal, it cost U.S.$500 000 for new stationery, signs, and so forth.

A key goal of firms is to develop brand loyalty, which allows them to maximize sales and maintain a strong brand image. As one expert noted:

> Brands work by facilitating and making more effective the customer's choice process. Every day an individual makes hundreds of consumer decisions. He or she is besieged by countless products and messages competing for attention. To make life bearable and to simplify this decision-making process, the individual looks for shortcuts. The most important of these is to rely on habit—buy brands that have proved satisfactory in the past.[5]

Sometimes, brands do so well that they gain "power" status—they are both well known and highly esteemed. At present, according to a survey of 25 300 people in sixteen nations, the world's ten most powerful brands are (in order) Coca-Cola, Kodak, Sony, Mercedes-Benz, Pepsi-Cola, Nestlé, Gillette, Colgate, Adidas, and Volkswagen. The ten brands with the greatest "vitality"—global growth potential—are Coca-Cola, Nike, Adidas, Sony, Ferrari, Reebok, Disney, Porsche, Pepsi-Cola, and Mercedes-Benz.[6] See Figure 14-1.

Brand rankings do differ by region. Thus, in China, six of the top ten brands are from Japan, led by Hitachi; three are from the United States—Coca-Cola, Mickey Mouse, and Marlboro; and one is from China—Tsing Tao (beer).[7] Europeans favour such brands as BMW, Porsche, and Rolls-Royce. Sony is the most powerful brand for Japanese consumers.

---

[5]Peter Doyle, "Building Successful Brands: The Strategic Options," *Journal of Consumer Marketing*, Vol. 7 (Spring 1990), p. 7.
[6]Laurel Wentz, "Upstart Brands Steal Spotlight from Perennials," *Advertising Age* (September 19, 1994), pp. I-13–I-14.
[7]Kevin Goldman, "U.S. Brands Lag Behind Japanese in Name Recognition by Chinese," *Wall Street Journal* (February 16, 1995), p. B8.

In North America, the top brands include Coca-Cola, Campbell, Disney, Pepsi-Cola, Kodak, NBC, Black & Decker, Kellogg, McDonald's, and Hershey.

The use of popular brands can also speed up public acceptance and gain reseller cooperation for new products. For instance, here's a product that gained quick public approval and dealer enthusiasm:

> In mid-1992, Gillette Company unveiled its Sensor for Women razor. Within six months, the stout green-and-white gadgets—designed to give women a better shave in the shower, had a 36 per cent dollar share of the total North American women's razor market. Gillette followed this up by launching SensorExcel for Women in 1996. The SensorExcel represents Gillette's best effort yet to pitch shavers to women. Although Gillette also sells such products as Oral-B toothbrushes and Soft & Dri deodorant, to many consumers, its name is synonymous with razors and blades.[8]

KELLOGG
www.kelloggs.com/

Today, annual sales of Sensor for Women exceed U.S.$50 million. And it is by far the leading product in its category—with foreign revenues growing rapidly.

Gaining and maintaining brand recognition is a top priority for all kinds of firms. As an example, the national TV networks in Canada (CBC and CTV) and the U.S. (ABC, CBS, Fox, and NBC) "are facing increasing competition and are very conscious of the need to get their brands out there. As more choices are given to consumers, networks have to make sure their viewers understand who they are and what they offer. That can mean anything from a logo subtly popping up in the corner of the viewer's TV screen to a major cross-promotion with some big-name packaged-goods marketers."[9]

In recent years, a new branding concept—which more concretely recognizes the worth of brands—has emerged. It is known as **brand equity** and measures the "financial impact associated with an increase in a product's value accounted for by its brand name above and beyond the level justified by its quality (as determined by its configuration of brand attributes, product features, or physical characteristics)."[10] As one expert noted:

Brand equity *represents a brand's worth.*

> In a general sense, brand equity is defined in terms of the marketing effects uniquely attributable to the brand—for example, when certain outcomes result from the marketing of a good or service because of its brand name that would not occur if the same good or service did not have that name. A brand is said to have positive (negative) customer-based brand equity if consumers react more (less) favourably to the product, price, promotion, or distribution of the brand than they do the same marketing-mix element when it is attributed to a fictitiously named or unnamed version of the good or service.[11]

According to *Financial World*, the fifteen most valuable brands in the world—based on sales, profitability, and growth potential—are Coca-Cola, Marlboro, IBM, Motorola, Hewlett-Packard, Microsoft, Kodak, Budweiser, Kellogg, Nescafé, Intel, Gillette, Pepsi-Cola, GE, and Levi's.[12]

Here is an example of how the brand equity concept can be applied. When Cadbury Schweppes acquired the Hires and Crush soda lines from Procter & Gamble, it paid U.S.$220 million. Twenty million dollars of that amount was for physical assets and the balance was for "brand value."[13] Brand equity is even higher when licensing royalties can

---

[8]Kathleen Deveny, "Sensor Gets Big Edge in Women's Razors," *Wall Street Journal* (December 17, 1992), pp. B1, B10. See also Laurie Freeman, "Sensor Still Helping Gillette Fend Off Razor Challenges," *Advertising Age* (September 28, 1994), p. 21; and Barbara Carton, "Gillette Looks Beyond Whiskers to Big Hair and Stretchy Floss," *Wall Street Journal* (December 14, 1994), pp. B1, B4.

[9]Cyndee Miller, "Stay Tuned for TV Networks as Brands," *Marketing New* (October 9, 1995), pp. 1, 10; and Canadian Media Directors' Council, *23rd Annual Media Digest* (Toronto: Marketing Magazine, 1995), p. 8.

[10]Morris B. Holbrook, "Product Quality, Attributes, and Brand Names as Determinants of Price: The Case of Consumer Electronics," *Marketing Letters*, Vol. 1 (1992), p. 72.

[11]Kevin Lane Keller, "Conceptualizing, Measuring, and Managing Customer-Based Brand Equity," *Journal of Marketing*, Vol. 57 (January 1993), pp. 1, 8. See also David A. Aaker, *Managing Brand Equity* (New York: Free Press, 1991); and David C. Bello and Morris B. Holbrook, "Does an Absence of Brand Equity Generalize Across Product Categories? *Journal of Business Research*, Vol. 34 (October 1995), pp. 125–131.

[12]"Coke Is Still It," *Advertising Age* (July 17, 1995), p. 8.

[13]Peter H. Farquhar, Julia Y. Han, and Yuji Ijiri, "Brands on the Balance Sheet," *Marketing Management*, Vol. 1 (Winter 1992), pp. 16–22.

FIGURE 14-2
Differentiated Marketing Through the DeWalt Brand
When Black & Decker determined that professional tool users did not have a high enough regard for the Black & Decker tool line (which appealed mostly to the do-it-yourself market), the firm introduced a new tool line under the DeWalt name. DeWalt tools are bright yellow and black, have more features, and are sturdier than Black & Decker tools. They are also very popular with their chosen target market.
Reprinted by permission.

Branding creates identities, assures quality, and performs other functions. **Brand images** *are the perceptions that consumers have of particular brands.*

be generated from other firms' use of the brand, such as occurs with trade characters like Walt Disney's Mickey Mouse. Nonetheless, there are no widely approved techniques for assessing overall brand equity.

These reasons summarize why branding is important:

- Product identification is eased. A customer can order a product by name instead of description.

- Customers are assured that a good or service has a certain level of quality and that they will obtain comparable quality if the same brand is reordered.

- The firm responsible for the product is known. The producer of unbranded items cannot be as directly identified.

- Price comparisons are reduced when customers perceive distinct brands. This is most likely if special attributes are linked to different brands.

- A firm can advertise (position) its products and associate each brand and its characteristics in the buyer's mind. This aids the consumer in forming a **brand image**, which is the perception a person has of a particular brand. It is "a mirror reflection (though perhaps inaccurate) of the brand personality or product being. It is what people believe about a brand—their thoughts, feelings, expectations."[14]

- Branding helps segment markets by creating tailored images. Multiple market segments can be attracted by using two or more brands. Figure 14-2 highlights Black & Decker's DeWalt brand and the image it presents.

- For socially-visible goods and services, a product's prestige is enhanced by a strong brand name.

- People feel less risk when buying a brand with which they are familiar and toward which they have a favourable attitude. This is why brand loyalty occurs.

- Cooperation from resellers is greater for well-known brands. A strong brand also may let its producer exert more control in the distribution channel.

---

[14]Bennett, *Dictionary of Marketing Terms*, p. 28. See also Ernest Dichter, "What's in an Image," *Journal of Product & Brand Management*, Vol. 1 (Spring 1992), pp. 54–60.

International Marketing in Action

Will Owens-Corning's Panther Be Pink in Europe?

To boost its brand image in Europe, Owens-Corning Fiberglass Corporation recently acquired the global rights to the Pink Panther through the year 2000. The Pink Panther has been the firm's U.S. trade character since 1980 and is well known in Canada due to the "spillover" effect of the firm's U.S. advertising.

Owens-Corning was able to secure these rights after IBM let its exclusive global rights to the character expire in 1994. IBM decided to create and reinforce a single image for its PC line (not tied to a trade character) throughout the world. Owens-Corning's director for global branding programs noted that, "The money IBM spent on the Panther could help us in the notoriety of our character."

According to Owens-Corning's director for global branding programs, "The Panther has been very strong for us; he's catchy, he's different, and he's been a terrific ambassador for us in the United States." To coordinate its overall branding program with the Pink Panther, Owens-Corning even trademarked the colour pink for its insulation material.

Although the Pink Panther is well known in Europe due to its use by IBM, Owens-Corning decided to thoroughly research the Pink Panther's image. It also studied the attitudes of European contractors and homeowners regarding the use of the colour pink for its insulation. Market analysts estimate that the home improvement market in Europe is worth U.S.$73 billion a year, as compared to Canada with U.S.$9.7 billion in home improvement expenditures and the United states where U.S.$125 billion is spent annually.

Some marketing experts say it is common for trade characters, such as Snoopy, to be used by many different firms. And using a single trade character in multiple markets can reduce production costs for advertising and increase the spillover of promotions from one market area to another (as happened with the Pink Panther in Canada).

As a marketing consultant to Owens-Corning, evaluate the decision to use the Pink Panther as its trade character on a worldwide basis.

Source: Based on material in Kim Cleland, "Owens Takes Brand Abroad," *Business Marketing* (December 1994), p. 2; and "Do-It-Yourselfers Spawn Home-Specialty Shopping Centres" *Profit* (January/February 1991), p. 7.

- A brand may help sell an entire line of products, as with Kellogg cereals.
- A brand may help a company enter a new product category, like Reese's peanut butter.
- "A product is something made in a factory [or offered by a service firm]; a brand is something bought by a customer. A product can be copied by a competitor; a brand is unique. A product can be quickly outdated; a successful brand is timeless."[15]

Figure 14-3 illustrates the four basic branding decisions firms must make: choosing their corporate symbols, creating their branding philosophy, selecting a brand name, and deciding whether or not to use trademarks.

---

[15] Stephen King, WPP Group, London, as quoted in Aaker, *Managing Brand Equity*, p. 1.

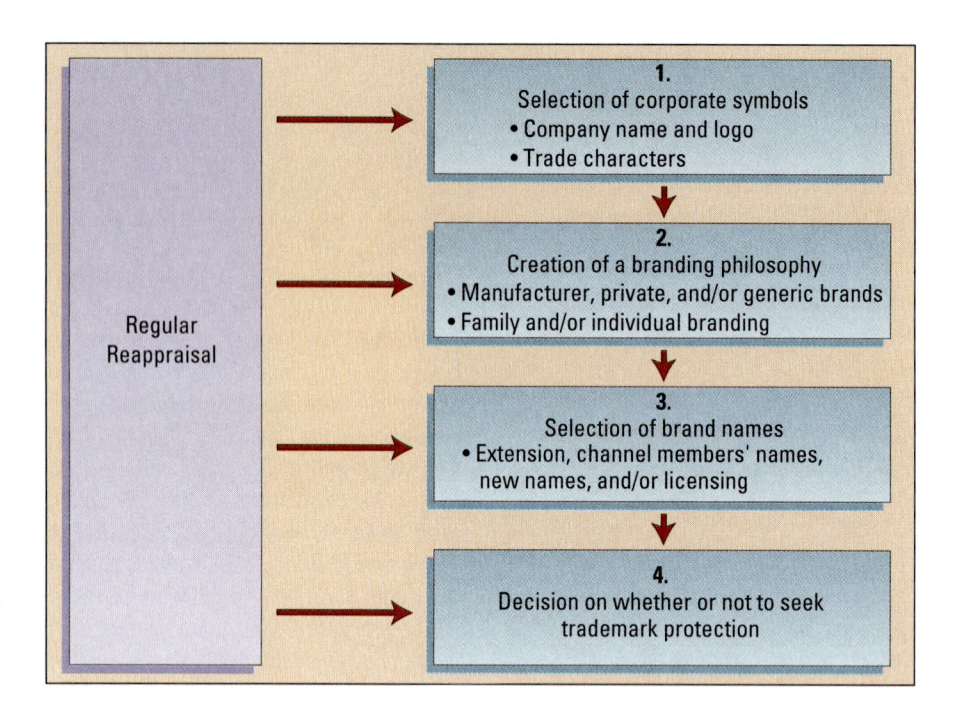

FIGURE 14-3
Branding Decisions

Corporate Symbols

Corporate symbols *help establish a companywide image.*

Corporate symbols are a firm's name (and/or divisional names), logo(s), and trade characters. They are significant parts of an overall company image. If a firm begins a business; merges with another company; reduces or expands product lines; seeks new geographic markets; or finds its name to be unwieldy, nondistinctive, or confusing, it needs to evaluate and possibly change its corporate symbols. Here are examples of each situation.

Fifteen years ago, a new PC maker hired a consultant to devise a company name. It wanted a name that "would be memorable and at the same time take command of the idea of portableness; something that would distinguish it from all other IBM PC compatibles." The consultant recommended a name combining two syllables representing "communications" and "small but important." Today, Compaq is one of the 100 largest firms in North America.[16]

As a result of mergers, pharmaceutical firms Glaxo Canada Inc. and Burroughs Wellcome Inc., are now Glaxo Wellcome Inc.; computer-makers Burroughs and Sperry are now Unisys; publishers Time Inc. and Warner Communication are Time Warner; and General Cinema and Harcourt Brace & Company are Harcourt General.

Because the nature of its business changed, International Harvester is now Navistar International (after selling its farm equipment business) and General Shoe Corporation is Genesco (a diversified retailer). To save money and streamline operations (for example by merging their salesforces) Lever, Canada and Chesebrough-Ponds Canada were merged by their parent company, Unilever, to become Lever Ponds.

In 1995, Nike acquired Canstar Sports, a Canadian company which is well known for making hockey equipment. Rather than bringing in the Nike name, which is well known for shoes and other sports apparel but not for hockey equipment, Nike kept the Canstar name. Further, Canstar had been making hockey equipment under the Lange, Micron, Cooper, and Bauer brand names. A decision was made to consolidate all of the firm's brand names under the Bauer brand because Bauer was the best known hockey brand and had the strongest image in Canada.

Federal Express now promotes the FedEx name, since it is easier to say. United Telecommunications converted its nondistinctive name to Sprint, in recognition of its leading brand. When Corel software of Ottawa acquired the rights to WordPerfect, a lead-

---

[16]Robert A. Mamis, "Name-Calling," *Inc.* (July 1984), pp. 67–74; and "Fortune 500," *Fortune* (May 15, 1995), pp. F-3–F-4.

ing word processing product from Novell of Orem, Utah in January 1996, they wanted to link their corporate name with this new brand. WordPerfect is now marketed as Corel WordPerfect, linking the product and its producer together.[17]

Developing and maintaining appropriate corporate symbols are not easy tasks. For example, when Nissan Motor Corporation changed the name of its North American car division from Datsun to Nissan (to have a global brand), sales fell dramatically despite a major ad campaign. It took years for the Nissan name to reach the level of brand awareness that Datsun had attained. Along the way, Nissan had numerous clashes with dealers not wanting the name change.

CORL
www.corel.com/

Branding Philosophy

While developing a brand strategy, a firm needs to determine its branding philosophy. This philosophy outlines the use of manufacturer, private, and/or generic brands, as well as the use of family and/or individual branding.

MANUFACTURER, PRIVATE, AND GENERIC BRANDS[18] **Manufacturer brands** use the names of their makers. They generate the vast majority of North American revenues for most product categories: over 85 per cent of food, all autos, 75 per cent of major appliances, and over 80 per cent of gasoline. They appeal to a wide range of people who desire low risk of poor product performance, good quality, routine purchases, status, and convenience shopping. The brands are often well known and trusted because quality control is strictly maintained. They are identifiable and present distinctive images. Producers may have a number of product alternatives under their brands.

Manufacturer brands *are well known and heavily promoted.*

Manufacturers have better channel control over their own brands, which may be sold through many competing intermediaries. Yet individual resellers can have lower investments if the brands' pre-sold nature makes turnover high—and if manufacturers spend large sums promoting their brands and sponsor cooperative ads with resellers (so costs are shared). Prices are the highest of the three brands, with the bulk going to the manufacturer (which also has the greatest profit). The marketing goal is to attract and retain loyal consumers for these brands, and for their makers to direct the marketing effort for the brands.

Private (dealer) brands use names designated by their resellers, usually wholesalers or retailers—including service providers. They account for sizable North American revenues in many categories: 50 per cent of shoes, one-third of tires, 14 per cent of food items, and one-quarter of major appliances. And unit market shares are even higher. Some firms, such as Bata Shoes and McDonald's, derive most revenues from their own brands. Private brands account for 20 per cent of unit food sales in supermarkets. In the Canadian grocery-store soft drink market (worth about $1.6 billion per year), private brands have captured 25 per cent of the market. The dominant manufacturer is Cott Corporation, who makes 90 per cent of the private label sodas; and Cott is expanding its efforts into the United States where they have agreements with the Wal-Mart and Safeway chains as well as many others . Private-brand foods are more popular in Europe than in North America but the North American market is catching up fast, with Canada leading the way. In Europe, private labels generate 28 per cent of revenues in British grocery stores and about 20 to 24 per cent in French and German ones.[19]

Private brands *enable channel members to gain loyal customers.*

---

[17]James Pollock, "Glaxo Wellcome Reviews Operations," *Marketing Magazine* (July 17, 1995), p. 4; James Pollock, "Unilever Reorganizes Canadian Operations, *Marketing Magazine* (February, 12, 1996), p. 4; "Canstar Consolidates Brand-Name Lineup," *Marketing Magazine* (December 11, 1995), p. 5; and Sean Eckford, "Corel Plans Big Marketing Relaunch for WordPerfect," *Marketing Magazine* (February 19, 1996), p. 5.

[18]For a good overview of this topic, see John A. Quelch and David Harding, "Brands Versus Private Labels," *Harvard Business Review*, Vol. 74 (January–February 1996), pp. 99–109; Marcia Mogelonsky, "When Stores Become Brands," *American Demographics* (February 1995), pp. 32–38; and "Special Report: Brand Power," *Progressive Grocer* (October 1994), supplement.

[19]Chad Rubel, "Price, Quality Important for Private Label Goods," *Marketing News* (January 2, 1995), p. 24; E. S. Browning, "Europeans Witness Proliferation of Private Labels," *Wall Street Journal* (October 20, 1992), pp. B1, B5; Laurel Wentz, "Private Labels March in Europe Too," *Advertising Age* (May 9, 1994), p. 53; Tara Parker-Pope, "U.K. Grocer Aims to Bag U.S. Customers," *Wall Street Journal* (May 16, 1995), p. A14; Mark Stevenson, "The Hired Hand Waves Goodbye," *Canadian Business* (August 1994), p. 12–22; and Laura Medcalf, "Club Monaco Cola Highlights New Trend in Private-Label Pop," *Marketing Magazine* (March 18, 1996), p. 4.

384 Part 4 *Product Planning*

Private brands appeal to price-conscious people who buy them if they feel the brands offer good quality at a lower price. In the past Canadians used to accept some risk with regards to quality, but brands like President's Choice from Loblaws, Master Choice from A&P, Our Best from Sobey's and Life Brands from Shopper's Drug Mart have caused people to view the private brands as comparable to national brands. In some cases, such as President's Choice Decadent Chocolate Chip Cookies, private brands are even considered superior. Private brands are usually presented as of similar quality to manufacturer brands, with less emphasis on packaging, and are often made to dealer specifications. In the past brand assortments were smaller and the reseller's private brand was unknown to people who did not shop there. However, the President's Choice brand has transcended this case. It is closely associated with Loblaw's in Canada but it is also being carried by competing retailers and is being sold in the United States as a manufacturer's brand.

Resellers have more exclusive rights for these brands, and are more responsible for distribution and larger purchases. Inventory turnover may be lower than for manufacturer brands; and promotion and pricing are the reseller's job. Due to lower per-unit packaging and promotion costs, resellers can sell private brands at lower prices and still have better per-unit profits (due to their higher share of the selling price). The marketing goal is to attract people who become loyal to the reseller and for that firm to exert control over marketing. Large resellers advertise their brands widely and essentially every major Canadian retailer sells some type of private brand. Loblaw's President Choice brand is even more popular than some manufacturer brands; and in Loblaw's stores, private label products represent a remarkable 33 per cent of the products purchased by customers.[20]

Generic brands *are low-priced items with little advertising.*

Generic brands emphasize the names of the products themselves and not manufacturer or reseller names. They started in the drug industry as low-cost alternatives to expensive manufacturer brands. Today, generics have expanded into cigarettes, batteries, motor oil, and other products. In Canada, the pharmaceutical industry is worth $5.9 billion and the generic manufacturers have about 10 per cent of this market. However, the prescription volume for generic drugs is closer to 40 per cent; the low prices of the drugs results in significantly lower dollar volume. Virtually all of Canada's supermarkets stock some generic products but they only account for about one per cent of supermarket revenues. Generics appeal to price-conscious, careful shoppers, who perceive them as being a very good value, are sometimes willing to accept lower quality, and often purchase for large families or large organizations.

Generics are seldom advertised and receive poor shelf locations; consumers must search them out. Prices are lower than those of other brands by anywhere from 10 to 50 per cent, due to quality, packaging, assortment, distribution, and promotion economies. The major marketing goal is to offer low-priced, lower-quality items to consumers interested in price savings. Table 14-1 compares the three types of brands.

A **mixed-brand strategy** *combines brand types.*

Many companies—including service firms—use a **mixed-brand strategy**. This strategy involves producing products which are sold under both manufacturer and private brands (and maybe generic brands). For example, apple juice producers often put many different brand labels on their juice cans. Mixed branding benefits manufacturers and resellers: it gives the firm associated with the brand name a chance to gain a customer franchise. Multiple segments may be targeted. Loyalty to manufacturers and loyalty to dealers can be fostered separately. In addition, mixed branding means a producer firm is given more shelf space (under different brand names), gets more cooperation in the distribution channel (when they supply products branded in the reseller's cheaper juice) and allows producers to offer a wider assortment (sweeter apple juice, cheaper juice). Selling more means producing more, which stabilizes production and uses excess capacity. As such, sales are maximized for manufacturing firms and profits are shared more equitably between producers and resellers. Planning is better too. For example, in Japan, Kodak markets its own brand of film and COOP private-brand film (for the 2500-store Japanese Consumer

---

[20]Mark Stevenson, "The Hired Hand Waves Goodbye," *Canadian Business* (August 1994), p. 12–22; Laura Medcalf, "Club Monaco Cola Highlights New Trend in Private-Label Pop," *Marketing Magazine* (March 18, 1996), p. 4; Donalee Moulton, "Sobeys Launches Premium House Brand," *Marketing Magazine* (December 11, 1995), p. 4; James Pollock, "A&P Expands No-Frills Food Basics Division," *Marketing Magazine* (November 27, 1995), p. 2.

Table 14-1
Manufacturer, Private, and Generic Brands

CHARACTERISTIC	MANUFACTURER BRAND	PRIVATE BRAND	GENERIC BRAND
Target market	Risk avoider, quality conscious, brand loyal, status conscious, quick shopper	Price conscious, comparison shopper, quality conscious, moderate risk taker, dealer loyal	Price conscious, careful shopper, willing to accept lower quality, large family or organization
Product	Well known, trusted, best quality control, clearly identifiable, deep product line	Same overall quality as manufacturer, less emphasis on packaging, less assortment, not known to nonshoppers of the dealer	Usually less overall quality than manufacturer, little emphasis on packaging, very limited assortment, not well known
Distribution	Often sold at many competing dealers	Usually only available from a particular dealer in the area	Varies
Promotion	Manufacturer-sponsored ads, cooperative ads	Dealer-sponsored ads	Few ads, secondary shelf space
Price	Highest, usually suggested by manufacturer	Moderate, usually controlled by dealer	Lowest, usually controlled by dealer
Marketing	To generate brand loyalty and manufacturer control	To generate dealer loyalty and control	To offer a low-priced, lesser-quality item to those desiring it

Cooperative Union). By doing this, it hopes to make a dent in Fuji's 75 per cent share of the Japanese market.[21]

Manufacturer, private, and generic brands also repeatedly engage in a **battle of the brands**, in which each strives to gain a greater share of the consumer's dollar, control over marketing strategy, consumer loyalty, product distinctiveness, maximum shelf space and locations, and a large share of profits. In recent years, this battle has been intensifying:

*In a **battle of the brands**, the three brand types compete.*

> You know the old joke: Just because you're paranoid doesn't mean that they're not out to get you. In a nutshell, that describes how manufacturers of brand-name products react to competition from private labels. On one hand, manufacturers have the right to be concerned: There are more private labels on the market than ever before. Collectively, private labels in North America command higher unit shares than the strongest national brands in 77 of 250 supermarket product categories. But on the other hand, many manufacturers have overreacted to the threat posed by private labels without fully recognizing two essential points. First, private-label strength generally varies with economic conditions. Second, through their actions, manufacturers of brand-name products can temper the challenge posed by private labels.[22]

FAMILY AND MULTIPLE BRANDING in **family (blanket) branding**, one name is used for two or more individual products. Many firms selling industrial goods and services (such as Boeing and IBM), as well as those selling consumer services (such as Bell Canada), use some form of family branding for all or most of their products. Other companies employ a family brand for each category of products. For example, Sears has Kenmore ap-

Family branding uses a single name for many products.

---
[21] Lara Mills, "The new Rx for Drug Marketing," *Marketing Magazine* (September 11, 1995), p. 15; Rob McKenzie, "A Hard Pill To Swallow," *Canadian Business* (February 1994), p. 44–50; and Wendy Bounds, "Kodak Pursues a Greater Market Share in Japan with New Private-Label Film," *Wall Street Journal* (March 7, 1995), p. B9.
[22] Quelch and Harding, "Brands Versus Private Labels," pp. 99–100.

386 Part 4 *Product Planning*

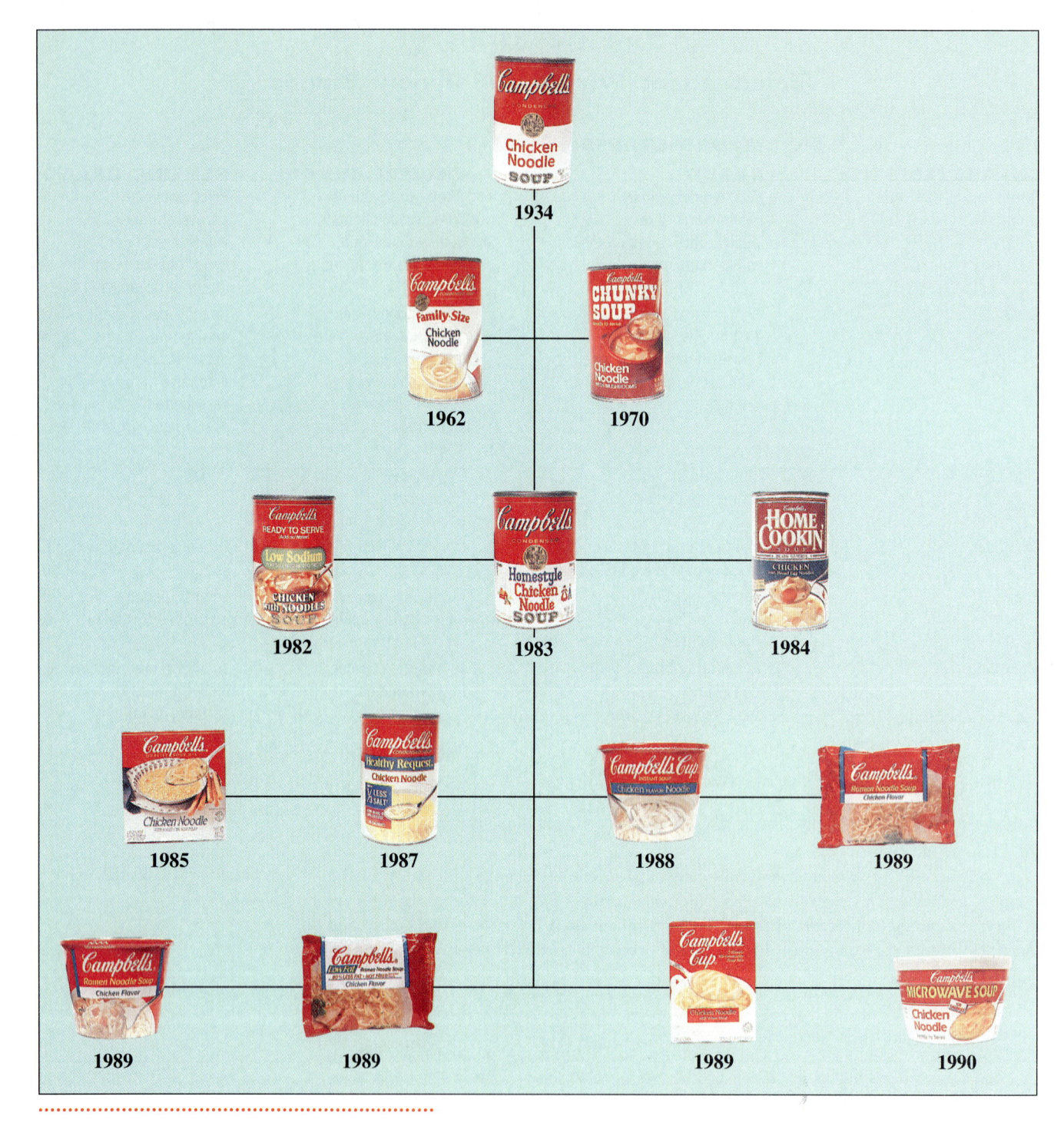

FIGURE 14-4
How Campbell's Soup Stays on Top Through Brand Extension
Reprinted by permission of Campbell Soup Company.

CANADIAN TIRE CORPORATION
www.cyberplex.com/hr/

pliances and Craftsman tools and Canadian Tire Corporation has Mastercraft tools and parts. Family branding can be applied to both manufacturer and private brands, and to both domestic and international (global) brands.

Family branding is best for specialized firms or those with narrow product lines. Companies capitalize on a uniform, well-known image and promote the same name regularly—keeping promotion costs down. The major disadvantages to family branding are that differentiated marketing opportunities may be low (if only one brand is used to target all of a firm's customers), company image may be adversely affected if vastly different products (such as men's and women's cologne) carry one name, and innovativeness may not be projected to consumers.

Brand extension, whereby an established name is applied to new products, is an effective use of family branding. It is a way of gaining quick customer acceptance, since people are familiar with existing products having the same name. Figure 14-4 shows how Campbell has applied brand extension to its chicken noodle soup line. Keep in mind that brand extension may have a negative effect if people do not see some link between the original product and a new one. Most new products now use some form of brand extension.

Brand extension *gains quick acceptance.*

These are seven situations in which brand extension could be effective:

1. The same product is produced in a different form—for example, Jell-O Pudding Pops.
2. A distinctive taste/ingredient/component is presented in a new item—for example, Arm & Hammer detergent.
3. A new companion product is introduced—for example, Colgate Plus toothbrush.
4. A different product is offered to the same target market—for example, Visa travellers cheques aimed at Visa credit-card customers.
5. A brand's perceived expertise is conferred on a new product—for example, Canon bubble-jet printers.
6. An existing benefit/attribute/feature is conferred on a new product—for example, Ivory shampoo (which connotes mildness).
7. A designer image/status is conveyed to a new product—for example, Pierre Cardin sunglasses.[23]

With **individual (multiple) branding**, separate brands are used for different items or product lines sold by a firm. For example, ConAgra is a multinational company serving Canada and the United States and it has a wide and deep product mix of twenty-one food brands, each of which chalk up annual retail sales of U.S.$100 million or more. See Figure 14-5.

Individual branding *uses distinct brands.*

Through individual branding, a firm can create multiple product positions (separate brand images), attract various market segments, increase sales and marketing control, and offer both premium and low-priced brands. Individual branding also lets manufacturers secure greater shelf space in retail stores.

However, each brand incurs its own promotion costs and there is no positive brand-image rub-off. Economies from mass production may be lessened and new products may not benefit from an established identity. And there may be some cannibalization among company brands. Consumer products firms are more likely than industrial products firms to engage in individual branding.

FIGURE 14-5
Individual Branding by ConAgra
Reprinted by permission.

[23]Edward M. Tauber, "Brand Leverage: Strategy for Growth in a Cost-Controlled World," *Journal of Advertising Research*, Vol. 28 (August–September 1988), pp. 26–30.

To gain the benefits of family and individual branding, many firms combine the approaches, perhaps by having a flagship brand and other secondary brands. For example, one-third of Heinz's products have the Heinz name; the rest have names like StarKist, 9-Lives, Ore-Ida, and Weight Watchers. Or, a family brand could be used together with individual brands: Honda markets the upscale Acura and mainstream Honda auto lines. The Honda line includes the Honda Accord, Honda Civic, Honda Del Sol, Honda Odyssey, and Honda Prelude. It has an overall image and targets a specific market. New models gain from the Honda name, and there is a relationship among models. Individual brands are used with each model so differences can be highlighted.

Choosing a Brand Name

A firm may choose a brand name from several potential sources. Under brand extension, an existing name is employed with a new product (Kid Fresh Flushable Wipes from Baby Fresh Wipes, Hewlett-Packard Deskjet printers). For a private brand, the reseller specifies the name (BayCrest—a traditional clothing and soft goods brand name of The Bay).

If a new name is sought, these alternatives are available:

- Initials (YTV, A&W).
- Invented name (Kleenex, Compaq).
- Numbers (Boeing 777, Century 21).
- Mythological character (Atlas tires, Samsonite luggage).
- Personal name (Labatt, Ford).
- Geographical name (Texas Instruments, Air Canada).
- Dictionary word (Close-Up toothpaste, Airlift water-based release agents—Air Products and Chemicals, Inc.'s way for its industrial customers to reduce or eliminate solvent emissions).
- Foreign word (Nestlé, Lux).
- Combination of words, initials, numbers, etc. (General Foods International Coffee, Head & Shoulders shampoo).

*Brand sources range from existing names to **licensing agreements** and **co-branding**.*

Under a **licensing agreement**, a company pays a fee to use a name or logo whose trademark rights are held by another firm. Due to the high consumer recognition of many popular trademarks, sales for a product may be increased by paying a royalty fee to use one. Examples of names used in licensing are Coca-Cola, Montreal Canadiens, and Anne of Green Gables. Two hundred Coca-Cola licensees make and market 3000 products in thirty nations. Annually, sports merchandise licensing generates a total of U.S.$12 billion in worldwide retail sales alone.[24]

In **co-branding**, two or more brand names are used with the same product to gain from the brand images of each. Typically, a company uses one of its own brand names in conjunction with another firm's—often under a licensing agreement. For instance, credit card companies have embraced this idea, and there are now Canadian Tire MasterCards and GM-Visa cards; and Zeller's and the Canadian Imperial Bank of Commerce have launched a Club Z Visa Card. Other examples of co-branding include the Pillsbury Deluxe Bar with M&M's, and the Seiko Mickey Mouse Alarm Chronograph. See Figure 14-6.

Brand names should be suggestive, easy to remember, and flexible.

A good brand name has several attributes, depending on the situation. It suggests something about a product's use or attributes (Sleep-Eze, Wash 'n Dry); is easy to spell and remember and is pronounceable in only one way (Bic, Tang); can be applied to a whole line of products (Deere tractors, Calvin Klein clothing); is capable of legal protection from use by others (Perrier, Equal artificial sweetener); has a pleasant or at least neutral meaning internationally (Esso, Kodak); and conveys a differential advantage (Pert Plus, Acutrim).

---

[24]Carolyn Shea, "Taking License," *Promo* (June 1995), pp. 33–34; Donalee Moulton, "Green Gables Grows Greener," *Marketing Magazine* (November 6, 1995), p. 14–16; and Lara Mills, "From Boxer Shorts to Beach Towels," *Marketing Magazine* (November 6, 1995), p. 11.

FIGURE 14-6
Co-Branding: The Seiko Mickey Mouse Alarm Chronograph
Reprinted by permission.

As firms expand globally, branding takes on special significance. Regardless of whether brands are "global" or tailored to particular markets, their meanings must not have negative connotations or violate cultural taboos. To avoid this, specialized firms such as NameLab (which can devise names that are acceptable around the world) can be hired. But brands must also reflect cultural and societal differences. This example illustrates why:

> The Lewis Woolf Griptight company makes infant and toddler products such as pacifiers. These products are sold in Great Britain, and the United States. When it talked to parents in Great Britain about the Griptight brand name being used before a new line was launched, the company discovered that it was 'the most un-user-friendly name.' People thought it was a carpet glue, a denture fixative, a kind of tire. The brand name became Kiddiwinks, a British word for children. In the United States, however, recognition of the name Binky was high, with some consumers using it as a generic term for pacifiers— hence, the name Binkykids.[25]

When branding, a firm should plan for the stages in the **consumer's brand decision process**, as displayed in Figure 14-7. For a new brand, a consumer begins with nonrecognition of the name, and the seller must make the person aware of it. He or she then moves to recognition, wherein the brand and its attributes are known, and the seller stresses persuasion. Next, the person develops a preference (or dislike) for a brand and buys it (or opts not to buy); the seller's task is to gain brand loyalty. Last, some people show a brand insistence (or aversion) and become loyal (or never buy); the seller's role is to maintain loyalty. Often times, people form preferences toward several brands but do not buy or insist upon one brand exclusively.

Using brand extension, a new product begins at the recognition, preference, or insistence stage of the brand decision process because of the carryover effect of the established

The **consumer's brand decision process** *moves from nonrecognition to insistence (or aversion).*

---

[25]Cyndee Miller, "Kiddi Just Fine in the U.K., But Here It's Binky," *Marketing News* (August 28, 1995), p. 8. See also Martin S. Roth, "The Effects of Culture and Socioeconomics on the Performance of Global Brand Image Strategies," *Journal of Marketing Research*, Vol. 32 (May 1995), pp. 163–175.

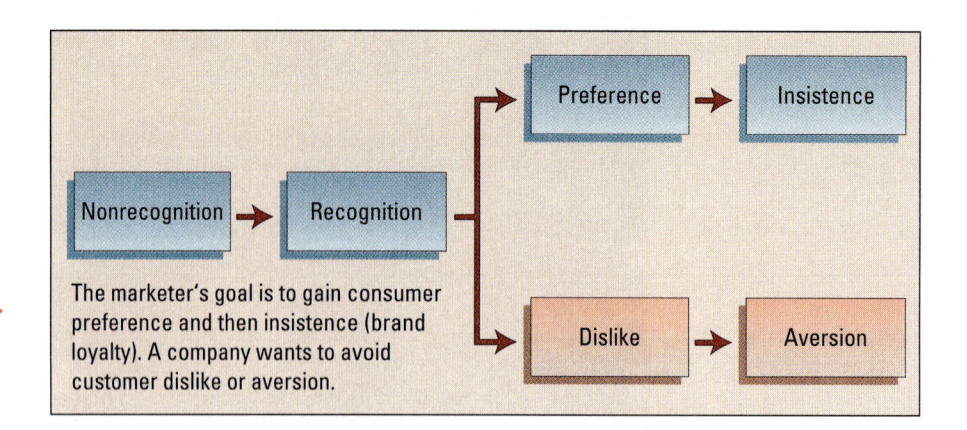

FIGURE 14-7
The Consumer's Brand Decision Process

The marketer's goal is to gain consumer preference and then insistence (brand loyalty). A company wants to avoid customer dislike or aversion.

Nonrecognition → Recognition → Preference → Insistence
Recognition → Dislike → Aversion

name. However, consumers who dislike the existing product line would be unlikely to try a new product under the same name; but they might try another company product under a different brand.

The Use of Trademarks

Trademark protection grants exclusive use of a brand or mark for as long as it is marketed.

Finally, a firm must decide whether to seek trademark protection.[26] In Canada, the Canadian Trademarks Act is administered by Industry Canada through the Competition Bureau. Trademarking gives a firm the exclusive use of a word, name, symbol, combination of letters or numbers, or other devices—such as distinctive packaging—to identify the goods and services of that firm and distinguish them from others for as long as they are marketed. Both trademarks (for goods) and service marks (for services) are covered by trademark law.

Trademarks are voluntary and require registration and implementation procedures that can be time consuming and expensive (challenging a competitor may mean high legal fees and many years in court). A multinational firm must register trademarks in every nation in which it operates; even then, trademark rights may not be enforceable. For a trademark to be legally protected in Canada, it must have a distinct meaning that does not describe an entire product category, be used in interprovincial commerce (for federal protection), not be confusingly similar to other trademarks, and not imply attributes a product does not possess. A surname by itself cannot be registered because any person can generally do business under his or her name; it can be registered if used to describe a specific business (for example, McDonald's restaurants).

When U.S. retailer Wal-Mart entered Canada in 1994 it became embroiled in a couple of trademark disputes, one of which is yet to be resolved. One of the issues involved Wal-Mart putting up "Canada Proud" signs in their stores. Tom Shaw, President of Canada Proud Inc. was not amused and Wal-Mart was forced to remove these signs. However, Wal-Mart has a more serious trademark issue on their hands. Wool-mart Inc. of Nepean is taking Wal-Mart to court over trademark infringement. Wool-mart registered its trade name in 1990 before Wal-Mart came to Canada. Wool-mart's owner, Teresa de Vries, offered to change the name if Wal-Mart would give her a fee of $1 million. Wal-Mart refused, believing this to be a situation of trademark piracy and, recognizing that Wool-Mart is a very small firm (annual sales of $1 million versus Wal-Mart 's annual sales of U.S.$82 billion) who might not be able to afford a long legal battle. The $1 million dollar fee may look cheap by comparison because Wool-mart is suing for $105 million and the Federal Court of Canada has ruled in a preliminary hearing that the case should go to trial.

[26]See Dorothy Cohen, *Legal Issues in Marketing Decision Making* (Cincinnati: South-Western, 1995), pp. 111–136.

Ethics AND TODAY'S MARKETER

Controversial Brand Names On Not-So-Controversial Products

Sometimes it seems that the marketplace is plagued by products with controversial brand names on products that are accepted in society. Products like beer and perfume could certainly be consumed in front of children and their usage explained fairly easily. But having to explain the meanings behind brands like: Nude Beer, Lakeport Truly Naked Beer, Opium perfume, and Sexual perfume could present a lot more difficulty. Although many people feel that these brand names are in questionable taste, and most people would agree that a name alone does not really make a product, the fact is that many of these brands sell very well.

Lakeport brewing company is having success with Truly Naked beer; the beer's name ostensibly comes from the fact that it is a filtered beer and thus pure, or "naked." The beer has nothing to hide and is pioneering a new category of beers. One has to wonder though, if it is merely a coincidence that the brand has a "sexy" name and is being targeted at young males, 18–25 years old.

It is usually the case that the consumers of these brands with controversial names use them because of their shock value. Once this wears off, the brands tend to fade away.

Branding is one of the key strategic marketing decisions that relates to the target market. A sexy or risqué name is selected with the express intent of appealing to a certain type of customer. Contrary to popular belief, offending people is not necessarily something marketers wish to avoid. Market experience with controversial brands clearly proves this. Of course, for products with broad appeal, like Pepsi-Cola, offending people is of great concern. This is why Pepsi-Cola quickly stopped running ads featuring Madonna and Mike Tyson when some consumers responded very negatively to the images of these celebrities.

When a brand presents an unwholesome image, like Death Cigarettes (shocking name but it clearly reflects the actual nature of the product) or Nude Beer (which featured women on its containers who became nude when the containers got wet with condensation), and Opium perfume (which would be addictive to your lover), then it is clear that some segments will be offended. Have marketers crossed the line of decency in these cases? It is not simply a matter of selling "smut" (a product in itself) or being shocking, which falls under freedom of speech, but a matter of using "smut" or shock value to sell a product which is, of itself, not particularly smutty or shocking.

Beer, cigarettes, and perfumes can be branded and promoted on the basis of their own inherent benefits and characteristics. However, a large number of sexual appeals are associated with the products, even if the brand names themselves are not "sexy." For example, Molson Canadian Beer, Alfred Sung's Sung Perfume, and Virginia Slim's cigarettes are not brand names that bring to mind anything particularly controversial. Yet advertising associated with these brands has featured prominent sexual appeals. Perhaps, the overt appeals presented by brand names like Sexual perfume, Death cigarettes and Truly Naked beer are simply more honest.

Research and identify some "controversial" brand names associated with non-controversial products and try to determine how long these "brands" have lasted. Discuss the advantages and disadvantages of controversial branding for a firm's product strategy.

Source: Based on material in "The Naked and the Dinosaur in Brewing," *Marketing* (September 4, 1995), p. 3; Gail Chiasson, "Canadian Sexual Goes National," *Marketing* (May 22, 1995), p. 4.

Aside from any punitive damages that Wal-Mart might have to pay, the simple costs of changing signs and stationery in Canada alone are estimated at over $3 million.[27]

When brands become too popular or descriptive of a product category, they run the risk of becoming public property. A firm then loses its trademark position. Brands fighting to remain exclusive trademarks include L'eggs, Rollerblade, Xerox, Levi's, Plexiglas, Formica, Kleenex, and Teflon. Former trademarks that are now considered generic—and, thus, public property—are cellophane, aspirin, shredded wheat, cola, linoleum, monopoly, and lite beer.

Trademark rulings can have wide implications. For example, a ruling in Ontario on a trademark infringement case involving Orkin pest control affected a ruling in India on a trademark case involving Calvin Klein. In the Ontario situation, Orkin of America tried to force an Ontario company named Orkin to change its name. Orkin was an unregistered foreign trademark in Canada. If the trademark is unregistered, a firm needs a local reputation acquired through doing business locally to gain protection. The problem was that Orkin of America had no history of doing business in Canada under the name Orkin. The court ruled, however, that Orkin of America did have a local reputation acquired by virtue of "spillover" advertising and by the fact that millions of Canadians were exposed to the brand in the Southern U.S. when they travelled there. Consequently, Ontario Court ruled in favour of Orkin of America.

A similar situation cropped up in India where International Apparel Syndicate (IAS) sought to market "Calvin Klein" brand jeans in India. The real Calvin Klein company did not have a distribution relationship with IAS, had not registered its trademark in India, and was not selling any jeans there at the time. However, Calvin Klein sought trademark protection from IAS. The justice of the High Court of Calcutta looked for legal precedents for the case in jurisdictions throughout the British Commonwealth and came upon the Orkin decision in Ontario. As a result, a ruling was made in favour of Calvin Klein and trademark protection in India was granted.

Packaging

Packaging *involves decisions as to a product's physical container, label, and inserts.*

Packaging is the part of product planning where a firm researches, designs, and produces packages. As noted at the beginning of the chapter, a package consists of a product's physical container, label, and/or inserts.

The physical container may be a cardboard, metal, plastic, or wooden box; a cellophane, waxpaper, or cloth wrapper; a glass, aluminium, or plastic jar or can; a paper bag; styrofoam; some other material; or a combination of these. Products may have more than one container: Cereal is individually packaged in small cardboard boxes, with inner waxpaper wrapping, and shipped in large corrugated boxes; and watches are usually covered with cloth linings and shipped in plastic boxes. The label indicates a product's brand name, the company logo, ingredients, promotional messages, inventory codes, and/or instructions for use. Inserts are (1) instructions and safety information placed in drug, toy, and other packages or (2) coupons, prizes, or recipe booklets. They are used as appropriate.

Prior to the advent of the modern supermarket and department store, manufacturers commonly shipped merchandise in bulk containers such as: cracker barrels, sugar sacks, and butter tubs. Retail merchants repackaged the contents into smaller, more convenient units to meet customer needs. With the growth of mass merchants and self-service, manufacturers came to realize the value of packaging as a marketing tool. Today, it is a vital part of a firm's product development strategy; a package may even be the product itself (such as the Reynolds Wrap shown in Figure 14-8) or an integral part of the product (such as the aerosol can for shaving cream).

Packaging plays a key role in helping consumers form perceptions about a product (brand). As one packaging expert noted, "Our experience, supported by research, indicates that the consumer does not conceptually strip away the packaging and consider the ac-

---

[27]Brian Banks and David North, "Ticked off: Wal-Mart's Infuriating Ways," *Canadian Business* (January 1996), pp. 23–24; Eric Swetsky, "Wool-Mart Versus Wal-Mart," *Marketing Magazine* (June 24, 1996), p. 20; and Eric Swetsky, "Corporate Reputations," *Marketing Magazine* (October 2, 1995), p. 24.

FIGURE 14-8
The Package as the Product
Reprinted by permission.

tual product when making a buying decision. For instance, in the case of food and beverages, the package communicates a promise of quality, taste, and enjoyment, and the consumer expects the product inside to measure up. If it does not, or if the package fails to deliver on the product's promise, another product failure is the likely result."[28]

About 10 per cent of a typical product's final selling price goes for its packaging. The amount is higher for such products as cosmetics (up to 40 per cent and more). The complete package redesign of a major product might cost millions of dollars for machinery and production. Packaging decisions must serve both resellers and consumers. Plans are often made in conjunction with production, logistics, and legal personnel. Errors in packaging can be costly.

Package redesign may occur when a firm's current packaging receives a poor response from channel members and customers or becomes too expensive; the firm seeks a new market segment, reformulates a product, or changes or updates its product positioning; or new technology becomes available. For instance:

> When Hostess Frito-Lay "reinvented" their flat potato chip they wanted to inform consumers in a unique and interesting way. They approached the Thomas Pigeon Design Group which specializes in packaging design. Thomas Pigeon is somewhat biased in his view, but he is a believer in the power and importance of packaging on brand identification and sales. Hostess Frito-Lay asked Pigeon's company to "redesign" their potato chip package so it would reflect the "redesign" of the chips inside. What Pigeon's company came up with was a "newspaper bag." The initial idea was to run a short-term trial of the "newspaper bag" to announce the change in the Hostess brand chips. The initial results of the packaging change were a 200 per cent increase in sales in a number of regions. The group product manager of potato chips at Hostess Frito-Lay, Rob Carscadden, gives a lot of credit to the package design as he states "the relaunch of Hostess Potato Chips has become the most successful made-in-Canada marketing project Hostess Frito-Lay has ever undertaken." [29]

---

[28]Primo Angeli, "Thinking Out of the Box: A New Approach to Product Development," *Business Horizons*, Vol. 38 (May–June 1995), p. 18.

[29]Thomas Pigeon, "Read All About It," *Marketing Magazine* (May 6, 1996), p. 10; and Rob Carscadden, "Trash the Flash," *Marketing Magazine* (May 6, 1996), p. 12.

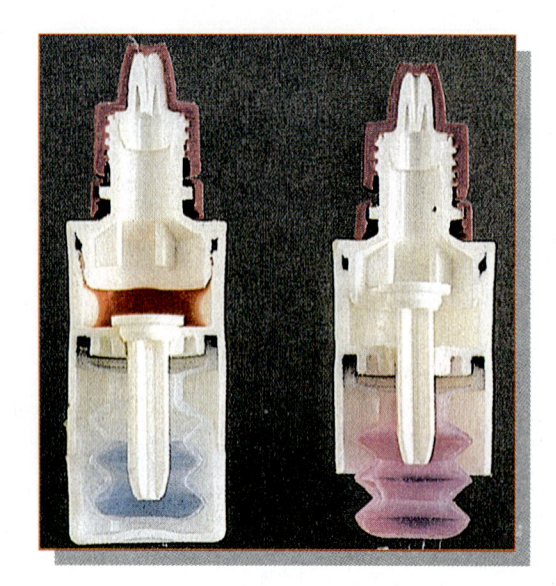

394 Part 4 *Product Planning*

FIGURE 14-9
Using Packaging to Facilitate Product Use
Timpilo, a product for control of glaucoma, is packaged in a unique, award-winning dual-chambered vial. A sight-threatening disease, glaucoma can be controlled with regular applications of two medications, one taken twice a day and the other four times a day. This regimen can be hard for patients to follow; and the medications cannot be combined because the two substances must be stored in different solutions to prevent their deterioration. To solve the problem Merck's packaging engineers designed a bottle with separate chambers for the two substances (photo on left), which are not mixed together until a patient presses the bottom of the vial, displacing a plug (photo on right).
Reprinted by permission.

Packaging functions range from containment and protection to product planning.

The basic functions of packaging, factors considered when making packaging decisions, and criticisms of packaging are described next.

Basic Packaging Functions

The basic **packaging functions** are containment and protection, usage, communication, segmentation, channel cooperation, and new-product planning:

- *Containment and protection*—Packaging enables liquid, granular, and other divisible products to be contained in a given quantity and form. It also protects a product while it is shipped, stored, and handled.
- *Usage*—Packaging lets a product be easily used and re-stored. It may even be reusable after a product is depleted. Packaging must also be safe to all who use it, from the youngest child to the oldest senior. See Figure 14-9.
- *Communication*—Packaging communicates a brand image, provides ingredients and directions, and displays the product. It is a major promotion tool.
- *Segmentation*—Packaging can be tailor-made for a specific market group. If a firm offers two or more package shapes, sizes, colours, or designs, it may employ differentiated marketing.
- *Channel cooperation*—Packaging can address wholesaler and retailer needs with regard to shipping, storing, promotion, and so on.
- *New-product planning*—New packaging can be a meaningful innovation for a firm and stimulate its sales.

What image is sought?

Factors Considered in Packaging Decisions

Several factors must be weighed in making packaging decisions. Colour, shape, and material all influence consumer perceptions. For example:

> After 115 years, Listerine Antiseptic changed from glass to plastic in its most popular bottle sizes, as well as redesigned the classic barbell-shaped package that signified amber mouthwash—and 'medicine-y' taste to generations of consumers. The product inside is the same. But, we wanted to update and modernize it from the package in your grandmother's medicine cabinet.[30]

---

[30]Glenn Collins, "New Looks for Two Staples of the Medicine Cabinet," *New York Times* (July 19, 1994), p. D4.

FIGURE 14-10
Innovative Packaging from Sonoco
Sonoco's consumer packaging operations are known around the world for innovative packaging solutions. These products include composite canisters, plastic tennis ball containers, capseals, plastic and fibre caulk cartridges, carry-out plastic bags for supermarkets and high volume retail stores, plastic produce roll bags, agricultural film, pressure-sensitive labels, promotional coupons, screen process printing for vending machine graphics, screen printing for fleet graphics, flexible packaging, specialty folding cartons, coasters, and glass covers.
Reprinted by permission.

In family packaging, a firm uses a common element on each package in a product line. This approach parallels family branding. Campbell has virtually identical packages for its traditional soups, distinguished only by flavour or content identification. Proctor and Gamble, the maker of Head & Shoulders and Pert Shampoo, does not use family packaging with the two brands; they have distinct packages to attract different segments.

An international firm must determine if a standardized package can be used worldwide (with only a language change on the label). Standardization boosts global recognition. Thus, Coke and Pepsi have standard packages when possible. Yet some colours, symbols, and shapes have negative meanings in some nations. For example, white can mean purity or mourning, two vastly different images.

Package costs must be considered on both a total and per-unit basis. As noted earlier, total costs can run into the millions of dollars; and per-unit costs can go as high as 40 per cent of a product's selling price—depending on the purpose and extent of the packaging.

A firm has many packaging materials from which to select, such as paperboard, plastic, metal, glass, styrofoam, and cellophane. In making the choice, trade-offs are often needed: cellophane allows products to be attractively displayed, but it is highly susceptible to tearing; paperboard is relatively inexpensive, but it is hard to open. A firm must also decide how innovative it wants its packaging to be. Figure 14-10 displays some of the innovative packaging from Sonoco.

There is a wide range of package features from which to choose, depending on the product. These features include pour spouts, hinged lids, screw-on tops, pop-tops, see-through bags, tuck- or seal-end cartons, carry handles, product testers (for items like batteries), and freshness dating. They may provide a firm with a differential advantage.

A firm has to select the specific size(s), colour(s), and shape(s) of its packages. In picking a package size, shelf life (how long a product stays fresh), convenience, tradition, and competition must be considered. In the food industry, new and larger sizes have captured high sales. The choice of package colour depends on the image sought. Mello Yello, a citrus soft drink by Coca-Cola, has a label with bright orange and green lettering on a lemon-yellow background. Package shape also affects a product's image. Hanes created a mystique for L'eggs pantyhose by packaging them in an egg-shaped package. The number of packages used with any one product depends on competition and the firm's use of differentiated marketing. By selling small, medium, and large sizes, a firm may ensure maximum

Should family packaging be used?

Should standard packages be used worldwide?

What should costs be?

What materials and innovations are right?

What features should the packaging incorporate?

What size(s), colour(s), and shape(s) are used?

How should the label and inserts appear?

shelf space, appeal to different consumers, and make it difficult and expensive for a new company to gain channel access.

The placement, content, size, and prominence of the label must be determined. Both company and brand names (if appropriate) need to appear on the label. The existence of package inserts and other useful information (some of which may be required by law) should be noted on the label. Sometimes, a redesigned label may be confusing to customers and hurt a product's sales. As one analyst noted, "Marketers are always trying to improve things, and they may end up causing problems for themselves."[31]

Should multiple packaging be used?

Multiple packaging couples two or more product items in one container. It may involve the same product (such as razor blades) or combine different ones (such as a comb and a brush or a first-aid kit). The goal is to increase usage (hoarding may be a problem), get people to buy an assortment of items, or have people try a new item (such as a new toothpaste packaged with an established toothbrush brand). Many multiple packs, like cereal, are versatile—they can be sold as shipped or broken into single units.

Should items be individually wrapped?

Individually wrapping portions of a divisible product may offer a competitive advantage. This may be weighed against the fact that it is often costly and contributes to environmental waste. Kraft has done well with its individually wrapped cheese slices. Alka-Seltzer sells tablets in individually wrapped tin-foil containers, as well as in a bottle without wrapping.

Should a package have a pre-printed price and use the **Universal Product Code***?*

For certain items (such as shirts, magazines, watches, and candy), some resellers want pre-printed prices. They then have the option of charging those prices or adhering their own labels. Some resellers prefer only a space for the price on the package and insert their own price labels automatically. Because of the growing use of computer technology by resellers in monitoring their inventory levels, more of them are insisting on pre-marked inventory codes on packages. The **Universal Product Code (UPC)**, is a voluntary marking standard used by retailers and manufacturers in Canada and the United States. Using the UPC, manufacturers pre-mark items with a series of thick and thin vertical lines. Price and inventory data codes are represented by these lines, which appear on outer package labels— but are not readable by employees and customers. The lines are "read" by computerized optical scanning equipment at the checkout counter. The cashier does not have to ring up a transaction manually and inventory data are instantly transmitted to the main computer of the retailer (or the manufacturer). In the UPC system, human-readable prices must still be marked on items, either by the manufacturer or the reseller.[32]

The Product Code Council of Canada, located at 885 Don Mills Rd., Ste. #301, Don Mills, Ontario, M3C 1V9 is responsible for assigning and administering Universal Product Codes in Canada. In 1995, the Product Code Council of Canada would assign a six digit manufacturer's code number for a sum of $321.

How does the package interrelate with other marketing variables?

Last, a firm must be sure the package design fits in with the rest of its marketing mix. A well-known perfume brand may be extravagantly packaged, distributed in select stores, advertised in upscale magazines, and sold at a high price. In contrast, a firm making perfumes that imitate leading brands has more basic packaging, distributes in discount stores, does not advertise, and uses low prices. The two perfume brands may cost an identical amount to make, but the imitator would spend only a fraction as much on packaging.

Criticisms of Packaging

Packaging is faulted for waste, misleading labels, etc.

The packaging practices of some industries and firms have been heavily criticized and regulated in recent years due to their impact (or potential impact) on the environment and scarce resources, the high expenditures on packaging, questions about the honesty of labels and the

---

[31] Stuart Elliott, "Advertising," *New York Times* (January 28, 1993), p. D20.
[32] See Barry Berman and Joel R. Evans, *Retail Management: A Strategic Approach*, Sixth Edition (New York: Prentice Hall, 1995), pp. 232–234; and *U.P.C. Guidelines Manual* (Don Mills, Ontario: Product Code Council of Canada), p. 1–4.

TECHNOLOGY & MARKETING

Why Hasn't Milk in a Box Made It in North America?

Several years ago, Parmalat (Italy's largest milk producer) developed a superheated milk product that is packaged in special aseptic cartons (also known as drink boxes). The major advantage of Parmalat's processed milk is that it can be kept without refrigeration for at least six months. As a result, Parmalat milk accounts for 70 per cent of the total fresh milk consumed by Europeans; and annual sales are almost U.S.$2 billion. In contrast, the product accounts for less than one per cent of North American fresh milk sales.

Parmalat has learned that North Americans like to purchase their milk fresh and cold. This means they are suspicious of Parmalat milk. Many consumers think the milk is irradiated or produced from specially treated cows. And Parmalat's higher price (twenty per cent more than regular milk) may also reduce consumer demand. Although North American consumers may be suspicious of the taste, a test by a noted food critic found only subtle differences between Parmalat and regular whole milk.

To broaden its appeal in the North American market, Parmalat has given out leaflets explaining that it uses heat (not radiation) to preserve the milk, its process does not destroy nutrition, and its milk tastes the same as traditional milk. To underscore the point, some Parmalat packages even contain the wording "Not Irradiated" and "No Preservatives" in large letters.

Parmalat has spent millions of dollars to promote its product to North American consumers. Its TV ads highlight the convenience of nonrefrigerated milk and stress the ease of children handling the package. It has distributed discount coupons and free samples. Parmalat even added a two-quart carton to appeal to the larger-sized refrigerators and kitchen cabinets found in North American homes. To date, none of these strategies has significantly increased sales.

As a branding and packaging consultant to Parmalat, develop a marketing strategy to increase its market penetration in the Canadian market.

Sources: Based on material in John Tagliabue, "Unchilled Milk: Not Cool Yet," *New York Times* (June 10, 1995), pp. 33–34, and Carolyn Shea, "Parmalat Pours It On," *Promo* (October 1995), pp. 94–99.

---

confusion caused by inconsistent designations of package sizes (such as large, family, super), and critics' perceptions of inadequate package safety.

Yet, consumers—as well as business—must bear part of the responsibility for the negative results of packaging. Throwaway bottles (highly preferred by consumers) use almost three times the energy of returnable ones. Shoplifting annually adds to packaging costs because firms must add security tags and otherwise alter packages.

In planning their packaging programs, firms need to weigh the short-term and long-term benefits and costs of providing environmentally safer ("green"), less confusing, and more tamper-resistant packages. Generally, firms are responding quite positively to the criticisms raised here. These issues were examined in Chapter 5.

MARKETING IN A CHANGING WORLD
Marketers Aren't Only Building Brands, They're Branding Buildings!

The task of building up a firm's brand name image is often thought of as monumental. However, a number of firms have chosen to make their brand names literally monumental, by sponsoring buildings. At first thought, this might not seem like a particularly new idea, since most large companies do have a corporate headquarters named after the company. And benefactors have been getting their names on university buildings for years in response to generous donations.

However, the new trend now emerging in Canada and the United States is to brand public sports and entertainment venues in response to major donations by corporations. Examples include Vancouver's GM Place, the Canadian Airlines Saddle Dome in Calgary, the United Centre in Chicago (United Airlines is the sponsor), the Corel Centre in Ottawa (formerly the Palladium), the Molson Centre in Montreal, and the Air Canada Toronto Raptors stadium. The hockey teams located in the Corel Centre and the Molson Centre are owned by their corporate sponsors, although they are not the main businesses of their owners. But this is not always the case: Ford has its name on performing arts centres in both Toronto and Vancouver.

What possible advantages accrue to these companies by virtue of "branding" these buildings? For starters, the exposure of the firm's name is linked with the entertainment taking place at the venue—not just the 17 000 to 22 000 fans who pack the various arenas and concert halls, but the millions who watch on TV and the millions more who see the sports highlights later or read about the event in the newspaper the next day. This "free" publicity goes on game-in, game-out, year-after-year. The degree of exposure is also extremely high. Whereas thousands may use your university building or visit your corporate headquarters, millions hear about the events that occurred in your sports arena.

A couple of possible problems with branding a building are that the teams using your venue may be losers, and over time the building may begin to look disreputable. Both of these reflect negatively on the sponsor. In the case of Molson and Corel some of the disaffection for the team's performance and the sponsor might be justified because of the ownership relation. However, it is doubtful that anyone will blame Canadian Airlines for an early playoff exit by the Calgary Flames. As for the second problem, one can remove sponsorship, make it conditional on the structure being maintained, or even ante up to renovate and rebuild, thus garnering more positive public relations.[33]

SUMMARY

1. *To define and distinguish among branding terms and to examine the importance of branding* Branding is the procedure a firm follows in planning and marketing its brand(s). A brand is a name, term, design, or symbol (or combination) that identifies a good or service. A brand name is a word, letter (number), or group of words or letters (numbers) that can be spoken. A brand mark is a symbol, design, or distinctive colouring or lettering. A trade character is a personified brand mark. A trademark is a brand name, brand mark, or trade character given legal protection.

There are millions of brand names in circulation worldwide. Ad spending on them is many billions of dollars annually. Through strong brands, brand loyalty can be secured. Popular brands also speed up the acceptance of new products. Gaining and keeping brand recognition is a top priority, as are the development of brand equity and a brand image. Branding benefits all parties: manufacturers, distribution intermediaries, and consumers.

2. *To study the key branding decisions that must be made* Four fundamental decisions are necessary in branding. First, corporate symbols are determined and, if applicable, revised. The company's name (and/or divisional names), logo(s), and trade characters set its overall image. Second, a branding philosophy is set, which includes the proper use of manufacturer, private, and/or generic brands, as well as family and/or individual branding. At this stage, a mixed-brand strategy, the battle of the brands, and brand extension (a popular approach) are also assessed.

Third, a brand name is chosen from one of several sources, including brand extension from existing names, private brands, licensing a name from another firm, and co-branding. With a new brand, the consumer's brand decision

---

[33]Nimisha Raja, "Branded Buildings," *Marketing Magazine* (May 27, 1996), p. 20.

process moves from nonrecognition to recognition to preference (or dislike) to insistence (or aversion). With a continuing name applied to a new product, the brand decision process would begin at recognition, preference (or dislike), or insistence (or aversion). Fourth, the use of trademarks is evaluated and planned.

3. *To define and distinguish among packaging terms and to examine the importance of packaging* Packaging is the procedure a firm follows in planning and marketing their product package(s). A package consists of a physical container, label, and/or inserts. Today, packaging is an integral part of a firm's new-product planning strategy.

Ten per cent of a typical product's final selling price goes for packaging. Package redesign can be quite expensive. Both channel-member and final-consumer needs must be taken into consideration. Errors can be quite costly.

4. *To study the basic functions of packaging, key factors in packaging decisions, and criticisms of packaging* There are six basic packaging functions: containment and protection, usage, communication, market segmentation, channel cooperation, and new-product planning.

Packaging decisions involve image; family packaging; standardization; package costs; packaging materials and innovation; package features; package size(s), colour(s), and shape(s); the label and package inserts; multiple packaging; individual wrapping; pre-printed prices and inventory codes (such as the UPC); and integration with the marketing plan.

Packaging has been criticized on the basis of environmental, safety, and other issues. Both business and consumers must assume some responsibility for unsatisfactory packaging practices.

KEY TERMS

brand (p. 377)
package (p. 377)
brand name (p. 377)
brand mark (p. 377)
trade character (p. 377)
trademark (p. 377)
brand equity (p. 379)
brand image (p. 380)

corporate symbols (p. 382)
manufacturer brands (p. 383)
private (dealer) brands (p. 383)
generic brands (p. 384)
mixed-brand strategy (p. 384)
battle of the brands (p. 385)
family (blanket) branding (p. 385)
brand extension (p. 387)

individual (multiple) branding (p. 387)
licensing agreement (p. 388)
co-branding (p. 388)
consumer's brand decision process (p. 389)
packaging (p. 392)
packaging functions (p. 394)
Universal Product Code (UPC) (p. 396)

Review Questions

1. Differentiate among these terms: brand, brand mark, trade character, brand name, and trademark.
2. Distinguish between brand equity and brand image.
3. Why do manufacturer brands have such a large percentage of sales in so many product categories? Will private brands and generic brands eventually displace manufacturer brands? Explain your answer.
4. In which circumstances is brand extension most effective? Least effective?
5. "Even though a company wants a brand to be popular, it must not be used to describe an entire product category." Explain why.
6. What are the three components of a package?
7. Describe the six major functions of packaging. Give an example of each.
8. Compare family packaging and standardized packaging.
9. What are the major goals of multiple packaging? The major problem?
10. How does the Universal Product Code (UPC) assist channel members, such as wholesalers and retailers?

Discussion Questions

1. An office-supply company, Horizon Paper Corporation, recently changed its name to Horizon Products Corporation. Why do you think this name change was necessary? Do you think this is a good name? Explain your answer.
2. Present two successful and two unsuccessful examples of brand extension. Discuss why brand extension worked or did not work in these cases.
3. How would you protect Levi's jeans from losing its trademark status? What would you recommend if the brand does become a generic term?
4. Evaluate the recent package redesigns of three products. Base your analysis on several specific concepts covered in this chapter.
5. Comment on this statement: "In planning packaging programs, firms need to weigh the short-term and long-term benefits and costs of environmentally safer, less confusing, and more tamper-resistant packages."

VIDEO CASE

Windows 95: Going for the World's Number One Brand

Coca Cola was the world's number one brand in 1995 and has been number one since at least 1990 according to recent surveys. However, Microsoft is fast approaching, moving up from number seven in 1994 to number six in 1995. Bill Gates has unabashedly stated that it is his goal to make Microsoft the number one known company on the planet. In 1995, companies opened up commercial Internet domains at the rate of 150 businesses a day. This produced a frenzied wave of stories about the Internet and the equipment to use it in the media, and by word of mouth. Consequently, computer firms like IBM, Motorola, Hewlett-Packard, Microsoft, and Intel became very prominent in the minds of people, eclipsing packaged-goods brands like Kodak, Budweiser, Kellogg, Nescafé, Gillette, Pepsi and Levi's.

Of course, it is quite likely that Microsoft itself fuelled this with the mega-launch of Windows 95, which had an estimated U.S.$150–$200-million budget. The launch was accompanied by demonstrations at convention centres, testing by 400 000 trial users, and special promotions by retailers. At its Redmond, Washington headquarters, Microsoft sponsored a carnival and trade show for 2500 people. Microsoft paid between $4 and $12 million to get the rights to use the Rolling Stone's hit song "Start Me Up" as their theme music. Microsoft booked the CN Tower in Toronto for a four-day event party. The crowning event was having Stuart Leggett, president of the Canadian School of Rescue Training, suspended in the air at the top of the Tower while demonstrating Windows 95 on a notebook after which he rappeled the 447 metres (1,465 ft.) from the Tower's Space Deck to the ground.

The impact of the campaign was certainly massive and, combined with the stories in the news and popular press, made it the most momentous new-product launch in marketing history. If money can buy anything in the field of marketing, brand awareness is it.

Rex Murphy comments in his CBC report that computers are the indispensible product of the 90s, and the invention of our time that is shaping the global economy. Clearly, there is more than hype driving Microsoft, there is a real and strong need. Filling this need is what will make Windows 95 the standard for the computing industry and potentially make Microsoft the world's number one brand. Still, one cannot help but wonder how many people are sitting at their computers and sipping away on a Coke while they surf the Net!

QUESTIONS

1. Review the branding theory of the chapter. What do you think accounts for the popularity of brands like Coca-Cola and Microsoft?
2. Do you think Microsoft will become the world's number one brand? Why, or why not? In branding terminology, what kind of a brand is Microsoft? Windows? and Windows 95? Evaluate the Windows 95 brand name according to the Chapter's criteria on what makes a "good" brand name.
3. Discuss the needs and wants that are filled by computers and their operating systems. Do you think the computer phenomenon is just a fad, or is it "for real"? Justify your answer.
4. Consider the branding strategies employed by various computer firms. Identify and present examples of: manufacturer's brands, private label brands, and generic brands. Consider the product life cycle in computers and discuss the relationship between product life cycles and branding strategies.

VIDEO QUESTIONS ON WINDOWS 95

1. The positioning strategy of computer manufacturers and software producers presented in the video is fairly clear: If you do not own and operate a computer with the latest technology, life is passing you by. First, discuss this positioning strategy from a computer software producer's standpoint. Next, consider the statement from the consumer's perspective. Is this statement true? Evaluate the criticisms presented in the video, give your opinion, and then conclude whether the strategy is appropriate or not.
2. Clifford Stoll commented that people are becoming so focused on computing and computing technologies that they will not be able to cope when change occurs in the future. This fear of rapid change keeps a lot of people from entering the market, for fear they will be stuck with obsolete equipment (a very real fear). Discuss how "branding" would play a role in dealing with these fears.

Video Source: "Software-Hardsell," *The National Magazine* (November 7, 1995). *Other Sources:* The data in this case are drawn from Jo Marney, "Top of Mind, Top of Market," *Marketing Magazine* (November 27, 1995), p. 13; Angela Kryhul, "Companies Embrace the Internet Big Time as a Legitimate Mainstream Marketing Option," *Marketing Magazine* (January 1–8, 1996), p. 4; Stan Sutter, "The Win-Win Promise of Windows 95," *Marketing Magazine* (August 14, 1995), p. 8; "Microsoft's Magic Moment," *Marketing Magazine* (September 4, 1995), p. 27; and "Canadian Rescuer Stu Leggett Will Rappel from the CN Tower August 24th in Celebration of the Launch of Windows 95!" *Canada NewsWire* (August 23, 1995).

CASE STUDY

Ralcorp: Is Its Imitation Strategy Really Flattery?

Ralcorp, a recent spin-off of Ralston Purina, dominates the "knockoff" market for ready-to-eat cereals. Unlike some makers of private brands that produce their own cereal formulations and use standard packaging supplied by a retailer, Ralcorp seeks to produce cereals that look and taste almost exactly like the best-selling manufacturer brands. For example, Ralcorp's Tasteeos cereal mimics General Mills' Cheerios in the use of a yellow carton, the "O" shape of its toasted oats, and its taste. Ralcorp uses the same strategy with its Fruit Rings multigrain cereal that has similar elements to Kellogg's Fruit Loops and with its own Corn Flakes.

And Ralcorp plans to market up to four new knockoff cereals per year—aiming at brands such as Shredded Wheat and Trix that do not have knockoff equivalents. The leading cereal makers certainly do not view Ralcorp's approach from the perspective that "imitation is the sincerest form of flattery."

Ralcorp generally prices its cereals at a dollar or so less than the leading cereal makers (Kellogg, General Mills, and Quaker Oats). In addition, its brands typically offer retailers twice the profit margins of manufacturer brands. Nonetheless, despite the price savings to consumers and the higher profits to retailers, until recently, private and knockoff cereals garnered only six per cent of cereal sales. In contrast, private brands account for double that amount for total grocery sales.

The slow market penetration of knockoff and private brands in the cereal market has finally changed. During 1994, these brands of cereals averaged 8 per cent year-to-year growth, while manufacturer brands grew only 3 per cent—a trend that continues.

Some market analysts expect even more growth in knockoff and private brands due to the aggressive marketing by Ralcorp and others. Ralcorp has even invested in new plant technology to help it better copy major brands. Legal experts say the copying of leading cereal brands is legal because these brands are produced with standard manufacturing processes that are not patented.

However, all is not rosy for Ralcorp and other manufacturers of knockoff cereal brands. Potential problems that exist relate to the need for costly equipment, trademark registration by manufacturer brands, potential price competition, and market saturation.

Although Ralcorp can legally copy technology that is not proprietary, in some cases a manufacturer's brand uses cereal equipment that is too costly for Ralcorp to purchase or lease. For example, General Mills' Cheerios cereal is produced through a costly "gun puffing" process that cannot be duplicated with Ralcorp's current equipment. As a result, Cheerios is more uniform and has a different colour from Ralcorp's Tasteeos.

All manufacturer brands have registered their brand names, brand marks, and trade characters as trademarks. The trademark owners have won legal suits (on the basis of their trademark ownership) over promotional claims made by knockoff and private brand manufacturers. In a recent case, General Mills won a case against Malt-O-Meal Company, another knockoff cereal maker that compared the firm's Toasty O's cereal to Cheerios.

Large manufacturer brands could also temporarily cut their prices to destroy the cost advantage that drives the knockoff brands' retail sales. In addition, some analysts believe that since most of the larger manufacturer brands have already been copied, opportunities for knockoff brand manufacturers are now limited to lesser-known manufacturer brands with lower market shares. In other words, they question whether the price-sensitive segment of the cereal market is close to its saturation point.

QUESTIONS

1. Explain how a trademark owner can use its trademark as protection in comparative advertising.
2. Evaluate the pros and cons of Ralcorp's knockoff branding strategy versus a traditional private brand from Ralcorp's perspective.
3. Evaluate the pros and cons of Ralcorp's knockoff branding strategy versus a traditional private brand from a supermarket's perspective.
4. How can a knockoff brand of cereal be sold for a dollar less and at the same time provide a retailer with twice its traditional profit margin?

GENERAL MILLS
www.genmills.com/

Source: The data in this case are drawn from Greg Burns, "A Fruit Loop by Any Other Name," *Business Week* (June 26, 1995), pp. 72, 76.

DISTRIBUTION PLANNING

PART 5

Part 5 deals with the second major element of the marketing mix, distribution.

15 Considerations in Distribution Planning and Physical Distribution

Here, we broadly study distribution planning, which involves the physical movement and transfer of ownership of a product from producer to consumer. We explore the functions of distribution, types of channels, supplier/distribution intermediary contracts, channel cooperation and conflict, the industrial channel, and international distribution. We also look at physical distribution, in particular at transportation and inventory management issues.

16 Wholesaling

In this chapter, we examine wholesaling, which entails buying and/or handling goods and services and their subsequent resale to organizational users, retailers, and/or other wholesalers. We show the impact of wholesaling on the economy, its functions, and its relationships with suppliers and customers. We describe the major types of company-owned and independent wholesalers and note recent trends in wholesaling.

17 Retailing

Here, we concentrate on retailing, which consists of those business activities involved with the sale of goods and services to the final consumer. We show the impact of retailing on the economy, its functions in distribution, and its relationship with suppliers. We categorize retailers by ownership, store strategy mix, and nonstore operations. We also describe several retail planning considerations and note recent trends in retailing.

Part 5 Vignette
Goods and Services Distribution

The exchange process of marketing requires a physical transfer from producer to consumer of both goods and services and the transaction requirements associated with the transfer. Transaction requirements usually involve the title to goods or rights to services.

The first video case discusses how Canada's busiest shipping port operates. The Port of Vancouver is a hub of intermodal transportation activity with containers full of imported products waiting to be loaded for shipment to Ontario and Quebec; it also handles exports of softwood lumber, wood pulp, grain, coal, potash and sulphur. The logistics of the port's operations are demonstrated with stories on two ships that dock there for loading. The *Saga Spray* was constructed to transport wood and wood products from British Columbia to Japan. The *Golden Empire* is a general cargo vessel contracted to carry grain to Mexico. It is very illuminating to see how goods that were made in Japan, Hong Kong, Singapore or China are shipped into Canada for our use and how goods produced here are transported to offshore markets.

The second case examines a characteristically Canadian form of distribution, the producer co-op. Cooperative enterprises were founded on the pioneer spirit and are managed on the principle of democracy, with members voting on important decisions. The Saskatchewan Wheat Pool is one of the largest and most successful cooperative enterprises in Canada; it has 57 000 farmer members and is a publicly traded company on the Toronto Stock Exchange. Like most producer cooperatives, it handles all distribution and product marketing for its members. It operates a grain handling system of storage elevators and fish farms, markets livestock and other grains, makes available 27 farm service centres, operates a flour mill, and publishes a newspaper for farmers. Finally, the Saskatchewan Wheat Pool acts as a lobby interest group to the provincial and federal governments on behalf of its farmer members. The marketplace is fast-paced and more volatile than ever, however, which requires faster decision making for enterprises to survive. Cooperatives are threatened by the fact that democracy is a slow decision making process and cooperative managers need to make expedient decisions to keep pace with the environment. This cooperative is viewed as the one that is adapting best to this situation.

Finally, the Canadian retail landscape has been undergoing a number of fundamental shifts. One of the major stories in retailing is considered in the third video case. Wal-Mart's entry into Canada was seen as a form of retail revolution, a revolution for which there was a U.S. precedent. Canada is an attractive new market for American retailers because of its close geographic proximity and the fact that cross-border shopping, combined with the powerful spillover effect of retail advertising, have made Canadians familiar with, and well disposed to, U.S. retailers. For these reasons, it was only natural for Wal-Mart, the world's largest retailer, to select Canada as its first major site for international expansion. The video case illustrates the general state of Canadian retailing at the time and the threat that Wal-Mart presented, and still presents, to non-responsive retailers. Convincing retailers that they must have a complete marketing mix to be successful is the objective of Dr. Ken Stone, a consultant who advises small retailers on how to cope with Wal-Mart. Understanding the competition and your customers and then responding appropriately to them both are key to retail survival.

However, Wal-Mart recognizes that it is involved in face-to-face, direct contact with customers. As a marketing organization, Wal-Mart sees itself as the leader in the channel of distribution, and they work for their customers backwards through the channel of distribution to the producers to lower costs and raise quality. This constant interaction with suppliers helps Wal-Mart to build relationships and lower costs, to the detriment of their competitors and the satisfaction of their customers.

> *Distribution is part of the exchange process of marketing and involves the physical transfer of goods and services from producer to consumer.*

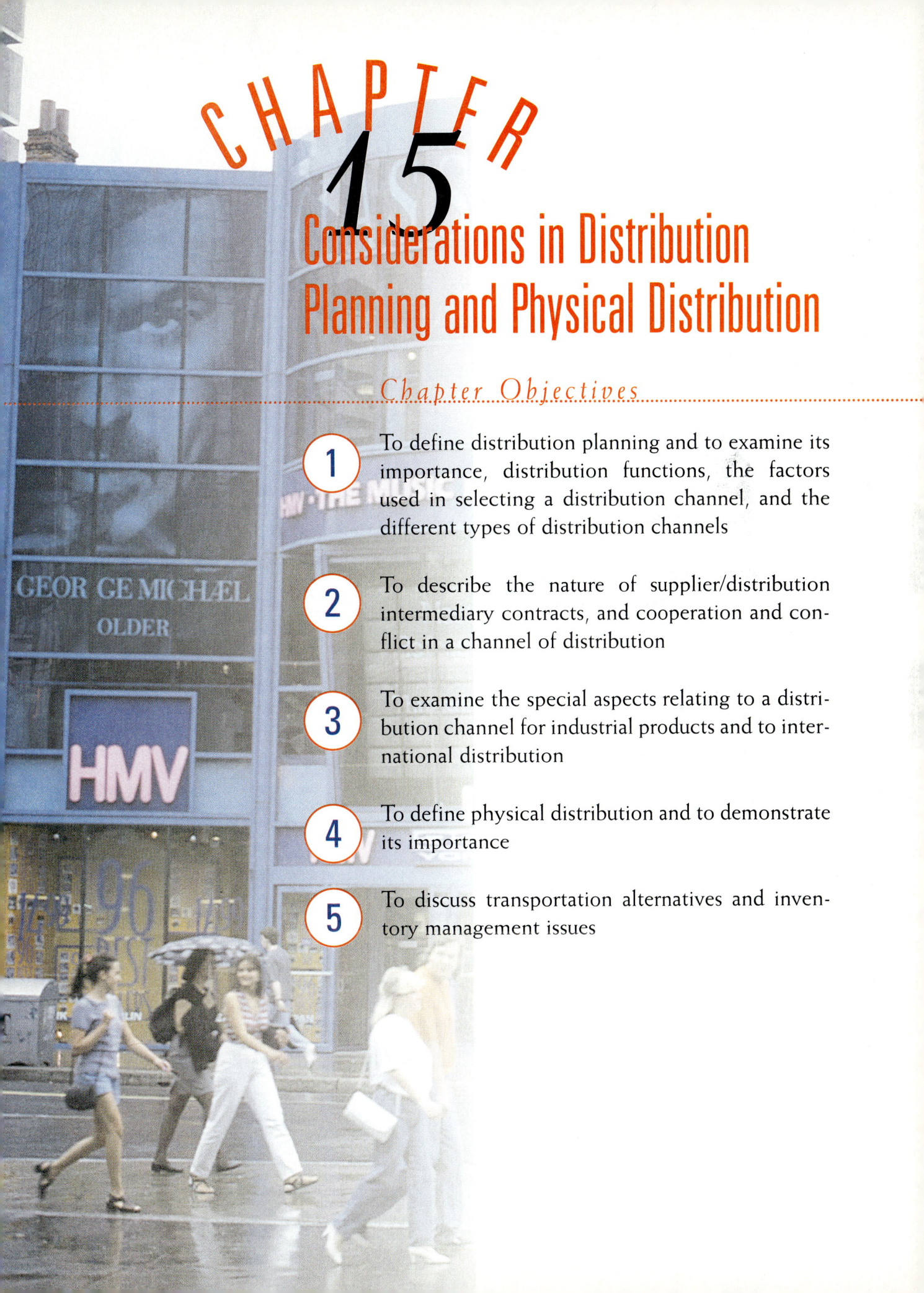

CHAPTER 15
Considerations in Distribution Planning and Physical Distribution

Chapter Objectives

1. To define distribution planning and to examine its importance, distribution functions, the factors used in selecting a distribution channel, and the different types of distribution channels

2. To describe the nature of supplier/distribution intermediary contracts, and cooperation and conflict in a channel of distribution

3. To examine the special aspects relating to a distribution channel for industrial products and to international distribution

4. To define physical distribution and to demonstrate its importance

5. To discuss transportation alternatives and inventory management issues

> *A pivotal battle in the war over the distribution of recorded music is taking place in Canada and it is being fueled by changes in technology and demographics. The following statement sums up the situation: "Nowhere in the world is music retailing more brutally competitive than Canada."*

HMV
www.hmv.ca/cdn_music/

Reprinted by permission of Bob Carroll

Traditional music retailers like Music World, HMV Records, and Sam the Record Man are in a life-and-death struggle with the record clubs such as BMG and Columbia House, who sell ten CDs for a penny. It's not just music clubs who are bothering these retailers. Now hardware retailers of stereos and computers, like Future Shop and A&B Sound, are selling music. In addition, Tower Records/Video of Sacramento, California opened up a record store in Toronto in December 1995 and Virgin Records, part of a Beverly Hills, California conglomerate, was awaiting approval from the federal government to open up a store in Vancouver. Both retail outlets represent the front-end entry of these retail chains and these stores promise to appeal to customers by their unusual presentation and display of the merchandise.

The distribution channels for recorded music are undergoing a rapid change and the future promises more of the same. Currently, the major Canadian music retailers are: HMV Canada (19 per cent market share), Music World (17 per cent market share), Sam the Record Man (12 per cent market share), BMG and Columbia House music clubs (25 per cent market share) with the remainder of the market going to an assortment of: independent record retailers, department stores (like the Bay, Eatons, Sears, K-Mart, Zellers, and Wal-Mart), and sound equipment outlets like the Future Shop and A&B Sound. However, these players are about to be blind sided.

The dominant medium for music these days is the compact disk (CD). People can carry personal CD players, play them in their cars, play them in multi-CD players in a home stereo, and in CD-equipped home computers. Technology for "recordable" CDs is still very expensive, but it is only a matter of time before the costs fall dramatically. The existence of copyright piracy has always been a thorn in the side of the recording industry, and the thorn is getting sharper. The CD's utility as a storage medium combined with its link to the computer has opened up the potential for another channel of distribution: direct from producer (the musician) to the consumer.

John Parry Barlow, a co-founder of the Electronic Frontier Foundation, believes that in the future, copyright and intellectual property will not exist. Recordings, technology designs, video games, books, and videos will be "free." He claims that the interchange of information and technology brought about by the computer's ability to copy and transfer digital images will mean that enforcing copyright and intellectual property rights will be impossible and this will mean that collecting royalties and fees will be impossible too. Barlow sees a world in which people will browse through an online catalogue and then download the music or entertainment they see to their computers. From there, they may permanently record the entertainment (music, video, game, computer software, etc.) on a recordable CD or on their mega-megabyte hard drives.

If you think Barlow is just speculating, think again. CDnow! is a commercial service with an online catalogue (look out music clubs) which allows browsers to sample the products from their computers, place a mail order, and even download items for a fee. Cerberus Sound + Vision in Britain has a license to sell music online. Meanwhile, Cyberspace Promotions in Los Altos, California offers "Virtual Radio." Bands can pay to have their demo music played on virtual radio, which is accessed through the Internet. Listeners can download the music free of charge. According to Barlow, it is only a matter of time before the artists will be selling music directly to the listeners, by-passing the record companies and their distributors. At the moment, Internet music products are only half CD quality. However, this technological issue will likely be resolved in the future. From the marketing standpoint, reaching out directly to the customer is the key. If the customer wants "full CD" quality now, they will order an actual CD through their computer and get it in the mail.

HMV Canada is considering an Internet marketing approach for their products. The key will be the database information that will be provided. It is expected that users will sample and order products by computer but still receive conventional media (CDs, music cassettes, videos and computer software) through mail order. The music clubs, BMG (started up in 1995) and Columbia House (in business since 1955) have depended primarily on mail order for their operations but direct ordering on the Internet is a natural extension for them.

Will there be a growth in Internet purchases and a fall-off in music store buying? The demographics appear to say yes. Apparently the older crowd, people in their late 20s up through their 40s (a crowd which is getting older and represents the largest market potential) is not buying as much music as they once did. The most likely reason is that they have been mostly ignored by the music industry in favour of the younger crowd. They do not feel at home in music stores, which play "heavy metal" rock music and prominently display and feature price the artists targeted at the teenage group. This older 20- to 40-year-old segment also represents the Internet types who just might be more likely to respond to mail order and Internet appeals and shun music stores. The future of distribution in the music industry will be interesting to watch. As for predicting the winners and losers, one winner has already emerged: the consumers.[1]

In this chapter, we will learn more about the decisions made in distribution planning and the activities involved in physical distribution, including quick response inventory systems.

Overview

Distribution planning is systematic decision making regarding the physical movement of goods and services from producer to consumer, as well as the related transfer of ownership (or rental) of them. It encompasses such diverse functions as transportation, inventory management, and customer transactions.

Functions are carried out via a **channel of distribution**, which is comprised of all the organizations or people involved in the distribution process. Those organizations or people are known as **channel members** and may include manufacturers, service providers, wholesalers, retailers, marketing specialists, and/or consumers. When the term **distribution intermediaries** is used, it refers to wholesalers, retailers, and marketing specialists (such as transportation firms) that act as facilitators (links) between manufacturers/service providers and consumers.

Distribution planning *involves movement and ownership in a* **channel of distribution**. *It consists of* **channel members**.

Distribution intermediaries *often have a channel role.*

---

[1] Christian Allard, "Loony Tunes," *Canadian Business* (August 1995), pp. 73–74; Michael McCullough, "The Changing Sounds of Music Marketing," *Marketing Magazine* (June 19, 1995), p. 20; James Pollock, "Luckhurst Rising Fast on HMV's Charts," *Marketing Magazine* (February 5, 1996), p. 7; James Pollock, "Tower Entry Stokes up TO Record Market," *Marketing Magazine* (January 22, 1996), p. 5; Michael McCullough, "Virgin Awaits Approval for First Canadian Store," *Marketing Magazine* (February 19, 1996), p. 5; and Laura Medcalf, "Music Industry Tests Ways to Reach Grown-Up Consumers," *Marketing Magazine* (August 21–28, 1995), p. 3.

This chapter presents an in-depth look at distribution planning and looks at the role of physical distribution. Chapter 16 covers wholesaling's role in the distribution process. Chapter 17 discusses retailing.

Distribution Planning

Distribution arrangements vary widely.

A channel of distribution can be simple or complex. It can be based on a handshake agreement between a small manufacturer and a local reseller or require detailed written contracts among numerous manufacturers, wholesalers, and retailers. Some firms seek widespread distribution and need independent wholesalers and/or retailers to carry their merchandise and improve cash flow. Others want direct customer contact and do not use independent resellers. Industrial channels usually have more direct contact between manufacturers/service providers and customers than final-consumer channels. International channels also have special needs.

The importance of distribution planning, the range of tasks performed in the distribution process, the criteria to consider in picking a distribution channel, supplier/distribution intermediary contracts, channel cooperation and conflict, the industrial channel of distribution, and international distribution are discussed next.

The Importance of Distribution Planning

Distribution decisions have a great impact on a company's marketing efforts. Because intermediaries can perform a host of functions, a firm's marketing plan will differ if it sells direct rather than through intermediaries; and a decision to sell in stores rather than through the mail or the World Wide Web requires a different marketing orientation and tasks.

The choice of a distribution channel is one of the most critical decisions a firm will make. Close ties with intermediaries and/or customers may take time to develop; if there are existing bonds among channel members, it may be hard for a new firm to enter. Once channel alliances are achieved, suitable new products can be put into distribution more easily. Channel members need to act in a coordinated way. Strong resellers enhance manufacturers' marketing abilities. Consumers like to buy products the same way over time.

Through relationship marketing, companies strive for ongoing ties with suppliers, intermediaries, and customers.

Today, more companies recognize the value of having good relationships throughout the distribution channel. As a result, many firms now engage in **relationship marketing**, whereby they seek to develop and maintain continuous long-term ties with suppliers, distribution intermediaries, and customers. By doing so, these firms ensure a more consistent flow of goods and services from suppliers, encourage intermediaries to act more as partners than adversaries, and increase the likelihood of having loyal customers. They improve employee morale by empowering them to respond positively to reasonable requests—in the employees' judgment—from suppliers, intermediaries, and/or customers. They get earlier and better data on prospective new products and the best strategies for continuing ones. They also lower operating and marketing costs, thus improving efficiency. As one expert noted, with relationship marketing, it is "traumatic to leave someone who you believe is responsive to your personal needs. We don't change doctors, lawyers, or accountants at the drop of a hat. Firms want to build the same relationships with suppliers, distribution intermediaries, and customers so they won't leave every time they get a better offer."[2] See Figures 15-1 and 15-2.

---

[2]Aimee L. Stern, "Courting Consumer Loyalty with the Feel-Good Bond," *New York Times* (January 17, 1993), Section 3, p. 10. For further information on relationship marketing, see Barry Berman, *Marketing Channels* (New York: Wiley, 1996), pp. 201–239; "Special Issue on Relationship Marketing," *Journal of the Academy of Marketing Science*, Vol. 23 (Fall 1995); Robert M. Morgan and Shelby D. Hunt, "The Commitment-Trust Theory of Relationship Marketing," *Journal of Marketing*, Vol. 58 (July 1994), pp. 20–38; Robert D. Buzzell and Gwen Ortmeyer, "Channel Partnerships Streamline Distribution," *Sloan Management Review*, Vol. 36 (Spring 1995), pp. 85–96; and Gregory T. Gundlach, Ravi S. Achrol, and John T. Mentzer, "The Structure of Commitment in Exchange," *Journal of Marketing*, Vol. 59 (January 1995), pp. 78–92.

Chapter 15 Considerations in Distribution Planning and Physical Distribution 409

FIGURE 15-1
Relationship Marketing and Digital Equipment
To illustrate its commitment to relationship marketing, Digital Equipment Corporation discusses its partnerships and willingness to cooperate. Firms are encouraged to phone or visit Digital's Web site.
Reprinted with permission of Digital Equipment Corporation.

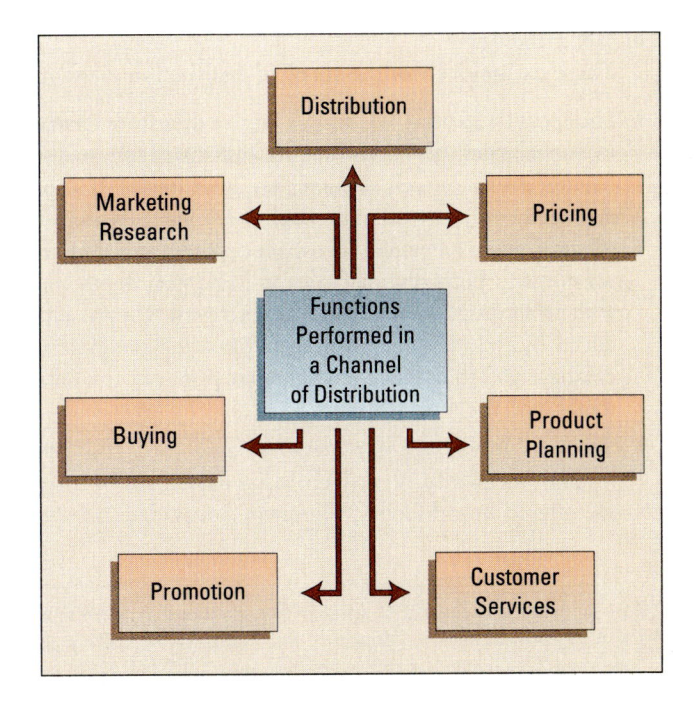

FIGURE 15-2
Channel Functions

These are several recommendations as to how effective relationship marketing in a distribution channel may be achieved:

- Relationship marketing should be conducted as a continuous and systematic process that incorporates both buyer and seller needs.
- Relationship marketing needs top management support; and its principles should permeate a firm's corporate culture.
- At a minimum, relationship marketing means understanding consumer expectations, building service partnerships, empowering employees, and total quality management (from buyer and seller perspectives).
- Suppliers, intermediaries, and customers should be surveyed—by category—to determine the aspects of relationship marketing to be emphasized for them.
- Although increased profitability is a desirable result from relationship marketing, other important measures of success are customer satisfaction, customer loyalty, and product quality.
- Both positive and negative feedback (going far beyond just passively receiving customer complaints) can provide meaningful information.
- Sellers need to communicate to their customers that relationship marketing involves responsibilities, as well as benefits, for both parties.
- Mutually agreeable (by buyers and sellers) contingency plans should be devised in case anything goes awry.[3]

Costs, as well as profits, are affected by the selection of a particular type of distribution channel. A firm doing all functions must pay for them itself; in return, it reaps all profits. A firm using intermediaries reduces per-unit distribution costs; it also reduces per-unit profits because those resellers receive their share. With intermediaries, a firm's total profits would rise if there are far higher sales than the firm could attain itself.

Distribution formats are long-standing in some industries. For example, in the beverage and food industry, manufacturers often sell through wholesalers that then deal with retailers. Auto makers sell through franchised dealers. Mail-order firms line up suppliers, print catalogues, and sell to consumers. So, firms must frequently conform to the channel patterns in their industries.

A firm's market coverage is often influenced by the location and number, market penetration, image, product selection, services, and marketing plans of the wholesalers, retailers, and/or marketing specialists with which it deals. In weighing options, a firm should note that the more intermediaries it uses, the less customer contact it has and the lower its control over marketing.

These examples show the scope of distribution planning:

- Shoppers Drug Mart is Canada's largest drugstore chain with 850 stores and $4 billion in annual sales. Shoppers doesn't just distribute and sell prescription and over-the-counter drugs (as well as numerous other items). It also distributes customized health management information through the "Health Watch" system. Each prescription customer is given a detailed fact sheet on their prescription medications, which provides warnings to both pharmacists and customers about the dangers of drug interactions with other drugs, food, beverages, and even types of activities. The information is produced by linking the customer information database with a large drug information database and then having a computer print out the details on the medicines, the customer, and their physicians.[4]
- Shoppers Advantage is a member-based shopping service that operates exclusively through the World Wide Web. It has a database of 250 000 brand-name products that are offered at a discount. Shoppers Advantage "acts as an online broker, displaying

---

[3]Joel R. Evans and Richard L. Laskin, "The Relationship Marketing Process: A Conceptualization and Application," *Industrial Marketing Management*, Vol. 23 (December 1994), p. 451.
[4]Lara Mills, "Drug Retail Rumble," *Marketing Magazine* (March 4, 1996), p. 11.

Ethics AND TODAY'S MARKETER

Can New Firms Use an Honour System to Gain Distribution?

McAfee Associates markets two computer software packages: VirusScan, which protects PCs from viruses, and Netshield, which monitors security in local area networks. The firm's annual sales revenues exceed US$30 million.

Unlike many other similar firms, both of McAfee's products are shareware. Thus, these programs can be downloaded from electronic bulletin boards by anyone with a modem and a personal computer. In theory, consumers are given a sixty-day trial period. Those who wish to continue using the products are expected to pay a US$100 fee for access to technical support and for future upgrades. However, in practice, most consumers do not pay the fee, realizing that it is quite difficult for any shareware provider to enforce payment.

About 100 000 potential customers download McAfee's software packages each month. Of this group, about 20 per cent eventually remit the US$100 fee. In some cases, McAfee's technical support people have fielded questions from nonpaying users. Why? The firm is careful not to offend nonpayers, hoping they will pay for the programs they use. McAfee also realizes that many of these "freeloaders" are responsible for publicizing its software within their firms.

Unlike hobbyists, almost all corporate users are quick to pay for the shareware they use. As a result, the majority of McAfee's actual sales are from corporate users. Ford Motor Company, for instance, has a license for 52 000 users and Mobil Corporation has one for over 36 000 computers.

Shareware is typically marketed by small software firms that cannot afford to get distribution through traditional channels. These companies typically concentrate on the hobbyist market. In many cases, shareware authors also do not have the resources to properly test and refine their products.

As a channels manager for McAfee, evaluate the pros and cons of the firm's continued use of shareware. What would you do next? Why?

Source: Based on material in Julie Pitta, "Honour System," *Forbes* (October 24, 1994), pp. 258–260.

---

wares and taking orders and payment. Orders are passed on to distributors, manufacturers, and vendors, which ship products to, or book reservations for, customers."[5]

- Century 21 is the world's largest residential real-estate broker. It relies on 6000 franchisee-operated offices in eleven countries.[6]
- Singer and its affiliates operate 1300 stores throughout the globe. Of these, nearly 600 are in Asia, more than 250 are in Latin America, and about 30 are in Africa and the Middle East. Independent dealers and mass merchants represent another 59 000 Singer distribution points. In developing nations, a total of 13 000 door-to-door salespeople are used in conjunction with retail stores.[7]

McAFEE ASSOCIATES
www50.dt.navy.mil/code521/Virus/McAfee.html

---

[5] Peter H. Lewis, "Online Middleman Opens for Business," *Wall Street Journal* (October 2, 1995), p. D5.
[6] Suzanne Woolley, "I Want My Century 21!" *Business Week* (January 15, 1996), pp. 72–73.
[7] *Singer Company 1995 Annual Report.*

Channel Functions and the Role of Distribution Intermediaries

Intermediaries can perform **channel functions** *and reduce costs, provide expertise, open markets, and lower risks.*

For most goods and services, the **channel functions** shown in Figure 15-2 and described here must be undertaken somewhere in the distribution channel and responsibility for them assigned.

Distribution intermediaries can play a vital role in marketing research. Due to their closeness to the market, they generally have good insights into the characteristics and needs of customers.

In buying products, intermediaries sometimes pay as items are received; other times, they accept items on consignment and do not pay until after sales are made. Purchase terms for intermediaries may range from net cash (payment due at once) to net sixty days (payment not due for sixty days) or longer. If intermediaries do not pay until after resale, manufacturers risk poor cash flow, high product returns, obsolescence and spoilage, multiple transactions with the intermediaries, and potentially low sales to customers.

Manufacturers and service firms like H&R Block often take care of national (and international) ads when assigning promotion roles. Wholesalers may help coordinate regional promotions among retailers and may motivate and train retail salespeople. Most retailers use local ads, personal selling, and special events as forms of promotion.

Customer services include delivery, credit, in-office and in-home purchases, training programs, warranties, and return privileges. Again, these services can be provided by one channel member or a combination of them.

Distribution intermediaries can contribute to product planning in several ways. They often provide advice on new and existing products; test marketing requires their cooperation; and intermediaries can be helpful in positioning products against competitors and suggesting which products to drop.

Wholesalers and retailers often have strong input into pricing decisions. They state their required markups and then price-mark products or specify how they should be marked. Court rulings limit manufacturers' control over final prices. Intermediaries thus have great flexibility in setting prices.

Distribution incorporates three major factors: transportation, inventory management, and customer contact. Goods must be shipped from a manufacturer to consumers; intermediaries often provide this service. Because production capabilities and customer demand frequently differ, inventory levels must be properly managed (and items may require storage in a warehouse before being sold). Consumer transactions may require a store or other selling location, long hours of operation, and store fixtures (such as dressing rooms).

Manufacturers typically like to make a limited variety of items in large quantities and have as few transactions as possible to sell their entire output. On the other hand, consumers tend to want a variety of brands, colours, sizes, and qualities from which to select—and opt to buy a small amount at a time. Manufacturers might also prefer to sell products from the factory, have nine to five hours and spartan fixtures, and use a limited sales force. Yet organizational consumers may want salespeople to come to their offices and final consumers may want to shop at nearby locations and visit attractive, well-staffed stores on weekends and evenings.

The **sorting process** *coordinates manufacturer and consumer goals.*

To resolve these differences, intermediaries can be used in the **sorting process**, which consists of four distribution functions: accumulation, allocation, sorting, and assorting. Accumulation is collecting small shipments from several firms so shipping costs are lower. Allocation is apportioning items to various consumer markets. Sorting is separating products into grades, colours, and so forth. Assorting is offering a broad range of products so the consumer has many choices.

Selecting a Channel of Distribution

In choosing a distribution channel, several key factors must be considered:

Channel choice depends on consumers, the company, the product, competition, existing channels, and legalities.

- *The consumer.*
  Characteristics—number, concentration, average purchase size.
  Needs—shopping locations and hours, assortment, sales help, credit.
  Segments—size, purchase behaviour.

- *The company.*
    Goals—control, sales, profit, timing.
    Resources—level, flexibility, service needs.
    Expertise—functions, specialization, efficiency.
    Experience—distribution methods, channel relationships.
- *The product.*
    Value—price per unit.
    Complexity—technical nature.
    Perishability—shelf life, frequency of shipments.
    Bulk—weight per unit, divisibility.
- *The competition.*
    Characteristics—number, concentration, assortment, customers.
    Tactics—distribution methods, channel relationships.
- *Distribution channels.*
    Alternatives—direct, indirect.
    Characteristics—number of intermediaries, functions performed, tradition.
    Availability—exclusive arrangements, territorial restrictions.
- *Legalities*—current laws, pending laws.

While assessing the preceding factors, a firm would make decisions about the type of channel used, contractual arrangements or administered channels, channel length and width, channel intensity, and whether to use dual channels.

There are two basic types of channels: direct and indirect. A **direct channel of distribution** involves the movement of goods and services from producer to consumers without the use of independent intermediaries. An **indirect channel of distribution** involves the movement of goods and services from producer to independent intermediaries to consumers. Figure 15-3 shows the transactions necessary for the sale of 200 000 men's umbrellas under direct and indirect channels. Figure 15-4 shows the most common indirect channels for final consumer and organizational consumer products.

If a manufacturer or service provider sells to consumers via company-owned outlets (for example, Imperial Oil's Esso gas stations), this is a direct channel. In an indirect channel, a manufacturer may employ several layers of independent wholesalers (for example, regional, provincial, and local) and sell through different kinds of retailers (such as discount, department, and specialty stores). A direct channel is most used by firms that want control over their entire marketing programs, desire close customer contact, and have limited markets. An indirect channel is most used by firms that want to enlarge their markets, raise sales volume, and give up distribution functions and costs, and that are willing to surrender some channel control and customer contact.

Because an indirect channel has independent members, marketing responsibilities may be assigned in different ways. With a *contractual channel arrangement*, all the terms regarding distribution tasks, prices, and other factors are stated in writing for each member. A manufacturer and a retailer could sign an agreement citing promotion support, delivery and payment dates, and product handling, marking, and displays. In an *administered channel arrangement*, the dominant firm in the distribution process plans the marketing program and itemizes and coordinates each member's duties. Depending on their relative strength, a manufacturer/service provider, wholesaler, or retailer could be a channel leader. Accordingly, a manufacturer with a strong brand could set its image, price range, and selling method.

Channel length refers to the levels of independent members along a distribution channel. In Figure 15-3, *A* is a short channel and *B* is a long channel. Sometimes, a firm shortens its channel by acquiring a company at another stage, as when a manufacturer merges with a wholesaler. Doing so allows the firm to be more self-sufficient, ensure supply, control channel members, lower distribution costs, and coordinate timing throughout the channel. However, it may also limit competition and foster inefficiency, and may not result in lower consumer prices.

In a **direct channel** *one firm performs all tasks. An* **indirect channel** *has multiple firms.*

Channel length *describes the number of levels of independent members.*

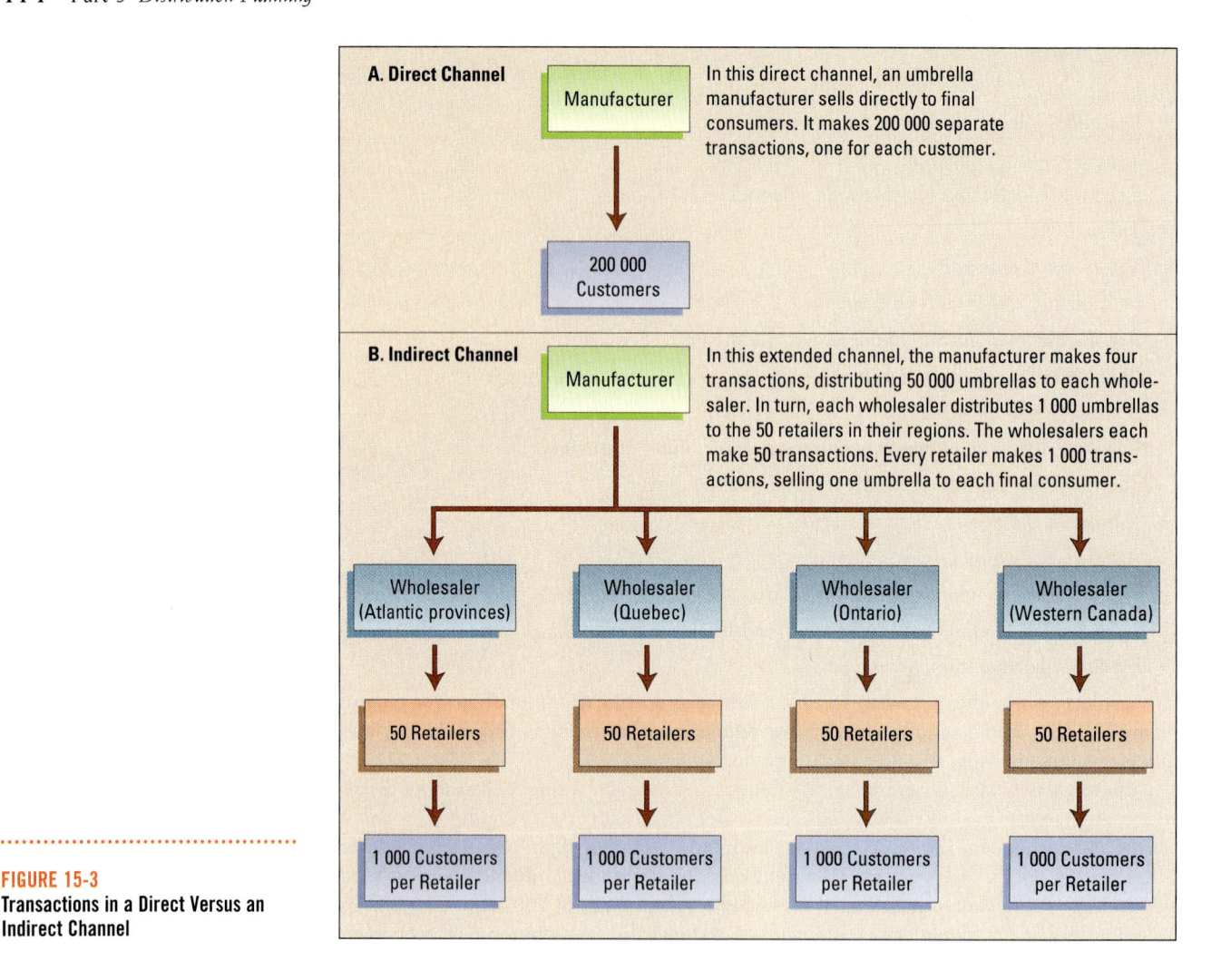

FIGURE 15-3
Transactions in a Direct Versus an Indirect Channel

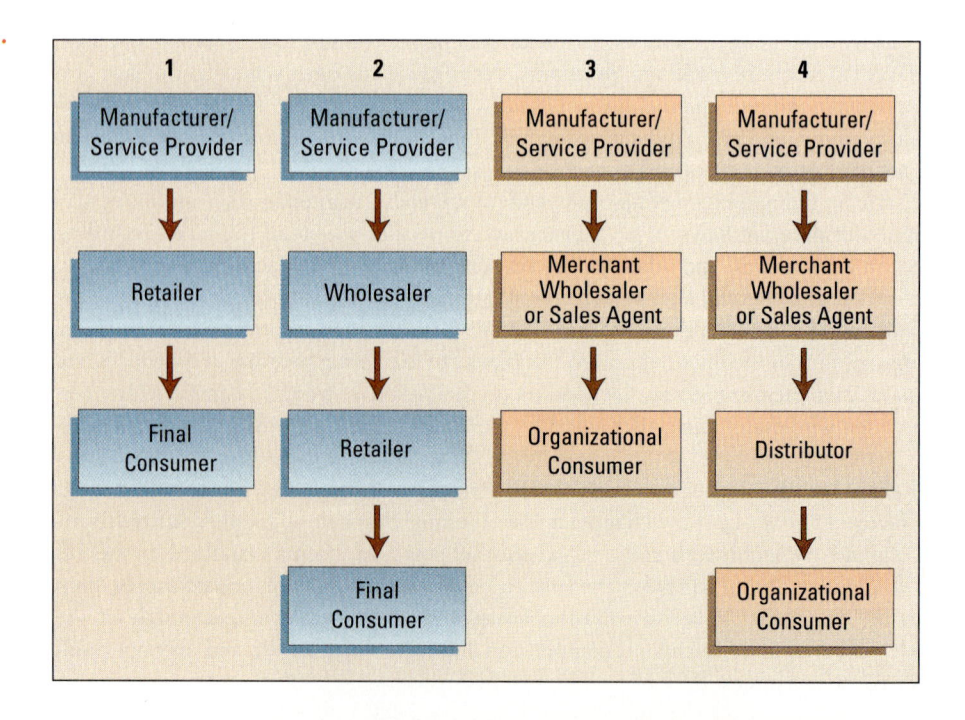

A. Direct Channel

Manufacturer → 200 000 Customers

In this direct channel, an umbrella manufacturer sells directly to final consumers. It makes 200 000 separate transactions, one for each customer.

B. Indirect Channel

Manufacturer → Wholesaler (Atlantic provinces), Wholesaler (Quebec), Wholesaler (Ontario), Wholesaler (Western Canada) → 50 Retailers (each) → 1 000 Customers per Retailer

In this extended channel, the manufacturer makes four transactions, distributing 50 000 umbrellas to each wholesaler. In turn, each wholesaler distributes 1 000 umbrellas to the 50 retailers in their regions. The wholesalers each make 50 transactions. Every retailer makes 1 000 transactions, selling one umbrella to each final consumer.

FIGURE 15-4
Typical Indirect Channels of Distribution

1. Manufacturer/Service Provider → Retailer → Final Consumer
2. Manufacturer/Service Provider → Wholesaler → Retailer → Final Consumer
3. Manufacturer/Service Provider → Merchant Wholesaler or Sales Agent → Organizational Consumer
4. Manufacturer/Service Provider → Merchant Wholesaler or Sales Agent → Distributor → Organizational Consumer

Table 15-1
Intensity of Channel Coverage

ATTRIBUTES	EXCLUSIVE DISTRIBUTION	SELECTIVE DISTRIBUTION	INTENSIVE DISTRIBUTION
Objectives	Prestige image, channel control and loyalty, price stability and high profit margins	Moderate market coverage, solid image, some channel control and loyalty, good sales and profits	Widespread market coverage, channel acceptance, volume sales and profits
Resellers	Few in number, well-established, reputable firms (outlets)	Moderate in number, well-established, better firms (outlets)	Many in number, all types of firms (outlets)
Customers	Final consumers: fewer in number, trend setters, willing to travel to store, brand loyal. Organizational consumers: focus on major accounts, service expected from manufacturer	Final consumers: moderate in number, brand conscious, somewhat willing to travel to store. Organizational consumers: focus on many types of accounts, service expected from manufacturer or intermediary	Final consumers: many in number, convenience-oriented. Organizational consumers: focus on all types of accounts, service expected from intermediary
Marketing	Final consumers: personal selling, pleasant shopping conditions, good service. Organizational consumers: availability, regular communications, superior service	Final consumers: promotional mix, pleasant shopping conditions, good service. Organizational consumers: availability, regular communications, superior service	Final consumers: mass advertising nearby location, items in stock. Organizational consumers: availability, regular communications, superior service
Major weakness	Limited sales potential	May be difficult to carve out a niche	Limited channel control
Examples	Autos, designer clothes, capital equipment, complex services	Furniture, clothing, mechanics' tools, industrialized services	Household products, groceries, office supplies, routine services

Channel width refers to the number of independent members at any stage of distribution. In a narrow channel, a manufacturer or service provider sells through few wholesalers or retailers; in a wide channel, it sells through many. If a firm wants to enhance its position at its stage of the channel, it may buy other companies like itself, such as one janitorial-services firm buying another. This lets a firm increase its size and share of the market, improve bargaining power with other channel members, enlarge its market, and utilize mass promotion and distribution techniques more efficiently.

In selecting a distribution channel, a firm must decide on the intensity of its coverage. Under **exclusive distribution**, a firm severely limits the number of resellers utilized in a geographic area, perhaps having only one or two within a specific shopping location. It seeks a prestige image, channel control, and high profit margins, and accepts lower total sales than it would attain using another type of distribution. With **selective distribution**, a firm employs a moderate number of resellers. It tries to combine some channel control and a solid image with good sales volume and profits. A firm uses a large number of resellers in **intensive distribution**. Its goals are to have wide market coverage, channel acceptance, and high total sales and profits. Per-unit profits are low. It is a strategy aimed at the greatest number of consumers. See Table 15-1.

Some additional factors are noteworthy in selecting a channel. First, a firm may use a **dual channel of distribution**, which allows it to appeal to different market segments or diversify business by selling through two or more separate channels. A company could use

Channel width refers to the independent members at one level.

Exclusive, selective, and intensive distribution depend on goals, sellers, customers, and marketing.

*A **dual channel** lets a company reach different segments or diversify.*

selective distribution for a prestige brand of watches and intensive distribution for a discount brand, or use both direct and indirect channels (such as an insurance firm selling group health insurance directly to large businesses and individual life insurance indirectly to final consumers via independent agents). Kodak uses a three-tiered distribution approach for microfilm, supplies, and imaging systems and software: (1) Kodak's own sales representatives concentrate on complex document-imaging systems. (2) Well-trained brokers market such Kodak equipment as reader-printers and other stand-alone components; they must be certified to sell and service each product line carried. (3) Other intermediaries handle film sales, film processing, and delivery to all business clients in their territories.

Second, a firm may go from exclusive to selective to intensive distribution as a product passes through its life cycle. However, it would be hard to go in the opposite direction, from intensive to selective to exclusive distribution. For example, designer jeans rapidly moved from prestige stores to better stores to all types of outlets. This process would not have worked in reverse. Third, a firm may distribute products in a new way and achieve great success. The sale of women's hosiery was revolutionized when L'eggs products were placed in supermarkets.

Supplier/Distribution Intermediary Contracts

Supplier/distribution intermediary contracts cover prices, sale conditions, territories, commitments, timing, and termination.

Supplier/distribution intermediary contracts focus on price policies, conditions of sale, territorial rights, the services/responsibility mix, and contract length and conditions of termination. The highlights of a basic contract follow.

Price policies largely deal with the discounts given to intermediaries for their functions, quantity purchases, and cash payments and with commission rates. Functional discounts are deductions from list prices given to intermediaries for performing storage, shipping, and other jobs. Quantity discounts are deductions for volume purchases. Cash discounts are deductions for early payment. Some intermediaries are paid commissions for their tasks.

Conditions of sale cover price and quality guarantees, payment and shipping terms, reimbursement for unsold items, and return allowances. A guarantee against a price decline protects one intermediary from paying a high price for an item that is then offered to others at a lower price; if prices are reduced, the original buyer receives a rebate so its product costs are like competitors'. Otherwise, it could not meet the prices that competitors charge customers. Suppliers sometimes employ full-line forcing, whereby intermediaries are required to carry an entire line of products. This is legal if they are not prevented from also buying items from other suppliers.

Territorial rights outline the geographic areas (such as greater Paris) in which resellers may operate and/or the target markets (such as small business accounts) they may contact. In some cases, they have exclusive territories, as with McDonald's franchisees; in others, many firms are granted territorial rights for the same areas, as with retailers selling Sharp calculators.

The services/responsibility mix describes the role of each channel member. It outlines such factors as who delivers products, stores inventory, trains salespeople, writes ad copy, and sets up displays; and it sets performance standards. If included, a hold-harmless clause specifies that manufacturers or service providers—and not resellers—are accountable for lawsuits arising from poor product design or negligence in production.

Contract length and conditions of termination protect an intermediary against a manufacturer or service provider prematurely bypassing it after a territory has been built up. The manufacturer or service provider is shielded by limiting contract duration and stating the factors that may lead to termination.

Not all relationships among channel members are so formal. Some firms rely on handshake agreements. However, without a contract, the danger exists that there will be misunderstandings regarding goals, compensation, tasks to be performed, and the length of the agreement. The one constraint of a written contract may be its inflexibility under changing market conditions.

Channel Cooperation and Conflict

All firms in a distribution channel have similar general goals: profitability, access to goods and services, efficient distribution, and customer loyalty. Yet, the way these and other goals are achieved often leads to differing views, even if the parties engage in relationship marketing. For example, how are profits allocated along a channel? How can manufacturers sell products through many competing resellers and expect the resellers not to carry other brands? Which party coordinates channel decisions? To whom are consumers loyal—manufacturers/service providers, wholesalers, or retailers?

There are natural differences among the firms in a distribution channel by virtue of their channel positions, the tasks performed, and the desire of each firm to raise its profits and control its strategy. A successful channel will maximize cooperation and minimize conflict. Table 15-2 cites causes of channel conflict. Table 15-3 shows how channel cooperation can reduce these conflicts.

In the past, manufacturers dominated channels because they had the best market coverage and recognition; resellers were small and localized. Now, with the growth of large national (and international) wholesalers and retailers, the volume accounted for by them, and the popularity of private brands, the balance of power has shifted more to resellers. As one expert said:

Channel member goals need to be balanced.

Table 15-2
Potential Causes of Channel Cooperation

FACTOR	MANUFACTURER'S/ SERVICE PROVIDER'S GOAL	DISTRIBUTION INTERMEDIARY'S GOAL
Pricing	To establish final price consistent with product image	To establish final price consistent with the intermediary's image
Purchase terms	To ensure prompt, accurate payments and minimize discounts	To defer payments as long as possible and secure discounts
Shelf space	To obtain plentiful shelf space with good visibility so as to maximize brand sales	To allocate shelf space among multiple brands so as to maximize total product sales
Exclusivity	To hold down the number of competing brands each intermediary stocks while selling through many intermediaries	To hold down the number of competing intermediaries carrying the same brands while selling different brands itself
Delivery	To receive adequate notice before deliveries are required	To obtain quick service
Advertising support	To secure ad support from intermediaries	To secure ad support from manufacturers/service providers
Profitability	To have adequate profit margins	To have adequate profit margins
Continuity	To receive orders on a regular basis	To receive shipments on a regular basis
Order size	To maximize order size	To have order size conform with consumer demand to minimize inventory investment
Assortment	To offer a limited variety	To secure a full variety
Risk	To have intermediaries assume risks	To have manufacturers/service providers assume risks
Branding	To sell products under the manufacturer's/service provider's name	To sell products under private brands as well as manufacturers'/service providers' brands
Channel access	To distribute products wherever desired by the manufacturer/service provider	To carry only those items desired by intermediaries
Importance of account	To not allow any one intermediary to dominate	To not allow any one manufacturer/service provider to dominate
Consumer	To have consumers loyal to the manufacturer/service provider	To have consumers loyal to the intermediary
Channel control	To make key channel decisions	To make key channel decisions

Table 15-3
Methods of Channel Cooperation

FACTOR	MANUFACTURER'S/SERVICE PROVIDER'S ACTIONS	DISTRIBUTION INTERMEDIARY'S ACTIONS
New-product introduction	Thorough testing, adequate promotional support	Good shelf location and space, enthusiasm for product, assistance in test marketing
Delivery	Prompt filling of orders, adherence to scheduled dates	Proper time allowed for delivery, shipments immediately checked for accuracy
Marketing research	Data provided to resellers	Data provided to manufacturers/service providers
Pricing	Prices to intermediaries let them gain reasonable profits, intermediary flexibility encouraged	Infrequent sales from regular prices, maintaining proper image
Promotion	Training reseller's salespeople, sales force incentives, developing appropriate ad campaign, cooperative ad programs	Attractive store displays, knowledgeable salespeople, participation in cooperative programs
Financing	Liberal financial terms	Adherence to financial terms
Product quality	Product guarantees	Proper installation and servicing of products for customers
Channel control	Shared and specified decision making	Shared and specified decision making

In highly competitive markets, with so many manufacturers competing for the same customers, distributors and dealers can afford to be choosy about which firms' products they will push. Getting them to push your products is what motivation in marketing channels is all about. With so many [North American] manufacturers interested in marketing products overseas, and needing foreign dealers and distributors to do so, the motivation of channel partners needs to be addressed from an international perspective, as well as a domestic one.[8]

If conflicts are not resolved cooperatively, confrontations may occur. A manufacturer or service provider may then ship late, refuse to deal with certain resellers, limit financing, withdraw promotional support, or use other tactics. Similarly, a reseller may make late payments, give poor shelf space, refuse to carry items, return many products, and apply other tactics. A channel cannot function well in a confrontational framework. Here is an example of channel conflict:

In March 1996, 100 members of the Retail Music Association of Canada boycotted the 1996 Juno awards. They refused to put up posters promoting the awards, would not distribute ballots so fans could vote on entertainer of the year and refused to sponsor or be represented at the awards. The only major retailer not to comply was Sam the Record Man, which has incurred the disapproval of other retailers for breaking ranks.

Why would music retailers boycott the big show that promotes the performers whose products they sell? Because Columbia House, a mail-order record club, was the main sponsor of the event and the music stores did not want to be involved in anything that allied them with one of their most hated competitors. Record clubs used to get delayed music releases, products that had already been selling in music stores for a few months. It was a concession the large record companies made to the traditional music retailers. This concession is no longer given, and music clubs now have the newest music releases, which they sell as loss leaders (ten CDs for a penny). Music stores cannot compete with this and they are rebelling against the industry.[9]

---

[8]Bert Rosenbloom, "Motivating Your International Channel Partners," *Business Horizons*, Vol. 33 (March–April 1990), p. 53.
[9]Anita Lahey, "Music Retailers Boycott Junos Over Club Sponsorship," *Marketing Magazine* (March 4, 1996), p. 2.

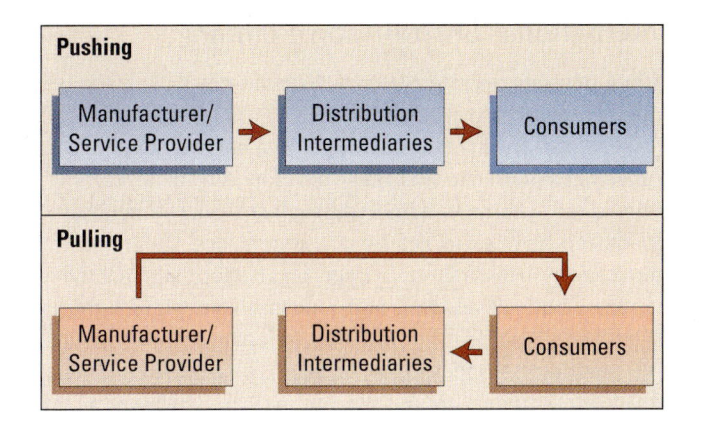

FIGURE 15-5
Pushing Versus Pulling Strategies

A thriving existing manufacturer or service provider can often secure reseller support and enthusiasm when introducing new products and continuing popular ones. This occurs because resellers know the manufacturer's or service provider's past track record, the promotion support that will be provided, and the manufacturer's or service provider's reliability in future deliveries. Thus, a **pushing strategy** is used, whereby the various firms in a distribution channel cooperate in marketing a product. With this approach, a manufacturer or service provider uses relationship marketing.

As a rule, it is harder for a new manufacturer or service provider to break into an existing channel. Resellers are unfamiliar with the firm, not able to gauge its sales potential, and wonder about its support and future deliveries. So, a new firm would need a **pulling strategy**, whereby it first stimulates consumer demand and then gains dealer support. This means heavy promotion expenses, fully paid by the manufacturer or service provider; it must often offer guarantees of minimum sales or profits to resellers, and make up shortfalls. Figure 15-5 contrasts pushing and pulling strategies.

In today's competitive environment, with so many new domestic and foreign products being introduced each year, even market-leading firms must sometimes use pulling strategies. They have to convince resellers that consumer demand exists for their products, before the resellers agree to tie up shelf space.

In a pushing strategy, there is cooperation among channel members. With pulling, a firm generates demand before receiving channel support.

The Industrial Channel of Distribution

The distribution channel for industrial products differs from that for consumer products in the following key ways:

1. Retailers are typically not utilized.
2. Direct channels are more readily employed.
3. Transactions are fewer and orders are larger.
4. Specification selling is more prevalent.
5. Intermediaries are more knowledgeable.
6. Team selling (two or more salespeople) may be necessary.
7. Distinct intermediaries specialize in industrial products.[10]
8. Leasing, rather than selling, is more likely.
9. Customer information needs are more technical.
10. Activities like shipping and warehousing may be shared.

An industrial channel has unique characteristics.

---

[10]See Kris Frieswick, "Surviving the Mass Merchant Diagnosis," *Industrial Distribution* (September 1995), pp. 28–35.

International Distribution Planning

International distribution requires particular planning.

When devising an international distribution plan, a number of factors should be kept in mind. Here are several of them.

Channel length often depends on a nation's stage of economic development and consumer behaviour patterns. Less-developed and developing nations tend to use shorter, more direct channels than industrialized ones. They have many small firms marketing goods and services to nearby consumers; and the more limited transportation and communications networks encourage local shopping. At the same time, cultural norms in nations—both developing and industrialized—affect the expected interactions between sellers and consumers. For instance, in Japan, people treasure personal attention when making purchases, especially of expensive products. Unlike North American shoppers, Japanese consumers are not used to making purchases by telephone.

International Marketing in Action

How Do Mexican Distributors Rate Foreign Manufacturers?

To answer this question, a survey was mailed to Mexican distributors in four industries: industrial machinery, parts and components, chemicals and allied products, and office equipment. A total of one hundred distributors responded. By using distributor *importance* ratings for several attributes, as well as ratings of manufacturer *performance* on these same attributes, the study researchers developed performance "gap" measures.

Respondents were first asked to evaluate the importance of eleven types of support that manufacturers typically provide to distributors. Two of the eleven items related to distributors' terms: adequacy of profit margins and territorial exclusivity. The others related to the manufacturer support provided (such as financial assistance, sales force training, and advertising assistance). According to study results, "quick responses to requests for information" and "adequate profit margins" were the most important factors.

The distributors then assessed the manufacturers on each of the eleven factors and gap measures were generated by subtracting the performance ratings from the importance ratings. Where importance ratings were higher than performance ratings, manufacturers were deemed "underperforming." The opposite results would be categorized as "overperforming." For items rated as important, manufacturers should have high performance ratings. Very high ratings on items viewed as less important indicated that resources could be allocated to other support activities.

In the study, all performance ratings were lower than their importance ratings. This indicates underperformance by manufacturers. Items of high importance with large performance gaps included: "quick responses to requests for information," "training for your salespeople," "materials to assist your salespeople," "advertising to your customers," and "exclusive territories."

As a sales manager for a firm selling products through Mexican distributors, integrate these findings into your overall distributors' sales strategy.

Source: Based on material in Lance Leuthesser, Douglas W. LaBahn, and Katrin R. Harich, "Assessing Cross-National Business Relationships," *Industrial Marketing Management*, Vol. 24 (January 1995), pp. 61–68.

Distribution practices and formats vary by nation, as these examples show:

- Great Britain has the largest retail chains in Europe. The other nations have more independent retailers; but with the opening of European borders the growth of chains will accelerate in the future.
- Some Mexican supermarkets shut off their electricity overnight to hold down costs. Thus, items such as dairy products have a much shorter shelf life and must be more frequently delivered than in Canada.
- Large Japanese firms often set up *keiretsus*. A vertical keiretsu is an integrated network of suppliers, manufacturers, and resellers. A horizontal keiretsu typically consists of a money-centre bank, an insurance company, a trust banking company, a trading company, and several major manufacturers. North American firms have some channels that resemble vertical keiretsus, but they do not have networks that emulate horizontal keiretsus.[11]
- Although it has about three times as many people as both Canada and the United States, India has roughly the same number of retail establishments; and just one-quarter of them are in metropolitan areas. "Pan-bidi" are the popular neighbourhood grocery and general stores that offer very low prices.[12]

If a firm enters a foreign market for the first time, it must resolve various questions, including: Should products be made domestically and shipped to the foreign market or made in the foreign market? If products are made domestically, what form of transportation is best? What kind of distribution intermediaries should be used? Which specific intermediaries should be used?

Industry Canada and the Department of Foreign Affairs and International Trade are only too willing to help Canadian businesses who wish to distribute products internationally. They have set up a a network of Canada Business Service Centres in each province in Canada, with the Northwest Territories being served out of Manitoba and the Yukon Territory being served out of Alberta. Currently, each centre can be contacted by toll-free number or fax. The purpose of these centres is to provide small businesses with one-stop-shopping convenience for information on provincial and federal government programs and services, as well as private programs and services. Canada Business Service Centres offer their users: Business Information Systems (a database of information on programs and services offered by federal, provincial, and private sector organizations), pathfinders (which describe services and programs by topic), toll-free telephone information and referral services, and leading-edge business products (such as videos, how-to manuals, CD-ROM products and external database access).[13]

Through these centres, or through a personal computer with an Internet feed, you can access *Strategis*, Industry Canada's and the Department of Foreign Affairs and International Trade's online database and information system. *Strategis* has computerized market data on industries in many foreign nations and names of contacts in many of these industries as well. Legal requirements regarding distribution differ by country—and some have strict laws as to hours, methods of operation, and sites. In France, there are severe limits on Sunday retail hours. In Germany, there are strict limits on store size and Sunday hours. And many nations have complex procedures for foreign firms wishing to distribute products there. Thus, firms interested in standardized (global) distribution may be stymied in their efforts.

What is likely to cause a company to be more or less satisfied with its international distribution channel? According to one study:

---

[11]Roy L. Simerly, "Should U.S. Companies Establish Keiretsus?" *Journal of Business Strategy*, Vol. 13 (November–December 1992), pp. 58–61.

[12]Janet Zhang, "Asia: Opportunities Large and Small," *Chain Store Age Executive* (January 1995), Section 3, p. 7.

[13]Industry Canada & Department of Foreign Affairs and International Trade, "Canada Business Service Centre Network,", Industry Canada *Strategis* Web site (1996).

- The better a firm's domestic channel performs relative to its international channel, the lower its satisfaction with the international channel.
- The more experience a firm has in foreign markets, the greater its satisfaction with its existing international channel.
- A firm is more satisfied with an existing international channel if it believes it has the ability to change channels.
- A firm has less satisfaction with its existing international channel if environmental uncertainty is high.
- A firm is less satisfied with its existing international channel if it is difficult to monitor the behaviour of channel members.[14]

Physical Distribution

Physical distribution involves the location, timing, and condition of deliveries. An **order cycle** covers many activities.

Physical distribution (also known as **logistics**) encompasses the broad range of activities concerned with efficiently delivering raw materials, parts, semifinished items, and finished products to designated places, at designated times, and in proper condition. It may be undertaken by any member of a channel, from producer to consumer.

Physical distribution involves such functions as customer service; shipping; warehousing; inventory control; private trucking-fleet operations; packaging; receiving; materials handling; and plant, warehouse, and store location planning. The physical distribution activities involved in a typical **order cycle**—the period of time from when the customer places an order to its receipt—are illustrated in Figure 15-6.

The Importance of Physical Distribution

Physical distribution is important for a number of reasons: its costs, the value of customer service, and its relationship with other functional areas.

Cost control is a major goal.

COSTS Physical distribution costs amount to 10 to 12 per cent of the Canadian GDP, with transportation (freight) and storage accounting for almost one-half of that total. To contain costs, firms have been working hard to improve efficiency. Today, physical distribution tasks are completed faster, more accurately, and with fewer people than twenty years ago. Due to computerization and improved transportation, firms have reduced their inventory levels by hundreds of millions of dollars, thus saving on warehousing and interest expenses.

Distribution costs vary widely by industry and company type. At individual firms, total physical distribution costs depend on such factors as the nature of the business, the geographic area covered, the tasks done by other channel members, and the weight/value

FIGURE 15-6
Selected Physical Distribution Activities Involved in a Typical Order Cycle

[14]Saul Klein and Victor J. Roth, "Satisfaction with International Marketing Channels," *Journal of the Academy of Marketing Science*, Vol. 21 (Winter 1993), pp. 39–44.

Table 15-4
Selected Symptoms of a Poor Physical Distribution System

SYMPTOM	COST RAMIFICATIONS
1. Slow-turning and/or too-high inventory	Excessive capital is tied up in inventory. The firm has high insurance costs, interest expenses, and high risks of pilferage and product obsolescence. Merchandise may be stale.
2. Inefficient customer service	Costs are high relative to the value of shipments; warehouses are poorly situated; inventory levels are not tied to customer demand.
3. A large number of interwarehouse shipments	Merchandise transfers raise physical distribution cost because items must be handled and verified at each warehouse.
4. Frequent use of emergency shipments	Extra charges add significantly to physical distribution costs.
5. Peripheral hauls and/or limited backhauling	The firm uses its own trucking facilities; but many hauls are too spread out and trucks may only be full one way.
6. A large number of small orders	Small orders often are unprofitable. Many distribution costs are fixed.

ratio of the items involved. For example, while many retailers spend 2 to 3 per cent of their revenues on transportation from vendors and receiving, marking, storing, and distributing goods, petroleum refiners spend almost one-quarter of their sales just on inbound and outbound transportation. And whenever Canada Post raises rates, shipping costs are dramatically affected for all kinds of firms.

Firms must identify the symptoms of poor distribution systems and strive to be more efficient. Up to one-fifth of the perishable items carried by Canadian grocers, like fish and dairy items, are lost to spoilage due to breakdowns in shipping or too much time on store shelves. To reduce losses, many grocers now insist on smaller, more frequent deliveries and have upgraded their storage facilities. Table 15-4 shows several cost ramifications of poor distribution.

CUSTOMER SERVICE A major concern in planning a firm's physical distribution program is the level of customer service it should provide. Decisions involve delivery frequency, speed, and consistency; emergency shipments; whether to accept small orders; warehousing; coordinating assortments; whether to provide order progress reports; and other factors. Weak performance may lose customers.

Accordingly, distribution standards—clear and measurable goals as to service levels in physical distribution—must be devised. Examples are filling 90 per cent of orders from existing inventory, responding to customer requests for order information within two hours, filling orders with 99 per cent accuracy, and limiting goods damaged in transit to 2 per cent or less.

One way to set the proper customer service level is the **total-cost approach**, whereby the distribution service level with the lowest total costs—including freight (shipping), warehousing, and lost business—is the best service level. An ideal system seeks a balance between low expenditures on distribution and high opportunities for sales. Seldom will that be at the lowest level of distribution spending; lost sales will be too great. Figure 15-7 illustrates the total-cost approach.

By offering superior customer service, a firm may establish a significant competitive advantage. The opposite is also true: "Customers increasingly demand on-time delivery from their suppliers. If they don't get it, they go elsewhere. The standard delivery window in supermarkets used to be four hours. Now, top suppliers deliver within an hour of their

*The **total-cost approach** considers both costs and opportunities.*

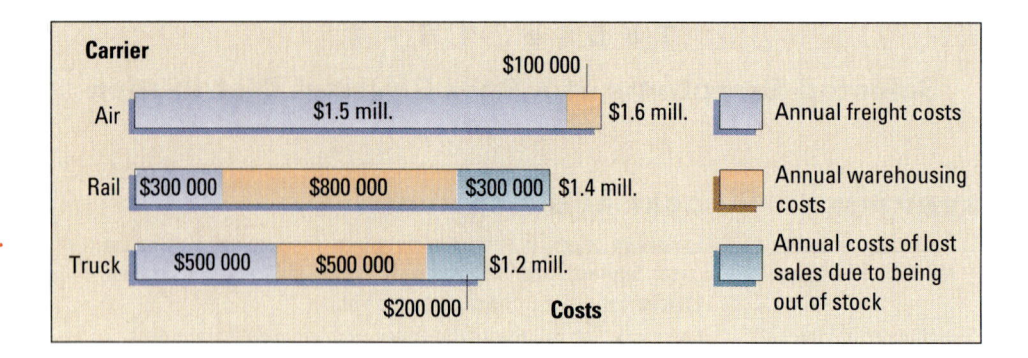

FIGURE 15-7
An Illustration of the Total-Cost Approach in Distribution

Carrier	Annual freight costs	Annual warehousing costs	Annual costs of lost sales due to being out of stock	Total
Air	$1.5 mill.	$100 000	—	$1.6 mill.
Rail	$300 000	$800 000	$300 000	$1.4 mill.
Truck	$500 000	$500 000	$200 000	$1.2 mill.

promised times, sometimes within fifteen minutes. The trend toward more reliable delivery times reaches across all industries."[15]

Physical distribution must be coordinated with other areas.

PHYSICAL DISTRIBUTION AND OTHER FUNCTIONAL AREAS There is an interaction between physical distribution and every aspect of marketing, as well as other functional areas in the firm, as the following indicate.

Product variations in colour, size, features, quality, and style impose a burden on a firm's distribution facilities. Greater variety means lower volume per item, which increases unit shipping and warehousing costs. Stocking a broader range of replacement parts also becomes necessary.

Physical distribution is related to an overall channel strategy. A firm seeking extensive distribution needs dispersed warehouses. One involved with perishables needs to be sure that most of a product's selling life is not spent in transit.

Because promotion campaigns are often planned well in advance, it is essential that distribution to resellers be done at the proper times to ensure ample stocks of goods. Resellers may get consumer complaints for not having sufficient quantities of the items they advertise, even if the manufacturer is at fault. Some new products fail due to poor initial distribution.

Physical distribution also plays a key part in pricing. A firm with fast, reliable delivery and an ample supply of replacement parts—that ships small orders and provides emergency shipments—may be able to charge higher prices than one providing less service.

A distribution strategy has a link with production and finance functions. High freight costs inspire firms to put plants closer to markets. Low average inventories in stock allow firms to reduce finance charges. Warehouse receipts may be used as collateral for loans.

Overall, there are many decisions to be made and coordinated in planning a physical distribution strategy: the transportation form(s) used, inventory levels and warehouse form(s), and the number and sites of plants, warehouses, and shopping facilities. A strategy can be simple: A firm can have one plant, focus on one geographic market, and ship to resellers or customers without the use of decentralized warehouses. On the other hand, a strategy can include multiple plants, assembly and/or warehouse locations in each market, thousands of customer locations, and several transportation forms.

The rest of this chapter looks at two central aspects of a physical distribution strategy: transportation and inventory management.

Transportation

Transportation is rated on speed, availability, dependability, capability, frequency, losses, and cost.

There are five basic transportation forms: railroads, motor carriers, waterways, pipelines, and airways. Table 15-5 ranks them on seven operating characteristics. Because the range of products that can be shipped by pipeline is so restricted, business firms typically ship products using one or a combination of railroads, motor carriers, waterways and airways. Table 15-6 shows the share of Canadian cargo tonnage and revenue for these four most commonly employed forms of transportation. Each transportation form and three transport services will now be presented.

---

[15] Anil Kumar and Graham Sharman, "We Love Your Product, But Where Is It?" *Sloan Management Review*, Vol. 33 (Winter 1992), p. 92. See also Ronald Henkoff, "Delivering the Goods," *Fortune* (November 28, 1994), pp. 64–78.

Table 15-5
The Relative Operating Characteristics of Five Transportation Forms

OPERATING CHARACTERISTICS	RANKING BY TRANSPORTATION FORM[a]				
	Railroads	Motor Carriers	Waterways	Pipelines	Airways
Delivery speed	3	2	5	4	1
Number of locations served	2	1	4	5	3
On-time dependability[b]	3	2	4	1	5
Range of products carried	1	2	3	5	4
Frequency of shipments	4	2	5	1	3
Losses and damages	5	4	2	1	3
Cost per tonne-mile	3	4	1	2	5

[a] 1 = highest ranking.
[b] Relative variation from anticipated delivery time.

Sources: Adapted by the authors from Donald J. Bowersox and David J. Closs, *Logistical Management: The Integrated Supply Chain Process* (New York: McGraw-Hill, 1996); Ronald H. Ballou, *Business Logistics Management: Planning and Control*, Third Edition (Englewood Cliffs, N.J.: Prentice Hall, 1992); and James C. Johnson and Donald F. Wood, *Contemporary Logistics*, Fourth Edition (New York: Macmillan, 1990).

Table 15-6
The Relative Share of Canadian Cargo Tonnage and Revenue by Transportation Form

TRANSPORTATION FORM	% SHARE OF TONNAGE SHIPPED	% SHARE OF SHIPPING REVENUE
Railroads	22.42	13.11
Motor carriers	47.58	73.35
Waterways	29.96	12.67
Airways	.04	00.87

Sources: Adapted by the authors from Bernd Zechel, "Transportation Industries—Overview," *Industry Canada, Strategis Web site* (1996), http://strategis.ic.gc.ca; Statistics Canada, "For-Hire Motor Carriers of Freight, All Carriers, First and Second Quarters 1995," *The Daily* (Thursday, June 6, 1996); Statistics Canada, "Port Activity 1995," *The Daily* (Thursday, June 4, 1996); "Air Canada Reports Record Operating Income for Second Consecutive Year, Earnings of $52 Million For 1995," *Canada NewsWire* (February 23, 1996), http://www.newswire.ca; and John Robert Colombo, *The 1996 Canadian Global Almanac* (Toronto:Macmillan Canada, 1996).

RAILROADS Railroads usually carry heavy, bulky items that are low in value (relative to weight) over long distances. They ship items too heavy for trucks. Canada has 146 444 km of railway connecting the nation from coast to coast. Because of the fact that Canada's economy is commodity-based, railways will always have a unique position as a transportation mode. Despite this, railroads have had various problems. Canadian Pacific lost $823 million in 1995 and Crown corporation Canadian National lost over $1 billion on their operations. Railway operations are risky because fixed costs are high due to investments in facilities. Shippers face rail car shortages in high-demand months for agricultural goods. Some tracks and rail cars are in serious need of repair. Trucks are faster, more flexible, and are more

Railroads *ship mostly heavy items over long distances.*

CANADIAN PACIFIC RAILWAYS
www.cprailways.com/

easily packed. In response to these problems, railroads are relying on new shipping techniques and operating flexibility to improve efficiency.[16]

Motor carriers *handle small shipments for short distances.*

MOTOR CARRIERS **Motor carriers** predominantly transport small shipments over short distances. They handle about 80 per cent of Canadian shipments weighing less than 500 kilograms. Seventy per cent of all motor carriers are used for local deliveries and two-thirds of total truck miles are local. For these reasons, motor carriers account for a large share of shipping revenue. Motor carriers are more flexible than rail because they can pick up packages at a factory or warehouse and deliver them to the customer's door. They are often used to supplement rail, air, and other forms of transportation that cannot deliver direct to customers. In addition, trucks are faster than rail for short distances. In Canada, statistics for for-hire motor carriers are reported by Statistics Canada but the majority of truck freight is hauled by private carriers (business firms have their own truck fleets which carry their own goods and raw materials). It is estimated that private motor carriers have an economic value of $20 billion per year and they carry 227 million tonnes of merchandise, compared to 173 million tonnes by for-hire carriers who take in about $13 billion in revenues. In the for-hire carrier motor transport segment, carriers had an operating ratio of .97 in 1995 (the ratio of operating expenses divided by revenues). A ratio of .95 is considered a sign of a healthy industry. Ratios near 1 indicate problems while ratios over 1 mean the industry is losing money.[17]

Waterways *specialize in low-value, high-bulk items.*

WATERWAYS In Canada, **waterways** involve the movement of goods on barges via inland rivers and on tankers and general-merchandise freighters through the Great Lakes, intercoastal shipping, and the St. Lawrence Seaway. They are used primarily for transporting low-value, high-bulk freight (such as coal, iron ore, gravel, grain, and cement). Waterways are slow, and may be closed by ice in winter, but rates are quite low. Various improvements in vessel design have occurred over the last several years. For example, many "supervessels" now operate on the Great Lakes and other waterways. Their conveyor systems are twice as efficient as the ones on older boats. Navigation is computer-controlled.

In 1995 Canada's 200 ports handled a total of 360.8 million tonnes of goods (259.8 million tonnes of foreign goods and 101 million tonnes of domestic goods), the most tonnage on record. Canada's ports employ 30 000 people. The busiest port is Vancouver, which handled about 26 per cent of all the foreign tonnage.[18]

Pipelines *centre on liquids, gases, and semiliquids.*

PIPELINES Within **pipelines**, there is continuous movement and there are no interruptions, inventories (except those held by a carrier), and intermediate storage sites. Handling and labour costs are minimized. Although pipelines are very reliable, only certain commodities can be moved through them. In the past, emphasis was on gas and petroleum-based products. Pipelines have now been modified to accept coal and wood chips, which are sent as semiliquids. Still, the lack of flexibility limits their potential. Some pipelines carry enormous volumes of products. For example, TransCanada Pipelines is a leading transporter of natural gas in North America. In the first three months of 1996, its main line in Canada delivered 651 billion cubic feet (166 billion cubic metres) of natural gas. In addition, TransCanada moved 28.4 million barrels of crude oil through its oil pipeline holdings in the first three months of 1996.[19]

Airways *handle valuable, perishable, and emergency items.*

AIRWAYS **Airways** are the fastest, most expensive transportation form. High-value, perishable, and emergency goods dominate air shipments. For example, flowers from the Caribbean can be flown north to Canada during the winter; electronics parts and emergency repair items or high-fashion clothing items might also be shipped airfreight. Although air transit is costly, it may lower other costs, such as the need for outlying or even

---

[16]John Robert Colombo, *The 1996 Canadian Global Almanac* (Toronto:Macmillan Canada, 1996); and Performance 500, "Biggest Money Losers," *Canadian Business* (June 1996), p. 151.

[17]Bernd Zechel, "Transportation Industries: Overview," Industry Canada, *Strategis* Web site (1996); and Statistics Canada, "For-Hire Motor Carriers of Freight, All Carriers, First and Second Quarters 1995," *The Daily* (Thursday, June 6, 1996).

[18]Statistics Canada, "Port Activity 1995," *The Daily* (Thursday, June 4, 1996).

[19]"TransCanada Earnings Rise in First Quarter 1996," *Canada NewsWire* (April 23, 1996), http://www.newswire.ca.

TECHNOLOGY & MARKETING

How Are Carriers Weblike in Tracking Shipments?

According to experts, the role of the Internet has gone from being a library of data (phase one) to a provider of important customer services (phase two). In its third phase, the Internet will enable customers to better handle financial transactions. Evidence of the transition from phase one to phase two is the use of the Internet's World Wide Web by business customers to track packages shipped by Federal Express and United Parcel Service (UPS).

Since November 1994, all Federal Express customers have been able to log on to the FedEx home page on the World Wide Web and enter their bill-tracking numbers into online package-tracking forms. Within minutes, the Internet server connects with Federal Express' main computer and returns reports to customers on the locations of their packages. As packages move through the FedEx distribution system, the data passed on to clients are constantly updated by Federal Express personnel.

Although Federal Express had to design special software and contract with an Internet provider, the overall costs of implementing its system have been very low. In addition, the FedEx site—which receives over 4500 inquiries per day—saves money for the firm by reducing the need for customer service personnel. All customers have access to this Internet-based service, but larger ones can also access the firm's private network. According to a Federal Express spokesperson, 60 per cent of all package tracking is now done through automated procedures.

Likewise, UPS has begun to offer package tracking on the Internet. As with Federal Express, UPS's site was not started to save money for the firm, but is less costly than other package tracking methods.

As a customer service supervisor for Federal Express, outline the pros and cons of using the World Wide Web to automate package tracking.

Source: Based on material in Laurie Flynn, "Companies Use Web Hoping to Save Millions," *New York Times* (July 17, 1995), p. D5.

---

regional warehouses. The costs of packing, unpacking, and preparing goods for shipment are lower than for other transportation forms. Modern communications and sorting equipment have also been added to airfreight operations to improve their efficiency. Firms specializing in air shipments have done well by stressing speedy, guaranteed service at acceptable prices. In 1994, Canadian Airlines transported 395 000 tonnes of goods. However, in terms of volume, air freight represents a minuscule amount of goods shipped.[20]

TRANSPORTATION SERVICES Transportation service companies are marketing specialists that chiefly handle the shipments of small and moderate-sized packages. Some pick up at the sender's office and deliver direct to the addressee. Others require packages to be brought to a service company outlet. The major kinds of transportation service firms are parcel post (Canada Post's service), private parcel, and express.

Canada Post's parcel post service operates out of post offices and has rates based on shipping weight and distance shipped. Parcel post can be insured or sent COD (collect on delivery). Regular service is completed in a few days. Special handling is available to expedite shipments. Priority Post mail is available at post offices for next-day service between major Canadian cities.

Private parcel services specialize in small-package delivery, usually less than twenty-kilogram shipments. Most shipments go from businesses to their customers. Regular ser-

CANADIAN AIRLINES INTERNATIONAL
www.cdnair.ca/

These transportation service companies ship packages: government parcel post, private parcel, and express.

---

[20]Colombo, *The 1996 Canadian Global Almanac.*

FIGURE 15-8
1-800-PICK-UPS
Reprinted by permission

PUROLATOR COURIER LTD.
www.purolator.com/

Containerization and freight forwarding simplify intermodal shipping.

vice usually takes two to three days. More expensive next-day service is also available from many carriers. The largest private firm is United Parcel Service (UPS), a multibillion-dollar, international company. See Figure 15-8.

Specialized express companies, such as Federal Express and Purolator (majority-owned by Canada Post), typically provide guaranteed nationwide delivery of small packages for the morning after pickup. The average express delivery is under four kilograms.

COORDINATING TRANSPORTATION Because a single shipment may involve a combination of transportation forms—a practice known as *intermodal shipping*—coordination is needed. A firm can enhance its ability to coordinate shipments by using containerization and freight forwarding.

With **containerization**, goods are placed in sturdy containers that can be loaded on trains, trucks, ships, or planes. The marked containers are sealed until delivered, thereby reducing damage and pilferage. Their progress and destination are monitored. The containers are mobile warehouses that can be moved from manufacturing plants to receiving docks, where they remain until the contents are needed.

In **freight forwarding**, specialized firms (freight forwarders) collect small shipments (usually less than 200 kilograms each) from several companies. They pick up merchandise at each shipper's place of business and arrange for delivery at buyers' doors. Freight forwarders prosper because less-than-carload (lcl) shipping rates are sharply higher than carload (cl) rates. They also provide traffic management services, such as selecting the best transportation form at the most reasonable rate.

Inventory Management

Inventory management deals with the flow and allocation of products.

The intent of **inventory management** is to provide a continuous flow of goods and to match the quantity of goods kept in inventory as closely as possible with customer demand. When production or consumption is seasonal or erratic, this can be particularly difficult.

Inventory management has broad implications: A manufacturer or service firm cannot afford to run out of a crucial part that could put a halt to its business. Yet inventory on hand should not be too large because the costs of storing raw materials, parts, and/or finished products can be substantial. If models change yearly, as with autos, large inventories can adversely affect new-product sales or rentals. Excessive stock may also lead to stale goods, cause a firm to mark down prices, and tie up funds.

To improve their inventory management, a lot of companies are now applying either or both of two complementary concepts: a just-in-time inventory system and electronic data interchange. With a **just-in-time (JIT) inventory system**, a purchasing firm reduces the amount of inventory it keeps on hand by ordering more often and in lower quantity. This requires better planning and information on the part of the purchaser, geographically closer sellers, improved buyer-seller relationships, and better production and distribution facilities. To retailers, a JIT system is known as a **quick response (QR) inventory system**—a cooperative effort between retailers and suppliers to reduce retail inventory while providing a merchandise supply that more closely addresses the actual buying patterns of consumers.[21]

JIT and QR inventory systems closely monitor inventory levels.

JIT and QR systems are being used by auto makers, Hewlett-Packard, Canon, DuPont, Ryder, Whirlpool, Levi Strauss, Wal-Mart, Motorola, General Electric, Deere, Black & Decker, Boeing, and many other large and small firms. For example, Raymond Industrial Equipment, a forklift truck manufacturer in Brantford, Ontario, implemented a JIT system to replace their batch production system. They benefited by reducing their inventory by 60 per cent, they released warehouse space and they reduced the manufacturing time to make a forklift truck from fifteen days to only four.[22]

Through **electronic data interchange (EDI)**, suppliers and their manufacturers/service providers, wholesalers, and/or retailers exchange data through computer linkups. This lets firms maximize revenues, reduce markdowns, and lower inventory carrying costs by speeding the flow of data and products. For EDI to work well, each firm in a distribution channel must use the Universal Product Code (UPC) and electronically exchange data. Although all major food makers use the UPC, many makers of general merchandise do not. However, the number of general merchandise manufacturers using the UPC on their products has been rising; and more will begin using the UPC in the near future.

With EDI, computers are used to exchange information between suppliers and their customers.

Four specific aspects of inventory management are examined next: stock turnover, when to reorder, how much to reorder, and warehousing.

STOCK TURNOVER **Stock turnover**—the number of times during a stated period (usually one year) that average inventory on hand is sold—shows the relationship between a firm's sales and the inventory level it maintains. It is calculated in units or dollars (in selling price or at cost):

Stock turnover shows the ratio between sales and average inventory.

$$\text{Annual rate of stock turnover} = \frac{\text{Number of units sold during year}}{\text{Average inventory on hand (in units)}}$$

$$\text{or}$$

$$= \frac{\text{Net yearly sales}}{\text{Average inventory on hand (valued in sales dollars)}}$$

$$\text{or}$$

$$= \frac{\text{Cost of goods sold}}{\text{Average inventory on hand (valued at cost)}}$$

---

[21] See Jitendra Chhikara and Elliott N. Weiss, "JIT Savings—Myth or Reality?" *Business Horizons*, Vol. 38 (May–June 1995), pp. 73–78; Susan R. Helper and Mari Sako, "Supplier Relations in Japan and the United States: Are They Converging?" *Sloan Management Review*, Vol. 36 (Spring 1995), pp. 77–84; Lisa Phillips and Cornelia Dröge, "Quick Response: A Theoretical Framework" in David W. Stewart and Naufel J. Vilcassim (Eds.), *1995 AMA Winter Educators' Proceedings* (Chicago: American Marketing Association, 1995), pp. 295–302; Paul F. Christ and Jack Gault, "The Benefits, Costs, and Strategic Implications of Quick Response Systems" in Barbara B. Stern and George M. Zinkham (Eds.), *1995 AMA Educators' Proceedings* (Chicago: American Marketing Association, 1995), pp. 485–491; and "The Next Industrial Revolution: Canada's Manufacturers Are Hard at Work Turning Today's Factories Into Tomorrow's Success Stories," *Canadian Business* (June, 1992), pp. 96–101.

[22] Marcia Berss, "Watizzit?" *Forbes* (August 28, 1995), p. 100.

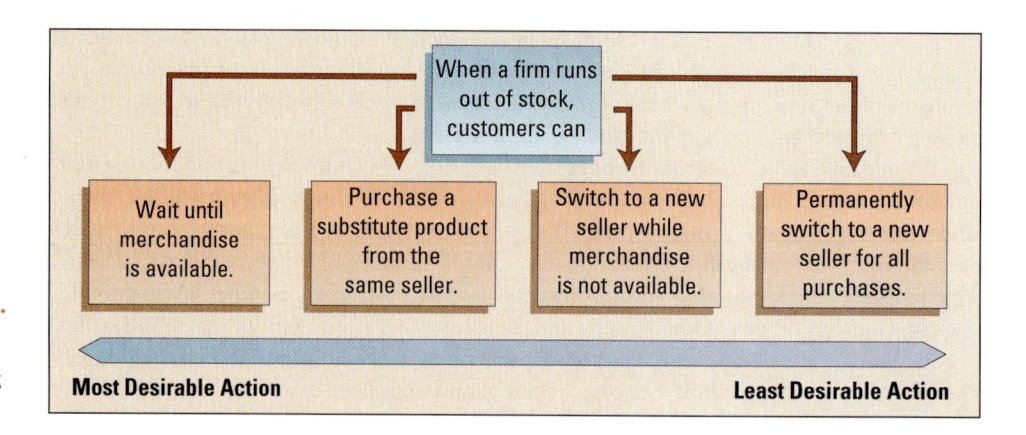

FIGURE 15-9
What Happens When a Firm Has Stock Shortages

When a firm runs out of stock, customers can:
- Wait until merchandise is available.
- Purchase a substitute product from the same seller.
- Switch to a new seller while merchandise is not available.
- Permanently switch to a new seller for all purchases.

Most Desirable Action ⟶ Least Desirable Action

For example, in retailing, average annual stock turnover ranges from less than three in jewellery stores to more than thirty in gasoline service stations.

A high stock turnover rate has many advantages: inventory investments are productive, items are fresh, losses from style changes are reduced, and inventory costs (such as insurance, breakage, warehousing, and credit) are lower. Turnover can be improved by reducing assortments, dropping slow-selling items, keeping only small amounts of some items, and buying from suppliers that deliver on time. On the other hand, too high a turnover rate may have adverse effects: small purchases may cause a loss of volume discounts, low product assortment may reduce sales volume if consumers do not have enough choice or related items are not carried, discounts may be needed to lift sales volume, and chances of running out of stock go up when average inventory size is low. Figure 15-9 shows how people can act should a firm run out of stock.

Knowing when to reorder merchandise helps protect against stockouts while minimizing inventory investments.

The **reorder point** *is based on lead time, usage, and safety stock.*

WHEN TO REORDER INVENTORY By having a clear reorder point for each of its products (or raw materials or parts), a firm sets the inventory levels for new orders. A reorder point depends on order lead time, the usage rate, and safety stock. Order lead time is the period from the date an order is placed until the date items are ready to sell or use (received, checked, and altered, if needed). Usage rate is the average unit sales (for a reseller) or the rate at which a product is used in production (for a manufacturer). Safety stock is extra inventory kept to guard against being out of stock due to unexpectedly high demand or production and delivery delays.

The reorder point formula is:

Reorder point = (Order lead time x Usage rate) + (Safety stock).

For instance, a wholesaler that needs four days for its purchase orders to be placed and received, sells ten items per day, and wants to have ten extra items on hand in case of a supplier's delivery delay of one day, has a reorder point of fifty [(4 x 10) + (10)]. Without safety stock, the firm would lose ten sales if it orders when inventory is forty items and the items are received in five days.

HOW MUCH TO REORDER A firm must decide its order size—the right amount of products, parts, and so on, to buy at one time. Order size depends on volume discounts, the firm's resources, the stock turnover rate, the costs of processing each order, and the costs of holding goods in inventory. If a firm places large orders, quantity discounts are usually available, a large part of its finances are tied up in inventory, its stock turnover rate is relatively low, per-order processing costs are low, and inventory costs are generally high. The firm is also less apt to run out of goods. The opposite is true for small orders.

EOQ *balances ordering and inventory costs.*

Many companies seek to balance their order-processing costs (filling out forms, computer time, and product handling) and their inventory-holding costs (warehouse expenses, interest charges, insurance, deterioration, and theft). Processing costs per unit fall as orders get bigger, but inventory costs rise. The **economic order quantity (EOQ)** is the order volume corresponding to the lowest sum of order-processing and inventory-holding costs.

Table 15-7

Computing an Economic Order Quantity

A.

AVERAGE ORDER QUANTITY (UNITS)	INVENTORY MAINTAINED (UNITS)[a]	ANNUAL INVENTORY-HOLDING COSTS[b]	ANNUAL ORDER-PROCESSING COSTS[c]	ANNUAL TOTAL COSTS
100	50	$10	$90	$100
200	100	20	45	65
EOQ → 300	150	30	30	60
400	200	40	24	64
500	250	50	18	68

B.

[Graph showing Total costs, Holding costs, and Order-processing costs plotted against Order quantity (Units) from 100 to 500, with EOQ arrow pointing to 300.]

C.

$$EOQ = \sqrt{\frac{2DS}{IC}} = \sqrt{\frac{2(3{,}000)(\$3)}{0.20(\$1)}} = 300$$

where EOQ = Order quantity (units)
D = Annual demand (units)
S = Costs to place an order ($)

I = Annual holding costs (as a % of unit costs)
C = Unit cost of an item ($)

[a] The average inventory on hand = ½ × Order quantity.

[b] Inventory-holding costs = Annual holding costs as a per cent of unit cost × Unit cost × Average inventory.

[c] Order-processing costs = Number of annual orders × Costs to place an order. Number of orders = Annual demand/Order quantity.

Table 15-7 demonstrates three ways to compute EOQ. In this illustration, a firm has an annual demand of 3000 units for a product; the cost of each unit is $1; order-processing costs are $3 per order; and inventory-holding costs equal 20 per cent of each item's cost. As shown in the table, the economic order quantity is 300 units. Thus, the firm should place orders of 300 units and have 10 orders per year.

WAREHOUSING Warehousing involves the physical facilities used to store, identify, and sort goods in expectation of their sale and transfer within a distribution channel. Warehouses can be used to store goods, prepare goods for shipment, coordinate shipments, send orders, and aid in product recalls.

Private warehouses are owned and operated by firms that store and distribute their own products. They are most likely to be used by those with stable inventory levels and long-run plans to serve the same geographic areas.

Public warehouses provide storage and related distribution services to any interested firm or individual on a rental basis. They are used by small firms that do not have the resources or desire to have their own facilities, larger firms that need more storage space (because their own warehouses are full), or any size of firm entering new geographic areas. Public warehouses offer shipping economies for users by receiving carload shipments from factories or distribution centres; and then allowing short-distance, smaller shipments to be made from these warehouses to customers. Firms can also reduce their investments in facilities and maximize flexi-

Warehousing involves storing and dispatching goods.

bility by using public warehouses. If products must be recalled, these warehouses can be used as collection points, where items are separated, disposed of, and/or salvaged. There are hundreds of public warehouses in Canada.

Public warehouses can accommodate both bonded warehousing and field warehousing. In bonded warehousing, imported or taxable goods are stored and can be released for sale only after applicable taxes are paid. This enables firms to postpone tax payments until they are ready to make deliveries to customers. Cigarettes and liquor are often stored in bonded warehouses. In field warehousing, a receipt is issued by a public warehouse for goods stored in a private warehouse or in transit to consumers. The goods are put in a special area, and the field warehouser is responsible for them. A firm may use field warehousing because a warehouse receipt serves as collateral for a loan.

MARKETING IN A CHANGING WORLD
Being Aware of the Problem of Export Diversion[23]

As companies expand globally, they face a greater chance of dealing with unscrupulous foreign distributors. Why? There are two major reasons: One, it is difficult to do the proper background checks on such distributors—and less is known about them than about domestic distributors. Two, it is hard to monitor distributor performance in distant markets.

A particularly troublesome distribution practice for North American manufacturers is known as "export diversion." This hypothetical example shows how it works:

1. A North American manufacturer sells 100 000 widgets to Europe-based ABC Distributors for $10 each (half the wholesale price) so as to gain access to Kazakhstan.
2. The manufacturer ships the widgets to Rotterdam, while ABC secretly pre-sells them to Canadian or U.S. supermarket chains and wholesalers for $15 apiece. In Rotterdam, the widgets are repackaged and sent back to Canada or the U.S. duty-free as "goods returned."
3. ABC earns $500 000—the difference between the manufacturer's export price and the price paid by the Canadian or U.S. supermarkets and wholesalers.
4. The returned widgets are sold in North America, and the manufacturer cannot understand why some of its supermarket customers are no longer buying from it.

Johnson & Johnson, a very sophisticated U.S.-based manufacturer, recently learned that export diversion is not just "hypothetical":

> It seemed like the perfect opportunity to break into an important emerging market. At least that's what LifeScan Inc., a Johnson & Johnson subsidiary, thought when it agreed to sell U.S.$400 000 worth of glucose test strips at half its wholesale price. The buyer, Swiss-based Anglo-American Foundation, promised to distribute LifeScan's devices to needy diabetics in the former Soviet Union. But the deal was costly—particularly when LifeScan discovered that its strips never even left U.S. shores. Instead, they allegedly were diverted by Anglo-American to a New Jersey warehouse and then resold to local wholesalers for a tidy profit.

Because of export diversion, international companies now have one more illegal and unethical business practice to worry about—and to police.

[23] The material in this section is based on Amy Borrus, "Exports That Aren't Going Anywhere," *Business Week* (December 4, 1995), pp. 121, 124.

SUMMARY

1. *To define distribution planning and to examine its importance, distribution functions, the factors used in selecting a distribution channel, and the different types of distribution channels* Distribution planning is systematic decision making as to the physical movement of goods and services from producer to consumer, as well as the related transfer of ownership (or rental). A channel of distribution consists of the organizations or people—known as channel members or distribution intermediaries—involved in the distribution process.

Distribution decisions often affect a firm's marketing plans. For many firms, the choice of a distribution channel is one of the most important decisions they make. More companies now realize the value of relationship marketing and work for long-term relations with suppliers, intermediaries, and customers. Both costs and profits are affected by the channel chosen. Firms may have to conform to existing channel patterns; and their markets' size and nature are also influenced by the channel employed.

No matter who does them, channel functions include research, buying, promotion, customer services, product planning, pricing, and distribution. Intermediaries can play a key role by doing various tasks and resolving differences in manufacturer and consumer goals through the sorting process.

In selecting a method of distribution, these factors must be considered: the consumer, the company, the product, the competition, the distribution channels themselves, and legal requirements.

A direct channel requires that one party do all distribution tasks; in an indirect channel, tasks are done by multiple parties. In comparing methods, a firm must weigh its costs and abilities against control and total sales. An indirect channel may use a contractual or an administered agreement. A long channel has many levels of independent firms; a wide one has many firms at any stage. A channel may be exclusive, selective, or intensive, based on company goals, resellers, customers, and marketing. A dual channel lets a company use two or more distribution methods.

2. *To describe the nature of supplier/distribution intermediary contracts, and cooperation and conflict in a channel of distribution* In contracts between suppliers and distribution intermediaries, price policies, sale conditions, territorial rights, the services/responsibility mix, and contract length and termination conditions are specified.

Cooperation and conflict may both occur in a distribution channel. Conflicts must be settled fairly because confrontation can cause hostility and negative acts by all parties. Frequently, a pushing strategy—based on channel cooperation—can be employed by established firms. But a pulling strategy—based on proving that consumer demand exists prior to gaining intermediary support or acceptance—must be used by many new companies.

3. *To examine the special aspects relating to a distribution channel for industrial products and to international distribution* An industrial channel normally does not use retailers; it is more direct, entails fewer transactions and larger orders, requires specification selling and knowing resellers, uses team selling and special intermediaries, includes more leasing, provides more technical data, and embraces shared activities.

Channel length depends on a nation's stage of economic development and consumer behaviour. Distribution practices and structures differ by nation. International decisions must be made as to shipping and intermediaries. Each country has distinct legal provisions pertaining to distribution.

4. *To define physical distribution and to demonstrate its importance* Physical distribution (logistics) involves efficiently delivering products to designated places, at designated times, and in proper condition. It may be undertaken by any member of a channel, from producer to consumer.

There are various reasons for studying physical distribution: its costs, the value of customer service, and its relationship with other functional areas in a firm. With the total-cost approach, the service level with the lowest total cost (including freight, warehousing, and lost business) is the best one. In a physical distribution strategy, decisions are made as to transportation, inventory levels, warehousing, and facility locations.

5. *To discuss transportation alternatives and inventory management issues* Railroads typically carry bulky goods for long distances. Motor carriers dominate small shipments over short distances. Waterways primarily ship low-value freight. Pipelines provide ongoing movement of liquid, gaseous, and semiliquid products. Airways offer fast, expensive movement of perishables and high-value items. Transportation service firms are specialists that mostly handle small and medium-sized packages. Coordination can be improved through containerization and freight forwarding.

Inventory management is needed to provide a continuous flow of goods and to match the stock kept in inventory as closely as possible with demand. In a JIT or QR system, the purchasing firm reduces the stock it keeps on hand by ordering more often and in lower quantity. With electronic data interchange, channel members exchange information via computer linkages.

The interplay between a firm's sales and the inventory level it keeps is expressed by its stock turnover. A reorder point shows the inventory level when goods must be reordered. The economic order quantity is the optimal amount of goods to order based on order-processing and inventory-holding costs. Warehousing decisions include selecting a private or public warehouse and examining the availability of public warehouse services.

KEY TERMS

distribution planning (p. 407)
channel of distribution (p. 407)
channel members (p. 407)
distribution intermediaries (p. 407)
channel functions (p. 412)
sorting process (p. 412)
direct channel of distribution (p. 413)
indirect channel of distribution (p. 413)
channel length (p. 413)
channel width (p. 415)
exclusive distribution (p. 415)
selective distribution (p. 415)

intensive distribution (p. 415)
dual channel of distribution (p. 417)
pushing strategy (p. 419)
pulling strategy (p. 419)
physical distribution (logistics) (p. 422)
order cycle (p. 422)
total-cost approach (p. 423)
railroads (p. 425)
motor carriers (p. 426)
waterways (p. 426)
pipelines (p. 426)

airways (p. 426)
containerization (p. 428)
freight forwarding (p. 428)
inventory management (p. 428)
just-in-time (JIT) inventory system (p. 429)
quick response (QR) inventory system (p. 429)
electronic data interchange (EDI) (p. 429)
stock turnover (p. 429)
reorder point (p. 430)
economic order quantity (EOQ) (p. 430)
warehousing (p. 431)

Review Questions

1. What is relationship marketing?
2. Explain the sorting process. Provide an example in your answer.
3. Which factors influence the selection of a distribution channel?
4. Under what circumstances should a company engage in direct distribution? Indirect distribution?
5. What is meant by a short, narrow channel of distribution?
6. Explain how a product could move from exclusive to selective to intensive distribution.
7. Compare motor carrier and waterway deliveries on the basis of the total-cost approach.
8. The average stock turnover rate in jewellery stores is less than three. What does this mean? How could a jewellery store raise its turnover rate?
9. Two wholesalers sell identical merchandise. Yet, one plans a safety stock equal to 20 per cent of expected sales, while the other plans no safety stock. Comment on this difference.
10. Why would a firm use both private and public warehouses?

Discussion Questions

1. What distribution decisions would a new firm that rents vans to small, seasonal businesses have to make?
2. Devise distribution channels for the sale of a daily newspaper, pianos, and cellular phones. Explain your choices.
3. Present a checklist that a firm could use in making international distribution decisions on a country-by-country basis.
4. Develop a list of distribution standards for a firm delivering fresh fruit to supermarkets.
5. Are there any disadvantages to a JIT or QR system? Explain your answer.

VIDEO CASE

Physical Distribution at Vancouver's Port

Efficient physical distribution of goods and services is one of the keys to success in international trade. This must be combined with some type of comparative advantage or absolute advantage in production of goods to enable a nation to trade effectively and not run a trade deficit. As a nation, Canada had a merchandise trade surplus of $11 billion in 1994. The majority of the natural resources exported from Canada now go through the port of Vancouver since there has been tremendous growth in international trade with Pacific Rim nations while trade with European nations has been declining.

The port of Vancouver is one of the busiest ports in North America, and the busiest in Canada. It is a virtual hub of intermodal transportation activity.

The logistical activities associated with visiting ships gives a perspective on the activities that go on in Vancouver's port. For example, the Saga Spray is a Norwegian-owned vessel that was constructed at a cost of U.S.$70 million in Japan. This ship was built for one purpose, to carry wood and wood pulp products. The vessel is self-loading and unloading with its own roofed, double gantry system. Because the operating/depreciation costs for this vessel are approximately US$30 000 a day, the owners do not like it to stand awaiting either loading or unloading for very long. However, the labour agreement associated with the Port of Vancouver requires that only Port of Vancouver teamster union workers be involved in the loading and unloading work. This can present some problems if a crew of teamsters fails to show up for work, something the Saga Spray experienced during one trip to Vancouver.

In contrast, the vessel Golden Empire is a much older general freight vessel planning to take on a cargo of grain for Mexico. The daily cost for this vessel is only $10 000 a day. The crew is from Greece and, like the Saga Spray, the captain is anxious to have as fast a loading and unloading process as possible. However, the Golden Empire is not a self-loading vessel and must depend on the facilities of Vancouver's port. With respect to grain loading, rainy weather can present a major problem when loading grain. Moisture can cause germination of the grain in the hold of a ship, which effectively ruins the entire cargo. Therefore, during loading, the hold must be covered to keep moisture out of the grain cargo. This requires rigging up tarpaulins and creates delays in ship loading, which of course costs the ship owners more money.

A second logistical matter for the ships is the matter of provisions for the vessel and crew. On the high seas, a ship cannot stop for food and fuel as trucks are able to do with ease on the highway. Arya Marine is a $15 million/year ship stocking company that provides provisions to ships in Vancouver. Ship schedules are constantly changing and this means that Arya must handle the provisions quickly and carefully so they do not spoil and waste before being loaded onto a ship. Furthermore, the provisions must arrive on time so that they can be loaded before a ship has to depart port. For example, the Saga Spray ordered bread and chicken burgers as part of their provision order. Ship chandler Nick Jacic was able to load the bread, but the chicken burger order arrived after the vessel had sailed. Although changing schedules and hurried deadlines are a problem for Arya Marine, its customers do pay in cash. This is a tremendous business advantage because Arya Marine's suppliers likely wait for their payments. For example, Arya Marine was paid U.S.$10 000 by the Saga Spray, even without the chicken burgers.

QUESTIONS

1. Define the term *multi-modal* and discuss it with respect to the operations of Vancouver's Port.
2. If you were the owner of the Saga Spray ship, estimate the total "shipping" fees you would have to charge per trip to make owning this ship "reasonably profitable" on an annual basis, considering operating costs, frequency of visits, building costs, and competition.
3. Compare the advantages and disadvantages of owning a specialized ship like the Saga Spray versus a general freighter like the Golden Empire.
4. Identify as many logistical problems as you can that were presented in this case. Categorize these problems into two types: facility related and non-facility related. Suggest some potential solutions for one facility related problem and one non-facility related problem.

VIDEO QUESTIONS ON VANCOUVER'S PORT

1. Identify as many of the "named" people as possible who were working in physical distribution and describe the kind of work they were doing and their job titles. For at least three of these people, speculate on what type of educational background a person would have to have to qualify for their job.
2. Look at Table 15-5, the comparison of transportation modes. Discuss how this video has reinforced, refuted, or did not address these comparisons. How would you evaluate the overall rating of ships as a mode of transportation based on the information in this video?

Video Source: "Vancouver Port," *Venture* (August 6, 1995).
Other Sources: Statistics Canada, "Port Activity 1995," *The Daily* (June 4, 1996), www.statcan.ca; Statistics Canada, *Market Research Handbook 1995*.

CASE STUDY
CSX: An Intermodal Shipping Strategy

CSX Corporation is a diversified international transportation company that offers a variety of container shipping, intermodal shipping (ship to truck to train), waterway barging, and distribution services. The firm has annual revenues of U.S.$10 billion and an operating income of U.S.$1.2 billion.

CSX Corporation operates CSX, North America's largest railroad in terms of revenues. CSX has a 30 046-kilometre rail system that links twenty states in the eastern, midwestern, and southern United States and Ontario. The firm also operates American Commercial Lines (a leading inland barge line), Sea-Land Service (the largest U.S. flag container shipping company), and CSX Intermodal Inc. (CSXI), which is the only full-service coast-to-coast intermodal transportation company in the U.S.

All of CSX Corporation's units are involved with containerization and intermodal shipping. Among the types of intermodal transportation offered are fishyback (waterways and motor carriers), piggyback (rail and motor carriers), COFC (container on flat cars), rail–water, airtruck, and trainship. For example, Sea-Land owns ninety-three container ships (and about 188 000 containers) that serve 120 ports in eighty nations and territories. It features the world's largest container fleet, with standard-sized twenty-foot and forty-foot containers, as well as forty-five-foot containers, refrigerated containers, specialized containers (that house garments on hangers), and open-top containers for oversized loads.

A major advantage of intermodal transportation is that it enables the most efficient transportation mode to be used for each part of an overall transportation system. For instance, using piggyback, a firm could combine the advantages of the low-cost operations of a railroad with the flexibility (in terms of the number of pickup and delivery locations served) of a motor carrier. In addition, containerization also reduces pilferage, allows loading and unloading to be automated, and reduces handling and storage costs at terminals. As a result of these benefits, demand for piggybacking services is increasing. An Association of American Railroads study found that a record 7 million trailers and their containers now "hitch a ride" on U.S. railroads. And 90 per cent of intermodal piggyback services are from five firms: CSX, Conrail, Union Pacific, Santa Fe, and Norfolk Southern.

One major drawback in using piggyback-based intermodal transportation is that there are wide swings between peak and minimum demand for containers and their trailers. Because a new container costs an average of U.S.$10 400 and the trailer costs an additional U.S.$8000, most shipping firms cannot afford to have enough containers and trailers to accommodate peak demand—since this would result in idle equipment during periods of slow demand.

One way to facilitate the use of containers is to boost the container turnover rate. A recent study tracked the percentage of a container's turnaround time accounted for by activity: in-transit (29 per cent), delivery (23 per cent), awaiting dispatch (18 per cent), destination awaiting delivery (13 per cent), pickup (11 per cent), loading (4 per cent), and out of service (2 per cent). To reduce nonproductive container time, some firms are providing an incentive to truckers who turn in containers prior to the posted deadline. In addition, all carriers charge truckers a penalty if they turn in containers late.

CSX Intermodal has increased its supply of containers by privatizing (owning) its trailer fleet. Privatizing ensures that the newest and best parts of CSX's fleet will be available to its own customers.

QUESTIONS
1. Discuss the pros and cons of an intermodal transportation system.
2. Explain how container usage facilitates inventory management.
3. How can freight forwarders utilize intermodal transportation through containerization?
4. Describe other measures that can be used by CSX Corporation to increase the turnover rate of containers.

CSX TRANSPORTATION INC.
www.csxt.com/

Source: The data in this case are drawn from "Balancing Supply and Demand," *Distribution* (January 1995), p. 18; "Capacity Dampens Intermodal Growth," *Distribution* (February 1994), p. 14; *CSX Corporation 1994 Annual Report and Form 10-K*; and Gregory D. L. Morris, "CSX Practices the Art of Tracking," *Chemical Week* (May 4, 1994), p. 34.

CHAPTER 16
Wholesaling

Chapter Objectives

1. To define wholesaling and show its importance

2. To describe the three broad categories of wholesaling (manufacturer/service provider wholesaling, merchant wholesaling, and agents and brokers) and the specific types of firms within each category

3. To examine recent trends in wholesaling

{ *Retailers often advertise their low prices to customers with the statement, "We've eliminated the middleman and that's why our prices are low." The "middleman" that is being referred to is usually some type of wholesaler. One organization that does not want to see the middleman eliminated is the International Federation of Pharmaceutical Wholesalers (IFPW), a global organization designed to represent and advance the global institution of pharmaceutical wholesaling.* }

INTERNATIONAL FEDERATION OF PHARMACEUTICAL WHOLESALERS

Reprinted with permission of International Federation of Pharmaceutical Wholesalers.

IFPW is very interested in the commercial and professional relationships that wholesalers have with manufacturers, pharmacies, hospitals, and any other health professionals involved in the distribution and sale of pharmaceuticals. The need for a global pharmaceutical wholesale organization exists because the channel power of pharmaceutical wholesalers has been eroded by a shift in how pharmaceutical products are distributed. Independent pharmacies are using computer technology to deal directly with pharmaceutical manufacturers, often bypassing wholesalers. Through the IFPW, pharmaceutical wholesalers are trying to redefine their role and work to maintain their position as members of the channel of distribution for pharmaceuticals.

One of the key undertakings of the IFPW is to keep an eye on the industry and on the role of their institution in the industry. As such, they have undertaken a number of initiatives to understand their role in the channel of distribution and to be proactive in making and adjusting to changes brought about by market forces. The IFPW understands that goods have their greatest value when they are close to the point of sale and that these goods gain value as they approach this point. As such, wholesalers have been moving closer to customers. The IFPW also understands that wholesaling is a very low profit-margin business (from 1.5 to 2.5 per cent) and that dollar profits come from high volumes and operating efficiencies. The high value of pharmaceutical products, modern information systems, and improved physical distribution facilities have undermined the position of pharmaceutical wholesalers throughout the world. This is because both manufacturers and retailers have sought to lower costs by dealing directly with manufacturers. For example, in the past four years U.S. wholesalers have seen their independent pharmacy customer base shrink from 41 per cent of their business to only 34 per cent, and this has put a squeeze on already small wholesale margins, pushing the majority of them below 2 per cent. Pharmaceutical wholesalers have to be more competitive or their pharmacy customer base will shrink even further.

These factors have caused a significant decrease in the number of wholesalers worldwide. Since 1991, the number of U.S. pharmaceutical wholesalers has fallen from 84 firms to 63, while the number of Japanese wholesalers has declined from 491 to 310 since 1986. These trends are consistent in all countries throughout the world. At the same time, pharmaceutical product sales have been increasing worldwide, indicating that the change is clearly due to a shift in channel activity rather than an industry-wide downward trend.

However, not all of the trends have been negative. The remaining wholesalers have captured a larger share of sales of the hospital market, a market formerly dominated by direct sales from manufacturers. Turnover order sales are another area of increasing revenue. Products are shipped direct from manufacturer to retailer but "billed" through wholesalers. This enables the manufacturer to keep retail costs low by eliminating the costs of wholesaler handling while not incurring the information handling costs involved in billing retail accounts. The billing is left to the wholesaler who makes a small profit margin. This margin is less than it would be if the goods were handled.

The areas of growth for pharmaceutical firms are in sales to pharmacy chains, hospitals, and clinics, but these are large customers who demand more services and lower prices—which means lower profit margins. This change in customer base means pharmaceutical wholesalers will have to work hard to cut costs while figuring out new ways to earn money. One thing is certain, the pharmaceutical wholesalers will not be alone in their quest to stay viable. The kinds of problems besetting them are besetting wholesalers in almost every industry. These days, it seems like everyone is out to get the middleman![1]

---

[1] International Federation of Pharmaceutical Wholesalers, "Pharmaceutical Wholesalers & Manufacturers Relationship," International Federation of Pharmaceutical Wholesalers Web site (July 12, 1996), http://www.ifpw.com.

In this chapter, we will further study wholesalers' relationships with their suppliers and customers. We will also examine the different types of firms that perform wholesaling activities and the strategies they use to compete in the marketplace.

Overview

Wholesaling encompasses the buying and/or handling of goods and services and their subsequent resale to organizational users, retailers, and/or other wholesalers—but not the sale of significant volume to final consumers. Wholesaling undertakes many vital functions in a channel of distribution, particularly those in the sorting process.

Manufacturers and service providers sometimes are their own wholesalers; other times, independent firms are employed. Independents may or may not take title to or possession of products, depending on the type of wholesaling. Some independents have limited tasks; others perform a wide range of functions.

Wholesaling is the buying/handling of products and their resale to organizational buyers.

Industrial, commercial, and government institutions are wholesalers' leading customers, followed closely by retailers. Sales from one wholesaler to another also represent a significant proportion of wholesaling activity. The following examples show the diversity of transactions that are considered wholesaling:

- Sales of goods and services to manufacturers, service providers, oil firms, fisheries, railroads, public utilities, and government departments.
- Sales of office or laboratory equipment, supplies, and services to such professionals as doctors and dentists.
- Sales of building materials and services to contractors, except when they buy on behalf of homeowners.
- All purchases of farm products for sale to other than individual consumers, regardless of whether purchases are made from farmers or intermediaries.
- All sales by supply houses, as long as purchases are not by final consumers.
- Sales to grocery stores, restaurants, hotels, clothing stores, shoe repair firms, video rental stores, and all other retailers.
- Manufacturer/service provider sales to wholesalers, and wholesaler sales to other wholesalers.[2]

In this chapter, the importance of wholesaling, the different types of wholesaling, and recent trends in wholesaling are all discussed in depth.

The Importance of Wholesaling

Wholesaling is an important aspect of distribution because of its impact on the economy, its functions in the distribution channel, and its relationships with suppliers and customers.

Wholesaling's Impact on the Economy

In Canada, there are about 65 000 wholesale merchant establishments with total annual sales exceeding $240 billion. There are about 1700 agents and brokers who function as wholesalers with annual sales near $40 billion. These revenues are higher than retail revenues, yet there are three times as many retail establishments (206 000) as wholesale.[3]

Wholesale sales are high; and wholesalers greatly affect final prices.

Revenues are high because wholesaling involves any purchases made by organizational consumers. Some products also move through multiple levels of wholesalers (e.g., regional, then local); an item can be sold twice or more at the wholesale level. There are more retailers because they serve individual, geographically dispersed final consumers; wholesalers handle fewer, larger, more concentrated customers.

---

[2]Adapted by the authors from C. Glenn Walters and Blaise J. Bergiel, *Marketing Channels*, Second Edition (Hinsdale, Ill.: Scott, Foresman, 1982), p. 108.

[3]Statistics Canada, *1995 Market Research Handbook* (Ottawa: Minister of Supply Services Canada) pp. 95–96; and Statistics Canada, "Wholesale Trade," *The Daily* (Thursday, April 25, 1996).

Table 16-1
Selected Performance Data for Wholesalers by Product Category[a]

PRODUCT CATEGORY OF WHOLESALER	GROSS PROFIT (AS PER CENT OF SALES)[b]	OPERATING EXPENSES (AS PER CENT OF SALES)	ALL OTHER EXPENSES (AS PER CENT OF SALES)	PROFIT BEFORE TAXES (AS PER CENT OF SALES)
Building materials	25.3	22.5	0.4	2.3
Chemicals and allied products	28.8	25.7	0.3	2.8
Coffee, tea, and spices	29.0	25.4	1.1	2.5
Drugs, drug proprietaries, and druggists' supplies	29.3	25.0	0.5	3.8
Electronic parts and equipment	29.7	26.5	0.5	2.6
Fish and seafoods	15.2	12.9	0.4	1.8
Flowers, nursery stock, and florists' supplies	33.7	30.3	0.9	2.4
General groceries	18.2	16.4	0.4	1.5
General merchandise	31.3	28.4	0.7	2.2
Hardware and paints	29.9	26.8	0.6	2.4
Jewellery	28.2	24.6	0.9	2.7
Motor vehicle supplies and new parts	30.9	27.3	0.7	2.9
Petroleum bulk stations and terminals	14.8	13.7	0.0	1.2
Wine, liquor, and beer	23.7	20 N.9	0.4	2.4

[a] In interpreting these data, RMA cautions that the Studies be regarded only as a general guideline and not as an absolute industry norm. This is due to limited samples within categories, the categorization of firms by their primary Standard Industrial Classification (SIC) number only, and different methods of operations by firms within the same industry. For these reasons, RMA recommends that the figures be used only as general guidelines in addition to other methods of financial analysis.
[b] Total costs of wholesaling, which include expenses and profit. There are some rounding errors.

Source: Adapted from *RMA Annual Statement Studies 1995* (Philadelphia: Robert Morris Associates, 1995). Copyright © 1995, Robert Morris Associates; reprinted by permission.

From a cost perspective, wholesalers have a great impact on prices. Table 16-1 shows the per cent of wholesale selling prices that go to selected wholesalers to cover their operating expenses and pretax profits. For example, 31 per cent of the price that a general merchandise wholesaler charges its retailers covers that wholesaler's operating and other expenses (29 per cent) and pretax profit (2 per cent). Operating costs include inventory charges, sales force salaries, advertising, and rent.

Wholesaler costs and profits depend on inventory turnover, the dollar value of products, the functions performed, efficiency, and competition.

The Functions of Wholesalers

Wholesalers perform tasks ranging from distribution to risk taking.

With regard to functions performed, wholesalers can:

- Enable manufacturers and service providers to distribute locally without making customer contacts.
- Provide a trained sales force.
- Provide marketing and research assistance for manufacturers, service providers, and retail or institutional consumers.

- Gather assortments for customers and let them make fewer transactions.
- Purchase large quantities, thus reducing total physical distribution costs.
- Provide warehousing and delivery facilities.
- Offer financing for manufacturers and service providers (by paying for products when they are shipped, not when they are sold) and retail or institutional consumers (by granting credit).
- Handle financial records.
- Process returns and make adjustments for defective merchandise.
- Take risks by being responsible for theft, deterioration, and obsolescence of inventory.[4]

Wholesalers that take title to and possession of products usually perform several or all of these tasks. Agents and brokers that facilitate sales, but do not take title or possession, tend to concentrate on more limited duties.

The use of independent wholesalers varies by industry. Most consumer products, food items, replacement parts, and office supplies are sold through independent wholesalers. In other industries, including heavy equipment, mainframe computers, gasoline, and temporary employment, manufacturers and service providers may bypass independent resellers.

Without independent wholesalers, organizational consumers would have to develop supplier contacts, deal with a number of suppliers and coordinate shipments, do more distribution functions, stock greater quantities, and place more emphasis on an internal purchasing agent or department. Many small retailers and other firms might be avoided as customers because they might not be profitably reached by a manufacturer or service provider; and they might not be able to buy necessary items elsewhere.

An illustration of the value of wholesaling is found in the North American auto parts industry, in which there used to be thousands of firms making a wide range of products and marketing them through a multitude of sales organizations. At that time, customers (mostly specialty stores and service stations) faced constant interruptions by salespeople; and manufacturers' sales costs were high. A better system exists today, with the organized use of a moderate number of independent distributors.

Wholesalers' Relationships with Suppliers and Customers

Independent wholesalers are often very much "in the middle," unsure whether their allegiance should be to manufacturers/service providers or their own customers. These comments show the dilemma many wholesalers face:

Wholesalers have obligations to both suppliers and customers.

> The challenge is to find ways individually, and as an industry, to show our customers and manufacturers exactly where and how we do and can add value. Our roles and performance are in a state of flux. The new theory is to cut out the wholesaler to reduce costs.[5]

Many wholesalers feel they get scant support from manufacturers/service providers. They desire training, technical assistance, product literature, and advertising. They dislike it when vendors alter territory assignments, shrink territory size, add new distributors to cover an existing geographic area, or decide to change to a direct channel and perform wholesale tasks themselves. Wholesalers want manufacturers/service providers to sell to them and not through them. Selling to the wholesaler means a distributor is viewed as a customer to be researched and satisfied. Selling through the wholesaler means retailers or

---

[4]Adapted by the authors from Walters and Bergiel, *Marketing Channels*, p. 109; and Louis W. Stern, Adel L. El-Ansary, and James R. Brown, *Management in Marketing Channels* (Englewood Cliffs, N.J.: Prentice Hall, 1989), pp. 98–99.

[5]Craig MacClaren, "Squeezed Brokers Position for Value-Added Services," *Promo* (February 1995), p. 36; and Stephen Bennett, "Working the Middle Ground," *Progressive Grocer* (August 1995), p. 147.

Ethics AND TODAY'S MARKETER

What Responsibility Do Big Customers Have to Their Suppliers?

According to a Dun & Bradstreet (D&B) survey, companies with 500 or more employees have begun to pay their small suppliers' bills more slowly. And a study by the U.S.-based National Association of Credit Management found that almost two-thirds of its members cited slow-paying customers as a moderate to severe problem.

A D&B spokesperson says that some large firms are paying their bills sixty days late, and that many smaller suppliers accept the late payments "out of desperation to get business." In many cases, however, the small suppliers are unaware that continued late payments by major accounts can significantly reduce the small firms' cash flow, as well as the capital they need to expand. For example, one firm, Earthly Elements, a small manufacturer of dried floral gifts and accessories, ultimately closed down due to the cash crunch from a late-paying customer. By the time the customer paid (close to three months past due), it was too late.

In response to large customers not only paying late, but also deducting a discount for early payment, Caruthers Raisin Packing Company was forced to stop offering its time-based discounts to anyone (even those paying within the stipulated time). Other small firms are being even more aggressive. Truck Brokers Inc., a transportation brokerage company, demands cash payments from customers with a reputation or track record of late payment. Says the owner of the firm, "If there's any question about payment, we're saying, make it cash."

To better cope with slow-paying accounts, Dun & Bradstreet recommends that small firms reduce their reliance on large accounts, develop cash reserves, and arrange to stretch out their own accounts payable.

As the sales manager for a small manufacturer, develop a policy for dealing with a major account that repeatedly pays late.

Sources: Based on material in Michael Selz, "Big Customers' Late Bills Choke Small Suppliers," *Wall Street Journal* (July 22, 1994), p. B1; and Christina Duff, "Big Stores' Outlandish Demands Alienate Small Suppliers," *Wall Street Journal* (October 27, 1995), pp. B1, B5.

---

final consumers are objects of manufacturers'/service providers' interest and wholesaler needs are less important. See Figure 16-1.

To remedy the situation, this is how many wholesalers are reacting:

Wholesalers have traditionally viewed themselves as extensions of either their suppliers or customers. Wholesalers that saw themselves as extensions of suppliers adopted the mind set of their suppliers, structured operations to best assist suppliers, and viewed customers as "outside" this relationship. And wholesalers that saw their role as extensions of their customers adopted that mind set and business structure and viewed the supplier as "outside." In short, wholesalers have typically viewed themselves as "distributors."

Today, more wholesalers feel they are in the "marketing support business." They view themselves as marketing *with* their suppliers and customers, not just being distributors. They recognize their primary role is to help both suppliers and customers devise better marketing programs. The marketing-support oriented wholesaler is willing to perform any task, activity, or function for either suppliers or customers that will result in more effective and efficient marketing for the entire channel.[6]

---

[6] Robert F. Lusch, Deborah Zizzo, and James M. Kenderdine, "Strategic Renewal in Distribution," *Marketing Management*, Vol. 2 (Number 2, 1993), p. 25.

Selling to the wholesaler

Manufacturer/Service Provider → Wholesaler → Retailer

The wholesaler is viewed as a customer who is researched and satisfied.

Selling through the wholesaler

Manufacturer/Service Provider → Wholesaler → Retailer

The retailer (or final customer) is the object of the manufacturer's/service provider's interests. The needs of the wholesaler are considered unimportant.

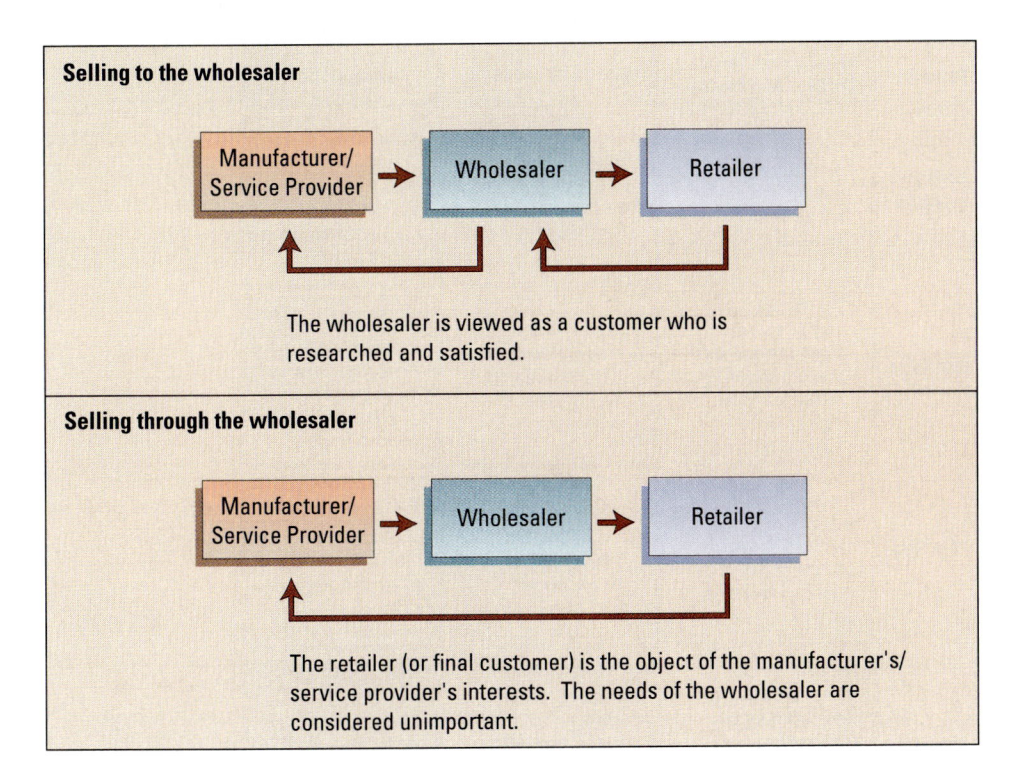

FIGURE 16-1
Selling to Versus Selling Through the Wholesaler

Types of Wholesaling

The three broad categories of wholesaling are outlined in Figure 16-2: manufacturer/service provider wholesaling, merchant wholesaling, and agents and brokers. Table 16-2 contains detailed descriptions of every type of independent wholesaler and shows their functions and special features.

Manufacturer/Service Provider Wholesaling

In **manufacturer/service provider wholesaling**, a producer does all wholesaling functions itself. This occurs if a firm feels it is best able to reach retailers or other organizational customers by being responsible for wholesaling tasks itself. Manufacturer/service provider wholesalers include General Motors, IBM, Frito-Lay, Pitney Bowes, Prudential, and public utilities.

Wholesale activities by a manufacturer or service provider may be carried out via sales offices and/or branch offices. A sales office is located at a firm's production facilities or a site close to the market. No inventory is carried there. In contrast, a branch office has facilities for warehousing products, as well as for selling them.

Manufacturer/service provider wholesaling is most likely if independent intermediaries are unavailable, existing intermediaries are unacceptable to the manufacturer or service provider, the manufacturer or service provider wants control over marketing, customers are relatively few in number and each is a key account, customers desire personal service from the producer, customers are near to the firm or clustered, a computerized order system links a firm with customers, and/or laws (particularly in foreign markets) limit arrangements with independent resellers.

For instance, because Boeing makes multimillion-dollar aircraft and individual customer orders can be in the billions of dollars, manufacturer wholesaling is a must. When Boeing recently sold $3 billion in jets to General Electric, the complex negotiations took over a year.[7] And at Chrysler, manufacturer wholesaling means closer relationships with its auto dealers. Chrysler distributes its Mopar brand replacement parts directly to the retailers and works with them to market the parts. See Figure 16-3.

In **manufacturer/service provider wholesaling**, *a firm acts via its own sales or branch offices.*

BOEING
www.boeing.com/

[7]Jeff Cole and Susan Carey, "Boeing Co. to Get GE Job Valued at Over $3 Billion," *Wall Street Journal* (January 8, 1996), pp. A3–A4.

FIGURE 16-2
The Broad Categories of Wholesaling

Factors	Manufacturer/Service Provider Wholesaling	Merchant Wholesaling	Agents and Brokers
Control/Functions	• The manufacturer/service provider controls wholesaling and performs all functions.	• The wholesaler controls wholesaling and performs many or all functions.	• The manufacturer/service provider and wholesaler each have some control and perform some functions.
Ownership	• The manufacturer/service provider owns products until they are bought by retailers or other organizational consumers.	• The wholesaler buys products from the manufacturer/service provider and resells them.	• The manufacturer/service provider owns the products and pays the wholesaler a fee/commission.
Cash Flow	• The manufacturer/service provider does not receive payment until the retailer or other customer buys products.	• The manufacturer/service provider is paid when the wholesaler purchases products.	• The manufacturer/service provider does not receive payment until products are sold.
Best Use(s)	• The manufacturer/service provider deals with a small group of large and geographically concentrated customers; rapid expansion is not a goal.	• The manufacturer/service provider has a large product line that is sold through many small and geographically dispersed customers; expansion is a goal.	• The manufacturer/service provider is small, has little marketing expertise, and is relatively unknown to potential customers; expansion is a goal.

FIGURE 16-3
Manufacturer Wholesaling by Chrysler
Reprinted by permission.

Table 16-2
Characteristics of Independent Wholesalers

MAJOR FUNCTIONS

WHOLESALER TYPE	Provides Credit	Stores and Delivers	Takes Title	Provides Merchandising and Promotion Assistance	Provides Personal Sales Force	Performs Research and Planning	SPECIAL FEATURES
I. Merchant wholesaler							
A. Full service							
1. General merchandise	Yes	Yes	Yes	Yes	Yes	Yes	Carries nearly all items a customer normally needs.
2. Specialty	Yes	Yes	Yes	Yes	Yes	Yes	Specializes in a narrow product range
3. Rack jobber	Yes	Yes	Yes	Yes	Yes	Yes	Furnishes racks and shelves, consignment sales
4. Franchise	Yes	Yes	Yes	Yes	Yes	Yes	Use of common business format, extensive management services
5. Cooperative							
a. Producer-owned	Yes	Yes	Yes	Yes	Yes	Yes	Farmer controlled, profits divided among members
b. Retailer-owned	Yes	Yes	Yes	Yes	Yes	Yes	Wholesaler owned by several retailers
B. Limited service							
1. Cash and carry	No	Stores, no delivery	Yes	No	No	No	No outside sales force, wholesale store for business needs
2. Drop shipper	Yes	Delivers, no storage	Yes	No	Yes	Sometimes	Ships items without physically handling them
3. Truck/wagon	Rarely	Yes	Yes	Yes	Yes	Sometimes	Sales and delivery on same call
4. Mail order	Sometimes	Yes	Yes	No	No	Sometimes	Catalogues used as sole promotion tool
II. Agents and brokers							
A. Agents							
1. Manufacturers' (service providers')	No	Sometimes	No	Yes	Yes	Sometimes	Sells selected items for several firms
2. Selling	Sometimes	Yes	No	Yes	Yes	Yes	Markets all the items of a firm
3. Commission (factor) merchants	Sometimes	Yes	No	No	Yes	Yes	Handles items on a consignment basis
B. Brokers							
1. Food	No	Sometimes	No	Yes	Yes	Yes	Brings together buyers and sellers
2. Stock	Sometimes	Sometimes	No	Yes	Yes	Yes	Brings together buyers and sellers

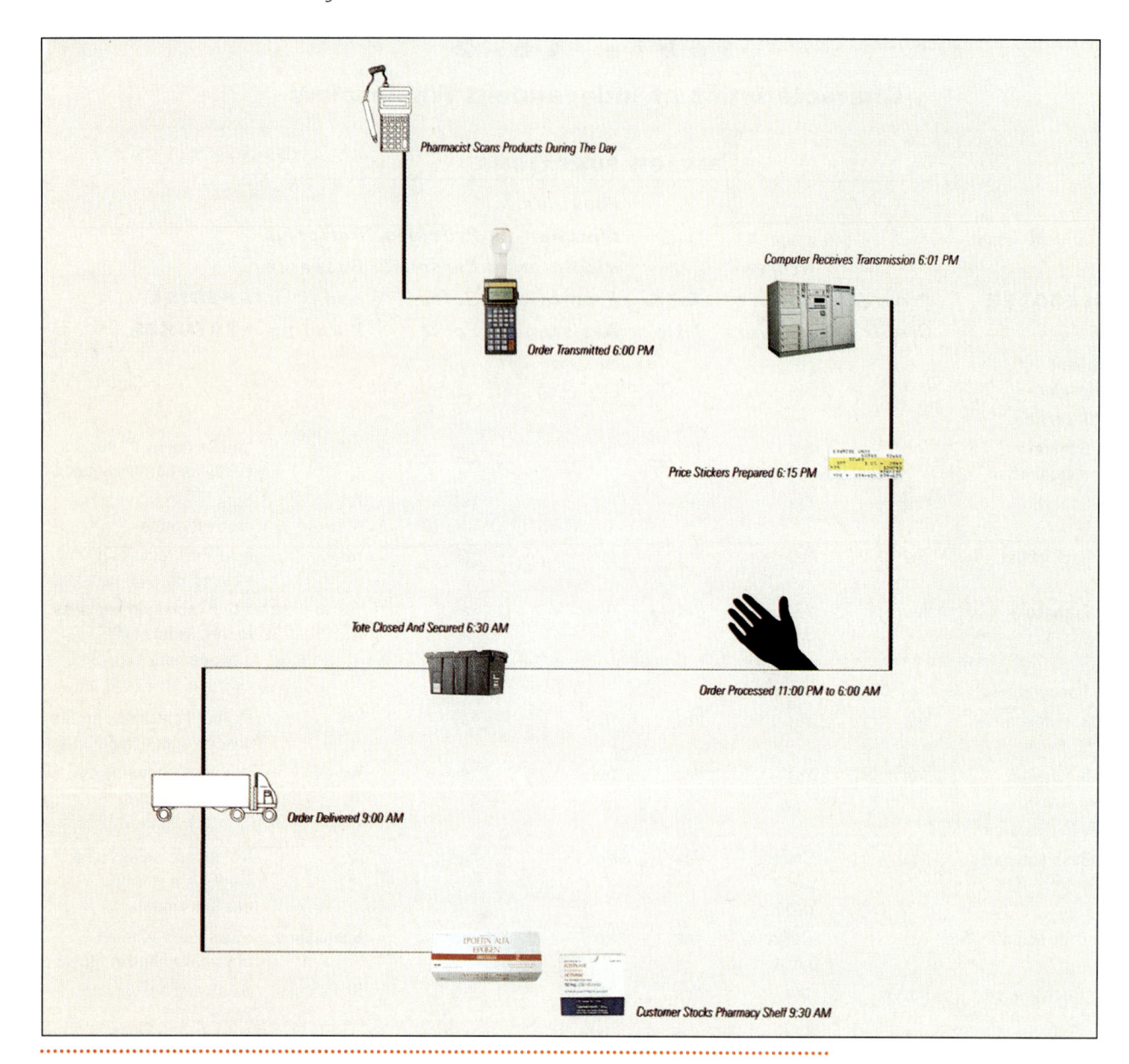

FIGURE 16-4
Bergen Brunswig Corporation: A Full-Service Merchant Wholesaler
Bergen Brunswig Corporation is a pharmaceutical wholesaler. It provides a wide range of services for customers, including automated order processing. The firm's computer network is linked to drugstores and hospitals. In general, a customer prepares an order during the day for transmission in the late afternoon. The order is filled at night and delivered early the next morning.
Reprinted by permission.

Wholesale Merchants

Wholesale merchants *buy products and may offer* **full** *or* **limited** *service.*

Wholesale merchants buy, take title, and take possession of products for further resale. This is the largest wholesale category in sales—over $240 billion per year in Canada. As an example, Sysco is a merchant wholesaler that buys and handles 150 000 products from 3000 producers of food and related products from around the world. It resells these products and offers many customer services to its 250 000 clients—restaurants, hotels, schools, hospitals, fast-food chains, and other organizations in both Canada and the United States.[8]

[8]Gary Hoover, Alta Campbell, and Patrick J. Spain (Eds.), *Hoover's Handbook of American Business 1995* (Austin, Texas: Reference Press, 1994), pp. 1004–1005.

Full-service merchant wholesalers perform a full range of distribution tasks. They provide credit, store and deliver products, offer merchandising and promotion assistance, have a personal sales force, offer research and planning support, pass along information to suppliers and customers, and provide installation and repair services. They are frequently used for grocery products, pharmaceuticals, hardware, plumbing equipment, tobacco, alcoholic beverages, and television program syndication. See Figure 16-4.

Limited-service merchant wholesalers do not perform all the functions of full-service merchant wholesalers. For instance, they may not provide credit, merchandising assistance, or marketing research data. They are popular for construction materials, coal, lumber, perishables, equipment rentals, and specialty foods.

On average, full-service merchant wholesalers require more compensation than limited-service ones because they perform more functions.

FULL-SERVICE MERCHANT WHOLESALERS Full-service merchant wholesalers can be divided into general merchandise, specialty merchandise, rack jobber, franchise, and cooperative types.

General-merchandise (full-line) wholesalers carry a wide product assortment—nearly all the items needed by their customers. Thus, some general-merchandise hardware, drug, and clothing wholesalers stock many products, but not much depth in any one line. They seek to sell their retailers or other organizational customers all or most of their products and develop strong loyalty and exclusivity with them.

Specialty-merchandise (limited-line) wholesalers concentrate on a rather narrow product range and have an extensive selection in that range. They offer many sizes, colours, and models—and provide functions similar to other full-service merchant wholesalers. They are popular for health foods, seafood, retail store displays, frozen foods, and video rentals.

Rack jobbers furnish the racks or shelves on which products are displayed. They own the products on the racks, selling them on a consignment basis—so their clients pay after goods are resold. Unsold items are taken back. Jobbers set up displays, refill shelves, price mark goods, maintain inventory records, and compute the amount due from their customers. Rack jobbers usually handle heavily advertised, branded merchandise that is sold on a self-service basis. Included are magazines, health and beauty aids, cosmetics, drugs, hand tools, toys, housewares, and stationery.

In **franchise wholesaling**, independent retailers affiliate with an existing wholesaler to use a standardized storefront design, business format, name, and purchase system. Many times, suppliers produce goods and services according to specifications set by the franchise wholesaler. This form of wholesaling is utilized for hardware, auto parts, and groceries. Franchise wholesalers include Independent Grocers Alliance (IGA), Independent Druggists Association (IDA), Western Auto, and Home Hardware Stores. At IGA, affiliated retailers are supplied with such services as site selection, store engineering, interior design, and merchandising assistance.

Wholesale cooperatives are owned by member firms to economize functions and provide broad support. Producer-owned cooperatives are popular in farming. They market, transport, and process farm products—as well as make and distribute farm supplies. These cooperatives often sell to stores under their own names, such as Blue Diamond, Ocean Spray, Sunkist, and Welch's. With retailer-owned cooperatives, independent retailers form associations that purchase, lease, or build wholesale facilities. The cooperatives take title to merchandise, handle cooperative advertising, and negotiate with suppliers. They are used by hardware and grocery stores.

LIMITED-SERVICE MERCHANT WHOLESALERS Limited-service merchant wholesalers can be divided into cash-and-carry, drop shipper, truck/wagon, and mail-order types.

In **cash-and-carry wholesaling**, small businesspeople drive to wholesalers, order products, and take them back to a store or business. These wholesalers offer no credit or delivery, no merchandising and promotion help, no outside sales force, and no research or planning assistance. They are good for fill-in items, have low prices, and allow immediate product use. They are common for construction materials, electrical supplies, office supplies, auto supplies, hardware products, and groceries.

General-merchandise wholesalers sell a range of items.

Specialty-merchandise wholesalers sell a narrow line of products.

Rack jobbers set up displays and are paid after sales.

With franchise wholesaling, retailers join with a wholesaler.

INDEPENDENT GROCERS ALLIANCE (IGA) INC.
www.igainc.com/

HOME HARDWARE
www.pagemaker.com/~home/overview.html

Producers or retailers can set up wholesale cooperatives.

In cash-and-carry wholesaling, the customer drives to a wholesaler.

International Marketing in Action

Malofilm: International Distributor of Canadian Entertainment

Malofilm Distribution, a unit of Malofilm Communications Inc., is one of Canada's leading distributors of Canadian films and video cassettes. It's parent firm, Malofilm Communications, is an integrated entertainment company with average annual sales between $30 to $40 million and earnings between $2 to $3 million. Pure distribution accounts for about 95 per cent of the firm's revenues. Aside from domestic and international distribution, Malofilm's business consists of development and production of programming for theatre, video, television, and multimedia (such as video games for the Sony Play Station). Malofilm is also one of Canada's largest distributors of home videos and has an investment in TotalNet, one of the nation's largest providers of Internet services.

In the past, the main source of products and income for Malofilm has been the distribution of foreign-made films (mostly U.S. productions) in Canada. Malofilm has been very successful in this regard, acquiring the rights to distribute and sell entertainment titles such as: *Braveheart* (Best Picture Winner at the 1996 Academy Awards), *Highlander 3*, and *Margaret's Museum*..

However, for real growth and diversity, Malofilm needs access to markets much larger than Canada. This means controlling the rights to worldwide distribution of original productions. According to René Malo, CEO of Malofilm Communications Inc., plans to make production and international distribution account for more of the firm's revenue in the future. Malofilm plans to produce four feature films in 1996 (*J'en Suis*, *Scanners IV*, *Turning Blue*, and *The Last Chocolate Maker*), along with its involvement in the production of children's television programs (*Little Star*, *Mighty Machines* and *Turtle Island*) and interactive digital media ("Jersey Devil" Game for Sony's Playstation, and the Montreal Canadiens 1909–1995 CD-ROM). The future in entertainment will quite likely be linked to Internet distribution, so Malofilm is looking ahead there as well.

In early 1996, Malofilm distribution began the process of expanding international distribution by becoming the international distributor for Toronto-based Associated Producers, a firm known for making award-winning and hard-hitting documentaries.

MALOFILM
www.malo.com/
TOTALNET
www.infobahnos.com/beta/francais/english.html

Drop shippers *buy goods, but do not take possession.*

Truck/wagon wholesalers *offer products on a sales route.*

Drop shippers (desk jobbers) buy goods from manufacturers or suppliers and arrange for their shipment to retailers or industrial users. They have legal ownership, but do not take physical possession of products and have no storage facilities. They purchase items, leave them at manufacturers' plants, contact customers by phone, set up and coordinate carload shipments from manufacturers directly to customers, and are responsible for items that cannot be sold. Trade credit, a personal sales force, and some research and planning are provided; merchandising and promotion support are not. Drop shippers are often used for coal, coke, and building materials. These goods have high freight costs, in relation to their value, because of their weight. Thus, direct shipments from suppliers to customers are needed.

Truck/wagon wholesalers generally have a regular sales route, offer items from a truck or wagon, and deliver goods while they are sold. They do provide merchandising and promotion support; however, they are considered limited service because they usually do not extend credit and offer little research and planning help. Operating costs are high due to

International Marketing in Action

Malofilm: International Distributor of Canadian Entertainment (continued)

President of Malofilm Distribution, Yves Dion, believes the worldwide explosion of news and information programming such as CNN (Cable News Network) and Headline News will lead to greater interest in documentary-type products.

Malofilm also distributes internationally the firm's own productions, like *Mojave Frankenstein*, a family film starring Burt Reynolds. To promote the film and get international distribution, Malofilm had Burt Reynolds interviewed on the syndicated TV show "Entertainment Tonight." Malofilm International is also handling world rights for the family film, *Kids of the Round Table*, which they have sold to over thirty countries, including the key market, the United States.

The control of all worldwide distribution rights is critical to international sales success. With control, Malofilm has the ability to allocate the rights on a nation-by-nation basis and in all media. Being able to subdivide rights by broadcast, theatrical release, and videocassette distribution allows Malofilm to maximize the revenue from film distribution. For example, the television rights for *Kids of the Round Table* in the U.S. were sold to The Disney Channel, while the U.S. video distribution rights were sold to Cabin Fever. In another example, Malofilm acquired international sales rights in all media to two movies launched at the 1996 Cannes Film Festival. One of the films, entitled *Sous-sol*, was produced in Quebec; the second, *The Interview*, was a combined Brazilian and American production. However, the Canadian production's domestic distribution rights were sold to another distributor, not Malofilm.

As a market analyst, discuss Malofilm's strategy and plans for sales growth based on international distribution.

Sources: "Malofilm Communications Inc. Picks Up International Sales Rights To Hard-Hitting, Controversial Documentaries From Award-Winning Associated Producers," *Canada NewsWire* (February 19, 1996), http://www.newswire.ca:80 ; "Malofilm Distribution Inc. Executive Producer And Foreign Distributor of 'Mojave Frankenstein'; Entertainment Tonight to Interview Burt Reynolds," *Canada NewsWire* (August 9, 1995), http://www.newswire.ca:80; "Second Quarter Profit Up 59 Per Cent at Malofilm Communications Inc.," *Canada NewsWire* (May 27, 1996), http://www.newswire.ca:80; and "Feature Film, Children's TV, And Multimedia Production Spur Growth Strategy at Malofilm Communications Inc.," *Canada NewsWire* (March 20, 1996), http://www.newswire.ca:80.

---

the services performed and low average sales. These wholesalers often deal with goods requiring special handling or with perishables—such as bakery products, tobacco, meat, candy, potato chips, and dairy products.

Mail-order wholesalers use catalogues, instead of a personal sales force, to promote products and communicate with customers. They may provide credit but do not generally give merchandising and promotion support. They store and deliver goods, and offer some research and planning assistance. These wholesalers are found with jewellery, cosmetics, auto parts, specialty food product lines, business supplies, and small office equipment.

Mail-order wholesalers *sell through catalogues.*

Agents and Brokers

Agents and **brokers** perform various wholesale tasks, but do not take title to products. Unlike merchant wholesalers, which make profits on the sales of products they own, they work for commissions or fees as payment for their services. In Canada there are about 1700

Agents *and* **brokers** *do not take title to products.*

brokers and agents and these account for almost $40 billion in sales each year. The main difference between agents and brokers is that agents are more apt to be used on a permanent basis.[9]

Agents and brokers let a manufacturer or service provider expand sales volume despite limited resources. Their selling costs are a predetermined per cent of sales; and they have trained salespeople. There are manufacturers'/ service providers' agents, selling agents, and commission (factor) merchants.

Manufacturers'/service providers' agents *work for many firms and carry noncompeting items.*

Manufacturers'/service providers' agents work for several manufacturers or service providers and carry noncompetitive, complementary products in exclusive territories. By selling noncompetitive items, the agents eliminate conflict-of-interest situations. By selling complementary products, they stock a fairly complete line of products for their market areas. They do not offer credit but may store and deliver products and give limited research and planning aid. Merchandising and promotional support are provided. These agents may supplement the sales efforts of their clients, help introduce new products, enter dispersed markets, and handle items with low average sales. They may carry only some of a firm's products; a manufacturer or service provider may hire many agents; larger firms may hire a separate one for every product line. Agents have little say on marketing and pricing. They earn commissions of 5 to 10 per cent of sales, and are popular for auto products, iron, steel, footwear, textiles, and commercial real-estate and insurance. See Figure 16-5.

Selling agents *market all the products of a manufacturer or service provider.*

Selling agents are responsible for marketing the entire output of a manufacturer/service provider under a contractual agreement. They become the marketing departments for their clients and can negotiate price and other conditions of sale, such as credit and delivery. They perform all wholesale tasks except taking title. While a firm may use several manufacturers'/service providers' agents, it may employ only one sales agent. These agents are more apt to work for small firms than large ones. They are common for textile manufacturing, canned foods, metals, home furnishings, apparel, lumber, and metal products. Because they perform more tasks, they often get higher commissions than manufacturers'/service providers' representatives.

Commission merchants *assemble goods from local markets.*

Commission (factor) merchants receive goods on consignment, accumulate them from local markets, and arrange for their sale in a central location. They may offer credit; they do store and deliver goods, provide a sales force, and offer research and planning help. They normally do not assist in merchandising and promotion; but, they can negotiate prices with buyers, provided the prices are not below sellers' stated minimums. They may act in an auction setting; commissions vary. These wholesalers are used for agricultural and seafood products, furniture, and art.

Brokers are common for food and financial services. They are well informed about market conditions, terms of sale, sources of credit, price setting, potential buyers and sellers, and the art of negotiating. They do not take title and usually are not allowed to complete a transaction without approval.

Food brokers *and* **commercial stock brokers** *unite buyers and sellers to conclude sales.*

Food brokers introduce buyers and sellers of food and related general-merchandise items to one another and bring them together to complete a sale. They operate in specific locales and work for a limited number of food producers. Their sales forces call on chain-store buyers, store managers, and purchasing agents. Food brokers work closely with ad agencies. They generally represent the seller, who pays the commission; they do not actually provide credit but may store and deliver. Commissions are 3 to 5 per cent of sales.

Commercial stock brokers are licensed sales representatives who advise business clients, take orders, and then acquire stocks and/or bonds for the clients. They may aid the firms selling the stocks or bonds, represent either buyers or sellers (with both buyers and sellers paying commissions), and offer some credit. Although operating in particular areas, they typically sell the stocks and bonds of firms from throughout Canada, the United States, and around the world. They deal a lot over the phone and may help publicize new stock or bond offerings. The average commission for commercial stock brokers is 1 to 10 per cent of sales, depending on volume and stock prices.

---

[9]Statistics Canada, *1995 Market Research Handbook* (Ottawa: Minister of Supply Services Canada), p. 96.

FIGURE 16-5
Promoting the Purchase of Life Insurance Through Professional Agents
Reprinted by permission

Anything Can Happen.

Citizens has all the insurance coverage. Group life and health. Worker's comp and financial planning. Plus lots more. So drop by or give us a call. Because the best time to protect your business from a disaster is before one happens.

CITIZENS Business Insurance
111 S.E. Third Street · Post Office Box 99 · Evansville, Indiana 47701 · 812-428-2830

Recent Trends in Wholesaling

During the last fifteen years, wholesaling has changed dramatically, with independent wholesalers striving to protect their place in the channel. Among the key trends are those related to the evolving wholesaler mix, productivity, customer service, international opportunities, and target markets.

Since the early 1980s, the proportion of total sales volume contributed by merchant wholesaling, agents, and brokers has remained steady. However, there are fewer agent and broker wholesaler establishments and more merchant wholesaler establishments. The most recent Statistics Canada Census Data (1992) estimates that 63 000 companies engaged in merchant wholesaling in 1992, up from 49 000 in 1982. The average annual sales of these wholesalers was $3.9 million in 1992 compared to $2.9 million in 1982. In that same year, an estimated 5015 brokers and agents had average sales of $5.4 million, compared to 1758 agents and brokers in 1992 with average sales of $22 million. In the wholesaling business an astonishing 0.6 per cent of the firms accounted for 44 per cent of the sales.[10]

Firms are becoming larger and more productive.

[10]Industry Canada, "Wholesale Trade-Industry Profile, 1992," Industry Canada *Strategis* Web site (1994), http://www.ic.gc.ca/strategis.

Wholesalers are emphasizing customer service and looking to international markets.

WW GRAINGER
www.grainger.com/

Since wholesalers' profit margins are small (1.5 per cent of sales for food wholesalers and less than 3 per cent of sales for general merchandise wholesalers), they are constantly seeking gains in productivity. For example, VWD Distributors, a Western Canadian pharmaceutical wholesaler, installed a $400 000 electronic carousel order-filling system, the first of its kind in Canada, in their Burnaby, B.C. facility. The new system allows one person to fill fourteen orders simultaneously. The system holds almost 80 per cent of VWD's inventory and the company hopes the new system will reduce handling and shipping errors, provide better inventory control, and reduce labour expenses. One of the driving forces for all members of the pharmaceutical industry in Canada are the provincial drug plans. These plans have been reducing their payouts and this is forcing all members of the pharmaceutical distribution channel to try and lower costs so they can maintain their profitability.[11]

Wholesalers have learned that customer service is extremely important in securing a competitive advantage, developing client loyalty, and attaining acceptable profit margins. For example, W.W. Grainger, a wholesaler of maintenance, repair, and operating supplies—offers a "value package" that includes electronic ordering and payment, cost-reduction consulting services, and so forth. As a Grainger vice-president says, "On sales calls these days, we seldom talk about why the motor we sell is better than someone else's motor; we talk about value-added services."[12]

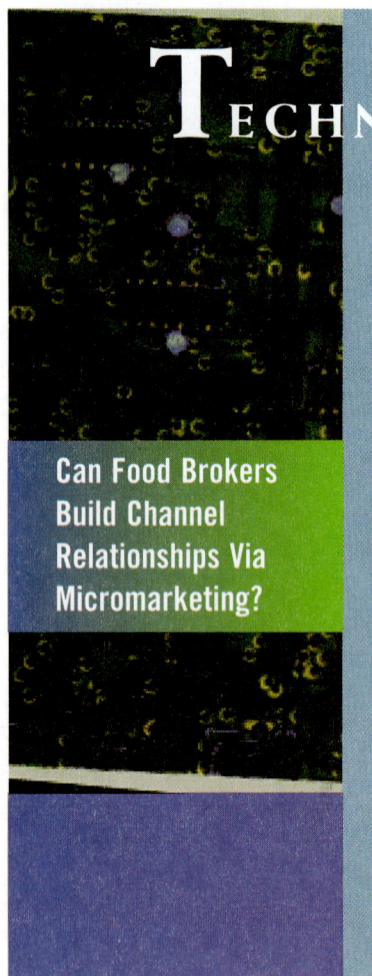

TECHNOLOGY & MARKETING

Can Food Brokers Build Channel Relationships Via Micromarketing?

The micromarketing approach recognizes that different marketing strategies may be necessary on a store-by-store basis to maximize a reseller's sales and profitability. Micromarketing opportunities are facilitated when retailers and suppliers are able to share vital information. This process increases trust between both parties. According to Ed Fargo, a vice-president of Eisenhart & Associates, a food brokerage firm, "When we can show a food retailer what's selling, who's buying, where those buyers live and what they like, we have won that food retailer's attention."

As a service to customers, Eisenhart & Associates compiles and evaluates research data on product sales, consumer demographics, lifestyles, and local advertising expenditures. Eisenhart's analysis relies on its computer-generated profiles of the typical users and heavy users of each account's product line. Thus, it can estimate a chain's market share in selected merchandise categories as compared with local supermarkets, mass merchandisers, and drug stores. Although a chain can develop similar analyses, Fargo realizes that "not all retailers can afford the time and effort to analyze hundreds of categories in this manner."

On the basis of this analysis, Eisenhart & Associates determines which stores in a chain would most benefit from special displays and in-store demonstrations, and which ones should be sold together using joint promotions. In many cases, Eisenhart is able to show that a product's contribution to sales and profits is greater than its proportionate use of shelf space.

Eisenhart & Associates then seeks to increase product positions on shelves (from ankle to eye level) or to add new items to a product line. For example, in one case, Fargo was able to convince a supermarket to add seven new items to a line of light yogurt.

As a food broker, what other opportunities exist for the building of channel relationships via micromarketing?

Source: Based on material in "Building Bridges," *Promo/ Progressive Grocer Special Report* (October 1994), p. 9.

---

[11] "VWD Installs Canada's First Computerized Carousel System For Wholesale Drug Operations," *Canada NewsWire* (August 9, 1995), http://www.newswire.ca:80.

[12] Thomas A. Stewart, "The Information Wars: What You Don't Know Will Hurt You," *Fortune* (June 12, 1995), pp. 120–121.

And the Canadian Council of Grocery Distributors is trying to anticipate the needs of shoppers in the future. The Council expects that soon we will not have to shop during store hours, or even step into a store. Instead, we will visit virtual supermarkets, which retailers will present along with physical supermarkets. A pilot project of grocery shopping on the Web has already been launched.[13]

More wholesalers are turning to foreign markets for growth. Finning Ltd., a British Columbia based wholesaler of Caterpillar and allied equipment, is concentrating on international expansion. Finning sells, finances, and provides customer service for this equipment. The company serves geographic markets in Western Canada, Britain, Poland, and Chile. The firm has over 4000 employees in its worldwide operations and sells heavy equipment to industry market segments such as mining, agricultural, petroleum, construction, and forestry. To service this equipment Finning has a hydraulic rebuild company and a component remanufacturing centre, both located in Edmonton. In order to be accepted more readily by international customers, Finning has sought and received certification under International Quality Standard ISO-9002.

Finning's efforts to improve international sales have paid off: international business accounted for 44 per cent of their 1995 sales of $1.75 billion and a total profit of $77.5 million or 4.4 per cent. European sales accounted for 24 per cent and Chilean sales represented 20 per cent of this total. In contrast, in 1994, Canadian sales represented 60 per cent of the company's total $1.46 billion in sales, while European sales accounted for 23 per cent and Chilean sales for 17 per cent. An important factor to consider is that European profit margins were 5 per cent of sales in 1995 and 4.6 per cent in 1994. In contrast, Canadian profit margins were lower, at 4.5 per cent in 1995 and 4.1 per cent in 1994. Although Chilean sales had the greatest increase, the associated profit margins are lower than in Canada with 1995 profit margins falling to 3.7 per cent from a 1994 profit margin of 3.9 per cent. Still, international sales increased at a rate of 33 per cent, while Canadian sales increased at only 12 per cent, indicating the best growth potential for Finning is in international markets.[14]

In large numbers, wholesalers are diversifying the markets they serve or the products they carry: Farm and garden machinery wholesalers now sell to florists, hardware dealers, and garden supply stores. Plumbing wholesalers have added industrial accounts, contractors, and builders. Grocery wholesalers deal with hotels, airlines, hospitals, schools, and restaurants. Some food wholesalers have moved into apparel retailing and opened auto-parts stores.

Yet, some wholesalers are taking the opposite approach and seeking to appeal to one customer niche or need. Thus, Prudential Steel focuses on supplying line pipe for the oil industry and gas industry in Western Canada through its wholesale operation, Oil Country Tubular Goods. Like all wholesalers, Prudential has to manage its incoming goods costs carefully while remaining price competitive on outgoing goods. The price of steel has a major impact on acquisition costs and Prudential cannot control this cost. Likewise, the price of oil and gas affect exploration and oil and gas well operations and these greatly affect Prudential's demand. Prudential had sales of $177 million in 1995, down from 1994 sales of $215 million because of low prices for oil and gas in 1995. Despite this, the firm is committed to its niche as a supplier of steel line pipes, which carry the products of oil and gas producers. In fact, Prudential management feels customer service is so critical that despite a fall in sales, the company kept a large inventory of finished goods on hand in 1995. This decision anticipated expanding sales in 1996 as oil and gas prices were rebounding in late 1995.[15]

FINNING LTD.
www.finning.ca/

Target market strategies are more complex.

---

[13]"Canadian Council Of Grocery Distributors, "Grocery Shopping From Your Own Home," *Canada NewsWire* (May 27, 1996), http://www.newswire.ca.

[14]"Finning Ltd.: Revenue And Profits," *Canada NewsWire* (October 16, 1995), http://www.newswire.ca:80; "Finning Ltd. Reports Record Revenue And Net Income," *Canada NewsWire* (February 1, 1996), http://www.newswire.ca:80; and "Finning Ltd: New Chairman," *Canada NewsWire* (April 19, 1996), http://www.newswire.ca:80.

[15]"Prudential Steel Ltd. Second Quarter Results Reflect More Normal Seasonal Downturn In Oil Patch Activity," *Canada NewsWire*, http://www.newswire.ca:80 (July 27 1995); and "Prudential Reports Strong Fourth Quarter," *Canada NewsWire* (February 21, 1996), http://www.newswire.ca:80

MARKETING IN A CHANGING WORLD

How Manufacturers'/Service Providers' Agents Are Staying the Course[16]

For some time now, many manufacturers'/service providers' agents (MSPAs) have been on the endangered species list. Why? Some large retail chains such as Wal-Mart insist on interacting face-to-face with manufacturers/service providers and will not even schedule appointments with MSPAs. And because of the competition for their shelf space, loads of retailers have stopped buying from small manufacturers/service providers—the same firms that the MSPAs represent. Finally, the technological advances (particularly, electronic data interchange) that make today's distribution so efficient are also reducing the MSPAs' role—or at least greatly modifying it.

The initial MSPAs appeared in the mid-1880s. Since it was inconvenient and expensive to send salespeople and samples to distant locales, MSPAs were hired locally by railroad manufacturers to market equipment to railroad builders. In some regards, MSPAs have not changed much; they still offer localized customer attention. Since a set commission is specified in advance, sales costs are predictable. Health benefits, training, and turnover are also eliminated.

Nonetheless, MSPAs are adapting to their current situation. And the most far-sighted ones are performing very well. Here are some examples of what they are doing:

- They are becoming more technologically knowledgeable, learning and applying everything from EDI to computerized inventory controls. This benefits the small firms that they represent (which do not have these capabilities themselves) and lets them gain entry to big retailers.
- They are helping to develop new products, based on feedback from their own customers.
- They are hiring their own support staff, providing marketing services, and turning into product specialists—an even narrower niche than being industry specialists.
- They are offering such marketing services as telemarketing and direct-mail programs for the firms they represent.

In sum, as one MSPA expert says, "The focus of the MSPA has been modified. MSPAs no longer peddle products in the traditional sense. They work closely with the manufacturers they serve, identify the needs of their customers, and then provide the product and service solutions to meet those needs."

SUMMARY

1. To define wholesaling and show its importance Wholesaling involves the buying and/or handling of goods and services and their resale to organizational users, retailers, and/or other wholesalers but not the sale of significant volume to final consumers. In Canada, about 65 000 wholesale establishments distribute over $280 billion in goods and services annually.

Wholesale functions encompass distribution, personal selling, marketing and research assistance, gathering assortments, cost reductions, warehousing, financing, returns, and risk taking. These functions may be assumed by manufacturers/service providers or shared with independent wholesalers. The latter are sometimes in a precarious position because they are located between manufacturers/service providers and customers and must determine their responsibilities to each.

2. To describe the three broad categories of wholesaling (manufacturer/service provider wholesaling, merchant wholesaling, and agents and brokers) and the specific types of firms within each category In manufacturer/service provider wholesaling, a producer undertakes all wholesaling functions itself. This form of wholesaling can be conducted through sales or branch offices. The sales office carries no inventory.

Merchant wholesalers buy, take title, and possess products for further resale. Full-service merchant wholesalers gather assortments of products, provide trade credit, store and deliver products, offer merchandising and promotion assistance, provide a personal sales force, offer research and planning support, and complete other functions as well. Full-service merchant wholesalers fall into general merchandise, specialty merchandise, rack jobber, franchise, and cooperative types. Limited-service merchant wholesalers take title to

---

[16] The material in this section is based on Melissa Campbell, "Agents of Change," *Sales & Marketing Management* (February 1995), pp. 71–75.

products but do not provide all wholesale functions. Limited-service merchant wholesalers are divided into cash-and-carry, drop shipper, truck/wagon, and mail-order types.

Agents and brokers provide various wholesale tasks, such as negotiating purchases and expediting sales; but, they do not take title. They are paid commissions or fees. Agents are used on a more permanent basis than brokers. Types of agents are manufacturers'/service providers' agents, selling agents, and commission (factor) merchants. Food brokers and commercial stock brokers are two key players in wholesale brokerage.

3. *To examine recent trends in wholesaling* The nature of wholesaling has changed over the last several years. Trends involve the evolving wholesaler mix, productivity, customer service, international openings, and target markets.

KEY TERMS

wholesaling (p. 439)
manufacturer/service provider wholesaling (p. 443)
wholesale merchants (p. 446)
full-service merchant wholesalers (p. 446)
limited-service merchant wholesalers (p. 446)
general-merchandise (full-line) wholesalers (p. 447)
specialty-merchandise (limited-line) wholesalers (p. 447)

rack jobbers (p. 447)
franchise wholesaling (p. 447)
wholesale cooperatives (p. 447)
cash-and-carry wholesaling (p. 447)
drop shippers (desk jobbers) (p. 448)
truck/wagon wholesalers (p. 448)
mail-order wholesalers (p. 449)

agents (p. 449)
brokers (p. 449)
manufacturers'/service providers' agents (p. 450)
selling agents (p. 450)
commission (factor) merchants (p. 450)
food brokers (p. 450)
commercial stock brokers (p. 450)

Review Questions

1. Why does wholesale sales volume exceed retail sales volume?
2. Differentiate between selling to a wholesaler and selling through a wholesaler.
3. Under what circumstances should a manufacturer or service provider undertake wholesaling?
4. Distinguish between a manufacturer's/service provider's branch office and a manufacturer's/service provider's sales office.
5. Which wholesaling functions are performed by merchant wholesalers? Which are performed by agents and brokers?
6. Distinguish between limited-service merchant wholesalers and full-service merchant wholesalers.
7. What are the unique features of cash-and-carry and truck/wagon merchant wholesalers?
8. Why are drop shippers frequently used for coal, coke, and building materials?
9. How do manufacturers'/service providers' agents and selling agents differ?
10. What is the role of the commercial stock broker?

Discussion Questions

1. "Wholesalers are very much in the middle, often not fully knowing whether their first allegiance should be to the manufacturer/service provider or the customer." Comment on this statement. Can they rectify this situation? Why or why not?
2. The marketing vice-president of Canada Trust MasterCard has asked you to outline a support program to improve relations with the retailers that accept its cards. Prepare this outline.
3. As a member of a producer-owned wholesale cooperative, what factors would you study to determine whether your firm is being well served?
4. Develop a short checklist that Malofilm Communications Inc. (see the *International Marketing* box in this chapter) could use in determining whether to use merchant wholesalers or agents/brokers in different countries around the world to distribute its videocassette movies intended for retail sale.
5. Discuss how and why a perfume manufacturer would use a combination of manufacturer/service provider wholesaling, merchant wholesaling, and agents/brokers.

VIDEO CASE

Uniquely Canadian: The Saskatchewan Wheat Pool and Other Co-ops

On a drive through almost any city in the Prairie provinces one sees many retail signs for gasoline, food, hardware, and convenience stores all ending with the word Co-op. Co-op, short for cooperative, usually identifies a business as being a community-owned enterprise. Cooperative enterprises are more common in Canada than anywhere else in the world and were founded on the pioneer spirit. Originally, cooperatives were an idea implemented by settlers where communities got together to operate businesses and share in the profits. This enabled communities to build needed distribution facilities that private operators could not or would not otherwise provide.

One of the largest cooperative businesses in Canada is the Saskatchewan Wheat Pool with annual sales of $3.9 billion. The Wheat Pool was founded in 1923 by Saskatchewan farmers who were tired of being paid so poorly for their crops because control of the physical distribution and the agency of sales for their grain was held by a few grain elevator companies. They banded together to form the Saskatchewan Wheat Pool, a farmer's cooperative which today has 57 000 farmer-members. The Saskatchewan Wheat Pool operates a grain-handling system of storage elevators in over 400 locations in Canada (including ship-loading facilities at the ports of Vancouver and Thunder Bay) and handles 60 per cent of the grain produced in Saskatchewan. In addition, the Wheat Pool operates fish farms, markets livestock and other grains, serves the needs of farmers with twenty-seven farm service centres, operates a flour mill, co-owns the Robin's Donuts chain, and publishes a newspaper for farmers. Finally, the Saskatchewan Wheat Pool acts as a lobby group to the provincial and federal governments on behalf of its farmer members.

Like many other cooperatives, the Wheat Pool runs on democratic principles. The Saskatchewan Wheat Pool has nearly 500 local committees, a board of sixteen directors and 126 delegates who are elected. The elected delegates of the various co-ops have several major challenges ahead of them. The deregulation of many industries (transportation for one) combined with NAFTA and the attractiveness of the Canadian market, has resulted in powerful international competition. The co-ops have to be able to deal with this quickly and efficiently, and this means adopting new methods and approaches in which "democratic" decision making may not be possible.

The Saskatchewan Wheat Pool is facing powerful competition from new, well financed, and super-efficient American Grain Elevator facilities. Coupled with a deregulated transportation industry where grain shipment costs will rise because government-funded subsidies for rail shipments have ended, this means doing business will be more expensive. To combat this, the Saskatchewan Wheat Pool needs a large infusion of cash, in the hundreds of millions of dollars, to build more cost-efficient facilities. To acquire this cash, on April 2, 1996 the Wheat Pool, through its underwriters, sold 12.8 million Class B non-voting shares valued at $153 million on the Toronto Stock Exchange. According to Lyle Spencer, the Chief Financial Officer of the Saskatchewan Wheat Pool, all of the co-ops are watching and waiting to see how the success of the Wheat Pool's stock offering and the resultant marketing strategy will turn out. Everyone believes that what happens to the Saskatchewan Wheat Pool will point to the future of co-ops in general.

QUESTIONS

1. Discuss the advantages and disadvantages co-op organizations have in comparison with privately owned enterprises.
2. Identify as many of the issues facing co-ops as you can. Which issues are unique to co-ops and which are common to all wholesalers? Discuss the reasoning behind your classification of these issues.
3. The initial share offering by the Saskatchewan Wheat Pool valued the Class B non-voting shares at $12.00 each. The stock market code on the Toronto Stock Exchange (TSE) for these shares is: Sask Wht B. Take a look at the most recent financial page of the TSE and find the trading price of these shares. Report on it and then use this information as part of a discussion as to whether the share offering approach could be and should be adopted by other co-ops.

VIDEO QUESTIONS ON UNIQUELY CANADIAN

1. Based on the video, discuss the future of Co-ops as a wholesale institution.
2. Evaluate the Saskatchewan Wheat Pool. What kinds of things seem to account for its success? Consider the specific threats that are facing the Wheat Pool and discuss how the Wheat Pool is responding to these threats.

Video Source: "Co-ops," *Venture* (February 11, 1996).

Other Sources: Material in this case is based upon "Pool's Board Ratifies Reorganization," *Canadian Corporate News* (March 29, 1996); "About the Pool," Saskatchewan Wheat Pool Website (June 15, 1996); "Pool History," Saskatchewan Wheat Pool Website (July 15, 1996); "On Receipt Pool Places $153 Million in Shares," Saskatchewan Wheat Pool Website (March 25, 1996).

CASE STUDY

The Home-Market Dominance of Japanese Wholesalers

The Japanese distribution system has often been knocked as restricting the entry of foreign goods into Japanese channels. Due to their great channel power, Japanese wholesalers are often cited as critical factors in this restrictiveness by experts.

Japanese wholesalers ("tonya") have three traits that are different from typical Western wholesalers. One, besides the marketing functions generally offered by Western wholesalers, tonya provide financing, insurance, and management consulting services for manufacturers. Two, Japanese wholesaling is more multitiered than in the West; a typical Japanese distribution channel has two or more levels of wholesalers between manufacturers and retailers. Three, tonya supply Japan with critical imports. Today, Japanese wholesalers have taken on a significant new role through "supervised exports," in which the production processes of foreign companies are controlled. Collectively, these factors give wholesalers a large degree of channel power.

Tonya have been criticized as having so much power that foreign goods are at a disadvantage in Japan. Their power is rooted in historical, political, and economic forces. Therefore, the tonya's modern role is better understood by examining the history of the Japanese distribution system.

In the 1100s, a rigid four-tier caste system evolved in Japan. The system placed the samurai (whose status was inherited) at the top, followed by farmers, artisans, and then merchants. The samurai were not permitted to engage in any form of business. Thus, even though Japanese wholesalers had low prestige as members of the merchant class, they rapidly gained power and wealth through political protection and patronage. Part of their power was also due to their high wealth in comparison to the state government.

The power of wholesalers was consolidated in the 1600s, due to three factors: the functions performed by tonya for the state, the development of trade associations that represented tonya, and the financial dependence of the samurai class on wealthy wholesalers. At that time, wholesalers in Western Japan were responsible for storing, transporting, and marketing the rice tax for the state. Samurai were still restricted from business activities. Trade associations enhanced the power of wholesalers by offering insurance and extending credit to members, through their lobbying activities, and by granting control of trade routes. The samurai class also needed the services of wholesalers, since the latter maintained the price of rice against the price levels of other commodities (as a means of protecting the samurai's income stream).

During the 1870s, Japan's defence, manufacturing, and finance sectors were modernized. Yet its distribution system hardly changed. As a result, many small manufacturers stayed dependent on powerful wholesalers for capital, materials, and marketing. Even today, the Japanese distribution system still bears some resemblance to the feudal system.

The power of the tonya has continued into modern times, even with the increased presence of foreign businesses. For example, retail distribution in Japan is still characterized by single-product-line stores. These small independent retailers have little channel power relative to their wholesalers. And foreign firms must use a number of strategies to penetrate a Japanese distribution system that is dominated by strong wholesalers. Thus, Schick bypassed the traditional Japanese distribution channel by using a major cutlery wholesaler to market its razor blades. Johnson & Johnson piggybacked onto the distribution system of a manufacturer selling noncompeting goods to the same market. And Maxwell House used a partnership arrangement to gain access to the strong distribution network controlled by a major food company.

QUESTIONS

1. Describe the notion of a wholesaler being "in the middle" with reference to the role of Japanese wholesalers.
2. What types of wholesalers are described in this case? Refer to Table 16-2.
3. The case quotes one researcher as saying: "The power of wholesalers in Japan is based on historical, political, and economic forces, not culture." Discuss the validity and relevance of this statement.
4. Evaluate each of the different types of channel strategies used by foreign firms to penetrate the Japanese distribution system.

Source: The data in this case are drawn from Barry Berman, *Marketing Channels* (New York: John Wiley & Sons, 1996), p. 614; and Susan Kitchell, "Tonya, the Japanese Wholesalers: Why Their Dominant Position?" *Journal of Macromarketing*, Vol. 15 (Spring 1995), pp. 21–31.

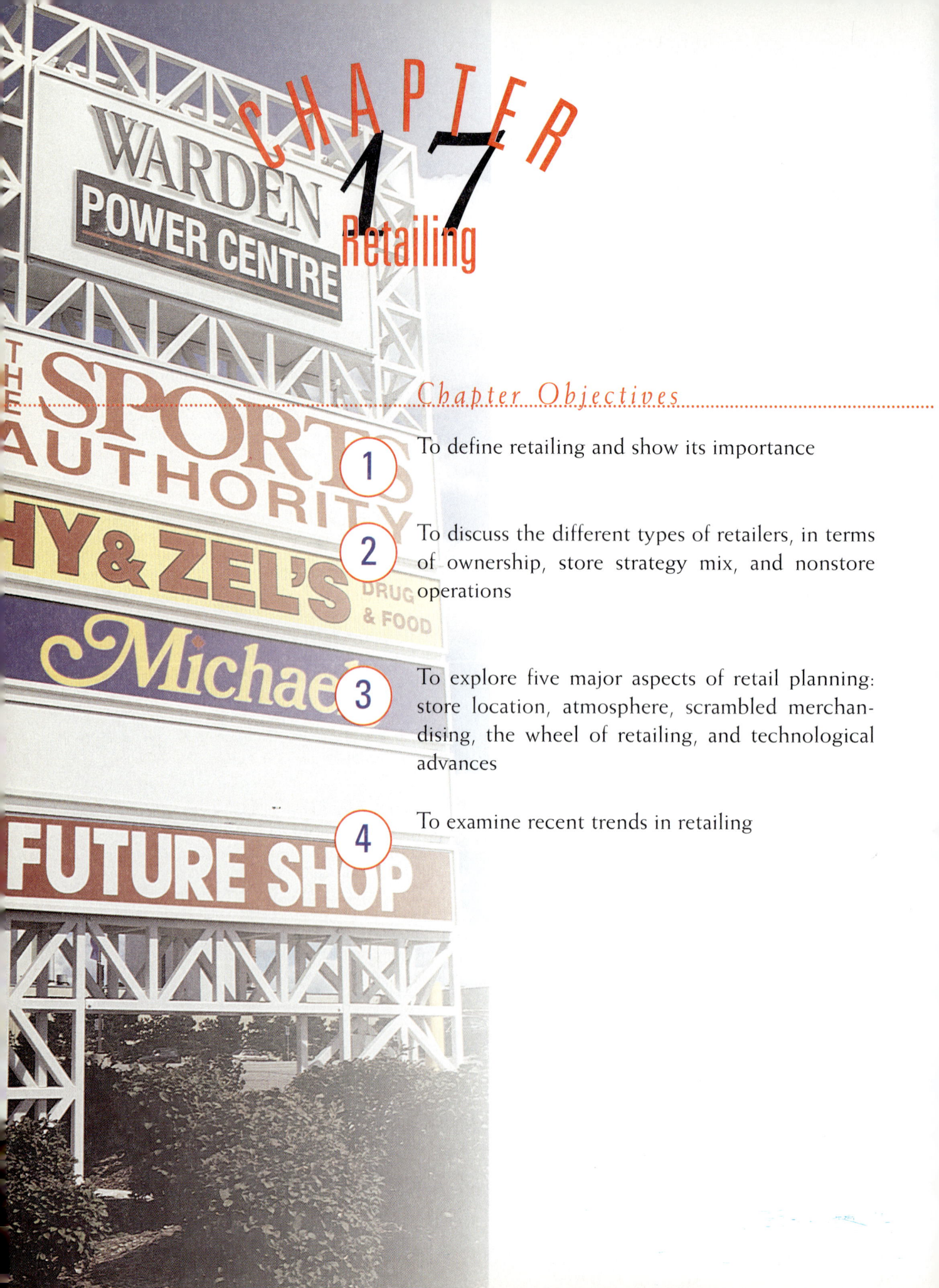

CHAPTER 17
Retailing

Chapter Objectives

1. To define retailing and show its importance

2. To discuss the different types of retailers, in terms of ownership, store strategy mix, and nonstore operations

3. To explore five major aspects of retail planning: store location, atmosphere, scrambled merchandising, the wheel of retailing, and technological advances

4. To examine recent trends in retailing

> *Retailing in Canada in the 1990s is undergoing a revolution. One sign of this revolution is the widespread advent of so called "category killer" stores, which are locating close to one another in groups, to create "power malls." A power mall is created when large product-specific retail stores such as Toys 'R' Us and The Home Depot (referred to as category killers) locate near stores like Wal-Mart or a Price Club/Costco warehouse (referred to as big box stores).*

In early 1995, retail estimates indicated that the U.S. market had about 250 power malls while Canada had between fifteen and twenty with more on the way. So far, these large competitors have chosen to locate in large metropolitan areas such as Metro Toronto, Montreal, Vancouver, and Ottawa. However, all of Canada's twenty-five CMA's (census metropolitan areas) represent potential markets for power malls. For example, in Moncton, New Brunswick, Price Club/Costco opened up a 120 000-square-foot warehouse in late 1995 as part of a power mall. This mall also includes a 100 000-square-foot Kent Building supply warehouse, a 110 000-square-foot oversized K-Mart store, and a 60 000-square-foot Real Atlantic Superstore (owned by Loblaws).

These new power malls are threatening the existence of one of the traditional mainstays of retailing, the shopping mall. The regional and super-regional malls (like the West Edmonton Mall) are particularly at risk. Says Carl Steidtmann, director of research at Management Horizons, a retail consulting division of Price Waterhouse: "Regional malls clearly have a life cycle, and a lot of them are in their last throes."

Those that survive will have to reinvent themselves somehow. They will have to become primary destinations once again, catering to a consumer generation no longer willing to drift through loads of boutiques while slowly annihilating the family budget. Ironically, the malls that are falling victim may respond by taking on category killers as allies. In Toronto, the Warden Woods shopping centre was in deep trouble. It had lost half of its tenants and was losing one of its anchor stores, the Bay. The response: create a power mall with some category-killer stores. Warden Woods attracted the Sports Authority, Michaels (a craft store), Petstuff, and the Future Shop. In addition, a six-screen Odeon movie theatre was put in and there is room for sixty other stores as well.

Offering shoppers on-premises entertainment is another way shopping malls are hoping to entice customers. Many centres have added movie theatres, video arcades, and fancy restaurants to enhance the shopping experience. Even some factory outlet malls now offer festivals, concerts, and book signings as a means of attracting greater consumer traffic. As one real estate executive says, "The idea is to give people multiple reasons to come to your centre."

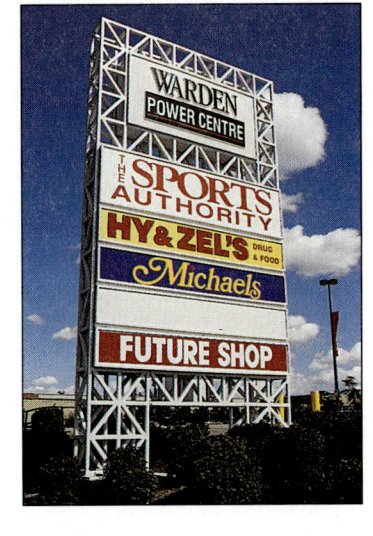

Cambridge Shopping Centres of Toronto, owners and operators of a large number of Canadian malls, has certainly not surrendered to the power malls. In 1995 they committed to spending $500 million to renovate their forty-five Canadian malls, adding two million square feet of retail space to their existing 28.5 million square feet of mall space. They recognize that big box stores and category killers that combine to form power malls are going to have an impact, but traditional malls have a loyal customer base that they can serve. New malls are probably not going to arise very often but the existing ones plan to stay.[1]

In this chapter, we will examine various aspects of retailing—including trends affecting shopping centres—and consider their ramifications.

Overview

Retailing, *the last channel stage, entails selling to final consumers.*

Retailing encompasses those business activities involved with the sale of goods and services to the final consumer for personal, family, or household use. It is the final stage in a channel of distribution. Manufacturers, importers, and wholesalers act as retailers when they sell products directly to the final consumer.

Surveys undertaken for the Grocery Products Manufacturers of Canada and the Canadian Council of Grocery Distributors indicated the following about Canadian shoppers: The average spending on groceries by individual shoppers was about $100/week. The shoppers were mostly female (82 per cent) and 80 per cent of the shoppers bought brands with which they were familiar. Approximately 66 per cent of the shoppers purchased store brands but these store brands only accounted for 14 per cent of all products they purchased. Studies of shopping behaviour in North America indicate that the average retail sale per shopping trip is small, about $40 for department stores and $50 for specialty stores. Convenience stores, such as 7-Eleven, have average sales of just a few dollars (not including gasoline).

Chain supermarkets average nearly $20 per customer transaction.[2] Accordingly, retailers try to increase their sales volume by using one-stop shopping appeals, broadening merchandise and service assortments, increasing customer shopping frequency, and encouraging more family members to go shopping. Inventory controls, automated merchandise handling, and electronic cash registers enable retailers to reduce their transaction costs.

Despite the low average size of customer transactions, about one-half of sales for such retailers as department stores involve some form of customer credit. This means these retailers must pay a percentage of each transaction to a bank or other credit-card service company or absorb the costs of their own credit programs—in return for increased sales.[3] For example, The Bay and Eatons each have millions of holders of their own credit cards; these people buy hundreds of millions of dollars in goods and services every year.

Whereas salespeople regularly visit organizational consumers to initiate and conclude transactions, most final consumers patronize stores. This makes the location of the store, product assortment, store hours, store fixtures, sales personnel, delivery, customer service, and other factors critical tools in drawing customers. See Figure 17-1.

Final consumers make many unplanned purchases. In contrast, those that buy for resale or use in production (or operating a business) are more systematic in their purchasing. Therefore, retailers need to place impulse items in high-traffic locations, organize store layout, train sales personnel in suggestion selling, place related items next to each other, and sponsor special events to stimulate consumers.

In this chapter, the importance of retailing, the various types of retailers, considerations in retail planning, and recent trends in retailing are all discussed in detail.

---

[1] Kenneth Labich, "What It Will Take to Keep People Hanging Out at the Mall," *Fortune* (May 29, 1995), pp. 102–106; James Pollock, "Attack of the Killer Malls!" *Marketing Magazine*, (February 20, 1995), p. 11; James Pollock, "Cambridge Investment a Sign of Mall Revival," *Marketing Magazine*, (July 24, 1995), p. 5; and Mark Higgins, "Price Club Opens Two Atlantic Warehouse Stores," *Marketing Magazine* (November 6, 1995), p. 15.

[2] "Retailing: Basic Analysis," *Standard & Poor's Industry Surveys* (June 15, 1995), p. R82; Jo Marney, "North American Shoppers," *Marketing Magazine* (April 24, 1995), p. 41; and "Canadian Council of Grocery Distributors: Supermarket Loyalty Up, Switching Down—Trends in Canada Survey," *Canada NewsWire* (July 18, 1995), http://www.newswire.ca:80.

[3] "Survey of Retail Payment Systems," *Chain Store Age* (January 1996), Section Two.

FIGURE 17-1
Customer Service at Radio Shack
To provide excellent customer service, Radio Shack has thousands of convenient locations, 20 000 well-trained employees, and "simple" answers to "complicated" questions—all backed by a seventy-year company tradition.
Reprinted by permission.

The Importance of Retailing

Retailing is a significant aspect of distribution because of its impact on the economy, its functions in the distribution channel, and its relationships with suppliers.

Retailing's Impact on the Economy

Retail sales and employment account for substantial amounts of sales and employment. In 1995 Canadian retail-store sales volume exceeded $211 billion. This figure does not include nonstore retail activities such as vending machines, mail-order, electronic shopping, and other forms of direct selling. In 1995, Canada's ten largest retail organizations were George Weston Ltd. ($13 billion in sales), Loblaws Cos. Ltd. ($9.8 billion in sales), Oshawa Group Ltd. ($6.1 billion in sales), Hudson's Bay Co. ($6.0 billion in sales), Provigo Inc. ($5.7 billion in sales), Canada Safeway Ltd. ($4.8 billion in sales), Sears Canada Inc. ($3.9 billion in sales), Canadian Tire Corporation Ltd. ($3.7 billion in sales), Westfair Foods Ltd. ($3 billion in sales), and the Great Atlantic and Pacific Co. of Canada Ltd. ($2.5 billion in sales). Globally, the world's top 100 retailers generate U.S.$1.3 trillion in total annual revenues and include firms from fourteen different nations. The largest retailer on the planet, by far, is U.S.-based Wal-Mart—with annual sales approaching U.S.$100 billion (more than 95 per cent in the United States), nearly 3000 stores, and multiple store formats (such as Wal-Mart and Sam's Clubs).[4]

The retailing sector employed 1 384 000 Canadians in 1995, which is approximately 10 per cent of all working Canadians. Within the Canadian market and around the globe,

Retailing embodies high annual sales, employment, and costs.

GEORGE WESTON LTD.
www.weston.ca/default.htm

LOBLAWS
www.loblaws.ca/

SEARS CANADA INC.
www.yellowpages.ca/sears/

---

[4]Statistics Canada, "Retail Sales, by Trade Group, and Total Retail Sales, Canada, The Provinces And Territories," CANSIM matrix 2400 (Ottawa: Minister of Supply Services Canada); "Performance 500," *Canadian Business* (June 1996), pp. 152–155; "State of the Industry," *Chain Store Age* (August 1995), Section Two; "The Shopping Spree That Wasn't," *Wall Street Journal* (January 5, 1996), p. B1; and Coopers & Lybrands, "Global Powers of Retailing," *Chain Store Age* (December 1995).

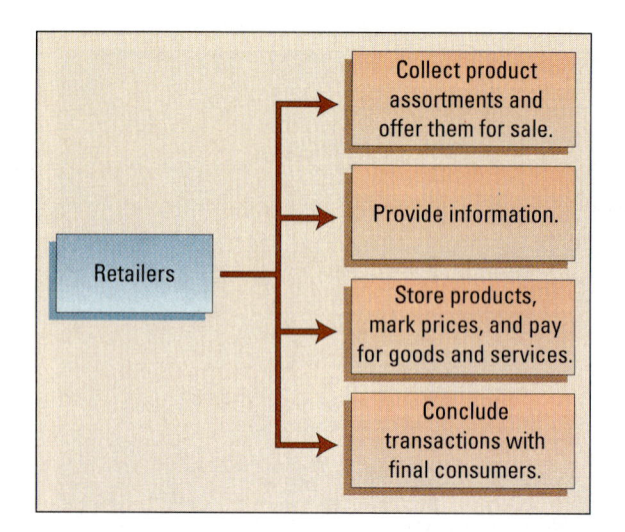

FIGURE 17-2
Key Retailing Functions

Retailers undertake four key functions.

a wide range of retailing career opportunities are available, including store management, merchandising, and owning one's own retail business.[5]

From a cost perspective, retailing is a significant field in North America. For example, on average, 38 to 40 cents of every dollar a consumer spends in a department or specialty store pays for the functions it performs. The corresponding figure is 22 cents for a supermarket. This compensation—known as gross margin—is for rent, taxes, fuel, advertising, management, personnel, and other retail costs, as well as profits. One of the reasons Wal-Mart is the world's leading retailer is that its operating costs are so low (16 per cent of sales) compared to its close competitors like K-mart, whose operating costs are 22 per cent.[6]

Retailing Functions in Distribution

As highlighted in Figure 17-2, retailers generally perform four distinct functions. They:

- Engage in the sorting process by assembling an assortment of goods and services from a variety of suppliers and offering them for sale. The width and depth of assortment depend on the individual retailer's strategy.
- Provide information to consumers via ads, displays and signs, and sales personnel. And marketing research support (feedback) is given to other channel members.
- Store products, mark prices, place items on the selling floor, and otherwise handle products. Retailers usually pay for items before selling them to final consumers.
- Facilitate and complete transactions by having appropriate locations and hours, credit policies, and other services (like delivery).

The Relationship of Retailers and Suppliers

Retailers deal with two broad supplier categories: those selling goods or services for use by the retailers and those selling goods or services that are resold by the retailers. Examples of goods and services purchased by retailers for their use are store fixtures, computer equipment, management consulting, and insurance. Resale purchases depend on the lines sold by the retailer.

Suppliers must have knowledge of their retailers' goals, strategies, and methods of business operation to sell and service accounts effectively. Retailers and their suppliers may have divergent viewpoints, which must be reconciled. For example:

---

[5]A discussion of careers in retailing can be found in Barry Berman and Joel R. Evans, *Retail Management: A Strategic Approach*, Sixth Edition (New York: Prentice Hall, 1995), pp. A1–A13; and Statistics Canada, "Employment, Transportation, Communications, and Trade Industries, By Industry," (Ottawa: Minister of Supply Services), Catalogue No. 72F0002.

[6]*Stores*, various issues; "Progressive Grocer Annual Report," *Progressive Grocer* (April 1996); and Mary Kuntz, et al., "Reinventing the Store," *Business Week* (November 27, 1995), p. 92.

Ethics AND TODAY'S MARKETER

Green Products: Retailing's Endangered Species

In the late 1980s and early 1990s store shelves were awash with "green" products. Retailers were actively promoting the availability and the importance of using products that were environmentally friendly. At the time many environmentalists chalked up the responses of marketers to this trend as commercialism. They may have been right because now finding products promoted and labelled as "green" is almost as difficult as it was before they were hyped. In Canada, one of the leaders of the "green" product revolution was Loblaw, which brought more than 100 "Green" products to market alone. But consumers are no longer willing to pay a premium price for a "green" product and with sales slowing, many of these products have been removed from the shelves.

A lot of "product greening" revolved around the way products were being packaged and how the packaging was disposed of. Many retailers and their suppliers say that the "green" revolution really changed the way they do things in this regard. For them, the concept of "green" is now engendered in their products in terms of packaging, recycling, and environmental impact. They have found that concentrating marketing effort on "green" does not have the appeal to consumers it once did. People will not pay more for "green" but they will select "green" products over others if the price and quality are comparable and the only point of difference is "green" or not.

Patrick Carson of Loblaws was one of the main proponents behind Green products and their success. He sees "green" as an attitude not a label. Any products or services that contribute to a society or healthier humans can be considered, "green" and do not necessarily have to carry that label. Therefore, low cholesterol and low fat foods could be considered "green" products. Since many producers and retailers have embraced the ideals brought about by the "green" revolution, they are still "green" even if they do not say so.

However, the original charge by environmentalists that environmental friendliness was a guise for crass commercialism remains valid. When asked about the future of green products, Carson replied, "Environmental initiatives are normally economic issues for us." Still, Loblaw is committed to its Green products, which have had a steady level of sales at 0.3 per cent of the chain's total revenues. It seems clear that what it takes to "survive" in the intensely competitive environment of retailing is often at odds with what it takes to survive in the natural environment.

Develop a definition of a "green" product, and on your next visit to a food store try to find three different product categories of labelled "green" products. Identify some brands in the same product category that are not labelled as "green." Compare the labelled "green" products and the brands not labelled as "green" to see if they meet your definition and discuss why.

Source: Based on material in James Pollock, "The Green Devolution," *Marketing Magazine* (April 15, 1996), p. 9.

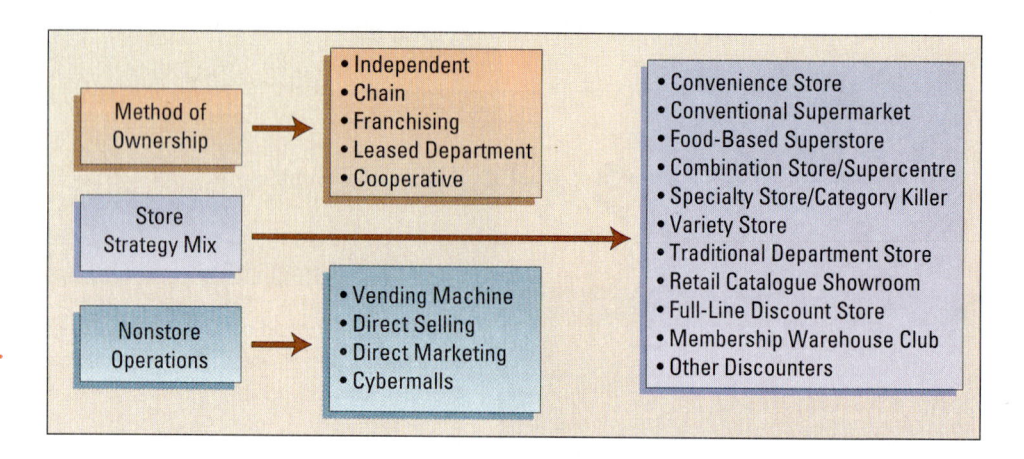

FIGURE 17-3
Categorizing Retailers

Current and former Reebok insiders say the toughest fight with Nike is being waged at Woolworth Corporation's Foot Locker unit—and Reebok is losing. With little fanfare, the shoe retailer has grown into a behemoth: Its 2800 outlets chalk up about 23 per cent of North American sneaker sales. When a retailer achieves such dominance in a product category, it expects to get preferred terms from manufacturers, early looks at new models, and speedy shipments. Nike has been playing the game. Reebok has not. Thus, in 1995, Foot Locker's Nike sales were U.S.$750 million, while Reebok's were only U.S.$172 million.[7]

Types of Retailers[8]

Retailers can be categorized by ownership, store strategy mix, and nonstore operations. See Figure 17-3. The categories overlap; that is, a firm can be correctly placed in more than one grouping. For example, 7-Eleven is a chain, a franchise, and a convenience store. The study of retailers by group provides data on their traits and orientation, and the impact of environmental factors.

Ownership

An independent retailer has one store, while a retail chain has multiple outlets.

An **independent retailer** operates only one outlet and offers personal service, a convenient location, and close customer contact. Nearly 80 per cent of North American retail establishments (including those staffed solely by the owners and their families)—and an even higher percentage in some foreign nations—are operated by independents, including many dry cleaners, beauty salons, furniture stores, gas stations, and neighbourhood stores. This large number is due to the ease of entry because various kinds of retailing require low investments and little technical knowledge. Therefore, competition is plentiful. Numerous retailers do not succeed because of the ease of entry, poor management skills, and inadequate resources. About one-third of new retailers do not last one full year and two-thirds do not make it past the first three years.

A **retail chain** involves common ownership of multiple outlets. It usually has central purchasing and decision making. Although independents have simple organizations, chains tend to rely on specialization, standardization, and elaborate control systems. Chains can serve a large, dispersed target market and have a well-known company name. There are approximately 1100 chains in Canada operating about 36 500 stores. They represent 17 per cent of Canadian retail establishments and account for 40 per cent of all retail

---

[7] Joseph Pereira, "In Reebok-Nike War, Big Woolworth Chain Is a Major Battlefield," *Wall Street Journal* (September 22, 1995), p. A1.

[8] Unless otherwise indicated, the statistics in these subsections are the authors' current projections, based on data from Statistics Canada, "Retail Sales, by Trade Group, and Total Retail Sales, Canada, The Provinces And Territories," CANSIM matrix 2400 (Ottawa: Minister of Supply Services Canada); Leonard Kubas, "Navigating the New Retail Landscape," *Marketing Magazine* (July 31/August 7, 1995) pp. 11–12; *1992 Census of Retail Trade* (Washington, D.C.: U.S. Bureau of the Census); *Stores; Progressive Grocer; Discount Store News, Inc.; Vending Times Census of the Industry* (1995); *Direct Marketing*; and Berman and Evans, *Retail Management: A Strategic Approach*.

FIGURE 17-4
Pizza Hut: A Leader in Franchising
PepsiCo serves as the franchiser for Pizza Hut, KFC, and Taco Bell—the big guns in their respective market niches. Of the 12 000 Pizza Hut restaurants around the world, over 4000 are franchised; the rest are owned and operated by PepsiCo.
Reprinted by permission.

store sales. Chains are common for department stores, supermarkets, and fast-food outlets, among others. Examples of chains are The Bay, Loblaws, Wal-Mart, and Foot Locker.

Retail franchising is a contractual arrangement between a franchiser (a manufacturer, wholesaler, or service sponsor) and a retail franchisee, which allows the latter to run a certain form of business under an established name and according to specific rules. It is a form of chain retailing that lets a small businessperson benefit from the experience, buying abilities, and name of a large multi-unit retailer. Many times, the franchisee gets management training and engages in cooperative buying and advertising. The franchiser benefits by obtaining franchise fees and royalties, faster payments, strict operating controls, consistency among outlets, and motivated owner-operators. There is an estimated 25 000 franchise outlets in Canada. The total sales statistics for Canadian franchises are not accurately known but estimates range from a low of $13 billion[9] up to $90 billion.[10] Franchising is popular for auto and truck dealers, gasoline stations, donut shops, fast-food outlets, hotels and motels, service firms, and convenience-foods stores. Examples of retail franchises include: Chevrolet dealers, Petro Canada Service Stations, Tim Horton's Donuts, Pizza Hut, and H&R Block. See Figure 17-4.

Retail franchising *uses an established name and operates under certain rules.*

---

[9]Donna Jean MacKinnon, "Franchising Shrugs Off Recession," *The Toronto Star* (November 19, 1992), pp. B1, B3.

[10]Canadian Franchise Association, "Franchising Has Come of Age," Advertising Supplement to *Canadian Business* (January, 1994), pp. 79–84.

A **leased department** is a section of a retail store rented to an outside party. The lessee operates a department—under the store's rules—and pays a percentage of sales as rent. Lessors gain from the reduced risk and inventory investment, expertise of lessees, lucrative lease terms, increased store traffic, and appeal to one-stop shopping. Lessees gain from the location in established stores, lessor name awareness, overall store traffic, one-stop customers attracted to stores, and whatever services (such as ads) lessors provide. Leased departments are popular for beauty salons, jewellery, photo studios, shoes and shoe repairs, cosmetics and food service. Radio Shack and Rogers Cantel of Toronto reached an agreement whereby Radio Shack will sell Cantel mobile phones through in-store boutiques called "Wireless Specialists." In return, Radio Shack will manage 150 Cantel stores, which will devote 25 per cent of their floor space to Radio Shack products.[11]

A leased department is one rented to an outside party.

With a **retail cooperative**, independent retailers share purchases, storage and shipping facilities, advertising, planning, and other tasks. Individual stores remain independent—but agree on broad, common policies. Cooperatives are growing due to chains' domination of independents. They are popular for pharmacies, hardware stores, and grocery stores. An example of a well-known retail cooperative is IDA Pharmacies (Independent Druggists Association). *Retail cooperative* and *retailer-owned wholesale cooperative* are synonymous terms.

With a retail cooperative, stores organize to share costs.

Table 17-1 compares the various forms of retail ownership.

Store Strategy Mix

Firms can be classed by the store strategy mix they choose. A typical **retail store strategy mix** consists of an integrated combination of hours, location, assortment, service, advertising, prices, and other factors retailers employ. Store strategy mixes vary widely, as the following indicate.

A retail store strategy mix combines the hours and products, etc. offered.

A **convenience store** is usually a well-situated, food-oriented store with long hours and a limited number of items. In Canada, these stores have annual sales of $4.1 billion, including gasoline, and account for about 7.5 per cent of total grocery sales. The average store has yearly sales that are a fraction of those of a conventional supermarket. Consumers use a convenience store for fill-in merchandise, often at off-hours. Gasoline, milk, groceries, newspapers, soda, cigarettes, beer, and fast food are popular items. 7-Eleven and Beckers operate convenience stores.

A convenience store stresses fill-in items.

A **conventional supermarket** is a departmentalized food store with minimum annual sales of $2 million; it emphasizes a wide range of food and related products—general merchandise sales are limited. It originated in the 1930s, when food retailers realized a large-scale operation would let them combine volume sales, self-service, low prices, impulse buying, and one-stop grocery shopping. The car and refrigerator aided the supermarket's success by lowering travel costs and adding to perishables' life spans. Loblaws, A&P, Provigo, Sobey's and Safeway are among the large chains operating conventional supermarkets.

A conventional supermarket is a large, self-service food store.

A **food-based superstore** is a diversified supermarket that sells a broad range of food and nonfood items. A food-based superstore typically has greeting cards, floral products, VCR tapes, garden supplies, some apparel, film developing, and small household appliances—besides a full line of supermarket items. A food-based superstore typically has about twice the floor space of a conventional supermarket and generates about $16 million in average sales. Several factors have caused many conventional supermarkets to switch to superstores: consumer interest in one-stop shopping, the levelling of food sales due to population stability and competition from fast-food stores and restaurants, and higher margins on general merchandise (double those of food items). For large food chains, the superstore is now the preferred supermarket format.

A food-based superstore stocks food and other products for one-stop shoppers.

A **combination store** unites food/grocery and general merchandise sales in one facility, with general merchandise providing 25 to 40 per cent or more of sales. It goes further than a food-based superstore in appealing to one-stop shoppers and occupies 30 000 to 100 000 square feet or more. It lets a retailer operate efficiently, expand the number of people drawn to a store, raise impulse purchases and the size of the average transaction,

A combination store offers a large assortment of general merchandise, as well as food. One type is a supercentre.

---

[11]News Line, "Cantel, Radio Shack Team in Retail Concept," *Marketing Magazine* (May 6, 1996), p. 3.

Table 17-1
Key Characteristics of Retail Ownership Forms

OWNERSHIP FORM	CHARACTERISTICS		
	Distinguishing Features	*Major Advantages*	*Major Disadvantages*
Independent	Operates one outlet, easy entry	Personal service, convenient location, customer contact	Much competition, poor management skills, limited resources
Retail chain	Common ownership of multiple units	Central purchasing, strong management, specialization of tasks, larger market	Inflexibility, high investment costs, less entrepreneurial
Retail franchising	Contractual arrangement between central management (franchiser) and independent businesspersons (franchisees) to operate a specified form of business	To franchiser: investments from franchisees, faster growth, entrepreneurial spirit of franchisees. To franchisee: established name, training, experience of franchiser, cooperative ads	To franchiser: some loss of control, franchisees not employees, harder to maintain uniformity. To franchisee: strict rules, limited decision-making ability, payments to franchisers
Leased department	Space in a store leased to an outside operator	To lessor: expertise of lessee, little risk, diversification. To lessee: lower investment in store fixtures, customer traffic, store image	To lessor: some loss of control, poor performance reflects on store. To lessee: strict rules, limited decision-making ability, payments to store
Retail cooperative	Purchases, advertising, planning, and other functions shared by independent retailers	Independence maintained, efficiency improved, enhances competitiveness with chains	Different goals of participants, hard to control members, some autonomy lost

sell both high-turnover/low-profit food items and lower-turnover/high-profit general merchandise, and offer fair prices. A supercentre is a combination store that integrates an economy supermarket with a discount department store, with at least 40 per cent of sales from nonfood items. It is 75 000 to 150 000 square feet in size, and carries 50 000 or more items. Among the firms with combination stores are Loblaws Superstore Atlantic, Real Canadian Superstore, Price/Costco warehouse, and France's Carrefour.

A **specialty store** concentrates on one product line, such as stereo equipment or hair-care services. Consumers like these stores since they are not faced with racks of unrelated products, do not have to search through several departments, are apt to find informed

*A **specialty store** emphasizes one kind of product, with a **category killer** store being a large version.*

FIGURE 17-5
The Body Shop: A Focused Specialty Store Chain
Around the world, The Body Shop offers a deep selection of goods and services—all related to its natural cosmetics and personal-care products. Shown here is Anita Roddick, the founder and managing director.
Reprinted by permission.

salespeople, can select from tailored assortments, and may avoid crowding. Specialty stores are quite successful with apparel, appliances, toys, electronics, furniture, personal care products, and personal services. Specialty stores include Tip Top Tailors, LensCrafters, and The Body Shop. See Figure 17-5.

A rather new type of specialty store—the category killer—is now gaining strength. The **category killer** is an especially large specialty store. It features an enormous selection in its product category and relatively low prices; and consumers are drawn from wide geographic areas. Toys "R" Us and Staples/Business Depot are among the many specialty store chains that are opening new category killer stores to complement their existing stores. Blockbuster Video, Sports Authority, and Home Depot are among the chains fully based on the category-killer store concept.

A **variety store** *sells an assortment of lower-priced items.*

A **variety store** sells a wide assortment of inexpensive and popularly priced merchandise. It features stationery, gift items, women's accessories, toiletries, light hardware, toys, housewares, and confectionery items. With the growth of other retail store strategy mixes, variety stores have lost a lot of ground in recent years. The Biway store and Army and Navy Stores are examples of this type of store.

A department store employs at least fifty people and usually sells a general line of apparel for the family, household linens and textile products, and some mix of furniture, home furnishings, appliances, and consumer electronics. It is organized into separate departments for purposes of buying, promotion, service, and control. There are two types of department store: the traditional department store and the full-line discount store.

A **traditional department store** *is a fashion leader with many customer services.*

A **traditional department store** has a great assortment of goods and services, provides many customer services, is a fashion leader, and often serves as an anchor store in a shopping district or shopping centre. Prices are average to above average. It has high name recognition and uses all forms of media in ads. In recent years, traditional department stores have set up more boutiques, theme displays, and designer departments to compete with other firms. They face intense competition from specialty stores and discounters and consequently annual sales in 1995 were $6.5 billion, down from a high of $7.1 billion in 1991. Canada has essentially three department store chains: Sears, The Bay, and Eaton's, with estimated market shares of 41 per cent, 31 per cent and 28 per cent respectively.[12]

A **full-line discount store** *has self-service and popular brands.*

A **full-line discount store** is a department store with lower prices, a broad product assortment, a lower-rent location, more emphasis on self-service, brand-name merchandise, wide aisles, shopping carts, and more goods displayed on the sales floor. In 1995 Canadian full-line discounters annually sold over $7 billion in goods and services. They are among the largest retailers of apparel, housewares, electronics, health and beauty aids, auto supplies, toys, sporting goods, photographic products, and jewellery. Wal-Mart, K-mart, and Zellers are examples of these kinds of retail operations.[13]

[12]Ian McGugan, "Eaton's On The Brink," *Canadian Business* (March 1996), pp. 38–73.
[13]Leonard Kubas, "Navigating the New Retail Landscape," *Marketing Magazine* (July 31–August 7, 1995) pp. 11–12.

With a **membership warehouse club**, final consumers and businesses pay small yearly dues for the right to shop in a huge, austere warehouse. Products are often displayed in their original boxes, large sizes are stocked, and some product lines vary by time period (since clubs purchase overruns and one-of-a-kind items that cannot always be replaced). Consumers buy items at deep discounts. In the United States, this retailing format, whose annual sales skyrocketed from U.S.$2.5 billion in 1985 to U.S.$20 billion (excluding sales to business customers) in 1995, was the fastest-growing form of retailing. The advent of the free trade agreement in 1989 and a slowing of U.S. growth due to marketplace saturation and overexpansion led to the expansion of this format into Canada. And it seems that this approach is having the same kind of impact in Canada as in the United States. Presently, Canada's most significant retailer using the club format is Price/Costco, with estimated annual sales of $4.5 billion.[14]

*A **membership warehouse club** offers deep discounts to its member customers.*

In recent years, other forms of low-price retailing have also grown. Among them are warehouse-style food stores, off-price specialty chains, discount drugstore chains, and factory outlet stores. These retailers all hold their prices down by maximizing inventory turnover, using plain store fixtures, locating at inexpensive sites, running few ads, and offering less customer service. They appeal to price-sensitive consumers. Examples of these retailers include Loblaws-owned No Frills (a warehouse-style food store) and A Buck or Two (an off-price specialty chain).

Table 17-2 shows the differences between discount store and traditional department store strategies.

Table 17-2
Typical Retail Strategy Mixes: A Discount Store Versus a Traditional Department Store

DISCOUNT STORE STRATEGY	DEPARTMENT STORE STRATEGY
1. Less expensive rental location—lower level of pedestrian traffic. (Note: Some discount stores are using more expensive locations.)	1. More expensive rental location in shopping centre or district—higher level of pedestrian traffic.
2. Simpler fixtures, linoleum floor, central dressing room, fewer interior and window displays.	2. More elaborate fixtures, carpeted floor, individual dressing rooms, many interior and exterior displays.
3. Promotional emphasis on price. Some discounters do not advertise brand names, but say "famous brands."	3. Promotional emphasis on full service, quality brands, and store image.
4. Fewer alterations, limited phone orders, delivery, and gift wrapping; less availability of credit.	4. Many alterations included in prices, phone orders accepted, and home delivery at little or no fee; credit widely available.
5. More reliance on self-service, plain displays with piles of merchandise; most merchandise visible.	5. Extensive sales assistance, attractive merchandise displays, a lot of storage in back room.
6. Emphasis on branded products; selection may not be complete (not all models and colours). Some discounters feature "seconds," remove labels from goods if asked by manufacturers, and stock discontinued lines.	6. Emphasis on a full selection of branded and privately branded high-quality products; does not stock closeouts, low-price, nonbranded items.
7. Year-round use of low prices.	7. Sales limited to end-of-season clearances and special events.

---

[14]"Price Costco Gets Even Bigger," *Marketing Magazine* (September 11, 1995), p. 3.

Nonstore Operations

Nonstore retailing *is nontraditional.*

With **nonstore retailing**, a firm uses a strategy mix that is not store-based to reach consumers and complete transactions. It does not involve conventional store facilities.

Vending machines *allow twenty-four-hour, self-service sales.*

A **vending machine** uses coin- or card-operated machinery to dispense goods (such as beverages) or services (such as video rentals). It eliminates the need for salespeople, allows twenty-four-hour sales, and can be placed outside rather than inside a store. Its sales are concentrated in a few products—beverages, food items, and cigarettes yield 99 per cent of the Canadian total. Machines may need intensive servicing due to breakdowns, stock-outs, and vandalism. Improved technology lets vending machines make change for bills, "talk" to consumers, use video screens to show products, brew coffee, and so on. Canadian sales through vending machines were $376.8 million in 1994, a fall from $393.3 million in 1993. This occurred despite the fact that Canada has a one dollar coin. Vending machine retailers are hopeful that the availability of the $2 coin will improve the sales picture.[15]

Direct selling *encompasses personal contacts with consumers in nonstore settings.*

Direct selling involves personal contact with consumers in their homes (and other nonstore locations) and phone solicitations initiated by the retailer. Cosmetics, vacuum cleaners, household services (like carpet cleaning), dairy products, and newspapers are sometimes marketed via direct selling. In a cold canvass, a salesperson calls people or knocks on doors to find customers. With referrals, past buyers recommend friends to the salesperson. In the party method, one consumer acts as host and invites people to a sales demonstration in his or her home (or other nonstore site). To some consumers, direct selling has a poor image. In addition, sales force turnover is high and many people are not home during the day. To increase business, salespeople for firms such as Avon now target working women using office presentations during breaks and lunch hours. Direct selling has yearly revenues of $3 billion.[16] Avon, Tupperware, and Kids Only Clothing are direct selling organizations.

In **direct marketing**, *a seller first communicates with consumers via nonpersonal media.*

Direct marketing occurs when a consumer is first exposed to a good or service by a nonpersonal medium (such as direct mail, TV, radio, magazine, newspaper, or PC) and then orders by mail, phone, or PC. Many people find this a convenient way to shop because they do not have to leave their home. Although they do have to wait to receive their goods, express transportation services have offset some of the delay in delivery and made this form of retailing even more attractive.

In the U.S. more than one-half of households make such purchases each year but the Canadian market is less responsive with only 15 per cent of Canadians ordering every year. Despite the low level of response in Canada compared with the U.S., the sales growth in direct marketing is from 7 to 10 per cent each year in Canada and it is one of the faster growing sectors of Canadian retailing. Its growth is being fuelled by the popularity of both manufacturer brands and the private brands of many direct marketing firms (and consumer confidence in them), the large number of working women, and the belief that direct marketing is a good way to shop.[17]

For retailers, direct marketing offers low operating costs, coverage of a wide geographic area, and new market segments. Direct marketing is used by specialized firms, as well as store retailers that apply it to supplement their regular business. Among the most popular direct-marketing items are books; tapes and CDs; clothing; magazines; insurance; home accessories; and sports equipment. Yearly Canadian direct marketing retail sales are about $3.2 billion, with about $1.8 billion of that in catalogue sales. Some examples of Canadian direct marketers include: Sears Canada (with half of Canadian catalogue sales), Regal Greetings & Gifts, and the Winnipeg Fur Exchange. See Figure 17-6. Hoping to expand their sales, a large number of American catalogue direct marketers have been ser-

---

[15]Statistics Canada, *1995 Market Research Handbook* (Ottawa: Minister of Supply Services Canada), p. 90.
[16]Statistics Canada, "Vending Machine Operators, 1994," *The Daily* (Wednesday April 3, 1996).
[17]Lara Mills, "Foreign Cataloguers Still Puzzling Over Canada," *Marketing Magazine* (June 12, 1995), p. 8; and David Napier, "Northern Exposure: Why Competing Cataloguers Are Welcoming Spiegel's Entry Into Canada," *Marketing Magazine* (April 29, 1996), pp. 12–13.

FIGURE 17-6
Regal Greetings and Gifts: A Canadian Tradition of Catalogue Retailing for Sixty-Eight Years
Reprinted with permission of REGAL Greetings & Gifts Inc.

vicing the Canadian market, including: Land's End, L.L. Bean, Victoria's Secret, Walt Disney, and the most recent entrant, Spiegel.[18]

Globally, the United States, Europe, and Japan account for 95 per cent of the world's mail-order business. The United States alone is responsible for 47 per cent of the total. These global markets represent excellent opportunities for sales growth of Canadian direct marketers. Curiously, despite its size and a favourable exchange rate, Canadian catalogue retailers have not focused on the the U.S. market because they believe it is overexposed and too competitive. For this reason many Canadian catalogue marketers are looking to Japan, an underexposed market with a favourable exchange rate. In March 1996, catalogue retailers Regal Greetings and Gifts, Kindred Spirits of Prince Edward Island, the Winnipeg Fur Exchange, Canadian Geographic Enterprises, B.C. Placings of Vancouver and Cows Prince Edward Island of Charlottetown promoted themselves at the Tokyo Convention Centre in hopes of getting a piece of the U.S.$1 billion dollar foreign-catalogue sales market in Japan.[19]

LAND'S END
www.landsend.com/

L.L. BEAN
www.llbean.com/

Considerations in Retail Planning

There are many factors for retailers to weigh in devising marketing plans—and for manufacturers, service providers, and wholesalers to keep in mind. Five key factors are store location, atmosphere, scrambled merchandising, the wheel of retailing, and technological advances.

---

[18] James Pollock, "Lists of Opportunity," *Marketing Magazine* (May 22, 1995), pp. 14–15; James Pollock, "Pushing the Envelope," *Marketing Magazine* (November 20, 1995), pp. 14–15; and "Mail-Order Shopping: Which Catalogs Are Best?" *Consumer Reports* (October 1994), p. 621.

[19] James Pollock, "Eastward Ho!" *Marketing Magazine* (April 29, 1996), pp. 12–14; For an in-depth look at the global opportunities available to direct marketers, see Richard Miller, *Multinational Direct Marketing: The Methods and the Markets* (New York: McGraw-Hill, 1995).

Store Location

Store location is meaningful because it helps determine the customer mix and competition faced. Once selected, it is also inflexible. The basic forms of store location are the isolated store, the unplanned business district, and the planned shopping centre.

*An **isolated store** is a freestanding outlet on a highway or side street.*

An **isolated store** is a freestanding retail outlet located on a highway or street. There are no adjacent stores with which the firm competes; but, there are also no stores to help draw shoppers. Customers may hesitate to travel to an isolated store unless it has a good product assortment and an established image. This site may be used by discount stores due to low rent and to accommodate suppliers who prefer them to be far enough away from stores selling goods and services at full prices. Some K-mart and 7-Eleven stores are isolated.

*In an **unplanned business district**, stores locate together with no prior planning.*

An **unplanned business district** exists where multiple stores are located close to one another without prior planning as to the number and composition of stores. The four unplanned sites are central business district, secondary business district, neighbourhood business district, and string.

A central business district (CBD) is the hub of retailing in a city and is sometimes called "downtown." It has the most commercial, employment, cultural, entertainment, and shopping facilities in a city—with at least one major department store and a broad grouping of specialty and convenience stores. CBDs have had some problems with crowding, a lack of parking, older buildings, limited pedestrian traffic when offices close, nonstandardized store hours, and crime. Yet in many urban areas CBD sales remain strong. Among the tactics being used to strengthen CBDs are modernizing storefronts and equipment, improving transportation, closing streets to vehicular traffic, developing strong merchant associations, planting trees to make areas more attractive, and integrating the commercial and residential environment.

A secondary business district (SBD) is a shopping area bounded by the intersection of two major streets. Cities tend to have several SBDs, each with at least one branch department store, a variety store, and/or some larger specialty stores, as well as several smaller shops. Compared to a CBD, an SBD has less assortment, a smaller trading area (the geographic area from which customers are drawn), and sells more convenience-oriented items.

A neighbourhood business district (NBD) satisfies the convenience-shopping and service needs of a neighbourhood. It has a number of small stores, with the major retailer being a supermarket, a large drugstore, or a variety store. An NBD is located on the major street in a residential area.

A string is ordinarily composed of a group of stores with similar or compatible product lines that situate along a street or highway. Because this location is unplanned, various store combinations are possible. Car dealers, antique stores, and clothing stores often locate in strings.

*A **planned shopping centre** is centrally planned and has balanced tenancy.*

A **planned shopping centre** has centrally owned or managed facilities; it is planned and operated as an entity, ringed by parking, and based on balanced tenancy. With balanced tenancy, the number and composition of stores are related to overall shopper needs—stores complement each other in the variety and quality of their offerings. To ensure balance, a centre may limit the products a store carries. The three types of planned centre are regional, community, and neighbourhood.

A regional shopping centre sells mostly shopping goods to a geographically dispersed market. It has at least one or two department stores and up to a hundred or more smaller stores. People will drive as much as a half hour to reach such a centre. As with CBDs, many regional centres (especially those built a while ago) need renovation. Enhancements include bringing in "hot" new retailers, enclosing more malls, erecting new store directories, redesigning storefronts, adding trees and plants, and replacing concrete in parking lots.

A community shopping centre has a branch department store, a variety store, and/or a large specialty store as its major retailer, with several smaller stores. It sells both convenience- and shopping-oriented items. A neighbourhood shopping centre sells mostly convenience-oriented goods and services. It has a supermarket and/or drugstore, and a few smaller stores.

Atmosphere

Atmosphere is the sum total of the physical attributes of a retail store or group of stores that are used to develop an image and draw customers. It affects the target market attracted, the customer's shopping mood and time spent in the store, impulse purchases, and store positioning; and is related to the strategy chosen. As was shown in Table 17–2, a discount store would have simple fixtures, linoleum floors, and crowded displays. A full-service store would have elaborate fixtures, carpeted floors, and attractive displays.

There are four basic components of a store's atmosphere:

- *Exterior*—elements such as the storefront, the marquee, entrances, display windows, store visibility, store design, the surrounding area, and traffic congestion.
- *General interior*—elements such as flooring, colours, scents, lighting, fixtures, wall textures, temperature, aisle width, vertical transportation, personnel, cash register placement, and overall cleanliness.
- *Store layout*—elements such as the floor space allotted for customers, selling, and storage; product groupings; and department locations.
- *Interior (point-of-sale) displays*—elements such as merchandise cases and racks, mobiles, in-store ads, posters, and mannequins.

Canada's West Edmonton Mall—the world's largest planned shopping centre—uses an innovative atmosphere to draw millions of people annually, some from over 1200 kilometres away. It has eleven department stores, more than 800 other shops, a mile-long concourse, and fifty-eight entrances. Its size equals 115 football fields. The mall contains an amusement park, an ice-skating rink, a miniature golf course, and other attractions. It has parking for 20 000 vehicles. Total construction costs exceeded $700 million and the mall is estimated to bring $1.2 billion into Alberta each year.[20] See Figure 17-7.

Atmosphere *consists of a store's exterior, general interior, layout, and displays.*

WEST EDMONTON MALL
www.westedmall.com/

FIGURE 17-7
The World's Largest Mall
Canada's West Edmonton Mall is the world's largest planned shopping centre.
Reprinted by permission of West Edmonton Mall.

[20]Brian Hutchinson, "Trouble In Big Mall Country," *Canadian Business* (September 1994), pp. 68–76; and Triple Five Corporation Ltd. correspondence.

FIGURE 17-8
The Self-Perpetuating Nature of Scrambled Merchandising

Scrambled Merchandising

In **scrambled merchandising**, *a retailer adds items to obtain one-stop shopping, higher margins, and impulse purchases.*

Scrambled merchandising occurs when a retailer adds goods and services that are unrelated to each other and to the firm's original business. Examples are supermarkets adding videocassette rentals, department stores offering theatre ticket services, restaurants carrying newspapers, and car washes stocking postcards.

There are several reasons for the popularity of scrambled merchandising: Retailers seek to convert their stores to one-stop shopping centres. Scrambled merchandise is often fast selling, generates store traffic, and yields high profit margins. Impulse purchasing is increased. Different target markets can be attracted. And the effects of seasonality and competition may be lessened.

On the other hand, scrambled merchandising can spread quickly and cause competition among unrelated firms. For instance, when supermarkets branch into nonfood personal-care items, drugstore sales fall. This forces the drugstores to scramble into stationery and other product lines, which has a subsequent impact on specialty store sales. The situation is illustrated in Figure 17-8.

There are limits to how far a firm should go with scrambled merchandising, especially if adding unrelated items would reduce buying, selling, and service effectiveness. Furthermore, stock turnover might be low for certain product lines should a retailer enter too many diverse product categories. Finally, scrambled merchandising may make a firm's image fuzzy to consumers.

The Wheel of Retailing

The **wheel of retailing** *shows how strategies change, leaving opportunities for new firms.*

The **wheel of retailing** describes how low-end (discount) strategies can evolve into high-end (full service, high price) strategies and thus provide opportunities for new firms to enter as discounters. Retail innovators often first appear as low-price operators with low profit-margin requirements and low costs. As time passes, the innovators look to increase their sales and customer base. They upgrade product offerings, facilities, and services and turn into more traditional retailers. They may expand the sales force, move to better sites, and usher in delivery, credit, and alterations. The improvements lead to higher costs, which in turn cause higher prices. This creates openings for a new generation of retailers to emerge by appealing to the price-conscious shoppers who are left behind as existing firms move along the wheel. Figure 17-9 shows the wheel in action.

There are some limitations in applying the wheel-of-retailing theory too literally. In particular, many retailers do not follow the pattern suggested; and trying to move along the wheel may cause a firm to lose its loyal customers. The best use of the wheel is in understanding that retailers can pursue distinct low-end, medium, and high-end strategies.

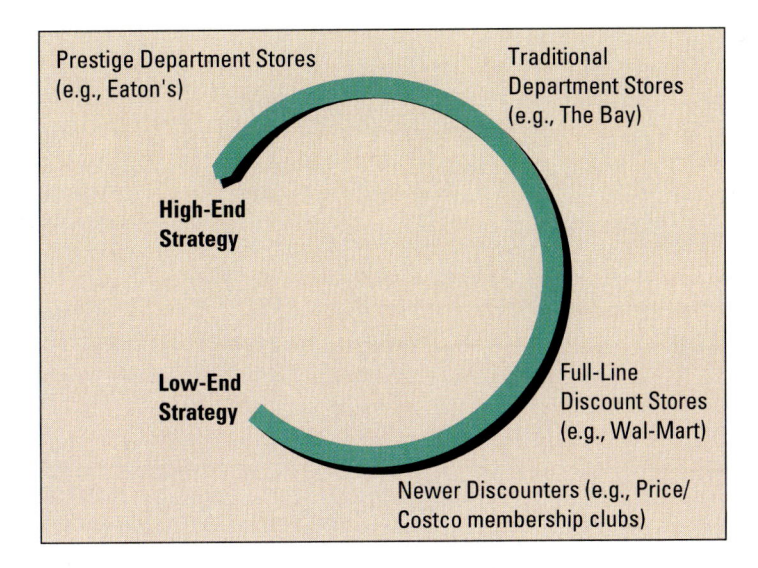

FIGURE 17-9
The Wheel of Retailing in Action

(Diagram showing: Prestige Department Stores (e.g., Eaton's) — High-End Strategy; Traditional Department Stores (e.g., The Bay); Full-Line Discount Stores (e.g., Wal-Mart); Newer Discounters (e.g., Price/Costco membership clubs) — Low-End Strategy)

Technological Advances

Over the last several years, a number of technological advances related to retailing have emerged. The most dramatic are the computerized checkout system, video shopping services, data warehousing, computer-aided site selection, electronic banking, and operating efficiency.

In a computerized-checkout (electronic point-of-sale) system, a cashier manually rings up a sale or passes an item over or past an optical scanner; a computerized register instantly records and displays a sale. The customer gets a receipt, and inventory data are stored in the computer's memory bank. Such a system reduces checkout time, employee training, misrings, and the need for price marking on all products. It also generates a current listing of the merchandise in stock without taking a physical inventory, improves inventory control, reduces spoilage, and aids ordering.

Video shopping services let retailers efficiently, conveniently, and promptly present information, receive orders, and process transactions. These services can be divided into two basic categories: merchandise catalogues, and in-store and in-home ordering systems.

Video catalogues (shown on special monitors or via disc players/VCRs using conventional TV sets) allow consumers to view pre-recorded product and sales presentations in store and nonstore settings without the seller having to set up costly displays. With such catalogues (sometimes called kiosks), supermarkets can market appliances, airports can market watches, department stores can market gourmet foods, and mail-order firms can make their offerings come to life.

With an in-store video-ordering system, a consumer orders products by entering data into a self-prompting computer, which processes the order. After placing the order, the consumer usually goes to a checkout area where the item can be picked up and an invoice received. The consumer then pays a cashier. For an in-home system, goods and services are listed or displayed and then consumers order directly on special toll-free 800 phone numbers or through their PCs. To date, most in-home ordering has been from consumer phone responses to TV shows offered by such firms as the Canadian Home Shopping Network.

One area of massive retail growth is expected to be shopping on the Internet in **cybermalls**. Many retailers have set up independent Internet Web sites and e-mail sites (e.g., Toronto's Cookbook Store), but a cybermall is a shared Web site. The Malls of Canada shopping site has ninety storefronts including firms such as: Bell Mobility, Carnival Cruiselines, and The Jewellery Archives. Growth of these malls had been expected to accelerate at a tremendous rate, but online sales have been disappointing. This is because only an estimated 8 per cent of Canadians are using online shopping. A major concern for

Technological advances range from computerized-checkout systems to enhanced operating efficiency.

Cybermalls are one of the new forms of retailing spawned by the computer age.

TECHNOLOGY & MARKETING

Self-Scanning: Will Consumers Pass the Honesty Test?

Several supermarket chains are now testing a scanning system that lets consumers scan their groceries as they shop and then ring up and total their purchases. In most of the tests, shoppers receive a hand-held scanner as they enter the supermarket. They then scan items as they are picked and deposited into their shopping carts. If a shopper wishes to return an item to the shelf, it can easily be deducted from the bill.

At the end of the shopping trip, the scanner system prints out a shopper's total bill. In some stores, a customer can pay the bill on his or her credit card by swiping the card through the scanner. Many stores are also providing a take-home container that fits compactly into the shopping cart. This container eliminates the need to unpack and then repack the shopping cart.

According to market analysts, the real test of self-scanning is of consumers' honesty, not the equipment. Although tests of this system in the Netherlands showed that retail shoplifting actually dropped because of self-scanning, many experts feel that the Dutch experience may not be replicated in North America. Other potential problems relate to using self-scanning with fruits and vegetables (consumers must know the proper variety and then weigh the foods selected), dealing with items that do not properly scan, and the embarrassment to shoppers who, during a random check by a store employee, discover they inadvertently forgot to scan an item or two.

Supermarkets hope that self-scanning will attract shoppers interested in reducing the time spent on checkout lines. Other advantages include the ability to calculate their total bill during the shopping process (to stay within budget) and better access to price information.

As the manager of an independent supermarket, would you recommend self-scanning? Why or why not?

Source: Based on material in Tara Parker-Pope, "New Devices Add Up Bill, Measure Shoppers' Honesty," *Wall Street Journal* (June 6, 1995), pp. B1, B6; and Emily Nelson, "Finast Tests Scanners to Shorten Time Needed for Customers to Check Out," *Wall Street Journal* (October 25, 1995), p. B5.

---

consumers is the security of transactions and currency exchanges on the Internet when credit cards or bank debit cards are used for payment.[21]

Through "data warehousing," more retailers are embracing database marketing. For example:

> Regal Greetings & Gifts of Toronto acquired a new catalogue entitled the *Jacarandra Tree*. Regal then used two years' worth of purchase behaviour information from its Disney Catalogue to match up buyers from this list with potential buyers for items from the *Jacarandra Tree*. Keeping detailed information on customers enables Regal's managers to find and analyze data by customer, product, and transaction. The transaction information available to Regal includes not only purchases, but also requests for catalogues, shipping dates, and orders for merchandise that was not in stock.[22]

The availability of inexpensive computerized site-selection software is so prevalent that retailers of any size and type can now use it. For as little as U.S.$500, a retailer can buy geographic information systems (GIS) software that graphically depicts population characteristics, location attributes, roadways, and so on—for numerous potential or existing store sites. Canadian retail firms interested in locating in the U.S. can buy a CD-ROM diskette that lists 400 000 retail tenants in 34 000 U.S. shopping centres for U.S.$1795.[23]

---

[21] Deborah Stokes, "Take Two for Cybermalls," *Marketing Magazine* (June 10, 1996), pp. 16, 19.
[22] James Pollock, "Lists of Opportunity," *Marketing Magazine* (May 22, 1995), pp. 14–15.
[23] See Greg Hano, "Back to Basics," *Marketing Tools* (October 1995), pp. 10–15; and Michael Hartnett, "New Technologies Simplify Retail Site Selection," *Stores* (October 1995), pp. 45–46.

Electronic banking involves the use of automatic teller machines (ATMs) and the instant processing of purchases. It provides central record keeping and lets customers conduct transactions twenty-four hours a day, seven days a week at many locations (such as banks and supermarkets). Deposits, withdrawals, and other banking and retailing tasks can be completed. ATMs are widely available in Canadian banks and trust companies, shopping centres, stores, airports, and other sites. To allow customers to make financial transactions over wider geographic areas, many banks have formed ATM networks. In North America there are hundreds of local and regional networks and half a dozen national (international) systems. The Cirrus and Plus networks allow customers to make transactions at tens of thousands of ATMs throughout North America and the world. There are 100 000 ATMs respectively in each of North America, Japan, and Europe.

As electronic banking spreads, more firms will participate in **debit transactions**, in which the amount of a sale is immediately charged against a buyer's bank account at the point of sale. A debit-card system is different from current credit-card policy, whereby consumers are sent bills and then remit payment. Debit cards will receive wide acceptance as a substitute for cheques. In 1995, approximately 7.5 per cent of all retail purchases were made with debit cards, compared to 3.5 per cent in 1994. One of the well-known brands of debit cards used in Canada is Interac.[24]

*With **debit transactions**, payments are immediately deducted from customers' accounts.*

Technological advances are also leading to greater retailer efficiency by:

- Increasing the use of self-service operations by firms marketing gasoline, airline tickets, and rental cars, and for hotel registrations and payment.
- Linking manufacturers, warehouses, and transportation firms.
- Introducing anti-shoplifting tags that set off an alarm if not properly removed by employees.
- Automating energy-control systems to monitor store temperature carefully and reduce fuel costs.
- Computerizing order entry in restaurants.

Furthermore, "The good news is that small retailers can also use technology as a tool in achieving greater efficiency. And the technology that's used doesn't have to be the highly complicated or expensive *Star Wars* variety."[25] It is essentially the same technology found in the home computers owned by millions of Canadians.

Recent Trends in Retailing

Retailing is in a great state of flux, particularly in Canada, as firms strive to defend or expand their positions in the marketplace. Many consumers no longer want to spend as much time shopping as they once did, various retail sectors have become saturated, a number of large retailers are operating under high levels of debt (typically caused by leveraged buyouts or overexpansion), and some retailers—after running frequent sales—have found it difficult to maintain regular prices. Here's what has been happening:

This is a tough period for many retailers, due to changing consumer lifestyles, competition, and other factors.

> The new rules of retailing include coping with nonstore competition, technology, and consolidation, as well as entertaining customers. Traditional jewellers are increasingly threatened by TV home shopping and catalogues. Hosiery manufacturers may sell pantyhose and socks on the Internet; perfumers are already doing so with scents. Small family nurseries are giving way to conglomerates in the bulb-and-seed business. Shoppers will soon see entertainment-retail destinations at which they can play tennis before buying a racquet or see a show about Julius Caesar's coronation. Virtually every retail business is involved with at least one of these issues.[26]

To succeed in the long run, Canadian retailers must respond to the trends they are facing. Among the most prominent are those relating to consumer demographics and

---

[24]"Interac Promotion to Boost Debit Cards," *Marketing Magazine* (October 9, 1995), p. 3.
[25]"Using Technology to Achieve Critical Success Factors," *Chain Store Age* (October 1995), Section Three, p. 8A.
[26]Fanglan Du and Ira Apfel, "The Future of Retailing," *American Demographics* (September 1995), p. 28.

CLUB MONACO
www.clubmonaco.com

lifestyles, competitive forces, operating costs, the labour force, and opportunities in foreign markets. Here is how various retailers are dealing with them.

The aging Canadian population, the increasing size of ethnic markets, and the saturation of many prime markets have resulted in various innovative retailing strategies. Club Monaco, a youth oriented clothier owned by Dylex of Toronto, has chosen to expand by opening outlets in Japan, Korea, and Thailand where the youth markets are larger and growing much faster than in Canada. Leon's Furniture of Toronto has targeted the multicultural population of Toronto with specially designed ads for the Chinese, Italian, and Portuguese communities. Locations that have been underserved are being used—Price/Costco opened up a store in Moncton, New Brunswick, a relatively small population centre, in hopes of drawing customers from all of New Brunswick and the neighbouring Atlantic Provinces.[27]

Retailers are adapting to the shopping needs and time constraints of working women and dual-earner households, and the increased consumer interest in quality and customer service. They are stocking such laboursaving products as ready-to-eat foods and pre-loaded PCs; lengthening store hours and opening additional days; expanding catalogue and phone sales efforts; reemphasising personal selling; pre-wrapping gift items to eliminate waiting lines; setting up comprehensive specialty boutiques to minimize the number of departments a consumer must visit; adding special services, such as fashion coordinators; marketing high-quality private brands; and creating more attractive displays.

Retailing's intense competition has led to a wide spectrum of company responses. These are two illustrations: Market analysts believed that Canadian Tire would become a retail casualty as a result of the entrance of Wal-Mart and Home Depot into Canada. Canadian Tire chose to respond by expanding and modernizing stores in small and mid-size Canadian markets. In addition, it improved customer service with a no-hassle returns policy, a frequent purchaser points program for credit-card users and more training for sales staff. And it focused on its three core product areas of autos, housewares, and sports and leisure.

Building customer loyalty is the philosophy of Co-op Atlantic stores. Co-op Atlantic operates member-only stores which have two approaches to building customer loyalty. Some stores charge weekly fees of $3 to $5 no matter how much a member spends. After paying their fee, members can then make their purchases at essentially no markup. A second approach allows both members and non-members to shop at the store. At the end of the year, members receive a dividend cheque. Developing a loyal customer franchise ensures the stores operating profits and efficiency, while the consumers benefit from low prices.[28]

Because of the level of competition in many sectors of retailing, the price sensitivity of a large segment of consumers, and their general interest in improving efficiency (and profit margins), retailers are more concerned with cost control than ever before. For instance, several fast-food companies now use a format whereby different outlets occupy the same building (as food courts have done for years in shopping malls). This format lets them share common costs and even some employees. Most small hardware stores participate in buying cooperatives that enable them to secure quantity discounts and "buy smarter." Many supermarkets have increased their use of bulk selling, by which consumers select exact quantities of items such as candy and dried fruit from open displays. A number of mail-order firms are better targeting customers and containing their catalogue costs. United Furniture Warehouse of Coquitlam, B.C. has chosen a no-frills approach to keep costs down. United Furniture's strategy is to sell at warehouse prices, operate without commission sales staff, and finally, "We keep the overhead down." Literally. "We don't even have ceilings—just rafters like in a regular warehouse."[29]

---

[27]James Pollock, "Club Monaco Continues Asian Expansion," *Marketing Magazine* (November 13, 1995), p. 7; Andrea Haman, "Chinese Market: Leon's Furniture's TV Spots," *Marketing Magazine* (November 6, 1995), p. 21; and Mark Higgins, "Price Club Opens Two Atlantic Warehouse Stores," *Marketing Magazine* (November 6, 1995), p. 15.

[28]John Lorinc, "Road Warriors," *Canadian Business* (October 1995), pp. 26–43; and Mark Higgins, "Owners and Consumers," *Marketing Magazine* (November 6, 1995), pp. 14–15.

[29]Katrina Onstad, "Armchair Quarterback," *Canadian Business* (December 1995), pp. 80–81.

International Marketing in Action

What's Next for Retailing in China?

Retail experts predict that China's retail sales will more than double between 1995 and the year 2000. In 1993, the latest year for which data are available, the sales of China's state-owned department store chain, Shanghai No. 1, rose by 44 per cent and after-tax profit rose by 78 per cent over 1992.

State retailers are working hard to deal with China's increasingly sophisticated consumers. Thus, to better compete against domestic and international competitors, state-owned retailers are teaming up with foreign partners. Generally, China's retailers are trading their land-rights usage (as a state enterprise they have rent-free status) and their ability to cut through China's bureaucracy in return for their foreign partners' superior management skills and financial resources.

One significant joint venture is Nextage Shanghai (short for next stage), a partnership of Shanghai No. 1 Department Store Company and Japan's Yaohan Group. Nextage Shanghai is a U.S.$200-million complex that features department and specialty stores, an ice-skating rink, an automobile dealership, fast-food outlets, and sports and entertainment facilities. One marketing characteristic of Nextstage Shanghai is its focus on higher-fashion clothing. To appeal to fashion-oriented firms such as Esprit, Donna Karan, Ralph Lauren, and Yves Saint Laurent, Nextstage Shanghai will provide manufacturers with greater control over merchandise presentation by offering them consignment sales opportunities. Nextstage Shanghai hopes to attract these designers, many of whom shunned state-owned department stores in previous years.

High growth prospects and the easing of government investment restrictions have also accelerated the growth of foreign retailer competition. Among the retailers that have recently announced plans to enter China or have already entered are Wal-Mart, Walt Disney, Esprit, Jusco (Japan), and Au Printemps (France).

As a marketing consultant to a Canadian retailer, assess Nextstage's strategy.

Source: Based on material in Sally D. Goll, "China's Big State-Owned Retail Stores Form New Ventures with Foreign Firms," *Wall Street Journal* (March 13, 1995), p. A11C.

Some Canadian retailers are having trouble attracting and retaining a quality labour force. According to surveys, retailers rank the labour shortage as one of the most crucial issues for them to address. Among the reasons why the shortage exists are that the number of available young people has declined; full-time career opportunities in other industries have attracted a number of part-time retail workers; many retail workers are inexperienced and have overly high job expectations, leading to employee dissatisfaction and turnover; hours can be long and irregular; some people do not like the pressure of interacting with customers on a regular basis; and the pay in other industries has been relatively higher.

A few of the actions retailers are taking to resolve the labour shortage are to recruit more at high schools, community colleges and universities, hire retired persons, offer child-care services for working mothers, raise starting salaries (sometimes to double the minimum wage or more), rotate employees among tasks to reduce boredom, reward good performance with bonuses, and encourage the best employees to pursue full-time career paths in retailing.

Foreign opportunities are plentiful.

For firms with proper resources and management prowess, there are numerous retailing opportunities in foreign markets. These are several examples:

- Toys "R" Us does well in Europe and Japan because of the wide merchandise selection in its stores, especially compared to local retailers.[30]
- "Direct marketing is in its infancy in Russia. In the decade ahead, and based on what has been accomplished in a short time, we expect to witness a commercial environment intertwined with direct marketing applications. That process is certain to become more important and a more integrated function in the new Russian economy. This is especially true in view of the large distances and great span of the country, requiring the vital communication function that direct marketing can provide."[31]
- Because of the lack of discounters in South Korea, the Seoul Price Club has attracted 100 000 members. In contrast, the typical North American Price Club has 45 000 members.[32]
- McDonald's is building hundreds of restaurants in Central Europe, an underserved area for fast-food outlets. It is also expanding rapidly in Latin America and Asia.[33]
- Annual worldwide direct selling revenues are estimated to be U.S.$50 billion (including Canada). This form of retailing was traditionally more popular in North America but is now significantly more popular outside North America, due to consumer demographics and other factors.[34]
- France's Carrefour is the leading retailer in Argentina, with U.S.$1.5 billion in annual revenues.[35]

MARKETING IN A CHANGING WORLD

Invasion of the U.S. Retailers[36]

Recently, many large U.S. retail operations, many of them category killers, have begun to enter Canada. From the consumer's perspective, selection has never been so good while prices have never seemed so low. But for thousands of retailers competing against U.S. invaders, the news is not so good. Take Wal-Mart, for example. In the U.S. Wal-Mart seems virtually unstoppable with its low prices and large assortments. Wal-Mart stores and Sam's Clubs blanket the United States. In addition to its rapid expansion into Canada with the acquisition of 122 Woolco stores from Woolworth, Wal-Mart is also expanding into Mexico, Hong Kong, and elsewhere. In its wake, vulnerable (unprepared) retailers have been falling by the wayside. Category killers such as Home Depot, Price/Costco, and Business Depot are wiping out smaller independent businesses that once thrived as small specialists competing against department stores.

The current American invasion has not had its full impact yet, and it is expected that more foreign retail competition from both the United States and Europe will arise. Wal-Mart's entry has had an effect on retailers that are not positioned against it. For example, Eaton's Department Store is trying to remake itself by downsizing and there are questions about its survival. After the entry of Spiegel on the heels of a number of other U.S. catalogue retailers, Sears Canada says its catalogue

---

[30] Carla Rapoport and Justin Martin, "Retailers Go Global," *Fortune* (February 20, 1995), pp. 104, 106.
[31] Mark D. Mariska, "Direct Marketing in Russia," *Direct Marketing* (January 1995), p. 41.
[32] Gale Eisenstodt, "Park Gui-Sook's Reading List," *Forbes* (September 11, 1995), pp. 72–76.
[33] Jeanne Whalen, "McDonald's Cooks Worldwide Growth," *Advertising Age* (July 17, 1995), pp. l–4.
[34] Direct Selling Education Foundation.
[35] Jonathan Friedland, "Big Discounters Duel Over Hot Market," *Wall Street Journal* (August 23, 1995), p. A8.
[36] James Pollock, "Canada Tougher Than U.S. Stores Thought," *Marketing Magazine* (July 3–10, 1995), p. 4; Andrea Haman, "By the Book," *Marketing Magazine* (November 27, 1995), pp. 9–10; Leonard Kubas, "Navigating the New Retail Landscape," *Marketing Magazine* (July 31–August 7, 1995), pp. 11–12; Eric Swetsky, "Wool-Mart versus Wal-Mart," *Marketing Magazine* (June 24, 1996), p. 20; and James Pollock, "A&P Expands No-frills Food Basics Division," *Marketing Magazine* (November 27, 1995), p. 2.

operations are no longer particularly profitable. Sears Canada is considering following the lead of its U.S. parent, which discontinued catalogue operations a few years ago.

However, U.S. retailers have not steamrolled into Canada without trouble. Wal-Mart is embroiled in a trademark suit over its name with Wool-Mart. Home Depot purchased Aikenhead's from Molson Cos. Ltd. but slowed the pace of its store openings in 1995. Borders books had its entry stalled by the Canadian government, responding to lobbying efforts by Canadian booksellers. Finally, Target Stores of Minneapolis decided not to enter at all given the size of the Canadian market and the level of competition that was being demonstrated.

Price/Costco's focus on the food market has caused expansion and repositioning of grocery retailers throughout Canada. For example, Sobey's, an Atlantic Canada-based retailer, has opened some stores in Ontario and has plans to enter the Quebec market. Meanwhile, A&P has opened some Food Basics stores in southern Ontario, which emphasize low prices. These stores are smaller than traditional grocery stores, do not have delis or bakeries, ask consumers to bag their own groceries, and carry more private labels.

Add the unknown impact of cybermalls and marketing on the Internet to the American invasion and one thing is clear: the Canadian retail market is, and will remain, a highly contested and unstable retailing environment. Nonetheless, as we have noted throughout *Marketing*, when companies follow sound marketing principles, they greatly increase their chances of success. And this is just as true of retailers in the age of the U.S. invasion.

SUMMARY

1. *To define retailing and show its importance* Retailing encompasses those business activities involved with the sale of goods and services to the final consumer for personal, family, or household use. It is the final stage in a distribution channel. Average retail sales are small, yet the use of credit is widespread. Final consumers generally visit a retail store to make a purchase and they also make many unplanned purchases.

Retailing has an impact on the economy because of its total sales and the number of people employed. Retailers provide a variety of functions, including gathering a product assortment, providing information, handling merchandise, and completing transactions. Retailers deal with suppliers that sell products the retailers use in operating their businesses as well as suppliers selling items the retailers will resell.

2. *To discuss the different types of retailers, in terms of ownership, store strategy mix, and nonstore operations* Retailers may be categorized in several ways. The basic ownership formats are independent—a retailer operating only one outlet; chain—a retailer operating two or more outlets; franchise—a contractual arrangement between a franchiser and a franchisee to conduct a certain business; leased department—a department in a store that is leased to an outside party; and retail cooperative—an enterprise shared by retail owners. The ease of entry into retailing fosters competition and results in many new firms failing.

Different strategy mixes are used by convenience stores—well-situated, food-oriented retailers; conventional supermarkets—departmentalized food stores with minimum annual sales of $2 million; food-based superstores—diversified supermarkets that sell a broad range of food and non-food items; combination stores (including supercentres)—outlets that go further than food-based superstores in carrying both food and general merchandise; specialty stores (including category killers)—outlets that concentrate on one merchandise or service line; variety stores—outlets selling a wide assortment of inexpensive and popularly priced merchandise; traditional department stores—outlets that have a great assortment, provide customer services, are fashion leaders, often dominate surrounding stores, and have average to above-average prices; full-line discount stores—department stores with a low-price, moderate-service orientation; membership warehouse clubs—stores that offer very low prices in austere settings; and other discounters—including limited-line stores and off-price chains.

Nonstore retailing occurs when a firm uses a strategy mix that is not store-based. Vending machines use coin- or card-operated machinery to dispense goods and services. Direct selling involves both personal contact with consumers in their homes (or other places) and phone solicitations initiated by retailers. Direct marketing occurs when consumers are exposed to goods and services through non-personal media and then order by mail, phone or computer. Cybermalls and sales through Web sites are among the newest approaches to direct marketing. Nonstore retailing is now a large part of retailing.

3. *To explore five aspects of retail planning: store location, atmosphere, scrambled merchandising, the wheel of retailing, and technological advances* A firm may select from among three forms of store location: an isolated store—a freestanding outlet located on a highway or street; an unplanned business district—in which two or more stores locate close to one another without prior planning as to the number and composition of stores; and a planned shopping centre—which is centrally

managed, as well as planned and operated as an entity. Only planned shopping centres utilize balanced tenancy, thus relating the store mix to consumer needs.

Atmosphere is the sum total of a store's physical characteristics that help develop an image and attract customers. It depends on the store's exterior, general interior, layout, and interior displays.

Scrambled merchandising occurs when a retailer adds products unrelated to its original business. The goals of scrambled merchandising are to encourage customer one-stop shopping, increase sales of high-profit items and impulse purchases, attract different target markets, and balance sales throughout the year.

The wheel of retailing explains low-end and high-end retail strategies and how they emerge. As low-cost, low-price innovators move along the wheel, they leave opportunities for newer, more cost-conscious firms to enter the market.

A number of technological advances have emerged over the past several years. These include computerized checkouts, video shopping services, data warehousing, computerized site selection, electronic banking, and techniques to improve operating efficiency.

4. *To examine recent trends in retailing* The nature of retailing has changed dramatically in recent years. Among the key trends retailers are adapting to are those relating to consumer demographics and lifestyles, competitive forces, operating costs, the labour force, and international opportunities.

KEY TERMS

retailing (p. 460)
independent retailer (p. 464)
retail chain (p. 464)
retail franchising (p. 465)
leased department (p. 466)
retail cooperative (p. 466)
retail store strategy mix (p. 466)
convenience store (p. 466)
conventional supermarket (p. 466)
food-based superstore (p. 466)

combination store (p. 466)
supercentre (p. 466)
specialty store (p. 467)
category killer (p. 467)
variety store (p. 468)
traditional department store (p. 468)
full-line discount store (p. 468)
membership warehouse club (p. 469)
nonstore retailing (p. 470)
vending machine (p. 470)

direct selling (p. 470)
direct marketing (p. 470)
isolated store (p. 472)
unplanned business district (p. 472)
planned shopping centre (p. 472)
atmosphere (p. 473)
scrambled merchandising (p. 474)
wheel of retailing (p. 474)
cybermalls (p. 475)
debit transactions (p. 477)

Review Questions

1. Describe the four basic functions performed by retailers.
2. What are the disadvantages of an independent retailer in competing with retail chains?
3. What are the benefits of retail franchising to the franchisee? To the franchiser?
4. Why would a store want to have leased shoe departments rather than operate these departments itself?
5. Compare the strategies of full-line discount stores and membership warehouse clubs.
6. Distinguish between direct marketing and direct selling. Which has greater sales? Why?
7. What are the pros and cons of scrambled merchandising?
8. Explain the wheel of retailing from the perspective of the battle between traditional department stores and full-line discount stores for market share.
9. Differentiate between credit cards and debit cards. What is the benefit of debit cards to retailers?
10. Why is attracting and retaining a quality labour force so difficult for many Canadian retailers?

Discussion Questions

1. The typical retailer earns a profit of three per cent or less on its sales revenues. How can this amount be so low if 38 to 40 cents of every customer dollar spent in department stores and specialty stores go to the retailers?
2. As a prospective franchisee for a Robin's Donuts outlet, what criteria would you use in deciding whether Robin's Donuts is right for you? What criteria do you think Robin's Donuts should use in assessing potential franchisees? Explain the differences in your answers to these two questions.
3. Develop a discount-store strategy for an art gallery. How would the strategy differ from that for an upscale art gallery?
4. Select a planned shopping centre near your college or university and evaluate it with respect to its size and the size of its trading area. (Note that the term "size" can have several definitions—take as many of them into account as possible when answering this question.)
5. How can a nonstore retailer create a good shopping atmosphere for its customers?

VIDEO CASE

Wal-Mart: The World's Largest Retailer Comes to Canada

When the Canada-U.S. free trade agreement was signed in 1987 it allowed Wal-Mart, the world's largest retailer, to select Canada as its first major site for international expansion. In 1994, Wal-Mart bought 122 Woolco stores from Woolworth Canada. How could Canadian retailers compete with the world's largest retailer? They had some advantages over their U.S. counterparts. Canada is similar to the United States, but it is still a different country with different laws and a different political system. Secondly, with the acquisition of the Woolco chain, Canadian competitors knew where Wal-Mart was going to locate physically. Since the Woolco stores were going concerns, the market was not really absorbing another competitor, just a newer one, albeit a much leaner and meaner one.

Finally, Canadian retailers could get advice on dealing with Wal-Mart by looking at its U.S. history and by hiring Wal-Mart's nemesis, Dr. Ken Stone, an Economics professor from the University of Iowa. Ken Stone lectures and advises retailers on how to challenge Wal-Mart. The two main essentials of Ken Stone's advice are "Know thy competitor" and "Change the way you do business to respond to Wal-Mart."

"Know thy competitor" means knowing as much as possible about the way Wal-Mart operates. For example, Wal-Mart is really only heavily price competitive on 500 to 600 of the 75 000 to 80 000 items it carries. And with the second largest computer system in the United States, sales and inventory levels are communicated to head office and the factories of suppliers. Head office can then order from a central location from its suppliers and get the maximum quantity discounts possible.

Wal-Mart approaches suppliers directly, dealing from a position of great strength as the world's largest retailer and the fourth largest firm in the United States. In fact, it often re-engineers its suppliers, investigating the manufacturing costs of suppliers' products and asking them to justify the prices they charge. This constant interaction with suppliers help Wal-Mart build relationships and lower costs, to the detriment of their competitors.

So how can you compete against Wal-Mart? Ken Stone believes that with knowledge, competing stores can survive and thrive. The key is finding a niche that Wal-Mart is not filling and being price competitive on the particular retailer's share of the 500 to 600 items about which consumers are price conscious. If a retailer cannot be price competitive, it should abandon products and concentrate on others. For example, a hardware store cannot compete against Wal-Mart when it comes to small appliances and commonly used cleaning items. However, Wal-Mart has very little in the way of plumbing supplies or specialty items. The local hardware retailer can position itself as an advisor to its customers. Wal-Mart salespeople will unlikely be trained to fulfil this function.

Some firms have been successful by working with Wal-Mart, contracting for their repair business. Finally, competing retailers must give cash refunds, the same as Wal-Mart.

So how has it turned out? In 1995, Wal-Mart was operating 129 stores in Canada and claiming to have a 40 per cent share of the sales of the discount department store market. However, the firm was not turning a profit and projections are that Wal-Mart will not achieve a profit on Canadian operations by the end of 1996 either. The firm is embroiled in a lawsuit over its name with a Canadian firm named Wool-Mart. Whatever the outcome, it will involve costs that Wal-Mart would prefer to have going to the bottom line. Finally, one of Wal-Mart's expected victims, Canadian Tire, reacted to Wal-Mart by repositioning themselves. You might say they took Ken Stone's advice. Since Wal-Mart has opened stores in Mexico, Brazil, Argentina, and Asia, it would appear that Ken Stone may just find himself in for some international travel.

QUESTIONS

1. Discuss how Wal-Mart's store location and market entry strategy in Canada differ from its typical U.S. approach. What implications might these differences have for its Canadian competitors?
2. Discuss the validity of this statement: Wal-Mart's success is built on logistics, pure and simple.
3. Discuss why it is so difficult for other firms to match Wal-Mart's success.
4. Evaluate Wal-Mart's international expansion strategy. What suggestions could Wal-Mart managers implement to make Canada a profitable market?

VIDEO QUESTIONS ON WAL-MART

1. Evaluate the pros and cons of Wal-Mart's low-price marketing strategy.
2. Consider yourself as a Canadian counterpart of Dr. Ken Stone. Is there anything unique to Canada which retailers could employ to compete successfully against Wal-Mart?

Video Sources: "Wal-Mart Wizard," *Venture* (December 5, 1993) and "Wal-Mart Update," *Venture* (January 16, 1994).

Other Sources: The data in this case are drawn from Mark Stevenson, "The Store to End All Stores," *Canadian Business* (May 1994), pp. 20–29; James Pollock, "Retreaded," *Marketing Magazine* (July 31–August 7, 1995), pp. 1, 11; Michael Treacy, "Success Through Cannibalism," *Marketing Magazine* (September 4, 1995), p. 17; James Pollock, "Retailers in Scramble to Reposition Stores," *Marketing Magazine* (November 20, 1995), p. 4; Patricia Sellers, "Can Wal-Mart Get Back the Magic?" *Fortune Magazine* (April 29, 1996), pp. 130–136; and Eric Swetsky, "Wool-Mart versus Wal-Mart," *Marketing Magazine* (June 24, 1996), p. 20.

CASE STUDY

At Woodworkers Warehouse Stores: No One's Afraid of Home Depot

At one time, Stanley Black (a high school dropout from a poor family) had two small businesses. One sold metal fasteners; the other sold tools used by furniture makers, repairpersons, and upholsters. In 1982, Black realized that much of the demand for his products came from shops selling to woodworking hobbyists. So, he rented mailing lists of such hobbyists and produced a mail-order catalogue called *Trend-lines*.

In 1986, Stanley Black opened his first Woodworkers Warehouse store. During 1994, Trend-lines raised U.S.$22 million by selling 35 per cent of the company's stock. Black and his wife own 65 per cent of the company. Their stock ownership in Trend-lines is valued at about U.S.$55 million.

Today, Massachusetts-based Trend-lines Inc. owns seventy-five woodworking stores, a *Trend-lines* catalogue that goes to 1.5 million customers, and Golf-Day (a golf-supply retail chain and mail-order catalogue division). In fiscal 1995, Trend-lines had sales of U.S.$128 million and after-tax profits of U.S.$5 million. For fiscal 1996, sales were expected to reach U.S.$185 million; and profits of U.S.$7.5 million were forecast.

Many of Trend-lines' 5000-square-foot Woodworkers Warehouse stores are located within a few blocks of Home Depot (whose stores are up to ten times larger) and other major home improvement stores. But in comparison to Home Depot (which carries a much wider product assortment), Woodworkers Warehouse has a more extensive selection within its chosen product lines—woodworking tools and supplies. For example, Home Depot stores typically carry thirty or so power drills; Woodworker Warehouse stores carry about seventy. And many of the specialty items carried by Woodworkers Warehouse, such as a dovetail jig, are not even available at Home Depot. As a result, many Home Depot salespeople refer customers to Woodworkers Warehouse for specialty items. According to a top executive at Black & Decker, "Woodworkers Warehouse typical customers are like avid fishermen, hunters, and golfers. They want the best and newest products in their hobby. It's a toy store for these people."

There is plenty of untapped growth in this niche market. The magazine *American Woodworker* estimates that there are now 17 million woodworking hobbyists. To capitalize on this demand, Black wants to open another forty stores per year. And Trend-lines' new 286 000-square-foot warehouse has the capacity to supply 375 stores, five times the current level.

Trend-lines acquired Golf-Day in 1989 for U.S.$100 000. Golf-Day complements the firm's woodworking business because sales of golf supplies (such as clubs and golf-cart seat covers) are busiest in the spring and summer—when woodworking sales are slowest. The division's opposite seasonal sales pattern from woodworking supplies and tools (whose sales are busiest in the fall and winter) increases the efficiency of Trend-lines' warehouse operations and sales staff. Golf-Day's ten stores and 700 000-customer mailing list account for over 20 per cent of Trend-lines companywide revenues.

Although Stanley Black is very aggressive in pursuing sales, he is also known for his desire to reduce operating and other costs. For example, Black initially rejected purchasing Golf-Day for U.S.$600 000. A year later he was able to purchase the firm and its then 200 000-person mailing list for U.S.$100 000. In outfitting Trend-lines' new offices, Black selected used partitions, purchased at 15 per cent of the cost of comparable new fixtures. He even buys surplus and misprinted cartons to save money. Thus, some merchandise is delivered to customers in cartons imprinted with a frozen food manufacturer's name.

QUESTIONS

1. Contrast Woodworkers Warehouse's overall retail strategy with Home Depot's.
2. How can an independent retailer effectively compete against Woodworker's Warehouse?
3. What type of store location is most suitable for Woodworkers Warehouse stores? Explain your answer.
4. Explain the strategic fit of the Golf-Day acquisition to Trend-lines.

Source: The data in this case are drawn from Matthew Schifrin, "What Do Woodworkers Do in the Summer?" *Forbes* (May 22, 1995), pp. 116–117.

PROMOTION PLANNING

PART 6

Part 6 covers the third major element of the marketing mix, promotion.

18 The Context of Promotion Planning

Here, we broadly discuss promotion planning, which involves all communication used to inform, persuade, and/or remind people about an organization's or individual's goods, services, image, ideas, community involvement, or impact on society. We describe the basic types of promotion and the stages in a channel of communication. Next, we present the steps in developing an overall promotion plan. We conclude the chapter with international promotion considerations, and the legal environment and criticisms of promotion.

19 Advertising and Public Relations

In this chapter, we examine two of the four types of promotion: advertising and public relations. We define advertising as paid, nonpersonal communication by an identified sponsor; and public relations as any form of image-directed communication by an identified sponsor or the independent media. We detail the scope of advertising and public relations and their attributes, and describe the role of publicity. We discuss the development of advertising and public relations plans in depth.

20 Personal Selling and Sales Promotion

Here, we focus on the two other key elements of a promotion mix: personal selling and sales promotion. We define personal selling as oral communication with one or more prospective buyers by paid representatives for the purpose of making sales; and sales promotion as the paid marketing communication activities (other than advertising, publicity, or personal selling) that stimulate consumer purchases and dealer effectiveness. We describe the scope, characteristics, and stages in planning for both personal selling and sales promotion.

Part 6 Vignette
Promotion: Stimulating Marketplace Demand with Information

Promotion involves communicating information to help people find goods and help marketers find customers. In addition, it establishes and reinforces the product positioning image that has been selected for a good or service. The first video case deals with the use of promotion in image positioning by the Bank of Montreal, the second focuses on how advertising commercials are developed as part of an advertising campaign and the third shows a number of activities that a good salesperson can employ to be successful.

Canadian banks have been enjoying record profits throughout the mid-1990s, a fact that is viewed negatively by the Canadian public given that these profits have occurred at a time when banks have been instituting transaction fees, paying low deposit interest rates and charging high interest rates on bank credit cards. As a result, a lot of people feel that banks are greedy and untrustworthy. Aware of their image problems, Canadian banks have been trying to become more customer oriented by changing their way of doing business.

The Bank of Montreal is taking one of the most innovative approaches with its campaign slogan: "It Is Possible."™

Promotion involves communicating information to help customers find goods and help marketers find customers.

The Radio Shack video case provides insight into one way in which the commercials we see on television are created. Vice-president Laurie Ross hired advertising agent Vaughan Weilland to create a high-impact, humorous campaign as part of a pre-Christmas promotional effort.

Weilland believes that effective advertising involves using humorous ads that cut through the clutter and command attention among an overexposed audience. The creative approach uses comedian Peter McCormick, who created impromptu humorous situation ads built around the slogan "This Place Is Completely Wired." The use of improvisation and on site filming is an extremely risky approach to take in advertising, and resulted in some very unusual circumstances for McCormick and Weilland. However, this approach also produced entertaining advertising.

The RE/MAX video case spotlights Craig Procter, an agent in Newmarket, Ontario. A top performing salesperson, Procter shows how real estate agents must work to create both ends of a home sale transaction. Agents must find sellers, who pay the agent's commission, and buyers, from whose proceeds the seller pays the agent. Procter believes that the first key to success in real estate sales involves creating awareness and interest in the agent's name. To make his name and real estate synonymous, Procter puts his name on billboards, bus shelters and bus stop benches and on special promotional materials such as key chains, pens, pencils, business cards, and even plastic milk jugs! He also provides people in Newmarket with a toll-free line to make personal calls to Toronto. The "catch" in this goodwill freebie is that before the call can be completed, the caller must listen to a Craig Procter phone pitch. The second key to his successful selling involves a "team selling" approach. Procter hires telemarketers and doorknockers who call people to see if they are thinking of selling their homes. When he gets a listing, Procter has a customer service agent contact sellers and let them know how their homes are being perceived by potential buyers. Finally, Procter hires associate agents who work for him and do the basic tasks so he can be free to sign up new listings and to present offers on homes. A salesperson functions as a source of personal communication of information, but the basic objective of helping customers find goods that fulfil their needs and wants remains, regardless of the form of communication.

CHAPTER 18

The Context of Promotion Planning

Chapter Objectives

1. To define promotion planning and show its importance

2. To describe the general characteristics of advertising, public relations, personal selling, and sales promotion

3. To explain the channel of communication and how it functions

4. To examine the components of a promotion plan

5. To discuss international promotion considerations, and the legal environment and criticisms and defences of promotion

You have to have something that sets you apart from the competition— whether it be a particular product, quality, or service. And, burned by the foibles of human celebrity spokespeople, more and more companies are turning their corporate images (and fortunes) over to animated characters. After all, you have almost no chance of being embarrassed by Fred Flintstone, the Pink Panther, or Snoopy. These characters can help you maintain visibility, to stay favourably in the public eye.

In particular, says John Lister (chief executive officer of Lister Butler, a corporate and brand identity consultant), animated characters can bring warmth and feeling to an otherwise boring category of products: "The goal of using a cartoon is to complement the product, not eclipse it, take top billing, or conflict with the intended message." Let's look at how Owens-Corning and Metropolitan Life use animated characters—the Pink Panther and the *Peanuts* group of figures—in their advertising programs.

For a decade and a half, Owens-Corning has utilized the Pink Panther in ads for its insulation products. The character is especially effective in reassuring people that insulating their attics is a task they can easily accomplish. This is an important message since marketing research studies have found that many consumers view this project as too difficult for the typical do-it-yourselfer.

The Pink Panther is a natural communicator because of its affable nature and colour. And Owens-Corning is the only firm that markets a pink-coloured insulation. The Pink Panther-based campaign is instrumental in allowing Owens-Corning to maintain an eight-to-one brand preference over its closest competitor. According to John Lister, Owens-Corning's success is due to the "masterful job of integrating the character into the product's identity."

In the mid-1980s, Metropolitan Life Insurance chose to hire *Peanuts* characters to help generate more warmth and feeling towards the company and its products. As a Metropolitan Life account executive noted, "We wanted to convey a warm and friendly personality, which we think we have. The characters convey a kind of trust and goodwill."

The MetLife *Peanuts* campaign continues to this day, with the characters used in everything from print media to TV ads. The firm believes the feelings that the *Peanuts* characters engender, "particularly of security," are a part of the insurance firm's solid positioning in the marketplace.

OWENS-CORNING

www.owenscorning.com/

As with live actors, a company using animated characters as endorsers needs to safeguard its interests. A major concern is that a popular character could be used in so many product categories that its image becomes blurry. To avert this potential problem, MetLife has "an exclusive in the financial services market." According to a senior vice-president at Young & Rubicam, the advertising agency that handles the MetLife account, "We have an equity in the characters, and we can't afford to have that equity diluted."[1]

In this chapter, we will study many dimensions of promotion planning, including the usefulness of celebrities (human or animated) as sources in the channel of communication. Our discussion will also cover how the channel of communication works and the roles of the source, encoding, the message, the media, decoding, the audience, and feedback.

Overview

Promotion is any communication used to inform, persuade, and/or remind people about an organization's or individual's goods, services, image, ideas, community involvement, or impact on society. **Promotion planning** is systematic decision making relating to all aspects of an organization's or individual's communications efforts.

Promotion planning focuses on a total promotion effort—informing, persuading, and reminding.

Communication occurs through brand names, packaging, company marquees and displays, personal selling, customer service, trade shows, sweepstakes, and messages in mass media (such as newspapers, television, radio, direct mail, billboards, magazines, and transit). It can be company sponsored or controlled by independent media. Messages may emphasize information, persuasion, fear, sociability, product performance, humour, and/or comparisons with competitors.

In this chapter, the context of promotion planning is provided. Included are discussions on promotion's importance, the basic promotion types, the channel of communication, promotion planning, international considerations, the legal environment, and general criticisms and defences of promotion. Chapter 19 covers advertising and public relations. Chapter 20 deals with personal selling and sales promotion.

The Importance of Promotion

Promotion is a key element of the marketing mix. For new products, people must be informed about items and their features before they can develop favourable attitudes toward them. For products with some consumer awareness, the focus is on persuasion: converting knowledge to preference. For very popular products, the focus is on reminding: reinforcing existing consumer beliefs.

The people and/or organizations to whom a firm's promotional efforts are aimed may fall into various categories: consumers, shareholders, consumer advocacy groups, government, channel members, employees, competitors, and the general public. Firms often communicate with each of these audiences, not just with consumers. In addition, communication with each may be different because each category has distinct goals, knowledge, and needs.

Within an audience category (like consumers), a firm needs to identify and appeal to opinion leaders—those who influence others' decisions. It also should understand **word-of-mouth communication**, the process by which people express opinions and product-related experiences to one another. Unless a product or service has a sustained positive word-of-mouth reputation, it is hard to succeed.[2]

Word-of-mouth communication occurs as people state opinions to others.

A company's promotion plan usually stresses individual goods and services, with the intent of moving people from awareness to purchase. Yet the firm may also convey its overall image (industry innovator), views on ideas (nuclear energy), community service (fund-

---

[1]Christine Unruh, "Snap, Crackle, Pop," *Journal of Business Strategy*, Vol. 16 (March–April 1995), pp. 39–43.
[2]See Paula Fitzgerald Bone, "Word-of-Mouth Effects on Short-Term and Long-Term Product Judgments," *Journal of Business Research*, Vol. 32 (March 1995), pp. 213–223; and Chip Walker, "Word of Mouth," *American Demographics* (July 1995), pp. 38–44.

Table 18-1

The Value of Promotion

PROMOTION

- *Establishes an image for a company and its goods and services.*
- *Communicates features of goods and services.*
- *Creates awareness for new goods and services.*
- *Keeps existing goods and services popular.*
- *Can reposition the images or uses of faltering goods and services.*
- *Generates enthusiasm from channel members.*
- *Notes where goods and services can be purchased.*
- *Can persuade consumers to trade up from one product to a more expensive one.*
- *Alerts consumers to sales.*
- *Justifies (rationalizes) the prices of goods and services.*
- *Answers consumer questions.*
- *Closes transactions.*
- *Provides service for consumers after transactions are completed.*
- *Reinforces loyal consumers.*
- *Places the firm and its goods and services in a favourable light, relative to competitors.*

---

ing a new hospital), or impact on society (the size of its work force). Table 18-1 shows many valuable promotion functions.

A good promotion plan complements the product, distribution, and price aspects of the marketing mix. For example, Waterman—a maker of pens—distributes its products to finer stores and sets premium prices. It advertises in magazines such as *Canadian Business*, and expects retailers to provide first-rate personal selling. Ads are in colour and refer to product features, not prices. See Figure 18–1.

Well-conceived promotion plans are feasible even if companies have limited resources. For instance:

> Until 1989, Straight Arrow Products, a twenty-five-year old company, couldn't afford to do much marketing. Sales at the time were only $675 000 annually. Fast-forward five years: Sales reached $67 million and current owner W. Roger Dunavant was running a $4.8 million ad campaign. What happened? During 1989, without a bundle to spend on advertising, Dunavant (then the firm's director of sales and marketing) began to hit the road to sell the company's wares. The goods: grooming products that horse owners use on their animals—and themselves. The strategy: play up the novelty for all it was worth. Dunavant attended horse shows and handed out samples of Mane 'n Tail shampoo and conditioner and a cream called Hoofmaker (for equestrians' hands, not feet). He encouraged horse owners to use Mane 'n Tail on both themselves and their horses. One person he met at a show turned out to be a radio announcer who invited him for an interview. Once the show aired, other journalists from print and radio began calling. Dunavant bought Straight Arrow in 1993. He handled his own bookings until that year, when he hired a public relations firm. In 1994 alone, he gave 140 radio interviews. The result: skyrocketing sales and *Wall Street Journal* coverage.[3]

Promotion's importance is also evident from the expenditures and jobs it generates. The world's fifty largest advertising agencies have overall annual billings of U.S.$20 billion. The International Advertising Association's thousands of members are from ninety nations. In Canada alone, each year, business firms spend $9.2 billion on media advertis-

INTERNATIONAL ADVERTISING ASSOCIATION

www1.usa1.com/~ibnet/iaahp.html

---

[3] Jeffrey A. Tannenbaum, "Priceless Promotions," *Wall Street Journal* (May 22, 1995), p. R20.

Chapter 18 *The Context of Promotion Planning* 493

FIGURE 18-1
The Consistent, High-Quality Promotional Emphasis of Waterman Pens
Reprinted by permission of Waterman.

ing; 1.3 million people work in sales; 17.1 billion coupons are given out; and Canadian firms participate in the 4000 North American trade shows.[4]

Types of Promotion

In their communications programs, organizations use one or more of four basic types of promotion:

- **Advertising** is paid, nonpersonal communication regarding goods, services, organizations, people, places, and ideas that is transmitted through various media by business firms, government, and other nonprofit organizations, and individuals who are identified in the advertising message as the sponsor. The message is generally controlled by the sponsor.

Advertising, public relations (publicity), personal selling, and sales promotion are the four key promotion types.

---

[4]Statistics Canada,*1995 Market Research Handbook* (Ottawa: Minister of Supply Services Canada), p. 164; Jim McElgunn, "CARD Releases New Figures on Ad Spending," *Marketing Magazine* (September 25, 1995), p. 6; Lara Mills, "In-ad Promos Lift Total Coupon Distribution," *Marketing Magazine* (February 12, 1996), p. 2; "The 1995 Annual Report on the Promotion Industry," *Promo Magazine's SourceBook '96*, p. 15; and Srinath Gopalakrishna, Gary L. Lilien, Jerome D. Williams, and Ian K. Sequeira, "Do Trade Shows Pay Off?" *Journal of Marketing*, Vol. 59 (July 1995), p. 75.

- **Public relations** includes any communication to foster a favourable image for goods, services, organizations, people, places, and ideas among their publics—such as consumers, investors, government, channel members, employees, and the general public. It may be nonpersonal or personal, paid or nonpaid, and sponsor controlled or not controlled. **Publicity** is the form of public relations that entails nonpersonal communication passed on through various media but not paid for by an identified sponsor. Wording and placement of publicity messages are generally media controlled.
- **Personal selling** involves oral communication with one or more prospective buyers by paid representatives for the purpose of making sales.
- **Sales promotion** involves paid marketing communication activities (other than advertising, publicity, or personal selling) that are intended to stimulate consumer purchases and dealer effectiveness. Included are trade shows, premiums, incentives, giveaways, demonstrations, and various other efforts not in the ordinary promotion routine.[5]

The general characteristics of each type of promotion are shown in Table 18–2. As discussed later in the chapter, many firms in some way combine them into an integrated promotional blend. This lets them reach their entire target market, present both persuasive and believable messages, have personal contact with customers, sponsor special events, and balance the promotional budget.

Table 18-2
Characteristics of Promotional Types

FACTOR	ADVERTISING	PUBLICITY FORM OF PUBLIC RELATIONS[a]	PERSONAL SELLING	SALES PROMOTION
Audience	Mass	Mass	Small (one-to-one)	Varies
Message	Uniform	Uniform	Specific	Varies
Cost	Low per viewer or reader	None for media space and time; can be some costs for media releases and publicity materials	High per customer	Moderate per customer
Sponsor	Company	No formal sponsor in that media are not paid	Company	Company
Flexibility	Low	Low	High	Moderate
Control over content and placement	High	None (controlled by media)	High	High
Credibility	Moderate	High	Moderate	Moderate
Major goal	To appeal to a mass audience at a reasonable cost, and to create awareness and favorable attitudes	To reach a mass audience with an independently reported message	To deal with individual consumers, to resolve questions, to close sales	To stimulate short-run sales, to increase impulse purchases
Example	Television ad for a Sony CD player for use in cars	Magazine article describing the unique features of a Sony CD player for cars	Retail sales personnel explaining how a Sony CD player for cars works	A Sony CD player for cars exhibited at trade shows

[a] When public relations embodies advertising (an image-related message), personal selling (a salesperson describing the firm's public service efforts to college students), and/or sales promotion (distributing special discount coupons to low-income consumers), it takes on the characteristics of those promotional types. However, the goal would be more image-related than sales-related.

[5] Adapted by the authors from Peter D. Bennett (Ed.) *Dictionary of Marketing Terms*, Second Edition (Chicago: American Marketing Association, 1995), pp. 6, 206, 231, 232, and 253.

The Channel of Communication

To develop a proper promotion mix and interact effectively with a target audience, the **channel of communication (communication process)** shown in Figure 18–2 must be understood. Through such a channel, a source develops a message, transmits it to an audience by some medium, and gets feedback from the audience. The components of a communication channel are discussed next.

A message is sent to an audience through a **channel of communication**.

The Source

The **source** of communication is usually a company, an independent institution, or an opinion leader seeking to present a message to an audience. A firm communicates through a spokesperson, celebrity, actor playing a role, representative consumer, and/or salesperson.

A company spokesperson is typically a long-time employee who represents it in communications. The spokesperson has an aura of sincerity, commitment, and expertise. Sometimes, the spokesperson is a top executive, such as Loblaws' Dave Nichol, who pitched President's Choice products for years. Other times, front-line employees are used, such as a Shoppers Drug Mart pharmacist or a sales clerk from the Subway Sandwich shop. In general, this source has been quite effective.

A celebrity is used when the goal is to gain the audience's attention and improve product awareness. Problems can arise if the celebrity is perceived as insincere or unknowledgeable. Popular celebrities include hockey player Wayne Gretzky for Sharp, basketball player Michael Jordan for Nike, singer Celine Dion for the Bay, sprinter Donovan Bailey for Air Canada, and Snoopy and other *Peanuts* characters for Metropolitan Life Insurance.

Many ads have actors playing roles rather than celebrity spokespeople. In these commercials, the emphasis is on presenting a message about a good, service, or idea—rather than on the consumer recognizing a celebrity. The hope is that the consumer will learn more about product attributes.

A representative consumer is one who likes a product and recommends it in an ad. The person is shown with his or her name and hometown. The intent is to present a real consumer in an actual situation. A hidden camera or blind taste test is often used with this source. Today, viewers are more skeptical about how representative the endorser is.

Finally, a firm may use a salesperson to communicate with consumers. Many salespeople are knowledgeable, assertive, and persuasive. However, consumers may doubt their objectivity and tactics. Auto salespeople rate particularly low in consumer surveys.

An independent institution is not controlled by the firms on which it reports. It presents information in a professional, nonpaid (by the firms) manner. The Canadian Automobile Association and the local newspaper restaurant critic are examples of independent sources. They have great credibility for their readers because they discuss both good and bad points, but some segments of the population may not be exposed to these sources. The information presented may differ from that contained in a firm's commercials or sales-force presentations.

A **source** *presents a message.*

HUDSON'S BAY COMPANY

www.sd35.bc.ca/schools/ae/FL/hbc.html

CANADIAN AUTOMOBILE ASSOCIATION (BC)

www.bcaa.bc.ca/value/consumer/

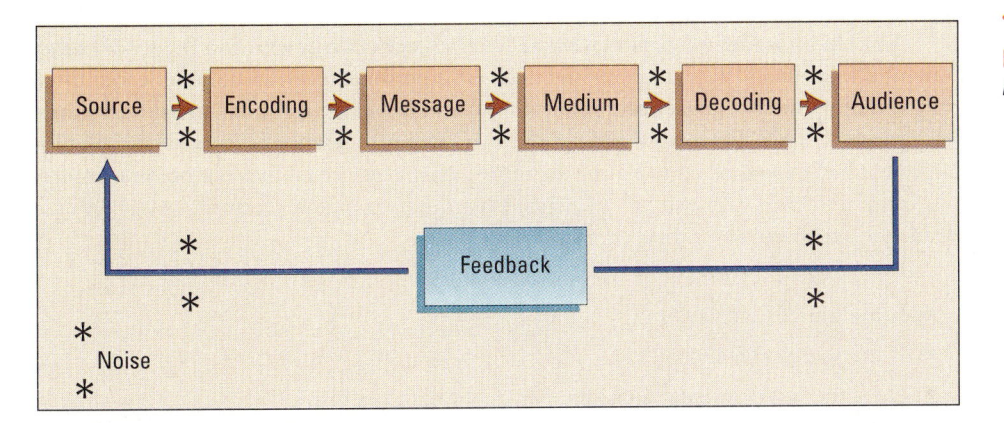

FIGURE 18-2
A Channel of Communication

Source → Encoding → Message → Medium → Decoding → Audience → Feedback → Source

Noise

Ethics AND TODAY'S MARKETER

Is It Getting Harder to Tell the TV Programs from the Ads?

A product placement occurs when a branded product is shown during a TV show or movie, often being used by an actor—such as when James Bond (Pierce Brosnan) drove a new BMW Z3 roadster in the movie *GoldenEye*.

It is important to note that if a program is going to air in the United States, a frequently sought market for Canadian entertainment vehicles, the U.S. Federal Communications Commission requires full disclosure of all product placement fees that are paid directly by companies to TV show producers. However, companies can bypass this provision by paying product-placement firms, instead. To protect themselves from legal action, all TV networks require producers to sign a statement indicating that they have not received a product-placement fee.

Marketers favouring the use of product placements feel this is a relatively inexpensive way of gaining recognition for a new product or reinforcement for an existing one. A $20 000 product placement, for example, can reach more people for a longer time period than a $250 000, thirty-second commercial. Networks also benefit from product placements by getting free props.

Those that question the use of product placements cite both implementation and societal concerns. On an implementation level, product placements can be hit or miss. Product visibility can be poor if a camera pans too quickly or if a brand name is out of focus. Like publicity, a firm cannot overly rely on product placement. There are also concerns when too many brands are placed on the same show.

On a societal level, product placements can blur the distinction between advertising and program content. According to the executive director of the Center for Science in the Public Interest, "You can zap a commercial. But you can't zap something that's on a program."

As an advertising consultant, give a strategy for using product placements on *Seinfeld*, the popular TV comedy. In the past, Snapple iced tea, Rold Gold pretzels, Diet Coke, and Columbo frozen yogurt were featured on the show.

Sources: Based on material in Fara Warner, "Why It's Getting Harder to Tell the Shows From the Ads," *Wall Street Journal* (June 15, 1995), pp. B1, B11; and Daniel Shannon, "Nobody Does It Better," *Promo* (January 1996), p. 10.

An opinion leader is a person who has face-to-face contact with and influences other potential consumers. Because he or she deals on a personal level, an opinion leader often has strong persuasive impact and believability; and he or she can offer social acceptance for followers. Thus, firms often address initial messages to opinion leaders, who then provide word-of-mouth communication to others. Many marketers believe opinion leaders not only influence, but also are influenced by, others (opinion receivers); even opinion leaders need approval for their choices.

In assessing a source, these questions are critical:

- Is the source believable?
- Is the source convincing?
- Does the source present an image consistent with the firm?

- Do consumers value the message of the source?
- Is the source seen as knowledgeable?
- Does the source complement the product he/she communicates about—or overwhelm it?
- Do significant parts of the market dislike the source?

Encoding

Encoding is the process whereby a thought or idea is translated into a message by the source. At this stage, preliminary decisions are made as to message content, such as the use of symbolism and wording. It is vital that the thought or idea be translated exactly as the source intends. For example, a firm wanting to stress its product's prestige would include the concepts of status, exclusive ownership, and special features in a message. It would not emphasize a price lower than competitors, availability in discount stores, or the millions of people who have already purchased.

In encoding, a source translates a thought into a message.

The Message

A **message** is a combination of words and symbols transmitted to an audience. Its thrust depends on whether a firm's goal is to inform, persuade, or remind its audience. Almost all messages include some information on the company name, the product name, the desired image, differential advantages, and product attributes. A firm would also give information about availability and price at some point during the consumer's decision process.

A message combines words and symbols.

Most communication involves one-sided messages, in which only the benefits of a good, service, or idea are cited. Fewer firms use two-sided messages, in which both benefits and limitations are noted. Firms are not anxious to point out their shortcomings, although consumer perceptions of honesty may be improved by two-sided messages. For example, in June 1996, Standard Life ran an ad in *Canadian Business* admitting they were headquartered in Scotland and had not been listed as one of the top insurance companies in Canada. However, the ad pointed out that the rankings of Canadian firms included worldwide assets, while foreign firms were ranked only by their Canadian assets. Standard Life's ad stated they had $90 billion in assets and that Canadian policyholders were fully protected.[6]

Many messages use symbolism and try to relate safety, social acceptance, or sexual appeal to a purchase. In symbolic messages, a firm stresses psychological benefits rather than tangible product performance. Clothing ads may offer acceptance by peers; and toothpaste may brighten teeth and make a person more sexually attractive. One type of symbolism, the use of fear appeals, has had mixed results. Although people respond to moderate fear appeals, strong messages may not be as well received.

Fear appeals can be useful. Ads alerting people to potential natural resource depletion, the danger of forest fires, ramifications of drunk driving, and the potential health hazards of permissive sexual behaviour are examples. The public good and advertisers' self-interest are compatible. In addition, these ads have an educational value which may prove useful over an extended period. However, marketers must avoid creating too much anxiety or discomfort among recipients, or the message may backfire.[7]

Humour is sometimes used to gain audience attention and retain it. Two popular examples are the Leon's Furniture "Ho, Ho, Hold The Payments" commercials and NBA

---

[6]Ayn E. Crowley and Wayne D. Hoyer, "An Integrative Framework for Understanding Two-Sided Persuasion," *Journal of Consumer Research*, Vol. 20 (March 1994), p. 561; and Advertisement for Standard Life, "We're All For Comparisons . . . But Not of Apples and Oranges," *Canadian Business* (June 1996), p. 147.

[7]Michael S. LaTour and Shaker A. Zahra, "Fear Appeals as Advertising Strategy: Should They Be Used?" *Journal of Consumer Marketing*, Vol. 6 (Spring 1989), p. 67. See also Tony L. Henthorne, Michael S. LaTour, and Rajan Nataraajan, "Fear Appeals in Print Advertising: An Analysis of Arousal and Ad Response," *Journal of Advertising*, Vol. 22 (June 1993), pp. 59–69; and James B. Hunt, John F. Tanner, Jr., and David P. Eppright, "Forty Years of Fear Appeal Research: Support for the Ordered Protection Motivation Model" in David W. Stewart and Naufel J. Vilcassim (Eds.), *1995 AMA Winter Educators' Proceedings* (Chicago: American Marketing Association, 1995), pp. 147–153.

FIGURE 18-3
A Humorous U.S. Ad: There's a New Grandma in Town
Reprinted by permission.

basketball player Larry Johnson as "Grandma" in Converse shoe ads. However, a firm needs to be careful to get across the intended message when using humour—which should not make fun of the company, its goods, or its services; and humour should not dominate a message so the brand name or product's attributes go unnoticed. Figure 18-3 shows a Larry Johnson ad. Figure 18-4 has a Netherlands Vegetarian Council ad. Because humour has cultural underpinnings, the Dutch ad would probably not work well in North America, and it is likely that the Larry Johnson ad would not be appreciated in the Netherlands.

Comparative messages *position a firm in relation to its competitors.*

Comparative messages implicitly or explicitly contrast a firm's offerings with those of competitors. Implicit comparisons use an indirect brand X or leading brand approach ("Our industrial glues are more effective than other leading brands"). Explicit comparisons use a direct approach (such as the Nissan print ad, "We can see by your face that you've priced the new Camry" from Toyota). Comparative messages, in one form or another, are used in various TV and radio commercials, print ads, and other media. In addition, salespeople often compare their products' attributes with competitors'. When using comparative messages, a firm has to be quite careful not to turn off consumers, place too much emphasis on a competitor's brand, or lose sight of its own differential advantages that should be promoted.

A message must be presented in a desirable, exclusive, and believable way. The good, service, or idea must be perceived as something worth buying or accepting. It also must be seen as unique to the seller—that is, it cannot be gotten elsewhere. Finally, the message must make believable claims.

Massed *or* **distributed promotion** *and the* **wearout rate** *must be carefully planned.*

Message timing must also be carefully planned. First, during what times of the year should a firm advertise, seek publicity, add salespeople, or run sales promotions? In **massed promotion**, communication efforts are concentrated in peak periods, like holidays. In **distributed promotion**, communication efforts are spread throughout the year. Figure 18–5 compares massed and distributed promotion.

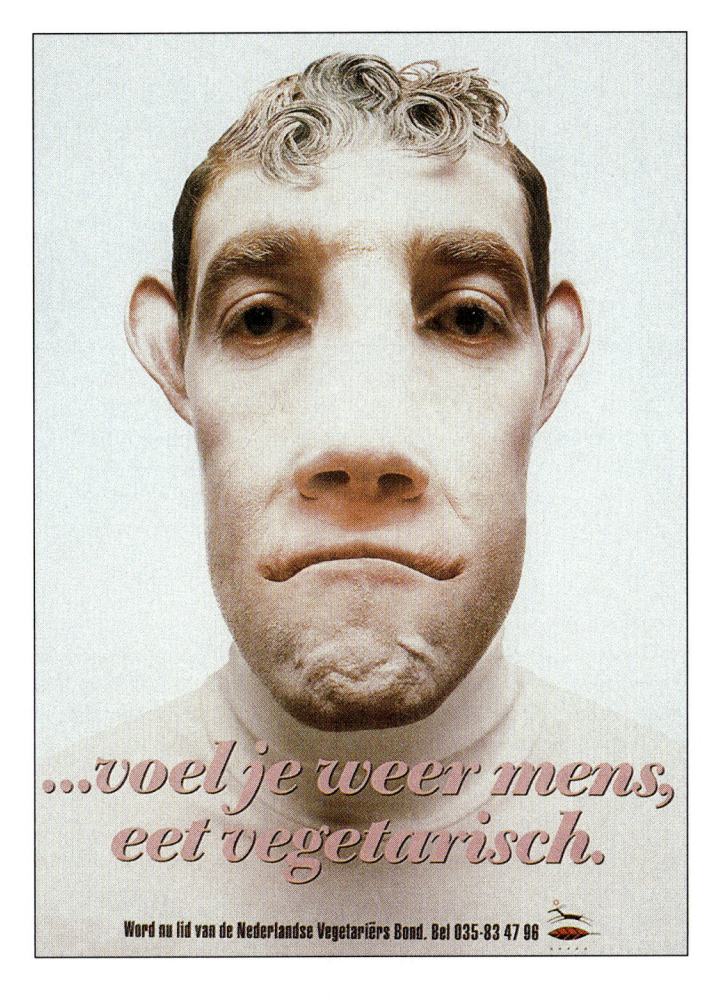

FIGURE 18-4
A Humorous Dutch Ad: Feel Human Again, Eat Vegetarian
Reprinted by permission.

Second, the **wearout rate**—the time it takes for a message to lose its effectiveness—must be determined. Some messages wear out quickly; others last for years. The wearout rate depends on the frequency of communications, message quality, the number of different messages used by a firm, and other factors. Ford has done such a good job with its "Quality is Job 1" message that it is still strong after many years.

The Medium

The **medium** is the personal or nonpersonal means used to send a message. Personal media are company salespeople and other representatives, as well as opinion leaders. Nonpersonal (mass) media include newspapers, television, radio, direct mail, billboards, magazines, and transit.

Personal media offer one-to-one audience contact. They are flexible, can adapt messages to individual needs, and can answer questions. They appeal to a small audience and are best with a concentrated market. Nonpersonal media have a large audience and low per-customer costs. They are not as flexible and dynamic as one-to-one contacts. They work best with a dispersed target market.

In deciding between personal and nonpersonal media, a firm should consider both total and per-unit costs, product complexity, audience attributes, and communication goals. The two kinds of media go well together since nonpersonal media generate consumer interest and personal media help close sales.

*A **medium** is a personal or nonpersonal channel for a message.*

Decoding

Decoding is the process by which a message sent by a source is interpreted by an audience. The interpretation is based on the audience's background, and on the clarity and

*In **decoding**, the audience translates the message sent by the source.*

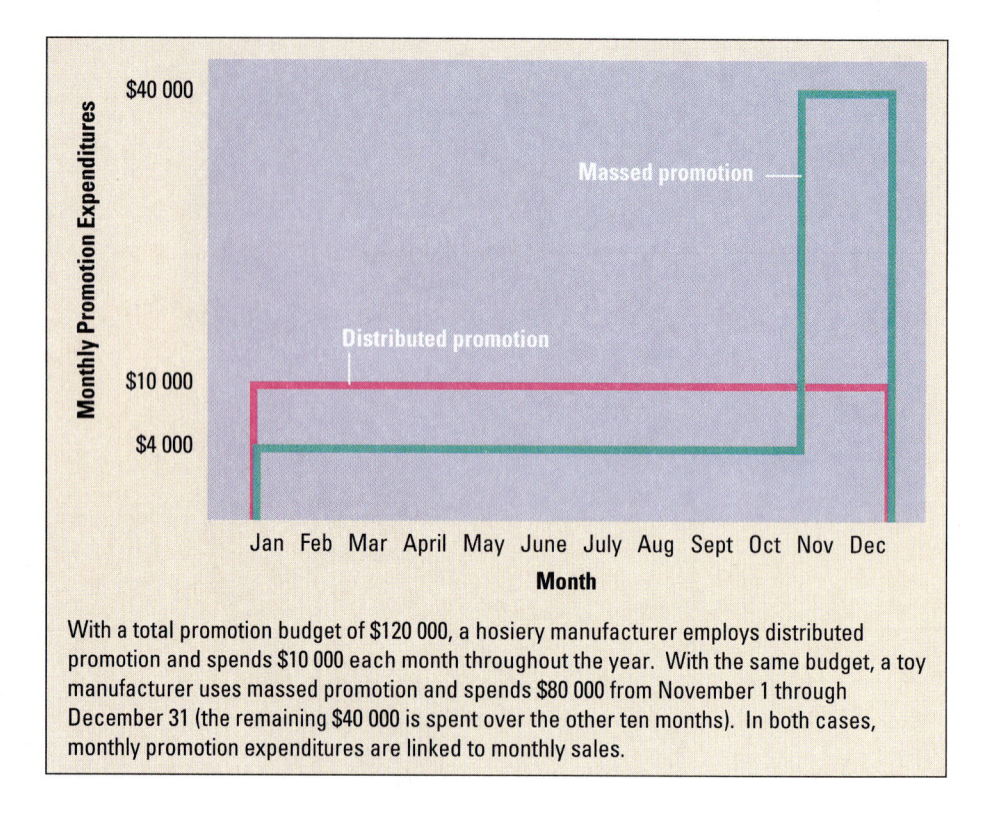

FIGURE 18-5
Massed Versus Distributed Promotion

With a total promotion budget of $120 000, a hosiery manufacturer employs distributed promotion and spends $10 000 each month throughout the year. With the same budget, a toy manufacturer uses massed promotion and spends $80 000 from November 1 through December 31 (the remaining $40 000 is spent over the other ten months). In both cases, monthly promotion expenditures are linked to monthly sales.

complexity of the message. For example, a woman who works in the home and a woman who works in an office might have different interpretations of a message on the value of child-care centres. Usually, as symbolism and complexity increase, clarity decreases. "*National Geographic*: Connect. Convince." is not as understandable a message as "Yellow Pages. It Pays. We'll Prove It." As noted earlier, it is essential that a message be decoded in the manner intended by the source (encoding = decoding). Is the business-to-business ad depicted in Figure 18-6 too provocative or merely attention grabbing? Is the serious message buried in the imagery or quite clear to the targeted audience?

Subliminal advertising aims at a consumer's subconscious.

Subliminal advertising is a highly controversial kind of promotion because it does not enable the audience to consciously decode a message. Instead, visual or verbal messages are presented so quickly that people do not see, hear, or remember them. Yet, the assumption is that they will buy goods and services because of subconscious impulses stimulated by these messages. The overwhelming evidence shows that subliminal ads cannot get people to buy things they do not want. In addition, subliminal ads are often misinterpreted; clear, well-labelled ads are much more effective. In Canada subliminal advertising is illegal.[8]

The Audience

The audience is usually the target market, but it can also include others.

An **audience** is the object of a source's message. In most marketing situations, it is the target market. However, a source may also want to communicate an idea, build an image, or give information to shareholders, independent media, the public, government officials, and others.

The way a communication channel is used by a firm depends on the size and dispersion of the audience, demographic and lifestyle audience traits, and the availability of appropriate media. Because the communication process should be keyed to the audience, AIDS prevention groups have had a tough time getting their message across to teens and young adults:

---

[8] See Carl L. Witte, Madhavan Parthasarathy, and James W. Gentry, "Subliminal Perception Versus Subliminal Persuasion: A Re-Examination of the Basic Issues" in Barbara B. Stern and George M. Zinkham (Eds.), *1995 AMA Educators' Proceedings* (Chicago: American Marketing Association, 1995), pp. 133–138.

FIGURE 18-6
Is This Business-to-Business Ad Easily Decoded?
Reprinted by permission.

Past AIDS-related public service announcements have defined the problem as one of HIV/AIDS awareness, the assumption being that once young people are aware of AIDS, they will be motivated to practice APBs (AIDS preventive behaviours). However, this definition is outdated. It is now evident that AIDS awareness has been accomplished among teens and young adults. They are already aware that sexual intercourse and IV drug use represent the major modes of AIDS transmission. The challenge facing communicators is how to convert AIDS awareness into APBs. Although there is some need to keep generic AIDS messages before the public, rudimentary information/awareness-based appeals are of little use to a market that knows the elementary facts or when there is little evidence that basic knowledge leads to adoption of APBs.[9]

And to make matters still tougher for marketers, a recent global consumer survey found that people are rather down on promotion messages:

- 72 per cent believe marketers exaggerate health benefits.
- 70 per cent do not believe marketers respect consumers' intelligence.
- 70 per cent believe marketers brainwash children.
- 62 per cent do not believe marketers give accurate information.
- 55 per cent do not believe marketers sponsor worthwhile events.
- 40 per cent do not believe ads are creative and entertaining.[10]

Feedback

Feedback is the response an audience has to a message. It may be a purchase, an attitude change, or a nonpurchase. A firm must understand that each of these responses is possible and devise a way of monitoring them.

Feedback *consists of purchase, attitude, or nonpurchase responses to a message.*

---

[9] Kristina D. Frankenberger and Ajay S. Sukhdial, "Segmenting Teens for AIDS Preventive Behaviors with Implications for Marketing Communications," *Journal of Public Policy & Marketing*, Vol. 13 (Spring 1994), p. 134.
[10] Roper Starch, "The World's View of Marketers," *Advertising Age* (January 15, 1996), pp. I–10.

The most desirable kind of feedback occurs if a consumer buys a good or service (or accepts an idea) after communication with or from the firm. This means a message is effective enough to stimulate a transaction.

A second type of feedback takes place if a firm finds its promotion efforts elicit a favourable audience attitude toward it or its offerings. For new goods or services, positive attitudes must usually be formed before purchases (awareness → favourable attitude → purchase). With existing products, people may have bought another brand just before receiving a message or be temporarily out of funds; generating their favourable attitudes may lead to future purchases.

The least desirable feedback is if the audience neither makes a purchase nor develops a favourable attitude. This may happen for one of several reasons: The audience does not recall the message; the audience is content with another brand; the audience did not believe the message; or no differential advantage is perceived.

Noise

Noise may interfere with the communication process at any stage.

Noise is interference at any point along a channel of communication. Because of it, messages are sometimes encoded or decoded incorrectly or weak audience responses are made. Examples of noise are:

- A phone call interrupting a company's marketing manager while he or she is developing a promotional theme.
- A salesperson misidentifying a product and giving incorrect information.
- An impatient customer interrupting a sales presentation.
- A conversation between two consumers during a TV commercial.
- A direct-mail ad being opened by the wrong person.
- A consumer seeing a sale on a competitor's item while waiting at an office-supply store's checkout counter.

Promotion Planning

After a firm gains an understanding of the communication process, it is ready to develop an overall promotion plan. Such a plan consists of three parts: objectives, budgeting, and the promotion mix.

Objectives

Promotion objectives can be divided into two main categories: stimulating demand and enhancing company image.

The **hierarchy-of-effects model** *outlines demand goals.*

In setting demand goals, the **hierarchy-of-effects model** should be used. It outlines the sequential short-term, intermediate, and long-term promotion goals for a firm to pursue—and works in conjunction with the consumer's decision process that was discussed in Chapter 8:

1. *Provide information*—Obtain consumer product recognition, then gain consumer knowledge of product attributes.
2. *Develop positive attitudes and feelings*—Obtain favourable attitudes, then gain preference for the company's brand(s) over those of competitors.
3. *Stimulate purchases and retain desires*—Obtain strong consumer preference, gain purchase of good or service, encourage continued purchases (brand loyalty).

Primary demand *is for a product category;* **selective demand** *is for a brand.*

By applying the hierarchy-of-effects model, a company can move from informing to persuading and then to reminding consumers about its offerings. At the early stages of the model, when a good or service is little known, **primary demand** should be sought. This is consumer demand for a product category. At later stages, with preference the goal, **selective demand** should be sought. This is consumer demand for a particular brand. Sometimes, organizations may try to sustain or revitalize interest in mature products and

FIGURE 18-7
Institutional Advertising by CanWest Global Communications
Reprinted with permission of CanWest Global Communications Corp.

revert to a primary demand orientation. If promotion goals are image-oriented, a firm engages in public relations efforts—using suitable advertising, publicity, personal selling, and/or sales promotion (as noted in Table 18-2). **Institutional advertising** is used when the advertising goal is to enhance company image—and not to sell goods or services. This is illustrated in Figure 18-7, an ad for CanWest Global. Many of the leading advertisers in Canada run institutional ads.

Institutional advertising is involved with image goals.

Budgeting

There are five basic ways to set a total promotion budget: all you can afford, incremental, competitive parity, percentage of sales, and objective and task. The choice depends on the requirements of the individual firm. Budgets can range from 1 to 5 per cent of sales for industrial-products firms to up to 20 to 30 per cent of sales for consumer-products firms.[11]

In the **all-you-can-afford method**, a firm first allots funds for other elements of marketing; any remaining marketing funds then go to the promotion budget. It is the weakest

Budgeting methods are **all you can afford, incremental, competitive parity, percentage of sales,** *and* **objective and task**.

[11]See Cyndee Miller, "Marketing Industry Report: Who's Spending What on Biz-to-Biz Marketing," *Marketing News* (January 1, 1996), pp. 1, 7.

International Marketing in Action

What Kind of Communication Strategy Should Be Used in Tanzania?

Tanzania, located in the southern tier of Africa, has a population of 30 million people. After years of socialism, high import restrictions, and very low per capita income, conditions in Tanzania have recently improved. Several large firms have recently been drawn to Tanzania (such as PepsiCo, Coca-Cola, and Sterling Health)—based on the country's good resource base, stable political government, and fast-growing economy.

According to the executive chairman of ScanAd, Tanzania's largest advertising agency, when the company opened in 1990, "The Tanzanian population was literally starved of basic consumer needs. In the rural areas, people didn't know how to use toothpaste and they ate their bread dry."

Despite the recent growth, marketers in Tanzania still face various challenges. Tanzania's annual per-capita GDP is around U.S.$600. Total yearly advertising expenditures are currently under U.S.$3 million (versus U.S.$32 million in Kenya with a population of 26 million, and U.S.$30 million in Zimbabwe with a population of 14 million).

Promotional media are also very limited. For example, Radio Tanzania is the only real national medium because the country's two television stations only reach the two million inhabitants of Dar es Salaam. And though Tanzania's national literacy rate is about 45 per cent, its national newspaper's sales are hampered by its basic printing techniques and by road conditions so poor that newspapers can take four days to arrive. Even the most popular English-language daily newspaper, *The Daily News*, sells only 22 000 copies per day.

ScanAd does business in Tanzania with such large international clients as Swiss-Air, Toyota, and Sterling Health—while other agencies are content to plan advertising campaigns from nearby Nairobi, Kenya.

As the advertising manager for SwissAir (the international airline), develop a communication strategy to be used for the Tanzanian market.

Source: Based on material in Karen Yates, "Advertising's Heart of Darkness," *Advertising Age* (May 15, 1995), p. I-10–I-15.

---

technique and used most often by small, production-oriented firms. It gives little importance to promotion, spending is not linked to goals, and there is a risk of having no promotion budget if finances are low.

With the **incremental method**, a company bases its new promotion budget on the previous one. A percentage is added to or subtracted from this year's budget to determine next year's. The technique is also used by small firms. It has these advantages: it gives the firm a reference point, it bases the budget on a firm's feelings about past performance and future trends, and it is easy to calculate. Important disadvantages do exist: budget size is rarely tied to goals, "gut feelings" are overemphasized, and it is hard to evaluate success or failure.

In the **competitive parity method**, a firm's promotion budget is raised or lowered according to competitors' actions. It is useful to both large and small firms. The benefits are that it is keyed to a reference point, market-oriented, and conservative. The shortcomings are that it is a follower and not a leadership approach, it is difficult to get competitors' promotion data, and it assumes a similarity between the firm and its competitors (as to years in business, goods or services, image, prices, and so on) which may not exist.

With the **percentage-of-sales method**, a firm ties its promotion budget to sales revenue. In the first year, a promotion-to-sales ratio is set. During succeeding years, the ratio of promotion to sales dollars is constant. The benefits of this method are that it uses sales as a base, it is adaptable, and it links revenues and promotion. However, it bears no relation to promotion goals; promotion is a sales follower, not a sales leader; and promotion cuts occur in poor sales periods (when increases could help). The technique yields too large a budget in high sales periods and too small a budget in low sales periods.

Under the **objective-and-task method**, a firm sets promotion goals, determines the activities needed to satisfy them, and then establishes the proper budget. This is the best method. The advantages are that goals are clearly stated, spending is related to goal-oriented tasks, adaptability is offered, and it is easy to evaluate performance. The major weakness of objective and task is the complexity of setting goals and specific tasks, especially for small firms. Most large companies use some form of objective-and-task technique.

During promotional budgeting, a firm should keep the concept of marginal return in mind. The **marginal return** is the amount of sales each increment of promotion spending will generate. When a product is new, the marginal return is high because the market is expanding. When a product is established, the marginal return is lower because each additional increment of promotion has less of an impact on sales (due to a saturated target market).

*The **marginal return** is the sales generated by incremental promotional spending.*

The Promotion Mix

After establishing a total promotion budget, a company must determine its **promotion mix**. This is the firm's overall and specific communication program, including its involvement with advertising, public relations (publicity), personal selling, and/or sales promotion. Seldom does a company use just one type of promotion—such as a mail-order firm relying on ads, a hospital on publicity, or a flea-market vendor on selling. Typically, a promotion mix is used.

When a well-coordinated promotion mix is involved, a firm is undertaking **integrated marketing communications (IMC)**. An IMC program would be defined as one that "recognizes the value of a comprehensive plan that evaluates the strategic roles of a variety of communication disciplines—advertising, public relations, personal selling, and sales promotion—and combines them to provide clarity, consistency, and maximum communication impact."[12] For example, Frito-Lay has a sales force that visits every store stocking its products, advertises in papers and magazines and on TV, and distributes cents-off coupons. Hitachi has a large technical sales force, advertises in business and trade publications, and sends representatives to trade shows.

*A **promotion mix** somehow combines advertising, public relations, personal selling, and/or sales promotion. When done well, **integrated marketing communications** results.*

Each type of promotion has a distinct function and complements the other types. Ads appeal to big audiences and create awareness; without them, selling is more difficult, time consuming, and costly. The publicity aspect of public relations provides credible information to a wide audience, but content and timing cannot be controlled. Selling has one-to-one contact, flexibility, and the ability to close sales; without it, the interest caused by ads might be wasted. Sales promotion spurs short-run sales and supplements ads and selling.

The selection of a promotion mix depends on company attributes, the product life cycle, media access, and channel members. A small firm is limited in the kinds of ads it can afford or use efficiently; it may have to stress personal selling and a few sales promotions. A large firm covering a sizable geographic area could combine many ads, personal selling, and frequent sales promotions. As products move through the life cycle, promotion emphasis goes from information to persuasion to reinforcement; different media and messages are needed at each stage. Some media may not be accessible (no cigarette ads on TV) or require lengthy lead time (Yellow Pages). In addition, channel members may demand special promotions, sales support, and/or cooperative advertising allowances.

It is the job of a firm's marketing director (or vice-president) to set up a promotion budget and a promotion mix, as well as to allocate resources to each aspect of promotion.

---

[12]Adapted by the authors from Janet Smith, "Integrated Marketing," *Marketing Tools* (November-December 1995), p. 64.

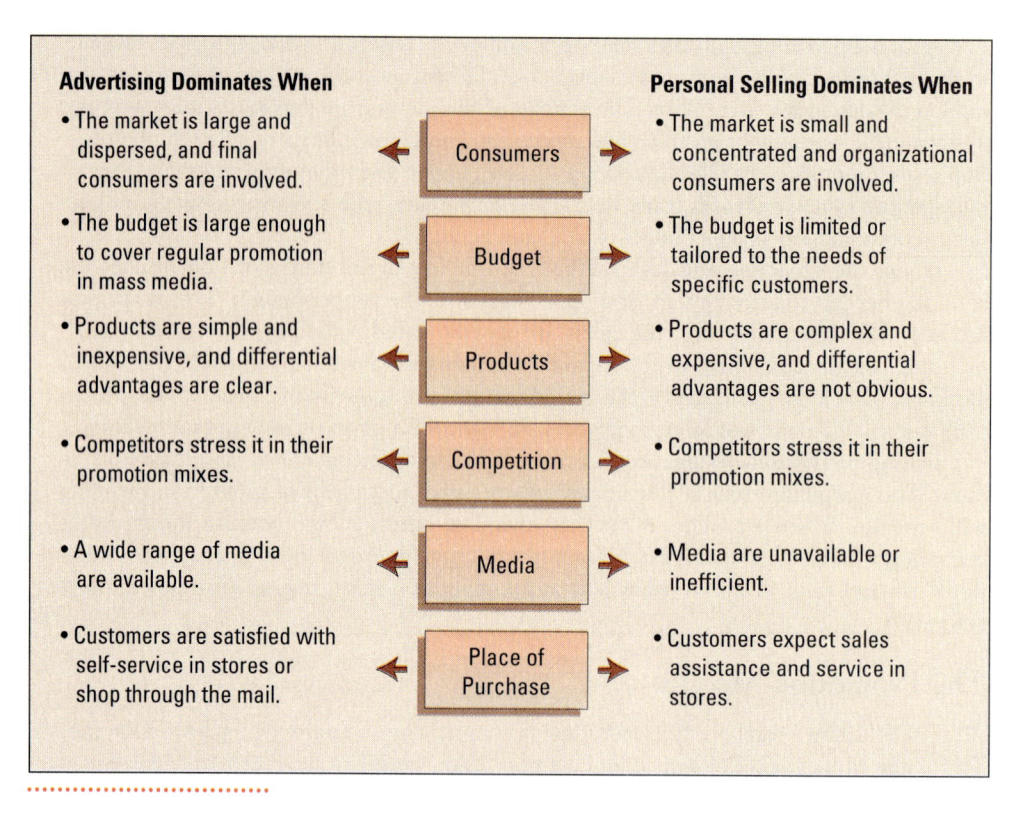

Advertising Dominates When		Personal Selling Dominates When
• The market is large and dispersed, and final consumers are involved.	← Consumers →	• The market is small and concentrated and organizational consumers are involved.
• The budget is large enough to cover regular promotion in mass media.	← Budget →	• The budget is limited or tailored to the needs of specific customers.
• Products are simple and inexpensive, and differential advantages are clear.	← Products →	• Products are complex and expensive, and differential advantages are not obvious.
• Competitors stress it in their promotion mixes.	← Competition →	• Competitors stress it in their promotion mixes.
• A wide range of media are available.	← Media →	• Media are unavailable or inefficient.
• Customers are satisfied with self-service in stores or shop through the mail.	← Place of Purchase →	• Customers expect sales assistance and service in stores.

FIGURE 18-8
Contrasting Promotion Mixes

In large firms, there may be separate managers for advertising, public relations, personal selling, and sales promotion. They report to, and have their efforts coordinated by, the marketing director.

Figure 18-8 contrasts promotion mixes in which advertising and personal selling would dominate.

International Promotion Considerations

International promotion decisions should not be made until each market is carefully studied.

SPRINT CANADA
www.sprintcanada.ca/english/text/index.html

While preparing a promotion strategy for foreign nations, the channel of communication, promotion goals, budgeting, and the promotion mix should be carefully reviewed as they pertain to each market.

With regard to the channel of communication, a firm should recognize that:

- Source recognition and credibility vary by nation or region. In Canada, celebrities who are popular in English Canada may not be popular in Quebec. For example, Sprint Canada was using Candace Bergen as their advertising spokesperson in both languages. Candace Bergen was married to the late French film director Louis Malle and is fluently bilingual in both of Canada's official languages. Yet she was not well received in Quebec so Sprint replaced her with three spokespersons who are well known in Quebec: Jean-Luc Brassard, an Olympic gold medal-winning aerial skier; actor Dominique Michel; and Jacques Languirand, a well-known radio host. Actors from Hollywood are rarely received well in Quebec: "they always look like they've been dubbed, even if they haven't." [13]

---

[13]"Sprint Uses Local Stars in New Quebec Effort," *Marketing Magazine* (March 27, 1995), p. 3; and George Morris, "Homegrown Icons," *Marketing Magazine* (June 3, 1996), p. 14.

- Encoding messages can be quite challenging, particularly if the messages must be translated into another language.
- Because the effects of message symbolism depend on the nation or region, care must be taken if fear, humorous, and/or sexual messages are used. Themes have to correspond to local customs. For example, for firms targeting the Canadian youth market it is important that approaches to advertising recognize regional differences. "In Toronto there's more stress on uniformity. A key to teens is 'Let's be different together,' but there's less of that in Quebec. You'll see more flexibility in terms of being unique." [14]
- In some locales, few residents have TVs, a limited number of newspapers and magazines are printed, and programs (channels) limit or do not accept ads.
- Ensuring that messages are decoded properly can be demanding: "To promote its Wash & Go shampoo, Procter & Gamble blanketed Polish TV and mailed samples. Poles found the dubbed ad culturally out of touch: It showed a woman popping out of a swimming pool and into a shower. 'We don't have swimming pools, and most of us don't have showers. We have baths,' sniffed Eugeniusz Smilowski, president of a Warsaw research group."[15]
- Making assumptions about audience traits in foreign markets without adequate research may lead to wrong assumptions: Western marketers entered the Indian market believing well-known brands would be accepted in India just like they had been accepted elsewhere. What they found out was that in India, "the consumer does not buy a global brand just because it is global... International brands have to be relevant in terms of perceived image, performance, and value if they are to succeed locally."[16]
- Global techniques for measuring promotion effectiveness are emerging.

In terms of promotion goals, budgeting, and the promotion mix, these points should be considered:

- For nations where a firm and its brands are unknown, a firm should have a series of promotion goals to lead people through the hierarchy-of-effects model. For nations in which a product category is new, primary demand must be created before selective demand is gained. To show goodwill, image ads may be even more important in foreign than in domestic markets.
- The promotion budgets in foreign countries must be keyed to the size of the markets and the activities required to succeed there. The objective-and-task method is highly recommended in setting international promotion budgets.
- Due to cultural, socioeconomic, infrastructure, and other differences, promotion mixes must be consistent with the countries served. In Western Europe, Germans listen to the most radio; the Dutch and British watch the most TV. And when Procter & Gamble mailed free samples (a form of sales promotion) of Wash & Go shampoo to people's homes in Poland, thieves broke into mailboxes to get the samples—which they resold. As a Procter & Gamble manager said, "The tools we were using were new to that area."[17]

---

[14]Gail Chiasson, "Quebec 13 to 24," *Marketing Magazine* (February 20, 1995), p. 13.
[15]Gail E. Schares, "Colgate-Palmolive Is Really Cleaning Up in Poland," *Business Week* (March 15, 1993), p. 56.
[16]Tom Duncan, "Standardized Global Marketing Communication Campaigns Are Possible, They're Just Hard to Do" in Robert P. Leone and V. Kumar (Eds.), *1992 AMA Educators' Proceedings* (Chicago: American Marketing Association, 1992), p. 355; and Dilip Subramanian, "Western Marketers Join India's Economic Boom," *Marketing Magazine* (March 11, 1996), p. 5.
[17]"Data Watch," *Advertising Age* (October 26, 1992), p. I-10; and E. S. Browning, "Eastern Europe Poses Obstacles for Ads," *Wall Street Journal* (July 30, 1992), p. B6.

Table 18-3

Selected Canadian Regulations (Federal & Provincial) Affecting Promotion

MARKETING PRACTICE	LEGAL CONSIDERATIONS
Access to media	Cigarette, liquor, and drug manufacturers have restricted access.
Deception	It is illegal to make false statements or use messages that would mislead reasonable consumers and potentially harm them.
Bait-and-switch	It is illegal to lure a customer with an ad for a low-priced item and then, once the customer talks to a salesperson, to use a strong sales pitch intended to switch the shopper to a more expensive item.
Door-to-door selling	Many locales restrict door-to-door sales practices. A cooling-off period allows a person to cancel an in-home sale up to seven days after an agreement is reached.
Promotional allowances	Such allowances must be available to channel members in a fair and equitable manner.
Comparative advertisements	Claims must be substantiated. Federal and provincial regulators favour naming competitors in ads (not citing a competitor as brand X).
Testimonials or endorsements	A celebrity or expert endorser must actually use a product if he or she makes such a claim.
Contests	Advertisers must disclose the chances of winning and the manner in which prizes are to be distributed.

Source: Ed Ratushny, Q.C., "Report of the Consultative Panel on Amendments to the Competition Act," *Strategis*, Industry Canada, http://strategis.ic.gc.ca. Ottawa: Competition Bureau (April 15, 1996); and Keith J. Tuckwell, *Canadian Advertising*, Third Edition, Prentice-Hall: Scarborough, Ontario, (1995), pp. 20, 635–654.

The Legal Environment of Promotion

Federal, provincial, and local governmental bodies in Canada—and similar bodies in other nations around the globe—have laws and rules regarding promotion practices. These regulations range from banning billboards in some locales to requiring celebrity endorsers to use products if they say they do. The Canadian federal agencies most involved with promotion are Industry Canada's Competition Bureau and the Canadian Radio-television and Telecommunications Commission (CRTC). Table 18-3 shows selected promotional practices that are subject to regulation.

The CRTC regulates all broadcast advertising but delegates some of this authority to other governmental bodies responsible for specific products. For example, Health Canada's Health Protection Branch regulates promotion for the Canadian pharmaceutical and cosmetic industry. Five regulatory tools are available to protect consumers and competing firms from undesirable promotion practices: full disclosure, substantiation, cease-and-desist orders, corrective advertising, and fines.

Full disclosure requires that all data necessary for a consumer to make a safe and informed decision be provided in a promotion message. That is why Alka-Seltzer must mention that its regular version contains aspirin, and diet products must note how many calories they contain. In this way, consumers can assess the overall benefits and risks of a purchase.

CRTC
www.crtc.gc.ca/

Full disclosure, substantiation, cease-and-desist orders, corrective advertising, *and fines are major governmental limits on promotion activities.*

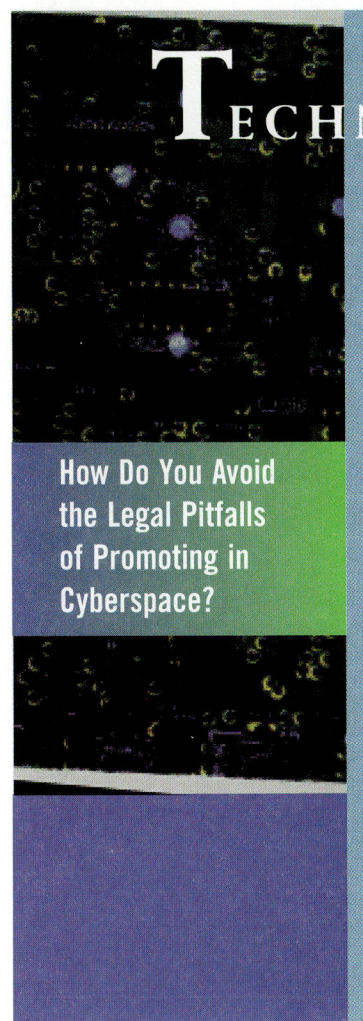

TECHNOLOGY & MARKETING

How Do You Avoid the Legal Pitfalls of Promoting in Cyberspace?

According to experts in the field, there are many legal risks associated with using the Internet for promotions. They advise marketers to keep this seven-point checklist in mind when planning and evaluating Internet-based promotions:

1. All Internet domain names and e-mail addresses are trademarks that must be cleared to ensure they are not owned by others and then legally protected.
2. A firm operating a bulletin board may be liable for the information showing up there. In a case involving slanderous information, Prodigy was held responsible for the same standards as traditional publishers.
3. The Screen Actors Guild claims jurisdiction over the employment of actors used in the production of online and CD-ROM programs. This affects videos that were initially made for television that are now used on the Internet.
4. As with other media, an individual's name, photograph, or likeness cannot be used in connection with any promotion, without his or her written permission.
5. Because the Internet is worldwide in terms of distribution, its use is subject to the laws in countries where the messages are reproduced.
6. The rights of photographers and freelance photographers may be affected by use of their materials on the Internet.
7. Marketers should reserve the right to cancel any Internet-based promotion in the event it is infected with a virus or otherwise cannot properly run.

As the advertising manager for Aiwa, you are responsible for devising an Internet-based promotion for a new line of surround-sound stereo receivers. How can you best assure that your promotion meets the above legal guidelines?

Source: Based on material in Douglas J. Wood and Linda A. Goldstein, "Seven Legal Pitfalls of Promoting in Cyberspace," *Promo* (July 1995), p. 21.

Substantiation requires that a firm be able to prove all the claims it makes in promotion messages. This means thorough testing and evidence of performance are needed before making claims. In a recent Ontario court case, Unilever, maker of Dove soap, sued Proctor and Gamble, maker of Oil of Olay, for an injunction against their comparative ads. Proctor and Gamble ran an ad claiming Oil of Olay helped retain more skin moisture than Dove soap. The case hinged on the ability of Proctor and Gamble to prove their claim with verifiable test results. Because they were able to do so, Unilever was denied an injunction.[18]

Under a **cease-and-desist order**, a firm must discontinue a promotion practice that is deemed deceptive and modify a message accordingly. The firm is usually not forced to admit guilt or pay fines, as long as it obeys the order.

Corrective advertising requires a firm to run new ads to correct the false impressions left by previous ones. Several years ago, Listerine was told to spend U.S.$10.2 million on ads in Canada and the U.S. to correct prior messages claiming it was a cold remedy. Listerine decided to run the ads (with the phrase "Listerine will not help prevent colds or sore throats or lessen their severity") after learning it would not otherwise be permitted to continue any advertising.

The last major remedy is **fines**, which are dollar penalties for deceptive promotion. A company may have to pay a sum to the government, as when K-mart was fined $200 000

---

[18] Angela Di Padova, "Moisture and Misleading Advertising," *Marketing Magazine* (March 18, 1996), p. 20.

FIGURE 18-9
A Strong Defence of Promotion by the American Association of Advertising Agencies
Reprinted by permission.

for misleading advertising related to advertised sale prices of mattresses. K-mart promoted a sale on mattresses by claiming the price during the sale was 50 per cent less than the price would be *after* the sale. The advertising was judged to be misleading because the mattresses had been specially purchased for the sale, and would not be available afterwards. Therefore, promoting a discount price based on an after-the-sale price was misleading.[19]

In addition to government legislation, trade and professional associations often have rules or guidelines governing the use of promotion by their members. The International Advertising Association sets guidelines for the self-regulation of promotion throughout the world. Within Canada, marketers are asked to voluntarily abide by the Canadian Code of Advertising Standards, which is administered by the Canadian Advertising Foundation (CAF). The CAF delegates its responsibilities to various bodies in each of the provinces. For example, in Ontario, the Standards Division of the Canadian Advertising Foundation handles all English-language complaints about national advertising in Canada and any

---

[19]Industry Canada, "K-mart Canada Limited Fined $200 000 for One Count of Misleading Advertising Under the Competition Act," Industry Canada *Strategis* Web site (April 13, 1995).

complaints in Ontario, while le Conseil des Normes de la Publicité handles all of the complaints on national advertising in French and all complaints in Quebec. In the Atlantic provinces and the Western provinces there are regional councils that handle complaints on advertising in these regions.[20]

Some cities have their own advertising councils to handle complaints. For example, the Windsor Media Council (Windsor, Ontario) places ads in the local media informing the community where they can register complaints and seek resolution concerning local advertising and media programming. Another important local body involved in self-regulation is the Better Business Bureau. The Better Business Bureau usually deals with more product and service complaints but complaints about promotional practices are handled as well.

Criticisms and Defences of Promotion

For many years, various industry trade groups have campaigned to improve the overall image of promotion, as illustrated in Figure 18–9. According to the general director of the International Advertising Association, "There's been enough talk about the bad—the clutter, the obtrusiveness, the stuffed mailboxes. It's time that people know about the good."[21]

Promotion controversies centre on materialism, honesty, prices, symbolism, and consumer expectations.

Nonetheless, promotion is the most heavily criticized area of marketing. Here are a number of criticisms and the defences of marketers to them:

DETRACTORS FEEL THAT PROMOTION:	MARKETING PROFESSIONALS ANSWER THAT PROMOTION:
Creates an obsession with material possessions.	Responds to consumer desires for material possessions. In affluent societies, these items are plentiful and paid for with discretionary earnings.
Is basically dishonest.	Is basically honest. The great majority of companies abide by all laws and set strict self-regulations. A few dishonest firms give a bad name to all.
Raises the prices of consumer goods and services.	Holds down prices. By increasing demand, promotion enables firms to use mass production and mass distribution and reduce per-unit costs. Employment is higher when demand is stimulated.
Overemphasizes symbolism and status.	Differentiates goods and services through symbolic and status appeals. Consumers desire distinctiveness and product benefits.
Causes excessively high expectations.	Keeps expectations high; it thereby sustains consumer motivation and worker productivity in order to satisfy expectations.

---

[20]Keith J. Tuckwell, *Canadian Advertising, Third Edition*, Prentice-Hall: Scarborough, Ontario (1995), pp. 20, 635–654.
[21]Cyndee Miller, "The Marketing of Advertising," *Marketing News* (December 7, 1992), p. 2.

MARKETING IN A CHANGING WORLD
What's Ahead for Integrated Marketing Communications?

According to Don E. Schultz, Stanley Tannenbaum, and Robert F. Lauterborn (in their best-selling book, *Integrated Marketing Communications: Pulling It All Together and Making It Work*), IMC has four fundamental goals:

- To ensure that all communications with consumers are coordinated.
- To make the consumer—not the product—the focal point of communication.
- To foster one-on-one communication with consumers.
- To engender two-way communication between a firm and its consumers.[22]

These sound like admirable objectives, so what's the problem? In a word: implementation. Says one expert, "Integrated marketing communications is the buzz in today's business world. Unfortunately, it usually ends there—a buzz lacking a bite." In fact, one survey of business marketers found that only one-quarter of the respondents had developed an annual IMC plan.[23]

Let us see why implementation is so rough and how it may be worked out:

At a recent Marketing Sciences Institute conference on marketing communications, one firm after another recounted various attempts to overcome vertical silos [departmental turfs] and to create cross-organizational marketing integration. IBM told of multiple experiments, moving from centralized communications to a decentralized team approach, and then to a marketing services "account manager" approach. Currently, the company is attempting to dismantle its vertical marketing functions completely in favour of cross-functional teams that reside in and work for sponsoring companies.

Organizational resistance is a common impediment because marketing departments—whether arranged by product or by function—are accustomed to autonomy and see IMC as a threat to their resources and decision-making power. Some firms try to tackle this problem by creating marketing service functions that gradually build on some small successes. As the company demonstrates the value of cooperation to marketing or product managers, resistance gradually gives way to rising demand for further integration.[24]

SUMMARY

1. To define promotion planning and show its importance Promotion involves any communication that informs, persuades, and/or reminds people about an organization's or individual's goods, services, ideas, community involvement, or impact on society. Promotion planning is systematic and relates to all aspects of communication.

Promotion efforts are needed for both new products and existing ones. The audience for promotion may be consumers, shareholders, consumer advocacy groups, government, channel members, employees, competitors, and the public. With word-of-mouth communication, people express opinions and product-related experiences to one another. A firm may communicate its image, views on ideas, community involvement, or impact on society—as well as persuade people to buy. Good promotion enhances the other elements of the marketing mix. Promotion is a major activity around the world.

2. To describe the general characteristics of advertising, public relations, personal selling, and sales promotion Advertising is paid, nonpersonal communication transmitted through various media by organizations and individuals who are in some way identified as the sponsor. Public relations includes any communication (paid or nonpaid, nonpersonal or personal, sponsored by a firm or reported by an independent medium) designed to foster a favourable image. Publicity is the nonpaid, nonpersonal, nonsponsored form of public relations. Personal

---

[22]Don E. Schultz, Stanley Tannenbaum, and Robert F. Lauterborn, *Integrated Marketing Communications: Pulling It All Together and Making It Work* (Lincolnwood, Ill.: NTC Business Books, 1993).
[23]Kim Cleland, "Few Wed Marketing, Communications," *Advertising Age* (February 27, 1995), p. 10.
[24]Smith, "Integrated Marketing," p. 65.

selling involves oral communication with one or more prospective buyers by paid representatives for the purpose of making sales. Sales promotion involves paid marketing activities to stimulate consumer purchases and dealers.

3. *To explain the channel of communication and how it functions* A source sends a message to its audience through a channel of communication. A channel consists of a source, encoding, the message, the medium, decoding, the audience, feedback, and noise.

A source is a company, an independent institution, or an opinion leader that seeks to present a message to an audience. Encoding is the process by which a thought or an idea is translated into a message by the source. A message is a combination of words and symbols transmitted to the audience. A medium is a personal or nonpersonal channel used to convey a message. Decoding is the process by which a message sent by a source is translated by the audience. The audience is the object of a source's message. Feedback is the response the audience makes to a message: purchase, attitude change, or nonpurchase. Noise is interference at any stage.

4. *To examine the components of a promotion plan* Promotion goals may be demand- or image-oriented. Demand goals should correspond to the hierarchy-of-effects model, moving a consumer from awareness to purchase. Primary demand is total consumer demand for a product category; selective demand refers to consumer interest in a particular brand. Institutional advertising is used to enhance company image.

Five ways to set a promotion budget are: all you can afford (the weakest method), incremental, competitive parity, percentage of sales, and objective and task (the best method). Marginal return should be considered when budgeting.

A promotion mix is the overall and specific communication program of a firm, including its use of advertising, public relations (publicity), personal selling, and/or sales promotion. The mix can be well-rounded through integrated marketing communications. Many factors need to be considered in developing a promotion mix.

5. *To discuss international promotion considerations, and the legal environment and criticisms and defences of promotion* When devising an international promotion plan, the channel of communication, promotion goals, budgeting, and promotion mix should be studied for and applied to each market.

There are many laws and rules affecting promotion. The major ways to guard against undesirable promotion are full disclosure, substantiation, cease-and-desist orders, corrective advertising, and fines.

Critics are strong in their complaints about promotion practices and their effects. Marketers are equally firm in their defences.

KEY TERMS

promotion (p. 491)
promotion planning (p. 491)
word-of-mouth communication (p. 491)
advertising (p. 493)
public relations (p. 493)
publicity (p. 493)
personal selling (p. 493)
sales promotion (p. 493)
channel of communication (communication process) (p. 495)
source (p. 495)
encoding (p. 497)
message (p. 497)

comparative messages (p. 498)
massed promotion (p. 498)
distributed promotion (p. 498)
wearout rate (p. 498)
medium (p. 499)
decoding (p. 499)
subliminal advertising (p. 500)
audience (p. 500)
feedback (p. 501)
noise (p. 502)
hierarchy-of-effects model (p. 502)
primary demand (p. 502)
selective demand (p. 502)

institutional advertising (p. 503)
all-you-can-afford method (p. 503)
incremental method (p. 503)
competitive parity method (p. 503)
percentage-of-sales method (p. 503)
objective-and-task method (p. 503)
marginal return (p. 505)
promotion mix (p. 505)
integrated marketing communications (IMC) (p. 505)
full disclosure (p. 508)
substantiation (p. 508)
cease-and-desist order (p. 508)
corrective advertising (p. 508)

Review Questions

1. Why is promotion planning important?
2. Distinguish among advertising, public relations, personal selling, and sales promotion.
3. What is the role of an opinion leader in a channel of communication?
4. What is a two-sided message? Why do few companies use such messages?
5. What should be the relationship between encoding and decoding messages? Why?
6. A consumer listens to a sales presentation but does not make a purchase. Has the presentation failed? Explain your answer.
7. Explain the hierarchy-of-effects model. How is it related to demand objectives?
8. Describe each of the methods of promotional budgeting.
9. When should personal selling dominate the promotion mix?
10. State the basic criticisms and defences of promotion.

Discussion Questions

1. What are the advantages and disadvantages of changing messages (themes) infrequently?
2. Present a promotion campaign to increase APBs (AIDS preventive behaviours) among teens.
3. As the marketing manager for a small Canadian-based Portuguese book publisher that is entering the Brazilian market for the first time, devise a promotion budget relying on the objective-and-task method.
4. Develop a promotion mix for:
   a. A global restaurant chain.
   b. A small janitorial service.
   c. A four-person dental practice.
   d. A medium-sized sporting-goods manufacturer.
5. Comment on this statement: "Full disclosure confuses consumers by giving them too much information. It also raises costs."

VIDEO CASE

Changing the Negative Image of Banks: Is It Possible?

The Canadian banking industry has developed an image problem in the eyes of the public. In 1995 six of the top ten most profitable firms in Canada were banking institutions. In 1994 and 1995 Canadian banks had record profits at a time when the Canadian economy had been relatively sluggish. Meanwhile, banks were imposing a host of transaction fees on their customers, paying low interest rates on deposits, and charging high interest rates on bank cards, which resulted in Canadians having record levels of personal debt.

The mood of the public in Canada with respect to banks in the mid-90s can be characterized as "angry." Newspaper editorial columnists and cartoonists have been having a field day criticizing the banks, further tarnishing the public image of banking. Of course, Canadian banks are fully aware of the fact that they have an image problem. Almost 60 percent of the earnings of the banks come from "corner" branches who transact with individual customers and small businesses as opposed to large businesses.

When an institution is faced with a serious image problem it is important that it respond to the situation to stay in touch with its customers. In addition, banks need to stand in good favour with consumers because they will be competing in businesses they are relatively new to. For example, because of banking deregulation, banks are starting to market a lot of new products including life insurance and automobile leasing.

As a result, most of the major banks in Canada are using image campaigns to win back the favour of the public. The Royal Bank of Canada has developed an imaging position of "One customer at a time." The Canadian Imperial Bank of Commerce hopes to tap into the psyche of everyday Canadians with the position "We see what you see." Toronto Dominion Bank is taking the friendly approach: "We're here to help make it easier." However, one of the most innovative approaches to remaking the image of a bank is being undertaken by the Bank of Montreal.

The Bank of Montreal believes that customers matter but sees its competitors as offering the same kind of message. The Bank of Montreal elected to undergo a radical image change and put a budget of $13 million behind it. They hired the Vickers and Benson Advertising agency to come up with a campaign. The creative geniuses behind the campaign are Philippe Garneau and Michael Wurstlin. The major theme of the campaign developed from the notion "Can a Bank Learn"? The tag line associated with the campaign became "It is possible™" at the Bank of Montreal.

The theme was developed to show that the Bank of Montreal could adapt to change and to set up specific promotional appeals for a host of new banking products.

The key to the campaign is that it addresses ordinary concerns and fears of most Canadians and then presents the Bank of Montreal as a solution. The campaign features black-and-white ads of Canadians holding up signs with statements like: "I'm buying mutual funds" and "This year I'm going to retire" and questions like "Will I ever own my own home?" and "Can a bank help?" The ending line for these ads is "It is possible™", the idea being that with the help of the Bank of Montreal ordinary Canadians will be able to achieve their financial goals. To reinforce the image on a local level, branches are sponsoring local events and working more closely with their communities.

The Bank of Montreal's image campaign has been considered the most successful within the industry so far. It seems to have had a strong impact because it has tapped into the needs of consumers, and doing this successfully is considered one of the hallmarks of a good marketing strategy.

QUESTIONS

1. Since the negative perception of banks applies to the industry as a whole, perhaps the banking industry should develop an "industry" campaign as opposed to promoting separate institutions. Suggest some campaign themes for this approach and justify them.
2. Apply the stages in the channel of communication to the Bank of Montreal's image campaign.
3. Relate the stages in promotion planning—objectives, budgeting, and the promotion mix—to the "It is possible™" campaign undertaken by the Bank of Montreal.
4. Describe how the Bank of Montreal, or any bank, can evaluate the effectiveness of their image campaign.

VIDEO QUESTIONS ON BANKS

1. Evaluate the appeal of the Bank of Montreal's campaign. Does it have staying power or is it just the hot campaign of the month? Explain your answer.
2. Compare the four campaign themes of the various banks presented in the video and this case in terms of their effectiveness as positioning statements. Discuss whether the banks can really hope to live up to these statements.

Sources: The data in this case are drawn from Laura Medcalf, "It's Even Possible at BMO," *Marketing Magazine* (October 23, 1995), p. 4; Michael Valpy, "Yours Sincerely, Your Soothing Bank," *Marketing Magazine* (March 25, 1996), p. 8; and "Performance 500 Indicators," *Canadian Business* (June 1996), p. 151.

Video Source: "Bank of Montreal," *Venture* (January 7, 1996).

CASE STUDY

Can a Firm Succeed by Poking Fun at Itself?

An increasing number of firms have begun to mock their past behaviour in their advertising. Examples of self-deprecating ads include those for Thom McAn shoes and 7-Eleven stores. For example, a recent ad for Thom McAn said, "Please excuse some of our shoe styles in the past. Through a fluke computer error, the office-supply store repeatedly sent us the wrong desk calendar and we still thought it was 1976." Another ad even stated, "Please excuse some of our shoe styles in the past. For years, our new and updated shoes were rerouted by a disgruntled worker and abandoned under a bridge near Chicago."

7-Eleven's ads have poked fun at the stores' past high prices, cramped interiors, and food that wasn't always fresh. In one ad, comedian Louie Anderson remarked, "They're so small that there's barely room for me and a Big Gulp." Another ad featuring Brett Butler (of the TV series *Grace Under Fire*) expressed surprise at the gourmet coffee and frozen yogurt at a 7-Eleven. She also said, "Are women running 7-Eleven now? Pork rinds and Perrier. Is this heaven or what?"

After tough times, both Thom McAn and 7-Eleven poked fun at their past strategies as a way of promoting their new images. For example, in 1981, Thom McAn had sales of $440 million through 1200 outlets, but 1995 sales had sunk to $275 million from 400 stores. And 7-Eleven had difficulty convincing consumers that its grocery products were delivered daily, versus every four to five days. The chain also had a blue-collar male image that was not attractive to females and higher-income professionals. As 7-Eleven's director of advertising and sales promotion noted, "We needed to communicate the magnitude of our changes."

Marketing analysts have mixed views on the effectiveness of advertising that makes fun of a firm's past. Advocates of this technique feel this approach is perceived as honest. They also say this strategy is most effective when a company's/brand's image has hit rock-bottom and when the current reality is better than the public's perceptions. According to the head of Thom McAn's advertising agency, "There's nothing new in just saying, 'Come see us, we have changed.' A lot of people do that, and there's no reason to believe them. So you have to use a bit of self-deprecation to get people to take you seriously."

Those who question this technique, however, have a different viewpoint. One marketing expert suggests that, "It's foolish to talk about the past and remind people of things that may have not made a difference. Consumers want to know what's in your stores now." Another cautions advertisers about using this technique: "You had better be certain that your product or service fulfils the promise of the apologizing advertising."

Most marketing observers do agree that poking fun at oneself will work only when a firm has made meaningful changes in its overall marketing strategy. Therefore, in addition to changing its advertising, Thom McAn introduced more contemporary shoe styles, a spiffy new logo, more modern store colours, and a private label that offers fashionable shoes targeted at younger, more fashion-conscious shoppers.

An example of an ineffective self-deprecating ad was Oldsmobile's, "This is not your father's Oldsmobile" campaign, which aired in the late 1980s. Although the campaign lured a young target market to Oldsmobile dealerships, few browsers actually bought a car resembling their "father's Oldsmobile."

QUESTIONS

1. How does a self-deprecating ad differ from a two-sided message?
2. What are the similarities between a self-deprecating ad and a two-sided message?
3. What are the pros and cons of the use of humour in advertising?
4. Explain how Thom McAn can develop a budget for its advertising using the objective-and-task technique.

Source: The data in this case are drawn from Joshua Levine, "Please Excuse Our Shoe Styles of the Past," *Forbes* (January 2, 1995), p. 64; and Fara Warner, "'We Goofed, Forgive Us,' New Ads Plead," *Wall Street Journal* (May 25, 1995), pp. B1, B8.

CHAPTER 19
Advertising and Public Relations

Chapter Objectives

1. To examine the scope, importance, and characteristics of advertising

2. To study the elements in an advertising plan

3. To examine the scope, importance, and characteristics of public relations

4. To study the elements in a public relations plan

{ *Infomercials represent a powerful marketing vehicle that is not limited by geographic borders. New cable and distribution systems are exploding around the globe. The kinds of products that sell on TV appeal to a mass market and fall into categories that many cultures buy, such as cosmetics, personal care items, fitness equipment, and kitchen supplies.* }

An infomercial is a full-length TV advertising program (typically thirty minutes) that airs on cable television—or on broadcast media at a fringe time. While watching infomercials, consumers call in orders and items are then delivered directly to their homes or offices. An infomercial is especially useful for products requiring demonstrations to show their benefits.

Infomercials are successfully promoting a variety of goods and services—including food preparation devices (such as juice preparation machines and pasta makers), cosmetics, exercise equipment, instructional videos on computer software, and car waxes. Through a French-language infomercial running twice a day on Infopub, an infomercial channel which is part of Le Groupe Videotron Ltee of Montreal, Royal Diamond Cookware received 2000 calls and generated $200 000 in sales in less than three weeks.

There are several factors behind a good infomercial. They relate to the use of testimonials, program length, product pricing, two-step offers, and production considerations. Let's now review each.

A key to the success of any infomercial is the proper use of testimonials. A testimonial is particularly important with two types of infomercials—those that sell a product replacing an "earlier generation" item and the "I made a ton of money and so can you" types of programs. Testimonials do not have to come from a celebrity; they can come from satisfied customers. Some celebrity testimonials can be very effective; however, celebrities can also double an infomercial's production cost.

Even though most infomercials are thirty minutes long, most viewers watch only part of a show. Therefore, infomercial sponsors often divide their programs into self-sustaining parts (such as three ten-minute segments) and give people a chance to order merchandise during each portion of the program.

According to one industry expert, the price of a product appearing on an infomercial should exceed $40 to $50, due to the high production costs and media expenditures. If an appropriate item is priced at a lower amount, sponsors may sell the product as a package of three for $49.95 or as part of a "buy two for $49.95, get one free" promotion.

Some products require a two-step offer, in which a sponsor first generates a list of prospects from an infomercial and then makes separate calls to try to close sales. Two-step offers are appropriate to screen prospects by getting additional information about the prospects' needs, product use, or company size. A negative element of the two-step approach is that the sponsor needs to sell the potential consumer twice, on both the initial inquiry and close.

Producers must include several production considerations in planning and implementing infomercials: The offer should be listed as available for a limited time only to increase sales responses. A toll-free number should be clearly listed. Humour can be used in establishing rapport with the customer, but infomercial experts warn against using humour when promoting a product. And lastly, the qualifications of an "expert host" should be mentioned in the infomercial to enhance credibility.[1]

In this chapter, we will study both the advertising and public relations aspects of promotion.

---

[1] Andrea Haman, "Powerful Pitches," *Marketing Magazine* (December 4, 1995), p. 14; Kim Cleland, "Infomercial Audience Crosses Over Cultures," *Advertising Age* (January 15, 1996), pp. I–8; Hershell Gordon Lewis, "Information on Infomercials," *Direct Marketing* (March 1995), pp. 30–32; and Zachary Schiller and Ron Grover, "And Now, A Show from Your Sponsor," *Business Week* (May 22, 1995), pp. 100–104.

Overview

This chapter covers two promotion forms: advertising and public relations. As defined in Chapter 18, advertising is paid, nonpersonal communication regarding goods, services, organizations, people, places, and ideas; it may be used by businesses, government, and other nonprofit organizations, and individuals. Its distinguishing features are that a sponsor pays for its message, a set format is sent to an entire audience through mass media, the sponsor's name is clearly presented, and the sponsor controls the message.

In contrast, public relations involves communication that fosters a favourable image for goods, services, organizations, people, places, and ideas among their various publics. Its unique features are that it is more image- than sales-oriented it includes image-oriented advertising, personal selling, and sales promotion; and it often seeks favourable publicity for a firm. As an aspect of public relations, publicity entails nonpersonal communication that is transmitted via mass media but not paid for by an identified sponsor. The media usually control the wording and placement of publicity messages.

The distinctions between advertising and publicity are in part revealed by this statement: "Advertising is paid for, publicity is prayed for."

The scope and importance, characteristics, and planning considerations for both advertising and public relations are examined in this chapter.

Advertising and public relations are two of the major forms of promotion.

The Scope and Importance of Advertising

In 1996 alone, it is estimated that U.S.$375 billion was spent on advertising around the world—U.S.$6.7 billion in Canada (equivalent to about $9.2 billion in Canadian funds); nearly U.S.$175 billion in the United States, and just about U.S.$200 billion outside North America (half in Western Europe).[2] Table 19-1 shows per cent of expenditures by medium for Canada, the United States, and Western Europe. In Canada, catalogues and direct mail command the largest expenditure while newspapers and television are the next most used media. In the United States and Western Europe, newspapers and TV are the preferred media; but, newspapers are more popular for Western European advertisers, partly due to greater vehicle choice relative to television. Direct mail is also a key and growing medium in all three areas. The largest media difference between Canada, the U.S., and Western Europe is with magazines, which are more popular in Western Europe.

The per cent of sales devoted to advertising varies by industry and firm; and company advertising as a per cent of sales is usually very low. See Tables 19-2 and 19-3. During 1995, expenditures were less than 2.0 per cent of sales in 40 per cent of North American industries; 2.0 to 3.9 per cent of sales in 35 per cent of North American industries; and at least 4.0 per cent of sales in 25 per cent of North American industries.[3] Among the leading advertisers in the world, such as Procter & Gamble, the percentages often far exceed industry averages.

An advertising emphasis is most likely if products are standardized, have easily communicated features, appeal to a large market, have low prices, are marketed through independent resellers, and/or are new. Leading brands often get large ad budgets to hold their positions. For example, Zurich Canada, a large insurance company, runs ads positioning itself with two themes: customer focused and responsive. Zurich believes people see insurance companies as cold and impersonal and wants to change this perception for their firm. To fulfil this positioning change the firm has set up Zurich-Assist, a twenty-four-hour help line to deliver advice and guidance to Zurich policy holders, and is advertising this fact. Zurich uses an external advertising agency and its ads are placed on television and in magazines; in addition, Zurich has paid to have its logo displayed at Maple Leaf Gardens in

Three-quarters of North American firms spend less than 4 per cent of sales on advertising. Ads are most important for standardized products aimed at large markets.

ZURICH CANADA
www.zurcan.com/

---

[2] Jim McElgunn, "CARD Releases New Figures on Ad Spending," *Marketing Magazine* (September 25, 1995), p. 6; Stuart Elliott, "Advertising," *New York Times* (December 5, 1995), p. D10; and Sally Goll Beatty, "Agencies See Record Ad Spending in '96, Slowing Growth Thereafter," *Wall Street Journal* (December 5, 1995), p. B12.

[3] Computed by the authors from Schonfeld & Associates, "1995 Advertising to Sales Ratios for the 200 Largest Ad Spending Industries," *Advertising Age* (August 14, 1995), p. 26.

Table 19-1

Advertising Expenditures by Medium: Canada, the United States, and Western Europe

MEDIA	Canada[a]	PER CENT OF TOTAL EXPENDITURES United States[a]	Western Europe[a]
Direct Mail Catalogue	22.6	19.7	16.2
Newspapers	20.0	22.9	32.0
Television	19.2	22.8	25.0
Magazines	9.5	5.3	17.4
Yellow Pages	9.2	6.6	—
Outdoor	8.6	0.8	4.7
Radio	8.1	7.0	3.5
Business publications	1.8	2.2	—
Cinema	—	—	0.7
Farm publications	—	0.2	—
Miscellaneous	1.0	12.5	0.5
Total	100.0	100.0	100.0

[a]The media designations in the three areas differ because the sources for the Canadian, U.S., and European data are different.

Sources: Estimated by the authors from data reported in various issues of *Advertising Age;* and Jim McElgunn, "CARD Releases New Figures on Ad Spending," *Marketing Magazine* (September 25, 1995), p. 6.

Table 19-2

Advertising in Selected North American Industries, 1995

INDUSTRY	ADVERTISING AS PER CENT OF SALES	INDUSTRY	ADVERTISING AS PER CENT OF SALES
Games and toys	13.3	Hospitals	4.1
Hand tools	9.7	Books	3.6
Soaps and detergents	9.7	Financial services	3.0
Perfume	8.2	Paper mills	1.9
Beverages	8.2	Security brokers	1.2
Mail-order catalogues	7.7	Grocery stores	1.1
Educational services	7.4	Lumber	1.0
Food products	6.5	Computer & office equipment	0.9
Adhesives and sealants	5.4	Electronic components	0.9

Source: Derived from Schonfeld & Associates, "1995 Advertising to Sales Ratios for the 200 Largest Ad Spending Industries," *Advertising Age* (August 14, 1995), p. 26.

Table 19-3

The Leading Advertisers in Canada, the United States, and the World (1994 data)

IN CANADA ($C)

Company	Advertising Expenditures	Advertising as Per Cent of Sales
General Motors	$121 000 000	.48
Procter and Gamble	$81 670 000	7.35
Hudson's Bay	$71 400 000	1.22
BCE	$57 500 000	.27
Sears Canada	$56 450 000	1.41
Chrysler Canada	$51 210 000	.33
Molson	$50 100 000	1.69
Eaton's	$40 000 000	2.19
Vycom Electronics	$39 320 000	NA
John Labatt Ltd.	$35 600 000	1.53

IN THE UNITED STATES ($U.S.)

Company	Advertising Expenditures	Advertising as Per Cent of Sales
Procter and Gamble	$2 698 800 000	16.6
Philip Morris	$2 413 300 000	5.9
General Motors	$1 929 400 000	1.6
Ford	$1 186 000 000	1.3
Sears	$1 134 100 000	NA
AT&T	$1 102 700 000	1.6
PepsiCo	$1 097 800 000	5.4
Chrysler	$971 600 000	2.1
Walt Disney	$934 800 000	12.1
Johnson & Johnson	$933 700 000	12.0

THE WORLD (OUTSIDE NORTH AMERICA $U.S.)

Company	Advertising Expenditures	Advertising as Per Cent of Sales
Unilever	$2 208 800 000	6.1
Procter & Gamble	$2 199 500 000	12.8
Nestlé	$1 216 800 000	3.6
Philip Morris	$778 300 000	3.2
Peugeot-Citroën	$773 300 000	3.0
Toyota	$697 400 000	NA
Volkswagen	$696 900 000	1.5
General Motors	$650 500 000	2.0
Nissan	$611 000 000	NA
Mars	$604 200 000	NA

NA = Not available.

Sources: 1995 Annual Report On Form 10-K, THE PROCTER & GAMBLE COMPANY AND SUBSIDIARIES; "Performance 500," *Canadian Business* (June, 1995), p. 104–126; "Top Ten Advertisers Boosted Spending in '95," *Marketing Magazine* (April 15, 1996), p. 1; Derived from "100 Leading National Advertisers," *Advertising Age* (September 27, 1995); and "Top 50 Non-U.S. Spenders," *Advertising Age* (November 20, 1995), p. I-20. Reprinted by permission of *Advertising Age*. Copyright 1995 by Crain Communications, Inc. All rights reserved.

Toronto. Through advertising, Zurich wants to be seen as a different kind of insurance company that is there to help.[4]

As a senior executive at the J. Walter Thompson advertising agency once noted, "Advertising works on television and it works in print. What's more, it especially pays to advertise during recessions. All too often, by focusing on the bottom line, firms sacrifice the long-term, brand-building gains advertising makes possible. In our view, this is a serious mistake."[5]

J. WALTER THOMPSON COMPANY
www.jwtworld.com/

[4]News Line, "Zurich Backs Help Line with TV Campaign," *Marketing Magazine* (February 26, 1996), p. 1.
[5]Peter Kim, "Does Advertising Work: A Review of the Evidence," *Journal of Consumer Marketing*, Vol. 9 (Fall 1992), p. 5.

International Marketing in Action

Which Soft Drink Is the Real Thing in Brazil?

With U.S.$6 billion in annual sales, Brazil has the world's fourth-largest soft-drink consumption after the United States, Mexico, and Germany. About 45 million of the country's residents are aged 10 to 24, the prime soda-drinking age group. Brazil's average per capita consumption is about twenty-four litres.

In a effort to gain additional market share in the Brazilian market, PepsiCo has invested more than U.S.$500 million in advertising and distribution facilities since 1994. Because of this initiative, Pepsi has increased its overall market share of the Brazilian soda market from 5 per cent to 6 per cent. During the same period Coca-Cola's overall soda market share has dropped by 1.5 per cent—to 38 per cent. In the cola segment, Pepsi has a 7 per cent share; Coca-Cola's is nearly 88 per cent share.

Pepsi has devised twenty different TV commercials targeted specifically at the Brazilian market. One of these commercials shows Coca-Cola executives worrying about Pepsi's revised look, reformulated taste, and new distribution prowess. In response, Coca-Cola is increasing its advertising budget and running a new campaign—with a photocopy salesperson, who while demonstrating the world's most advanced copy machine, says that no one can copy Coca-Cola.

Royal Crown Cola (RC), owned by Cott Corporation of Canada, is entering the Brazilian market in alliance with a local distributor. Using the firm's "Shake things up" international advertising slogan, RC invested U.S.$750 000 in a promotional campaign aimed at three Brazilian test market areas. After a national rollout, RC hopes to go from 0 per cent to 3 per cent market share in the cola segment by the end of 1997.

As the advertising manager for RC, what would you do to compete with Coke and Pepsi in Brazil?

Source: Based on material in Claudia Penteado, "Pepsi Challenges Coke in Brazil," *Advertising Age* (January 16, 1995), p. 12.

Due to low-involvement purchases, consumer behaviour may be easier to change than attitudes. One ad can have a strong effect on brand awareness. By advertising, it is easier to raise people's opinions of a little-known product than a well-known one. Ad effectiveness often rises over long-term campaigns.

The Characteristics of Advertising

Advertising attracts an audience, has low per-customer costs, offers varied media, is surrounded by information, and aids selling.

On the positive side, advertising reaches a large, geographically dispersed market; and, for print media, circulation is supplemented by the passing of a copy from one reader to another. The costs per viewer or listener are low. For example, a single TV ad may cost $25 000 to air on the CBC network and reach 2 million people—a cost of $0.0125 per person (for media time). A broad range of media is available: from national (international) television to local newspapers and even the Internet. Thus, a firm's goals and resources may be matched with the most appropriate medium.

A sponsor has control over message content, graphics, timing, and size or length, as well as the audience targeted. A uniform message is sent to the whole audience. With print media, people can study and restudy messages. Editorial content (a news story or segment of a broadcast show) often borders an ad. This can raise readership or viewing/listening, enhance an image, and create the proper mood for an ad. A firm may even seek specialized media or sections of media (like a paper's sports section for a sports equipment ad).

Ads ease the way for personal selling by creating audience awareness and liking for brands. They also enable self-service wholesalers and retailers to operate, and they sustain an industry—mail order. With a pulling strategy, advertising enables a firm to show its resellers that consumer demand exists.

On the negative side, because messages are standardized, they are rather inflexible and not responsive to consumer questions. This makes it hard to satisfy the needs of a diverse audience. And since many media appeal to broad audiences, a large portion of viewers or readers may be wasted for a sponsor. For instance, a single-unit health spa or a local roofing-materials firm might find that only one-fifth of a newspaper's readers live in its shopping area.

Advertising is inflexible and can be wasteful, costly, and limit information and feedback.

Advertising sometimes requires high total expenditures, although costs per viewer or reader are low. This may keep smaller firms from using some media. In the example earlier in this section, it was said that a TV ad might cost only $0.0125 per viewer. Yet, media time alone for that ad would be $25 000— for one ad, placed once. Also, because high costs lead to brief messages, most ads do not provide much information. TV commercials are very short, averaging 30 seconds or less; few are as long as one minute. Further, because ads are impersonal, feedback is harder to get and it may not be immediately available.

Mass media are used by many people who do not view or listen to ads. They watch TV, read print media, and so on, but ignore ads and discard direct mail. Of concern to television advertisers is "zapping," whereby a viewer uses a remote-control device to switch programs when an ad comes on.

Developing an Advertising Plan

The process of developing an advertising plan consists of the nine steps shown in Figure 19-1 and discussed below.

Setting Objectives

An organization's advertising goals relate either to the demand for its product or service or to its image, with image-oriented ads being part of the firm's public relations effort. Table 19-4 cites several possible goals. Usually, a number of them are pursued in an advertising plan.

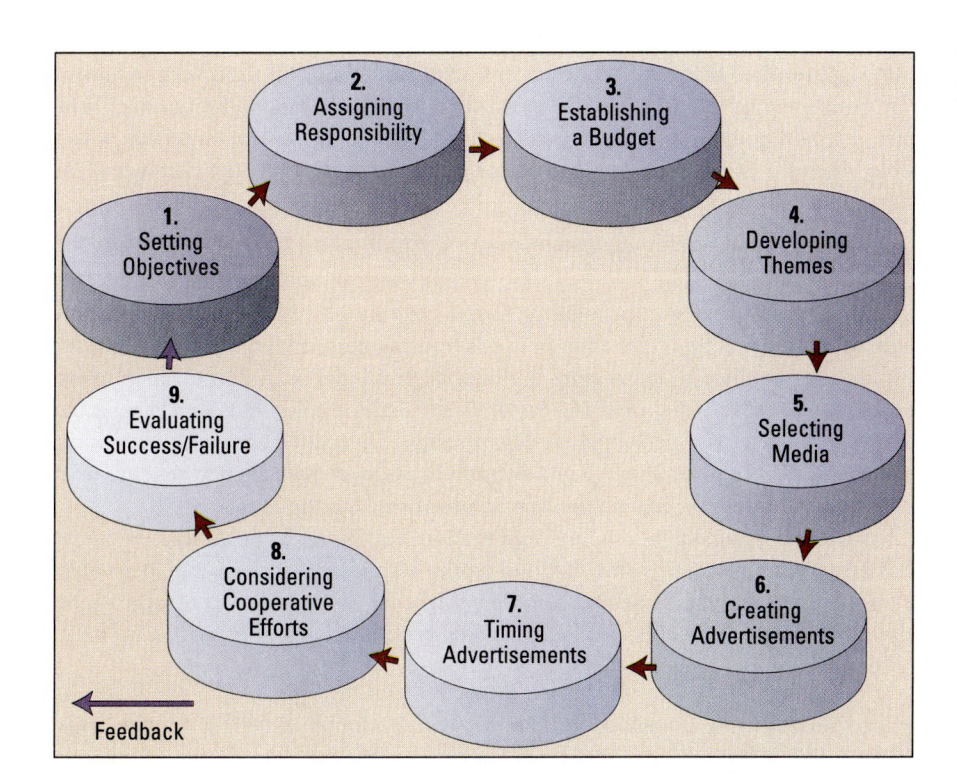

FIGURE 19-1
Developing an Advertising Plan

Table 19-4
Illustrations of Specific Advertising Objectives

TYPE OF OBJECTIVE	ILLUSTRATIONS
Demand-Oriented	
Information	To create target market awareness for a new brand
	To acquaint consumers with new business or store hours
	To reduce the time salespeople take to answer basic questions
Persuasion	To gain brand preference
	To increase store traffic
	To achieve brand loyalty
Reminding (retention)	To stabilize sales
	To maintain brand loyalty
	To sustain brand recognition and image
IMAGE-ORIENTED	
Industry	To develop and maintain a favourable industry image
	To generate primary demand
Company	To develop and maintain a favourable company image
	To generate selective demand

As an example, in late 1995 and early 1996 the Bank of Montreal decided to run an image-oriented ad campaign with very clear goals: to allay consumer concerns and to reduce anti-bank sentiments. Anti-bank sentiments were strong because bank profits were at record levels in 1994 and 1995, just after banks had significantly raised existing transaction fees and imposed new ones on their customers. In addition, bank credit card interest rates were very high at a time when prime interest rates were falling to twenty-five-year lows. One of the concerns expressed by consumers was that banks did not appear to be changing in response to the social and economic changes occurring around them. To tap into these sentiments, the Bank of Montreal decide to run an "It is possible" campaign. The campaign featured black and white ads of Canadians holding up signs with statements like: "I'm buying mutual funds" and "This year I'm going to retire" and questions like "Will I ever own my own home?" and "Can a bank help?". The ending line for these ads is "It is possible," the idea being that with the help of the Bank of Montreal the consumers' financial situation would be all right.[6]

Assigning Responsibility

In assigning advertising responsibility, a firm can rely on its internal personnel involved with marketing functions, use an in-house advertising department, or hire an outside advertising agency. Although many firms use internal personnel or in-house departments, most involved with advertising on a regular or sizable basis employ outside agencies (some in addition to their own personnel or departments). Diversified firms may hire a different agency for each product line. A firm's decision to use an outside agency depends on its own expertise and resources and on the role of advertising for the firm.

An **advertising agency** is an organization that provides a variety of advertising-related services to client firms. It often works with clients in devising their advertising plans—including themes, media choice, copyrighting, and other tasks. A large agency may also offer market research, product planning, consumer research, public relations, and other services.

An advertising agency may work with a firm to develop its ad plan, conduct research, or provide other services.

[6]Laura Medcalf, "It's even possible at BMO," *Marketing Magazine* (October 23, 1995), p. 4; Michael Valpy, "Yours Sincerely, Your Soothing Bank," *Marketing Magazine* (March 25, 1996), p. 8.

Establishing a Budget

After figuring its overall advertising spending by the all-you-can-afford, incremental, competitive parity, percentage-of-sales, or objective-and-task method, a firm sets a detailed ad budget—to specify the funds for each type of advertising (such as product and institutional messages) and each medium (such as newspapers and radio). Because demand-oriented ads generate revenues, firms should be cautious about reducing these budgets. A better campaign, not a lower budget, may be the answer if performance does not reach goals.

These points should be addressed: What do various alternatives cost for time or space (a thirty-second TV spot versus a full-page magazine ad)? How many placements are needed for an ad to be effective? (If it takes four telecasts of a single ad to make an impact, a budget must allow four placements.) Have media prices risen recently? How should a firm react during an industry sales slump? What channel members are assigned to which promotion tasks? Do channel members require contributions toward advertising? What does it cost to produce an ad? How should a budget be allocated for domestic versus international ads?

According to a recent survey of international advertising executives, 28 per cent of firms allow personnel in each pan-geographic region to determine their own needs and then petition headquarters for a budget; 28 per cent allow each individual market to have its own advertising strategy and budget; and 20 per cent control budgeting decisions from their world headquarters. Airlines are most likely to use the pan-geographic approach. Consumer products and high-tech companies are most apt to have individual market budgeting.[7]

Developing Themes

A firm next develops **advertising themes**, the overall appeals for its campaign. A good or service appeal centres on the item and its attributes. A consumer appeal describes a product in terms of consumer benefits rather than features. An institutional appeal deals with a firm's image. Table 19–5 presents a full range of advertising themes from which a firm may select. Figures 19–2 and 19–3 show thematic ads from The Canadian Dairy Bureau and Ombrelle sunscreens.

*Basic **advertising themes** are product, consumer, and/or institutional appeals.*

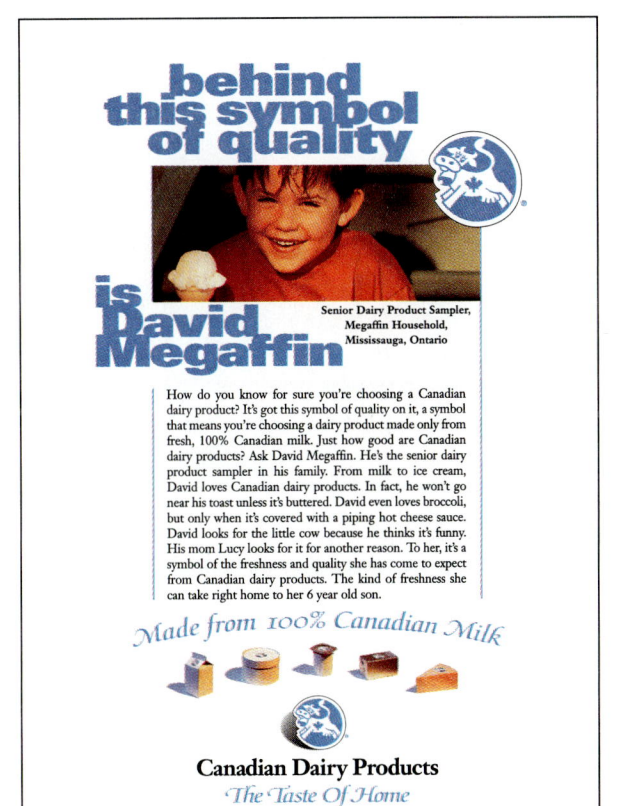

FIGURE 19-2
The Canadian Dairy Bureau: Seeking Primary Demand
Reprinted with permission of Dairy Farmers of Canada.

---

[7]Jan Jaben, "Ad Decision Makers Favor Regional Angle," *Advertising Age* (May 15, 1995), pp. I-3, I-16.

Table 19-5
Advertising Themes

THEME	EXAMPLE
Good or Service-Related	
Dominant features described	Maytag washers emphasize dependability and durability.
Competitive advantages cited	Aiwa stresses the superior quality of its portable stereos.
Price used as dominant feature	Suave beauty products advertise low prices.
News or information domination	New-model laser printers point out enhancements in colour and fonts.
Size of market detailed	Chrysler emphasizes its leading position as a mini-van maker.
Primary demand sought	The Dairy Bureau, Canadian Dairy Product symbol.
Consumer Related	
Good or service uses explained	Pillsbury ads have cake recipes.
Cost benefits of good or service shown	Owens-Corning states how consumers reduce heating bills with Fibreglas insulation.
Emphasis on how good or service helps consumer	Canadian Pacific hotels mentions how its rooms are set to accommodate all the needs of business travellers with new work centres.
Threatening situation	Ombrelle sunscreen talks about the threat of skin cancer and how the product can help reduce the risk.
Incentives given to encourage purchases	An ad mentions $1 off the purchase as an introductory offer for a new brand of coffee.
Institutional Related	
Favourable image sought	The Bank of Montreal talks about how a bank can help Canadians plan their future with their "It is possible" campaign.
Growth, profits, and potential described to attract investors	Companies regularly take out full-page ads in business sections of major newspapers.

FIGURE 19–3
Ombrelle Sunscreens: How a Product Can Help with a Threatening Situation
Reprinted with permission of Dermtek Pharmaceuticals Ltd.

Selecting Media

There are many media available, as noted in Table 19–6. In selecting them, costs, reach, waste, narrowcasting, frequency, message permanence, persuasive impact, clutter, lead time, and media innovations should be reviewed.

Advertising media costs are outlays for media time or space. They are related to ad length or size, as well as media attributes. First, the total cost to place an ad in a given medium should be computed—for example, $30 000 for a full-page colour ad in a magazine. Second, per-reader or viewer costs should be derived (stated on a per-thousand basis). If a $30 000 ad goes in a magazine with a 500 000 circulation, the cost per thousand is $60.

Reach refers to the number of viewers, readers, or listeners in a medium's audience. For TV and radio, it is the total number of people who watch or listen to an ad. For print media, it has two aspects: circulation and passalong rate. Circulation is the number of copies sold or distributed to people. The passalong rate is the number of times each copy is read by another reader. For instance, each copy of *Maclean's* is read by several people. The magazine passalong rate is much higher than that for daily papers.

Waste is the part of a medium's audience not in a firm's target market. Because media appeal to mass audiences, it can be a big factor. This can be shown by continuing the magazine example noted in media costs. If the magazine is a special-interest one for amateur photographers, a film producer would know that 450 000 readers might have an interest in a new fast-speed film; 50 000 would have no interest. The latter represents the wasted audience for its ad. So, the real cost is $66.67 ($30 000/450 000 x 1000 = $66.67) per thousand circulation. The firm also knows a general-interest magazine runs ads for film. That magazine sells one million copies and a full-page ad costs $40 000—$40 per thousand. Yet, the firm expects only 200 000 people to have an interest in photography. Thus, the real cost is $200 ($40 000/200 000 x 1000 = $200) per thousand circulation. See Figure 19-4.

Narrowcasting, which presents advertising messages to rather limited and well-defined audiences, is a way to reduce the audience waste with mass media. It may be achieved using direct mail, local cable TV, specialty magazines, and other targeted media. In narrowcasting, a firm gets less waste in return for a smaller reach. Given that 74.1 per

Advertising media costs *are total and per person.*

Reach *includes circulation and passalongs.*

Waste *is the audience segment not in the target market.*

In **narrowcasting,** *advertisers seek to reduce waste.*

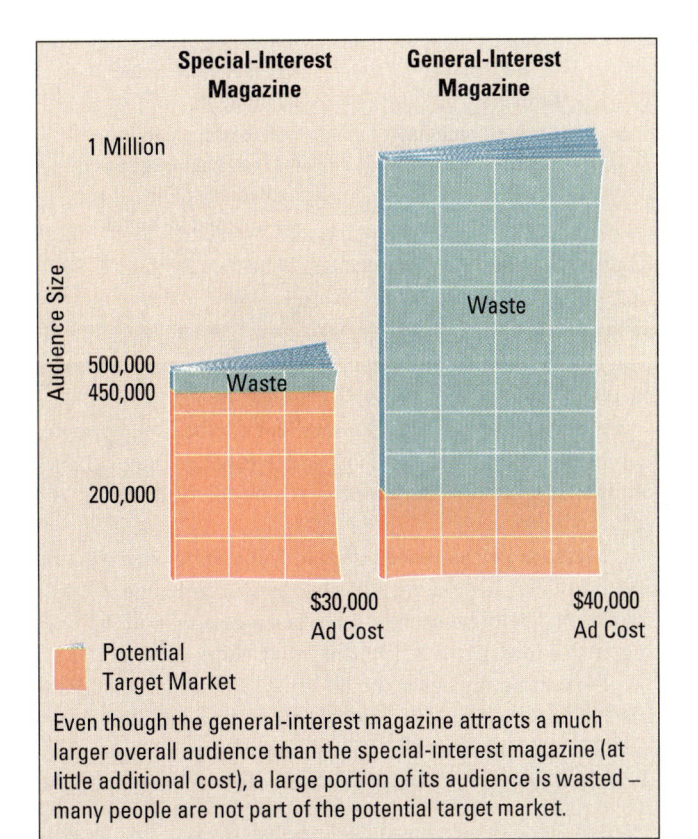

FIGURE 19-4
Waste in Advertising

Even though the general-interest magazine attracts a much larger overall audience than the special-interest magazine (at little additional cost), a large portion of its audience is wasted — many people are not part of the potential target market.

Table 19-6
Advertising Media

MEDIUM	MARKET COVERAGE	BEST USES	SELECTED ADVANTAGES	SELECTED DISADVANTAGES
Daily newspaper	Entire metropolitan area; local editions used sometimes	Medium and large firms	Short lead time, concentrated market, flexible, high frequency, passalongs, surrounded by content	General audience, heavy ad competition, limited colour, limited creativity
Weekly newspaper	One community	Local firms	Same as daily	Heavy ad competition, very limited colour, limited creativity, small market
Commercial television	Regional, national, or international	Regional manufacturers and large retailers; national, large manufacturers and largest retailers	Reach, low cost per viewer, persuasive impact, creative options, flexible, high frequency, surrounded by programs	High minimum total costs, general audience, lead time for popular shows, short messages, limited availability
Cable television	Local, regional, national, or international	Local, regional, and national manufacturers and retailers	More precise audience and more creative than commercial television	Not all consumers hooked up; ads not yet fully accepted on programs
Direct mail	Advertiser selects market	New products, book clubs, financial services, catalogue sales	Precise audience, flexible, personal approach, less clutter from other messages	High throwaway rate, receipt by wrong person, low credibility
Magazines	Local, national, or international (with regional issues)	Local service retailers and mail-order firms; major manufacturers and retailers	Colour, creative options, affluent audience, permanence of messages, passalongs, flexible, surrounded by content	Long lead time, poor frequency (if monthly), ad clutter, geographically dispersed audience
Radio	Entire metropolitan area	Local or regional firms	Low costs, selective market, high frequency, immediacy of messages surrounded by content	No visual impact, commercial clutter, channel switching, consumer distractions

cent of Canadian homes get cable TV programs, this medium has great potential for local narrowcasting.[8]

Frequency is highest for daily media.

Frequency is how often a medium can be used. It is greatest for papers, radio, and TV. Different ads may appear daily and a strategy may be easily changed. Phone directories, outdoor ads, and magazines have the poorest frequency. A Yellow Pages ad may be placed only once per year.

Message permanence refers to exposures per ad.

Message permanence refers to the number of exposures one ad generates (repetition) and how long it remains available to the audience. Outdoor ads, transit ads, and phone directories yield many exposures per message; and many magazines are retained by consumers for long periods. On the other hand, radio and TV ads last only 5 to 60 seconds.

Persuasive impact is highest for TV.

Persuasive impact is the ability of a medium to stimulate consumers. Television often has the highest persuasive impact because it is able to combine audio, video, colour, and animation. Magazines also have high persuasive impact. Many newspapers are improving their technology in order to feature colour ads and increase their persuasive impact.

[8]Statistics Canada, *1995 Market Research Handbook* (Ottawa: Minister of Supply Services), p. 229.

Table 19-6 (Con't)

MEDIUM	MARKET COVERAGE	BEST USES	SELECTED ADVANTAGES	SELECTED DISADVANTAGES
Business publications	National, regional, or international	Corporate advertising, industrial firms	Selective market, high readability, surrounded by content, message permanence, passalongs	Restricted product applications, may not be read by proper decision maker, not final-consumer oriented
Outdoor	Entire metropolitan area or one location	Brand-name products, nearby retailers, reminder ads	Large size, colour, creative options, repetition, less clutter, message permanence	Legal restrictions, consumer distractions, general audience, inflexible, limited content, lead time
Transit	Urban community with a transit system	Firms located along transit route	Concentrated market, message permanence, repetition, action-oriented messages, colour, creative options	Clutter of ads, consumer distractions, geographically limited audience
Telephone directories	Entire metropolitan area (with local supplements)	All types of retailers, professionals, service companies	Low costs, permanence of messages, repetition, coverage of market, specialized listings, action-oriented messages	Clutter of ads, limited creativity, very long lead time, low appeal to passive consumers
Internet	Local, national, or international	All types and sizes of firms	Low costs, huge potential audience, vast geographic coverage and amount of information conveyed, interactivity	Clutter of ads, viewed as a novelty by some, goals unclear (advertising vs. entertainment and education), no set rate structure
Flyers	Single neighbourhood	Local firms	Low costs, market coverage, little waste, flexible	High throwaway rate, poor image

Clutter involves the number of ads found in a single program, issue, and so forth of a medium. It is low when few ads are presented, such as Hallmark placing only scattered commercials on the TV specials for which it is the exclusive sponsor. It is high when there are many ads, such as the large amount of supermarket ads in a newspaper's Wednesday issue. Overall, magazines have the highest clutter. And TV is criticized for allowing too much clutter, particularly for assigning more time per hour to commercials and for letting firms show very brief messages (e.g., 15 seconds or shorter). About one-third of all television ads are 15-second spots.[9]

Lead time is the period required by a medium for placing an ad. It is shortest for newspapers and longest for magazines and phone directories. Popular TV shows may also require a lengthy lead time since the number of ads they can carry is limited. With a long

Clutter *occurs when there are many ads.*

Lead time *is needed for placing an ad.*

[9]Robert J. Kent, "Competitive Clutter in Network Television Advertising: Current Levels and Advertiser Responses," *Journal of Advertising Research*, Vol. 35 (January–February 1995), pp. 49–57.

TECHNOLOGY & MARKETING

How the World Wide Web Is Affecting Interactive Kiosks

Prior to the ascension of the World Wide Web as an interactive medium between marketers and consumers, a different interactive technology was being embraced. Interactive kiosks were seen as having tremendous potential. Kiosks are machines that stand alone, usually in a business location, and allow users to interact with them for specific purposes, such as providing information, processing transactions, and collecting information. Kiosks usually have "touch" screens, which makes them very easy to use.

Many firms that have experimented with kiosks are financial institutions. Customers could use them to apply for loans, check their credit card or account balances, and look up information. For example, Toronto-Dominion tested kiosks in some of their bank branches. Although a large number of people used the kiosks for information, very few completed transactions on them. Now with the wider access of the World Wide Web, firms are not spending much on kiosk development for mass customer use, preferring instead to spend money on development of Web sites.

However, the kiosk has not died. Toronto Dominion uses kiosks at trade shows to promote their services and interact with customers. Kiosks are always open and ready to interact with customers, unlike people, who take breaks or get tied up doing many different tasks. In addition, kiosks can collect information at trade shows in a less intrusive manner than direct interaction involves. People feel less rushed and less self-conscious answering questions from a machine than they do answering questions from a person.

Consumers Distributing and Canadian Tire are retailers who have set up kiosks in their stores. Consumer's kiosks are designed to allow shoppers to place merchandise orders from their catalogue, while Canadian Tire's kiosks are designed as merchandise directories. Shoppers Drug Mart has used kiosks as part of a cross promotion to allow customers to select seats and dates for NBA tickets purchased for the Toronto Raptors or Vancouver Grizzlies. Another use involves placing kiosks in places where people are normally waiting for service and they can serve as an amusement and information gathering device at the same time. Hotel lobbies are seen as a good place for having interactive kiosks.

Finally, kiosks could be set up to interact with and display elaborate Web sites and thus provide users with a more delightful experience of using the World Wide Web.

As the marketing manager of a Canadian Hotel chain, discuss the various ways your firm could employ kiosks to serve your guests more effectively.

Source: Based on material in Anita Lahey, "Life After the Web," *Marketing Magazine* (March 18, 1996), p. 19.

AMERICA ONLINE
www.aol.com/

COMPUSERVE
www.compuserve.com/

lead time, because a firm must place ads well in advance, it risks improper themes in a changing environment.

There have been many media innovations in advertising in recent years. These include commercial online computer services such as Compuserve, America Online Canada and the other fast-emerging services that let people "surf the Web;" regional editions and special one-sponsor issues ("advertorials") to revitalize magazines; specialized Yellow Pages; televised ads in supermarkets, movie theatres, and aircraft; more radio stations handling ads in stereo; better quality in outdoor signs; full-length televised advertising programs ("infomercials"); and direct-mail ads with CD-ROM diskettes.

FIGURE 19-5
Sony's Use of a Long-Time Advertising Message
Reprinted by permission

Creating Advertisements

There are four fundamental decisions that the advertiser must make when creating advertisements:

1. Determining the message content and devising the ads. Each ad needs a headline or opening to create consumer interest and copy that presents the message. Content decisions also involve the use of colour and illustrations, ad size or length, the source, the use of symbolism, and the adaptations needed for foreign markets. The role of these factors depends on a firm's goals and resources.
2. Outlining a promotion schedule. This should allow for all copy and artwork and be based on the lead time needed for the chosen media.
3. Specifying each ad's location in a broadcast program or print medium. As costs have risen, more firms have become concerned about ad placement.
4. Choosing how many variations of a basic message to use. This depends on the frequency of presentations and the ad quality. Sony has been able to run its "There's Nothing Like a Real Trinitron" message for years (see Figure 19-5).

Ad creation involves content, scheduling, media placement, and variations.

Timing Advertisements

Potential advertisers must make two major decisions about the timing of advertisements: how often a given ad will be shown and when to advertise during the year. First, a firm must balance audience awareness and knowledge with the danger of irritating the audience if it places an ad a number of times in a short period. Thus, McDonald's runs its ads repeatedly, but changes them often. Second, a firm must choose whether to advertise through the year or in concentrated periods. Distributed ads maintain brand recognition and increase sales in nonpeak periods. They are used by most manufacturers and general-

Timing refers to how often an ad is shown and when to advertise during the year.

merchandise retailers. Massed ads are concentrated in peak periods to generate short-run consumer enthusiasm; they ignore sales in nonpeak periods. Specialty manufacturers and retailers use this method.

Other timing considerations include when to advertise new products, when to stop advertising existing products, how to coordinate advertising and other promotional tools, when to change basic themes, and how to space messages during the hierarchy-of-effects process.

Considering Cooperative Efforts

In **cooperative advertising**, *costs are shared by multiple parties.*

To stimulate advertising by channel members and/or to hold down its own ad budget, a firm may consider cooperative efforts. With **cooperative advertising**, two or more firms share some advertising costs. In a vertical cooperative-advertising agreement, firms at different stages in a distribution channel (such as a manufacturer and a wholesaler) share costs. In a horizontal cooperative-advertising agreement, two or more independent firms at the same stage in a distribution channel share costs (such as retailers in a mall).

Good cooperative agreements state the share of costs paid by each party, the functions and responsibilities of each party, the advertisements to be covered, and the basis for termination. They also benefit each participant.

Each year, manufacturers offer millions of dollars in vertical-cooperative advertising support in Canada. Yet distribution intermediaries typically use only about two-thirds of the money offered. The nonuse by so many resellers is due to their perceptions of manufacturer inflexibility involving messages and media, the costs of cooperative advertising to the resellers, restrictive provisions (such as high minimum purchases to be eligible), and the emphasis on the manufacturer's name in ads. To remedy this, more manufacturers are now flexible as to the messages and media they will support, pay a larger share of advertising costs, have eased restrictive provisions, and feature reseller names more prominently in ads.

Evaluating Success or Failure

Advertising's success or failure depends on how well it helps an organization to achieve promotion goals. Creating customer awareness and increasing sales are distinct goals; success or failure in reaching them must be measured differently. In addition, advertising can be quite difficult to isolate as the single factor leading to a certain image or sales level.

Here are various examples dealing with the evaluation of advertising's success or failure:

- The typical consumer is bombarded with 300 advertising messages each day—about 110 000 per year. According to one major research study, two-thirds of people believe a nationally advertised brand creates the perception that it is of better quality than brands that are not heavily advertised; and in choosing among two unfamiliar brands, two-thirds of people will select the one that is advertised most.[10]

- A survey of consumers in twenty-two nations found that advertising is favourably regarded, although opinions differ by country: "Individuals in former Communist nations are among the most enthusiastic supporters of advertising, apparently reflecting their current desire to embrace consumer-oriented Western capitalism. Egypt was the only market where respondents were consistently anti-advertising."[11]

- Young adults (those 18 to 34) account for one-third of all Yellow Pages use. They are more apt than older adults to rely on information in display ads and less likely to have a specific company name in mind when consulting the Yellow Pages.[12]

---

[10]Michael J. McCarthy, "Mind Probe," *Wall Street Journal* (March 22, 1991), p. B3; and "Advertising Makes the Difference," *Advertising Age* (January 15, 1996), p. 30.

[11]Laurel Wentz, "Major Global Study Finds Consumers Support Ads," *Advertising Age* (October 11, 1993), pp. I-1, I-21.

[12]Jeffrey Casey, "How Do We Get Into This Person's Head?" *Link* (October–November 1995), pp. 37–45.

- A study for the Association of National Advertisers indicates that advertising is a reliable way to boost sales but less consistent in raising market share and profits.[13]
- *Business Marketing* annually honours the best business-to-business ads. It uses criteria like these in picking winners: visual magnetism, the target audience, the message, readability, and the firm's character.

The Scope and Importance of Public Relations

Each firm would like to foster the best possible relations with its publics and to receive favourable publicity about its offerings or the firm itself. Sometimes, as with restaurant or theatre reviews, publicity can greatly increase sales or virtually put a firm out of business. For example, Tout Sweet Chocolates went bankrupt when letters were sent to some of the retailers carrying its products claiming they had been poisoned. Retailers pulled all of the products off their shelves and consumers balked at buying any newly produced chocolates even though no tampering was discovered in any of the recalled products. The negative publicity associated with this incident undermined Tout Sweet with its creditors and they put the firm into receivership despite the fact that Tout Sweet chocolate products were of the highest quality.[14]

In Canada, The Canadian Public Relations Society has 1600 members, and many of the larger business firms in Canada and trade associations have their own public relations departments. Worldwide, the International Public Relations Association has 1000 members from sixty nations; yet, the role of public relations varies greatly by nation: "In many foreign areas, the term *public relations* really means *press relations*. Working with the press abroad is not easy; there may be a language barrier, and many times, government controls the media."[15]

The competition to gain media attention for publicity is intense. After all, in Canada, television broadcasting is done on only two national television networks, with fourteen regional commercial networks and eighteen cable specialty networks available as well. In terms of print media there are only ten consumer magazines with circulations of 500 000 or more. Nonetheless, there are many opportunities for publicity—with 361 AM radio stations, 432 FM radio stations, 136 originating commercial television stations covering 41 television markets, 108 daily newspapers, and 939 community newspapers around Canada.[16]

Some firms have poor policies to deal with their publics and the media, and fail to develop a sustained public relations effort. Table 19-7 shows several public relations-related situations and how a firm could deal with them. Since unfavourable publicity can occur, a firm must be ready to deal with it in the best way possible. Negative publicity can happen to any firm; a successful one will have a plan to handle it. A firm may get the media on its side by being candid and acting promptly; media may be used to help explain complex issues; and by cooperating with reporters, preconceived notions may be dispelled.

The interrelationship of public relations and other promotion forms must be understood. If advertising, personal selling, and sales promotion are image-oriented, public relations is involved. If they are demand-oriented, it is not. Figure 19-6 shows the interface between public relations and other promotion tools. Figures 19-7 and 19-8 show two effective institutional ads.

Public relations efforts can have a major impact.

CANADIAN PUBLIC RELATIONS SOCIETY
www.cprs.ca/

Public relations encompasses image-directed ads, selling, and sales promotion—as well as publicity.

---

[13]Gary Levin, "Ads Show Power to Help Sales," *Advertising Age* (December 13, 1993), p. 28.
[14]Michael McCullough, "Poison Threat Sinks Tout Sweet Chocolates," *Marketing Magazine* (May 6, 1996), p. 4.
[15]Nancy Boomer, "CPRS Toughens Up Accreditation Standards," *Marketing Magazine* (June 17, 1996), p. 4; and Fraser P. Seitel, *The Practice of Public Relations*, Sixth Ed. (Englewood Cliffs, New Jersey: Prentice Hall, 1995), various pages.
[16]Canadian Media Directors' Council, *Media Digest 1995-96*, (Toronto, Ontario: Marketing Magazine), various pages.

Table 19-7
Public Relations-Related Situations and How a Firm Could Respond to Them

SITUATION	POOR RESPONSE	GOOD RESPONSE
Fire breaks out in a company plant	Requests for information by media are ignored.	Company spokesperson explains the fire's causes and the precautions to avoid it and answers questions.
New product introduced	Advertising is used without publicity.	Pre-introduction news releases, product samples, and testimonials are used.
News story about product defects	Media requests for information are ignored, blanket denials are issued, and there is hostility to reporters.	Company spokesperson says tests are being done, describes the procedure for handling defects, and takes questions.
Competitor introduces new product	A demand-oriented advertising campaign is stepped up.	Extensive news releases, statistics, and spokespeople are made available to media to present firm's competitive features.
High profits reported	Profits are justified and positive effects on the economy are cited.	Profits are explained, comparative data are provided, and profit uses are noted: research and community development.
Overall view of public relations	There is an infrequent need for public relations; crisis fighting is used when bad reports are circulated.	There is an ongoing need for public relations, strong planning, and plans to counter bad reports.

FIGURE 19-6
The Relationship Between Public Relations and the Other Elements of the Promotion Mix

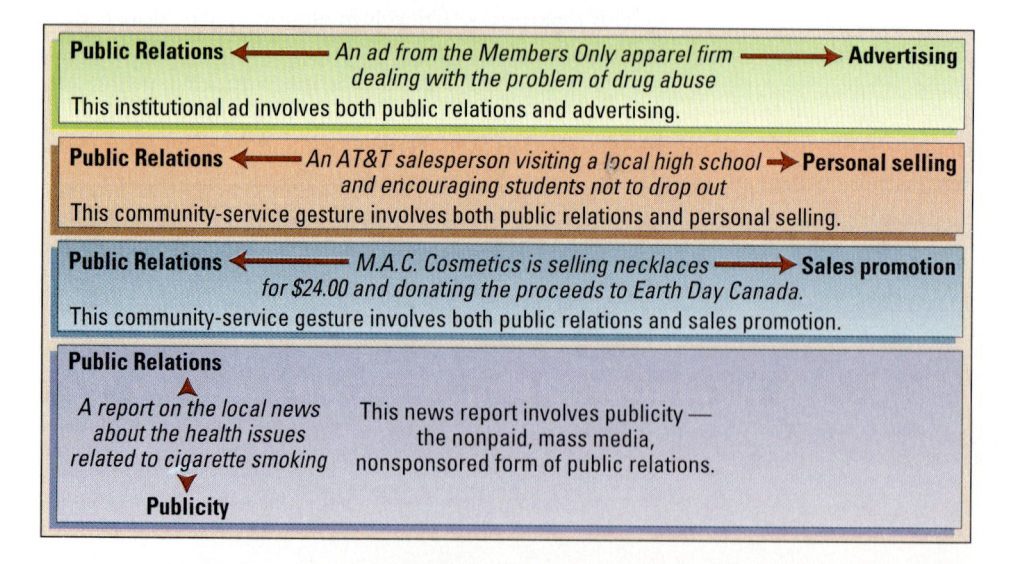

Public Relations ← An ad from the Members Only apparel firm dealing with the problem of drug abuse → **Advertising**
This institutional ad involves both public relations and advertising.

Public Relations ← An AT&T salesperson visiting a local high school and encouraging students not to drop out → **Personal selling**
This community-service gesture involves both public relations and personal selling.

Public Relations ← M.A.C. Cosmetics is selling necklaces for $24.00 and donating the proceeds to Earth Day Canada. → **Sales promotion**
This community-service gesture involves both public relations and sales promotion.

Public Relations
↑
A report on the local news about the health issues related to cigarette smoking
↓
Publicity

This news report involves publicity — the nonpaid, mass media, nonsponsored form of public relations.

FIGURE 19-7
A Socially Responsible Public Relations Campaign
Reprinted by permission.

FIGURE 19-8
A Community-Oriented Public Relations Campaign
Reprinted by permission.

The Characteristics of Public Relations

Public relations engenders good feelings; publicity has no time costs, a large audience, high credibility, and attentiveness.

Public relations offers several benefits. Since it is image-oriented, good feelings toward a firm by its external publics can be fostered. In addition, employee morale (pride) is enhanced if the firm is community and civic minded.

When publicity is involved, there are no costs for message time or space. A prime-time television ad may cost $50 000 to $80 000 or more per minute of media time; a five-minute report on a network newscast does not cost anything for media time. However, there are costs for news releases, a public relations department, and so on. As with advertising, publicity reaches a mass audience. In a short time, new products or company policies are well known.

Message believability is higher with publicity because stories appear in independent media. A newspaper's movie review is more credible than an ad in the same paper—the reader links independence with objectivity. Similarly, people may pay more attention to news than to ads. *Canadian Living* has both cooking advice and food ads; people read the stories, but flip through ads. There are a dozen or more ads in a half-hour TV show and hundreds of them in a typical magazine; feature stories are fewer in number and stand out more.

Public relations may be downplayed by some firms; publicity cannot be controlled or timed accurately by a company.

Public relations also has limitations, compared to other promotion forms. Some firms question the value of image-oriented communications and are disinterested in activities not directly tied to sales and profits. They may give the poor responses that were indicated in Table 19-7.

With publicity, a firm has less control over messages and their timing, placement, and coverage by the media. It may issue detailed press releases and find only parts cited in the media; and media may be more critical than a firm would like. Media tend to find disasters, scandals, and product recalls more newsworthy than press releases. And the accessibility of the Internet for disgruntled consumers provides another outlet for bad publicity. This shows how bad publicity can be intense and spread quickly:

> When Rich Koch, a computer salesperson from Florida, bought a new U.S.$13 000 Dodge Neon, it quickly developed glitches. The driver's door latch sometimes refused to release, the plastic liners inside both fenders rattled, and sealant oozed from around the rear window. So, Koch posted an electronic memo on Prodigy detailing his car's woes for the online service's 1.2 million subscribers. "I'd never buy another," he wrote in disgust. Unfortunately for Chrysler, Koch wasn't the only one taking aim at its quality problems. In its annual survey of auto quality, J.D. Power & Associates ranked Chrysler cars below industry averages. And *Consumer Reports* warned readers to be wary of the Dodge Intrepid, Jeep Cherokee pickup, and Dodge Ram pickup—which all had above-average chances of landing in the repair shop.[18]

A firm may want publicity during certain periods, such as when a new product is introduced or a new store opened, but the media may not provide coverage until much later. Similarly, the media determine a story's placement; it may follow a crime or sports report. Finally, the media choose whether to cover a story at all and the amount of coverage devoted to it. A firm-sponsored jobs program might go unreported or get three-sentence coverage in a local paper.

---

[17]Gene Koprowski, "Extra: Smart Companies Use Public Relations Tactics to Get Good Ink," *Marketing Tools* (October 1995), p. 48.

[18]David Woodruff, "An Embarrassment of Glitches Galvanizes Chrysler," *Business Week* (April 17, 1995), p. 76.

Publicity may be hard to plan in advance because newsworthy events occur quickly and unexpectedly. Thus, short-run and long-run public relations plans should differ in approach. Publicity must complement advertising and not be a substitute. The assets of each (credibility and low costs for publicity, control and coverage for ads) are needed for a good communications program.

To optimize their public relations efforts, at many companies:

- Public relations personnel have regular access to senior executives.
- The publicity value of annual reports is recognized.
- Public relations messages are professionally prepared (with the same care used in writing ad copy) and continuously given to media.
- Internal personnel and media personnel interaction is fostered.
- Public-service events are planned to obtain maximum media coverage.
- Part of the promotion budget goes to publicity-generating tasks.
- There is a better understanding of the kinds of stories the media are apt to cover and how to present stories to the media.

Developing a Public Relations Plan

Developing a public relations plan is much like devising an advertising plan. It involves the seven steps shown in Figure 19-9, and which are described next.

Setting Objectives

Public relations goals are image-oriented (firm and/or industry). The choice of goals guides the entire public relations plan.

These are some goals that could be set:

- To gain placement for news releases and coverage of company spokespersons with a variety of media.
- To have the media report on the accomplishments of the company.
- To have the company's position presented when controversy arises.
- To coordinate publicity with advertising.
- To gain more media coverage than competitors.

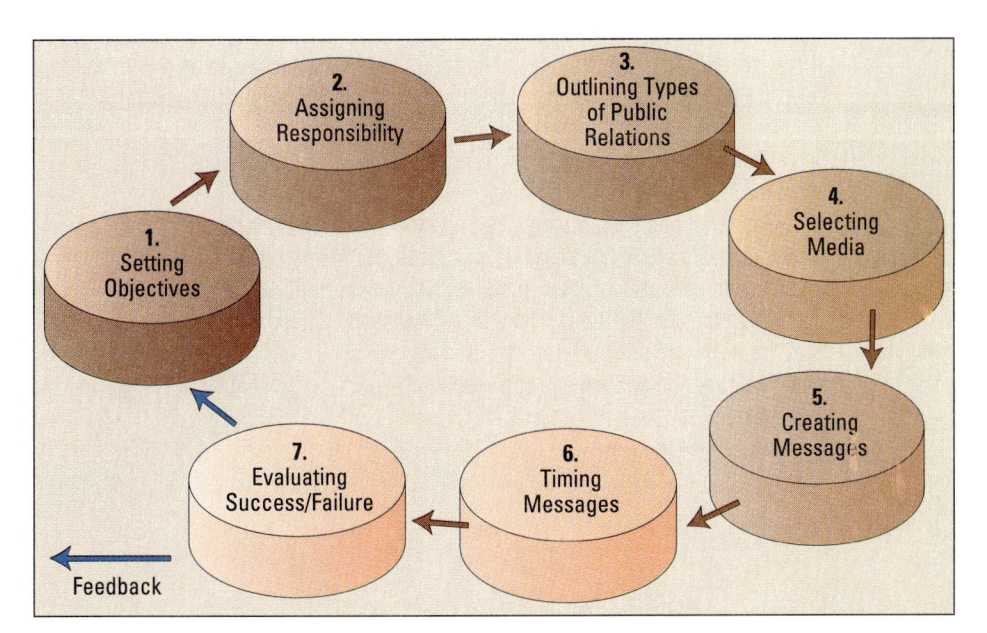

FIGURE 19–9
Developing a Public Relations Plan

Ethics AND TODAY'S MARKETER

Sexual Appeals in Advertising: Where is the Line of Acceptability?

It is one of the oldest controversies in advertising and is likely to remain so: sexual appeals in advertising. There is no question that marketers want their products to be attractive to their target market. There is also no question that sexual motivations are among the most powerful. Tapping into these powerful motivations and catering to them with a product or linking them directly to a product or product appeal is very alluring for marketers and as natural as sexual attraction itself.

Some products are developed for the specific purpose of catering to sexual motivations; even talking about such products may be offensive to some people. For example, there is essentially one purpose for condoms, so the mere existence of advertising for this product is upsetting to some people. As for whether the advertising itself is distasteful, that is a matter of social consensus. One television ad features a young man ranting and raving about being forced to do something he does not want to do. He is approached by an attractive girlfriend who hands him a condom and says: "Use one, or get none." His reply is, "I can live with that." Perhaps he can, but many parents are uncomfortable about having to explain to their preteen children what is going on in this ad. Does it cross the line? For some people it does.

Aside from products directly related to sex, a large number of products are related to sex *appeal*. Perfumes, cosmetics, lingerie, clothing, beer, and even food are often tied into the basic natural attraction between men and women. The advertising associated with these products arouses some strong feelings and ethical concerns about whether their appeals are appropriate or not. Calvin Klein has been at the centre of this storm for over fifteen years. In 1981, Calvin Klein put a young and controversial actress/model named Brooke Shields in an ad. A television ad supported by a print campaign showed her lying in a provocative prone position from which she proclaimed: "Nothing comes between me and my Calvins." Although the ads were controversial, the product sold very well.

Since then, Klein has continued to use provocative advertising, not only for CK jeans but also for Obsession, a cologne. One of the first ads for this cologne was particularly shocking, as it showed two naked males and one naked female in bed together. In contrast, other scent makers simply show the product in an ad and include a scratch and sniff sample. However, comparing the sales associated with the two forms of advertising shows that Calvin Klein's approach pays off.

One thing seems certain, the line of acceptability may shift in the future, but firms operating on or near the line seem to be rewarded with sales, and this means the controversy over sex in advertising will remain an issue.

Search through some magazines and identify three print ads for three different product types that are not designed specifically for the purpose of sex yet which have clear sexual appeals (e.g. beer, perfume, clothing, cosmetics, etc.). Find some ads for competing brands that do not have sexual appeals. Compare the ads and how well they work. Recommend whether the sex appeal ads should be dropped or the products with the non-sex appeal ads should use more sex appeal. Justify your recommendation.

Source: Based on material in Greg Farrell, "Over the Line," *Marketing Magazine* (January 1–8, 1996), p. 11.

- To sustain favourable publicity as long as possible.
- To reach out to community groups.
- To have publics view the firm and its industry favourably.

While setting goals, this truism should be kept in mind: "PR involves both *performance* and *recognition*. It is possible to boast excellent performance without being properly recognized, but it is not possible to earn recognition that is not based on solid performance. Woe to the firm that tries to get the R (recognition) without the P (performance)."[19]

Assigning Responsibility

A firm has three options in assigning public relations responsibility: it may use its existing marketing personnel, an in-house public relations department, or an in-house publicity department; it may have an outside advertising agency handle public relations; or it may hire a specialized public relations firm. Internal personnel or an in-house department ensure more control and secrecy. An outside firm often has better contacts and expertise. Each approach is popular; and they may be combined.[20]

Procter & Gamble has an in-house publicity department and several outside public relations agencies. In contrast, some smaller firms rely on the services of specialists, which may charge retainers fees of $25 000 to $50 000 per year. Computer software, such as PRpower, can also let smaller firms easily set up media mailing lists.

A firm can use an in-house department, hire an outside ad agency, or hire a specialist.

Outlining the Types of Public Relations to Be Used

In this step, a firm first chooses the mix of institutional advertising, image-oriented personal selling, image-oriented sales promotion, and publicity to incorporate into an overall promotion plan. Next, public relations efforts must be coordinated with the demand-oriented promotion activities of the firm.

Finally, the general **publicity types** must be understood and envisioned. Each can play a role in an integrated public relations program:

Publicity types *involve news, features, releases, background material, and emergency information.*

- *News publicity* deals with international, national, regional, or local events. Planned releases can be prepared and regularly given out by a firm.
- *Business feature articles* are detailed stories about a company or its offerings that are given to business media.
- *Service feature articles* are lighter stories focusing on personal care, household items, and similar topics, and are sent to newspapers, cable TV stations, and magazines.
- *Finance releases* are stories aimed at the business sections of newspapers, TV news shows, and magazines.
- *Product releases* deal with new products and product improvements; they aim at all media forms.
- *Pictorial releases* are illustrations or pictures sent to the media.
- *Video news releases* are videotaped segments supplied to the media.
- *Background editorial material* is extra information given to media writers and editors; it enhances standard releases and provides filler for stories (like the biography of the chief executive of a company).
- *Emergency publicity* consists of special spontaneous news releases keyed to unexpected events.[21]

---

[19]Nat B. Read, "Sears PR Debacle Shows How Not to Handle a Crisis," *Wall Street Journal* (January 11, 1993), p. A16.
[20]See Gene Koprowski, "Hiring an Agency," *Marketing Tools* (October 1995), pp. 48–49.
[21]H. Frazier Moore, *Public Relations: Principles, Cases, and Problems*, Eighth Ed. (Homewood, Ill.: Richard D. Irwin, 1981), pp. 163–167.

Selecting the Media for Public Relations Efforts

For institutional ads, personal selling, and sales promotion, traditional nonpersonal and/or personal media would be used. For publicity, a firm would typically focus on newspapers, television, magazines, radio, and business publications. Due to the infrequent publication schedule of many magazines and some business publications, publicity-seeking efforts may be aimed at daily or weekly media.

Public relations executives rank newspapers and business publications the highest. The *Globe and Mail, The Toronto Star, The Vancouver Sun,* and *Le Journal de Montreal* are preferred newspapers. *Canadian Business, The Financial Post,* and *En Route* are preferred business publications. *Maclean's* and *Time* magazine are preferred general news magazines.

FINANCIAL POST
www.canoe.ca/FP/

Creating Messages

The creation of public relations messages involves the same factors as other promotion forms—deciding on content and variations, and drawing up a production schedule. Messages can be conveyed in one or a combination of forms, such as news conferences, media releases, phone calls or personal contacts, media kits (a combination of materials on a story), special events (the Molson Grand Prix in Toronto), or videos.

Because it is essential that the media find a firm's publicity messages to be useful, these points need to be kept in mind:

1. Messages should be newsworthy.
2. Reporter deadlines should be respected.
3. Appropriate company representatives should be accessible to reporters.
4. "Mind-fogging" jargon should be avoided.
5. The phrase "no comment" should not be used.
6. Attribution rules (making the source and the content of a story "on" or "off" the record) should be set in advance.
7. A reporter should not be asked to kill a story.
8. Releases should be both easy to read (or view or hear), and easy to use.
9. There should be no hesitancy to volunteer a "bad" story (it will probably get out anyway).
10. Attention should be paid to the needs of each type of medium.[22]

Timing Messages

Public relations efforts should precede new-product introductions and generate excitement for them. For emergencies, media releases and spokespeople should be made available immediately. For ongoing public relations, messages should be properly spaced through the year. As already noted, a firm may find it hard to anticipate media coverage for both unexpected and planned publicity because the media control the timing.

Evaluating Success or Failure

There are several straightforward ways to rate a public relations campaign's success or failure. With institutional ads, image-oriented personal selling, and image-oriented sales promotion, a firm can conduct simple surveys to see how well these communications are received and their impact on its image. With publicity, a firm can count the stories about it, analyze coverage length and placement, review desired with actual timing of stories, evaluate audience reactions, and/or compute the cost of comparable advertising.

---

[22]Christel K. Beard and H. J. Dalton, Jr., "The Power of Positive Press," *Sales & Marketing Management* (January 1991), pp. 37–43. See also Daniel P. Dern, "News That's Fit to Print," *Marketing Tools* (October 1995), pp. 52–53.

Here are some measures of public relations' success:

- Labatt ran a print campaign offering their thoughts on beer and asking readers to share some of theirs. Respondents were offered a free bottle opener for responding. In a two-week period almost 100 000 letters and phone calls came in. The information from these letters and calls provided Labatt with insights into their customers and the perception of beer marketing.[23]
- Wal-Mart now tracks the *quality*, as well as the quantity of their media coverage. It classifies items as news stories, letters to the editor, editorials, or opinion articles—for each market area.[24]
- According to various surveys, many chief executive officers feel effective public relations contribute to profits.[25]

MARKETING IN A CHANGING WORLD
Dos and Don'ts for Using the Web[26]

Since October 1994, HotWired has operated a Web site—complete with advertising—on the Internet. These are some of the lessons it has learned and wants to pass along:

The most important decision. A company must be clear about why it wants to be on the Web. Is the goal brand building, publicity, selling products, giving information, customer service, or order tracking?

- *The only valid measure is response.* An actual customer has much more value than an anonymous impression.
- *Bandwidth is still limited.* Because so many people are joining the Web, the average access speed is slowing. Thus, a company should keep its image, video, and text files small—and not waste customers' time.
- *Bigger is not always better.* A 1000-page Web site may not be better than a one-page site. The best Web sites are quick, personalized, and user-friendly.
- *Static sites are toxic.* The easiest way to lose traffic is to set up a site and not change its look often enough.
- *It's more than advertising.* "Marketing on the Web is about providing information and entertainment, and about fostering community. Many companies have also discovered that Web-based customer service functions are improving customer relations and saving money."
- *If it's not part of your media mix, you lose.* To succeed, a company must commit itself to the Web as an integral part of its media mix.
- *Don't ignore demographics or lifestyles.* "All sites are not equal, any more than all magazines or TV shows are equal."
- *No "Under Construction" signs.* "Vaporware is not appreciated. Don't open your site until it's ready."
- *No shovelware.* "TV isn't just radio with pictures, and the Net isn't just a brochure with buttons. It's a whole new medium, with a whole new dynamic."

---

[23]Terry Zuk, "Closing in on the Customer," *Marketing Magazine* (February 13, 1995), p. 14.
[24]Don E. Shinkle, "PR Measurement Is the Answer," *Public Relations Quarterly*, Vol. 39 (Fall 1994), pp. 16–17.
[25]Bristol Voss, "Measuring the Effectiveness of Advertising and PR," *Sales & Marketing Management* (October 1992), p. 123; Catherine B. Campbell, "Does Public Relations Affect the Bottom Line?" *Public Relations Journal*, Vol. 49 (October 1993), pp. 14–17; and Koprowski, "Extra: Smart Companies Use Public Relations Tactics to Get Good Ink," pp. 46–53.
[26]The material in this section is based on HotWired, "How *Not* to Advertise on the Web," *Advertising Age* (December 4, 1995), p. 17.

SUMMARY

1. To examine the scope, importance, and characteristics of advertising Advertising is paid, nonpersonal communication sent through various media by identified sponsors. Canadian ad spending is $9.2 billion annually and non-Canadian spending exceeds U.S.$375 billion per year in such media as newspapers, TV, direct mail, Yellow Pages, radio, magazines, business publications, and outdoor ads. In many industries, advertising is under 2.0 per cent of sales.

It is most apt with standardized products and when features are easy to communicate, the market is large, prices are low, resellers are used in distribution, and/or products are new. In general, behaviour is easier to change than attitudes; one ad can have an impact; ads do well with little-known products; and effectiveness rises during extended campaigns.

Among advertising's advantages are its appeal to a geographically dispersed audience, low per-customer costs, the availability of a broad variety of media, the firm's control over all aspects of a message, the surrounding editorial content, and how it complements personal selling. Disadvantages include message inflexibility, the fact that some viewers or readers are not in the target audience, high media costs, limited information provided, difficulty in getting audience feedback, and low audience involvement.

2. To study the elements in an advertising plan An advertising plan has nine steps: setting goals—demand and image types; assigning duties—internal and/or external; setting a budget; developing themes—good/service, consumer, and institutional; selecting media—based on costs, reach, waste, narrowcasting, frequency, message permanence, persuasive impact, clutter, lead time, and media innovations; creating ads—including content, placement, and variations; timing ads; considering cooperative efforts—both vertical and horizontal; and evaluating success or failure.

3. To examine the scope, importance, and characteristics of public relations Public relations includes any communication that fosters a favourable image among a firm's various publics. It is more image- than sales-oriented; embodies image-oriented ads, personal selling, and sales promotion; and seeks favourable publicity—the nonpersonal communication sent via various media but not paid for by identified sponsors. There are thousands of companies with their own public relations departments and many specialized public relations firms. Companies try to get positive publicity and to avoid negative publicity. Competition is intense for placing publicity releases. Some firms have ineffective policies to deal with independent media or develop a sustained publicity campaign.

Among its advantages are its image orientation, its positive effects on employee morale, and—for publicity—its lack of cost for message time, its high credibility, and audience attentiveness. The disadvantages of public relations—compared with other promotion forms—include the lack of interest by some firms in image-oriented communications and the lack of control over publicity placements by the firm, the media's interest in negative events, and the difficulty in planning publicity in advance.

4. To study the elements in a public relations plan A public relations plan has seven steps: setting goals—company and/or industry; assigning duties—internally and/or externally; outlining types of public relations—the mix of image-oriented promotion forms and the categories of publicity (news publicity, business and service feature articles, finance releases, product and pictorial releases, video news releases, background editorial releases, and emergency publicity); choosing media; creating messages; timing messages; and weighing success or failure.

KEY TERMS

advertising agency (p. 524)
advertising themes (p. 525)
advertising media costs (p. 527)
reach (p. 527)
waste (p. 527)
narrowcasting (p. 527)
frequency (p. 528)
message permanence (p. 528)
persuasive impact (p. 528)
clutter (p. 529)
lead time (p. 529)
cooperative advertising (p. 532)
publicity types (p. 539)

Review Questions

1. Explain the statement "Advertising is paid for, publicity is prayed for."
2. Under what circumstances is advertising most likely to be used?
3. List five objectives of advertising and give an example of how each may be accomplished.
4. A small firm has an overall annual budget of $50 000 for advertising. What specific decisions must it make in allocating the budget?
5. Differentiate among these advertising concepts: reach, narrowcasting, waste, clutter, and frequency.
6. What are the pros and cons of cooperative advertising?
7. Explain several ways that public relations as practised in both Canada and the U.S. may differ from public relations in other countries.
8. What is a video news release?
9. According to public relations executives, which are the two most preferred media for receiving publicity?
10. State three ways for a firm to evaluate the success or failure of its public relations efforts.

Discussion Questions

1. Devise an advertising plan for generating primary demand for domestically-made TVs.
2. A hotel chain knows a full-page ad in a general-interest magazine like *Maclean's* would cost $25 000; the magazine's total audience is 550 000, 200 000 of whom are part of the chain's target market. A full-page ad in *Ski Canada* magazine would cost $5000; its total audience is 50 000, 40 000 of whom are part of the chain's target market. Which magazine should the hotel chain select? Why?
3. Present and evaluate current examples of companies using institutional advertising, image-oriented personal selling, image-oriented sales promotion, and publicity.
4. Why do you think so many firms handle public relations-related situations poorly?
5. How would you obtain publicity for a small company that has developed a "talking" computer—one that gives instructions on how to set up the computer, how to use various software, and how to diagnose and correct computer errors.

VIDEO CASE

Creating Advertising for Radio Shack: "This Place Is Completely Wired"

Radio Shack is an electronic-products retailer with over 850 stores and 2300 employees in Canada. Radio Shack's Canadian home office is located in Barrie, Ontario and the firm has been in business in Canada since opening their first store in Rexdale, Ontario in 1970.

At one time Radio Shack only carried their own exclusive brand name products. However, because of the strong competition they have changed this policy and now carry competing brands. The main positioning for Radio Shack is now as a specialty retailer that carries name brand electronic products and hard to find "electronic" hardware and specialty products. To support this positioning the current promotional slogan for Radio Shack is "You've Got Questions? We've Got Answers." Much of Radio Shack's promotional effort is concentrated on flyers and direct mail to existing customers. However, at Christmas time, they like to do some media advertising to create extra sales volume.

In 1994, Radio Shack wanted to create a unique television advertising campaign as part of their pre-Christmas promotional effort. Laurie Ross, Radio Shack's vice-president, wanted a campaign that would look real, be funny, and draw attention. She decided to hire Vaughan Weilland to create this campaign for Radio Shack, with a budget of $3.5 million. Vaughan's premise was that advertising must get attention, and people enjoy watching advertising that is fun. Weilland states quite pointedly that dull advertising is useless because it is invisible. Basically, consumers hate commercials so advertisers must work hard to provide commercials people like.

Vaughan's experience with the effectiveness of a humorous campaign appeal came with a unique radio campaign he created for Labatt's Blue Star beer in Atlantic Canada. With unemployment a major issue in the region, Vaughan created a special "Take This Job And Shove It" campaign whereby a lucky winner would be given a ten-week job at Labatt and thus qualify for Unemployment Insurance. The campaign was a success, in that it doubled Blue Star's market share. In one other respect it had some success because the government took a dim view of offering UIC qualification as a prize. Consequently, a lot of publicity surrounded the campaign and Labatt was forced to offer an alternative prize.

Vaughan Weilland decided to start the Radio Shack campaign in Atlantic Canada as well. His creative approach was very simple, employing comedian Peter McCormick to create impromptu humorous situation ads built around the Christmas campaign slogan "This Place Is Completely Wired." Weilland decided to take McCormick and a film crew into Radio Shack stores all across Canada and film twenty-seven different thirty-second spots, with a different ad being aired each day up until Christmas.

The use of improvisation and on-site filming was an extremely risky approach to take in advertising and resulted in some very unusual circumstances for McCormick and Weilland. However, this approach also produced some interesting advertising. For example, in one mall the store was located near a fountain that was interfering with the sound recording. They used the problem to demonstrate a "universal" remote from Radio Shack to "zap" the fountain. Sometimes the interplay with the managers and staff of the stores was not particularly funny so customers were invited to help create the ads. McCormick created all kinds of different sight gags in the various stores and locations.

The campaign was begun in November and the ads ran 250 times on television all across Canada. In January 1995, Radio Shack found their sales had increased 3 per cent over the previous year. In the face of increased competition they evaluated the campaign as being effective but were not ecstatic over its impact on sales. The general conclusion drawn was that the campaign was effective in communicating the message, "This Place Is Completely Wired."

QUESTIONS

1. Discuss the steps presented in the text for creating a promotional campaign. Evaluate Radio Shack's method of campaign creation in relation to these steps.
2. It is often said that a relationship between sales and advertising cannot be established. Why might this be true?
3. Find and explain a situation where it is appropriate and possible to relate advertising efforts to sales response. Discuss this situation relative to your answer to question 2.
4. From a marketing perspective discuss the advantages and disadvantages of using humour as part of an advertising campaign. Identify two products/services for which the use of humorous promotional appeals would not be appropriate and explain why.

VIDEO QUESTIONS ON RADIO SHACK

1. What measures of success could Radio Shack have used to evaluate the television advertising campaign? What measure do you think Weilland would prefer be used and why?
2. Evaluate the "creativity" of the Radio Shack campaign created by Vaughan Weilland. Explain why you thought the campaign was particularly creative or why you did not. Suggest one alternative creative approach.

Video Source: "Radio Shack," *Venture* (January 16, 1994).

Other Source: The data in this case are drawn from the Radio Shack Web site (August, 1996); http://www.Radioshack.ca/.

CASE STUDY

Intuit and Intel: Two Different Reactions to Negative Publicity

When a California sculptor found a serious error in MacIn-Tax, the version of TurboTax software for Apple Macintosh users, he complained to Intuit (the software's developer). After the firm brushed off the complaint, the sculptor took his story to the *San Francisco Chronicle*.

Right after a newspaper story appeared, Scott D. Cook, Intuit's chairperson, admitted the firm's tax software had a number of errors that could produce inaccurate calculations. And Intuit offered to replace the diskettes of all 1.7 million MacIn-Tax customers, even though the calculation errors affected less than one per cent of them. Those consumers who wanted to correct their software quickly were given the opportunity to download the corrected version from commercial online services. Along with the replacement software, Cook sent an apology letter to registered users. In addition, Intuit complied with consumer requests for refunds.

According to experts, errors in tax packages are inevitable due to the short time a firm has to adapt its software to the latest changes in tax legislation. In total, only 75 000 of Intuit's 1.4 million registered users requested the new diskette, and about 3000 consumers downloaded the corrected program from online services.

Intuit's handling of the problem was in sharp contrast to Intel's reaction to the flawed Pentium chip, which generated division errors in complex mathematical calculations. Although the flaw was discovered in November 1994, only after weeks of pressure from final and intermediate customers (including IBM and Gateway 2000) did Intel offer to replace the flawed chips. At first, Intel asked customers to prove they were affected by the flaw. The firm also took the position that errors would occur in only one of nine billion calculations. Furthermore, Intel knowingly sent defective chips to customers prior to correcting the problem, instead of immediately stopping production.

Because of its unpopular approach, Intel was berated in an almost endless stream of negative TV, newspaper, and Internet reports. Then, on December 12, 1994, IBM announced it was temporarily stopping the sale of Pentium-based computers (based on IBM's estimate that errors could occur as frequently as once every twenty-four days for heavy users). IBM also pledged to replace defective Pentium chips free-of-charge. Soon thereafter, other manufacturers of PCs agreed to "no questions asked" free replacements.

Eventually, Intel capitulated. As Andrew Grove, Intel's chief executive officer, said then, "We got caught between our mindset, which is a fact-based, analysis-based engineer's mindset, and the customers' mindset, which is not so much emotional but accustomed to making their own choice. I think the kernel of the issue we missed was that we presumed to tell somebody what they should or shouldn't worry about, or should or shouldn't do."

Although Intel will not disclose actual numbers, analysts estimate the total Pentium chip return rate was less than 10 per cent, compared with initial estimates of about 25 per cent. Market analysts estimated that half of corporate users and 10 per cent of final consumers would ask for replacement chips. However, the actual replacement rate was 25 per cent for corporate users and between 1 and 3 per cent for final consumers.

Some marketing experts say the high initial customer outcry, followed by such a low return rate, was a sign that people were more concerned with Intel's attitude than with the actual defect.

QUESTIONS

1. Develop appropriate public relations objectives for both Intuit and Intel in handling their product recalls.
2. Why do you think that Intuit acted so much more quickly than Intel to recall its defective product?
3. Do you think the barrage of media criticism that Intel faced was "fair?" Explain your answer.
4. How can Intel ensure that a similar situation (in terms of negative publicity) does not happen again?

INTEL
www.intel.com/index.htm

Sources: The data in this case are drawn from Jim Carlton and Stephen Kreider Yoder, "Humble Pie: Intel to Replace Its Pentium Chips," *Wall Street Journal* (December 21, 1994), pp. B1, B6; Dean Foust, "Good Instincts and Intuit," *Business Week* (March 27, 1995), p. 46; and G. Christian Hill, "Despite Furor, Most Keep Their Pentium Chips," *Wall Street Journal* (April 13, 1995), pp. B1–B2.

CHAPTER 20
Personal Selling and Sales Promotion

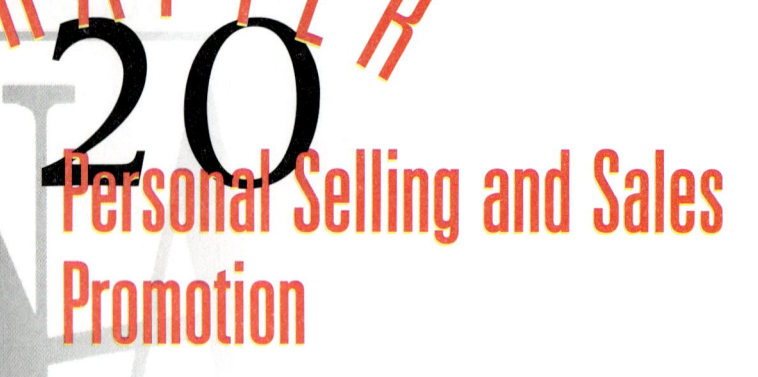

Chapter Objectives

1. To examine the scope, importance, and characteristics of personal selling

2. To study the elements in a personal selling plan

3. To examine the scope, importance, and characteristics of sales promotion

4. To study the elements in a sales promotion plan

{ *Timothy C. Gercke, who lectures on behalf of the National Automobile Dealers Association, is part of an industry-wide effort to turn salespeople into "sales professionals" and buff the business's greasy image. The auto companies have inaugurated numerous training programs because they believe that as quality gaps narrow, the salesperson is the key to keeping customers loyal in a market jammed with competitors selling what Gercke, with typical sweep, refers to as "this thing called a car."* }

The training program sponsored by the National Association of Auto Dealers consists of an eight-hour class and twelve hours of home study. After passing a multiple-choice exam, working for six months at a dealership, and completing product training for the vehicles they sell, salespeople become certified as members of the Society of Automobile Sales Professionals.

The program suggests some dos and don'ts for car salespeople:

- Do tell the truth.
- Do greet customers with a handshake, eye contact, and a genuine smile, not exaggerated.
- Do carefully check your appearance in a full-length mirror before leaving for work.
- Do promise to find the answer to a customer's question if you do not know it. You should never fake an answer.
- Do answer questions posed by a customer's children.
- Don't swear, or use expressions such as "you know" or "yeah."
- Don't treat men and women differently.
- Don't refer to women as "babe," "honey," or "sweetheart."
- Don't use high-pressure tactics.
- Don't display cartoons that could be considered offensive.

Although the ideals of the National Automobile Dealers Association are laudatory, it recognizes the difficulties in accomplishing its goals. Among the major problems are the continued use of commissions and the difficult environment facing many salespeople.

With few exceptions, auto dealers pay their salespeople on the basis of the gross profit of each transaction, with most salespeople receiving between 20 and 25 per cent of the dealer's gross profit. Thus, salespeople have an incentive to overcharge an unknowing customer, offer a customer lower value for his or her trade-in, and even disregard a dealer's advertised price when speaking with an unsuspecting customer.

On the other hand, not all of the gamesmanship comes from the salespeople. Auto salespeople are also confronted with customers who overestimate the condition of their trade-in (some trade-ins that customers say have never been in an accident have more dimples than a golf ball) and lie about the best deal they've been offered elsewhere. And after completing reams of paperwork, a salesperson could also find that a customer's credit rating is much poorer than stated by that person. One salesperson completing the training program told of having seventeen credit rejections in a row. These experiences can make a salesperson quite cynical.

So far, the association has signed up only 350 of its 19 400 members to attend the program. The fee for the program is U.S.$1295 per dealership and an additional U.S.$295 per attendee.[1]

Next, we will study the personal selling and sales promotion aspects of promotion and see how these tools (including sales training) can be used effectively.

Overview

This chapter looks at the two other major promotion forms: personal selling and sales promotion. As defined in Chapter 18, personal selling involves oral communication with one or more prospective buyers by paid representatives for the purpose of making sales. It relies

Personal selling is one-on-one with buyers. Sales promotion includes paid supplemental efforts.

---

[1] James Bennet, "A Charm School for Car Salesmen," *New York Times* (March 29, 1995), pp. D1, D8.

on personal contact, unlike advertising and the publicity aspect of public relations. Its goals are similar to other promotion forms: informing, persuading, and/or reminding.

Sales promotion involves paid marketing communication activities (other than advertising, publicity, or personal selling) that stimulate consumers and dealers. Among the kinds of promotions classed as sales promotions are coupons, trade shows, contests and sweepstakes, and point-of-purchase displays.

The scope and importance, characteristics, and planning considerations for both personal selling and sales promotion are examined in this chapter.

The Scope and Importance of Personal Selling

In Canada, 1.3 million people work in sales positions. In addition, 15 million people work in sales in the United States and millions more in other nations are also employed in sales jobs. Professional salespeople generate new customer accounts, ascertain needs, interact with consumers, emphasize knowledge and persuasion, and offer substantial service. They include stockbrokers, insurance agents, manufacturer sales representatives, and real-estate brokers. Top salespeople can earn $100 000+ per year. Clerical salespeople answer simple queries, retrieve stock from inventory, recommend the best brand in a product category, and complete transactions by receiving payments and packing products. They include retail, wholesale, and manufacturer sales clerks.

From a marketing perspective, personal selling really goes far beyond the people in identified sales positions because every contact between a company representative and a customer entails some personal interaction. Lawyers, plumbers, hairdressers, and cashiers are not defined as salespeople, yet each comes in contact with the customer. The CPSA Sales Institute is one organization that knows the value of customer contact. See Figure 20-1.

CANADIAN PROFESSIONAL SALES ASSOCIATION
cpsa.medius.com/

FIGURE 20-1
The CPSA Sales Certification Program
The value of customer contact with organizational consumers is high, so it requires highly trained salespeople.
Reprinted by permission of CPSA Sales Institute, photo by Chuck Davis/Tony Stone Images.

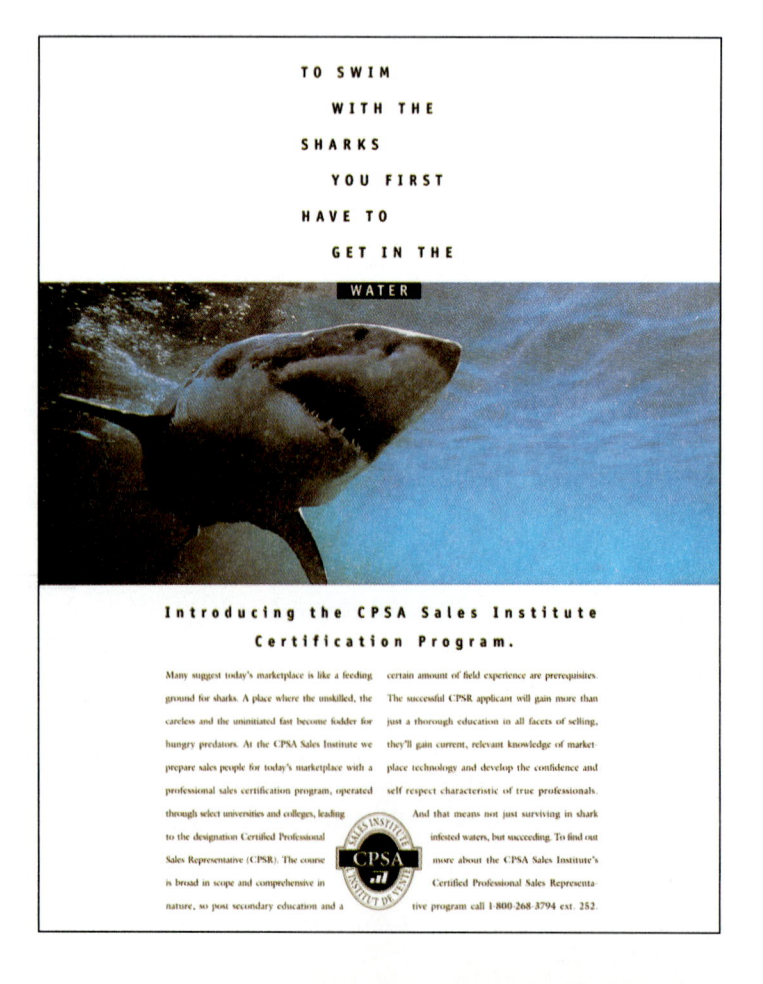

In some situations, a strong personal-selling emphasis may be needed. Large-volume customers require special attention. Geographically concentrated consumers may be more efficiently served by a sales force than by ads in mass media. Custom-made, expensive, and complex goods or services require in-depth consumer information, demonstrations, and follow-up calls. Tangential sales services—like gift wrapping and delivery—may be requested. If ads are not informative enough, questions can be resolved only by personal selling. New products may need personal selling to gain reseller acceptance. Entering a foreign-market may best be achieved by personal contact with prospective resellers and/or consumers. Finally, many organizational customers expect a lot of personal contact. Generally, a decision to stress personal selling depends on such factors as cost, audience and needs, and a desire for flexibility.

Selling is stressed when orders are large, consumers are concentrated, items are expensive, and service is required.

Selling costs are often greater than advertising costs. For example, Fuller Brush sales commissions range up to 50 per cent of sales and auto parts firms, office and equipment firms, and appliance makers all spend far more on selling than on ads. The average cost of a single business-to-business field sales call is several hundred dollars; and it may take several visits to make a sale.[2]

A number of strategies have been devised to keep selling costs down and improve the efficiency of the sales force, as these examples show:

- Many firms are routing salespeople more effectively to minimize travel time and expenses. Some firms are bypassing smaller customers in their personal selling efforts and specifying minimum order sizes for personalized service. This means opportunities for sellers willing to serve small accounts.

- With **telemarketing**, telephone communications are used to sell or solicit business or to set up an appointment for a salesperson to sell or solicit business. By using it, salespeople can talk to several consumers per hour, centralize operations and lower expenses, screen prospects, process orders and arrange shipments, provide customer service, assist the field sales staff, speed communications, and increase repeat business. A lot of companies rely on telephone personnel to contact customers; outside sales personnel (who actually call on customers) are then more involved with customer service and technical assistance. A broad range of both small and large firms use some form of telemarketing.

*High selling costs have led to a concern for efficiency. In **telemarketing**, phone calls initiate sales or set up sales appointments.*

- Computerization is improving sales efficiency by providing salespeople with detailed—and speedy—data, making ordering easier, coordinating orders by various salespeople, and identifying the best prospects and their desires (such as preferred brands)—based on prior purchases. Thousands of Canadian salespeople now have notebook PCs: "Anything that allows reps to squeeze a couple more hours out of their day has great benefits."[3] Figure 20-2 illustrates the value of computerization in sales.

- A lot of firms now view computerized customer databases as among their most valuable sales resources. These databases enable the firms to focus their efforts better, make sure their key accounts are regularly serviced, and use direct mailings to complement telephone calls and salesperson visits.

The Characteristics of Personal Selling

On the positive side, personal selling provides individual attention for each consumer and passes on a lot of information. There is a dynamic interplay between buyer and seller. This lets a firm use a **buyer-seller dyad**, the two-way flow of communication between both parties (see Figure 20-3.) That is not possible with advertising. Thus, personal selling can be

*Selling uses a **buyer-seller dyad** and is flexible and efficient, closes sales, and provides feedback.*

---

[2]Allison Lucas, "Portrait of a Salesperson," *Sales & Marketing Management* (June 1995), p. 13; and Richard T. Hise and Edward L. Reid, "Improving the Performance of the Industrial Sales Force in the 1990s," *Industrial Marketing Management*, Vol. 23 (October 1994), pp. 273–279.
[3]Tom Dellecave, Jr., "Getting the Bugs Out," *Sales & Marketing Management* (December 1995), Part 2, p. 27.

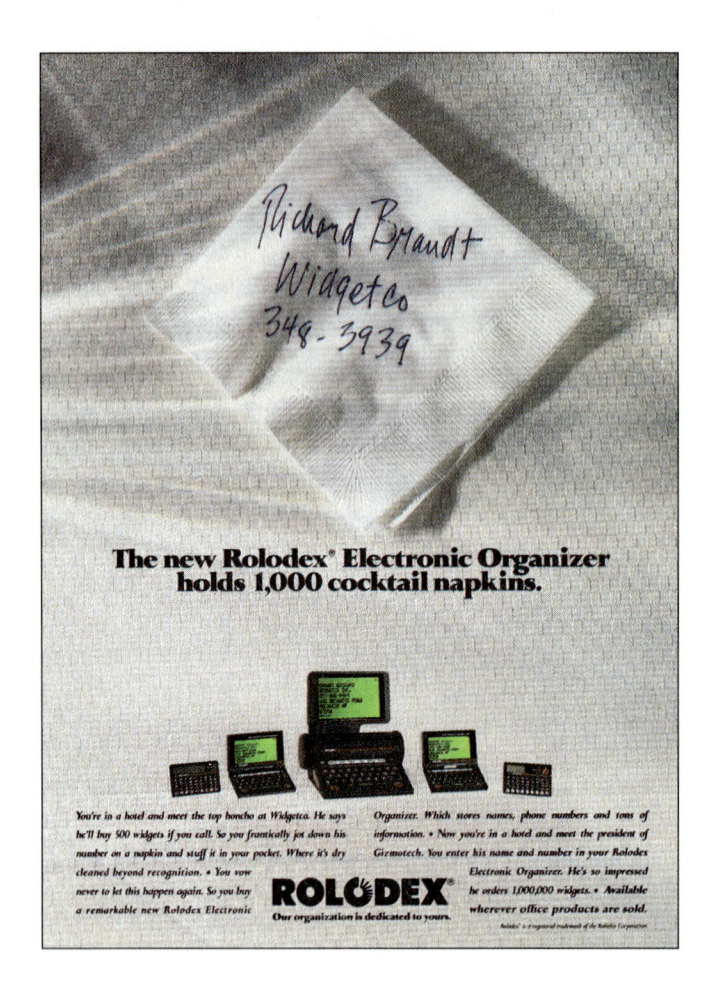

FIGURE 20-2
Why Should Salespeople Carry Portable Computers?
Reprinted by permission

flexible and adapted to specific consumer needs. For example, a real-estate broker can use one sales presentation with a first-time buyer and another with a person who has already bought a home. A salesperson can also apply as much persuasion as needed and balance it against the need for information. Furthermore, through the buyer-seller dyad, a "relationship selling" approach is possible, whereby customer friendships may be developed.[4]

Personal selling targets a more defined and concentrated audience, which means less waste than with advertising. In addition, people who enter a store or who are contacted by a salesperson are more apt to buy a product than those watching an ad on TV. Because ads stimulate interest, those who make it to the personal selling stage are often key members of the target market. When unsolicited, direct selling has the most waste in personal selling.

Personal selling often clinches a sale and is usually conducted during the purchase stage of the consumer's decision process, taking place after an information search and

FIGURE 20-3
The Buyer-Seller Dyad

---

[4]See John J. Withey and Eric Panitz, "Face-to-Face Selling: Making It More Effective," *Industrial Marketing Management*, Vol. 24 (August 1995), pp. 239–246.

International Marketing in Action

Door-to-Door Car Sales—the Japanese Way

According to the Japan Automobile Dealers Association, as many as half of all cars in Japan are bought through direct selling. Toyota alone has over 100 000 door-to-door salespeople. This is equivalent to almost 50 per cent of the sales force for all brands of cars in North America. Toyota's sales force in Japan is so strong that many Japanese car buyers never have to go into a dealership.

Eiko Shiraishi is a typical Toyota salesperson. He represents Toyota in a southwest Tokyo territory, comprised of 3000 households. He has already sold cars to 370 of these prospects. And he has many repeat customers. Shiraishi sells about seven cars a month and earns a salary of $70 000 per year. Almost all of his income is from a salary; very little is due to sales commissions.

Shiraishi times his visits so that he stops by his customers' homes just before their cars reach three years old. He also calls on customers every two years thereafter. Why? At these times, car owners must replace several costly parts as part of the Japanese government's inspection system.

He is careful not to call on housewives early in the morning (when children are being sent off to school) or in late afternoon (when dinner is being prepared). As with most door-to-door car salespeople, Eiko Shiraishi personally delivers his customers' new vehicles right to their homes. He even drives trade-in vehicles back to the dealership.

Shiraishi's job does not end with the sale of a car. Afterwards, he always calls to see how well the car is running, writes handwritten greeting cards, and sends out special invitations for low-cost oil changes and other services.

As a sales manager for Ford, evaluate the pros and cons of using direct selling. Could it be used in Canada? Why or why not?

Source: Based on material in Valarie Reitman, "In Japan's Car Market, Big Three Face Rivals Who Go Door-to-Door," *Wall Street Journal* (September 28, 1994), pp. A1, A13.

---

exposure to ads. It holds repeat customers and those already convinced by advertising—and resolves any concerns of undecided consumers by answering questions about price, warranty, and other factors. It settles service issues, like delivery and installation. Feedback is immediate and clear-cut: Consumers may be asked their feelings about product features or they may complain; and salespeople may unearth a marketing program's strengths and weaknesses.

On the negative side, selling is ineffective for generating awareness because salespeople can handle only a limited number of consumers. A retail furniture salesperson may be able to talk to fewer than twenty people per day if the average length of a customer contact is fifteen minutes to a half hour. Sales personnel who call on customers can handle even fewer accounts, due to travel time. In addition, many consumers drawn by advertising may want self-service. This is discouraged by some aggressive salespeople.

Personal selling costs per customer can be very high due to the one-on-one nature of selling. An in-store furniture salesperson who talks to twenty customers daily might cost a firm $7 per presentation ($140/day compensation divided by 20), an amount much higher than an ad's cost per-customer contact. For outside salespeople, hotel stays, meals, and transportation can amount to $250 or more daily per salesperson, and compensation must be added to these costs.

Selling has a limited audience, high costs per customer, and a poor image.

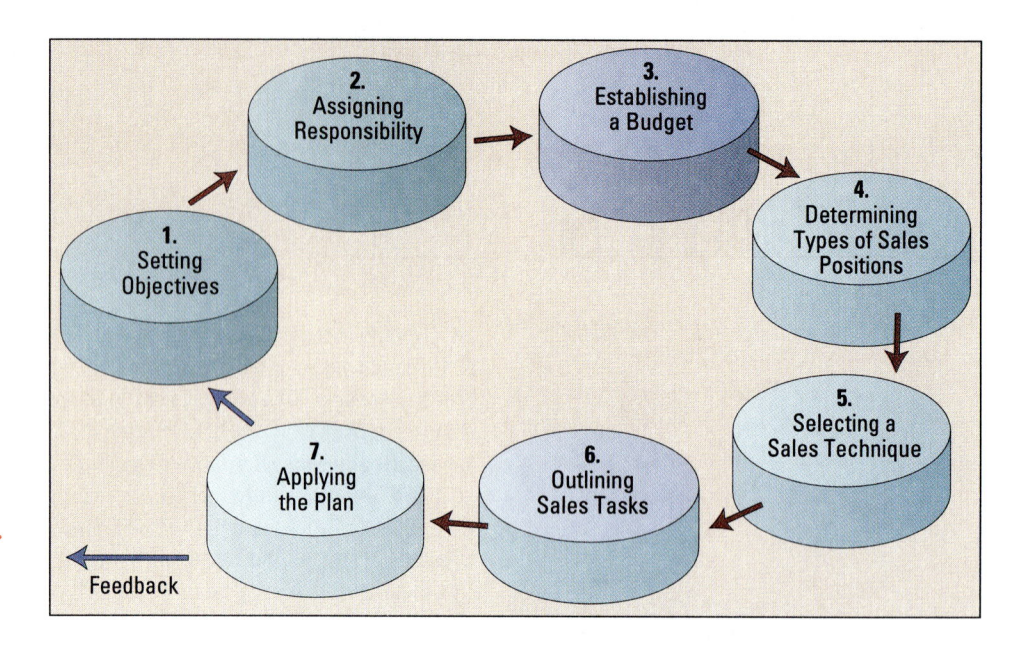

FIGURE 20-4
Developing a Personal Selling Plan

Finally, personal selling, especially among final consumers, has a poor image. It is criticized for a lack of honesty and pressure tactics:

> The public's consistent interpretation of the term *salesperson* has provided fodder for many dramatic works, anecdotes, and jokes that reflect the widely held negative stereotype of salespeople. As a result, people may avoid them deliberately. The consumer practice of visiting car dealerships after business hours [indicates the common distrust] of salespeople. This practice may be due to beliefs that consumers can evaluate alternative cars better in the absence of the "dreaded" salesperson. Sometimes, salespeople may even inhibit, rather than facilitate, mutually satisfying exchanges.[5]

The situation can be improved by better sales-force training and the use of consumer-oriented rather than seller-oriented practices.

Developing a Personal Selling Plan

A personal selling plan can be divided into the seven steps shown in Figure 20-4 and highlighted here.

Setting Objectives

Selling goals can be demand- and/or image-oriented. When image-oriented, they involve public relations. Although many firms have some interest in information, reminder, and image goals, the major goal usually is persuasion: converting consumer interest into a sale. Examples appear in Table 20-1.

Assigning Responsibility

A manager must oversee selling functions.

The personal selling function may be assigned to a marketing or sales manager who oversees all areas of selling, from planning to sales force management. A small or specialized firm is likely to have its marketing manager oversee selling or use one general sales manager. A large or diversified firm may have multiple sales managers—assigned by product line, customer type, and/or region.

---

[5]Barry J. Babin, James S. Boles, and William R. Darden, "Salesperson Stereotypes, Consumer Emotions, and Their Impact on Information Processing," *Journal of the Academy of Marketing Science*, Vol. 23 (Spring 1995), p. 94.

Table 20-1
Specific Personal Selling Objectives

TYPE OF OBJECTIVE	ILLUSTRATIONS
Demand-Oriented	
Information	To fully explain all attributes of goods and services
	To answer any questions
	To probe for any further questions
Persuasion	To distinguish attributes of goods or services from those of competitors
	To maximize the number of purchases relative to the presentations made
	To convert undecided consumers into buyers
	To sell complementary items—e.g., a telephoto lens with a camera
	To placate dissatisfied customers
Reminding	To ensure delivery, installation, etc.
	To follow-up after a good or service has been purchased
	To follow-up when a repurchase is near
	To reassure previous customers as they make a new purchase
Image-Oriented	
Industry and company	To have a good appearance for all personnel having customer contact
	To follow acceptable (ethical) sales practices
	To be respected by customers, employees, and other publics

These are the basic responsibilities of a sales manager:

- To understand the firm's goals, strategies, market position, and basic marketing plan and to convey them to the sales force.
- To determine and outline a sales philosophy, sales force characteristics, selling tasks, a sales organization, and methods of customer contact.
- To prepare and update sales forecasts.
- To allocate selling resources based on sales forecasts and customer needs.
- To select, train, assign, compensate, and supervise sales personnel.
- To synchronize selling tasks with advertising, product planning, distribution, marketing research, production, and other activities.
- To assess sales performance by salesperson, product, product line, customer, customer group, and geographic area.
- To continuously monitor competitors' actions.
- To make sure the sales force acts in an ethical manner.
- To convey the image sought by the company.

Establishing a Budget

A **sales-expense budget** allots selling costs among salespeople, products, customers, and geographic areas for a given period. It is usually tied to a sales forecast and relates selling tasks to sales goals. It should be somewhat flexible in case expected sales are not reached or are exceeded.

These items should be covered in a budget: sales forecasts, overhead (manager's compensation, office costs), sales force compensation, sales expenses (travel, lodging, meals,

*A **sales-expense budget** assigns spending for a specific time.*

Table 20-2
A Sales-Expense Budget for a Small Manufacturer Specializing in Business Machinery, 1997

ITEM	ESTIMATED ANNUAL COSTS (REVENUES)
Sales forecast	$1 950 000
Overhead (1 sales manager, 1 office)	$ 100 000
Sales force compensation (2 salespeople)	90 000
Sales expenses	40 000
Sales meetings	5 000
Selling aids	15 000
Sales management costs	10 000
Total personal-selling budget	$ 260 000
Personal selling costs as a percentage of sales forecast	13.3

entertainment), sales meetings, selling aids (including computer equipment), and sales management (employee selection and training) costs. Table 20–2 shows a budget for a small maker of business machinery.

The budget will be larger if customers are geographically dispersed and a lot of travel is required. Complex products need costly, time-consuming sales presentations and result in fewer calls per salesperson. An expanding sales force needs expenditures for recruiting and training salespeople.

Determining the Type(s) of Sales Positions

Salespeople can be broadly classed as order takers, order getters, or support personnel. Some firms employ one type of salesperson, others a combination.

An **order taker** processes routine orders and reorders. This person is involved more with clerical than creative selling, typically for pre-sold goods or services. He or she arranges displays, restocks items, answers simple questions, writes up orders, and completes transactions. He or she may work in a warehouse (manufacturer clerk) or store (retail clerk) or call on customers (a field salesperson). An order taker has these advantages: compensation is rather low, little training is required, both selling and nonselling tasks are performed, and a sales force can be expanded or contracted quickly. However, an order taker is improper for goods and services that need creative selling, or where extensive information must be available for customers. Personnel turnover is high and enthusiasm may be limited due to the low salary and routine tasks.

An **order getter** generates customer leads, provides information, persuades customers, and closes sales. He or she is the creative salesperson used for high-priced, complex, and/or new products. There is less emphasis on clerical work. The person may be inside (jewellery store salesperson) or outside (Xerox salesperson).[6] He or she is expert and enthusiastic, expands sales, and can convince undecided customers to buy or decided customers to add peripheral items—such as carpeting and appliances along with a newly built house. Yet, for many people, the order getter has a high-pressure image. He or she may also need expensive training. Such nonsales tasks as writing reports may be avoided because they take away from a seller's time with customers and are seldom rewarded. Compensation can be very high for salespersons who are effective order getters. Figure 20-5 contrasts order takers and order getters.

An order taker handles routine orders and sells items that are pre-sold.

An order getter obtains leads, provides information, persuades customers, and closes sales.

[6]See Kris Frieswick, "Inside Sales Takes Centre Stage," *Industrial Distribution* (October 1995), pp. 24–27.

Order Takers	Order Getters
• Process routine orders and reorders.	• Generate customer leads and persuade consumers.
• Provide clerical functions.	• Are creative.
• Handle pre-sold items and maintain sales.	• Handle high-priced/complex items and increase sales.
• Arrange displays, restock items, answer simple questions, and complete transactions.	• Are less involved with routine tasks.
• Require little training and compensation.	• Require a lot of training and compensation.
• Have limited expertise and enthusiasm.	• Are highly expert and enthusiastic.

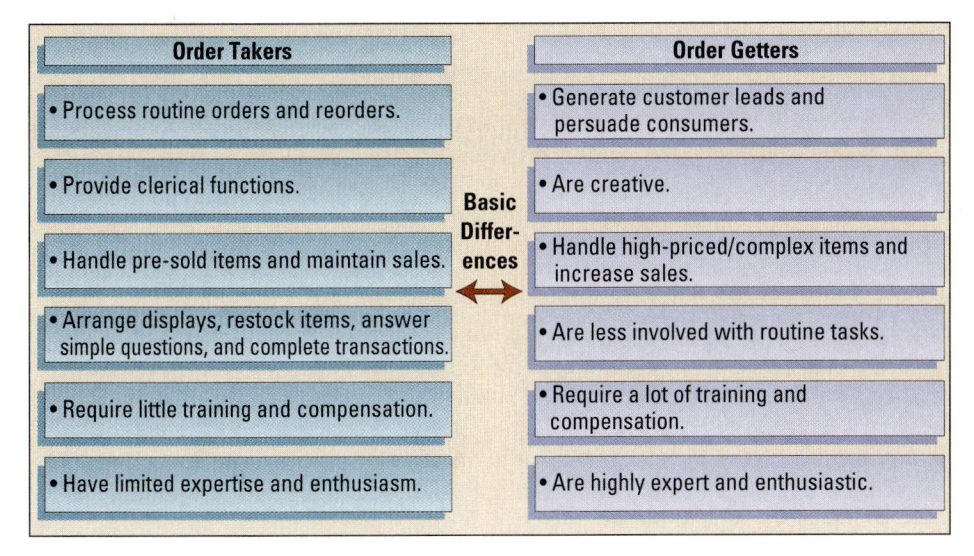

Basic Differences ↔

FIGURE 20-5
Contrasting Order Takers and Order Getters

Support personnel supplement a sales force. A **missionary salesperson** gives out information on new goods or services. He or she does not close sales but describes items' attributes, answers questions, and leaves written matter. This paves the way for later sales and is commonly used with prescription drugs. A **sales engineer** accompanies an order getter if a very technical or complex item is involved. He or she discusses specifications and long-range uses, while the order getter makes customer contacts and closes sales. A **service salesperson** ordinarily deals with customers after sales. Delivery, installation, and other follow-up tasks are done.

Missionary salespersons, sales engineers, and service salespersons are support personnel.

Selecting a Sales Technique

The two basic techniques for selling are the canned sales presentation and the need-satisfaction approach. The **canned sales presentation** is a memorized, repetitive presentation given to all customers interested in a given item. It does not adapt to customer needs or traits but presumes a general presentation will appeal to everyone. Although criticized for its inflexibility and nonmarketing orientation, it does have some value:

The canned sales presentation is memorized and nonadaptive.

> Inexperienced salespeople who are lacking in selling instinct and confidence will benefit from the professionalism, anticipation of questions and objections, and other fail-safe mechanisms often inherent in a company-prepared, memorized, audiovisual or flip-chart presentation. Consequently, this method should be considered when qualified new salespeople are scarce and when brevity of training is essential.[7]

The **need-satisfaction approach** is a high-level selling method based on the principle that each customer has different attributes and wants, and therefore the sales presentation should be adapted to the individual consumer. With this technique, a salesperson first asks such questions of the consumer as: What type of product are you looking for? Have you ever purchased this product before? What price range are you considering? Then the sales presentation is more responsive to the particular person; and a new shopper is treated quite differently from an experienced one. The need-satisfaction approach is more popular and customer-oriented; however, it requires better training and skilled sales personnel. This approach includes:

The need-satisfaction approach adapts to individual consumers.

- Using the buyer-seller dyad to generate two-way respect.
- Listening well.
- Making presentations based on a good grasp of the facts.

---

[7]Marvin A. Jolson, "The Underestimated Potential of the Canned Sales Presentation," *Journal of Marketing*, Vol. 39 (January 1975), p. 78.

- Spending time on pre-sales research ("homework").
- Being punctual for appointments (and willing to leave when the allotted time is over).
- Allowing the customer to talk.
- Offering "solutions," not goods and services.
- Showing competence.
- Acknowledging if a question cannot be answered, but getting back to the customer immediately with the correct answer.
- Not wasting a prospect's time.
- Providing superior service after the sale.[8]

The canned sales presentation works best with inexpensive, routine items that are heavily advertised and relatively pre-sold. The need-satisfaction approach works best with more expensive, more complex items that have moderate advertising and require substantial additional information for consumers.

Outlining Sales Tasks

*The **selling process** consists of seven steps.*

The tasks to be performed by the personal sales force need to be outlined. The **selling process** consists of prospecting for leads, approaching customers, determining consumer wants, giving a sales presentation, answering questions, closing the sale, and following up. See Figure 20-6.

***Prospecting** creates customer leads.*

Outside selling requires a procedure, known as **prospecting**, to generate a list of customer leads. Blind prospecting uses phone directories and other general listings of potential customers; a small percentage of those contacted will be interested in a firm's offering. Lead prospecting depends on past customers and others for referrals; thus, a greater percentage of people will be interested because of the referral from someone they know. Inside selling does not involve prospecting because customers have already been drawn to a store or office through ads or prior purchase experience.

*The pre-approach and greeting are part of **approaching customers**.*

Approaching customers is a two-stage procedure: pre-approach and greeting. During pre-approach, a salesperson tries to get information about the customer from the firm's database, census materials, and/or other secondary data—as well as from referrals. The salesperson is then better equipped to interact with that customer. Inside retail salespeople may be unable to use a pre-approach; they often know nothing about a consumer until he or she enters the store. During the greeting, a salesperson begins a conversation. The intention is to put the customer at ease and build rapport.

The next step is to ascertain customer wants by asking the person a variety of questions regarding past experience, price, product features, intended uses, and the kinds of information still needed.

FIGURE 20-6
The Selling Process

Prospecting for Leads → Approaching Customers → Determining Customer Wants → Giving a Sales Presentation → Answering Questions → Closing the Sale → Following Up

---

[8]Adapted by the authors from James E. Lukaszewski and Paul Ridgeway, "To Put Your Best Foot Forward, Start by Taking These 21 Simple Steps," *Sales & Marketing Management* (June 1990), pp. 84–86. See also Fiona Gibb, "The New Sales Basics," *Sales & Marketing Management* (April 1995), p. 81.

The **sales presentation** includes a verbal description of a product, its benefits, options and models, price, associated services like delivery and warranty, and a demonstration (if needed). A canned sales presentation or need-satisfaction method may be used. The purpose of a sales presentation is to convert an undecided consumer into a purchaser.

*The **sales presentation** converts an uncertain consumer.*

After a presentation, the salesperson usually must answer questions from the consumer. Questions are of two kinds: the first kind request more information; the second kind raise objections that must be settled before a sale is made.

Once any questions have been answered, a salesperson is ready for the **closing**. This means getting a person to agree to a purchase. The salesperson must be sure no major questions remain before trying to close a sale. In addition, a salesperson must not argue with a consumer.

*The **closing** clinches a sale.*

For a large purchase, the salesperson should follow up after the sale to make sure the customer is pleased. Doing so achieves three goals: the customer is better satisfied; referrals are stimulated; and, repurchases are more likely. "Relationship selling is not about getting an order; it is about convincing customers that you will be there after an order, no matter what. Relationships are based on doing what is right, not doing what you can get away with."[9]

Besides the tasks in the selling process, a firm must clearly enumerate the nonselling tasks it wants sales personnel to perform. Among the nonselling tasks that may be assigned are setting up displays, writing up information sheets, marking prices on products, checking competitors' strategies, doing test marketing analysis and consumer surveys, and training new employees.

Applying the Plan

Sales management—planning, implementing, and controlling the personal sales function—should be used in applying a personal selling plan. Sales management covers employee selection, training, territory allocation, compensation, and supervision.

***Sales management** tasks range from employee selection to supervision.*

In selecting sales personnel, a combination of personal attributes should be assessed: mental (intelligence, ability to plan), physical (appearance, speaking ability), experiential (education, sales/business background), environmental (group memberships, social influences), personality (ambition, enthusiasm, tact, resourcefulness, stability), and willingness to be trained and to follow instructions.[10] Contrary to earlier beliefs, it is now pretty much accepted that good salespeople are not necessarily born; they are carefully selected and trained: "How would you describe the ideal salesperson? Extroverted, aggressive? Quick to develop a rapport? A good sense of humour, a competitive spirit, charisma? This has been a popular stereotype, to be sure, and no doubt there are some excellent sales professionals out there who actually do possess these qualities. On the other hand, it's also a popular misconception. The truth is, these factors aren't always the most important ones to consider when selecting and training top salespeople."[11]

The traits of potential salespeople must be compatible with the customers with whom they will interact and the requirements of the good or service being sold. The buyer-seller dyad operates better when there are some similarities in salesperson and customer characteristics. And certain product categories require much different education, technical training, and sales activities than others (such as jewellery versus computer sales).

Once these factors are studied, the firm would develop a formal selection procedure that specifies the personal attributes sought, sources of employees (such as colleges and employment agencies), and methods for selection (such as interviews and testing). It would be based on the firm's overall selling plan.

Salesperson training may take one or a combination of forms. A formal program uses a trainer, a classroom setting, lectures, and printed materials. It may also include role play-

---

[9]Michael Collins, "Breaking into the Big Leagues," *Marketing Tools* (January–February 1996), p. 28.

[10]Adapted by the authors from William J. Stanton, Richard H. Buskirk, and Rosann L. Spiro, *Management of a Sales Force*, Ninth Edition (Homewood, Ill.: Richard D. Irwin, 1995).

[11]Thomas Rollins, "How to Tell Competent Salespeople from the Other Kind," *Sales & Marketing Management* (September 1990), p. 116.

ing (in which trainees act out parts) and case analysis. Field trips take trainees out on actual calls so they can observe skilled salespeople in action. On-the-job training places trainees in their own selling situations under the close supervision of the trainer or a senior salesperson. Training often covers a range of topics; it should teach selling skills and include information on the firm and its offerings, the industry, and employee duties. At Caterpillar (the industrial and farm equipment manufacturer), "We train our sales force to understand why our customers buy our products, what their needs are, the importance of follow-up, the need to let a customer vent his/her anger, and how to help a customer resolve problems without passing the responsibility on to someone else in the company."[12] Besides initial training, continuous training or retraining of sales personnel may teach new techniques, explain new products, or improve performance.

Territory size and salesperson allocation are decided next. A **sales territory** consists of the geographic area, customers, and/or product lines assigned to a salesperson. If territories are assigned by customer type or product category, two or more salespeople may cover the same geographic area. Territory size depends on customer locations, order size, travel time and expenses, the time per sales call, the yearly visits for each account, and the amount of hours per year each salesperson has for selling tasks. The mix of established versus new customer accounts must also be considered. Allocating salespeople to specific territories depends on their ability, the buyer-seller dyad, the mix of selling and nonselling functions (such as one salesperson training new employees), and seniority. Proper territory size and allocation provide adequate coverage of customers, minimize territory overlap, recognize geographic boundaries, minimize travel expenses, encourage solicitation of new accounts, provide enough sales potential for good salespeople to be well rewarded, and are fair to the whole sales force.

A **sales territory** *contains the area, customers, and/or products assigned to a salesperson.*

Salespeople can be compensated by straight salary, straight commission, or a combination of salary and commission or bonus. With a **straight salary plan**, a salesperson is paid a flat amount per time period. Earnings are not tied to sales. The advantages are that both selling and nonselling tasks can be specified and controlled, salespeople have security, and expenses are known in advance. The disadvantages are the low incentive to increase sales, expenses not being tied to productivity, and the continuing costs even if there are low sales. Order takers are usually paid straight salaries.

Sales compensation may be **straight salary**, **straight commission**, *or a* **combination** *of the two.*

With a **straight commission plan**, a salesperson's earnings are directly related to sales, profits, customer satisfaction, or some other type of performance. The commission rate is often keyed to a quota, which is a productivity standard. The advantages of this plan are the motivated salespeople, the elimination of fixed sales compensation costs, and the fact that expenses are tied to productivity. The disadvantages are the firm's lack of control over nonselling tasks, the instability of a firm's expenses, and salesperson risks due to variable pay. Insurance, real estate, and direct-selling order getters often earn straight commissions. Typically Canadian real-estate salespersons receive a 6 per cent commission of $9000 for selling a $150 000 house.

To gain the advantages of both salary- and commission-oriented methods, many firms use elements of each in a **combination compensation plan**. Such plans balance company control, flexibility, and employee incentives; and some award bonuses for superior individual or company performance. All types of order getters work on a combination basis. According to various studies, about two-thirds of North American firms compensate sales personnel via some form of combination plan, one-fifth use a straight-salary plan, and the rest use straight commissions. Smaller firms are more apt to use a straight-salary plan and less apt to use a combination plan.

Supervision encompasses four aspects of sales management:

Supervision involves motivation, performance measures, nonselling tasks, and behaviour modification.

1. Sales personnel must be motivated. Their motivation depends on such factors as the clarity of the job (what tasks must be performed), the salesperson's desire to achieve, the variety of tasks performed, the incentives for undertaking each task, the style of the sales manager, flexibility, and recognition.

---

[12] Geoffrey Brewer, "Caterpillar Inc.: Industrial & Farm Equipment," *Sales & Marketing Management* (September 1993), p. 61.

Ethics AND TODAY'S MARKETER

Do Life Insurance Agents "Churn" So Much to Earn So Much?

Prudential and other agents have recently been scrutinized for "churning" insurance policies. Under this practice, agents recommend that customers use the built-in cash value from old policies to purchase new ones. Churning is often practiced by agents as a way of increasing their commission income from loyal accounts. Because a new policy often generates a sales commission equal to half of the first year's premium, churning is highly profitable to agents.

Unfortunately, people are often not fully briefed about the consequences of switching policies. In one instance, a unsuspecting consumer was advised by an agent to borrow against the cash value in an existing policy so that the customer could purchase more insurance coverage. However, in such instances, the cash value of the old policy could run out, while the interest on the loan increases. The customer would then be forced to pay off the debt.

Churning is also generally not profitable for the insurance company. It often takes at least six years of payments for a new policy to be profitable due to the company's cost of sales commissions, administrative costs, and medical testing fees.

Despite these problems, it is hard to reduce churning activity. In many sales offices, monitoring this activity falls under the jurisdiction of junior managers. Because these managers are evaluated on the basis of the sales revenues of their agents, churning increases their income. In addition, many insurance agents represent multiple firms. An independent agent can easily churn a policyholder from one insurance provider to another. Finally, many insurance firms do not want to come down too hard on productive independent agents, since they can easily switch their loyalty from one insurance company to another.

As a Prudential marketing executive, how would you discourage independent agents from churning?

Source: Based on material in Leslie Scism, "Some Agents Churn Life-Insurance Policies, Hurt Their Customers," *Wall Street Journal* (January 3, 1995), pp. 1, 4.

2. Performance must be measured. To do this, achievements must be gauged against such goals as sales and calls per day. The analysis should take into account territory size, travel time, and experience. The failure of a salesperson is often related to poor listening skills, a lack of concentration on priorities, a lack of effort, the inability to determine customer needs, a lack of planning for presentations, overpromising on product performance, and inadequate knowledge.

3. The sales manager must ensure that all nonselling tasks are completed, even if sales personnel are not rewarded for them.

4. If a salesperson's performance does not meet expectations, then some action may be needed to modify behaviour.[13]

PRUDENTIAL INSURANCE CO.
www.prudential.com/

---

[13]Thomas N. Ingram, Charles H. Schwepker, Jr., and Don Hutson, "Why Salespeople Fail," *Industrial Marketing Management*, Vol. 21 (August 1992), pp. 225–230; and "Pipe Down," *Sales & Marketing Management* (January 1994), p. 22. See also Goutam N. Challagalla and Tasadduq A. Shervani, "Dimensions and Types of Supervisory Control: Effects on Salesperson Performance and Satisfaction," *Journal of Marketing*, Vol. 60 (January 1996), pp. 89–105.

There are more women in sales than ever before, and international markets require special decisions.

In sales management, these key factors should also be taken into account: the evolving role of women in selling and the special nature of selling in foreign markets.

One of the major changes in industrial sales forces over the last twenty years is "the accelerated recruitment of women into traditionally male-dominated sales positions."[14] According to Statistics Canada[15], women hold 46 per cent of the sales positions in Canada and industry observers expect that even more women will be recruited into sales forces in the future. Two researchers have noted:

> Sales managers do not have to provide special considerations or training programs for female salespersons to facilitate their socialization into the industrial sales force. Consequently, sales managers should not be concerned with incurring additional training expenses for females, nor do they need to behave more solicitously in their management practices toward women than men. To do otherwise will probably result in the demotivation of male salespersons, and will probably handicap females by intimating that they are deficient in some way and require additional assistance. Instead, sales managers should include women equally in all sales training, motivation, and socialization activities, just as these opportunities are extended to men.[16]

When firms go international, "they are faced with the task of establishing and managing sales forces in foreign markets. Once in place, they must decide how much home-office influence to exert on subsidiary sales policies. When faced with the diversity of the international marketplace, top marketing management is often uncertain about how much it should influence its overseas sales forces. Management benefits from knowing which sales decisions are suited to home-office input and, just as important, which are not."[17] In particular, the attributes of salespeople; salesperson training, compensation, and supervision; the dynamics of the buyer-seller dyad; and the selling process may need to be tailored to different foreign markets. For example, in many Arab countries, negotiations—particularly bargaining—are viewed as an enjoyable activity or even as a social event. Foreign salespeople need to respect the religious traditions of their Arab customers and recognize that Arab personnel may not be available at all times. In addition, they are known to refrain from saying "no" and to engage in contract renegotiations if the need arises. Arabs end negotiations by orally committing themselves, rather than doing so in writing.

The Scope and Importance of Sales Promotion

Sales promotion efforts are now quite extensive.

Due to intense competition in their industries, numerous firms are aggressively seeking every marketing edge possible. Thus, sales promotion activities worldwide are at their highest level. In the Canadian food and beverage industry, sales promotion expenditures are estimated to be $6.7 for every $1 spent on advertising. In comparison, in the United States the ratio is $2.57 for every $1 spent on advertising.[18]

The extent of sales promotion activities are illustrated in the following examples:

- In Canada, households receive about 400 coupons every year—a drop in the bucket compared to the U.S., where each household receives an average of 3000 coupons per year! Virtually all coupons have an expiry date to encourage faster redemption and to allow marketers to evaluate their effectiveness. In a typical year, most Canadian households use coupons, half on a regular basis. Yet, all told people redeem only two per cent of distributed coupons.[19]

---

[14] Patrick L. Schul and Brent M. Wren, "The Emerging Role of Women in Industrial Selling: A Decade of Change," *Journal of Marketing*, Vol. 56 (July 1992), p. 38.

[15] Statistics Canada, *1995 Market Research Handbook* (Ottawa: Minister of Supply Services), p. 164.

[16] Judy A. Siguaw and Earl D. Honeycutt, Jr., "An Examination of Gender Differences in Selling Behaviors and Job Attitudes," *Industrial Marketing Management*, Vol. 24 (January 1995), p. 51. See also Nancy Arnott, "It's a Woman's World," *Sales & Marketing Management* (March 1995), pp. 54–59.

[17] John S. Hill, Richard R. Still, and Onal O. Boya, "Managing the Multinational Sales Force," *International Marketing Review*, Vol. 8 (Number 1, 1991), pp. 19–31. See also Earl D. Honeycutt and John B. Ford, "Guidelines for Managing an International Sales Force," *Industrial Marketing Management*, Vol. 24 (March 1995), pp. 135–144.

[18] Andrea Haman, "Causes of the Conundrum," *Marketing Magazine* (August 21–28, 1995), p. S7.

[19] Lara Mills, "1995 Coupon Calendar," *Marketing Magazine* (August 21–28, 1995), p. 12; and "The 1995 Annual Report on the Promotion Industry," *Promo* (July 1995), p. 38.

- Business-to-business firms spend about 13 per cent of their marketing budgets on trade shows and exhibits. Fifty per cent of industrial trade show attendees report signing a purchase order as a result of a trade show visit.[20]
- According to International Events Group, North American firms spend U.S.$4.5 billion annually to sponsor special events—two-thirds on sports-related events. For example, Air Canada spent $8 million to be a sponsor of the 1996 Olympics in Atlanta, and agreed to be a sponsor for the 1998 Winter Olympics. A promotion related to their sponsorship was a special "Go Canada Go" promotion, which involved a chance for participants to win one of six private jet flights with thirty-nine of their friends to the Olympics.[21]
- Zellers has been operating a frequent shopper program for over 10 years called Club Z. Currently, there are over 9.4 million members, 7.6 million of which make purchases on a monthly basis and are considered active. Club Z allows customers to build up points which can be redeemed for merchandise from a special catalogue, and in some cases, merchandise in the Zellers stores themselves. Customers get rewarded with special discounts and Zellers is able to build its customer data base.[22]
- Point-of-purchase displays (P.O.Ps) are categorized as instore media and are estimated to represent about $150 million in spending each year in Canada.[23] These displays stimulate impulse purchases and provide information. Besides traditional cardboard, metal, and plastic displays, more stores are now using digital electronic signs and video displays. Figure 20-7 shows a sales-oriented display by Revlon of Canada.

REVLON
www.revlon.com/

FIGURE 20-7
Lip Blitz: Revlon's Towering 3D Display
In-store displays can have a dramatic impact on sales. Revlon's Lip Blitz display sold millions of lipsticks in its first two weeks.
Reprinted courtesy of Revlon Canada Inc.

---

[20]Cyndee Miller, "Marketing Industry Report: Who's Spending What on Biz-to-Biz Marketing," *Marketing News* (January 1, 1996), p. 1; and John F. Tanner, Jr. and Lawrence B. Chonko, "Trade Show Objectives," *Industrial Marketing Management*, Vol. 24 (August 1995), pp. 257–264.
[21]"The 1995 Annual Report on the Promotion Industry," p. 40; and News Line, "Air Canada launches Atlanta promotion," *Marketing Magazine* (May 6, 1996), p. 1.
[22] News Line, "CIBC and Zellers launch Club Z Visa card," *Marketing Magazine* (October 23, 1995), p. 1.
[23]Lara Mills, "The Biggest Fish," *Marketing Magazine* (April 8, 1996), p. 9.

COLGATE PALMOLIVE
www.colgate.com/

- In rural India (with its 650-million population), fewer than 15 per cent of the people use toothpaste. So, Colgate-Palmolive hires "video vans" to regularly visit local villages. The vans show a twenty-seven-minute infomercial on the value of toothpaste; free samples are then given out and tooth brushing demonstrations are provided.[24]

Several factors account for the strength of sales promotion as a marketing tool. As noted at the beginning of this section, firms are looking for any competitive edge they can get and this often involves some kind of sales promotion; sales promotions are more acceptable to firms and consumers than in the past; many firms want to improve short-run profits, and promotions allow for quick returns; more consumers look for promotions before buying (especially in economic downturns) and resellers put pressure on manufacturers to provide them; advertising and personal selling have become more expensive relative to sales promotion; and technology advances make aspects of sales promotion, like coupon redemption, easier to administer.

The Characteristics of Sales Promotion

Sales promotion lures customers, maintains loyalty, creates excitement, is often keyed to patronage, and appeals to channel members.

Sales promotion has many advantages. It helps attract customer traffic, for example, with new-product samples and trial offers, and it helps keep brand or company loyalty. A manufacturer can retain brand loyalty by giving gifts to regular customers and coupons for its brands. A reseller can retain loyal customers by offering incentives to frequent shoppers and using store coupons.

Rapid results can be gained from some promotions. Calendars, matchbooks, T-shirts, pens, and posters with the firm's name provide consumer value and are retained; thus, they remind the consumer of the company name every time they are used. Impulse purchases can be stimulated by in-store displays. For example, an attractive supermarket display for batteries can dramatically raise sales. In addition, a good display may lead a shopper to a bigger purchase than originally intended.

Excitement can be created by short-run promotions involving gifts, contests, or sweepstakes; and high-value items or high payoffs encourage consumers to participate. Contests offer the further benefit of customer involvement (through the completion of some skill-oriented activity). Many promotions are keyed to customer patronage—with the awarding of coupons, frequent-shopper gifts, and referral gifts directly related to purchases. In these cases, promotions can be a fixed percentage of sales and their costs not incurred until transactions are completed. And resellers may be stimulated if sales-promotion support is provided in the form of displays, manufacturer coupons, manufacturer rebates, and trade allowances.

Sales promotion may hurt image, cause consumers to wait for special offers, and shift the focus from the product.

Sales promotion also has limitations. A firm's image may be tarnished if it always runs promotions. People may view discounts as representing a decline in product quality and believe a firm could not sell its offerings without them. Profit margins are often lower for a firm if sales promotion is used. When coupons, rebates, or other special deals are employed frequently, people may not buy when products are offered at regular prices; they will stock up each time there is a promotion. Some consumers may even interpret a regular price as an increase for items that are heavily promoted.

Some promotions shift the marketing focus away from the product itself to secondary factors. People may be lured by calendars and sweepstakes instead of product quality and features. In the short run, this generates consumer enthusiasm. In the long run, it may adversely affect a brand's image and sales because a product-related advantage has not been communicated. Sales promotion can enhance—not replace—advertising, personal selling, and public relations.

---

[24] Miriam Jordan, "In Rural India, Video Vans Sell Toothpaste and Shampoo," *Wall Street Journal* (January 10, 1996), pp. B1, B5.

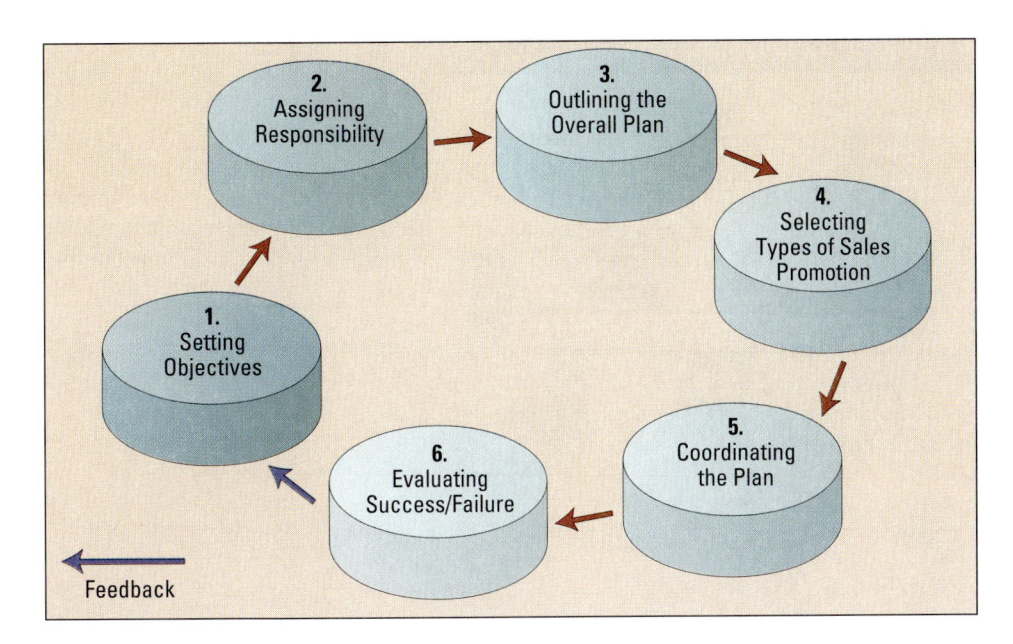

FIGURE 20-8
Developing a Sales Promotion Plan

Developing a Sales Promotion Plan

A sales promotion plan consists of the steps shown in Figure 20-8 and explained next.

Setting Objectives

Sales promotion goals are usually demand-oriented. They may be related to channel members and to consumers.

Objectives associated with channel-member sales promotions include gaining distribution, receiving adequate shelf space, increasing dealer enthusiasm, raising sales, and getting cooperation in sales promotion expenditures. Objectives pertaining to consumer sales promotions include boosting brand awareness, increasing product trials, hiking average purchases, encouraging repurchases, obtaining impulse sales, emphasizing novelty, and supplementing other promotional tools.

Assigning Responsibility

Sales promotion duties are often shared by advertising and sales managers, with each directing the promotions in his or her area. Thus, an advertising manager would work on coupons, customer contests, calendars, and other mass promotions. A sales manager would work on trade shows, cooperative promotions, special events, demonstrations, and other efforts involving individualized attention directed at channel members or consumers.

Some companies have their own specialized sales-promotion departments or hire outside promotion firms. Outside sales-promotion firms tend to operate in narrow areas—such as coupons, contests, or gifts—and generally can develop a sales promotion campaign at less expense than the user company could. These firms offer expertise, swift service, flexibility, and, when requested, distribution.

Outlining the Overall Plan

Next, a sales promotion plan should be outlined and include a budget, an orientation, conditions, media, duration and timing, and cooperative efforts. In setting a sales promotion budget, it is important to include all costs. For example, the average face value of a grocery coupon is over 65 cents; supermarkets receive a handling fee for each coupon they redeem; and there are costs for printing, mailing, and advertising coupons.

Sales promotion orientation refers to the focus of the promotion—channel members or consumers—and its theme. Promotions for channel members should raise their product knowledge, provide sales support, offer rewards for selling a promoted product, and seek

Sales promotion orientation *may be toward channel members and/or final consumers.*

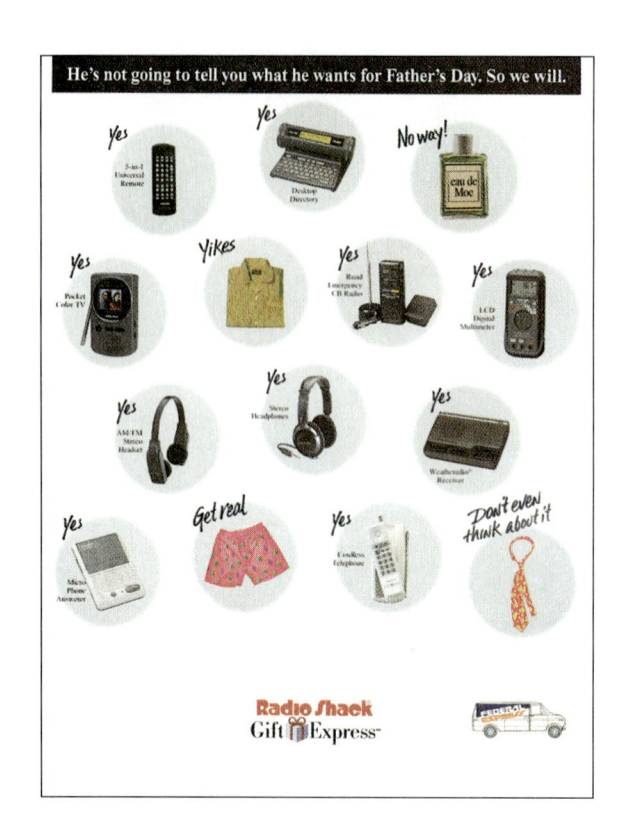

FIGURE 20-9
Happy Father's Day
Reprinted by permission

TECHNOLOGY & MARKETING

What's Ahead for Electronic Frequent-Shopper Programs?

According to Brian P. Woolf, president of the Retail Strategy Centre, a retailer should "treat all customers equally, but reward them differently." He bases this advice on the fact that a firm's frequent customers can spend fifty times the amount of occasional customers.

One way to enact a differential reward strategy is to use an electronic frequent-shopper program. Such programs rely on the use of shopper information that has been captured by retailers at the point of sale.

There are various types of frequent-shopper programs. Some are price-based, with frequent shoppers getting price reductions on their total bill or special offers not available to the general public. In another type of program, retailers contribute money to charities based on frequent-shopper purchases. Other programs offer different point values keyed to the products purchased. Some state-of-the-art programs even automatically accumulate shopper transactions. Until recently, retailers had to design and implement frequent-shopper programs on their own.

According to Brian Woolf, in over 90 per cent of the instances where retailers have introduced frequent-shopper programs, they have achieved a 6 per cent increase in same-store sales. However, to achieve these results, a frequent-shopper program must be at the centre of the retailer's overall marketing strategy.

Recently, Safeway Stores Eastern Division announced a simple program available to marketers of packaged goods. These marketers can now participate in special targeted promotions aimed at Safeway's 1.2-million-member Savings Club database. This database contains purchase histories of consumers all the way down to the individual item level.

As marketing manager for Heinz ketchup, how would you tie into Safeway's Savings Club database?

Source: Based on material in R. Craig MacClaren, "The Future Is in the Cards," *Promo* (July 1995), p. 56.

better cooperation and efficiency. Promotions for consumers should induce impulse and larger-volume sales, sustain brand-name recognition, and gain participation. A promotion theme refers to its underlying channel-member or consumer message—such as a special sale, store opening, new-product introduction, holiday celebration, or customer recruitment. See Figure 20-9.

Sales promotion conditions are requirements channel members or consumers must meet to be eligible for a specific sales promotion. These may include minimum purchases, performance provisions, and/or minimum age. A channel member may have to stock a certain amount of merchandise to receive a free display case from a manufacturer. A consumer may have to send in proofs of purchase to get a refund or gift. In some cases, strict time limits are set as to the closing dates for participation in a sales promotion.

Sales promotion conditions are eligibility requirements.

The media are the vehicles through which sales promotions reach channel members or consumers. They include direct mail, newspapers, magazines, television, the personal sales force, trade shows, and group meetings.

A promotion's duration may be short or long, depending on its goals. Coupons usually have quick closing dates because they are used to increase store traffic. Frequent-shopper points often can be redeemed for at least one year; their goal is to maintain loyalty. As noted earlier, if promotions are lengthy or offered frequently, consumers may come to expect them as part of a purchase. Some promotions are seasonal, and for these timing is crucial. They must be tied to such events as fall school openings or model or style changes.

Finally, the use of shared promotions should be decided. With cooperative efforts, each party pays some costs and gets benefits. These promotions can be sponsored by industry trade associations, manufacturers and/or service firms, wholesalers, and retailers. For example, "McDonald's realizes the strength of the Walt Disney Co. and its strength with animated films, and Disney made a conscious decision to work with us, to our mutual advantage. So, in March 1996, McDonald's headlined a two-tier promotion that included an instant-win trivia game for adults and a kid-targeted Happy Meals promotion. The entire effort surrounded Walt Disney Home Video's top-selling Masterpiece Collection of thirteen videos, including *The Lion King* and *Pocahontas*."[25]

Selecting the Types of Sales Promotion

There is a wide range of sales promotion tools available. The attributes of several promotion tools oriented to channel members are shown in Table 20-3. The attributes of several consumer-oriented sales-promotion tools are noted in Table 20-4. Examples for each tool are also provided in these tables.

The selection of sales promotions should be based on such factors as company image, company goals, costs, participation requirements, and the enthusiasm of channel members or customers.

Coordinating the Plan

It is essential that sales promotion activities be well coordinated with other elements of the promotion mix. In particular:

Advertising and sales promotion should be integrated.

- Advertising and sales promotion plans should be integrated.
- The sales force should be notified of all promotions well in advance and trained to implement them.
- Publicity should be generated for special events, such as the appearance of a major celebrity.
- Sales promotions should be consistent with channel members' activities.

Evaluating Success or Failure

Measuring the success or failure of many types of sales promotions is straightforward, since the promotions are so closely linked to performance or sales. By analyzing before-and-after

The success or failure of some sales promotions is simple to measure.

[25] Kate Fitzgerald, "McDonald's Scores Big Promo Role with Disney," *Advertising Age* (January 8, 1996), p. 8.

Table 20-3
Selected Types of Sales Promotion Directed at Channel Members

TYPE	CHARACTERISTICS	ILLUSTRATION
Trade shows or meetings	One or a group of manufacturers invites channel members to attend sessions where products are displayed and explained.	The annual National Home Centre Show attracts more than one thousand exhibitors and tens of thousands of attendees.
Training	The manufacturer provides training for personnel of channel members.	Compaq trains retail salespeople in how to operate and use its computers.
Trade allowances or special offers	Channel members are given discounts or rebates for performing specified functions or purchasing during certain time periods.	A local distributor receives a discount for running its own promotion for GE light bulbs.
Point-of-purchase displays	The manufacturer or wholesaler gives channel members fully-equipped displays for its products and sets them up.	Coca-Cola provides refrigerators with its name on them to retailers carrying minimum quantities of Coca-Cola products.
Push money	Channel members' salespeople are given bonuses for pushing the brand of a certain manufacturer. Channel members may not like this if their salespeople shift loyalty to the manufacturer.	A salesperson in an office-equipment store is paid an extra $50 for every desk of a particular brand that is sold.
Sales contests	Prizes or bonuses are distributed if certain performance levels are met.	A wholesaler receives $2500 for selling 1000 microchips in a month.
Free merchandise	Discounts or allowances are provided in the form of merchandise.	A retailer gets one case of ballpoint pens free for every 10 cases purchased.
Demonstration	Free items are given to channel members for demonstration purposes.	A hospital-bed manufacturer offers demonstrator models to its distributors.
Gifts	Channel members are given gifts for carrying items or performing functions.	During one three-month period, a book publisher gives computerized cash registers to bookstores that agree to purchase a specified quantity of its books.
Cooperative	Two or more channel members share the cost of a promotion.	A manufacturer and retailer each pay part of the cost for T-shirts with the manufacturer's and retailer's names embossed.

data, the impact of these promotions is clear. Trade show effectiveness can be gauged by counting the number of leads generated from a show, examining the sales from those leads and the cost per lead, getting customer feedback about a show from the sales force, and determining the amount of literature given out at a show. Companies can verify changes in sales as a result of dealer-training programs. Firms using coupons can review sales and compare redemption rates with industry averages. Surveys of channel members and consumers can indicate satisfaction with promotions, suggestions for improvements, and the effect of promotions on image.

Some sales promotions—such as event sponsorships and T-shirt giveaways—are more difficult to evaluate. Objectives are less definitive.

Here are three examples relating to the effectiveness of sales promotion:

- About two-thirds of supermarket shoppers say that end-aisle displays and circular coupons "frequently" catch their attention.[26]

[26]"Impact in the Aisles: The Marketer's Last Best Chance," *Promo* (January 1996), p. 26.
[27]Blair R. Fischer, "Making Your Product the Star Attraction," *Promo* (January 1996), p. 88.

Table 20-4
Selected Types of Sales Promotion Directed at Consumers

TYPE	CHARACTERISTICS	ILLUSTRATION
Coupons	Manufacturers or channel members advertise special discounts for customers who redeem coupons.	P&G mails consumers a 50-cents-off coupon for Sure deodorant, which can be redeemed at any supermarket.
Refunds or rebates	Consumers submit proofs of purchase (usually to the manufacturer) and receive extra discount.	First Alert provides rebates to consumers submitting proofs of purchase for its fire alarms.
Samples	Free merchandise or services are given to consumers, generally for new items.	Health clubs offer a free one-month trial.
Contests or sweepstakes	Consumers compete for prizes by answering questions (contests) or filling out forms for random drawings of prizes (sweepstakes).	Publishers Clearing House sponsors annual sweepstakes and awards cash and other prizes.
Bonus packs or multipacks	Consumers receive discounts for purchasing in quantity.	An office-supply store runs a "buy one, get one free" sale on desk lamps.
Shows or exhibits	Many firms co-sponsor exhibitions for consumers.	The Canadian National Exhibition is annually scheduled for the public in Toronto.
Point-of-purchase displays	In-store displays remind customers and generate impulse purchases.	*TV Guide* sales in supermarkets are high because displays are placed at checkout counters.
Special events	Firms sponsor the Olympics, fashion shows, and other activities.	Air Canada is a worldwide sponsor of the Olympics.
Product placements	Branded goods and services depicted in movies and TV shows.	Nike sneakers appears in the movie *Forrest Gump*.
Gifts	Consumers get gifts for making a purchase or opening a new account.	Savings banks offer a range of gifts for consumers opening new accounts or expanding existing ones.
Frequent-shopper	Consumers get gifts or special discounts, based on cumulative purchases. Points are amassed and exchanged for gifts or money.	Airline travellers can accumulate gifts and receive free trips or mileage gifts when enough miles have been earned.
Referral gifts	Existing customers are given gifts for referring their friends to the company.	Tupperware awards gifts to the hosts of their Tupperware parties.
Demonstrations	Goods or services are shown in action.	Different models of Apple computers are demonstrated in a complimentary lesson.

- BMW received 6000 pre-orders for its Z3 roadster after it was seen in the James Bond thriller *GoldenEye*. The car wasn't commercially available until several months after the movie opened.[27]
- A study by the Canadian Congress of Advertising indicated that for non-personal sources of purchase information, 42 per cent of Canadians would rely on flyers and circulars as a source of information. This rating was barely behind newspapers, which were mentioned by 44 per cent of Canadians, and way ahead of the third-ranked source of information, television, which was mentioned by 35 per cent of respondents.[28]

CANADIAN CONGRESS OF ADVERTISING
www.vrx.net/congress95/cong5.htm

---

[28] Jim McElgunn, "Study Says Nothing Beats Word of Mouth," *Marketing Magazine* (May 1, 1995), p. 9.

MARKETING IN A CHANGING WORLD
Sales Training the 3M Way[29]

3M is taking a very novel approach to sales training for its veteran salespeople, and others can learn from its experiences. As one observer noted, "While innovation was long a part of the research, product development, and manufacturing processes at 3M, it wasn't as conspicuous in sales. 3M sales training, although always high-quality, was not focused as well as it might have been on customer needs. That's changed. Three years ago, innovation struck sales training: the firm started asking customers to tell it where salespeople needed to improve skills or get additional training."

The new sales-training approach is a big departure from prior 3M practice, when the company relied on broad customer satisfaction surveys rather than specific measures of salesperson performance. 3M now surveys customers to determine how its sales representatives are performing in terms of specific skills. In a typical year, 1000 or so business customers are surveyed.

The new program is called A.C.T.—assessment and analysis, curriculum content, and training transfer. It provides "customer-focused, just-in-time, on-demand sales training." This is how A.C.T. works:

- A written questionnaire assesses selling skills in six areas: knowledge of products and services, strategic skills critical to best using the time spent with the customer, interpersonal selling, sales negotiation, internal influence and teamwork, and customer-focused quality.
- Each participating salesperson personally gives the questionnaire to a select group of about six customers. The customers then rate the importance of each of the skill areas, and how well the salesperson is performing them.
- Completed questionnaires go to an outside tabulation firm. (Sales managers only receive composite scores for their salespeople, but not the results of individual salespeople.) Results are computed and the gaps in salesperson performance are derived.
- Each salesperson works with his or her sales manager to set up a training curriculum to correct key weaknesses, and to undergo appropriate training.
- The last step is transfer, whereby each salesperson applies what he or she has learned to actual customer situations.

SUMMARY

1. To examine the scope, importance, and characteristics of personal selling Personal selling involves oral communication with one or more prospective buyers by paid representatives for the purpose of making sales. About 1.3 million Canadians work in selling jobs; millions more work in sales jobs throughout the world. Yet these numbers understate the value of personal selling because every contact between a company employee and a customer involves some degree of selling.

Selling is emphasized with high-volume clients, geographically concentrated customers, expensive and/or complex products, customers wanting sales services, and entries into foreign markets. Selling also resolves questions and addresses other issues. Selling costs are higher than advertising costs at many firms. An average business-to-business sales call costs several hundred dollars. Thus, efficiency is important.

Selling fosters a buyer-seller dyad (a two-way communication flow), offers flexibility and adaptability, adds to relationships with customers, results in less audience waste, clinches sales, and provides immediate feedback. Yet, personal selling can handle only a limited number of customers, is rather ineffective for creating consumer awareness, has high costs per customer, and has a poor image for some consumers.

2. To study the elements in a personal selling plan A selling plan has seven steps: setting goals—demand- and/or image-related; assigning responsibility—to one manager or to several managers; setting a budget; choosing the type(s) of sales positions—order takers, order getters, and/or support salespeople; selecting a sales technique—the canned sales presentation or the need-satisfaction approach; outlining tasks—including each of the relevant steps in the selling process and nonselling tasks; and applying the plan—which centres on sales management.

3. To examine the scope, importance, and characteristics of sales promotion Sales promotion encompasses paid marketing communi-

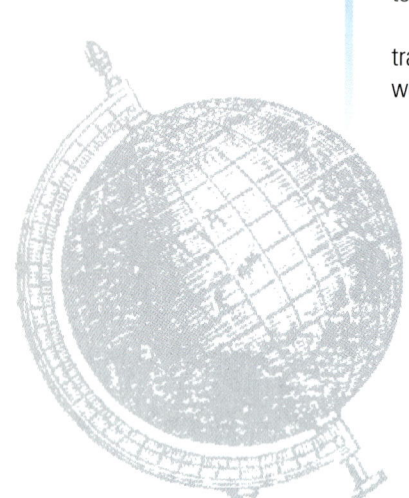

---

[29]The material in this section is based on William Keenan, Jr., "Getting Customers into the A.C.T.," *Sales & Marketing Management* (February 1995), pp. 58–63.

cation activities (other than advertising, publicity, or personal selling) that stimulate consumer purchases and dealer effectiveness. In the Canadian food and beverage industry, sales promotion expenditures are estimated to be $6.7 for every $1 spent on advertising.

The rapid growth of sales promotion is due to firms aggressively looking for a competitive edge, the greater acceptance of sales promotion tools by both firms and consumers, quick returns, the pressure by consumers and channel members for promotions and their popularity during economic downturns, the high costs of other promotional forms, and technological advances that make them easier to administer.

A sales promotion helps attract customer traffic and loyalty, provides value and may be retained by consumers, increases impulse purchases, creates excitement, is keyed to patronage, and improves reseller cooperation. However, sales promotions may also hurt a firm's image, encourage consumers to wait for promotions before making purchases, and shift the focus away from product attributes. Sales promotion cannot replace other forms of promotion.

4. *To study the elements in a sales promotion plan* A promotion plan has six steps: setting goals—ordinarily demand-oriented; assigning responsibility—to advertising and sales managers, company departments, and/or outside specialists; outlining the overall plan—including orientation, conditions, and other factors; selecting the types of sales promotion; coordinating the plan with the other elements of the promotion mix; and evaluating its success or failure.

KEY TERMS

telemarketing (p. 549)
buyer-seller dyad (p. 549)
sales-expense budget (p. 553)
order taker (p. 554)
order getter (p. 554)
missionary salesperson (p. 555)
sales engineer (p. 555)
service salesperson (p. 555)

canned sales presentation (p. 555)
need-satisfaction approach (p. 555)
selling process (p. 556)
prospecting (p. 556)
approaching customers (p. 556)
sales presentation (p. 557)
closing the sale (p. 557)

sales management (p. 557)
sales territory (p. 558)
straight salary plan (p. 558)
straight commission plan (p. 558)
combination compensation plan (p. 558)
sales promotion orientation (p. 563)
sales promotion conditions (p. 565)

Review Questions

1. Statistics Canada lists 1.3 million people in sales positions in Canada. Why does this figure understate the importance of personal selling?
2. Under what circumstances should personal selling be emphasized? Why?
3. Draw and explain the buyer-seller dyad.
4. Distinguish among order-taker, order-getter, and support sales personnel.
5. When is a canned sales presentation appropriate? When is it inappropriate?
6. Outline the steps in the selling process.
7. Why is sales promotion growing as a marketing tool?
8. What are the limitations associated with sales promotion?
9. Differentiate between sales promotion orientation and sales promotion conditions.
10. Why is the success or failure of many types of sales promotion relatively easy to measure?

Discussion Questions

1. Comment on this statement: "Although its role may differ, telemarketing may be successfully used during the selling process for any type of good or service."
2. How would you handle these objections raised at the end of a sales presentation?
   a. "I saw the price of the same item at a competing store for 10 per cent less than what you are asking."
   b. "Your warranty period is much too short."
   c. "None of the alternatives you showed me is satisfactory."
3. Present a checklist for a medium-sized apparel manufacturer to use in setting up a sales force in a foreign market.
4. List several sales promotion techniques that would be appropriate for a university. List several that would be appropriate for a minor league baseball team. Explain the differences in your two lists.
5. How could a sales promotion be *too* successful?

VIDEO CASE

Craig Procter: A Super Salesperson

Craig Procter is a real estate agent for the Re/Max firm in Newmarket, a city of 50 000 people in the suburbs of Toronto. He is a top performing salesperson. In a typical year Craig is responsible for the sale of 200 homes, while most real estate agents average about ten homes. Craig Procter appears to have adopted the marketing philosophy of wanting to help his customers buy.

In the mid-1990s Canadians have been seeing both low mortgage rates and low prices. In fact, in the Toronto area where Craig works, housing prices were 25 per cent below their 1989 values in 1995. The implication is that the selling job will be tough because homeowners who were selling resale homes that were purchased between the late 1980s and 1995 would likely be asked to sell at a loss.

How do real estate agents like Craig Procter make sales, especially in this kind of economic environment? It requires an all-out marketing effort. The task of real estate agents is twofold. They must create both ends of a transaction. First, they must find people who wish to sell their homes. This is called getting a "listing." Next, the agent needs to find buyers. There is an informal agreement in the real estate industry that an agent who finds a buyer for a home listed by another agent will split the commission.

The task of finding sellers and buyers and bringing them together is onerous. Craig Procter pursues this with a vengeance. He spends about $250,000 a year to get his name in the public eye in Newmarket. Craig has used some very traditional approaches, like putting his name on billboards, bus shelters, and benches; and giving out special promotional materials like key chains, pens, pencils, business cards, and even plastic milk jugs! But he has also tried some innovative ideas. His phone line allows residents of Newmarket to call Toronto toll free—after listening to his sales pitch. It has cost Craig about $40 000 a year but the line is very popular: Craig has already rewarded the two millionth caller.

These techniques create awareness of Craig's name. He also has his own team of cold callers, who knock on doors and call people in the Newmarket area to see if they are thinking about selling their homes. The team uses Craig's name and tries to find prospective listings for him.

Craig realizes that word-of-mouth is important to his image. He must do a good job for his customers, who will then tell other customers. Craig also has a plan to overcome the slightly soft economy. If he lists your home and it does not sell as fast as you would like, he will buy the home from you and sell it himself. This guarantees the seller that a transaction will take place and gives Craig an advantage when it comes to getting listings. Craig has a team of people on his payroll and they perform basic tasks, freeing Craig's time to sign up new listings and to present offers on homes. His reward is $1.2 million in commissions earned—but after expenses, he takes home $150 000.

Craig offers these guidelines for aspiring salespeople: (1) Don't waste your time. Be organized and understand prospects. Customers may be unrealistic in what they want. If you cannot help them, move on. (2) Stay in touch with customers. Maintain your relationship before, during, and after a sale. (3) Practice self-marketing. Get your name out.

QUESTIONS

1. Personal selling seems to be the key promotional element in real estate sales; discuss the role of the other elements of the promotion mix. Calculate a "cost per thousand" for Craig's free phone line based on the information in the case and the assumption that the line has been running for one year. Research the reach, frequency, and advertising costs for some local newspapers, television, and magazines. How would you rate Craig's phone line as an advertising medium in comparison?
2. Successful real estate agents will often make two sales for every house sold. Discuss this statement within the context of the stages of the personal selling process and the nature of real estate transactions. Identify the stage you think would be most important to the success of a "new" real estate agent and explain why.
3. Develop two sales presentations for Craig to acquire new listings of resale homes for his real estate firm.
4. What are the pros and cons of Craig Procter's guaranteed sale program (I'll sell your house in sixty days or I'll buy it myself)? What kinds of limits would you suggest for this program to overcome or reduce the risk associated with its disadvantages?

VIDEO QUESTIONS ON CRAIG PROCTER

1. Identify and evaluate the attributes which seem to set Marshall Redden and Craig Procter apart from other salespeople. Discuss whether these attributes can be learned or not and the implications for sales managers with respect to hiring and training.
2. Discuss the concept of "backending" presented in the video with respect to the real estate market. What would a real estate agent have to know to develop an effective strategy? Take an example of backending from the video applicable to real estate and recommend a marketing strategy to Craig Procter and Marshall Redden.

Video Source: "Top Seller," *Venture* (June 12, 1994).

Other Sources: The data in this case are drawn from George Vasic, "Today's Millstones, Tomorrow's Castles," *Canadian Business* (August 1995), p. 87; Andrea Haman, "Re/Max Ads Aim to Lure First-Time Buyers," *Marketing Magazine* (July 24, 1995), p. 4.

CASE STUDY

Sales Promotion in the United States: Does a Free Lunch Work?

According to Donnelley Marketing's *Survey of Promotional Practices*, marketers cite these as their top reasons for product sampling: introducing a new product, launching line extensions, building a customer franchise, defending against brand competition, adding consumer value, gaining retail distribution, and defending against private label competition.

Among the well-known firms that have developed major sampling promotions are Taco Bell, Dunkin' Donuts, and Keebler. Each of these firms has recently used product sampling to increase trial rates and to convert nonusers to product users. Let's now examine each of their strategies.

In 1995, Taco Bell, a division of PepsiCo, decided to offer free samples of its new Border Lights low-fat foods for an entire day. The company's goal was to quickly generate trial and use of this line of foods. According to Taco Bell's chair and chief executive officer, "We knew that once consumers took their first bite, they would love the taste." Taco Bell expected sales of its Border Lights products to reach U.S.$800 million by the end of 1995.

Dunkin' Donuts used sampling to increase the trial of its coffee. During summer 1995, it used four custom vans (which travelled to beaches, festivals, and other high-traffic locations) to give out free samples of its new flavoured Hazelnut and Vanilla Nut coffees. Unlike Taco Bell, which handled its own sampling distribution, Dunkin' Donuts hired a sampling firm to plan and implement its sampling effort. Dunkin' Donuts' also decided to go to its customers (rather than to provide the coffee samples in its stores) to increase the trial rate.

As Dunkin' Donuts marketing development manager said, "Today, people live in the here and now. Even getting a coupon for a free product is considered a lot of work because they have to go to the store to get it. Sampling is intrusive and is a way to create awareness of our brands and get them into the consumers' mouths immediately."

After reformulating its Pizzarias snack product, Keebler realized that product sampling was the fastest and most efficient way to make its teenage customer market aware of the improvements. Working with a promotion agency, Keebler distributed a million free Pizzarias samples at over 200 arcades, tying its sampling activity to *Brutal Paws of Fury* (GameTek's new video game). In addition to the free sample, teenagers received tear pads inviting them to a special offer upon purchasing a regular size bag of Pizzarias. The offer included a free demo of *Brutal Paws*, as well as a chance to win various prizes. Keebler's integrated marketing program even included retail displays, shelf talkers, and local radio tie-ins.

To date, Keebler has been "extremely pleased" with the results of this marketing effort. However, according to Keebler's brand manager, if the firm were to use product sampling again for Pizzarias, he would use more in-store sampling. This would facilitate the consumer's purchase of a desired product.

One way to assess the effectiveness of product sampling is to compute the break-even conversion rate. The conversion rate represents how many consumers buy a product after trying a free sample.

Mathematically, this is equal to a product's distribution costs (including the cost of manufacturing the samples) divided by the annual profit per user. Thus, if these costs equal U.S.$1 per unit and 750 000 samples are distributed, the firm's investment would equal U.S.$750 000. The annual profit per user can be calculated by multiplying the average annual use of the product by its profit margin. If the average annual use is 12 and the profit per unit is U.S.$1, the annual profit per user is U.S.$12. Thus, the break-even conversion rate is 62 500 (the U.S.$750 000 investment divided by the $12 profit per user).

QUESTIONS

1. Under what conditions should a firm employ an outside agency to handle its sampling effort?
2. Evaluate Dunkin' Donuts' strategy to sample its flavoured coffees from vans rather than from its stores.
3. Discuss the pros and cons of product sampling versus coupons.
4. If a product's distribution costs are $3, one million samples are distributed, and the annual usage rate is 6, what is the break-even conversion rate? Is this good or bad? Why?

DUNKIN' DONUTS
www.franchise1.com/comp/dunkin1.html

Source: The data in this case are drawn from Kerry J. Smith, "Free Lunch," *Promo* (September 1995), pp. 93–96, 105.

PART 7
PRICE PLANNING

Part 7 covers the fourth and final element of the marketing mix, pricing.

21 Considerations in Price Planning

In this chapter, we study the role of price, its importance in transactions, and its interrelationship with other marketing variables. We contrast price-based and nonprice-based approaches. We also look at each of the factors affecting price decisions in depth: consumers, costs, government, channel members, and competition.

22 Developing and Applying a Pricing Strategy

Here, we explain how to construct and enact a pricing strategy. First, we distinguish among sales, profit, and status quo objectives. Next, we discuss the role of a broad price policy. Then, we introduce three approaches to pricing (cost-, demand-, and competition-based) and show how they may be applied. We also explain why these three pricing methods should be integrated. We examine a number of pricing tactics, such as customary and odd pricing. We conclude the chapter by noting methods for adjusting prices.

Part 7 Vignette
Pricing for Competition

> *Price planning means ensuring that the marketplace values a firm's offerings at a price that is greater than the costs of providing them.*

For marketers, the value of goods and services is created by the choice of target market combined with the product, promotion and distribution decisions. Capturing the value created and recovering the costs incurred from being in business is an objective of the pricing strategy. Marketers must ensure that the marketplace confers greater value to their offerings than it costs to provide them. The first video case looks at Canadian energy exports and demonstrates how cost-based pricing can become a problem for organizations with a price umbrella when they suddenly find themselves faced with price-based competition in a commodity market. The second video case discusses the start-up of two new airlines seeking to be profitable while occupying the low price position for air travel in Canada.

A rapid expansion in the need for energy in the 1970s, coupled with an oil embargo by middle eastern oil producers, spawned strong government support for innovative approaches to new energy development in Canada and, simultaneously, a strong impetus towards energy conservation and efficiency. Consequently, Ontario and Quebec Hydro, government regulated and supported electricity producers, embarked on a number of "mega-projects" to supply more energy. At the same time, the marketplace responded with energy conservation behaviour and electrical appliances were redesigned to become more energy efficient. Ontario and Quebec Hydro went to considerable expense to develop facilities that turned out to be excessive for their markets. The solution seemed simple: sell the power to the United States, where there was a big market and a "shortage" of electrical power.

Then the price of fossil fuels began to fall, and since Canadian natural gas producers had been very active in developing natural gas wells and building pipelines to eastern markets in both Canada and the United States, and gas-based power plants had been springing up all over the eastern seaboard of the United States, these lower-cost plants were able to provide electricity for one third of the price of electricity provided by Ontario and Quebec Hydro. This cut in revenue for Ontario and Quebec Hydro meant that current customers were asked to pay more, which forced more of the current customers to consider alternative suppliers.

When it comes to market competition, price can be the toughest way to compete for customers, especially when your competitors undersell you. So why would any organization choose this approach? A business competes on price because it is the easiest way to differentiate products in the marketplace. And in the air carrier business, the comparison is very clear. If one air carrier can transport a person from Vancouver to Toronto for a lower fare than another, the choice is obvious. People will choose the cheaper carrier since the distance between Vancouver and Toronto remains the same no matter who does the flying.

The trick in the airline business is to offer lower fares than the competition while remaining profitable. That's not easy, since no domestic discount airline in Canada has been able to survive trying this trick. In fact, very few of the world's airlines are profitable, even without using discount positioning. The one exception has been Southwest Airlines in the United States. Southwest has been able to combine a low cost structure with high capacity utilization of its aircraft. Two Canadian airlines, WestJet and Greyhound Air, are planning to try to duplicate Southwest's formula for success. Both firms seem to have excellent plans and prospects for achieving the low cost approach. The problem for these two airlines will be to achieve the capacity utilization that a low price position should confer. The key marketing issue for all firms that choose to compete on price is price demand elasticity.

CHAPTER 21
Considerations in Price Planning

Chapter Objectives

1. To define the terms price and price planning

2. To demonstrate the importance of price and study its relationship with other marketing variables

3. To differentiate between price-based and nonprice-based approaches

4. To examine the factors affecting pricing decisions

{ *"We have been slowly pricing ourselves out of the competition with our biggest competitors, which are the old airplanes in the fleets,"* says Ronald Woodward, president of commercial-jetliner manufacturing for Boeing. The pressure on airfares is taking root and appears *"irreversible,"* he adds. *"Deregulation is hitting the manufacturers now."* }

What does this mean? According to some experts, aircraft pricing is finally reflecting the deregulation of airline fares, airlines' preoccupation with reducing costs, and many airlines' delay in purchasing new aircraft. And it is a good thing, since the list price of smaller jetliners reached U.S.$50 million in 1995, and that for the largest jumbo jets hit U.S.$175 million.

Today, there is much greater flexibility in the pricing of commercial aircraft as manufacturers are more willing to offer substantial discounts from a plane's list price. Even Boeing, the world's leading commercial aircraft manufacturer and the United States' largest exporter, has embarked on a new pricing strategy. Gordon Bethune, the chief executive of Continental Airlines and a former senior executive at Boeing, says that Boeing has changed from its "fair price" notion to offering planes at prices airlines will pay.

Central to Boeing's current pricing strategy is its massive cost-reduction program. It consists of reduced staffing requirements, reduced cycle times (the time from the beginning of work on a plane to a plane's delivery), and standardized parts.

During one recent two-year period, Boeing laid off thousands of production and managerial personnel. It has lowered its cycle time by 45 per cent and plans an another 20 per cent reduction. The firm has also begun standardizing parts on all of its planes. Previously, each part was individually engineered. Boeing estimates the parts standardization program will save it between U.S.$2 billion and U.S.$5 billion when the program is fully implemented.

Boeing's pricing program has increased interest among airlines in newer planes that are more fuel efficient, have better seat configurations, and fully meet new noise abatement standards at major airports. Airlines that might not have considered buying or leasing new planes are expressing greater enthusiasm. Furthermore, the pace of negotiations with such firms as International Lease Corp., the largest lessor of new aircraft, has increased. The firm plans to buy forty to fifty new 737 jets from Boeing.

An example of Boeing's new aggressiveness can be seen in how it won an order for forty-one planes from Scandinavian Airlines System (SAS). By some accounts, Boeing and its engine supplier, General Electric, agreed to sell the 100-passenger 737-600 jets for about U.S.$20 million each, a 38 per cent discount from the list price. The sale was particularly disheartening to McDonnell Douglas because SAS had been that firm's most loyal customer. Boeing's Robert Woodward remarked that his firm won the sale because "the value of our product was better."

And Boeing is so committed to its value pricing plan that it intends to give up some of the escalator clauses it has placed in long-term aircraft contracts (to protect itself against the effects of inflation).[1]

In this chapter, we will learn more about the importance of price and its relationship with other marketing variables. We will also examine factors affecting pricing decisions: consumers, costs, government, channel members, and competition.

Overview

Through **price planning**, *each* **price** *places a value on a good or service.*

A **price** represents the value of a good or service for both the seller and the buyer. **Price planning** is systematic decision making by an organization regarding all aspects of pricing.

The value of a good or service can involve both tangible and intangible factors. An example of a tangible factor is the cost saving to a soda distributor from buying a new bottling machine; and an example of an intangible factor is a consumer's pride in owning a Porsche rather than another brand of car.

---

[1] Jeff Cole, "Boeing Is Offering Cuts in Prices of New Jets, Rattling the Industry," *Wall Street Journal* (April 24, 1995), pp. A1, A6; and Lawrence M. Fisher, "Boeing Beats Rival for $12.7 Billion Order," *New York Times* (November 15, 1995), pp. D1, D7.

FIGURE 21-1
The Role of Price in Balancing Supply and Demand

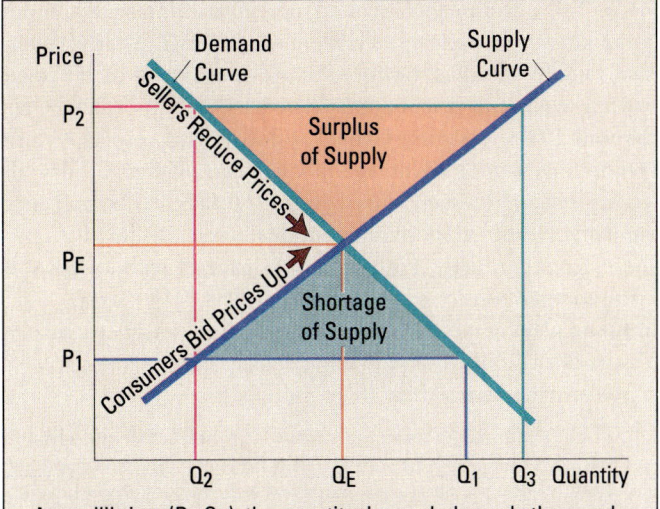

At equilibrium (P_E Q_E), the quantity demanded equals the supply. At price P_1, consumers demand Q_1 of an item. However, at this price, suppliers will make available only Q_2. There is a shortage of supply of Q_1 - Q_2. The price is bid up as consumers seek to buy greater quantities than offered at P_1.

At price P_2, suppliers will make available Q_3 of an item. However, at this price, consumers demand only Q_2. There is a surplus of supply of Q_3 - Q_2. The price is reduced by sellers in order to attract greater demand by consumers.

For an exchange to take place, both buyer and seller must feel that the price of a good or service provides an equitable ("fair") value. To the buyer, the payment of a price reduces the purchasing power available for other items. To the seller, the receipt of a price is a source of revenue and a key determinant of sales and profit levels.

Many words are substitutes for the term *price*, including admission fee, membership fee, rate, tuition, service charge, donation, rent, salary, interest, retainer, and assessment. No matter what it is called, a price refers to all the terms of purchase: monetary and nonmonetary charges, discounts, handling and shipping fees, credit charges and other forms of interest, and late-payment penalties.

A nonmonetary exchange would be a department store awarding a gift to a person who gets a friend to shop at that store, or an airline offering tickets as payment for advertising space and time. Monetary and nonmonetary exchanges may be combined. This is common with autos, where the buyer gives the seller money plus a trade-in. That combination leads to a lower monetary price.

From a broader perspective, price is the mechanism for allocating goods and services among potential buyers and for ensuring competition among sellers in an open marketplace. If demand exceeds supply, prices are usually bid up by consumers. If supply exceeds demand, prices are usually reduced by sellers. See Figure 21-1.

In this chapter, the importance of price and its relationship to other marketing variables, price-based and nonprice-based approaches, and the factors affecting price decisions are studied. Chapter 22 deals with devising and enacting a price strategy, and applying techniques for setting prices.

The Importance of Price and Its Relationship to Other Marketing Variables

The importance of price decisions has risen considerably over the last thirty years. First, because price in a monetary or nonmonetary form is a component of the exchange process, it appears in every marketing transaction. More firms now realize the impact of price on

The stature of price decisions has risen because more firms recognize their far-reaching impact.

image, sales, and profits. Second, deregulation in several industries has led to more price competition among firms. Third, in the 1970s and early 1980s, Canadian costs and prices rose rapidly—leading both firms and consumers to be price-conscious. In some other nations, costs and prices continue to escalate very quickly. Fourth, in the 1970s through the mid-1980s, a strong Canadian dollar with respect to other currencies gave foreign competitors a price advantage in Canadian markets. Today, the Canadian dollar is much weaker relative to such currencies as the U.S. dollar and the Japanese yen; and a larger number of firms monitor international currency fluctuations and adapt their marketing strategies accordingly. Fifth, the rapid pace of technological advances has caused intense price competition for such products as PCs, CD players, and VCRs. Sixth, service-based firms are placing more emphasis on how they set prices. Seventh, in slow economic times, it is hard for firms to raise prices.

Many marketers share this view:

> Pricing is a manager's biggest marketing headache. It's where they feel the most pressure to perform and the least certain that they are doing a good job. The pressure is intensified because, for the most part, managers believe they don't have control over price: It is dictated by the market. Moreover, pricing is often seen as a difficult area in which to set goals and measure results. Ask managers to define the firm's manufacturing function, and they will cite a concrete goal, such as output and cost. Ask for a measure of productivity, and they will refer to cycle times. But pricing is hard to pin down. High unit sales and increased market share sound promising, but they may in fact mean a price is too low. And foregone profits do not appear on any scorecard.[2]

Inasmuch as a price places a value on the overall marketing mix offered to consumers (such as product features, product image, store location, and customer service), pricing decisions must be made in conjunction with product, distribution, and promotion plans. For instance, Parfums de Coeur makes imitations of expensive perfumes from Chanel, Estée Lauder, and Giorgio and sells them for one-third to one-fifth the price of those perfumes. It uses similar ingredients but saves on packaging, advertising, and personal selling costs. It distributes through such mass merchandisers as K-mart.

These are some basic ways in which pricing is related to other marketing and company variables:

- Prices ordinarily vary over the life of a product category, from high prices to gain status-conscious innovators to lower prices to lure the mass market.
- Customer service is affected since low prices are often associated with less customer service.
- From a distribution perspective, the prices charged to resellers must adequately compensate them for their functions, yet be low enough to compete with other brands at the wholesale or retail level.
- There may be conflict in a distribution channel if a manufacturer tries to control or suggest final prices.
- Product lines with different features—and different prices—can attract different market segments.
- A sales force may need some flexibility in negotiating prices and terms, particularly with large business accounts.
- The roles of marketing and finance personnel must be coordinated. Marketers often begin with the prices that people are willing to pay and work backward to ascertain acceptable company costs. Finance people typically start with costs and add desired profits to set prices.
- As costs change, the firm must decide whether to pass these changes on to consumers, absorb them, or modify product features.

[2] Robert J. Dolan, "How Do You Know When the Price Is Right?" *Harvard Business Review*, Vol. 73 (September–October 1995), p. 174.

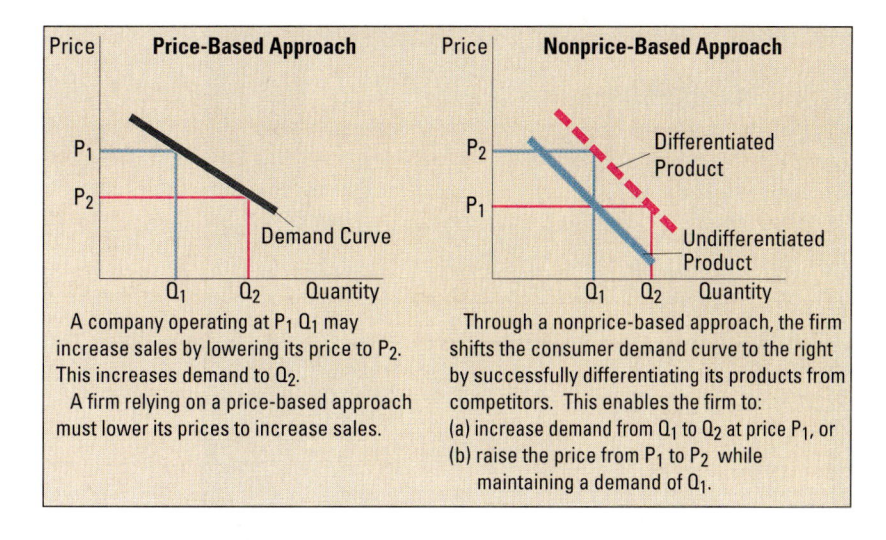

FIGURE 21-2
Price-Based and Nonprice-Based Approaches

For firms marketing products in foreign countries, "One of the most significant and perplexing of decisions has to do with pricing. Determining what prices to charge and when to change those prices are almost always tough decisions, but they become even more complicated when a company begins offering products to customers in several international markets." The greater complexity is typically due to the divergent company goals in different markets, the varying attributes of each market, and other factors. Furthermore, the ability to set prices in foreign markets may be affected by variations in government rules, competition, currency exchange rates, anti-dumping laws, operating costs, the rate of inflation, the standard of living, and so on.[3]

Pricing internationally can be quite complicated.

Price-Based and Nonprice-Based Approaches

With a **price-based approach**, sellers influence consumer demand primarily through changes in price levels. With a **nonprice-based approach**, sellers downplay price as a factor in consumer demand by creating a distinctive good or service by means of promotion, packaging, delivery, customer service, availability, and other marketing factors. The more unique a product offering is perceived to be by consumers, the greater a firm's freedom to set prices above competitors'. See Figure 21-2.

In a price-based approach, sellers move along a demand curve by raising or lowering prices. This is a flexible marketing technique because prices can be adjusted quickly and easily to reflect demand, cost, or competitive factors. Yet, of all the controllable marketing variables, price is the easiest for a competitor to copy. This may result in "me-too" strategies or even in price wars. Furthermore, the government may monitor anti-competitive aspects of price-based strategies.

In a nonprice-based approach, sellers shift consumer demand curves by stressing the distinctive attributes of their products. This lets firms increase unit sales at a given price or sell their original supply at a higher price. The risk with a nonprice strategy is that consumers may not perceive a seller's product as better than a competitor's. People would then buy the lower-priced item.

These are examples of price- and nonprice-oriented strategies:

- It was called "Grape Nuts Monday," April 15, 1996, the day that Post cereals in the United States rolled back the retail prices of its cereals by 20 per cent in response to severe price competition from private label brands. Canadian consumers were anxiously awaiting a similar move in Canada but were disappointed. When asked about

*A **price-based approach** occurs when sellers stress low prices; a **nonprice-based approach** emphasizes factors other than price.*

---

[3]James K. Weekly, "Pricing in Foreign Markets: Pitfalls and Opportunities," *Industrial Marketing Management*, Vol. 21 (May 1992), pp. 173–179.

FIGURE 21-3
Lenox's Nonprice-Oriented Strategy
Reprinted by permission. Not to be reproduced without authorization of Lenox China and Crystal.

the situation, one manager said, "we have no plans to reduce prices. In fact, the U.S. reduction, generally speaking, brings U.S. list prices in line with (ours)." An independent industry observer supported this statement by commenting that U.S. price points are now comparable to Canadian price points. Private label competition has always been strong in Canada, holding about 10 per cent of the market; consequently the market impact on prices had already been registered here.[4]

- Lenox makes fine china and crystal, which are elegant and expensive. Ads rarely mention price, but focus on product quality and design. "Lenox—Because art is not an extravagance" is one of its slogans. See Figure 21-3.

- Gucci is the Italian designer/manufacturer of upscale fashion accessories. ("Everyone in Hollywood has to have Gucci's velvet hip-huggers—and the suede loafers with the classic horse's bit on top of a lug sole are selling as fast as Gucci can deliver them.") Its shoes are priced from $160 to $1050, handbags go for $335 to $8995, and women's apparel prices are $110 to $9000. The company recently scrapped some of its cheaper items, such as canvas and plastic handbags.[5]

Factors Affecting Pricing Decisions

Before a firm develops a pricing strategy (which is described in Chapter 22), it should analyze the outside factors affecting decisions. Like distribution planning, pricing depends heavily on elements external to the firm. This contrasts with product and promotion decisions, which, with the exception of publicity, are more controlled by a firm. Sometimes,

---

[4]James Pollock, "Canada Skips Cereal Cuts," *Marketing Magazine* (April 29, 1996), p. 6.
[5]John Tagliabue, "Gucci Gains Ground with Revival of Style," *New York Times* (December 14, 1995), pp. D1, D6.

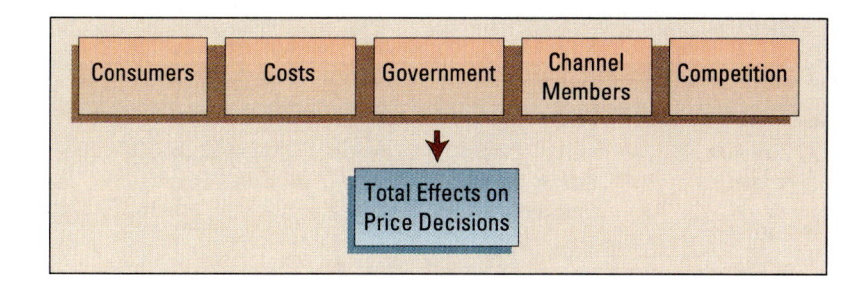

FIGURE 21-4
Factors Affecting Price Decisions

outside elements greatly influence the firm's ability to set prices; in other cases, they have little impact. Figure 21-4 outlines the major factors, which are discussed next.

Consumers

Company personnel involved with pricing decisions must understand the relationship between price and consumer purchases and perceptions. This relationship is explained by two economic principles—the law of demand and the price elasticity of demand—and by market segmentation.

The **law of demand** states that consumers usually purchase more units at a low price than at a high price. The **price elasticity of demand** indicates the sensitivity of buyers to price changes in terms of the quantities they will purchase.[6]

Price elasticity represents the percentage change in the quantity demanded relative to a specific percentage change in the price charged. This formula shows the percentage change in demand for each one per cent change in price:

$$\text{Price elasticity} = \frac{\dfrac{\text{Quantity 1} - \text{Quantity 2}}{\text{Quantity 1} + \text{Quantity 2}}}{\dfrac{\text{Price 1} - \text{Price 2}}{\text{Price 1} + \text{Price 2}}}$$

*According to the **law of demand**, more is bought at low prices; **price elasticity** explains reactions to changes.*

Because the quantity demanded usually falls as price rises, elasticity is a negative number. However, for purposes of simplicity, elasticity calculations are usually expressed as positive numbers.

Elastic demand occurs if relatively small changes in price result in large changes in quantity demanded. Numerically, price elasticity is greater than 1. With elastic demand, total revenue goes up when prices are decreased and goes down when prices rise. **Inelastic demand** takes place if price changes have little impact on the quantity demanded. Price elasticity is less than 1. With inelastic demand, total revenue goes up when prices are raised and goes down when prices decline. **Unitary demand** exists if price changes are exactly offset by changes in the quantity demanded, so total sales revenue remains constant. Price elasticity is 1.

*Demand may be **elastic, inelastic,** or **unitary** depending on the availability of substitutes and urgency of need.*

Demand elasticity is based mostly on two criteria: availability of substitutes and urgency of need. If people *believe* there are many similar goods or services from which to choose or have no urgency to buy, demand is elastic and greatly influenced by price changes: Price increases lead to purchases of substitutes or delayed purchases, and decreases expand sales as people are drawn from competitors or move up the date of their purchases. For some people, the airfare for a vacation is highly elastic. If prices go up, they may travel to a nearer location by car or postpone a trip.

---

[6] See N. Carroll Mohn, "Price Research for Decision Making," *Marketing Research* (Winter 1995), pp. 11–19; Stephen J. Hoch, Byung-Do Kim, Alan L. Montgomery, and Peter E. Rossi, "Determinants of Store-Level Price Elasticity," *Journal of Marketing Research*, Vol. 32 (February 1995), pp. 17–29; and Francis J. Mulhern and Robert P. Leone, "Measuring Market Response to Price Changes: A Classification Approach," *Journal of Business Research*, Vol. 33 (July 1995), pp. 197–205.

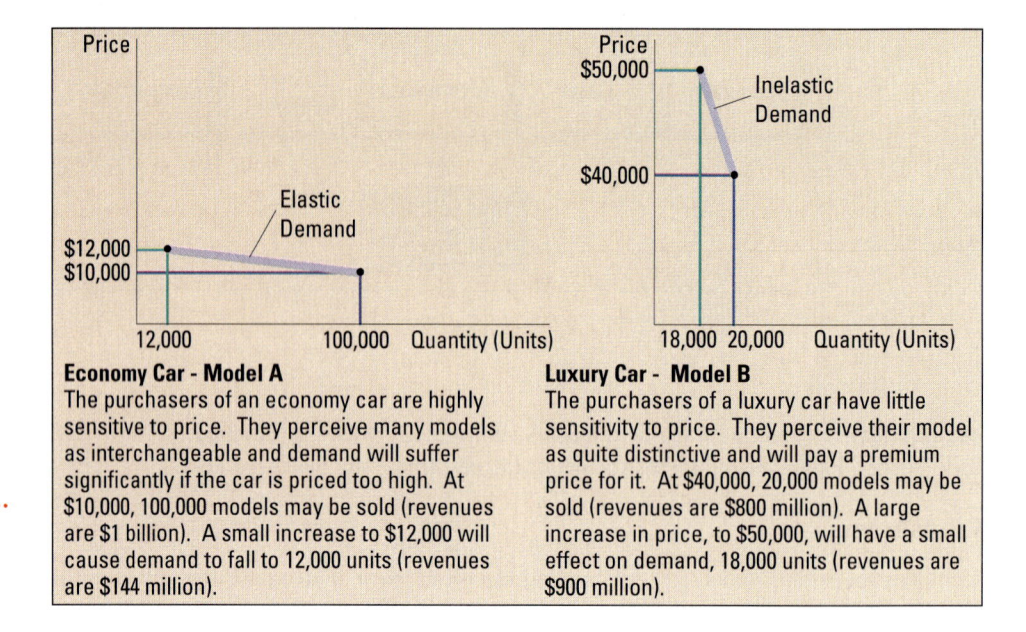

FIGURE 21-5
Demand Elasticity for Two Models of Automobiles

Economy Car - Model A
The purchasers of an economy car are highly sensitive to price. They perceive many models as interchangeable and demand will suffer significantly if the car is priced too high. At $10,000, 100,000 models may be sold (revenues are $1 billion). A small increase to $12,000 will cause demand to fall to 12,000 units (revenues are $144 million).

Luxury Car - Model B
The purchasers of a luxury car have little sensitivity to price. They perceive their model as quite distinctive and will pay a premium price for it. At $40,000, 20,000 models may be sold (revenues are $800 million). A large increase in price, to $50,000, will have a small effect on demand, 18,000 units (revenues are $900 million).

If consumers believe a firm's offering is unique or there is an urgency to buy, demand is inelastic and little influenced by price changes: neither price increases nor declines will have much impact on demand. In most locales, when heating oil prices go up or down, demand remains relatively constant because there is often no feasible substitute—and homes and offices must be properly heated. Brand loyalty also generates inelastic demand; consumers then feel their brands are distinctive and do not accept substitutes. Finally, emergency conditions increase demand inelasticity. A truck driver with a flat tire would pay more for a replacement than a driver with time to shop around. Figure 21-5 illustrates elastic and inelastic demand.

It should be noted that demand elasticity usually varies over a wide range of prices for the same good or service. At very high prices, even revenues for essential goods and services may fall (mass-transit ridership would drop a lot if fares rose from $1.50 to $3; driving would become a more reasonable substitute). At very low prices, demand cannot be stimulated further; market saturation is reached and consumers may begin to perceive quality as inferior.

Table 21-1 shows the price-elasticity calculations for an office-equipment repair business. There is a clear relationship between price and demand. At the lowest price, $60, daily demand is greatest: ten service calls. At the highest price, $120, demand is lowest: five service calls. Demand is inelastic between $60 and $84; total service-call revenues (price x quantity) rise as price increases. Demand is unitary between $84 and $96; total service-call revenues remain the same ($672). Demand is elastic between $96 and $120; total service-call revenues decline as the price rises within this range.

Although a fee of either $84 or $96 yields the highest total service-call revenues, $672, other criteria must be evaluated before selecting a price. The repair firm in Table 21-1 should consider costs per service call; the number of servicepeople required at different levels of demand; the overall revenues generated by each service call, including parts and additional labour charges; travel time; the percentage of satisfied customers at different prices, as expressed by repeat business; and the potential for new-customer referrals.

Consumers can be segmented in terms of their price orientation.

Price sensitivity varies by market segment because all people are not equally price-conscious. Consumers can be divided into such segments as these:

- *Price shoppers*—They are interested in the "best deal" for a product.
- *Brand-loyal customers*—They believe their current brands are better than others and will pay "fair" prices for those products.
- *Status seekers*—They buy prestigious brands and product categories and will pay whatever prices are set; higher prices signify greater status.

Table 21-1
Price Elasticity for Service Calls by an Office-Equipment Repair Business

PRICE OF SERVICE CALL	SERVICE CALLS DEMANDED PER DAY	REVENUES FROM SERVICE CALLS	PRICE ELASTICITY OF DEMAND[a]	TYPE OF DEMAND
$60.00	10	$600.00		
			$E = \frac{(10-9)}{(10+9)} / \frac{(\$60-\$72)}{(\$60+\$72)} = 0.58$	Inelastic
$72.00	9	$648.00		
			$E = \frac{(9-8)}{(9+8)} / \frac{(\$72-\$84)}{(\$72+\$84)} = 0.76$	Inelastic
$84.00	8	$672.00		
			$E = \frac{(8-7)}{(8+7)} / \frac{(\$84-\$96)}{(\$84+\$96)} = 1.00$	Unitary
$96.00	7	$672.00		
			$E = \frac{(7-6)}{(7+6)} / \frac{(\$96-\$108)}{(\$96+\$108)} = 1.31$	Elastic
$108.00	6	$648.00		
			$E = \frac{(6-5)}{(6+5)} / \frac{(\$108-\$120)}{(\$108+\$120)} = 1.73$	Elastic
$120.00	5	$600.00		

[a]Expressed as positive numbers.

- *Service/features shoppers*—They place a great value on customer service and/or product features and will pay for them.
- *Convenience shoppers*—They value ease of shopping, nearby locations, long hours by sellers, and other approaches that make shopping simple; they will pay above-average prices.

A firm must determine which segment or segments are represented by its target market and plan accordingly.

The consumer's (market segment's) perception of the price of a good or service as being high, fair, or low—its **subjective price**—may be more important than its actual price. For example, a consumer may feel a low price represents a good buy or inferior quality—or a high price represents status or poor value.

The following factors affect a consumer's (market segment's) subjective price:

- *Purchase experience with a particular good or service*—"How much have I paid in the past?"
- *Purchase experience with other, similar goods or services*—"What's a fair price for an item in the same or adjacent product category that I bought before?"

A consumer's perception of a price level is the **subjective price**.

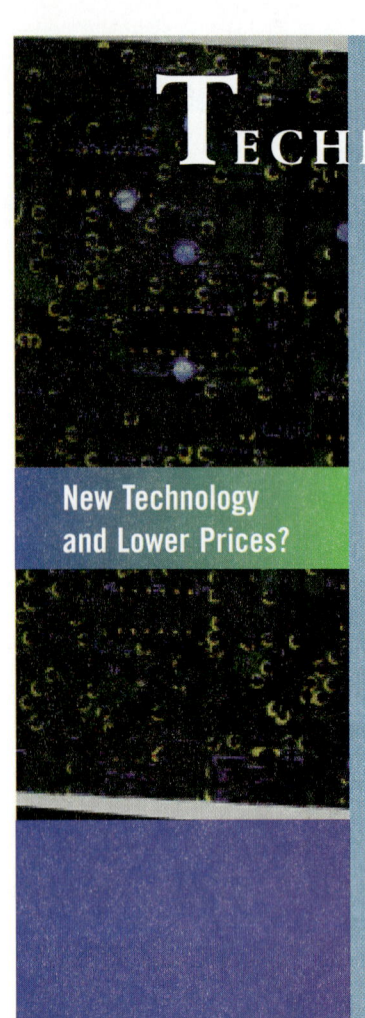

TECHNOLOGY & MARKETING

New Technology and Lower Prices?

Three years ago, when Computer Associates introduced its *Simply Money* accounting software, the firm decided to offer the package free of charge to consumers. Computer Associates correctly assumed the favourable publicity that a no-cost offer would generate was worth much more than the cost of producing the diskettes. Furthermore, Computer Associates felt the zero-price strategy would increase its database of customers, creating a ready-made market for upgrades and other programs.

According to marketing experts, the massive cost reductions attributable to new technologies now call for a redefinition of value. These experts say that companies need to establish long-term relationships with customers—even if it means giving the first generation of a product away for free.

Companies are reacting to the combination of declining costs and better product quality by using radically different marketing strategies. For example, due to their market dominance, Intel and Microsoft have kept above-average prices compared to smaller competitors. And while clone makers like Packard Bell compete mostly on price, firms such as Compaq and Dell look to differentiate their products by offering superior customer service, distinctive product features, and more competitive prices.

In many instances, technological growth has been so great that it has played havoc with pricing. For example, the sound quality of inexpensive CD players is so good that some consumers use them instead of costly audio systems. And a five-dollar quartz watch is as accurate as a model costing 100 times its price.

An executive with the Japan Institute of Office Automation says these advances create real pricing dilemmas. He asks, "How do you assign prices or value in a world where quality is perfect and nothing breaks?"

As a Computer Associates marketing executive, under what conditions would you recommend another product giveaway? When would you avoid giveaways? Why?

Source: Based on material in Neil Gross, Peter Coy, and Otis Port, "The Technology Paradox," *Business Week* (March 6, 1995), pp. 76–84.

DELL
www.us.dell.com/

CANTEL
www.rogers.com/

- *Self-image*—"How much should a person like me pay for something like this?"
- *Social situation*—"How much do the people around me expect me to pay for something like this?"
- *Context of the purchase*—"What should this cost in these circumstances?"[7]

Consumers have generally perceived cellular phones as expensive luxury items. To change this perception Cantel has promoted its "Amigo" brand phone with 10-cent-a-minute calling during off-peak phone hours. The idea is to make consumers perceive cellular phones as being more affordable. In fact, Cantel and Bell Mobility have been hammering the affordability point so hard that people can now get the actual cellular phones for "free" with 100 minutes of free air time. With the phone in hand customers need only pay monthly charges and for any calling time after the first 100 minutes.[8]

Costs

The costs of raw materials, supplies, labour, transportation, and other items are commonly beyond a firm's control. Yet, they have a great impact on prices.

---

[7]Ray Funkhouser, "Using Consumer Expectations as an Input to Pricing Decisions," *Journal of Product & Brand Management*, Vol. 1 (Spring 1992), p. 48. See also Richard W. Olshavsky, Andrew B. Aylesworth, and DeAnna S. Kempf, "The Price-Choice Relationship: A Contingent Processing Approach," *Industrial Marketing Management*, Vol. 33 (July 1995), pp. 207–218; and John R. Johnson, "How Valuable Is Value Added?" *Industrial Distribution* (May 1995), pp. 35–38.

[8]News Line, "Cantel Plays Up Affordability in Promo," *Marketing Magazine* (April 17, 1995), p. 3.

In Canada, from the early 1970s into the 1980s, many costs rose rapidly and pushed prices to high levels, before levelling off. For example:

- The federal minimum wage rose from $2.00 per hour in 1972 to $4.00 per hour in 1996 (Although 1996 provincial minimum wages range from a low of $4.75 in Newfoundland to a high of $6.85 in Ontario). Minimum wage rates have their greatest impact on fast-food retailers and other firms relying on semiskilled and unskilled labour.
- Mortgage interest rates more than doubled between 1977 and 1981, severely dampening the housing market, before starting to decline in 1983. Since 1993, they have been at twenty-five-year lows.
- The cost of prime-time TV ads has gone up dramatically. For example, the most expensive commercial broadcast time on earth is an ad on the NFL's championship, the Super Bowl. A thirty-second ad on the 1972 Super Bowl cost U.S.$100 000. In 1996, the cost was U.S.$1.3 million.
- Fuel costs went up almost 500 per cent, before falling considerably in 1985 and 1986. This placed pressure on airlines, the trucking industry, and the auto industry. Since then, with scattered fluctuations, fuel costs have increased only a little—and, sometimes even declined.
- Silver and gold prices were very volatile. Silver went from U.S.$6 per ounce to more than U.S.$50 per ounce, before dropping down. This caused problems for the photography industry, which uses silver as an ingredient in film. In 1996, silver was selling for U.S.$5 to U.S.$7 per ounce. Gold went from U.S.$45 per ounce to U.S.$1000 per ounce, before settling at U.S.$300 to U.S.$500 per ounce. This affected dentists and jewellers.

Over the past fifteen years, overall Canadian cost increases have been rather low. Although the 1980 inflation rate was 15 per cent, the 1996 rate was under 5 per cent. This means better cost control and more stable prices for most firms. Yet, unexpected events can still strike specific industries. As an example, a few years ago, the price of rhodium, a precious metal used to make catalytic converters for cars, rose rapidly from U.S.$1750 to U.S.$7000 per ounce due to problems at a refinery. Rhodium's cost per car went from U.S.$15 to U.S.$60.[9]

During periods of rapidly rising costs, firms can react in several ways: they can leave products unchanged and pass along all of their cost increases to consumers; leave products unchanged and pass along part of the cost increases and absorb part of them; modify products to hold down costs and maintain prices (by reducing size, using lesser-quality materials, or offering fewer options); modify products to gain consumer support for higher prices (by increasing size, using better-quality materials, offering more options, or upgrading customer service); and/or abandon unprofitable products. For instance, in response to a 50 to 60 per cent increase in the cost of pulp paper, Scott decided to reduce the number of sheets in the smallest roll of Scott Clean paper towels from 96 to 60—and *lower* the price by 10 per cent.[10]

When costs rise, companies pass along increases, alter products, or delete some items.

Despite a firm's or an industry's best efforts, it sometimes takes years to get runaway costs (and prices) under control. A good illustration is the North American auto industry, where costs and prices have risen substantially since 1970. The average new car had a retail price of under U.S.$3500 then; the average price now is over U.S.$17 000. Among the costs that auto executives have had to deal with are billions of dollars in retooling from large to small cars; high fixed costs for plant, equipment, and unionized labour; hundreds of millions of dollars for anti-pollution and safety devices; and investments of up to U.S.$1 billion or more to develop each major new model. Therefore, pricing decisions have to be made far in advance; and flexibility is limited.

If costs decline, firms can drop selling prices or raise profit margins, as these examples show: the use of microchips has reduced PC costs by requiring less wiring and assembly time in production, improving durability, and enlarging information-processing capability.

Cost decreases have mostly positive benefits for marketing strategies.

---

[9] "Scarce Metal Hits $7000 an Ounce," *New York Times* (July 4, 1990), pp. 43, 48.
[10] Chad Rubel, "Marketers Try to Ease Sting of Price Increases," *Marketing News* (October 9, 1995), pp. 5–6.

PC prices have gone down steadily, thus expanding the market. On the other hand, low sugar prices let candy makers increase package size (and profits) without raising prices.

Sometimes, low costs can actually have a negative long-run impact:

> Since the oil price collapse of 1986, years of relatively cheap energy prices have brought the march toward greater efficiency to a virtual halt. And that has stymied the efforts to temper the indirect social and economic costs associated with energy use: increased dependence on foreign oil, which retards progress in cutting the trade deficit, and pollution and environmental damage—including the uncertain but potentially catastrophic effects of global warming.[11]

Government[12]

Canada's Competition Act regulates pricing behaviour with criminal and non-criminal provisions.

Canadian federal government actions related to pricing are set out in the Competition Act and fall into two major areas: criminal provisions and non-criminal provisions, as shown in Figure 21-6. The Competition Act became law in June 1986 and replaced the former Combines Investigation Act. Criminal provisions related to pricing include: conspiracy, bid-rigging, discriminatory and predatory pricing, price maintenance, and misleading advertising (with respect to price). Non-criminal matters include: refusal to deal, consignment selling, exclusive dealing, tied selling, and delivered pricing. Criminal provisions mean that matters with respect to these practices are normally dealt with through the court system. Non-criminal matters go before the Competition Tribunal which is empowered to issue injunctions. Finally, individuals or firms can file civil suits if they have suffered damages due to anti-competitive behaviour in the market place.

Criminal Provisions

Conspiracy to price fix *results from agreements among companies at the same stage in a channel to control resale prices.*

CONSPIRACY TO PRICE FIX There are restrictions on price fixing among competitors. Often referred to as horizontal price fixing, it results from agreements among manufacturers, among wholesalers, or among retailers to set prices at a given stage in a channel of distribution. Such agreements are illegal according to the Competition Act, regardless of how "reasonable" prices are.

When violations are found, federal penalties can be severe: For example the legislation allows maximum penalties of fines as high as $10 million or imprisonment of up to five years, or both. In practice the penalties are usually less. For example, in 1994–95 the average fine for violations of the Competition Act was $61 191 per case, or $39 094 for each person accused. These fines were twice the level of those levied in the previous five years.[13]

In January 1996, thirteen individuals and ten companies in Edmonton were charged with price fixing on real estate property reports for resale homes. These reports were required before real estate transactions could be completed and prior to the price fixing arrangement the base price was $250 and negotiable. It was alleged that after the price fixing agreement, prices rose to $325 for these reports and they were not negotiated.[14]

To avoid price-fixing charges, a firm must be careful not to:

- Coordinate discounts, credit terms, or conditions of sale with competitors.
- Talk about price levels, markups, and costs at trade association meetings.
- Plan with competitors to issue new price lists on the same date.
- Plan with competitors to rotate low bids on contracts.
- Agree with competitors to limit production to keep high prices.
- Exchange information with competitors, even informally.

---

[11]"Why Lower Energy Prices Can Be a Mixed Blessing," *Business Week* (February 8, 1993), p. 16.

[12]Unless otherwise stated, information in this section is based on: Industry Canada, "Canada's Competition Act: An Overview," Industry Canada *Strategis* Web site (1996), http://strategis.ic.gc.ca/sc_mrksv/competit/engdoc/homepage.html.

[13]Industry Canada, "Strategic Approach to Marketing Practices Matters Yields Results," Industry Canada *Strategis* Web site (July 12, 1996), http://strategis.ic.gc.ca/sc_mrksv/competit/engdoc/homepage.html; and Industry Canada, "Canada's Competition Act: An Overview," Industry Canada *Strategis* Web site (June 12, 1996), http://strategis.ic.gc.ca/sc_mrksv/competit/engdoc/homepage.html.

[14]Industry Canada, "Enforcement: Current Activities," Industry Canada *Strategis* Web site (May 22, 1996), http://strategis.ic.gc.ca/sc_mrksv/competit/engdoc/homepage.html.

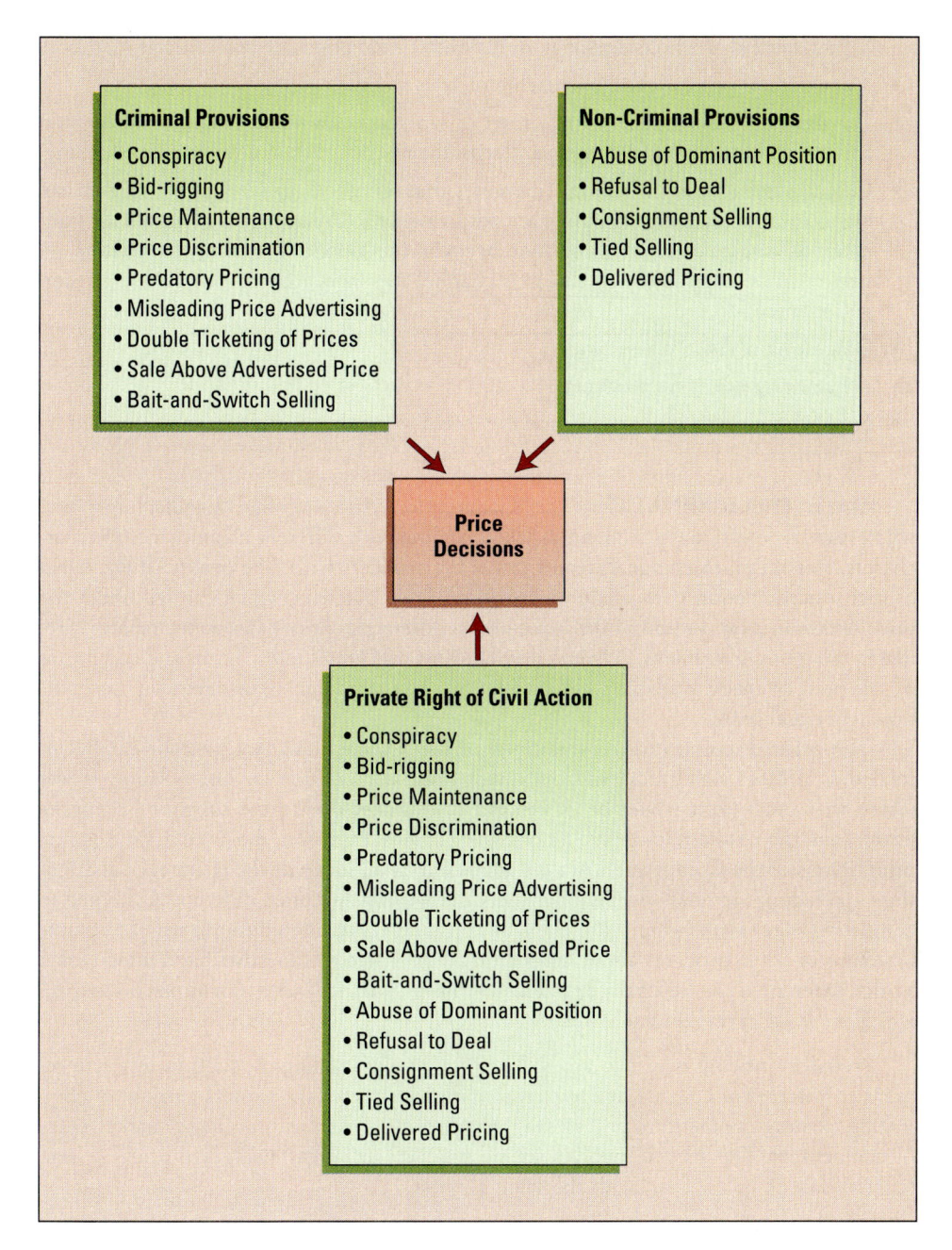

FIGURE 21-6
Canadian Legislative Regulations Affecting Price Decisions

Criminal Provisions
- Conspiracy
- Bid-rigging
- Price Maintenance
- Price Discrimination
- Predatory Pricing
- Misleading Price Advertising
- Double Ticketing of Prices
- Sale Above Advertised Price
- Bait-and-Switch Selling

Non-Criminal Provisions
- Abuse of Dominant Position
- Refusal to Deal
- Consignment Selling
- Tied Selling
- Delivered Pricing

Private Right of Civil Action
- Conspiracy
- Bid-rigging
- Price Maintenance
- Price Discrimination
- Predatory Pricing
- Misleading Price Advertising
- Double Ticketing of Prices
- Sale Above Advertised Price
- Bait-and-Switch Selling
- Abuse of Dominant Position
- Refusal to Deal
- Consignment Selling
- Tied Selling
- Delivered Pricing

→ **Price Decisions**

Bid-rigging is very much akin to conspiracy. Bidders collude together or collude with the party offering the bid tender to restrain competition or to inflate bids. It may result in some competitors not submitting bids or in one competitor being given preferential bid treatment.

Price maintenanc occurs when manufacturers or wholesalers seek to control the final selling prices of their goods or services. Price maintenance is also known as fair trade, resale price maintenance, and vertical price fixing. It originated out of a desire by manufacturers and wholesalers to protect small resellers and maintain brand images by forcing all resellers within a given area to charge the same price for affected products. Price maintenance was criticized by consumer groups and many resellers and manufacturers as being noncompetitive, keeping prices too high, and rewarding reseller inefficiency.

The use of price maintenance has been illegal in Canada since 1951. Under the Competition Act, resellers cannot be forced to adhere to manufacturer or wholesaler list prices.

*With **bid-rigging**, bidders collude with tendering parties to inflate bids.*

Price maintenance *occurs when manufacturers or wholesalers seek to control final retail selling prices.*

Manufacturers or wholesalers may only control final prices by one of these methods:

- Manufacturer or wholesaler ownership of sales facilities.
- Consignment selling. The manufacturer or wholesaler owns items until they are sold and assumes costs normally associated with the reseller, such as advertising and selling.
- Careful screening of the channel members that sell goods or services. A supplier can bypass or drop distributors if they are not living up to the supplier's performance standards, as long as there is no collusion between the supplier and other distributors. (A firm must be careful not to threaten channel members that do not adhere to suggested prices).
- Suggesting realistic selling prices.
- Pre-printing prices on products.
- Establishing customary prices (such as 50 cents for a newspaper) that are accepted by consumers.

Price discrimination *involves charging different prices to different channel members for products of "like quality."*

PRICE DISCRIMINATION The Competition Act prohibits manufacturers and wholesalers from **price discrimination** when dealing with different channel-member purchasers. It is illegal to charge different prices for products with "like quality" if the effect of such discrimination is to injure competition. Price practices which can fall under the price discrimination portion of the Act include: differential prices, discounts, rebates, premiums, coupons, guarantees, delivery, warehousing, and credit rates. Terms and conditions of sale must be made available to all competing channel-member customers on a proportionately equal basis.

The price discrimination prohibitions of the Competition Act were originally intended to protect small retailers from unfair price competition by large chains. It was feared that small firms would be driven out of business due to the superior bargaining power (and the resultant lower selling prices) of chains. However, the price discrimination prohibitions of the Competition Act are applicable at all levels of the channel of distribution—including the retail level. Under the Competition Act price differences charged to competing purchasers (whether resellers or consumers) are limited to quantity or volume discounts or when products are of different quality. There are no other bases upon which a price differential can be legally granted and this includes so-called "functional discounts," which are legal in the United States.

Predatory pricing *involves setting low prices with the purpose of driving competitors out of business.*

Predatory pricing is of two types. The first involves selling products in different regions at different prices (not due to transportation costs) for the express purpose of eliminating existing competitors or lessening competition—such as preventing market entry of competitors. The second involves selling products at unreasonably low prices (essentially at cost or below cost) with the same purpose.

Regulations on **double ticketing** *ensure that when a product has two different prices, consumers pay the lowest price.*

DOUBLE PRICE TICKETING The **double ticketing** provision states that when two prices are marked on an item (as often occurs with sale products) it is illegal to charge the higher price.

Marketers are not allowed to make **sales above advertised prices.**

SALE ABOVE ADVERTISED PRICE When an item is advertised in the media at a special price (assuming the price was not a misprint), the marketer is obliged to honour that price according to the terms of the advertising. Charging higher prices to individuals who have not heard of the sale or refusing to honour the price for individuals who have heard of the sale is a violation of the Competition Act.

Under **bait-and-switch selling,** *sellers illegally draw customers by deceptive pricing.*

Bait-and-switch selling is the intended practice of advertising a bargain price on a sale item and then not carrying a sufficient supply to satisfy the created demand. The intention is to "switch" customers to other, higher priced items. Signs of bait-and-switch are a refusal to demonstrate sale items, the belittling of sale items, inadequate quantities of sale items on hand, a refusal to take orders, demonstrations of defective items, and the use of compensation plans encouraging salespeople to use the tactic. However, advertisers can avoid violating this regulation by stating the quantity available, offering rainchecks during the sale, or making a reasonable attempt to obtain a large enough quantity.

Ethics ETHICS AND TODAY'S MARKETER

Can Pricing Be More Consumer Friendly?

Some marketing critics compare the buying of products such as liquid detergent to tricky high school math problems. For example, which is cheaper, a 1.5-litre bottle of regular liquid detergent at $4.99 or a 900 mL bottle of concentrated liquid detergent at $3.49?

If the concentrated detergent washes the same amount of clothes as the regular version, it is cheaper. Unfortunately, many consumers still mistakenly buy the regular detergent, incorrectly believing that a larger-sized bottle washes more clothes. This matter is significant since concentrated liquid detergent now accounts for 60 per cent of the total liquid and powder detergent market.

In stores with unit pricing, only the price per ounce may been shown on supermarket shelves—despite the fact that the 1.5-litre bottle and the 900-mL bottle each clean sixteen laundry loads. Thus, although the 1.5-litre bottle's unit price is .33 cents per mL versus .38 cents per mL for the concentrated version, by the washload, the larger bottle costs 31 cents as compared with 22 cents for the concentrated version. This means that in addition to encouraging consumers to purchase a more costly product, the larger size package is also worse for the environment.

Resolving this problem is not easy because it requires that the members of the Soap and Detergent Association set a standard to define exactly what constitutes a "washload." Some supermarket chains have tried to compute unit prices on the basis of washloads despite the absence of standards, but most of the chains continue to compute unit prices based on ounces. The genesis of the problem seems to be the manufacturers themselves, who keep changing their products and the packaging. These constant changes make it hard for consumers to establish a frame of reference for comparing products and makes it hard for supermarkets to set unit pricing standards.

As a vice-president of consumer affairs for a major supermarket chain, develop a strategy for the unit pricing of detergents.

Source: Based on material in "Consumer-Friendly Labels Sought for Laundry Soap," *Marketing News* (January 30, 1995), p. 9.

MISLEADING PRICE ADVERTISING For consumers, the Competition Act has its most visible impact with respect to **misleading price advertising**. In particular, regulating advertising with respect to regular prices is a key consideration in the Competition Act.

The Competition Bureau offers a Program of Advisory Opinions from which marketers can receive advice on their approach to pricing and price advertising. In addition, price advertising guidelines have been developed by various trade associations, such as the Better Business Bureau. Here are some price advertising guidelines that a firm could follow to avoid contravening the Competition Act:

- Do not claim or imply that a price has been reduced from a former level unless the original price was offered to the public on a regular basis during a reasonable, recent period of time.

Regulation of **misleading price advertising** *is one of the most frequently enforced provisions of the Competition Act.*

The Program of Advisory Opinions provides advice to marketers on pricing and price advertising.

- Do not claim a price is lower than that of competitors or the manufacturer's list price without verifying, through price comparisons involving large quantities of merchandise, that an item's price at other companies in the same trading area is in fact higher.
- A suggested list price or a pre-marked price cannot be advertised as a reference point for a sale or a comparison with other products unless the advertised product has really been sold at that price.
- Bargain offers (such as "free," "buy one, get one free," and "half-price sale") are considered deceptive if their terms are not disclosed at the beginning of a sales presentation or in an ad, the stated regular price of an item is inflated to create an impression of savings, or the quality or quantity of a product is lessened without informing the consumer. A firm may not continuously advertise the same product as being on sale.

Complaints about pricing are normally made to the Competition Bureau. The director of the Competition Bureau determines whether a suspected violation of the Competition Act has occurred. The director then decides whether the suspected violation involves criminal or non-criminal provisions. Violations of any of the previously discussed criminal provisions are referred to the Attorney General of Canada for prosecution under the Act. Prosecution of firms and individuals under the criminal provisions require that strict rules of evidence be applied and cases proved beyond a reasonable doubt. However, the suspected violation may be considered under one of the non-criminal provisions which will now be discussed.

NON-CRIMINAL PROVISIONS Non-criminal matters go before the Competition Tribunal, which is empowered to issue injunctions to stop the practices. The normal rules of evidence which apply in court cases do not apply in proceedings undertaken by the Competition Tribunal, although firms do have recourse through the court system if they so desire. Let's look at some of the pricing practices subject to the non-criminal provisions of the Competition Act.

Large firms who sell products below cost to eliminate competition are guilty of **abuse of dominant position**.

ABUSE OF DOMINANT POSITION The competitive actions of firms who have a dominant position in sectors of the Canadian marketplace can adversely affect their competitors and lessen competition in the marketplace. Pricing considerations that involve **abuse of dominant position** include purchasing products to prevent the reduction of existing price levels and selling articles at a price lower than the acquisition cost to discipline or eliminate a competitor. When this practice involves a sale to a foreign market, it is referred to as product dumping. Before this provision can be enacted, it must be established that an individual or a firm does have substantial control of a class of business in Canada.

The Competition Tribunal can recommend almost any remedy that can restore the level of competition to the marketplace, including prohibiting any actions that have been lessening competition and divesting a firm of its assets to reduce its market power.

Refusal to deal *is an illegal practice that may be used to force channel members to maintain prices.*

REFUSAL TO DEAL Retailers or wholesalers might encounter a situation where a supplier will refuse to supply a product to them even though they are willing to deal under the supplier's usual trade terms and the supplier has an ample amount of products. If this **refusal to deal** is related to a dispute between the supplier and the retailer or wholesaler over price maintenance it is a violation of the Competition Act. In this case, the Competition Tribunal can order the supplier to accept the customer under the usual trade terms.

Consignment selling *is a way of ensuring price maintenance and can be used to practice price discrimination.*

Consignment selling occurs when a dealer is supplied products and only pays for what is sold, when it is sold. The dealer can return unsold goods to the supplier without any penalty. If the practice is undertaken so the supplier is able to price-discriminate between consignees and other dealers or to insure price maintenance, then it is a violation of the Competition Act. The Competition Tribunal can make an order to force the supplier to discontinue the practice.

Tied sales *are a problem when the "tied" product is unwanted.*

Tied selling is the practice wherein a supplier will only provide a product wanted by a customer on the condition that the customer agrees to purchase another type of product or refrain from purchasing a second product from another firm—in effect, tying one transaction to a second. If the tying results in less competition the Competition Tribunal can issue a prohibition order to stop the practice. Tied selling is a common approach in marketing and usually only becomes a problem when the tie is "unwanted." In this case, a firm may want only one product and find their supplier refuses to deal unless the firm accepts or rejects a second product too.

A recent case of tied selling in Canada occurred in 1992, when Digital Equipment of Canada Ltd. came under investigation by the Competition Bureau. Digital Equipment presented a stated policy that buyers could obtain lower hardware and software prices if they used the company as their sole computer service provider. The reason the situation became a tied selling case was that many of the buyers had no recourse but to use Digital because of the proprietary nature of their equipment. As such, the policy had the effect of lessening competition, particularly when competing service providers had "lower" prices for maintenance services. Digital agreed to stop the practice and since it was a matter involving a non-criminal provision, there was no admission of guilt and no further action on the part of the Competition Bureau.[15]

DIGITAL EQUIPMENT OF CANADA LTD.
www.digital.ca/

DELIVERED PRICING The practice of refusing a customer delivery on the same trade terms as similar customers in essentially the same location is a violation of **delivered pricing**. This regulation applies only if the customers have a comparable ability to receive delivery. For example, if a supplier had to make major capital investments or other accommodations to serve a customer, they could legitimately demand different trade terms. Another situation might involve products that are customarily supplied in bulk quantities on skids and off-loaded with a forklift truck to save labour. If a customer required that the product be broken down from the skids and handled manually, differential trade terms could be applied. Once again, the Competition Tribunal would make an order prohibiting the practice.

Delivered pricing *means that customers in the same geographic area should be charged the same price.*

Channel Members

Each channel member seeks to play a significant role in setting prices so as to generate sales volume, obtain adequate profit margins, create a suitable image, ensure repeat purchases, and meet specific goals.

A manufacturer can gain greater control over prices by using an exclusive distribution system or avoiding price-oriented resellers; premarking prices on products; owning sales outlets; offering products on consignment; providing adequate margins to resellers; and, most importantly, by having strong brands to which people are brand loyal and for which they will pay premium prices.

A wholesaler or retailer can gain better control over prices by stressing its importance as a customer to the supplier, linking resale support to the profit margins allowed by the supplier, refusing to carry unprofitable items, stocking competing items, having strong private brands so people are loyal to the seller and not the supplier, and purchasing outside traditional channels.

Wholesalers and retailers may engage in **selling against the brand**, whereby they stock well-known brands at high prices, and then sell other brands for lower prices to increase sales of their private brands. This practice is disliked by manufacturers since sales of their brands decline.

To increase private brand sales, some channel members **sell against the brand**.

Sometimes, wholesalers and retailers go outside traditional distribution channels and buy **grey market goods**—foreign-made products imported by distributors (suppliers) that are not authorized by the products' manufacturers. Personal stereos, VCRs, car stereos, watches, and cameras are just some of the items handled in this way.

Grey market goods *bypass authorized channels.*

If wholesalers and retailers buy grey market goods, their purchase prices are less than they would be otherwise and they have greater control over their own selling prices. The result is often discounted prices for consumers, which may be upsetting to manufacturers and authorized dealers.[16]

To maximize channel-member cooperation on pricing decisions, these factors should be considered: channel-member profit margins, price guarantees, special deals, and the

---
[15]"Digital Agrees to Change Its Ways: Government Alleges 'Tied Selling'" *Globe & Mail* (October 31, 1992), p. B5.
[16]See Gert Assmus and Carsten Wiese, "How to Address the Gray Market Threat Using Price Coordination," *Sloan Management Review*, Vol. 36 (Spring 1995), pp. 31–41.

impact of price increases. Wholesalers and retailers require appropriate profit margins to cover their costs (such as shipping, storage, credit, and advertising) and earn reasonable profits. Thus, the prices that are charged to them must take these profit margins into account. An attempt to reduce traditional margins for channel members may lose their cooperation and perhaps make them unwilling to carry a product. Pricing through a distribution channel is discussed further in Chapter 22.

Channel members may seek price guarantees to maintain inventory values and profit. **Price guarantees** assure resellers that the prices they pay are the lowest available. Any discount given to competitors will also be given to the original purchasers. Guarantees are most frequently requested for new firms or new products that want to gain entry into an established channel.

Price guarantees *reassure channel members.*

Special deals—consisting of limited-time discounts and/or free products— are often used to stimulate purchases by resellers. The deals may require channel members to share their savings with final consumers to increase the latter's demand. For example, soda bottlers normally give retailers large price discounts on new products to encourage them to make purchases and then offer low introductory prices to consumers.

The effects of price increases on channel members' behaviour must also be assessed. When firms raise prices to resellers, these increases tend to be passed along to consumers. This practice is more difficult for items with customary prices, such as candy, where small cost rises may be absorbed by the resellers. In any event, cooperation depends on an equitable distribution of costs and profit within the channel.

Competition

Another factor contributing to the degree of control a firm has over prices is the competitive environment within which it operates. See Figure 21–7.

A **market-controlled price environment** is characterized by a high level of competition, similar goods and services, and little control over prices by individual firms. Those trying to charge much more than the going price would attract few customers because demand for any single firm is weak enough that customers would switch to competitors. There would similarly be little gained by selling for less because competitors would match price cuts.

A firm may face a **market-controlled, company-controlled,** *or* **government-controlled price environment**.

A **company-controlled price environment** is characterized by moderate competition, well-differentiated goods and services, and strong control over prices by individual firms. Companies can succeed with above-average prices because people view their offerings as unique. Differentiation may be based on brand image, features, associated services, assortment, or other elements. Discounters also can carve out a niche in this environment by attracting consumers interested in low prices.

A **government-controlled price environment** is characterized by prices being set or strongly influenced by some level of government. Examples are public utilities, mass transit, insurance, and publicly funded colleges and universities. In each case, government bodies determine or affect prices after obtaining input from the relevant companies, institutions, and/or trade associations, as well as other interested parties (such as consumer groups).

FIGURE 21-7
The Competitive Environments of Pricing

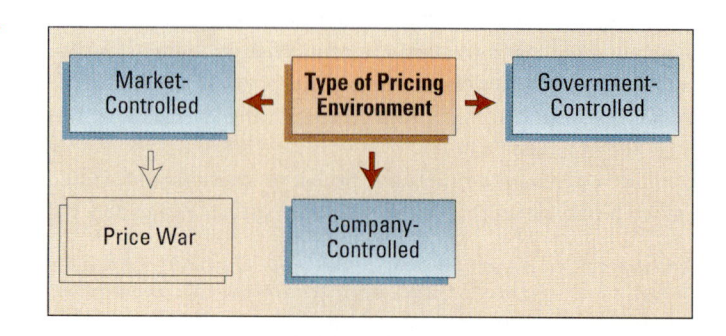

International Marketing in Action

Will the Euro Ever Come to Pass?

For several years, most leaders of the European Union have agreed that a uniform currency should be established to further unify Europe. This would also eliminate currency losses among EU members, make it unnecessary for travellers to exchange currencies in each European country, and reduce the cross-border shopping that results when products have different prices due to fluctuating currency values.

Plans now call for the new common currency to be called "Euro" and for it to be fully adopted by the year 2002. These are some of the major events scheduled for the Euro:

- *Early 1998*—Decision on which nations qualify for the monetary union. A European Central Bank is created.
- *January 1, 1999*—Permanent exchange rates set for qualifying nations. The European Central Bank takes over monetary policy. Government debt is issued in Euros.
- *Early 2002*—Circulation of Euro notes begins. Stores price goods and services in Euros.
- *June 2002*—Old national currencies no longer legal tender. Only Euros used in member countries.

But several experts question whether the Euro will ever be the currency of Europe. They point out that very few EU members meet eligibility requirements in terms of the inflation rate, total government debt as a percentage of Gross Domestic Product, and the annual budget deficit as a percentage of Gross Domestic Product. In addition, the governments of some EU members, especially the British government, look at a unified currency as an infringement on national sovereignty, and it will not be easy to re-educate the citizens in member countries.

As a consultant to the EU, develop a strategy for resolving these difficulties.

Source: Based on material in Nathaniel C. Nash, "Europeans Agree on New Currency," *New York Times* (December 16, 1995), pp. 1, 40.

Companies may have to adapt to a changing competitive environment in their industries. Firms in the transportation, telecommunications, and financial industries have seen their price environment shift from government- to market-controlled—although some strong firms in these industries have managed to develop a company-controlled price environment.

Price strategies are easy and quick to copy, so marketers must view price from both short- and long-run perspectives. Excessive price competition may lead to lengthy and costly **price wars**, in which various firms continually try to undercut each other's prices to draw customers. These wars often result in low profits or even losses for the participants, and in some companies being forced out of business.

In recent years, there have been price wars among some car-rental firms, airlines, blank videocassette tape manufacturers, PC makers, semiconductor manufacturers, supermarkets, insurance companies, and others. Although price wars have been more common in Canada and the United States (due to fierce competition in some industries), they are now spreading overseas—particularly to Europe and, to a lesser extent, Japan.

Price wars *occur when competitors constantly lower prices.*

MARKETING IN A CHANGING WORLD
Will "Pre-Owning" Catch On?[17]

As the prices of such products as in-line skates ($170 for a pair of Rollerblade Lightning), guitars ($550 to $650 for a Fender Stratocaster), and cribs ($250 to $325 for a Simmons model) keep creeping up, some consumers are turning to "pre-owned" versions of these items.

Here's how:

Retailing, meet recycling. Regional and national chains of thrift boutiques are doing a brisk business in used but perfectly usable stuff, from golf clubs to baby cribs, at 20 per cent to 60 per cent below the prices charged by discounters on new items. (Hagglers can sometimes do even better.) In 1995, Grow Biz International, a Minneapolis-based franchiser, had 814 outlets around North America, including Play It Again Sports, Once Upon a Child, Music-Go-Round, and Disc Go Round—with another 400 more stores planned for 1996.

Much of the merchandise comes from local individuals who sell it outright or on consignment or trade it in for other products. (Most shops pay sellers 25 to 35 per cent of the price of the item when new or about 60 per cent of the take for a consignment item, or exchange the item for a store credit worth about 40 per cent of its original price).

Despite the seeming popularity of shopping for pre-owned items—after all, we have been buying used cars for decades—questions still remain. Is this a fad that will fade away in a short time? If someone's old Rollerblade skates are priced at $122 when new ones (fresh out of the box) sell for $170, will very many people really want the pre-owned ones? What types of pre-owned products will sell best? Will status seekers be drawn to pre-owned goods because they still have prestige names (which the consumers might not otherwise be able to afford)? Should traditional retailers think about stocking both new and pre-owned items? What kinds of warranties and return policies should be made available?

SUMMARY

1. To define the terms price and price planning A price represents the value of a product for both the seller and the buyer. Price planning is systematic decision making relating to all aspects of pricing by a firm; it involves both tangible and intangible factors, purchase terms, and the nonmonetary exchange of goods and services. Exchange does not take place unless the buyer and seller agree a price represents an equitable value. Price also balances supply and demand.

2. To demonstrate the importance of price and study its relationship with other marketing variables Price (monetary or nonmonetary) is part of every type of exchange. During the last three decades, price decisions have become more important to business executives. This is due to factors such as deregulation, cost increases, currency rates, technological advances, the greater price emphasis by service companies, and periodic economic slowdowns.

Price decisions must be made in conjunction with other marketing-mix elements. And pricing is often related to the product life cycle, customer service levels, and other specific marketing and company variables. Setting prices for international markets can be complex and influenced by factors specific to the country.

3. To differentiate between price-based and nonprice-based approaches Under a price-based approach, sellers influence demand primarily by means of changes in price levels; they move consumers along a demand curve by raising or lowering prices. With a nonprice-based approach, sellers downplay price and emphasize such marketing attributes as image, packaging, and features; they shift the demand curves of consumers by stressing product distinctiveness.

4. To examine the factors affecting pricing decisions Several factors affect pricing decisions: consumers, costs, government, channel members, and competition. The law of demand states that consumers usually buy more units at a low price than at a high price. The price elasticity of demand explains the sensitivity of buyers to price changes in terms of the amounts they buy. Demand may be elastic, inelastic, or unitary. It is impacted by the availability of substitutes and

---

[17]The material in this section is based on Kerry Hannon, Sally Deneen, Melanie Mavrides, and Jill Jordan Sieder, "Think of It as 'Pre-Owned,'" *U.S. News & World Report* (June 5, 1995), pp. 61–64.

urgency of need. Consumers can be divided into segments based on their level of price sensitivity. Subjective price may be more important than actual price.

The costs of raw materials, supplies, labour, ads, transportation, and other items affect prices. Large increases often lead firms to raise prices, modify products, or abandon some offerings. Cost declines benefit marketing strategies by improving firms' ability to plan prices.

Government restrictions affect a broad variety of pricing areas. The Competition Act has criminal provisions for pricing activities involving: conspiracy to price fix, bid-rigging, price maintenance, price discrimination, predatory pricing, misleading price advertising, double ticketing, sales above the advertised price, and bait-and-switch selling. Maximum fines of $10 million and/or imprisonment of up to five years are penalties which can be imposed if a firm or individual is found guilty of violating these provisions. Non-criminal provisions of the Act govern practices such as abuse of dominant position, refusal to deal, consignment selling, tied selling, and delivered pricing. Business firms can pursue complaints with respect to these activities in civil courts as well. The Competition Bureau and Better Business Bureau are willing to provide businesspeople with guidelines for price advertising.

Often, each channel member seeks a role in pricing. Manufacturers exert control through exclusive distribution, pre-ticketing, opening their own outlets, offering goods on consignment, providing adequate margins, and having strong brands. Resellers exert control by making large purchases, linking sales support to margins, refusing to carry items, stocking competing brands, developing private brands, and purchasing outside traditional channels. Reseller profit margins, price guarantees, special deals, and the ramifications of price increases all need to be considered.

A market-controlled price environment has a high level of competition, similar products, and little control over prices by individual firms. A company-controlled price environment has a moderate level of competition, well-differentiated products, and strong control over prices by individual firms. In a government-controlled price environment, the government sets or influences prices. Some competitive actions may result in price wars, in which firms try to undercut each other's prices.

KEY TERMS

price (p. 576)
price planning (p. 576)
price-based approach (p. 579)
nonprice-based approach (p. 579)
law of demand (p. 581)
price elasticity of demand (p. 581)
elastic demand (p. 581)
inelastic demand (p. 581)
unitary demand (p. 581)
subjective price (p. 583)
conspiracy to price fix (p. 586)

bid-rigging (p. 587)
price maintenance (p. 587)
price discrimination (p. 588)
predatory pricing (p. 588)
double ticketing (p. 588)
sale above advertised price (p. 588)
bait-and-switch selling (p. 588)
misleading price advertising (p. 589)
abuse of dominant position (p. 590)
refusal to deal (p. 590)
consignment selling (p. 590)

tied sales (p. 590)
delivered pricing (p. 591)
selling against the brand (p. 591)
grey market goods (p. 591)
price guarantees (p. 592)
market-controlled price environment (p. 592)
company-controlled price environment (p. 592)
government-controlled price environment (p. 592)
price wars (p. 593)

Review Questions

1. Cite at least three reasons why price decisions are so important today.
2. Explain the role of price in balancing supply and demand. Refer to Figure 21-1.
3. What is the risk of using a nonprice-oriented strategy?
4. Distinguish between elastic and inelastic demand. Why is it necessary for a firm to understand these differences?
5. At a price of $40, a firm could sell 900 units. At a price of $25, it could sell 1200 units. Calculate the elasticity of demand and state what price the firm should charge—and why.
6. If costs rise rapidly, how could a company react?
7. Is conspiracy to price fix always illegal? Explain your answer.
8. Does the buyer have any potential liability under the Competition Act? Why or why not?
9. In what way are loss leaders different from bait-and-switch advertising?
10. How can a firm turn a market-controlled price environment into a company-controlled one?

Discussion Questions

1. How could a firm estimate price elasticity for a new industrial product? A mature industrial product?
2. When would you pass along a cost decrease to consumers? When would you not pass the decrease along?
3. You are the marketing vice-president of a telemarketing firm that sells chimney cleaning services at prices ranging from $200 to $600 (depending on the size and condition of the chimney). What would you do to persuade consumers that you offer fair prices?
4. Present five examples of price advertising for a hardware store that would violate the price advertising guidelines mentioned in the chapter.
5. Describe several advantages and disadvantages of a government-controlled price environment.

VIDEO CASE

Price Competition in the Energy Business

The Northeastern United States is one of the most lucrative markets for Canadian energy. Free trade has opened up these markets for Canadian energy producers.

In terms of heating efficiency natural gas is the best value for consumers and electricity the least economical. Natural gas has a tremendous price advantage as a fuel. Between 1985 and 1995 the importation of Canadian natural gas into the United States increased threefold. This increase has been facilitated by natural gas pipelines, which enable the transmission of natural gas from Alberta to California and to New York and New England.

The increased use of natural gas as a fuel for electric power generation is a major reason for this threefold increase. Independent power suppliers are able to produce electricity for one third the price of hydroelectric producers by using natural gas. The cost advantage of natural gas is conferred by its ease of transmission and inexpensive methods of conversion to electricity.

Natural gas is an easy-to-use source of energy. Since it is transported in its basic form, there is no loss of "energy" during transmission. Because of this ease of use, large U.S. customers have built their own Non-Utility Generation plants (NUGs). This has become a chief concern of both Ontario and Quebec Hydro. Large customers have found they can acquire natural gas directly from the pipeline and both build and operate their own electrical generation plants for less money than buying electricity.

Large customers creating their own power generation units is just one of the worries for Ontario and Quebec Hydro. In Ontario, the electrical power industry is about to be deregulated. Ontario Hydro recognizes the new reality that its monopoly is on the verge of ending. Its 1995 mission statement reads as follows: "To make Ontario Hydro a leader in energy efficient and sustainable development, and to provide its customers with safe and reliable energy services at competitive prices." The fact that pricing is overtly acknowledged in this mission statement is testament to its importance.

Stating competitive pricing as a part of the mission is a lot easier for Ontario Hydro than actually achieving it. Being price competitive with gas generated electricity, which is about 4¢ per kilowatt hour less than the cost of the electricity generated by both Quebec and Ontario Hydro—is going to be difficult. Quebec Hydro has already lost a power contract in New York State.

Ontario and Quebec Hydro have high costs due to excessive debt loads (taking about 30¢ of every $1 Ontario Hydro earns for servicing), expensive facilities, and large workforces. Natural gas operated power plants are relatively cheap, easy to operate, do not require a lot of labour and can be built and brought online in less than a year. Were it not for the monopolies granted to both Ontario and Quebec Hydro, many NUG plants would have been in operation in Eastern Canada before 1996. They have been prevented so far because Ontario Hydro and Quebec Hydro have excess capacity and have used their monopoly position to argue that NUGs are not needed. Given the huge cost differentials, it will become harder and harder to argue that the public interest is being served by maintaining a monopoly. Allowing NUGs and private power plants will bring the Ontario and Quebec energy markets into line with other markets in North America. However, the price competition may mean the death of Ontario and Quebec Hydro as they now exist.

QUESTIONS

1. As the CEO of Ontario or Quebec Hydro, how would you undertake to deal with the competitive situation?
2. Describe the kind of market environment you would envision for electrical power companies in a deregulated market where consumers have a choice of electric companies. What would be the bases for competition?
3. The comparative cost of fossil fuel energy in the U.S. has always been cheaper than electricity. What is it about the current market that is putting so much pressure on Ontario and Quebec Hydro? Do they really have to change, or do they merely have to ride out a storm?
4. Evaluate the advantages and disadvantages of dealing with a large power utility supplier versus a small NUG supplier. Who is more to be price sensitive, large industrial customers or household consumers?

VIDEO QUESTIONS ON THE ENERGY BUSINESS

1. Characterise the kind of pricing strategies used by both Quebec and Ontario Hydro. What kind of pricing strategies will they have to use in the future?
2. Discuss and present some short-term pricing strategy alternatives for Ontario and Quebec Hydro to deal with their current competitive situations

---

Video Source: "Natural Gas Versus Hydro Sales," *Venture* (March 13, 1994).

Other Sources: Randall Litchfield, "The Never-Never Land of a Public Utility: There Are Lots of Schemes to Reform Ontario Hydro. Letting It Wither and Die Is Probably the Smartest," *Canadian Business* (November, 1992) p 19; "Power Failure: Botched Megaprojects and Bungling Management Have Put Ontario Hydro Billions In Debt," *Canadian Business* (November, 1992), pp 50–58; "The Politics of Power," *Canadian Business* (March, 1993), pp 41–42; Ontario Hydro Web site (August 1996), http://www.hydro.on.ca/; New York City Web site (August 1996), http://www.ci.nyc.ny.us/; United States Department of Energies Web site (August 1996), http://www.eia.doe.gov/emeu/mer/mer.html.

CASE STUDY

Here Come $20 Eyeglasses

Optometrist Robert Morrison and his son Jim own Morrison International, a firm specializing in the manufacture and sale of inexpensive prescription eyeglasses. The firm's main product, Instant Eyeglasses, is especially easy to assemble and retails for about U.S.$20 a pair. Morrison's most expensive product—bifocal sunglasses with an anti-scratch coating—sells for U.S.$39.95.

To keep its costs low, Morrison International has re-invented the way eyeglasses are made. Although traditional eyeglasses are custom ground to accommodate the different sizes and shapes of various frames, Morrison's eyeglasses utilize pre-molded lenses. These lenses can be snapped into frames and adjusted to fit any size face. They can also be rotated to one of 180 positions in the frame. Each position accommodates a different prescription. Thus, Morrison can fill 26 000 prescriptions from an inventory of 152 lenses.

From a cost perspective, Instant Eyeglasses are not only inexpensive to produce, but they are also efficient to store (due to the high inventory turnover of lenses and their frames). This enables Instant Eyeglasses to be sold at rock-bottom prices.

Morrison has two target markets: consumers who want a spare pair of inexpensive glasses (and would not pay the average retail price of U.S.$135), and charities that provide glasses for the needy in North America and other international markets. Eyeglasses sold to the spare pair market are sold through mail order and through kiosks. Morrison markets the glasses to the spare-frame market as a profit-making venture, but sells to the poor on a nonprofit basis.

In the U.S., Morrison is reaching the poor through a U.S.$500 000 laboratory on wheels. The equipment and supplies for this lab have been paid through a grant from the Hershey Foods Corporation. In one recent eighteen-month period, the lab travelled throughout the United States and provided eye examinations and eyeglasses to 18 000 people free of charge.

The company also rents mobile clinics to charities in Atlanta and Tampa. These clinics can evaluate a person's vision and then make a pair of Instant Eyeglasses in minutes. In a typical arrangement, Morrison provides the eyeglasses at cost (between U.S.$10 and U.S.$12) to the charities, which then sell the glasses at cost to the poor. Morrison is negotiating similar arrangements in foreign markets.

According to Dean Butler, the founder of LensCrafters, the world's largest optical retailer, "Doggone, he is onto something." Butler, who sold LensCrafters in 1988, is on the board of Optical Care Ltd., which has the right to distribute Instant Eyeglasses in the former Soviet Union, Eastern Europe, India, and Pakistan. As Optical Care's chair says, "The need is enormous." For instance, 40 per cent of the Russian adults who need glasses do not have them. In nations where there are few eye doctors, Optical Care plans to put equipment in stores to test people's vision. Optical Care estimates that it will sell U.S.$55 million worth of Instant Eyeglasses per year in the former Eastern Bloc markets over the next five years.

Instant Eyeglasses is not Robert Morrison's first invention. In 1963, he worked with Czech scientists to develop the first soft contact lens. And briefly in the 1960s, Morrison's lab manufactured every soft lens that was sold in the United States. He later sold his share in the business to his partners in exchange for royalty income. According to the chair of the ophthalmology department at Penn State University, "He dramatically refined contact lenses from an experimental concept into a successful product."

QUESTIONS

1. Apply the concept of price and nonprice competition to Instant Eyeglasses.
2. Describe the impact of price elasticity of demand for Instant Eyeglasses' spare eyeglasses market.
3. How does a consumer's subjective price affect Instant Eyeglasses' market strategy?
4. If Morrison's costs go up by 15 per cent, should he pass along the full increase? Why or why not?

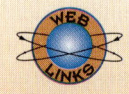

LENSCRAFTERS
www.lenscrafters.com/

Source: The data in this case are drawn from Amy Borrus, "Eyeglasses for the Masses," *Business Week* (November 20, 1995) pp. 104–105.

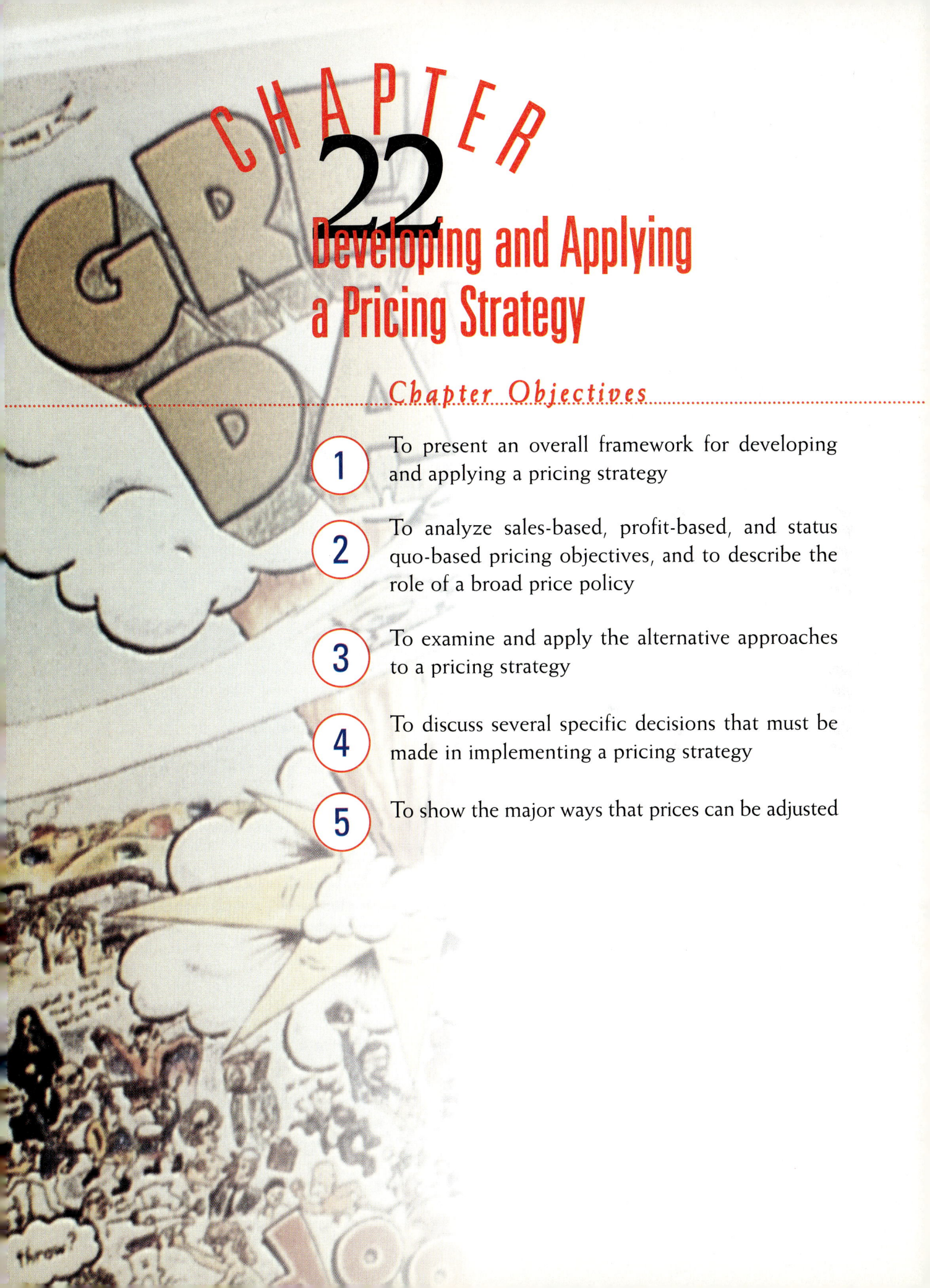

CHAPTER 22
Developing and Applying a Pricing Strategy

Chapter Objectives

1. To present an overall framework for developing and applying a pricing strategy

2. To analyze sales-based, profit-based, and status quo-based pricing objectives, and to describe the role of a broad price policy

3. To examine and apply the alternative approaches to a pricing strategy

4. To discuss several specific decisions that must be made in implementing a pricing strategy

5. To show the major ways that prices can be adjusted

> *Recent growth in the music business has been set off by an explosion of new recording talent, the coming of age of Walkman-toting Generation Xers, and ever more ways to deliver tunes. "Music is a more important part of more people's lives than ever before," explains David Geffen, billionaire record impresario and co-founder of DreamWorks SKG. "Young people listen to more music than [baby boomers] did. They buy more music than we did. And we're still buying it, too."*

MUCH MUSIC
www.muchmusic.com/

VIACOM
www.viacom.com/

MCA
www.mca.com/

The total sales of pre-recorded music in Canada, the United States, and around the world have increased dramatically in recent years. Globally, annual pre-recorded music sales are approaching U.S.$40 billion. In Canada the music retail business is worth $1.5 billion (Canadian). In 1994, Canadian pre-recorded music sales rose by 19.6 per cent and were on track for a 23 per cent growth rate in 1995.

The largest firm in the recording business is Warner Brothers, with over 22 per cent market share. Warner has many established recording artists, as well as such newer stars as Hootie & the Blowfish and Green Day.

Although close to 80 per cent of new releases fail, successful recordings are *very* profitable. A CD is relatively inexpensive to produce, usually costing less than U.S.$500 000. And besides the profits from CD sales, there are proceeds from catalogue and music publishing sales.

It once took a group several years—and many road tours—to obtain a following. But now, through rock videos on Much Music and the Internet, a group can receive incredible recognition and sales from its first recorded effort. The debut albums *Dookie* and *Cracked Rear View*, from Green Day and Hootie & the Blowfish, respectively, each sold more than six million copies. *Cracked Rear View* remained on the music charts for well over a year.

The high sales and profit potential have generated increased attention for the CD business. Both the News Corporation and Viacom have been looking at opportunities in the recording industry. Existing recording companies such as MCA and Warner Bros. are also launching new labels—at a cost of U.S.$50 to U.S.$100 million per label (the same amount needed to bankroll a major action movie).

Let's look at the economics of producing and marketing a typical CD. A CD usually sells for $15.98 to $16.98 at retail. Since the standard wholesale cost for a major release is $10.00, the retailer's markup (at retail selling price) is as high as 40 per cent [($16.98 - $10.00)/$16.98]. The $10.00 wholesale price represents the sales revenue to a recording company per CD.

From its $10.00, the recording company must pay for overhead and profits, artist royalties and copyright fees, marketing expenses, and CD manufacturing costs. Of these items, overhead (comprising record company administration expenses, recording costs,

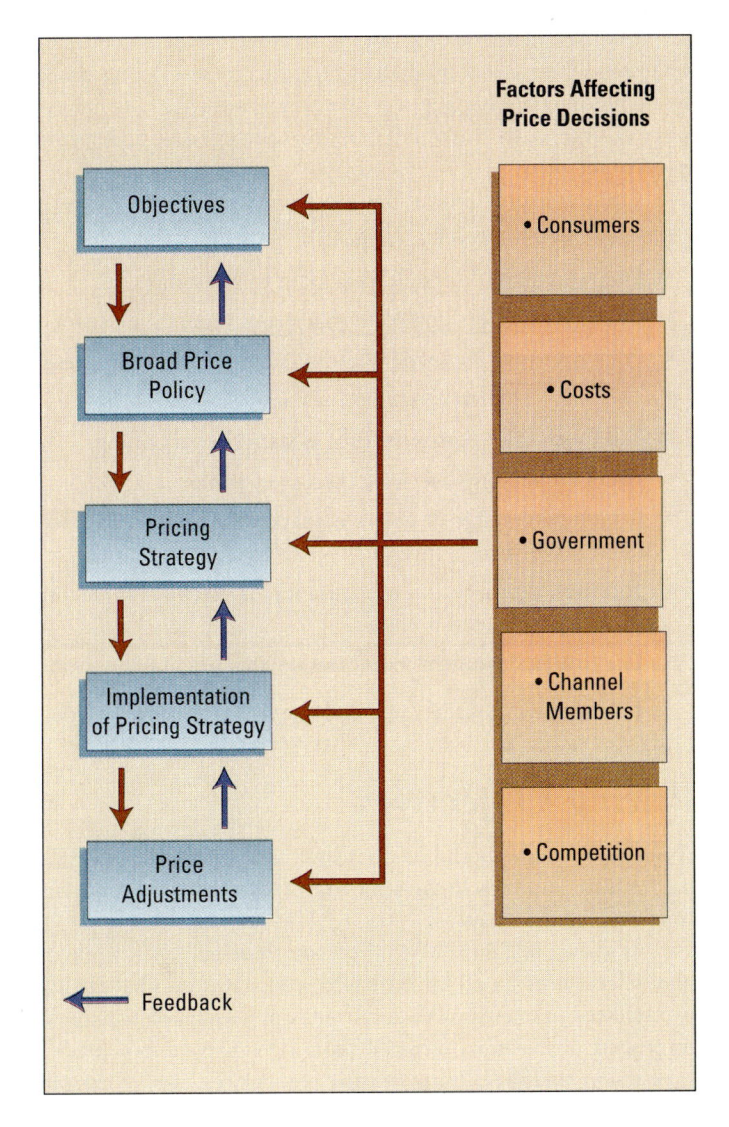

FIGURE 22-1
A Framework for Developing and Applying a Pricing Strategy

returns, and profits) is the largest category, amounting to $4.25 to $5.25 per CD. The next largest expense, artist royalties and copyright fees, is $2.00 to $3.00 per CD. Marketing expenses for advertising, public relations, and physical distribution activities total $1.45. Lastly, manufacturing costs are $1.30; this consists of CD production ($0.75), the jewel box container ($0.30), and the printed booklet ($0.25) that accompany the CD.[1]

In this chapter, we will look at the overall process of developing and applying a pricing strategy—including the setting of pricing objectives, the use of various pricing approaches, how a pricing strategy is implemented, and how prices can be adjusted.

Overview

As Figure 22-1 shows, a pricing strategy has five steps: objectives, broad policy, strategy, implementation, and adjustments. All of them are affected by the outside factors noted in Chapter 21. Like any planning activity, a pricing strategy begins with a clear statement of goals and ends with an adaptive or corrective mechanism. Pricing decisions are integrated with the firm's overall marketing program during the broad price-policy step.

---

[1]Thom Geier, Betsy Streisand, and Kevin Whitelaw, "Recording Sound Sales," *U.S. News & World Report* (September 25, 1995), pp. 67–72; and Christian Allard, "Loony Tunes," *Canadian Business* (August 1995), pp. 73–74.

The development of a pricing strategy is not a one-time occurrence. It needs to be reviewed when a new product is introduced, an existing product is revised, the competitive environment changes, a product moves through its life cycle, a competitor initiates a price change, costs rise or fall, the firm's prices come under government scrutiny, and other events take place.

These are some indications a pricing strategy may be performing poorly:

- Prices are changed too frequently.
- Pricing policy is difficult to explain to consumers.
- Channel members complain that profit margins are inadequate.
- Price decisions are made without adequate marketing-research information.
- Too many different price options are available.
- Too much sales personnel time is spent in bargaining.
- Prices are inconsistent with the target market.
- A high percentage of goods is marked down or discounted late in the selling season to clear out surplus inventory.
- Too high a proportion of customers is price-sensitive and attracted by competitors' discounts. Demand is elastic.
- The firm has problems conforming with pricing legislation.

This chapter describes in detail the pricing framework outlined in Figure 22–1.

Pricing Objectives

A pricing strategy should be consistent with and reflect overall company goals. It is possible for different firms in the same industry to have dissimilar objectives and, therefore, distinct pricing strategies.

As shown in Figure 22–2, there are three general pricing objectives from which a firm may select: sales-based, profit-based, and status quo-based. With sales-based goals, a firm is interested in sales growth and/or maximizing market share. With profit-based goals, it is interested in maximizing profit, earning a satisfactory profit, optimizing the return on investment, and/or securing an early recovery of cash. With status quo-based goals, it seeks to avoid unfavourable government actions, minimize the effects of competitor actions, maintain good channel relations, discourage the entry of competitors, reduce demands from suppliers, and/or stabilize prices.

A company may pursue more than one pricing goal at the same time, such as increasing sales by 5 to 10 per cent each year, achieving a 15 per cent return on capital investments, and keeping prices near those of competitors. It may also set distinct short- and long-run goals. In the short run, it may seek high profit margins on new products; in the long run, these profit margins would drop to discourage potential competitors.

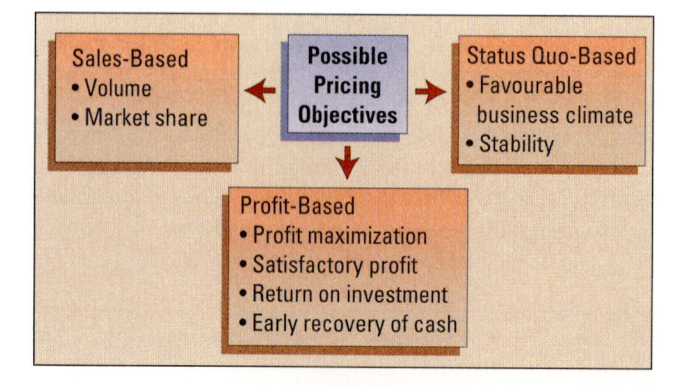

FIGURE 22-2
Pricing Objectives

Sales-Based	Possible Pricing Objectives	Status Quo-Based
• Volume • Market share	← → ↓	• Favourable business climate • Stability

Profit-Based
• Profit maximization
• Satisfactory profit
• Return on investment
• Early recovery of cash

Sales-Based Objectives

A firm with **sales-based pricing objectives** is oriented toward high sales volume and/or expanding its share of sales relative to competitors. The company focuses on sales-based goals for either (or all) of three reasons: It sees market saturation or sales growth as a major step leading to market control and sustained profits. It wants to maximize unit sales and will trade low per-unit profits for larger total profits. It assumes greater sales will enable it to have lower per-unit costs.

To gain high sales volume, **penetration pricing** is often employed—whereby low prices are used to capture the mass market for a good or service. It is a proper approach if customers are highly sensitive to price, low prices discourage actual and potential competitors, there are economies of scale (per-unit production and distribution costs fall as sales rise), and a large consumer market exists. Penetration pricing also recognizes that a high price may leave a product vulnerable to competition.

Penetration pricing is used by such companies as Compaq and Malt-O-Meal. Compaq now markets a $1500 "entry level" PC whose price includes a monitor, a 100-megahertz Pentium chip, a one-gigabyte hard drive, eight megabytes of memory, and a fast modem. As one observer says, "The closer you get to $1000, the bigger the market will be." Malt-O-Meal makes no-frills cereals and sells them in bags rather than boxes. Its prices are half those of better-known brands.[2]

Penetration pricing may even tap markets not originally anticipated. For example, few people forecast that cordless phones would reach the sales volume attained during their peak. The market expanded rapidly after prices fell below $100. It grew again as new models were introduced for $60 and less.

Profit-Based Objectives

A company with **profit-based pricing objectives** orients its strategy toward some type of profit goals. With profit-maximization goals, high dollar profits are sought. With satisfactory-profit goals, stability over time is desired; rather than maximize profits in a given year (which could result in declines in nonpeak years), steady profits for a number of years are sought. With return-on-investment goals, profits are related to investment costs; these goals are often pursued by regulated utilities as a way of justifying rate increases. With early-recovery-of-cash goals, high initial profits are sought because firms are short of funds or uncertain about their future.

Profit may be expressed in per-unit or total terms. Per-unit profit equals the revenue a seller receives for one unit sold minus its costs. A product like custom-made furniture has a high unit profit. Total profit equals the revenue a seller receives for all items sold minus total costs. It is computed by multiplying per-unit profit times the number of units sold. A product like mass-marketed furniture has a low unit profit; success is based on the number of units sold (turnover). Products with high per-unit profits may have lower total profits than ones with low per-unit profits if the discount prices of the latter generate a much greater level of consumer demand. However, this depends on the elasticity of demand.

Skimming pricing uses high prices to attract the market segment more concerned with product quality, uniqueness, or status than price. It is proper if competition can be minimized (by means of patent protection, brand loyalty, raw material control, or high capital requirements), funds are needed for early cash recovery or further expansion, consumers are insensitive to price or willing to pay a high initial price, and unit costs remain equal or rise as sales increase (economies of scale are absent).

Skimming prices are used by such firms as Genentech, Canondale, and British Airways. Genentech is the maker of Activase, a patented brand of TPA (tissue plasminogen activator), a product that quickly clears the blood clots associated with heart attacks and effectively treats certain kinds of strokes. It sells Activase for about $1500 per dose.

Sales-based objectives *seek high volume or market share.*

Penetration pricing *aims at the mass market.*

COMPAQ
www.compaq.com/

Profit-based objectives *range from maximization to recovery of cash. Goals can be per unit or total.*

Skimming pricing *is aimed at the segment interested in quality or status.*

BRITISH AIRWAYS
www.british-airways.com/bans/checkin.htm

GENENTECH
www.gene.com/

---

[2]Jim Carlton, "Compaq and Acer Are Slashing Prices on Entry-Level PCs to Expand Market," *Wall Street Journal* (November 17, 1995), pp. A3, A8; Richard Gibson, "Quaker Oats Co. Will Begin Marketing Value-Priced Cereals Under Its Brand," *Wall Street Journal* (January 23, 1995), pp. 88, 90.

Canondale's Super V bikes retail for $3500 each. They have rear shock absorbers to boost comfort, rear frames that pivot vertically to keep the back wheels in constant contact with bumpy roads, light aluminium frames to maximize pedalling efficiency, and front suspensions that ease steering and ensure smoother rides. British Airways recently overhauled its first-class cabins to provide passengers with fully reclining seats, greater privacy, and more room. It is targeting those willing to pay U.S.$6600 for a round trip ticket between London and New York.[3]

Firms sometimes first employ skimming pricing and then penetration pricing, or they market both a premium brand and a value brand. High prices may be charged when competition is limited, or when a product is new. The first group of customers to buy a new product is usually less price sensitive than later groups. High initial prices may also be used to portray a high-quality image. Another advantage of starting a product off with high prices is the fact that it is always easier to lower prices than it is to raise them. After the initial market segment is saturated, penetration pricing can be used to appeal to the mass market and expand total sales volume. Thus, multiple segments can be reached with one product simply by altering pricing strategy.

Status Quo-Based Objectives

Status quo-based objectives *seek good business conditions and stability.*

Status quo-based pricing objectives are sought by a firm interested in continuing a favourable or stable business climate for its operations.

The pricing strategy is used to minimize the impact of such outside parties as government, competitors, and channel members—and to avoid sales declines.

One should not infer that status quo goals require no effort. A firm must instruct salespeople not to offer different terms to competing channel members or else the government may accuse it of a Competition Act violation. It may have to match competitors' price cuts to keep customers—while striving to avoid price wars. It may have to accept lower profit margins in the face of rising costs to hold channel cooperation. It may have to charge penetration prices to discourage competitors from also marketing certain product lines.

Broad Price Policy

A **broad price policy** *links prices with the target market, image, and other marketing elements.*

A **broad price policy** sets the overall direction (and tone) for a firm's pricing efforts and makes sure pricing decisions are coordinated with the firm's choices as to a target market, an image, and other marketing-mix factors. It incorporates short- and long-term pricing goals, as well as the role of pricing. Pricing can play a passive role—with customer purchases based on superior service, convenience, and quality—or it can play an active role—with purchases based on discount prices. Thus, a high-income segment buying status brands at upscale stores would expect premium prices. A moderate-income segment buying private brands at flea markets would expect low prices.

A firm outlines a broad price policy by placing individual decisions into an integrated format. It then decides on the interrelationship of prices for items within a product line, how often special discounts are used, how prices compare to competition, the frequency of price changes, and the method for setting new-product prices. As such, "marketing strategies attempt to define where the firm wants to be in the marketplace, and how it plans to get there. They provide the larger framework within which pricing and other programs are developed. Correspondingly, there should be a clear link between strategies and individual programs."[4]

---

[3]Ralph T. King, Jr., "TPA Scores Big in Treatment of Stroke," *Wall Street Journal* (December 14, 1995), p. 8; Ron Stodghill II, "Joe Montgomery's Wild Ride," *Business Week* (April 19, 1993), pp. 50, 52; and Charles Goldsmith, "Jet Ahoy! First-Class Fliers Go 'Yachting,'" *Wall Street Journal* (December 4, 1995), pp. B1, B10.

[4]Michael H. Morris and Roger J. Calantone, "Four Components of Effective Pricing," *Industrial Marketing Management*, Vol. 19 (November 1990), p. 327.

International Marketing in Action

Can Reebok's Global Hopscotching Pay Off in Lower Costs?

Ten years ago, most of Reebok's shoes and sneakers were produced in South Korea and Taiwan. However, as labour costs in these nations rose, Reebok sought new production facilities. Now, China and Indonesia account for 60 per cent of Reebok's annual worldwide production. That is almost 170 million pairs of sneakers and shoes. Only 9 per cent of Reebok footwear is still produced in South Korea.

Reebok is not alone in changing production sites on the basis of costs. According to the Athletic Footwear Association, a pair of sneakers costs about $27 to manufacture in East Asia and sells for $96 in North America. Nonetheless, after deducting operating expenses, a sneaker manufacturer is left with an average profit of just over $8 per pair. Thus, most manufacturers play a game of global hopscotching in their vendor sourcing.

Different parts of the same shoe are often produced in different countries. For Reebok's Kamikaze II sneaker, a basketball high top, cushioning materials are made in Southern California and then shipped along with moulded shoes to Reebok plants in South Korea and China for final assembly. Different types of sneakers are also made in different countries. Generally, a new production facility first produces a simple version of a running shoe or an aerobic shoe. After workers perfect their skills, more costly lines of shoes are manufactured there.

All of its Asian factories are evaluated through the six-point Reebok Supplier Certification Program that ranks suppliers on the basis of such attributes as the number of defective sneakers returned by retailers and on-time delivery. In addition, suppliers must comply with the firm's human-rights production standards.

As a consultant to Reebok, discuss the pros and cons of its global hopscotching approach.

Source: Based on material in David Fischer, "Global Hopscotch," *U.S. News & World Report* (June 5, 1995), pp. 43–45.

Pricing Strategy

A pricing strategy may be cost-, demand-, and/or competition-based. When the three approaches are integrated, combination pricing is involved. See Figure 22-3.

Cost-Based Pricing

In **cost-based pricing**, a firm sets prices by computing merchandise, service, and overhead costs and then adding an amount to cover its profit goal. Table 22-1 defines the key concepts in cost-based pricing and how they may be applied to big-screen television sets.

Cost-based prices are rather easy to derive because there is no need to estimate elasticity of demand or competitive reactions to price changes. There is also greater certainty about costs than demand or competitor responses to prices. Finally, cost-based pricing seeks reasonable profits since it is geared to covering all types of costs. It is often used by firms whose goals are stated in terms of profit or return on investment. A **price floor** is the lowest acceptable price a firm can charge and attain its profit goal.

Under **cost-based pricing**, *expenses are computed, profit is projected, and a* **price floor** *set.*

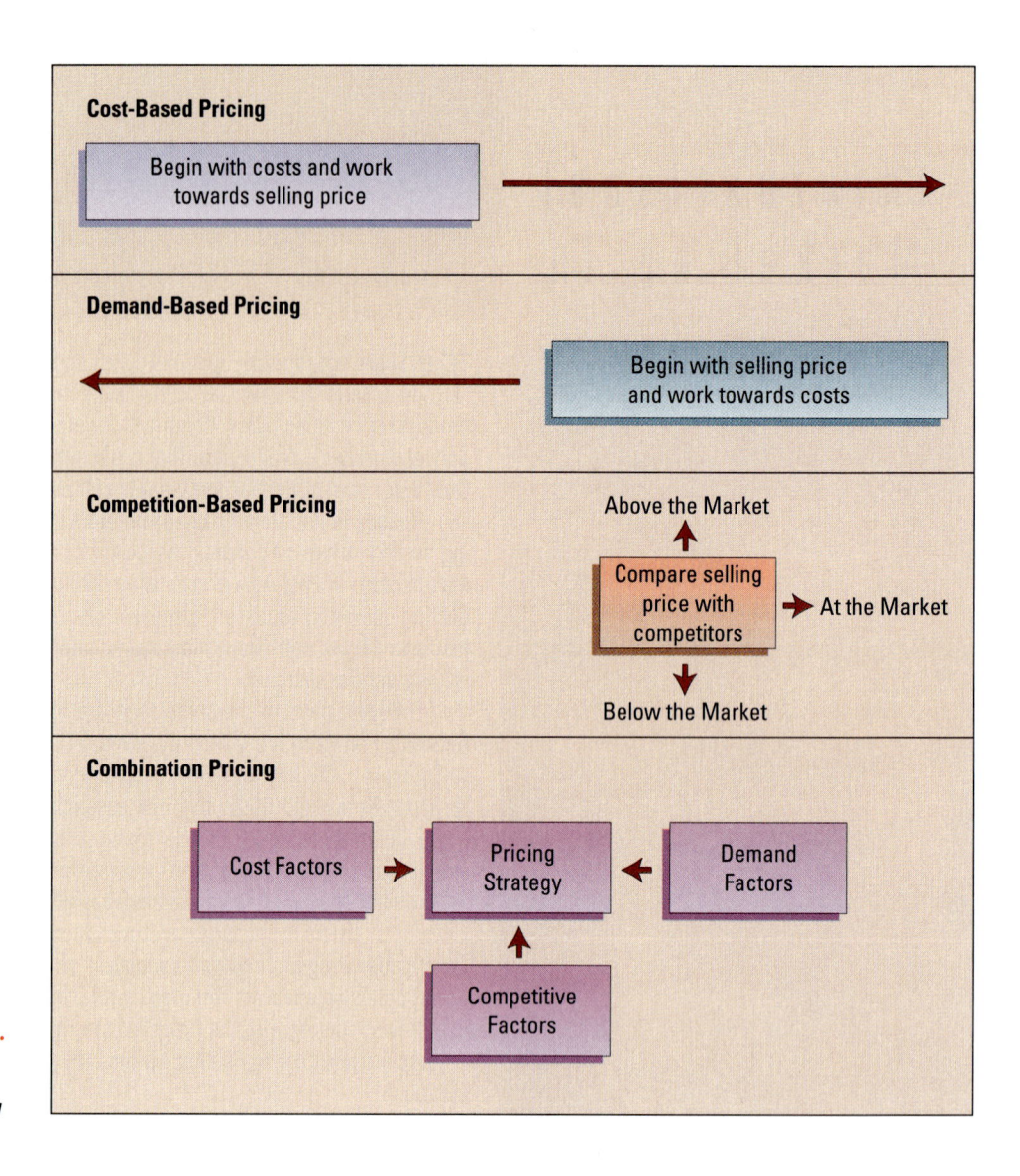

FIGURE 22-3
Ways of Developing a Pricing Strategy

Cost-Based Pricing
Begin with costs and work towards selling price

Demand-Based Pricing
Begin with selling price and work towards costs

Competition-Based Pricing
Compare selling price with competitors → Above the Market / At the Market / Below the Market

Combination Pricing
Cost Factors → Pricing Strategy ← Demand Factors
Competitive Factors ↑

When used by itself, cost-based pricing does have some significant limitations. It does not consider market conditions, the full effects of excess plant capacity, competitive prices, the product's phase in its life cycle, market share goals, consumers' ability to pay, and other factors.

Sometimes, it is hard to figure how such overhead costs as rent, lighting, personnel, and other general expenses should be allocated to each product. These costs are often assigned on the basis of product sales or the personnel time associated with each item. For instance, if product A accounts for 10 per cent of sales, it might be allotted 10 per cent of overhead costs. If product B receives 20 per cent of personnel time, it might be allotted 20 per cent of overhead costs. Yet, problems may arise since different methods for assigning costs may yield different results: How would costs be allocated if product A yields 10 per cent of sales and requires 20 per cent of personnel time?

In the following subsections, five cost-based pricing techniques are covered: cost-plus, markup, target, price-floor, and traditional break-even analysis. Figure 22-4 gives a synopsis of each technique. And Table 22-2 contains numerical examples of each.

Table 22-1
Key Cost Concepts and their Application to Big-Screen Television Sets

COST CONCEPT	DEFINITION	EXAMPLES[a]	SOURCES OF INFORMATION	METHOD OF COMPUTATION
Total fixed costs	Ongoing costs not related to volume. They are usually constant over a given range of output for a specified time.	Rent, salaries, electricity, real-estate taxes, plant, and equipment.	Accounting data, bills, cost estimates.	Addition of all fixed cost components.
Total variable costs	Costs that change with increases or decreases in output (volume).	Parts (such as tuners and speakers), hourly employees who assemble sets, and sales commissions.	Cost data from suppliers, estimates of labour productivity, sales estimates.	Addition of all fixed and variable cost components.
Total costs	Sum of total fixed and total variable costs.	See above.	See above.	Addition of all fixed and variable cost components.
Average fixed costs	Average fixed costs per unit.	See above under total fixed costs.	Total fixed costs and production estimates.	Total fixed costs/Quantity produced in units.
Average variable costs	Average variable costs per unit.	See above under total variable costs.	Total variable costs and production estimates.	Total variable costs/Quantity produced in units.
Average total costs	Sum of average fixed costs and average variable costs.	See above under total fixed and total variable costs.	Total costs and production estimates.	Average fixed costs + Average variable costs or Total costs/Quantity produced in units.
Marginal costs	Costs of making an additional unit.	See above under total fixed and total variable costs.	Accounting data, bills, cost estimates of labour and materials.	(Total costs of producing current quantity + one unit) − (Total costs of producing current quantity).

[a]Such marketing costs as advertising and distribution are often broken down into both fixed and variable components.

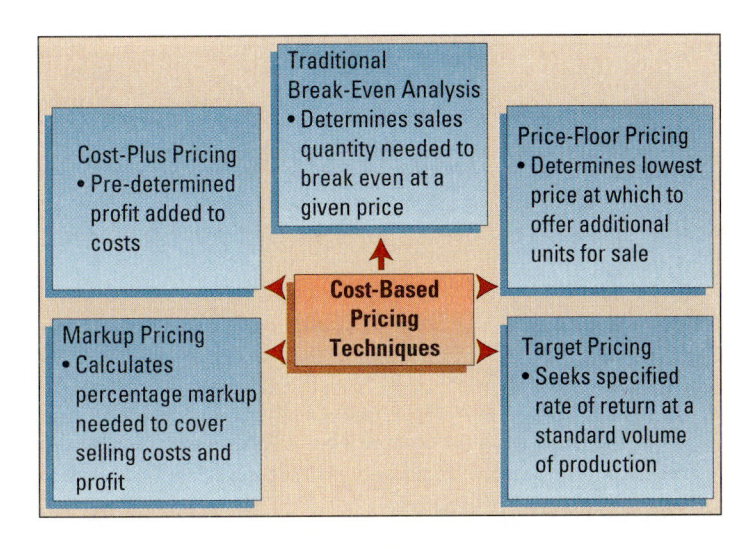

FIGURE 22-4
Cost-Based Pricing Techniques

- **Cost-Plus Pricing**
  - Pre-determined profit added to costs
- **Traditional Break-Even Analysis**
  - Determines sales quantity needed to break even at a given price
- **Price-Floor Pricing**
  - Determines lowest price at which to offer additional units for sale
- **Markup Pricing**
  - Calculates percentage markup needed to cover selling costs and profit
- **Target Pricing**
  - Seeks specified rate of return at a standard volume of production

Cost-Based Pricing Techniques

Table 22-2
Examples of Cost-Based Pricing Techniques

Cost-Plus Pricing—A custom-sofa maker has total fixed costs of $50 000, variable costs of $500 per sofa, desires $10 000 in profits, and plans to produce 100 couches. What is the selling price per couch?

$$\text{Price} = \frac{\text{Total fixed costs} + \text{Total variable costs} + \text{Projected profit}}{\text{Units produced}}$$

$$= \frac{\$50\ 000 + \$500(100) + \$10\ 000}{100} = \underline{\underline{\$1\ 100}}$$

Markup Pricing—A retailer pays $30 for touch-tone phones and wants a markup on selling price of 40 per cent (30 per cent for selling costs and 10 per cent for profit). What is the final selling price?

$$\text{Price} = \frac{\text{Merchandise costs}}{(100 - \text{Markup per cent})/100} = \frac{\$30}{(100 - 40)/100} = \underline{\underline{\$50}}$$

Target Pricing—A specialty auto maker has spent $160 million for a new plant. It has a 25 per cent target return on investment. Standard production volume for the year is 5 000 units. Average total costs, excluding the new plant, are $14 000 for each car (at a production level of 5 000 cars). What is the selling price to the firm's retail dealers?

$$\text{Price} = \frac{\text{Investment costs} \times \text{Target return on investment (\%)}}{\text{Standard volume}}$$
$$+ \text{Average total costs (at standard volume)}$$

$$= \frac{\$160\ 000\ 000 \times .25}{5\ 000} + \$14\ 000 = \underline{\underline{\$22\ 000}}$$

Price-Floor Pricing—A big-screen TV manufacturer's plant capacity is 1 000 units. Its total fixed costs are $500 000 and variable costs are $375 per unit. At full production, average fixed costs are $500 per unit. The firm sets a price of $1 100 to retailers and gets orders for 800 TVs at that price. It must operate at 80 per cent of capacity, unless it re-evaluates its pricing strategy. With price-floor pricing, it can sell the 200 additional sets to retailers. How?

The firm could let resellers buy one TV at $425 for every four they buy at $1 100. Then, it earns a profit of $90 000 [revenues of ($1 100 × 800) + ($425 × 200) less costs of ($875 × 1 000)]. If it just makes and sells 800 TVs at full price, it earns $80 000 [revenues of ($1 100 × 800) less variable costs of ($375 × 800) and fixed costs of $500 000]. The higher profits are due to the fact that marginal revenue > marginal cost.

Traditional Break-Even Analysis—A small candy maker has total fixed costs of $150 000 and variable costs per unit of $0.25. It sells to retailers for $0.40 per bar. What is the break-even point in units? In sales dollars?

$$\frac{\text{Break-even point}}{(\text{units})} = \frac{\text{Total fixed costs}}{\text{Price} - \text{Variable costs (per unit)}} = \frac{\$150\ 000}{\$0.40 - \$0.25} = \underline{\underline{1\ 000\ 000}}$$

$$\frac{\text{Break-even point}}{(\text{sales dollars})} = \frac{\text{Total fixed costs}}{1 - \dfrac{\text{Variable costs (per unit)}}{\text{Price}}} = \frac{\$150\ 000}{1 - \dfrac{\$0.25}{\$0.40}} = \underline{\underline{\$250\ 000}}$$

Cost-plus pricing is the easiest form of pricing, based on units produced, total costs, and profit.

COST-PLUS PRICING For **cost-plus pricing**, prices are set by adding a predetermined profit to costs. It is the simplest form of cost-based pricing.

Generally, the steps for computing cost-plus prices are to estimate the number of units to be produced, calculate fixed and variable costs, and add a desired profit to costs. The formula for cost-plus pricing is:

$$\text{Price} = \frac{\text{Total fixed costs} + \text{Total variable costs} + \text{Projected profit}}{\text{Units produced}}$$

This method is easy to compute; yet, it has shortcomings. Profit is not expressed in relation to sales but in relation to costs, and price is not tied to consumer demand. Adjustments for rising costs are poorly conceived, and there are no plans for using excess capacity. There is little incentive to improve efficiency to hold down costs, and marginal costs are rarely analyzed.

Cost-plus pricing is most effective when price fluctuations have little influence on sales and when a firm is able to control prices. For example, the prices of custom-made furniture, ships, heavy machinery, and extracted minerals typically depend on the costs incurred in producing these items; thus, companies set prices by computing costs and adding a reasonable profit. Cost-plus pricing often allows firms to get consumer orders, produce items, and then derive prices after total costs are known. This protects sellers.

MARKUP PRICING In **markup pricing**, a firm sets prices by computing the per-unit costs of producing (buying) goods and/or services and then determining the markup percentages needed to cover selling costs and profit. It is most commonly used by wholesalers and retailers, although it is employed by all types of organizations. The formula for markup pricing is:[5]

Markup pricing considers per-unit product costs and the markups required to cover selling costs and profits. Markups should be expressed in terms of price rather than cost.

$$\text{Price} = \frac{\text{Product cost}}{(100 - \text{Markup per cent})/100}$$

There are several reasons why markups are commonly stated in terms of selling price instead of cost. One, since expenses, markdowns, and profits are computed as percentages of sales, citing markups as percentages of sales also aids in profit planning. Two, firms quote their selling prices and trade discounts to channel members as percentage reductions from final list prices. Three, competitive price data are more readily available than cost data. Four, profitability appears smaller if based on price rather than cost. This can be useful in avoiding criticism over high earnings.

Markup size depends on traditional profit margins, company selling and operating expenses, suggested list prices, inventory turnover, competition, the extent to which products must be serviced, and the effort needed to complete transactions. Due to differences in selling costs among products, some firms use a **variable markup policy**, whereby separate categories of goods and services receive different percentage markups. Variable markups recognize that some items require greater personal selling, customer service, alterations, and end-of-season markdowns than others. For example, expensive cosmetics need more personal selling and customer service than paperback books, suits need greater custom alterations than shirts, and fashion items are marked down more than basic clothing late in the selling season.

A variable markup policy responds to differences in selling costs among products.

Markup pricing, while having many of cost-plus pricing's limitations, is popular. It is fairly simple, especially for firms with uniform markups for several items. Channel members get fair profits. Price competition is less if firms have similar markups. Resellers can show their actual prices compared to suggested prices. Adjustments can be made as costs rise. Variable markups are responsive to selling-cost differences among products or channel members.

TARGET PRICING In **target pricing**, prices are set to provide a particular rate of return on investment for a standard volume of production—the level of production a firm anticipates achieving. For example, in the paper industry, the standard volume of production is usually set at around 90 to 92 per cent of plant capacity.[6] For target pricing to operate properly, a company must sell its entire standard volume at specified prices.

Target pricing enables a rate of return on investment to be earned for a standard volume of production.

---

[5]Markup can be calculated by transposing the formula above into:

$$\text{Markup percentage} = \frac{\text{Price} - \text{Product cost}}{\text{Price}} \times 100$$

[6]*Industrial Outlook 1994* (Washington, D.C.: U.S. Department of Commerce, 1994), pp. 10-1–10-2.

Target pricing is used by capital-intensive firms (like auto makers) and public utilities (like water companies). The prices charged by utilities are based on fair rates of return on invested assets and must be approved by regulatory commissions. Mathematically, a target price is computed as:

$$\text{Price} = \frac{\text{Investment costs} \times \text{Target return on investment (\%)}}{\text{Standard volume}}$$
$$+ \text{Average total costs (at standard volume)}$$

Target pricing has five major shortcomings. First, it is not useful for firms with low capital investments; it understates selling price. Second, because prices are not keyed to demand, the entire standard volume may not be sold at the target price. Third, production problems may hamper output and standard volume may not be attained. Fourth, price cuts to handle overstocked inventory are not planned under this approach. Fifth, if the standard volume is reduced due to expected poor sales performance, the price would have to be raised under a target-pricing calculation.

Price-floor pricing *may be used if there is excess capacity.*

PRICE-FLOOR PRICING A firm's usual goal is to set prices to cover the sum of average fixed costs, average variable costs, and profit per unit. But, when a firm has excess (unused) capacity, it may use **price-floor pricing** to determine the lowest price at which it is worthwhile to increase the amount of goods or services it makes available for sale.

The general principle in price-floor pricing is that the sale of additional units can be used to increase profits or help pay for fixed costs (which exist whether or not these items are made), as long as marginal revenues are greater than marginal costs. Although a firm cannot survive in the long run unless its average total costs are covered by prices, it may improve performance through price-floor pricing. The formula is:

$$\text{Price-floor price} = \text{Marginal revenue per unit} > \text{Marginal cost per unit}$$

Traditional break-even analysis *computes the sales needed to break even at a specific price.*

TRADITIONAL BREAK-EVEN ANALYSIS Like target pricing, **traditional break-even analysis** looks at the relationship among costs, revenues, and profits. While target pricing yields the price that results in a specified return on investment, traditional break-even analysis finds the sales quantity in units or dollars that is needed for total revenues (price × units sold) to equal total costs (fixed and variable) at a given price. If sales exceed the break-even quantity, a firm earns a profit. If sales are less than the break-even quantity, it loses money. Traditional break-even analysis does not consider return on investment, but can be extended to take profit planning into account. It is used by all kinds of sellers.

The break-even point can be computed in terms of units or sales dollars:

$$\text{Break-even point (units)} = \frac{\text{Total fixed costs}}{\text{Price} - \text{Variable costs (per unit)}}$$

$$\text{Break-even point (sales dollars)} = \frac{\text{Total fixed costs}}{1 - \dfrac{\text{Variable costs (per unit)}}{\text{Price}}}$$

These formulas are derived from the equation: Price × Quantity = Total fixed costs + (Variable costs per unit × Quantity).

Break-even analysis can be adjusted to take into account the profit sought by a firm:

$$\text{Break-even point (units)} = \frac{\text{Total fixed costs} + \text{Projected profit}}{\text{Price} - \text{Variable costs (per unit)}}$$

$$\text{Break-even point (sales dollars)} = \frac{\text{Total fixed costs} + \text{Projected profit}}{1 - \dfrac{\text{Variable costs (per unit)}}{\text{Price}}}$$

There are limitations to traditional break-even analysis. First, as with all forms of cost-based pricing, demand is not considered. The presumption is that wide variations in quantity can be sold at the same price; this is highly unlikely. Second, it is assumed that all costs can be divided into fixed and variable categories. Yet, some, like advertising, are difficult to define; advertising can be fixed or a per cent of sales. Third, it is assumed that variable costs per unit are constant over a range of quantities. However, purchase discounts or overtime wages may alter these costs. Fourth, it is assumed that fixed costs remain constant; but increases in production may lead to higher costs for new equipment, new full-time employees, and other items.

By including demand considerations, each of the cost-based techniques can be improved. Demand-based pricing techniques are discussed next.

Demand-Based Pricing

With **demand-based pricing**, a firm sets prices after studying consumer desires and ascertaining the range of prices acceptable to the target market. This approach is used by companies that believe price is a key factor in consumer decision making. These companies identify a **price ceiling**, which is the maximum amount consumers will pay for a given good or service. If the ceiling is exceeded, consumers will not make purchases. Its level depends on the elasticity of demand (availability of substitutes and urgency of need) and consumers' subjective price regarding the particular good or service.

Under **demand-based pricing**, *consumers are researched and a* **price ceiling** *set.*

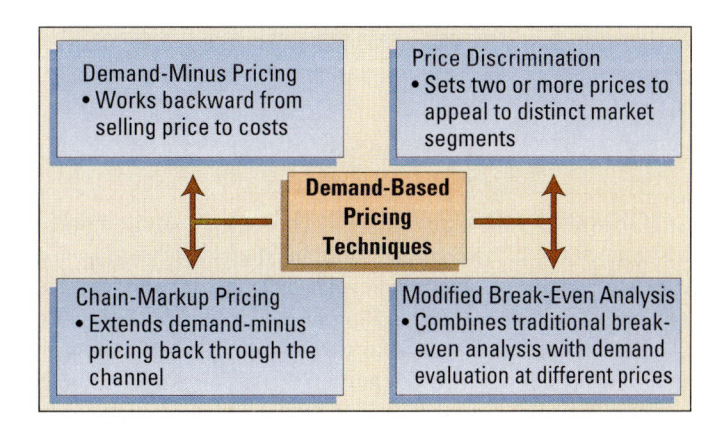

Demand-based techniques require that the firm research the quantities that consumers will purchase at various prices, sensitivity to price changes, the existence of market segments, and consumers' ability to pay. Demand estimates tend to be less precise than cost estimates. Also, firms that do inadequate cost analysis and rely on demand data may end up losing money if they make unrealistically low cost assumptions.

Under demand-based pricing, very competitive situations may lead to small markups and lower prices because consumers will purchase substitutes. In these cases, costs must be held down or prices will be too high—as might occur with cost-based pricing. For noncompetitive situations, firms can set large markups and high prices since demand is rather inelastic. There is less emphasis on costs when setting prices in these situations. With cost-based pricing, firms are more apt to set overly low prices in noncompetitive markets.

Four demand-based pricing techniques are reviewed next: demand-minus, chain-markup, modified break-even, and price discrimination. Figure 22-5 gives a synopsis of each technique, and Table 22-3 contains numerical examples of each.

Two aspects of competition-based pricing are discussed in the following subsections: price leadership and competitive bidding.

FIGURE 22-5
Demand-Based Pricing Techniques

Table 22-3
Examples of Demand-Based Pricing Techniques

Demand-Minus Pricing—A mail-order CD-ROM encyclopedia publisher has done consumer research and found people are willing to spend $60.00 for its brand. Its selling expenses and profits are expected to be 35 per cent of the selling price. What is the maximum it can spend to develop and produce each encyclopedia CD-ROM?

$$\text{Maximum merchandise costs} = \text{Price} \times [(100 - \text{Markup per cent})/100]$$
$$= \$60.00 \times [(100 - 35)/100] = \underline{\$39.00}$$

Chain-Markup Pricing—A ladies' shoe maker knows women will pay $50.00 for a pair of its shoes. It sells via wholesalers and retailers. Each requires a markup of 30 per cent; the manufacturer wants a 25 per cent markup. (a) What is the maximum price that retailers and wholesalers will spend for a pair of shoes? (b) What is the maximum the manufacturer can spend to make each pair of shoes?

(a) $\text{Maximum selling price to retailer} = \text{Final selling price} \times [(100 - \text{Retailer's markup})/100]$
$= \$50.00 \times [(100 - 30)/100] = \underline{\$35.00}$

$\text{Maximum selling price to wholesaler} = \text{Selling price to retailer} \times [(100 - \text{Wholesaler's markup})/100]$
$= \$35.00 \times [(100 - 30)/100] = \underline{\$24.50}$

(b) $\text{Maximum merchandise costs to manufacturer} = \text{Selling price to wholesaler} \times [(100 - \text{Manufacturer's markup})/100]$
$= \$24.50 \times [(100 - 25)/100] = \underline{\$18.38}$

Modified Break-Even Analysis—An aspirin maker has total fixed costs of $2 000 000 and variable costs of $1.50 per bottle. Research shows the following demand schedule. At what price should the company sell its aspirin?

Selling Price	Quantity Demanded	Total Revenue	Total Cost	Total Profit (Loss)	
$3.00	2 000 000	$ 6 000 000	$5 000 000	$1 000 000	Maximum
2.50	3 200 000	8 000 000	6 800 000	1 200 000 ←	profit at
2.00	5 000 000	10 000 000	9 500 000	500 000	price of $\underline{\$2.50}$

Price Discrimination—A sports team knows people will pay different prices for tickets, based on location. It offers 10 000 tickets at $30 each, 25 000 at $20 each, and 20 000 at $12 each. What are profits if total costs per game are $750 000?

$$\text{Profit} = (\text{Revenues from Segment A} + \text{Segment B} + \text{Segment C}) - \text{Total costs}$$
$$= (\$300\,000 + \$500\,000 + \$240\,000) - \$750\,000 = \underline{\$290\,000}$$

In demand-minus pricing, selling price, then markup, and finally maximum product costs are computed.

DEMAND-MINUS PRICING Through **demand-minus (demand-backward) pricing**, a firm finds the proper selling price and works backward to compute costs. This approach stipulates that price decisions revolve around consumer demand rather than company operations. It is used by firms selling directly to consumers.

Demand-minus pricing has three steps: first the selling price is determined by consumer surveys or other research; then the required markup percentage is set, based on selling expenses and desired profits; finally, the maximum acceptable per-unit cost for making or buying a product is computed. This formula is used:

$$\text{Maximum product cost} = \text{Price} \times [(100 - \text{Markup per cent})/100]$$

It shows that product cost is derived after selling price and markup are set.

The difficulty in demand-minus pricing is that marketing research may be time-consuming or complex, particularly if many items are involved. Also, new-product pricing research may be particularly inaccurate.

CHAIN-MARKUP PRICING **Chain-markup pricing** extends demand-minus calculations all the way from resellers back to suppliers (manufacturers): the final selling price is determined, markups for each channel member are examined, and the maximum acceptable costs to each member are computed.

Chain-markup pricing traces demand-minus calculations from channel members to suppliers.

In a traditional consumer-goods channel, the markup chain is composed of:

1. Maximum selling price to retailer = Final selling price × [(100 − retailer's markup)/100]

2. Maximum selling price to wholesaler = Selling price to retailer × [(100 − wholesaler's markup)/100]

3. Maximum product cost to manufacturer = Selling price to wholesaler × [100 − manufacturer's markup)/100]

By using chain-markup pricing, price decisions can be related to consumer demand and each reseller is able to see the effects of price changes on the total distribution channel. The interdependence of firms becomes more clear; they cannot set prices independently of one another.

MODIFIED BREAK-EVEN ANALYSIS **Modified break-even analysis** combines traditional break-even analysis with an evaluation of demand at various levels of price. Traditional analysis focuses on the sales needed to break even at a given price. It does not indicate the likely level of demand at that price, examine how consumers respond to different levels of price, consider that the break-even point can vary greatly depending on the price the firm happens to select, or calculate the price that maximizes profits.

Melding traditional break-even analysis with demand evaluation at various prices is **modified break-even analysis**.

Modified analysis reveals the price-quantity mix that maximizes profits. It shows that profits do not inevitably rise as the quantity sold increases because lower prices may be needed to expand demand. It also verifies that a firm should examine various price levels and select the one with the greatest profits. Finally, it relates demand to price, rather than assuming that the same volume could be sold at any price.

PRICE DISCRIMINATION With a **price discrimination** approach, a firm sets two or more distinct prices for a product so as to appeal to different final consumer or organizational consumer segments. Higher prices are offered to inelastic segments and lower prices to elastic ones. Price discrimination can be customer-based, product-based, time-based, or place-based.

Setting distinct prices to reach different market segments is **price discrimination**.

In customer-based price discrimination, prices differ by customer category for the same good or service. Price differentials may relate to a consumer's ability to pay (lawyers and accountants partially set prices in this manner), negotiating ability (the price of an office building is usually set by bargaining), or buying power (discounts are given for volume purchases).

Through product-based price discrimination, a firm markets a number of features, styles, qualities, brands, or sizes of a product and sets a different price for each product version. Price differentials are greater than cost differentials for the various versions. For example, a dishwasher may be priced at $400 in white and $450 in brown, although the brown colour costs the manufacturer only $10 more. There is inelastic demand by customers desiring the special colour, and product versions are priced accordingly.

Under time-based price discrimination, a firm varies prices for day versus evening (movie theatre tickets), peak versus off-peak hours (telephone and utility rates), or season (hotel rates). Consumers who insist on prime-time use pay higher prices than those who are willing to make their purchases at other times.

For place-based price discrimination, prices differ by seat location (sports and entertainment events), floor location (office buildings, hotels), or geographic location (resort cities). The demand for locations near the stage, elevators, or warm climates drives the

Ethics AND TODAY'S MARKETER

When Is a Sale Price Really a Sale Price?

In 1995, the Retail Council of Canada expressed concern over how the Competition Bureau was interpreting the regulations of misleading advertising with respect to sale prices. Regulation of misleading advertising is a criminal provision of the Competition Act so violations must be referred to the Attorney General of Canada and prosecuted through the court system. Many of the prominent members of the council had either been convicted, or were facing charges of misleading advertising related to prices, including K-mart Canada, which had a conviction over a mattress sale, and Hudson's Bay Company, which was facing seventeen separate charges related to activities in 1994.

The contention of the Retail Council is that the law does not reflect the current state of retail competition in the marketplace and needs to be changed. The focus of changes of interest to the Retail Council is on the definition of a "sale" price in relation to what constitutes a "regular" price. Under the current definition used by the Competition Bureau, the price at which 51 per cent of the volume of goods is sold is considered the regular price. However, when products go on sale, the intention of retailers is to make volume sales, and it is hard to predict what these volumes will be. The retailers would like the interpretation of regular price to be: the price set for 51 per cent of the time for which the item is available. Retailers contend that they cannot control sales volumes but they can control the amount of time for which a product is offered for sale at a specific price.

According to the Retail Council of Canada, when the Competition Act was written, most retailers held sales for the purpose of inventory clearance so the 51 per cent volume rule was quite reasonable. In today's competitive environment, sales are used to create instore traffic and to introduce new products. Pricing "new" products is particularly troublesome for retailers when they have to establish a "regular" price using the 51 per cent volume rule.

One other part of the argument for change presented by the Retail Council is based on a market research survey which was undertaken by Thompson Lightstone & Company Ltd. of Toronto. A key finding of the survey was that consumers are generally very skeptical about sale prices. This finding would imply that in practice, using the term "sale" is less likely to be misleading since consumers are skeptical. This argument could be used to ask legislators to ease up a bit. However, the survey also noted that consumers are also strongly attracted to sales. This finding would support the contention that regulators should remain vigilant with respect to retail activity in the marketplace to protect consumers from unscrupulous and manipulative pricing practices.

As a consultant to the Director of The Competition Bureau, debate the merits of the Retail Council of Canada's Argument and make a policy recommendation on how the Bureau should define a "regular" price.

Sources: Based on material in James Pollock, "RCC Wants Law Changed," *Marketing Magazine* (June 19, 1995), p. 3.

---

prices of these locations up. General admission tickets, basement offices, and moderate-temperature resorts are priced lower to attract consumers to otherwise less desirable purchases.

When a firm engages in price discrimination, it should use **yield management pricing**—whereby it determines the mix of price-quantity combinations that generates the highest level of revenues for a given period. A company wants to make sure that it gives itself every opportunity to sell as many goods and services at full price as possible, while also seeking to sell as many units as it can. It does not want to sell so many low-price items that it jeopardizes full-price sales. Thus, a 1000-seat theatre offering first-run plays must determine how many tickets to sell as orchestra (at $50 each) and how many to sell as general admission (at $25 each). If it tries to sell too many orchestra tickets, there may be empty seats during a performance. If it looks to sell too many general admission tickets, the theatre may be full—but total revenues may be unsatisfactory.[7]

Yield management pricing lets firms optimize price discrimination efforts.

Before using price discrimination, a firm should consider these questions: Are there distinct market segments? Do people communicate with each other about product features and prices? Can product versions be differentiated? Will some consumers choose low-priced models when they might otherwise buy high-priced models if they are the only ones available? How do the marginal costs of adding product alternatives compare with marginal revenues? Will channel members stock all models? How difficult is it to explain product differences to consumers? Under what conditions is price discrimination legal?

Competition-Based Pricing

In **competition-based pricing**, a firm uses competitors' prices rather than demand or cost considerations as its primary pricing guideposts. The company may not respond to changes in demand or costs unless they also have an effect on competitors' prices. It can set prices below the market, at the market, or above the market, depending on its customers, image, marketing mix, consumer loyalty, and other factors. This approach is applied by firms contending with others selling similar items (or those perceived as similar).

Competition-based pricing is setting prices relative to other firms.

Competition-based pricing is popular. It is simple, with no reliance on demand curves, price elasticity, or costs per unit. The ongoing market price level is assumed to be fair for both consumers and companies. Pricing at the market level does not disrupt competition, and therefore does not lead to retaliation. However, it may lead to complacency; and different firms may not have the same demand and cost structures.

PRICE LEADERSHIP Price leadership exists in situations where one firm (or a few firms) is usually the first to announce price changes and others in the industry follow. The price leader's role is to set prices that reflect market conditions, without disrupting the marketplace—it must not turn off consumers with price increases perceived as too large or precipitate a price war with competitors by excessive price cuts.

Price leadership occurs when one or a few firms initiate price changes in an industry; they are effective when others follow.

Price leaders are generally firms that have significant market shares, well-established positions, respect from competitors, and the desire to initiate price changes. As an illustration, a frequent price leader in the newsprint industry has been Canada's Abitibi-Price. It is the world's largest newsprint maker, has the largest production capacity, and has the dominant market share. Because over one-half of its revenues are in newsprint, the firm has a strong commitment to maintain stable prices.

Over the last several years, the role of price leaders has been greatly reduced in many industries, including steel, chemical, glass container, and newsprint, as many smaller firms have sought to act more independently. Even Abitibi-Price has been affected by this trend. At various times, it has announced higher newsprint prices and then has had to backtrack after competitors decided not to go along.

Announcements of price changes by industry leaders must be communicated through the media. It is illegal for firms in the same industry or in competing ones to confer with one another regarding the setting of prices.

COMPETITIVE BIDDING Through competitive bidding (discussed in Chapter 9), two or more firms independently submit prices to a customer for a specific good, project, and/or service. Sealed bids may be requested by some government or organizational consumers; each seller then has one chance to make its best offer.

---

[7]See Edwin McDowell, "His Goal: No Room at the Inns," *New York Times* (November 23, 1995), pp. D1, D8.

It is essential that companies integrate cost, demand, and competitive pricing techniques through **combination pricing**.

Various mathematical models have been applied to competitive bidding. All use the expected profit concept, which states that as the bid price increases, the profit to a firm increases but the probability of its winning a contract decreases. Although a firm's potential profit (loss) at a given bid amount can usually be estimated accurately, the probability of getting a contract (underbidding all other qualified competitors) can be hard to determine.

Combination Pricing

Although cost-, demand-, and competition-based pricing methods have been discussed separately, aspects of the three approaches are usually integrated into a **combination pricing** approach. A cost-based approach sets a price floor and outlines the various costs incurred in doing business. It establishes profit margins, target prices, and/or break-even quantities. A demand-based approach finds out the prices consumers will pay and the ceiling prices for each channel member. It develops the price-quantity mix that maximizes profits and allows a firm to reach different market segments (if it so desires). A competition-based approach examines the proper price level for the firm in relation to competitors.

Unless the approaches are integrated, critical issues may be overlooked. Table 22–4 shows a list of questions a firm should consider in setting prices.

Table 22-4
Selected Issues to Consider When Combining Pricing Techniques

Cost-Based
What profit margin does a price level permit?
Do markups allow for differences in product investments, installation and servicing, and selling effort and merchandising skills?
Are there accurate and timely cost data by good, service, project, process, and/or store?
Are cost changes monitored and prices adjusted accordingly?
Are there specific profit or return-on-investment goals?
What is the price-floor price for each good, service, project, process, and/or store?
What are the break-even points for each good, service, project, process, and/or store?

Demand-Based
What type of demand does each good, service, project, process, and/or store face?
Have price elasticities been estimated for various price levels?
Are demand-minus, chain-markup, and modified break-even analyses utilized?
Has price discrimination been considered?
How loyal are customers?

Competition-Based
How do prices compare with those of competitors?
Is price leadership used in the industry? By whom?
How do competitors react to price changes?
How are competitive bids determined?
Is the long-run expected profit concept used in competitive bidding?

Implementing a Pricing Strategy

Implementing a pricing strategy involves a wide variety of separate but related specific decisions, besides the broader concepts just discussed. The decisions involve whether and how to use customary versus variable pricing, a one-price policy versus flexible pricing, odd pricing, the price-quality association, leader pricing, multiple-unit pricing, price lining, price bundling, geographic pricing, and purchase terms.

Customary Versus Variable Pricing

Customary pricing occurs when a firm sets prices and seeks to maintain them for an extended time. Prices are not changed during this period. Customary pricing is used for items like candy, gum, magazines, restaurant food, and mass transit. Rather than modify prices to reflect cost increases, firms may reduce package size, change ingredients, or have a more restrictive transfer policy among bus lines. The assumption is that consumers prefer one of these alternatives to a price hike.

Variable pricing allows a firm to intentionally alter prices in response to cost fluctuations or differences in consumer demand. When costs change, prices are lowered or raised accordingly; the fluctuations are not absorbed and product quality is not modified to maintain customary prices. Through price discrimination, a firm can offer distinct prices to appeal to different market segments. In this way, the prices charged to diverse consumers are not based on costs, but on consumer sensitivity to price. Many firms use some form of variable pricing.

It is possible to combine customary and variable pricing. For example, a magazine may be $3 per single copy and $24 per year's subscription ($2 an issue)—two customary prices are charged; and the consumer selects the offer he or she finds most attractive.

*With **customary pricing**, one price is maintained over an extended period. Under **variable pricing**, prices reflect costs or differences in demand.*

A One-Price Policy Versus Flexible Pricing

A **one-price policy** lets a firm charge the same price to all customers seeking to purchase a good or service under similar conditions. Prices may differ according to the quantity bought, time of purchase, and services obtained (such as delivery and installation); but all consumers are given the opportunity to pay the same price for the same combinations of goods and services. This builds consumer confidence, is easy to administer, eliminates bargaining, and permits self-service and catalogue sales. Today, throughout Canada, one-price policies are the rule for most retailers. In industrial marketing, a firm with a one-price policy would not allow sales personnel to deviate from a published price list.

With **flexible pricing**, a firm sets prices based on the consumer's ability to negotiate or on the buying power of a large customer. For instance, people who are knowledgeable or are good bargainers would pay lower prices than those who are not knowledgeable or are weaker bargainers. Jewellery stores, car dealers, flea markets, real-estate brokers, antique shops, and many types of industrial marketers frequently use flexible pricing. In some cases, salesperson commissions are keyed to the profitability of orders; this encourages salespeople to solicit higher prices. Flexible prices to resellers are subject to the Competition Act restrictions explained in Chapter 21. Flexible pricing is much more prevalent outside North America, where this practice (sometimes known as "haggling") may be culturally ingrained.

One result of flexible pricing is the practice whereby consumers gather information from full-service sellers, shop around for the best available price, and then challenge discount sellers to "beat the lowest price." This practice is detrimental to full-service firms and allows discounters to hold down selling costs (and encourage further bargaining).

*All buying the same product pay the same price under a **one-price policy**. Different customers may pay different prices with **flexible pricing**.*

Odd Pricing

Odd pricing is used when selling prices are set at levels below even dollar values, such as 49 cents, $4.95, and $199. It has proven popular for several reasons. For one thing, people like getting change. Because the cashier must make change, employers ensure that transactions are properly recorded and money is placed in the cash register. Consumers gain the impression that a firm thinks carefully about its prices and sets them as low as possible. They may also believe that odd prices represent price reductions; a price of $8.95 may be viewed as a discount from $10.

Odd prices one or two cents below the next even price (29 cents, $2.98) are common up to $4 or $5. Beyond that point and up to $50 or so, five-cent reductions from the highest

***Odd prices** are those set below even-dollar values.*

even price ($19.95, $49.95) are more usual. For expensive items, odd endings are in dollars ($499, $5995).

Odd prices may help consumers stay within their price limits and still buy the best items available. A shopper willing to spend "less than $20" for a tie will be attracted to a $19.95 tie and might be as likely to purchase it as a $17 tie because it is within the defined price range. Yet, the imposition of the federal Goods and Services Tax combined with provincial sales taxes in nine Canadian provinces has the effect of raising odd prices into higher dollar levels and may reduce the impact of odd pricing as a selling tool.

The Price-Quality Association

The **price-quality association** *deals with perceptions.* **Prestige pricing** *indicates that consumers may not buy when a price is too low.*

According to the **price-quality association**, consumers may believe high prices represent high quality and low prices represent low quality. This association tends to be most valid when quality is difficult to judge on bases other than price, buyers perceive large differences in quality among brands, buyers have little experience or confidence in assessing quality (as with a new product), high prices are used to exclude the mass market, brand names are unknown, or brand names require certain price levels to sustain their images.

If brand names are well-known and/or people are confident of their ability to compare different brands in terms of nonprice factors, the price-quality association may be less valid. Then, many consumers may be more interested in the perceived value they receive for their money—and not necessarily believe a higher price represents better quality. It is essential that prices properly reflect both the quality and the image a firm seeks for its offerings.

With **prestige pricing**, a theory drawn from the price-quality association, it is assumed that consumers will not buy goods or services at prices they consider to be too low. Most people set their own price floors and will not purchase at prices below those floors—because they feel quality and status would be inferior at extremely low prices. Most people also set ceilings with regard to the prices they consider acceptable for particular goods or services. Above those ceilings, items would be seen as too expensive. For each good or service, a firm should set its prices in the target market's acceptable range between the floor and ceiling. See Figure 22–6 for an example using designer jeans.

FIGURE 22-6
Demand for Designer Jeans under Prestige Pricing

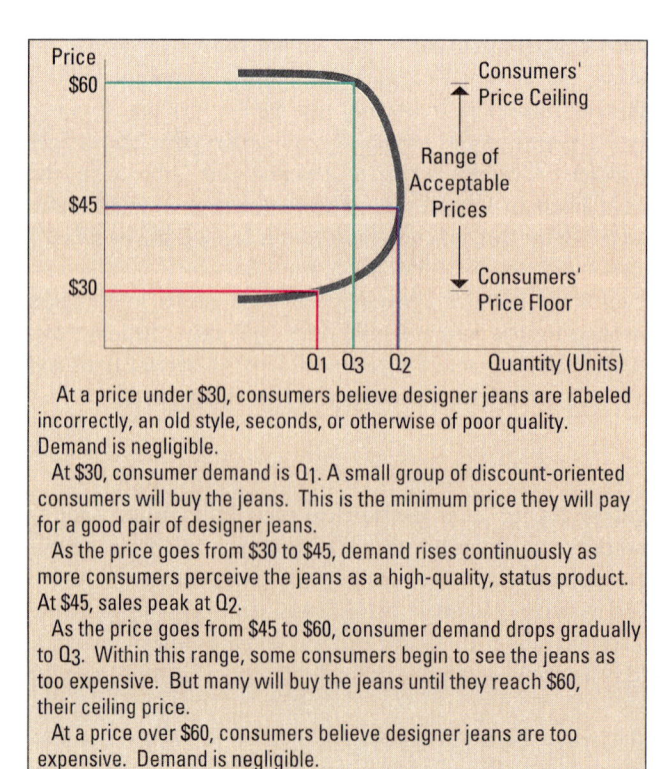

At a price under $30, consumers believe designer jeans are labeled incorrectly, an old style, seconds, or otherwise of poor quality. Demand is negligible.
At $30, consumer demand is Q1. A small group of discount-oriented consumers will buy the jeans. This is the minimum price they will pay for a good pair of designer jeans.
As the price goes from $30 to $45, demand rises continuously as more consumers perceive the jeans as a high-quality, status product. At $45, sales peak at Q2.
As the price goes from $45 to $60, consumer demand drops gradually to Q3. Within this range, some consumers begin to see the jeans as too expensive. But many will buy the jeans until they reach $60, their ceiling price.
At a price over $60, consumers believe designer jeans are too expensive. Demand is negligible.

Leader Pricing

With **leader pricing**, a firm advertises and sells key items in its product assortment at less than their usual profit margins. For a wholesaler or retailer, the goal is to increase customer traffic. For a manufacturer, the goal is to gain greater consumer interest in its overall product line. In both cases, it is hoped that consumers will buy regularly priced merchandise in addition to the specially priced items that attract them.

Leader pricing is most used with well-known, high-turnover, frequently bought products. For example, in some drugstores, one of the best-selling items in terms of dollar sales is Kodak film. To stimulate customer traffic into these stores, film may be priced very low; in some cases, it is sold at close to cost. Film is a good item for leader pricing because consumers are able to detect low prices and they are attracted into a store by a discount on the item, which regularly sells for several dollars.

There are two kinds of leader pricing: loss leaders and prices higher than cost but lower than regular prices. The use of loss leaders must be undertaken carefully to avoid violating the Competition Act.

Leader pricing is used to attract customers to low prices.

Multiple-Unit Pricing

Multiple-unit pricing is a practice whereby a firm offers discounts to consumers to encourage them to buy in quantity, so as to increase overall sales volume. By offering items at two for 89 cents or six for $1.39, a firm attempts to sell more units than at 50 cents or $.25 each.

There are four major benefits from multiple-unit pricing: customers may increase their immediate purchases if they feel they get a bargain; they may boost long-term consumption if they make larger purchases, as occurs with soda pop; competitors' customers may be attracted by the discounts; and a firm may be able to clear out slow-moving and end-of-season merchandise.

Multiple-unit pricing will not be successful if consumers merely shift their purchases and do not hike their consumption. For example, multiple-unit pricing for Heinz ketchup may not result in consumers using more ketchup with their meals. Thus, it would not raise total dollar sales; consumers would simply buy ketchup less frequently because it can be stored. However, it does have the benefit of protecting against competitive activity because consumers are carrying an inventory of ketchup and although they are not buying more Heinz ketchup, they are also not in the market for the competitor's ketchup either.

*With **multiple-unit pricing**, quantity discounts are intended to result in higher sales volume.*

Price Lining

Price lining involves selling products at a range of prices, with each representing a distinct level of quality (or features). Instead of setting one price for a single version of a good or service, a firm sells two or more versions (with different levels of quality or features) at different prices. Price lining involves two decisions: prescribing the price range (floor and ceiling) and setting specific price points in that range.

A price range may be low, intermediate, or high. For example, inexpensive radios may be priced from $8 to $20, moderately priced radios from $22 to $50, and expensive radios from $55 to $120. After the range is chosen, a limited number of price points is set. The price points must be distinct and not too close together. Inexpensive radios could be priced at $8, $12, and $20. They would not be priced at $8, $9, $10, $11, $12, $13, $14, $15, $16, $17, $18, $19, and $20. This would confuse consumers and be inefficient for the firm. Figure 22-7 illustrates how MacWarehouse uses price lining to sell its Apple Computers.

When price lining, a firm must consider these factors: Price points must be spaced far enough apart so customers perceive differences among product versions—otherwise, consumers might view the price floor as the price they should pay and believe there is no difference among models. Price points should be spaced farther apart at higher prices because consumer demand becomes more inelastic. Relationships among price points must be kept when costs rise, so clear differences are retained. If radio costs rise 25 per cent, prices should be set at $10, $15, and $25 (up from $8, $12, and $20).

Price lining offers benefits for both sellers and consumers. Sellers can offer a product assortment, attract market segments, trade up shoppers within a price range, control inven-

Price lining sets a range of selling prices and price points within that range.

FIGURE 22-7
Price Lining at MacWarehouse
By offering products at several different price points, MacWarehouse addresses the needs of all of its customers.
Reprinted by permission.

tory by price point, reduce competition by having versions over a price range, and increase overall sales volume. Consumers gain because choices are greater, confusion is lessened, comparisons are easier, and quality options are available within a given price range.

Price lining does have constraints. Consumers may feel price gaps are too large—a $25 handbag may appear cheap, while the next price point of $100 may be too expensive. Rising costs may squeeze individual prices and make it hard for a firm to keep the proper relationships in its line. And markdowns or special sales may disrupt the balance in a price line, unless all items in the line are proportionately reduced in price.

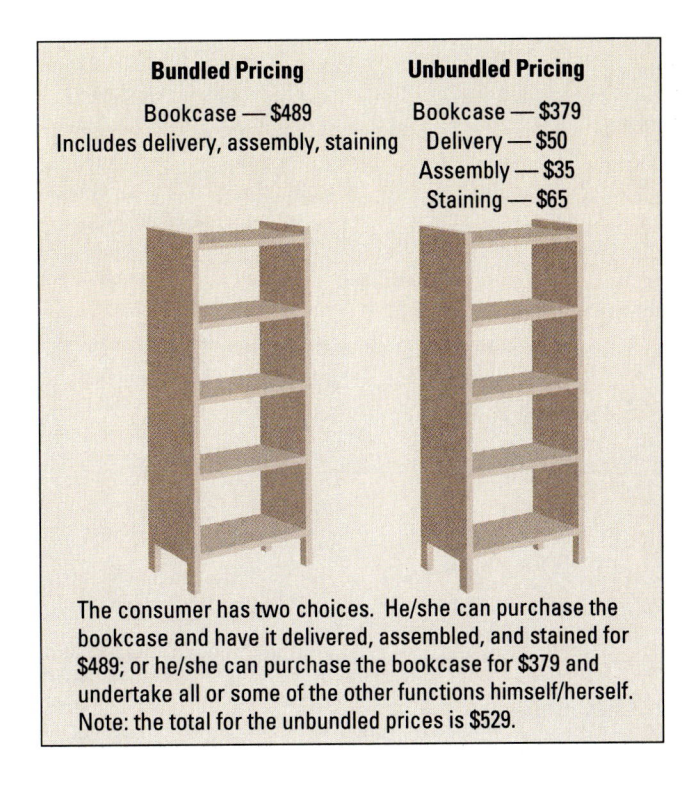

FIGURE 22-8
Price Bundling for a Bookcase

Bundled Pricing
Bookcase — $489
Includes delivery, assembly, staining

Unbundled Pricing
Bookcase — $379
Delivery — $50
Assembly — $35
Staining — $65

The consumer has two choices. He/she can purchase the bookcase and have it delivered, assembled, and stained for $489; or he/she can purchase the bookcase for $379 and undertake all or some of the other functions himself/herself. Note: the total for the unbundled prices is $529.

Price Bundling

Some form of price bundling can be used in a strategy. With **bundled pricing**, a firm sells a basic product, options, and customer service for one total price. An industrial-equipment manufacturer may have a single price for a drill press, its delivery, its installation, and a service contract. Individual items, such as the drill press, would not be sold separately.

With **unbundled pricing**, a firm breaks down prices by individual components and allows the consumer to decide what to purchase. A discount appliance store may have separate prices for a refrigerator, its delivery, its installation, and a service contract.

Many companies choose to offer consumers both pricing options and allow a slight discount for bundled pricing. See Figure 22-8.

A firm can use **bundled** *or* **unbundled pricing**.

Geographic Pricing

Geographic pricing outlines responsibility for transportation charges. Many times, it is not negotiated but depends on the traditional practices in the industry in which the firm operates; and all companies in the industry normally conform to the same geographic pricing format. Geographic pricing often involves industrial marketing situations.

These are the most common methods of geographic pricing:

- *FOB mill (factory) pricing*—The buyer picks a transportation form and pays all freight charges, the seller pays the costs of loading the goods (hence, "free on board"), and the delivered price to the buyer depends on freight charges.
- *Uniform delivered pricing*—All buyers pay the same delivered price for the same quantity of goods, regardless of their location; the seller pays for shipping.
- *Zone pricing*—It provides for a uniform delivered price to all buyers within a geographic zone; through a multiple-zone system, delivered prices vary by zone.
- *Base-point pricing*—Firms in an industry establish basing points from which the costs of shipping are computed; the delivered price to a buyer reflects the cost of transporting goods from the basing point nearest to the buyer, regardless of the actual site of supply.

Geographic pricing *alternatives are FOB mill (factory), uniform delivered, zone, and base-point pricing.*

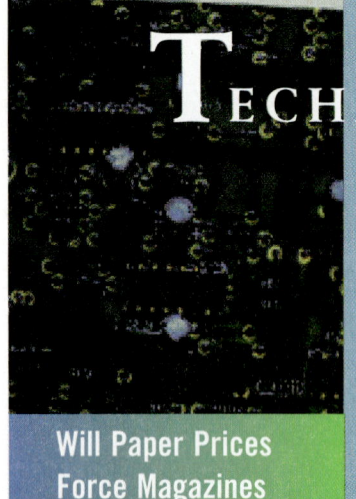

TECHNOLOGY & MARKETING

Will Paper Prices Force Magazines to Go "Online"?

It almost seems like the industry is committing economic suicide but in the last couple of years paper prices have been escalating at unprecedented rates. World prices for paper have nearly doubled since 1994 and were forecasted to be almost U.S.$785 per tonne by the end of 1996. This makes it very hard on firms in the printing and publishing industry. To stay in business media publishers are forced to hike advertising rates and newsstand prices while book publishers are forced to hike trade prices. All of these increases make their way to consumers, who pay more for their reading material and more for the products advertised in the media.

Curiously, these price hikes are coming at a time when demand for paper could well undergo a major decline due to increased use of electronic publishing and electronic media through home computers and the Internet. It is even conceivable that some paper producers are seeing the handwriting on the wall and the high prices are due to their desire to get some big profits before they are wiped out.

Traditional publishers have coped with the increases in a couple of basic ways. They have passed on some of the costs by raising product prices and in the case of paid media, raising advertising rates. In the newspaper industry one response has been a reduction in the actual size of the papers coupled with moderate price increases.

However, another response is to simply go "paperless." A large number of popular Canadian magazines have already established online electronic products. Magazines like *Maclean's*, *Canadian Business*, *L'actualite'*, *Saturday Night* and *Canadian Living* have online versions. Southam and Torstar have joined in a partnership to launch an online classified ad service. Even the government has reduced its dependence on paper by providing more online services and fewer print publications. For example, Statistics Canada no longer publishes its daily information release (appropriately called *The Daily*), on paper but offers it as a free online information service on the Statistics Canada Website.

The longest running online magazine in Canada is *Vancouver Village*, which is found on the World Wide Web. Much of the content of *Vancouver Village* was culled from *Vancouver Magazine* and *Western Living Magazine*. Currently revenue for Vancouver Village is derived from sponsorships and classified advertising. The current thinking is that online publishing targeted at consumers will have to earn its revenues from the advertisers, while providing the consumers the information for free. The circulation potential for online publishing has tremendous potential and the cost of publishing will not be affected by "paper" prices.

As a consultant to the paper industry, what recommendations would you make concerning their current pricing strategies? Explain your answer.

Sources: Based on material in Jim McElgunn, "Paper Prices Still Rising," *Marketing Magazine* (January 29, 1996), p. 3; Jim McElgunn, "Southam, Torstar Join for Online Classifieds," *Marketing Magazine* (January 29, 1996), p. 3; Andrea Haman, "Surviving on Paper," *Marketing Magazine* (June 26, 1995), p. 16; and Michael McCullough, "The Tricky Jump to Cyberspace," *Marketing Magazine* (August 14, 1995), p. 20.

Purchase terms *outline pricing provisions.*

VANCOUVER VILLAGE
www.vanmag.com/Welcome.html

Purchase Terms

Purchase terms are the provisions of price agreements. They include discounts, the timing of payments, and credit arrangements.

Discounts are the reductions from final selling prices that are available to resellers and consumers for performing certain functions, paying cash, buying large amounts, buying in off-seasons, or enhancing promotions. As an example, a wholesaler may buy goods at 40 per cent off the manufacturer's suggested final list selling price. This 40 per cent covers the wholesaler's expenses, profit, and discount to the retailer. The retailer could buy goods for 25 per cent off list (the wholesaler keeping 15 per cent for its costs and profit). In giving discounts, firms must make them proportionately available to all competing channel members, to avoid violating the Competition Act.

Payment timing must be specified in a purchase agreement. Final consumers may pay immediately or after delivery. In credit transactions, payments are not made until bills are received; they may be made over time. Organizational consumers are also quite interested in the timing of payments and negotiate for the best terms. For example, terms of net 30 mean products do not have to be paid for until 30 days after receipt. They must then be paid for in full. Terms of 2/10, net 30 mean a buyer receives a 2 per cent discount if the full bill is paid within 10 days after merchandise receipt. The buyer must pay the face value of a bill within 30 days after the receipt of products. Various time terms are available.

When marketing internationally, sellers must sometimes be prepared to wait an extended period to receive payments. At one time, it took North American firms an average of 337 days to get paid by Iranian businesses, 129 days to get paid by Kenyan businesses, 123 days to get paid by Argentine businesses, and 119 days to get paid by Brazilian clients.[8]

A firm that allows credit purchases may use open accounts or revolving accounts. With an **open credit account**, the buyer receives a monthly bill for the goods and services bought during the preceding month. The account must be paid in full each month. With a **revolving credit account**, the buyer agrees to make minimum monthly payments during an extended period of time and pays interest on outstanding balances. Today, various types of organizations (from Xerox to some physicians offering laser eye corrective surgery) offer some form of credit plan. Auto makers provide their own cut-rate financing programs to stimulate sales and leasing.

Open *and* **revolving credit accounts** *are possible.*

Price Adjustments

After a price strategy is enacted, it often requires continuous fine-tuning to reflect changes in costs, competitive conditions, and demand. Prices can be adjusted by alterations in list prices, escalator clauses and surcharges, added markups, markdowns, and rebates.

List prices are the regularly quoted prices provided to customers. They may be preprinted on price tags, in catalogues, and in dealer purchase orders. Modifications in list prices are necessary if there are sustained changes in labour costs, raw material costs, and market segments and as a product moves through its life cycle. When these events are long term in nature, they enable customary prices to be revised, new catalogues to be printed, and adjustments to be completed in an orderly fashion.

Costs or economic conditions may sometimes be so volatile that revised list prices cannot be printed or distributed efficiently. Escalator clauses or surcharges can then be used. Both allow prices to be adjusted quickly. With **escalator clauses**, a firm is contractually allowed to raise the prices of items to reflect higher costs in those items' essential ingredients without changing printed list prices. It may even be able to set prices at the time of delivery. **Surcharges** are across-the-board published price increases that supplement list prices. These may be used with catalogues because of their simplicity; an insert is distributed with the catalogue.

When list prices are not involved, **additional markups** can be used to raise regular selling prices if demand is unexpectedly high or costs are rising. There is a risk to this. For example, supermarkets get bad publicity for relabelling low-cost existing items at higher prices so they match those of newer merchandise purchased at higher costs.

Markdowns are reductions from items' original selling prices. All types of sellers use them to meet the lower prices of competitors, counteract overstocking of merchandise, clear out shopworn merchandise, deplete assortments of odds and ends, and increase customer traffic.

Although manufacturers regularly give discounts to resellers, they may periodically offer cash **rebates** to customers to stimulate the purchase of an item or a group of items. Rebates are flexible, do not alter basic prices, involve direct communication between consumers and manufacturers (since rebates are usually sent to consumers by manufacturers),

List prices, **escalator clauses**, **surcharges**, **additional markups**, **markdowns**, *and* **rebates** *are key pricing tools.*

---

[8]"Your Check Is in the Mail," *Wall Street Journal* (December 8, 1992), p. 2.

and do not affect resellers' profits (as regular price reductions do). Price cuts by individual resellers may not generate the same kind of consumer enthusiasm. Rebate popularity can be traced to their usage by the auto industry to help cut down on inventory surpluses. Rebates have also been offered by Canadian Tire, Sega, Gillette, Polaroid, Minolta, and a number of others. The major disadvantage is that so many firms have used rebates that their impact may be lessened.

Whenever adjustments are needed, channel members should cooperatively agree on their individual roles. Price hikes or cuts should not be unilateral.

MARKETING IN A CHANGING WORLD
Dealing with Non-Paying Customers[9]

An interesting situation facing many business people today is when customers use services that are paid for by third parties, usually insurers. People have eyeglass plans, drug plans, medical plans, and other company benefits. Car warranty repairs and car insurance repairs are also situations where third-party payments occur. In these circumstances the exchange of value between the service provider, the customer, and the paying insuring party gets distorted because the benefit of the service is separated from the price of the service.

The interests of the three parties are all different in these exchanges. For example, the service provider is chiefly concerned with getting paid a fair value, the customer wants fast, efficient, and high-quality service, and finally, the third-party provider wants low costs but strong revenues. Problems can occur when the interests of the different parties come into conflict as a result of the exchange, which they often do. And when competition gets added to the mix, the situation can get very confused.

Take the case of pharmaceutical marketing in Canada. In most provinces, senior citizens and welfare recipients are covered by provincial drug plans. Unlike private drug plans, which are profit-making enterprises, provincial drug plans are operated on a cost-recovery basis. Consequently, provincial drug plans have tended to focus on providing medications at the lowest possible cost. This means patients are often given generic drugs as opposed to name-brand drugs. In some cases, the patients and physicians have expressed concern that the generics were not up to the quality standards of name-brand medications. And many patients are not even aware of the fact that they may not be receiving the "best" quality product on the market, because by law, pharmacies are required to fill prescriptions with the lowest cost medication to keep costs down and save patients money.

The distortion in values has another unfortunate aspect. Physicians prescribe medications that are very expensive, knowing that the patient will not have to pay for them directly. Patients have prescriptions filled knowing they will not have to pay directly for the medication and then decide not to take the medication. Because the monetary exchange of values has been separated, this situation ends up costing the system a lot of money and the users are none the wiser.

As one pharmacist commented, "I once had a patient receive three prescriptions worth $200 and then had to listen to a complaint about how his insurance company had raised his co-pay from 35¢ a prescription to $1. Later he returned one of the prescriptions, valued at $100, and asked for $1 back, saying he decided not to take it. When I told him that I could not give him a refund because of the risk of product tampering he became so angry I was afraid of violence and my staff were about to call the police. He eventually calmed down but insisted I transfer his medical file to one of my competitors. All of this, over one lousy dollar. I shudder to think how he would have behaved if he had paid the full price!"

One way of bringing the exchange of values back into focus is to have co-pay and reimbursement types of insurance plans. In these instances, the consumer pays a portion of the cost of the service directly or pays for the complete service and then receives a reimbursement from the insurance company. The value of the service is duly registered by the consumer and the risk of loss if there is no reimbursement is also borne by the consumer. In this way, the balance in the exchange of values gets returned and all of the parties tend to act more responsibly towards one another.

....

[9] The material in this section is based on: Gail Chiasson, "Quebec Drug Marketers Take the Offensive," *Marketing Magazine* (September 25, 1995), p. 6; and the experiences of author William J. Wellington as a pharmaceutical representative.

SUMMARY

1. *To present an overall framework for developing and applying a pricing strategy* A pricing strategy has five stages: objectives, broad policy, strategy, implementation, and adjustments. The stages are affected by outside factors and must be integrated with a firm's marketing mix.

2. *To analyze sales-based, profit-based, and status quo-based pricing objectives, and to describe the role of a broad price policy* Sales goals centre on volume and/or market share. In penetration pricing, a company sets low prices to capture a mass market. Profit goals focus on profit maximization, satisfactory profits, optimum return on investment, and/or early cash recovery. In skimming pricing, a firm seeks to capture the segment less concerned with price than with quality or status. Status quo goals are geared toward minimizing the impact of outside parties and ensuring stability. Two or more pricing objectives may be combined.

   A broad price policy sets the overall direction for a firm's pricing efforts. Through it, a firm decides if it is price- or nonprice-oriented.

3. *To examine and apply the alternative approaches to a pricing strategy* A price strategy may be cost-based, demand-based, competition-based, or a combination of these.

   With cost-based pricing, a firm computes merchandise, service, and overhead costs and then adds an amount to cover profit. Cost-plus pricing adds costs and a desired profit to set prices. In markup pricing, a firm sets prices by calculating the per-unit costs of producing (buying) goods and/or services and then determining the markup percentages needed to cover selling costs and profit; a variable markup policy allows different markups for distinct products. In target pricing, prices are set to provide a specified rate of return on investment for a standard volume of production. When a firm has excess capacity, it may use price-floor pricing, in which prices are set at a level above variable costs rather than total costs. Traditional break-even analysis determines the sales quantity at which total costs equal total revenues for a chosen price.

   With demand-based pricing, a firm sets prices after doing consumer research and learning the range of acceptable prices to the target market. In demand-minus pricing, a firm determines the proper selling price and works backward to compute costs. Chain-markup pricing extends demand-minus calculations all the way from resellers back to suppliers (manufacturers). Modified break-even analysis combines traditional break-even analysis with an evaluation of demand at various levels of price. Price discrimination is a technique whereby a firm sets two or more distinct prices for a product so as to appeal to different market segments.

   In competition-based pricing, a firm uses competitors' prices as its main guideposts. Prices may be below, at, or above the market. A firm would determine whether it has the ability and the interest to be a price leader or price follower. Under competitive bidding, two or more firms independently submit prices in response to precise customer requests.

   These three pricing approaches should be integrated using combination pricing, so that a firm includes all necessary factors in its pricing strategy. Otherwise, critical decisions are likely to be overlooked.

4. *To discuss several specific decisions that must be made in implementing a pricing strategy* Enacting a price strategy involves a variety of interlocking specific decisions. Customary pricing is employed when a firm sets prices for an extended period. With variable pricing, a firm alters prices to coincide with cost or consumer demand fluctuations.

   In a one-price policy, all consumers purchasing under similar conditions pay the same price. Flexible pricing allows a firm to vary prices based on a shopper's ability to negotiate or the buying power of a large customer.

   Odd-pricing is used if selling prices are set below even-dollar values. According to the price-quality association, consumers may believe there is a correlation between price and quality. With prestige pricing, it is assumed that consumers do not buy products at prices that are considered too low. They set price floors, as well as price ceilings.

   Under leader pricing, key items are sold at less than their usual profit margins to increase consumer traffic. Multiple-unit pricing is a practice in which a company offers discounts to consumers for buying in quantity.

   Price lining involves the sale of goods and services at a range of prices, with each embodying a distinct level of quality (or features). In bundled pricing, a firm offers a basic product, options, and customer service for one total price; through unbundled pricing, it breaks down prices by individual components and lets consumers decide what to buy.

   Geographic pricing outlines the responsibility for transportation. Purchase terms are the provisions of price agreements, including discounts, timing of payments, and credit.

5. *To show the major ways that prices can be adjusted* Once a pricing strategy is implemented, it usually needs regular fine-tuning to reflect cost, competition, and demand changes. Prices can be adjusted by changing list prices, including escalator clauses and surcharges in contracts, marking prices up or down, and offering direct rebates.

KEY TERMS

sales-based pricing objectives (p. 603)
penetration pricing (p. 603)
profit-based pricing objectives (p. 603)
skimming pricing (p. 603)
status quo-based pricing objectives (p. 604)
broad price policy (p. 604)
cost-based pricing (p. 605)
price floor (p. 605)
cost-plus pricing (p. 608)
markup pricing (p. 609)
variable markup policy (p. 609)
target pricing (p. 609)
price-floor pricing (p. 610)
traditional break-even analysis (p. 610)
demand-based pricing (p. 611)
price ceiling (p. 611)

demand-minus (demand-backward) pricing (p. 612)
chain-markup pricing (p. 613)
modified break-even analysis (p. 613)
price discrimination (p. 613)
yield management pricing (p. 615)
competition-based pricing (p. 615)
price leadership (p. 615)
combination pricing (p. 616)
customary pricing (p. 617)
variable pricing (p. 617)
one-price policy (p. 617)
flexible pricing (p. 617)
odd pricing (p. 617)
price-quality association (p. 618)
prestige pricing (p. 618)
leader pricing (p. 619)

multiple-unit pricing (p. 619)
price lining (p. 619)
bundled pricing (p. 621)
unbundled pricing (p. 621)
geographic pricing (p. 621)
purchase terms (p. 622)
open credit account (p. 623)
revolving credit account (p. 623)
list prices (p. 623)
escalator clauses (p. 623)
surcharges (p. 623)
additional markups (p. 623)
markdowns (p. 623)
rebates (p. 623)

Review Questions

1. Explain this statement: "It should not be inferred that status quo objectives require no effort on the part of the firm."
2. When should a firm pursue penetration pricing? Skimming pricing?
3. Why are markups usually computed on the basis of selling price?
4. A firm requires a 14 per cent return on a $700 000 investment in order to produce a new electric garage-door opener. If the standard volume is 50 000 units, fixed costs are $500 000, and variable costs are $48 per unit, what is the target price?
5. A company making office desks has total fixed costs of $2 million per year and variable costs of $450 per desk. It sells the desks to retailers for $750 apiece. Compute the traditional break-even point in both units and dollars.
6. Discuss chain-markup pricing from the perspective of a retailer.
7. What is yield management pricing? Why is it important for sellers to understand this concept?
8. Contrast customary pricing and variable pricing. How may the two techniques be combined?
9. Under what circumstances is the price-quality association most valid? Least valid?
10. How does price lining benefit manufacturers? Retailers? Consumers?

Discussion Questions

1. A movie theatre has weekly fixed costs (land, building, and equipment) of $3500. Variable weekly costs (movie rental, electricity, ushers, etc.) are $1800. From a price-floor pricing perspective, how much revenue must a movie generate during a slow week for it to be worthwhile to open the theatre? Explain your answer.
2. A retailer determines that customers are willing to spend $27.95 on a new John Grisham (author of *The Client* and other best-sellers in the legal arena) novel. The publisher charges the retailer $22.50 for each copy. The retailer wants a 30 per cent markup. Comment on this situation.
3. a. A wholesaler of small industrial tools has fixed costs of $350 000, variable costs of $20 per tool, and faces this demand schedule from its hardware-store customers:

Price	Quantity Demanded
$24	100,000
$27	85,000
$30	65,000
$33	40,000

    At what price is profit maximized?

    b. If the company noted in Question 3a decides to sell 40 000 small tools at $33 and 45 000 of these tools at $27, what will its profit be? What are the risks of this approach?
4. Develop a price-lining strategy for each of these firms:
    a. A restaurant.
    b. A CA firm specializing in large-business accounts.
    c. A video-rental firm.
5. A wholesaler of plumbing supplies recently added a new line of kitchen sinks and priced them at $109 each (to plumbers). The manufacturer has just announced a 10 per cent price increase on the sinks—due to higher materials and labour costs. Yet, for this wholesaler, the initial response of plumbers to the sinks has been sluggish. Also, some competing wholesalers are selling the sinks for $99—$30 under the manufacturer's new suggested list price. What should the wholesaler do next?

VIDEO CASE

Another Discount Priced Airline in Canada? Are You Crazy?

Throughout the world one of the toughest businesses to operate in and make money in is the airline business. In Canada, the two major airlines are Air Canada and Canadian Airlines International. In 1995 Air Canada earned $52 million on sales of $4.5 billion, a paltry 1.2 per cent profit margin. Its closest competitor, Canadian Airlines International, lost $194.7 million on sales of $3.1 billion.

Surprisingly, two new discount airlines ventured into this environment in 1996. If the battle between Air Canada and Canadian Airlines International was not daunting enough, the history of discount airlines in Canada most certainly is. Discount airlines have a zero success rate in Canada.

Who are these airlines and why have they entered a business with so much competition and so little profit? The first, WestJet, is headed by Clyde Beadows and is based in Calgary. The second is Greyhound Air, which is headed by John Munro and based in Kelowna, B.C., but has its hub in Winnipeg. WestJet's initial plans are modest, with service to six Western cities. Greyhound is an operating partner of Greyhound bus lines and operates in eight cities connecting Ontario and Western Canada.

The discount positioning of these two competitors involves offering low airfares. For example, WestJet has advertised fares as low as $29 one way between Calgary and Edmonton and $59 from Calgary to Vancouver. But a low price positioning in the airline business makes it difficult to make a profit. WestJet and Greyhound are trying to duplicate the success formula of Southwest Airlines, the eighth largest airline in the U.S. (1995 sales of U.S.$2.8 billion) with the highest profit margin (6.4 per cent). This means having a low cost structure and high capacity utilization of its aircraft (typical airlines require an average of 65 per cent capacity on each plane, called the load factor, to break even).

WestJet is aiming to achieve this low cost structure by owning its fleet of aircraft and by instituting "ticketless" travel. Almost 35 per cent of employees of a typical airline are involved in ticketing. Another way costs are reduced is by not having connecting baggage handling. There is no inflight meal service, which reduces operating costs as well as the number of flight attendants required.

Greyhound is using a similar strategy: ticketless travel, limited inflight meals and service. They are not operating the aircraft themselves, but have formed a partnership with a courier airline. They are also offering passengers an air or bus option for travel, including connections to bus transportation to 1100 Canadian destinations. The existing ticketing system used by Greyhound is being used, and Greyhound also has a frequent user program.

WestJet was first to get off the ground in February 1996, and in response both Air Canada and Canadian Airlines International matched prices. In response to WestJet's entry, Greyhound waited until July 1996 to launch their service.

One important difference between the Canadian and U.S. air travel market is the phenomenon of winter tourism. High volumes of winter air travel result in high load factors year round for U.S. airlines. But history indicates that Canadians tend to fly across the country less in the winter.

The key issue for survival and profitability for all airlines is load factor. It seems clear that in Canada someone will come up short, given all the competition and the nature of the Canadian airline market.

QUESTIONS

1. Upon which main bases did WestJet and Greyhound select their pricing strategies? Discuss possible alternatives.
2. Identify WestJet's and Greyhound Air's competitors. Over which competitors do they not have a price advantage? On what basis will they be able to compete against them?
3. Discuss why Greyhound may have waited on the sidelines before entering the market. Compare their strategy to WestJet's.
4. Use the following information to determine what price air carrier discounters need to charge to break even: A typical aircraft holds a maximum of 160 passengers, costs $10 million and has a useful life of twenty years. The airline has twenty planes, overhead costs of $250 000 per month and investors expect an annual before-tax profit of $250 000 per month. Each aircraft can make two return flights a day and is grounded for servicing and inspection at least one day a week. A typical flight costs $5000 in variable costs (e.g., to pay flight attendants, pilots, fuel, etc.). The airline will fly with a load factor of 70 per cent.

Video Source: "New Airlines," *Venture* (February 18, 1996).
Other Sources: The data in this case are drawn from "Performance 500," *Canadian Business* (June 1996), pp. 152–155; "The Fortune 1000 Ranked Within Industries," *Fortune Magazine* (April 29, 1996), p. F44; Terry Bullick, "No-Frills Airline Takes Flight in Western Canada," *Marketing Magazine* (February 19, 1996), p. 2; Cecil Foster, "Tough Guys Don't Cuss," *Canadian Business* (February 1995), pp. 23–28; Anita Lahey, "Airlines Launch Shuttle Service Ad Dogfight," *Marketing Magazine* (February 26, 1996), p. 2; Nimisha Raja, "CAI and Second Cup Link Up With Service Offering," *Marketing Magazine* (February 19, 1996), p. 4; and "New Air Service Destined to Dog Competition," *Canada NewsWire* (July 8, 1996), http://www.newswire.ca:80.

VIDEO QUESTIONS ON DISCOUNT PRICED AIRLINES

1. Suggest some strategies that WestJet could pursue to keep its load factor up during the winter months.
2. The video presents demand for air travel as being an essentially price-responsive situation. What other key factors may enter into the selection of mode of transportation for consumers?

CASE STUDY

The Pricing of Beef at Supermarkets

According to *Progressive Grocer*, meat and seafood together account for 16 per cent of sales in an average supermarket. (The industry does not break out data for beef.) This case discusses two major developments affecting the sales and profitability of beef in supermarkets: the use of vitamin E supplements for cattle and the sales of ready-to-cook meat.

Vitamin E, when given to cattle in the final days of their feeding, has been shown to be effective in retarding the oxidation of beef. At the same time, Vitamin E does not affect beef's tenderness, juiciness, or flavour. With oxidation, beef loses its desirable "cherry red" colour and becomes brown; and brown-coloured beef generally has to be marked down in order to be sold.

A recent study compared markdowns for two samples of beef: one from cattle fed with vitamin E and the other from cattle fed in a traditional manner. Both samples were graded Choice and Select, vacuum packaged, and aged for a twelve-day period. Table 1 outlines the price reductions by cut for both samples during the first four days of sale in a chain supermarket.

As shown in the table, Vitamin E beef required much lower markdowns than traditional beef. Customers also reported that the Vitamin E beef retained its "bright cherry red" colour longer than traditional beef. The results of this study indicated that the use of Vitamin E could save the retail industry about $1 billion per year in markdowns.

Supermarkets are also considering expanded sales of ready-to-cook meats as a way to raise profits. And in devising a marketing strategy for ready-to-cook meats, supermarket managers need to evaluate sourcing (whether items should be purchased from a supplier, prepared on the premises, or prepared at a central kitchen for a chain operation), as well as the variety of meats offered for sale. For example, too few items could lead to low sales while too much choice could result in consumer confusion and waste due to poor sales of some items. Market analysts familiar with ready-to-cook items also note that there are high labour costs associated with this department.

One chain that has done well with ready-to-cook meats is Giant Foods. Giant monitors what products sell best by examining the chain's scanning data. Among its best-selling items are marinated London broil, beef for stir fry, chicken cutlet with lemon and herb seasoning, and marinated beef kabobs. To ensure uniformity, one person from each store's meat department is responsible for its prepared meats. That employee decides how much to produce daily, taking into account the product's high perishability. For example, sales of some meats expand significantly during weekends.

Although ready-to-cook meat prices are very high on a cost-per-gram basis, most consumers look at prices on a per-serving basis. Thus, a well-run ready-to-cook department can be extremely profitable. One supplier of ready-to-cook foods estimates that its products sell for $8.79 to $12.99 per kilogram and that most retailers use 20 to 30 per cent markups with its products. Most of its packages range in weight from 450 to 590 grams.

Table 1
Necessary Price Reductions by Cut for Vitamin E-Treated and Traditional Beef

Cut	PRICE REDUCTION NEEDED DURING FIRST FOUR DAYS Vitamin E– Treated Beef	Traditional Beef
Top Loin	0.0%	7.1%
Tenderloin	0.0	12.5
Cross Rib Steak	3.5	39.1

QUESTIONS

1. What other factors should be examined before a supermarket decides whether to purchase Vitamin-E treated beef?
2. Present additional strategies to reduce markdowns on beef.
3. Describe the costs associated with producing ready-to-cook meat on the premises versus costs for marketing outsourced meat.
4. How can a supermarket utilize price discrimination in its meat department?

Sources: The data in this case are drawn from Stephen Bennett, "Ready for Ready-to-Cook," *Progressive Grocer* (September 1995), pp. 133–136; and "Annual Report of the Grocery Industry" *Progressive Grocer* (April 1995), pp. 26, 37.

MARKETING MANAGEMENT

PART 8

In Part 8, we tie together the concepts introduced in earlier chapters and discuss planning for the future.

23 Pulling It All Together: Integrating and Analyzing the Marketing Plan

We first note the value of developing and analyzing integrated marketing plans. Next, we examine the elements in a well-integrated marketing plan: clear organizational mission, long-term competitive advantages, precisely defined target market, compatible subplans, coordination among SBUs, coordination of the marketing mix, and stability over time. Then, we study five types of marketing plan analysis: benchmarking, customer satisfaction research, marketing cost analysis, sales analysis, and the marketing audit. These are important tools for evaluating the success or failure of marketing plans. We conclude with a look at why and how firms should anticipate and plan for the future.

Part 8 Vignette
Integrated Marketing Plans

Marketing involves putting together component parts to produce a result. Marketers therefore need to realize that optimization of any particular element of the marketing mix may not work well and that weakness in a particular element does not have to lead to disaster; in short, marketers must always see the big picture. Refer back to Figure 1-5 for the marketing concept, which includes these elements: a consumer orientation, a market driven approach, a value-based philosophy, a goal orientation and an integrated marketing focus. The preceding video cases have focused on a number of organizations that, to varying degrees, have implemented the marketing concept in their lines of business. When we looked at these organizations, we focused on a particular element of marketing. However, to assume that these firms were ignoring the other elements of the marketing mix would be a mistake. In fact, in most instances there was discussion of the other elements of the marketing mix in relation to the element of focus, and often the overall strategy of the organization was considered as well.

> *Marketers who view the marketing mix as a totality know that it usually is not beneficial to optimize particular elements.*

The Part 8 video case examines M.A.C., an innovative Canadian cosmetics firm that does not have a formal marketing plan, but does have an overall marketing strategy. The president, Frank Toskan, discusses the firm's strategy, which is a form of product differentiation combined with intuitive management. Although he indicates that decision making for M.A.C. has been based on "what feels good," this approach has produced a company that has an articulated segmentation, target market and positioning strategy for its products. In terms of M.A.C.'s marketing mix, there are clear product, distribution, promotion and pricing strategies. The long-term outlook for M.A.C. is also fairly clear since its acquisition by Estee Lauder, one of the world's largest cosmetic companies. M.A.C. was acquired because it was a case of Estee Launder either owning M.A.C. or creating a firm to compete with it. M.A.C.'s success to date has stemmed from using a push marketing strategy in an industry where the standard approach to marketing has been the use of strong pull strategies for products with well-established images.

In terms of Estee Lauder's marketing strategy, M.A.C. is one brand name in a portfolio that includes the Estee Lauder, Aramis, Clinic and Prescriptis cosmetic product lines. The need for a comprehensive integrated marketing plan on the part of Estee Lauder to manage all of these brands is paramount. At the moment, this plan allows M.A.C. to continue to act freely even as Estee Lauder controls the activities of its other divisions. Whether M.A.C. will have this freedom in the future will depend on Estee Lauder's future plans.

CHAPTER 23
Pulling It All Together: Integrating and Analyzing the Marketing Plan

Chapter Objectives

1. To show the value of an integrated marketing plan

2. To discuss the elements of a well-integrated marketing plan

3. To present five types of marketing plan analysis: benchmarking, customer satisfaction research, marketing cost analysis, sales analysis, and the marketing audit

4. To see the merit of anticipating and planning for the future

> *Today's Canadian corporate planners, ravaged by the modern scourges of globalization, downsizing, and technological change, look for solutions and security at the American firms of Motorola, Microsoft, and Springfield ReManufacturing (the guru of open book management). Some 2000 devotees stream through AT&T Universal Card's super-efficient telephone customer service centre in Jacksonville, Florida, every year, at U.S.$375 a pop. More than 5000 supplicants have sojourned at Federal Express' expansive overnight package facility in Memphis for a U.S.$250 midnight hub tour and all-day seminar. USAA, the San Antonio-based insurer, has drawn more than 2100 seekers to its monthly program from such far-flung locales as Australia, Italy, Japan, South Korea, and South Africa.*

MOTOROLA
www.mot.com/

AT&T
www.att.com/

Firms such as Motorola, AT&T, and Federal Express are now viewed as "management meccas." And business visitors are drawn to these meccas to gain benchmarking insights, so they can better set performance standards for their own organizations. Benchmarking is becoming a more widely recognized component of a firm's integrated marketing program.

Each mecca company has been publicly recognized for its excellence in a specific aspect of business—by winning the Baldridge Award for quality in the U.S., by being lauded in the media, and/or by constantly increasing sales and profits:

- Motorola offers an eight-hour seminar on its famed "six sigma" quality program, which aims for only one defect per 1 000 000-unit production run. The seminar also includes material on how to reduce the time from when a new product idea is approved to when the product is commercialized, as well as Motorola's total customer satisfaction philosophy.
- AT&T's Universal Card walks executives through its customer service centre, which handles 1.5 million calls per month. A standout portion of its session features the high-technology system that lets AT&T employees retrieve a customer's bill and payment record even before the phone is picked up.
- Federal Express' session features a full tour of its package-handling facility, a discussion of its customer service policies, and its measurement of service quality.

Visits to management meccas are growing, since more management consulting firms are including them as part of their client training. In contrast to other techniques, such visits enable managers to see how concepts are really enacted, instead of evaluating different theories. "You get a real sense for the culture of the company, for what the people are like, and what the place looks like," says Jay Michaud, a vice-president with CSC Consulting. It also allows executives to talk with others who have had similar experiences.

By visiting such management meccas as General Electric, Lands' End, and Fidelity Investments, GTE found a better way to handle customer service—based on the technology these three firms were utilizing. As a result of its new methods, GTE can now complete a customer order in less than two hours, versus the three to four days it took using the previous technology. And the student has become the professor, as hundreds of managers from other firms visit GTE each year to learn about its high-tech customer service methods.[1]

In this chapter, we will study how a firm can integrate and analyze its marketing plan—and see the value of developing and implementing a clear, forward-looking, cohesive, and adaptable strategy.

Overview

Chapters 1 and 2 introduced basic marketing concepts and described the marketing environment. Chapters 3 and 4 presented the strategic planning process as it applies to marketing and the role of marketing information systems and marketing research. Chapters 5 and 6 broadened our scope to include the societal, ethical, and consumer implications of marketing and international marketing efforts. Chapters 7 to 22 centred on specific aspects of marketing: describing and selecting target markets, and the marketing mix (product, distribution, promotion, and price planning).

This chapter ties things together, and describes how a marketing plan can be integrated and evaluated. It builds on the discussion of strategic planning in Chapter 3—particularly, the total quality approach (whereby a firm strives to fully satisfy customers in an effective and efficient manner). With an integrated marketing effort, individual marketing components are synchronized and everyone is "on the same page." And when an organization wants to appraise performance, capitalize on strengths, minimize weaknesses, and plan for the future, marketing analysis (including benchmarking and customer satisfaction) is necessary.

This is the challenge, as one expert sees it:

> Do you know where your marketing plan is? In a world where competitors observe and rapidly imitate each other's advancements in product development, pricing, packaging, and distribution, internal and external communication is more important than ever as a way of differentiating your business from those of competitors. At its most basic level, a marketing plan defines a business niche, summarizes objectives, and presents strategies for getting from point A to point B. But roadmaps need constant updating to reflect the addition of new routes. Likewise, in a decade in which technology, international relations, and the competitive landscape are constantly changing, the concept of a static marketing plan has to be reassessed.
>
> Two of today's hottest buzzwords are "interactive" and "integrated." A successful marketing plan has to be both. "Interactive" means your marketing plan should be a conversation between your business and your customers. It's your chance to tell customers about your business and to listen and act on their responses. "Integrative" means the message in your marketing is consistently reinforced by every department within your company. Marketing is as much a function of the finance and manufacturing areas as it is the advertising and public relations areas.[2]

Thus, every organization can learn from the focused management rules of Wal-Mart, the world's leading retailer. These principles were developed by the late Sam Walton, the firm's founder, and are in his words:

Wal-Mart's ten basic rules are applied to a wide range of firms.

1. "Commit to your business. Believe in it more than anybody else."

2. "Share your profits with all your associates [workers] and treat them as partners. In turn, they will treat you as a partner."

---
[1] John A. Byrne, "Management Meccas," *Business Week* (September 18, 1995), pp. 122–132.
[2] Shelly Reese, "The Very Model of a Modern Marketing Plan," *Marketing Tools* (January–February 1996), pp. 56–59.

3. "Motivate your partners [workers]. Constantly, day by day, think of new and more interesting ways to motivate and challenge. Set high goals, encourage competition, and keep score."

4. "Communicate everything you possibly can to your partners [workers]. The more they know, the more they'll understand. The more they understand, the more they'll care. Once they care, there's no stopping them."

5. "Appreciate everything your associates do for the business. Nothing else can quite substitute for a few well-chosen, well-timed, sincere words of praise. They're absolutely free and worth a fortune."

6. "Celebrate your successes. Find humour in your failures. Don't take yourself so seriously. Loosen up and everybody around you will loosen up."

7. "Listen to everyone in your company. The folks on the front lines—the ones who actually talk to the customer—are the only ones who really know what's going on out there. You'd better find out what they know. This is really what total quality is all about."

8. "Exceed your customers' expectations. If you do, they'll come back over and over. Make good on all your mistakes, and don't make excuses—apologize. The two most important words I ever wrote were on the first Wal-Mart sign: SATISFACTION GUARANTEED."

9. "Control your expenses better than your competition. This is where you can always find the competitive advantage. You can make a lot of different mistakes and still recover if you run an efficient operation. Or you can be brilliant and still go out of business if you're inefficient."

10. "Swim upstream. Ignore the conventional wisdom. If everybody else is doing it one way, there's a good chance you can find your niche by going in exactly the opposite direction."[3]

Integrating the Marketing Plan

From a total quality perspective, the many parts of a marketing plan should be unified, consistent, and coordinated.

When a marketing plan is properly integrated, all of its various parts are unified, consistent, and coordinated; and a total quality approach can be followed. Although this appears a simple task, it is important to recall that a firm may have long-run, moderate-length, and short-run plans; the different strategic business units in an organization may require separate marketing plans; and each aspect of the marketing mix requires planning. For example:

- An overall plan is poorly integrated if short-run profits are earned at the expense of moderate- or long-term profits. This could occur if marketing research or new-product planning expenditures are reduced to raise profits temporarily. A firm could also encounter difficulties if plans are changed too frequently, leading to a blurred image for consumers and a lack of focus for executives.

- Resources need to be allocated among SBUs, so funds are given to those with high potential. The target markets, product images, price levels, and so on, of each SBU must be distinctive—yet not in conflict with one another. Physical distribution efforts and channel member arrangements need to be timed so the system and its role in a total quality program are not strained by two or more SBUs making costly demands simultaneously.

[3] Sam Walton and John Huey, *Made in America* (New York: Doubleday, 1992).

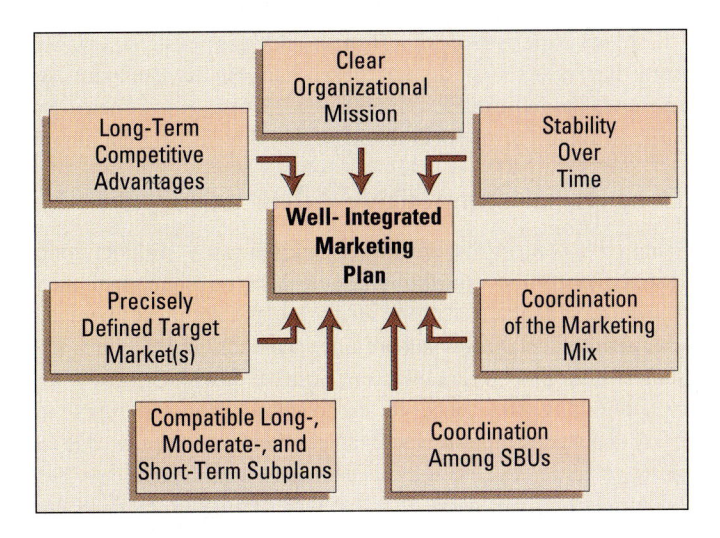

FIGURE 23-1
Elements Leading to a Well-Integrated Marketing Plan

- Even though a promotion plan primarily deals with one strategic element, it must also be integrated with product, distribution, and pricing plans. It must reflect the proper image for a firm's products, encourage channel cooperation, and demonstrate that products are worth the prices set.

A well-integrated marketing plan incorporates the elements shown in Figure 23-1. These elements are explained next.

Clear Organizational Mission

A clear organizational mission outlines a firm's commitment to a type of business and a place in the market. It directs the company's total quality efforts. The organizational mission is involved whenever a firm seeks new customer groups or abandons existing ones, adds or deletes product lines, acquires other firms or sells part of its own business, performs different marketing functions, and/or shifts technological focus (as noted in Chapter 3). Both top management and marketing personnel must be committed to an organizational mission for it to be achieved; and the mission must be communicated to customers, company employees, suppliers, and distribution intermediaries. For example, PHH has a directive yet flexible organizational mission with a total quality approach:

The organizational mission should be clear and directive.

> PHH is in the service business. We don't make cars. We don't own real-estate companies. We aren't a traditional bank. We specialize in business processes that are not an organization's primary focus, but are essential to top performance.
> *Vehicle Management Services*—Companies which operate fleets of vehicles turn to PHH for expert assistance in selecting, purchasing, managing, and remarketing their cars, vans, and trucks. Our consultative, information, and administrative services, as well as our extensive national networks of suppliers, help keep a client's drivers safely and productively on the road, while efficiently managing expenses through process improvements and valuable information. And PHH's fuel and service cards mean added driver convenience and client cost-savings through the world's largest fuel, vehicle repair, and maintenance network.
> *Relocation and Real-Estate Services*—Mobility for organizations and their employees is a critical factor in business success. PHH companies are dedicated to helping clients manage the complex process of relocating employees where they can be most effective. With comprehensive high-quality services and extensive real estate-related supplier networks, PHH facilitates the process of home selling, home finding, moving, and settling into the new area for the relocating family. PHH also provides property management and marketing services to financial institutions, and location planning and strategic management consulting to businesses and municipalities.
> *Mortgage Banking Services*—Finding the right home financing is a complicated business. PHH works with corporations, credit unions, real-estate brokers, and affinity groups to provide a full range of residential first mortgages and casualty insurance-related products. Via customer-focused services, centralized management, and extensive telecommunications and computer capabilities, PHH has grown into one of the top 20 mortgage originators in [North America].[4]

[4]*PHH Corporation: Your Connection to Quality Business Services* (n.d.).

Many experts believe a firm should reappraise its organizational mission if the company has values that do not fit a changing environment, its industry undergoes rapid changes, its performance is average or worse, it is changing size (from small to large or large to small), or opportunities unrelated to its original mission arise.

Long-Term Competitive Advantages

Competitive advantages should centre on company, product, and marketing attributes with long-range distinctiveness.

Long-term competitive advantages are company, product, and marketing attributes whose distinctiveness and appeal to consumers can be maintained over an extended period of time. A firm must capitalize on the attributes that are most important to consumers and prepare competitive advantages accordingly. For competitive advantages to be sustainable, consumers must perceive a consistent positive difference in key attributes between the company's offerings and those of competitors; that difference must be linked to a capability gap that competitors will have difficulty in closing (due to patents, superior marketing skills, customer loyalty, and other factors); and the company's offerings must appeal to some enduring consumer need. While concentrating on its competitive advantages, a company should not lose sight of the importance of customer service and its role in a total quality program.

As Michael Treacy and Fred Wiersema say in their best-selling book, *The Discipline of Market Leaders*:

> Today's market leaders understand the battle they're in. They know they have to redefine value by raising customer expectations in the one component of value they choose to highlight. Casio, for instance, establishes new affordability levels for familiar products such as calculators; Hertz makes car rental nearly as convenient as taking a cab; Lands' End shows individuals that they're not just a number; and Home Depot proves that old-fashioned, knowledgeable advice hasn't gone the way of trading stamps.
>
> But wait a minute. These companies don't shine in every way. A successful company like Wal-Mart doesn't peddle haute couture; Lands' End doesn't sell clothing for the lowest possible cost; and Starbucks, the Seattle coffee chain, doesn't slide a cup of java under your nose any faster or more conveniently than anyone else. Yet, all of these companies are thriving because they shine in a way their customers care most about. They have honed at least one component of value to a level of excellence that puts all competitors to shame. Our research shows that no company can succeed today by trying to be all things to all people. It must instead find the unique value that it alone can deliver to a chosen market.[5]

STARBUCKS
www.occ.com/starbucks/history.html

Because smaller firms often cannot compete on the basis of low prices, they tend to concentrate on other competitive advantages, such as:

- Targeting underserved market niches, including international ones.
- Having unique offerings through specialization. Firms can be innovative, process customized orders, or otherwise adapt products for particular customers.
- Stressing product quality and reliability. "The more crucial the performance of a product to customer needs, the lower will be the concern with pricing."
- Engaging in extra efforts to gain customer loyalty by making the purchase process easy, giving superior service, and promising the long-term availability of goods and services. As one small-firm manager said, "We know our products are reliable and do not require visits. But when our clients see us physically inspecting machines, sometimes merely dusting them, they have a sense of security and comfort." This is a total quality approach.
- Emphasizing relationship marketing, whereby personal relationships with their suppliers are viewed as important by customers.[6]

---

[5] Michael Treacy and Fred Wiersema, *The Discipline of Market Leaders* (Reading, Mass.: Addison-Wesley, 1995).
[6] Peter Wright, "Competitive Strategies for Small Business," *Collegiate Forum* (Spring 1983), pp. 3–4; Steven P. Galante, "More Firms Quiz Customers for Clues about Competition," *Wall Street Journal* (March 3, 1986), p. 21; "Hot Growth Companies," *Business Week* (May 27, 1991), pp. 78–84; and Donna Fenn, "Leader of the Pack," *Inc.* (February 1996), pp. 31–38.

International Marketing in Action

Does Korea's Samsung Represent the Conglomerate of the Future?

Under chair Lee Kun, Samsung is expanding from its traditional businesses—electronics, chemicals, finance, and heavy machinery—into autos, aerospace, transportation, and entertainment. It has also begun to negotiate strategic alliances with such firms as Boeing, Walt Disney, and Nissan. According to its chair, Samsung Group plans to more than quadruple its 1994 sales level to reach U.S.$200 billion in annual sales as of 2001.

More than one-half of its expansion projects are being financed through Samsung Electronics, the firm's semiconductor manufacturing division. If the worldwide demand for memory chips continues, Samsung can become a major conglomerate, on the level of a General Electric. If not, Samsung could be remembered as a firm that gambled with large stakes but lost.

In the past, Samsung's success confounded some critics. For instance, it became the world's top producer of semiconductors in just ten years. However, Samsung now plans on being a major player in some of the world's most competitive and capital-intensive industries. Among its planned projects are:

- A U.S.$4.5 billion investment over a three-year period to develop a new line of cars with Nissan.
- A U.S.$3 billion investment for three more semiconductor plants (one in North America and two in Europe and Southeast Asia).
- A U.S.$150 million investment as a partner in a Sino-Korean venture to build a 100-seat jetliner.

Besides being successful in these ventures, some analysts believe Samsung needs to move away from its present discount image. In some markets, Samsung products sell for as much as 30 per cent less than other brands; this reduces the firm's overall profitability.

As a marketing consultant to Samsung, evaluate its strategic plan.

Sources: Based on material in Steve Glain, "Korea's Samsung Plans Very Rapid Expansion into Autos, Other Lines," *Wall Street Journal* (March 2, 1995), pp. A1, A5; and Laxmi Nakami, Kevin Kelly, and Larry Armstrong, "Look Out World—Samsung is Coming," *Business Week* (July 10, 1995), pp. 52–53.

When implementing a marketing strategy, a firm should note that its competitive advantages may not apply in all situations. For instance, an advantage can lose its value when transferred to another nation. This can occur because an advantage is not relevant in a different context or because it can easily be countered by local competitors: "Products that are superior in the home market may not offer customer-perceived value in the target country because the price is too high or the degree of sophistication is excessive. The value of well-known brand names and trademarks can be reduced by piracy and imitation. Technological advantages can be neutralized by the weakness of intellectual property law and laxity in enforcing the law. Whether an advantage retains its value depends on the fit between conditions in the target country and the nature of the advantage."[7]

---

[7] Yao-Su Hu, "The International Transferability of the Firm's Advantages," *California Management Review*, Vol. 37 (Summer 1995), p. 83.

638 Part 8 *Marketing Management*

Precisely Defined Target Market(s)

The target market(s) should be identified precisely.

By precisely defining its target market(s), a firm identifies the specific customers to be addressed in its marketing plans. This guides the firm's current marketing efforts and future direction. For example, as noted in Figure 23–2, IBM is focused on business customers interested in computer networking. IBM has been repositioning its image away from being a company that provides "hardware" to businesses to being a company that provides "expertise" to businesses on a global basis. The "Solutions for a small planet™" slogan is so critical to this new positioning that IBM has trademarked it. The theme in this ad is "Connect," but IBM runs a number of ads with different themes to appeal to different business needs. In one ad the theme is "Secure" and the focus of the ad is how IBM can help protect businesses who have system networks from hackers and other people who might break in. Another ad uses the theme "Merge" and talks about how IBM can help a firm's various offices around the world work as a team even if the various offices have different

FIGURE 23-2
Target Marketing and IBM
IBM is targeting businesses by positioning itself as a firm that provides expertise for networking around the world.
Reprinted with permission of IBM Canada Ltd.

computer platforms such as :"Windows, UNIX, Mac or OS/2."[8] Whenever a firm such as IBM engages in differentiated marketing (multiple segmentation), it is essential that each segment be described fully.

A firm's target market approach may have to be fine-tuned due to changing demographics and lifestyles—or falling sales. Today, a lot of consumers are more demanding:

> The balance of power between producers and buyers has shifted to the latter. Most industries today are no longer constrained by supply. In fact, an overabundance of suppliers is crowding every part of the market. Customers, who are becoming more astute in their buying practices every day, have tremendous choice in deciding who will get their business. The 1990s have become the "value decade"; buyers carefully examine total offerings to find out which one yields the best overall value compared to alternatives. The challenge is to give customers all of what they want, and none of what they don't want: the best quality *and* the best prices, served quickly *and* with a smile![9]

In this context, a total quality approach is especially crucial in attracting and retaining consumers.

Compatible Long-, Moderate-, and Short-Term Subplans

The long-, moderate-, and short-term marketing subplans of a firm need to be compatible with one another. Long-term plans are the most general and set a broad framework for moderate-term plans. Short-term plans are the most specific; but they need to be derived from both moderate- and long-term plans. At Motorola, this means "placing farsighted bets on a wide array of technologies while expanding in fast-growing, developing markets. We think we're making balanced investments for the future."[10]

Long-, moderate-, and short-term subplans must be compatible.

Unfortunately, adequate plans and subplans are not always set—or are not communicated to employees. According to one study of employees at small and midsized firms, 77 per cent say their firms have a clear organizational mission; 55 per cent feel top management actions support the organizational mission; 57 per cent believe all departments, branches, and divisions have specific and measurable goals; 38 per cent feel all employees understand what is expected of them; and 22 per cent say all employees are held accountable for daily performance.[11] For a total quality program to work, these percentages must be considerably higher.

One important current trend among many companies is the shrinking time frame of marketing plans:

> Because customer priorities are constantly changing, a marketing plan should change with them. For years, conventional wisdom was "prepare a five-year marketing plan and review it every year." But change happens a lot faster than it did twenty or even ten years ago. For that reason, Bob Dawson of The Business Group, a consulting firm, recommends that firms prepare three-year plans and review them every quarter. Frequent reviews enable companies to identify potential problems and opportunities before the competition does. "Preventative maintenance for a company is as important as putting oil in a car," Dawson says. "You don't wait a whole year to do it. You can't change history, but you can anticipate what's going to happen."[12]

Coordination Among SBUs

Coordination among an organization's SBUs is enhanced when the functions, strategies, and resources allocated to each are described in long-term, moderate-term, and short-term plans. For instance, at GE (General Electric), the firm from which the SBU concept was first derived, there are now twelve SBUs (in technology, services, and manufacturing)—

SBUs should be coordinated.

---

[8]IBM Advertisement, "Timbuktu," *Canadian Business Technology* (Spring 1996), p. 1; IBM Advertisement, "Connect," *Canadian Business* (August 1996), pp. 34–35; and IBM Advertisement, "Hacker," *Canadian Business Technology* (Summer 1996), p. 1.
[9]William A. Band, "Customer-Accelerated Change," *Marketing Management* (Winter 1995), pp. 47–48.
[10]Peter Coy and Ron Stodghill II, "Is Motorola a Bit Too Patient?" *Business Week* (February 5, 1996), pp. 150–151.
[11]Oechsli Institute, "Reality Check," *Inc.* (March 1993), p. 34.
[12]Reese, "The Very Model of a Modern Marketing Plan," pp. 60–61.

down from 350 several years ago: "Only businesses that were number one or number two in their markets could win in the increasingly global arena. Those that were not leaders were fixed, closed, or sold." Today, GE's goal is to "attain competitive advantages that let it rank first or second in every market it serves." And its planning and resource allocation are structured accordingly.

Virtually all of GE's SBUs are market leaders, including aircraft engines, circuit breakers, electric motors, engineering plastics, industrial and power systems, nonbank financial services, major appliances, lighting, locomotives, and medical diagnostic imaging. Problematic SBUs are singled out for special attention by top management, which coordinates plans and assigns resources. Thus, when GE decided to hold onto its broadcasting SBU (even though the NBC TV network had fallen to a weak third in audience ratings as of 1993), a renewed commitment was pledged. By 1996, NBC was again number one with such popular shows as *ER*, *Seinfeld*, and *Friends*.[13]

The coordination of SBUs by large multinational firms can be particularly complex. For example, ABB (Asea Brown Boveri) has 175 global managers at its Swiss headquarters. They oversee 200 000 employees and 1000+ companies that operate in 140 countries around the globe: "ABB isn't Japanese, nor is it Swiss or Swedish. It is a global firm without a national identity, though its mailing address is in Zurich. The company's top thirteen managers hold frequent meetings in different countries. Since they share no common first language, they speak only English, a foreign tongue to all but one."[14]

Coordination of the Marketing Mix

The marketing mix within each SBU has to be coordinated.

The components of the marketing mix (product, distribution, promotion, and price) need to be coordinated and consistent with a firm's organizational mission. As an example, Intuit Inc. is a computer software maker, founded in 1984. It specializes in user-friendly personal-finance programs for PCs. From 1984 to 1986, sales were very low—due to a lack of startup capital: "Without money, there were no distribution channels and no customers. What computer store would carry an unknown software product, unsupported by advertising?" The firm then invested $170 000 in advertising and sales took off. By 1996, Intuit products were carried by virtually every type of computer software store and it had 1.7 million loyal customers.[15] Its current marketing mix is outstanding and adheres to a total quality philosophy:

- *Product*—Intuit's Quicken software is the leading personal-finance program on the market. It helps consumers balance their chequebooks, set up budgets, and monitor investments. Quicken has been upgraded and improved a number of times. New programs, such as QuickBooks bookkeeping software, are heavily tested before they are introduced.

- *Distribution*—Intuit products are sold by all types of retailers across North America and a number of other countries, including Wal-Mart, major computer chains, a number of bookstores, and mail-order firms. Some of Intuit's software is even bundled with computer hardware; for example, the Quicken program is often included with the Macintosh Performa line of computers.

- *Promotion*—Although ad expenditures are modest, Intuit runs ads in such magazines as PC and ComputerLife, and it seeks out publicity. The firm is also quite clever. In one recent ad campaign, it used this approach: "Stop Cheating—yourself out of legitimate, money-saving tax deductions. That's why you need TurboTax . . . Complete Satisfaction—We guarantee you'll be satisfied with TurboTax or your money back."

---

[13]Stephen W. Quickel, "CEO of the Year: Welch on Welch," *Financial World* (April 3, 1990), p. 62; Al Ries, "The Discipline of the Narrow Focus," *Journal of Business Strategy*, Vol. 13 (November–December 1992), p. 5; Noel M. Tichy and Stratford P. Sherman, *Control Your Own Destiny or Someone Else Will* (New York: Doubleday, 1993); and Gary Hoover, Alta Campbell, and Patrick J. Spain (Eds.), *Hoover's Handbook of American Business 1996* (Austin, Texas: Reference Press, 1996), pp. 544–545.

[14]Carla Rappoport, "A Tough Swede Invades the U.S.," *Fortune* (June 29, 1992), p. 76; Rich Karlgaard, "Percy Barnevik," *Forbes ASAP* (January 2, 1995), pp. 65–68; and Patrick J. Spain and James R. Talbot (Eds.), *Hoover's Handbook of World Business 1995-1996* (Austin, Texas: Reference Press, 1995), pp. 94–95.

[15]John Case, "Customer Service: The Last Word," *Inc.* (April 1991), pp. 88–93; and Intuit advertisement, *ComputerLife* (January 1996).

The firm does spend about 10 per cent of revenues on customer service personnel, including technical-support people who handle 800-number telephone calls.

- *Price*—Quicken, Quicken for Windows, TurboTax, and MacIn-Tax have "street prices" (the discounted prices offered by resellers) of $40 to $45. Included in purchases are a detailed owner's manual, the right to upgrades at a modest price, and telephone support service. Most competing programs are much more expensive than Quicken.

Stability Over Time

A marketing plan must have a certain degree of stability over time for it to be implemented and evaluated properly. This does not mean a plan should be inflexible and therefore unable to adjust to a dynamic environment. Rather, it means a broad marketing plan, consistent with a firm's organizational mission and total quality approach, should guide long-term efforts and be fine-tuned regularly; the basic plan should remain in effect for a number of years. Short-run marketing plans can be much more flexible, as long as they conform to long-term goals and the organizational mission. Thus, low prices might be part of a long-term marketing plan, but in any particular year, prices might have to be raised in response to environmental forces.

The stability of the basic plan should be maintained over time.

An example of a firm striving to maintain a stable—but flexible—approach is Bell Canada. It has been serving Canadians since the 1880s and up until July 1994, when it faced full competition in the long distance phone market, it was "the" phone company. Today, Bell is in a battle to hold its customer base in the face of severe competition, which has seen its market share fall from 100 per cent to 73 per cent in two years. Despite this rapid fall, Bell has been stemming the tide of defections and hopes to stabilize the market.

Where Unitel and Sprint, Bell's competitors, use price as their main weapon to attract customers, Bell focuses on service, support, and reliability. In addition, Bell has been appealing to the business market with affordable 1-800 and 1-888 toll free numbers to expand their market. Bell Canada set its corporate mission in its 1995 annual report as follows: "To be a pivotal player in the global economy, helping people and organizations realize their potential by connecting them with ease and imagination to the individuals and ideas that they need to grow and prosper."

To fulfil this corporate mission Bell Canada has chosen to embark on what they term an "aggressive three-year business plan." The goals of the plan are threefold: to make sure Bell Canada "survives, thrives and meets customers' needs in an increasingly competitive environment." The plan recognizes the firm's loss of revenues (estimated at $700 million), market share, and net income and the need to invest in new technologies to fight competition and to maintain Bell's place in the market. In light of these changes, according to John McLennan, Bell's CEO, the specific objective is to return Bell Canada to historic levels of financial performance by the end of 1997 and then maintain them. The plan put forward is designed to have a combined operating impact of $1 billion in terms of increased revenues and decreased costs.

The activities that will be undertaken in the plan include the following:

- Investment in technology, including a broadband network.
- Increasing revenues through price increases on local rates and adding new services such as interactive multimedia, personal communications services, Internet access and cable television.
- Business transformation in terms of how Bell does business. This will involve an initial investment of $1.7 billion. The outcome of this investment will be improved customer service with fewer resources. Employee training will be undertaken to make sure Bell employees have the skills to compete in the marketplace New revenue-generating opportunities will be researched.
- Workforce downsizing of 10 000 employees.
- Priority placed on marketing and sales.[16]

---

[16]*Bell Canada 1995 Annual Report*; Harvey Schachter, "Ma Bell, Femme Fatale," *Canadian Business* (June 1996), p. 121–124; and Bell Canada, "Overview," Bell Canada Web site, http://www.bell.ca.

FIGURE 23-3
Bell Advantage 800 Service for Business
Marketing is a key priority in Bell Canada's business plan.
Reprinted with permission of Bell Canada.

An important aspect of Bell Canada's marketing effort is illustrated in Figure 23-3, which advertises Bell's Advantage 800 service.

Analyzing the Marketing Plan

Marketing plan analysis *compares actual and targeted achievements.*

Marketing plan analysis involves comparing actual performance with planned or expected performance for a specified period of time. If actual performance is unsatisfactory, corrective action may be needed. Also, plans must sometimes be revised because of the impact of uncontrollable variables.

Five techniques used to analyze marketing plans are discussed in the following sections: benchmarking, customer satisfaction research, marketing cost analysis, sales analy-

DIRECT ACCESS TO MUTUAL FUNDS.
DIRECT ACCESS TO COMPARISON.

Compare the long and short term performance numbers of Canada's ten most popular equity funds.

10 LARGEST CANADIAN EQUITY FUNDS ranked by one year returns*

Fund	Load	1 year	3 years	5 years	10 years	Assets (,000)
Altamira Equity	N	24.4%	15.1%	24.7%	n/a	2,516,842
Investors Retirement Mutual	Y	19.7%	11.9%	9.5%	8.2%	2,258,800
Industrial Growth	Y	19.5%	11.7%	9.5%	8.1%	1,366,001
Investors Canadian Equity	Y	19.2%	11.9%	12.2%	8.3%	2,555,400
Investors Retirement Gth Portfolio	Y	19.1%	11.6%	9.9%	n/a	1,489,400
Ivy Canadian	Y	18.3%	12.1%	n/a	n/a	1,373,735
Trimark Canadian	Y	18.2%	13.8%	13.6%	11.2%	1,461,911
Trimark RSP Equity	Y	16.6%	12.6%	11.8%	n/a	2,726,997
Trimark Select Canadian Growth	Y	15.9%	12.4%	n/a	n/a	2,757,447
MD Equity	N	15.4%	11.1%	10.3%	8.9%	1,465,555

Funds shown represent 46.4% of all Canadian equity funds.

Now to make the comparison even more impressive, remember that because you can access Altamira's No-Load Mutual Funds directly, you pay no commission, only a one time forty dollar set up fee. Once you make the comparison, the phone call is that much easier.

Call and ask for a free information kit,
or if you have any specific questions, ask to speak to
one of Altamira's Mutual Fund Specialists.

Altamira
Helping you take control

Call 1-800-263-7396, ext. 55
e-mail: advice@altamira.com   net: http://www.altamira.com

The rates of return are the historical annual compounded returns for the periods ended April 30, 1996, including changes in unit value and reinvestment of all distributions and do not take into account any optional charges payable by any unitholder which would have reduced returns. Past performance is not necessarily indicative of future performance. Mutual Funds are sold by prospectus only. The simplified prospectus contains important information which you should read carefully before investing, also note pages two and three of our prospectus for all fees pertaining to our funds. As with all Altamira Mutual Funds there is no front or back-end load; only a one time forty dollar set up fee. *Source: Globe Information Services, using Globe HySales. The information shown compares the performance of the ten largest Canadian equity funds by one year returns.

FIGURE 23-4
Altamira: Benchmarking Versus the Competition
Reprinted with permission of Altamira Investment Services Inc.

sis, and the marketing audit. Though our discussion of these tools is limited to their utility in evaluating marketing plans, they may also be employed when developing and modifying these plans.

Benchmarking

For a firm to properly assess the effectiveness of its marketing plans, it must set performance standards. That is, it must specify exactly what constitutes "success." One way to do this is to utilize **benchmarking**, whereby a firm sets its own marketing performance standards based on the competence of the best companies in its industry, innovative companies in other industries anywhere around the world, the prowess of direct competitors, and/or prior actions by the firm itself. Xerox, a leader in this area, uses benchmarking to

*In **benchmarking**, specific points of comparison are set so performance can be measured.*

MARRIOTT INTERNATIONAL
www.marriott.com/

ALTAMIRA
www.altamira.com/

There are three steps in the benchmarking ladder: novice, journeyman, and master.

ERNST & YOUNG
tax.ey.ca/

measure its goods, services, and practices "against the toughest competitors or those recognized as industry leaders."[17] Among the growing number of other firms now using benchmarking are Bell Canada, DuPont, Ford, IBM, Kodak, Marriott, Motorola, and Altamira Mutual Funds. As Figure 23-4 illustrates, the benchmark for Altamira Mutual Funds is the "ten largest Canadian equity funds."

Benchmarking may be divided into two main categories:

> Strategic benchmarks for business performance are measures which set overall direction, and show managers how others have succeeded in similar circumstances. Process benchmarks, in contrast, usually indicate standards which should be achievable in day-to-day operations, given the willingness to learn.[18]

According to one worldwide study of over 580 companies in four industries (computer, auto, health care, and banking), a greater percentage of North American firms regularly engage in benchmarking than their Japanese and German counterparts. Nonetheless, there are some universal truths about total quality that can aid any firm. Those that do best communicate the corporate strategic plan to employees, customers, suppliers, and channel members; upgrade and simplify development and production processes; set up formal practices to certify suppliers; and scrutinize and reduce cycle time (how long it takes a firm to get from designing to delivering a good or service).[19]

The sponsors of the just-mentioned study, Ernst & Young and the American Quality Foundation, recommend that a benchmarking program be approached in three stages. Firms can hurt themselves by setting unrealistic goals if they compare themselves to those at a later stage:

- *Novice*—A firm in this category should strive to emulate direct competitors, not world-class companies. It should rely on customers for new-product ideas and choose suppliers mostly on price and reliability criteria. There should be a focus on cost-reduction potential, with a "don't develop it, buy it" thrust. Workers should be rewarded for teamwork and quality. The firm should identify processes that add value, simplify those processes, and move faster in responding to the marketplace.

- *Journeyman*—A firm in this category should encourage workers to find ways to do their jobs better and to simplify operations. It should strive to emulate market leaders and selected world-class companies. Consumer input, formal marketing research, and internal ideas should be used in generating new products. The firm should select suppliers having good quality, and then look at their prices. Compensation for both workers and managers should be linked to teamwork and quality. The firm should refine practices to improve the value added per employee, the time to market, and customer satisfaction.

- *Master*—A firm in this category relies on self-managed, multiskilled teams that emphasize horizontal processes (like product development and logistics). It measures its product development, distribution, and customer service against the world's best. Consumer input, benchmarking, and internal research and development should be used in generating new products. The firm should select suppliers that are technologically advanced and offer superior quality. Strategic partnerships are employed to diversify production. Compensation for senior executives should be linked to teamwork and quality. The firm should continue to refine its practices to improve the value added per employee, the time to market, and customer satisfaction.[20]

---

[17]Beth Enslow, "The Benchmarking Bonanza," *Across the Board* (April 1992), p. 17. See also Thomas C. Powell, "Total Quality Management as Competitive Advantage: A Review and Empirical Study," *Strategic Management Journal*, Vol. 16 (January 1995), pp. 15–37; and Roland T. Rust, Anthony J. Zahorik, and Timothy L. Keiningham, "Return on Quality (ROQ): Making Service Quality Financially Accountable," *Journal of Marketing*, Vol. 59 (April 1995), pp. 58–70.

[18]Tony Clayton and Bob Luchs, "Strategic Benchmarking at ICI Fibres," *Long Range Planning*, Vol. 27 (June 1994), p. 56.

[19]Jeremy Main, "How to Steal the Best Ideas Around," *Fortune* (October 1992), p. 102–106; Cyndee Miller, "'TQM's Value Criticized in New Report," *Marketing News* (November 9, 1992), pp. 1, 16; and Gilbert Fuchsberg, "'Total Quality' Is Termed Only a Partial Success," *Wall Street Journal* (October 1, 1992), pp. B1, B7.

[20]Otis Port, John Carey, Kevin Kelly, and Stephanie Anderson Forest, "Quality: Small and Midsize Companies Seize the Challenge—Not a Moment Too Soon," *Business Week* (November 30, 1992), pp. 66–72.

Some useful benchmarks for Canadian firms are award achievements like the Canada Export Awards, the Entrepreneur of the Year Award, and The Award for Canadian-American Business Achievement. For Canadian firms who do business in the United States, the Malcolm Baldridge National Quality Award criteria and Fortune's Corporate Reputations survey criteria are good benchmarks.

Every year the Department of Foreign Affairs and International Trade sponsors a set of Export Awards for the Canadian firms who are the leading exporters in their industries in terms of growth. In 1995 the Export Development Corporation and the Canadian Imperial Bank of Commerce became official sponsors too.

The Entrepreneur of the Year Award is sponsored by Air Canada, The Bank of Montreal, Ernst & Young, Nesbitt Burns, McCarthy Tetrault Law Firm and *Canadian Business* magazine. It is granted to firms in five regions in Canada (Pacific Canada, the Prairies, Ontario, Quebec, and Atlantic Canada). Within each of these regions, an entrepreneur of the year is chosen and then the best entrepreneurs in ten business categories are identified. The categories are manufacturing, agriculture and food, retailing, services, emerging entrepreneurs, turnaround entrepreneurs, master entrepreneurs, high technology, supporters of entrepreneurship, and socially responsible entrepreneurs.

The award for Canadian-American Business Achievement is sponsored by Nortel (Northern Telecom), FHS International, The Canadian-American Business Council, *Profit* magazine and *Canadian Business* magazine.. This award is focused on rewarding cooperative ventures between a Canadian and American firm that "demonstrate business success, innovation, and community contribution."[21]

A firm does not have to actually participate in any of these competitions to benefit from the benchmarks. Any organization can assess itself and compare its results with others. Canadian firms can benchmark themselves against competitors by applying the criteria used for the various awards.

For example, the criteria used for the Baldridge Award involve rating companies in seven areas: leadership; information and analysis (such as competitive comparisons and benchmarks); strategic quality planning; human resource development and management; management of process quality; quality and operational results; and customer focus and satisfaction. Of the maximum 1000 points a company can score, 300 are for customer focus and satisfaction. Fortune's Corporate Reputations survey rates companies in eight areas: quality of management; quality of goods or services; innovativeness; long-term investment value; financial soundness; the ability to attract, develop, and keep talented people; responsibility to the community and the environment; and wise use of corporate resources. Companies are rated within their own industry.

Customer Satisfaction Research

As defined in Chapter 1, **customer satisfaction** is the degree to which there is a match between a customer's expectations of a good or service and the actual performance of that good or service, including customer service. Today more than ever, companies realize they must measure the level of customer satisfaction through regular research:

Research is needed to gauge customer satisfaction. ACSI is a broad project that is doing so.

> How little we know about these indispensable strangers, our customers. Are they happy? Restless? Was it good for them, too? Will they come back tomorrow? The answers to these questions profoundly affect any business. Indeed, one could say they define a business. They also define the meaning of economic activity, for in the largest sense an economy cannot be described by adding up how many passenger-miles of air travel it logs or how much wood its woodchucks chuck per hour. All these count (and we count them). But in the final analysis, what matters is how well an economy satisfies its customers' needs and wants.[22]

---

[21]"Mohawk Oil Honored in Vancouver," *Marketing Magazine* (March 20, 1995), p. 3; "Entrepreneur of the Year," *Canadian Business*, advertising feature (June 1996), p. 95; "Once Again A Pair of Winners," *Canadian Business*, advertising feature (June 1996), p. 111; and "The 1995 Canada Export Awards," *Canadian Business*, advertising supplement (November 1995), pp. 69–76.

[22]Thomas A. Stewart, "After All You've Done for Your Customers, Why Are They Still Not Happy?" *Fortune* (December 11, 1995), p. 179.

MERCEDES-BENZ
www.mercedes.com/

The largest ongoing research project on customer satisfaction in the world is undertaken annually in the United States. The American Customer Satisfaction Index (ACSI) is a joint effort by the University of Michigan and the American Society for Quality Control. To compute ACSI, 30 000 consumers are surveyed about 3900 goods and services. The surveys cover "perceptions of service, quality, value, how well the good or service lived up to expectations, how it compared to an ideal, and how willing people were to pay more for it." With a maximum score of 100, these were the highest-rated firms in 1995: Dole (90), Mars (89), Clorox (88), CPC International (88), Hershey (88), American Tobacco (87), Heinz (87), Maytag (87), PepsiCo (87), Procter & Gamble (87), Borden (86), Colgate-Palmolive (86), Honda (86), Mercedes-Benz (86), Nestlé (86), Pillsbury (86), Cadbury Schweppes (85), Coca-Cola (85), Dial (85), and Federal Express (85). The average score for all companies was 73.7.[23]

Any firm can measure its own customer satisfaction. Here is an eight-step procedure to do so:

1. "Institute a process to tap management, employees, outside consultants, and industry sources for input on the dimensions critical to customer satisfaction. Environmental scanning of trade publications and competitors and a regular program of internal focus groups can accomplish this."

2. "Use this feedback to develop an ongoing program of customer focus groups and personal interviews to identify critical customer satisfaction dimensions."

3. "Work with a professional staff to develop telephone and/or mail survey instruments to reliably and validly incorporate identified dimensions."

4. "Regardless of whether the people developing the survey are internal or external, make sure they understand the theoretical basis of the instruments and are familiar with standard procedures for developing and testing reliable, valid items. Keep in mind that customer satisfaction survey results that simply describe what was found provide no guidance for developing an action plan to improve satisfaction."

5. "Regularly do surveys and re-evaluate their reliability and validity."

6. "From these data, develop a customer satisfaction metric that not only relates the level of satisfaction of your customers, but also analyzes the importance of the various dimensions of that satisfaction."

7. "Use the dimensional information to develop an action plan for improving each dimension and communicating these improvements to customers. Remember: delivery of customer satisfaction is not a reality if the customer does not notice it."

8. "Tie the performance evaluation and compensation of each employee involved in the action plan to its accomplishment. This will ensure that the customers' goals match employees' goals. Remember: what gets measured gets rewarded, and what gets rewarded gets done."[24]

---

[23] Jaclyn Fierman, "Americans Can't Get No Satisfaction," *Fortune* (December 11, 1995), pp. 186–194.
[24] John T. Mentzer, Carol C. Bienstock, and Kenneth B. Kahn, "Benchmarking Satisfaction," *Marketing Management* (Summer 1995), pp. 41–46. See also Dominique V. Turpin, "Japanese Approaches to Customer Satisfaction: Some Best Practices," *Long Range Planning*, Vol. 28 (June 1995), pp. 84–90; Abbie Griffin, Greg Gleason, Rick Preiss, and Dave Shevenaugh, "Best Practice for Customer Satisfaction in Manufacturing Firms," *Sloan Management Review*, Vol. 36 (Winter 1995), pp. 87–98; and William Keenan, Jr., "Customer Service," *Sales & Marketing Management* (January 1996), pp. 63–66.

Ethics AND TODAY'S MARKETER

How Far Should Customer Satisfaction Guarantees Go?

A money-back guarantee can be an especially strong competitive advantage in attracting skeptical customers. It can also function as an early warning system about potential problems and serve as a motivator to employees. For example, after studying its returns, mail-order retailer L.L. Bean found that "the wrong size" was the most frequent reason for returns. As a result, it revised the size information in all of its catalogues. And besides providing information to correct its operations, the president of Hampton Inns believes the hotel's service guarantee motivates its maids to be sure rooms are especially clean.

An example of an effective satisfaction guarantee is Xerox's "Total Satisfaction Guarantee." It covers the firm's equipment for three years from the date of purchase. Says a Xerox spokesperson, "We're putting the customer in charge. The customer is the sole arbiter and decision maker." Crest toothpaste also offers consumers their money back if they are not satisfied with the results of their dental examinations after six months of use.

Yet, not all companies openly embrace guarantees as a means of building customer loyalty. Some fear that too many customers will ask for a refund on the basis of a trivial complaint. And some companies that promote guarantees extensively in their advertising make it difficult to collect: "A guarantee program can either be the centrepiece of a service company's entire operation or simply a promotional tool. Many businesses continue to make shallow promises with slogans because they are not prepared to guarantee what their customers want, or because the process for getting the company to make good on its offer is overly complicated."

As a marketing manager for a leading hotel chain, develop a money-back guarantee policy that is designed both to reimburse dissatisfied guests and to reduce lost revenues due to trivial complaints.

Source: Based on material in Jonathan Barsky, "Guarantee; Warranty; Loyalty," *Marketing Tools* (September 1995), pp. 72–75.

Marketing Cost Analysis

Marketing cost analysis is used to evaluate the cost efficiency of various marketing factors, such as different total quality configurations, product lines, order sizes, distribution methods, sales territories, channel members, salespersons, advertising media, and customer types. Although a firm may be very profitable, it is highly unlikely that all of its products, distribution methods, and so on are equally cost efficient (or profitable).

With marketing cost analysis, a firm can determine which factors (classifications) are the most efficient and which are the least efficient, and make appropriate adjustments. It can also generate information that may be needed to substantiate price compliance with the Competition Act.

For this type of analysis to work properly, a firm needs to obtain and to use continuous and accurate cost data. Table 23-1 presents several examples of marketing cost analysis.

Cost efficiency is measured in **marketing cost analysis**.

Table 23-1
Examples of Marketing Cost Analysis

MARKETING FACTOR	STRATEGY/TACTICS STUDIED	PROBLEM/OPPORTUNITY DISCOVERED	ACTION APPLIED
Customer type	What are the relative costs of selling X-rays to dentists, doctors, and hospitals?	Per-unit costs of hospital sales are lowest (as are prices); per-unit costs of dentist and doctor sales are highest (as are prices).	Current efforts are maintained. Each customer is serviced.
Product	Should a manufacturer accept a retailer's proposal that the firm make 700 000 private-label sneakers?	Substantial excess capacity exists; the private label would require no additional fixed costs.	A contract is signed. Different features for private and manufacturer labels are planned.
Distribution	Should a men's suit maker sell directly to consumers, as well as through normal channels?	Startup and personal selling costs would be high. Additional sales would be minimal.	Direct sales are not undertaken.
Order size	What is the minimum order size a hardware manufacturer should accept?	Orders below $30 do not have positive profit margins; they are too costly to process.	Small orders are discouraged through surcharges and minimum order size.
Advertising media	Which is more effective, TV or magazine advertising?	TV ads cost $0.05 for every potential customer reached; magazine ads cost $0.07.	TV ads are increased.
Personal selling	What are the costs of making a sale?	15 per cent of sales covers compensation and selling expenses, 2 per cent above the industry average.	Sales personnel are encouraged to phone customers before visiting them, to confirm appointments.

Table 23-2
A Natural-Account Expense Classification

Net sales (after returns and discounts)	$1 000 000	
Less: Costs of goods sold	450 000	
Gross profit		$550 000
Less: Operating expenses (natural account expenses)		
Salaries and fringe benefits	220 000	
Rent	40 000	
Advertising	30 000	
Supplies	6 100	
Insurance	2 500	
Interest expense	1 400	
Total operating expenses		300 000
Net profit before taxes		$250 000

Marketing cost analysis consists of three steps: studying natural account expenses, reclassifying natural accounts into functional ones, and allocating functional accounts by marketing classification.

Table 23-3
Reclassifying Natural Accounts into Functional Accounts

FUNCTIONAL ACCOUNTS

NATURAL ACCOUNTS	TOTAL	Marketing Administration	Personal Selling	Advertising	Transportation	Warehousing	Marketing Research	General Administration
Salaries and fringe benefits	$220,000	$30,000	$50,000	$15,000	$10,000	$20,000	$30,000	$65,000
Rent	40,000	3,000	7,000	3,000	2,000	10,000	5,000	10,000
Advertising	30,000			30,000				
Supplies	6,100	500	1,000	500			1,100	3,000
Insurance	2,500		1,000			1,200		300
Interest expense	1,400							1,400
Total	$300,000	$33,500	$59,000	$48,500	$12,000	$31,200	$36,100	$79,700

STUDYING NATURAL ACCOUNT EXPENSES The first step is to determine the level of expenses for all **natural accounts**, which report costs by the names of the expenses and not by their purposes. Such expense categories include salaries, rent, advertising, supplies, insurance, and interest. These are the names most often entered in accounting records. Table 23-2 shows a natural-account expense classification.

RECLASSIFYING NATURAL ACCOUNTS INTO FUNCTIONAL ACCOUNTS Natural accounts are then reclassified into functional accounts, which indicate the purposes or activities for which expenditures have been made. Included as functional expenses are marketing administration, personal selling, advertising, transportation, warehousing, marketing research, and general administration. Table 23-3 reclassifies the natural accounts of Table 23-2 into functional accounts.

Once functional accounts are established, cost analysis becomes clearer. For instance, if salaries and fringe benefits increase by $25 000 over the prior year, natural account analysis cannot allocate the rise to a functional area. Functional account analysis can pinpoint the areas of marketing that have higher personnel costs.

ALLOCATING FUNCTIONAL ACCOUNTS BY MARKETING CLASSIFICATION The third step assigns functional costs by product, distribution method, customer, or another marketing classification. This reports each classification as a profit centre. Table 23-4 shows how costs can be allocated among different products, using the data in Tables 23-2 and 23-3. From Table 23-4, it is clear that product A has the highest sales and highest total profit. However, product C has the greatest profit as a per cent of sales.

In assigning functional costs, these points should be kept in mind. One, assigning some costs—such as marketing administration—to different products, customers, or other classifications is usually somewhat arbitrary. Two, the elimination of a poorly performing classification would lead to overhead costs—such as general administration—being allotted among the remaining product or customer categories. This may actually result in lower overall total profit. Thus, a firm should distinguish between those separable expenses that are directly associated with a given classification category and can be eliminated if a category is dropped, and those common expenses that are shared by various categories and cannot be eliminated if one is dropped.[25]

Natural accounts are reported as salaries, rent, and insurance.

Functional accounts denote the purpose or activity of expenditures.

Functional costs are assigned with each marketing classification becoming a profit centre.

---

[25] See Joseph A. Ness and Thomas G. Cucuzza, "Tapping the Full Potential of ABC," *Harvard Business Review*, Vol. 73 (July–August 1995), pp. 130–138.

Table 23-4
Allocating Functional Expenses by Product

	TOTAL	PRODUCT A	PRODUCT B	PRODUCT C
Net sales	$1 000 000	$500 000	$300 000	$200 000
Less: Cost of goods sold	450 000	250 000	120 000	80 000
Gross profit	$550 000	$250 000	$180 000	$120 000
Less: Operating expenses (functional account expenses)				
Marketing administration	33 500	16 000	10 000	7 500
Personal selling	59 000	30 000	17 100	11 900
Advertising	48 500	20 000	18 000	10 500
Transportation	12 000	5 000	5 000	2 000
Warehousing	31 200	20 000	7 000	4 200
Marketing research	36 100	18 000	11 000	7 100
General administration	79 700	40 000	23 000	16 700
Total operating expenses	300 000	149 000	91 100	59 900
Net profit before taxes	$250 000	$101 000	$88 900	$60 100
Profit as per cent of sales	25.0	20.2	29.6	30.1

A firm must differentiate between order-generating and order-processing costs (described in Chapter 3) before making any strategic changes suggested by marketing cost analysis:

> After a decade of frantic cost-cutting, the downside of downsizing is beginning to take its toll: decimated sales staffs turn in lousy numbers. "Survivor syndrome" takes hold, and overburdened staffers just go through the motions of working. New-product ideas languish. Risk-taking dwindles because the culture of cost-cutting emphasizes the certainties of cutting costs over the uncertainties—and expense—of trying something new."[26]

In making cost cuts, a company must be especially sure to judge the effects of those cuts on the total quality of its goods and services.

Sales Analysis

Sales analysis *looks at sales data to assess the effectiveness of a marketing strategy.*

Sales analysis is the detailed study of sales data for the purpose of appraising the appropriateness and effectiveness of a marketing strategy. Without adequate sales analysis, a poor response to the total quality offered by a firm may not be seen early enough, the value of certain market segments and territories may be overlooked, sales effort may be poorly matched with market potential, trends may be missed, or support for sales personnel may not be forthcoming. Sales analysis enables plans to be set in terms of revenues by product, product line, salesperson, region, customer type, time period, price line, method of sale, and so on. It also compares actual sales against planned sales. More firms engage in sales analysis than in marketing cost analysis.

The main source of sales analysis data is the sales invoice, which may be written, typed, or computer generated. An invoice may contain such information as the customer's name and address, the quantity ordered, the price paid, purchase terms, all the different

---

[26]Bernard Wysocki, Jr., "Some Companies Cut Costs Too Far, Suffer 'Corporate Anorexia,'" *Wall Street Journal* (July 5, 1995), p. A1. See also Robin Cooper and W. Bruce Crew, "Control Tomorrow's Costs Through Today's Designs," *Harvard Business Review*, Vol. 74 (January–February 1996), pp. 88–97.

items bought at the same time, the order date, shipping arrangements, and the salesperson. Summary data are generated by adding invoices. The use of computerized marking, cash register, and inventory systems speeds data recording and improves their accuracy.

In conducting sales analysis, proper control units must be selected. **Control units** are the sales categories for which data are gathered, such as boys', men's, girls', and women's clothing. Although a marketing executive can broaden a control system by adding several sales categories together, wide categories cannot be broken down into components. Thus, a narrow sales category is preferable to one that is too wide. It is also helpful to select control units consistent with other company, trade association, and government data. A stable classification system is necessary to compare data from different time periods.

Control units are an essential aspect of sales analysis.

A key concept in undertaking sales analysis is that summary data, such as overall sales or market share, are usually insufficient to diagnose a firm's areas of strength and weakness. More intensive investigation is needed. Two sales analysis techniques that offer in-depth probing are the 80-20 principle and sales exception reporting.

According to the **80-20 principle**, in many organizations, a large proportion of total sales (profit) is likely to come from a small proportion of customers, products, or territories. Thus, to function as efficiently as possible, firms need to determine sales and profit by customer, product, or territory. Marketing efforts can then be allocated accordingly. Firms that do not isolate and categorize data are acting in error. Through faulty reasoning, they would place equal effort into each sale instead of concentrating on key accounts. These errors are due to a related concept, the **iceberg principle**, which states that superficial data are insufficient to make sound evaluations.

The 80-20 principle notes that a large share of sales (profits) often comes from few customers, products, or territories. Analysis errors may be due to the iceberg principle.

This is how one firm is using the 80-20 principle in its sales analysis:

> In April 1996, Pepsi undertook a massive promotion to bolster youth loyalty and encourage frequent purchasing by young Canadians. At the time, the Pepsi "Get Stuff" promotion was described as "one of the largest consumer-loyalty programs ever run by a packaged-goods company in Canada." The approach of the campaign involved consumers collecting points off specially marked packages of Pepsi, Diet Pepsi, and Pepsi max. The points could be collected and redeemed for merchandise from a Pepsi Get Stuff catalogue. Described as a consumer "outreach" campaign, the promotion was designed to help Pepsi identify the heaviest product users through point redemption. Furthermore, the product usage of these users could be assessed as Pepsi Points associated with different packages were slightly different too. For example, 7-Eleven has Pepsi points on their Big Gulp cups and these points are different in value and shape from the Pepsi points carried on other packages. Pepsi planned to run the promotion for a six-month period and distributed 460 million points on 175 million packages with $92 million in premiums available.[27]

Analysis can be further enhanced by **sales exception reporting**, which highlights situations where sales goals are not met or sales opportunities are present. A slow-selling item report cites products whose sales are below forecasts. It could suggest such corrective actions as price reductions, promotions, and sales incentives to increase unit sales. A fast-selling item report cites items whose sales exceed forecasts. It points out openings, as well as items that need more inventory on hand to prevent stockouts. Finally, sales exception reporting enables a firm to evaluate the validity of forecasts and make the proper modifications in them. Figure 23-5 presents examples of the 80-20 principle, the iceberg principle, and sales exception reporting.

Sales exception reporting centres on unmet goals or special opportunities.

Organizations also may use sales analysis to identify and monitor consumer buying patterns by answering such questions as these:

- Who purchases? Organizational vs. final consumer, geographic region, end use, purchase history, customer size, customer demographics.
- What is purchased? Product line, price category, brand, country of origin, package size, options purchased.
- Where are purchases made? Place of customer contact, purchase location, warehouse location.

---

[27] Jeff Lobb, "The Right (Pepsi) Stuff," *Marketing Magazine* (July 8, 1996), p. 15.

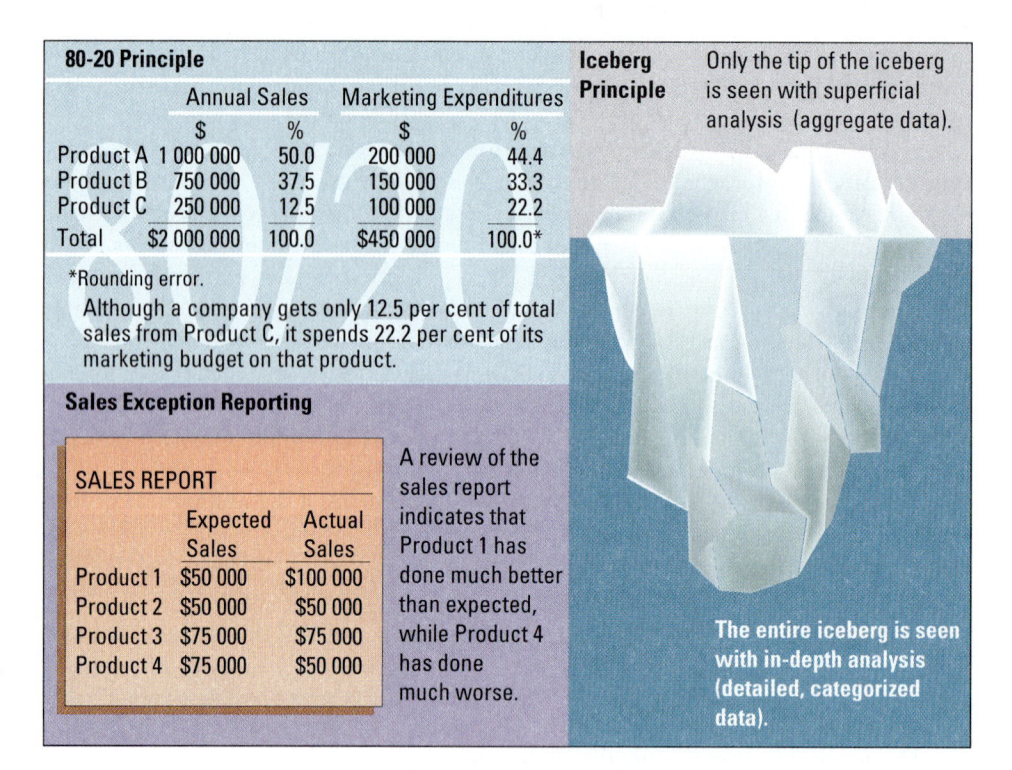

FIGURE 23-5
Sales Analysis Concepts

80-20 Principle				
	Annual Sales		Marketing Expenditures	
	$	%	$	%
Product A	1 000 000	50.0	200 000	44.4
Product B	750 000	37.5	150 000	33.3
Product C	250 000	12.5	100 000	22.2
Total	$2 000 000	100.0	$450 000	100.0*

*Rounding error.
Although a company gets only 12.5 per cent of total sales from Product C, it spends 22.2 per cent of its marketing budget on that product.

Sales Exception Reporting

SALES REPORT		
	Expected Sales	Actual Sales
Product 1	$50 000	$100 000
Product 2	$50 000	$50 000
Product 3	$75 000	$75 000
Product 4	$75 000	$50 000

A review of the sales report indicates that Product 1 has done much better than expected, while Product 4 has done much worse.

Iceberg Principle Only the tip of the iceberg is seen with superficial analysis (aggregate data).

The entire iceberg is seen with in-depth analysis (detailed, categorized data).

- How are items purchased? Form of payment, billing terms, delivery form, packaging technique.
- When are purchases heaviest and lightest? Season, day of week, time of day.
- How much is purchased? Unit sales volume, dollar sales volume, profit margin.
- What types of promotion get the best sales results? Advertising, personal selling, sales promotion.
- What prices are paid? List prices vs. discounted prices.

The Marketing Audit

A marketing audit examines a firm in a systematic, critical, and unbiased manner.

A **marketing audit** is a systematic, critical, impartial review and appraisal of the basic goals and policies of the marketing function, and of the organization, methods, procedures, and personnel employed to implement the policies and achieve the goals.[28] The purpose of a marketing audit is to determine how well a firm's marketing efforts are being conducted and how they can be improved. Audits should be conducted on a regular basis.

The marketing audit process involves the six steps shown in Figure 23-6:

1. A marketing audit may be conducted by company specialists, by company division or department managers, or by outside specialists. Expertise, access to information, costs, and potential biases are some of the factors to be considered when choosing audit personnel.

2. An audit may be undertaken at the end of a calendar year, at the end of a firm's annual reporting year, or when conducting a physical inventory. An audit should be performed at least annually, although some firms prefer more frequent analysis. It should be completed during the same time period each year to allow comparisons. In some cases, unannounced audits are useful to keep employees alert and to ensure spontaneous answers.

[28]Christopher H. Lovelock and Charles A. Weinberg, *Public & Nonprofit Marketing*, Second Edition (Redwood City, Calif.: Scientific Press, 1989), pp. 47–48. See also Peter Spillard, Matthew Moriarty, and John Woodthorpe, "The Role Matrix: A Diagnostic of Marketing Health," *European Journal of Marketing*, Vol. 28 (Number 7, 1994), pp. 55–76; and Robert S. Kaplan and David P. Norton, "Using the Balanced Scorecard as a Strategic Management System," *Harvard Business Review*, Vol. 74 (January–February 1996), pp. 75–85.

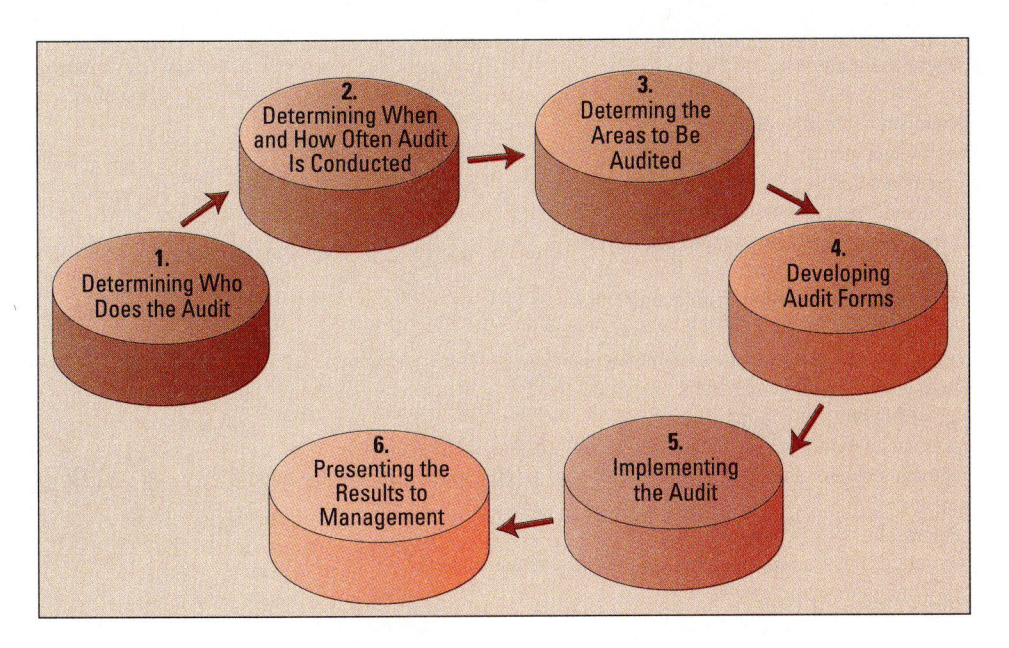

FIGURE 23-6
The Marketing Audit Process

3. A **horizontal audit** (also known as a marketing-mix audit) studies the overall marketing performance of a firm with particular emphasis on the interrelationship of variables and their relative importance. A **vertical audit** (also known as a functional audit) is an in-depth analysis of one aspect of a firm's marketing strategy, such as product planning. The two audits should be used in conjunction with one another because a horizontal audit often reveals areas needing further study.

4. Audit forms list the topics to be examined and the exact information required to evaluate each topic. Forms usually resemble questionnaires, and they are completed by the auditor. Examples of audit forms are contained in Figures 23-7 and 23-8.

5. When implementing an audit, decisions need to be made with regard to its duration, whether employees are to be aware of the audit, whether the audit is performed while a firm is open or closed for business, and how the final report is to be prepared.

6. The last step in an audit is to present findings and recommendations to management. However, the auditing process is complete only after suitable responses are taken by management. It is the responsibility of management, not the auditor, to determine these responses.

Despite the merits, many firms still do not use formal marketing audits. Three factors mostly account for this. First, success or failure is difficult to establish in marketing. A firm may have poor performance despite the best planning if environmental factors intervene. On the other hand, good results may be based on a firm's being at the right place at the right time. Second, if marketing audits are completed by company personnel, they may not be comprehensive enough to be considered audits. Third, the pressures of other activities often mean that only a small part of a firm's marketing strategy is audited or that audits are done irregularly.

*A **horizontal audit** studies overall marketing performance; a **vertical audit** analyzes one aspect of marketing.*

Anticipating and Planning for the Future

The next decade promises to be a complex one for marketers everywhere, as they try to anticipate trends and plan long-run strategies. On the positive side, this period should see increasing consumer affluence in many countries, improvements in technological capabilities, expanding worldwide markets, greater deregulation of industry, and other opportunities. On the negative side, the period will probably witness greater competition among firms based in different countries, relatively slow to moderate growth in North American and European markets, some resource instability, and an uncertain worldwide economy.

Does Your Department, Division, or Firm . . .	Answer Yes or No to Each Question
Planning, Organization, and Control	
1. Have specific objectives?	_____
2. Devise objectives to meet changing conditions?	_____
3. Study customer needs, attitudes, and behaviour?	_____
4. Organize marketing efforts in a systematic way?	_____
5. Have a market planning process?	_____
6. Engage in comprehensive sales forecasting?	_____
7. Integrate buyer behaviour research in market planning?	_____
8. Have strategy and tactics within the marketing plan?	_____
9. Have clearly stated contingency plans?	_____
10. Monitor environmental changes?	_____
11. Incorporate social responsibility as a criterion for decision making?	_____
12. Control activities via marketing cost analysis, sales analysis, and the marketing audit?	_____
Marketing Research	
13. Utilize marketing research for planning, as well as problem solving?	_____
14. Have a marketing information system?	_____
15. Give enough support to marketing research?	_____
16. Have adequate communication between marketing research and line executives?	_____
Products	
17. Utilize a systematic product-planning process?	_____
18. Plan product policy relative to the product life-cycle concept?	_____
19. Have a procedure for developing new products?	_____
20. Periodically review all products?	_____
21. Monitor competitive developments in product planning?	_____
22. Revise mature products?	_____
23. Phase out weak products?	_____
Distribution	
24. Motivate channel members?	_____
25. Have sufficient market coverage?	_____
26. Periodically evaluate channel members?	_____
27. Evaluate alternative shipping arrangements?	_____
28. Study warehouse and facility locations?	_____
29. Compute economic order quantities?	_____
30. Modify channel decisions as conditions warrant?	_____
Promotion	
31. Have an overall promotion plan?	_____
32. Balance promotion components within the plan?	_____
33. Measure the effectiveness of advertising?	_____
34. Seek out favourable publicity?	_____
35. Have a procedure for recruiting and retaining sales personnel?	_____
36. Analyze the sales-force organization periodically?	_____
37. Moderate the use of sales promotions?	_____
Prices	
38. Have a pricing strategy that is in compliance with government regulations?	_____
39. Have a pricing strategy that satisfies channel members?	_____
40. Estimate demand and cost factors before setting prices?	_____
41. Plan for competitive developments?	_____
42. Set prices that are consistent with image?	_____
43. Seek to maximize total profits?	_____

FIGURE 23-7
A Horizontal Marketing Audit Form

Total Quality Health Check-up Questionnaire

After filling out questionnaire, return to: _____

The purpose of this questionnaire is to provide a means for companies to conduct a study of their employees, to determine the degree of involvement and commitment to the principles and practices of Total Quality Management.

The questionnaire is based on the criteria embodied in the Baldridge Quality Award categories (Being employed by many companies as an integrated management system and to conform to requirements in attaining the award).

INDIVIDUAL INSTRUCTIONS

Identify your position title and company department in the spaces below, then respond to each of the following ten statements, indicating your personal opinion as to the degree of compliance with the criteria in company operations. When completed, return to the individual identified at the top of the sheet for tabulation and reporting of results.

Your Position: _____ Department: _____

QUALITY HEALTH CRITERIA (Circle numbers at right to indicate agreement)	HOW ARE WE DOING? Not true → Very true
1. External customer expectations define the quality of our goods and services.	0 1 2 3 4 5
2. Cross-functional and inter-departmental cooperation are encouraged and supported.	0 1 2 3 4 5
3. There is active leadership for quality improvement at all levels of management.	0 1 2 3 4 5
4. Employees have the authority to act on goods and service quality problems.	0 1 2 3 4 5
5. A team approach is used to solve quality problems and to meet customer expectations.	0 1 2 3 4 5
6. Measures of internal and external customer expectations are well understood.	0 1 2 3 4 5
7. Employees are brought into decisions that affect the quality of their work.	0 1 2 3 4 5
8. There is major emphasis on the prevention and solving of quality problems.	0 1 2 3 4 5
9. Individuals and teams are given recognition for contributions to quality improvement.	0 1 2 3 4 5
10. Systems are in place to assess and respond to changing customer expectations and needs.	0 1 2 3 4 5

FIGURE 23-8
A Total-Quality Vertical-Audit Form
Source: Dick Berry, "How Healthy Is Your Company?" *Marketing News* (February 15, 1993), p. 2. Reprinted by permission of the American Marketing Association.

Long-range plans must take into account both the external variables facing a firm and its capacity for change. Specifically, what variables will affect the firm? What trends are forecast that might affect the firm? Is the firm able to respond to these trends (for example, does it have the necessary resources and lead time)? A firm that does not anticipate and respond to future trends has a good possibility of falling into Levitt's marketing myopia trap and losing ground to more farsighted competitors:

> Most managers manage for yesterday's conditions because yesterday is where they got their experiences and had their successes. But management is about tomorrow, not yesterday. Tomorrow concerns what should be done, not what has been done. "Should" is determined by the external environment—what competitors (old, new, and potential) can and might do, the

Planning efforts for the future must consider external factors and company abilities.

TECHNOLOGY & MARKETING

Can You Predict Where Communications Technology Is Heading?

According to many technology experts, new applications for the "boring" telephone are going to explode in the near future. Here are some predictions:

- Appliances will soon will be equipped with phones that are programmed to automatically dial a service centre when an internal sensor detects a malfunction.
- Air conditioners will have phones that let people turn them on or off from remote locations.
- Cars will have phones that automatically dial the police or an ambulance in the event an air bag is deployed.

One of the major reasons for the expected increase in phone applications is that through research, AT&T has been able to reduce the size of a phone to a computer chip that is the size of a finger nail. This unit can be mass produced at a cost of a few dollars. Accordingly, the small size and low cost will allow phones to be easily installed in household appliances, auto dashboards, and other places.

In the long term, Compaq envisions marketing a central personal computer for the home into which consumers could plug all of their major appliances. And the computer would be connected to a phone line. According to Compaq's vice-president of corporate development, "You might be able to call home and tell 'home' to turn on the oven or to change the code of the security system."

Some analysts caution that consumers may reject innovations that phone designers feel are the most promising. A vice-president at Sony Electronics says that avant garde prototypes become actual products "about as often as concept cars do—not never, but never often."

As vice-president of long-range planning for Camco Inc, a Canadian home appliance firm with $444 million in sales, plan a major appliance strategy based on the information just provided.

Source: Based on material in Bart Ziegler, "Anytime, Anywhere," *Wall Street Journal* (March 20, 1995), p. R18.

---

choices this will give customers and those who advise or direct customers, the rules constantly being made by governments and other players, demographic changes, advances in generalized knowledge and technology, changing ecology and public sentiments, and the like.

The most precious thing a manager brings to a job is the wisdom conferred by experience—precisely so that he or she can operate decisively and effectively with limited information, with dispatch and confidence. But when change accelerates, when it comes unexpectedly from constantly unexpected directions, when new technologies and social and environmental conditions occur so disjunctively, the wisdom conferred by experience needs help. That is one reason professional staffs and consultants proliferate. It is also why, in this age of rapid acceleration, this hazardous new age of fast history, managers must take time to carefully think for themselves.[29]

Many North American middle managers think they've beaten the Japanese. They think they've won. They think they're smarter. But they don't understand the nature of the competition. The Japanese have a proven ability to cope with crisis. Japanese companies are, of neces-

[29] Theodore Levitt, "The Thinking Manager," *Across the Board* (June 1992), pp. 11, 13.

sity, becoming world-class experts at managing through tough times. Today, their customers won't spend enough, their currency won't fall enough, and their government won't—or can't—do enough. So Japanese managers are going back to the drawing board, sometimes literally. They are redesigning products, redeploying workers, reconfiguring distribution systems, and generally retooling some of their most storied management practices—from just-in-time production to consensus decision-making, from flexible manufacturing to continuous improvement.[30]

3M illustrates what a firm can do to prepare for the uncertain future. It recently decided to divest itself of businesses with annual sales of U.S.$3 billion (including computer diskettes, videotape, and audiotape). 3M believed its long-term prospects in those businesses were not strong. The firm is expanding its efforts in "microreplication" technologies that can "refract light or transport it, strip adhesive from plastic film or serve as a fastener, reduce water drag on boat hulls or polish golf clubs." 3M is more aggressive in obtaining ideas from business customers; and it is extremely interested in gaining insights into the unarticulated needs of those customers. As 3M's chief executive says, "We're going to do two principal things: be very innovative and satisfy our customers in all respects."[31]

To prepare for the future, companies can do the following:

- *Company vision planning*—This articulates the firm's future mission.
- *Scenario planning*—This identifies the range of events that may occur in the future.
- *Contingency planning*—This prepares alternative strategies, each keyed to a specific scenario (such as a slow-growth economy).
- *Competitive positioning*—This outlines where a firm will be positioned in the future versus competitors.
- *Competitive benchmarking*—This keeps the firm focused on how well it is doing versus its competitors.
- *Ongoing marketing research*—This entails consumer and other relevant research.[32]

As we look ahead, it is clear that the role of marketing will take on greater importance at many companies. Here is why:

> Marketing is responsible for more than the sale, and its responsibilities differ depending on the level of organization and strategy. It is the management function responsible for making sure that every aspect of the business is focused on delivering superior value [total quality] to customers in the competitive marketplace. The business is increasingly likely to be a network of strategic partnerships among designers, technology providers, manufacturers, distributors, and information specialists. The business will be defined by its customers, not its products or factories or offices. This is a critical point: in network organizations, it is the ongoing relationship with a set of customers that represents the most important business asset. Marketing as a distinct management function will be responsible for being expert on the customer and keeping the rest of the network organization informed about the customer. At the corporate and business unit levels, marketing may merge with strategic planning or, more generally, the strategy development function, with shared responsibility for information, environmental scanning, and coordination of the network activities.[33]

---

[30]Ronald Henkoff, "New Management Secrets from Japan: Really," *Fortune* (November 27, 1995), p. 136.
[31]Thomas A. Stewart, "3M Fights Back," *Fortune* (February 5, 1996), pp. 94–99.
[32]Adapted by the authors from Bernard Taylor, "The New Strategic Leadership: Driving Change, Getting Results," *Long Range Planning*, Vol. 28 (October 1995), pp. 71–81.
[33]Frederick E. Webster, Jr., "The Changing Role of Marketing in the Corporation," *Journal of Marketing*, Vol. 56 (October 1992), p. 14.

MARKETING IN A CHANGING WORLD
Stemming the Tide of Customer Defections[34]

As discussed in this chapter, measuring customer satisfaction is a key task for marketing-oriented firms. Yet, too many companies assume that satisfied customers will automatically be loyal customers. What these companies fail to recognize is that other firms may offer better choices and lure "defectors."

For example, even if you are satisfied with Air Canada, might you fly with WestJet Airlines, a new no-frills airline that started up in Calgary in February 1996, promising fares 50 to 70 per cent lower than Air Canada's? Even if you are pleased with a Jeep Cherokee, might you still switch to the more luxurious Range Rover the next time you buy? Of course, the answer to both questions is yes. Customer defections are always possible, and companies must learn to deal with them.

These are among the mistaken impressions that some firms have:

First, it is sufficient merely to satisfy a customer; as long as a customer responds with at least a satisfied rating, the company-customer relationship is strong. In other words, a level of satisfaction below complete or total satisfaction is acceptable. After all, this is the real world, where goods and services are rarely perfect and people are hard to please. Second, the investment required to change customers from satisfied to completely satisfied will not provide an attractive financial return and probably is not a wise use of resources. There may even be instances—most notably, when competing in a cut-throat commodity market—where it doesn't pay to try to satisfy any customers. Third, each division with a relatively high average rating should focus on the customers in the lowest-satisfaction categories. Striving to understand the causes of their dissatisfaction and concentrating efforts on addressing them is the best use of resources.

To stem the tide of customer defections, instead of relying on the preceding flawed assumptions, firms must see that:

- With rare exceptions, complete customer satisfaction is the key to gaining customer loyalty and superior long-term financial results.

- Even in relatively noncompetitive markets, providing customers with outstanding value may be the most reliable way to secure sustained customer satisfaction and loyalty.

- Very poor goods and services are not the sole cause—and may not even be the main one—of high customer dissatisfaction. A company may be attracting the wrong customers or have an inadequate process for turning around the right customers after they have bad experiences.

- Different satisfaction levels require different kinds of actions.

- Customer satisfaction surveys alone are insufficient marketing feedback.

---

[34]The material in this section is based on: Terry Bullick, "No-Frills Airline Takes Flight in Western Canada," *Marketing Magazine*, (February 19, 1996), p. 2; and Thomas O. Jones and W. Earl Sasser, Jr., "Why Satisfied Customers Defect," *Harvard Business Review*, Vol. 73 (November–December 1995), pp. 88–95.

Chapter 23 Pulling It All Together: Integrating and Analyzing the Marketing Plan 659

SUMMARY

1. *To show the value of an integrated marketing plan* Integrated planning builds upon a firm's strategic planning efforts and its use of a total quality approach. In this way, everyone is "on the same page." An integrated marketing plan is one in which all of its various parts are unified, consistent, and coordinated.

2. *To discuss the elements of a well-integrated marketing plan* There are several major elements in an integrated marketing plan. A clear organizational mission outlines a firm's commitment to a type of business and a place in the market. Long-term competitive advantages are company, product, and marketing attributes—whose distinctiveness and appeal to consumers can be maintained over an extended period of time. A precisely defined target market enables a firm to identify the specific consumers it addresses in a marketing plan.

The long-, moderate-, and short-term marketing subplans of a firm need to be compatible with one another. Coordination among SBUs is enhanced when the functions, strategies, and resources of each are described and monitored by top management. The components of the marketing mix need to be coordinated within each SBU. The plan must have a certain degree of stability over time.

3. *To present five types of marketing plan analysis: benchmarking, customer satisfaction research, marketing cost analysis, sales analysis, and the marketing audit* Marketing plan analysis compares a firm's actual performance with its planned or expected performance for a specified period of time. If actual performance is unsatisfactory, corrective action may be needed. Plans may have to be revised because of the impact of uncontrollable variables.

Through benchmarking, a company can set its own marketing performance standards by studying the best firms in its industry, innovative firms in any industry, direct competitors, and/or the company itself. There are strategic benchmarks and process benchmarks. In general, firms progress through three stages as they engage in benchmarking: novice, journeyman, and master. Awards such as the Canada Export Awards, the Entrepreneur of the Year Award and The Award for Canadian-American Business Achievement are good benchmarks. Surveys using criteria such as those used to award the Malcolm Baldridge National Quality Award and measure Fortune's Corporate Reputations are good benchmarking tools.

In customer satisfaction research, a firm determines the degree to which customer expectations regarding a good or service are actually satisfied. The world's largest research project in this area is the American Customer Satisfaction Index (ACSI), which rates thousands of goods and services. In 1995, the average ACSI score for all companies was 73.7 (out of 100).

Marketing cost analysis evaluates the cost efficiency of various marketing factors, such as different total quality configurations, product lines, order sizes, distribution methods, sales territories, channel members, salespersons, advertising media, and customer types. Continuous and accurate cost data are needed. Marketing cost analysis involves studying natural account expenses, reclassifying natural accounts into functional accounts, and allocating accounts by marketing classification.

Sales analysis is the detailed study of sales data for the purpose of appraising the appropriateness and effectiveness of a marketing strategy. Sales analysis enables plans to be set in terms of revenues by product, product line, salesperson, region, customer type, time period, price line, or method of sale. It also monitors actual sales against planned sales. More firms use sales analysis than marketing cost analysis. The main source of sales data is the sales invoice; control units must be specified. Sales analysis should take the 80-20 principle, the iceberg principle, and sales exception reporting into account.

The marketing audit is a systematic, critical, impartial review and appraisal of a firm's marketing objectives, strategy, implementation, and organization. It contains six steps: determining who does the audit, establishing when and how often the audit is conducted, deciding what the audit covers, developing audit forms, implementing the audit, and presenting the results. A horizontal audit studies the overall marketing performance of a firm. A vertical audit is an in-depth analysis of one aspect of marketing strategy.

4. *To see the merit of anticipating and planning for the future* Long-range plans must take into account both the external variables facing a firm and its capacity for change. A firm that does not anticipate and respond to future trends has a good chance of falling into Levitt's marketing myopia trap—which should be avoided.

KEY TERMS

marketing plan analysis (p. 642)
benchmarking (p. 643)
customer satisfaction (p. 645)
marketing cost analysis (p. 647)
natural accounts (p. 649)

functional accounts (p. 649)
sales analysis (p. 650)
control units (p. 651)
80-20 principle (p. 651)
iceberg principle (p. 651)

sales exception reporting (p. 651)
marketing audit (p. 652)
horizontal audit (p. 653)
vertical audit (p. 653)

Review Questions

1. State five of Wal-Mart's ten focused management rules.
2. Explain Figure 23–1, which deals with a well-integrated marketing plan.
3. Why might competitive advantages not travel well internationally?
4. What is benchmarking? How should a novice firm use it differently from a master firm?
5. Discuss the value of measuring customer satisfaction with studies like the American Customer Satisfaction Index (ACSI).
6. Why is functional account cost analysis more useful than natural account analysis?
7. Distinguish between marketing cost analysis and sales analysis.
8. When conducting sales analysis, why is it necessary that control units not be too wide?
9. Differentiate between a vertical and a horizontal marketing audit.
10. What are some of the positive and negative trends firms are likely to face over the coming decade?

Discussion Questions

1. Do you think your college or university is applying an integrated marketing approach? Why or why not? What marketing recommendations would you make for your school?
2. Develop a customer satisfaction survey for your local bank. Discuss the kinds of information you are seeking.
3. What data could a manufacturer obtain from a monthly analysis of its sales to wholesalers? How could this information improve marketing plans?
4. Develop a vertical marketing audit form for Sony to appraise its relationship with the retailers that carry its products.
5. As the marketing vice-president for a small book publisher, how would you prepare for the future? What key trends do you foresee over the next decade? How would you address them?

VIDEO CASE

Make-up Art Cosmetics (M.A.C.): A Marketing Strategy of No Strategy

Make-Up Art Cosmetics is an innovative Canadian company which is having a significant impact in the $2-billion Canadian cosmetics market. M.A.C. employs approximately 1000 people and had 1995 sales of $150 million. M.A.C.'s approach to marketing earned the firm a Special Citation in 1995 from *Canadian Business* as Entrepreneur of the Year for Marketing Excellence.

Frank Toskan, president of M.A.C., says that he doesn't take make-up seriously. The philosophy driving M.A.C. is extremely simple: "Make a good product, and people will come to you," and "All races, all sexes, all ages." M.A.C.'s approach sounds heretical in the age of target marketing: something for everyone, and a production orientation. However, the secret of success for M.A.C. is that their approach is different in an industry that has been dominated by slick marketing approaches. Dictating what women should look like and wear is something M.A.C. does not do.

Frank Toskan used to be a fashion photographer and he approached Frank Angelo to help him develop new products for make-up shoots. They employed make-up artists to help them with product development and sold the products to others at a discount. The demand for their products began to build on word-of-mouth. These sources of personal influence built M.A.C.'s image and product. The firm has received unsolicited support from users such as Madonna, Princess Di, and Michael Jackson.

Now that M.A.C. is growing they have acquired a black spokesmodel, RuPaul, a seven-foot transvestite. Frank Toskan sees RuPaul as an excellent representative of M.A.C. because he is "a stunningly beautiful woman and strikingly handsome man [who] represents M.A.C.'s belief that beauty is genderless [and because] we couldn't find anyone who wore more make-up and had so much fun doing it."

At first, M.A.C. was taken very lightly by its competitors. When the firm started in 1984 there was no advertising, no promotional giveaways, and the approach was to push the products to make-up artists. In fact, Frank Toskan admits that M.A.C. was unaware of the actions of competitors. The decision making for M.A.C. was based on what felt right.

The most significant difficulty for M.A.C. is one faced by all business firms who have excellent products, good pricing strategies, and positive images: access to distribution. When Toronto Bay store buyer Rod Ulmer saw the product and agreed to give M.A.C. some showcases in his store, sales exploded, generating $300 000 in one year. Results like this prompted U.S. retail chains like Saks Fifth Avenue and Henri Bendel to give M.A.C. selling space in their stores too.

The product was so well received that a grey market was developing in overseas markets for M.A.C. products. Frank Toskan and Frank Angelo needed to find a partner to give them access to distribution and capital for market expansion.

They approached Estee Lauder, a leading cosmetic manufacturer in North America with a 40 per cent market share and U.S.$3 billion in sales. Faced with developing its own line of products to compete with M.A.C, Estee Lauder purchased a 51 per cent controlling interest. The partnership is very specific: Lauder provides the financing and M.A.C. management controls the creative approach and management strategy, as the company expands into European and Asian markets.

M.A.C.'s founder Frank Toskan seems to want to avoid formal approaches to marketing strategy. For example, the firm does not have a formal media relations strategy and has not been pursuing media attention. This contrary approach has worked well so far, as media outlets have been actively pursuing M.A.C. to do stories and have been promoting the firm very favourably.

As for M.A.C.'s position with its new parent firm, Estee Lauder is shooting for $1 billion in sales by the year 2000. Will M.A.C. continue on its present course? Don't all $1 billion dollar companies have formal marketing strategies?

QUESTIONS

1. Evaluate M.A.C.'s current "marketing" strategy.
2. As a consultant wishing to sell your services, develop an argument you would present to Frank Toskan and Frank Angelo as to why they need a formal marketing plan and your help to prepare it.
3. As a consultant, write a mission statement for M.A.C. and recommend some overall short- and long-range goals to fit with this mission.
4. What factors have accounted for M.A.C.'s success? How might M.A.C. be at risk in the future? Explain.

VIDEO QUESTIONS ON M.A.C.

1. Discuss the apparent segmentation and positioning strategy of M.A.C. in using spokesmodel RuPaul rather than the female supermodel used by competitors. Compare these approaches and discuss some implications for current and future marketing strategies.
2. The video presents a lot of M.A.C.'s history. Discuss this history and then forecast its future as part of Estee Lauder's portfolio. Where do you think M.A.C. will go as part of this portfolio, and where do think it should go?

Video Source: "M.A.C. Cosmetics," *Venture* (March 3, 1996).

Other Sources: The data in this case are drawn from Lara Mills, "Fantasy's End," *Marketing Magazine* (April 17, 1995), p. 11; Lara Mills, "M.A.C. Finds the Ideal Spokesperson," *Marketing Magazine* (March 20, 1995), p. 9; Lara Mills, "That Old M.A.C. Magic," *Marketing Magazine* (February 5, 1996), p. 1; Doug Forster, "In Your Face," *Canadian Business* (December 1995), p. 54.

CASE STUDY
Full Speed Ahead?

Some experts suggest that speed in all phases of marketing strategy—from receiving orders to delivering products to answering customer questions—may be replacing total quality management as the latest competitive advantage. Michael Porter, Harvard Business School's strategy guru, says "It's gone from a game of resources to a game of rate-of-progress." The chair of a software firm concurs, "It's not the big companies that eat the small; its the fast that eat the slow."

Firms in a variety of industries are seeking to boost the speed of their marketing operations. IBM can now build and ship a customized PC within twenty-four hours of taking an order. Gillette has reduced its new-product development process from three to two years, while Toyota's development process has been cut from twenty-seven months to nineteen months. And Westinghouse Electric is aiming to reduce the time it takes to issue an invoice.

There are various approaches to speeding up marketing processes. One technique is to enumerate all of the steps in the process, determine which steps add value to the customer, and then eliminate most of the others. In an application of this approach, a firm found that just filling an order for its business forms took ninety separate steps. The company re-engineered the ordering process so sales taxes are automatically calculated (based on the postal code of the customer) and credit checks are no longer required (unless a new order exceeds the previous order by a certain amount). Because of these activities, the company was able to cut the steps required to fill an order to twenty. In addition, the firm can now quote an order in one week versus three weeks under the old process.

A second approach to speeding up processes is to use interfunctional teams to design products as units, rather than to work in separate units. With this technique, Chrysler has been able to reduce the number of engineers it needs to develop a new car model (such as the LH design for the Dodge Intrepid, Chrysler Concorde, and Eagle Vision) from 1400 to 741. Chrysler estimates that its next new cars will be planned by 540 engineers.

Today, Chrysler even chooses outside suppliers before starting work on the design of new cars; and many of its suppliers lease space near Chrysler's design centre to facilitate cooperation. Under the old system, Textron, a big supplier to Chrysler, took five days to estimate the costs of alternative dashboard designs. According to the president of the Textron unit, "Now, we can develop a price within 5 per cent inside of a day. We're trying to get it down to half a day."

A third approach involves using computers to speed up processes. For example, PC software can enable a salesperson to determine parts availability and receive price quotes while sitting in a customer's office. Previously, the salesperson had to write down information by hand, travel back to his or her office, and then look up price and item availability information.

Despite all of the excitement associated with speed, managers need to be aware of the potential limitations of speeding up processes. Managers may feel they are under constant pressure to work faster. A slow delivery of crucial inventory may cause the temporary shutdown of a plant using just-in-time production. Still worse, the emphasis on speed may result in products being commercialized before they are fully tested.

QUESTIONS
1. Discuss the overall advantages and disadvantages of speed in marketing strategy.
2. How can a firm employ benchmarking to assess and revise its speed of operations?
3. Do smaller firms have an advantage in speed over larger ones? Explain your answer.
4. Is speed an aid or inhibitor to integrating a marketing strategy? Why?

Source: The data in this case are drawn from William M. Bulkeley, "The Latest Big Thing at Many Companies Is Speed, Speed, Speed," *Wall Street Journal* (December 23, 1994), pp. A1, A4; and Valerie Reitman and Robert L. Simpson, "Japanese Car Makers Speed Up Car Making," *Wall Street Journal* (December 29, 1995), pp. B1-B2.

Appendix

Computer-Based Marketing Exercises

This appendix and an accompanying computer diskette allow you to engage in marketing decision making under simulated conditions and to apply many of the concepts studied during your introduction to or survey of marketing course. To use *Computer-Based Marketing Exercises*, you need a blank 3-1/2 inch formatted computer diskette to make a personal copy of the master exercise disk, which is available to your instructor.

The exercises described in this appendix are designed to reinforce text material; to allow you to manipulate controllable marketing factors and to see their impact on costs, sales, and profits; to have you understand better the influence of uncontrollable factors; and to have you gain experience in using a computer to assess marketing opportunities and to solve marketing problems. All 18 exercises are designed either to be handed in for class assignments or for your own use. The exercises are balanced in terms of subject and level.

These are among the features of *Computer-Based Marketing Exercises*:

- The exercises are linked to key concepts covered throughout *Marketing*, Canadian Edition. Text page references are provided for each exercise both on the computer diskette and in this appendix.
- Although exercises closely parallel the text, they allow great flexibility in data input. You are encouraged to manipulate data and compare the results attained under different assumptions. This provides "hands-on" experience.
- The format of the exercises is very user-friendly. All directions are contained on screens that introduce each exercise, and the exercises are self-prompting. No knowledge of computer programming or computers is needed.
- There is a broad variety of applications.
- All exercises are as realistic as possible.
- The graphics quality is high. Although some exercises use spreadsheet-type analyses, spreadsheet software (such as Lotus or Excel) is not required.
- The software operates on either IBM personal computers or compatibles and with either a colour or monochrome monitor. The exercise diskette is available in a 3-1/2 inch format and requires Windows 3.1 or higher.
- After setting up your personal copy of the exercise diskette, your name will appear at the top of each screen and on any pages you print from the screen.

How to Use the Computer-Based Exercise Diskette

Computer Requirements

This version of *Computer-Based Marketing Exercises* requires that users have the following minimum hardware requirements:

- A personal computer that has a 386, 486, or Pentium microprocessor.
- An operating system that runs Windows 3.1 or higher.
- At least 4 MB of RAM (performance increases with 8 MB of memory).
- A hard drive with sufficient space for this program (about 800 KB).
- At least one 3-1/2 inch floppy drive.
- A graphics card that is compatible with Windows 3.1 or later.
- A high-resolution monitor (VGA or SVGA).
- A printer that is supported by Windows.

Although this program can be operated through either traditional keys or a mouse (or trackball), a mouse is preferable.

Program Installation and Operation

This section explains how to install and operate your copy of the *Computer-Based Marketing Exercises* diskette and how to permanently place your name, class, and section on your diskette (so that assignments may be submitted with your name printed on them). Separate directions are provided for a computer with a hard drive and a network. Since the program contains compressed files, it must be copied onto a hard drive or used on a network.

Using a Computer with a Hard Drive To run *Computer-Based Marketing Exercises* from a computer with a hard drive, your instructor or college or university computer centre must make a copy of the master diskette for you or have you make your own copy of the master diskette (using the proper disk copy command). The instructions below assume you have your own student copy of *Computer-Based Marketing Exercises*, Windows 3.1 or higher is pre-loaded on your hard drive, and "A" or "B" is a 3-1/2 inch drive.

Switch on your computer and then initialize the Windows environment. Insert your *Computer-Based Marketing Exercises* disk into the 3-1/2 inch floppy drive (either A or B). From the Program Manager window, pull down FILE and then choose RUN. In the COMMAND LINE field, type "A:Setup" (without the quotes). (If your 3-1/2 inch drive is designated as B:, type "B:Setup".) Press [ENTER] or click OK with your mouse. (If you get a message to close any running applications before continuing, use the [ALT] + [TAB] keys to switch to other applications and then close them.)

On the CBME Exercise setup screen, click on the underscored C (or hold down the [Alt] key and then press the [C] key if you do not have a mouse or trackball) to transfer the exercise files to your hard disk. The program automatically creates the directory "C:\EXERCISE" for this program. If a directory currently exists with this designation, you will be asked to designate a new drive and path. Use the [Backspace] key to remove the "C:\EXERCISE" drive and/or path. Then, type a new drive and/or path. Click on the underscored C (or hold down the [ALT] key and then press the [C] key) to accept the new drive and/or path that you designated.

A dialog box then appears telling you that your installation is complete. Now click on the OK box (or hold down the [Enter] key). You can remove your disk from the floppy drive. Please store this disk in a location that is not subject to heat or a magnetic field.

You can now run *Computer-Based Marketing Exercises* from your hard drive. If you are still in the Windows environment, open the EXERCISE application by double clicking on the CBME exercises group icon and then double click on the exercises icon. If you do not have a mouse or trackball, you can open this program by pulling down FILE, choosing RUN and typing "C:\EXERCISE\EXERCISE.EXE". If you have designated a different drive or path, use that designation. If you have exited your computer and then return at another time, switch on the computer and initialize the Windows environment. Then, simply adhere to the instructions just cited.

The first time you run *Computer-Based Marketing Exercises*, you will be asked to insert your name, class, and section. Once you enter this information, it will appear on every computer screen and printout—and become a permanent part of your "exercise" program. It will not have to be repeated. The program will do the rest and guide you to the main menu.

Using a Network Some colleges and universities have PC networks for student use. Because there are many differences in the way these networks are set up and operated, please consult with your professor or someone in the computer lab with regard to using *Computer-Based Marketing Exercises*.

How to Use the Main Menu

When running *Computer-Based Marketing Exercises*, all exercises can be accessed from the MAIN MENU. Use the mouse to select an exercise and then double-click at the desired exercise. You can also choose an exercise by repeatedly hitting the tab key until the desired exercise is highlighted; then press the ENTER key. Selecting EXIT (or holding down the [ALT] key and then pressing the [E] key) will enable you to quit the program.

The menu is arranged in the order the topics appear in the text and shows page references so you may review concepts before or while doing an exercise. See Table 1.

How to Operate Each Exercise

At the bottom of each exercise screen, there are a number of commands. They include the EXIT button [E] to quit the program, the MENU button [M] to return to the main menu, the NEXT button [N] to proceed to the following screen, the BACK button [B] to return to the prior screen, the PRINT SCREEN button [P], the ANALYSIS button [A], and the TABLE button [T]. All commands can be executed by either double-clicking your mouse (or trackball) or by holding down the [ALT] key and then hitting the respective letter key. All decisions can be entered by clicking your mouse (or trackball) or by using the [TAB] key and appropriate cursor key.

How to Print from the Exercise Diskette

While using the exercise diskette, you may print any screen for your own reference or for the submission of a class assignment. Simply turn on the printer (either dot-matrix, letter-quality, or laser) that is connected to the computer you are using. Then,

Table 1
Computer-Based Marketing Exercises Main Menu

Part 1: An Introduction to Marketing
 1 Marketing Orientation (p. 11)
 2 Boston Consulting Group Matrix (p. 63)
 3 Questionnaire Analysis (p. 100)

Part 2: Broadening an Organization's/Individual's Marketing Scope
 4 Ethics in Action (p. 123)
 5 Standardization in International Marketing Strategy (p. 161)

Part 3: Consumer Analysis
 6 Vendor Analysis (p. 232)
 7 Segmentation Analysis (p. 270)

Part 4: Product Planning
 8 Product Positioning (p. 302)
 9 Services Strategy (p. 325)
 10 Product Screening Checklist (p. 358)

Part 5: Distribution Planning
 11 Economic Order Quantity (p. 423)
 12 Wholesaler Cost Analysis (p. 443)

Part 6: Promotion Planning
 13 Advertising Budget (p. 525)
 14 Salesperson Deployment (p. 554)

Part 7: Price Planning
 15 Price Elasticity (p. 581)
 16 Key Cost Concepts (p. 605)

Part 8: Marketing Management
 17 Performance Ratios
 18 Optimal Marketing Mix

Appendix *Computer-Based Marketing Exercises* **A-3**

double-click on the PRINT SCREEN button [P] located at the bottom of each exercise screen (or hold down the [ALT] key and then press the [P] key). The screen appearing on your computer monitor will automatically be printed—including your name, class, and section.

The Exercises

In the following sections, each exercise is discussed. For every exercise, we present objectives, a list of the relevant key terms and concepts from the text, an explanation of the exercise, and questions/assignments to be answered or completed.

Exercise 1: Marketing Orientation

Objectives

1. To demonstrate selling versus marketing philosophies
2. To see the importance of customer service
3. To illustrate the components of a marketing orientation
4. To show how changes in attitudes affect a marketing orientation

Key Terms and Concepts

production era
sales era
marketing department era
marketing company era
marketing concept
customer service
empowering employees
customer satisfaction
relationship marketing

Explanation of Exercise

As the owner of a local florist, a table allows you to enter your degree of agreement to ten questions (on a five-point scale ranging from strongly agree to strongly disagree). These questions relate to such areas as the importance of various markets, planning for seasonality, forecasting sales and profits, assessing customer needs, understanding the strategies of competitors, and selling flowers with a limited shelf life.

A summary table then rates your overall marketing orientation. For each of the ten questions, the most appropriate answer receives a +2 score, while the least appropriate response generates a score of −2. The total score can vary from +20 to −20, with +20 being the maximum marketing orientation and −20 the lowest.

By responding differently to the various statements, you can determine an optimal philosophy in terms of the firm's total marketing orientation score.

The exercise is keyed to pages 10-16 in the text.

Questions/Assignments

1. Print out and evaluate your responses to the ten-question marketing orientation checklist.
2. Explain how the checklist is used to compute a firm's overall marketing orientation. Use your response to question/assignment 1 in answering this question.
3. Develop five additional questions that can be used to rate a retailer's overall marketing orientation.
4. What are the difficulties in measuring the overall marketing orientation of a firm through the use of this checklist?

Exercise 2: Boston Consulting Group Matrix

Objectives

1. To apply the Boston Consulting Group matrix to a firm's marketing planning activities
2. To see how a product category's relative market share and industry growth rate affect its placement as a star, cash cow, question mark, or dog
3. To consider the appropriate balance of stars, cash cows, question marks, and dogs for a firm

Key Terms and Concepts

strategic business unit (SBU)
Boston Consulting Group matrix
star
cash cow
question mark
dog

Explanation of Exercise

As a marketing executive for Packard Athletic Shoe Company, a table allows you to enter revised values for the relative market shares and industry growth rates for any or all of Packard's product categories (SBUs). The products are then displayed in a Boston Consulting Group matrix.

In this exercise, the dividing lines between high and low relative market shares, as well as high and low industry growth rates, are the average market share and the average industry growth rate for all of Packard's product categories. The averages change when you vary relative market shares and industry growth rates for individual product categories.

When examining the Boston Consulting Group matrix, study the balance of products in each grouping. For example, are there enough cash cows to support question marks? Also consider the balance of products for future periods. For example, where will future stars come from?

The exercise is keyed to pages 63-65 in the text.

Questions/Assignments

1. Print and evaluate a Boston Consulting Group matrix with these current percentage values for Packard Athletic Shoe Company: All-purpose sneakers—70 (share) and 4 (growth); Tennis sneakers—100 (share) and 6 (growth); Soccer shoes—20 (share) and 10 (growth); Bowling shoes—15 (share) and 3 (growth); Running shoes—250 (share) and 15 (growth); Low-impact aerobic shoes—75 (share) and 5 (growth); Walking shoes—125 (share) and 5 (growth); and Basketball sneakers—50 (share) and 15 (growth).
2. Print and evaluate a Boston Consulting Group matrix with these 2005 projections for Packard Athletic Shoe Company: All-purpose sneakers—150 (share) and 2 (growth); Tennis sneakers—70 (share) and 7 (growth); Soccer shoes—150 (share) and 10 (growth); Bowling shoes—50 (share) and 10 (growth); Running shoes—125 (share) and 7 (growth); Low-impact aerobic shoes—20 (share) and 5 (growth); Walking shoes—35 (share) and 10 (growth); and Basketball sneakers—50 (share) and 15 (growth).
3. Compare the current and projected matrixes. Will Packard Athletic Shoe Company be in a stronger, weaker, or equal position in 2005 than it is now? Explain your answer.
4. What should an ideal projected Boston Consulting Group matrix for Packard Athletic Shoe Company look like? Print the matrix and explain your answer.

5. What additional data do you need to better advise Packard Athletic Shoe Company in its strategic planning efforts?

Exercise 3: Questionnaire Analysis

Objectives

1. To implement a survey dealing with consumer attitudes, usage, and purchase behavior
2. To explore the differences between market segments via a survey
3. To see how data analysis is undertaken
4. To present recommendations based upon survey results

Key Terms and Concepts

marketing research
marketing research process
primary data
research design
survey
data analysis

Explanation of Exercise

In this exercise, you are a market researcher who is requested to collect data for a consumer survey on boom boxes (portable self-contained stereos with multiple speakers). The exercise screens explain how blank copies of the survey may be printed, as well as how the survey may be administered at the computer.

After interviewing respondents, you input their answers into the computer, and a summary of the responses is provided automatically—separated into boom box buyer and nonbuyer segments. The questionnaire consists of several questions and varies slightly for the two segments. For the analysis to be meaningful, you should interview at least 20 respondents; the program will accept as many as 50 respondents.

The exercise is keyed to pages 91-101 in the text.

Questions/Assignments

1. Prepare ten blank questionnaires each for boom box buyers and nonbuyers. Then interview ten boom box buyers and ten nonbuyers. Record their answers on the blank questionnaires (one per respondent) and enter these answers on your exercise program. Print a boom box questionnaire analysis screen summarizing the responses.
2. Analyze the data generated from question/assignment 1. Write a two-page report recapping the findings of your study. Make sure your analysis covers each question (including features, record option pricing, and colour and brand preference).
3. Develop specific recommendations for the marketing of boom boxes.
4. Develop specific recommendations for the pricing of the record option, based upon your analysis in question/assignment 2.
5. Evaluate the questionnaire used in this exercise.
   a. Is the wording clear? Why?
   b. What additional questions should be asked?
   c. How else could the attitudes/behaviour of recent boom box buyers versus nonbuyers be studied?

Exercise 4: Ethics in Action

Objectives

1. To study ethical behaviour in detail
2. To distinguish between process-related and product-related ethical issues
3. To examine ethics from business, consumer, and international perspectives
4. To evaluate marketing strategies on the basis of ethical criteria
5. To see the range of business responses to consumer issues

Key Terms and Concepts

ethical behaviour
process-related ethical issues
product-related ethical issues
product recall

Explanation of Exercise

As a marketing executive for an industrial-goods manufacturer, a table allows you to enter your degree of agreement to ten questions (on a five-point scale ranging from strongly agree to strongly disagree). These questions present a variety of ethical situations relating to salespersons, marketing managers, buyers, retailers, and importers.

A summary table indicates your firm's overall ethical orientation. For each of the ten questions, the most ethical answer receives a +2 score, with the least appropriate response generating a score of −2. The total score can vary from +20 to −20, with +20 being the maximum possible ethical score and −20 being the lowest possible score.

By responding differently to the various statements, you can affect the ethical nature of the industrial-goods manufacturer.

The exercise is keyed to pages 121-128 in the text.

Questions/Assignments

1. Print out and evaluate your responses to the ten-question ethics checklist.
2. Explain how the checklist is used to compute an overall ethics score. Use your response to question/assignment 1 to answer this question.
3. Develop five additional questions that can be used to measure the ethical behavior of a marketer.
4. How could you improve the overall ethical orientation of the industrial-goods manufacturer?
5. Do small firms have a greater difficulty being ethical than large firms? Explain your answer.

Exercise 5: Standardizing Marketing Plans

Objectives

1. To see the dynamics of international marketing
2. To study several components of an international marketing strategy: brand name, product design, manufacturing adaptation, advertising, and pricing
3. To consider the conditions under which a standardized (global), a nonstandardized, or a glocal marketing approach to international marketing is preferred
4. To demonstrate how specific changes in an international marketing strategy affect the overall level of standardization

Key Terms and Concepts

international marketing
global marketing
standardized (global) marketing
  approach
nonstandardized marketing approach
glocal marketing approach

Explanation of Exercise

By answering a series of questions, you—as an international marketing consultant—are able to make decisions regarding the level of standardization for five factors: a product's brand name, its design, its manufacturing process, its advertising, and its pricing. You can vary each factor from pure standardized (global) to glocal to nonstandardized.

Each time you change a factor's level of standardization, the graph on the bottom of the exercise screen automatically moves to reflect the overall degree of standardization for your marketing strategy. All of the five factors are weighted equally. The graphic scale has fifteen gradation points.

This exercise is keyed to pages 161-168 in the text.

Questions/Assignments

1. A small U.S. detergent manufacturer that never exported its products to Mexico is now seeking entry into the Mexican market. The firm hopes that free trade due to the North American Free Trade Agreement (NAFTA) will stimulate demand for its products. Preliminary market research by the firm suggests that many upper-middle-class Mexicans employ domestic help to purchase detergents and wash clothes. These workers generally speak little or no English. The low current value of the Mexican peso relative to the U.S. dollar places many U.S. products out of the price range of low-income Mexican consumers. What do you recommend as the detergent manufacturer's level of standardization for each of the factors covered in this exercise? Print out and comment on your decisions.

2. You have been asked to develop a marketing strategy for a U.S.-based car maker that wants to begin selling four-wheel drive vehicles in Japan.
   a. What important questions regarding consumers, competition, distribution channels, and the legal and economic environment should you resolve prior to recommending a marketing strategy for the firm?
   b. Select an appropriate level of standardization for each of the factors covered in this exercise. Print out and comment on your decisions.

3. a. Under what conditions should a firm adopt a pure standardized marketing strategy? Why?
   b. Under what conditions should a firm adopt a pure nonstandardized marketing strategy? Why?

4. a. What problems would confront a PC maker with a pure standardized approach in all markets? Explain your answer.
   b. What problems would confront a PC maker with a pure nonstandardized approach in all markets? Explain your answer.

Exercise 6: Vendor Analysis

Objectives

1. To show the value of vendor analysis
2. To apply vendor analysis in an organizational consumer purchase situation
3. To show how changes in attribute weights can affect a company's overall vendor rating

Key Terms and Concepts

organizational consumer
vendor analysis
organizational consumer's decision process

Explanation of Exercise

As the purchasing director for a firm, you are to assign weights to eight important vendor attributes: delivery speed, delivery reliability, product quality, quality of final customer support, quality of intermediate customer support, purchase terms, pricing, and availability of styles and colours in all sizes.

A table allows you to enter revised weights for each vendor attribute. The sum of your weights is then converted to 100 per cent automatically by the computer program. In addition, after you enter new weights, the program computes total rating scores for ten potential vendors, as well as the average total score for all vendors. Each vendor is also rated from unsatisfactory to excellent on the basis of its total score.

Mathematically, each vendor's total score equals your assigned weight (in per cent) for each attribute times the pre-assigned evaluation for each attribute (these evaluations cannot be changed by you), summed for all attributes. Attributes with higher assigned weights have the greatest impact on vendor analysis. One of the computer screens enables you to see the pre-assigned evaluations for all ten vendors.

The exercise is keyed to pages 229-234 in the text.

Questions/Assignments

1. Develop vendor analysis weights for the eight attributes for a photography specialty retailer seeking to evaluate multiple vendors. Assume that the retailer appeals to a sophisticated clientele, has high seasonality, and is concerned about product quality (particularly the handling of defective merchandise during the warranty period). Prepare a report evaluating all the vendors, keyed to the vendor data base and your attribute weights.

2. Develop vendor analysis weights for an auto maker that purchases steering wheels (which include airbags and wiring for horns) as complete units. A defective steering wheel can cause consumer dissatisfaction, a major product recall, and dealer service difficulties. Unreliable delivery schedules can cause a major production tie-up. Prepare a report evaluating all the vendors, keyed to the vendor data base and your attribute weights.

3. How do your weights for the vendors in questions/assignments 1 and 2 in this exercise differ? Explain your answer.

4. Develop specific recommendations showing how a poorly rated vendor can improve its evaluation.

5. Evaluate the vendor analysis technique used in this exercise.
   a. Are attributes appropriate? Why or why not? What specific attributes should be added?
   b. Are attributes equally appropriate for manufacturers, wholesalers, and retailers as customers?
   c. Comment on the information shown in the data-base screen.

Exercise 7: Segmentation Analysis

Objectives

1. To better understand the alternatives for developing a target market strategy: undifferentiated marketing (mass marketing), concentrated marketing, and differentiated marketing (multiple segmentation)
2. To show how the choice of a target market approach and alternative marketing budget levels affect a firm's sales and profitability
3. To relate such concepts as product differentiation, demand patterns, the majority fallacy, sales penetration, and diminishing returns to marketing budget allocations

Key Terms and Concepts

market
market segmentation
target market strategy
undifferentiated marketing
 (mass marketing)
concentrated marketing
differentiated marketing (multiple
 segmentation)
product differentiation
demand patterns
majority fallacy
sales penetration
diminishing returns

Explanation of Exercise

A table allows you, the vice-president of marketing for a medium-sized local company, to allocate a $3-million annual marketing budget between final and organizational market segments. By varying the budget, unit sales, sales revenues, manufacturing costs, total costs, and profit are affected. Different levels of marketing expenditures are required to be successful in each market segment.

The final consumer segment is large and very competitive. Consumers have many brands from which to choose. Although the organizational segment is much smaller, it has less competition. Selling prices and manufacturing costs also differ between the segments.

The exercise is keyed to pages 270-276 in the text.

Questions/Assignments

1. At what marketing budget level would you be most profitable in the final consumer segment? Print your optimal budget level for this market and explain your answer.

2. At what marketing budget level would you be most profitable in the organizational segment? Print your optimal budget level for this market and explain your answer.

3. Describe the basic differences between the final and organizational segments in terms of the relationship among sales, profits, and marketing expenditures. What does this mean to marketers?

4. At what marketing budget allocation levels would your firm's total profits be maximized? Print your optimal budget allocation and explain your answer. *NOTE:* You may use a differentiated marketing approach.

5. Explain how these concepts relate to the exercise:
   a. Product differentiation.
   b. Demand patterns.
   c. Majority fallacy.
   d. Sales penetration.
   e. Diminishing returns.

Exercise 8: Product Positioning

Objectives

1. To demonstrate the use of a product-positioning map as a tool for studying and evaluating consumer product perceptions
2. To show how a product position can be changed through price and nonprice factors
3. To illustrate how competitive and company product positioning are affected by modifications in marketing strategy
4. To consider which competitive product positioning strategies maximize the market share for a company's brand

Key Terms and Concepts

product positioning
ideal points

Explanation of Exercise

A product positioning map lets you—acting as an outside consultant—evaluate Hewlett Packard's (HP's) personal computer positioning relative to other major brands (Apple, IBM, Packard Bell, Compaq, and Dell). By rating HP's updated image on the basis of a series of statements, a revised product-positioning map for HP and five other brands is generated and displayed. In addition, the computer program calculates revised market shares for HP and the other brands, leading to an adjusted market-share table.

By responding differently to the various product-positioning statements, you can determine the optimal product-positioning strategy for HP, in terms of HP's market share and the market share for the other brands.

The exercise is keyed to pages 302-305 in the text.

Questions/Assignments

1. What series of responses to the statements on the exercise screens would result in HP being positioned in the prestige brands segment? Why? Print your input screens and the related product-positioning map.

2. What series of responses to the statements on the exercise screens would result in HP being positioned in the high-value brands segment? Why? Print your input screens and the related product-positioning map.

3. Which product position for HP results in its achieving a maximum market share? Why? Print your input screens and the related positioning map.

4. Which product position for HP results in its achieving a minimum market share? Why? Print your input screens and the related positioning map.

5. a. Evaluate the series of statements used in this exercise.
   b. Make specific recommendations to improve these statements.

Exercise 9: Services Strategy

Objectives

1. To distinguish between core and peripheral services
2. To explore the characteristics of services
3. To illustrate the development of a service marketing strategy

Key Terms and Concepts

service marketing
core services
peripheral services
intangibility of services
perishability of services
inseparability of services
variability in service quality

Explanation of Exercise

By making a number of marketing decisions, you—as a manager of a hotel chain—are able to develop an overall services strategy. You are seeking to increase your hotel's occupancy rate and profits by looking into free breakfasts, exercise facilities, and the use of a print shop. Each of these strategies can be offered at four different levels; cost data are provided for each level. By varying the level of each strategy, total revenues, costs, operating profit, and the hotel's occupancy rate are affected. You can revise your overall strategy by re-entering a new strategy.

This exercise is keyed to pages 318-328 in the text.

Questions/Assignments

1. Which overall strategy maximizes the hotel's sales revenues?
2. Which overall strategy maximizes the hotel's overall profit?
3. Explain the differences in these strategies.
4. The hotel chain is seeking to attract convention customers. Explain your choice of a services strategy for this segment.

5. The hotel chain plans to use a differentiated marketing strategy to attract both businesspersons and tourists. Explain your choice of services strategy for each segment.

Exercise 10: Product Screening Checklist

Objectives

1. To demonstrate the use of a new-product screening checklist as a product evaluation tool
2. To show how the importance of various product characteristics can be denoted
3. To illustrate how different assumptions regarding the importance of product characteristics and the ratings of individual attributes affect a product's overall rating
4. To consider what minimum overall evaluation score would be necessary for a product to successfully pass the product-screening stage of new-product planning

Key Terms and Concepts

modifications
minor modifications
major modifications
new-product planning process
product screening

Explanation of Exercise

A new-product screening checklist lets you—acting as an outside consultant who specializes in new-product concepts—weight the importance of various general, marketing, and production characteristics; and then rate a new product idea in terms of each of these characteristics. The computer program then computes separate indexes for general, marketing, and production factors—as well as an overall evaluation index.

Mathematically, every specific index equals the average of all of its attributes' weights times their ratings. Thus, the general characteristics index equals

$$\frac{\text{The sum of (Each attribute's weight} \times \text{That attribute's rating)}}{\text{The total weights assigned to general characteristics}}$$

The exercise is keyed to pages 356-363 in the text.

Questions/Assignments

1. As a new-product planning analyst at a major computer manufacturer, you have been asked to explore the feasibility of producing an inexpensive desktop computer designed especially for Internet users. Like traditional computers, this model comes complete with a keyboard, modem, floppy disk, and a color monitor. However, unlike traditional desktop units, it is priced at $500 retail—since it contains a slow microprocessor and no hard drive. In comparison, the least expensive computer currently produced by the firm is priced at $2000 at retail. Preliminary market research reports indicate a large market potential for consumers who would like to "surf the net" but who do not wish to spend $2000 or more for a computer. Print both the individual weights and ratings that you assign to the product, as well as the overall analysis screen.

2. **a.** Explain your choice of weights and ratings for each of the criteria in the new-product screening checklist for question/assignment 1.
   b. How should the computer manufacturer use concept testing with this product?
   c. Would you recommend that the manufacturer skip test marketing? Why or why not?

3. As a product manager for radios at Electrohome, you have been carefully following the new products produced by competitors. The most innovative clock radio of the 1990s is Bose's Wave Radio. Despite its small size, this radio provides sound that is comparable in clarity and richness to many full-sized stereos. Bose has accomplished this via a patented speaker design. In addition to its fine sound, the Bose Wave has features generally not found on a clock radio. These include a remote control device, a consumer's ability to fall asleep listening to one station and to wake up listening to another (also at different volumes), and twin alarms to accommodate different work schedules. Electrohome currently makes clock radios priced from $15 to $75 at retail and is considering producing a $150 unit that incorporates some Wave Radio features. Print both the individual weights and ratings that you assign to Electrohome's proposed new product, and the overall analysis screen.

4. **a.** Explain your choice of weights and ratings for each of the criteria in the new-product screening checklist in question/assignment 3.
   b. Should Electrohome proceed further with this product? Why or why not?
   c. Comment on the risks inherent in marketing the new clock radio. Compare these to the risks in marketing a new personal computer.

Exercise 11: Economic Order Quantity

Objectives

1. To consider the overall ramifications of order size for a firm when it makes purchases
2. To examine the individual components of economic order quantity (EOQ): annual demand, wholesale unit costs, order-processing costs, and inventory-holding costs
3. To calculate economic order quantities
4. To see the impact of different assumptions on economic order quantity

Key Terms and Concepts

just-in-time (JIT) inventory system
quick response (QR) inventory system
stock turnover
economic order quantity (EOQ)

Explanation of Exercise

As the purchasing manager for a firm, you can determine its economic order quantity under various assumptions by answering questions about expected annual demand for a product, its unit cost at wholesale, order-processing costs, and inventory-holding costs (as a percentage of a unit's wholesale cost). The computer program uses the EOQ formula, and a screen graphically displays the results.

Mathematically,

$$EOQ = \sqrt{\frac{2 \times \text{Annual demand} \times \text{Order-processing costs}}{\text{Inventory-holding costs \%} \times \text{Unit cost}}}$$

The exercise is keyed to pages 428-432 in the text.

Questions/Assignments

1. **a.** How can order-processing and inventory-holding costs be estimated by a company?
   b. Explain how a just-in-time (JIT) inventory system can reduce a firm's order-processing costs.

c. Explain how a just-in-time (JIT) inventory system can reduce a firm's inventory-holding costs.

2. A mail-order office-supply retailer wishes to apply the EOQ concept to its purchases of key items to minimize the sum of its order-processing and inventory-holding costs. For example, it annually buys 2,000 units of an automatic electric stapler. The cost at wholesale is $8.00. Each order the retailer places with its supplier costs the retailer $10.00. Inventory-holding costs are 20 per cent of unit cost. Print and comment on the economic order quantity for the retailer.

3. Determine how each of the following (one at a time) impacts on the EOQ of the mail-order firm noted in question/assignment 2. Discuss these changes and print the relevant screens.
  a. Reduce annual demand from 2,000 to 1,500 units.
  b. Increase the cost at wholesale from $8.00 to $10.00.
  c. Reduce order-processing costs from $10.00 to $7.00.
  d. Raise inventory-holding costs from 20 per cent to 25 per cent.

4. Describe three situations in which the economic order quantity model would be inappropriate for the mail-order retailer.

Exercise 12: Wholesaler Cost Analysis

Objectives

1. To study the functions of wholesalers
2. To consider the characteristics of manufacturer wholesaling
3. To review the characteristics of merchant wholesaling
4. To determine under what circumstances manufacturer wholesaling or merchant wholesaling should be used

Key Terms and Concepts

wholesaling
manufacturer/service provider wholesaling
merchant wholesalers

Explanation of Exercise

As a consultant for a manufacturer, you have been retained to review that firm's selection of manufacturer wholesaling versus merchant wholesaling. The total costs of each wholesaling alternative differ on the basis of sales.

The costs for manufacturer wholesaling and merchant wholesaling are provided. These are based upon estimates of salesperson productivity, salesperson salaries, warehouse administrative costs, functional discounts, and channel manager costs for each wholesaler alternative. In computing these costs, note that some are fixed, while others are based upon sales volume. In addition, some cost elements are unique to the type of wholesaler used. For example, there are no channel manager costs under manufacturer wholesaling and no sales manager costs under merchant wholesaling.

After you enter your sales-volume forecast, the computer program automatically generates a screen showing total planned distribution costs under each alternative.

The exercise is keyed to pages 438-449 in the text.

Questions/Assignments

1. Calculate total distribution costs under manufacturer wholesaling and merchant wholesaling for projected sales volumes of $1 million and $3 million. Print and assess the results.

2. Calculate total distribution costs under manufacturer wholesaling and merchant wholesaling for projected sales volumes of $5 million and $10 million. Print and assess the results.

3. Under what conditions should a manufacturer use manufacturer wholesaling even though merchant wholesaling would be less costly?

4. Under what conditions should a manufacturer use merchant wholesaling when manufacturer wholesaling would be less costly?

Exercise 13: Advertising Budget

Objectives

1. To practice setting an advertising budget—using such concepts as reach, waste, and cost per thousand
2. To examine the characteristics of alternative magazines as advertising media
3. To see how the allocation of an advertising budget among various magazines affects promotion effectiveness
4. To study the match between magazine readership and the target market

Key Terms and Concepts

advertising media costs
reach
waste
cost per thousand
effective cost per thousand
narrowcasting
frequency
clutter
lead time

Explanation of Exercise

As the advertising director for Sunshine Cruise Lines, a leading cruise ship operator, you have been asked to develop an advertising campaign for the U.S. market.

You make decisions with regard to the number of insertions (full-page 4-colour ads) that Sunshine should make in these magazines during the year and the per cent of each magazine's audience that would be wasted for Sunshine. You are provided with the names of the magazines, their cost per full-page ad (equal to one insertion), and their reach. These data are from *Standard Rate & Data Service*. Based on your decisions, the computer program calculates the budget allocated to each magazine, its cost per thousand, and the effective cost per thousand. For instance, the effective cost per thousand for a specific magazine equals

$$\frac{\text{Advertising budget for a magazine}}{\text{Reach for that magazine} \times (100 - \text{Per cent waste})} \times 1000$$

The program also derives company totals, using weighted averages. As an example, the total waste for Sunshine's magazine advertising equals

(% of magazine ad budget allocated to magazine A × % waste for magazine A)

+ (% of magazine ad budget allocated to magazine B × % waste for magazine B)

+ (other magazines, based on individual budgets and waste)

When choosing among the magazines, note that the number of placements is limited by each magazine's frequency. The computer program limits your placements to match each magazine's frequency. It is also important that your decisions be based upon the target market for Sunshine. Important target markets for the firm are newlyweds, retired couples, and singles.

The exercise is keyed to pages 525-530 in the text.

Questions/Assignments

1. a. Evaluate each of the magazines shown on the computer screen for this exercise in terms of cost per 1-page ad and reach. These are the full titles of the magazines: *Cruise Travel*,

Ladies Home Journal, Modern Bride, Modern Maturity, People, Travel & Leisure, Travel Holiday, and *TV Guide.*
   - **b.** Estimate waste as a percentage of reach for each magazine and explain your answer.
   - **c.** Allot a $2 million advertising budget roughly equally among all the magazines. Print and comment upon the results.
2. Sunshine's marketing vice-president has given you these guidelines in making your actual magazine budget expenditure decisions: You should spend as close to your entire $2 million magazine advertising budget as possible. You should use no fewer than five magazines. You should allocate no more than 40 per cent of the budget to any one magazine. The effective cost per thousand should be minimized.
   - **a.** Develop an advertising budget that meets these guidelines.
   - **b.** Print and explain your budget allocations.
   - **c.** What is the role of reach in your decision making?
3. Sunshine's marketing vice-president has decided to modify two of the guidelines stated in question/assignment 2. First, you may use as few magazines as you deem proper (you may even use just one magazine). Second, there are no restrictions on the maximum per cent of the $2 million budget that may be spent on any single magazine.
   - **a.** Develop an advertising budget that meets these guidelines.
   - **b.** Print and explain your budget allocations.
   - **c.** What are the pros and cons of concentrating your budget on fewer magazines?
4. Explain how each of these factors would affect your magazine advertising budget decisions:
   - **a.** Passalong rates (as a part of reach).
   - **b.** Narrowcasting.
   - **c.** Frequency.
   - **d.** Clutter.
   - **e.** Message permanence.
   - **f.** Lead time.

Exercise 14: Salesperson Deployment

Objectives

1. To practice setting a sales-expense budget
2. To see how the mix of accounts in a territory affects the required number of salespeople
3. To show how the level of customer service affects the required number of salespeople
4. To study how the use of telemarketing and catalog sales reduces the required number of salespeople

Key Terms and Concepts

sales-expense budget   sales management
order taker   sales territory
order getter

Explanation of Exercise

As a regional sales manager, one of your more important responsibilities is to determine the required number of salespeople in your territory. Your firm has four types of industrial accounts ("A", "B", "C", and "D"). "A" accounts are key customers; "B" accounts have high potential but only moderate sales; "C" accounts are smaller firms with lower sales potential; and "D" are the smallest accounts. First, you make decisions on the number of accounts in each group: "A," "B," "C," and "D." Next, you can set the required call frequency for each account type. Finally, you need to determine the desired level of customer service: limited, regular, or intensive.

After you enter your decisions, the computer program generates a screen showing the required number of sales calls per year, the number of calls per salesperson per year, and the required number of salespersons. The required number of salespersons equals

$$\frac{\text{Required number of sales calls per year}}{\text{Number of calls per salesperson per year}}$$

The exercise is keyed to pages 554-560 in the text.

Questions/Assignments

1. Calculate the required number of salespeople when the firm has 50 "A" accounts, 150 "B" accounts, 1,000 "C" accounts, and 2,000 "D" accounts. The required call frequencies per year for "A," "B," "C," and "D" accounts are 50, 25, 10, and 3 respectively. Assume that the firm desires intensive service. Print and assess the results.
2. Calculate the required number of salespeople when the firm has 50 "A" accounts, 150 "B" accounts, 1,000 "C" accounts, and 2,000 "D" accounts. The required call frequency per year for "A," "B," "C," and "D" accounts are 50, 25, 10, and 3 respectively. Assume that the firm desires limited service. Print and compare the results to your answer in question/assignment 1.
3. Under what conditions would you recommend that a firm use limited service? Intensive service?
4. Describe the specific assumptions of the salesperson deployment model used in this exercise.

Exercise 15: Price Elasticity

Objectives

1. To illustrate the law of demand
2. To distinguish among elastic, inelastic, and unitary demand
3. To see how a firm can estimate demand at different price levels
4. To further explore the interrelationship among price, demand, total revenue, and price elasticity

Key Terms and Concepts

law of demand   inelastic demand
price elasticity of demand   unitary demand
elastic demand   subjective price

Explanation of Exercise

As the owner-operator of an auto-repair firm specializing in tune-ups, you are concerned about what price to charge for a basic tune-up. First, you answer a series of questions about the price range to be considered and the expected average amount of consumer demand (which may be expressed in fractions) at various prices. The computer program then calculates elasticity of demand for the various price intervals and graphically displays it.

Your answers affect the type of demand the firm would face at different prices. Demand may be elastic, inelastic, or unitary—based on the price elasticity formula discussed in the text.

The exercise is keyed to pages 581-584 in the text.

Questions/Assignments

1. You are considering the implementation of one of two price strategies: The low-end strategy involves traditional spark plugs and a one-year or 20 000-mile warranty (whichever comes first). In contrast, the high-end strategy involves platinum-tipped spark plugs and a two-year or 30 000-mile warranty. You have done some preliminary demand analysis and estimate the following demand schedule:

Price	Average Low-End Demand (Tune-Ups per Day)	Average High-End Demand (Tune-Ups per Day)
$ 50	12	15
$ 60	10	12
$ 70	7	10
$ 80	3	7
$ 90	0	5
$100	0	0

Determine the price elasticities at the various prices for the two strategies. Print the computer-generated tables and assess them. Hint: Enter the numbers in two groups (one for low-end demand and another for high-end demand).

2. **a.** Could your firm utilize both a low-end and a high-end marketing strategy? Explain your answer.
   b. Based on the information provided for question/assignment 1, could you determine the most profitable price level for the firm? If yes, what is it? If no, why not?
   c. How could you improve your ability to estimate the demand at various price levels?

3. **a.** Present average customer demand levels so that price elasticity at every interval between $50 and $80 (at $10 intervals) is elastic. Print and discuss your answer.
   b. Present average customer demand levels so that price elasticity at every interval between $70 and $100 (at $10 intervals) is inelastic. Print and discuss your answer.
   c. Is it realistic that demand would always be elastic or always be inelastic over a broad price range? Explain your answer.

4. **a.** Under what conditions would the price elasticity of demand equal 0? Why?
   b. Under what conditions would the price elasticity of demand equal 1? Why?
   c. Print a demand curve screen showing both 0 and 1 price elasticities.

Exercise 16: Key Cost Concepts

Objectives

1. To study fixed and variable cost concepts in detail
2. To distinguish between total and average fixed costs and total and average variable costs
3. To show the effects of changes in fixed and variable costs on a variety of cost components
4. To see how fixed, variable, and total costs are related to the level of production

Key Terms and Concepts

total fixed costs
total variable costs
total costs
average fixed costs
average variable costs
average total costs
marginal costs

Explanation of Exercise

As a pricing consultant for Ultimate Audiovision, you answer questions about the fixed and variable costs of making the home-entertainment system at various production levels. Ultimate Audiovision contains a state-of-the-art 46-inch rear projection TV, a VCR, an AM/FM tuner, two tape decks, a CD player, a turntable, an amplifier, an equalizer, and two 200-watt speakers. The system has an oak-wood look and may be operated via an infrared remote control or manually.

First, you set the total fixed costs at two different production levels. Next, you set the average (per-unit) variable costs at four different production levels. *NOTE:* You should reduce per-unit variable costs as the production volume increases. After you enter your decisions, the computer program automatically generates a screen showing production levels; total fixed, variable, and overall costs; average fixed, variable, and overall costs; and the change in per-unit costs as volume increases.

The exercise is keyed to pages 605-609 in the text.

Questions/Assignments

1. You have been asked to prepare an analysis of home-entertainment system production costs for the purpose of gathering background data to be used in the development and implementation of Ultimate Audiovision's pricing strategy. You estimate that fixed costs would be $180 000 if 100 to 499 units are produced and $225 000 if production involves 500 or more units. You further estimate that average (per-unit) variable costs would be $3000 if 100 to 299 units are produced, $2700 if 300 to 599 units are produced, $2400 if 600 to 899 units are produced, and $2200 if 900 or more units are produced. Print and analyze a key cost calculations screen based on these data.

2. Use the same variable costs as in question/assignment 1, but assume that fixed costs are $195 000 for all production levels. Print the key cost calculations screen based on these data and compare it to the one you generated for question/assignment 1.

3. Using all the data from question/assignment 1, what would be the price-floor price at each production level (100 units, 200 units, 300 units, etc.)? Would you be willing to sell your full production of 1000 units at the price-floor price? Explain your answers.

4. How could you use the information from this exercise to undertake traditional break-even analysis? Modified break-even analysis? What additional data would be needed to complete these analyses?

Exercise 17: Performance Ratios

Objectives

1. To evaluate company efficiency and effectiveness by using performance ratios
2. To apply several company performance ratios: sales efficiency, cost-of-goods-sold, gross margin, operating expense, net profit, stock turnover, and return on investment
3. To show the relationship between profit-and-loss statement values and company performance ratios

Key Terms and Concepts

profit-and-loss (income) statement
performance ratios
sales efficiency ratio (percentage)
cost-of-goods-sold ratio (percentage)
gross margin ratio (percentage)
operating expense ratio (percentage)
net profit ratio (percentage)
stock turnover ratio
return on investment (ROI)

Appendix *Computer-Based Marketing Exercises* **A-11**

Explanation of Exercise

As a General Toy Company executive vice-president, you are quite interested in using performance ratios to measure your company's relative success or failure across several criteria.

By entering new data onto a profit-and-loss screen, you can see the impact of changes in General Toy's sales efficiency, cost of goods sold, gross margin, operating expenses, net profit, stock turnover, and return on investment on the company's related performance ratios. For example, what would happen to ROI if General Toy's assets rise by 5 per cent?

After you input the new data, the computer calculates revised performance ratios and shows a screen summarizing all the ratios. The screen also stipulates whether each ratio is excellent, good, or poor—based on criteria that you may access via the exercise diskette.

Questions/Assignments

1. **a.** Evaluate General Toy's performance on the basis of the preset data appearing on the exercise screens. Print the relevant screens.
   b. What recommendations would you make to General Toy?
2. Enter the following data on the profit-and-loss screen: assets—$1 120 000; gross sales—$1 000 000; returns—$200 000; ending inventory—$100 000; and operating expenses—$400 000. The other data categories should retain the pre-set values. Print the relevant screens and comment on General Toy's performance. Compare your answers with those in question/assignment 1.
3. Enter these revised data on the profit-and-loss screen: assets—$800 000; gross sales—$1 050 000; returns—$50 000; beginning inventory—$150 000; and operating expenses—$300 000. The other data categories should retain the pre-set values. Print the relevant screens and comment on General Toy's performance. Compare the answers with those in questions/assignments 1 and 2.
4. Enter these revised data on the profit-and-loss screen: gross sales—$1 050 000; returns—$50 000; beginning inventory—$50 000; purchases (new merchandise)—$300 000; and ending inventory—$50 000. The other data categories should retain the pre-set values. Print the relevant screens and comment on General Toy's performance. Compare your answers with those in questions/assignments 1, 2, and 3.

Exercise 18: Optimal Marketing Mix

Objectives

1. To apply and compare mass marketing, selective marketing, and exclusive marketing strategies
2. To determine the impact of specific marketing-mix factors on mass, selective, and exclusive marketing strategies
3. To see how the optimal marketing mixes for mass, selective, and exclusive marketing strategies may be calculated
4. To demonstrate the value of sales response curves

Key Terms and Concepts

alternative marketing mixes *opportunity costs*
optimal marketing mix *sales response curves*

Explanation of Exercise

A table allows you—the marketing director for a small industrial manufacturer—to make decisions regarding your firm's $3 million annual marketing budget. You have the ability to make decisions regarding the expenditures for advertising, personal selling, and distribution and to set the price for your product for each of three strategy alternatives: mass marketing, selective marketing, and exclusive marketing. Thus, you are involved with two distinct areas of decision making: (1) For each strategy alternative (mass marketing, selective marketing, and exclusive marketing), what is the best marketing mix? (2) Which strategy alternative should your firm pursue?

In setting prices, you must use penetration pricing (a range of $10 to $15) with mass marketing, moderate pricing ($20 to $34) with selective marketing, and skimming pricing (a range of $35 to $99) with exclusive marketing. When allocating the $3 million marketing budget, you assign values to advertising and personal selling; the computer subtracts these figures from $3 million and displays the amount you want to spend on distribution. The costs of making the product depend on which strategy alternative is involved. For example, an exclusive-marketing strategy requires a much higher cost to make the product than a mass-marketing strategy.

Once you enter decisions, the computer program automatically calculates and displays unit sales, revenues, total product costs, total costs, and profit. The results will differ substantially for the three alternative strategies.

Questions/Assignments

1. For each strategy alternative (mass marketing, selective marketing, and exclusive marketing), what is the best marketing mix? Print the relevant table and explain it.
2. Which strategy alternative should your firm pursue? Why?
3. If you could reduce your product costs by 10 per cent, which strategy alternative would you choose? Why? *NOTE:* This question/assignment requires you to make some computations with a calculator and should be answered after you respond to questions/assignments 1 and 2.
4. **a.** Develop separate sales response curves for price, advertising, personal selling, and distribution under a mass-marketing strategy.
   b. Develop separate sales response curves for price, advertising, personal selling, and distribution under an exclusive-marketing strategy.
   c. Compare the curves in a and b.

   NOTE: In deriving each sales response curve, vary only the factor for which you are devising that response curve (for example, price). Otherwise, you will not be able to trace the response to the single factor you are studying.

Company and Name Index

Aamco, 331
A&B sound, 406
A&P, 272, 384, 466, 481
Abitibi-Price, 615
A Buck or Two, 263
A.C. Nielsen Canada, 94, 105
Acton, 76
Adidas, 50
Advanced Neurotechnologies, 91
Advantis, 319
Aerospatiale, 158
Aikenhead's, 199-200
Airbus Industrie, 158
Air Canada, 305, 306, 319, 398, 495, 567, 627, 658
Aiwa, 526
Allied Signal, 233, 378
AlphaNet Telecom, 361
Altamira, 643, 644
Aluminum Corporation of America (Alcoa), 254
American Airlines, 38
American Business Information (ABI), 83
American Express, 85, 346
American Tobacco, 646
America Online, 83, 530
Amoco, 364
Andersen consulting, 229
Anderson, Louie, 516
Apple Computer, 4, 567
Arbitron, 282
Arm & Hammer , 315
Arthritis Society, 340
Arthur Andersen & Co., 229
Arya Marine, 435
Asatsu/BBDO, 221
Asea Brown Boveri (ABB), 640
Astoria Airlines, 67
AT&T, 13, 38, 347, 632
Athlete's World, 224
Atlantic Canada Inns, 331
Atomic Energy Canada, 336
Avon Products, 143, 470

Bank America, 324
Bank of Montreal, 38, 324, 515, 524, 526
Bank of Nova Scotia, 327
Barkley, Charles, 50
Barlow, John Parry, 406
Bata Ltd., 37
Bata Shoes, 383
Bata, Thomas, 37
Batelle, 21
Bausch & Lomb, 66, 161, 290
BC Hydro, 341
B.C. Placings, 471
BC Sugar Refinery Limited, 38, 58
Beadows, Clyde, 627
Bell Canada, 26, 124, 641, 644
Bell Mobility, 475, 584
Bell South, 13
Bergen, Candice, 506

Bergum, Doug, 16
Bethune, Gordon, 577
Betty Crocker, 151
Biddulph, Jennifer, 351
Biway, 273
Black & Decker, 302, 350, 380, 485
Black, Stanley, 485
Blockbuster Video, 468
BMG, 406, 407
BMW, 113, 114, 566
Body Shop, 140, 468
Boeing, 274, 385, 443, 576
Bombardier Inc., 228, 234, 241, 299-300
Borden, 646
Brahma Beer and Soda Company, 164
Brassard, Jean-Luc, 506
Brewers Warehousing corporation, 72
Bristol-Myers, 38
Bristol-Myers Squibb, 347
British Aerospace, 158
British Airways, 14, 15, 132, 183, 603-604
Brosnan, Pierce, 496
Brownies and Girl Guides of Canada, 332
Brunk, Fred, 227
Burke International Research, 94
Burke Marketing Services, 95
Burroughs Wellcome Inc., 382
Bush, George, 373
Business Depot, 468, 480
Butler, Brett, 516
Butler, Dean, 598

Cadbury Schweppes, 379, 646
Calgary Philharmonic Orchestra, 334
Calvin Klein, 294, 392, 538
Cambridge Shopping Centres, 460
Campbell Soup, 302, 386, 395
Campofrío, 176
Canada Life, 38
Canada Post, 332, 336, 339-40, 423, 428
Canada Proud Inc., 390
Canada Safeway Ltd., 461
Canada Trust, 38, 346
Canadian Airlines, 38, 398, 627
Canadian Council on Smoking and Health, 338
Canadian Dairy Bureau, 525
Canadian Facts, 94
Canadian Geographic Enterprises, 471
Canadian Home Shopping Network, 475
Canadian National Railways, 336, 425
Canadian Pacific, 425
Canadian Pacific Hotels, 526
Canadian Tire Corporation Ltd., 346, 386, 461, 478, 624
Canon Corporation, 55, 118
Canondale, 603-604
Canstar Sports, 382
Cantel, 584
CanWest Global Communications, 158, 503
Carling-O'Keefe, 38
Carnival Cruiselines, 475

Carrefour, 467, 480
Carscadden, Rob, 393
Carson, Patrick, 463
Caruthers Raisin Packing Company, 442
Caterpillar Tractor, 67, 113, 292, 297, 453
CDnow, 407
Century 21, 411
Cerberus Sound + Vision, 407
Charoen Pokphand, 158
Chesebrough-Ponds Canada, 382
Chevron, 364
Choice Hotels, 265
Christie Brown, 302
Chrysler, 38, 145, 167, 254, 364, 443, 444, 526, 536, 662
Church, Austin, 315
City of Thunder Bay, 338
Clairborne, Liz, 368
Clairol, 263
Clinton, Bill, 171
Clorox, 646
Club Med, 265
Club Monaco, 65
Coalition for Environmentally Responsible Economies (CERES), 117
Coca-Cola, 52, 145, 159, 162, 165, 168, 354, 388, 401, 522, 566, 646
Coca-Cola Canada, 363
Coca-Cola de Argentina, 99
Colgate-Palmolive, 165, 562
Columbia/HCA Healthcare, 347
Columbia House, 406, 418
Compaq, 383, 566, 584, 603
CompuServe, 83, 530
Computer Associates, 584
ConAgra, 298, 299, 387
Connell, Grant, 50
Construcciones Aeronauticas, 158
Cookbook Store, 475
Cook, Scott D., 545
Co-op Atlantic Stores, 478
Corcoran, Terence, 140
Cordiant, 17
Corel, 382-83
Cott Corporation, 383, 522
CPC International, 162, 646
CP Rail, 341
Credit Suisse, 158
Crest, 183, 647
CSC Cosulting, 633
CS First Boston, 158
CSX Corporation, 436
CSX Intermodal Inc., 436
Cubanacan SA, 159
Cummins Engine, 292
Cyberspace Promotions, 407
Cyrix, 27

Darsey Masius Benton & Bowles (DMB&B), 286
Dawson, Bob, 63
de Havilland Inc., 228

I-1

I-2   Company and Name Index

Dell, 584
Delphi, 83
Delta Hotels, 159
Delta Hotels and Resorts, 165
de Silva, Eliana Maria Machado, 143
Deutsche Airbus, 158
Deutsche Telekom, 13
de Vries, Teresa, 390
Digital Equipment Corporation, 371
Dion, Celine, 495
Dion, Yves, 449
Dole, 646
Donnelley Marketing, 571
Dover, 59
Dow Chemical, 168
Dreamworks SKG, 600
Drucker, Peter, 73-74
Dun & Bradstreet Canada, 94, 442
Dunavant, W. Roger, 493
Dunkin' Donuts, 571
DuPont, 368, 644
Dwight, John, 315
Dylex Ltd., 65, 273, 478
Dynamics Group, 99

Easter Seal Society, 336
Eaton's Department Store, 4, 460, 468, 480
Ebara Corporation, 117
Equifax Canada Inc., 4
Eurotel, 150
Exxon Corporation, 160, 364

Fairweather and Braemar, 65, 273
Fallows, James, 171
Federal Express, 4, 67, 339, 355, 382, 428, 632, 646
FHS International, 645
Fidelity Investment, 633
Finning Ltd., 453
Fireman, Paul, 50
First Alert, 567
Fluid Management, 227
Ford, Henry, 271
Ford Motor Company, 38, 145, 163, 254, 364, 398, 411, 499, 644
Ford Motor Company of Canada, 135
Four Seasons, 265
Frank Perdue, 272
Frito-Lay, 68, 443, 505
Fuji, 118
Future Shop, 133, 406

Garneau, Philippe, 515
Gates, Bill, 49, 401
Gateway 2000, 545
GD Express Worldwide, 339
Geffen, David, 600
Gemstar Corporation, 371
Genentech, 69, 603
General Cinema, 383
General Electric (GE), 59, 159, 229, 302, 347, 443, 576, 633, 637, 639-40
General Mills, 61, 402
General Motors (GM), 38, 145, 254, 273, 290, 331, 346, 364, 365, 369, 443
General Motors Spain, 176
General Shoe Corporation, 382
Genesco, 382

Gennum Corporation, 146
George Weston Ltd., 661
GE Plastics, 244
Gerber Canada, 301
Gercke, Timothy C., 546
Gerrie, Bob, 277
GfK, 17
Giant Foods, 628
Gillette Company, 379, 624, 662
Glaxo Canada Inc., 382
Glaxo Wellcome Inc., 382
Global Environmental Management Initiative (GEMI), 117
Global Express Airplane, 234, 234
Goizueta, Roberto, 52
Gold, Christina A., 143
Golf-Day, 485
Goodyear, 350
Great Atlantic and Pacific Co. of Canada Ltd., 461
Great Plains Software, 16
Grench, Bruce, 102
Gretsky, Wayne, 495
Greyhound Air, 627
Greyhound Courier Express, 327
Griffey, Ken Jr., 50
Grove, Andy, 27, 545
Grow Biz International, 594
GTE, 633
Gucci, 580

Hamilton, 273
H&R Block, 412, 465
Harcourt General, 382
Harry Rosen, 65, 67
Harvard Capital Corporation, 355
Harvey's, 32
HDIS, 102
Heineken, 166, 183
Heinz, 359, 388
Hellmann's, 295
Herman Miller, 141
Hershey, 646
Hewlett-Packard, 113, 351
Hitachi, 355, 505
H.J. Heinz Co., 300
HMV Canada, 407
HMV Records, 406
Home Depot, 199-200, 459, 478, 485
Home Shopping Budapest, 130
Honda, 38, 183, 254, 274, 388
Hostess Frito-Lay, 304, 393
Hudson's Bay Co., 461, 461, 614
Humpty-Dumpty Foods Ltd., 304

IBM, 113, 165, 217, 225, 275, 319, 327, 381, 382, 385, 443, 545, 638-39, 644, 662
IBM Canada, 30
IDA Pharmacies, 466
Imperial Oil Ltd., 124, 160, 413
Information Resources Inc. (IRI), 17, 105
Integrated Systems Solution, 319
Intel, 27, 545
Interbrew S.A., 72, 160
International Apparel Syndicate (IAS), 392
International Harvester, 382
International Lease Corp., 576
International Surveys Ltd. (ISL), 89
Interpublic Group, 17

Intuit Inc., 545, 640-41
Investors Group, 38
IP Constructors Ltd., 158
ISM Information Systems Management, 319
Izatt, James, 67

Jackson, Bo, 224
Jackson, Marie, 5
Jackson, Michael, 661
J.C. Penny, 163
Jergens, 300
Jiffy Lube, 331
Jim Scharf Holdings Ltd., 314
Johnson & Johnson, 59, 87, 135, 295, 302, 432
Johnson Controls, 59, 353
Johnson, Larry, 498
Jordan, Michael, 50, 495
Jostens Learning Corporation, 58
J. Walter Thompson, 521

Karan, Donna, 368
Keebler, 571
Kellogg Canada Inc., 124
Kemp, Shawn, 50
Kennedy, John F., 128
Kids Only Clothing, 470
Kindred Spirits, 471
K-mart, 468, 614
Knorr Products, 162
Koch, Rich, 536
Kodak, 91, 113, 118, 352, 359, 384, 416, 6404
Konica, 305, 306
Koss Corporation, 10-11
Kraft General Foods, 302
Kreb, 76
Kun, Lee, 637
Kwoh, Daniel, 371

Labatt Brewing Company, 38, 71, 147, 160, 302, 541, 544
Lakeport, 391
Land's End, 58, 130, 471, 633
Languirand, Jacques, 506
La Red Television, 158
Lauterborn, Robert F., 512
Learjet Inc., 228
Lee, Orville, 224
Leggett, Stuart, 401
Le Group Videotron Ltee of Montreal, 518
Lenox, 580
LensCrafters, 468, 598
Leon's Furniture, 497
Lever Brothers, 176
Levi Strauss, 225
Lewis Woolf Griptight company, 389
LifeScan, 135
Lister Butler, 490
Lister, John, 490
L.L. Bean, 471, 647
Loblaws, 135, 384, 459, 463, 466, 469, 495
Loblaws Superstore Atlantic, 467
Loewen Group Inc., 164
Louis Vuitton Malletier, 376

McAfee Associates, 411
McCormick, Peter, 544
McDonald's, 160, 168, 183, 354, 362, 383, 390, 416, 480, 565

McDonald's Restaurants of Canada, 14
McDonnell Couglas, 576
MacLean Hunter, 274
McLennan, John, 641
McMath, Robert, 373
McWarehouse, 620
Madonna, 391, 661
Magna International Corporation, 160
Mail Boxes Etc., 63
Makeup Art Cosmetics (M.A.C.), 661
Malle, Louis, 506
Malofilm communications, 448-49
Malo, René, 449
Malt-O-Meal, 603
Maritz Marketing Research, 89
Mars, 646
Mary Kay Cosmetics, 124
MasterCard, 346
Maxwell, Brian, 351
Maxwell House, 150
Maytag, 526, 646
Meca Software, 324
Meditrust Pharmacy Inc., 340
Mercedes-Benz AG, 172, 646
Metlife, 297, 490-41, 495
Michel, Dominique, 506
MicroAge, 90
Microsoft, 6, 49, 217, 401, 584, 632
Midas, 331
Miller, Herman, 141
Minolta, 624
Miss Vickie's, 304
Mobil Corporation, 364, 411
Molson Cos. Ltd., 481, 38, 72, 147, 398, 481
Moosehead, 72
Morrison International, 598
Morrison, Robert, 598
Motorola, 232, 632, 639
Munro, John, 627
Murphy, Rex, 401
Music World, 406

Naganuma, Koichiro, 221
NameLab, 389
National Semiconductor, 4
Nations Bank, 324
Navistar International, 382
NBC TV, 640
Neilsen-Cadbury's, 352
Nestlé, 38, 145, 154, 646
Netherlands Vegetarian Council, 498
New Product Showcase and Learning Centre, 373
News Corporation, 600
Nextage Shanghai, 479
Nichol, Dave, 495
Nielsen, 17
Nike, 50, 382, 495
Nintendo, 295, 324
Nissan Motor Corporation, 383, 498
Nitkin, David, 140
No Frills, 469
Nolan, Norton & Co., 317
Northern Telecom, 87-88, 645
Novel, 383
NutraSweet, 87
Nynex, 158

Office Angels, 347

Oil Country tubular goods, 453
Okanagan Spring Brewery, 72
Old Dutch Foods Ltd., 304
Olsen, Kenneth, 371
Olsten Corporation, 347
Olsten Kimberly Quality Care, 347
Olsten STAFF, 347
Olympus, 34-35
Ombrelle, 526
Omnicom Group, 17
O'Neal, Shaquille, 50
One Step Tree and Lawn Care, 102
Onex Corp, 38
Ontario Hydro, 597
Ontario Lottery Corporation, 302
Orkin of America, 392
Ottley, Bob, 102
Owens-Corning Fiberglass Corporation, 381, 490, 526

Pacific Western Brewery, 72
Packard Bell, 584
Panasonic, 265
Paradigm Simulation, 353
Parfums de Coeur, 578
Parmalat, 397
PepsiCo, 52, 154, 159, 162, 164, 234, 302, 354, 391, 522, 571, 646, 651
Pepsodent, 150
Perrier, 38
Perry, Michael, 370
PHH, 635
Philips Electronics, 146, 355
Pigeon, Thomas, 393
Pillsbury, 526, 646
Pitney Bowes, 265, 443
Pizza Hut, 150, 354, 465
Polaroid Corporation, 228, 229, 624
Porter, Michael, 662
Powell, Hugo, 73
Powerfood Inc., 351
Price Club, 45
Price/Costco, 467, 469, 478
Princess Di, 661
Pro CD Inc., 83
Procter & Gamble (P&G), 263, 274, 291, 302, 370, 379, 395, 507, 519, 567, 646
Procter, Craig, 570
Prodigy, 83
Provigo, 461, 466
Prudential, 443, 559
Prudential Steel, 453
Publishers Clearing House, 567
Purolator Courier, 339, 428

Quaker Oats Company, 60, 350
Quebec Hydro, 597
Queen's University, 341

Raab, Kirk G., 69
Radio Shack, 466, 544
Ralcorp, 402
Ralston Purina, 368, 402
RCA, 355
Reader's Digest Association, 79
Real Atlantic Superstores, 45
Real Canadian Superstore, 467
Reebok International, 50, 605

Regal Greetings & Gifts, 470, 476
Re/Max, 570
Research International, 17
Revlon, 166, 297, 352, 561
Revson, Charles, 292
Reynolds Metals, 353
Rider Group Inc., 38
R.J. Reynolds, 354
Robert Bosch Corporation, 295
Roberts Express Inc., 14
Rogers Cable, 133
Rogers Cantel, 466
Rolex, 292
Roper Starch Worldwide, 256
Ross, Laurie, 544
Royal Airlines, 67
Royal Bank of Canada, 219, 515
Royal Crown Cola (RC), 522
Royal Diamond Cookware, 518
Royal Plastics, 353
RuPaul, 661

Safeway, 383, 466, 564
Saga Spray, 435
Sampras, Pete, 50
Sampson, Albert, 5
Samsung, 67, 151, 637
Sam the Record Man, 406, 418
Saskatchewan Wheat Pool, 456
ScanAd, 504
Scandinavian Airlines System (SAS), 576
Scharf, Jim, 314
Schering-Plough (SP), 77
Schultz, Don E., 512
Scott Paper Company, 369, 585
Scouts Canada, 336, 338
Scudder Funds of Canada, 326
Seagate, 177
Seagram Company Ltd., 145, 297
Sears, 385, 468
Sears Canada Inc., 461, 470, 480
Second Cup Coffee, 224
Sega, 49, 624
Seiko, 67, 307, 350
Seoul Price Club, 480
7-Eleven, 464, 516
7-Eleven Japan, 135
Sextant Avionique, 234
Shanghai No. 1 Department Store Company, 479
Sharp, 495
Shaw, Tom, 390
Sherwin-Williams, 305
Shiraishi, Eiko, 551
Shoppers Advantage, 410
Shoppers Drug Mart, 183, 384, 410, 495
Short Brothers PLC, 228
Siemens AG, 146
Silicon Graphics, 353
Simmons, Richard, 373
Simon Fraser University, 341
Simpson, Bruce, 14
Singer, 411
SKF, 118
Sleeman Brewery, 72
SMH, 273, 374
Smilowski, Eugeniusz, 507
Smith Corona, 370

Smith, Emmitt, 50
Snapple, 32
Sobey's, 466
Soft Image, 49
Sonoco, 395
Sony, 294, 359
Southam Inc., 154
Southwest Airlines, 627
Spencer, Lyle, 456
Spiegel, 471
Sports Authority, 468
Springfield ReManufacturing, 632
Sprint Canada, 26, 382, 506, 641
Squibb, 38
SRG International Ltd., 91
SRI International, 268
Standard Life, 497
Steidtmann, Carl, 459
Sterling Health, 504
Stone, Ken, 484
Straight Arrow Products, 492
Stroh, 166
Subway Sandwich, 495
SwissAir, 504

Taco Bell, 571
Tannenbaum, Stanley, 512
TelePizza, 176
Telology, Inc., 106
Texaco, 364
Texas Instruments, 233
The Bay, 460, 468, 495
The Business Group, 639
The Jewellery Archives, 475
Thermalux, 355
Thomas, Frank, 50
Thomas Pigeon Design Group, 393
Thom McAn, 516
Thompson Lightstone & Company Ltd., 614
Thrifty's, 273
Time Warner, 382
Timex, 374
Tim Horton's Donuts, 465
Timken Company, 292, 350
Tip Top Tailors, 468, 65, 273, 468

Toronto Dominion Bank, 32, 264, 285, 324, 346
Toskan, Frank, 661
Tout Sweet Chocolates, 533
Tower Records/Video, 406
Toyota, 38, 311-12, 498, 551, 662
Toys 'R' Us, 459, 468, 480
TransCanada Pipelines, 426
Treacy, Michael, 636
Trend-lines Inc., 485
Trillium Cable, 133
Truck Brokers Inc., 442
True Value Hardware, 314
TRW, 301
Turner Broadcasting System, 314
Tyson, Mike, 391

Unilever, 305, 352, 370, 383
Union Carbide, 350
Unique Tire Recycling Inc., 117
Unisys, 383
United Airlines, 398
United Cigar Stores, 87, 88
United Communications, 382
United Furniture Warehouse, 478
United Parcel Service (UPS), 62, 258, 339, 428
United Way-Centraides, 341-43
United Way of Canada, 341-42
Unitel, 26, 38, 641
University of Calgary, 341
University of Western Ontario, 341
University of Windsor, 341
Upper Canada Brewing, 60-61
Upplysnigs Centralen (UC Research), 87
UUNET Canada, 83

Vaaler, Johan, 367
Viacom, 600
Victoria's Secret, 471
Videotron, 133
Virgin Records, 406
Visa, 166, 183, 346
Volkswagon, 172
VWD Distributors, 452

Wahl Clipper Corporation, 12

Wahle, Elliott, 65
Wahl, Jack, 12
Walker Group, 89
Wal-Mart, 38, 67, 135, 227-28, 314, 383, 390-92, 454, 459, 461, 462, 468, 478, 480, 481, 484, 541, 633
Walt Disney, 380, 471, 565
Walton, Sam, 633
Warden Woods, 459
Warner Brothers, 600
Waterman, 492, 493
WC Wood, 120
Weilland, Vaughan, 544
Werner, Helmut, 172
West Edmonton Mall, 473
Westinghouse Electric, 662
WestJet Airlines, 627, 658
Weyerhauser, 114
Whirlpool, 89, 186, 274
Wiersema, Fred, 636
Winnipeg Blue Bombers, 14
Winnipeg Fur Exchange, 470, 471
Woodward, Ronald, 575
Woodworkers Warehouse, 485
Woolco, 38, 484
Woolf, Brian P., 564
Wool-mart Inc., 390, 481
World Linx Telecommunications, 83
WPP group, 17
Wrigley, 299, 305
Wurstlin, Michael, 515
W.W. Grainger, 90, 452
Wyman, Georgina, 37

Xerox, 113, 232, 302, 643, 647
Xpresspost, 339

Yankelovich, Daniel, 125
Young & Rubicam, 491
Yuen, Henry, 371

Zarrella, Ronald L., 290
Zellers, 32, 219, 468, 561
Zurich Canada, 519

Subject Index

Absolute product failure, 354
Abuse of dominant position, 590
Accelerator principle, 232
Accessory equipment, 296
Accumulation, sorting process, 412
A.C.T., 568
Adaptation, 28, 45
Administered channel arrangement, 413
Adoption process
    defined, 363
    stages of, 363-65
Advertising
    audience, 522
    billboard, 277
    characteristics of, 494, 522-23
    costs of, 520, 523, 525, 527, 585
    creation of, 531
    defined, 493
    direct-to-consumer, 77
    institutional, 503
    media, 527-30
    misleading, 124, 130, 589-90
    product placements, 496
    public relations distinguished from, 591
    relationship with sales promotion, 565
    schoolbus, 192
    scope and importance of, 519-23
    sexual appeals in, 538
    and social responsibility, 113
    subliminal, 500
    themes, 525-26
    timing, 531
    tobacco industry, 110-11
Advertising agencies, 17
    defined, 524
Advertising media costs, 527
Advertising plan
    assigning responsibility, 524
    cooperative efforts, 532
    creating advertisements, 531
    developing themes, 525-26
    establishing a budget, 525
    selecting media, 527-30
    setting objectives, 523
    success or failure of, 532-33
    timing of advertisements, 531-32
Age
    consumer demographics, 181, 193, 478
    marketing to seniors, 196
Agents, *see* Wholesalers
Airways, 426-27
Allocation, 412
All-you-can-afford method, budgeting, 503-504
Aluminum industry, 254
American Customer Satisfaction Index (ACSI), 646
American Demographics, 179
American Marketing Association, 94
    Code of Ethics, 122
    Survey of Marketing Research, 89
Andean Pact, 156

Annual Survey of Manufacturers, 237
Anti-Counterfeiting Coalition, 376
Approaching customers, 556
Argentina, market segmentation for, 269
Association of Canadian Advertisers, 136
Association of South East Asian Nations, 156
Assorting, 412
Atmosphere, store, 473
Attitudes, 206
Audience, 500-501
Augmented product, 292
Automated Teller machines (ATMs), 477
Automobile repair industry, 331
Award for Canadian-American Business
    Achievement, 645

Baby boomers, 193
Background editorial material, 539
Backward invention, 162-63
Bait-and-switch selling, 588
Balanced product portfolio, 307
Banking
    electronic, 477
    image campaigns, 515
    interactive kiosks, 530
    and World Wide Web, 530
Bargaining, 247
Barter era, 8
Base-point pricing, 621
Battle of the brands, 385
BehaviourScan, 90
Benchmarking, 632, 657
    award achievements, 645
    defined, 643
    process, 644
    strategic, 644
    vs. the competition, 643
Benefit segmentation, 266
Better Business Bureau (BBB), 136
Bidding
    competitive, 232
    open vs. closed, 247
Bid-rigging, 587
Billboard advertising, 277
Bill C–2, 40
Bipolar adjective scales, 96
Blanket branding, *see* Family branding
Blurring gender roles, 209, 212
Bonus packs or multipacks, promotion, 567
Book publishing, marketing and, 31-32
Boot industry, 76
Bottom-up plans, 56
Brand equity, 379-81
Brand extension, 387, 388, 389
Brand images, 380, 394
Branding
    battle of the brands, 385
    brand extension, 387, 388, 389
    choosing a brand name, 388-90
    defined, 377
    family, 385-87, 388

    generic brands, 384
    history of, 377
    individual (multiple), 387, 388
    manufacturer brands, 383
    mixed-brand strategy, 384-85
    philosophy of, 383-88
    power status, 378
    private brands, 383-84
Brand loyalists, 256
Brand loyalty, 32, 85, 218-19
    and demand elasticity, 582
    and mature products, 366-67
    sustaining, 219-20
Brand mark, 377
Brand names, 377
    choosing, 388-91
    controversial, 391
Brand recognition, 379
Brazil, advertising in, 522
Break-even analysis, 610-11
Brief concept test, 360
Broad price policy, 604
Brokers, *see* Wholesalers
Budgeting
    advertising plan, 525
    all-you-can-afford method, 503-504
    personal selling, 553-54
    promotion, 503-505
    sales-expense, 553-54
Bundled pricing, 621
Bureau of Broadcast Measurement, 210
Bureau of the Census (U.S.), 181
Business analysis, new-product planning, 359
Business feature articles, 539
Business organizations
    cooperatives, 456
    corporate culture, 29-31
    corporate symbols, 382-83
    international, 144-45
    line of business, 28-29
    mecca companies, 632-33
    organization of, 157-60
    overall objectives, 28
    role of marketing in, 29
Business perspective, 5
Business publications, advertising in, 529
Bust cycle, 307
Buyer-seller dyad, 549
Buying process, organizational consumer, 246-47

Cable TV industry, specialty channels, 133
Canada Business Service Centres, 421
Canada Export Awards, 645
Canada Phone, 83
Canada-U.S. Autopact, 148
Canada-U.S. Free Trade Agreement, 148, 484
Canada Yearbook, 179
Canadian Advertising Foundation (CAF), 510
Canadian Automobile Association, 495
Canadian Business Information, 265

I-5

I-6 Subject Index

Canadian Chamber of Commerce, 135-36, 149
Canadian Code of Advertising Standards, 510
Canadian Council of Grocery Distributors, 453, 460
Canadian Direct Marketing Association (CDMA), 85, 135, 338
Canadian Global Almanac, 179
Canadian International Merchandise Trade Database, 149
Canadian Markets, 179
Canadian Professional Sales Association (CPSA), 548
Canadian Public Relations Society, 533
Canadian Radio-Television and Telecommunications Commission (CRTC), 133, 508
Canadian Socio-Economic Information Management System (CANSIM), 180
Canadian Standard Industrial Classification Manual, 237
Canadian Standards Association (CSA), 85
Canadian Tobacco Manufacturers' Council, 136
Canadian Trade Index, 265
Canadian Trademarks Act, 390
Canned sales presentation, 555
Caribbean Common Market, 156
Cash-and-carry wholesaling, 447
Cash cow, 63, 64
Category killer, 467, 468
Cause-related marketing, 124
Cease-and-desist order, 509
Census Agglomeration Areas, 182
Census Metropolitan Areas (CMAs), 182, 260, 459
Census Summary Data Service, 180
Central American Common Market, 156
Central business district (CBD), 472
Central Fax Retrieval Hotline, 149
Chain-markup pricing, 613
Chain-ratio method, sales forecasting, 280
Chains, *see* Retail chains
Channel competition, 36
Channel cooperation, packaging and, 394
Channel functions, 412
Channel length, 413, 420
Channel members, 407
    role in price setting, 591-92
Channel of communication
    audience, 500-501
    decoding, 499-500
    defined, 495
    feedback, 501-502
    medium, 499
    message, 497-99
    source, 495-97
Channel of distribution, 407
Channel width, 415
China, retailing, 479
Chinese Canadians, Feng Shui, 285
Churning, 559
Cigarettes, *see* Tobacco industry
Class, *see* Social class
Class-action suit, 131
Class consciousness, 206
Clean Air Act (U.S.), 119, 141
Clients, nonprofit organizations, 336
Closed bidding, 247
Closing, personal selling, 557
Clustered demand, 258
Clutter, 529

Co-branding, 388
Cocooning, 46
Cognitive dissonance, 216
Combination compensation plan, 558
Combination pricing, 616-17
Combination store, 466
Combines Investigation Act, 586
Commercial cue, 214
Commercial databases, 83
Commercialization
Commercial stock brokers, 451
Commission merchants (factor merchants), 451
Community shopping centre, 472
Compact disk (CD), 406-407
Company-controlled price environment, 592
Company organization, 157-60
Company product positioning, 303
Company-specific buying factors, 246
Company vision planning, 657
Comparative advantage, 146
Competition, 9, 10, 11
    channel, 36
    foreign, 38
    generic, 36, 39
    and international expansion, 146
    monopolistic, 38
    part of marketing environment, 36-39
    and pricing, 579-80
    pure, 38
    in retailing, 478
Competition Act, 40-41, 129, 130, 586-91, 604, 647
Competition-based pricing, 615-16
Competition Bureau, 40, 41, 105, 129, 234, 304, 390, 614
    Marketing Practices Branch, 130
    Program of Advisory Opinions, 589
Competitive advantage, long-term, 636-37
Competitive bidding, 232, 246, 615-16
Competitive parity method, 504
Competitive positioning, 657
Competitive product positioning, 303, 305
Competitive structures, 38
Component lifestyle, 209, 212
Component materials, 296
Computers. *See also* Technology
    database services, 83
    check-out systems, 475
    for marketing intelligence network, 82
    purchasing, 253
    sales, 349, 549
    system obsolescence, 253
    user friendliness of, 217
Concentrated marketing, 270, 271, 272-73
Concept testing, new-product planning, 359
Conclusive research (quantitative research), 92
Confirmation, adoption process, 365
Conflict resolution, 247
Conseil des Normes de la Publicité, 510
Consignment selling, 590
Consolidated Metropolitan Statistical Areas (CMSAs), 182
Conspiracy to price fix, 586
Consumer analysis, 18, 177
Consumer and Corporate Affairs Canada, 129, 133
Consumer behaviour
    active vs. passive, 219

adoption process, 363-65
part of marketing environment, 35-36
teenagers, 286
Consumer bill of rights (U.S.), 128
Consumer brand decision process, 389
Consumer decision process
    brand decisions, 389
    defined, 213
    factors affecting, 216
    freedom of choice, 224
    marketing implications, 220
    organizational consumer, 245-50
    post-purchase behaviour, 216
    stages of, 213-16
    types of, 216-20
Consumer demand, 7
    analyzing, 258-70
Consumer demographics
    defined, 178
    ethnicity/race, 188-90
    income and expenditures, 183-86
    limitations of, 191-92
    location, housing and mobility, 182-83
    marital status, 188
    and market segmentation, 262-65
    occupations and education, 186-88
    population, 180-82
    use of, 191
Consumerism
    current role of, 136
    defined, 128
    history of, 128-29
Consumer lifestyles
    analysis of, 210-13
    defined, 200
    and market segmentation, 265-69
    studies of, 210
    types of, 208-210
Consumer needs, 11
Consumer perspective, 5
    on social responsibility, 125
Consumer price index, 184-85
Consumer products, 293-95
Consumer rights
    choice, 132-33
    information and education, 130
    right to be heard, 133
    safety, 131-32
Consumers, 7. *See also* Final consumers; Organizational consumers
    active vs. passive, 219
    decision process, *see* Consumer decision process
    pricing decisions and, 581-84
    psychological characteristics of, 206-208
    social characteristics of, 201-206
    unethical behaviour by, 202
Consumers' Association of Canada, 129, 130, 133
Consumer spending, 46
Consumers' Research, 128
Consumers Union, 128
Containerization, 428
Contests or sweepstakes, sales promotion, 567
Context of the purchase, 584
Contingency planning, 657
Continuous improvement, total quality, 54
Continuous monitoring, 82
Contractual channel arrangement, 413, 422

Controllable factors, 28. *See also* Marketing environment
Control units, 651
Convenience products, 293-94, 583
Convenience store, 466
Conventional supermarket, 466
Cooperative efforts, 532
Cooperatives, 456
Core services, 320
Corporate culture, 29-31
　ethics and, 30
Corporate Ethics Monitor, 140
Corporate symbols, 382-83
Correlation techniques, 280
Cost-based pricing, 605-611
　defined, 605
　examples of, 607-608
Cost-leadership strategy, 66-67
Cost of living, 184
Cost-plus pricing, 608-609
Costs
　of advertising, 520, 523, 525, 527
　and choice of distribution channel, 410
　effect of on pricing, 584-86
　of marketing, 16
　order-generating, 68
　personal selling, 549, 551
　of physical distribution, 422-23
　pricing based on, 605-611
　product development, 361
Council for Mutual Economic Assistance, 156
Counterfeiting, 376
Coupons, sales promotion, 567
Cross Classified Database, 180
Crown Corporations, 242
Culture
　and consumer social profile, 201
　defined, 150
　and international marketing, 150-51, 166-67
　Japanese, 221
　and organizational consumers, 234
Currency stability, and international marketing, 153
Current Business Reports, 237
Customary pricing, 617
Customer focus, total quality, 54
Customer satisfaction, 14-16, 177
　defined, 645
　factors affecting, 15
　and guarantees, 647
　research on, 645-46
　total quality and, 54, 639
Customer service
　defined, 12-14
　employee empowerment and, 14
　and physical distribution program, 423
Cybermalls, 475

Daily, *see Statistics Canada Daily*
Data
　government sources, 94
　primary, 94-100
　for sales forecasting, 278
　secondary, 93-94
Data analysis, 100-101
Database marketing, 83-86
　fully integrated, 84
Databases

　commercial, 83
　Telogy example, 106
Data collection, 81. *See also* Marketing research
　experiment research, 98, 100
　grocery-store scanners, 105
　internal vs. outside personnel for, 95
　observation method, 98, 100
　research design for, 95
　sampling techniques, 96
　semantic differentials for, 96
　simulation method, 98-99, 100
　single-source, 90
　survey method, 96, 100
　technological innovations in, 89-91
Data storage, 82
Data warehousing, 476
Dealer brands, *see* Private brands
Deal makers, 256
Debit transactions, 477
Decision, adoption process, 365
Decline stage, product life cycle, 309
Decoding, 499-500
Delivered pricing, 591
Demand
　anticipating, 7
　clustered, 258
　consumer, 7
　derived, 232, 244-45
　diffused, 258-59
　elastic, 581-82
　homogeneous, 258, 271-72
　inelastic, 581-82
　law of, 81
　primary vs. selective, 502
　publics', 7
　unitary, 581
Demand-based pricing, 611-15
　defined, 611
　examples of, 612
Demand-minus pricing, 612-13
Demographic profile, 178. *See also* Consumer demographics
Demographic trends, 146
Demographic Yearbook, 179
Demonstrations, sales promotion, 567
Department stores, traditional, 468
Deregulation, 575-76, 578
Derived demand, 232
　as constraint on purchase behaviour, 244-45
Design for Disassembly (DFD), 113
Desk jobbers, *see* Drop shippers
Developing countries, 152-53
　distribution channels, 420
Differential advantages, 32, 39, 257, 302
Differentiated marketing, 257, 270, 271, 273-75
Differentiation strategy, 67
Diffused demand, 259-60
Diffusion process, new-product acceptance, 365-66
Diminishing returns, 281
Direct channel, 413
Direct mail, 519, 528
Direct marketing, 470
Direct ownership, 160
Direct selling, 470
Direct-to-consumer advertising, 77
Discretionary income, 186
Disposable income, 186

Distribution channel(s)
　competition, 36
　cooperation, 394, 417-19
　defined, 407
　direct, 412, 413
　indirect, 412, 413
　industrial, 408, 419
　length of, 323, 413, 420
　members, 407, 417, 591-92
　for organizational consumers, 233
　relationship marketing in, 408-410
　selecting, 412-13
　simple vs. complex, 408
　width of, 415
Distribution decisions, 34
Distribution intermediaries, 407
　channel functions performed by, 412
　contracts, 416
　retailing, 462
　in sorting process, 412, 462
Distribution planning, 18. *See also* Physical distribution
　defined, 407
　importance of, 408-411
　intensity of channel coverage, 415-16
　for international markets, 164-65, 420-22
　pushing vs. pulling strategy, 419
　scope of, 410-11
　supplier/intermediary contracts, 416
Distribution promotion, 498
Diversification, 63
Dockers Authentics, 225
Dog, 63, 65
Domestic firm, 144
Domestic marketing, 144
Donors, 336
Double price ticketing, 588
Drop shippers (desk jobbers), 448
Dual channel of distribution, 415
Dumping, 167-68
Dun's Latin America's Top 25 000, 237
Duty-based theory of ethics, 122-23

Early adopters, 365
Early majority, 365
Early-recovery-of-cash goals, 603
Eastern Europe, consumer behaviour in, 211
Economic Community of West African States, 156
Economic environment, 42
　and international marketing, 146, 151-53
　organizational consumers and, 234
　stages of economic development, 152-53, 234
Economic order quantity (EOQ), 430-31
Economies of scale, 64, 67
Editor & Publisher Market Guide, 179
Education, demographics, 186-87
Effectiveness, 54
Efficiency, 54
Egoism, 122
80-20 principle, 651
Elastic demand, 581
Electronic data interchange (EDI), 429
Embargoes, 154
Emergency publicity, 539
Employee empowerment
　and customer service, 14
　and total quality, 54

Employee interpersonal skills, in services, 327
Encoding, 497
End-use analysis, 237
    applying to sales forecasting, 238
End-user demand, 232
Energy business, pricing, 597
Entrepreneur of the Year Award, 645
Environmental analysis, 18
Environmental pollution, 117
Environment Canada, 117
Escalator clauses, 623
Ethical behaviour, defined, 121
Ethics, 6, 19. *See also* Social responsibility
    in advertising, 538
    in branding, 391
    and cause-related marketing, 124-25
    consumer, 125, 126
    and contemporary marketing, 136-37
    corporate culture and, 30
    database marketing and, 85
    Genentech example, 69
    in international setting, 125-27
    process-related issues, 123
    product-related issues, 123
    purchasing agents, 249
    schoolbus advertising, 192
    teachability of, 127-28
    theories of, 122-23
    tobacco industry, 110-11
    unethical consumer behaviour, 202
Ethnicity, demographics, 188-89
Euromonitor, 149
European Marketing Data and Statistics, 149
European Union (EU), 149, 155, 156
    common currency, 593
Evaluation of alternatives, consumer decisions, 215
Exchange, 7
Exclusive distribution, 415
Expectations, consumer, 245-46
Experiment, 98
Exploratory research (qualitative research), 92
Export Development Corporation, 154
Export diversion, 432
Exporting, 157
Exporting firm, 145
Export Yellow Pages, 149
Extended consumer decision making, 216-17
Extended fad cycle, 307
External secondary data, 93-94
E-ZEEWRAP dispenser, 314
Fabricated parts, 296
Factor merchants, *see* Commission merchants
Fad cycle, 307
Family branding (blanket branding), 385-87
Family, defined, 188
Family life cycle, 204-205
    defined, 204
Family values, 208, 212
Fashion cycle, 307
Fax machines, 349
Federal Trade Commission (FTC), 41, 128
Feedback, 28, 45
    defined, 501
    organizational consumer decisions, 247
    types of, 502
Feng Shui, 285
FIDO (First In Defeats Others), 149

Final consumer lifestyles, *see* Consumer lifestyles
Final consumers. *See also* Consumers
    defined, 178
    organizational consumers contrasted to, 230, 248
    segmentation strategy and, 262-64
Finance function, and physical distribution, 424
Finance releases, 539
Fines, 509-510
Flexible pricing (haggling), 617
Flyers, 529
FOB mill (factory) pricing, 621
Focus strategy, 67
Food and Drug Act, 131
Food-based superstore, 466
Food brokers, 451
Forecasts, *see* Sales forecasting
Foreign Corrupt Practices Act (U.S.), 126
Foreign markets, entry decisions, 160-61. *See also* International marketing
Fortune's Corporate Reputations, 645
Forward invention, 163
Franchise wholesaling, 447
Franchising, *see* Retail franchising
Freedom of choice, consumer decision process, 224
Freight forwarding, 428
Frequency, 528
Frequent shopper programs, 564, 567
Full disclosure, 508
Full-line discount store, 468
Full-line wholesalers, 447
Full-service merchant wholesaler, 447
Fully integrated database marketing, 84
Functional accounts, 649
Functional areas, relationships among, 56-57

Gasoline and Automotive Services Association, 331
Gender, demographics, 181
Gender roles, blurring of, 209, 212
General Agreement on Tariffs and Trade (GATT), 72, 76, 149, 155
General Electric business screen, 65-66
General-merchandise (full-line) wholesalers, 447
Generation Xers, 193, 225
Generic brands, 384
Generic competition, 36
Generic product, 292
Geographic demographics, market segmentation, 260-61
Geographic information systems (GIS), 476
Geographic pricing, 621
GeoVALS, 268
Germany
    changes in, 201
    international marketing and, 172
Getting by, 208, 212
Gifts, sales promotion, 567
Global firm, 145
Global marketing, 144. *See also* International marketing
Global Trade and Economic Outlook, 237
Glocal
    marketing plan, 161-62, 165
    promotion campaigns, 165, 167
Goal-oriented firms, 11
Goods

    classification of, 321-23
    government regulation of, 322-23
    high and low value-added, 321-22
Goods and Services Tax (GST), 199
Goods marketing, 292
    defined, 318
Goods/services continuum, 319
Government
    anti-pollution legislation, 119
    as consumer, 240
    effect of on pricing, 586
    legislation affecting marketers, 40, 154
    marketing environment, 40-42
    regulation, 120
    stability of, 154
    tax revenue from cigarettes, 110
Government-controlled price environment, 592-93
Great Britain, retailing, 421
Green marketing, 119
Green products, 463
Grey market goods, 591
Gross Domestic Product (GDP), 42, 151-52
    services, 318
Gross margin, 462
Growth stage, product life cycle, 309
Guarantees, 647
    price, 592
Guidestar system, 295
Gulf Cooperation Council, 156

Haggling, *see* Flexible pricing
Hard technologies, 327
Hazardous Products Act, 131
Health Canada, 508
Health care services, 344-45
Heavy-usage segments, 265-66
Heritage Inns Marketing Association, 330-31
Hidden service sector, 319
Hierarchy-of-effects model, 502
Homogeneous demand, 258, 271
Hoover's Masterlist of Major Latin American Companies, 265
Horizontal marketing audit, 653
    form, 654
Hotel industry, use of marketing, 329-31
Household
    defined, 188
    size by country, 189
Household life cycle, 204
Housing, demographics, 183
Hybrid technologies, 327

Iceberg principle, 651
Idea generation, new products, 357
Ideal points, 303
Implementation, adoption process, 365
Importance of a purchase, 208
Income
    demographics, 183-86
    discretionary, 186
    disposable, 186
    real, 42, 184
Incremental method, 504
Independent media, 44-45
Independent retailer, 464
India, retailing, 421
Indirect channel, 413

Subject Index I-9

Individual branding (multiple branding), 387-88
Industrial channel of distribution, 419
Industrialization, 8-9
    of services, 327-28
Industrialized countries, 152
Industrial marketing. *See also* Organizational consumers
    defined, 228
Industrial products, 295-97
    characteristics of, 296
    defined, 295
Industrial Revolution, 8
Industrial services, 297
Industrial supplies, 297
Industry Canada, Strategis, 94
Industry forecasts, 278
Inelastic demand, 581
Infomercial, 517, 518
Information search, decision process, 215
Innovativeness, 208
Innovators, 365
Inseparability, of services, 325
Installations, 296
Institute of Canadian Advertisers, 136
Institutional advertising, 503
Insurance, third-party payments, 624
Intangibility, 324
Integrated marketing communications (IMC), 505, 512
Integrated marketing focus, 11
Intensive distribution, 415
Interactive kiosks, 530
Intermodal shipping, 428, 435, 436
Internal secondary data, 93
International Advertising Association, 492, 511
International Federation of Pharmaceutical Wholesalers (IFPW), 437, 438
International firm, 145
International Hardwood Products Association (IHPA), 141
International marketing
    cultural environment, 150-51
    defined, 144
    distribution channels, 420-22
    economical environment, 151-53
    global marketing, 144
    and international codes of conduct, 163
    organizational consumers, 234-36
    PC sales in Chile, 157
    personal selling, 560
    political and legal environment, 153-56
    pricing, 579
    and product positioning, 311
    promotion strategy, 506-507
    reasons for, 146-48
    resources dealing with, 149
    retailing and, 480
    scope of, 148
    technological factors affecting, 156
International Marketing Data and Statistics, 179
International marketing strategy
    company organization, 157-60
    distribution planning, 164-65
    market entry decisions, 160-61
    price planning, 167-68
    product planning, 162-63
    promotion planning, 165-67
    standardizing plans, 161-62

International Public Relations Association, 533
Internet
    advertising, 529
    and marketing, 44, 244, 401
Introduction stage, product life cycle, 308
Inventory management
    electronic data interchange (EDI), 429
    just-in-time (JIT) systems, 429
    quick response (QR) systems, 429
    reordering inventory, 430-31
    stock turnover, 429-30
    warehousing, 431-32
Isolated store, 472
Issue definition, research, 91-92
Item price removal, 135

Jacarandra Tree, 476
Japan
    culture of, 221
    international marketing and, 171
    keiretsus, 421
    personal selling in, 551
    wholesalers (tonya), 457
Joint decision making, 204
    conflict resolution, 247
Joint ventures, 158-60
Journeyman, benchmarking, 644
Jury of executive opinion, 279-80
Just-in-time inventory system, 429

Keiretsus, 421
Knowledge, product adoption process, 363

Labelling, misleading, 124
Laboratory-oriented sources, new-product ideas, 257
Laggards, 366
Late majority, 365
Law of demand, 581
Law, Order, and Good Government, 201
Law Society of Upper Canada, 331-32
Lawsuits, consumer, 131
Lawyers, use of marketing, 331-32
Leader pricing, 619
Lead time, 529-30
Leased department, 466
Leasing, automobiles, 124-24
Legal environment, *see* Political (and legal) environment
Less-developed countries, 153
Licensing agreement, 388
Life insurance, selling, 559
Lifestyle, 200. *See also* Consumer lifestyles
Limited consumer decision making, 217-18
Limited-service merchant wholesaler, 447
Line of business, 28
List prices, 623
Local content laws, 154
Long-term subplans, 639
Looking at the Sun, 171
Low-involvement purchasing, 218
Luxury innovators, 256

Macroenvironment, 28
Magazines, 528
    online, 622
Mailing lists, privacy issues, 134
Mail-order wholesalers, 449

Major innovations, new products, 350
Majority fallacy, 272-73, 275
Malcolm Baldridge National Quality Award, 645
Malls, 459-60
Management meccas, 632-33
Management, top, 28-31
Manufacturer brands, 383
Manufacturers
    as consumers, 237-38
    defined, 237
    response to consumer issues, 135
Manufacturers'/service providers' agents (MSPAs), 450, 454
Marginal return, 505
Marital status, demographics, 188
Markdowns, 623, 628
Market buildup method, sales forecasting, 280
Market-controlled price environment, 592
Market development, 63
Marketing
    business perspective, 5
    consumer perspective, 5-6
    costs of, 16
    defined, 4-5, 7
    evolution of, 8-10
    importance of, 16-17
    relation to other functional areas, 56-57
    socioeconomical view of, 112
Marketing audit, 652
    horizontal, 653
    vertical, 653, 655
Marketing company era, 8, 10
Marketing concept, 10
Marketing cost analysis
    defined, 647
    examples of, 648
    steps in, 649-50
Marketing department
    era of, 8, 9
    role of in firm, 29
Marketing environment
    adaptation, 28
    competition, 36-39
    consumer behaviour, 35-36
    controllable factors, 27-35
    economic factors, 42
    feedback, 45
    government, 40-42
    independent media, 44-45
    international marketing, 149-56
    marketing personnel decisions, 31-34
    suppliers and distributors, 39-40
    technology, 43-44
    top management decisions, 28
    uncontrollable factors, 35-45
Marketing functions, 17-20
Marketing information, 79-80
Marketing information system (MIS). *See also* Marketing research
    basic system, 82-83
    commercial databases, 83
    defined, 80
    uses of, 81
Marketing intelligence network, 82, 87
Marketing Magazine, 94
Marketing management, 18
Marketing manager system, 301-302
Marketing match, 6-7

Marketing mix, 68
  coordination of, 640-41
  defined, 34
  and packaging decisions, 396
Marketing mix plan
  outlining, 276-77
  for PC firm, 277
Marketing myopia, 45-46
Marketing objectives, 59-61
  Labatt case, 72
Marketing organizations
  defined, 32
  illustrations of, 33
Marketing performers, 20
Marketing plan. *See also* Strategic planning
  analyzing, 642-653
  integrating, 634-42
  organizational mission, 635-36
  stability of, 641-42
Marketing research, 80, 657. *See also* Data collection; Marketing information system (MIS)
  costs of, 100
  defined, 82, 88
  exploratory vs. conclusive, 92
  issue (problem) definition, 91-92
  primary data, 94-100
  process, 91, 92
  scope of, 89-91
  secondary data, 93-95
Marketing strategy
  defined, 61
  Labatt case, 73
  Schering-Plough, 77
Market-oriented sources, new-product ideas, 357
Market penetration, 62
Market Research Handbook, 179
Market segmentation
  bases for, 259-70
  benefit segmentation, 266
  concentrated marketing, 270, 271, 272-73
  defined, 31, 257
  differentiated marketing, 257, 270, 271, 273-75
  final consumers, 262-64
  and geographic demographics, 260-61
  heavy-usage segments, 265-66
  majority fallacy, 272-73, 275
  organizational consumers, 264-65
  packaging and, 394
  Social Styles model, 266, 268-69
  undifferentiated marketing, 257, 271-72
  VALS program, 266-68
Market share analysis, 279
Market share, in Boston Consulting Group matrix, 63-64
Markup pricing, 608, 609
Massed promotion, 498
Mass marketing, 257. *See also* Undifferentiated marketing
Master, benchmarking, 644
Maturity stage, product life cycle, 309, 366-69
Media, 499
  for advertising, 527-30
  independent, 44-45
  for public relations, 540
"Me" generation, 210, 212
Membership warehouse, 469

Men, shopping habits, 210
Mercosur, 156
Message
  believability, 536
  comparative, 498
  defined, 497
Message performance, 528
Mexico
  distribution, 420
  population profile, 191
Microbreweries, 72
Microenvironment, 28
Micromarketing, 452
MindTrack, 91
Minor innovations, new products, 350
Misleading price advertising, 589-90
Missionary salesperson, 555
Mixed-brand strategy, 384-85
Mobility, demographics, 183
Modifications, new products, 350
Modified break-even analysis, 613
Modified-rebuy purchase process, 247-48
Monitoring results, 68. *See also* Strategic planning
  Labatt case, 73
Monopolistic competition, defined, 38
Monopoly, defined, 38
Moody's Industry Review, 237
Mosaic, 180
Motivation, 207
Motives, 207
Motor carriers, 426
Moving targets, 46
Multinational firms, 145
  coordination of SBUs, 640
Multiple branding, *see* Individual branding
Multiple-buying responsibility, 231
Multiple segmentation, *see* Differentiated marketing
Multiple-unit pricing, 619

Narrowcasting, 527-28
National Association of Auto Dealers, 547
National Association of Temporary Staffing Services (NATSS), 347
Nationalism, 154
National Trade Data Bank (NTDB), 149
Natural accounts, 648-49
Natural resources, depletion of, 114-16, 117
Need-satisfaction approach, 555
Negotiation, 232
Neighbourhood business district (NBD), 472
NewMedia Pathfinder Study, 282
New-product manager system, 302
New-product planning
  business analysis, 359-61
  commercialization, 362-63
  concept testing, 359
  defined, 356
  idea generation, 357
  packaging and, 394
  product development, 361-62
  product screening, 357-59
  test marketing, 362
  3M approach to, 356, 357
New products
  adoption of, 363-65
  defined, 349
  diffusion of, 365-66

  failure of, 354-56
  importance of, 350-54
  major innovations, 350
  minor innovations, 350
  modifications, 350
  patenting, 358
Newspapers, 528
News publicity, 539
New-task decision process, 247
Noise, 502
Noncommercial cue, 214
Nondurable goods, 318
Nongoods services, 318
Nonpersonal media, 499
Nonprice-based strategies, 579
Nonprofit institutions, as consumers, 242
Nonprofit marketing
  classifying, 336-37
  clients, 336
  defined, 332
  donors, 336
  extent of in economy, 337-39
  illustrations of, 339-43
  vs. profit-oriented marketing, 332-36
Non-Utility Generation plants (NUGs), 597
North American Free Trade Agreement (NAFTA), 148, 149, 155, 156, 237, 456
North American Industrial Classification System (NAICS), 237
Nostalgia cycle, 307
Novice, benchmarking, 644

Objective-and-task method, 505
Observation, 98
Occupations, demographics, 186-87
Odd pricing, 617-18
Oligopoly, defined, 38
One-on-one marketing, 46
One-price policies, 617
Open bidding, 247
Open credit account, 623
Opinion leaders, 203, 496
Order getter, 554
Order taker, 554
Organizational consumers
  buying objectives, 242-43
  buying structure, 243-44
  constraints on purchases, 244-45
  contrasted with final consumers, 230, 248
  decision process, 245-50
  defined, 178
  demand, 232
  ethical concerns of, 249
  international differences among, 234-36, 248
  nature of market, 232-34
  nature of purchases, 231-32
  perceptions of quality, 235
  purchases, 247-48
  segmentation strategy and, 264-65
  types of, 236-42
Organizational mission, 58, 74
  example, 635
  Labatt case, 72
Organization for Economic Cooperation and Development (OECD), 85, 149, 151, 179
Organizations, 8-9. *See also* Business organizations
Outdoor advertising, 529

Output-related philosophy, total quality approach, 54
Overall objectives, of firm, 28
Owned-goods services, 318

Packaging
    criticisms of, 397
    decisions, 394-96
    defined, 392
    functions of, 394
    importance of, 392-93
Pan-bidi, 421
Paper clip, 367
Partnership for a New Generation of Vehicles, 254
Patent, 358
Patent rights, 133
PC Meter, 89
Penetration pricing, 603
Perceived risk, 208
Percentage-of-sales method, 505
Performance, 28
    variability, 325, 327
Performance assessment, 34
Peripheral services, 320
Perishability, of services, 324-25
Personal demographics, market segmentation, 261-65
Personality, 206
Personal media, 499
Personal selling, 494
    buyer-seller dyad, 550
    characteristics of, 549-52
    costs of, 549, 551
    distinguished from sales promotion, 547-48
    in Japan, 551
    sales personnel, 557-60
    scope and importance of, 548-49
    techniques, 555-56
Personal selling plan
    applying, 557-60
    assigning responsibility, 552-53
    determining sales position types, 554-55
    establishing a budget, 553-54
    outlining sales tasks, 556-57
    selecting sales technique, 555-56
    setting objectives, 552, 553
Persuasion, 247
    adoption process, 363
Persuasive impact, advertising, 528
Pharmaceutical industry, 77
Physical distribution
    costs of, 422-23
    customer service provided by, 423-24
    defined, 422
    importance of, 422-24
    inventory management, 428-32
    relation to other functional areas, 424
    symptoms of poor system, 423
    transportation, 424-28
    at Vancouver port, 435
Physical drives, 214
Pictorial releases, 539
Pipelines, 426
Planned obsolescence, 117-18
    functional, 118
    style, 118
Planned shopping centre, 472

Point-of-purchase displays (POPs), 561, 566
Political (and legal) environment, 41-42, 153-56
    effect on pricing, 586-91
    promotion practices, 508-511
Political marketing, 333
Politicking, 247
Population, 180-82, 317, 478
Porter generic strategy model, 66-67
Positioning, *see* Product positioning
Post-purchase behaviour, 216
Poverty of time, 209, 212
Predatory pricing, 588
Predicasts F&S Index Europe, 237
Predicast's Forecasts, 237
pre-owning, 594
Prestige pricing, 618
Price bundling, 621
Price ceiling, 611
Price decisions, 34
    competition and, 592-93
    and consumer sensitivity, 581-84
    effect of costs on, 584-86
    government/legal restrictions affecting, 586-91
    organizational consumers, 243
    role of channel members, 591-92
    supplier/intermediary contracts, 417
Price discrimination, 588
    customer-based, 613
    place-based, 613-14
    time-based, 613
    and yield management pricing, 615
Price elasticity, 581, 582
Price fixing, 133
Price floor, 605
Price-floor pricing, 608, 610
Price guarantees, 592
Price leadership, 615
Price lining, 619-20
Price maintenance, 587
Price planning, 18
    defined, 576
    dumping, 167
    for international markets, 579
    and physical distribution, 424
    price- vs. nonprice-based strategies, 579-80
    standardization, 167-68
Price-quality association, 618
Price(s)
    defined, 576
    deregulation and, 575-76, 578
    fixing, *see* Conspiracy to price fix
    importance of, 577-79
    role of in balancing supply and demand, 577
    sale, 614
Price seekers, 256
Price shoppers, 582
Price wars, 593
Pricing strategy
    broad policy, 604
    combination, 616-17
    competition-based, 615-16
    cost-based, 605-611, 616
    customary vs. variable, 617
    demand-based, 611-15, 616
    geographic pricing, 621
    implementing, 616-23
    leader pricing, 619

    multiple-unit pricing, 619
    odd pricing, 617-18
    one-way vs. flexible pricing, 617
    penetration pricing, 603
    price bundling, 621
    price lining, 619-20
    price-quality association, 618
    profit-based objectives, 603
    sales-based objectives, 603
    skimming pricing, 603
    status quo-based objectives, 604
    steps in, 601
Primary data, 94-100. *See also* Data collection; Marketing research
    defined, 94
Primary demand, 502
Principal International Businesses, 237
Privacy, mailing lists, 134
Private brands (dealer brands), 383-84
Privatization, 42
PRIZM (Potential Rating Index by Zip Market), 210
Problem awareness, consumer decision process, 214-15
problem solving, 247
Process philosophy, total quality approach, 54
Product-adaptation, 162
Product Code Council of Canada, 396
Product decisions, 34
Product deletion, 369-70
Product development, 63
    new-product planning process, 361-62
Product differentiation, 257, 302
Production era, or marketing, 8, 9
Product item, 297
Product life cycle
    defined, 307
    evaluation of, 309
    mature products, 366-69
    stages in, 307-308
Product line, 297
Product management organizations, 301-302
Product manager system, 302
Product/market opportunity matrix, 61-63
Product mix
    consistency of, 299
    defined, 297
    depth of, 299
    effects on companies, 299-301
    elements of, 297-301
    width of, 297, 298
Product placement, 496
Product planning, 18
    defined, 291
    international, 162-63, 310-11
    and physical distribution, 424
    and product life cycle, 307
Product planning committee, 302
Product positioning
    company, 303
    competitive, 303
    defined, 302
    GM products, 290-91
    illustration of, 303-305, 315
Product recall, 131-32
Product releases, 539
Products
    consumer, 293-95
    goods vs. services, 292-93

I-12 Subject Index

ideal points, 303
industrial, 295-97
new, *see* New products
Product screening, new product planning, 357-59
Product-specific buying factors, 246
Product warranty, *see* Warranty
Profit-based objectives, pricing, 603-604
Promotion. *See also* Advertising; Public relations; Sales promotion
    channel of communication, 494-502
    criticisms and defences of, 511
    defined, 491
    importance of, 491-93
    legal environment, 508-511
    product placements, 496
    types of, 493-94
Promotion decisions, 34, 491
Promotion planning, 18
    budgeting, 503-505
    defined, 491
    for international markets, 165-67, 506-507
    objectives, 502-503
    and physical distribution, 424
    promotion mix, 505-506
Prospecting, 556
Publicity, 494, 536-37
    negative, 533
    types, 539
Public relations
    advertising distinguished from, 519
    characteristics of, 536-37
    defined, 494
    scope and importance of, 533-36
    and social responsibility, 535
Public relations plan
    assigning responsibility, 539
    creating messages, 540
    evaluating success or failure, 540-41
    outlining PR types to use, 539
    selecting media, 540
    setting objectives, 537-39
    timing messages, 540
Publics' demand, 7
Pulling strategy, 419
Purchase act, 215-16, 247
Purchases, organizational consumer, 247-48
Purchase terms, price agreements, 622-23
Purchasing agents, 248, 249. *See also* Organizational consumers
Purchasing partnerships, 250
Pure competition, 38
Pushing strategy, 419
Push money, 566

Qualitative research, *see* Exploratory research
Quantitative research, *see* Conclusive research
Quebec Association of Forest Industries, 120
Quebec Manufacturers Association, 120
Quebec Mining Association, 120
Quebec referendum, 154
Question mark, 63, 64
Quick response (QR) inventory, 429

Rack jobbers, 447
Radio advertising, 528, 533
Railroads, 425-26
Rand McNally Commercial Atlas & Market Guide, 179

Raw materials, 296
Reach, advertising, 527
Reader's Digest, marketing information, 79
Real income, 42, 184
Rebates, 623
Reciprocity, 233-34
Recycling, 115-16
Reference groups, 203
Referral gifts, 567
Refusal to deal, 590
Regression techniques, 280
Relationship managers, 327
Relationship marketing, 408-409
    defined, 16
    and digital equipment, 409
Relative market share, 63
Relative product failure, 354
Remote Emergency Satellite Cellular Unit (RESCU), 295
Rented-goods services, 318
Reorder point, 430
Research design, 95
Resellers, 384
Resource allocation, 68
Retail chains, 464-65
Retail cooperative, 466
Retail Council of Canada, 614
Retailers, 241
    as consumers, 240
    defined, 240
    functions performed by, 462
    independent, 464
    relationship to suppliers, 462
    response to consumer issues, 135
    role in price setting, 591
    slotting fees, 240
    types of, 464-71
Retail franchising, 465
Retailing
    defined, 460
    impact on economy, 461-62
    labour force, 479
    nonstore operations, 470-71
    ownership, 464-66, 467
    recent trends in, 477-81
    scrambled merchandising, 474
    store atmosphere, 473
    store location, 472
    store strategy mix, 466-69
    technological advances, 475-77
    wheel of, 474
Retail store strategy, 466
Revival cycle, 307
Revolving credit account, 623
Risk, perceived, 208
Roper Reports Americas, 269
Routine consumer decision making, 218
Russia, ethical values, 127
Ryoshiki, 268

Salability, 243
Sale above advertised price, 588
Sale price, 614
Sales analysis, 650-52
Sales & Marketing Management, 179
Sales-based objectives, pricing, 603
Sales contests, 566
Sales engineer, 555

Sales era, of marketing, 8, 9
Sales exception reporting, 651
Sales-expense budget, 553-54
Sales forecasting
    data needed for, 278
    defined, 278
    methods of, 278-80
    for new items, 280-81
    and sales exception reporting, 651
    and sales penetration, 281
Sales invoice, 650
Sales management, 557
Sales penetration, 281
Sales personnel, 557-60
Sales positions, types of, 554-55
Sales presentation, 557
Sales promotion, 494
    characteristics of, 562
    conditions, 565
    distinguished from personal selling, 547-48
    orientation, 565
    relationship with advertising, 565
    scope and importance of, 560-62
    types of, 566-67
Sales promotion plan
    assigning responsibility, 563
    coordinating, 565
    evaluating success or failure, 565-67
    outlining, 563-65
    selecting types of, 565
    setting objectives, 563
Sales territory, 558
Samples, for sales promotion, 567
Sampling, 96
Scenario planning, 657
Scientific method, 80
Scott's Directories, 265
Scrambled merchandising, 474
Seasonal cycle, 307
Secondary data
    defined, 93
    external, 93-94
    internal, 93
Selective demand, 502
Selective distribution, 415
Self-fulfilling prophesy, 309
Self-image, 584
Self-scanning, supermarkets, 476
Sell against the brand, 591
Sellers, 7
Selling agents, 451
Selling process, 556
Selling, vs. marketing philosophy, 11-12
Semantic differential, 96
Seniors, marketing to, 196
Service blueprint, 328
Service/features shoppers, 583
Service gaps, 328
Service marketing, 292
    in auto repair, 331
    defined, 318
    in hotel industry, 329-31
    use of by lawyers, 331-32
Services
    classification of, 322
    consumer expectations, 328
    credit cards, 346
    and goods/services continuum, 319

health care, 344-45, 347
industrialization of, 327-28
inseparability, 325
intangibility of, 324, 325
perishability of, 324-25
positioning of, 325
use of marketing by, 329-32
variability in quality of, 325, 327
Service salesperson, 555
Services/responsibility mix, 417
Shopping malls (shopping centres), 459-60, 472
cybermalls, 475
Shopping products, 294
Short-run plans, 55
Short-term subplans, 639
Simulation, 98-99
for sales forecasting, 280
Single-source data collection, 90
Situational factors, consumer decisions, 247
Situation analysis (SWOT analysis), 61
Labatt case, 72
Skimming pricing, 603
Slotting fees, 240
Social class, 202
structure, 203
Social marketing, 335
Social mission, 249
Social performance, 203
Social responsibility. *See also* Ethics
benefits and costs of, 118-19
defined, 112
environmental pollution, 117
illustrations of, 115
and landscape, 116
and natural resources, 114-16
planned obsolescence, 117-18
Social situation, 584
Social Styles model, 266, 268-69
Society of Automobile Sales Professionals, 547
Soft technologies, 327
Sorting process, 412
wholesaling and, 439
Source of communication, 495-97
Special Olympics, marketing of, 8
Specialty-merchandise (limited-line) wholesalers, 447
Specialty products, 295
Specialty store, 467
Spud Stop machines, 355
Standard & Poor's Industry Surveys, 237
Standard Industrial Classification (SIC), 236-37
Standardization, 421, 519
of marketing plans, 161-62
of prices, 167-68
of promotion campaigns, 165, 167
Standard of living, 151
Stars, 63, 64
Statistical Yearbook, 149, 179
Statistics Canada
international marketing resources, 149
website, 94
Statistics Canada Daily, 180
Status quo-based objectives, 604
Status seekers, 582
Staying alive, future trend, 46
Steel industry, 254
Stimulus, 213-14
St. Lawrence Seaway, 426

Stock brokers, 450
Stock turnover, 429-30
Straight commission plan, 558
Straight-extension strategy, 162
Straight-rebuy purchase process, 248
Straight salary plan, 558
Strategic alliance, *see* Joint ventures
Strategic business plan, 53
Strategic business units (SBUs), 58-59, 61, 634
Boston Consulting Group matrix, 63-65
coordinating among, 639-40
General Electric business screen, 65-66
Labatt case, 72
Porter generic strategy model and, 66-67
product/market opportunity matrix and, 61-63
Strategic marketing plan, 53, 82
glocal (think global act local), 161-62, 165
nonstandardized, 162
standardized, 161
Strategic planning
Boston Consulting Group matrix approach, 63-65
bottom-up vs. top-down, 56
evaluation of approaches to, 67
General Electric business screen approach, 65-66
integrating the marketing plan, 634-42
Labatt example, 71-73
long-term competitive advantage, 636-37
organizational mission, 635-36
Porter generic strategy model approach, 66-67
product/market opportunity matrix approach, 61-63
sample of written plan, 69-71
scope of, 55-56
short-run plans, 55
subplans, 639
and tactical plans, 68
total quality approach to, 53-55, 639
types of, 55-56
Strategic planning process, 57
defining organizational mission, 58
developing marketing strategy, 61
establishing strategic business units, 58-59
implementing tactical plans, 68
monitoring results, 68
performing situation analysis, 61, 72
setting marketing objectives, 59-61
Strategis, 94, 421
String, of stores, 472
Subjective price, 583
Subliminal advertising, 500
Substantiation, 509
Suppliers and distributors, 39-40. *See also* Wholesalers; Retailers
relationship to retailers, 462-63
and total quality, 54
Surcharges, 623
Survey
disguised vs. nondisguised, 96
mail, 96
personal, 96
for sales forecasting, 280
Survey of Buying Power, 179
Swatch, marketing strategy for, 374
SWOT analysis, *see* Situation analysis

Systems selling, 233

Tactical plans, 68
Labatt case, 73
Taiwan, 197
Tangential sales services, 549
Tangible product, 292
Tanzania, communication strategy, 504
Target Mail, 210
Target market, defined, 31
Target market strategy. *See also* Market segmentation
defined, 257
determining demand patterns, 258-59
establishing segmentation bases, 259-70
outlining the marketing mix plan, 276-77
positioning the company's offering, 276
steps in planning, 257
targeting the market, 270-76, 638-39
Target pricing, 608, 609-610
Tariffs, 154-55
Technology, 7
automobile industry, 295
and banking, 324, 477
hard vs. soft, 327
hybrid, 327
internet, 44, 244, 401
and marketing environment, 43, 156-57
and marketing research, 89-91
micromarketing, 452
in next decade, 21
online census data, 180
online magazines, 622
Parmalat milk, 397
and pricing, 584
privacy issues, 134
promoting cyberspace, 509
in retailing, 475-77
in service industry, 329
Soft Image case, 49
telephone, 656
V-Chip, 354
virtual reality, 353
World Wide Web, 530, 541
Teen behaviour, global perspective, 286
Telemarketing, 549
Telephone directory, advertising, 529
Television advertising, 528, 533
costs of, 522, 585
and zapping, 523
Territorial rights, supplier/intermediary contracts, 417
Test marketing, new-product planning, 362
The International Member & Marketing Services Guide, 94
3M
and preparing for the future, 657
sales training, 568
Tied selling, 590-91
TIERS — Trade Information and Enquiry Retrieval System, 149
Timber Trade Organization, 141
Time expenditures, 206
Time Series Database, 180
Tobacco industry, ethical issues and, 110-11
Tobacco Products Control Act, 110
Tonya, 457
Top-down plans, 56

Top management
  commitment to total quality, 54
  decisions, 28
Total-cost approach, 423, 424
Total quality approach, 53-55, 639
Total-quality vertical-audit form, 655
Tourism industry, Middle East, 334
Trade allowances, 566
Trade associations, response to consumer issues, 135-36
Trade character, 377
Trade Commissioner Service, 154
Trade deficit, 148
Trademarks, 377
  use of, 390-92
Trade quotas, 154
Trade shows, 566
Trade surplus, 148
Traditional break-even analysis, 608, 610-11
Traditional cycle, 307
Traditional department store, 468
Transit, advertising, 529
Transportation
  airways, 426-27
  containerization, 428
  coordinating, 428
  freight forwarding, 428
  intermodal shipping, 428, 435, 436
  motor carriers, 426
  pipelines, 426
  railroad, 425-26
  service companies, 427-28
  waterways, 426
Trend analysis, 278-79
Truck/wagon wholesalers, 448-49
TV Guide, 272

Unbundled pricing, 621
Uncontrollable factors, 35. *See also* Marketing environment
Undifferentiated marketing, 257, 271-72
Unemployment rates, 186
Uniform delivered pricing, 621
Unitary demand, 581
United Nations (UN), 338
  resources published by, 149
United States
  culture of, 201
  ethical values, 127
  legislative environment, 41
  population profile, 191
Universal Product Code (UPC), 105, 396, 429
Universities, marketing by, 340-41
Unplanned business district, 472
U.S. Federal Trade Commission, 41
U.S. Industrial Outlook, 237
Utilitarianism, 122

VALS (Values and Lifestyles) program, 210
  GeoVALS, 268
  VALS 2 Network, 266-68
Value analysis, 231
Value-based philosophy, 11
Variable markup pricing, 609
Variable pricing, 617
Variety store, 468
V-Chip, 354
VCRs, 371, 475
Vending machines, 470
Vendor analysis, 231
Venezuela, market segmentation, 269
Venture team, 302
Vertical marketing audit, 653
  form, 655
Video catalogues, 475
Video conferencing, 329
Video news releases, 539
Video shopping services, 475
Virtual Reality, 353
Virtue ethics, 123
Voluntary simplicity, 208

Warehousing, 431-32
  private, 431
  public, 431-32
Warranty
  and consumer rights, 130
  express vs. implied, 130
  full vs. limited, 130
Waste, advertising, 527
Waterways, 426
Wearout rate, 499
Weekly Bulletin of Business Opportunities, 241
Wellington County Board of Education, 192
Wheelchair advertising, 277
Wheel of retailing, 474
Wholesale cooperatives, 447
Wholesale merchants, 446
Wholesalers
  agents and brokers, 449-50, 454
  as consumers, 238-40
  costs, 440-41
  defined, 238
  full-service merchant, 447
  functions of, 440-41
  independent, 445
  manufacturer/service provider, 443-46
  performance data for, 440
  relationship with suppliers and customers, 441-42
  role in price setting, 591
  selling to vs. selling through, 441-42
Wholesaling
  cash-and-carry, 447-48
  defined, 439
  examples of, 439
  impact on economy, 439-40
  recent trends in, 451-53
  sales volume contributed by, 451
  types of, 443-51. *See also* Wholesalers
Wildering, 46
Windows 95, 6
Women
  in personal selling, 560
  population, 181
  shopping habits, 210
  in workforce, 176, 186, 188
Word-of-mouth communication, 496
World Factbook, 149
World Index of Economic Forecasts, 149
World Tourism Organization, 334
World Trade Database, The, 149
World Trade Organization (WTO), 155
World Wide Web, 408, 410, 530, 541

Yankelovich Monitor, 210
Yearbook of International Trade Statistics, 149
Yellow Pages, advertising, 532
Yield management pricing, 615

Zambia, economy, 185
Zap Mail, 355
Zone pricing, 621

MARKETING AROUND THE GLOBE

(Continued from front endpapers)

AUSTRALIA
News Corporation Ltd. owns the *New York Post, TV Guide*, and Fox Broadcasting.

BOTSWANA
Debswana is a joint mining venture between De Beers (South Africa) and the government of Botswana.

CHINA
Kraft Foods International markets Philadelphia cream cheese, Oscar Mayer meats, Miracle Whip salad dressing, and Jell-o gelatin.

CZECH REPUBLIC
Budejovicky Budvar is a 100-year-old Czech beer maker with the European rights to the name Budweiser.

EGYPT
Orascom Foods and Mansour Foods (both of Egypt) have joint ventures with McDonald's (United States) to operate fast-food outlets.

FINLAND
Nokia is a leader in mobile telephones.

FRANCE
Club Méditerranée operates vacation villages around the globe.

GERMANY
Hoescht AG is the world's largest chemical manufacturer.

GREAT BRITAIN (UNITED KINGDOM)
The Body Shop International, featuring natural personal-care products, has more than 1,000 stores in 45 nations.

INDIA
Baja Auto is a leading maker of motor scooters.

INDONESIA
Indofood exports noodles to China, Chile, and Poland.

IRELAND
Waterford Wedgwood PLC makes glassware, crystal, and fine china.

ISRAEL
Osem is the largest food producer in the Middle East.

ITALY
Benetton Group SPA produces the United Colors of Benetton clothing.

JAPAN
Matsushita Electric has such brands as JVC and Panasonic, and owns the Spencer Gifts retail chain.

KENYA
Nuave Motor is the nation's first national vehicle manufacturer.

KOREA
Daewoo Group operates 19 member companies, ranging from shipbuilding to international trading.

LATVIA
Kellogg has a factory that produces Corn Flakes.

MOZAMBIQUE
Mozambique Airlines has purchased Boeing (United States) 737 and 767 jets.

NETHERLANDS
KPMG Peat Marwick, the accounting and consulting firm, is headquartered here.

NEW ZEALAND
H.J. Heinz (United States) now owns Watties Industries, Ltd., a leading food processor.

NIGERIA
Elf Nigeria is developing the Ibewa natural gas field.

PHILIPPINES
San Miguel Corporation is a beverage company distributing such brands as Coca-Cola, Sprite, and San Miguel Pale Pilsen.

POLAND
General Motors has a joint venture with Fabryka Samachodow Osobowych.

RUSSIA
Russkoye Bistro is a chain of fast-food restaurants featuring borscht, pirogi (pastries stuffed with vegetables or meat), and vodka.

SAUDI ARABIA
Heineken (Netherlands), Stroh (United States), and others market nonalcoholic beer brands because alcohol is forbidden.

SOUTH AFRICA
Vodacom has "phone shops" in areas where people do not have private phones.

SWEDEN
Electrolux AB makes Electrolux, Frigidaire, Tappan, and Gibson appliances.

SWITZERLAND
Nestlé brands include Nescafé coffee, Perrier water, Baby Ruth candy, Carnation milk, and Alpo dog food.

THAILAND
Nynex (United States) has a joint venture with TelecomAsia to build two million main phone lines.

TURKEY
Koç Holding AS makes Döktas auto parts, Otoyol trucks, and Tofas autos (under license from Italy's Fiat).